Educational Psychology

Windows on Classrooms

Eighth Edition

Paul Eggen
University of North Florida

Don Kauchak
University of Utah

Merrill
Upper Saddle River, New Jersey
Columbus, Ohio

Library of Congress Cataloging-in-Publication Data

Eggen, Paul D.
Educational psychology : windows on classrooms / Paul Eggen, Don Kauchak.—8th ed.
p. cm.
Includes bibliographical references and index.
ISBN-13: 978-0-13-501668-8
ISBN-10: 0-13-501668-1
1. Educational psychology—Study and teaching (Higher)—United States. 2. Learning, Psychology of–Case studies. I. Kauchak, Donald P. II. Title.
LB1051.E463 2010
370.15—dc22

2008038797

Vice President and Editor in Chief: Jeffery W. Johnston
Assistant Vice President and Publisher: Kevin M. Davis
Development Editor: Christina Robb
Editorial Assistant: Lauren Reinkober
Senior Managing Editor: Pamela D. Bennett
Production Editor: Sheryl Glicker Langner
Art Director: Diane C. Lorenzo
Cover Design: Rokusek Design
Photo Coordinator: Lori Whitley
Production Manager: Laura Messerly
Vice President, Director of Sales and Marketing: Quinn Perkson
Marketing Manager: Quinn Perkson
Marketing Coordinator: Brian Mounts

This book was set in Minion by S4Carlisle Publishing Services. It was printed and bound by Courier Kendallville, Inc. The cover was printed by Phoenix Color Corp.

Photo Credits: Photo credits are on page xxiv.

Pearson Education Ltd., London
Pearson Education Singapore, Pte. Ltd.
Pearson Education Canada, Ltd.
Pearson Education—Japan
Pearson Education Australia PTY. Limited
Pearson Education North Asia Ltd., Hong Kong
Pearson Educación de Mexico, S.A. de C.V.
Pearson Education Malaysia, Pte. Ltd.
Pearson Education Upper Saddle River, New Jersey

Merrill
is an imprint of

10 9 8 7 6 5 4 3 2 1
ISBN 13: 978-0-13-501668-8
ISBN 10: 0-13-501668-1

To Judy and Kathy,
teachers who have changed many lives.

preface

Our core goal in writing *Educational Psychology: Windows on Classrooms* has always been to prepare teachers to be able to use educational psychology in their teaching—to bring educational psychology into classrooms and into the work teachers and students do together every day. *Application, application, application* are three of the most important words that can be used to describe our book. Its subtitle—*Windows on Classrooms*—reflects how we attempt to accomplish our goal of bringing the theory and research of educational psychology into the practice of teaching. Every topic in our book is presented in the context of classrooms; we immerse educational psychology in the P–12 world of teaching and learning. This is why each chapter begins with a real story from a real classroom; this is why we carry and elaborate on that story throughout the chapter; and this is why we provide elementary, middle school, and secondary examples with the wealth of teaching guidelines found in features such as *Theory to Practice* and *Classroom Connections.* This is the driving force behind everything you will find in our book.

We have spent and continue to spend a great many hours in P–12 classrooms, and we know that a deep understanding of educational psychology and an ability to apply it in practice are fundamental to being a great teacher. We believe that *Educational Psychology: Windows on Classrooms* can help provide you with this practicable knowledge and that this knowledge will serve you and your students for years to come.

New to This Edition

Expanded Coverage of Theory and Research

Theory and application exist in a synergistic relationship; theory informs practice, and application demonstrates how theory is applied in classrooms. In our ongoing effort to provide readers with a firm conceptual foundation, we have significantly expanded our coverage of theory—placing the book on the cutting edge of theory and research—while retaining our focus on application. Topics that receive increased coverage in this new edition include:

- Recent brain research including a discussion of the cerebral cortex and its role in thinking, problem solving, and language
- Urie Bronfenbrenner's bioecological theory of development
- The social processes involved in the construction of knowledge
- Current theories of cognitive development including socio-cultural and neo-Piagetian approaches
- The implications of student diversity for our understanding of topics such as development, learning, and motivation
- Assessment *for* learning, including informal and formal assessment, and issues involved with assessing English language learners and members of cultural minorities
- The latest perspectives on memory and their implications for teaching and learning
- Qualitative research and the controversies surrounding scientifically based research in education

Features New to This Edition

We have also added several new features to this edition:

- **Theory to Practice:** Applying theories of learning, development, and motivation in the classroom can be challenging. In addition to the numerous existing applications in the book, we have added a feature called *Theory to Practice.* This feature offers an extended example of a teacher putting educational psychology theory and research into practice. The *Theory to Practice* feature appears in every chapter and illustrates how teachers can use educational psychology to help students learn and develop.
- **Exploring Diversity:** Student diversity in the United States is rapidly increasing. We have expanded our coverage of diversity throughout the book. A new feature in every chapter, *Exploring Diversity,* shows how diversity influences learning and teaching and how teachers can capitalize on student diversity to increase learning for all students.
- **Developmentally Appropriate Practice:** Children in elementary, middle, and high schools think differently and have different social and emotional needs. To help teachers address this diversity, a *Developmentally Appropriate Practice* feature in each chapter provides guidelines for adapting the application of chapter content to the appropriate developmental level of students.
- **MyEducationLab:** A new online learning tool, MyEducationLab, offers quizzes to test mastery of chapter objectives: *Review, Practice, and Enrichment* exercises to deepen understanding, *Activities and Applications* to foster application of chapter concepts, and *Building Teaching Skills and Dispositions* exercises to provide interactive practice applying the core principles and concepts of educational psychology. The video clips of real children and classrooms formerly available on the DVD set accompanying the textbook are now located on MyEducationLab.

the most applied educational psychology book in the field

As the most applied text in the field, the book aims to increase learning for all students by capturing the realities of learning and teaching with written and video case studies and a number of features that provide concrete examples of P–12 teachers using educational psychology in their classrooms.

Authentic Case Studies. Each chapter begins with a brief case study that provides a concrete illustration of the application of educational psychology. The case is weaved through the chapter to provide repeated connections between the case and the chapter content. For an example, check out the case of eighth grade science teacher, Karen Johnson, in Chapter 2 on pages 29, 36, and 42.

To see how Karen responds to this problem, let's sit in on another conversation she has with Ken the Tuesday following their Friday discussion.

"What's that for?" Ken asks, seeing Karen walking into the teachers' lounge with a plastic cup filled with cotton balls.

"I just had the greatest class," Karen replies. "You remember how frustrated I was on Friday when the kids didn't understand basic concepts like *mass* and *density*, and all they wanted to do was memorize a formula. . . . I thought about it over the weekend, and decided to try something different, even if it seemed sort of elementary.

"See," she goes on, compressing the cotton in the cup. "Now the cotton is more dense. And now it's less dense," she points out, releasing the cotton.

"Then, I made some different-sized blocks out of the same type of wood. Some of the kids believed the density of the big block was greater. But then we weighed the blocks, measured their volumes, and computed their densities, and the kids saw they were the same. They gradually began to understand that size is only one factor influencing density.

"This morning," she continues with increasing animation, "I had them put equal volumes of water and vegetable oil on our balances, and when the balance

Classroom Connections at the Elementary, Middle School, and High School Levels. These boxed features in each chapter offer strategies for applying content to specific learning and teaching situations. Each strategy is illustrated with a classroom example, derived from our experiences working in classrooms at the elementary, middle, and high school levels. For examples see the *Classroom Connections* in Chapter 3 on pages 66, 74, 78, and 88.

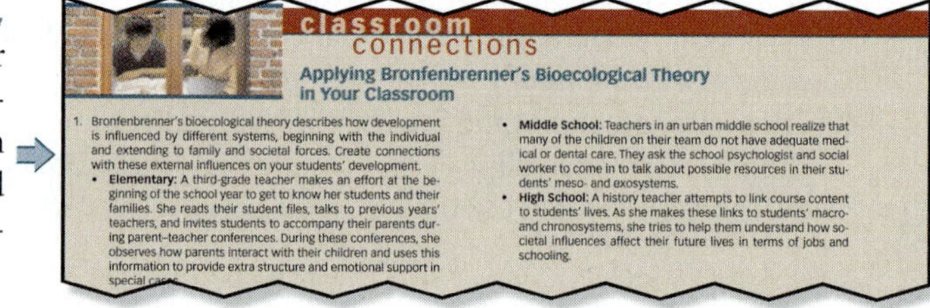

classroom connections

Applying Bronfenbrenner's Bioecological Theory in Your Classroom

1. Bronfenbrenner's bioecological theory describes how development is influenced by different systems, beginning with the individual and extending to family and societal forces. Create connections with these external influences on your students' development.
   - **Elementary:** A third-grade teacher makes an effort at the beginning of the school year to get to know her students and their families. She reads their student files, talks to previous years' teachers, and invites students to accompany their parents during parent–teacher conferences. During these conferences, she observes how parents interact with their children and uses this information to provide extra structure and emotional support in special
   - **Middle School:** Teachers in an urban middle school realize that many of the children on their team do not have adequate medical or dental care. They ask the school psychologist and social worker to come in to talk about possible resources in their students' meso- and exosystems.
   - **High School:** A history teacher attempts to link course content to students' lives. As she makes these links to students' macro- and chronosystems, she tries to help them understand how societal influences affect their future lives in terms of jobs and schooling.

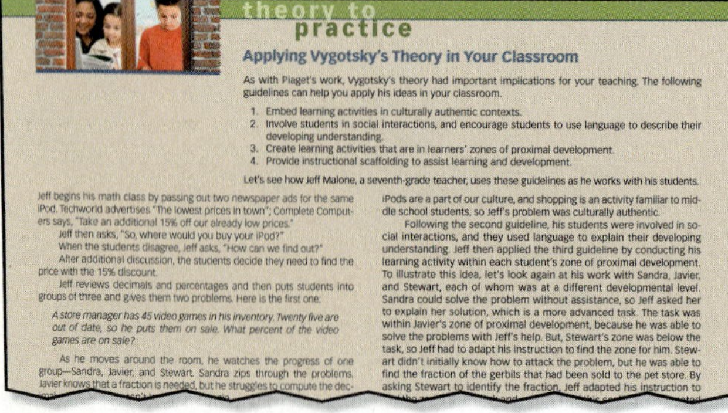

theory to practice

Applying Vygotsky's Theory in Your Classroom

As with Piaget's work, Vygotsky's theory had important implications for your teaching. The following guidelines can help you apply his ideas in your classroom.

1. Embed learning activities in culturally authentic contexts.
2. Involve students in social interactions, and encourage students to use language to describe their developing understanding.
3. Create learning activities that are in learners' zones of proximal development.
4. Provide instructional scaffolding to assist learning and development.

Let's see how Jeff Malone, a seventh-grade teacher, uses these guidelines as he works with his students.

Jeff begins his math class by passing out two newspaper ads for the same iPod. Techworld advertises "The lowest prices in town"; Complete Computers says, "Take an additional 15% off our already low prices."

Jeff then asks, "So, where would you buy your iPod?"

When the students disagree, Jeff asks, "How can we find out?"

After additional discussion, the students decide they need to find the price with the 15% discount.

Jeff reviews decimals and percentages and then puts students into groups of three and gives them two problems. Here is the first one:

A store manager has 45 video games in his inventory. Twenty five are out of date, so he puts them on sale. What percent of the video games are on sale?

As he moves around the room, he watches the progress of one group—Sandra, Javier, and Stewart. Sandra zips through the problems. Javier knows that a fraction is needed, but he struggles to compute the dec-

iPods are a part of our culture, and shopping is an activity familiar to middle school students, so Jeff's problem was culturally authentic.

Following the second guideline, his students were involved in social interactions, and they used language to explain their developing understanding. Jeff then applied the third guideline by conducting his learning activity within each student's zone of proximal development. To illustrate this idea, let's look again at his work with Sandra, Javier, and Stewart, each of whom was at a different developmental level. Sandra could solve the problem without assistance, so Jeff asked her to explain her solution, which is a more advanced task. The task was within Javier's zone of proximal development, because he was able to solve the problems with Jeff's help. But, Stewart's zone was below the task, so Jeff had to adapt his instruction to find the zone for him. Stewart didn't initially know how to attack the problem, but he was able to find the fraction of the gerbils that had been sold to the pet store. By asking Stewart to identify the fraction, Jeff adapted his instruction to

Theory to Practice. The *Theory to Practice* feature offers specific guidelines for applying the theories and research covered in the book with students. The feature includes case studies taken from classroom practice that illustrate the guidelines being applied in classroom settings. For examples see pages 21, 42, 72, 220, 256, and 312.

clearly identifying and reinforcing key ideas in every chapter

This text is designed to increase students' learning with a *Guided Learning System* that matches learning objectives to the chapter outline, reinforces main ideas with *Check Your Understanding* questions at the end of every section, and organizes each chapter's summary around the learning objectives.

Clear Alignment of Learning Objectives and the Chapter Outline. Like the previous edition, the eighth edition begins every chapter with learning objectives and links the specific learning objectives to each of the major headings in the chapters. By aligning the learning objectives and the chapter outline, the key ideas are clearly identified and highlighted to help students maximize their learning. See pages 195, 225, and 253 for examples.

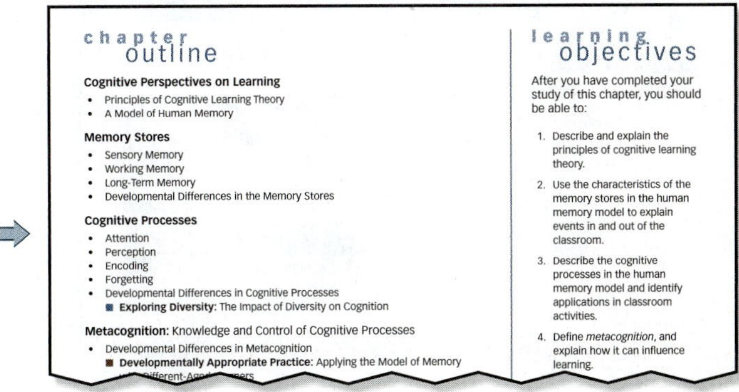

chapter outline

Cognitive Perspectives on Learning
- Principles of Cognitive Learning Theory
- A Model of Human Memory

Memory Stores
- Sensory Memory
- Working Memory
- Long-Term Memory
- Developmental Differences in the Memory Stores

Cognitive Processes
- Attention
- Perception
- Encoding
- Forgetting
- Developmental Differences in Cognitive Processes
  - **Exploring Diversity:** The Impact of Diversity on Cognition

Metacognition: Knowledge and Control of Cognitive Processes
- Developmental Differences in Metacognition
  - **Developmentally Appropriate Practice:** Applying the Model of Memory

learning objectives

After you have completed your study of this chapter, you should be able to:

1. Describe and explain the principles of cognitive learning theory.
2. Use the characteristics of the memory stores in the human memory model to explain events in and out of the classroom.
3. Describe the cognitive processes in the human memory model and identify applications in classroom activities.
4. Define *metacognition*, and explain how it can influence learning.

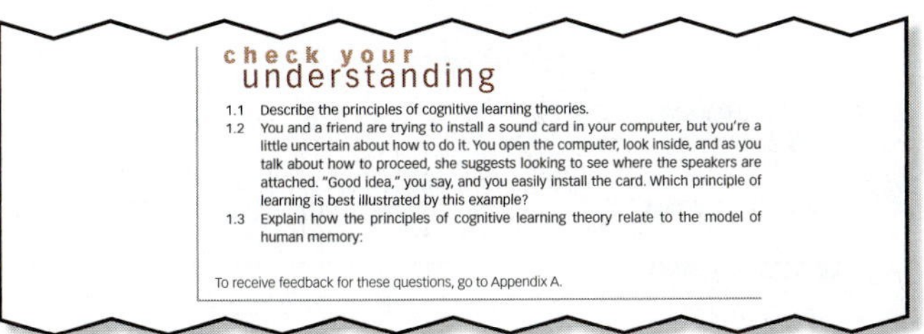

check your understanding

1.1 Describe the principles of cognitive learning theories.
1.2 You and a friend are trying to install a sound card in your computer, but you're a little uncertain about how to do it. You open the computer, look inside, and as you talk about how to proceed, she suggests looking to see where the speakers are attached. "Good idea," you say, and you easily install the card. Which principle of learning is best illustrated by this example?
1.3 Explain how the principles of cognitive learning theory relate to the model of human memory.

To receive feedback for these questions, go to Appendix A.

Check Your Understanding. *Check Your Understanding* questions at the end of every major section are aligned with learning objectives and reinforce the essential ideas of that section. These *Check Your Understanding* questions put students in cognitively active roles and provide formative feedback to help students deepen their understanding of chapter content. Check out the *Check Your Understanding* questions in Chapter 7 on pages 198, 206, 217, and 220 for examples. Feedback for all the *Check Your Understanding* questions is provided in Appendix A.

Meeting Your Learning Objectives. The end-of-chapter *Meeting Your Learning Objectives* review section restates the learning objectives and provides a bulleted summary of the most important topics discussed in each chapter. Organizing the chapter summary around specific learning objectives, reminds students of the key ideas presented in the chapter and reinforces the most important information. For examples, see pages 221, 248, and 279.

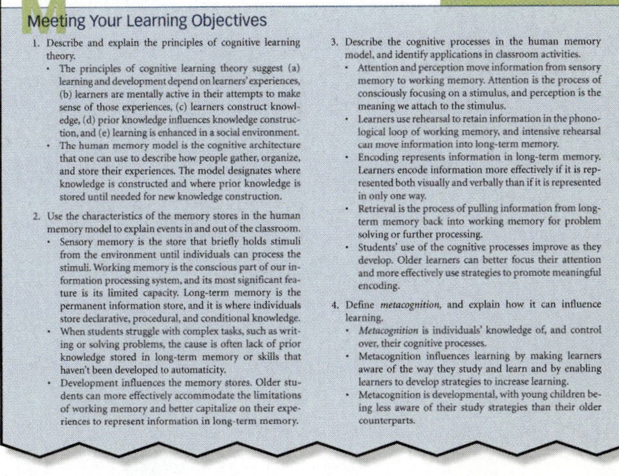

Meeting Your Learning Objectives

1. Describe and explain the principles of cognitive learning theory.
   - The principles of cognitive learning theory suggest (a) learning and development depend on learners' experiences, (b) learners are mentally active in their attempts to make sense of those experiences, (c) learners construct knowledge, (d) prior knowledge influences knowledge construction, and (e) learning is enhanced in a social environment.
   - The human memory model is the cognitive architecture that one can use to describe how people gather, organize, and store their experiences. The model designates where knowledge is constructed and where prior knowledge is stored until needed for new knowledge construction.
2. Use the characteristics of the memory stores in the human memory model to explain events in and out of the classroom.
   - Sensory memory is the store that briefly holds stimuli from the environment until individuals can process the stimuli. Working memory is the conscious part of our information processing system, and its most significant feature is its limited capacity. Long-term memory is the permanent information store, and it is where individuals store declarative, procedural, and conditional knowledge.
   - When students struggle with complex tasks, such as writing or solving problems, the cause is often lack of prior knowledge stored in long-term memory or skills that haven't been developed to automaticity.
   - Development influences the memory stores. Older students can more effectively accommodate the limitations of working memory and better capitalize on their experiences to represent information in long-term memory.
3. Describe the cognitive processes in the human memory model, and identify applications in classroom activities.
   - Attention and perception move information from sensory memory to working memory. Attention is the process of consciously focusing on a stimulus, and perception is the meaning we attach to the stimulus.
   - Learners use rehearsal to retain information in the phonological loop of working memory, and intensive rehearsal can move information into long-term memory.
   - Encoding represents information in long-term memory. Learners encode information more effectively if it is represented both visually and verbally than if it is represented in only one way.
   - Retrieval is the process of pulling information from long-term memory back into working memory for problem solving or further processing.
   - Students' use of the cognitive processes improve as they develop. Older learners can better focus their attention and more effectively use strategies to promote meaningful encoding.
4. Define *metacognition*, and explain how it can influence learning.
   - *Metacognition* is individuals' knowledge of, and control over, their cognitive processes.
   - Metacognition influences learning by making learners aware of the way they study and learn and by enabling learners to develop strategies to increase learning.
   - Metacognition is developmental, with young children being less aware of their study strategies than their older counterparts.

Expanded content reflecting issues of student diversity has been added, including the implications of student diversity for understanding topics such as development, learning, and motivation as well as increased information on assessing English Language Learners.

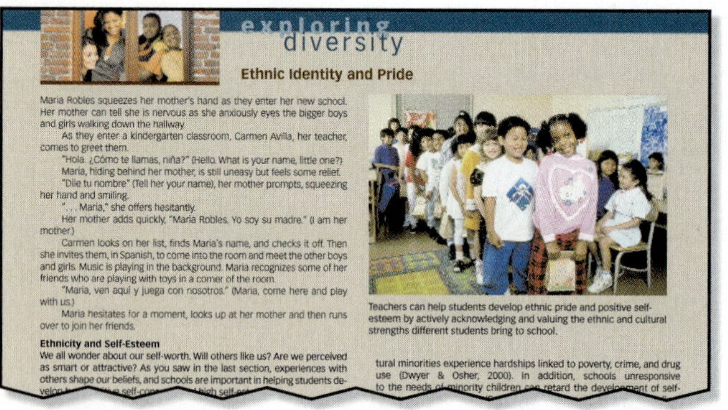

exploring diversity

Ethnic Identity and Pride

Maria Robles squeezes her mother's hand as they enter her new school. Her mother can tell she is nervous as she anxiously eyes the bigger boys and girls walking down the hallway.

As they enter a kindergarten classroom, Carmen Avila, her teacher, comes to greet them.

"Hola. ¿Cómo te llamas, niña?" (Hello. What is your name, little one?)

Maria, hiding behind her mother, is still uneasy but feels some relief.

"Dile tu nombre" (Tell her your name), her mother prompts, squeezing her hand and smiling.

". . . Maria," she offers hesitantly.

Her mother adds quickly, "Maria Robles. Yo soy su madre." (I am her mother.)

Carmen looks on her list, finds Maria's name, and checks it off. Then she invites them, in Spanish, to come into the room and meet the other boys and girls. Music is playing in the background. Maria recognizes some of her friends who are playing with toys in a corner of the room.

"Maria, ven aquí y juega con nosotros." (Maria, come here and play with us.)

Maria hesitates for a moment, looks up at her mother and then runs over to join her friends.

Ethnicity and Self-Esteem

We all wonder about our self-worth. Will others like us? Are we perceived as smart or attractive? As you saw in the last section, experiences with others shape our beliefs, and schools are important in helping students de-

Teachers can help students develop ethnic pride and positive self-esteem by actively acknowledging and valuing the ethnic and cultural strengths different students bring to school.

tural minorities experience hardships linked to poverty, crime, and drug use (Dwyer & Osher, 2000). In addition, schools unresponsive to the needs of minority children can retard the development of self-

Exploring Diversity. A new feature in every chapter, *Exploring Diversity,* shows how diversity influences learning and teaching. This feature illustrates how teachers can capitalize on student diversity to increase learning for all students. For examples, see pages 73, 274, and 420.

Developmentally Appropriate Practice. New to this edition, the *Developmentally Appropriate Practice* feature helps teachers accommodate developmental differences in their students and provides suggestions for adapting the application of key chapter content to the developmental levels of their students. For examples, see pages 55, 89, and 219.

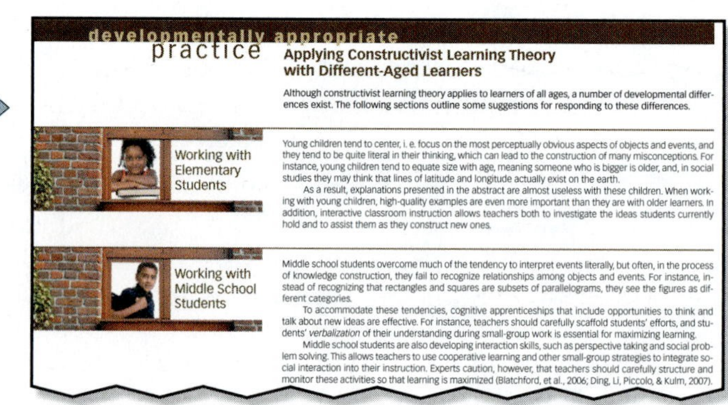

developmentally appropriate practice

Applying Constructivist Learning Theory with Different-Aged Learners

Although constructivist learning theory applies to learners of all ages, a number of developmental differences exist. The following sections outline some suggestions for responding to these differences.

Working with Elementary Students

Young children tend to center, i. e. focus on the most perceptually obvious aspects of objects and events, and they tend to be quite literal in their thinking, which can lead to the construction of many misconceptions. For instance, young children tend to equate size with age, meaning someone who is bigger is older, and, in social studies they may think that lines of latitude and longitude actually exist on the earth.

As a result, explanations presented in the abstract are almost useless with these children. When working with young children, high-quality examples are even more important than they are with older learners. In addition, interactive classroom instruction allows teachers both to investigate the ideas students currently hold and to assist them as they construct new ones.

Working with Middle School Students

Middle school students overcome much of the tendency to interpret events literally, but often, in the process of knowledge construction, they fail to recognize relationships among objects and events. For instance, instead of recognizing that rectangles and squares are subsets of parallelograms, they see the figures as different categories.

To accommodate these tendencies, cognitive apprenticeships that include opportunities to think and talk about new ideas are effective. For instance, teachers should carefully scaffold students' efforts, and students' *verbalization* of their understanding during small-group work is essential for maximizing learning.

Middle school students are also developing interaction skills, such as perspective taking and social problem solving. This allows teachers to use cooperative learning and other small-group strategies to integrate social interaction into their instruction. Experts caution, however, that teachers should carefully structure and monitor these activities so that learning is maximized (Blatchford, et al., 2006; Ding, Li, Piccolo, & Kulm, 2007).

MyEducationLab

PEARSON
MyEducationLab
Where the Classroom Comes to Life

> Teacher educators who are developing pedagogies for the analysis of teaching and learning contend that analyzing teaching artifacts has three advantages: it enables new teachers time for reflection while still using the real materials of practice; it provides new teachers with experience thinking about and approaching the complexity of the classroom; and in some cases, it can help new teachers and teacher educators develop a shared understanding and common language about teaching. . . .[1]

As Linda Darling-Hammond and her colleagues point out, grounding teacher education in real classrooms—among real teachers and students and among actual examples of students' and teachers' work—is an important, and perhaps even an essential, part of training teachers for the complexities of teaching today's students in today's classrooms. We have created a Website that provides you and your students with the context of real classrooms and artifacts that research on teacher education tells us is so important. Through authentic in-class video footage, interactive skill-building exercises, and more, MyEducationLab offers you and your students a uniquely valuable teacher education tool.

MyEducationLab is easy to use! Wherever the MyEducationLab logo appears in the margins or elsewhere in the text, you and your students can follow the simple link instructions to access the MyEducationLab resource that corresponds with the chapter content.

MyEducationLab
To examine different teacher's attempts to attract their students' attention, go to the *Activities and Applications* section in Chapter 7 of MyEducationLab at www.myeducationlab.com, and watch the episode *Applying Information Processing: Attracting Students' Attention*. Answer the questions following the episode.

MyEducationLab resources include:

- **Video:** Videos formerly available on the DVD set accompanying the seventh edition are now available on MyEducationLab. These clips allow students to analyze video relating to concepts and principles described in the text. Viewing videos and discussing and analyzing them not only deepen understanding of concepts presented in the book, but also build skills in observing and analyzing children and classrooms.
- **Individualized Study Plan:** Your students have the opportunity to take a quiz to test their mastery of chapter objectives. Detailed feedback is presented to explain why answers are correct or incorrect. Results automatically generate a personalized study plan, identifying areas of the chapter that need to be reread to fully understand chapter concepts. Students are also presented with Review, Practice, Enrichment exercises to help ensure learning and to deepen understanding of chapter concepts.
- **Activities and Applications:** These activities, designed to be assigned by instructors or used by students on their own, help students apply what they have learned in each chapter by analyzing real classrooms through video clips, artifacts, and case studies. Feedback for these exercises is available *only to instructors.*
- **Building Teaching Skills and Dispositions:** These assignments help students practice and strengthen skills that are essential to quality teaching. Students are given practice applying a specific skill and are scaffolded through several opportunities to practice the skill. The final task tests the mastery of the skill. Feedback for the final task is available *only to instructors.*

MyEducationLab is easy to assign. Visit www.myeducationlab.com for a demonstration of this exciting new online teaching resource.

---

[1] Darling-Hammond, l., &Bransford, J., Eds.(2005). *Preparing Teachers for a Changing World.* San Francisco: John Wiley & Sons.

supplementary materials

The following supplements to the textbook are available for download on www.pearsonhighered.com. Simply click on "Educators"; enter the author, title, or ISBN; and select this textbook. Click on the "Resources" tab to view and download the available supplements detailed next.

Online Instructor's Manual

The *Instructor's Manual* (ISBN 0-13-501670-3) includes chapter overviews and objectives, listings of available PowerPoint® slides, presentation outlines, teaching suggestions for each chapter, and questions for discussion and analysis including feedback.

Online Test Bank and Test Gen

The *Test Bank* (ISBN 0-13-501691-6) provides a comprehensive but flexible assessment package. The *Test Bank* for this edition has been *completely reorganized* to make it more accessible and usable. To provide complete coverage of the content in each chapter, all multiple-choice and essay items are grouped under the chapters' main headings, and they are balanced between knowledge/recall items and those that require analysis and application. The computerized test bank software, *TestGen* (ISBN 0-13-501672-X), allows instructors to create and customize exams. *TestGen* is available in both Macintosh and PC/Windows versions.

Online PowerPoint Slides

The *PowerPoint Slides* (ISBN 0-13-501671-1) highlight key concepts and summarize text content. "Presentation Guides," now included with the slides, contain detailed outlines of each major section along with "Check Your Understanding" questions to stimulate discussion about chapter content. These guides are designed to provide structure to instructor presentations and give students an organized perspective on each chapter's content.

Online Course Content Cartridges

Available for both BlackBoard (ISBN 0-13-501676-2) and WebCT (ISBN 0-13-501675-4), the *online course cartridges* contain the content of the Test Bank available for use on either online learning application.

MyEducationLab

MyEducationLab, the new online learning tool discussed earlier in this preface, is available at www.myeducationlab.com.

Computer Simulation Software

Simulations in *Educational Psychology and Research, version 2.1* (ISBN 0-13-113717-4), features five psychological/educational interactive experiments on a CD-ROM: (1) Piaget's developmental stages, (2) misconceptions and the role of prior knowledge in learning, (3) schemas and the construction of meaning, (4) Kohlberg's stages of moral development, and (5) mental models and assessment. Instructors should contact their local sales representative to order a copy of these simulations.

The Video Package

An extensive video package is offered, including: *Double-Column Addition: A Teacher Uses Piaget's Theory* (ISBN 0-13-751413-1), *Windows on Classrooms Video Case Studies* (ISBN 0-02-0-13-118642-6), *Secondary Video Case Studies* (ISBN 0-13-118641-8), and *Video Workshop for Educational Psychology: Student Learning Guide with CD-ROM, Second Edition* (ISBN 0-205-45834-3). Instructors should contact their local sales representative to order a copy of these videos.

acknowledgments

Every book reflects the work of a team that includes the authors, the staff of editors, and the reviewers. We appreciate the input we've received from professors and students who have used previous editions of the book, and we gratefully acknowledge the contributions of the reviewers who offered us constructive feedback to guide us in this new edition:

Seth Alper, Florida Atlantic University; Lynley Anderman, The Ohio State University; Katherine H. Greenberg, The University of Tennessee; Brian K. Leavell, Texas Woman's University; Kathy Nakagawa, Arizona State University; Larry Nucci, University of California, Berkeley; Rayne A. Sperling, Pennsylvania State University; and Mary Styers, North Carolina State University.

In addition, we acknowledge with our thanks, the reviewers of our previous editions:

Patricia Barbetta, Florida International University; David Bergin, University of Toledo; Scott W. Brown, University of Connecticut; Kay S. Bull, Oklahoma State University; Barbara Collamer, Western Washington University; Jerome D'Agostino, University of Arizona; Betty M. Davenport, Campbell University; Ronna F. Dillon, Southern Illinois University; Oliver W. Edwards, University of Central Florida; Thomas G. Fetsco, Northern Arizona University; Leena Furtado, California State University, Dominguez Hills; Newell T. Gill, Florida Atlantic University; Charles W. Good, West Chester University; Robert L. Hohn, University of Kansas; Dov Liberman, University of Houston; Hermine H. Marshall, San Francisco State University; Tes Mehring, Emporia State University; Luanna H. Meyer, Massey University–New Zealand; Nancy Perry, University of British Columbia; Evan Powell, University of Georgia; Anne N. Rinn, Western Kentucky University; Jay Samuels, University of Minnesota; Gregory Schraw, University of Nebraska, Lincoln; Dale H. Schunk, Purdue University; Rozanne Sparks, Pittsburgh State University; Rayne A. Sperling, Pennsylvania State University; Robert J. Stevens, Pennsylvania State University; Julianne C. Turner, Notre Dame University; Nancy Vye, University of Washington; Glenda Wilkes, University of Arizona; and Karen M. Zabrucky, Georgia State University.

In addition to the reviewers who guided our revisions, our team of editors gave us support in many ways. Kevin Davis, our Publisher, continues to guide us with his intelligence, insight, and understanding of the field. Christie Robb, our development editor, has been available whenever we had questions or needed help, and she has provided us with invaluable support. Working with her has been a pleasure in every way. Luanne Dreyer Elliott, our copyeditor, has been thoroughly professional in her efforts to make the content of the book clear and understandable. Sheryl Langner, our production editor, has been with us for 7 editions; her professionalism and commitment to excellence are appreciated more than we can say. Special thanks go to Suzanne Schellenberg, who did the PowerPoint® slides and *Instructor's Manual* for this edition. She has also provided us with many ideas and examples over the years that have been incorporated into our writing.

Our appreciation goes to all of these fine people who have taken our words and given them shape. We hope that all of our efforts will result in increased learning for students and more rewarding teaching for instructors.

Finally, we would sincerely appreciate any comments or questions about anything that appears in the book or any of its supplements. Please feel free to contact either of us at any time. Our e-mail addresses are: peggen@unf.edu and don.kauchak@gmail.com.

Good luck.

Paul Eggen

Don Kauchak

brief contents

chapter 1 Educational Psychology: Developing a Professional Knowledge Base 2

part 1 the learner

chapter 2 The Development of Cognition and Language 28

chapter 3 Personal, Social, and Moral Development 60

chapter 4 Learner Diversity 94

chapter 5 Learners with Exceptionalities 124

part 2 learning

chapter 6 Behaviorism and Social Cognitive Theory 162

chapter 7 Cognitive Views of Learning 194

chapter 8 Constructing Knowledge 224

chapter 9 Complex Cognitive Processes 252

part 3 classroom processes

chapter 10 Theories of Motivation 282

chapter 11 Motivation in the Classroom 318

chapter 12 Creating Productive Learning Environments: Classroom Management 350

chapter 13 Creating Productive Learning Environments: Principles and Models of Instruction 388

chapter 14 Assessing Classroom Learning 430

chapter 15 Assessment Through Standardized Testing 470

appendix A Feedback for "Check Your Understanding" Questions A-1

appendix B Feedback for "Preparing for Your Licensure Exam" Questions B-1

appendix C Using This Text to Practice for the Praxis™ *Principles of Learning and Teaching* Exam C-1

glossary G-1

references R-1

name index I-1

subject index I-9

contents

chapter 1
Educational Psychology: Developing a Professional Knowledge Base 2

Educational Psychology and Becoming a Professional 4
- Characteristics of Professionalism 4

Professional Knowledge and Learning to Teach 6
- Knowledge of Content 8
- Pedagogical Content Knowledge 9
- General Pedagogical Knowledge 10
- Knowledge of Learners and Learning 11
- Professional Knowledge: Reform and Accountability 13

The Role of Research in Acquiring Professional Knowledge 14
- Descriptive Research 15
- Correlational Research 16
- Experimental Research 17
- Qualitative Research 18
- Scientifically-Based Research in Education 19
- Action Research 19
- Research and the Development of Theory 20

The Use of Case Studies in Educational Psychology 22

part 1 the learner

chapter 2
The Development of Cognition and Language 28

What Is Development? 30
- Principles of Development 30
- The Human Brain and Cognitive Development 31

Piaget's Theory of Intellectual Development 34
- The Drive for Equilibrium 34
- Organization and Adaptation: The Development of Schemes 35
- Factors Influencing Development 35
- Stages of Development 37
- Putting Piaget's Theory into Perspective 42
- Current Views of Cognitive Development 43

A Sociocultural View of Development: The Work of Lev Vygotsky 45
- Learning and Development in a Cultural Context 45
- Zone of Proximal Development 47
- Scaffolding: Interactive Instructional Support 47
- Piaget's and Vygotsky's Views of Knowledge Construction 49

Language Development 50
- Theories of Language Development 50
- Early Language Development 51
- Language Development in the School Years 52

chapter 3
Personal, Social, and Moral Development 60

Bronfenbrenner's Bioecological Theory of Development 62
- The Microsystem: Proximal Influences on Development 62
- Additional Systems in Bronfenbrenner's Model 65
- Evaluating the Theory 65

The Development of Identity and Self-Concept 66
- Erikson's Theory of Psychosocial Development 66
- The Development of Identity 68
- The Development of Self-Concept 70

Social Development 75
- Perspective Taking: Understanding Others' Thoughts and Feelings 75
- Social Problem Solving 76
- Violence and Aggression in Schools 76

Development of Morality, Social Responsibility, and Self-Control 79
- Increased Interest in Moral Education and Development 79
- Moral, Conventional and Personal Domains 80
- Piaget's Theory of Moral Development 81
- Kohlberg's Theory of Moral Development 81
- Emotional Factors in Moral Development 85
- Learning Contexts: Promoting Personal, Social, and Moral Development in Urban Environments 86

chapter 4
Learner Diversity 94

Culture 96
- Ethnicity 96
- Culture and Classrooms 97

Linguistic Diversity 101
- English Dialects 101
- English Language Learners 102

Gender 108
School-Related Gender Differences 108
Gender Differences in Classroom Behavior 109
Gender Stereotypes and Perceptions 109

Socioeconomic Status 111
How SES Influences Learning 112
SES: Some Cautions and Implications for Teachers 114
Students Placed at Risk 114
Resilience 115

chapter 5
Learners with Exceptionalities 124

Intelligence 126
Intelligence: One Trait or Many? 127
Intelligence: Nature Versus Nurture 130
Ability Grouping 130
Learning Styles 131

Changes in the Ways Teachers Help Students with Exceptionalities 133
Individuals with Disabilities Education Act (IDEA) 133
Amendments to the IDEA 137

Students with Learning Problems 137
The Labeling Controversy 138
Learning Disabilities 138
Attention Deficit/Hyperactivity Disorder (ADHD) 140
Mental Retardation 141
Behavior Disorders 143
Autism Spectrum Disorder 145
Communication Disorders 146
Visual Disabilities 147
Hearing Disabilities 147

Students Who Are Gifted and Talented 149
Characteristics of Students Who Are Gifted and Talented 149
Identifying Students Who Are Gifted and Talented 150
Programs for the Gifted and Talented 151

The Teacher's Role in Inclusive Classrooms 152
Collaborative Consultation: Help for the Classroom Teacher 152
Identifying Students with Exceptionalities 152
Modifying Instruction to Meet Students' Needs 153
Promote Social Integration and Student Growth 154

part 2
learning

chapter 6
Behaviorism and Social Cognitive Theory 162

Behaviorist Views of Learning 164
What Is Behaviorism? 164
Classical Conditioning 164
Operant Conditioning 167
Applied Behavior Analysis 175
Putting Behaviorism into Perspective 176

Social Cognitive Theory 179
Comparing Behaviorism and Social Cognitive Theory 180
Modeling 181
Vicarious Learning 182
Nonoccurrence of Expected Consequences 182
The Effects of Modeling 183
Processes Involved in Learning from Models 184
Effectiveness of Models 184
Self-Regulation 185
Putting Social Cognitive Theory into Perspective 188

chapter 7
Cognitive Views of Learning 194

Cognitive Perspectives on Learning 196
Principles of Cognitive Learning Theory 196
A Model of Human Memory 198

Memory Stores 199
Sensory Memory 199
Working Memory 199
Long-Term Memory 201
Developmental Differences in the Memory Stores 205

Cognitive Processes 207
Attention 207
Perception 208
Encoding 209
Forgetting 214
Developmental Differences in Cognitive Processes 216

Metacognition: Knowledge and Control of Cognitive Processes 217
Developmental Differences in Metacognition 218
Putting the Memory Model into Perspective 220

chapter 8
Constructing Knowledge 224

What Is Constructivist Learning Theory? 226
Cognitive Constructivism 226
Social Constructivism 227

Characteristics of Constructivist Learning Theory 230
Learners Construct Understanding That Makes Sense to Them 230
New Learning Depends on Current Understanding 230
Social Interaction Facilitates Learning 231

Meaningful Learning Occurs Within Real-World Tasks 233

When Learners Construct Invalid Knowledge: Misconceptions and Conceptual Change 234

Misconceptions in Teaching and Learning 235

The Origin of Misconceptions 236

Misconceptions' Resistance to Change 236

Teaching for Conceptual Change 236

Constructivist Learning Theory in Classrooms 238

The Teacher's Role in Constructivist Classrooms 238

Constructivism and Human Memory 238

Suggestions for Classroom Practice 240

Learning Contexts: Knowledge Construction in Urban Environments 242

Putting Constructivist Learning Theory into Perspective 245

chapter 9

Complex Cognitive Processes 252

Concept Learning 254

Theories of Concept Learning 255

Learning and Teaching Concepts: The Need for Examples 256

Problem Solving 258

Well-Defined and Ill-Defined Problems 259

A Problem-Solving Model 259

Expert-Novice Differences in Problem-Solving Ability 262

Creativity in Problem Solving 263

Problem-Based Learning 264

Using Technology to Promote Problem Solving 265

The Strategic Learner 267

Metacognition: The Foundation of Strategic Learning 267

Study Strategies 268

Critical Thinking 271

Transfer of Learning 275

General and Specific Transfer 275

Factors Affecting Transfer 276

part 3

classroom processes

chapter 10

Theories of Motivation 282

What Is Motivation? 284

Extrinsic and Intrinsic Motivation 285

Motivation to Learn 285

Theoretical Views of Motivation 286

The Influence of Needs on Motivation to Learn 290

Maslow's Hierarchy of Needs 290

The Need for Self-Determination 291

The Need to Preserve Self-Worth 294

The Influence of Beliefs on Motivation to Learn 296

Expectations: Beliefs About Future Outcomes 297

Beliefs About Intelligence 297

Self-Efficacy: Beliefs About Capability 298

Beliefs About Value 299

Attributions: Beliefs About Causes of Performance 300

The Influence of Goals on Motivation to Learn 303

Mastery and Performance Goals 304

Social Goals 305

Work Avoidance Goals 306

Goals, Motivation, and Achievement 306

Using Goals Effectively 307

The Influence of Interest and Emotion on Motivation to Learn 309

The Influence of Interest on Motivation to Learn 309

The Influence of Emotion on Motivation to Learn 310

chapter 11

Motivation in the Classroom 318

Class Structure: Creating a Mastery-Focused Environment 320

Self-Regulated Learners: Developing Student Responsibility 322

Developing Self-Regulation: Applying Learners' Needs for Self-Determination 322

Teacher Characteristics: Personal Qualities That Increase Motivation to Learn 325

Personal Teaching Efficacy: Beliefs About Teaching and Learning 326

Modeling and Enthusiasm: Communicating Genuine Interest 327

Caring: Meeting Needs for Belonging and Relatedness 327

Teacher Expectations: Increasing Perceptions of Competence 328

Climate Variables: Creating a Motivating Environment 332

Order and Safety: Classrooms as Secure Places to Learn 332

Success: Developing Learner Self-Efficacy 333

Challenge: Increasing Perceptions of Competence 333

Task Comprehension: Increasing Feelings of Autonomy and Value 334

The TARGET Program: Applying Goal Theory in Classrooms 334

Instructional Variables: Developing Interest in Learning Activities 336

Introductory Focus: Attracting Students' Attention 336
Personalization: Links to Students' Lives 338
Involvement: Increasing Intrinsic Interest 339
Feedback: Meeting the Need to Understand 341
Assessment and Learning: Using Feedback to Increase Interest and Self-Efficacy 343
Learning Contexts: Increasing Motivation in Urban Classrooms 343

chapter 12
Creating Productive Learning Environments: Classroom Management 350

The Importance of Well-Managed Classrooms 352
Public and Professional Concerns 352
The Complexities of Classrooms 353
Influence on Motivation and Learning 354
Goals of Classroom Management 354

Planning for Effective Classroom Management 356
Principles of Planning for Classroom Management 356
Planning for Effective Management in Elementary Schools 359
Planning for Effective Management in Middle and Secondary Schools 361
Learning Contexts: Classroom Management in Urban Environments 364

Communication with Parents 367
Benefits of Communication 368
Strategies for Involving Parents 368

Intervening When Misbehavior Occurs 371
Principles of Successful Interventions 372
Cognitive Interventions 374
Behavioral Interventions 376
An Intervention Continuum 377

Serious Management Problems: Violence and Aggression 382
School Violence and Aggression 382
Long-Term Solutions to Violence and Aggression 383

chapter 13
Creating Productive Learning Environments: Principles and Models of Instruction 388

Planning for Instruction 390
Selecting Topics 390
Preparing Learning Objectives 391
Preparing and Organizing Learning Activities 393
Planning for Assessment 394
Instructional Alignment 394
Planning in a Standards-Based Environment 395

Implementing Instruction: Essential Teaching Skills 399
Attitudes 400
Organization 401
Communication 401
Focus: Attracting and Maintaining Attention 402
Feedback 402
Questioning 404
Review and Closure 406
Learning Contexts: Instruction in Urban Environments 406

Models of Instruction 409
Direct Instruction 409
Lecture-Discussion: Developing Integrated Schemas 413
Guided Discovery 417
Cooperative Learning 419

Assessment and Learning: Using Assessment as a Learning Tool 424

chapter 14
Assessing Classroom Learning 430

Classroom Assessment 434
Assessment for Student Learning 434
Validity: Making Appropriate Assessment Decisions 435
Reliability: Consistency in Assessment 436

Informal Assessment 437
Informal Assessment During Learning Activities 438
Informal Assessment in the Larger School Context 439
Reliability of Informal Assessments 439

Formal Assessment 440
Paper and Pencil Items 441
Commercially Prepared Test Items 446
Performance Assessments 446
Portfolio Assessment: Involving Students in the Assessment Process 449
Putting Formal Assessment Formats into Perspective 451

Effective Assessment Practices 453
Planning for Assessment 453
Preparing Students for Assessments 454
Administering Assessments 457
Analyzing Results 457

Grading and Reporting: The Total Assessment System 459
Formative and Summative Assessment 460
Designing a Grading System 460
Assigning Grades: Increasing Learning and Motivation 462

chapter 15
Assessment Through Standardized Testing 470

Standardized Tests 473
Functions of Standardized Tests 473
Types of Standardized Tests 475
Evaluating Standardized Tests: Validity Revisited 478

Understanding and Interpreting Standardized Test Scores 479
Descriptive Statistics 480
Interpreting Standardized Test Results 482

Accountability Issues in Standardized Testing 486
Standards-Based Education and Accountability 486
Testing Teachers 487
Accountability Issues in Standardized Testing: Implications for Teachers 488

Diversity and Standardized Testing 489
Student Diversity and Test Bias 489
Standardized Testing and English Language Learners 490

appendix A
Feedback for "Check your Understanding" Questions A-1

appendix B
Feedback for "Preparing for Your Licensure Exam" Questions B-1

appendix C
Using This Text to Practice for the Praxis™ *Principles of Learning and Teaching* Exam C-1

glossary G-1

references R-1

name index I-1

subject index I-9

special features and topics

Exceptional Applications and a Wealth of Classroom Examples

Authentic, Integrated Cases

Chapter 1 "*Professional Knowledge and Decision Making in Middle School Math*" Case Study begins on page 3 and is elaborated and/or referenced on pages 4, 6, 8, 10, 11, and 15.

Chapter 2 "*Promoting Learner Development in Eighth-Grade Science*" Case Study begins on page 29 and is elaborated and/or referenced on pages 34, 36, and 41.

Chapter 3 "*Examining Personal and Social Development in Middle School*" Case Study begins on page 61 and is elaborated and/or referenced on pages 68, 75, and 79.

Chapter 4 "*Dimensions of Learner Diversity in 3rd Grade*" Case Study begins on page 95.

Chapter 5 "*Learners with Exceptionalities in Elementary School*" Case Study begins on page 125 and is elaborated and/or referenced on pages 141 and 143.

Chapter 6 "*Behaviorist and Social Cognitive Principles in Algebra II*" Case Study begins on page 163 and is elaborated and/or referenced on pages 164, 165, 166, 167, 179, 180, 181, 182, 183, 185, and 187.

Chapter 7 "*Processing Information in Early Science*" Case Study begins on page 195 and is elaborated and/or referenced on pages 196, 197, 200, 201, 202, 203, 204, 205, 208, 209, 210, 211, 212, 214, and 216.

Chapter 8 "*Constructing Knowledge of Balance Beams in 4th Grade*" Case Study begins on page 225 and is elaborated and/or referenced on pages 226, 230, 231, 232, 233, 235, 236, 239, 240, 241, 242, 244, and 246.

Chapter 9 "*Solving an Area Problem in 5th-Grade Math*" Case Study begins on page 253 and is elaborated and/or referenced on pages 258, 259, 261, 262, 264, 266, 272, and 273.

Chapter 10 "*Increasing Learner Motivation in High School History*" Case Study begins on page 283 and is elaborated and/or referenced on pages 285, 287, 289, 293, 295, 298, 303, 304, 309, 310, and 312.

Chapter 11 "*Classroom Applications of Motivation in 5th Grade*" Case Study begins on page 319 and is elaborated and/or referenced on pages 330, 336, 337, 340, and 341.

Chapter 12 "*Classroom Management in Middle School*" Case Study begins on pages 351–352 and is elaborated and/or referenced on pages 353, 355, 361, 362, 366, 371, 373, 375, 378, and 381.

Chapter 13 "*Effective Instruction in Seventh Grade*" Case Study begins on page 389 and is elaborated and/or referenced on pages 391, 392, 393, 394, 395, 397, 399, 400, 401, 402, 404, 405, 406, 417, 418, 419, 424, and 425.

Chapter 14 "*Using Assessment to Increase Learning for 5th Graders*" Case Study begins on page 432 and is elaborated and/or referenced on pages 434, 438, 439, 440, 454, 455, 456, 457, and 458.

Chapter 15 "*Standardized Assessments in 4th Grade*" Case Study begins on page 471 and is elaborated and/or referenced on pages 474, 475, 483, 484, and 495.

Classroom Connections at Elementary, Middle, and High School Levels

Applying an Understanding of Piaget's Views of Development in Your Classroom 44

Applying Vygotsky's Theory of Development in Your Classroom 50

Promoting Language Development in Your Classroom 54

Applying Bronfenbrenner's Bioecological Theory in Your Classroom 66

Promoting Psychosocial and Self-Concept Development in Your Classroom 74

Applying an Understanding of Social Development in Your Classroom 78

Promoting Moral Development in Your Classroom 88

Working Effectively with Culturally and Linguistically Diverse Students in Your Classroom 105

Eliminating Gender Bias in Your Classroom 111

Using Effective Teaching Practices for Students Placed at Risk in Your Classroom 118

Applying an Understanding of Ability Differences in Your Classroom 132

Teaching Students with Exceptionalities in the General Education Classroom 156

Applying Classical Conditioning in Your Classroom 166

Applying Operant Conditioning in Your Classroom 178

Applying Social Cognitive Theory in Your Classroom 187

Applying an Understanding of Memory Stores in Your Classroom 206

Applying an Understanding of Cognitive Processes in Your Classroom 215

Applying an Understanding of Metacognition in Your Classroom 218

Promoting Conceptual Change in Your Classroom 238

Applying Constructivist Views of Learning in Your Classroom 245

Promoting Concept Learning in Your Classroom 257

Developing Your Students' Problem-Solving Abilities 267

Promoting Strategic Learning and Critical Thinking in Your Classroom 275

Promoting Transfer in Your Classroom 277

Applying an Understanding of Learners' Needs in Your Classroom 296

Applying an Understanding of Learners' Beliefs in Your Classroom 302

Capitalizing on Goals to Increase Motivation to Learn in Your Classroom 308

Capitalizing on Interest and Emotion to Promote Motivation to Learn in Your Classroom 311

Promoting Self-Regulation in Your Classroom 325
Demonstrating Personal Characteristics in the Model for Promoting Student Motivation in Your Classroom 331
Applying the Climate Variables in Your Classroom 335
Applying the Instructional Variables in the Model for Promoting Student Motivation in Your Classroom 345
Planning for Effective Classroom Management 367
Communicating Effectively with Parents 371
Using Interventions Successfully in Your Classroom 379
Applying an Understanding of Expert Planning in Your Classroom 398
Demonstrating Essential Teaching Skills in Your Classroom 407
Using Models of Instruction Effectively in Your Classroom 422
Capitalizing on Informal Assessments in Your Classroom 440
Creating Valid and Reliable Assessments in Your Classroom 453
Conducting Effective Assessment Practices in Your Classroom 459
Designing an Effective Assessment System in Your Classroom 464
Using Standardized Tests Effectively in Your Classroom 485
Eliminating Test Bias in Your Classroom 493

Theory to Practice

Conducting Research in Classrooms 21
Applying Piaget's Work in Your Classrooms 42
Applying Vygotsky's Theory in Your Classroom 48
Promoting Identity and Self-Concept Development in Your Classroom 72
Promoting Social Development in Your Classroom 77
Promoting Moral Development in Your Classroom 87
Teaching Culturally and Linguistically Diverse Students in Your Classroom 106
Responding to Gender Differences in Your Classroom 110
Teaching Students Placed at Risk in Your Classroom 116
Teaching Students Who Are Gifted and Talented 150
Teaching Students with Exceptionalities 155
Using Behaviorism in Your Classroom 177
Applying Social Cognitive Theory in Your Classroom 186
Applying an Understanding of the Human Memory Model in Your Classroom 220
Applying Constructivist Learning Theory in Your Classroom 244
Promoting Concept Learning in Your Classroom 256
Helping Learners Develop Their Problem-Solving Abilities 266
Helping Students Become Strategic Learners 273
Capitalizing on Learner's Needs to Increase Motivation to Learn 295
Capitalizing on Students' Beliefs, Goals, and Interests to Increase Motivation to Learn 312
Personal Qualities That Increase Motivation to Learn 330
Capitalizing on Climate and Instructional Variables to Increase Student Motivation to Learn 342
Creating and Teaching Classroom Rules 366
Responding Effectively to Misbehavior 381
The Theoretical Framework for Essential Teaching Skills 408
Increasing the Quality of Your Assessments 458
The Teacher's Role in Standardized Testing 492

Extensive Coverage of Diversity

Chapter Content Reflecting Issues of Student Diversity

Gender Differences: The Morality of Caring 85
Learning Contexts: Promoting Personal, Social, and Moral Development in Urban Environments 86
Chapter 4: Learner Diversity 94
Chapter 5: Learners with Exceptionalities 124
Developmental Differences in Memory Stores 205
Developmental Differences in Cognitive Processes 216
Developmental Differences in Metacognition 218
Sociocultural Learning Theory 228
Learning Contexts: Constructing Knowledge in Urban Environments 242
Learning Contexts: Increasing Motivation in Urban Classrooms 343
Developmental Differences Influence Classroom Management 356
Learning Contexts: Classroom Management in Urban Environments 364
Learning Contexts: Effective Instruction in Urban Classrooms 406
Diversity and Standardized Testing 489
Student Diversity and Assessment Bias 489
Standardized Testing and English Language Learners 490

Exploring Diversity

Teaching and Learning in Urban Environments 14
Language Development for Non-Native English Speakers 53
Ethnic Identity and Pride 73
Teaching and Learning in Urban Schools 120
Pursuing Equity in Special Education 151
Capitalizing on Behaviorism and Social Cognitive Theory with Learners from Diverse Backgrounds 190
The Impact of Diversity on Cognition 216
The Impact of Diversity on Knowledge Construction 237
Learner Differences in Complex Cognitive Processes 274
Learner Differences in Motivation to Learn 309
Personalizing Content to Increase Motivation to Learn in Students with Diverse Backgrounds 340
Classroom Management in Diverse Environments 380
Using Cooperative Learning to Capitalize on Diversity in Your Classroom 420
Effective Assessment Practices with Students from Diverse Backgrounds 463

Developmentally Appropriate Practice

Knowledge of Learners and Learning 12
Promoting Cognitive and Linguistic Development with Different-Aged Learners 55
Personal, Social, and Moral Development with Different-Aged Learners 89
Diversity in Students at Different Ages 119
Students with Exceptionalities at Different Ages 157
Applying Behaviorism and Social Cognitive Theory with Different-Aged Learners 189
Applying the Model of Memory with Different-Aged Learners 219
Applying Constructivist Learning Theory with Different-Aged Learners 246
Developing Complex Cognitive Skills with Different-Aged Learners 278
Motivation to Learn at Different Ages 313
Applying the Model for Promoting Student Motivation with Learners at Different Ages 346
Classroom Management with Different-Aged Learners 384
Using Models of Instruction for Different-Aged Learners 423
Assessment of Learning with Different-Aged Students 465
Standardized Testing with Different-Aged Learners 494

Innovative Learning Technology

Activities and Applications Exercises That Foster the Application of Chapter Concepts Are Integrated with Text Content Through Margin Notes

Demonstrating Knowledge in Classrooms 10
The Principal's View of Professionalism 13
Increasing Professional Knowledge with Research 21
Developmental Differences: Studying Properties of Air in First Grade 36
Examining Learner Thinking: Piaget's Conservation Tasks 39
Advancing Cognitive Development in Middle School Students 49
Friendships 64
Moral Reasoning: Examining a Moral Dilemma 84
Social and Moral Development in Middle School Students 88
Culturally Responsive Teaching 101
The Effective Teacher 105
Reviewing an IEP 137
Analyzing Exceptionalities in a First-Grade Class 153
Using Peer Tutoring with Students Having Exceptionalities 155
Behaviorism in the Workplace 172
Behaviorism in the Classroom 178
Demonstrating Problem Solving in High School Chemistry 188
The Number 3 200
Applying Information Processing: Attracting Students' Attention 208
Five Brain Coral 213
Teaching the Solar System 220
Constructing Knowledge of Balance Beams 233
Constructivist Instruction in Fifth Grade 243
The Scarlet Letter in High School English 244
Constructing Concepts: Using Concrete Examples 256
Using a Problem-Solving Model: Finding Area in Elementary Math 262
Video 1: Memory and Cognition: Early and Middle Childhood 271
Video 2: Memory and Cognition: Early and Late Adolescence 271
Finding Areas of Irregular Figures 274
Pig Dissection 287
Classroom Environments and Motivation 289
Motivation 310
Introductory Focus: Attracting Students' Attention 338
Guiding Students' Problem Solving: Graphing in Second Grade 341
Instruction and Motivation to Learn 347
Establishing and Practicing Classroom Rules 361
Establishing Rules and Procedures at the Beginning of the School Year 363
Using a Behavioral Management System 377
Analyzing Instructional Alignment 395
Guided Discovery in the Elementary Classroom 419
Models of Instruction in Elementary Math 420
Pig Lungs Dissection 451
Using Assessment in Decision Making 451
Assessment in Middle School Math 459
Validity in Standardized Testing 479
Descriptive Statistic in Standardized Testing 482
Analyzing Standardized Testing 491

Building Teaching Skills and Dispositions Exercises Provide Interactive Practice Applying the Core Principles and Concepts of Educational Psychology. These Exercises Are Integrated with Text Content Through Margin Notes.

Improving Teaching with Research and Theory 22
Constructing Knowledge of Balance Beams 53
The Scarlet Letter in High School English 76
Creating an Inclusive Classroom 155
Applied Behavior Analysis in Elementary Schools 176
Applying Information Processing: Organizing Content 210
Author's Chair 229
Designing Experiments 279
Applying Cognitive Motivation Theory: Writing Paragraphs in Fifth Grade 308
Applying the Motivation Model: Studying Arthropods in Fifth Grade 343
Communicating Effectively with Parents 370
Essential Teaching Skills in an Urban Classroom 409
Colonial America Exam 446
Interpreting Standardized Test Results 486

photo credits

Comstock Royalty Free Division, p. 2; Bill Aron/PhotoEdit Inc., pp. 14, 240, 430; David Young–Wolff/PhotoEdit Inc., pp. 15, 128, 227; Katelyn Metzger/Merrill, pp. 20, 147, 329; Myrleen Ferguson Cate/PhotoEdit Inc., p. 28; Richard Hutchings/PhotoEdit Inc., pp. 30, 404; Ken Karp/Prentice Hall School Division, p. 37; Anthony Magnacca/Merrill, pp. 38, 78, 79, 85, 134, 153, 259, 277, 358, 360, 462; © Jose Luiz Pelaez, Inc./CORBIS, p. 41 (top); Michael Newman/PhotoEdit Inc., pp. 41 (bottom), 73, 181, 224, 237, 304, 350, 364, 368, 412, 463; Laura Dwight/Corbis/Bettmann, p. 43; George Dodson/PH College, p. 50; © Richard Hutchings/CORBIS All Rights Reserved, p. 60; Mary Kate Denny/PhotoEdit Inc., pp. 68, 80, 86, 333; David Grossman/The Image Works, p. 69; T. Lindfors/Lindfors Photography, pp. 71, 318, 353; Patrick White/Merrill, p. 76; Will Hart/PhotoEdit Inc., pp. 82, 102, 265, 417, 419; Robin Sachs/PhotoEdit Inc., p. 94; Rhoda Sidney/PH College, p. 98; Scott Cunningham/Merrill, pp. 106, 109, 204, 449; Getty Images, Inc., p. 107; PunchStock, p. 115; Bob Daemmrich/PhotoEdit Inc., pp. 124, 388; Realistic Reflections/Getty Images – Creative Express Royalty Free, p. 135 (top); Spencer Grant/PhotoEdit Inc., p. 135 (bottom), 166; Will & Deni McIntyre/Photo Researchers, Inc., p. 139; Catherine Ledner/Getty Images, Inc. – Stone Allstock, p. 141; Todd Yarrington/Merrill, p. 144; Paul Conklin/PhotoEdit Inc., p. 145; Tony Freeman/PhotoEdit Inc., pp. 150, 154, 470; Spencer Grant/Photo Researchers, Inc., pp. 162, 456, 474; Christina Kennedy/PhotoEdit Inc., p. 169; © Ellen B. Senisi/Ellen Senisi, p. 173; Masterfile Royalty Free Division, p. 174; Andy Sacks/Getty Images Inc. – Stone Allstock, p. 185; Jim West/The Image Works, p. 194; Tom Watson/Merrill, pp. 200, 266, 374; David Mager/Pearson Learning Photo Studio, pp. 211, 254; Peter Skinner/Photo Researchers, Inc., p. 213; Bob Daemmrich/The Image Works, p. 216; Elizabeth Crews/Elizabeth Crews Photography, pp. 228, 345; Frank Siteman, p. 231; Murray Lee/AGE Fotostock America, Inc., p. 252; Frank Siteman/PhotoEdit Inc., p. 272; Adrian Weinbrecht/Getty Images – DK Stock, p. 282; Getty Images – Stockbyte, pp. 285, 287; Bob Daemmrich Photography, Inc., pp. 288, 292, 327; Mary Kate Denny/Getty Images Inc. – Stone Allstock, p. 289; Liz Moore/Merrill, p. 294; © Royalty-Free/CORBIS, p. 300; Corbis Royalty Free, pp. 302, 437, 451; GeoStock/Getty Images, Inc. – Photodisc, pp. 306, 447; Valerie Schultz/Merrill, p. 310; Robert Harbison, p. 337; Lori Whitley/Merrill, pp. 341, 401; Pearson Scott Foresman, p. 357; SW Productions/Getty Images–Photodisc, p. 362; Bob Daemmrich/Bob Daemmrich Photography, Inc., pp. 373, 493; KS Studios/Merrill, p. 378; Elena Rooraid/PhotoEdit Inc., p. 382; Davis Barber/PhotoEdit Inc., p. 402; Image 100, p. 403; © Tim Pannell/Corbis, p. 409; Doug Menuez/Getty Images, Inc. – Photodisc, p. 415; David Buffington/Getty Images, Inc. – Photodisc, p. 444; Steve Lyne, Rex Interstock/Stock Connection/Picture Quest, p. 487; Photos.com, p. 490.

chapter 1

Educational Psychology

Developing a Professional Knowledge Base

chapter outline

Educational Psychology and Becoming a Professional

- Characteristics of Professionalism

Professional Knowledge and Learning to Teach

- Knowledge of Content
- Pedagogical Content Knowledge
- General Pedagogical Knowledge
- Knowledge of Learners and Learning
  - **Developmentally Appropriate Practice:** Knowledge of Learners and Learning
- Professional Knowledge: Reform and Accountability
  - **Exploring Diversity:** Teaching and Learning in Urban Environments

The Role of Research in Acquiring Professional Knowledge

- Descriptive Research
- Correlational Research
- Experimental Research
- Qualitative Research
- Scientifically Based Research in Education
- Action Research
- Research and the Development of Theory
  - **Theory to Practice:** Conducting Research in Classrooms

The Use of Case Studies in Educational Psychology

learning objectives

After you have completed your study of this chapter, you should be able to:

1. Describe the characteristics of professionalism, and identify examples of these characteristics in teachers' actions.
2. Describe the different kinds of knowledge professional teachers possess, and identify examples of professional knowledge in teachers' actions.
3. Describe different types of research, and analyze applications of these types.
4. Explain how using case studies that place educational psychology in real-world contexts makes it meaningful.

"Demanding," "challenging," "exciting," and "rewarding" are just a few of the many adjectives used to describe teaching. Think about these descriptions as you read the following case study, and ask yourself how educational psychology might be related to both the descriptions of teaching and the experiences of the teachers in the case study.

> As Keith Jackson, in his first year as a math teacher at Lakeside Middle School, walks into the work room, Jan Davis, a veteran who has become Keith's confidant, asks, "Hi, Keith. How's it going?"
>
> "My last period class is getting to me," Keith replies. "The students are okay when we stick to mechanics, but they simply can't do word problems. . . . They just try to memorize formulas.
>
> "I have a good math background, and I was going to be so great when I got here. . . . I'm not so sure any more. . . . I explain the stuff so carefully, but some of the kids just sit with blank looks on their faces.
>
> "Then, there's Kelly. She disrupts everything I do. I gave her a referral, and I even called her mother. . . . The only thing that seemed to work was taking her aside and asking her straight out why she was giving me such a hard time."
>
> "You're becoming a *teacher*," Jan smiles. "There are few easy answers for what we do. . . . But then, that's what makes it so challenging, . . . and rewarding when we succeed.
>
> "Like working with Kelly. She might not have another adult she can talk to, and she may simply need someone to care about her.

"And, for the blank looks, I'm taking a class at the university. The instructor emphasizes involving the kids, and he keeps talking about research that says how important it is to call on all the kids as equally as possible.

"So, here's an example of what I'm trying to do more of now. We were reviewing decimals and percents, so I brought in a 12-ounce soft drink can from a machine, a 20-ounce bottle, and a 6-pack with price tags on them.

I put the kids into pairs and told them to figure out a way to determine which one was the best buy. I helped them along, and we created a table, so we could compare the groups' answers. They're beginning to see how math relates to their lives. . . . And, now that they're all used to being called on, they really like it. It's one of the most important things I do.

"When I think about it, I realize that I sometimes jump in too soon when they can figure it out themselves, and at other times I let them stumble around too long and they waste time. So, then I adapt for the next lesson."

"I hate to admit this," Keith says, "but some of my university courses suggested just what you did. It was fun, but I didn't think it was real teaching."

"You couldn't relate to it at the time. You didn't have a class with live students who 'didn't get it.'

"Hang in there," Jan smiles. "You're becoming what teaching needs—a pro."

Educational psychology. The academic discipline that focuses on human teaching and learning.

Welcome to **educational psychology**, the academic discipline that focuses on human teaching and learning (Berliner, 2006). Let's begin our study of this discipline by considering three questions.

1. What does it mean to be a "professional"?
2. What characteristics did Jan and Keith demonstrate that suggested they are professionals?
3. How might educational psychology help you meet the demands and challenges of teaching while also increasing the rewards and excitement?

We answer these and other questions about teaching and learning in this chapter. We begin with a discussion of teacher professionalism and how educational psychology contributes to it.

Educational Psychology and Becoming a Professional

Teacher professionalism and its impact on student learning are receiving increasing attention in American education. Policy makers are raising the standards for teachers and are asking teachers to become professionals who know and can do more (Bransford, Darling-Hammond, & LePage, 2005; Darling-Hammond & Baratz-Snowdon, 2005).

Let's see what *professionalism* means.

Characteristics of Professionalism

Definitions of professionalism vary, but most include the following characteristics (Ingersoll, 2003):

- A commitment to learners that includes a code of ethics
- The ability to make decisions in complex and ill-defined contexts
- Reflective practice
- A body of specialized knowledge

These characteristics help answer our first question, "What does it mean to be a 'professional'?" They are outlined in Figure 1.1 and discussed in the sections that follow.

Commitment to Learners

Keith and Jan both demonstrated professionalism in their commitment to their students. Keith began their conversation by describing his concerns about both his last-period class and Kelly,

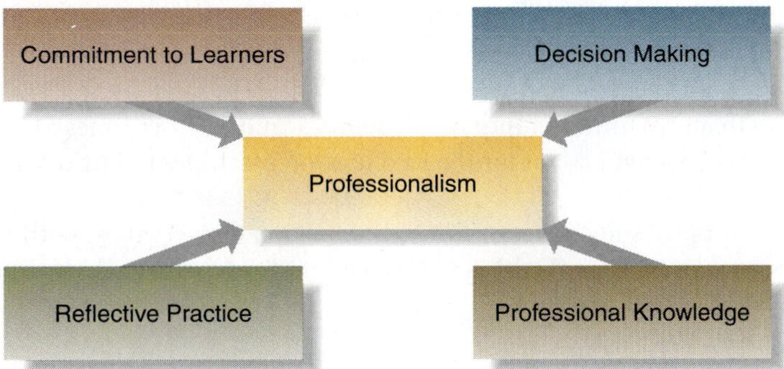

Figure 1.1 Characteristics of professionalism

who was giving him a hard time. Someone less professional might have abandoned word problems and written Kelly off as incorrigible, doing whatever it took to eliminate her distractions and letting it go at that.

Jan was equally committed, and because of her experience, her comments were more sophisticated than Keith's. For instance, she modified her instruction to increase student involvement and motivation, and she attempted to grow professionally by studying and taking extra courses.

Some authors describe commitment as *professional caring*. "A professional doesn't view his or her profession as just a job, but rather sees it as a *calling* that is all about caring for children" (Kramer, 2003, p. 23).

Decision Making

Professionals also have the ability to make decisions in complex and ill-defined situations. As Jan commented to Keith, "There are few easy answers for what we do. . . . But then, that's what makes it so challenging, . . . and rewarding when we succeed."

In her lesson on decimals and percents, Jan made decisions about the following:

- The learning objectives for her lesson
- The strategy she would implement to help students reach the objectives
- The examples she would use
- The sequence of activities she would follow during the lesson
- Which students she would call on and the order in which she would call on them
- The specific questions she would ask
- How she would respond to students after they answered or failed to answer a question

Teachers make a staggering number of decisions; some historical research suggests as many as 800 per day (Jackson, 1968). And, no one helps them make the decisions; teachers are essentially on their own. As they acquire knowledge and experience, however, they learn to make these decisions routinely and efficiently (Berliner, 1994, 2000).

Reflective Practice

Every professional decision we make is designed to increase learning and learner development. So the process of decision making centers on one simple question: "Did this decision increase learning as much as possible?" If it did, it was a good decision; if it didn't, we need to make changes in the future.

The question, though simple, isn't easy to answer, because teachers receive little feedback about the effectiveness of their work. Administrators observe them a few times a year at most, and teachers receive only vague and sketchy feedback from students and parents. In addition, they get virtually no feedback from their colleagues, unless the school has a peer-coaching or mentoring program. To improve, teachers must be able to answer the question by assessing their own classroom performance.

The ability to conduct this self-assessment can be developed, but it requires a willingness to critically examine our actions. This is the essence of a powerful idea called **reflective practice**, the process of conducting a critical self-examination of one's teaching (Clarke, 2006).

Reflective practice. The process of conducting a critical self-examination of one's teaching.

Research suggests that reflective practice can help teachers become more sensitive to individual student differences (Berrill & Whalen, 2007) and can make them more aware of the impact of their instruction on learning (Gimbel, 2008). For example, Jan's comment, "When I think about it, I realize that sometimes I jump in too soon . . . and at other times I let them stumble around too long. . . . So, then I adapt for the next lesson," illustrates reflection and its influence on her instruction.

Her ability to improve her practice through reflection depended on both her experience and her professional knowledge (Helsing, 2007). Let's look at this knowledge in more detail.

Professional Knowledge

Professionals make decisions in ill-defined situations and reflect on those decisions to improve their teaching. But, a professional like Jan didn't make and reflect on her decisions based on intuition, whim, or emotion; they were grounded in a vast store of professional knowledge (Hogan, Rabinowitz & Craven, 2003). For example, her decision to call on all her students equally was based on research indicating that this practice increases student achievement. And, her decision to use the containers of soft drinks as the framework for her lesson was grounded in theory and research indicating that real-world applications increase both learning and motivation (Putnam & Borko, 2000). The fact that Keith was less knowledgeable helps explain some of his difficulties. Making decisions based on knowledge and using that knowledge as a basis for reflection is the core of professionalism.

> The accumulation of richly structured and accessible bodies of knowledge allows individuals to engage in expert thinking and action. In studies of teaching, this understanding of expertise has led researchers to devote increased attention to teachers' knowledge and its organization. (Borko & Putnam, 1996, p. 674)

This is the reason you're studying educational psychology; it provides a professional knowledge base that will help you make decisions that maximize student learning. It also helps answer the third question we asked at the beginning of the chapter: "How might educational psychology help you meet the demands and challenges of teaching while also increasing the rewards and excitement?" The more knowledgeable you are, the better able you will be to meet the demands and challenges of teaching, and the better able you will be to capitalize on its excitement and rewards. We examine this knowledge base in more detail in the next section.

check your understanding

1.1 Describe and explain the characteristics of professionalism.

1.2 Identify three ways in which Keith demonstrated the characteristics of professionalism in his conversation with Jan.

1.3 Explain how Jan demonstrated each of the characteristics of professionalism in her conversation with Keith.

1.4 Using the characteristics of professionalism as a basis, describe the primary difference between Keith's and Jan's level of professional behavior.

To receive feedback for these questions, go to Appendix A.

Professional Knowledge and Learning to Teach

In the previous section, we emphasized the importance of knowledge as an essential element of professionalism. Now, we want to examine this knowledge in more detail.

To begin, complete the following Learning and Teaching Inventory, designed to provide a brief introduction to the different kinds of knowledge needed to understand students, ourselves, and the way learning occurs. Decide if each item is true or false.

Learning and Teaching Inventory

1. The thinking of children in elementary schools tends to be limited to the concrete and tangible, whereas the thinking of middle and high school students tends to be abstract.
2. Students generally understand how much they know about a topic.
3. Experts in the area of intelligence view knowledge of facts (e.g., "On what continent is Brazil?") as one indicator of intelligence.
4. Effective teaching is essentially a process of presenting information to students in succinct and organized ways.
5. Preservice teachers who major in a content area, such as math, are much more successful than nonmajors in providing clear examples of the ideas they teach.
6. To increase students' motivation to learn, teachers should praise as much as possible.
7. Teachers who are the most successful at creating and maintaining orderly classrooms are those who can quickly stop disruptions when they occur.
8. Preservice teachers generally believe they will be more effective than teachers who are already in the field.
9. Teachers learn by teaching; in general, experience is the primary factor involved in learning to teach.
10. Testing detracts from learning, because students who are tested frequently develop negative attitudes and usually learn less than those who are tested less often.

Let's see how you did. The answers for each item are outlined in the following paragraphs. As you read the answers, remember that they describe students or other people in general, and exceptions will exist.

1. *The thinking of children in elementary schools tends to be limited to the concrete and tangible, whereas the thinking of middle and high school students tends to be abstract.*
   False: Research indicates that middle school, high school, and even university students think effectively in the abstract only when they have considerable experience and expertise related to the topic they're studying (P. Alexander, 2006; M. Cole, Cole, & Lightfoot, 2005). When you study the development of students' thinking in Chapter 2, you'll see how understanding this research can improve your teaching.
2. *Students generally understand how much they know about a topic.*
   False: Learners in general, and young children in particular, often cannot accurately assess their own understanding (Hacker, Bol, Horgan, & Rakow, 2000; Schommer, 1994). Students' awareness of what they know and how they learn strongly influences understanding, and cognitive learning theory helps us understand why. (You will study cognitive learning theory in Chapters 7 to 9.)
3. *Experts in the area of intelligence view knowledge of facts (e.g., "On what continent is Brazil?") as one indicator of intelligence.*
   True: The Wechsler Intelligence Scale for Children—Fourth Edition (Wechsler, 2003), the most popular intelligence test in use today, has several items similar to this example. Theories of intelligence, which you will study in Chapter 5, examine issues and controversies related to learner intelligence.
4. *Effective teaching is essentially a process of presenting information to students in succinct and organized ways.*
   False: As we better understand learning, we find that simply explaining information to students is often ineffective for promoting understanding (Bransford, Brown, & Cocking, 2000; R. Mayer, 2008). Learners construct their own knowledge based on what they already know, and their emotions, beliefs, and expectations all influence the process (Bruning, Schraw, Norby, & Ronning, 2004; Schunk, Pintrich, & Meese, 2008). (You will examine the processes involved in constructing knowledge in Chapter 8.)
5. *Preservice teachers who major in a content area, such as math, are much more successful than nonmajors in providing clear examples of the ideas they teach.*
   False: One of the most pervasive misconceptions about teaching is the idea that knowledge of subject matter is all that is necessary to teach effectively. In one study of teacher candidates, math majors were no more capable than nonmajors of effectively illustrating and representing math concepts in ways that learners could understand (National Center for Research on Teacher Learning, 1993). Knowledge of content is essential, but

understanding how to make that content meaningful to students requires an additional kind of knowledge (Darling-Hammond & Baratz-Snowdon, 2005). (You will study ways of making knowledge accessible to learners in Chapters 2, 6–9, and 13.)

6. *To increase students' motivation to learn, teachers should praise as much as possible.*
   False: Although appropriate use of praise is important, overuse detracts from its credibility. This is particularly true for older students who discount praise if they believe it is unwarranted or invalid. Older students may also interpret praise given for easy tasks as indicating that the teacher thinks they have low ability (Schunk, et al., 2008). Your study of motivation in Chapters 10 and 11 will help you understand this and other factors influencing students' desire to learn.
7. *Teachers who are the most successful at creating and maintaining orderly classrooms are those who can quickly stop disruptions when they occur.*
   False: Research indicates that classroom management, one of the greatest concerns of beginning teachers, is most effective when teachers prevent management problems from occurring in the first place, instead of responding to problems when they occur (Brophy, 2006b; Emmer, Evertson, & Worsham, 2006; Evertson, Emmer, & Worsham, 2006). (You will study classroom management in Chapter 12.)
8. *Preservice teachers generally believe they will be more effective than teachers who are already in the field.*
   True: Preservice teachers (like yourself) are often optimistic and idealistic. They believe they'll be effective with young people, and they generally believe they'll be better than teachers now in the field (Feiman-Nemser, 2001; Ingersoll & Smith, 2004). They are also sometimes "shocked" when they begin work and face the challenge of teaching on their own for the first time (Grant, 2006; S. Johnson & Birkeland, 2003). Keith's comments in the opening case study illustrate the experience of many beginning teachers: "I was going to be so great when I got here. . . . I'm not so sure anymore." The more knowledge you have about teaching, learning, and learners, the better prepared you'll be to cope with the realities of your first job.
9. *Teachers learn by teaching; in general, experience is the primary factor involved in learning to teach.*
   False: Experience is essential in learning to teach, but it isn't sufficient by itself (Darling-Hammond & Bransford, 2005; Helsing, 2007). In some cases, experience results in repeating the same actions year after year, regardless of their effectiveness. Knowledge of learners and learning, combined with experience, however, can lead to high levels of teaching expertise.
10. *Testing detracts from learning, because students who are tested frequently develop negative attitudes and usually learn less than those who are tested less often.*
    False: In comprehensive reviews of the literature on assessment, experts have found that frequent, thorough assessment is one of the most powerful and positive influences on learning (Bransford et al., 2000; Stiggins, 2007; Stiggins & Chappuis, 2006). (You will study assessment and its role in learning in Chapters 14 and 15.)

The items you've just examined give a brief sampling of the different kinds of knowledge teachers need to help students learn.

Let's examine this knowledge in more detail. Research indicates that four different kinds are essential for expert teaching:

- Knowledge of content
- Pedagogical content knowledge
- General pedagogical knowledge
- Knowledge of learners and learning (Darling-Hammond & Baratz-Snowdon, 2005; Shulman, 1987)

Knowledge of Content

We can't teach what we don't understand. This self-evident statement has been well documented by research examining the relationships between what teachers know and how they teach (Bransford et al., 2005; Darling-Hammond & Baratz-Snowdon, 2005; Shulman, 1986). To effectively teach about the American Revolutionary War, for example, a social studies teacher must know not only basic facts about the war but also how the war relates to other aspects of history, such as the French and Indian War, the colonies' relationship with England before the Revolution, and the unique characteristics of the colonies. The same is true for any topic in other content area.

Pedagogical Content Knowledge

Pedagogical content knowledge is an understanding of how to represent topics in ways that make them understandable to learners, as well as an understanding of what makes specific topics easy or hard to learn (Darling-Hammond & Bransford, 2005; Shulman, 1986). In addition, some experts suggest that understanding student motivation is also part of pedagogical content knowledge (Brophy, 2004; McCaughtry, 2004).

Pedagogical content knowledge. An understanding of how to represent topics in ways that make them understandable to learners, as well as an understanding of what makes specific topics easy or hard to learn.

Knowledge of content and pedagogical content knowledge are closely related, but they are not identical. For example, understanding the factors that led to the American Revolution reflects knowledge of content; knowing how to illustrate this content so students can understand it reflects pedagogical content knowledge. Both are needed to make topics meaningful (Loughran, Mulhall, & Berry, 2004; Segall, 2004).

To illustrate the role of pedagogical content knowledge in expert teaching, think about how you might help fifth graders understand the process of multiplying fractions, such as 1/4 × 1/3 = 1/12. This is neither easy to understand nor easy to teach. Experience indicates that the product of two numbers is larger than either (e.g., 6 × 5 = 30), but with fractions the product is smaller. As a result, students often simply memorize the process with little understanding.

Now, try the following activity. Fold a sheet of plain paper into thirds, and shade the center one third of the paper, as shown:

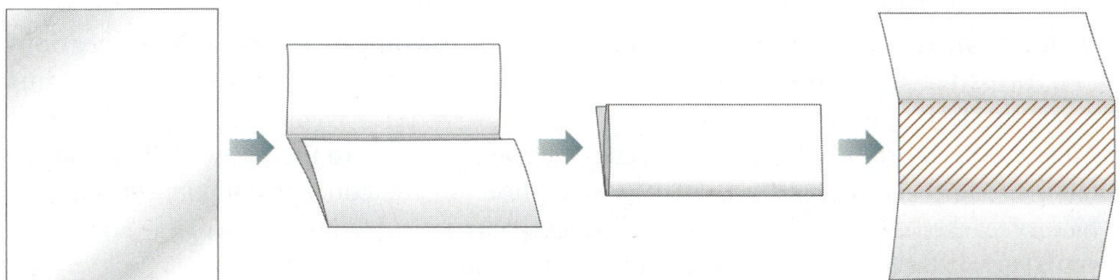

Now, refold your paper so that the shaded third is exposed:

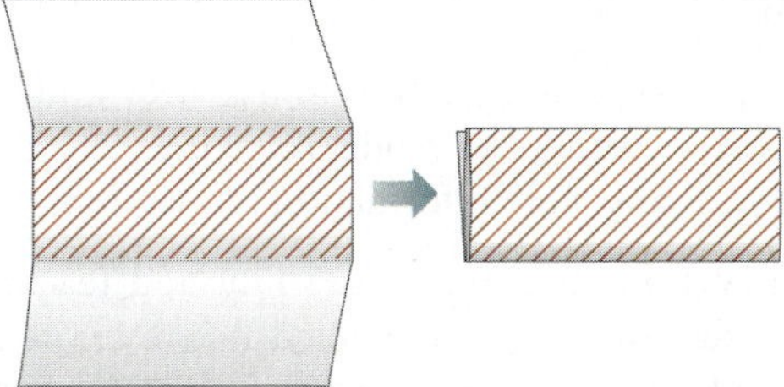

Now fold the paper in half, and in half again, so that one fourth of the shaded one third is visible. Put additional shading on that portion, and then unfold the paper, as shown:

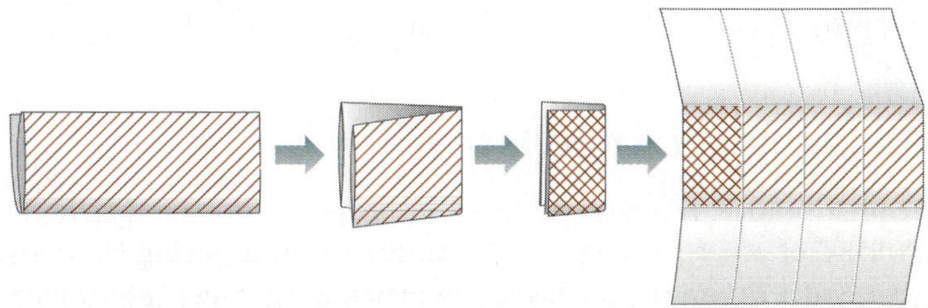

You've just prepared a concrete example demonstrating that 1/4 × 1/3 = 1/12 (the cross-hatched portion of the paper). This example helps students see that the product of multiplying two fractions results in a smaller number and also helps them apply their understanding in real-world settings (R. Mayer, 2008). This is why pedagogical content knowledge is so important. Without examples like this one, students grasp what they can, memorize as much as possible, and little understanding develops (Bransford et al., 2000; Donovan & Bransford, 2005).

As Keith's pedagogical content knowledge increases, he will better understand why "The students are okay when we stick to mechanics, but they simply can't do word problems." He tended to rely on verbal explanations—"I explain the stuff so carefully"—because he lacked the pedagogical content knowledge to illustrate topics so that his students could understand them. In contrast, Jan used real-world examples, the containers of soft drinks, to illustrate her topic, demonstrating her more advanced pedagogical content knowledge.

Teachers can represent content in several ways:

- *Examples.* A fifth-grade math teacher uses pieces of chocolate to illustrate equivalent fractions (demonstrated in the opening case study in Chapter 14). An eighth-grade physical science teacher compresses cotton in a drink cup to illustrate the concept *density* (shown in the opening case study of Chapter 2).
- *Demonstrations.* A first-grade teacher uses water to demonstrate that air takes up space and exerts pressure (illustrated in the closing case study of Chapter 2). A middle school teacher demonstrates the concept *force* by pushing on the board and blowing on an object on his desk (shown in the case study beginning on p. 399 in Chapter 13).
- *Case studies.* We use case studies throughout this text to illustrate the topics you're studying. Along with vignettes (short case studies), they illustrate complex and difficult-to-represent topics. For instance, an English teacher illustrated the concept *internal conflict* with this brief vignette:

  > *Andrea didn't know what to do. She was looking forward to the class trip, but if she went, she wouldn't be able to take the scholarship-qualifying test.*

  In addition, analysis of video cases, such as the ones you can access on MyEducationLab, helps teachers think about connections between teaching and student learning (Siegel, 2002).
- *Metaphors.* A world history teacher uses her students' loyalty to their school, their ways of talking, and their weekend activities as metaphors for the concept *nationalism.* Another history teacher uses her class's "crusade" for extracurricular activities as a metaphor for the actual Crusades (illustrated in the opening case study of Chapter 10).
- *Simulations.* An American government teacher creates a mock trial to simulate the workings of our country's judicial system, and a history teacher has students role-play delegates in a simulated Continental Congress to help his students understand forces that shaped our country.
- *Models.* A science teacher uses a model of an atom to help students visualize the organization of the nucleus and electrons. The model in Figure 7.1 (on page 198) helps us think about the ways we process and store information in memory.

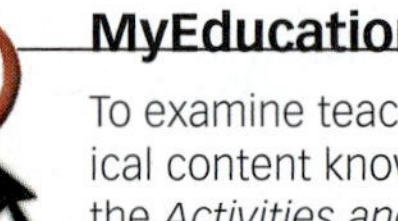

MyEducationLab

To examine teachers' pedagogical content knowledge, go to the *Activities and Applications* section in Chapter 1 of MyEducationLab at www.myeducationlab.com, and watch the episode *Demonstrating Knowledge in Classrooms*. Answer the questions following the episode.

From this list, we can see why item 5 on the Learning and Teaching Inventory is false. Majoring in math does not ensure that a teacher will be able to create examples like the one involving the multiplication of fractions, and majoring in history does not ensure that a social studies teacher will think of using a school's extracurricular activities as a metaphor for the Crusades. The ability to do so requires both a clear understanding of content and pedagogical content knowledge. If either is lacking, teachers commonly paraphrase information in learners' textbooks or provide abstract explanations that aren't meaningful to their students.

General Pedagogical Knowledge

General pedagogical knowledge. An understanding of essential principles of instruction and classroom management that transcends individual topics or subject matter areas.

Knowledge of content and pedagogical content knowledge are domain specific; that is, they are related to knowledge of a particular content area, such as multiplying fractions, the concept *density*, or the Crusades. In comparison, **general pedagogical knowledge** involves an understanding of essential principles of instruction and classroom management that transcends individual topics or subject matter areas (Borko & Putnam, 1996; Darling-Hammond & Bransford, 2005).

Instructional Strategies

Instructional strategies are important components of general pedagogical knowledge. Regardless of the content area or grade level, teachers need to know how to involve students in learning, check their understanding, and keep lessons running smoothly. For example, Jan applied an important strategy when she called on all her students as equally as possible (Good & Brophy, 2008). Though she was teaching middle school math, calling on students equally is important regardless of the topic or grade level. Similarly, teachers must communicate clearly, provide feedback, and perform a variety of other skills to maximize learning. You will study these aspects of general pedagogical knowledge in detail in Chapter 13.

Classroom Management

Classroom management is a second major component of general pedagogical knowledge. All teachers need to create classroom environments that are safe, orderly, and focused on learning (Emmer et al., 2006; Evertson et al., 2006). Creating these environments requires that teachers know how to plan, implement, and monitor rules and procedures; organize groups; and intervene when misbehavior occurs. The complexities of these processes help us see why item 7 in the Learning and Teaching Inventory is false. It is impossible to maintain an orderly classroom if we wait for misbehavior to occur. Classroom environments must be designed to prevent, rather than stop, disruptions. Chapter 12 describes how to do this in your classroom.

Knowledge of Learners and Learning

Knowledge of learners and learning is essential, "arguably the most important knowledge a teacher can have" (Borko & Putnam, 1996, p. 675). Let's see how this knowledge can influence the way we teach.

Knowledge of Learners

Items 1, 2, and 6 in the Learning and Teaching Inventory all involve knowledge of learners, and each has important implications for the way you teach. For instance, you learned from item 1 that students need to have abstract ideas illustrated with concrete examples, and this is true for older as well as for younger students. Chapter 2, which focuses on cognitive development, describes how understanding learners increases your pedagogical content knowledge and helps you provide meaningful representations, such as the example of multiplying fractions.

Item 2 suggests that learners often aren't good judges of either how much they know or the ways they learn. Chapter 7, which discusses the development of metacognition, helps you understand how to guide your students toward becoming more knowledgeable about themselves and more strategic in their approaches to learning (Bruning et al., 2004).

Item 6 has implications for the ways you interact with your students. Intuitively, it seems that providing as much praise as possible is both desirable and effective. However, research and theories of motivation, which you will study in Chapters 10 and 11, help you understand why this isn't always the case.

Knowledge of Learning

As we better understand the ways people learn, we can understand why item 4 on the Learning and Teaching Inventory is false. For example, evidence overwhelmingly indicates that people don't behave like tape recorders; they don't simply record in memory what they hear or read. Rather, in their attempt to make sense of it, they interpret information in personal and sometimes idiosyncratic ways (Bransford et al., 2000; R. Mayer, 2002). In the process, meaning can be distorted, sometimes profoundly. For instance, look at the following statements, actually made by students:

> "The phases of the moon are caused by clouds blocking out the unseen parts."
> "Coats keep us warm by generating heat, like a stove or radiator."
> "A triangle which has an angle of 135 degrees is called an obscene triangle."

developmentally appropriate practice

Knowledge of Learners and Learning

Developmental differences. Differences in students' thinking, memory, emotions, and social relationships that result from maturation and different kinds of experiences.

Developmentally appropriate practice. Instructional practice that matches teacher actions to the capabilities and needs of learners at different developmental levels.

While much of what we know about learners and learning applies to students of all ages, developmental differences exist. **Developmental differences** refer to differences in students' thinking, memory, emotions, and social relationships that result from maturation and different kinds of experiences.

Because of the important influence of development on learning, this edition of the text includes a new feature titled "Developmentally Appropriate Practice" that appears in each chapter. **Developmentally appropriate practice** refers to instructional practices that match teacher actions to the capabilities and needs of learners at different developmental levels. The feature describes ways to adapt the chapter's content to the different learning needs of elementary, middle school, and high school learners.

The following paragraphs briefly illustrate the feature as it appears in subsequent chapters.

FAMILY CIRCUS

"How do they fit so much water in that little spigot?"

Source: Family Circus © Bil Keane, Inc. King Features Syndicate.

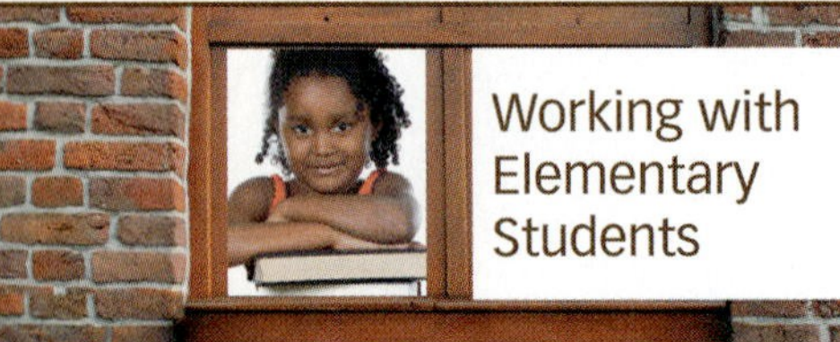

Working with Elementary Students

Young children's thinking differs from that of older students. As an example, look at the accompanying cartoon. Wondering how all the water could fit in the spigot is characteristic of the thinking of young children. Older students would of course realize that a vast reservoir of water exists that we can't see. Young children's personal and social characteristics also differ from those of older students. We examine these characteristics in each of the chapters in the book.

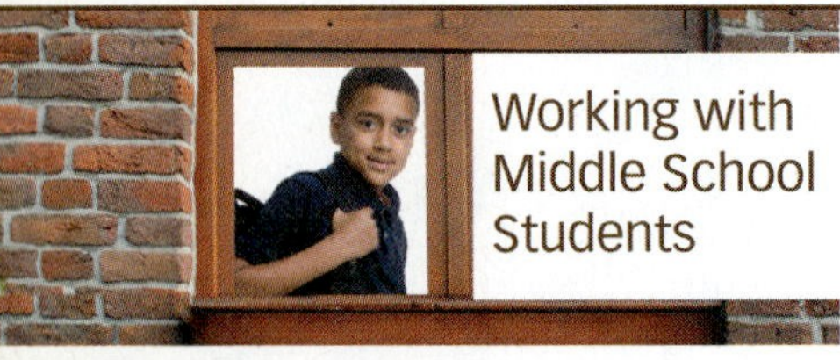

Working with Middle School Students

As a result of maturation and a variety of experiences, the thinking, social skills, and other characteristics of middle school students differ from those of young children. For example, middle school students are more likely than younger learners to realize that they don't understand an idea the class is discussing and raise their hands to ask for an explanation or clarification. Many other differences exist between middle school learners and their younger counterparts.

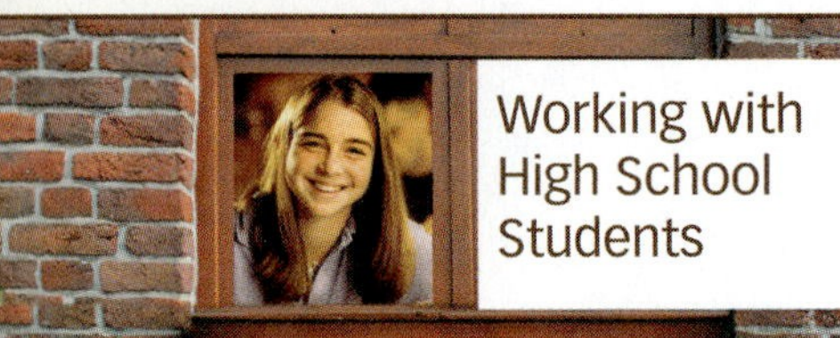

Working with High School Students

As with differences between elementary and middle school students, additional differences exist between learners in high school and their younger peers. For example, many high school students are quite mature, and speaking to them about personal and social issues on an adult-to-adult level can be more effective than it would be with younger students. They are capable of more abstract thinking than are their younger counterparts, although they still need concrete examples to understand new or difficult topics.

"Classroom Connections" is an additional feature that appears after major sections of Chapters 2–15. "Classroom Connections" is also organized by developmental levels and is designed to help you apply chapter topics to the developmental level of the students you'll be teaching.

Obviously, students didn't acquire these ideas from teachers' explanations. Rather, students interpreted what they heard, experienced, or read, related it to what they already knew, and attempted to make sense of both.

These examples help us see why "wisdom can't be told" (Bransford, 1993, p. 6) and why "I explain the stuff so carefully" usually isn't enough to maximize learning. Effective teaching is more complex than simply explaining, and expert teachers have a thorough understanding of the way learning occurs and what they can do to promote it. (We examine learning in detail in Chapters 6 to 9.)

We now can also understand why item 9 is false. Experience is essential in learning to teach, and no one suggests that it isn't necessary. However, you can already see that teachers won't acquire all the knowledge they need to be effective from experience alone. As we've said earlier in the chapter, acquiring this knowledge is the primary reason you're studying educational psychology.

Professional Knowledge: Reform and Accountability

The current focus on teacher knowledge and professionalism is part of a broader emphasis on **reforms**, suggested changes in teaching and teacher preparation intended to increase student learning. Establishing standards for student learning and accountability are important components of the current reform movement. **Accountability** is the process of requiring students to demonstrate that they have met specified standards and of holding teachers responsible for students' performance. (We discuss standards in more detail in Chapter 13, and we examine the relationship between accountability and standardized testing in Chapter 15.)

Reforms. Suggested changes in teaching and teacher preparation intended to increase student learning.

Accountability. The process of requiring learners to demonstrate that they possess specified knowledge and skills as demonstrated by standardized measures, and making teachers responsible for student performance.

As we moved into the 21st century, the reform movement in education received an important boost with the well-known and politically charged No Child Left Behind Act (NCLB), passed in 2001 by the administration of George W. Bush. Improved teacher quality is a major provision of NCLB, and increased teacher knowledge is an essential characteristic of "teacher quality" (Selwyn, 2007). The emphasis on teacher quality is a direct result of research indicating that teachers have a powerful effect on student achievement and that poor, minority, and urban students are often taught by underqualified teachers (Darling-Hammond & Baratz-Snowdon, 2005).

In an attempt to ensure that teachers possess the knowledge to teach effectively, a panel of educational leaders sponsored by the National Academy of Education called for a national teacher test with results incorporated into state licensing requirements (Bransford et al., 2005). Most states already require teachers to pass tests before they're licensed.

The Praxis™ Exam

Although some states have their own licensure exams, the Praxis™ Series, published by the Educational Testing Service, is the most widely used teacher test (*praxis* means putting theory into practice). Forty-four states plus the District of Columbia, Guam, and the U.S. Virgin Islands use this series (Educational Testing Service, 2008a).

The Principles of Learning and Teaching (PLT) tests are important parts of the Praxis Series. The PLT tests are designed for teachers seeking licensure in early childhood or grades K–6, 5–9, and 7–12 (Educational Testing Service, 2008b). This book addresses most topics covered on these tests, and a discussion of the Praxis exam and a correlation matrix linking test and text topics appear in Appendix C.

Each of the grade-level–specific PLT tests is 2 hours long and is composed of four case histories, each followed by three short-answer questions. In addition, the test includes 24 multiple-choice questions in two sections of 12 each (Educational Testing Service, 2008b). The "case histories" are similar to the case studies you see at the beginning and the end of each chapter of this book. In the section "Developing as a Professional: Preparing for Your Licensure Exam," which appears at the end of each chapter, you can practice preparing short-answer responses similar to those you will be expected to make on the PLT tests. The multiple-choice questions that you will respond to as you study the material in this book also ask you to apply your understanding to the real world of classrooms, and they are similar to the multiple-choice questions on the PLT exam.

The significance of the reform movement lies in its focus on professional knowledge. At no point in the history of education has the role of knowledge been more strongly emphasized. Helping you acquire this knowledge is the goal of this text.

check your understanding

2.1 Describe and give an example of each of the different kinds of knowledge that professional teachers possess.

2.2 Identify the statement Keith made in the opening case study that best indicates his lack of pedagogical content knowledge in trying to teach problem solving to his students. Explain why the statement shows that he lacks this knowledge.

2.3 A life science teacher holds up a sheet of bubble wrap and then places a second sheet of bubble wrap on top of the first to help her students visualize the way that cells are organized into tissue. What kind of knowledge does the teacher's demonstration best indicate? Explain.

To receive feedback for these questions, go to Appendix A.

MyEducationLab

To examine a school principal's view of the professional knowledge needed in teaching, go to the *Activities and Applications* section in Chapter 1 of MyEducationLab at *www.myeducationlab.com,* and watch the episode *The Principal's View of Professionalism*. Answer the questions following the episode.

exploring diversity

Teaching and Learning in Urban Environments

For a number of years, researchers have expressed concern about the education of students in urban environments. Consider the following statistics (Hoffman, 2003; Macionis & Parillo, 2007):

- The 100 largest school districts in the nation represent less than 1 percent of all districts but are responsible for the education of nearly a quarter of all students. These districts are overwhelmingly urban, and the New York City Public Schools and the Los Angeles Unified School District, the two largest in the nation, each have enrollments greater than the total enrollments of 27 states.
- The 100 largest districts employ more than a fifth of the nation's teachers.
- More than two thirds of students in urban environments are members of cultural minorities, and in some urban schools, more than 95 percent of the students are members of minorities.
- More than half of all urban students are eligible for free or reduced-price school lunch.

In addition, research indicates that in urban schools,

> Children are often taught by teachers who are the least prepared; children are less likely to be enrolled in academically challenging courses; they are too often treated differently in what they are expected to do and the kinds of assignments they are given and teachers often lack the resources needed to teach well. (Armour-Thomas, 2004, p. 113)

Unquestionably, teaching in urban schools differs from teaching in other settings. Urban schools are large, have large numbers of students from diverse backgrounds, and present challenges to both teaching and learning (Armour-Thomas, 2004; Goldstein, 2004, Rubinson, 2004).

Unfortunately, many negative stereotypes about urban students also exist, ranging from "All urban kids are in gangs" to "Urban children are mostly from poor, dysfunctional homes, homeless shelters, or foster homes and come to school 'just to grow up' and then drop out" (Goldstein, 2004, pp. 43–44). These stereotypes tend to create anxiety in people not familiar with the situation. This anxiety can then lead to actions that are damaging to everyone.

Urban environments present both challenges and opportunities for teachers who understand these instructional contexts.

> When I was in high school, we had the chance to host a group of students from the suburbs. . . . So, this girl comes with her friends, and they pair us up. Later on I find that they [the students from the suburbs] were told not to wear any jewelry or nice clothes or bring any money with them so they wouldn't get robbed. . . . All they saw when they visited us were people who might rob them. (Goldstein, 2004, p. 47)

Being a successful teacher in an urban environment isn't as simple as ignoring stereotypes or caring about and being committed to kids (Kincheloe, 2004). It takes context-specific knowledge that directly addresses essential aspects of teaching and learning, such as the influence of the social environment on learning and development, ways of organizing urban classrooms to promote learning, and teaching strategies that promote learning and motivation in urban students (Whitcomb, Borko, & Liston, 2006). We address these issues in special sections of Chapters 3, 4, 8, and 11 through 13.

The Role of Research in Acquiring Professional Knowledge

In the previous sections, we considered the different kinds of knowledge teachers use to help their students learn. Where did this knowledge originate, how does it accumulate, and how can we acquire it?

One answer is experience, sometimes called "the wisdom of practice" (Berliner, 2000; Munby, Russel, & Martin, 2001; Richardson & Placier, 2001). Effective teacher education programs help people like you acquire the beginnings of "the wisdom of practice" by integrating clinical experiences in schools with the topics you study in your classes.

Research. The process of systematically gathering information in an attempt to answer professional questions.

Research, the process of systematically gathering information in an attempt to answer professional questions, is a second important source of teacher knowledge. It is the process all professions use to develop their professional literature (Gall, Gall, & Borg, 2007; Van Horn, 2008). For example, in an effort to answer the question "How does teacher questioning influence student learning?" researchers have conducted many studies examining the numbers of questions, the patterns in their questioning, and the types of questions teachers ask (Good & Brophy, 2008). The influence of teacher questioning on student learning is part of the professional literature of educational psychology. Jan drew from it when she talked about the changes she made in her teaching based on the university class she is taking and her instructor who "keeps talking about research that says how important it is to call on all the kids as equally as possible." Jan is a veteran teacher, but she continues to grow professionally by staying up-to-date on current research.

Research exists in many forms. In this chapter, we consider five of the most common:

- Descriptive research
- Correlational research
- Experimental research
- Qualitative research
- Action research

Research provides valuable information that teachers can use in their instructional decision making.

Descriptive Research

Descriptive research. Research that uses tests, surveys, interviews, and observations to describe the status or characteristics of a situation or phenomenon.

Descriptive research, as the term implies, uses tests, surveys, interviews, and observations to describe the status or characteristics of a situation or phenomenon (B. Johnson & Christensen, 2008). For example, "How much are our students learning" is an important question facing all educators. In an attempt to answer this question, the National Assessment of Educational Progress (NAEP) administers math and reading achievement tests to samples of fourth, eighth, and twelfth graders every 2 years (Manzo, 2008). Advocates hope to use this descriptive research to: (1) measure the effectiveness of different math and reading programs, (2) hold states and districts accountable for student achievement, and (3) provide a comparative benchmark with other countries (Yeager, 2007).

Even something as seemingly innocuous as an examination of what students learn and know is controversial, however. Some critics, for example, worry that a national test will lead to a national curriculum (Nichols & Berliner, 2005). Critics also point to the low participation rates of twelfth graders and the exclusion of some students with disabilities. Even the content is criticized; critics question whether the NAEP overemphasizes academic skills at the expense of other important areas, such as critical thinking, social skills, appreciation of art and literature, and preparation for work (Manzo, 2008). These controversies illustrate the central role of educational research in framing and answering important questions about our schools.

A second form of descriptive research uses surveys to gauge the public's attitudes toward important issues in education. The annual *Phi Delta Kappan/Gallup Poll of the Public's Attitude Toward the Public Schools* is a well-known example. In the 2007 poll, for instance, researchers attempted to determine the public's attitude toward the NCLB Act and accountability. Researchers found that 26 percent of a national sample felt that NCLB was helping the performance of local public schools, 27 percent believed it was hurting, and 41 percent felt that it made no difference (L. Rose & Gallup, 2007). When asked about the current emphasis on achievement testing in the public schools, 43 percent of respondents said there was too much emphasis, while only 15 percent said "not enough." This descriptive research is likely to influence government officials at the state and national levels as well as state and district school board members governing the schools in which you'll teach.

Observations have also been used in descriptive research. Perhaps most significant is the work done by Jean Piaget (1952, 1959), a pioneer in the study of cognitive development, one of the cornerstones of educational psychology. Piaget studied the way learners' thinking develops by making detailed observations of his own children. Because of his observations, and a great deal of research conducted by others, we now know, for example, that 10-year-olds don't simply know more than 5-year-olds; they think differently. We understand these differences in children's thinking because of Piaget's and other researchers' systematic descriptive research. (We examine Piaget's work in detail in Chapter 2.)

Evaluating Descriptive Studies

A great deal of research exists, and teachers need to become proficient at evaluating different studies, not only for their validity but also for their applicability to specific teaching situations.

For instance, several studies reporting similar results provide information that is more likely to be valid than a single, or even a few, studies (Chatterji, 2008; H. Cooper, 2006).

For descriptive studies, two additional aspects are important. First, the subjects used should be well described (J. H. McMillan, 2008). This information allows the reader to judge how applicable the findings are to other populations. The Gallup poll described earlier provides a detailed analysis of the demographic breakdown of its respondents (L. Rose & Gallup, 2007).

The instrument used to gather data is a second aspect of descriptive research that should be scrutinized. For example, are questions asked in a straightforward manner, or are they designed to provide a skewed response? Again, the Gallup poll provides readers with actual copies of the questions so the reader can decide whether the data were gathered in a valid way.

Descriptive research can provide valuable information about the condition of education, but it doesn't allow us to predict future events, and it doesn't describe relationships. Finding relationships between variables leads us to correlational research.

Correlational Research

Consider the following questions: Does a relationship exist between

- Students' grade-point averages (GPAs) and their scores on the Scholastic Aptitude Test (SAT)?
- The use of cell phones while driving and car accidents?
- Students' absences and their grades in school?
- Students' heights and high school GPAs?

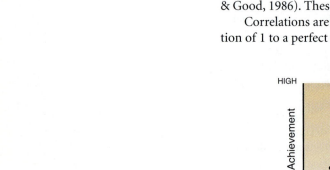

Correlation. A relationship, either positive or negative, between two or more variables.

A **correlation** is a relationship, either positive or negative, between two or more variables. In our examples, the variables are *grade-point averages* and *SAT scores, cell-phone usage* and *accidents, absences* and *grades, height* and *high school GPAs.* In the first two cases, the variables are positively correlated: In general, the higher students' GPAs, the higher their SAT scores; and the greater the use of cell phones while driving, the greater the number of accidents. In the third case, the variables are negatively correlated: The more school students miss, the lower their grades. No correlation exists in the fourth: Height and high school GPAs are not related.

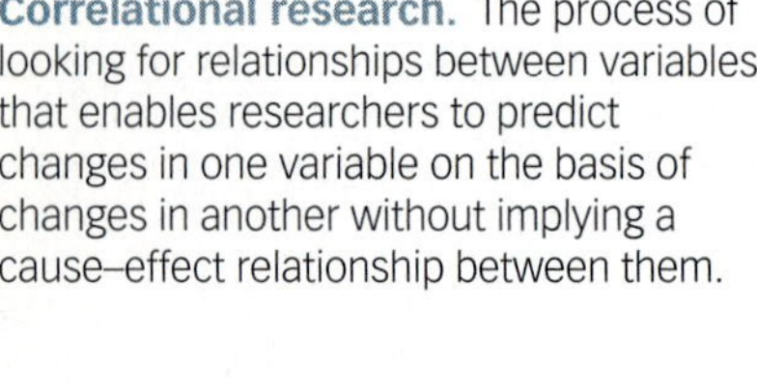

Correlational research. The process of looking for relationships between variables that enables researchers to predict changes in one variable on the basis of changes in another without implying a cause–effect relationship between them.

Much of what we know about learning and teaching is based on **correlational research**, the process of looking for relationships between variables that enables researchers to predict changes in one variable on the basis of changes in another without implying a cause–effect relationship between them. A great deal of this research attempts to find relationships between teachers' actions and student achievement. For example, researchers have found positive correlations between the number of questions teachers ask and their students' achievement (Shuell, 1996). They have also found negative correlations between achievement and the time teachers spend in noninstructional activities, such as taking roll or passing out papers (Brophy & Good, 1986). These relationships are illustrated in Figure 1.2.

Correlations are represented quantitatively and can range from a perfect positive correlation of 1 to a perfect negative correlation of −1. As a simple example, speed and distance have

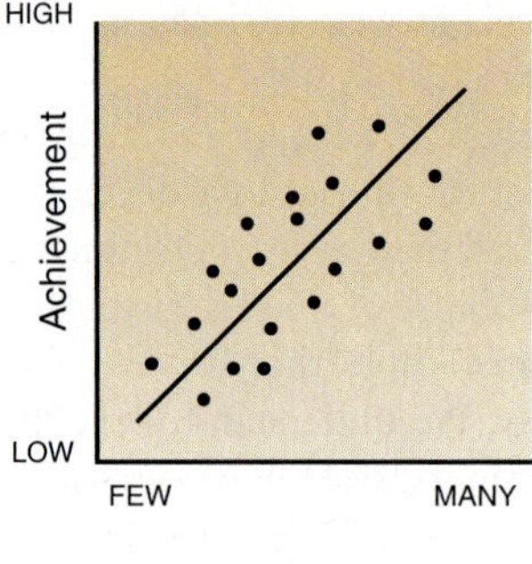

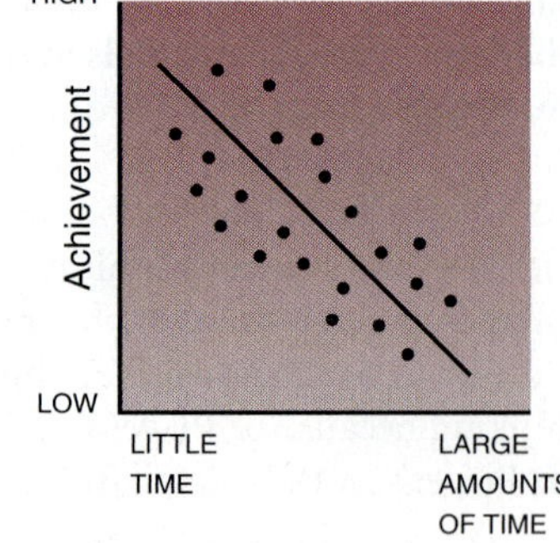

Figure 1.2 Examples of positive (left) and negative (right) correlations

a correlation of 1. For each mile per hour faster we travel, a corresponding increase occurs in the distance we cover in the same amount of time. Most correlations are less than a perfect 1 or −1. For instance, the correlation between the number of questions teachers ask and student achievement is about .5, and the correlation between time spent in noninstructional activities and achievement is about −.4 (Good & Brophy, 1986; Shuell, 1996).

Correlational research is valuable because it allows us to make predictions about one variable if we have information about the other (B. Johnson & Christensen, 2008; J.H. McMillan, 2008). For instance, because a positive correlation exists between teacher questioning and student achievement, we can predict that students will learn more in classrooms where teachers ask many questions than in those where teachers primarily lecture. Because of this, many of the instruments used to evaluate teacher effectiveness focus on teachers' questioning behaviors with students.

Evaluating Correlational Research

As with descriptive research, correlational studies have limitations. Most important, they do not suggest that one variable *causes* the other (Gall et al., 2007; J.H. McMillan, 2008). Consider the relationship between GPAs and SAT scores. Obviously, a high GPA doesn't cause a high SAT score. Other factors, such as time spent studying, effective study strategies, and general intelligence are likely to be causes of both. Also, obviously, a cell phone doesn't cause an accident; failing to pay attention to other cars while driving causes the accidents. The same kind of reasoning applies to our example of a negative correlation. Being absent, per se, doesn't cause low grades. Instead, missing opportunities to learn topics, not completing homework assignments, and losing chances to interact with peers are likely causes.

Experimental Research

Whereas correlational research looks for relationships in existing situations (e.g., the relationship between teacher questioning and student achievement), **experimental research** systematically manipulates variables in attempts to determine cause and effect (H. Cooper, 2006). Experimental studies commonly build on correlational research. For example, let's look again at the relationship between teachers' questioning and student achievement.

Experimental research. Research that systematically manipulates variables in attempts to determine cause and effect.

In an extension of earlier correlational studies, researchers randomly assigned teachers to a treatment and a control group. **Random assignment** means that an individual has an equal likelihood of being assigned to either group, and it ensures that the two groups are comparable. The researchers trained teachers in the treatment group to provide prompts and cues when students initially failed to answer a question; the researchers attempted to consciously manipulate the variable *frequency of teachers' prompts* through training. Teachers in the control group received no training; they taught as they normally did. Researchers compared the reading scores of the students in both groups at the end of the year. Students taught by teachers in the treatment group scored significantly higher on an achievement test than did students taught by teachers in the control group (L. Anderson, Evertson, & Brophy, 1979). In this case, researchers concluded that the ability to provide follow-up questions and cues to struggling students *causes* increases in achievement.

Random assignment. A process used to ensure that an individual has an equal likelihood of being assigned to either group within a study.

Evaluating Experimental Research

As with both descriptive and correlational research, teachers should read experimental studies with a critical eye. Factors to consider include

- Comparability of experimental and control groups
- Maximum control of extraneous variables
- Sample size
- Clearly described manipulation of the independent variable

For instance, let's consider the L. Anderson et al. (1979) study again. It would be possible to conclude that prompting caused higher reading achievement only if the treatment and the control groups were similar. If, for example, the students who received prompts had higher initial ability than students in the control group, conclusions about the effectiveness of the prompts would be invalid. Similarly, if the teachers who were trained to provide prompts had higher initial levels of expertise than teachers in the control group, conclusions about prompting also would be invalid.

Using random assignment and an adequate sample size helps ensure that experimental and control groups are comparable. For instance, if 30 teachers each have been randomly assigned to experimental and control groups, concluding that teacher expertise has been controlled is more valid than if only 10 teachers existed in each group.

Finally, experimental research must clearly describe the treatment of the experimental group. The questioning study gave explicit details about how researchers trained the teachers in the experimental group to provide cues and prompts. This clear description not only allows the reader to evaluate the research but also allows other researchers to replicate it, which is another way to increase validity.

Qualitative Research

Imagine picking up a research report and finding the following:

> A quiet early morning fog shrouds rolling hills blanketed by pine-green stands of timber, patched with fields of red clay. As the sun rises and burns off the fog, the blue sky is feathered with smoke let go from chimney stacks of textile mills: this is the Piedmont of the Carolinas. (Heath, 1983, p. 19)

Qualitative research. Research that attempts to describe a complex educational phenomenon in a holistic fashion using nonnumerical data, such as words and pictures.

If you're like most students, one of your first reactions might be, "Research? Where are the numbers?" **Qualitative research**, as its name implies, is an attempt to describe a complex educational phenomenon in a holistic fashion using nonnumerical data, such as words and pictures (B. Johnson & Christensen, 2008). The passage you just read is from a classic research study in education, Shirley Brice Heath's (1983) *Ways with Words*, a qualitative study of the development of language and literacy in two communities in the southeastern United States. It attempts to describe how children learn to speak, read, and write, both in and out of school, not through numerical or statistical analysis, but through a fine-grained description of what it's like to grow up poor in rural factory towns. The vivid picture it creates of life and learning in realistic settings is what makes this piece of research valuable.

Qualitative research differs from quantitative research in several ways (see Table 1.1). Its goal is to gain a holistic description of some unique phenomenon. Some things can't be quantified, and attempting to do so oversimplifies and trivializes them. Qualitative research relies on in-depth interviews, field notes, and artifacts, such as the books, newspapers, and magazines collected in the Heath (1983) study of literature development. In analyzing data, qualitative researchers search for patterns and themes, as do quantitative researchers, but publish their results in narrative reports with detailed descriptions of settings and participants. In contrast, quantitative studies typically result in statistical reports with correlations, comparisons of means, and effect sizes (L. Gay, Mills, & Airasian, 2006).

table 1.1 Qualitative Versus Quantitative Research

	Qualitative	Quantitative
Goal	To gain a holistic description of some complex phenomenon	To gain a specific, precise, and numerical description of some phenomenon
Form of data	In-depth interviews, field notes, artifacts, open-ended interviews	Numerical data using formal assessment instruments
Data analysis	Search for patterns or themes	Statistical procedures that address probability of occurrence
Final report	Narrative report with detailed descriptions of settings and participants	Statistical report with correlations, comparison of means, and statistical effect sizes

Source: Denzin & Lincoln, 2007; Gay, Mills, & Airasian, 2006; B. Johnson & Christensen, 2008; J.H. McMillan, 2008.

A classic qualitative study of teaching, *First-Year Teacher* (Bullough, 1989), further illustrates these characteristics. The researcher's goal was to describe what it's like to be a first-year teacher from a teacher's perspective. The researcher spent a year observing a first-year middle-school language arts teacher, interviewing her, and collecting artifacts such as lesson plans and assignments. A realistic account of the triumphs and difficulties encountered by one teacher emerged from the study. Like other qualitative studies, the researcher did not claim that this teacher's experience generalized to *all* first-year teachers' experiences. Instead, the researcher attempted to describe one teacher's experience in as much detail as possible and then allow readers to draw their own conclusions about the teacher's experiences.

So, which is better, qualitative or quantitative research? The question is controversial, with both qualitative and quantitative researchers supporting their approaches (H. Cooper, 2006; Eckardt, 2007; Nesbit & Hadwin, 2006). Let's look at this question in more detail.

Scientifically Based Research in Education

You are likely to encounter the term *scientifically based research* as you progress through your teacher education program and begin your first years of teaching. **Scientifically based research** emphasizes experimental research using classic techniques of the scientific method instead of descriptive or qualitative approaches. Responding to this emphasis, the U.S. Department of Education "has strongly advocated both expanding research on practical programs using rigorous methods, especially randomized experiments, and using the findings of this research to guide policy and practice" (Slavin, 2008, p. 5).

Scientifically based research. Research that emphasizes experimental research using classic techniques of the scientific method instead of descriptive or qualitative approaches.

However, the term *scientifically based* has sometimes been misinterpreted to mean only experimental research using randomized designs (Liston, Whitcomb, & Borko, 2007). While experimental research has and will continue to yield valuable insights into teaching and learning, overemphasis on it to the exclusion of other forms of research narrows and distorts our perspective about effective instructional practices.

Much of the support for this view comes from advocates citing parallels between education and medicine (Riehl, 2006). Both fields attempt to help people in complex situations, and practitioners in both areas are often forced to make decisions with less than a complete research base. In addition, the success of some randomized clinical trials in medicine has encouraged some to recommend that these should be the major (and sometimes only) way to determine best practices in education. Major differences exist between medicine and education, however, not the least of which is the feasibility of randomly assigning thousands of students to different educational conditions (Sloane, 2008).

As an alternative, experts advocate a more eclectic approach to research that uses a variety of methods (Ball & Forzine, 2007). This broader and more comprehensive approach begins with a question that is important to educators and then selects the research design that will best help them answer the question (Slavin, 2008). Educational research is a tool that helps answer questions about teaching and learning, and selecting a method before identifying the question research is supposed to answer is inconsistent with effective research methodology (H. Cooper, 2006). So, as a future consumer of educational research, treat claims that an approach is "scientifically based" with skepticism, and instead ask yourself three questions:

1. Does the research address a clear and important question?
2. Does the research method address the question?
3. Are the claims made about the results of the research justified by the data?

The research and its methodology are valid if the answer to each question is yes (H. Cooper, 2006).

Action Research

Earlier in the chapter, you saw that teacher knowledge is an essential element of professionalism. Understanding and critically examining others' research is one way to increase teacher knowledge. Another is for teachers to conduct research in their own classrooms. **Action research** is a form of applied research designed to answer a specific school- or classroom-related question (A. P. Johnson, 2005). It is conducted by teachers, school administrators, or other education professionals and can include descriptive, correlational, experimental, or qualitative methods. When they conduct

Action research. A form of applied research designed to answer a specific school- or classroom-related question.

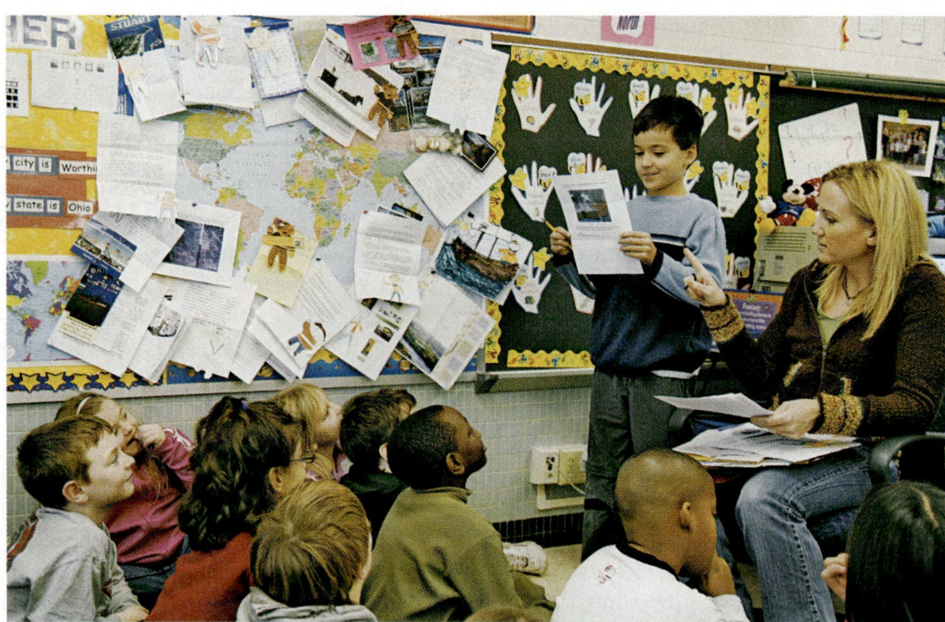

Action research allows teachers to investigate connections between their instruction and student learning and share their findings with other teachers.

action research projects (and share the results with others), teachers learn about research and begin to understand how self-assessment and reflection can link theory and practice in their own classrooms (Blumenreich & Falk, 2006). The intent in action research is to improve practice within a specific classroom or school (J.H. McMillan, 2008). It also increases the professionalism of teachers by recognizing their ability to contribute to the professional literature of learning and teaching (Bransford et al., 2000).

Research and the Development of Theory

As research accumulates, results are summarized and patterns emerge. After a great many studies, for instance, researchers have concluded that the thinking of young children tends to be dominated by their perceptions (Piaget, 1970, 1977; Wadsworth, 2004). For example, when first graders see an inverted cup of water with a card beneath it, as we see in the accompanying picture, they commonly explain that the card doesn't fall because the water somehow holds it against the cup. They focus on the most perceptually obvious aspect of the object—the water—and ignore atmospheric pressure, the actual reason the card stays on the cup.

The statement "The thinking of young children tends to be dominated by their perceptions" is considered a principle because it summarizes results consistently supported by large numbers of research studies. Some additional examples of research-based principles include

- Behaviors rewarded some of the time, but not all of the time, persist longer than behaviors rewarded every time they occur.
- People tend to imitate behaviors they observe in others.
- People strive for a state of order, balance, and predictability in the world.

Theory. A set of related principles derived from observations that are used to explain events in the world and make predictions.

As additional research is conducted, related principles are formed, which in turn generate further studies. As knowledge accumulates, theories are gradually constructed. A **theory** is a set of related principles, derived from observations, that are used to explain events in the world and make predictions (H. Cooper, 2006). In the everyday world, the term is used more loosely. For instance, one person will make a point in a conversation, and a second will respond, "I have a theory about that." In this case, the person is merely offering an explanation for the point. In science, theory has a more precise definition.

Theories help organize research findings, and they can provide valuable guidance for teachers (Gall et al., 2007). Let's look at a brief example. One research-based principle states that reinforced behaviors increase in frequency, and as mentioned earlier, a related principle

theory to practice

Conducting Research in Classrooms

If you decide to conduct action research in your own classroom, the following guidelines can help you plan and conduct your studies (A. P. Johnson, 2005):

1. Identify and diagnose a problem that is important to you.
2. Systematically plan and conduct a research study.
3. Implement the findings to solve or improve a local problem.
4. Use the results of the study to generate additional research.

Let's see how Tyra Forcine, an eighth-grade English teacher, attempts to implement these guidelines in her classroom.

Tyra is sitting in the teachers' lounge with a group of colleagues who are discussing problems they're having with homework. "My kids won't do it," Kim Brown laments. "A third of them blow it off on some days."

"I solved that problem. . . . I simply don't assign homework," Bill McClendon responds. "I give them a seat-work assignment, we do it after the lesson, and that's it. . . . I'm tired of fighting the homework battle."

"I've heard teachers say that homework doesn't help that much in terms of learning, anyway," Selena Cross adds.

The conversation bothers Tyra, so she decides to look at the effects of homework more systematically. She begins her study a week later, which is the start of the third grading period. She collects homework every day and gives students 2 points for having done it fully, 1 for partial completion, and 0 for minimal effort or not turning it in. She discusses the most frequently missed items on each assignment. On Fridays she quizzes the students on the content discussed Monday through Thursday, and she gives a midterm and final exam. She then looks for a relationship between students' homework averages and their quiz and test scores.

At the end of the grading period, Tyra summarizes the results. Each student has a homework score, a quiz average, and an average on the two tests.

She calls the district office to ask for help in summarizing the information, and together they find a correlation of .55 between homework scores and quiz averages, and a correlation of .44 between homework and test averages.

"I don't get it," Tyra says to Kim and Bill in a later conversation. "I can see why the correlation between the homework and tests might be lower than the one between homework and quizzes, but why aren't both higher?"

"Well," Kim responds. "You're only giving the kids a 2, 1, or 0 on the homework, you're not actually grading it. So I suspect that some of the kids aren't really thinking carefully about it."

"On the other hand," Bill acknowledges, "homework and quizzes and tests are positively correlated, so maybe I'd better rethink my stand on no homework."

"Well, I'm going to keep on giving homework," Tyra nods, "but I think I need to change what I'm doing, too. . . . It's going to be a ton of work, but I'm going to repeat my study next grading period to see if I get similar results, and then, starting in the fall, I'm going to redesign my homework so it's easier to grade. I'll grade every assignment, and we'll see if the correlations go up."

"Good idea," Kim nods. "If the kids see that it's important for learning, maybe they'll take it more seriously, and some of the not-doing-it problem will also get better. . . . I'm going to look at that in the fall."

Now let's look at Tyra's efforts to apply the guidelines for conducting action research projects. She applied the first when she identified a problem that was important to her—the relationship between homework and quizzes and tests. Addressing problems that are personally meaningful makes action research motivating for teachers (Mills, 2002; Quiocho & Ulanoff, 2002).

She applied the second guideline by systematically designing and conducting her study, and its efficiency was an important feature. School systems rarely provide extra time and resources for action research, so conducting projects that don't take inordinate amounts of teacher time is important (Bransford et al., 2000).

Tyra and her colleagues implemented the results of her project immediately, which applies the third guideline. Bill, for example, planned to give homework during the next grading period. Tyra applied the fourth guideline when her project prompted further studies. She planned another study to see if scoring the homework more carefully would increase the correlations between homework and quizzes and tests, and Kim planned to investigate whether more careful scoring would lead to students' more conscientiously doing their homework. (We discuss existing research examining the effectiveness of homework in Chapter 13.)

Perhaps Tyra and her colleagues will reap an additional benefit. As mentioned earlier, engaging in research increases teachers' feelings of professionalism; contributing to a body of literature that guides practice helps teachers grow professionally. And the results of well-designed studies can often be presented at professional conferences and published in professional journals. This allows the knowledge gained to be made public and integrated with other research, two important characteristics in the development of a professional body of knowledge (J. Hiebert, Gallimore, & Stigler, 2002).

indicates that intermittently reinforced behaviors persist longer than those that are continuously reinforced (Baldwin & Baldwin, 2001; Skinner, 1957). Further, too much reinforcement can actually decrease its effectiveness. A classroom application of these principles occurs in learning activities. If students are praised for their attempts to answer questions (reinforced), they are likely to increase their efforts, but they will persist longer if they are praised for some, but not all, of their attempts (intermittently reinforced). If they are praised excessively, they may actually reduce their efforts (R. Ryan & Deci, 1996).

These related principles are part of *behaviorism*, a theory that studies the effects of experiences on behavior. Our illustration, of course, is only a tiny portion of the complete theory. (We examine behaviorism in depth in Chapter 6.) The key feature of any theory is that a number of research-based principles integrates a comprehensive body of research.

MyEducationLab

To further examine professional knowledge and research, go to the *Activities and Applications* section in Chapter 1 of MyEducationLab at www.myeducationlab.com, and read the case study *Increasing Professional Knowledge With Research*. Answer the question following the case study.

Theories are useful in two important ways. First, they allow us to explain behaviors and events. For instance, look again at the cartoon on page 12. Piaget's theory of cognitive development (1970, 1977), which includes the principle mentioned earlier ("The thinking of young children tends to be dominated by their perceptions"), helps us explain why the child in the cartoon thinks the way he does. Using Piaget's theory, we can explain this behavior by saying that the child can see only the water and the faucet, and because his thinking is dominated by his perception—what he can see—he concludes that all the water is in the faucet. Similarly, using behaviorist theory, we can explain why casino patrons persist in playing slot machines, though coins infrequently fall into the trays, by saying that they are being intermittently reinforced.

MyEducationLab

To see how research and theory can improve instruction, go to the *Building Teaching Skills and Dispositions* section in Chapter 1 of MyEducationLab at www.myeducationlab.com, and read the case study *Improving Teaching With Research and Theory*. Complete the exercises following the case study to develop your skills in applying research and theory.

Theories also allow us to predict behavior and events. For instance, attribution theory, a theory of motivation, allows us to predict that students who believe they control their own grades try harder than those who believe their grades are due primarily to luck or the whim of the teacher (Brophy, 2004; Schunk, Pintrich, & Meese, 2008).

In all three instances, theories—cognitive development theory, behaviorist theory, and attribution theory—help us understand learning and teaching by allowing us to explain and predict people's actions. Throughout this book, you will study a number of theories, the applications of which can increase your students' learning.

check your understanding

3.1 Describe the major types of educational research.

3.2 Teachers who are high in personal teaching efficacy—who believe that they have an important positive effect on students—have higher-achieving students than teachers who are low in personal teaching efficacy (Bruning et al., 2004). Is this finding based on descriptive, correlational, or experimental research? Explain.

3.3 Suppose that Tyra and her colleagues concluded that doing homework caused an increase in student achievement. Would this be a valid conclusion? Explain why or why not.

To receive feedback for these questions, go to Appendix A.

The Use of Case Studies in Educational Psychology

The different forms of knowledge that teachers need for their professional decision making have important implications both for you, who are learning to teach, and for us, as we write texts to help you in this process. Our knowledge of learners and learning reminds us that students of all ages need concrete and real-world representations of the topics they study to make those topics meaningful.

Case studies (cases). Authentic stories of teaching and learning events in classrooms.

One of the most effective ways to provide concrete illustrations of the topics you will study in educational psychology is the use of **case studies**, authentic stories of teaching and learning events in classrooms, such as the one at the beginning of this chapter. Case studies will help you prepare for the events that will occur in your own classroom when you begin teaching (Fishman & Davis, 2006; Putnam & Borko, 2000). Long popular in other professional fields, such as law and medicine, cases are now commonly used in education. Research supports their value in clarifying ideas and showing how they can be applied in classrooms. Teacher candidates, such as yourself, not only retain more information when it is illustrated in cases, but are more likely to transfer ideas to their own unique teaching situation (Moreno & Valdez, 2007).

Because of the value of case studies in illustrating the complex processes involved in teaching and learning, we employ cases in this text in two ways: (1) we provide access to realistic video cases of classrooms through MyEducationLab and (2) we introduce and end each chapter in this book with a case study. Our students find the video case studies that you can access on MyEducationLab valuable because they realistically portray the complexities of classroom teaching.

The introductory case and the chapter closing case serve two different purposes. The beginning case provides a real-world introduction to the content and illustrates the topics pre-

table 1.2 Organization of this Book

Part and Chapter	Goal
Chapter 1: Educational Psychology: Developing a Professional Knowledge Base	To understand the role of knowledge in developing professionalism
Part I: The Learner	
Chapter 2: The Development of Cognition and Language	To understand how learners' intellectual capacities and language abilities develop over time
Chapter 3: Personal, Social, and Moral Development	To understand learners' personal, social, and moral development
Chapter 4: Learner Diversity	To understand how culture, socioeconomic status, and gender affect learning
Chapter 5: Learners with Exceptionalities	To understand how learner exceptionalities affect learning
Part II: Learning	
Chapter 6: Behaviorism and Social Cognitive Theory	To understand learning from behaviorist and social cognitive perspectives
Chapter 7: Cognitive Views of Learning	To understand learning from cognitive perspectives
Chapter 8: Constructing Knowledge	To understand the processes involved in constructing understanding
Chapter 9: Complex Cognitive Processes	To understand concept learning, problem solving, and the development of strategic learners
Part III: Classroom Processes	
Chapter 10: Theories of Motivation	To understand basic theories of motivation and how they apply to classrooms
Chapter 11: Motivation in the Classroom	To understand how to apply basic principles of motivation to classrooms
Chapter 12: Creating Productive Learning Environments: Classroom Management	To understand how to create learning-focused classrooms and develop learner self-regulation
Chapter 13: Creating Productive Learning Environments: Principles and Models of Instruction	To understand how to plan, and implement, different learning strategies
Chapter 14: Assessing Classroom Learning	To understand how teachers can use assessment to promote learning in the classroom
Chapter 15: Assessment Through Standardized Testing	To understand how standardized tests can be used to increase student learning

sented in the chapter. As topics are discussed, we often refer back to the case, in some instances taking dialogue directly from it, to make concepts more meaningful. We also present vignettes (short cases) throughout each chapter to further link content to real-world examples.

The closing cases, found in the "Developing as a Professional" feature, have an additional purpose. To encourage critical thinking, decision making, and reflection, we ask you to analyze each case and assess the extent to which the teacher applied the chapter content in his or her classroom. In some cases, the teacher's work was quite effective; in others it may not have been. The cases attempt to present the richness and complexity of actual classroom problems and provide opportunities to apply your understanding of the chapter content to an authentic teaching situation (Siegel, 2002). The cases and the format for your responses parallel the Praxis™ PLT tests, as well as many state-specific teacher exams.

We hope this introduction has provided a framework for the rest of your study of this book. Its organization and goals are outlined in Table 1.2

check your understanding

4.1 Explain how using case studies to place educational psychology in real-world contexts makes it more meaningful.

4.2 Identify the advantages of video case studies over those in written form.

To receive feedback for these questions, go to Appendix A.

Meeting Your Learning Objectives

1. Describe the characteristics of professionalism, and identify examples of these characteristics in the teachers' actions.
   - Professionals are committed to the people they serve, and their actions are guided by a professional code of ethics.
   - The characteristics of professionalism are illustrated in teachers' actions when they use their professional knowledge as a basis for their decision making.
   - Professionalism is also illustrated in teachers' actions when they reflect on their practice and can make decisions in complex and ill-defined contexts.
2. Describe the different kinds of knowledge professional teachers possess, and identify examples of professional knowledge in teachers' actions.
   - Professionals thoroughly understand the topics they teach, and their knowledge is illustrated in their actions when they use their pedagogical content knowledge to illustrate those topics in ways that make sense to learners.
   - Professionals' general pedagogical knowledge is illustrated when they organize learning environments and use basic instructional skills in ways that promote learning for their students.
   - Professionals' knowledge of learners and learning is illustrated in their actions when they design learning activities to involve students, promote motivation, to learn, and use developmentally appropriate practice.
3. Describe different types of research, and analyze applications of these types.
   - Descriptive research uses interviews, observations, and surveys to describe events. Correlational research looks for relationships between two variables. Experimental research manipulates variables in attempts to determine cause and effect.
   - Teachers and other school personnel sometimes conduct action research designed to answer school- or classroom-related questions.
4. Explain how using case studies to place educational psychology in real-world contexts makes it more meaningful.
   - Research indicates that topics embedded in authentic contexts is more meaningful than the same topics presented in the abstract.
   - Written and video case studies make the content of educational psychology meaningful by embedding its content in real-world classroom events.

Developing as a Professional: Preparing for Your Licensure Exam

To begin learning how to prepare short-answer responses similar to those you will encounter on your teacher exams, read the following case studies and answer the questions that follow.

The following episodes illustrate four teachers at different classroom levels working with their students. In the first, Rebecca Atkins, a kindergarten teacher, talks with her children about planting a garden. Richard Nelms, a middle school teacher, illustrates the concept of symmetry for his seventh-grade life science students in the second episode. In the third, Didi Johnson, a chemistry teacher, presents Charles's law to her 10th graders. Finally, in the fourth episode, Bob Duchaine, an American history teacher, is discussing the Vietnam War with his 11th graders.

As you read the episodes, think about the different types of professional knowledge that each teacher demonstrates as they attempt to help their students learn.

> Rebecca has the children seated on the floor in a semicircle in front of her. She sits on a small chair in front of them and begins, "We had a story about gardening the other day. Who remembers the name of the story?. . . Shereta?"
>
> " 'Together,' " Shereta softly responds.
>
> "Yes, 'Together,'" Rebecca repeats. "What happened in 'Together'?. . . Andrea?"
>
> "They had a garden."
>
> "They planted a garden together, didn't they?" Rebecca smiles. "The boy's father helped them plant the garden."
>
> She continues by referring the children to previous science lessons during which they had talked about plants and soil. She then asks them about helping their parents plant a garden.
>
> "I helped put the seeds in the ground and put the dirt on top of it," Robert offers.
>
> "What kinds of vegetables did you plant? . . . Kim?"
>
> "I planted lots of vegetables . . . tomatoes, carrots."
>
> "Shereta?"
>
> "I planted lettuce in my own garden."
>
> "Travis?"
>
> "I planted okra."
>
> "Raphael?"
>
> "I planted beans."
>
> She continues, "Tell about the story 'Together.' What did they have to do to take care of the garden? . . . Carlita?"
>
> "Water it."
>
> "Bengemar?"
>
> "Pull the weeds from it."

"Pull the weeds from it," Rebecca repeats enthusiastically. "What would happen if we left those weeds in there? . . . Latangela?"

"It would hurt the soil."

"What's another word for *soil*?"

"Dirt," several of the children say in unison.

"How many of you like to play in the dirt?"

Most of the children raise their hands.

"So, planting a garden would be fun because you get to play in the dirt," Rebecca says enthusiastically.

"I like to play in the mud," Travis adds.

"You like to play in the mud," Rebecca repeats, attempting to stifle a laugh.

Next is Richard Nelms's lesson on animal symmetry with his seventh graders.

Richard begins his discussion of symmetry by holding up a sponge as an example of an asymmetrical object; he demonstrates radial symmetry using a starfish; and he then turns to bilateral symmetry.

"We have one more type of symmetry," he says. "Jason, come up here. . . . Stand up here."

Jason comes to the front of the room and stands on a stool.

"Would you say," Richard begins, "that Jason is asymmetrical—that there is not uniformity in his shape?"

The students shake their heads.

He has Jason extend his arms out from his sides and then asks, "Would you consider this radial, because he has extensions that go out in all directions?. . . Jarrett?"

"No."

"Why not? Explain that for us."

"There's nothing there," Jarrett says, pointing to Jason's sides.

"There's nothing coming from here, is there, and the arms, legs and head are all different?" Richard adds.

"So, we move to the third type of symmetry," he continues, as Jason continues to stand with his arms extended. "Does anyone know what that is called? . . . Rachel?"

"A type of symmetry," Rachel responds uncertainly.

"Yes, it's a type of symmetry. . . . It's called bilateral. . . . *Bilateral* means that the form or shape of the organism is divided into two halves, and the two halves are consistent. . . . If I took a tree saw and started at the top," he says, pointing at Jason's head as the class laughs, "the two halves would be essentially the same."

"Now, tomorrow," he continues, "we're going to see how symmetry influences the ways organisms function in their environments."

Next, let's turn to Didi Johnson's chemistry lesson.

Didi wants her students to understand Charles's law of gases, the law stating that an increase in the temperature of a gas causes an increase in its volume when the pressure on the gas remains the same.

To illustrate that heat causes gases to expand, Didi prepares a demonstration in which she places three identical balloons filled with the same amount of air into three beakers of water. She puts the first into a beaker of hot water, the second into a beaker of water at room temperature, and the third into a beaker of ice water, as shown.

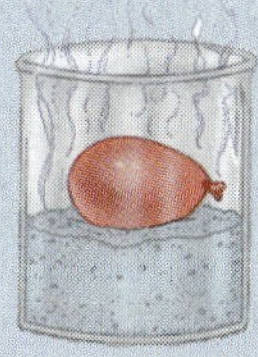

"This water is near boiling," Didi explains as she places the first balloon in the beaker. "This is room temperature, and this has had ice in it, so it is near the freezing point," she continues as she puts the other two balloons into the beakers.

"Now, today," she says as she begins writing on the board, "we're going to discuss Charles's law, but before we put it on the board and discuss it, we're going to see what happened to the balloons. . . . Look up here. . . . How is the size of the balloon related to the temperature of the water we placed it in?"

"The balloon in the hot water looks bigger," Chris responds.

"Can you see any difference in these two?" Didi continues, pointing to the other two balloons.

"The one in the cold water looks smaller than the one in the room temperature water," Chris adds.

"So, from what we see, if you increase temperature, what happens to the volume of the gas?"

"It increases," several students volunteer.

Didi writes, "Increase in temperature increases volume" on the board, emphasizes again that the amount of air and the pressure in the balloons were kept essentially constant, and then asks, "Who can state Charles's law based on what we've seen here?"

"Increased temperature will increase volume if you have constant pressure and mass," Jeremy offers.

Didi briefly reviews Charles's law, writes an equation for it on the board, and has the students solve a series of problems using the law.

Finally, let's look at Bob Duchaine's discussion of the Vietnam War.

Bob begins by saying, "To understand the Vietnam War, we need to go back to the beginning. Vietnam had been set up as a French colony in the 1880s, but by the mid-1900s, the military situation had gotten so bad for the French that they only controlled the little city of Dien Bien Phu."

Bob explains that the French surrendered in the summer of 1954, and peace talks followed. The talks resulted in Vietnam being split, and provisions for free elections were set up.

"These elections were never held," Bob continues. "Ngo Dinh Diem, in 1956, said there will be no free elections: 'I am in charge of the South. You can have elections in the north if you want, but there will be no elections in the south.'"

Bob continues by introducing the domino theory, which suggested that countries such as South Vietnam, Cambodia, Laos, Thailand, Burma, and even India would fall into communist hands much as dominos tip over and knock each other down. The way to prevent the loss of the countries, he explains, was to confront North Vietnam.

"And that's what we're going to be talking about throughout this unit," he says. "The war that we took over from the French to stop the fall of the dominos soon was eating up American lives at the rate of 12 to 15 thousand a year. . . . This situation went from a little simple plan—to stop the dominos from falling—to a loss of over 53,000 American lives that we know of.

"We'll pick up with this topic day after tomorrow. . . . Tomorrow you have a fun day in the library."

Short-Answer Questions

In answering these questions, use information from the chapter, and link your responses to specific information in the case.

1. What type or types of knowledge did Rebecca Atkins primarily demonstrate? Explain.
2. What type or types of knowledge did Richard Nelms demonstrate in his lesson? Explain.
3. What type or types of knowledge did Didi Johnson primarily demonstrate?
4. What type or types of knowledge did Bob Duchaine primarily demonstrate?

To receive feedback for these questions, go to Appendix B.

Now go to Chapter 1 of MyEducationLab, located at www.myeducationlab.com, where you can:

- Take a quiz to test your mastery of chapter objectives. Detailed feedback is provided to explain why your responses are correct or incorrect.
- Deepen your understanding of chapter concepts with *Review, Practice, Enrichment* exercises.
- Complete *Activities and Applications* that will help you apply what you have learned in the chapter by analyzing real classrooms through video clips, artifacts, and case studies. Your instructor will provide you with feedback for the *Activities and Applications.*
- Develop your professional knowledge and decision making in *Building Teaching Skills and Dispositions* exercises. Structured feedback will be available to you, providing you with support as you practice each skill. Your instructor will provide you with feedback on the final task that accompanies the exercise.

Important Concepts

accountability (p. 13)
action research (p. 19)
case studies (p. 22)
correlation (p. 16)
correlational research (p. 16)
descriptive research (p. 15)
developmental differences (p. 12)
developmentally appropriate practice (p. 12)
educational psychology (p. 4)
experimental research (p. 17)
general pedagogical knowledge (p. 10)
pedagogical content knowledge (p. 9)
qualitative research (p. 18)
random assignment (p. 17)
reflective practice (p. 5)
reforms (p. 13)
research (p. 14)
scientifically based research (p. 19)
theory (p. 20)

chapter

2

The Development of Cognition and Language

chapter outline

What Is Development?

- Principles of Development
- The Human Brain and Cognitive Development

Piaget's Theory of Intellectual Development

- The Drive for Equilibrium
- Organization and Adaptation: The Development of Schemes
- Factors Influencing Development
- Stages of Development
  - **Theory to Practice:** Applying Piaget's Work in Your Classroom
- Putting Piaget's Theory into Perspective
- Current Views of Cognitive Development

A Sociocultural View of Development: The Work of Lev Vygotsky

- Learning and Development in a Cultural Context
- Zone of Proximal Development
- Scaffolding: Interactive Instructional Support
  - **Theory to Practice:** Applying Vygotsky's Theory in Your Classroom
- Piaget's and Vygotsky's Views of Knowledge Construction

Language Development

- Theories of Language Development
- Early Language Development
- Language Development in the School Years
  - **Exploring Diversity:** Language Development for Non-Native English Speakers
  - **Developmentally Appropriate Practice:** Promoting Cognitive and Linguistic Development With Different-Aged Learners

learning objectives

After you have completed your study of this chapter, you should be able to:

1. Describe development, and explain why understanding cognitive development is important for teachers.
2. Use concepts from Piaget's theory of intellectual development to explain both classroom and everyday events.
3. Use Vygotsky's sociocultural theory to explain how language, culture, and instructional support influence development.
4. Use theories of language development to explain language patterns in children.

The way students think about the world they live in depends on their maturity, and perhaps even more significantly, on their experiences. Keep these factors in mind as you examine the thinking of the students in the following case study.

On Friday morning Karen Johnson, an eighth-grade science teacher, walks into the teachers' workroom with a disgusted look on her face.

"What's happening?" Ken, one of her colleagues, asks.

"I just had the most frustrating class," Karen replies. "You know how I told you the other day that my third-period students really struggle with basic science concepts. Well, today we were working on *density*. They memorize the formula and try to solve problems but don't really get it. They are confused about basic concepts such as *mass, weight, volume*—everything. To them, mass, weight, and density are all the same. If it's bigger, it's more dense. The class was a disaster."

"You know how these kids are; they just aren't used to thinking on their own," Ken responds.

"That's part of the problem, but there's more." Karen says, shaking her head. "They've never really done anything other than memorize some definitions and formulas. So what do we expect?"

We will return to the conversation between Karen and Ken later in the chapter, but for now, think about these questions:

1. Why did Karen's students struggle with a concept as basic as *density?*
2. What, specifically, can Karen do in response to their struggles?
3. How will an understanding of the way students think increase your effectiveness as a teacher?

Theories of cognitive development help answer these questions, and in this chapter you'll see how these theories can be applied to your teaching.

What Is Development?

Development. The changes that occur in human beings as we grow from infancy to adulthood.

Physical development. Changes in the size, shape, and functioning of our bodies.

Personal, social, and emotional development. Changes in our personality, the ways we interact with others, and our ability to manage our feelings.

Cognitive development. Changes in our thinking that occur as a result of learning, maturation, and experience.

Maturation. Genetically controlled, age-related changes in individuals.

Think back to when you were in elementary and middle school. What kinds of things can you do now that you couldn't do then? Who were your friends? How about your high school years? How has your thinking changed since you graduated?

These questions deal with the concept of **development,** which refers to the changes that occur in human beings as we grow from infancy to adulthood. **Physical development** describes changes in the size, shape, and functioning of our bodies. **Personal, social, and emotional development** refers to changes in our personalities, the ways we interact with others, and our ability to manage our feelings.

In this chapter, we focus on **cognitive development,** changes in our thinking that occur as a result of learning, maturation, and experience (Figure 2.1). This helps us understand differences in the ways that young children think compared to the thinking of older students and adults. It also helps us understand why students who have had a rich array of experiences think differently than those the same age whose experiences are limited. Karen was focusing on cognitive development when she lamented her students' inability to understand the concept *density.*

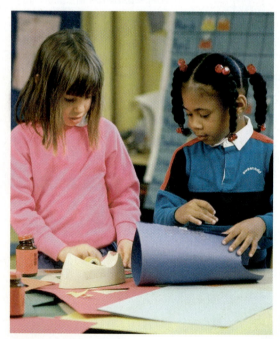

A variety of experiences contributes to learners' development.

Principles of Development

At least three general principles exist that apply to all people and all forms of development.

- *Development depends on both heredity and the environment.* **Maturation**, genetically controlled, age-related changes in individuals, plays an important role. High school students are more cognitively mature than elementary or middle school students, which helps us understand why we don't teach calculus or physics, for example, to younger students. While genetics are largely fixed, learners' experiences also influence their development. Genetics set an upper limit on what may be achieved, but the environment determines where individuals fall within the range.
- *Development proceeds in relatively orderly and predictable patterns.* Developmental psychologists generally agree that development is systematic (Lerner, 2006). We babble before we talk, crawl before we walk, and learn concrete concepts such as *mammal* and *car* before we learn abstract ones such as *density* and *democracy.*
- *People develop at different rates.* While progression from childhood to adolescence and ultimately to adulthood is generally orderly, the rate at which we progress varies dramatically. We have all heard phrases such as, "He's a late bloomer" or "She never quite grew up," which describe individual differences in people's rates of development.

With these general principles in mind, we now focus on cognitive development. We begin by considering research on the role of the brain in this process.

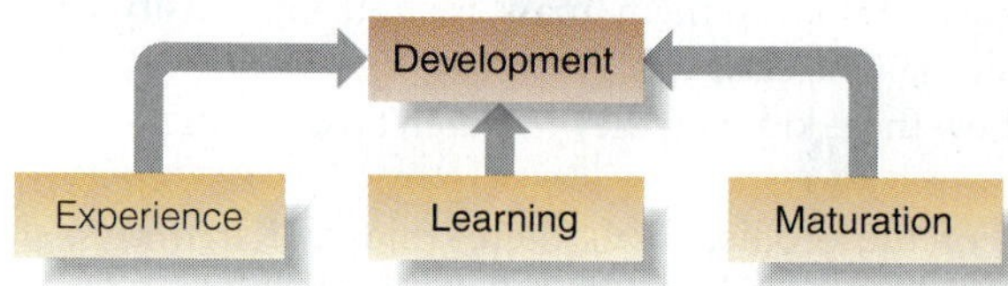

Figure 2.1 Factors influencing human intellectual development

The Human Brain and Cognitive Development

Our cognitive development is strongly influenced by physiological changes that occur in our brains. In recent years, neuroscience has developed new brain imaging techniques that allow changes in the brain to be studied as development occurs (Craig, 2003; Nelson, Thomas, & DeHaan, 2006). Understanding these changes can help you better guide the development of your students.

The Learning Physiology of the Brain

The human brain is incredibly complex. Estimates suggest that it is composed of between 100 and 200 billion nerve cells, called **neurons** (Berninger & Richards, 2002; Merzenich, 2001). The neuron is the learning unit of the brain. As you can see in Figure 2.2, a neuron is composed of a cell body, **dendrites,** which are branchlike structures that extend from the cell body and receive messages from other neurons, and **axons,** which transmit outgoing messages to other neurons (Craig, 2003).

Neurons don't actually touch one another; instead, signals are sent across **synapses,** tiny spaces between neurons that allow messages to be transmitted from one to another. When an electrical impulse is sent down an axon, it stimulates a chemical that crosses the synapse and stimulates the dendrites of neighboring neurons. Frequent transmissions of information between neurons can establish a permanent physical relationship between them (P. Howard, 2000).

Neurons. Nerve cells composed of cell bodies, dendrites, and axons, which make up the learning capability of the brain.

Dendrites. Branchlike structures in neurons that extend from the cell body and receive messages from other neurons.

Axons. Components of neurons that transmit outgoing messages to other neurons.

Synapses. The tiny spaces between neurons that allow messages to be transmitted from one neuron to another.

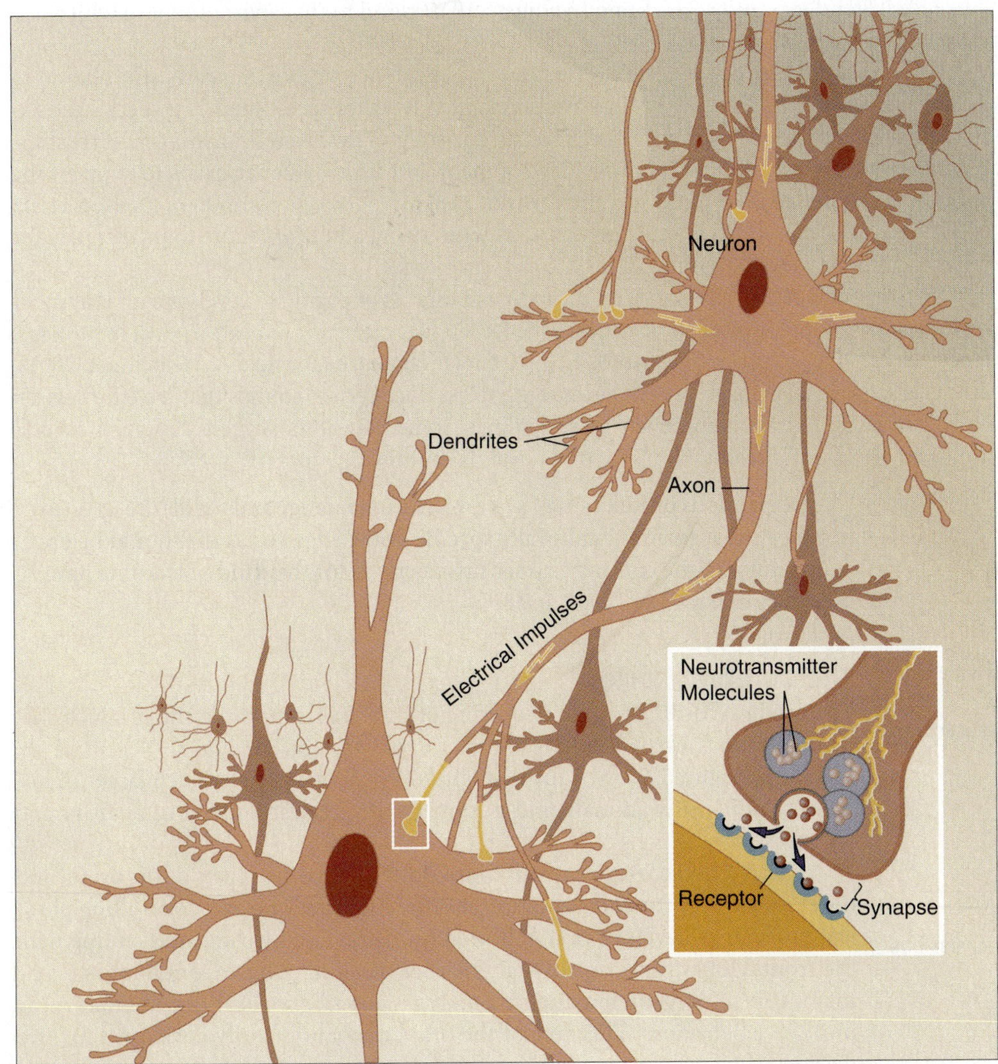

Figure 2.2 The learning physiology of the brain

Researchers once believed that we are born with all the neurons we will ever have, but newer research indicates that neurons are created throughout people's lives (Halpern, 2008). Each neuron has about 2,500 synapses, and cognitive development involves both creating and eliminating synaptic connections between neurons (Bruer & Greenough, 2001; Byrnes, 2001b). Evidence from animal studies indicates that learning experiences can increase the number of neurons and the number of synaptic connections per neuron (Berninger & Richards, 2002; Halpern, 2008). For example, laboratory rats given experiences with mazes and objects to manipulate develop and retain 25 percent more synapses than rats developed in sterile environments (Nelson et al., 2006). Age is also important; younger rats' brain development is more sensitive to this stimulation than are the brains of older rats. This research supports the contention that experience is essential for cognitive development (Bransford et al., 2000).

During the first 3 years of life, so many new synapses occur that they far exceed adult levels. Psychologists believe that generating more synapses than they will ever need allows children to adapt to a wide variety of circumstances (Bruer & Greenough, 2001). As they begin to experience orderly patterns in their environment, the large number of synapses become unnecessary, and two important processes, *myelination* and *synaptic pruning*, occur in the brain (Nelson et al., 2006). Myelination occurs when cells grow around neurons to give them structural support and form a fatty coating (myelin) that insulates axons and enables them to conduct electrical charges quickly and efficiently. Synaptic pruning, the second developmental trend, eliminates synapses that are infrequently used. At age 2 or 3, each neuron has around 15,000 synapses, but, as a result of synaptic pruning, this number is sharply reduced in adults. This "use it or lose it" tendency allows the brain to adjust and respond to the environment in which it is developing.

An understanding of synaptic connections and evidence supporting early stimulation in animals have resulted in some brain-based research advocates recommending specialized instruction during the early years. Other experts aren't so sure. Research confirms that early stimulus deprivation can impede cognitive development, but little evidence exists to support the application of added stimulation in the form of expensive toys or computers (Nelson et al., 2006). Pots and pans, blocks, and conversations with caring adults are more than adequate for normal cognitive development.

Whether or not critical periods exist for certain aspects of cognitive development is another controversial topic. For instance, a critical time for language learning appears to exist in humans, especially learning to pronounce words in a particular language (Bortfeld & Whitehurst, 2001). Adults who learn a language later in life struggle to produce certain sounds that are effortless for native speakers. Extrapolating from these findings, some educators suggest designing schools around these critical periods. However, other experts caution,

> The tremendous production of synapses during infancy and toddlerhood does not mean that teaching culturally specific knowledge and skills should begin at this time. To the contrary, no sensitive periods for this kind of learning have been identified. (Berk, 2003, p. 186)

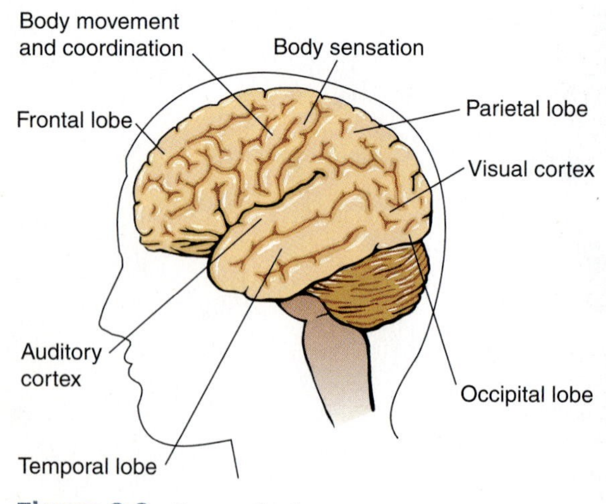

Figure 2.3 The cerebral cortex

The Cerebral Cortex

The cerebral cortex, the outer covering of the cerebrum, is the site of much that characterizes human thinking, problem solving, and language (Nelson et al., 2006) (see Figure 2.3). Not surprisingly, it is proportionately much larger in humans than in other animals, and it contains the greatest number of neurons and synapses.

The cerebral cortex develops more slowly than other parts of the brain, and different parts of the cortex mature at different rates. The part controlling physical movement develops first, followed by vision and hearing, and ending with the frontal lobes that control higher-order thinking. These frontal lobes play a major role in decision making, risk taking, delay of gratification, and managing impulsive behaviors. This area of the brain may not be fully developed for two decades.

The development in the frontal lobes helps explain several aspects of behavior, such as the temper tantrums of 2-year-olds and the impulsive and sometimes dangerous behaviors of teenagers, such as speeding, drinking and driving, drug use, and unprotected sex. While equipped with the bodies of adults, their abilities to assess risk and make sound decisions are still developing. Rules and limits that simplify decisions help teenagers through this often confusing period.

Brain-imaging research suggests that the cortex may develop more slowly in students with attention deficit/hyperactivity disorder (ADHD) (Shaw & Rapoport, 2007). This may explain why many students with ADHD outgrow the condition in their teen years.

The left and right hemispheres of the cortex specialize in different functions (Byrnes, 2001a). The right side controls the left side of your body and vice versa. In addition, in most people, the left hemisphere controls language and logical thinking, and the right hemisphere deals with synthesizing information—especially visual images—into meaningful patterns.

This hemispheric specialization has been misinterpreted by many in education and has resulted in expressions such as "He's a right-brain thinker" or "This task requires left-brain thinking." Despite their separate specialties, the two hemispheres are connected by neurons and function as an integrated whole, especially with most of the cognitive tasks found in school (N. Carlson, 1999). Experts generally believe that efforts to teach to the left or right brain are both overly simplistic and misguided (Byrnes & Fox, 1998; Stanovich, 1998).

Putting Research on the Brain into Perspective

"Brain-based learning," an attempt to directly apply research on the brain to instruction, is controversial, with proponents (e.g., Craig, 2003; Walsh & Bennett, 2004) lining up on one side and critics (e.g., Coles, 2004; A. Davis, 2004; Willis, 2007) on the other. Proponents promote the use of critical periods to maximize learning and development (Willis, 2006). They also emphasize the importance of deliberate practice and strategies such as guided discovery, problem solving, and hands-on learning.

Critics, on the other hand, acknowledge that critical periods probably do exist in humans but point out that our brains retain an enormous ability to benefit from stimulation throughout our lives (Bransford et al., 2000; Willingham, 2006). In addition, no evidence indicates the existence of critical periods in the development of traditional academic subjects, such as reading or math. Critics further argue that deliberate practice and the active learning strategies described by brain-based learning proponents have been widely accepted for years, and describing them as "brain-based" adds nothing new (Shaywitz & Shaywitz, 2004; Zull, 2004). "The brain based learning advocates . . . have [merely] repackaged progressive educational principles favoring active learning and constructivist methods" (Jorgenson, 2003, p. 365).

The critics' positions can be summarized in the following quote: "Neuroscience has only the broadest outline of principles to offer education at this time. And in a lot of cases, the principles suggest strategies that educators already know" (D'Arcangelo, 2000, p. 71).

Research does consistently indicate, however, that the stimulation that occurs in a healthy environment is essential to normal cognitive development, and parents and teachers play major roles in the process. At present, cognitive science, the area of research that examines how people learn and develop, offers the most valuable suggestions for teachers that presently exist. We discuss this research in detail throughout this text.

check your understanding

1.1 Describe development and explain why understanding cognitive development is important for teachers.

1.2 Describe the basic principles of development. Why are they important for teachers?

1.3 How does the physical development of the brain influence cognitive development?

To receive feedback for these questions, go to Appendix A.

Piaget's Theory of Intellectual Development

To begin this section, consider the following problem:

> *You have two identical containers of liquid. You then pour the contents of one into a third container, as shown here. Now, are the amounts of liquid in the first and third containers the same or different?*

Jean Piaget (1896–1980) was born in Switzerland, a precocious child with an initial interest in biology. As a young man, he taught at a school run by Alfred Binet, founder of the Binet intelligence test, and he became interested in the fact that young children gave consistently wrong answers to certain questions. This gradually led him to conclude that children's thought processes are inherently different from those of adults, and he began to focus on the development of thinking in children. His research began with detailed observations of his own three children. Initially, his ideas were not well received because his research procedures weren't viewed as scientifically rigorous. In time, as his ideas were accepted and became prominent, he changed the landscape of developmental psychology. During his career he wrote more than 60 books and hundreds of articles.

This task may seem ridiculous; the amounts are obviously the same, since you merely poured the contents of one container into the other. However, in the 1920s Jean Piaget used problems such as this to examine children's thinking. He found, for example, that young children, such as 4- or 5-year-olds, concluded that the third container has more liquid, whereas older children noted that the amounts are obviously the same. The differences in children's thinking proved fascinating to Piaget and resulted in one of the most widely studied theories of cognitive development (Inhelder & Piaget, 1958; Piaget, 1952, 1959, 1980). We examine his theory in this section.

The Drive for Equilibrium

Are you bothered when something doesn't make sense? Do you want the world to be predictable? Are you more comfortable in classes where the instructor specifies the requirements and outlines the grading practices? For most people, the answer to these questions is "Yes."

People want their experiences to make sense, and they have an intrinsic need for understanding, order, and certainty. This finding is widely accepted by sources ranging from philosophy to the popular media (e.g., van Gelder, 2005). "We inquire about the past, present, and future. We investigate every conceivable subject. Human beings want and need to make sense of things that happen—or don't happen—in the short run as well as over the long haul" (Marinoff, 2003, p. 3).

Equilibrium. A cognitive state in which we can explain new experiences by using existing understanding.

Piaget (1952, 1959, 1980) described this need for understanding as the drive for **equilibrium,** a cognitive state in which we're able to explain new experiences by using existing understanding (our experiences make sense to us). If we can explain new experiences, we remain at equilibrium; if we can't, our equilibrium is disrupted, and we are motivated to reestablish it. When our understanding advances as a result of regaining equilibrium, development occurs.

The drive for equilibrium can be a double-edged sword. Karen's students, for example, were at equilibrium when they equated the concepts *mass* and *density.* As you'll see in Chapters 8 and 9, people's need for equilibrium helps us understand why they retain misconceptions and why critical thinking is often difficult.

Organization and Adaptation: The Development of Schemes

To achieve and maintain equilibrium, people use two related processes: *organization* and *adaptation*.

Achieving Equilibrium: The Process of Organization

To make sense of our experiences and reach equilibrium, people create **schemes,** mental operations that represent our constructed understanding of the world. The process of creating and using schemes to make sense of experiences is called **organization.**

Schemes. Mental operations that represent our constructed understanding of the world.

Organization. The process of creating and using schemes to make sense of experiences.

For instance, when you learned to drive a car, you had a series of experiences with attempting to start the engine, maneuver in traffic, and make routine driving decisions. As you organized and came to understand these experiences, they became your "driving" scheme.

As suggested by our example with the containers of liquid, the schemes we construct vary with age. Infants develop psychomotor schemes such as reaching for and holding objects; school-age children develop more abstract schemes such as classification and proportional reasoning. Piaget used the idea of schemes to refer to a narrow range of operations, such as infants' *object permanence* scheme (the idea that an object still exists even when we can't see it) or children's conservation-of-volume scheme (the idea that the amount of liquid doesn't change if it is poured into a different-shaped container, as you saw in our example) (Piaget, 1952). However, teachers and some researchers (e.g., Wadsworth, 2004) find it useful to extend Piaget's idea to include content-related schemes, such as an *adding-fractions-with-unlike-denominators* scheme, a *creating-a-persuasive-essay* scheme, or a *reptile* scheme. As with our driving scheme, each represents our understanding of a piece of the world, and as you'll see in the chapters that focus exclusively on cognitive learning theories (Chapters 7–9), they are commonly described as *schemas* rather than schemes. We use this expanded view in our description of Piaget's work.

Adaptation. The process of adjusting schemes and experiences to each other to maintain equilibrium.

Accommodation. A form of adaptation during which individuals modify an existing scheme and create a new one in response to experience.

Assimilation. A form of adaptation during which individuals incorporate an experience in the environment into an existing scheme.

Maintaining Equilibrium: The Process of Adaptation

As we have new experiences, our existing schemes may become inadequate; that is, they can't explain the new experience, and our equilibrium is disrupted. To reestablish it, we adapt. **Adaptation** is the process of adjusting schemes and experiences to each other to maintain equilibrium. For example, if you learn to drive a car with an automatic transmission and then later buy one with a stick shift, you must adapt your "driving" scheme.

Adaptation consists of two reciprocal processes: *accommodation* and *assimilation* (Byrnes, 2001a). **Accommodation** is a form of adaptation during which individuals modify an existing scheme and create a new one in response to experience. For example, as you learn to drive with the stick shift, you modify your original *driving* scheme and create a *driving-with-a-stick-shift* scheme; you have accommodated your original *driving* scheme. Accommodation functions with its counterpart process, assimilation. **Assimilation** is a form of adaptation during which individuals incorporate an experience in the environment into an existing scheme. For instance, once you've learned to drive a car with a stick shift, you likely will also be able to drive a pickup truck with a stick shift. You will have assimilated the experience with the pickup truck into your *driving-with-a-stick-shift* scheme. The relationship between assimilation, accommodation, and equilibrium is illustrated in Figure 2.4.

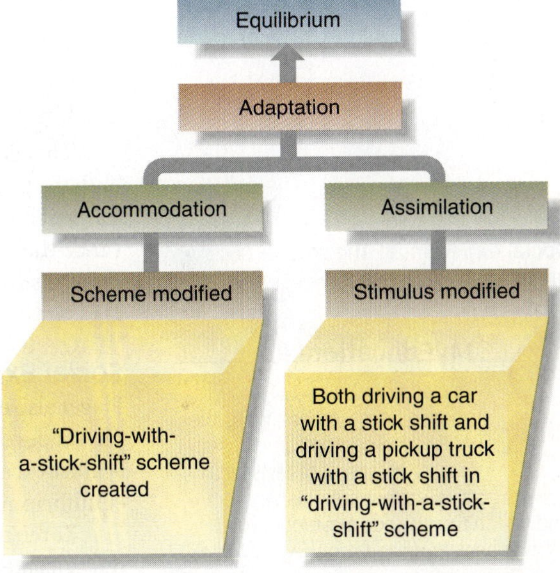

Figure 2.4 Maintaining equilibrium through the process of adaptation

Factors Influencing Development

As you saw in the preceding paragraphs, experience is the key to development. New experiences can require accommodation, and it is through accommodation that schemes are modified and thinking is advanced. Two forms of experience are important: (1) experience with the physical world and (2) social experiences. Let's look at them.

Experience with the Physical World

To see how experience with the physical world influences development, think again about your driving. Because of your driving experience, you had to accommodate your driving scheme, and your ability to drive developed. For young children, maturation is also important, but for older students and adults, experience is the key. Without it, development doesn't occur.

The central role that experience plays in cognitive development helps us answer the first question that we asked at the beginning of the chapter: "Why did Karen's students struggle with a concept as basic as *density?*" They struggled because they lacked the direct, concrete experiences they needed to understand the concept. For example, many of us have used the formula Density = Mass/Volume ($d = m/v$), plugged in numbers, and got answers that meant little to us.

To see how Karen responds to this problem, let's sit in on another conversation she has with Ken the Tuesday following their Friday discussion.

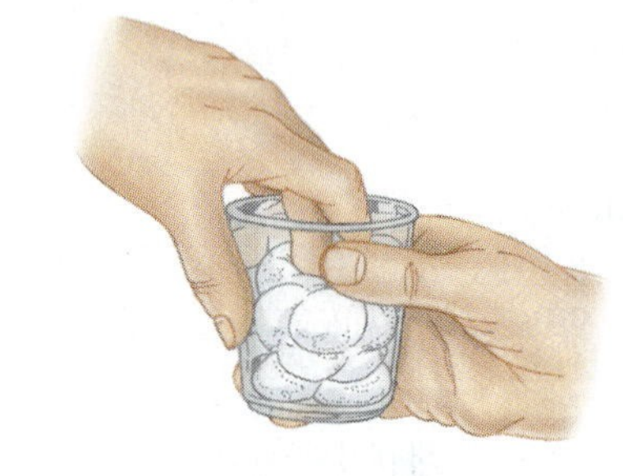

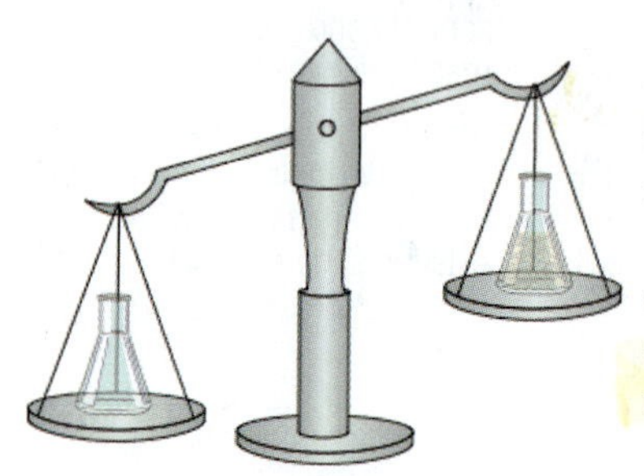

"What's that for?" Ken asks, seeing Karen walking into the teachers' lounge with a plastic cup filled with cotton balls.

"I just had the greatest class," Karen replies. "You remember how frustrated I was on Friday when the kids didn't understand basic concepts like *mass* and *density,* and all they wanted to do was memorize a formula. . . . I thought about it over the weekend, and decided to try something different, even if it seemed sort of elementary.

"See," she goes on, compressing the cotton in the cup. "Now the cotton is more dense. And now it's less dense," she points out, releasing the cotton.

"Then, I made some different-sized blocks out of the same type of wood. Some of the kids believed the density of the big block was greater. But then we weighed the blocks, measured their volumes, and computed their densities, and the kids saw they were the same. They gradually began to understand that size is only one factor influencing density.

"This morning," she continues with increasing animation, "I had them put equal volumes of water and vegetable oil on our balances, and when the balance tipped down on the water side, they saw that the mass of the water was greater, so water is more dense. I had asked them to predict which was more dense before we did the activity, and most of them said oil. We talked about that, and they concluded the reason they predicted oil is the fact that it's thicker.

"Here's the good part," she continues. "Calvin, he hates science, remembered that oil floats on water, so it made sense to him that oil is less dense. He actually got excited about what we were doing and came up with the idea that less-dense materials float on more-dense materials.

"You could almost see the wheels turning. We even got into population density and compared a door screen with the wires close together to one with the wires farther apart, and how that related to what we were studying. The kids were really into it. A day like that now and then keeps you going."

This description addresses the second question we asked at the beginning of the chapter: "What, specifically, can Karen do in response to their struggles?" She responded by providing the specific, concrete experiences they needed to understand the concept and ultimately advance their development. Now, her students are better equipped to explain why people float more easily in the ocean than in lakes, why hot-air balloons rise, and many others. Their thinking is more fully developed.

Social experience. The process of interacting with others.

Social Experience

Piaget also emphasized the role of **social experience,** the process of interacting with other people, on development (Wadsworth, 2004). Social experience allows learners to test their schemes against those of others. When schemes match, we remain at equilibrium; when they don't, our equilibrium is disrupted, we are motivated to adapt, and development occurs.

Karen's role in guiding the students' developing understanding was an essential aspect of this social experience. Most of the students had prior experiences with objects that sink and float, and through social interaction Karen helped them connect these experiences to a general principle about factors that influence buoyancy.

MyEducationLab

To examine the role of experience in development, go to the *Activities and Applications* section in Chapter 2 of MyEducationLab at www.myeducationlab.com, and watch the episode *Developmental Differences: Studying Properties of Air in First Grade.* Answer the questions following the episode.

Social experience encourages learners to examine their schemes by comparing them to the schemes of others.

Recognizing that social interaction is essential for development has strongly influenced both education and child-rearing practices. For example, parents organize play groups for their young children, classrooms utilize cooperative learning, and teachers encourage students to conduct experiments and solve problems in groups. The fact that these activities contribute to development illustrates the value of social interaction.

Stages of Development

Among the most widely known elements of Piaget's theory are his descriptions of stages of development. The stages describe general patterns of thinking for children at different ages and with different amounts of experience. As you study the characteristics of each stage, keep the following ideas in mind:

- Movement from one stage to another represents a qualitative difference in thinking; that is, a difference in the *way* children think about their experiences, not the *amount* that they know.
- Children develop steadily and gradually, and experiences in one stage form the foundation for movement to the next (P. Miller, 2002).
- Although rates vary, all people pass through each stage before progressing into a later one. Older children and even adults will process information in ways that are characteristic of young children if they lack experience in that area (Keating, 2004).
- Although approximate chronological ages are attached to the stages, children pass through them at different rates, and students at the same age may be at different stages (Brainerd, 2003; P. Miller, 2002).

Table 2.1 summarizes Piaget's stages of development, and we describe them in the sections that follow.

The Sensorimotor Stage (0 to 2 Years)

In the sensorimotor stage, children use their senses and motor capacities to understand the world. The schemes they develop, such as using eye–hand coordination to grab objects and bring them to their mouths, are based on their physical interactions with their environments.

table 2.1 Piaget's Stages and Characteristics

Stage	Characteristics	Example
Sensorimotor (0–2)	Goal-directed behavior	Makes jack-in-the-box pop up
	Object permanence (represents objects in memory)	Searches for object behind parent's back
Preoperational (2–7)	Rapid increase in language ability with overgeneralized language	We goed to the store."
	Symbolic thought	Points out car window and says, "Truck!"
	Dominated by perception	Concludes that all the water in a sink came out of the faucet (the cartoon in Chapter 1)
Concrete Operational (7–11)	Operates logically with concrete materials	Concludes that two objects on a "balanced" balance have the same mass even though one is larger than the other
	Classifies and serial orders	Orders containers according to decreasing volume
Formal Operational (11–Adult)	Solves abstract and hypothetical problems	Considers outcome of WWII if the Battle of Britain had been lost
	Thinks combinatorially	Systematically determines how many different sandwiches can be made from three different kinds of meat, cheese, and bread

Object permanence. The understanding that objects exist separate from the self.

Early in the sensorimotor stage, children do not mentally represent objects; for them, the objects are literally "out of sight, out of mind." Later in the stage, however, they acquire **object permanence,** the understanding that objects exist separate from the self. Children in this stage also develop the ability to imitate, an important skill that allows them to learn by observing others.

The Preoperational Stage (2 to 7 Years)

In the preoperational stage, perception dominates children's thinking. The name of this stage comes from the idea of "operation," or mental activity. A child who can classify different animals as dogs, cats, and bears, for example, is performing a mental operation.

Many changes occur in children as they pass through this stage. For example, they make enormous progress in language development, reflecting growth in the ability to use symbols. They also learn huge numbers of concepts. For example, a child will point excitedly and say, "Truck," "Horse," and "Tree," delighting in exercising these newly formed schemes. These concepts are concrete, however; the truck, horse, and tree are present or associated with the current situation. Children in this stage have limited notions of abstract ideas such as *fairness, democracy,* and *energy.* The powerful effect of perceptual dominance is also seen in another widely publicized idea from Piaget's theory: preoperational students' inability to conserve.

Conservation. The idea that the "amount" of some substance stays the same regardless of its shape or the number of pieces into which it is divided.

Conservation. **Conservation** refers to the idea that the "amount" of some substance stays the same regardless of its shape or the number of pieces into which it is divided. The thinking of young children can be demonstrated with a number of conservation tasks. The example with the containers of liquid that we used to introduce our discussion of Piaget's work is one example. A number of others exist, and Figure 2.5 outlines two conservation tasks.

In Figure 2.5 we see that preoperational children don't "conserve." That is, it makes sense to them that the amount of liquid (as we saw in the example at the beginning of our discussion of Piaget's work), the number of coins, or the amount of clay can somehow change without adding or subtracting anything from them. Let's see how this occurs using the example with the liquids on page 34. (Check Your Understanding question 2.2 asks you to explain how this occurs with the coins and clay.)

Centration (centering). The tendency to focus on the most perceptually obvious aspect of an object or event, neglecting other important aspects.

Transformation. The ability to mentally record the process of moving from one state to another.

Reversibility. The ability to mentally trace the process of moving from an existing state back to a previous state.

First, the children tend to center on the height of the liquid in the container. **Centration** (or centering) is the tendency to focus on the most perceptually obvious aspect of an object or event, and ignore other important aspects. The height is the most perceptually obvious feature of the liquids, so preoperational children conclude that the tall, narrow container has more liquid. Second, young children lack **transformation,** which is the ability to mentally record the process of moving from one state to another. They don't mentally record the process of pouring the liquid into the third container; they see it as new and different. Third, they lack **reversibility,** which is the ability to mentally trace the process of moving from an existing state

A nonconserver is influenced by appearances, believing that the flat pieces of clay have different amounts than the balls of clay even though they were initially the same.

Conservation Task	Initial Presentation by Observer	Change in Presentation by Observer	Typical Answer From Preoperational Thinker
Number	The observer shows the child two identical rows of objects. The child agrees that the number in each row is the same.	The observer spreads the bottom row apart while the child watches. The observer then asks the child if the two rows have the same number of objects or if there are more in one row.	The preoperational child typically responds that the row that has been spread apart has more objects. The child centers on the length, ignoring the number.
Mass	The observer shows the child two balls of clay. The child agrees that the amount of clay is the same in each. (If the child doesn't agree that they have the same amount, the observer then asks the child to move some clay from one to the other until the amount is the same.)	The observer flattens and lengthens one of the balls while the child watches. The observer then asks the child if the two have the same amount of clay or if one has more.	The preoperational child typically responds that the longer, flattened piece has more clay. The child centers on the length.

Figure 2.5 Conservation tasks for number and mass

back to a previous state, such as being able to mentally reverse the process of pouring the liquid from one container to another. When lack of transformation and reversibility are combined with their tendency to center, we can see why they conclude that the tall, narrow container has more liquid in it, even though no liquid was added or removed.

Egocentrism. **Egocentrism,** people's tendency to believe that other people view the world as they do, is another characteristic of preoperational children. Egocentric people don't consider the world from others' perspectives. As an example, imagine that you're looking at a chair from the front and you're asked to describe how it would look to a person seated on the opposite side. As with Piaget's conservation tasks, this task is easy for us. Piaget and Inhelder (1956), in another famous experiment, showed young children a model of three mountains and asked them to describe how the mountains would look to a doll seated on the opposite side. The children described the doll's view as identical to their own.

Egocentrism. The tendency to believe that other people look at the world as the individual does.

The Concrete Operational Stage (7 to 11 Years)

The concrete operational stage, which is characterized by the ability to think logically about concrete objects, marks another important advance in children's thinking (Flavell, Miller, & Miller, 2002). For instance, when facing the conservation-of-number task, concrete operational thinkers simply observe, "You just made the row longer" or "You just spread the coins apart," so the number must be the same. This represents logical thought.

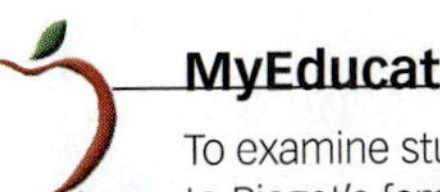

To examine students' responses to Piaget's famous conservation tasks, go to the *Activities and Applications* section in Chapter 2 of MyEducationLab at www.myeducationlab.com, and watch the episode *Examining Learner Thinking: Piaget's Conservation Tasks.* Answer the questions following the episode.

Concrete operational learners also overcome some of the egocentrism of preoperational thinkers. They are better able to understand the views of others and able to take on the roles and perspectives of their peers as well as storybook characters.

Classification and Seriation. Classification and seriation are two logical operations that develop during this stage (Piaget, 1977), and both are essential for understanding number concepts. **Classification** is the process of grouping objects on the basis of common characteristics. Before age 5, children can form simple groups, such as separating a pile of cardboard circles into one group of white and another group of black. When a black square is added, however, they typically include it with the black circles, instead of forming subclasses of black circles and black squares. By age 7, they can form subclasses, but they still have problems with more complex classification systems.

Classification. The process of grouping objects on the basis of common characteristics.

Seriation is the ability to order objects according to increasing or decreasing length, weight, or volume.

Seriation. The ability to order objects according to increasing or decreasing length, weight, or volume.

Transitivity. The ability to infer a relationship between two objects based on knowledge of their relationship with a third object.

Once children have acquired this ability, they can master **transitivity,** the ability to infer a relationship between two objects based on knowledge of their relationship with a third object. For example:

An experimenter has three sticks. He presents 1 and 2, as shown here:

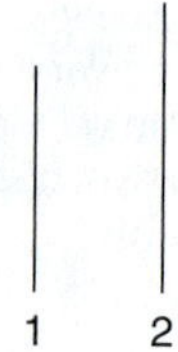

Now he removes Stick 2 and displays 1 and 3, as you see here:

He then asks, "What do you know about the relationship between Sticks 2 and 3?"

A concrete operational thinker concludes that 2 is longer than 3, reasoning that, because 2 is longer than 1, and 1 is longer than 3, then 2 must be longer than 3. This illustrates transitivity.

Though concrete operational thinkers have made dramatic progress compared to preoperational learners, their thinking is still limited. For instance, they interpret sayings, such as "Make hay while the sun shines," literally, with a conclusion such as "You should gather your crop before it gets dark."

Let's see how this compares to formal thinkers.

The Formal Operational Stage (Age 11 to Adult)

You're making sandwiches for a picnic. You have three different kinds of bread, four different kinds of meat, and three different kinds of cheese. How many different kinds of sandwiches can you make?

Although concrete operational thinkers are capable of logic, their thinking is tied to the real and tangible. Formal thinkers, in contrast, can think logically about the hypothetical and even the impossible. During formal operations, learners can examine abstract problems, such as the one above, systematically and generalize about the results. These abilities open a range of possibilities for thinking about the world that were unavailable to learners at the earlier stages.

Characteristics of Formal Thought. Formal thinking has three characteristics (P. Miller, 2002):

- Thinking abstractly
- Thinking systematically
- Thinking hypothetically

As an example of abstract thinking, formal thinkers would interpret "Make hay while the sun shines" to mean something more abstract, such as "Seize an opportunity when it exists." Their ability to consider the abstract and hypothetical makes the study of courses such as algebra, in which letters and symbols stand for numbers, meaningful on a different level from the concrete thinker. To the concrete operational child, $x + 2x = 9$ is meaningful only if it is represented concretely, such as:

Dave ate a certain number of cookies. His sister ate twice as many. Together they ate 9. How many did each one eat?

Formal operational learners can think logically about abstract and hypothetical ideas.

Formal operational learners, in contrast, can think about the equation as a general idea, just as they would in the transitivity problem by saying, "If *A* is greater than *B*, and if *B* is greater than *C*, then A is greater than *C*."

Formal thinkers also reason systematically and recognize the need to control variables in forming conclusions. A formal operational thinker would solve the sandwich problem by first taking one type of bread and systematically working through all the different variations of meat and cheese, and then do the same with a second type of bread. Concrete thinkers attack the problem haphazardly (e.g., "Well, you could make a roast beef with white bread and cheddar cheese. Then you could put salami on the rye bread with Swiss cheese.").

Formal operational learners can also think hypothetically. Examples of students' thinking hypothetically include American history students imagining what might have happened if the British had won the Revolutionary War, art students' thinking about multiple perspectives and light sources when they create drawings, and biology students' considering the possibilities when crossing different combinations of dominant and recessive genes.

The difficulties Karen's students had in understanding the concept *density* further illustrate the need for formal thinking in classrooms. When students cannot think abstractly, they revert to memorizing what they can, or, in frustration, give up altogether.

Formal Operational Thinking: Research Results. Much of the middle, junior high, and particularly the high school curriculum is geared toward formal operational thinking. Understanding *density,* for example, requires formal operations, and it was clear that the thinking of Karen's students was not formal operational with respect to the concept. Further, although we think of *centering* as characteristic of the thinking of young children, we see it in older students and even adults. For example, Karen's students were eighth graders, but they centered on the thickness of the oil, concluding that it is more dense than water. Many adults also do. Until they have concrete experiences demonstrating that water is more dense, they're likely to retain this belief.

Middle and high school curricula create a dilemma, because, as you saw illustrated with Karen's students, research indicates that the thinking of most middle, junior high, and high school students is still concrete operational (and even preoperational in some cases) (P. Alexander, 2006; M. Cole, Cole, & Lightfoot, 2005). Additional research indicates that almost half of all college students don't consistently reason at the formal operational stage, particularly in areas outside their majors (De Lisi & Straudt, 1980; Wigfield, Eccles, & Pintrich, 1996). Many individuals, including adults, never reach the stage of formal operations in some content domains (Niaz, 1997).

These findings have important implications for teachers, particularly those in middle schools, junior highs, and high schools (and even universities). Many students come to these settings without the concrete experiences needed to think at the level of abstraction often required. Effective teachers realize this and provide concrete experiences for them, as Karen did with her eighth graders. The many examples that we include in discussions of the topics presented in this book are

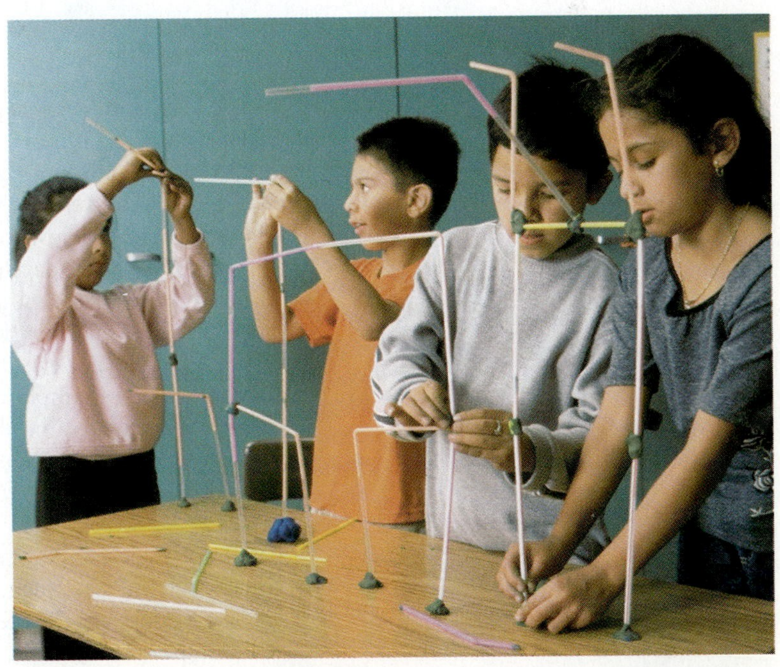
Concrete experiences provide opportunities for students to learn abstract concepts by modifying existing schemas.

theory to practice

Applying Piaget's Work in Your Classroom

Piaget's theory suggests that you keep the developmental needs of your students in mind as you design and implement instruction. The following guidelines can help you in your efforts:

1. Provide concrete experiences that represent abstract concepts and principles.
2. Help students link the concrete representations to the abstract idea.
3. Use social interaction to help students verbalize and refine their developing understanding.
4. Design learning experiences as developmental bridges to more advanced stages of development.

Let's review Karen's work with her students to see the extent to which she applied these guidelines in her teaching. She applied the first two with her demonstrations of the concept *density*. For instance, she showed the students the cotton balls in the cup, the blocks, and the balance with the water and oil, and discussed screens and population density.

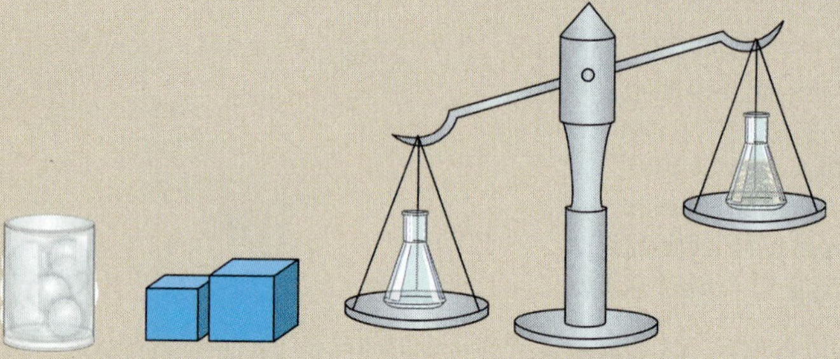

Karen didn't simply demonstrate the concept and then explain it, however. She combined the examples and demonstrations with detailed discussion. Without this discussion, Calvin probably wouldn't have been able to conclude that less-dense materials float on materials that are more dense, and Karen probably wouldn't have observed, "You could almost see the wheels turning." In leading this interaction, Karen applied the third guideline—use social interaction.

The discussion and the students' increased understanding then prepared them to understand additional concepts such as population density, buoyancy, and flotation. With this increased understanding, they would be better prepared to explain advanced ideas such as hot air balloons and massive oil tankers. These bridges applied the fourth guideline—design learning experiences as developmental bridges.

our effort to provide concrete experiences as you attempt to understand educational psychology. Without these experiences, students revert to whatever it takes for them to survive—in most cases, memorization without understanding.

Putting Piaget's Theory into Perspective

As with all theories, Piaget's work has critics. We look now at both the criticisms and strengths of his work. The following outline some of the criticisms:

- Piaget's descriptions of stages that affect all types of tasks aren't valid (K. Fischer & Bidell, 2006; Halford & Andrews, 2006; Siegler, 2006). For example, the development of concrete operational thinking typically begins with conservation of mass, proceeds through a range of other tasks, and ends with conservation of volume. Instead of discrete stages, many development psychologists now think that general developmental trends best describe the patterns of cognitive development (Halford & Andrews, 2006; Rogoff, 2003).
- Piaget underestimated the abilities of young children. Abstract directions and requirements cause children to fail at tasks they can do under simpler, more realistic conditions (Z. Chen & Siegler, 2000; Siegler, 2006). When 3-year-olds are given a simplified conservation-of-number task, for example, they succeed.
- Piaget overestimated the abilities of older learners. For example, middle and junior high teachers often assume that their students can think logically in the abstract, but as you saw in our discussion of research examining formal thinking, often they cannot (Flavell et al., 2002).
- Children's logical abilities depend more strongly on knowledge and experience in a specific area than Piaget suggested (P. Alexander, 2006; M. Cole et al., 2005). For example, if given adequate experiences, students can solve proportional reasoning problems, but without these experiences, they cannot (Fujimura, 2001).
- Piaget's work was essentially context-free and failed to adequately consider the influence of culture on development (M. Cole et al., 2005). Culture determines children's experi-

ences, values, language, and their interactions with adults and each other (Rogoff, 2003). (We examine the role of culture in development in our discussion of Lev Vygotsky's work in the next section.)

Despite these shortcomings, Piaget's work has been enormously influential. For instance, educators now see learning as an active process in which learners construct their own knowledge, instead of seeing it as students passively receiving information. Piaget strongly contributed to this constructivist view of learning.

Piaget's work has also influenced the curriculum (Tanner & Tanner, 2007). Lessons are now organized with concrete experiences presented first, followed by more abstract and detailed ideas. Piaget's influence is evident in the emphasis on "hands-on" experiences in science and the use of manipulatives in math; in children writing about their own experiences in language arts; and in students beginning social studies topics by studying their own neighborhoods, cities, states, cultures, and finally those of other nations.

In summary, some of the specifics of Piaget's theory are now criticized, but his emphasis on experience and his idea that learners actively construct their own understanding are unquestioned. He continues to have an enormous influence on curriculum and instruction in this country.

Current Views of Cognitive Development

As you've seen in this section, Piaget conducted his research many years ago, and subsequent research has both built on his theory and attempted to refine it. For example, more recent research views cognitive development in terms of specific strategies learners use as they become more efficient at processing information from the environment (Siegler, 2006).

Neo-Piagetian theory accepts Piaget's stages but attempts to explain developmental changes in terms of information processing efficiency and capacity. Robbie Case (1992, 1998), the most prominent researcher in this area, uses the acquisition of specific processing strategies to explain movement from one stage to the next. For example, as children play with water, they learn that water poured from a tall, thin glass to a short, wide one results in a lower water level and vice versa. After a number of trials, this knowledge becomes automatic and a regular part of the child's cognitive repertoire. As this knowledge combines with other areas of conservation such as mass and number, a central conceptual structure for conservation is created.

Neo-Piagetian theory. A theory of cognitive development that accepts Piaget's stages but explains developmental changes in terms of information processing efficiency and capacity.

Neo-Piagetian approaches contribute to our understanding of development by offering a clearer description of assimilation and accommodation. Practicing specific tasks such as pouring water into different containers is a form of assimilation that leads to automaticity. When demonstrating automaticity, the child no longer has to think about the results. This clears memory space to think about connections between water conservation and the conservation of other materials. When the child makes this connection, he or she constructs a new scheme that is more comprehensive and provides a more complete and accurate picture of how the world operates. This is a form of accommodation. This perspective is useful because it helps explain why development in an area such as conservation is uneven and depends on specific experiences. It also explains how specific areas of conservation are integrated into a comprehensive conservation scheme.

Information processing theory. A theory that explains development in terms of the increasingly sophisticated strategies that learners use to complete cognitive tasks, such as remembering and solving problems.

Practicing specific tasks is a form of assimilation that can lead to automaticity.

Information processing theory explains development in terms of the increasingly sophisticated strategies that learners use to complete cognitive tasks (Kuhn & Franklin, 2006; Munakata, 2006).

For example, look at the following list for 15 seconds, then cover it up and see how many items you can remember.

apple	bear	cat	grape
hammer	pear	orange	cow
chair	sofa	chisel	lamp
saw	table	elephant	pliers

Most adults organize a list like this into categories such as furniture, fruit, tools, and animals, and use these categories to remember specific items (Pressley & Hilden, 2006). In comparison, young

classroom connections

Applying an Understanding of Piaget's Views of Development in Your Classroom

1. Concrete experiences are essential to cognitive development. Provide concrete examples, particularly when abstract concepts are first introduced.
   - **Elementary:** A kindergarten teacher begins her unit on animals by taking her students to the zoo. She plans to spend a portion of the time at the petting zoo.
   - **Middle School:** An English teacher encourages students to role-play different characters in a novel they are reading. The class then discusses the feelings and emotions of the characters.
   - **High School:** An American government teacher involves his students in a simulated trial to help them understand the American court system. After the activity, he has participants discuss the process from their different perspectives.
2. Social interaction contributes to cognitive development. Use students' interactions to assess their present levels of development and expose them to the thought processes of more advanced thinking.
   - **Elementary:** After completing a demonstration on light refraction, a fifth-grade science teacher asks students to describe their understanding of what they saw. She encourages other students to ask questions of those offering the explanations.
   - **Middle School:** A science teacher gives his students a pretest at the beginning of the year on tasks that require controlling variables and proportional thinking. He uses this information to group students for cooperative learning projects, placing students with different levels of development in the same group. He models thinking aloud at the chalkboard and encourages students to do the same in their groups.
   - **High School:** A geometry teacher asks students to explain their reasoning as they demonstrate proofs at the chalkboard. She asks probing questions that require the students to clarify their explanations, and she encourages other students to do the same.
3. Development is encouraged when learning tasks both match and stretch the developmental capabilities of learners. Provide your students with developmentally appropriate practice in reasoning.
   - **Elementary:** A kindergarten teacher gives each pair of children a variety of geometric shapes. He asks the students to group the shapes and then has different pairs explain their grouping while he organizes the shapes on a flannel board.
   - **Middle School:** An algebra teacher has her students factor this polynomial expression: $m2 + 2m + 1$. She then asks, "If no 2 appeared in the middle term, would the polynomial still be factorable?"
   - **High School:** A history class concludes that people often emigrate for economic reasons. The teacher asks, "Consider a family named Fishwiera, who are upper-class Lebanese. What is the likelihood of them immigrating to the United States?" The class uses this and other hypothetical cases to test the generalizations it has formed.

children tend to use less efficient strategies such as repeating items verbatim. Simply repeating items is an inefficient strategy, and young children are less effective at remembering information.

We examine the use of strategies in more detail in Chapters 7–9, when we discuss cognitive learning theory.

check your understanding

2.1 The hands-on activities that we see in today's classrooms are applications of Piaget's theory. Explain specifically how hands-on activities apply his theory.

2.2 Use the concepts *centration, transformation*, and *reversibility* to explain why preoperational children don't "conserve" number and mass in the coins and clay tasks in Figure 2.5.

2.3 Read the following vignette, and explain in a paragraph how the concepts *accommodation*, *assimilation development*, *equilibrium*, *experience*, *organization*, and *scheme* are illustrated in it.

> You have learned word processing on an Apple McIntosh computer, and you're comfortable performing a variety of operations.
>
> Then, you go to college, and the only computers available run on Windows. You ask a friend to help you get started, and eventually you can use the new word processing system comfortably, and can perform a variety of operations on it.

To receive feedback for these questions, go to Appendix A.

A Sociocultural View of Development: The Work of Lev Vygotsky

Sociocultural theory of development. A theory of cognitive development that emphasizes the influence of social interactions and language, embedded within a cultural context, on cognitive development.

Piaget viewed developing children as busy and self-motivated individuals who, on their own, explore, form ideas, and test the ideas with their experiences. Lev Vygotsky, a Russian psychologist, provided an alternative view. Described as a **sociocultural theory of development,** his view emphasizes the role of language together with social and cultural influences on the child's developing mind (Vygotsky, 1978, 1986). Let's look at these factors.

Lev Vygotsky (1896–1934) was born in Belarus, then part of the Russian Empire. As a boy, Vygotsky was instructed by private tutors who used Socratic dialogue, a question-and-answer process that challenges current ideas, to promote higher levels of understanding. His research led him to conclude that cognitive development is strongly influenced by language and an individual's cultural and social environment. His seminal work, *Thought and Language*, was published in Russian in the same year as his death from tuberculosis. This book wasn't translated into English until 1962, so his ideas didn't begin to have an influence on developmental psychology until many years after his death.

Learning and Development in a Cultural Context

To begin this section, let's look at two examples of cognitive development being facilitated by social interaction and language embedded within a cultural context.

Suzanne is reading *The Little Engine That Could* to her 5-year-old daughter, Perri, who sits on her lap. "I think I can, I think I can," she reads enthusiastically from the story.

"Why do you think the little engine kept saying, 'I think I can, I think I can'?" Suzanne asks as they talk about the events in the story.

"We need to try . . . and try . . . and try," Perri finally says hesitantly and with some prompting.

Sometime later, Perri is in school, working on a project with two of her classmates.

"I don't get this," her friend Dana complains. "It's too hard."

"No, we can do this if we keep trying," Perri counters. "We need to work a little harder."

Limok and his father look out and see a fresh blanket of snow on the ground.

"Ahh, beautiful," his father observes. "Iblik, the best kind of snow for hunting, especially when it's sunny."

"What is iblik?" Limok wonders.

"It is the soft, new snow; . . . no crystals," his father responds, picking up a handful and demonstrating how it slides easily through his fingers. "The seals like it. They come out and sun themselves. Then, we only need the spear. Our hunting will be good today."

Sometime later, as Limok and his friend Osool hike across the ice, Limok sees a fresh blanket of snow covering the landscape.

"Let's go back and get our spears," Limok says eagerly. "The seals will be out and easy to find today."

Figure 2.6 outlines the developmental relationships between social interaction, language, and culture, and we discuss these relationships in the sections that follow.

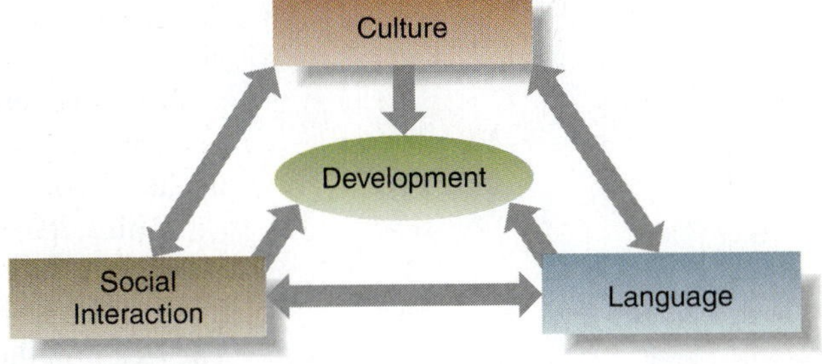

Figure 2.6 Learning and development in a cultural context

Social Interaction and Development

As you saw earlier in the chapter, Piaget (1970, 1977) saw social interaction as a mechanism for disrupting equilibrium. Then, as individuals adapt their schemes through accommodation and assimilation, cognitive development occurs. In contrast, Vygotsky (1978, 1986) believed development results directly from social interactions. To see how, let's look again at our two examples.

First, in each, learning occurred within the context of a social situation. Perri learned about perseverance as her mother read and talked to her, and Limok learned about hunting as he interacted with his father. According to Vygotsky, their thinking developed as a direct result of social interaction.

Second, the interactions were between the children and a "more knowledgeable other," an adult in these cases, and through these interactions, the children developed understanding that

Cognitive tools. The concepts and symbols (numbers and language) together with the real tools that allow people to think, solve problems, and function in a culture.

they wouldn't have been able to acquire on their own. This understanding exists in the form of **cognitive tools,** the concepts and symbols (numbers and language) together with the real tools that allow people to think, solve problems, and function in a culture. For example, the Yu'pik people, who live in the Bering Sea just west of Alaska, have 99 different concepts for ice. They have concepts describing wavy ice, shore fast ice, small cakes of ice, and thin ice overlapped like shingles (Block, 2007). These concepts help them function in their culture. In our culture, computers, iPods™, the Internet, and many others are real tools that help us operate effectively.

Internalization. The process through which learners incorporate external, society-based activities into internal cognitive processes.

Vygotsky suggested that children need not, and should not, reinvent the knowledge of a culture on their own. This knowledge has accumulated over thousands of years and should be appropriated (internalized) through social interaction (Leont'ev, 1981). **Internalization** is the process through which learners incorporate external, society-based activities into internal cognitive processes.

> Every function in the child's cultural development appears twice: first, on the social level, and later on the individual level; first between people . . . and then inside the child. . . . This applies equally to voluntary attention, to logical memory, and to the formation of concepts. All the higher functions originate as actual relationships between individuals. (Vygotsky, 1978, p. 57)

Internalization creates a link between the external and internal world of the child and is a primary mechanism for cognitive development.

Both of the children in our examples internalized specific cultural knowledge; Perri learned the value of perseverance, and Limok learned about the conditions for good hunting. Later, they incorporated their learning into a different and more complex context. Perri, for example, encouraged Dana, who wanted to quit, to keep trying; and Limok recognized the conditions for good hunting as he and Osool hiked across the ice. Incorporating their understanding into a new context represents an advanced level of development.

Finally, Perri and Limok didn't passively listen to the adults; they were active participants in the interactions. The concept of *activity* is essential in sociocultural theory (Roth & Lee, 2007). Vygotsky believed that children learn by doing and being involved in meaningful activities with more knowledgeable people. Activity provides a framework in which dialogue can occur; through dialogue driven by activity, ideas are exchanged and development is advanced.

Language and Development

Language is also central to Vygotsky's theory and plays three different roles in development. First, it gives learners access to knowledge others already possess. Second, as you saw in the previous section, language is a *cognitive tool* that allows them to think about the world and solve problems. For example, when Limok learned *iblik*, he didn't just learn the word and how to pronounce it; he also learned that it is soft, fresh, crystal-free snow and something that increases the likelihood of a successful hunt.

Third, language is a means for regulating and reflecting on our own thinking (Byrnes, 2001a; Winsler & Naglieri, 2003). We all talk to ourselves. For example, we grumble when we're frustrated, and we talk ourselves through uncertain situations: "Oh no, a flat tire. Now what? The jack is in the trunk. Yeah. I'd better loosen the wheel nuts before I jack up the car."

Children also talk to themselves. During free play, for example, you will often hear them muttering to no one in particular. If you listen more closely, you'll hear them talk as they attempt to complete a task: "Hmm, which button goes where? . . . I better start at the bottom."

Private speech. Self-talk that guides thinking and action.

Vygotsky believed this free-floating external speech is the precursor of internalized, **private speech,** which is self-talk that guides thinking and action. Piaget (1926) observed it in young children and termed it "egocentric speech," but Vygotsky (1986) instead believed that it indicates the beginnings of self-regulation. Private speech forms the foundation for cognitive skills such as remembering ("If I repeat the number, I'll be able to remember it"), and problem solving ("Let's see, what kind of answer is the problem asking for?") (Winsler & Naglieri, 2003).

As development advances, private speech becomes silent but it remains important. Research indicates that children who use it extensively learn complex tasks more effectively than those who don't (Emerson & Miyake, 2003; B. Schneider, 2002).

Culture and Development

Culture, the third essential concept in Vygotsky's sociocultural theory, provides a context in which development occurs (Glassman, 2001). The role of culture was illustrated most concretely in the example with Limok and his father. As they interacted, they used the term *iblik*, which represents a concept unique to Limok's culture. It provided a mechanism for both communication and thinking.

Zone of Proximal Development

As you saw earlier, children benefit from the experience of interacting with a more knowledgeable other. However, not all forms of interaction are equally effective. Learners benefit most from the interaction when they are working in their **zone of proximal development,** a range of tasks that an individual cannot yet do alone but can accomplish when assisted by others (Glassman & Wang, 2004; Gredler & Shields, 2004). Vygotsky (1978) described it as, "the distance between the actual developmental level as determined by independent problem solving and the level of potential development as determined through problem solving under adult guidance or in collaboration with more capable peers" (p. 86). Learners have a zone of proximal development for each task they are expected to master, and they must be in the zone to benefit from assistance.

Zone of proximal development. A range of tasks that an individual cannot yet do alone but can accomplish when assisted by the guidance of others.

Scaffolding: Interactive Instructional Support

More knowledgeable others, most commonly parents and teachers, play an essential role in helping learners progress through the zone of proximal development for the task they are attempting. For example, as small children learn to walk, their parents often walk behind them, holding onto their hands as they take their tentative steps. As the children's development advances, parents hold only one hand, and later, let the children walk on their own. This example illustrates the concept of **scaffolding,** which is assistance that helps children complete tasks they cannot complete independently (Puntambekar & Hübscher, 2005; D. Wood, Bruner, & Ross, 1976).

Scaffolding. Assistance that helps children complete tasks they cannot complete independently.

Just as toddlers' development with respect to walking is advanced by their parents' support, learners' development is enhanced by their teachers' support (Rogoff, 2003; Lutz, Guthrie, & Davis, 2006). Without this support, development is impaired. It is important to note, however, that effective scaffolding provides only enough support to allow learners to progress on their own. The parent provided the support, but the child actually did the walking. Doing tasks for learners delays development.

Table 2.2 outlines some different forms of instructional scaffolding.

table 2.2 Types of Instructional Scaffolding

Type of Scaffolding	Example
Modeling	An art teacher demonstrates drawing with two-point perspective before asking students to try a new drawing on their own.
Think-aloud	A physics teacher verbalizes her thinking as she solves momentum problems at the chalkboard.
Questions	After modeling and thinking aloud, the same physics teacher "walks" students through several problems, asking them questions at critical junctures.
Adapting instructional materials	An elementary physical education teacher lowers the basket while teaching shooting techniques and then raises it as students become proficient.
Prompts and cues	Preschoolers are taught that "the bunny goes around the hole and then jumps into it" as they learn to tie their shoelaces.

theory to practice

Applying Vygotsky's Theory in Your Classroom

As with Piaget's work, Vygotsky's theory had important implications for your teaching. The following guidelines can help you apply his ideas in your classroom.

1. Embed learning activities in culturally authentic contexts.
2. Involve students in social interactions, and encourage students to use language to describe their developing understanding.
3. Create learning activities that are in learners' zones of proximal development.
4. Provide instructional scaffolding to assist learning and development.

Let's see how Jeff Malone, a seventh-grade teacher, uses these guidelines as he works with his students.

Jeff begins his math class by passing out two newspaper ads for the same iPod. Techworld advertises "The lowest prices in town"; Complete Computers says, "Take an additional 15% off our already low prices."

Jeff then asks, "So, where would you buy your iPod?"

When the students disagree, Jeff asks, "How can we find out?"

After additional discussion, the students decide they need to find the price with the 15% discount.

Jeff reviews decimals and percentages and then puts students into groups of three and gives them two problems. Here is the first one:

A store manager has 45 video games in his inventory. Twenty five are out of date, so he puts them on sale. What percent of the video games are on sale?

As he moves around the room, he watches the progress of one group—Sandra, Javier, and Stewart. Sandra zips through the problems. Javier knows that a fraction is needed, but he struggles to compute the decimal, and Stewart doesn't know how to begin.

"Let's talk about how we compute percentages in problems like this," Jeff says, kneeling in front of the group. "Sandra, explain how you did the first problem."

Sandra begins, "Okay, the problem asks what percent of the video games are on sale. Now, I thought, how can I make a fraction? . . . Then I made a decimal out of it and then a percent. . . . So here's what I do first," and she then demonstrates how she solved the problem.

"Okay, let's try this one," Jeff then says, pointing to the second problem.

Joseph raised gerbils to sell to the pet store. He had 12 gerbils and sold 9 to the pet store. What percentage did he sell?

"The first thing," Jeff continues, "I need to find out is what fraction he sold. Why do I need to find a fraction? . . . Javier?"

". . . So we can make a decimal and then a percent."

"Good," Jeff smiles. "What fraction did he sell? . . . Stewart?"

". . . 9 . . . 12ths."

"Excellent. Now, Javier, how might we make a decimal out of the fraction?"

". . . Divide the 12 into the 9," Javier responds hesitantly.

"Good," and he watches Javier get .75. Stewart also begins hesitantly, as he begins to grasp the idea.

After the groups have finished the review problems, Jeff calls the class back together and has some of the other students explain their solutions. When they struggle to put their explanations into words, Jeff asks questions that guide both their thinking and their descriptions.

He then returns to the iPod problem and asks them to apply their knowledge of percentages to it.

Now let's look at Jeff's attempts to apply the guidelines. He applied the first (embed learning activities in culturally authentic contexts) when he began the lesson with a problem that was real for students. iPods are a part of our culture, and shopping is an activity familiar to middle school students, so Jeff's problem was culturally authentic.

Following the second guideline, his students were involved in social interactions, and they used language to explain their developing understanding. Jeff then applied the third guideline by conducting his learning activity within each student's zone of proximal development. To illustrate this idea, let's look again at his work with Sandra, Javier, and Stewart, each of whom was at a different developmental level. Sandra could solve the problem without assistance, so Jeff asked her to explain her solution, which is a more advanced task. The task was within Javier's zone of proximal development, because he was able to solve the problems with Jeff's help. But, Stewart's zone was below the task, so Jeff had to adapt his instruction to find the zone for him. Stewart didn't initially know how to attack the problem, but he was able to find the fraction of the gerbils that had been sold to the pet store. By asking Stewart to identify the fraction, Jeff adapted his instruction to find the zone for this task and, as a result of this scaffolding, promoted Stewart's development.

Jeff's instruction seems quite simple, but it was, in fact, very sophisticated. By observing and listening to the students, Jeff assessed their current understanding and then adapted the learning activity so it was within the zone of proximal development for each.

Finally, Jeff applied the fourth guideline by providing scaffolding for Javier and Stewart with his questioning. And, he only provided enough support to ensure that they made progress on their own. Effective scaffolding adjusts instructional requirements to learners' capabilities and levels of performance (Puntambekar & Hübscher, 2005). Figure 2.7 outlines the relationship between the students' zones of proximal development and the scaffolding Jeff provided.

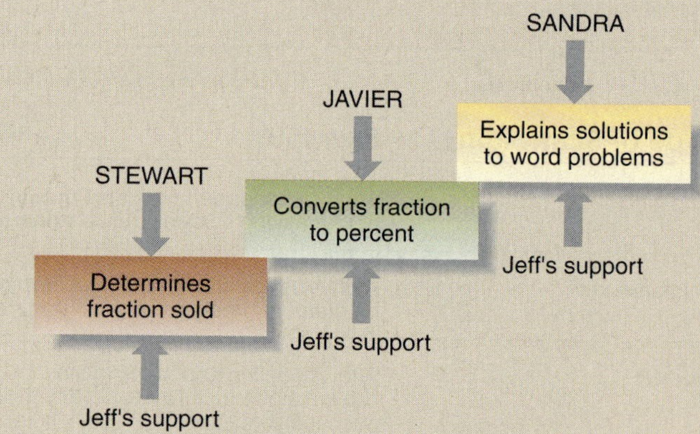

Figure 2.7 Scaffolding tasks in three zones of proximal development

table 2.3 A Comparison of Piaget's and Vygotsky's Views of Knowledge Construction

	Piaget	Vygotsky
Basic question	How is new knowledge created in all cultures?	How are the tools of knowledge transmitted in a specific culture?
Role of language	Aids in developing symbolic thought. Does not qualitatively raise the level of intellectual functioning. (The level of functioning is raised by action.)	Is an essential mechanism for thinking, cultural transmission, and self-regulation. Qualitatively raises the level of intellectual functioning.
Social interaction	Provides a way to test and validate schemes.	Provides an avenue for acquiring language and the cultural exchange of ideas.
View of learners	Active in manipulating objects and ideas.	Active in social contexts and interactions.
Instructional implications	Design experiences to disrupt equilibrium.	Provide scaffolding. Guide interaction.

Piaget's and Vygotsky's Views of Knowledge Construction

Important similarities and differences exist in Piaget's and Vygotsky's descriptions of cognitive development (Fowler, 1994). For example, both views are grounded in the widely accepted idea that learners, instead of passively receiving knowledge from others, actively construct it for themselves. They differ, however, in how the knowledge construction process occurs. Piaget believed that learners construct knowledge essentially on their own, whereas Vygotsky believed that it is first socially constructed and then internalized by individuals.

Also, they both view language and social interaction as important, but they differ in the role that it plays. For Piaget, language and social interaction are mechanisms for disrupting equilibrium that lead to individual reconstruction of knowledge. For Vygotsky, language and social interaction directly contribute to the construction of knowledge in a social environment (Rogoff, 2003).

Both views suggest that teachers limit lecturing and explaining as much as possible and move toward learning activities that put students in cognitively active roles. We examine the process of knowledge construction in detail in Chapter 8. Table 2.3 outlines the comparisons between Piaget's and Vygotsky's views of development.

MyEducationLab

To see how a middle school teacher attempts to promote cognitive development in her students, go to the *Activities and Applications* section in Chapter 2 of MyEducationLab at www.myeducationlab.com, and read the case study *Advancing Cognitive Development in Middle School Students*. Answer the questions following the case study.

check your understanding

3.1 You're a math teacher. What does the discussion in the section "Language and Development" suggest that you should encourage in your students as they study math?

3.2 In mainstream American culture, the concept of *ice* is relatively simple. In contrast, the Yu'pik people have 99 different concepts for ice. Use Vygotsky's theory to explain why this difference exists. How does this difference relate to learner development?

3.3 You are unsuccessfully trying to learn a new word processing program. A friend comes over. You do fine when she helps, but after she leaves, you again run into problems. Explain the difference between your zone of proximal development and your friend's zone. How does this difference relate to development?

To receive feedback for these questions, go to Appendix A.

classroom connections

Applying Vygotsky's Theory of Development in Your Classroom

1. Cognitive development occurs within the context of meaningful, culturally embedded tasks. Use meaningful activities and authentic tasks as organizing themes for your instruction.
   - **Elementary:** A fourth-grade teacher teaches graphing by having students graph class attendance. Students record information for both boys and girls, keep figures for several weeks, and discuss patterns.
   - **Middle School:** A science teacher structures a unit on weather around a daily recording of the weather conditions at her school. Each day, students observe the temperature, cloud cover, and precipitation; record the data on a calendar; graph the data; and compare the actual weather to that forecasted in the newspaper.
   - **High School:** Before a national election, an American government teacher has his students poll their parents and students around the school. Students then have a class election and compare their findings with national results.
2. Scaffolding is instructional support that assists learners as they progress through their zones of proximal development. Effective teachers provide enough scaffolding to ensure student success as they progress through each zone.
   - **Elementary:** When her students are first learning to print, a kindergarten teacher initially gives them dotted outlines of letters and paper with half-lines for gauging letter size. As students become more skilled, she removes these aids.
   - **Middle School:** A science teacher helps her students learn to prepare lab reports by doing an experiment with the whole class and writing the report as a class activity. Later, she provides only an outline with the essential categories in it. Finally, she simply reminds them to follow the proper format.
   - **High School:** An art teacher begins a unit on perspective by sharing his own work, showing slides, and displaying works from other students. As students work on their own projects, he provides individual feedback and asks the students to discuss how perspective contributes to each drawing.
3. Vygotsky believed social interaction to be a major vehicle for cognitive development. Structure classroom tasks to encourage student interaction.
   - **Elementary:** After fifth-grade students complete a writing assignment, their teacher has them share their assignments with each other. To assist them in the process, she provides them with focusing questions that students use to discuss their work.
   - **Middle School:** An English teacher uses cooperative learning groups to discuss the novel the class is studying. The teacher asks each group to respond to a list of prepared questions. After students discuss the questions in groups, they share their perspectives with the whole class.
   - **High School:** Students in a high school biology class work in groups to prepare for exams. Before each test, the teacher provides an outline of the content covered, and each group is responsible for creating one question on each major topic.

Language Development

A miracle occurs from birth to 5 years of age. Born with a limited ability to communicate, children enter school with an impressive command of language. Experts estimate that 6-year-olds know between 8,000 and 14,000 words, and by the sixth grade, children's vocabulary expands to 80,000 words (Biemiller, 2005). As important, they can use these words to read, talk, and write about the ideas they are studying.

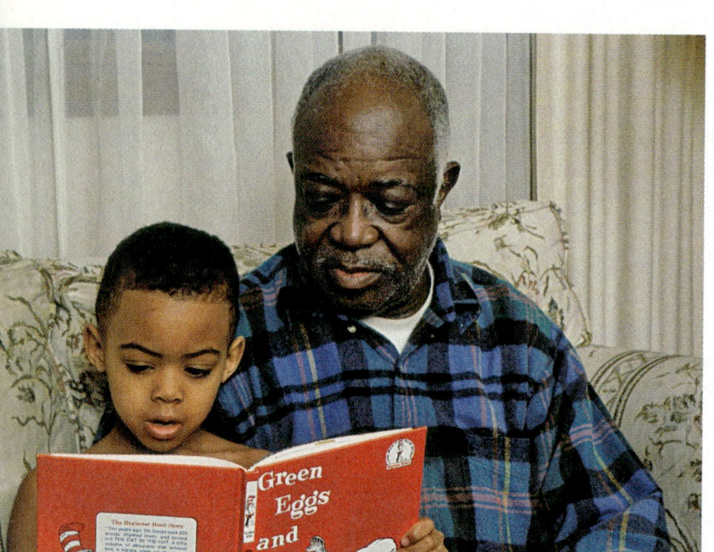

Language development is facilitated by experience and the opportunities to practice language.

As with all forms of development, experience with language is essential for language development. A long and consistent line of research examining success in school suggests that early language experiences in the home lay the foundation for later school success (C. Snow & Kang, 2006).

Understanding language development is important for at least two reasons. First, language is essential for learning to read and write, and it is a catalyst for all forms of cognitive development (E.H. Hiebert & Kamil, 2005). As students' language develops, their ability to learn abstract concepts also develops.

Second, language provides a tool for social and personal development, as you'll see in Chapter 3.

Theories of Language Development

Theories of language development differ, and these differences reflect varying emphases on heredity and environment.

Nativist theory focuses on heredity and asserts that all humans are genetically "wired" to learn language. Exposure to language triggers its development. Noam Chomsky (1972, 1976), the father of nativist theory, proposed that an innate, genetically controlled **language acquisition device (LAD)** predisposes children to learn the rules governing language. When children are exposed to language, the LAD analyzes patterns for the rules of grammar—such as the subject after a verb when asking a question—that govern a language.

Nativist theory. A theory of language development that focuses on heredity and asserts that all humans are genetically "wired" to learn language.

Language acquisition device (LAD). A genetically controlled set of processing skills that enables children to understand and use the rules governing language.

Other theories more strongly emphasize the environment. Behaviorism explains language development by suggesting that children are reinforced for demonstrating sounds and words (B. Skinner, 1953, 1957). For example,

A 2-year-old picks up a ball and says, "Baa."
Mom smiles broadly and says, "Good boy! Ball."
The little boy repeats, "Baa."
Mom responds, "Very good."

Mom's "Good boy! Ball" and "Very good" reinforce the child's efforts, and over time, language is shaped. (We examine behaviorism in Chapter 6.)

Social cognitive theory emphasizes the role of modeling and children's imitation of adult speech (Bandura, 1986, 2001). Children grow up in a language-rich environment; research suggests that 1- to 3-year-old children hear an average of 5,000 to 7,000 words per day (Tomasello, 2006). As children practice language, adults provide corrective feedback to help direct their developing speech. For example,

"Give Daddy some cookie."
"Cookie, Dad."
"Good. Jacinta gives Daddy some cookie."

The father modeled an expression, Jacinta attempted to imitate it, and he refined it by saying, "Good. Jacinta gives Daddy some cookie." (We also examine social cognitive theory in Chapter 6.)

Vygotsky's sociocultural theory provides an alternative perspective on language development. Children learn language by practicing it in their day-to-day interactions, and it appears effortless because it's embedded in everyday activities. In helping young children develop language, adults adjust their speech to operate within children's zones of proximal development (Tamis-LeMonda, Bornstein, & Baumwell, 2001). Baby talk and *motherese* use simple words, short sentences, and voice inflections to simplify and highlight important aspects of a message (Baringa, 1997). These adjustments provide a form of linguistic scaffolding that facilitates communication and language development. As a child's language skills advance, parents use bigger words and more complex sentences, which keeps the process in each child's zone of proximal development.

Early Language Development

Language development actually begins in the cradle when adults say "Ooh" and "Aah" and "Such a smart baby!" to encourage the infant's gurgling and cooing. The first words, spoken between ages 1 and 2, are holophrases, one- and two-word utterances that carry as much meaning for the child as complete sentences. For example:

"Momma car."	*That's Momma's car.*
"Banana."	*I want a banana.*
"No go!"	*Don't leave me alone with this scary babysitter!*

Children also learn to use intonation to convey meaning. For example, the same word said differently has a very different message for the parent:

"Cookie."	*That's a cookie.*
"Cookie!"	*I want a cookie.*

Differences in intonation indicate that the child is beginning to use language as a communication tool.

Two patterns emerge and continue with the child through later stages. **Overgeneralization** occurs when a child uses a word to refer to a broader class of objects than is appropriate, such

Overgeneralization. A language pattern that occurs when a child uses a word to refer to a broader class of objects than is appropriate.

Undergeneralization. A language pattern that occurs when a child uses a word too narrowly.

as using the word car to also refer to buses and trucks (Gelman & Kalish, 2006). **Undergeneralization,** which is harder to detect, occurs when a child uses a word too narrowly, such as using "Kitty" for her own cat but not for cats in general. Both are normal aspects of language development and in most instances are corrected through ordinary listening and talking. For example, parents frequently intervene, with, "No, that's a truck. See, it has more wheels and a big box on it."

The young child brings to school a healthy and confident grasp of the powers of language and how it can be used to communicate with others and think about the world. The importance of this foundation for learning in general, and particularly for learning to read and write, is impossible to overstate (Tompkins, 2006).

Language Development in the School Years

Language plays a central role in school learning. We want students to develop facility with language and also be able to use language as a learning tool. In short, cognitive and language development go hand in hand.

Developing Vocabulary

Before you read this chapter, it's likely that you didn't know the meaning of the terms *centration, object permanence, reversibility,* and *zone of proximal development,* but we hope that you do now. The concepts represented by these terms make up part of the knowledge base that helps you understand cognitive development, and practice with the terms deepens your understanding. In addition to acquiring subject-specific vocabulary, we also want students to understand abstract concepts such as *logic, fairness,* and *beauty,* which broaden their views of the world and enrich their lives.

Semantics. The study of the meanings of words and word combinations.

Semantics, which deals with the meanings of words and word combinations, is a central component of language development. Elementary students enter school knowing around 10,000 words; by the time they leave, they have mastered more than eight times that many, adding approximately 20 new words each day (Biemiller, 2005; S. Waxman & Lidz, 2006)!

This prodigious feat is accomplished in at least two ways. One is explicit instruction that focuses on key concepts, as this text does. Explicit instruction is especially useful when technical terms are introduced, precise definitions are required, and the term is unlikely to be learned incidentally (Reutzel & Cooter, 2008).

Encountering words in context, in both spoken and written language, is a second way new terms are learned. Reading is particularly valuable for learning new vocabulary, because written language contains a richer vocabulary than spoken language (Nagy & Scott, 2000).

Teachers can help students learn vocabulary by specifically emphasizing new terms during instruction and providing examples to illustrate the concepts being represented by the terms (Peregoy & Boyle, 2005; Reutzel & Cooter, 2008). Effective textbooks assist in this regard by putting important concepts in bold print, providing definitions, and listing key concepts at the end of chapters. Teachers also promote vocabulary development by encouraging students to use the new vocabulary in their discussions and responses to questions. Questioning, small-group work, and writing are all effective ways to develop vocabulary.

Development of Syntax

Syntax. The set of rules that we use to put words together into meaningful sentences.

Vocabulary makes up the building blocks of language. But just as a house is more than an accumulation of bricks, language development is more than learning words; it also involves an understanding of **syntax,** the rules of language that we use to put words together into meaningful sentences.

Learning the rules of grammar proceeds slowly and with practice (Tomasello, 2006). During the school years, children gradually learn different and more complex language constructions such as passive sentences (i.e., "The ball was thrown to him") and sentences with multiple clauses.

The introduction of more complex sentence forms begins at around age 6 and parallels other aspects of cognitive development. For instance, "Jackie paid the bill" and "She had asked him out" become "Jackie paid the bill because she had asked him out." The ability to use more complex sentences reflects the child's developing understanding of cause-and-effect relationships.

Teachers promote the development of syntax by having students read, listen to, and practice a variety of grammatical forms. Teachers should encourage students to talk and write about the new ideas they are learning in academic subjects.

Using Language to Learn

Language is also essential for learning all subjects, and it occurs through listening, reading, and writing.

A great deal of learning results from listening (Cuban, 1993). Students, and especially young ones, are not very good at it, however. Young children think that good listening means sitting quietly without interrupting (McDevitt, Spivey, Sheehan, Lennon, & Story, 1990). They don't know that listening is an active process, and they often don't realize that asking questions is both permitted and necessary to promote understanding.

You can address these problems by emphasizing the importance of listening (e.g., "Now, I want you to listen carefully, because we want to understand this idea."). In addition, you can ask questions both during and after presentations to check the extent to which students are listening and to demonstrate that the purpose of listening is learning. Encouraging students to ask questions, and assuring them that this is what effective listeners do can also be effective.

Reading is a second language-based vehicle for learning. In about second or third grade, the emphasis in reading shifts from learning to read to reading to learn (Reutzel & Cooter, 2008). As with listening, students need to learn that reading is an active, purposeful activity with understanding as its goal.

Other similarities exist between listening and reading. Both depend on prior knowledge; to make sense of new information, students must connect it to what they already know (R. Mayer, 2008). In addition, comprehension-monitoring strategies such as self-questioning (e.g. "What am I trying to learn here?") and summarizing convert reading from a passive to a cognitively active process. Finally, learner awareness, such as asking, "Do I understand what I just read?" is essential. Many children read passively, never realizing that they are understanding little of what they're reading.

Writing is the third language-related mechanism that students use to learn. Done well, it is a cognitively demanding and effective vehicle for increasing understanding, as anyone who has written a paper on a specific topic can attest. Like both listening and reading, effective writing requires learners to be active, purposeful, and strategic in their actions. Effective teachers provide students with frequent opportunities to write about their increasing understanding.

MyEducationLab

To see how developmental concepts are applied in instruction, go to the *Building Teaching Skills and Dispositions* section in Chapter 2 of MyEducationLab at www.myeducationlab.com, and watch the episode *Constructing Knowledge of Balance Beams.* Complete the exercises following the case study to develop your skills in advancing cognitive development.

exploring diversity

Language Development for Non-Native English Speakers

According to U.S. Census data, nearly 15 percent of the school-age population comes from homes where English is not the native language, and this number is increasing (U.S. Bureau of the Census, 2004). More than half of these English-language learners (ELLs) are found in the lower elementary grades, where they face the dual task of learning a new language while also learning to read and write (C. Snow et al., 2005).

Not all ELLs are alike, however (C. Snow & Kang, 2006). They vary considerably in the language backgrounds and skills they bring to our classrooms. Some come from literacy-rich homes where books and newspapers are accessible and parents regularly read to and speak with their children. Others come from homes where both parents work, and the opportunities for language development are limited.

Many children are bilingual, and for children growing up in bilingual households, learning both languages is an effortless process (Genese, 2004; Hakuta, 1999). However, when students grow up in households where English isn't the native language, the transition to English can be challenging.

Learning to pronounce words in a second language is easier for young children than for those who are older, especially if the second language differs fundamentally from the first, such as Chinese compared to Spanish for native English speakers. However, the advantage for young children may be offset by the advanced cognitive abilities of adolescents and adults. In short, students of all ages can learn a language when provided with the right kind of instruction.

This instruction doesn't differ fundamentally from effective language development activities in general, but at least three additional factors are important. First, you need to be patient with children who struggle with English. Impatience and criticism can create an emotional barrier, making children feel that they are inferior and not welcome in school. Second, the more concrete you can be when promoting language development with second language learners, the better. For example, when using the term *force*, actually demonstrating the concept, such as pushing a book across a desk, makes the term meaningful. When children have concrete reference points for English vocabulary, learning the vocabulary is made much easier. And finally, all children need practice using language to promote their language development.

We discuss different educational approaches for helping ELL students learn English in Chapter 4 when we discuss language diversity in greater depth.

classroom connections

Promoting Language Development in Your Classroom

1. Language development depends on opportunities to hear and use language. Provide students with activities in which they can practice language in the classroom.
   - **Elementary:** A fourth-grade teacher says to a student who has solved a problem involving the addition of fractions with unlike denominators, "Okay, explain to us exactly what you did. Be sure to include each of the terms in your description."
   - **Middle School:** An eighth-grade history teacher, in a study of the American Revolution, says to his class, "Now, go ahead and take a few moments to put into words the parallels we've discussed between the American, French, and Russian revolutions."
   - **High School:** A physics teacher, in a discussion of force and acceleration, says, "Describe what we mean by the 'net force' operating on this object."
2. Language development requires that students practice in emotionally supportive environments. Create an emotional climate that makes students feel safe as they practice language.
   - **Elementary:** When a third grader struggles to explain how he solved a problem, his teacher says, "That's okay. We all struggle to express ourselves. The more you practice, the better you'll get at it."
   - **Middle School:** In response to snickers as a student struggles to describe the parallels in the American, French, and Russian revolutions, the teacher states sternly, "We sit politely when a classmate is trying to explain his or her thoughts. We're here to support each other."
   - **High School:** In response to a student who says, "I know what 'net force' is, but I can't quite say it," the physics teacher says, "That's okay. We all struggle. Say as much as you can, and we'll take it from there."
3. Understanding teachers are an essential component of healthy language development. Provide scaffolding when students struggle with language.
   - **Elementary:** When a fifth grader says, "I tried to find for these numbers and, . . ." as he struggles to explain how he found a lowest common denominator, his teacher offers, "You attempted to find the lowest common denominator?"
   - **Middle School:** As the student hesitates in his attempts to describe differences in the American, Russian, and French revolutions, the history teacher says, "First, describe one thing the three revolutions had in common."
   - **High School:** In response to the student's struggles, the physics teacher says, "Go ahead and identify two forces that are acting on the block."

check your understanding

4.1 A child is talking with his friend and says, "Mine is gooder." Which theory of language acquisition best explains the use of "gooder"?

4.2 Is the use of "gooder" an example of under- or overgeneralization? Explain.

4.3 How are vocabulary and syntax development different? Which is more important for school learning?

To receive feedback for these questions, go to Appendix A.

developmentally appropriate practice

Promoting Cognitive and Linguistic Development with Different-Aged Learners

As you saw throughout this chapter, developmental differences have implications for the way we teach. We summarize some of them in this section.

Working with Elementary Students

Preoperational and concrete operational thinkers can learn a great many concepts, but they need concrete examples that connect abstract ideas to the real world. Effective teachers use concrete experiences such as squares of candy bars to illustrate fractions, real crabs to demonstrate exoskeletons in animals, experiences in their neighborhoods to illustrate the concept of *community*, and many others.

Elementary students need a great deal of scaffolding to help them progress through their zones of proximal development for each new skill. Effective teachers provide enough assistance to ensure success and then reduce scaffolding as development advances.

Language development is an essential goal for elementary students. Active participation in both whole-group and small-group activities—together with as much writing as possible—gives elementary students the practice with language that is essential for their development.

Working with Middle School Students

Though, chronologically, middle school students are on the border of formal operations, their thinking remains largely concrete operational. As a result, they still need the concrete experiences that make abstract concepts meaningful, such as Karen Johnson provided for her eighth graders when they struggled with the concept *density*.

Middle school students continue to need a great deal of scaffolding when working with topics that are becoming abstract, such as prealgebra and algebra. And, the more they practice putting their ideas into words, the more effective their learning will be.

Social interaction becomes even more important for middle school students. When well organized, group work can be effective for providing opportunities to experience different cognitive perspectives. When planning small-group work, effective teachers create groups that are developmentally and culturally diverse, providing rich opportunities to learn from each other.

Though high school students are chronologically at the stage of formal operations, the ability to think in the abstract depends on learners' prior knowledge and experiences. When new concepts are introduced, high school students still need concrete examples. Though widely used, lecture is a less effective teaching method than instruction that promotes discussion and interaction.

Writing provides valuable opportunities to develop both language and thinking skills. Using short writing assignments to help students learn vocabulary and develop syntactical fluency can be effective. Writing develops language skills, encourages deeper understanding, and prepares students for college.

Meeting Your Learning Objectives

1. Describe development, and explain why understanding cognitive development is important for teachers.
   - Development describes the physical, cognitive, social, and emotional changes that occur in people as they grow from infancy to adulthood.
   - Principles of development suggest that development depends on both heredity and environment, that it is continuous and relatively orderly, and that learners develop at different rates.
   - Understanding development is important for teachers because it allows them to adapt their instruction to meet the developmental needs of their students.
2. Use concepts from Piaget's theory of intellectual development to explain both classroom and everyday events.
   - Concepts from Piaget's theory help us explain why people want order and certainty in their lives, and how they adapt their thinking in response to new experiences.
   - According to Piaget, people organize their experiences into schemes that help them understand their world and achieve equilibrium. Compatible experiences are assimilated into existing schemes; incongruent experiences require an accommodation of these schemes to reestablish equilibrium.
   - Maturation and the quality of experiences in the physical and social world combine to influence development.
   - As children develop, they progress through stages that describe general patterns of thinking. Progress through the stages represents qualitative differences in the ways learners process information and think about their experiences; it does not describe simple accrual of knowledge.
3. Use Vygotsky's sociocultural theory to explain how language, culture, and instructional support influence learner development.
   - Vygotsky describes cognitive development as the interaction between social interaction, language, and culture.
   - Social interaction provides a mechanism to help children develop understandings that they wouldn't be able to acquire on their own.
   - Language is a tool people use for cultural transmission, communication, and reflection on their own thinking.
   - Social interaction and language are embedded in a cultural context that uses the language of the culture as the mechanism for promoting development.
4. Use theories of language development to explain language patterns in children.
   - Behaviorism describes language development by suggesting that children are reinforced for demonstrating sounds and words, and social cognitive theory focuses on the imitation of language that is modeled.
   - Nativist theory suggests that children are genetically predisposed to language.
   - Sociocultural theory suggests that language is developed through scaffolded practice that exists within children's zones of proximal development.
   - Children progress from an early foundation of one- and two-word utterances, to fine-tuning language that includes overgeneralizing and undergeneralizing, and finally to producing elaborate language use that involves complex sentence structures.
   - Language development during the school years focuses on word meanings (semantic); grammar (syntactic); and using language to learn through listening, reading, and writing.

Developing as a Professional: Preparing for Your Licensure Exam

In this chapter, you saw how Karen Johnson used her understanding of student development to help her students learn about the concept *density*. Let's look now at Jenny Newhall, a first-grade teacher who is working with her children in a lesson on the properties of air. Read the case study, and then answer the questions that follow.

> Jenny gathers her first graders around her on the rug in front of a small table to begin her science lesson. After they're settled, she turns to a fishbowl filled with water and an empty glass and asks students to make several observations of them. She then says, "I'm going to put this glass upside down in the water. What's going to happen? What do you think? . . . Michelle?"
>
> ". . . Water will go in the glass."
>
> "No, it'll stay dry," Samantha counters.
>
> Jenny then says, "Raise your hand if you think it will get water in it. . . . Okay, . . . raise your hand if you think it'll remain dry. . . . How many aren't sure? . . . Well, let's see if we can find out.
>
> "First, we have to be sure it's dry. Terry, because you're not sure, I want you to help me by feeling the inside of the glass. How does it feel? Is it dry?"

"Yeah," Terry replies after putting his hand into the glass.

Then Jenny asks students to watch carefully as she pushes the inverted glass under the water, as shown here:

Jenny pulls the glass carefully out of the water and asks Terry to check the inside.

"How does it feel?"

"Wet."

Jenny is momentarily taken aback. For students to begin to understand that air takes up space, the inside of the glass has to be dry. After a brief pause, she says, "Samantha, come up here and tell us what you feel."

Samantha touches the glass. "It's wet on the outside but dry on the inside."

"It's wet!" Terry asserts.

With a look of concern, Jenny says, "Uh, oh! We have two differing opinions. We've got to find out how to solve this problem."

She continues, "Let's dry this glass off and start again. Only this time, we're going to put a paper towel in the glass." She wads up a paper towel and pushes it to the bottom of the glass. "Now if water goes in the glass, what is the paper towel going to look like?"

The class agrees it will be wet and soggy.

She holds up the glass. "Okay, it's dry now. The paper towel is up in there. We're going to put it in the water again and see what happens."

The class watches as Jenny pushes the glass into the water again and, after a few seconds, pulls it back out.

"Okay, Marisse, come up here and check the paper towel and tell us whether it's wet or dry."

Marisse feels the towel, thinks for a moment, and says, "Dry."

"Why did it stay dry? . . . Raise your hand if you can tell us why it stayed dry. What do you think, Jessica?"

"Cause it's inside and the water is outside?"

"But why didn't the water go into the glass? What kept the water out? . . . Anthony?"

"A water seal."

"A water seal," Jenny repeats, forcing herself not to smile. "Hmm. . . . There's all that water on the outside. How come it didn't go inside? . . . How can the towel stay dry?"

A quiet voice volunteers, "Because there's air in there."

"Air. . . . Is that what kept the water out?" Jenny asks.

"Well, earlier Samantha said that when she was swimming in a pool and put a glass under the water, it stayed dry, but when she tipped it, it got wet inside. Now what do you think will happen if I put the glass under the water and tip it? . . . Devon?"

"It'll get wet."

Jenny removes the paper towel and returns the glass to the fishbowl.

"Let's see. Now watch very carefully. What is happening?" Jenny asks as she slowly tips the inverted glass, allowing some of the bubbles to escape. "Andrea?"

"There are bubbles."

"Andrea, what were those bubbles made of?"

"They're air bubbles."

"Now look at the glass. What do you see?" Jenny asked, pointing to the half-empty glass upside down in the water. "In the bottom half is water. What's in the top half?"

"It's dry."

"What's up in there?"

"Air."

"Air is up there. Well, how can I get that air out?"

"Tip it over some more," several students respond.

Jenny tips the glass, and additional bubbles float to the surface.

"Samantha, how does that work? When I tip the glass over, what's pushing the air out?"

". . . The water," Samantha offers.

"So, when I tip it this way (tipping it until more bubbles came out), what's pushing the air out?"

"Water," several students answer in unison.

Jenny then divides the class for small-group work. In groups of four or five, students use tubs of water, glasses, and paper towels to experiment on their own. After each student has a chance to try the activities, Jenny again calls the children together, and they review and summarize what they have found.

Short-Answer Questions

In answering these questions, use information from the chapter, and link your responses to specific information in the case.

1. At what level of cognitive development were Jenny's students likely to be? Was her instruction effective for that level? Explain.

2. Why was the medium of water important for Jenny's lesson? How does this relate to Piaget's levels of development?

3. When Samantha and Terry disagreed about the condition of the inside of the glass, how did Jenny respond? What other alternatives might she have pursued? What are the advantages and disadvantages of these alternatives?

4. Did Jenny conduct the lesson in the students' zones of proximal development? Explain why you do or do not think so. What forms of scaffolding did Jenny provide? How effective was the scaffolding?

For feedback on these responses, go to Appendix B.

Now go to Chapter 2 of MyEducationLab, located at www.myeducationlab.com, where you can:

- Take a quiz to test your mastery of chapter objectives. Detailed feedback is provided to explain why your responses are correct or incorrect.
- Deepen your understanding of chapter concepts with *Review, Practice, Enrichment* exercises.
- Complete *Activities and Applications* that will help you apply what you have learned in the chapter by analyzing real classrooms through video clips, artifacts, and case studies. Your instructor will provide you with feedback for the *Activities and Applications.*
- Develop your professional knowledge and decision making in *Building Teaching Skills and Dispositions* exercises. Structured feedback will be available to you, providing you with support as you practice each skill. Your instructor will provide you with feedback on the final task that accompanies the exercise.

Important Concepts

accommodation (p. 35)
adaptation (p. 35)
assimilation (p. 35)
axons (p. 31)
centration (p. 38)
classification (p. 40)
cognitive development (p. 30)
cognitive tools (p. 46)
conservation (p. 38)
dendrites (p. 31)
development (p. 30)
egocentrism (p. 39)
equilibrium (p. 34)
information processing theory of development (p. 43)
internalization (p. 46)
language acquisition device (LAD) (p. 51)
maturation (p. 30)
nativist theory (p. 51)
neo-Piagetian theory (p. 43)
neurons (p. 31)
object permanence (p. 38)
organization (p. 35)
overgeneralization (p. 51)
personal, social, and emotional development (p. 30)
physical development (p. 30)
private speech (p. 46)
reversibility (p. 38)
scaffolding (p. 47)
schemes (p. 35)
semantics (p. 52)
seriation (p. 40)
social experience (p. 36)
sociocultural theory of development (p. 45)
synapses (p. 31)
syntax (p. 52)
transformation (p. 38)
transitivity (p. 40)
undergeneralization (p. 52)
zone of proximal development (p. 47)

chapter

3

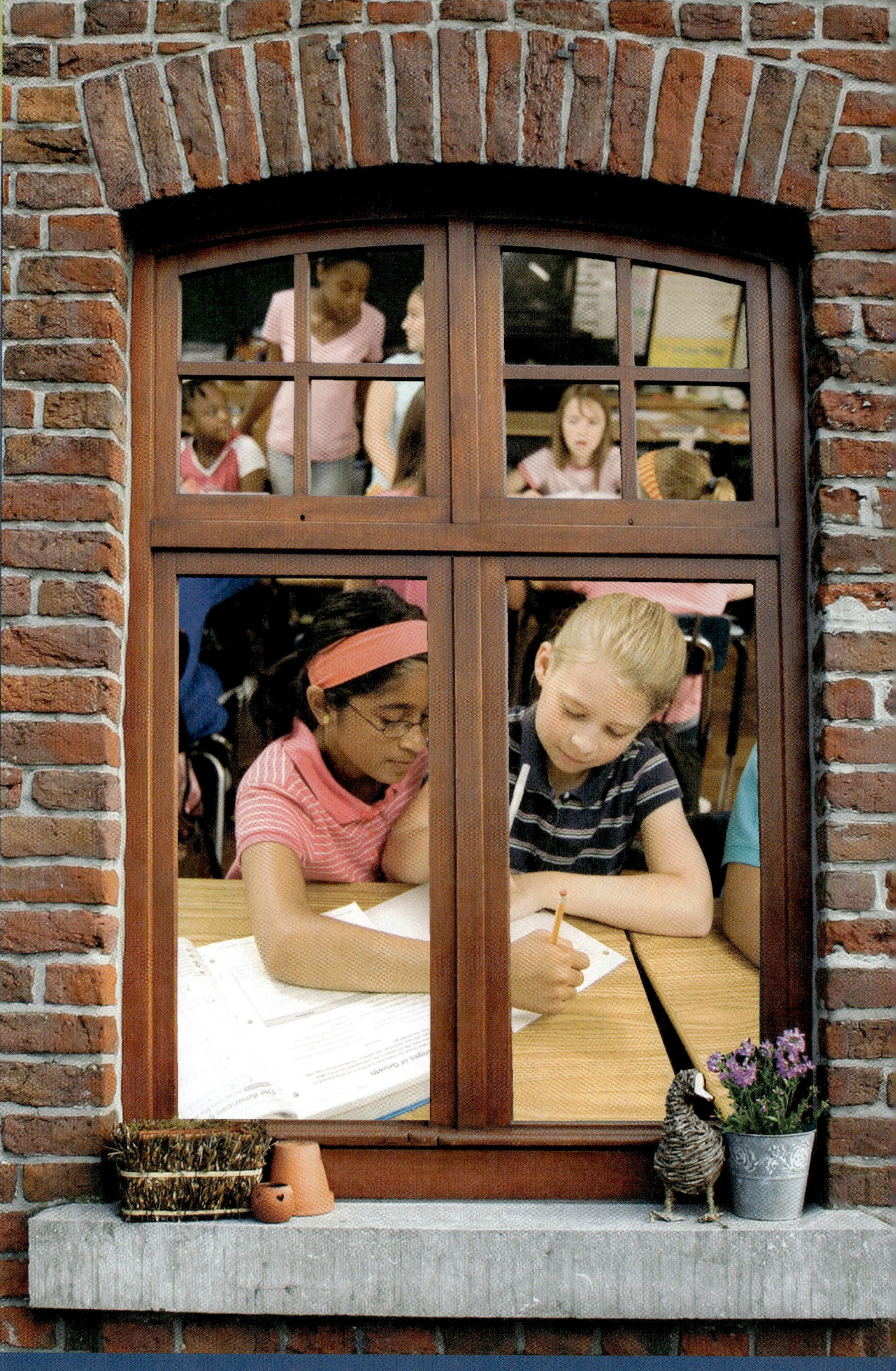

Personal, Social, and Moral Development

chapter outline

Bronfenbrenner's Bioecological Theory of Development

- The Microsystem: Proximal Influences on Development
- Additional Systems in Bronfenbrenner's Model
- Evaluating the Theory

The Development of Identity and Self-Concept

- Erikson's Theory of Psychosocial Development
- The Development of Identity
- The Development of Self-Concept
  - **Theory to Practice:** Promoting Identity and Self-Concept Development in Your Classroom
  - **Exploring Diversity:** Ethnic Identity and Pride

Social Development

- Perspective Taking: Understanding Others' Thoughts and Feelings
- Social Problem Solving
- Violence and Aggression in Schools
  - **Theory to Practice:** Promoting Social Development in Your Classroom

Development of Morality, Social Responsibility, and Self-Control

- Increased Interest in Moral Development
- Moral, Conventional, and Personal Domains
- Piaget's Theory of Moral Development
- Kohlberg's Theory of Moral Development
- Emotional Factors in Moral Development
- Learning Contexts: Promoting Personal, Social, and Moral Development in Urban Environments
  - **Theory to Practice:** Promoting Moral Development in Your Classroom
  - **Developmentally Appropriate Practice:** Personal, Social, and Moral Development with Different-Aged Learners

learning objectives

After you have completed your study of this chapter, you should be able to:

1. Describe the components of the bioecological model, and explain how they influence development.
2. Use descriptions of psychosocial, identity, and self-concept development to explain learner behavior.
3. Describe major components of social development, and explain how teachers can promote social development in the classroom.
4. Use theories of moral development to explain differences in people's responses to ethical issues.

If someone asked you to describe the kind of person you are, what would you say? What can people do to make and keep friends? How do you know if someone is moral or ethical? In this chapter, we address questions such as these by examining personal, social, and moral development. As you read the following case study, ask yourself how this development will influence your students' learning.

"Ahh," Amanda Kellinger, an eighth-grade English teacher, sighs as she slumps into a chair in the faculty lounge.

"Tough day?" her friend Beth asks.

"Yes, it's Sean again," Amanda nods. "I can't seem to get through to him. He won't do his work, and he has a bad attitude about school in general. I talked with his mother, and she said he's been a handful since birth. He doesn't get along with the other students, and when I talk with him about it, he says they're picking on him for no reason.

I don't know what's going to become of him. The funny thing is, I get the feeling that he knows he's out of line, but he just can't seem to change."

"I know what you mean," Beth responds. "I had him for English last year. He was a tough one, very distant. At times he would almost open up to me, but then the wall would go up again. . . . And his younger brother is so different, eager and cooperative, and he seems to get along with everyone. . . . Same home, same situation."

"Sean's a bright boy, too," Amanda continues, "but he seems to prefer avoiding work to doing it. I know that I can help him . . . if I can just figure out how."

Personal development. Age-related changes in personality and the ways that individuals react to their environment.

Social development. The advances people make in their ability to interact and get along with others.

Moral development. The development of prosocial behaviors and traits such as honesty, fairness, and respect for others.

As you begin your study of this chapter, think about three additional questions.

1. How might we explain why Sean and his younger brother are so different?
2. What impact, if any, will Sean's attitude have on his academic achievement?
3. What is a likely reason that Sean doesn't get along with the other students?

Personal development refers to age-related changes in people's personality and the ways that individuals react to their environments, **social development** describes the advances people make in their ability to interact and get along with others, and **moral development** describes advances in prosocial behaviors and traits such as honesty, fairness, and respect for others. Each affects learning and satisfaction with school and the ability to function effectively in later life. Promoting these forms of development is part of your role as a teacher.

Urie Bronfenbrenner (1917–2005) was born in Russia but came to the United States at the age of 6. Though educated as a traditional psychologist, he broadened his research focus to examine child psychology, sociology, and anthropology and became known as the father of the ecology of human development. He continually stressed the importance of applying research findings to our lives and was influential in creating Head Start, the federal child development program for low-income children and their families. He worked at Cornell University until his death.

Urie Bronfenbrenner, who was a renowned psychologist at Cornell University, developed a theory that describes the factors influencing each of these forms of development. We examine his theory in the next section.

B Bronfenbrenner's Bioecological Theory of Development

Cognitive development is influenced by both genetics and people's experiences. The same is true for personal, social, and moral development. Bronfenbrenner's bioecological model offers one of the most prominent and comprehensive descriptions of the factors that influence these forms of development (Bronfenbrenner & Morris, 2006). The *bio* in the theory's name reflects the influence of genetic makeup on development; the *ecological* component emphasizes that "development is a function of forces emanating from multiple settings and from the relations among these settings" (Bronfenbrenner & Morris, 2006, p. 817). As you can see in Figure 3.1, these influences include family, peers, social institutions such as church and school, and a person's community and culture.

Temperament. The relatively stable inherited characteristics that influence the way we respond to social and physical stimuli.

Individuals are at the center of Bronfenbrenner's model, and their development is shaped by both their genetic background and their environment. For example, genetics influence physical traits such as health and body build, as well as **temperament,** the relatively stable inherited characteristics that influence the way we respond to social and physical stimuli. Individuals vary in traits such as adventurousness, happiness, irritability, and confidence, and these differences persist over time (E. O'Connor & McCartney, 2007). Even siblings raised in the same environments often develop very different personalities. Knowledge of these genetic influences helps us answer our question about Sean and his brother in the opening case. Even though they were raised in the same family, their genetics likely resulted in different temperaments.

Next, we'll look at environmental influences on development.

Microsystem. In Bronfenbrenner's bioecological theory, the people and activities in a child's immediate surroundings.

The Microsystem: Proximal Influences on Development

The most powerful environmental influences on development occur in the **microsystem,** the people and activities in the child's immediate surroundings. They include family, peers, school,

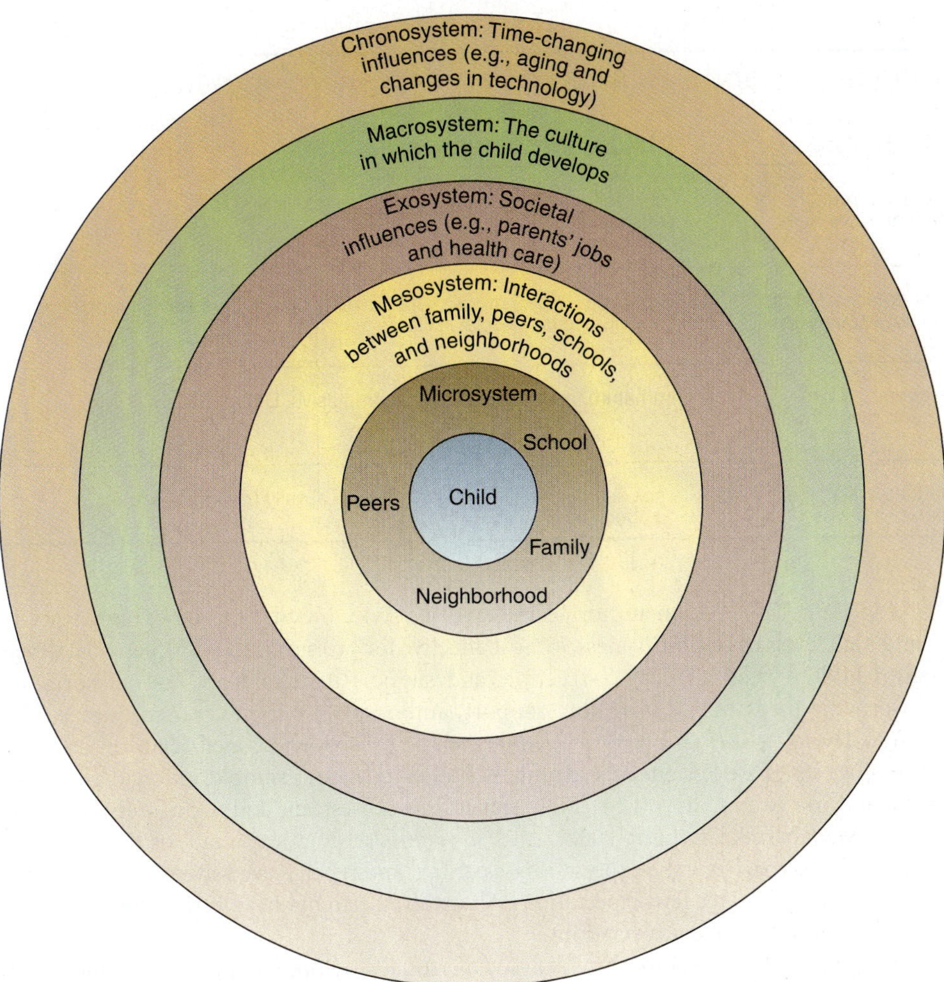

Figure 3.1 Bronfenbrenner's bioecological model of human development

and the child's immediate neighborhood (Pomerantz & Dong, 2006; Weigel, Martin, & Bennett, 2005), as well as the increasing influence of television, the Internet, and other forms of media (Comstock & Scharrer, 2006).

Parents

Parents and other caregivers are perhaps the most powerful influences on children's personal development (Landry, Smith, & Swank, 2006; Soenens et al., 2007). This makes sense given the amount of time children—and especially young children—spend with their parents. Experts estimate that children up to age 18 spend nearly 90 percent of their waking hours outside of school under the guidance of their parents (Kamil & Walberg, 2005).

Research indicates that certain **parenting styles,** general patterns of interacting with and disciplining children, promote more healthy personal development than others (Baumrind, 1991), and the effects of these styles can last into the college years, influencing motivation, achievement, and relationships with teachers (W. A. Collins, Maccoby, Steinberg, Hetherington, & Bornstein, 2000).

Parenting style. General patterns of interacting with and disciplining children.

Researchers have found two important differences among parents in the ways they relate to their children: their *expectations* and their *responsiveness.* Some set high expectations and insist that they're met; others expect little of their children and rarely try to influence them. Responsive parents, for example, accept their children and frequently interact with them; unresponsive parents tend to be rejecting, negative, or indifferent. Using expectations and responsiveness as a framework, researchers have identified four parenting styles and the patterns of personal development associated with them. These parenting styles are summarized in Table 3.1.

table 3.1 Parenting Styles and Patterns of Personal Development

Interaction Style	Parental Characteristics	Child Characteristics
Authoritative	Are firm but caring. Explain reasons for rules, and are consistent. Have high expectations.	High self-esteem. Confident and secure. Willing to take risks, and are successful in school.
Authoritarian	Stress conformity. Are detached, dont explain rules, and do not encourage verbal give-and-take.	Withdrawn. Worry more about pleasing parent than solving problems. Defiant, and lack social skills.
Permissive	Give children total freedom. Have limited expectations, and make few demands on children.	Immature, and lack self-control. Impulsive. Unmotivated.
Uninvolved	Have little interest in their child's life. Hold few expectations.	Lack self-control and long-term goals. Easily frustrated and disobedient.

As you see in Table 3.1, an authoritative parenting style, one that combines high expectations and high levels of responsiveness, is most effective for promoting healthy personal development. Children need challenge, structure, and support in their lives, and authoritative parents provide them. While providing support, authoritative parents also encourage their children to develop values and goals that guide their actions (Soenens et al., 2007).

The other styles are less effective. Authoritarian parents, for example, are rigid and unresponsive, and in extreme cases their children have low self-esteem and use aggressive coping behaviors (Maughan & Cicchetti, 2002). Also, if parents set high expectations but are unresponsive, children may view the expectations as unfair, and rebel. Permissive parents are emotionally responsive but set few expectations. Uninvolved parents have little interest in their children's lives and hold few expectations.

Healthy parent–child relationships promote personal development by helping children acquire a sense of autonomy, competence, and belonging (Christenson & Havsy, 2004). Such relationships also support the development of personal responsibility, the ability to control one's own actions based on developing values and goals.

Parenting styles depend, in part, on culture. For example, in one study, Puerto Rican parents, who deferred to teachers' authority in the classroom, were viewed by teachers as being uncaring and apathetic (Harry, 1992). These parents also wanted teachers to act like caregivers and provide more warmth and structure for students. Effective teachers are sensitive to these cultural differences and attempt to work with parents.

Other adults, most commonly teachers, also contribute to children's personal development. The interaction styles of effective teachers are similar to those of effective parents, and the description of authoritative parenting strongly parallels recommended classroom management practices for teachers (Emmer, Evertson, & Worsham, 2006; Evertson, Emmer, & Worsham, 2006).

Peers

Think back to the friends you had in middle and high school. How did they influence who you are today? Next to parents and other caregivers, peers exert the most powerful influence on personal development, especially for adolescents. This influence exists in three forms (Eisenberg, Fabes, & Spinrad, 2006; Rubin, Bukowski, & Parker, 2006).

- *Attitudes and Values.* Peers communicate attitudes and values about topics varying from the importance of school work to definitions of right and wrong (Kidron & Fleischman, 2006). Research indicates that choice of friends predicts grades, disruptive behaviors, and teachers' ratings of involvement in school (Benson, et al, 2006; Rubin et al., 2006). When students select academically oriented friends, for example, their grades improve; when they choose disruptive friends, their grades decline and behavior problems increase.

MyEducationLab

To examine the influence of peers on students' development, go to the *Activities and Applications* section in Chapter 3 of MyEducationLab at www.myeducationlab.com, and watch the episode *Friendships*. Answer the questions following the episode.

- *Social Development.* As you'll see later in the chapter, children's social skills develop over time. Peers, and especially close friends, provide opportunities to practice social skills and receive feedback.
- *Emotional Support.* Developing into a healthy, happy person isn't easy, and today's complex world makes the process even more challenging. Friends provide both emotional support and a sense of identity, sometimes through **cliques,** small groups of peers who provide support and temporary identities.

Clique. A small group of peers who act as friends, providing support and temporary identities.

The child's neighborhood and school are other important influences within the microsystem. Some neighborhoods are safe and nurturant, while others are dangerous and toxic (Fauth, Roth, & Brooks-Gunn, 2007; Stewart, Stewart, & Simons, 2007). Schools, like neighborhoods, can be caring and supportive or sterile and impersonal (Kozol, 2005; Mawhinney & Sagan, 2007).

Additional Systems in Bronfenbrenner's Model

According to Bronfenbrenner's model, the individual and the microsystem are embedded in and influenced by other systems in the environment. The **mesosystem** consists of the interactions between the elements of the microsystem, and healthy development depends on how effectively the elements work together. For example, research suggests that effective teachers involve parents in their children's education, creating links between two important elements of the microsystem (Epstein, 2001). In a similar way, effective schools open their doors to the community to create a web of support for the developing child (Comer, Joyner, & Ben-Avie, 2004).

Mesosystem. In Bronfenbrenner's bioecological theory, the interactions and connections between the different elements of children's immediate settings.

The **exosystem** includes societal influences that affect both the micro- and mesosystems, such as parents' jobs, health care, and other social services. For example, parents' jobs can affect family stability and the amount of time parents have to spend with their children. Community health and legal services, the larger community, and the school system are other elements of the exosystem. Like neighborhoods, school systems vary significantly in their ability to promote development (Biddle & Berliner, 2002; Kober, 2006). Wealthier school systems provide school nurses, psychologists, counselors, and small class sizes that allow teachers to know children as individuals. Not surprisingly, in smaller classes, teachers spend less time on classroom management and more on instruction (J. Finn, Gerber, & Boyd-Zaharias, 2005; Peevely, Hedges, & Nye, 2005).

Exosystem. In bioecological theory, societal influences that affect both the micro- and mesosystems.

The **macrosystem,** the fourth level in Bronfenbrenner's model, is the culture in which a child develops, and it influences all the other systems. For example, some cultures emphasize autonomy and independence, while others stress conformity (Chao, 1994, 2001).

Macrosystem. Bronfenbrenner's fourth level of influences on developing children, which includes cultural influences on development.

The macrosystem reflects the value a society places on its children and the resources necessary for healthy development. The national debate in our country about universal health care for children is an example. Children who are ill or injured won't develop congnitively, personally, or socially in the same way as will their healthier peers.

The **chronosystem** is the final level of the bioecological model. As the term implies, it includes time-dependent, changing influences on development. For example, family members grow older and change, we meet new people, experience different social institutions, and now live in a world strongly influenced by the Internet and other forms of technology. Children today are developing in a world very different from their grandparents' or parents' time.

Chronosystem. The final level in bioecological theory that includes temporal, or time-dependent, influences on development.

Evaluating the Theory

Bronfenbrenner's theory has made important contributions to our understanding of the influences on human development. We know that development depends on both genetics and the environment, and Bronfenbrenner's theory integrates these influences into a comprehensive model. In addition, it reminds us that development depends on a range of factors in the child's environment (E. O'Connor & McCartney, 2007).

The model has weaknesses, however. Its tendency to ignore the role of cognition in development is probably its primary weakness. As you'll see later in the chapter, the ways children think about themselves and their relationships with others also influence personal, social, and

classroom connections

Applying Bronfenbrenner's Bioecological Theory in Your Classroom

1. Bronfenbrenner's bioecological theory describes how development is influenced by different systems, beginning with the individual and extending to family and societal forces. Create connections with these external influences on your students' development.
   - **Elementary:** A third-grade teacher makes an effort at the beginning of the school year to get to know her students and their families. She reads their student files, talks to previous years' teachers, and invites students to accompany their parents during parent–teacher conferences. During these conferences, she observes how parents interact with their children and uses this information to provide extra structure and emotional support in special cases.
   - **Middle School:** Teachers in an urban middle school realize that many of the children on their team do not have adequate medical or dental care. They ask the school psychologist and social worker to come in to talk about possible resources in their students' meso- and exosystems.
   - **High School:** A history teacher attempts to link course content to students' lives. As she makes these links to students' macro- and chronosystems, she tries to help them understand how societal influences affect their future lives in terms of jobs and schooling.

moral development. In addition, the model ignores the idea of developmental stages, an idea you examined in your study of Piaget's work in Chapter 2.

check your understanding

1.1 Describe the components of the bioecological model, and explain how they influence development.

1.2 Why is the microsystem the most powerful influence on development?

1.3 How are the influences of teachers and schools reflected in Bronfenbrenner's bioecological model?

To receive feedback for these questions, go to Appendix A.

Identity. Individuals' sense of self, what their existence means, and what they want in life.

Self-concept. A cognitive assessment of one's physical, social, and academic competence.

The Development of Identity and Self-Concept

Individuals' responses to school and life in general are influenced by their identities in combination with their self-concepts. **Identity** is the sense of self, individuals' personal understanding of their own existence, and what they want in life. **Self-concept** is individuals' cognitive assessment of their physical, social, and academic competence. In this section, we consider how identity and self-concept develop, and what this development means for your teaching. We begin with a discussion of identity.

Erik Erikson (1902–1994). Erik Erikson's interest in identity can be traced to his own childhood. Born in Germany, Erikson was the product of an extramarital affair and the circumstances of his birth were concealed from him as a child. The development of identity became one of his greatest concerns, both in his own life and in his theory.

He worked with Anna Freud, daughter of the famous Sigmund Freud, who kindled his interest in becoming a psychoanalyst. He emigrated to the United States after the Nazis came to power in Germany in the 1930s, worked as a child psychoanalyst in Boston, and later held faculty positions at Yale and Berkeley. His work included research on diverse cultures including Sioux children and Yuroks, a Native American tribe in California.

He is also well known for coining the term "identity crisis."

Erikson's Theory of Psychosocial Development

Where are you going with your life? Do you feel you're on a positive career path? Are you in a relationship with someone "special"? Erik Erikson (1902–1994), a developmental psychologist and psychoanalyst, addressed questions such as these in his work with clients, and he personally wrestled with them in what he called a "crisis of identity" in his own life (Cross, 2001). Based on these experiences, he developed a theory of "psychosocial" development. The term *psychosocial* derives from the integration of identity and Erikson's belief that a primary motivation for human behavior is social and reflects a desire to connect with other people (Erikson, 1968, 1980). His theory is unique in the sense that he viewed developmental changes occurring throughout our lifespans.

Erikson believed that people have the same basic needs. He also believed that personal development occurs in response to those needs and depends on the quality of support provided by the social environment, particularly parents and other caregivers. Development proceeds in stages, each characterized by a **crisis,** a psychosocial challenge that presents opportunities for development. Although never permanently resolved, the positive resolution of a crisis at one stage increases the likelihood of a positive resolution at the next. The stages are summarized in Table 3.2.

Crisis. A psychosocial challenge that presents opportunities for development.

While positive resolution of the crisis at one stage better prepares people for a positive resolution at the next, Erikson didn't believe that it is always ideal. For instance, while learning to trust people is desirable, we cannot trust all people under all circumstances. However, when psychosocial development is healthy, the positive resolution predominates at each stage. In addition, when positive resolution doesn't occur at a particular stage, individuals often revisit earlier stages to rework these crises.

Putting Erikson's Work into Perspective

Erikson's work was popular and influential in the 1960s and 1970s, but since then, developmental theorists have taken issue with it on at least three points. First, some researchers argue that Erikson didn't adequately address the role of culture in personal and social development. For instance, some cultures discourage autonomy and initiative in children, perhaps as a way of protecting them from dangers in their environments (Dennis, Cole, Zahn-Waxler, & Mizuta, 2002).

table 3.2 Erikson's Eight Life-Span Stages

Stage	Description
Trust vs. Mistrust (Birth to 1 year)	Trust develops when infants receive consistently loving care. Mistrust results from unpredicatable or harsh care.
Autonomy vs. Shame (1–3 years)	Autonomy develops when children use their newly formed mental and psychomotor skills to explore their worlds. Parents support autonomy by encouraging exploration and accepting the inevitable mistakes.
Initiative vs. Guilt (3–6 years)	Initiative, a sense of ambition and responsibility, develops from encouragement of children's efforts to explore and take on new challenges. Overcontrol or criticism can result in guilt.
Industry vs. Inferiority (6–12 years)	School and home provide opportunities for students to develop a sense of competence through success on challenging tasks. A pattern of failure can lead to feelings of inferiority.
Identify vs. Confusion (12–18 years)	Adolescents experiment with various roles in an atmosphere of freedom with clearly established limits. Confusion results when the home environment fails to provide either the necessary structure or when it is overly controlling, failing to provide opportunities for individual exploration with different identity roles.
Intimacy vs. Isolation (Young adulthood)	Intimacy occurs when individuals establish close ties with others. Emotional isolation may result from earlier disappointments or a lack of developing identity.
Generativity vs. Stagnation (Adulthood)	Generativity occurs when adults give to the next generation through child rearing, productive work, and contributions to society or other people. Apathy or self-absorption can result from an inability to think about or contribute to the welfare of others.
Integrity vs. Despair (Old age)	Integrity occurs when people believe they've lived as well as possible and accept the inevitability of death. Remorse over things done or left undone leads to despair.

Early childhood and elementary classrooms should provide opportunities for students to develop personal independence and initiative.

Second, critics point out that some adolescents—and especially girls—establish a sense of intimacy with, or even before, a focus on personal identity (Kroger, 2000). This contrasts with Erikson's description of intimacy following the development of identity.

Third, as you'll see in our discussion of identity development in the next section, many people don't achieve a sense of identity as early as Erikson suggested.

Erikson's work is intuitively sensible, however, and it helps explain behaviors we often see in others. For example, we might explain Sean's contention in the opening case that the other students are "picking on him for no reason," by saying that he hasn't positively resolved the trust–distrust crisis. This has left him less able to develop a sense of autonomy, initiative, or industry, which helps us understand why he "won't do his work." We've all met people we admire because of their positive outlook, openness, and commitment to making the world better. We've also encountered those who believe that others are trying to take advantage of them or are somehow inherently evil. We see good minds sliding into lethargy because of a lack of initiative or even substance abuse. We become frustrated by people's apathy and lack of a zest for living. Erikson's work helps us understand these issues.

Supporting Psychosocial Development

Teachers support psychosocial development by encouraging and reinforcing initiative in young children. Then, during the elementary years, teachers provide the challenging experiences, support, and feedback that help children develop the sense of competence that leads to a positive resolution of the industry-inferiority crisis.

During adolescence, teenagers need firm, caring teachers who empathize with them and the uncertainties of this period in their lives, while providing the security of clear limits for acceptable behavior (Rudolph et al., 2001). In the opening case, you saw that Sean's teachers both tried to get him to "open up" to them. Most significant is the sensitivity they demonstrated in their efforts to reach him. This is essential for adolescents during this period.

The Development of Identity

Another perspective on identity development focuses on individual's efforts to define themselves through their lifestyle and career choices. Parents and a variety of social experiences contribute to this process (Trawick-Smith, 2003). For example, adolescents often identify with a peer group, rigidly adhering to a style of dress or way of wearing their hair (McCleo & Yates, 2006). Girls' bare-stomach tops and boys' baggy pants and reverse baseball caps, common in middle schools, are displays of these "temporary identities." In time they're replaced with a more individual sense of self and an awareness of lifelong goals.

Career Choices in Identity Development

Learners' attempts to make career choices also influence their identity development. Let's look at an example.

> Four seniors are talking about what they plan to do after high school:
>
> "I'm going into nursing," Taylor comments. "I've been working part-time at the hospital, and it feels really good to work with people and help them. I thought I wanted to be a doctor at one time, but I don't think I can handle the pressure. I've talked with the counselors, and I think I can do the chemistry and other science courses."
>
> "I'm not sure what I want to do," Sandy comments. "I've thought about veterinary medicine, and also about teaching. I've been working at the vet clinic, and I like it, but I'm not sure about doing it forever. Some of my parents' friends are teachers, so I hear what they say about it. I don't know."

"I wish I could do that," Ramon replies. "But I'm off to the university in the fall. I'm going to be a lawyer. At least that's what my parents think. It's not a bad job, and lawyers make good money."

"How can you just do that?" Nancy wonders. "You've said that you don't want to be a lawyer. . . . I'm not willing to decide yet. I'm only 18. I'm going to think about it for a while."

Conversations with caring adults provide opportunities for adolescents to think about and refine their developing personal identities.

As adolescents struggle with their identities, two processes occur (Luyckx, Goossens, & Soenens, 2006). The first, *identity formation*, involves the creation of commitments based on conviction or belief. This was illustrated in Taylor's comment, "it feels really good to work with people and help them." The second process, *evaluation*, occurs when they consider alternative identities and weigh the pros and cons of each. For example, you may have asked yourself whether or not you want to be a teacher or perhaps work instead in the business world. These deliberations are your attempt to evaluate different options.

To study the development of identity, researchers interviewed adolescents and found that young people's decisions can be generally classified into one of four states, which are outlined in Table 3.3 (Marcia, 1980, 1987, 1999). These states vary in their ability to produce healthy outcomes. *Identity moratorium*, for instance, is a positive state that may eventually lead to *identity achievement*, which is also positive. In contrast, *identity diffusion*, common in younger adolescents, reflects haphazard consideration of different career choices. If it persists over time, it can result in apathy and confusion (Berzonsky & Kuk, 2000). *Identity foreclosure*, another less productive path, occurs when adolescents adopt the goals and values of others—usually their parents—without thoroughly examining the implications for their future. Many adolescents experience both identity moratorium and diffusion before arriving at identity achievement. Teachers and other adults can assist in this search by openly discussing pressing issues with students.

In contrast with the predictions of Erikson's theory, research indicates that identity achievement more often occurs after, than during, high school (Berzonsky & Kuk, 2000; Marcia, 1980, 1987). This delay is especially true for college students, who have more time to consider what they want to do with their lives.

This research suggests that the uncertainty adolescents experience is related more to the demands of increased independence than to identity issues (Bettis & Adams, 2005; McLeod & Yates, 2006). Conflict with parents, teachers, and other adults peaks in early adolescence and then declines, as teenagers accept responsibility and adults learn how to deal with the new relationships

table 3.3 States in Identity Development

State	Description
Identity diffusion	Occurs when individuals fail to make clear choices. Characterized by haphazard experimentation with different career options. Choices may be difficult, or individuals aren't developmentally ready to make choices.
Identity foreclosure	Occurs when individuals prematurely adopt the positions of others, such as parents. This is an undesirable position because it is based on the identities of others.
Identity moratorium	Occurs when individuals pause and remain in a holding pattern. Long-range commitment is delayed.
Identity achievement	Occurs after individuals experience a period of crises and decision making. Identity achievement reflects a commitment to a goal or direction.

(Arnett, 2002). The challenges of early adolescence help explain why teaching middle and junior high students can be particularly challenging.

Sexual Identity

Sexual identity. Students' self-constructed definition of who they are with respect to gender orientation.

Sexual orientation. The gender to which an individual is romantically and sexually attracted.

Sexual identity, students' self-constructed definition of who they are with respect to gender orientation, is another important element of identity formation. Sexual identity influences student choices ranging from clothes and friends to the occupations they consider and ultimately pursue (Ruble, Martin, & Berenbaum, 2006). **Sexual orientation,** the gender to which an individual is romantically and sexually attracted, is an important dimension of sexual identity.

Homosexual students (students whose sexual orientations are directed toward members of their own gender) are estimated to make up about 3 to 10 percent of the school population, and this sexual orientation can be confusing and stressful for some of them (Macionis, 2006). Attempts to pinpoint the causes of homosexuality are controversial, with some believing that it is genetic and others attributing it to learning and choice (Gollnick & Chinn, 2006). Research suggests a definite genetic component; if one member of identical twins is homosexual, for example, the other is much more likely to also be homosexual than is the case with fraternal twins (Bailey, 1993).

Research also suggests that homosexuals experience a three-phase sequence in their attempts to understand who they are. The first is feeling different, a slowly developing awareness that they aren't like other children. The second is a feeling of confusion, which occurs during adolescence. In this phase, homosexuals attempt to understand their developing sexuality, looking for both social support and role models.

Finally, in the third phase, the majority of gay and lesbian teenagers accept their homosexuality and share it with those who are close to them.

One gay man described his experience in this way:

> It seems as if I always felt a little different. I don't ever remember having a crush on a girl, and then, when I got a little older, I began to have these feelings that scared me. I found myself physically attracted to, and even aroused by, some of my male friends. I didn't know who to talk to about it, so I just kept it to myself. I was really miserable. It took a long time, but finally I got okay with it all. My friends all know I'm gay, and it isn't a big deal. (Jim Pepperling, Personal Communication, January 28, 2008)

This information is important for teachers for at least two reasons. First, you may be one of the people with whom students share this information, and your reaction can have a major impact on students' acceptance of themselves. Second, research indicates that homosexual students are at greater risk for problems ranging from depression and substance abuse to suicide (M. Wood, 2005). Peer harassment is a major contributor to these problems. Teachers play an essential role in setting the moral tone of their classrooms, ensuring that they are safe places for all students.

The Development of Self-Concept

How athletic are you? How popular? How "smart" compared to your friends and fellow students?

Your responses reflect your self-concept, which, as we said in introducing this section, is a cognitive appraisal of your physical, social, and academic competence (Schunk, Pintrich & Meece, 2008). If you believe you're a good athlete, for example, you have a positive physical self-concept, or if you think you're good at getting along with people, you have a positive social self-concept. People who believe they are intellectually competent have positive academic self-concepts. Researchers believe that the formation of healthy self-concepts is central to both social and emotional development (Davis-Kean & Sandler, 2001).

Self-Concept and Self-Esteem

Self-esteem or **self-worth.** An emotional reaction to, or an evaluation of, the self.

The terms *self-concept* and *self-esteem* are often used interchangeably, but they are actually quite different. In contrast with self-concept, which is cognitive, **self-esteem,** or **self-worth,** is an emotional reaction to, or an evaluation of, the self (Schunk et al., 2008). People who have high self-esteem believe that they are inherently worthy people and feel good about themselves.

Self-esteem is important because low self-esteem during adolescence predicts poor health, criminal behavior, and limited economic prospects as adults (Baumeister, Campbell, Krueger, & Vohs, 2005; Trzesniewski et al., 2006).

Young children tend to have both high self-esteem and positive self-concepts—sometimes unrealistically so—probably because of few social comparisons and the support they receive from parents (Stipek, 2002). Self-esteem tends to drop during the transition from elementary to middle school (Eccles et al., 1989; Eccles et al., 2003). This decline, present in both males and females, is due to several factors, including the impersonal nature of middle schools and the physical changes brought on by puberty. Self-esteem then rises during the high school years, to a greater extent for boys than girls (Twenge & Campbell, 2001).

Self-concepts become more realistic as interactions with others give students more accurate measures of their performance compared to their peers (Schunk et al., 2008). As students move into adolescence, self-concept interacts with a developing sense of identity. Each influences the other, and both influence self-esteem.

Self-Concept and Achievement

The relationship between overall self-concept and achievement is positive but weak, and social and physical self-concepts are virtually unrelated to academic achievement (Marsh & Ayotte, 2003; Schunk et al., 2008). This makes sense; we've all known socially withdrawn students who are happy as academic isolates, as well as popular students who are modest achievers.

Students form their academic self-concepts on the basis of the experiences they have and the feedback they receive.

The relationship between achievement and academic self-concept is more robust, and they are interdependent (Choi, 2005). Each can lead to an increase in the other (Chapman, Tunmer, & Prochnow, 2000). This doesn't imply that all learning experiences can or should be successful, however; effective teachers help students learn from and manage their failures (Dweck, 2000).

An even stronger relationship exists between specific subject matter self-concepts and achievement in those areas (Choi, 2005). Researchers have also found that self-concepts in different subjects, such as math or English, become more distinct over time (Marsh & Ayotte, 2003; Yeung et al., 2000). We've all heard people make statements such as "I'm okay in English, but I'm no good in math." Some evidence suggests that comments such as these may not reflect actual competence; instead, people for whom societal expectations are low, such as girls in math, underestimate their abilities (D. A. Cole et al, 2001; Herbert & Stipek, 2005).

Extracurricular Activities

Research suggests that extracurricular activities can contribute to positive self-concepts (Mahoney, Larson, & Eccles, 2005). These activities provide both safe and supportive environments and opportunities for students to interact with others. These experiences can enhance both self-concept and self-esteem (Deutsch & Hirsch, 2001; Fredericks & Eccles, 2006).

The relationships between the different components of self-concept and achievement are illustrated in Figure 3.2.

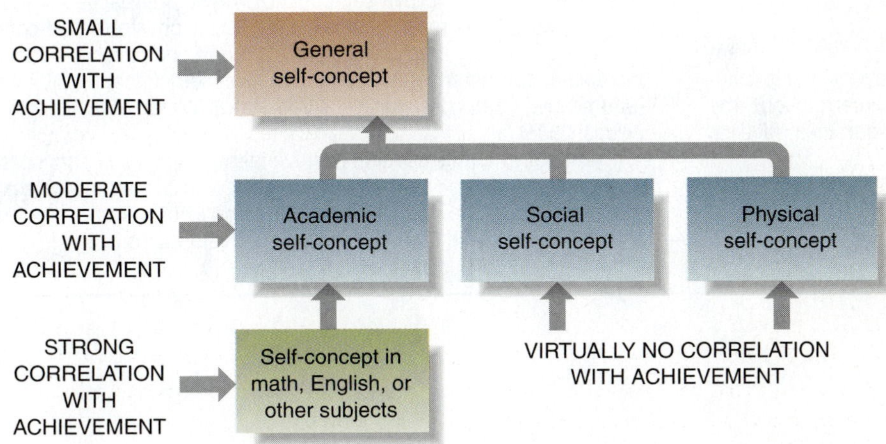

Figure 3.2 The relationships among the dimensions of self-concept and achievement

theory to practice

Promoting Identity and Self-Concept Development in Your Classroom

As a teacher, you strongly influence students' developing academic self-concepts. You design the learning activities and assessments and provide the feedback that students use to appraise their academic competence. The following guidelines can help you in your efforts to promote psychosocial and self-concept development:

1. Create a learning-focused classroom, and communicate genuine interest in all students.
2. Use an authoritative management style to help your students develop responsibility.
3. Reward autonomy and initiative in your students.
4. Establish appropriately high expectations for all learners, and provide evidence of increasing competence.
5. Design grading systems that emphasize learning progress and personal growth.

Let's see how John Adler, an eighth-grade English teacher, attempts to implement these guidelines with his students.

"Here are your papers," John announces on Friday as he hands back a set of quizzes from the day before. "You did a good job and I'm proud of you. Your writing is really improving. . . . I know I expect a lot, but you've always risen to the task.

"Put your scores in your logs, and add your improvement points."

"Who improved the most, Mr. Adler?" Jeremy asks.

"That's not important," John replies. "Remember, we're all in this together. You take responsibility for your learning, I help you as much as I can, and we all try to improve. . . . That's why I put your scores on the last page of the quizzes. They're your business, and no one else's."

"Now, I'd like to have a classroom meeting," he says, changing the direction of the discussion. "One of you came to me after school yesterday, concerned about the way some of you are treating each other outside of class. . . . She didn't name names; she simply expressed a concern, and I like it when someone takes the initiative to make our classroom better.

"I concur with her concern. . . . For instance, I saw one of you get tripped when you walked down the aisle, and another had water splashed on him at the water fountain. . . . I'm also seeing more litter on the floor.

"I'm disappointed at these behaviors. We're here to help one another. . . . So, I want to hear some ideas. What can we do to make our classroom better?"

The students offer comments, with suggestions ranging from kicking perpetrators out of class, to talking to them, to adding some more rules. The students agree that John has been attempting to enforce the rules fairly, but because he expects everyone to be responsible, perhaps he has perhaps been too lenient in some cases.

At the meeting's end, the students agree to be more responsible, and John agrees to renew his efforts to consistently enforce the rules.

Now, let's look at John's attempts to apply the guidelines. He applied the first by focusing on understanding and improvement in providing feedback on his quiz, and communicating concern about the students treatment of each other. When asked about their favorite teachers, students identify qualities such as

> Caring about them as individuals and seeking to help them succeed as learners. . . . However, students also say that they want teachers to articulate and enforce clear standards of behavior. They view this not just as part of the teacher's job but as evidence that the teacher cares about them. (Brophy, 2004, pp. 29–30)

Second, by being caring but firm and soliciting students' input into rules and procedures, John displayed an authoritative interaction style. Authoritative management, with opportunities for practicing independence within limits, is particularly valuable in middle schools where students are beginning the process of identity development.

Third, John realized that no psychosocial challenge is permanently resolved, so, even though his students were eighth graders, he reinforced one of them for taking the initiative to raise the issue of student behavior.

John's comment, "You did a good job and I'm proud of you. Your writing is really improving. . . . I know I expect a lot, but you've always risen to the task," communicated high expectations and emphasis on increasing competence, which is an attempt to apply the fourth guideline. These efforts also promote a sense of industry and positive academic self-concept.

Finally, he deemphasized competition, applying the fifth guideline, when he said, "That's not important. Remember, we're all in this together," in response to Jeremy's question about who improved the most. Also, by awarding points for improvement, he used his grading system to further emphasize increasing competence.

Research supports John's approach to developing his students' identity and self-concepts. An alternative approach uses strategies such as having minority students study multicultural learning materials, sending children to summer camps, and implementing support groups in attempts to directly improve self concept. These approaches are largely ineffective for two reasons. First, they focus on global self-concept, which is essentially unrelated to achievement, and second, evidence of increased competence is needed before self-concept will improve (Baumeister, Campbell, Krueger, & Vohs, 2005; O'Mara, Marsh, Craven, & Debus, 2006).

Helping students develop positive identities and self-concepts isn't easy, and efforts such as John's won't work with all students or with any student all the time. However, with time and effort, teachers can make a difference in these important areas of development.

exploring diversity

Ethnic Identity and Pride

Maria Robles squeezes her mother's hand as they enter her new school. Her mother can tell she is nervous as she anxiously eyes the bigger boys and girls walking down the hallway.

As they enter a kindergarten classroom, Carmen Avilla, her teacher, comes to greet them.

"Hola. ¿Cómo te llamas, niña?" (Hello. What is your name, little one?)

Maria, hiding behind her mother, is still uneasy but feels some relief.

"Dile tu nombre" (Tell her your name), her mother prompts, squeezing her hand and smiling.

". . . Maria," she offers hesitantly.

Her mother adds quickly, "Maria Robles. Yo soy su madre." (I am her mother.)

Carmen looks on her list, finds Maria's name, and checks it off. Then she invites them, in Spanish, to come into the room and meet the other boys and girls. Music is playing in the background. Maria recognizes some of her friends who are playing with toys in a corner of the room.

"Maria, ven aquí y juega con nosotros." (Maria, come here and play with us.)

Maria hesitates for a moment, looks up at her mother and then runs over to join her friends.

Teachers can help students develop ethnic pride and positive self-esteem by actively acknowledging and valuing the ethnic and cultural strengths different students bring to school.

Ethnicity and Self-Esteem

We all wonder about our self-worth. Will others like us? Are we perceived as smart or attractive? As you saw in the last section, experiences with others shape our beliefs, and schools are important in helping students develop both positive self-concepts and high self-esteem.

Our culture also influences the development of self-esteem, especially for minority youth. Researchers have found that the self-esteem of people from cultural minority groups often includes both a personal and a collective component (S. French, Seidman, Allen, & Aber, 2006).

Ethnic identity refers to an awareness of ethnic group membership and a commitment to the values and behaviors of that group, and **collective self-esteem** refers to individuals' perceptions of the relative worth of the groups to which they belong. When these groups are valued by society and perceived as having status, personal identities and self-esteem are enhanced. The opposite is also true.

Children as young as Maria know they are part of an ethnic minority, and research dating back to the 1930s indicates that minority children such as African Americans (K. Clark & Clark, 1939), Mexican Americans (Weiland & Coughlin, 1979), and Chinese Americans (Aboud & Skerry, 1984) evaluate their ethnic reference groups as less worthy than the White majority. As ethnic minority children develop, they become increasingly aware of problems with inequality and discrimination.

More recent research suggests that African American children who grow up in warm and supportive environments, both at home and school, actually possess higher levels of self-esteem than their Caucasian American counterparts (C. Carlson, Uppal, & Prosser, 2000; S. French et al., 2006; Gray-Little & Hafdahl, 2000). However, some cultural minorities experience hardships linked to poverty, crime, and drug use (Dwyer & Osher, 2000). In addition, schools unresponsive to the needs of minority children can retard the development of self-concept and self-esteem (Ferguson, 2003; Noguera, 2003a). These findings suggest that unique challenges can exist for students who are members of ethnic minorities.

Ethnic Pride and Identity Formation

Membership in an ethnic group also affects students' identities (M. Jones, 1999), and the messages children receive about their ethnic identities can be mixed or even negative (Lopez del Bosque, 2003; Trawick-Smith, 2003). However, children who are encouraged to explore their ethnicity and who adopt positive values from both the dominant and their native culture develop a clearer sense of self (D. Hughes, et al., 2006). Students with positive ethnic identities also achieve higher and have higher self-esteem and more positive beliefs about their ability to cope with their environments (Chavous et al., 2003; Spencer, Noll, Stoltzfus, & Harpalani, 2001). Minority students need to know that their cultures are valued and that the languages they bring to school are assets (S. French et al., 2006).

What can teachers do? We can make every effort to communicate to students that their ethnic heritage and language are both recognized and valued. Like Maria, many students come to school wondering if they will be welcome. The way a teacher reacts to these students, as Carmen Avilla did with Maria, has a powerful impact on their developing sense of self-worth.

Ethnic identity. An awareness of ethnic group membership and a commitment to the attitudes, values, and behaviors of that group.

Collective self-esteem. Individuals' perceptions of the relative worth of the groups to which they belong.

check your understanding

2.1 You are teaching a ninth-grade student with whom you can't "get going." He will do what is required of him and no more. He does a good job on his required work, however, and seems to be quite happy. Explain his behavior using Erikson's theory as a basis. What might a teacher do in response to this pattern of behavior?

2.2 Look again at the students' conversation at the beginning of the discussion of identity development. Use their statements to explain the state of identity development for each of the students.

2.3 "I know I can get this down the way I want to say it," a student says to his friend. "I've always been a decent writer. I'm not sure why I'm having a problem." Use the idea of self-concept and/or the idea of self-esteem to explain the student's comments. Describe the relationships between self-concept, self-esteem, and academic achievement.

To receive feedback for these questions, go to Appendix A.

classroom connections

Promoting Psychosocial and Self-Concept Development in Your Classroom

1. Erikson believed that social connections to others play a major role in promoting psychosocial development. Use social connection as an umbrella under which you conduct your interactions with students.
   - **Elementary:** A kindergarten student responsible for watering the classroom plants knocks one over on the floor. The teacher says evenly, "It looks like we have a problem. What needs to be done?" She pauses and continues, "Sweep up the dirt, and wipe up the water with some paper towels." When the student is done, the teacher gives her a hug and comments, "Everyone makes mistakes. The important thing is what we do about them."
   - **Middle School:** A math teacher designs her instruction so that all students can achieve success and develop a growing sense of industry. She spends extra time with students after school, and she lets students redo some of their assignments if they make an honest effort the first time. She frequently comments, "Math is for everyone—if you try!"
   - **High School:** A biology teacher pays little attention to the attire and slang of his students as long as offensive language isn't used, the rights of others are recognized, and learning occurs.
2. Success on challenging tasks is important for developing a sense of industry in students. Help students understand that effort leads to success and competence.
   - **Elementary:** A second-grade teacher carefully teaches a topic and provides precise directions before making seat-work assignments. She conducts "monitored practice" with the first few items to be sure all students begin correctly. When students encounter difficulties, she meets with them separately or in small groups so they don't fall behind.
   - **Middle School:** A sixth-grade teacher develops a grading system based partially on improvement so that each student can succeed by improving his or her performance. He meets with students periodically during each grading period to help them monitor their learning progress.
   - **High School:** An art teacher uses portfolios and individual conferences to help her students set goals and see their growth over the year. During conferences, she emphasizes individual growth and tries to help students understand how their effort and accomplishments are linked.

Developing Positive Self-Concepts in your Classroom

3. Self-concepts develop from the experiences students have in and outside of school. Make students feel wanted and valued in your class. Provide learning experiences that promote success.
   - **Elementary:** A fourth-grade teacher starts the school year by having students bring in pictures of themselves taken when they were preschoolers and write autobiographical sketches. They list their strengths, interests, and hobbies, and describe what they want to be when they grow up.
   - **Middle School:** A homeroom teacher for entering middle schoolers tries to make his classroom a place where students feel safe and secure. He begins the school year with classroom meetings where students get to know one another and form homeroom rules. As the year progresses, he uses these meetings to discuss issues and problems important to students.
   - **High School:** A ninth-grade English teacher begins each school year by announcing that everyone is important in her classes and that she expects everyone to learn. She structures her classrooms around success, minimizing competition. She also stays in her room after school and invites students who are having problems to come by for help.

Social Development

As we said at the beginning of the chapter, social development describes the advances people make in their ability to interact and get along with others, and it is an essential element of individuals' overall development. In a review of research in this area, experts concluded, "There is a growing body of scientifically based research supporting the strong impact that enhanced social and emotional behaviors can have on success in school and ultimately in life" (Zins, Bloodworth, Weissberg, & Walberg, 2004, p. 19). When students can make friends and get along with others, they feel better about themselves, feel more connected to school and their classmates, and have opportunities to practice and develop social skills (Rubin et al., 2006). Social development is also related to reduced dropout and substance abuse rates (Zins et al., 2004). This helps us answer the second question we asked at the beginning of the chapter: "What impact, if any, will Sean's attitude have on his academic achievement?" It is likely to decrease his achievement, and it will certainly have an adverse effect on his satisfaction with school. Students who are well developed personally and socially achieve more and enjoy school more than do their less well-developed peers. Understanding social development can help you contribute to this important process.

We turn now to perspective taking and social problem solving, two important dimensions of social development.

Perspective Taking: Understanding Others' Thoughts and Feelings

Perspective taking is the ability to understand the thoughts and feelings of others. To see an example, let's look at four fifth graders working on a project.

Perspective taking. The ability to understand the thoughts and feelings of others.

> Octavio, Mindy, Sarah, and Bill are studying American westward expansion in social studies. They'd been working as a group for 3 days and are preparing a report to be delivered to the class. There is some disagreement about who should present which topics.
>
> "So what should we do?" Mindy asks, looking at the others. "Octavio, Sarah, and Bill all want to report on the Pony Express."
>
> "I thought of it first," Octavio argues.
>
> "But everyone knows I like horses," Sarah counters.
>
> "Why don't we compromise?" Mindy suggests. "Octavio, didn't you say that you were kind of interested in railroads because your grandfather worked on them? Couldn't you talk to him and get some information for the report? And Sarah, I know you like horses. Couldn't you report on horses and the Plains Indians? . . . And Bill, what about you?"
>
> "I don't care . . . whatever," Bill replies, folding his arms and peering belligerently at the group.

These students differed significantly in their ability to understand the thoughts and feelings of others. When Mindy suggested that Octavio and Sarah switch assignments because of their interest in different topics, for example, she demonstrated this ability.

Research indicates that perspective taking develops slowly and is related to Piaget's stages of cognitive development (Burack et al., 2006). Children up to about age 8 typically don't understand events such as Bill's angry response or why Octavio might be happy reporting on railroads, but as they mature and acquire experiences, their perspective-taking abilities improve.

People skilled in perspective taking can handle difficult social situations, can display empathy and compassion, and are well liked by their peers (Eisenberg et al., 2006; Schult, 2002). Those less skilled tend to interpret others' intentions as hostile, which can lead to arguing and other antisocial acts. They also lack feelings of guilt and remorse when they hurt other people's feelings (Crick, Grotpeter, & Bigbee, 2002; Dodge et al., 2003).

This section addresses the third question we asked at the beginning of the chapter: "What is a likely reason that Sean doesn't get along with the other students?" His belief that the other kids are picking on him "for no reason" likely reflects underdeveloped perspective taking. He may also lack social problem-solving skills, the topic of our next section.

Social Problem Solving

Social problem solving. The ability to resolve conflicts in ways that are beneficial to all involved.

Social problem solving, the ability to resolve conflicts in ways that are beneficial to all involved, is closely related to perspective taking. Mindy displayed this ability when she suggested a compromise acceptable to everyone.

Research suggests that social problem solving is similar to problem solving in general (a topic presented in Chapter 9) and occurs in four sequential steps (Dodge, Coie, & Lynam, 2006; Eisenberg et al., 2006):

Perspective taking and social problem solving are important aspects of learners' social development.

1. Observe and interpret social cues. ("Bill seems upset, probably because he isn't getting his first choice.")
2. Identify social goals. ("If we are going to finish this project, everyone must contribute.")
3. Generate strategies. ("Can we find different topics that will satisfy everyone?")
4. Implement and evaluate the strategies. ("This will work if everyone agrees to shift their topic slightly.")

Social problem solving is a valuable tool, both in and out of school. Students who are good at it have more friends, fight less, and work more efficiently in groups than those who are less skilled (H. Patrick, Anderman, & Ryan, 2002).

Like perspective taking, social problem solving develops gradually and with practice (D. W. Johnson & Johnson, 2006). Young children, for example, are not adept at reading social cues, and they tend to create simplistic solutions that satisfy themselves but not others. Older children realize that persuasion and compromise can benefit everyone, and they're better at adapting when initial efforts aren't successful.

MyEducationLab

To see how teachers promote perspective taking and social problem solving in their students, go to the *Building Teaching Skills and Dispositions* section in Chapter 3 of MyEducationLab at www.myeducationlab.com, and watch the episode *The Scarlet Letter in High School English*. Complete the exercises following the episode to develop your skills in advancing social development.

Violence and Aggression in Schools

School violence and aggression are persistent problems, and experts link this trend to a lack of personal and social development (D.W. Johnson & Johnson, 2004; Lopes & Salovey, 2004). The widely publicized Columbine massacre in 1999, in which two students killed a teacher and 12 of their peers, and the Red Lake, Minnesota, tragedy in 2005 in which a student killed 5 of his peers, a teacher, and a security guard, together with other shooting incidents in schools around the nation, dramatically underscore this problem.

National statistics are also disconcerting; the homicide rate of juveniles under 18 increased by nearly 400% since 1965 (Dodge et al., 2006). This country continues to have the highest rates of youth suicides, homicides, and firearms-related deaths of any of the world's 26 wealthiest nations (Aspy et al., 2004).

Bully. A student who frequently threatens, harasses, or causes injury to peers.

Bullying, a more subtle form of school violence, is an ongoing problem, with up to one third of students saying they experience it frequently (D. Cooper & Snell, 2003; Viadero, 2003). A **bully** is a student who threatens, harasses, or causes injury to peers. Bullies often target peers who are immature, friendless, lacking in self-confidence, or have disabilities (Hyman et al., 2006; Newman & Murray, 2005), and bullying can have long-term negative effects on victims (Dodge et al., 2006). Experts estimate that boys bully more than girls by a ratio of three to one. This ratio may be misleading, however, since girls' bullying tends to be more verbal than physical and less likely to be reported (Ma, 2001).

Aggressive behavior in schools, which includes bullying, occurs in several forms. Some are:

- *Physical aggression.* Actions that that can cause injury (most common in boys)
- *Relational aggression.* Actions that can adversely affect interpersonal relationships, such as spreading rumors or ostracizing a peer (most common in girls) (Pellegrini, 2002)
- *Instrumental aggression.* Actions aimed at claiming an object, place, or privilege, such as a young child grabbing another's toy or cutting in line
- *Proactive aggression.* Hostile acts initiated by individuals and directed toward someone else
- *Reactive aggression.* Hostile acts in response to provocation or frustration

theory to practice

Promoting Social Development in Your Classroom

As with other aspects of learning, social development can be advanced through student understanding, practice, and feedback. You can make important contributions to social development by modeling social skills and by organizing your classroom in ways that contribute to this dimension of development (Elias, 2004). The following guidelines can assist you in your efforts:

1. Model and explicitly teach social skills to your students.
2. Establish rules governing acceptable classroom behavior.
3. Help students understand the reasons for rules by providing examples and rationales.
4. Have students practice social skills, and give them feedback.

Let's see how Teresa Manteras, a first-year teacher, uses these guidelines as she works with her sixth graders.

"How are you doing, Teresa?" Carla Ambergi, a veteran colleague asks as Teresa comes into the teachers' lounge.

"A little discouraged," Teresa sighs. "I learned about all those cooperative learning activities in my university classes, but when I try them with my kids, all they do is snip at each other. Maybe I should just lecture."

"They're not used to working in groups," Carla smiles, "and they haven't yet learned how to cooperate. They need some practice."

"Yes, I know, . . . but I don't even know where to start."

"Would you like me to come in during my planning period? Maybe I can help."

"That would be great!" Teresa replies with a big sense of relief.

Carla comes in the next day, and then she and Teresa sit down together after school. "First, I think you do an excellent job of modeling social skills," Carla comments. "You consider where the kids are coming from, you treat disagreements as an opportunity to solve problems, and you are supportive. . . . But, your modeling goes right over their heads. They don't notice what you're doing. So, I suggest that you be more specific; tell the kids what you're modeling, and give them some examples. Then, add a few rules that will help guide their interactions with each other. It will take some time, but it will make a difference."

"Good point," Teresa nods. "I hadn't quite thought about it that way before."

Carla then helps Teresa develop some rules that address behavior in groups:

1. Listen politely until other people are finished before speaking.
2. Treat other people's ideas with courtesy and respect.
3. Paraphrase other people's ideas in your own words before disagreeing.
4. Encourage everyone in the group to participate.

Teresa starts the next day. Before breaking the students into groups, she tells them that they are going to work on their social skills, and she models several examples, such as making eye contact, checking perceptions, and listening attentively. Then, she presents and explains the new rules, has volunteers role-play an example for each, and guides a discussion of the examples.

Students then begin their group work. Teresa monitors the groups, intervenes when they have difficulties, and reconvenes the class when she sees a similar problem in several groups. The students are far from perfect, but they are improving.

Now let's look at Teresa's attempts to apply the guidelines for promoting social development in her classroom. She applied the first by modeling and explicitly teaching her students the social skills she wanted them to develop. Just as learning to write, for example, involves understanding grammar and punctuation together with a great deal of practice, developing social skills involves both understanding and practice in interactions with others (Elias, 2004).

Teresa applied the second guideline by creating a set of rules designed to support the students as they worked together. She presented only four rules, first because they supplemented her general classroom rules, but also because a small number makes them easier to remember.

Third, Teresa provided concrete examples of the rules by having students role-play social situations and then discussing each to be sure the students understood what the role-playing illustrated. Her modeling provided additional examples of desirable social skills and behaviors.

Finally, Teresa provided opportunities for students to practice their social skills during group work, and she gave them feedback. Students won't become socially skilled in one or two activities, but with time, practice, and explicit instruction, students can develop these skills (Gillies, 2003; D. W. Johnson & Johnson, 2004, 2006).

Aggressive students have difficulty maintaining friendships and are at increased risk for engaging in delinquent activities (Berger, 2007). Aggressive tendencies cause problems both in school and in later life (Dodge et al., 2006).

The causes of aggressive behavior are complex, with both genetics and the environment playing roles. Bullies, for example, often come from homes where parents are authoritarian, hostile, and rejecting, and aggressive behavior is both modeled and reinforced (Barry & Wentzel, 2006; Brendgen et al., 2006). Their parents frequently have poor problem-solving skills and often advocate fighting as a solution to conflicts (Ma, 2001). These home environments can result in **hostile attributional bias,** a tendency to view others' behaviors as hostile or aggressive. Aggression is also linked to deficits in perspective taking, empathy, moral development, and emotional self-regulation (Crick et al., 2002).

Hostile attributional bias. A tendency to view others' behaviors as hostile or aggressive.

Aggressive behavior harms both the aggressor and the victim. It teaches the aggressor that force and coercion are acceptable ways to solve social problems, and victims often become

Programs designed to prevent violence and aggression in schools focus on developing social skills as substitutes for force.

depressed, anxious, or even suicidal (Hyman et al., 2006; Schwartz et al., 2005). Victims hesitate to tell teachers for fear of additional retribution (Newman & Murray, 2005).

Attempts to prevent aggression and violence in schools focus on peer mediation and programs designed to develop social problem-solving skills (San Antonio & Salzfass, 2007). In one of the best-known peer-mediation programs, designed by David and Roger Johnson (2004, 2006), a mediator guides peers through conflict-resolution steps in which students jointly define the conflict, exchange perspectives, reverse the perspectives, and invent solutions that are mutually agreed upon. The Johnson's research suggests that schools in which students were trained in conflict resolution had fewer management problems, both within classrooms and on school grounds, and students continued to use the strategies at home (D.W. Johnson & Johnson, 2004).

Programs designed to teach social problem-solving skills focus on substituting peaceful alternatives for force (Kress & Elias, 2006). With young children, teachers use puppet skits to present social dilemmas, which children discuss and try to solve. In programs for older children, teachers ask students to read and respond to scenarios such as the one involving Octavio, Mindy, Sarah, and Bill. Research indicates that students in these programs improve in both their social problem-solving abilities and their classroom behavior (Kress & Elias, 2006).

These strategies focus on violence and aggression at the individual level. A school climate that discourages violence and aggression and clearly communicates that they won't be tolerated is also essential (San Antonio & Salzfass, 2007). Parental involvement is important, and students need to know that teachers and administrators are committed to safe schools (Christenson & Havsy, 2004).

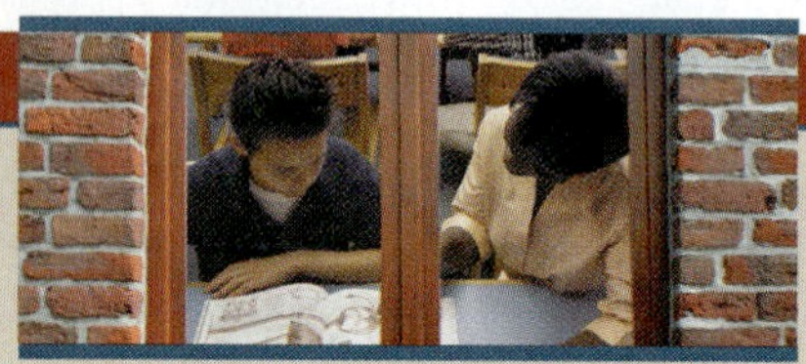

classroom connections

Applying an Understanding of Social Development in Your Classroom

1. Perspective taking, the ability to understand the thoughts and feelings of others, is an important part of social development. Provide opportunities for students to consider the perspectives of others.
   - **Elementary:** A fourth-grade teacher has her students analyze different characters' motives and feelings when they discuss a story they've read. She asks, "How does the character feel? Why does the character feel that way? How would you feel if you were that person?"
   - **Middle School:** A middle school science teacher stays after school to provide opportunities for students to ask questions about their work in his class. The conversations often drift to interpersonal problems the students are having with parents or friends. The teacher listens patiently, but also encourages students to think about the motives and feelings of the other people involved.
   - **High School:** A history teacher encourages her students to consider points of view when they read reports of historical events. For example, when her students study the Civil War, she reminds them that both sides thought they were morally right and asks questions such as, "Why was the topic of states' rights so controversial?" and "How did the different sides in the war interpret the Emancipation Proclamation?"
2. Social problem solving is the ability to resolve conflicts in ways that are beneficial to all involved. Provide opportunities for students to engage in social problem solving as they work with others.
   - **Elementary:** A third-grade teacher periodically has groups of four students check each others' math homework. He passes out two answer sheets to each group and asks each group to decide how to proceed. When the students don't accept equal responsibilities, or conflicts arise, he encourages students to work out the problems themselves and intervenes only if they cannot resolve the problems.
   - **Middle School:** An eighth-grade English teacher sometimes purposefully leaves decisions about individual assignments up to the groups in cooperative learning activities. When disagreements occur, she offers only enough assistance to get the group back on track. If the problem is widespread, she calls a whole-class meeting to discuss the problem.
   - **High School:** When art students argue about space and access to materials and supplies, their teacher calls a class meeting and requires them to discuss the problem and suggest solutions acceptable to everyone.

check your understanding

3.1 Describe and explain the major components of social development.

3.2 Two kindergarteners are arguing about who gets to play next at the water table. Their teacher approaches them and says, "Hmm. It looks like you both want to play at the water table at the same time. What could we do to make both of you happy?" What dimension of social development is this teacher trying to promote? Why?

3.3 Explain how school violence and aggression relate to social development. Describe the causes of violent and aggressive behaviors in children.

To receive feedback for these questions, go to Appendix A.

D Development of Morality, Social Responsibility, and Self-Control

To begin this section, let's return to Amanda Kellinger, our teacher at the beginning of the chapter, and her work with her eighth graders.

> "I need to go to the office for a moment," Amanda announces as her students work on a seat-work assignment. "You all have work to do, so work quietly until I get back. I'll only be gone for a few minutes."
>
> The quiet shuffling of papers can be heard for a few moments, and then Gary whispers, "Psst, what math problems are we supposed to do?"
>
> "Shh! No talking," Talitha says, pointing to the rules posted on the bulletin board.
>
> "But he needs to know so he can do his work," Krystal replies. "It's the evens on page 79."
>
> "Who cares?" Dwain growls. "She's not here. She won't catch us."

What influences our students' interpretation of classroom rules? For example, how might we explain the differences between Talitha's, Krystal's and Dwain's reactions to the rule about no talking? More importantly, as students move through life, how do they think about the laws and conventions that govern our society? The concept of morality deals with matters of right and wrong, and we now examine moral development, which, as you saw at the beginning of the chapter, is the development of prosocial behaviors and traits such as honesty, fairness, and respect for others.

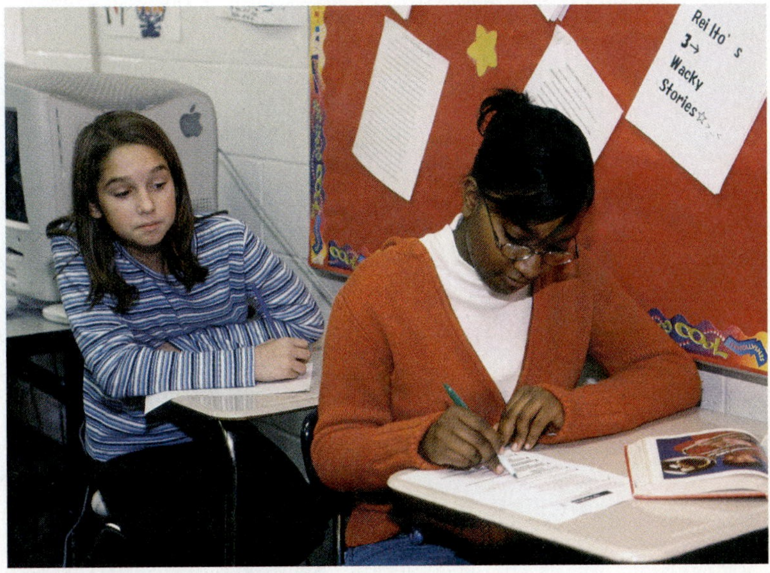

Cheating is a persistent problem in classrooms. How students think about this problem and how teachers respond to it depend on students' levels of moral development.

Increased Interest in Moral Development

Interest in moral development is increasing, partially due to disturbing trends in our country. For example, in our schools large numbers of students express concerns about being bullied (Raskauskas & Stoltz, 2007). Also, surveys indicate that as many as three fourths of high school students admit to cheating on tests, and cheating appears to be on the rise in elementary schools through college (Bracey, 2005; Murdock & Anderman, 2006). Outside of schools, corruption that led to the collapse of businesses such as Enron and WorldCom, and the loan scandals that resulted in the housing crisis in this country, in the latter part of the decade, have sent shock waves through the financial community and American society in general. The American public is increasingly looking to education for solutions to problems such as these (L. C. Rose & Gallup, 2007).

Moral issues are also embedded in the school curriculum. History is not a mere chronology of events; it is also a study of people's responses to moral issues, such as poverty, human suffering, peace, justice, and whether decisions to go to war are justified.

Ethical issues are also found in literature written for young people. For instance in E. B. White's (1974) children's classic *Charlotte's Web*, moral issues are involved when Charlotte, the spider, devises an ingenious plan to save Wilbur the pig from slaughter. And teachers commonly choose books such as *The Yearling* (Rawlings, 1938), *The Scarlet Letter* (Hawthorne, 1850), and *A Tale of Two Cities* (Dickens, 1859), not only because they are good literature but also because they examine moral issues.

Moral development is an integral part of development in general. Students' beliefs about right and wrong influence their behavior; incidents of cheating and vandalism, for example, decrease if students believe they are morally unacceptable. Socially and emotionally healthy learners have a moral compass that guides their behavior. Research also indicates that the moral atmosphere of a school (e.g., democratic and prosocial versus authoritarian) can influence motivation and the value students place on their learning experiences (Christenson & Havsy, 2004; Murdock, Miller, & Kohlhardt, 2004). Understanding moral development helps us better guide our students in this vital area.

Moral, Conventional, and Personal Domains

To begin this section, consider the following questions:

Is it all right to take a pencil that doesn't belong to you?
Is it okay to spread untrue rumors about another person?
Should young people call adults by their first names?
Is it all right to pierce your ears, eyebrows, nose, or navel?

Researchers investigating children's moral development differentiate between *moral, conventional,* and *personal* domains (Nucci, 2001, 2006; Turiel, 2006). Moral domains deal with basic principles of right, wrong, and justice; it's wrong, for example, to take someone's pencil or to hurt them by spreading false rumors.

Social conventions. Societal norms and ways of behaving in specific situations.

Social conventions, in contrast, are societal norms and ways of behaving in specific situations. They would suggest, for instance, that it's okay to yell at an athletic event but not in a classroom. Social conventions also vary according to culture and setting. For example, young people addressing adults by their first names is acceptable in some cultures, but in others it isn't.

Teachers can help students understand differences between moral, conventional, and personal domains with class discussions that focus on reasons for each.

Finally, the personal domain refers to decisions that are not socially regulated and do not harm or violate others' rights. Parents and other adults may object to tattoos and body piercing, but they aren't morally wrong, and they aren't usually addressed by social conventions such as dress codes.

Research suggests children as young as 2 or 3 years can distinguish among these domains (Nucci, 2001, 2006). Young children can understand that moral transgressions are generally wrong and do not depend on context; it's wrong to hit and hurt someone, for example, regardless of where you are, and whether or not rules prohibiting it exist.

Children learn to differentiate among the domains by observing the consequences of actions. For example, when children hit and hurt someone, they see the impact of their actions on others, and they are often reprimanded or punished by adults. Children also begin to realize that conventions are arbitrary and situation-specific, which can result in them questioning both school regulations and rules at home.

Teachers can help their students understand the differences among the domains by discussing them and emphasizing the reasons for each. For example, when moral rules are violated, teachers should encourage students to think about the effects of their actions on others. Similarly, the functional value of social conventions needs to be explained (e.g., "To give everyone a chance to participate, we need to raise our hands to speak.")

The lines between the moral, conventional, and personal domains are often blurred and depend on individuals' interpretations. Some preservice teachers, for example, view giving all students the opportunity to participate as a moral issue, whereas others are more likely to classify it in the conventional domain (Schellenberg & Eggen, 2008). Further, some researchers view reasoning about social conventions and society's rules as advances in moral development (Kohlberg, 1981, 1984).

Piaget's Theory of Moral Development

Although we usually think of Piaget in the context of cognitive development, he examined the development of ethics and morals as well. He studied cognitive and moral development in much the same way—by observing children, presenting them with tasks, and asking questions to probe their thinking (Krebs & Denton, 2005).

Piaget (1965) found that children's responses to moral problems can be divided into two broad stages. In the first stage, **external morality,** children view rules as fixed, permanent, and enforced by authority figures. When Talitha said, "Shh! No talking," and pointed to the rules, she was thinking at this stage. It didn't matter that Gary was only asking about the assignment; rules are rules. In responding "Who cares? She's not here. She won't catch us," Dwain demonstrated similar thinking; he was focusing on the fact that no authority figure was there to enforce the rule. External morality typically lasts to about age 10. Piaget believed that parents and teachers who stress unquestioned adherence to adult authority retard moral development and unintentionally encourage students to remain at this level.

External morality. A stage of moral development in which individuals view rules as fixed and permanent and enforced by authority figures.

Autonomous morality. A stage of moral development characterized by the belief that fairness and justice is the reciprocal process of treating others as they would want to be treated.

Moral dilemma. An ambiguous, conflicting situation that requires a person to make a moral decision.

When students advance to **autonomous morality,** the second stage, they develop rational ideas of fairness and see justice as a reciprocal process of treating others as they would want to be treated (Turiel, 2006). Children at this stage begin to rely on themselves instead of others to regulate moral behavior. Krystal's comment, "But he needs to know so he can do his work," demonstrates this kind of thinking; she viewed Gary's whispering as an honest request for assistance rather than an infraction of rules.

Kohlberg's Theory of Moral Development

Lawrence Kohlberg, a Harvard educator and psychologist, built on and extended Piaget's work. He used **moral dilemmas,** ambiguous, conflicting situations that require a person to make a moral decision, as the basis for his research. Let's look at an example.

Lawrence Kohlberg (1927–1987), born in New York, was a psychologist who became famous for his research in describing people's moral reasoning.

A brilliant student in psychology at the University of Chicago, he was inspired by, and built on, Piaget's work. His research focused on individuals' justifications for their actions when presented with moral dilemmas, and his dissertation described his six stages of moral reasoning. He taught at the University of Chicago and later held a faculty position in social psychology and education at Harvard. While at Harvard, he met Carol Gilligan, who later became a colleague and critic of his theory.

Based on criteria such as citations and recognition, Kohlberg was one of the 30 most eminent psychologists of the 20th century.

Discussing moral dilemmas provides students with oppurtunities to examine their thinking about moral issues.

Steve, a high school senior, works at a night job to help support his mother, a single parent of three. Steve is conscientious and works hard in his classes, but he doesn't have enough time to study.

Because of his night work, and because he isn't fond of history, he is barely passing. If he fails the final exam, he will fail the course and won't graduate. He isn't scheduled to work the night before the exam, so he has extra time to study. But, early in the evening his boss calls, desperate to have Steve come in and replace another employee who called in sick at the last moment. His boss pressures him, so Steve goes to work at 8:00 p.m. and comes home exhausted at 2:00 a.m. He tries to study but falls asleep on the couch with his book in his lap. His mother wakes him for school at 6:30 a.m.

Steve goes to his history class, looks at the test, and goes blank. Everything seems like a jumble. Clarice, one of the best students in the class, happens to have her answer sheet positioned so that he can clearly see every answer by barely moving his eyes.

Is he justified in cheating?

This is a moral dilemma because it deals with issues of right and wrong and because any decision Steve makes has both positive and negative consequences. If he cheats, he will pass the test, but cheating is morally wrong. On the other hand, if he doesn't cheat, he will likely fail the course and not graduate.

Kohlberg (1963, 1969, 1981, 1984) used responses to moral dilemmas, such as this one, as a basis of his research, which he later developed into his theory of moral development. Like Piaget, he concluded that moral reasoning exists in stages, and development occurs when people's reasoning advances to a higher stage. On the basis of research conducted in Great Britain, Malaysia, Mexico, Taiwan, and Turkey, Kohlberg concluded that the development of moral reasoning is similar across cultures.

Kohlberg originally described moral reasoning as occurring at three levels consisting of two stages each (Turiel, 2006). They are outlined in Table 3.4 and discussed in the sections that follow. As you read the descriptions, remember that the specific response to a moral dilemma isn't the primary issue; moral development is determined by the *reasons* a person gives for making the decision.

Level I: Preconventional Ethics

Preconventional morality. An egocentric orientation lacking any internalized standards for right and wrong.

Punishment–obedience. A stage of moral reasoning in which conclusions are based on the chances of getting caught and being punished.

Market exchange. A stage of moral reasoning in which conclusions are based on an act of reciprocity on someone else's part.

Preconventional morality is an egocentric orientation lacking internalized standards for right and wrong and focusing on the consequences of actions for the self. In the **punishment–obedience** stage, people make moral decisions based on their chances of getting caught and being punished; they reason that right or wrong is determined by the consequences of an action. For example, if a child is caught and punished, the act is morally wrong; if not, the act is right. A person who argues that Steve is justified in cheating because he is unlikely to get caught is reasoning at this stage.

At Stage 2, **market exchange,** people reason that an act is morally justified if it results in reciprocity, such as "You do something for me, and I'll do something for you." A person reasoning at Stage 2 might argue that Steve should go ahead and cheat, because if he doesn't, he'll have to repeat the course and quit his job. The focus remains on the self, and "The right thing to do is what makes me the happiest." Political patronage—the tendency of successful office seekers to give their supporters desirable jobs regardless of qualifications—is a common example of Stage-2 ethics.

Level II: Conventional Ethics

Conventional morality. A moral orientation linked to uncritical acceptance of society's conventions about right and wrong.

When moral reasoning has developed to the **conventional level of morality,** reasoning no longer depends on the consequences for the individual but instead is linked to acceptance of society's conventions about right and wrong. Values such as family expectations, obeying the

table 3.4 Kohlberg's Stages of Moral Reasoning

Level 1 Preconventional Ethics (*Typical of preschool and elementary students.*)	The ethics of egocentrism. Typical of children up to about age 10. Called preconventional because children typically don't fully understand rules set down by others.
Stage 1: Punishment–Obedience	Consequences of acts determine whether they're good or bad. Individuals make moral decisions without considering the needs or feelings of others.
Stage 2: Market Exchange	The ethics of "What's in it for me?" Obeying rules and exchanging favors are judged in terms of the benefit to the individual.
Level II Conventional Ethics (*Seen in older elementary and middle school students and many high school students.*)	The ethics of others. Typical of 10- to 20-year-olds. The name comes from conformity to the rules and conventions of society.
Stage 3: Interpersonal Harmony	Ethical decisions are based on concern for or the opinions of others. What pleases, helps, or is approved of by others characterizes this stage.
Stage 4: Law and Order	The ethics of laws, rules, and societal order. Rules and laws are inflexible and are obeyed for their own sake.
Level III Postconventional Ethics (*Rarely seen before college, and the universal principles stage is seldom seen even in adults.*)	The ethics of principle. Rarely reached before age 20 and only by a small portion of the population. The focus is on the principles underlying society's rules.
Stage 5: Social Contract	Rules and laws represent agreements among people about behavior that benefits society. Rules can be changed when they no longer meet society's needs.
Stage 6: Universal Principles	Rarely encountered in life. Ethics are determined by abstract and general principles that transcend societal rules.

law, and social order become prominent. In Stage 3, **interpersonal harmony,** people make decisions based on loyalty, living up to the expectations of others, and social conventions. For example, a teenager on a date who meets a curfew because she doesn't want to worry her parents is reasoning at this stage. A person reasoning at Stage 3 might offer two different perspectives on Steve's dilemma. One could argue that he needs to work to help his family and therefore is justified in cheating. A contrasting view, but still at this stage, would suggest that he should not cheat because people would think badly of him if they found out.

Interpersonal harmony. A stage of moral reasoning in which conclusions are based on loyalty, living up to the expectations of others, and social conventions.

At Stage 4, **law and order,** people follow laws and rules for their own sake. They don't make moral decisions to please other people as in Stage 3; rather, they believe that laws and rules exist to guide behavior, and they should be followed uniformly. A person reasoning at Stage 4 would argue that Steve should not cheat because "It's against the rules to cheat."

Law and order. A stage of moral reasoning in which conclusions are based on following laws and rules for their own sake.

Concern for the orderliness of society is also characteristic of Stage-4 ethics. For example, a person might argue that Steve should not cheat, because "What would our country be like if everybody cheated?" Concern for others is still the focus, but rules and order are key criteria. People reasoning at Stage 4 don't care whether the rest of the world cheats on their income taxes; they pay theirs because the law says they should.

Level III: Postconventional Ethics

Postconventional morality, also called *principled morality,* views moral issues in terms of abstract and self-developed principles of right and wrong. People reasoning at Level III have transcended both the individual and societal levels. They follow rules but, based on principle, they also see that rules sometimes need to be changed or ignored. Only a small portion of the population attains this level, and most of these don't reach it until their middle to late 20s.

Postconventional morality. A moral orientation that views moral issues in terms of abstract and self-developed principles of right and wrong.

Social contract. A stage of moral reasoning in which conclusions are based on socially agreed-upon principles.

In Stage 5, **social contract,** people make moral decisions based on socially agreed-upon rules. Stage 5 is the official ethic of the United States. The constitutional Bill of Rights is an example of a cultural social contract. For example, Americans agree in principle that people have the right to free speech (the First Amendment to the Constitution), and the legal profession is committed to interpreting the laws in this light. In addition, the American legal system has provisions for changing or amending laws when new values or conditions warrant it. A person reasoning at Stage 5 would say that Steve's cheating is wrong because teachers and learners agree in principle that grades should reflect achievement, and cheating violates this agreement.

Universal principles. A stage of moral reasoning in which conclusions are based on abstract and general principles that transcend society's laws.

At the sixth and final stage, **universal principles,** the individual's moral reasoning is based on abstract and general principles that transcend society's laws. People at this stage define right and wrong in terms of internalized universal standards. "The Golden Rule" is a commonly cited example. Because very few people operate at this stage, and questions have been raised about the existence of "universal" principles, Kohlberg deemphasized this stage in his later writings (Kohlberg, 1984).

MyEducationLab

To examine the influence of development on moral reasoning, go to the *Activities and Applications* section in Chapter 3 of MyEducationLab at www.myeducationlab.com, and watch the episode *Moral Reasoning: Examining a Moral Dilemma*. Answer the questions following the episode.

Putting Kohlberg's Theory into Perspective

As with most theories, Kohlberg's work has both proponents and critics. It has been widely researched, and this research has led to the following conclusions (Nucci, 2006; Turiel, 2006):

- Every person's moral reasoning passes through the same stages in the same order.
- People pass through the stages at different rates.
- Moral development is gradual and continuous, rather than sudden and discrete.
- Once a stage is attained, a person tends to reason at that stage instead of regressing to a lower stage.
- Intervention usually advances a person only to the next higher stage of moral reasoning.

These results are generally consistent with what Kohlberg's theory would predict.

Critics, however, point out that people's thinking, while tending to be at a certain stage, often shows evidence of reasoning at other stages. Also, although Stages 1 to 4 appear in most cultural groups, postconventional reasoning isn't seen in all cultures, suggesting that Kohlberg's theory more strongly focuses on Western thinking (Snary, 1995).

Moral reasoning also depends on context (Turiel, 2006). For example, people are more likely to believe that breaking a traffic law is immoral if it can cause someone harm. They would probably object to passing a parked school bus with the stop sign displayed, for example, but would likely view exceeding the speed limit on an interstate to be okay.

Although Kohlberg attempted to make his stages content free, thinking about moral dilemmas, like problem solving in general, is influenced by domain-specific knowledge (Nucci, 2006; Turiel, 2006). For example, a medical doctor asked to deliberate about an educational dilemma or a teacher asked to resolve a medical issue may be hampered by their lack of professional knowledge.

Researchers also question the self-reports of individuals' thought processes that Kohlberg used in his data-gathering methods. "Using interview data assumes that participants can verbally explain the workings of their minds. In recent years, this assumption has been questioned, more and more" (Rest et al., 1999, p. 295).

Finally, Kohlberg's work has been criticized for focusing on moral *reasoning* instead of moral *behavior.* People may reason at one stage and behave at another, influenced by context and personal history (Krebs & Denton, 2005). For example, an adolescent trying to decide whether to drink alcohol when out with friends will be influenced by family and cultural values as well as peer pressure. Kohlberg's work ignores these factors.

However, in support of a connection between moral reasoning and moral behavior, Kohlberg (1975) found that only 15 percent of students reasoning at the postconventional level cheated when given the opportunity to do so, as opposed to 55 percent of conventional thinkers and 70 percent of preconventional thinkers. In addition, adolescents reasoning at the lower stages are likely to be less honest and to engage in more antisocial behavior, such as delinquency and drug use (Comunian & Gielan, 2000). In contrast, reasoning at the higher stages is associated with altruistic behaviors, such as defending victims of injustice, the rights of minorities, and free speech (Kuther & Higgins-D'Alessandra, 1997; Turiel, 2006). Moral reasoning does influence behavior.

Gender Differences: The Morality of Caring

Some critics of Kohlberg's work also argue that it fails to adequately consider ways in which gender influences morality. Early research examining Kohlberg's theory identified differences in the ways men and women responded to moral dilemmas (Gilligan, 1982, 1998; Gilligan & Attanucci, 1988). Men were more likely to base their judgments on abstract concepts, such as justice, rules, and individual rights; women were more likely to base their moral decisions on interpersonal connections and attention to human needs. According to Kohlberg, these differences suggested a lower stage of development in women responding to moral dilemmas.

Gilligan (1977, 1982) argued that the findings, instead, indicate an "ethic of care" in women that is not inferior; rather, Kohlberg's descriptions don't adequately represent the complexity of female thinking. Gilligan suggests that a morality of caring proceeds through three stages. In the first, children are concerned primarily with their own needs. In the second, they show concern for others who are unable to care for themselves, such as infants and the elderly. And in the third, they recognize the interdependent nature of personal relationships and extend compassion to all of humanity. To encourage this development, Gilligan recommends an engaging curriculum with opportunities for students to think and talk about moral issues involving caring.

Nell Noddings (1992, 2002) has also emphasized the importance of caring, especially for teachers. Noddings argues that students should be taught the importance of caring through a curriculum that emphasizes caring for self, family and friends, and others throughout the world.

Gilligan makes an important point about gender differences, but additional research is mixed; some studies have found gender differences, whereas others have not (Turiel, 2006). Like cross-cultural studies, Gilligan's research reminds us of the complexity of the issues involved in moral development.

Emotional Factors in Moral Development

"Are you okay?" her mother asks as Melissa walks in the house after school.

"I feel really bad, Mom," Melissa answers softly. "We were working in a group, and Jessica said something sort of odd, and I said, 'That's dumb. Where did that come from?' . . . She didn't say anything for the rest of our group time. She doesn't get really good grades, and I know saying something about her being dumb really hurt her feelings. I didn't intend to do it. It just sort of came out."

"I know you didn't intend to hurt her feelings, Sweetheart. Did you tell her you were sorry?"

"No, when I realized it, I just sat there like a lump. I know how I'd feel if someone said I was dumb."

"Tell you what," her mom suggests. "Tomorrow, you go directly to her, tell her you're very sorry, and that it won't happen again."

"Thanks, Mom. I'll do it as soon as I see her. . . . I feel a lot better."

Shame. The painful emotion aroused when people recognize that they have failed to act or think in ways they believe are good.

Guilt. The uncomfortable feeling people get when they know they've caused distress for someone else.

Empathy. The ability to experience the same emotion someone else is feeling.

This exchange is about morality, but it doesn't involve reasoning; instead, it deals with emotions. Piaget and Kohlberg focused on cognitive aspects of moral development, but emotions are also important (Saarni, Campos, Camras, & Witherington, 2006). For instance, Melissa felt both **shame**, the painful emotion aroused when people recognize that they have failed to act or think in ways they believe are good, and **guilt**, the uncomfortable feeling people get when they know they've caused someone else's distress. Although unpleasant, experiencing shame and guilt indicates that moral development is advancing and future behavior will improve.

When Melissa said, "I know how I'd feel if someone said I was dumb," she was also describing feelings of **empathy**, the ability to experience the same emotion someone else is feeling. Empathy promotes moral and prosocial behavior even in the absence of wrongdoing (Eisenberg et al., 2006).

Although unpleasant, experiencing shame or guilt indicates that moral development is advancing.

Effective teachers in urban environments create relationships with students that foster personal and social development.

As children develop, they slowly acquire a **theory of mind**, an understanding that others have distinctive perceptions, feelings, desires, and beliefs. **Emotional intelligence**, the ability to understand emotions, such as shame, guilt, and empathy, in ourselves and others is an important part of this theory of mind. The term *emotional intelligence* has been popularized by Daniel Goleman (2006), who asserts that success in life is largely due to our ability to understand the role of emotions in our daily living. The development of emotional intelligence is important because it is related to positive self-esteem and social skills. In addition, low emotional intelligence and aggression are correlated (Lopes & Salovey, 2004).

As you see, moral development is complex, with both cognitive and emotional components. Kohlberg's work doesn't provide a complete picture, but combined with other information about personal, social, and emotional development, it helps us understand people's thoughts and feelings about moral issues. It also reminds us that moral reasoning and development aren't handed down from others. Rather, they are constructed from within by individuals as they attempt to make sense of their experiences.

Theory of mind. An understanding that other people have distinctive perceptions, feelings, desires, and beliefs.

Emotional intelligence. The ability to understand emotions in ourselves and others.

Learning Contexts: Promoting Personal, Social, and Moral Development in Urban Environments

Urban schools present unique challenges for students' personal, social, and moral development. They are often large and impersonal, "tough, confusing places where students can easily get lost" (Ilg & Massucci, 2003, p. 69).

Establishing meaningful relationships, so essential for personal and social development, is more challenging because of the diversity of urban neighborhoods and the distances students must travel, often using public transportation (Kincheloe, 2004). Extracurricular activities, which can serve as meeting points for students, may be inaccessible (R. Brown & Evans, 2002).

Establishing meaningful teacher–student relationships can also be a problem. From your study of Bronfenbrenner's bioecological theory, you saw that teachers are an important part of students' microsystems. Urban teachers commonly come from distant neighborhoods and cultures different from their students', making it more difficult for teachers to empathize with and connect to students' lives outside of school (Charner-Laird, Watson, Szczesuil, Kirkpatrick, & Gordon, 2004). As a result, the bond of mutual caring, an essential element in teacher–student relationships, is often missing. One study found that only 20 percent of urban African American boys and less than a third of African American girls felt that their teachers supported them and cared about their success (Noguera, 2003b). It is difficult for teachers to influence their students' personal, social, and moral development when trust and caring are absent.

The challenge is to create contexts in which urban students can interact in meaningful ways with both teachers and other students. One proposed solution is to create smaller schools, or schools within a school, that allow for the creation of more personal learning communities. Students in smaller schools "behave better, are more likely to be involved in extracurricular activities, . . . fight less, feel safe, and feel more attached to their schools" (Ilg & Massucci, 2003, p. 69).

While teachers, alone, can't create smaller schools, they can create a "small-school" feeling in their classrooms. Teachers can emphasize that they and the students are all there to learn and to support each other, both emotionally and academically. Effective urban teachers make a special effort to know students as people, and they're willing to spend extra time with them not only to listen but also to help with classroom-related tasks (B. L. Wilson & Corbett, 2001). They model courtesy and respect for their students and expect similar courtesy in return. And clear standards for behavior require that students treat each other the same way. This creates a sense of safety and attachment that students need for healthy development.

Effective urban teachers also scaffold their lessons to increase the likelihood of student success. One high school literature teacher commented:

> Sometimes for these stories, . . . they don't have the background knowledge to understand. They've never heard anything about Greek mythology. They're like "Polyphemus, Odysseus, what is that?" If they don't have the background knowledge, then it becomes harder for them to understand. So what I do is try to present information about Greek mythology in language they know. I use analogies or metaphors to help them make connections. (T. Howard, 2001, p. 192)

Urban teachers concerned about helping students develop positive academic self-concepts know that the process begins with achievement and that success comes from connecting with students' prior knowledge. This is only possible when teachers know their students and the world in which they live.

theory to practice

Promoting Moral Development in Your Classroom

Teachers have many opportunities to promote moral development in their students (Elias, 2004; Stengel & Tom, 2006). They do so primarily through the kinds of classroom environments they create and they way they guide students' interactions with each other. The following guidelines can assist you as you promote your students' moral development:

1. Model ethical thinking, behavior, and empathy in your interactions with students.
2. Use classroom management as a vehicle for promoting moral development.
3. Encourage students to understand and respect the perspectives of others.
4. Use moral dilemmas as concrete reference points for discussions of moral issues.

Let's see how Rod Leist, a fifth-grade teacher, uses these guidelines as he works with his students:

Rod begins language arts by saying, "Let's look in the story we've been reading and talk about Chris, the boy who found the wallet. He was broke, so would it be wrong for him to keep it, . . . and the money in it? . . . Jolene?"

"No, because it didn't belong to him."

"Ray?"

"Why not keep it? He didn't steal it; and . . . "

"That's terrible," Helena interrupts. "How would you like it if you lost your wallet?"

"Helena," Rod admonishes, "remember, we agreed that we would let everyone finish their point before we speak."

"Sorry for interrupting. . . . Please finish your point, Ray," Rod adds.

". . . It wasn't his fault that the person lost it. . . . And he was broke."

"Okay, Helena, go ahead," Rod says.

"Just . . . how would you feel if you lost something and somebody else kept it? Pretty bad, I think. . . . That's why I think he should give it back."

"That's an interesting point, Helena. When we think about these issues, it's good for us to try to put ourselves in someone else's shoes. . . . Of course, we would feel badly if we lost something and it wasn't returned.

"Go ahead, . . . Juan?"

"I agree. It was a lot of money, and Chris's parents would probably make him give it back anyway."

"And what if the person who lost the money really needed it?" Kristina adds.

After continuing the discussion for several more minutes, Rod says, "These are all good points. . . . Now, I want each of you to write a short paragraph saying whether or not you would keep the wallet and explaining why you feel it would be right or wrong. Then, we'll discuss your reasons some more tomorrow."

Now, let's look at Rod's attempts to apply the guidelines for promoting moral development in his classroom. He applied the first by modeling ethical thinking, behavior, and empathy in his interactions with his students. His simple and brief apology for interrupting the discussion communicated that he also obeyed their classroom rules. Also, in saying, "That's an interesting point, Helena. When we think about these issues, it's good for us to try to put ourselves in someone else's shoes," he reinforced Helena for being empathic and modeled his own empathy and prosocial behaviors.

Efforts to be fair, responsible, and democratic in dealings with students speak volumes about teachers' values and views of morality (Kohn, 2004). Rod's management system and his response to Helena applied the second and third guidelines. When he stopped Helena to remind her of the class agreement about interrupting, he was attempting to help his students understand fairness and tolerance for differing opinions. Acquiring this understanding is an important part of self-regulation, which can be developed only if students understand rules and why they are important, and agree to follow them. This type of learning environment promotes *autonomous morality* (Murdock et al., 2004).

Rod attempted to apply the fourth guideline by using the story of the lost wallet as a reference point for discussion. Effective teachers use moral dilemmas in literature to promote moral development and scaffold instruction so that the messages are meaningful (Goodman & Balamore, 2003; Koc & Buzzelli, 2004). During the discussion and in the writing exercise, Rod encouraged students to articulate and justify their moral positions on the issue.

Research supports this approach. Discussions that encourage students to examine their own moral reasoning combined with exposure to more advanced thinking promotes development (Nucci, 2006; Pyryt & Mendaglio, 2001).

MyEducationLab

To examine social and moral development in middle school students, go to the *Activities and Applications* section in Chapter 3 of MyEducationLab at www.myeducationlab.com, and read the case study *Social and Moral Development in Middle School Students*. Answer the questions following the case study.

check your understanding

4.1 Heavy traffic is moving on an interstate highway at a speed limit of 65. A sign appears that says "Speed Limit 55." The flow of traffic continues as before. How might a driver at Stage 3 and a driver at Stage 4 react? Explain each driver's reasoning.

4.2 According to Gilligan, how might a woman respond to the problem of Gary's not knowing the homework assignment (in the vignette at the beginning of this section)? How might her response differ from that of a man?

4.3 To which of Kohlberg's stages are empathy and prosocial behaviors most closely related? Explain.

To receive feedback for these questions, go to Appendix A.

classroom connections

Promoting Moral Development in Your Classroom

1. Moral development is enhanced by opportunities to think about concrete dilemmas and hear the positions of others. Openly discuss ethical dilemmas when they arise.
   - **Elementary:** The day before a new student with a learning disability joins the class, a second-grade teacher invites students to discuss how they would feel if they were new, how new students should be treated, and how they should treat one another in general.
   - **Middle School:** A seventh-grade math teacher has a classroom rule that students may not laugh, snicker, or make remarks of any kind when a classmate is trying to answer a question. In introducing the rule, she has the students discuss the reasons for it and the importance of the rule from other students' perspectives.
   - **High School:** A high school teacher's students view cheating as a game, seeing what they can get away with. The teacher addresses the issue by saying, "Because you feel this way about cheating, I'm going to decide who gets what grade without a test. I'll grade you on how smart I think you are." This provocative statement precipitates a classroom discussion on fairness and cheating.
2. Moral development is enhanced when students are exposed to moral behavior and moral reasoning at higher levels. Model moral and ethical behavior for your students.
   - **Elementary:** One election November, fifth-grade students jokingly ask if the teacher votes. The teacher uses this as an opportunity to discuss the importance of voting and each person's responsibilities in a democracy such as ours.
   - **Middle School:** A science teacher makes a commitment to students to have all their tests and quizzes graded by the following day. One day he is asked if he has the tests ready. "Of course," he responds. "I made an agreement at the beginning of the year, and people can't go back on their agreements."
   - **High School:** A group of tenth-grade business education students finishes a field trip sooner than expected. "If we just hang around a little longer, we don't have to go back to school," one student suggests. "Yes, but that would be a lie, wouldn't it?" the teacher counters. "We said we'd be back as soon as we finished, and we need to keep our word."

developmentally appropriate practice

Personal, Social, and Moral Development with Different-Aged Learners

Important differences exist in the personal, social, and moral development of elementary, middle school, and high school students. The following paragraphs outline some suggestions that will help you respond to these differences.

Working with Elementary Students

As children enter preschool, they are developing autonomy and taking the initiative to search for experiences. "Let me help!" and "I want to do it" are signs of this initiative. Criticism or overly restrictive directions detract from a sense of independence and, in extreme cases, lead to feelings of guilt and dependency. At the same time, children need the structure that helps them learn to take responsibility for their own behavior.

As children move through the elementary years, teachers attempt to help them succeed in learning experiences challenging enough to promote feelings of competence that lead to industry. This is demanding. Activities that are so challenging that students frequently fail can leave them with a sense of inferiority, but success on trivial tasks does little to make students feel competent (Brophy, 2004).

During the elementary years, student need opportunities to practice perspective taking and social problem solving. Discussions and group work where students can interact with others and practice these skills can be effective learning experiences.

The elementary grades also lay the foundation for students' moral growth and the development of social responsibility and self-control. Teachers who help students understand the impact of their actions on others help them make the transition from egocentric preconventional morality to conventional morality. Students who understand the importance of rules have attained this level of morality both in classrooms and in the world outside of school.

Working with Middle School Students

Adolescence is a time of physical, emotional, and intellectual changes, and adolescents are often uncertain about how to respond to new sexual feelings. They are concerned with what others think of them and are preoccupied with their looks. They want to assert their independence, yet long for the stability of structure and discipline. They want to rebel but need something solid to rebel against.

Most adolescents successfully negotiate this period, however, exploring different roles and maintaining positive relationships with their parents and other adults (W.A. Collins & Steinberg, 2006; Rudolph et al., 2001).

Students in middle and junior high schools need firm, caring teachers who empathize with them and their sometimes capricious actions while simultaneously providing the security of clear limits for acceptable behavior (Mawhinney & Sagan, 2007). Classroom management provides opportunities to advance moral reasoning from preconventional to conventional thinking. Effective teachers create classroom rules, discuss the reasons for them, and enforce them consistently.

Instruction in middle school classrooms should promote deep understanding of the topics being studied, while simultaneously giving students practice with prosocial behaviors, such as tolerance for others' opinions, listening politely, and avoiding hurtful comments. Effective instruction in middle schools is highly interactive, and lecture is held to a minimum.

Working with High School Students

High school students are beginning to wrestle with who they are and what they want to become. Peers become an increasingly important part of students' microsystems and have an important influence on both social and moral development.

Linking content to students' lives is particularly valuable at this age. For example, examining ideas about gender and occupational trends in social studies and showing how math and science will influence their futures are important for these students.

Like younger learners, high school students need opportunities to try out new ideas and link them to their developing sense of self. Discussions, small-group work, and focused writing assignments provide valuable opportunities for students to integrate new ideas into their developing self-identities.

Meeting Your Learning Objectives

1. Describe the components of the bioecological model, and explain how they influence development.
   - The components of the bioecological model include the individual and the systems that influence the individual's development.
   - The microsystem describes the people and activities in a child's immediate surroundings, and the mesosystem describes interactions among the elements of the microsystem.
   - The exosystem (societal influences), macrosystem (cultural influences), and chronosystem (time-dependent influences) also affect a child's development.
   - Each of the systems influence development through the experiences they provide for the developing learner.
2. Use descriptions of psychosocial, identity, and self-concept development to explain learner behavior.
   - Erikson's psychosocial theory integrates personal and social development.
   - Psychosocial development occurs in stages, each marked by a psychosocial challenge called a *crisis.* As people develop, the challenges change. Positive resolution of the crisis in each stage prepares the individual for the challenge at the next.
   - The development of identity usually occurs during high school and beyond. Identity moratorium and identity achievement are healthy developmental states; identity diffusion and identity foreclosure are less healthy.
   - Self-concept, developed largely through personal experiences, describes cognitive assessments of individuals' physical, social, and academic competence. Academic self-concept, particularly in specific content areas, is strongly correlated with achievement, and explains why learners who are generally successful persevere on challenging tasks.
   - Attempts to improve self-concept as an outcome of increased achievement in specific areas are often successful, but attempts to improve students' self-concepts by direct interventions are generally ineffective.
3. Describe major components of social development, and explain how teachers can promote social development in the classroom.
   - Perspective taking and social problem solving are major components of social development.
   - Perspective taking allows students to consider problems and issues from others' points of view.
   - Social problem solving includes the ability to read social cues, generate strategies, and implement and evaluate strategies for solving social problems.
   - Teachers promote social development when they provide examples and give students opportunities to practice social skills in the context of classroom learning experiences.
4. Use theories of moral development to explain differences in people's responses to ethical issues.
   - Piaget suggested that development represents individuals' progress from external morality, where rules are enforced by authority figures, to autonomous morality, where individuals see morality as rational and reciprocal.
   - Kohlberg's theory of moral development is based on people's responses to moral dilemmas. He developed a classification system for describing moral reasoning that had three levels.
   - At the preconventional level, individuals make egocentric moral decisions; at the conventional level, moral reasoning focuses on the consequences for others; and at the postconventional level, individuals base moral reasoning on principle.
   - The experience of the unpleasant emotions of shame and guilt and the development of empathy mark advances in the emotional component of moral development.
   - Teachers promote moral development by emphasizing personal responsibility and the functional nature of rules designed to protect the rights of others.

Developing as a Professional: Preparing for Your Licensure Exam

As you've studied this chapter, you've seen how personal and social development occur, as well as factors that influence the formation of identity and self-concepts.

Let's look now at a teacher working with a group of middle school students and see to what extent she contributes to these important aspects of development. Read the case study, and answer the questions that follow:

> "This is sure frustrating," Helen Sharman, a seventh-grade teacher, mumbles as she scores a set of quizzes in the teachers' workroom after school.
>
> "What's up?" her friend Natasha asks.
>
> "These students just won't think," Helen responds. "Three quarters of them put an apostrophe between the *r* and the *s* in *theirs.* The quiz was on using apostrophes in possessives. I warned them I was going to put some questions on the quiz that would make them think. Not only that, but I gave them practice problems that were just like those on the quiz. And I explained it so carefully," she sighs, shaking her head and returning to scoring her papers.

"What's really discouraging is that some of the students won't even try. Look at this one. Half of the quiz is blank. This isn't the first time Karl has done this, either. When I confronted him about it last time, he said, 'But I'm no good at English.' I replied, 'But you're doing fine in science and math.' He thought about that for a while and said, 'But that's different.' I wish I knew how to motivate him. You should see him on the basketball floor—poetry in motion—but when he gets in here, nothing."

"That can be discouraging. I've got a few like that myself," Natasha nods.

"What's worse, I'm almost sure some of the kids cheated. I left the room to go to the office, and when I returned, several of them were whispering and had guilt written all over their faces."

"Why do you suppose they did it?" Natasha replies.

"I'm not sure; part of it might be grade pressure, but how else am I going to motivate them? Some just don't see any problem with cheating. If they don't get caught, fine. I really am discouraged."

"Well," Natasha shrugs, "hang in there."

The next morning, as she returns the quizzes, Helen begins, "We need to review the rules again. You did so poorly on the quiz, and I explained everything so carefully. You must not have studied very hard.

"Let's take another look," she continues. "What's the rule for singular possessives?"

"Apostrophe *s*," Felice volunteers.

"That's right, Felice. Good. Now, how about plurals?"

"*S* apostrophe," Scott answers.

"All right. But what if the plural form of the noun doesn't end in *s*? . . . Russell?"

"Then it's like singular. . . . It's apostrophe *s*."

"Good. And how about pronouns?"

"You don't do anything," Connie adds.

"Yes, that's all correct," Helen nods. "Why didn't you do that on the quiz?"

". . ."

"Okay, look at number 3 on the quiz."

It appears as follows:

The books belonging to the lady were lost.

"It should be written like this," Helen explains, writing, "The lady's books were lost" on the chalkboard.

"Ms. Sharman," Nathan calls from the back of the room. "Why is it apostrophe *s*?"

"Nathan," Helen says evenly. "Remember my first rule?"

"Yes, Ma'am," Nathan says quietly.

"Good. If you want to ask a question, what else can you do other than shout it out?"

"Raise my hand."

"Good. Now, to answer your question, it's singular. So that's why it's apostrophe *s*.

"Now look at number 6." Helen waits a few seconds and then continues, "You were supposed to correctly punctuate it. But it's correct already because *theirs* is already possessive. Now that one was a little tricky, but you know I'm going to put a few on each quiz to make you think. You'd have gotten it if you were on your toes."

Helen identifies a few more items that were commonly missed and then hands out a review sheet.

"Now, these are just like the quiz," she says. "Practice hard on them, and we'll have another quiz on Thursday. Let's all do better. Please don't let me down again.

"And one more thing. I believe there was some cheating on this test. If I catch anyone cheating on Thursday, I'll tear up your quiz and give you a failing grade. Now go to work."

Short-Answer Questions

In answering these questions, use information from the chapter, and link your responses to specific information in the case.

1. How might Erikson explain Karl's behavior in Helen's class?
2. Using findings from the research on self-concept, explain Karl's behavior.
3. Using concepts from Kohlberg's theory, analyze Helen's cheating problem. From Kohlberg's perspective, how well did she handle this problem?
4. If you think Helen's teaching could have been improved on the basis of the information in this chapter, what suggestions would you make? Again, be specific.

For feedback on these responses go to Appendix B.

Now go to Chapter 3 of MyEducationLab, located at www.myeducationlab.com, where you can:

- Take a quiz to test your mastery of chapter objectives. Detailed feedback is provided to explain why your responses are correct or incorrect.
- Deepen your understanding of chapter concepts with *Review, Practice, Enrichment* exercises.
- Complete *Activities and Applications* that will help you apply what you have learned in the chapter by analyzing real classrooms through video clips, artifacts, and case studies. Your instructor will provide you with feedback for the *Activities and Applications.*
- Develop your professional knowledge and decision making in *Building Teaching Skills and Dispositions* exercises. Structured feedback will be available to you, providing you with support as you practice each skill. Your instructor will provide you with feedback on the final task that accompanies the exercise.

Important Concepts

autonomous morality (p. 81)
bully (p. 76)
chronosystem (p. 65)
clique (p. 65)
collective self-esteem (p. 74)
conventional morality (p. 82)
crisis (p. 67)
emotional intelligence (p. 86)
empathy (p. 85)
ethnic identity (p. 74)
exosystem (p. 65)
external morality (p. 81)
guilt (p. 85)
hostile attributional bias (p. 77)
identity (p. 66)
interpersonal harmony (p. 83)
law and order (p. 83)
macrosystem (p. 65)
market exchange (p. 82)
microsystem (p. 62)
mesosystem (p. 65)
moral development (p. 62)
moral dilemma (p. 81)
parenting style (p. 63)
personal development (p. 62)
perspective taking (p. 75)
preconventional morality (p. 82)
postconventional morality (p. 83)
punishment-obedience (p. 82)
self-concept (p. 66)
self-esteem (p. 70)
self-worth (p. 70)
sexual identity (p. 70)
sexual orientation (p. 70)
shame (p. 85)
social conventions (p. 80)
social contract (p. 84)
social development (p. 62)
social problem solving (p. 76)
temperament (p. 62)
theory of mind (p. 86)
universal principles (p. 84)

chapter

4

Learner Diversity

chapter outline

Culture

- Ethnicity
- Culture and Classrooms

Linguistic Diversity

- English Dialects
- English Language Learners
  - **Theory to Practice:** Teaching Culturally and Linguistically Diverse Students in Your Classroom

Gender

- School-Related Gender Differences
- Gender Differences in Classroom Behavior
- Gender Stereotypes and Perceptions
  - **Theory to Practice:** Responding to Gender Differences in Your Classroom

Socioeconomic Status

- How SES Influences Learning
- SES: Some Cautions and Implications for Teachers
- Students Placed at Risk
- Resilience
  - **Theory to Practice:** Teaching Students Placed at Risk in Your Classroom
  - **Developmentally Appropriate Practice:** Diversity in Students at Different Ages
  - **Exploring Diversity:** Teaching and Learning in Urban Schools

learning objectives

After you have completed your study of this chapter, you should be able to:

1. Describe culture and ethnicity, and explain how they can influence learning.
2. Explain why so much linguistic diversity exists in the United States, and describe ways that teachers can accommodate this diversity.
3. Explain how gender can influence learning, and describe steps for eliminating gender bias in classrooms.
4. Define socioeconomic status, and explain how it can affect learning.

The differences in our students are becoming ever more important. As you read the following case study, think about some of these differences and the influence they might have on learning in your classroom.

Jay Evans is a third-grade teacher in a large urban elementary school. He has 29 students—16 girls and 13 boys—in his class. It includes 8 African Americans, 7 students of Hispanic descent, 3 Asian Americans, and 2 Russian immigrants. English is not the native language for several, and most of his students come from low-income families.

He smiles as he walks by Katia's desk. She is his "special project," and she is blossoming in response to his efforts. When she first came to school, she was hesitant to participate because she came from Mexico, and Spanish is her native language. Initially, she could understand simple English sentences but struggled with speaking and reading English from textbooks. Jay made a point of involving her in classroom activities, paired her with students whose English was more developed, spent time with her after school, and gave her second-grade books to read at home. Her parents are supportive of Jay's efforts, and the home–school communication is very good. Her development since the beginning of the year has been remarkable.

As he steps past Angelo, his glow turns to concern. Angelo struggles to keep up with the rest of the class, and he is quiet and easily offended by perceived slights from his classmates. Because his parents are Mexican migrant workers, the family moves frequently, and he repeated first grade. His parents are separated, and his mother has settled in this area so the children can stay in the same school.

Jay consults with Jacinta Morales, a colleague who is bilingual, about additional things to try with Angelo. Together they develop a plan to help him with both his English and his academic work.

Learner diversity. The group and individual differences that we see in our students.

Learner diversity refers to both the group and individual differences that we see in our students. For instance, Jay has 16 girls and 13 boys in his class of 29; gender is one type of group difference. He also has students from different cultural backgrounds—African American, Hispanic, Asian American, and Russian. Some of his students are not native English speakers, and their socioeconomic status (SES) varies. Culture, language, and SES also describe common group differences. They are outlined in Figure 4.1.

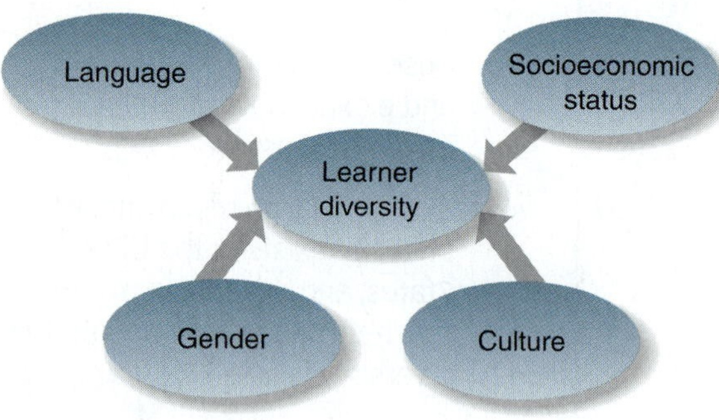

Figure 4.1 Sources of learner diversity

When we consider these differences, however, we should remember that they describe only general patterns, and a great deal of variation exists among the groups. For instance, both Katia and Angelo come from Mexico, so their cultural backgrounds are similar, and both are native Spanish speakers. However, Katia is thriving in Jay's class, while Angelo is struggling. Learner diversity also involves individual differences in our students.

They lead to two questions:

1. How might learner diversity influence learning?
2. How should teachers respond to this diversity?

Research helps us answer these and other important questions about our students. We begin by looking at studies focusing on the impact of culture on schooling.

Culture

Culture. The knowledge, attitudes, values, and customs that characterize a social group.

Think about the clothes you wear, the music you like, and the activities you share with your friends. These and other factors, such as family structure, are all part of your **culture**, which includes the knowledge, attitudes, values, and customs that characterize a social group (Banks, 2008). Culture pervades our lives and has a powerful influence on school success (see Figure 4.2).

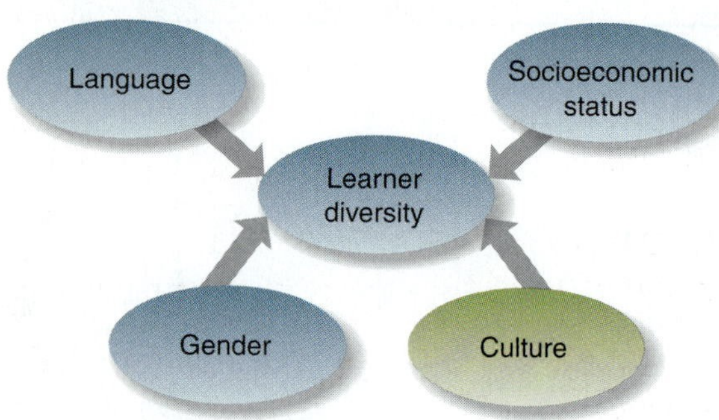

Figure 4.2 Sources of learner diversity: Culture

The cultural diversity in our country is rapidly increasing. Cultural minorities make up a third of the U.S. population, and the last census indicated that, for the first time, the Hispanic surnames Garcia and Rodriguez are among the 10 most common in our country (Roberts, 2007).

This trend is being reflected in our classrooms, where more than 4 of 10 students in the P–12 population are members of cultural minorities. Children of color currently make up the majority of public school enrollments in six states—California, Hawaii, Louisiana, Mississippi, New Mexico, and Texas—and make up over 90 percent of the student population in six major cities—Detroit, New York, Washington, D.C., Chicago, Los Angeles, and Baltimore (D. Short & Echevarria, 2004/2005; Padilla, 2006).

Ethnicity

Ethnicity. A person's ancestry and the way individuals identify with the nation from which they or their ancestors came.

Ethnicity, a person's ancestry and the way individuals identify with the nation from which they or their ancestors came, is an important part of culture (Banks, 2008). Members of an ethnic group have a common history, language (although sometimes not actively used), value system, and set of customs. Experts estimate that nearly 300 distinct ethnic groups live in the United States (Gollnick & Chinn, 2006).

Immigration and other demographic shifts have resulted in dramatic changes in the ethnic makeup of our country's school population. The Immigration Act of 1965, which ended quotas based on national origin, resulted in more immigrants coming to the United States from a wider variety of places. For example, while most during the early 1900s came from Europe, nearly 40 percent of more recent immigrants come from Mexico and Central America, about 25 percent come from Asia, and 10 percent come from the Caribbean. Less than 15 percent are now coming from Europe (U.S. Bureau of Census, 2004). This helps us understand why the backgrounds of Jay's students are so diverse.

By the year 2020, the school-age population will see more changes (see Figure 4.3). Researchers predict significant increases in all groups of students except those that are White, non-Hispanic, who will decrease to a little more than half of the total school population (U.S. Bureau of Census, 2003). By 2050, no one ethnic group will be a majority among adults. Each of these groups brings a distinct set of values and traditions that influences learning.

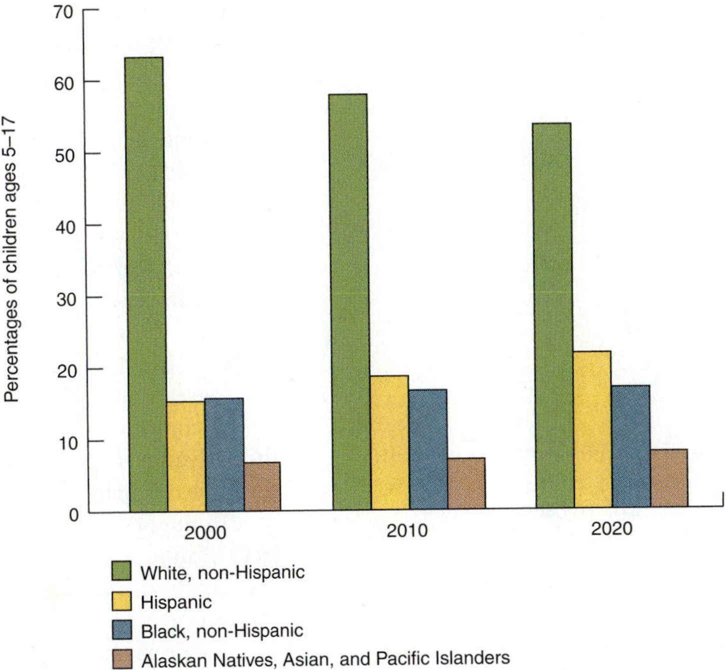

Figure 4.3 Changes in school-age population, 2000–2020
Source: U. S. Bureau of Census (2003).

Culture and Classrooms

When students enter our classrooms, they bring with them a set of values and beliefs from their home and neighborhood cultures, and these values often complement and reinforce classroom practices. Sometimes they don't, however, and when they don't, mismatches can interfere with learning (Greenfield et al., 2006). A **cultural mismatch** occurs when a child's home culture and the culture of the school create conflicting expectations for students' behavior. Awareness of these possible mismatches is a first step in dealing with them.

Cultural mismatch. A cultural clash that occurs when a child's home culture and the culture of the school create conflicting expectations for a student's behavior.

Let's look at an example.

> A second-grade class in Albuquerque, New Mexico, is reading *The Boxcar Children* and is about to start a new chapter. The teacher says, "Look at the illustration at the beginning of the chapter and tell me what you think is going to happen." A few students raise their hands. The teacher calls on a boy in the back row.
>
> He says, "I think the boy is going to meet his grandfather."
>
> The teacher asks, "Based on what you know, how does the boy feel about meeting his grandfather?"
>
> Trying to involve the whole class, the teacher calls on another student—one of four Native Americans in the group—even though she has not raised her hand. When she doesn't answer, the teacher tries rephrasing the question, but again the student sits in silence.
>
> Feeling exasperated, the teacher wonders if there is something in the way the lesson is being conducted that makes it difficult for the student to respond. She senses that the student she has called on understood the story and was enjoying it. Why, then, won't she answer what appears to be a simple question?
>
> The teacher recalls that this is not the first time this has happened, and that, in fact, the other Native American students in the class rarely answer questions in class discussions. She wants to involve them, wants them to participate in class, but can not think of ways to get them to talk. (Villegas, 1991, p. 3)

Why do students respond differently to our instruction, and how does culture influence these differences? We consider these questions in this section as we examine:

- Cultural attitudes and values
- Patterns of adult–child interactions
- Classroom organization and its match with students' home cultures

Cultural Attitudes and Values

Research helps us understand how cultural attitudes and values influence learning. For example, Asian Americans typically score higher on achievement tests and have higher rates of college attendance and completion than do other groups, including European Americans (Greenfield et al., 2006). Asian American parents typically have high expectations for their children and encourage them not only to attend college but also to earn graduate or professional degrees (Gollnick & Chinn, 2006). And Asian American parents translate these aspirations into academic work at home. For example, one study found that Chinese American parents were 10 times more likely to provide school-related practice activities at home for their children than were Caucasian American parents (Huntsinger, Jose, & Larsen, 1998).

Additional research has examined the remarkable successes of Vietnamese and Laotian refugee children in American classrooms. In spite of being in the United States less than 4 years, with vast language and cultural differences, these students earned better than B averages in school and high scores on standardized achievement tests (Caplan, Choy, & Whitmore, 1992). The researchers found that students' families strongly emphasized hard work, autonomy, perseverance, and pride. Parents reinforced these values with a nightly ritual of family homework—often doubling the amount of time spent by mainstream American counterparts—in which both parents and older siblings helped younger members of the family (Caplan et al., 1992).

Resistance cultures. Cultures with beliefs, values, and behaviors that reject the values of mainstream culture.

In contrast, some minorities, because of a long history of separatism and low status, defend themselves by forming **resistance cultures,** cultures with beliefs, values, and behaviors that reject the values of mainstream culture (Ogbu, 1992, 1999b, 2002, 2003; Ogbu & Simons, 1998).

To maintain their identity within their chosen group, members of resistance cultures reject attitudes and behaviors that lead to school success, such as doing homework, studying, and participating in class. To become a high achiever is to "become White," and students who study, want to succeed, and become actively involved in school risk losing the respect and friendship of their peers. Low grades, classroom management and motivation problems, truancy, and high dropout rates are often the result (Faiman-Silva, 2002).

John Ogbu (2002), a prominent researcher in this area, encourages teachers to help members of cultural minorities adapt to the dominant culture (including schools) without losing their cultural identities, a process he calls "accommodation without assimilation." The challenge for teachers is to help students understand the "culture of schooling"—the norms, procedures, and expectations necessary for success—while honoring the value and integrity of students' home cultures.

Minority role models are especially important in this process, as one African American doctor recalls:

> It all started in the second grade. One . . . Career Day at Jensen Scholastic Academy in my teacher, Mrs. F.'s room, an M.D. came to speak to the class about his career as a doctor. . . . I can't remember his name but from that day forward I knew I was destined to

Minority role models help members of cultural minorities understand that they can both succeed in mainstream culture and retain their cultural identity.

> be a doctor. From that point on I began to take my work seriously, because I knew to become a doctor grades were very important. Throughout my elementary career I received honors. In the seventh grade I really became fascinated with science, which I owe all to my teacher Mr. H. He made learning fun and interesting. I started to read science books even when it wasn't necessary, or I found myself watching the different specials on Channel 11 about operations they showed doctors performing. (Smokowski, 1997, p. 13)

Minority role models provide learners with evidence that they can both succeed in mainstream culture and retain their cultural identity (Stanton-Salazar & Spina, 2003).

Stereotype Threat. As cultural minorities struggle to adapt to and compete in schools, they sometimes experience **stereotype threat,** the anxiety experienced by members of a group resulting from concern that their behavior might confirm a stereotype (Aronson, Fried, & Good, 2002; Aronson & Inzlicht, 2004). It is most pernicious for cultural minority students who are high achievers in a domain such as math, but at some level it exists for many groups. For instance, stereotype threat is involved when women fear that they will do less well than men on tests involving math or computer science because they think that these are male domains, or when white males fear they will perform less well on math tests because they think they are competing with Asians who are better at math.

Stereotype threat. The anxiety experienced by members of a group resulting from concern that their behavior might confirm a stereotype.

Research suggests that stereotype threat can adversely affect performance through heightened anxiety. This anxiety reduces students' capacity for thinking and problem solving (Okagaki, 2006).

You can minimize the negative effects of stereotype threat for your students in at least three ways. First, communicate positive expectations for all students, and do so beginning the first day of class. Second, make individual improvement the theme of your teaching, and minimize comparisons between students. Third, emphasize the role of hard work and effort in learning success. As you'll see in Chapters 10 and 11, these suggestions are important for increasing student motivation to learn.

Cultural Differences in Adult–Child Interactions

Cultural interaction patterns acquired in the home can influence how teachers and students interact in school (Weigel, Martin, & Bennett, 2005). For example, when teachers said, "Let's put the scissors away now," White students, accustomed to this indirect way of speaking, interpreted it as a command; African American students did not (Heath, 1989). Failure to obey was then viewed as a management problem, which resulted from a mismatch between home and school cultures.

Similar disparities can cause problems during instruction. For example, research indicates that White children tend to respond comfortably to questions requiring specific answers, such as, "Who are the main characters in this story?" African American children, accustomed to questions that are more "open-ended," such as "What can you tell us about the story?" are sometimes confused by the specific questions because they aren't viewed as information givers in their interactions with adults (Rogoff, 2003). One parent reported, "Miss Davis, she complain 'bout Ned not answerin' back. He says she asks dumb questions she already know about" (Heath, 1982, p. 107).

Made aware of these cultural differences, teachers incorporated more open-ended questions in their lessons, and worded commands more directly, such as "Put your scissors away now." They also had all students practice answering factual questions and liberally praised their efforts to do so. In this way, teachers built bridges between the students' natural learning styles and the schools.

Cultural mismatches can also occur in interpretations of time and acceptable school-related behaviors. One principal's experience working with Pacific Island students is an example (Winitzky, 1994). The principal had been invited to a community awards ceremony honoring students from her school. She readily accepted, arrived a few minutes early, and was ushered to a seat on the stage. After an uncomfortable (to her) wait of over an hour, the ceremony began. The children received their rewards and returned to their seats, which led to an eye-opening experience:

> Well, the kids were fine for a while, but as you might imagine, they got bored fast and started to fidget. Fidgeting and whispering turned into poking, prodding, and open chatting. I became a little anxious at the disruption, but none of the other adults appeared to even notice, so I ignored it, too. Pretty soon several of the children were up and out of

> their seats, strolling about the back and sides of the auditorium. All adult faces continued looking serenely up at the speaker on the stage. Then the kids started playing tag, running circles around the seating area and yelling gleefully. No adult response—I was amazed, and struggled to resist the urge to quiet the children. Then some of the kids got up onto the stage, running around the speaker, flicking the lights on and off, and opening and closing the curtain! Still nothing from the Islander parents! . . . I suddenly realized then that when these children . . . come to school late, it doesn't mean that they or their parents don't care about learning. . . . that's just how all the adults in their world operate. When they squirm under desks and run around the classroom, they aren't trying to be disrespectful or defiant, they're just doing what they do everywhere else. (Winitzky, 1994, pp. 147–148)

Students from different cultures bring with them ways of acting and interacting with adults that may differ from the traditional teacher-as-authority-figure role (Trawick-Smith, 2003). Her experience with Pacific Island culture gave the principal insights into the reasons her students often acted as they did.

Classroom Organization and Culture

In many classrooms, teachers emphasize individual performance, which is reinforced by test scores and grades. This can lead to competition, which requires successes and failures, and the success of one student may be tied to the failure of another.

Contrast this orientation with the learning styles of the Hmong, a mountain tribe from Laos who immigrated to the United States after the Vietnam War. Their culture emphasizes cooperation, and Hmong students help and support each other (Vang, 2003). One teacher described it in this way:

> When Mee Hang has difficulty with an alphabetization lesson, Pang Lor explains, in Hmong, how to proceed. Chia Ying listens in to Pang's explanation and nods her head. Pang goes back to work on her own paper, keeping an eye on Mee Hang. When she sees Mee looking confused, Pang leaves her seat and leans over Mee's shoulder. She writes the first letter of each word on the line, indicating to Mee that these letters are in alphabetical order and that Mee should fill in the rest of each word. . . .
>
> Classroom achievement is never personal but always considered to be the result of cooperative effort. Not only is there no competition in the classroom, there is constant denial of individual ability. When individuals are praised by the teacher, they generally shake their heads and appear hesitant to be singled out as being more able than their peers. (Hvitfeldt, 1986, p. 70)

Students from other cultures, such as Native American, Mexican American, and Southeast Asian, may also experience difficulties in competitive classrooms (Aronson, Wilson, & Akert, 2005; Greenfield et al., 2006). They value cooperation and view competition as unnecessary or distasteful. A cultural mismatch then exists when they come to school and are asked to compete. Raising hands and jousting for the right to answer isn't congruent with the ways they interact at home. Also, the typical classroom sequence—teacher questions, student answers, teacher responds—isn't a normal part of family life in many cultures. Children aren't routinely asked questions for which adults already know the answer and instead are expected to quietly observe adult interactions (Greenfield et al., 2006).

This helps us understand the problem with the students who wouldn't respond to questions about the *Box Car Children* in the New Mexican classroom. The Native American children sat quietly because doing so was consistent with their culture.

This discussion also helps us answer the first question we asked at the beginning of the chapter: "How might learner diversity influence learning?" When cultural mismatches occur, less learning occurs. Sensitivity to these factors is essential for teachers.

Some Cautions About Culture and Classrooms

When encountering cultural mismatches, teachers sometimes conclude that parents of minority children don't value schooling or don't support their efforts. This couldn't be less true. Research consistently indicates that the parents of cultural minorities care deeply about their children and want them to succeed in school (Greenfield et al., 2006; Okagaki, 2006). However, the parents often don't understand how their home cultures influence learning or how to help their children succeed. This isn't surprising; most of us grew up tacitly assuming that all homes were like ours.

Research also reminds us of the need to bridge cultural differences and adapt our instruction to the backgrounds and needs of our students (Greenfield et al., 2006). This begins when we realize that that our students may enter our classrooms with different ways of acting and believing.

Also, as we said at the beginning of the chapter, it is important to remember that our discussion of culture has focused on group differences, and individuals within groups often vary. For example, our discussion of resistance cultures centered on Ogbu's work, which focuses on African American students. It is essential that we keep in mind that many African American students very much want to succeed in school and do so (Lewis & Kim, 2008). To conclude that they are all members of resistance cultures would be a dangerous form of stereotyping. Similarly, the successes of Asian American students as a group does not mean that they are all members of a "model minority," a stereotypic term that some Asian Americans reject (Asian-Nation, 2005). Many encounter difficulties in school, and language and poverty are obstacles for them (Lei, 2003; Lew, 2004).

You can help prevent cultural stereotyping by becoming informed about the characteristics of the cultural groups to which your students belong. Reading is helpful, but there is no substitute for direct interaction, both with your students and their caregivers. Parent–teacher conferences, phone calls, and e-mail if it exists in the home all help establish and maintain communication.

Paradoxically, some teachers respond to the possibility of stereotyping by assuming a position of **colorblindness,** the belief that students' ethnicity or culture should not be a consideration in teaching (L. Johnson, 2002; A. Lewis, 2001). When this occurs, teachers pretend that all students are alike and intentionally try to avoid any consideration of culture. This is also a mistake, because it ignores a powerful influence on students.

MyEducationLab

To examine one teacher's attempts to make her classroom culturally compatible, go to the *Activities and Applications* section in Chapter 4 of MyEducationLab at www.myeducationlab.com, and watch the episode *Culturally Responsive Teaching.* Answer the questions following the episode.

Colorblindness. The belief that students' culture of ethnicity should not be a consideration in teaching.

check your understanding

1.1 Describe *culture* and *ethnicity*, and explain how they can influence learning.
1.2 What is a resistance culture? How can teachers effectively deal with it?
1.3 Identify at least one way in which classroom organization can clash with the values of cultural minorities. What can teachers do about this problem?

To receive feedback for these questions, go to Appendix A.

Linguistic Diversity

One out of five children in U.S. schools—approximately 14 million students—are children of immigrant parents, and they bring with them a variety of languages and dialects (Kober, 2006; Padilla, 2006). Experts estimate that the number of students who speak a native language other than English increased 72 percent between 1992 and 2002 (Padilla, 2006; D. Short & Echevarria, 2004/2005). Increasingly, our students are bringing different native languages to school, and their facility with English varies widely (Abedi, Hofstetter, & Lord, 2004). Let's look at this linguistic diversity and its implications for teaching (see Figure 4.4).

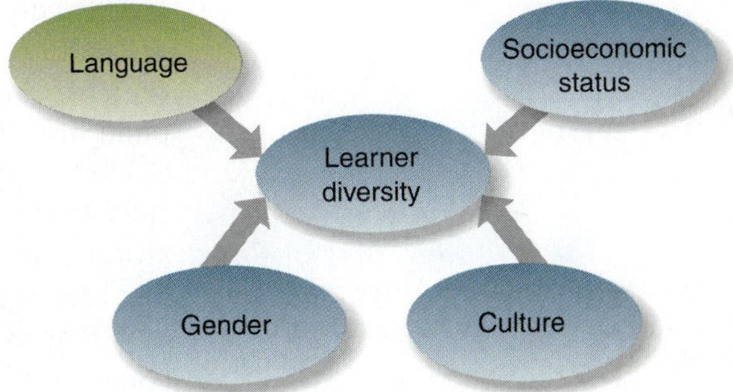

Figure 4.4 Sources of learner diversity: Language

English Dialects

Anyone who travels in the United States will notice that our country has many regional and ethnic dialects; experts identify at least 11 that are distinct (Owens, 2005). A **dialect** is a variation of standard English that is associated with a particular regional or social group and is unique in vocabulary, grammar, or pronunciation. Everyone speaks a dialect; people merely react to those

Dialect. A variation of standard English that is associated with a particular regional or social group and is distinct in vocabulary, grammar, or pronunciation.

Increasingly, our students are bringing different native languages to school.

different from their own. Some are more nearly accepted than others, however, and language is at the heart of what Delpit (1995) calls "codes of power," the cultural and linguistic conventions that control access to opportunity in our society.

Research suggests that teachers have lower expectations for students and assess their work accordingly when the students use nonstandard English (Godley, Sweetland, Wheeler, Minnici, & Carpenter, 2006). These language patterns are often confused with mistakes during oral reading (Snow, Griffin, & Burns, 2005), and some people believe that dialects, such as Black English, are substandard. Linguists, however, argue that these variations are just as rich and semantically complex as standard English (Godley et al., 2006; Labov, 1972).

Dialects in the Classroom: Implications for Teachers

Teachers who respond effectively to cultural diversity accept and value learner differences, and these responses are particularly important when working with students who use nonstandard English. Dialects are integral to the culture of students' homes and neighborhoods, and requiring students to eliminate their dialect communicates that differences are unacceptable.

Standard English, however, allows access to educational and economic opportunities, which is the primary reason for teaching it (Snow et al., 2005). Students realize this when they interview for a first job or when they plan for admission to college. So, what should teachers do when a student says, "I ain't got no pencil," or brings some other nonstandard dialect into the classroom? Opinions vary from "rejection and correction" to complete acceptance, but the most culturally sensitive approach is to first accept the dialect and then build on it (Padilla, 2006). For example, when a student says, "I ain't got no pencil," the teacher might say, "Oh, you don't have a pencil. What should you do, then?" Although results won't occur immediately, the long-range benefits, both for language development and attitudes toward learning, are worthwhile.

Bidialecticism. The ability to switch back and forth between a dialect and standard English.

Language differences don't have to form barriers between home and school. **Bidialecticism,** the ability to switch back and forth between a dialect and standard English, allows access to both (Gollnick & Chinn, 2006). For example, one high school teacher read a series of poems by Langston Hughes and focused on how Hughes used Black English to create vivid images. The class discussed contrasts with standard English and ways in which differences between the two dialects could be used to accomplish different goals (Shields & Shaver, 1990).

English Language Learners

English Language Learners. Students for whom English is not their first or home language.

English Language Learners (ELLs) are students whose first or home language is not English. As a result of immigration and high birth rates among immigrant families, the number of non-

English-speaking students and those with limited English has increased dramatically since the 1980s (Gray & Fleishman, 2005). In California alone, 1.6 million ELLs make up a fourth of that state's student population (Bielenberg & Fillmore, 2005). Projections indicate that by 2015 more than half of all P–12 students in our country will not speak English as their first language (Gray & Fleischman, 2005). The diversity is staggering; more than 450 languages other than English are spoken in our schools, with Spanish being the most common (Abedi et al., 2004; Kindler, 2002).

Let's see how language diversity can affect teaching.

> Ellie Barton, a language arts teacher at Northeast Middle School, is the school's ELL coordinator. Her job is challenging, as her students vary considerably in their knowledge of English. For instance, one group of Somali-Bantu children just arrived from a refugee camp in Kenya. They cannot read or write, because there is no written language for their native tongue. Language isn't their only challenge; many had never been in a building with more than one floor, and others found urinals and other aspects of indoor plumbing a mystery. At the other end of the continuum is a young girl from India who can read and write in four languages.
>
> To sort out this language diversity, the district uses a placement test that categorizes students into three levels: newcomer classrooms for students who have little or no expertise with English; self-contained ELL classrooms, where a primary emphasis is on learning to read and write English; and sheltered English, where students get help in learning academic subjects such as science and social studies. The process is problematic, however, because the school cannot communicate with some parents, and a few parents don't know the exact ages of their children. Ellie's principal deals with this information void in creative ways; he recently asked a dentist friend to look at a child's teeth to estimate one student's age. (Adapted from Romboy & Kinkead, 2005)

Being an ELL creates obstacles for students; they typically lag behind in achievement and are more likely to be referred for special education services. They are also much more likely to drop out of school (Bielenberg & Fillmore, 2005; D. Short & Echevarria, 2004/2005). How should schools respond to this linguistic challenge? Considerable controversy surrounds this question.

Types of ELL Programs

Have you ever tried to learn a foreign language? How proficient were you after 2 or 3 years? How successful would you have been if all the instruction in your other classes were in that language? Your answer to the last question provides some insight into the challenges faced by ELLs. Teaching English is the primary goal of ELL programs, but the way they attempt to reach the goal varies considerably (see Table 4.1).

Immersion Programs. **Immersion programs** place ELLs in regular classrooms to help them learn both English and academic content (Padilla, 2006). Pure immersion programs offer no extra assistance to ELLs; the idea is that continual exposure is sufficient to learn English.

Immersion programs. English language programs that place ELLs in regular classrooms without additional assistance to help them learn both English and academic content at the same time.

Structured immersion, in contrast, attempts to assist ELLs by teaching both English and introducing academic topics at a slower pace. You may have encountered a form of structured immersion in foreign language classes, where your teacher attempted to do as much instruction as possible in that language. Several states, including California and Arizona, have mandated a year of structured immersion as the beginning point for ELL instruction, which is followed by complete immersion (Padilla, 2006).

Structured immersion. A type of immersion program that attempts to assist ELLs by teaching both English and academic subjects at a slower pace.

Maintenance ELL Programs. **Maintenance ELL programs** build on students' native language by teaching in both English and the native language (Peregoy & Boyle, 2005). Found primarily at the elementary level, these programs have the goal of developing students who can speak, read, and write in two languages. They have the advantage of retaining and building on students' heritage language and culture, but they are difficult to

Maintenance ELL programs. Programs for English language learner (ELL) students that build on students' native languages by teaching in both English and the native languages.

table 4.1 ELL Programs

Type of Program	Description	Advantages	Disadvantages
Immersion	Places students in classrooms where only English is spoken, with few or any linguistic aids.	Increased exposure to new language and multiple opportunities to use it.	Sink or swim approach may be overwhelming and leave students confused and discouraged.
Maintenance	Students maintain first language through reading and writing activities in first language while teachers introduce English.	Students become literate in two languages.	Requires teachers trained in first language. Acquisition of English may not be as fast.
Transitional	Students learn to read in first language, and teachers give supplementary instruction in English as a Second Language. After mastering English, students enroll in regular classrooms and discontinue learning in first language.	Maintains first language. Transition to English is eased by gradual approach.	Requires teachers trained in first language. Literacy skills in first language not maintained and may be lost.
ESL Pullout Programs	Pullout programs in which students are provided with supplementary English instruction along with regular instruction in content classes.	Easier to administer when dealing with diverse language backgrounds because it requires only the pullout teachers to have ELL expertise.	Students may not be ready to benefit from content instruction in English. Pullout Programs segregate students.
Sheltered English	Teachers adapt content instruction to meet the learing needs of ELL students.	Easier for students to learn content.	Requires an intermediate level of English proficiency. Also requires teachers with ELL expertise.

implement because they require groups of students with the same native language and bilingual teachers who speak the students' first language.

Transitional ELL programs. English language learner (ELL) programs that attempt to use the native language as an instructional aid until English becomes proficient.

Transitional ELL Programs. **Transitional ELL programs** attempt to use the native language as an instructional aid until English becomes proficient. Transitional programs begin by teaching reading and writing in the first language and gradually develop learners' English skills. Often, the transition period is too short, leaving students inadequately prepared for learning in English (Echevarria & Graves, 2007). In addition, loss of the first language and lack of emphasis on the home culture can result in communication gaps between children who no longer speak the first language and parents who don't speak English.

ESL pullout programs. Programs for English language learner (ELL) students who receive most of their instruction in regular classrooms but are also pulled out for extra help.

ESL Pullout Programs. In **English as a Second Language (ESL) pullout programs,** students receive most of their instruction in regular classrooms but are also pulled out for extra help (Peregoy & Boyle, 2005). Instruction in these programs focuses on English language development, with emphasis on pronunciation, grammar, vocabulary, and oral comprehension. In addition, ESL teachers assist with the content, such as math or social studies, that is being taught in regular classrooms. The programs require students whose English skills are developed to the point that they can benefit from regular instruction. When this isn't the case, sheltered English classes are more effective.

Sheltered English. An approach to teaching ELL students in academic classrooms that modifies instruction to assist students in learning content.

Basic interpersonal communication skills. A level of proficiency in English that allows students to interact conversationally with their peers.

Academic language proficiency. A level of proficiency in English that allows students to handle demanding learning tasks with abstract concepts.

Sheltered English. **Sheltered English** classrooms modify instruction to assist students in learning content. Also called *Specially Designed Academic Instruction in English,* these classes require students with intermediate levels of English proficiency as well as instructors who know both content and ELL strategies.

When working with ELL students, teachers should avoid overestimating their English proficiency (Echevarria, Vogt, & Short, 2004; Padilla, 2006). After about 2 years in language-rich environments, students develop **basic interpersonal communication skills,** a level that allows them to interact socially with their peers (Cummins, 2000). Students may need an additional 5 to 7 years to develop **academic language proficiency,** a level that allows them to handle demanding learning tasks.

classroom connections

Working Effectively with Culturally and Linguistically Diverse Students in Your Classroom

1. Students' cultural attitudes and values can have a powerful effect on school learning. Communicate that you respect and value all cultures, and emphasize the contributions that cultural differences make to learning.
   - **Elementary:** A third-grade teacher designs classroom "festivals" that focus on different cultures and invites parents and other caregivers to help celebrate and contribute to enriching them. He also emphasizes values, such as courtesy and respect, which are common to all cultures. He has students discuss the ways different societies display these values.
   - **Middle School:** An art teacher decorates the room with pictures of Native American art. The teacher discusses how it contributes to art in general and how it communicates Native American values, such as a sense of harmony with nature and complex religious beliefs.
   - **High School:** An urban English teacher assigns students to read works written by African American and Middle Eastern, South Asian, and far Eastern authors. They compare both the writing approach and the different points of view that the authors represent.

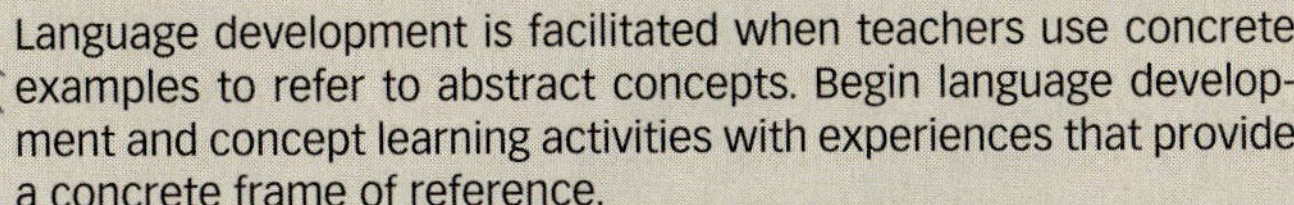

2. Language development is facilitated when teachers use concrete examples to refer to abstract concepts. Begin language development and concept learning activities with experiences that provide a concrete frame of reference.
   - **Elementary:** A fifth-grade teacher, in a unit on fractions, instructs students to fold pieces of paper into halves, thirds, fourths, and eighths. At each point, she asks them to state in words what the example represents, and she writes important terms on the board.
   - **Middle School:** A science teacher begins a unit on the skeletal and muscular systems by having students feel their own legs, arms, ribs, and heads. As they touch parts of their bodies, such as their Achilles tendon, she asks them to repeat the term *tendon* and say, "tendons attach bones to muscles."
   - **High School:** An English teacher stops whenever an unfamiliar word occurs in a reading passage or discussion and asks for a definition and example of it. He keeps a list of these words on a bulletin board and encourages students to use them in class and in their writing.

3. Learning a second language requires that students use the language in speaking, writing, and reading. Provide students with multiple opportunities to practice language in your classroom.
   - **Elementary:** The fifth-grade teacher who had the students fold the papers asks them to describe each step they take when they add fractions with both like and unlike denominators. When they struggle to put their understanding into words, she prompts them, in some cases providing essential words and phrases for them.
   - **Middle School:** A social studies teacher requires students to prepare oral reports in groups of four. Each student must make a 2-minute presentation to the other three members of the group. After students practice their reports with each other in groups, each person presents a part of a group report to the whole class.
   - **High School:** A history teacher calls on a variety of students to provide part of a summary of the previous day's work. As she presents new information, she frequently stops and asks other students to describe what has been discussed to that point and how it relates to topics discussed earlier.

Evaluating ELL Programs

ELL programs are controversial. For example, advocates of immersion programs claim that this approach teaches English more rapidly and efficiently; critics question whether this "sink or swim" approach is either effective or humane. They also argue that immersion dismisses the first language, resulting in a loss of **bilingualism,** the ability to speak, read, and write in two languages.

Bilingualism. The ability to speak, read, and write in two languages.

Maintenance and transitional ELL programs are also controversial. Critics contend that these programs are

- Divisive, encouraging groups of nonnative English speakers to remain separate from mainstream American culture
- Ineffective, slowing Ell students' development of English
- Inefficient, requiring expenditures for the training of bilingual teachers and materials that could be better spent on quality English programs (Schlesinger, 1992; U.S. English, 2007)

Proponents counter that the programs build on the student's first language and provide a smooth and humane transition to English. In addition, they argue that being able to speak two languages has practical benefits in today's world (Gutiérrez et al., 2002; Merisuo-Storm, 2007).

Research is also controversial. Some suggest that students in maintenance programs achieve higher in math and reading, students have more positive attitudes toward school and

theory to practice

Teaching Culturally and Linguistically Diverse Students in Your Classroom

Multicultural education. An approach to education that attempts to make classrooms welcoming for all students by recognizing, valuing, and building on the perspectives and experiences of all students' cultures.

It is a virtual certainty that you will teach students who are members of cultural minorities, and it is highly likely that English will not be the first language for some of them. **Multicultural education** attempts to make classrooms welcome places for all students by recognizing, valuing, and building on their perspectives and experiences (B. Gay, 2000; G. Gay, 2005).

You can implement aspects of multicultural education by being culturally responsive in your teaching (Zirkel, 2008). The following guidelines can help you in your efforts, and they begin to answer the second question we asked at the beginning of the chapter: "How should teachers respond to this diversity?"

1. Communicate that you respect all cultures and value the contributions that cultural differences make to learning.
2. Involve all students in learning activities.
3. Use concrete experiences as reference points for language development.
4. Target important vocabulary, and provide opportunities for all students to practice language.

Let's see how Gary Nolan, a fourth-grade teacher, uses these guidelines as he works with his students.

Of Gary's 28 students, 9 are Hispanic, 6 are African American, 4 are Asian, and 2 are from Morocco. Eight are ELLs.

"You're improving all the time," Gary smiles at his ELL students as the rest of the class files into the room. He spends a half hour with them each morning to help them keep up with their classmates.

"Good morning, Tu. . . . Nice haircut, Shah," Gary greets the other students as they come in the door.

"Who's up today?" he asks as the students settle down.

"Me," Anna says, raising her hand.

"Go ahead, Anna."

Anna moves to the front of the room. "I was born in Mexico, but my father is from Spain, and my mother is from Columbia," she explains, pointing to each of the countries on a map at the front of the room.

Every Friday morning, Gary has one of the students make a presentation. They bring food, costumes, art, and music that illustrate their backgrounds, and they place a push pin with their name on it on the map.

Gary frequently comments about how lucky they are to have classmates from so many parts of the world. "Remember when Shah told us about Omar Khayyam?" Gary had once asked. "He solved math problems that people in Europe didn't solve until many years later. If Shah weren't in our class, we would never have learned that."

Gary also has a chart displaying common words and phrases such as "Hello," "Goodbye," and "How are you?" in Spanish, Vietnamese, Arabic, and English. He has labeled objects around the room, like the clock, windows, and chairs, in the students' native languages and English. And he displays a calendar that identifies holidays in different cultures. Students make special presentations on the holidays, and parents are invited.

"Okay, story time," Gary says when Anna is finished. He reads a story from a book that is liberally illustrated with pictures. As he reads, he holds up the pictures and asks the students to identify the object or event being

Culturally responsive teachers build on the strengths that children bring to school.

themselves, and the knowledge and skills acquired in a native language transfer to the second language (Krashen, 2005; Slavin & Cheung, 2004). However, other research suggests that students in immersion programs learn English faster and achieve higher in other academic areas (Barone, 2000; K. Hayes & Salazar, 2001).

Making valid comparisons is difficult, because researchers use varying criteria for evaluating the merits of different programs (Padilla, 2006). Some researchers use the speed of English acquisition, while others use content-area achievement measures, such as standardized tests or grades, as criteria. The debate is likely to continue, because the issues are both complex and emotional (Hawkins, 2004).

illustrated. One picture shows a cave in a woods that the boy and girl in the story explore.

"Everyone say, 'cave,'" Gary directs, pointing at the picture, and the students say "cave" in unison. He does the same with other objects in the picture, such as tree, rock, and stream.

After finishing, he begins, "Tell us something you remember about the story. . . . Carmela?"

". . . A boy and a girl . . . are lost," Carmela responds in her halting English.

"Yes, good. . . . The story is about a boy and a girl who got lost in a cave," Gary says slowly and clearly, pointing again to each of the objects in the picture.

"Have any of you ever been in a cave?. . . How is a cave different from a hole?"

Gary asks the students to talk briefly to each other, and then asks them to share their experiences with digging holes and going into caves. When they struggle with a term, Gary provides it, asks the class to say it in unison, and he repeats the process with another student.

"Good, everyone," Gary smiles after they've discussed the story for several more minutes. "Let's get ready for math."

Now, let's look at Gary's efforts to apply the guidelines. He implemented the first by having students make presentations about their cultural heritage and emphasizing how lucky they are to have classmates from different parts of the world. His emphasis on the contributions of Omar Khayyam, for example, and comments such as, "If Shah weren't in our class, we probably would never have learned that," communicates that he respects and values students' cultures, which can promote pride and motivation (Banks, 2008; Gollnick & Chinn, 2006). The personal time he spent before school helping his non-native English speakers and his greeting as students enter his room also communicated that he cared for each one. These gestures are subtle but important with members of cultural minorities (Gollnick & Chin, 2006).

Effective teachers call on all students, regardless of students' backgrounds.

Gary applied the second guideline by calling on all his students. Doing so signaled that he expected each to participate, and when they struggled, he prompted them to help them answer.

Some teachers believe that students don't *want* to answer questions. This isn't true. A synthesis of research on learner motivation indicates that students, including those from cultural minorities, want to be called on if they believe they will be able to answer, and you emphasize that answering incorrectly is simply a part of learning (Eggen & Kauchak, 2002).

Gary further implemented the second guideline by combining whole-class and small-group instruction in an attempt to accommodate possible differences in cultural learning styles. (We examine strategies for involving all students in learning activities in Chapter 13.)

By using concrete experiences to facilitate language development, Gary implemented the third guideline. For example, as he read the story, he referred to pictures in the book, which provided concrete reference points for vocabulary (Echevarria & Graves, 2007). He also encouraged students to share their personal experiences with the concepts, and he linked language to them.

Gary applied the fourth guideline by specifically targeting key terms. Vocabulary, and especially the technical vocabulary found in many content areas, is challenging for ELL students (S. Baker, Gersten, Haager, & Dingle, 2006). Context clues together with specific strategies that differentiate closely related words, such as Gary did with *cave* and *hole*, are particularly important. He further applied both the third and fourth guidelines by labeling objects around the room in both English and students' native languages, he spoke slowly and clearly in rephrasing students' responses, and he had the students repeat terms in unison (Peregoy & Boyle, 2005).

Finally, Gary had all of his students practice language. Language is a skill, and students learn English by using it in their day-to-day lives. Open-ended questions, such as "Tell us something you remember about the story. . . . Carmela?" that allow students to respond without the pressure of giving specific answers are particularly effective (Echevarria & Graves, 2007).

As you saw in Gary's efforts, working with students whose first language is not English is challenging. However, these students respond very positively to displays of caring and genuine attempts to help them adapt to both school and mainstream American culture. Their responses will be among the most rewarding you will receive as a teacher.

check your understanding

2.1 Explain why so much linguistic diversity exists in the United States, and describe ways that teachers can accommodate this diversity.

2.2 What are English dialects? Explain why understanding them is important for teachers.

2.3 Describe the major approaches to helping ELL students. Explain how they are similar and different.

To receive feedback for these questions, go to Appendix A.

MyEducationLab

To examine another teacher's attempts to make her instruction effective for culturally and linguistically diverse students, go to the *Activities and Applications* section in Chapter 4 of MyEducationLab at www.myeducationlab.com, and watch the episode *The Effective Teacher.* Answer the questions following the episode.

Gender

What Marti Banes saw on the first day of her advanced-placement chemistry class was somewhat disturbing. Of her 26 students, only 5 were girls, and they sat quietly, responding only when she asked them direct questions. Sharing her interest in science was one reason she had chosen teaching as a career, but this situation gave her little opportunity to do so.

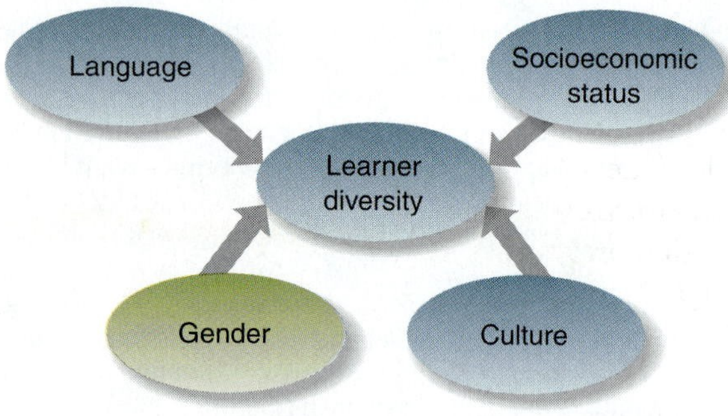

Figure 4.5 Sources of learner diversity: Gender

Why did you choose your current major? Did your gender play a role in the decision? If you are like students in other areas, there is a good chance it did. For example, research indicates that over 85 percent of all elementary teachers are female, as are more than 6 of 10 middle and secondary teachers (National Education Association, 2007).

Gender can also influence learning. The fact that some of our students are boys and others are girls is so obvious that we may not even think about it. When we're reminded, we notice that they often act and think differently. Many differences are natural and positive, but problems can occur if societal or school influences limit the academic performance of either girls or boys. Let's look at some of these differences (Figure 4.5).

Boys and girls *are* different. Girls tend to be more extroverted and anxious, and they're more trusting, less assertive, and have slightly lower self-esteem than boys of the same age and background (Halpern, 2006; Wigfield, Byrnes, & Eccles, 2006). Girls develop faster, acquire verbal and motor skills at an earlier age, and prefer activities with a social component. Boys are more oriented toward roughhouse play and playing with blocks, cars, or video games—activities that are physical and visual. Both prefer to play with members of the same sex. These tendencies, together with societal expectations, create **gender-role identities,** beliefs about appropriate characteristics and behaviors of the two sexes.

Gender-role identity. Beliefs about appropriate characteristics and behaviors of the two sexes.

Why do these gender-based differences exist? Most experts believe they result from an interaction between genetics and the environment (S. M. Jones & Dindia, 2004; Lippa, 2002). Genes control physical differences such as size and growth rate and probably differences in temperament, aggressiveness, and early verbal and exploratory behaviors. Girls and boys are also treated differently by parents, peers, and teachers, and this treatment influences how they view gender roles (Bleeker & Jacobs, 2004; Lippa, 2002; Rogoff, 2003).

Schools and curriculum also subtly influence gender-role identity (Garrahy, 2001; Lopez, 2003). For example, male characters in stories are typically presented as strong and adventurous, but seldom warm and sensitive (L. Evans & Davies, 2000). Video games and computer software programs are heavily oriented toward boys, with male heroes as the main characters (Meece, 2002). These messages influence the ways boys and girls view themselves.

How should teachers respond? Suggestions are controversial, with some people believing that most differences between boys and girls are natural and little intervention is necessary, whereas others argue that every attempt should be made to minimize gender differences.

School-Related Gender Differences

Gender differences are real and result in achievement differences between girls and boys. Some include the following:

- In the early grades, girls score as high or higher than boys on almost every standardized measure of achievement and psychological well-being. By the time they graduate from high school or college, they have fallen behind boys in some areas.
- Girls score lower on the Scholastic Aptitude Test (SAT) and American College Test (ACT), both of which are important for college admission. The greatest gaps are in science and math.
- Women score lower on all sections of the Graduate Record Exam, the Medical College Admissions Test, and admissions tests for law, dental, and optometry schools.
- Women still lag far behind men in traditionally male college majors, such as mathematics, physics, engineering, and computer science (Alperstein, 2005; Perkins-Gough, 2006).

On the other hand:

- Boys outnumber girls in remedial English and math classes, are held back in grade more often, and are more than twice as likely to be classified as special-needs students.
- Boys receive the majority of failing grades, drop out of school four times more often than girls, and are cited for disciplinary infractions as much as 10 times more often than girls.
- Boys score lower than girls on both direct and indirect measures of reading and writing ability, and with the addition of the writing component on the SAT, girls' and boys' performance has become essentially even.
- The proportion of both bachelor's and master's degrees earned favors women by a ratio of 53 to 47 (Gurian & Stevens, 2005; National Assessment of Educational Progress, 2001).

To put gender differences in perspective, we should note that the overlap between boys' and girls' performance is much greater than any differences; in any group of boys and girls, we are likely to see both struggling and excelling. On tests of general intelligence, gender differences are neglible, which is to be expected, because these tests are designed to be gender neutral. Boys' performance, however, exhibits greater variability on achievement tests, with more boys at the upper and lower ends of the spectrum (Halpern, 2006). In addition, boys perform better on visual-spatial tasks, a difference perhaps attributable to the kinds of toys they play with, participation in sports, or greater exposure to computers and computer games.

Some researchers explain these differences by suggesting that boys' and girls' brains are wired differently for learning (Gurian & Stevens, 2005; Lippa, 2002). Components of the brain that build word centers and fine-motor skills are a year ahead in girls, which gives them an advantage in reading, use of pencils, cursive writing, and other small-motor tasks. Centers in the brain that control emotions are also advanced for girls, making them calmer and more able to sit still for the long periods that school often requires (G. Gay, 2006). Some argue that school systems as a whole are more compatible with girls' genetic characteristics.

Gender Differences in Classroom Behavior

Given these differences, it is not surprising that boys and girls behave differently in classrooms. Boys participate in learning activities to a greater extent than girls, and they are more likely to ask questions and make comments (Brophy, 2004). Teachers also call on them more often (S. M. Jones & Dindia, 2004), probably because boys are more verbally assertive (Altermatt, Jovanovic, & Perry, 1998).

Gender-related differences are particularly pronounced in science and math (L. O'Brien & Crandall, 2003). Boys are more likely to lead in setting up science experiments, relegating girls to passive roles such as recording data (Sanders & Nelson, 2004). These experiences are important because they influence girls' perceptions of their ability to participate effectively in science. Differences become greater as students move through school, with a significant decrease in girls' participation in science and math activities during the middle school years. In addition, girls are more likely to attribute success in science to luck and failure to lack of ability. In general, girls are less confident about their abilities, even when aptitude and achievement are comparable (L. Hoffman, 2002; Nosek, Banaji, & Greenwald, 2002; Wigfield et al., 2006).

Although the areas of concern differ for boys and girls, evidence suggests that schools aren't effectively serving the needs of either boys or girls.

Involving girls in designing and conducting experiments helps combat stereotypes about the sciences being male domains.

Gender Stereotypes and Perceptions

Society and parents communicate, both directly and unconsciously, different expectations for their sons and daughters (Tenenbaum & Leaper, 2003). For example, researchers found that mothers' gender-stereotyped attitudes toward math and science adversely influenced their adolescent daughters entering these fields after high school (Bleeker & Jacobs, 2004). One woman recalled:

> It was OK, even feminine, not to be good in math. It was even cute. And so I locked myself out of a very important part of what it is

theory to practice

Responding to Gender Differences in Your Classroom

You can do a great deal to eliminate gender bias in your classroom (Ginsberg, Shapiro, & Brown, 2004). The following guidelines can assist you in your efforts:

1. Communicate openly with students about gender issues and concerns.
2. Eliminate gender bias in instructional activities.
3. Present students with nonstereotypical role models.

Let's return to Marti's work with her students to see how she attempts to apply these guidelines.

Marti decides to take positive steps to deal with the gender issue in her chemistry class. First, she initiates a discussion. "I almost didn't major in chemistry," she begins. "Some of my girlfriends scoffed, and others were nearly appalled. 'You'll be in there with a bunch of geeks,' some of them said. 'Girls don't major in chemistry,' others added. They all thought science and math were only for guys."

"It is mostly for guys," Amy shrugs. "Look at us."

"It isn't our fault," Shane responds. "Guys didn't try to keep you out of the class."

After several other students make comments, Marti continues. "I'm not blaming either you guys, or the girls. . . . It's a problem for all of us, and I'm not saying that just because I'm a woman. I'd be just as concerned if I were a man, because we're losing a lot of talented people who could be majoring in science."

As the discussion continues, she discusses historical reasons for gender stereotypes and encourages both the boys and the girls to keep their career options open. "There's no rule that says that girls can't be engineers or boys can't be nurses," she emphasizes. "In fact, there's a shortage of both."

She has similar discussions in her other classes. During learning activities, she makes a special effort to be sure that girls and boys participate as equally as possible, and she tells her students why she is doing so. For Career Week, Marti invites a female chemistry professor from a nearby university to come into her classes to talk about career opportunities for women in chemistry, and she invites a male nurse from one of the local hospitals to talk about the role of science in his job and his experiences in a female-dominated profession.

Marti also talks with other science teachers and counselors about gender stereotyping, and they work on a plan to encourage both boys and girls to consider career options in nonstereotypical fields.

Let's look now at Marti's attempts to apply the guidelines in her work. She implemented the first by openly discussing the issue of gender, and got responses from both boys and girls. The discussions increased their awareness of stereotyping subjects and career choices, and the discussions with her colleagues helped increase their sensitivity to gender issues in the school.

Second, Marti made a special effort to ensure equal treatment of boys and girls, and again she openly communicated why she was making the effort. She called on girls and boys equally, and she monitored lab activities to ensure that girls didn't slide into passive roles. She expected the same academic behaviors from both girls and boys.

Notice the term *academic behaviors*. No one suggests that boys and girls are the same in every way, and they shouldn't be expected to behave in the same ways. Academically, however, boys and girls should be given the same opportunities and encouragement, just as students from different cultures and socioeconomic backgrounds should be. In this way, Marti applied the second guideline, to eliminate gender bias in instructional activities.

Marti applied the third guideline by inviting a female chemistry professor and a male nurse into her classes to discuss careers in those fields. Seeing that both men and women can succeed and be happy in nonstereotypical fields can broaden the career horizons for both girls and boys (Sanders & Nelson, 2004).

> to be a human being, and that is to know all of oneself. I just locked that part out because I didn't think that was an appropriate thing for me to do. . . . [But] it was not OK for the men to not do well in math. It was not OK for them to not take calculus. It was not manly. (Weissglass, 1998, p. 160)

The perception that certain areas, such as math, science, and computer science, are male domains has a powerful effect on career choices (J. D. Lee, 2002). As you saw earlier, girls are much less likely than boys to major in math, physics, engineering, and computer science in college (Alperstein, 2005; American Association of University Women, 1998). The problem of gender-stereotypic views of math and science-related careers seems to be especially acute for low-SES and minority females (Bleeker & Jacobs, 2004). One study found that only 2 percent of new math faculty at U.S. colleges and universities were minority women (Herzig, 2004).

On the other hand, the fact that America's teaching force is primarily composed of white, middle-class women is also troublesome (National Education Association, 2007). Boys, and particularly members of cultural minorities, need male role models as they move through the school years, and these role models are presently lacking.

What does this information suggest to you as a teacher? We attempt to answer this question in the Theory to Practice section above.

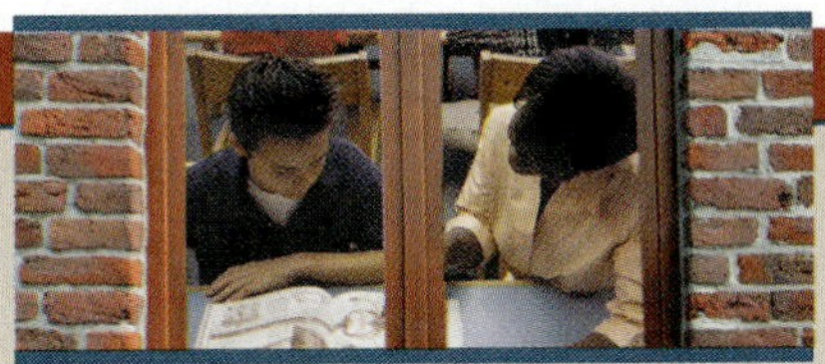

classroom connections

Eliminating Gender Bias in Your Classroom

1. Gender bias often results from a lack of awareness by both teachers and students. Actively attack gender bias in your teaching.
   - **Elementary:** A first-grade teacher consciously deemphasizes sex roles and differences in his classroom. He has boys and girls share equally in chores, and he eliminates gender-related activities, such as competitions between boys and girls and forming lines by gender.
   - **Middle School:** A middle school language arts teacher selects stories and clippings from newspapers and magazines that portray men and women in nontraditional roles. She matter-of-factly talks about nontraditional careers during class discussions about becoming an adult.
   - **High School:** At the beginning of the school year, a social studies teacher explains how gender bias hurts both sexes, and he forbids sexist comments in his classes. He calls on boys and girls equally, and emphasizes equal participation in discussions.

check your understanding

3.1. Explain how gender can influence learning, and describe steps for eliminating gender bias in classrooms.

3.2. What is gender-role identity, and why is understanding it important for teachers?

3.3. You're working with your students in a learning activity. What important factor that can help reduce gender bias should you attempt to apply as you conduct these activities? Hint: Think about the way Marti interacted with her students.

To receive feedback for these questions, go to Appendix A.

Socioeconomic Status

Were finances ever an important concern in your family? Did your parents go to college? What kinds of jobs do they have? These questions relate to your **socioeconomic status (SES)**, the combination of parents' income, level of education, and the kinds of jobs they have. It describes people's relative standing in society and is one of the most important factors that exists in influencing student achievement (see Figure 4.6).

Socioeconomic status (SES). The combination of parents' income, occupation, and level of education that describes the relative standing in society of a family or individual.

Sociologists divide families into four classes: upper, middle, working, and lower. Table 4.2 outlines some of the characteristics of these classes.

Socioeconomic status consistently predicts intelligence and achievement test scores, grades, truancy, and dropout and suspension rates (J. P. Byrnes, 2003; Macionis, 2006). It exerts its most powerful influence at the lower income levels. For example, low-SES fourth-graders are more than twice as likely as their higher-SES peers to fall below basic levels of reading, and dropout rates for students from the poorest families exceed 50 percent (Allington & McGill-Franzen, 2003). Students from families in the highest income quartile are eight times more likely to graduate from college than are their low-SES peers (B. Young & Smith, 1999).

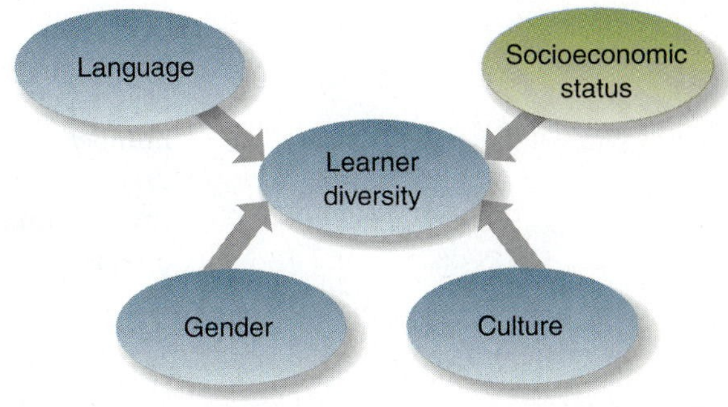

Figure 4.6 Sources of learner diversity: Socioeconomic status

Some disconcerting statistics exist in our country with respect to SES. The rate of childhood poverty in 2006 was more than 17 percent, and the percentage of U.S. families below the poverty level—defined in 2002 as an income of $20,614 for a family of four—is five times greater than in other industrialized countries. Minorities and single-parent families are overrepresented (Biddle,

table 4.2 Characteristics of Different Socioeconomic Levels

	Upper Class	Middle Class	Working Class	Lower Class
Income	$160.000+	$80,000–$160,000 (½) $40,000–80,000 (½)	$25,000–$40,000	Below $25,000
Occupation	Corporate or professional (e.g., doctor, lawyer)	White collar, skilled blue collar	Blue collar	Minimum wage unskilled labor
Education	Attended college and professional schools and expect children to do the same	Attended high school and college or professional schools.	Attended high school; may or may not encourage college	Attended high school or less; cost is a major factor in education
Housing	Own home in prestigious neighborhood	Usually own home	About half own a home	Rent

Source: Macionis, 2006; U. S. Bureau of Census, 2007.

2001; Education Vital Signs, 2005; U.S. Bureau of Census, 2007). Biddle (2001) describes the impact of poverty on this segment of our school population. These children

> are likely to be experiencing poverty-associated problems such as substandard housing, an inadequate diet, threadbare or hand-me-down clothes, lack of health insurance, chronic dental or health problems, deprivation and violence in their communities, little or no funds for school supplies, and whose overburdened parents subsist on welfare or work long hours at miserably paid jobs. These facts pose enormous problems for America's schools. (Biddle, 2001, p. 5)

The important effect that poverty can have on learning is reflected in integration-by-income programs implemented by a number of school districts in our country (Kahlenberg, 2006). These programs use a variety of ways to integrate students from different SES levels, including magnet schools, vouchers, and even busing. All are based on the belief that high concentrations of students from impoverished backgrounds detract from a school's ability to successfully meet students' learning needs. Initial results of these programs are promising; in North Carolina, for example, nearly two thirds of integrated-by-income students passed state-mandated, end-of-course exams compared to less than half in comparable surrounding areas (Kahlenberg, 2006).

How SES Influences Learning

SES influences learning in at least three ways:

- Basic needs and experiences
- Parental involvement
- Attitudes and values

Basic Needs and Experiences

Many low-SES children lack medical and dental care and live on inadequate diets in substandard housing (Rothstein, 2004a, 2004b). In 2006, over 35 million people in America went hungry, and cultural minorities and single-parent families make up a disproportionate share of this number (U.S. Department of Agriculture, 2007). Of the 35 million, over 12 million were children, and the figure did not include homeless families, because these families are hard to identify and count. Research also indicates that poor nutrition can affect attention and memory and even lead to lower intelligence test scores (Berk, 2008).

The school nurse in high-poverty schools often serves as a substitute for the family doctor, because many families in poverty don't have insurance and can't afford to seek medical care (F. Smith, 2005). One school nurse reported,

> Mondays we are hit hard. It's not like in the suburbs, where families call the pediatrician. When our kids get sick on the weekends, they go to the emergency room, or they wait. Monday morning, they are lined up, and they have to see the nurse. (F. Smith, 2005, p. 49)

It's hard to learn when you're sick.

Economic problems can also lead to family and marital conflicts, which result in less-stable and less-nurturant homes (Rainwater & Smeedings, 2003). Children of poverty often come to school without the sense of security that equips them to tackle school-related tasks. Research indicates that students from poor families have a greater incidence of depression and other emotional problems than do their more advantaged peers (G. W. Evans & English, 2002).

Children of poverty also relocate frequently; in some low-income schools, mobility rates exceed 100 percent (Rothstein, 2004a). Researchers have found that nearly a third of the poorest students attend at least three different schools by third grade compared to only 1 in 10 for middle-class students. These frequent moves are stressful for students and a challenge for teachers attempting to develop caring relationships with them (P. Barton, 2004).

The problem is particularly acute for the homeless. Experts estimate that between one-half to one million children make up 40 percent of the homeless population (National Law Center on Homelessness and Poverty, 2006). At least one fifth of homeless children fail to attend school regularly (U.S. Department of Education, 2005), and they are three times more likely to repeat a grade and four times more likely to drop out of school (Macionis & Parillo, 2007).

SES also influences the background knowledge that children bring to school (Orr, 2003; Wenner, 2003). High-SES parents are more likely to provide their children with educational activities, such as travel and visits to art galleries and science museums. They also have more computers, reference books, and other learning materials in the home, and they provide more formal training outside of school, such as music and dance lessons. These activities complement classroom learning (Lareau, 2003; V. E. Lee & Burkam, 2002).

Parental Involvement

Higher-SES parents tend to be more involved in their children's schooling and other activities (K. Brown et al., 2004; Diamond & Gomez, 2004). One mother commented, "When she sees me at her games, when she sees me going to open house, when I attend her Interscholastic League contests, she knows I am interested in her activities. Plus, we have more to talk about" (M. Young & Scribner, 1997, p. 12). Time spent working, often at two jobs or more, is a major obstacle to school involvement for low-SES parents (H. Weiss et al., 2003).

In general, high-SES parents talk to their children more and differently than do those who are low SES. They ask more questions, explain the causes of events, and provide reasons for rules. Their language is more elaborate, their directions are clearer, and they are more likely to encourage problem solving (Berk, 2008; Tomasello, 2006). Children expect the same in school and are more likely to pay attention and follow directions (Stright, Neitzel, Sears, & Hoke-Sinex, 2001). Sometimes called "the curriculum of the home," these rich interaction patterns, together with the background experiences already described, provide a strong foundation for future learning (Holloway, 2004; Lareau, 2003).

Attitudes and Values

The impact of SES is also transmitted through parental attitudes and values. For example, many high-SES parents encourage autonomy, individual responsibility, and self-control; low-SES parents are more likely to emphasis conformity and obedience (Greenfield et al., 2006; Macionis, 2006).

Values are also communicated by example. For instance, children who see their parents reading and studying learn that reading is valuable and are more likely to read themselves. And, as we would expect, students who read at home show higher reading achievement than those who don't (Weigel et al., 2005).

High-SES parents also have higher expectations for their children and encourage them to graduate from high school and attend college (K. Brown et al., 2004). They also know how to play the "schooling game," steering their sons and daughters into advanced high school courses and contacting schools for information about their children's learning progress (Lareau, 2003). Low-SES parents, in contrast, tend to have lower aspirations for their children, allow them to "drift" into classes, and rely on the decisions of others. Students often get lost in the shuffle, ending up in inappropriate or less challenging classes.

SES: Some Cautions and Implications for Teachers

As with culture, language, and gender, it's important to first remember that the research findings we report here describe group differences, and individuals within the groups will vary widely. For example, many low-SES parents read and talk to their children, encourage their involvement in extracurricular activities, and attend school events. Both of your authors come from low-SES families, and we were given all the enriching experiences we've discussed in reference to high-SES parents. Conversely, belonging to a high-SES family does not guarantee a child enriching experiences and caring, involved parents.

Second, although we know that certain home conditions make it more difficult for students to succeed in school (Rothstein, 2004a), we also know that schools and teachers can do much to overcome these problems (P. Barton, 2004; Darling-Hammond & Bransford, 2005). Schools that are safe, nurturing, and demanding, and teachers with high expectations who use effective instruction *can* make a significant difference in all students' lives.

Students Placed at Risk

Laurie Ramirez looks over the papers she has been grading and shakes her head. "Fourth grade, and some of these kids don't know what zero means or how place value affects a number. Some can't add, others can't subtract, and most don't understand multiplication. How am I supposed to teach problem solving when they don't understand basic math facts?"

"Reading isn't much better," she thinks. "I have a few who can actually read at a fourth-grade level, but others are still sounding out words like *dog* and *cat*. How can I teach them comprehension skills when they are struggling with ideas this basic?

Students placed at risk. Learners in danger of failing to complete their education with the skills necessary to succeed in today's society.

Failing students can be found in any school. Many reasons exist, but some students share characteristics that decrease their chances for success. **Students placed at risk** are learners in danger of failing to complete their education with the skills necessary to succeed in today's society. Educators used to call these students *underachievers*, but the term *at-risk* more clearly reflects the long-term consequences of school failure. Many jobs requiring few specialized skills no longer exist, and others are becoming rare in a world driven by technology. Research consistently indicates that high school dropouts earn less than their more educated peers and also have an increased incidence of crime, alcoholism, and drug abuse (Hardre & Reeve, 2003; Macionis, 2006).

Characteristics of students placed at risk include the following:

- *Poverty and Low SES.* As we saw earlier, poverty creates a number of stress factors that detract from learning (P. Barton, 2004; Biddle, 2001; V. E. Lee & Burkam, 2002, 2003).
- *Member of a Cultural Minority.* Being a member of a cultural minority can pose problems when schools are not responsive to cultural differences (Borman & Overman, 2004; Noguera, 2003a, 2003b).
- *Non-native English Speaker.* Learning is demanding for all students; struggling with both language and content can be overwhelming (Bielenberg & Fillmore, 2005; Zwiers, 2005).

These characteristics can result in a history of low achievement, which makes new learning even more challenging because students lack the knowledge and skills on which this learning depends (Barr & Parrett, 2001). A history of low achievement is often compounded by motivation and self-esteem problems (Dubois, 2001), disengagement from schools (R. Brown & Evans, 2002), and misbehavior (Barr & Parrett, 2001). The problem is often exacerbated by the fact that students who need quality education the most are often provided with substandard buildings and equipment as well as underqualified teachers (Crosnoe, 2005; Perkins-Gough, 2004; Thirunarayanan, 2004).

How do teachers react to these problems? Some are clearly overwhelmed:

> I just don't know what I'm going to do. Every year, my first grade class has more and more of these kids. They don't seem to care about right or wrong, they don't care about adult approval, they are disruptive, they can't read and they arrive at school absolutely unprepared to learn. Who are these kids? Where do they come from? Why are there

> more and more of them? I used to think that I was a good teacher. I really prided myself on doing an outstanding job. But I find I'm working harder and harder, and being less and less effective. (Barr & Parrett, 2001, p. 1)
>
> *Elementary Teacher, Atlanta, Georgia*

Other teachers respond differently,

> While visiting a small elementary school, I was walking down the halls with two teachers on our way to lunch. While passing an open classroom door, one of my friends stopped and called out to a fellow teacher, "Come and join us for lunch." The teacher left a small group of students sitting around her desk and walked over to the door and replied, "I really can't. I've got a group of kids here who are having real problems with their reading, and I've been working with them over part of their lunch period all year. . . . Before they leave my classroom I'm going to teach them to read. I can't do much about their home lives, but I can definitely teach them to read." (Barr & Parrett, 2001, p. 9)
>
> *Teacher, Sunrise Elementary School, Albany, Oregon*

Our goal in this section is to help you understand the nature of the problems for students placed at risk and how you can help students respond to the conditions they encounter.

Resilience

Research on students placed at risk is now focusing on the concept of **resilience**, a learner characteristic that, despite adversity, raises the likelihood of success in school and later life (Borman & Overman, 2004; Downey, 2003; Knapp, 2001). This research has studied young people who have survived and even prospered despite obstacles such as poverty, poor health care, and fragmented support services. Resilient children have well-developed self-systems, including high self-esteem, optimism, and feelings that they are in control of their destinies. They set personal goals, expect to succeed, and believe they are responsible for their success (Downey, 2003). They are motivated to learn and satisfied with school (Borman & Overman, 2004).

Resilience. A learner characteristic that, despite adversity, raises the likelihood of success in school and later life.

How do these skills develop? Resilient children come from nurturant environments, and one characteristic is striking. In virtually all cases, these children have one or more adults who have taken a special interest in them and hold them to high moral and academic standards, essentially refusing to let the young person fail (Reis, Colbert, & Hébert, 2005). These adults are often parents, but they could also be older siblings or other adults such as teachers who take a young person under their wing (E. Flores, Cicchetti, & Rogosch, 2005).

Schools also make important contributions to resilience. Next, we'll examine schools' impact on resilience.

Schools That Promote Resilience

Research has identified four school practices that promote resilience:

- *High and uncompromising academic standards.* Teachers emphasize mastery of content and do not accept passive attendance and mere completion of assignments (Jesse & Pokorny, 2001).
- *Strong personal bonds between teachers and students.* Teachers become the adults who refuse to let students fail, and students feel connected to the schools (Parish, Parish, & Batt, 2001).
- *High structure.* The school and classes are orderly and highly structured. Teachers emphasize reasons for rules and consistently enforce rules and procedures (Ilg & Massucci, 2003; Pressley, Raphael, & Gallagher, 2004).
- *Participation in after-school activities.* Activities such as clubs and athletics give students additional chances to bond with school and interact with caring adults (Wigfield et al., 2006).

Caring teachers promote resilience by forming personal relationships with students and supporting their academic work.

theory to practice

Teaching Students Placed at Risk in Your Classroom

In addition to the human element, what else can you do to ensure that students placed at risk will succeed? Research suggests that the same strategies that work for all students work for at-risk students (Borman & Overman, 2004; Brophy, 2004). You don't need to teach in fundamentally different ways; you need to do what works with all students, but you need to do it better. The following guidelines can assist you in your efforts:

1. Create and maintain a classroom environment with predictable routines.
2. Combine high expectations with frequent feedback about learning progress.
3. Use teaching strategies that involve all students and promote high levels of success.
4. Use high-quality examples that provide the background knowledge students need to learn new content.
5. Stress self-regulation and the acquisition of learning strategies.

Let's see how the principles guide Diane Smith, a fourth-grade teacher, as she works with her students.

Diane's students are studying adjectives in language arts, and she now wants them to be able to write using comparative and superlative forms of adjectives.

Students file into the room from their lunch break, go to their desks, and begin working on a set of exercises that has them identify all the adjectives and the nouns they modify in a paragraph displayed on the overhead. As they work, Diane identifies students who have pencils of different lengths and those whose hair color varies.

Diane reviews the passage, has students explain their choices, and provides feedback. When they finish, she directs, "Okay, very good, everyone. Look up here."

"Calesha and Daniel, hold your pencils up so everyone can see. What do you notice?. . . Naitia?"

Diane has the students make observations, among them the fact that Calesha's is longer.

Diane then goes to the board and writes:

Calesha has a long pencil.
Calesha has a longer pencil than Daniel does.

"Now, let's look at Matt and Leroy," she continues. "What do you notice about their hair?. . . Judy?"

Again the students make observations, and after hearing several, Diane asks, "Who's is darker?"

"LEROY!" several in the class blurt out.

"Good!" Diane again goes to the board and writes three more sentences so the list now appears as follows:

Calesha has a long pencil. *Calesha has a longer pencil than Daniel does.*	*Leroy has black hair.* *Matt has brown hair.* *Leroy has darker hair than Matt does.*

"Now, how do the adjectives in the sentences compare?. . . Heather?" Diane asks, pointing to the bottom sentences on each list.

". . . The ones at the bottom have an *er* on the end of them," Heather responds hesitantly.

"Yes, good. . . . And, what are we doing in each of the sentences?. . . Jason?"

Effective schools are both demanding and supportive; in many instances, they serve as homes away from home. The emphasis placed on school-sponsored activities reduces alienation and increases academic engagement and achievement (B. Davidson, et al., 2001; Jordan, 2001). School-sponsored activities also give teachers the chance to know students in contexts outside the classroom.

Teachers Who Promote Resilience

Schools are no more effective than the teachers who work in them. Becoming the adults who refuse to let students fail often means spending extra time before or after school, both helping students with their academic work or simply talking to them about issues important in their lives. Spending out-of-class time with students is demanding, but this kind of commitment is at the core of promoting resilience.

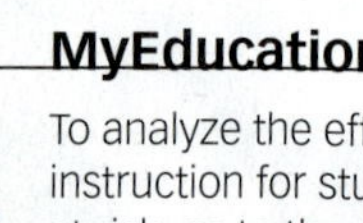

MyEducationLab

To analyze the effectiveness of instruction for students placed at risk, go to the *Activities and Applications* section in Chapter 4 of MyEducationLab at www.myeducationlab.com, and read the case study *Analyzing Instruction for Students Placed at Risk.* Answer the questions following the case study.

What else do we know about teachers who promote resilience? Research indicates that they interact frequently with students, learn about their families, and share their own lives (Doll, Zucker, & Brehm, 2004). They maintain high expectations, use interactive teaching strategies, and emphasize success and mastery of content (McCombs & Miller, 2007). They motivate students through personal contacts, instructional support, and attempts to link school to students' experiences (B. L. Wilson & Corbett, 2001).

Let's see what students say about these teachers. One middle school student commented,

"Sometimes a teacher don't understand what people go through. They need to have compassion. A teacher who can relate to students will know when something's going on

"We're comparing two things."

"Good thinking, Jason," Diane smiles.

She then repeats the process with the superlative form of adjectives by having students compare three pencils and three different hair colors, leading them to conclude that superlative adjectives have an *est* at the end.

"Very good, everyone. In describing nouns, if we're comparing two, we use the comparative form of the adjective, which has an *-er* on the end, and if we have three or more, we have an *-est* on the end of the adjective.

"Now," Diane says, pointing to a softball, tennis ball, and golf ball on her desk, "I have a little challenge for you. . . . Write two sentences each that use the comparative and superlative forms of adjectives, and tell about the sizes of these balls."

As the students work, Diane checks on their progress, and when they're finished, says, "Now let's look at your sentences. . . . Someone volunteer, and I'll write it on the chalkboard. . . . Okay, Rashad?"

"The tennis ball is bigger than the golf ball."

"Very good, Rashad. And why did you write *bigger* in your sentence?"

"We're comparing the size of two balls."

They continue discussing the comparative and superlative forms of adjectives and Diane then directs, "Now, I want you to write a paragraph with at least two sentences that use the comparative form of adjectives and at least two others that use the superlative form. Underline the adjectives in each case."

"And what do we always do after we write something?"

"We read it to be sure it makes sense!" several of the students say simultaneously.

"Very good," Diane smiles. "That's how we become good writers."

The students go to work, and Diane circulates among them, periodically stopping for a few seconds to comment on a student's work and to offer brief suggestions.

Now, let's look at Diane's attempts to apply the guidelines. She applied the first by creating a set of well-established routines. For example, when students came in from their break, they went to work on exercises on the overhead without being told to do so. Predictable routines maximize time available for learning and provide the structure that makes classrooms safe and comfortable.

Second, by calling on individuals and requiring that they explain their answers, Diane communicated that she expected all students to participate and learn. Maintaining high expectations is a simple idea but hard to put into practice (Haycock, 2001). Most students initially have trouble putting their understanding into words, and it is even more challenging for students placed at risk. Many teachers give up, concluding, "They can't, do it." They can't, because they haven't had enough practice and support. It isn't easy, but teachers can teach students placed at risk to increase their use of language.

Also, Diane provided detailed feedback for the beginning-of-class exercises and the sentences at the end of the lesson. This scaffolding promotes success, minimizes mistakes, and increases motivation (Brophy, 2004). These actions applied the second guideline.

Diane applied the third guideline with questioning that involved all students in the lesson. Open-ended questions such as "What do you notice?" and "How do the adjectives in the sentences compare?" virtually assured student success, an essential factor for both learning and motivation (Brophy, 2004). Interactive teaching methods are effective for all students and essential for students placed at risk (Barr & Parrett, 2001; B. L. Wilson & Corbett, 2001).

Diane applied the fourth guideline by developing her lesson around real-world examples. Teachers who promote resilience attempt to link school to students' lives, and using students' pencils and hair color to illustrate comparative and superlative adjectives was a simple application of this idea.

Finally, Diane emphasized self-regulation, and applied the fifth guideline, when she asked, "And what do we always do after we write something?" The fact that the students so quickly replied, "We read it to be sure it makes sense!" suggests that she emphasized student responsibility for their own learning.

The challenge for teachers who work with students placed at risk is how to help them succed while still presenting challenging activities. It isn't easy. However, seeing these students meet the challenges will be some of the most rewarding experiences you will have.

> with them. If like the student don't do work or don't understand, the teacher will spend a lot of time with them." (B. L. Wilson & Corbett, 2001, p. 5)

Effective teachers go the extra mile to ensure student success.

Teachers less effective in promoting resilience are more authoritarian and less accessible. They distance themselves from students and place primary responsibility for learning on them. They view instructional support as "babying students" or "holding students' hands." Lecture is a common teaching strategy, and motivation is the students' responsibility. Students perceive these teachers as adversaries, to be avoided if possible, tolerated if not. They also resent the teachers' lack of commitment:

> There's this teacher [over at the regular school] . . . you can put anything down and he'll give you a check mark for it. He doesn't check it. He just gives you a mark and says, 'OK, you did your work.' How you gonna learn from that? You ain't gonna learn nothing. (Dynarski & Gleason, 1999, p. 13)
>
> *Student, JFY Academy, Boston, Massachusetts*

As with culturally responsive teaching, much of promoting resilience lies in teachers' attitudes and commitment to students. Effective teachers care about students as people and accept nothing less than consistent effort and quality work (Gschwend & Dembo, 2001). Caring teachers are important for all students; for students placed at risk, they're essential.

MyEducationLab

To see how another teacher attempts to promote resiliency in her students go to the *Building Teaching Skills and Dispositions* section in Chapter 4 of MyEducationLab at www.myeducationlab.com, and read the case study *Building Resiliency in Students.* Complete the exercises following the case study to develop your skills in promoting resiliency in your students.

check your understanding

4.1. Define socioeconomic status (SES), and explain how it can affect learning.

4.2. As you work with your students, what important factor should you keep in mind when considering SES?

4.3. Describe characteristics of schools and teachers that promote resilience in students placed at risk.

To receive feedback for these questions, go to Appendix A.

classroom connections

Using Effective Teaching Practices for Students Placed at Risk in Your Classroom

1. Positive teacher expectations influence both motivation and achievement. Communicate positive expectations to both students and their parents.
   - **Elementary:** A fourth-grade teacher spends the first 2 weeks of school teaching students her classroom procedures and explaining how they promote learning and create a learning community. She makes short assignments, carefully monitors students to be certain the assignments are turned in, and immediately calls parents if an assignment is missing.
   - **Middle School:** A math teacher carefully explains his course procedures. He emphasizes the importance of attendance and effort and communicates that he expects all to do well. He also makes himself available before and after school for help sessions.
   - **High School:** An English teacher sends home an upbeat letter at the beginning of the year describing her work requirements and grading practices. She has students help translate the letter for parents whose first language is not English and asks parents to sign the letter, indicating they have read it. She also invites questions and comments from parents or other caregivers.
2. Interactive teaching strategies are essential for students placed at risk. Use teaching strategies that elicit high levels of student involvement and success.
   - **Elementary:** A fifth-grade teacher mixes students from different ethnic groups in his classroom seating. He combines small-group and whole-class instruction, and when he uses group work, he arranges the groups so they include high and low achievers, members of different ethnic groups, and boys and girls.
   - **Middle School:** An earth science teacher gives students a short quiz of one or two questions every day. She discusses the quiz with the students at the beginning of the following day, and students calculate their averages each day during the grading period. The teacher closely monitors these scores and spends time before school to work with students who are falling behind.
   - **High School:** An English teacher builds her teaching around questioning and examples. She comments, "My goal is to call on each student in the class at least twice during each lesson. I also use a lot of repetition and reinforcement as we cover the examples."

developmentally appropriate practice

Diversity in Students at Different Ages

While many aspects of diversity are similar across grade levels, important developmental differences exist. The following paragraphs outline some suggestions for responding to these differences.

Working with Elementary Students

The elementary grades pose developmental challenges for students learning a second language, as they face the dual tasks of learning to read and write while simultaneously learning English. Although some research suggests that young language learners may be more adaptable than older ones, they still need special assistance to succeed (Echevarria & Graves, 2007). Instruction that maximizes opportunities for students to practice and use language is essential for these children. The strategies Gary Nolan used in the *Theory to Practice* section on page 106 are effective for learners at all ages but are particularly important for elementary students (O'Donnell, 2006; Tomasello, 2006; S. Waxman & Lidz, 2006). Writing assignments that encourage ELLs to use their developing language skills are also important (Graham, 2006).

As you saw earlier in the chapter, boys develop slower than girls, and girls have more developed language abilities (Halpern, 2006; Ruble, Martin, & Berenbaum, 2006). Some experts suggest that developmental lags explain why boys outnumber girls in the number of special education placements (Hardman et al., 2008; Heward, 2009). Simple strategies, such as giving children a chance to get up and move around, providing concrete examples, and using strategies proven effective with second language learners are also effective with slower-developing boys.

Working with Middle School Students

Developmental changes, such as going through puberty, and making the move from self-contained elementary classrooms to the less personal nature of middle schools, can be more problematic for students who come from diverse backgrounds (Chumlea et al., 2003).

Communicating that all students' backgrounds are respected and valued is even more important in diverse middle schools than it is in elementary schools. In addition, creating safe and predictable environments is essential. Well-established routines, consistent enforcement of rules, and emphasis on treating all students with courtesy and respect are essential. Establishing personal relationships with students, emphasizing that learning is the purpose of school, and de-emphasizing competition and differences among students are also important.

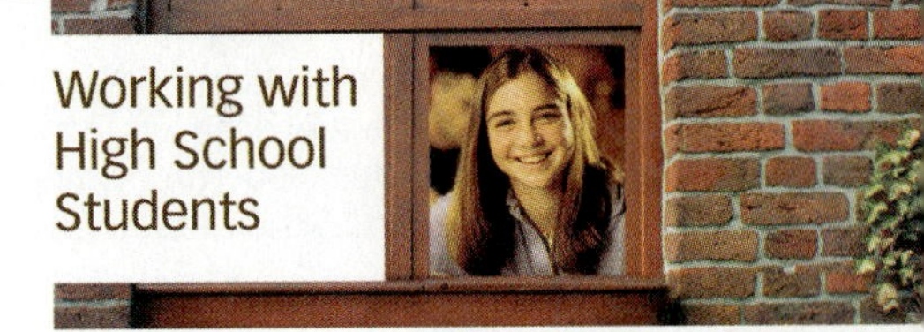

Working with High School Students

High school is not only the capstone of students' public school experience, it is also an increasingly important transition period for both college and careers (New Commission on the Skills of the American Workforce, 2007). Many students who come from low-SES backgrounds or are members of cultural minorities are unaware of the career and higher-education opportunities available to them. Connecting content to students' future lives is particularly important for these students. For example, science teachers can discuss career options in related fields, and social studies and English teachers can examine the impact of technology on our lives.

High school is also an important time for both girls and boys, who are trying to reconcile gender-role identities with societal expectations. For example, some high school girls are fearful that being intellectually assertive is not compatible with being feminine, whereas boys are struggling with decisions about whether to go to college or join the workforce. Openly discussing these topics with high school students can do a great deal to help them resolve the issues.

exploring diversity

Teaching and Learning in Urban Schools

Learner diversity and urban schools are in an interconnected relationship. For example, members of cultural minorities make up nearly 70 percent of the student population in urban schools, and in some they are more than 95 percent. Urban schools also have a disproportionate number of students who speak a first language other than English, as well as a disproportionate number of low-SES students; over half of urban students are eligible for free or reduced-price lunch (Macionis & Parillo, 2007).

Researchers often use the term *cultural minority* to refer to non-White cultural groups, but this term is a misnomer in many urban schools. In Adlai Stevenson high school in New York City, for example, nearly all the students are African American or Hispanic; only one-half of 1 percent are White (Kozol, 2005).

In addition, urban schools tend to be larger and less personal than their suburban counterparts. The nation's 100 largest school districts represent less than 1 percent of all districts in the nation, but they are responsible for the education of nearly one-fourth of all students.

Negative stereotypes about urban schools is another issue. Two of the most common are, "Students can't control themselves," and "Students don't know how to behave because the parents don't care" (R. A. Goldstein, 2004, p. 43). In response to these stereotypes, urban teachers often "teach defensively," "choosing methods of presentation and evaluation that simplify content and reduce demands on students in return for classroom order and minimal student compliance on assignments" (LePage et al., 2005, p. 331).

Urban schools don't have to be this way. Working with urban students can be challenging, but research provides some guidance and suggests that at least three factors are important:

- Caring and supportive teachers
- High structure
- Effective instruction

Caring and Supportive Teachers

We have emphasized the need for caring and supportive teachers throughout this chapter (and will continue to do so throughout the book). Teachers who care are important in all schools but are critical in urban environments. When students perceive their teachers as uncaring, disengagement from school often occurs, and disengaged students are much more likely to be disruptive than are their more-engaged peers (Charles & Senter, 2005; V. F. Jones & Jones, 2004).

High Structure

All people need order and structure in their lives, and students in urban schools sometimes come from environments that lack the stability that creates a sense of equilibrium. This makes order, structure, and predictability even more important in urban environments than in other kinds of classrooms. A predictable environment leads to an atmosphere of safety, which is crucial for developing the sense of attachment to school that is essential for learning and motivation. (We discuss ways of creating safe and orderly classrooms in Chapter 12.)

Effective Instruction

As you saw earlier, students in urban classrooms are often involved in low-level activities that detract from motivation and lead to feelings of disengagement from school.

> In my chemistry class, the teacher just keeps going and going and writing on the board. She never stops to ask the class, "Is everyone with me?" She's in her own little world. She never turns around, she just talks to the board, not to us. (Cushman, 2003, p. 8)

Exactly the opposite is needed. For example, in a comparison of more- and less-effective urban elementary teachers, researchers found that less-effective teachers interacted with students less than half of their instructional time compared to nearly three fourths of the time for their more effective counterparts (H. Waxman, Huang, Anderson, & Weinstein, 1997). Interactive teaching is characteristic of good instruction in general; with urban students, it is essential (Barr & Parrett, 2001; Rosenshine, 2006). (We discuss effective instruction in urban environments in Chapter 13.)

Meeting Your Learning Objectives

1. Describe culture and ethnicity, and explain how they can influence learning.
   - Culture refers to the attitudes, values, customs, and behavior patterns that characterize a social group. The match between a child's culture and the school has a powerful influence on school success.
   - *Ethnicity* refers to a person's ancestry and the way individuals identify with the nation from which their ancestors came.
   - Culture and ethnicity can influence learning through the cultural attitudes and values that students bring to schools. Some values support learning, whereas others can detract from it.
   - Culture and ethnicity can also influence learning through the interaction patterns characteristic of the cultural group. If the interaction patterns are similar to those found in school, they enhance learning. If they are dissimilar, they can detract from learning.
2. Explain why so much linguistic diversity exists in the United States, and describe ways that teachers can accommodate this diversity.
   - Federal legislation, which ended quotas based on national origin, resulted in more immigrants coming to the United States from a wider variety of places. This has resulted in much more cultural, ethnic, and linguistic diversity.

- Teachers can accommodate this diversity by first communicating that they value and respect all cultures, by involving all students in learning activities, and by representing topics as concretely as possible.
- Teachers also accommodate this diversity by providing students with opportunities to practice language and placing extra emphasis on important vocabulary.

3. Explain how gender can influence learning, and describe steps for eliminating gender bias in classrooms.
   - Gender can influence learning if either girls or boys adopt gender-stereotyped beliefs, such as believing that math or computer science is a male domain, or believing that girls are inherently better at English and writing than are boys.
   - Teachers can attempt to eliminate gender bias by openly discussing gender issues, expecting the same academic behaviors from both boys and girls, and inviting non-stereotypical role models to their classes to discuss gender issues.

4. Define socioeconomic status (SES), and explain how it can affect learning.
   - SES describes the relative standing in society resulting from a combination of family income, parents' occupations, and the level of education parents attain.
   - SES can affect learning through the extent to which students' basic needs are met. Children of poverty sometimes live in substandard housing, and often don't have access to medical care.
   - Low-SES children may also lack the school-related experiences they need to be successful, and lower-SES parents tend to be less involved in their children's education than are higher-SES parents.
   - SES can also influence learning through the attitudes and values of parents. Many high-SES parents encourage autonomy, individual responsibility, and self-control, whereas lower-SES parents tend to value obedience and conformity. High-SES parents also tend to have higher expectations for their children than do their lower-SES counterparts.

Developing as a Professional: Preparing for Your Licensure Exam

In this chapter, we've seen how culture, language diversity, gender, and SES can influence learning, and how certain combinations of these factors can place students at risk.

Let's look now at another teacher working with students having diverse backgrounds. Read the case study, and answer the questions that follow.

Teri Hall is an eighth-grade American history teacher in an inner-city middle school. Most of her students are from low-income families, many of them are from diverse cultures, and some speak English as a second language.

Today, her class is studying the colonization of North America. Teri takes roll as students enter the room, and she finishes entering the information into the computer on her desk just as the bell rings.

"What were we discussing yesterday?" Teri begins immediately after the bell stops ringing. "Ditan?"

". . . The beginning of the American colonies."

"Good. . . . Go up to the map, point out where we live, and show us the first British, French, and Spanish colonies. . . . Kaldya?"

Kaldya walks to the front of the room and points to four different locations on a large map of North America.

Teri reviews for a few more minutes and then displays the following on the overhead:

In the mid-1600s, the American colonists were encouraged to grow tobacco, because it wasn't grown in England. The colonists wanted to sell it to France and other countries, but were told no. In return for sending the tobacco to England, the colonists were allowed to buy textiles from England. They were forbidden, however, from making their own textiles. All the materials were carried on British ships.

Early French colonists in the New World were avid fur trappers and traders. They got in trouble with the French monarchy, however, when they attempted to make fur garments and sell them to Spain, England, and others. They were told that they had to buy the manufactured garments from dealers in Paris instead. The monarchy also told them that traps and weapons would be made in France and sent to them as well. One of the colonists, Jean Forjea, complied with the monarchy's wishes but was fined when he hired a Dutch ship to carry some of the furs back to Nice.

"Now let's take a look," she begins. "Take a few seconds to read the paragraphs you see on the screen. Then, with your partner, write down as many similarities as you can about the French and English colonists. You have 5 minutes."

Teri does a considerable amount of group work in her class. She sometimes has students work in pairs, and at other times in groups of four. The students are seated together, so they can move into and out of the groups quickly. Students initially protested the seating assignments, because they weren't sitting near their friends, but Teri emphasized that learning and getting to know and respect people different from themselves were important goals for the class. Teri persisted, and the groups became quite effective.

Teri watches as students work, and at the end of the 5-minute period, she says, "Okay, you've done a good job. . . . Turn back up here, and let's think about this."

The class quickly turns its attention to the front of the room, and Teri asks, "Serena, what did you and David come up with?"

". . . Both of the paragraphs deal with a colony from Europe."

"Okay, Eric, how about you and Kyo?"

". . . The colonies both produced something their countries, England and France, wanted—like tobacco or furs."

"Excellent observation, you two," Teri smiles. "Go on Gustavo. How about you and Pam?"

". . . They sent the stuff to their country," Gustavo responds after looking at his notes.

"And they couldn't send it anywhere else!" Tito adds, warming up to the idea.

"That's very good, all of you. Where do you suppose Tito got that idea?. . . Connie?"

"It says it right in the paragraphs," Connie responds.

"Excellent, everyone! Connie, good use of information to support your ideas."

Teri continues to guide the students as they analyze the paragraphs. She guides the class to conclude that, in each instance, the colonies sent raw materials to the mother country, bought back finished products, and were required to use the mother country's ships to transport all materials.

She then tells them that this policy, called *mercantilism,* was a strategy countries used to make money from their colonies. "Mercantilism helps us understand why Europe was so interested in imperialism and colonization," she adds. "It doesn't explain everything, but it was a major factor in the history of this period.

"Let's look at another paragraph. Does this one illustrate mercantilism? Be ready to explain why or why not when you've made your decision," she directs, displaying the following on the screen:

Canada is a member of the British Commonwealth. Canada is a large grain producer and exporter and derives considerable income from selling this grain to Great Britain, France, Russia, and other countries. This trade has also enhanced the shipping business for Greece, Norway, and Liberia, who carry most of the products. Canada, however, doesn't rely on grain alone. It is now a major producer of clothing, high-tech equipment, and heavy industrial equipment.

The class discusses the paragraph and, using evidence from the text, concludes that it does not illustrate mercantilism.

Short-Answer Questions

In answering these questions, use information from the chapter and link your responses to specific information in the case.

1. What strategies did Teri use to eliminate gender bias in her classroom? What else might she have done?
2. One of the principles of effective teaching for students placed at risk recommends the use of high-quality examples that supplement students' background knowledge. How well did Teri apply this principle?
3. Success and challenge are essential for effective instruction for students placed at risk. Evaluate Teri's attempts to provide these components.
4. What strategies did Teri use to actively involve her students?

For feedback on these responses, go to Appendix B.

Now go to Chapter 4 of MyEducationLab, located at www.myeducationlab.com, where you can:

- Take a quiz to test your mastery of chapter objectives. Detailed feedback is provided to explain why your responses are correct or incorrect.
- Deepen your understanding of chapter concepts with *Review, Practise, Enrichment* exercises.
- Complete *Activities and Applications* that will help you apply what you have learned in the chapter by analyzing real classrooms through video clips, artifacts, and case studies. Your instructor will provide you with feedback for the *Activities and Applications.*
- Develop your professional knowledge and decision making in *Building Teaching Skills and Dispositions* exercises. Structured feedback will be available to you, providing you with support as you practice each skill. Your instructor will provide you with feedback on the final task that accompanies the exercises.

Important Concepts

academic language proficiency (p. 104)
basic interpersonal communication skills (p. 104)
bidialecticism (p. 102)
bilingualism (p. 105)
colorblindness (p. 101)
cultural mismatch (p. 97)
culture (p. 96)
dialect (p. 101)
English Language Learners (ELLs) (p. 102)
ESL pullout programs (p. 104)
ethnicity (p. 96)
gender-role identity (p. 108)
immersion programs (p. 103)
learner diversity (p. 96)
maintenance ELL programs (p. 103)
multicultural education (p. 106)
resilience (p. 115)
resistance culture (p. 98)
sheltered English (p. 104)
socioeconomic status (SES) (p. 111)
stereotype threat (p. 99)
structured immersion (p. 103)
students placed at risk (p. 114)
transitional ELL programs (p. 104)

chapter 5

Learners with Exceptionalities

chapter outline

Intelligence

- Intelligence: One Trait or Many?
- Intelligence: Nature Versus Nurture
- Ability Grouping
- Learning Styles

Changes in the Ways Teachers Help Students with Exceptionalities

- Individuals with Disabilities Education Act (IDEA)
- Amendments to the IDEA

Students with Learning Problems

- The Labeling Controversy
- Learning Disabilities
- Attention-Deficit/Hyperactivity Disorder
- Intellectual Disabilities
- Behavior Disorders
- Autism Spectrum Disorders
- Communication Disorders
- Visual Disabilities
- Hearing Disabilities

Students Who Are Gifted and Talented

- Characteristics of Students Who Are Gifted and Talented
- Identifying Students Who Are Gifted and Talented
- Programs for the Gifted and Talented
  - **Theory to Practice**: Teaching Students Who Are Gifted and Talented
  - **Exploring Diversity**: Pursuing Equity in Special Education

The Teacher's Role in Inclusive Classrooms

- Collaborative Consultation: Help for the Classroom Teacher
- Identifying Students with Exceptionalities
- Modifying Instruction to Meet Students' Needs
- Promote Social Integration and Student Growth
  - **Theory to Practice**: Teaching Students with Exceptionalities
  - **Developmentally Appropriate Practice:** Students with Exceptionalities at Different Ages

learning objectives

After you have completed your study of this chapter, you should be able to:

1. Describe differences in the way intelligence is viewed, and explain how ability grouping can influence learning.
2. Describe the major provisions of the Individuals with Disabilities Education Act (IDEA) and the amendments to it.
3. Describe the most common learning problems that classroom teachers are likely to encounter.
4. Identify characteristics of learners who are gifted and talented, and describe methods for identifying and teaching these students.
5. Describe general education classroom teachers' roles in inclusive classrooms, and identify teaching strategies that are effective for working with students having exceptionalities.

Have you ever struggled in a class and received a D or an F? Or excelled and been the "smartest" one? How did it feel? How did other students in the class treat you? These are questions that students with exceptionalities face every day.

Virtually every classroom in our country includes learners who have exceptionalities. As you read the following case study, think about these issues and what teachers might do to accommodate the students who have them.

Celina Curtis, a beginning first-grade teacher in a large elementary school, has survived her hectic first weeks. She is beginning to feel comfortable, but at the same time, some things are bothering her.

"It's kind of frustrating," she admits, as she shares her lunch break with Clarisse, a veteran who has become her friend and confidante. "I think I'm teaching, but some of the kids just don't seem to get it."

"Maybe you're being too hard on yourself," Clarisse responds. "Students are different. Remember what you studied in college? One thing the profs emphasized was that we should be trying our best to treat students as individuals."

"Yes, . . . I understand that, but it seems too simple. For instance, there's Rodney. You've seen him on the playground. He's cute, but his engine is stuck on fast. I can barely get him to sit in his seat, much less work. The smallest distraction sets him off. He can usually do the work if I can get him to stick to it, but it's a challenge. I've talked to his mother, and he's the same way at home.

"Then there's Amelia; she's so sweet, but she simply doesn't get it. I've tried everything under the sun with her. I explain it, and the next time, it's as if it's all brand new. I feel sorry for her, because I know she gets frustrated when she can't keep up with the other kids. When I work with her one-on-one, it seems to help, but I don't have enough time to spend with her. She's falling farther and farther behind."

"Maybe it's not your fault. You're supposed to do your best, but you're going to burn yourself out if you keep this up," Clarisse cautions. "Check with the Teacher Assistance Team. Maybe these students need some extra help."

As you begin your study of this chapter, consider these questions:

1. What does the law say about our responsibilities in working with students having exceptionalities?
2. Are Rodney and Amelia displaying exceptionalities, and if so, how should they be described?
3. How can teachers accommodate students with exceptionalities in their classrooms?

Learners with exceptionalities. Students who need special help and resources to reach their full potential.

Disabilities. Functional limitations or an inability to perform a certain act.

Gifts and talents. Abilities at the upper end of the continuum that require additional support to reach full potential.

Special education. Instruction designed to meet the unique needs of students with exceptionalities.

Learners with exceptionalities are students who need special help and resources to reach their full potential (Kauffman, McGee, & Brigham, 2004). This category includes students with **disabilities**—functional limitations or an inability to perform a certain act, such as walk or listen—as well as students with **gifts and talents**—abilities at the upper end of the continuum that require additional support to reach full potential. Some students have both disabilities and gifts and talents. It is a virtual certainty that you will have students with exceptionalities in your classroom. **Special education** refers to instruction designed to meet the unique needs of these students.

Because it plays an important role in understanding, diagnosing, and helping students with exceptionalities, we begin by examining the concept of *intelligence.*

Intelligence

Intelligence. The ability to acquire and use knowledge, solve problems and reason in the abstract, and adapt to new situations in the environment.

Although experts don't totally agree on a definition, **intelligence** is often defined as the ability to acquire and use knowledge, solve problems and reason in the abstract, and adapt to new situations in the environment. Most experts also agree that it depends on culture (Ackerman & Lohman, 2006; J. Li, 2004; Sternberg, 2004).

From another perspective, intelligence is simply defined as the attributes that intelligence tests measure. Items such as the following are commonly found on these tests, and people's intelligence is inferred from their responses.

1. Cave:Hole:Bag: _________ (Cave is to hole as bag is to _________?)
   a. paper
   b. container
   c. box
   d. brown
2. Sharon had x amount of money, and this could buy 8 apples. How much money would it take to buy 4 apples?
   a. $8x$
   b. $2x$

c. $x/2$
d. x^2

3. Inspect the following list of numbers for 5 seconds:
9 7 4 6 2 1 8 3 9
Now cover them, and name the digits in order from memory.

As these items suggest, experience is an important factor in test performance (Ackerman & Lohman, 2006; Halpern & LaMay, 2000). Practice with vocabulary and analogies, for example, would improve the score on the first item. The second requires background in math, and even the third, a seemingly simple memory task, can be improved with training (A. Brown, Bransford, Ferrara, & Campione, 1983). Clearly, intelligence tests measure more than innate ability (Sternberg, 2007).

Intelligence: One Trait or Many?

Because scores on different measures of intelligence, such as verbal ability and abstract reasoning, are correlated, early researchers believed intelligence to be influenced by a single trait (W. Johnson & Bouchard, 2005; Waterhouse, 2006). For example, Charles Spearman (1927) described it as "g," or general intelligence, a basic ability that affects performance on all cognitive tasks but also includes task-specific abilities. This helps us understand why people who do well on verbal tests also do well on tests in math, but typically do better on one than the other.

A second perspective contrasts **fluid intelligence**, the flexible, culture-free mental ability to adapt to new situations, with **crystallized intelligence**, a form of intelligence that is culture-specific and depends on experience and schooling (Cattel, 1963, 1987). Fluid intelligence is often related to nonverbal abilities and is influenced by brain development, whereas crystallized intelligence increases throughout our lives as we acquire new knowledge and skills. Current conceptions of intelligence typically include a general component as well as specific knowledge that people use every day (Ackerman & Lohman, 2006; Phelps, McGrew, Knopik, & Ford, 2005).

Fluid intelligence. The flexible, culture-free mental ability to adapt to new situations.

Crystallized intelligence. Culture-specific mental ability, heavily dependent on experience and schooling.

Gardner's Theory of Multiple Intelligences

Howard Gardner, a Harvard psychologist, analyzed people's performance in different domains and concluded that intelligence is composed of eight relatively independent dimensions (Gardner, 1983; Gardner & Moran, 2006). Table 5.1 outlines the eight dimensions that currently exist, and he is also considering additional dimensions, called *existential* and *spiritual intelligences*, which deal with life's fundamental questions, such as "Who are we?" and "Where do we come from?" (Gardner & Moran, 2006).

The concept of multiple intelligences makes intuitive sense. We all know people who don't seem particularly "sharp" analytically but who excel in getting along with others, for example. This ability serves them well, and in some instances, they're more successful in life than their "brighter" counterparts. Others are extraordinary athletes or accomplished musicians. Gardner describes these people as high in interpersonal, bodily-kinesthetic, and musical intelligence, respectively.

Applications of Gardner's Theory. Gardner recommends that teachers present content in ways that capitalize on as many different intelligences as possible, and teachers' efforts should also focus on helping students understand their strengths and weaknesses in each (Denig, 2003; Kornhaber, Fierros, & Veenema, 2004). Table 5.2 outlines ways to differentiate instruction. Gardner warns, however, that not all topics can be adapted for each intelligence: "There is no point in assuming that every topic can be effectively approached in [multiple] ways, and it is a waste of effort and time to attempt to do this" (Gardner, 1995, p. 206).

Criticisms of Gardner's Theory. While popular with teachers (Cuban, 2004), Gardner's theory also has its critics. Some caution that the theory and its applications have not been validated by research (Corno et al., 2002; Waterhouse, 2006), and whether or not it even qualifies as a theory has been questioned (J. Chen, 2004). Others disagree with the assertion that abilities in specific domains, such as music, qualify as separate forms of intelligence (McMahon, Rose, & Parks, 2004; Sattler, 2001).

table 5.1 Gardner's Theory of Multiple Intelligences

Dimension	Example
Linguistic Intelligence Sensitivity to the meaning and order of words and the varied uses of language	Poet, journalist
Logical-Mathematical Intelligence The ability to handle long chains of reasoning and to recognize patterns and order in the world	Scientist, mathematician
Musical Intelligence Sensitivity to pitch, melody, and tone	Composer, violinist
Spatial Intelligence The ability to perceive the visual world accurately and to re-create, transform, or modify aspects of the world on the basis of one's perceptions	Sculptor, navigator
Bodily-Kinesthetic Intelligence A fine-tuned ability to use the body and to handle objects	Dancer, athlete
Interpersonal Intelligence The ability to notice and make distinctions among others	Therapist, salesperson
Intrapersonal Intelligence Access to one's own "feeling life"	Self-aware individual
Naturalist Intelligence The ability to recognize similarities and differences in the physical world	Naturalist, biologist, anthropologist

Source: Adapted from Gardner and Hatch (1989) and Chekley (1997).

Failure to account for the role that a centralized working memory system plays in intelligent behavior is one of the most important criticisms of Gardner's work (Lohman, 2001). (We examine working memory in detail in Chapter 7.) For example, when students solve word problems, they must keep the problems' specifics in mind as they search their memory for similar problems, select strategies, and find solutions. This cognitive juggling act occurs in all types of intelligent behavior. Because it views intelligence as consisting of separate dimensions, Gardner's theory ignores this factor (Lohman, 2001).

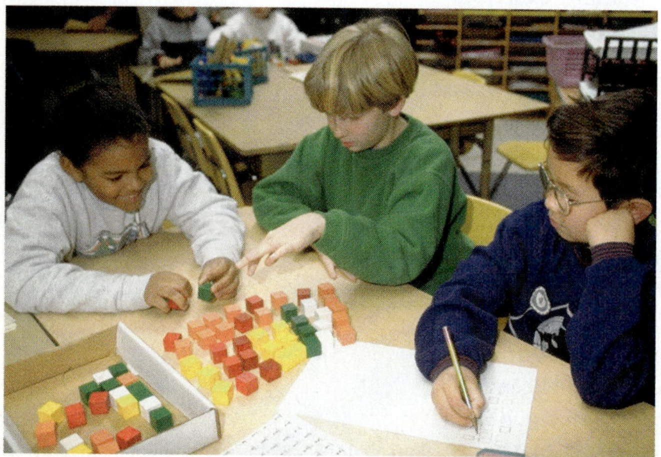

Sternberg believes that experiences requiring students to think analytically, creatively, and practically can increase intelligence.

Sternberg's Triarchic Theory of Intelligence

Robert Sternberg (Sternberg, 2003a, 2003b, 2004), another multitrait theorist, describes intelligence as existing in three dimensions:

- An *analytical* dimension, which is similar to traditional definitions of intelligence and is used in thinking and problem solving (Sternberg, 2003b).
- A *creative*, or experiential, dimension, which involves the ability to deal effectively with novel situations and solve familiar problems efficiently. Intelligent individuals quickly move from conscious learning in unfamiliar situations to performing tasks automatically as they become more familiar (Sternberg, 1998a, 1998b).
- A *practical*, or contextual, dimension, which is the ability to deal effectively with everyday tasks. Intelligent behavior involves adapting to the environment, changing the environment if adaptation isn't effective, or selecting a better environment if necessary (Sternberg, 2007).

table 5.2 Instructional Applications of Gardner's Multiple Intelligences

Dimension	Application
Linguistic	How can I get students to talk or write about the idea?
Logical-Mathematical	How can I bring in number, logic, and classification to encourage students to quantify or clarify the idea?
Spatial	What can I do to help students visualize, draw, or conceptualize the idea spatially?
Musical	How can I help students use environmental sounds or set ideas into rhythm or melody?
Bodily-Kinesthetic	What can I do to help students involve the whole body or to use hands-on experience?
Interpersonal	How can I use peer, cross-age, or cooperative learning to help students develop their interactive skills?
Intrapersonal	How can I get students to think about their capacities and feelings to make them more aware of themselves as persons and learners?
Naturalist	How can I provide experiences that require students to classify different types of objects and analyze their classification schemes?

Sternberg's emphasis on the creative and practical aspects of intelligence is what sets his theory apart from other views. He sees functioning effectively in the real world as intelligent behavior, and because of this emphasis, he believes that individuals considered intelligent in one setting or culture may be viewed as unintelligent in another (Sternberg, 2004, 2006, 2007).

Influenced by Piaget's emphasis on experience as essential for development, Sternberg believes that providing students with experiences in which they're expected to think analytically, creatively, and practically can increase intelligence. Some examples of applying Sternberg's theory are outlined in Table 5.3.

table 5.3 Applying Analytic, Creative, and Practical Thinking in Different Content Areas

Content Area	Analytic	Creative	Practical
Math	Express the number 44 in base 2.	Write a test question that measures understanding of three different number bases.	How is the base 2 used in our everyday lives?
Language Arts	Why is *Romeo and Juliet* considered a tragedy?	Write an alternative ending to *Romeo and Juliet* to make it a comedy.	Write a TV ad for the school's production of *Romeo and Juliet.*
Social studies	In what ways were the American and the French revolutions similar and different?	What would our lives be like today if the American revolution had not succeeded?	What lessons can countries take away from the study of revolutions?
Science	If a balloon is filled with 1 liter of air at room temperature, and it is then placed in a freezer, what will happen to the balloon?	How would the balloon filled with air behave on the moon?	Describe two common examples where heating or cooling affects solids, liquids, or gases.
Art	Compare and contrast the artistic styles of Van Gogh and Picasso.	What would the Statue of Liberty look like if it were created by Picasso?	Create a poster for the student art show using the style of one of the artists we studied.

Intelligence: Nature Versus Nurture

Nature view of intelligence. The assertion that intelligence is essentially determined by genetics.

Nurture view of intelligence. The assertion that emphasizes the influence of the environment on intelligence.

No aspect of intelligence has been more hotly debated than the influence of heredity versus environment, and this debate relates to our earlier discussion of crystallized and fluid intelligence. The extreme **nature view of intelligence** asserts that it is essentially determined by genetics; the **nurture view of intelligence** emphasizes the influence of the environment. Most experts take a position somewhere in the middle, believing that a person's intelligence is influenced by both (Coll, Bearer, & Lerner, 2004; Shepard, 2001). This view holds that a person's genes provide the potential for intelligence, and stimulating environments make the most of the raw material.

Evidence supports Sternberg's contention that experience can increase intelligence. For example, children exposed to enriched learning experiences, both in preschool and in later schooling, score higher on intelligence tests than those lacking the experiences (Christian, Bachnan, & Morrison, 2001; Ramey, Ramey, & Lanzi, 2001).

Ability Grouping

Ability grouping. The process of placing students of similar abilities into groups and attempting to match instruction to the needs of these groups.

Tracking. Placing students in different classes or curricula on the basis of achievement.

Schools most commonly respond to differences in students' capabilities by **ability grouping**, the process of placing students of similar abilities into groups, and attempting to match instruction to the needs of the groups (Chorzempa & Graham, 2006; McCoach, O'Connell, & Levitt, 2006). Though controversial, most elementary teachers endorse it, particularly in reading and math.

Ability grouping in elementary schools typically exists in three forms, described and illustrated in Table 5.4. In middle, junior high, and high schools, ability grouping goes further, with high-ability students studying college preparatory courses and lower-ability students receiving vocational or work-related instruction (Oakes, 2005). In some cases, students are grouped only in certain content areas, such as English or math; in others, ability grouping involves **tracking,** the process of placing students in different curricula on the basis of achievement. Some form of tracking exists in most middle, junior high, and high schools.

Ability Grouping: Research Results

Why is ability grouping so pervasive? Advocates argue that it is easier for teachers because it allows them to keep instruction uniform for each group, and it enables them to adjust the pace, methods, and materials to better meet learners' needs.

Critics counter by citing several problems:

- Within-class grouping creates logistical problems because different lessons and assignments are required, so monitoring students is difficult (Good & Brophy, 2008).
- Improper placements occur, which tend to become permanent. Members of cultural minorities and students with low socioeconomic status (SES) are underrepresented in high-ability classes and overrepresented in low-ability classes (McDermott, Goldman & Varenne, 2006; C. O'Conner & Fernandez, 2006).

table 5.4 Types of Ability Grouping in Elementary Schools

Type	Description	Example
Between-class grouping	Divides students at a certain grade into levels, such as high, average, and low	A school with 75 third graders divides them into one class of high achievers, one of average achievers, and one of low achievers.
Within-class grouping	Divides students in a class into subgroups based on reading or math scores	A fourth-grade teacher has three reading groups based on reading ability.
Joplin plan	Regroups across grade levels	Teachers from different grade levels place students in the same reading class.

- Members of low-ability groups are stigmatized by being labeled as low achievers (Oakes, 2005).
- Homogeneously grouped low-ability students achieve less than heterogeneously grouped students of similar ability (Good & Brophy, 2008).

The negative effects of grouping are related, in part, to the quality of instruction. Research indicates that presentations to low groups tend to be more fragmented and vague, and they focus on low-level tasks to a greater extent than those to high groups. Students in low-ability classes are often taught by teachers who lack enthusiasm and stress conformity instead of autonomy and the development of self-regulation (Chorzempa & Graham, 2006; Good & Brophy, 2008). As a result, self-esteem and motivation to learn decrease, and absentee rates increase. Tracking can also result in racial segregation of students, which negatively influences social development and opportunities to form friendships across cultural groups (Oakes, 2005).

Ability Grouping: Implications for Teachers

Suggestions for dealing with the issues involved in ability grouping vary. At one extreme, critics argue that its effects are so negative that the practice should be abolished. A more moderate position suggests that grouping may be appropriate in some areas, such as reading and math (Good & Brophy, 2008), but that every effort should be made to deemphasize groups in other content areas. In addition, the groups should be flexible, allowing students to move between groups as their skills increase (Castle, Deniz, & Tortora, 2005). Researchers have found that the **Joplin plan**, which uses homogeneous grouping in reading, but heterogeneous grouping in other areas, can increase reading achievement without negative side effects (Slavin, 1987). At the junior and senior high levels, between-class grouping should be limited to the basic academic areas.

Joplin plan. Homogeneous grouping in reading, combined with heterogeneous grouping in other areas.

When grouping is necessary, specific measures to reduce its negative effects should be taken. Some suggestions are outlined in Figure 5.1. These suggestions are demanding. Teachers must make careful decisions about group placements and closely monitor their students' progress. The need to maintain high expectations and instructional flexibility in this process is important.

Learning Styles

Historically, psychologists have used intelligence tests to measure mental abilities and have used concepts such as *introvert* and *extrovert* to describe different personality types. Researchers who study the interface between the two examine **learning styles**—students' personal approaches to processing information and problem solving (Denig, 2003). Researchers sometimes use the terms *learning style* and *cognitive style* interchangeably.

Learning styles. Students' personal approaches to learning, problem solving, and processing information.

One of the most common descriptions of learning style distinguishes between deep and surface approaches to processing information (C. J. Evans, Kirby, & Fabrigar, 2003; R. Snow, Corno, & Jackson, 1996). For instance, as you studied the Civil War in American history, did you relate it to the geography, economies, and politics of the Northern and Southern states? If so, you were using a deep-processing approach. On the other hand, if you memorized the dates

- Keep group composition flexible, and reassign students to other groups when their rate of learning warrants it.
- Make every effort to ensure that the quality of instruction is as high for low-ability students as it is for high-ability students.
- Treat student characteristics as dynamic rather than static; teach low-ability students appropriate learning strategies and behaviors.
- Avoid assigning negative labels to lower groups.
- Constantly be aware of the possible negative consequences of ability grouping.

Figure 5.1 Suggestions for reducing the negative effects of ability grouping

classroom connections

Applying an Understanding of Ability Differences in Your Classroom

1. Performance on intelligence tests is influenced by a number of factors, including genetics, experience, language, and culture. Use intelligence test scores cautiously when making educational decisions, keeping in mind that they are only one indicator of ability.
   - **Elementary:** An urban third-grade teacher consults with a school counselor in interpreting intelligence test scores, and she remembers that language and experience influence test performance.
   - **Middle School:** When making placement decisions, a middle school team relies on past classroom performance and grades in addition to standardized test scores.
   - **High School:** An English teacher uses grades, assessments of motivation, and work samples in addition to aptitude test scores in making placement recommendations.
2. Intelligence is multifaceted and covers a wide spectrum of abilities. Use instructional strategies that maximize student background knowledge, interests, and abilities.
   - **Elementary:** In a unit on the Revolutionary War, a fifth-grade teacher assesses all students on basic information but bases 25 percent of the unit grade on special projects, such as researching the music and art of the times.
   - **Middle School:** An eighth-grade English teacher has both required and optional assignments. Seventy percent of the assignments are required for everyone; the other 30 percent provide students with choices.
   - **High School:** A biology teacher provides students with choices in terms of the special topics they study in depth. In addition he allows students to choose how they will report on their projects, allowing either research papers, classroom presentations, or poster sessions.
3. Ability grouping has both advantages and disadvantages. Use ability grouping only when essential, view group composition as flexible, and reassign students when warranted by their performance. Attempt to provide the same quality of instruction for all group levels.
   - **Elementary:** A fourth-grade teacher uses ability groups only for reading. She uses whole-class instruction for other language arts topics such as poetry and American folktales.
   - **Middle School:** A seventh-grade team meets regularly to assess group placements and to reassign students to different groups based on their academic progress.
   - **High School:** A history teacher videotapes lessons to compare his teaching behaviors in high-ability compared to standard-ability groups. He reminds his standard classes that he will maintain high expectations for their performance.

of the war and dates and locations of important battles and prominent leaders, you were using a surface approach.

As you would expect, deep-processing approaches result in higher achievement if tests focus on understanding, but surface approaches can succeed if tests emphasize fact learning and memorization. Students who use deep-processing approaches also tend to be more intrinsically motivated and self-regulated, whereas those who use surface approaches tend to more motivated by high grades and their performance compared to others (Schunk, Pintrich, & Meece, 2008). (We examine motivation in detail in Chapters 10 and 11.)

Learning Styles and Learning Preferences

The concept *learning style* is popular in education, and many consultants use this label when they conduct in-service workshops for teachers. However, these workshops typically focus on students' *preferences* for different learning environments, such as lighting and noise level, and consultants encourage teachers to match classroom environments to students' preferences.

Research on these practices is controversial. Advocates claim the match results in increased achievement and improved attitudes (Farkas, 2003; Lovelace, 2005); critics counter by questioning the validity of the tests used to measure learning styles (preferences) (S. Stahl, 2002). They also cite research indicating that attempts to match learning environments to learning preferences have resulted in no increases in learning, and, in some cases, even decreases (Coffield, Moseley, Hall, & Ecclestone, 2004; Kratzig & Arbuthnott, 2006).

Learning Styles: Implications for Teachers

The concept of *learning style* has at least three implications for teachers. First, it reminds us of the need to vary instruction, because no instructional strategy will be preferred by all students (Brophy, 2004). Second, it suggests that we should help students understand how they learn most effectively. (We examine *metacognition*, the concept that describes learners' awareness of and control over their thinking and learning, in Chapter 7.) Third, awareness of learning style can increase our sensitivity to differences in our students, making it more likely that we will respond to our students as individuals.

Students' learning preferences unquestionably vary, and the idea of learning style is appealing, but many respected researchers are skeptical. "Like most other reviewers who pay close attention to the research literature, I do not see much validity in the claims made by those who urge teachers to assess their students with learning style inventories and follow with differentiated curriculum and instruction" (Brophy, 2004, pp. 343–344).

check your understanding

1.1 Describe differences in the way intelligence is viewed.

1.2 Describe ability grouping. What does research indicate about its potential impact on learning?

1.3 Describe the difference between the *nature view of intelligence* and the *nurture view of intelligence*. What does research say about these views?

To receive feedback for these questions, go to Appendix A.

Changes in the Ways Teachers Help Students with Exceptionalities

In the past, schools separated students with disabilities from their nondisabled peers and placed them in special classrooms or schools. Instruction in these placements was often inferior, achievement was no better than in general education classrooms, and students didn't learn the social and life skills needed in the real world (Karten, 2005; T. Smith, Polloway, Patton, & Dowdy, 2004). A series of federal laws redefined the way teachers assist these students. In this section, we attempt to answer the first question we asked at the beginning of this chapter, "What does the law say about our responsibilities in working with students having exceptionalities?"

Individuals with Disabilities Education Act (IDEA)

In 1975 Congress passed Public Law 94-142, which made a free and appropriate public education available for all students with disabilities in the United States (Sack-Min, 2007). This law, renamed the Individuals with Disabilities Education Act (IDEA), requires that educators working with students having exceptionalities do the following:

- Provide a free and appropriate public education (FAPE).
- Educate children in the least restrictive environment (LRE).
- Protect against discrimination in testing.
- Involve parents in developing each child's educational program.
- Develop an individualized education program (IEP) of study for each student.

IDEA has affected every school in the United States and has changed the roles of teachers in general education and special education. Let's look at its major provisions.

A Free and Appropriate Public Education (FAPE)

IDEA asserts that every student can learn and is entitled to a free and appropriate public education. Provisions related to FAPE are based on the 14th Amendment to the Constitution, which guarantees equal protection of all citizens under the law. The Supreme Court in 1982 defined an *appropriate education* as one specially and individually designed to provide educational benefits to a particular student (Hardman, Drew, & Egan, 2008).

Least Restrictive Environment: The Evolution Toward Inclusion

Educators attempting to provide FAPE for all students realized that segregated classes and services were not meeting the needs of students with exceptionalities. **Mainstreaming**, the practice

Mainstreaming. The practice of moving students with exceptionalities from segregated settings into general education classrooms.

The least restrictive environment helps students develop to their fullest potential.

Least restrictive environment (LRE). A policy that places students in as typical an educational setting as possible while still meeting the students' special needs.

Adaptive fit. The degree to which a school environment accommodates the student's needs and the degree to which a student can meet the requirements of a particular school setting.

Inclusion. A comprehensive approach to educating students with exceptionalities that advocates a total, systematic, and coordinated web of services.

of moving students with exceptionalities from segregated settings into general education classrooms was one of the first alternatives considered. Popular in the 1970s, it began the move away from segregated services and promoted interaction between students with and without exceptionalities. However, students with exceptionalities were often placed in classrooms without adequate support (Hardman et al., 2008).

As educators struggled with these problems, they developed the concept of the **least restrictive environment (LRE)**, one that places students in as typical an educational setting as possible while still meeting the students' special needs. Broader than the concept of *mainstreaming*, the LRE can consist of a continuum of services, ranging from full-time placement in the general education classroom to placement in a separate facility. Full-time placement in the general education classroom occurs only if parents and educators decide it best meets the child's needs.

The LRE provision ensures that you will have learners with exceptionalities in your classroom, and you will be asked to work with special educators to design and implement programs for these students. The LRE means that students with exceptionalities should participate as much as possible in the general education school agenda, ranging from academics to extracurricular activities. The form these programs take varies with the capabilities of the students. Figure 5.2 presents a continuum of services for implementing the LRE, starting with the least confining at the top and moving to the most restrictive at the bottom. If students don't succeed at one level, educators move them to the next.

The concept of **adaptive fit** is central to the LRE. It describes the degree to which a school environment accommodates each student's needs and the degree to which a student can meet the requirements of a particular school setting (Hardman et al., 2008). As educators examined mainstreaming, LRE, and adaptive fit, they gradually developed the concept of *inclusion*.

Inclusion is a comprehensive approach that advocates a total, systematic, and coordinated web of services for students with exceptionalities (Sailor & Roger, 2005; Sapon-Shevin, 2007). It has three provisions:

1. Students with special needs are placed on a general education school campus.
2. Students with special needs are placed in age- and grade-appropriate classrooms.
3. General and special education services are coordinated.

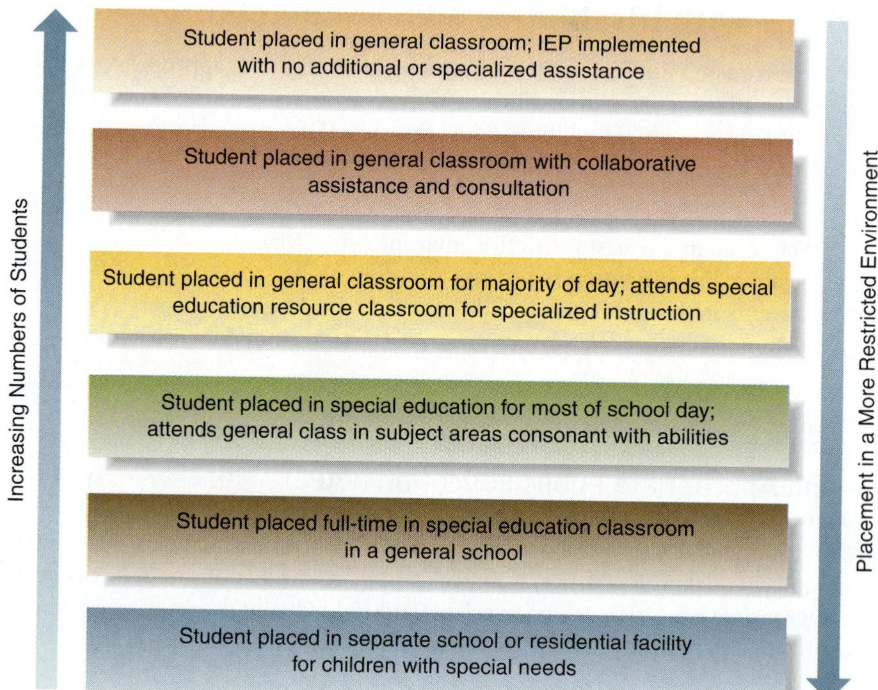

Figure 5.2 Educational service options for implementing the LRE
Source: U.S. Department of Education, 2002.

The practice of inclusion is controversial, with criticisms coming from general education classroom teachers, parents, and special educators themselves (Turnbull et al., 2007). Where inclusion works, general and special education teachers closely collaborate (Vaughn, Bos, Candace, & Schumm, 2006). Without this collaboration, inclusion isn't effective, and general education classroom teachers resent being expected to individualize instruction without adequate support (Kavale & Forness, 2000). Some parents, concerned that their children might become "lost in the shuffle," often favor special classrooms (J. Johnson & Duffett, 2002).

In the special education community, advocates of inclusion contend that placement in a general education classroom is the only way to eliminate the negative effects of segregation (Kluth, Villa, & Thousand, 2002). Opponents counter that inclusion is not for everyone and that some students are better served in special classes, at least for parts of the day (Holloway, 2001). Despite these controversies, inclusion is now widely accepted, and you are likely to encounter it in your teaching.

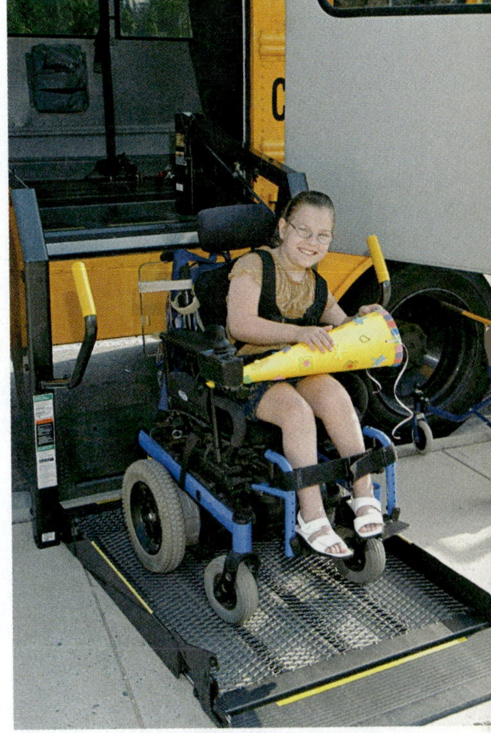

Inclusion creales a web of services to integrate students with exceptionalities into the educational system.

Fair and Nondiscriminatory Evaluation

In the past, students with disabilities were often placed in special education programs based on invalid information. IDEA requires that any testing used for placement be conducted in a student's native language by qualified personnel, and no single instrument, such as an intelligence test, can be used as the sole basis for placement. Recently, students' classroom performance and general adaptive behavior have been increasingly emphasized (Heward, 2009).

Due Process and Parents' Rights

Due process guarantees parents' rights to be involved in their children's placement in special programs, to access school records, and to obtain an independent evaluation if they're not satisfied with the school's evaluation. Parents often complain that they aren't being told about available services (J. Johnson, 2002). Legal safeguards are also in place for parents who don't speak English; they have the right to an interpreter, and their rights must be read to them in their native language.

Due process. The guarantee of parents' rights to be involved in identifying and placing their children in special programs, to access school records, and to obtain an independent evaluation if they're not satisfied with the school's evaluation.

Individualized Education Program

To ensure that inclusion works and learners with exceptionalities don't become lost in the general education classroom, educators prepare an **individualized education program (IEP)** after determining that a student is eligible for special education. An IEP is an individually prescribed instructional plan devised by special and general education teachers, resource professionals, and parents (and sometimes the student). It specifies the following:

Individualized education program (IEP). An individually prescribed instructional plan devised by special education and general education teachers, resource professionals, and parents (and sometimes the student).

- An assessment of the student's current level of performance
- Long- and short-term objectives
- Services or strategies to be used
- Schedules for implementing the plan
- Criteria to be used in evaluating the plan's success

A sample IEP is illustrated in Figure 5.3. It has three important features. First, the initials of all participants indicate that its development is a cooperative effort. Second, the information in sections 3 to 7 is specific enough to guide the classroom teacher and special education personnel as they implement the program. Third, the mother's signature indicates that a parent was involved in developing the program and agrees with its provisions. Computer software is now available to help teachers create effective IEPs by easing access to student records through current databases (Trotter, 2005).

The IEP performs four functions:

- Provides support for the classroom teacher, who may be uncertain about the suggested instructional adaptations.
- Creates a link between the general education classroom and the resource team.
- Helps parents monitor their child's educational progress.
- Provides a program to meet the individual needs of the student.

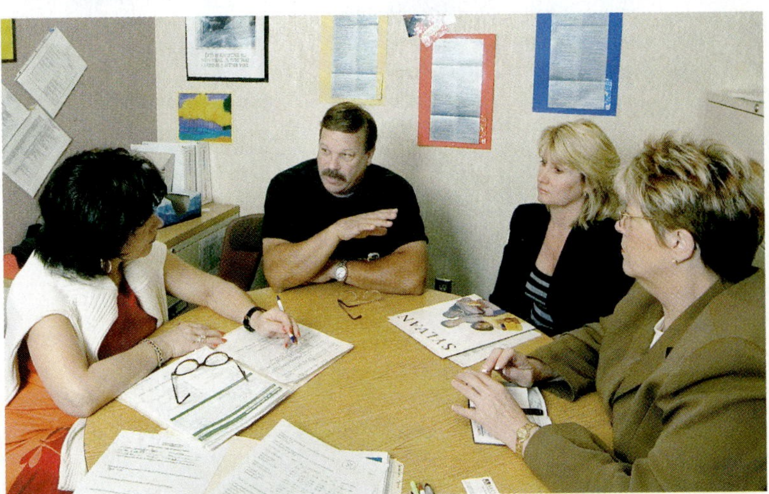

Teahers and other professionals meet with parents to design on IEP that meets a student's individual learning needs.

INDIVIDUAL EDUCATION PROGRAM

Date 3-1-09

(1) Student

Name: Joe S.
School: Adams
Grade: 5
Current Placement: Regular Class/Resource Room

Date of Birth: 10-1-97 Age: 11-5

(2) Committee

		Initial
Mrs. Wrens	Principal	D.A.W.
Mrs. Snow	General Education Teacher	AS
Mr. LaJoie	Counselor	SLJ
Mr. Thomas	Resource Teacher	M.T.
Mr. Ryan	School Psychologist	H.R.R.
Mrs. S.	Parent	J.S.
Joe S.	Student	Joe S.

IEP from 3-15-09 to 3-15-10

(3) Present Level of Educational Functioning	(4) Annual Goal Statements	(5) Instructional Objectives	(6) Objective Criteria and Evaluation
MATH Strengths 1. Can successfully compute addition and subtraction problems to two places with regrouping and zeros. 2. Knows 100 basic multiplication facts. Weaknesses 1. Frequently makes computational errors on problems with which he has had experience. 2. Does not complete seatwork. Key Math total score of 2.1 Grade Equivalent.	Joe will apply knowledge of regrouping in addition and renaming in subtraction to four-digit numbers.	1. When presented with 20 addition problems of 3-digit numbers requiring two renamings, the student will compute answers at a rate of one problem per minute and an accuracy of 90%. 2. When presented with 20 subtraction problems of 3-digit numbers requiring two renamings, the student will compute answers at the rate of one problem per minute with 90% accuracy. 3. When presented with 20 addition problems of 4-digit numbers requiring three renamings, the student will compute answers at a rate of one problem per minute and an accuracy of 90%. 4. When presented with 20 subtraction problems of 4-digit numbers requiring three renamings, the student will compute answers at a rate of one problem per minute with 90% accuracy.	Teacher-made tests (weekly) Teacher-made tests (weekly) Teacher-made tests (weekly)

(7) Educational Services to be provided

Services Required	Date initiated	Duration of Service	Individual Responsible for the Service
Regular reading-adapted	3-15-09	3-15-10	Reading Improvement Specialist and Special Education Teacher
Resource room	3-15-09	3-15-10	Special Education Teacher
Counselor consultant	3-15-09	3-15-10	Counselor
Monitoring diet and general health	3-15-09	3-15-10	School Health Nurse

Extent of time in the regular education program: 60% increasing to 80%
Justification of the educational placement:
It is felt that the structure of the resource room can best meet the goals stated for Joe, especially when coordinated with the general education classroom.
It is also felt that Joe could profit enormously from talking with a counselor. He needs someone with whom to talk and with whom he can share his feelings.

(8) I have had the opportunity to participate in the development of the Individual Education Program.
I agree with Individual Education Program (✓)
I disagree with the Individual Education Program ( )

Parent s Signature Mrs S.

Figure 5.3 Individualized education program (IEP)
Source: Adapted from *Developing and Implementing Individualized Education Programs* (3rd ed., pp. 308, 316) by B. B Strickfand and A. P. Turnbull, 1990, Upper Saddle River, NJ: Merrill/Pearson Education.

IEPs sometimes focus on adaptations in the general education classroom, and at others they provide for outside support, such as a resource room. They are most effective when the two are coordinated, such as when a teacher working on word problems in math asks the resource teacher to focus on the same type of problems.

Amendments to the IDEA

Since 1975, Congress has amended IDEA three times (Sack-Min, 2007). For example, amendments in 1986 held states accountable for locating young children who need special education.

Amendment 1997, known as IDEA 97, attempted to clarify and extend the quality of services to students with disabilities. This amendment clarified the features that you saw in the previous sections, such as protection against discrimination in testing and the requirements of the IEP. It also ensures that districts protect the confidentiality of children's records and share them with parents on request.

More recently, Congress enacted a change called IDEA 2004 (Council for Exceptional Children, 2005). It has the following elements:

- Reduce the special education paperwork burden by deleting short-term objectives and benchmarks from IEPs.
- Initiate a 15-state paperwork demonstration project to pilot 3-year IEPs.
- Create discipline provisions, which allow districts to remove students who "inflict serious bodily injury" from the classroom to an alternative setting during the appeals process.
- Establish methods to reduce the number of students from culturally and linguistically diverse backgrounds who are inappropriately placed in special education.
- Provide districts with more flexibility in meeting the highly qualified teacher requirements of the No Child Left Behind legislation of 2001. Special education teachers who teach more than one subject may prove their qualifications through HOUSSE (high, objective, uniform state standard of evaluation), which allows veteran teachers to demonstrate their qualifications by means other than a test.
- Provide professional development for special educators.
- Include students with disabilities in accountability systems.

The last provision is controversial, with some educators warning that testing students with exceptionalities in the standard ways harms them more than helps (Meek, 2006). Educators are still assessing the impact of these legislative changes on teaching.

check your understanding

2.1 Describe the major provisions of the IDEA.
2.2 Describe the amendments to IDEA.
2.3 Explain how mainstreaming and inclusion relate to the FAPE provision of IDEA.

To receive feedback for these questions, go to Appendix A.

MyEducationLab

To examine ways to involve parents in the construction of an IEP, go to the *Activities and Applications* section in Chapter 5 of MyEducationLab at www.myeducationlab.com, and watch the episode *Reviewing an IEP*. Answer the questions following the episode.

Students with Learning Problems

Educators often create labels to address student differences (Hardman et al., 2008). *Disorder, disability,* and *handicap* are common terms used to describe physical or behavioral differences. **Disorder**, the broadest of the three, refers to a general malfunction of mental, physical, or psychological processes. A disability, as you saw at the beginning of the chapter, is a functional limitation or an inability to perform a certain act. A **handicap** is a condition imposed on people's functioning that restricts their abilities, such as being unable to enter a building in a wheelchair. This condition could be imposed by society, the environment, or people's attitudes (V. Lewis, 2002). Some, but not all, disabilities lead to handicaps. For example, a student with a visual

Disorder. A general malfunction of mental, physical, or psychological processes.

Handicap. A condition imposed on a person's functioning that restricts the individual's abilities.

disability may be able to wear glasses or sit in the front of the classroom; if these measures allow the student to function effectively, the disability isn't a handicap.

About 6 million students with exceptionalities are enrolled in special programs, two thirds for relatively minor learning problems (Hardman et al., 2008). Slightly less than 10 percent of students in a typical school receive special education services, and their disabilities range from mild learning problems to physical impairments such as being deaf or blind (U.S. Department of Education, 2008). Federal legislation has created categories to identify learning problems, and educators use these categories in developing special programs to meet the needs of students in each.

The Labeling Controversy

The use of categories and their resulting labeling are controversial. Advocates argue that categories provide a common language for professionals and encourage specialized instruction that meets students needs (Heward, 2009). Opponents claim that categories are arbitrary, many differences exist within them, and categorizing encourages educators to treat students as labels instead of people (Cook, 2001; National Council on Disability, 2000). Despite the controversy, these labels are widely used, so you need to be familiar with them.

People-first language. Language in which a student's disability is identified after the student is named.

Regardless of their position, special educators agree that labels shouldn't focus attention on students' weaknesses, so they endorse **people-first language**, which first identifies the student and then specifies the disability. For example, they use the description *students with a learning disability* instead of *learning-disabled students.* People-first language reminds us that all students are human beings who need to be treated with respect and care.

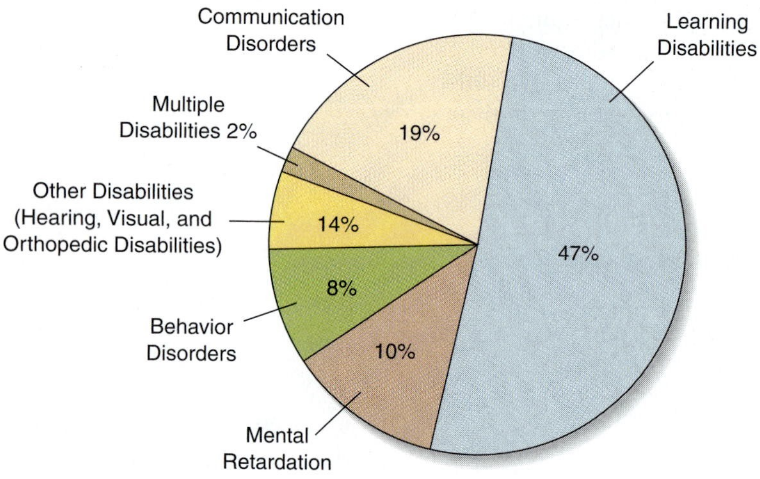

Figure 5.4 Poplation of students with disabilities
Source: U.S. Department of Education, 2004.

The percentage of students in each of the categories commonly used is outlined in Figure 5.4. The figure shows that a large majority (more than 80 percent) of the population of students with disabilities fall into four categories: *learning disabilities, communication disorders, intellectual disabilities,* and *behavior disorders.* In the following sections, we discuss these and other categories of disabilities you will likely encounter.

Learning Disabilities

Tammy Fuller, a middle school social studies teacher, is surprised when she scores Adam's first quiz. He seemed to be doing so well. He is rarely absent, pays attention, and participates in class. Why is his score so low? Tammy makes a mental note to watch him more closely, because his behavior and test performance are inconsistent.

In her second unit, Tammy prepares study guide questions and has students discuss their answers in groups. As she moves around the room, she notices that Adam's sheet is empty; when she asks him about it, he mumbles something about not having time the night before. Because the success of the group activity depends on students' coming to class prepared, Tammy asks Adam to come in after school to complete his work.

He arrives promptly and opens his book to the chapter. When Tammy stops to check on his progress, his page is blank; after another 10 minutes, it's still empty.

As she sits down to talk with him, he appears embarrassed and evasive. When they start to work on the questions together, she discovers that he can't read the text.

Learning disabilities. Difficulty in acquiring and using reading, writing, reasoning, listening, or mathematical abilities.

Some students, like Adam, have average or above-average intelligence but, despite their teachers' best efforts, struggle with learning. Students with **learning disabilities** (also called *specific learning disabilities*) encounter difficulties in acquiring and using reading, writing, reasoning, listening, or mathematical abilities (National Joint Committee on Learning Disabilities, 1994). Problems with reading, writing, and listening are most common (Shaywitz & Shaywitz, 2004), but math-related difficulties also receive attention (Hanich, Jordan, Kaplan, & Dick, 2001). Learning disabilities are believed to be due to central nervous system dysfunction and may exist along with, but are not caused by, other disabilities such as sensory impairment or attention problems. Experts stress that the term *learning disability* is broad and encompasses a range of problems (Berninger, 2006).

The concept of learning disabilities is related to the labeling controversy that we discussed earlier. Critics contend that *learning disability* is a catchall term for students who have learning problems (Sternberg & Grigorenko, 2001). Part of this criticism results from the rapid growth of the category. Nonexistent in the early 1960s, learning disability is now the largest category of exceptionality (U.S. Department of Education, 2008).

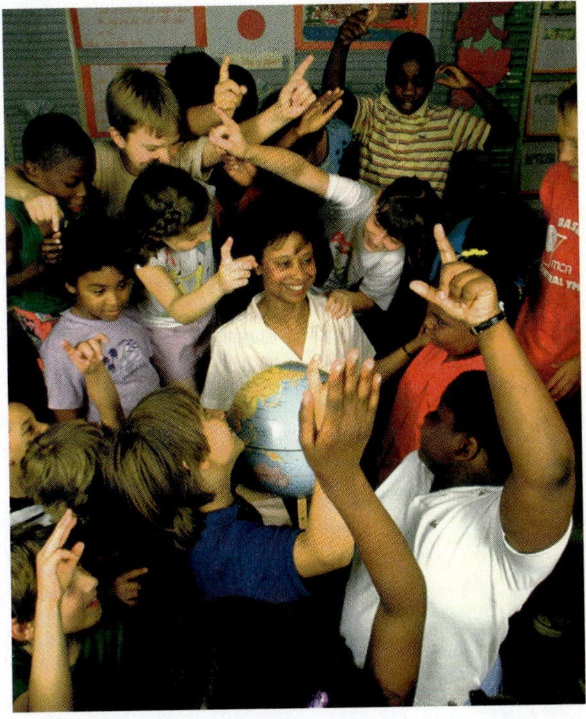

Although students with learning disabilities are found in almost every classroom, these students are often overlooked because they can be difficult to identify.

Characteristics of Students with Learning Disabilities

Students with learning disabilities often share a number of problems, which we outline in Table 5.5. Each student is unique, however, and teachers should individualize instructional adaptations.

Some of the characteristics in Table 5.5 are typical of general learning problems or immaturity. Unlike developmental lags, however, problems associated with learning disabilities often increase over time. Achievement declines, management problems increase, and self-esteem decreases (Hardman et al., 2008; Heward, 2009).

Identifying and Working with Students Who Have Learning Disabilities

As with all exceptionalities, identification is the first step, and early identification is important to prevent damaging effects from accumulating (Zambo, 2003). It isn't easy, however; uneven rates of development can be mistaken for learning disabilities, and classroom management issues can complicate identification (Vaughn et al., 2006). Students with learning disabilities often display

table 5.5 Characteristics of Students with Learning Disabilities

General Patterns	
Attention deficits	
Disorganization and tendency toward distraction	
Lack of follow-through and completion of assignments	
Uneven performance (e.g., capable in one area, extremely weak in others)	
Lack of coordination and balance	
Academic Performance	
Reading	Lacks reading fluency
	Reverses words (e.g., *saw* for *was*)
	Frequently loses place
Writing	Makes jerky and poorly formed letters
	Has difficulty staying on line
	Is slow in completing work
	Has difficulty copying from chalkboard
Math	Has difficulty remembering math facts
	Mixes columns (e.g., tens and ones) in computing
	Has trouble with story problems

inappropriate classroom behavior, and students who misbehave are referred for testing at a much higher rate than those who don't (Hunt & Marshall, 2002). Students with learning disabilities who comply with rules and complete assignments on time are often passed over for referral. This is likely the reason Adam, in Tammy's class, got to middle school before his difficulties with reading were discovered. These patterns can also be gender related; more boys than girls are identified because boys more commonly act out (Heward, 2009).

Discrepancy Versus Response to Intervention Models of Identification. Teachers play a central role in identifying and working with students who have learning disabilities. Information from teacher-made assessments as well as teachers' direct observations are combined with standardized test scores. Often, a **discrepancy model** is used, which looks for differences between the following:

Discrepancy model of identification. One method of identifying students with learning disabilities that focuses on differences between achievement and intelligence tests or subtests within either.

1. Intelligence and achievement test performance
2. Intelligence test scores and classroom achievement
3. Subtests on either intelligence or achievement tests (T. L. Hughes & McIntosh, 2002)
4. Performance in one area, such as an intelligence test, should predict performance in others; when the two are inconsistent, a learning disability may be the cause.

Many experts are dissatisfied with the discrepancy model. Critics argue that it identifies a disability only after a problem surfaces, sometimes after several years of failure and frustration (Brown-Chidsey, 2007). Instead, they argue, educators need early screening measures, so that teachers can prevent failure before it occurs. Critics also contend that the discrepancy model does not provide specific information about the nature of the learning problem and what should be done to correct it (Sternberg & Grigorenko, 2001; Stuebing et al., 2002).

Response to intervention model of identification. A method of identifying a learning disability that focuses on the specific classroom instructional adaptations that teachers use and their success.

The **response to intervention model of identification** attempts to address both of these problems (Vaughn & Fuchs, 2003). As soon as a learning problem surfaces, the classroom teacher attempts to adapt instruction to meet the student's needs. Some common adaptations include working with students one-on-one outside of regular school hours or while other students do seat work. The model emphasizes developing skills (e.g., highlighting important vocabulary) and developing study strategies (e.g., using a dictionary, reading assignments aloud, and finding a place to study that is free of distractions). If the adaptations do not suceed in modifying student achievement, the teacher suspects a learning disability. As the teacher adapts instruction, he or she also records what works and what doesn't. This provides valuable information for later interventions.

Attention-Deficit/Hyperactivity Disorder

Attention-deficit/hyperactivity disorder (ADHD). A learning problem characterized by difficulties in maintaining attention.

Attention-deficit/hyperactivity disorder (ADHD) is a learning problem characterized by difficulties in maintaining attention. ADHD has long been associated with learning disabilities; experts estimate an overlap of between 25 and 70 percent in the two conditions (Hardman et al., 2008). ADHD is relatively new as a described exceptionality, and it is not listed as a distinct category in IDEA. Students with ADHD may qualify for special education under the "other health impairments" disability category, however.

Characteristics of ADHD include

- Hyperactivity
- Inattention, difficulty in concentrating, and failure to finish tasks
- Impulsiveness, such as acting before thinking, calling out in class, and difficulty awaiting turns
- Forgetfulness and inordinate need for supervision

The disorder has received a great deal of media attention, and teachers see many students who seem to fit the ADHD description. High activity levels and inability to focus attention are characteristics of developmental lags—especially in young boys—however, so teachers should be cautious about drawing conclusions on the basis of these characteristics alone.

Brain-imaging research suggests that the sometimes impulsive behavior of students with ADHD may be due to slower rates of development in the frontal cortex area of the brain, which is responsible for monitoring and regulating behavior (Shaw & Rapoport,

Students with ADHD are impulsive and have difficulty concentrating.

2007). Experts caution, however, that a large percentage of students with ADHD don't "grow out" of the problem and will require special assistance in dealing with their disability (Viadero, 2007a).

ADHD usually appears early (at age 2 or 3) and, in at least half to nearly three fourths of the cases, it persists into adolescence (Purdie, Hattie, & Carroll, 2002). The American Psychiatric Association (2000) estimates that three to four times as many boys as girls are identified, although other experts estimate a higher ratio (Purdie et al., 2002; Whalen, Jamner, Henker, Delfino, & Lozano, 2002).

Treatments range from medication (e.g., the controversial medication Ritalin) to reinforcement programs and structured teaching environments (described later in this chapter) (J. Swanson & Volkow, 2002). Diagnosis and treatment of ADHD are usually conducted in consultation with medical and psychological experts.

Rodney, in the case study at the beginning of the chapter, shows symptoms of ADHD. He's hyperactive, easily distracted, and has difficulty focusing his attention. Celina is wise in seeking additional help for him. Before she does, however, she might try some adaptations in her classroom environment. For example, teachers sometimes find that moving a student like Rodney to a quieter part of the room can eliminate distractions and help him better focus on learning (Tannock & Martinussen, 2001). Teachers have also had success with behavioral interventions using principles of reinforcement for students with ADHD (Purdie et al., 2002). (We discuss reinforcement principles in detail in Chapter 6.) In addition, experts recommend teaching students how to break assignments into smaller components, requiring them to keep meticulously organized assignment books, and using flash cards and other drills to develop automaticity and confidence (Schlozman & Schlozman, 2000).

Intellectual Disabilities

To begin this section, let's return to Celina's work with her students.

> She watches her children as they work on a reading assignment. Most of the class works quietly. Amelia, in contrast, is out of her seat for the third time, supposedly sharpening her pencil. Celina has reminded her once to sit down and this time goes over to see what the problem is.
>
> "I can't do this! I don't get it!" Amelia responds in frustration when Celina asks her why she hasn't started her work.

After helping her calm down, Celina works with her for a few moments, but she can tell by Amelia's responses and her facial expression that she truly doesn't "get" the assignment.

Some students, like Amelia, learn less easily than others and become frustrated when they can't keep up with their peers. Unfortunately, this problem often isn't identified until students are several years into school. Many have mild intellectual disability. (You may also encounter the terms *educationally* or *intellectually handicapped*, and *intellectual* and *developmental disabilities*, which some educators prefer.) Intellectual disability is caused either by genetic factors, such as Down syndrome, or brain damage to the fetus during pregnancy (Fuchs, 2006; Nokelainen & Flint, 2002).

Intellectual disability. A disability characterized by significant limitations both in intellectual functioning and in adaptive behavior.

The American Association on Intellectual and Developmental Disabilities (AAIDD) defines **intellectual disability** as follows:

> Intellectual disability is a disability characterized by significant limitations both in intellectual functioning and in adaptive behavior as expressed in conceptual, social, and practical adaptive skills. This disability originates before the age of 18. A complete and accurate understanding of intellectual disability involves realizing that intellectual disability refers to a particular state of functioning that begins in childhood, has many dimensions, and is affected positively by individualized supports. (American Association on Intellectual and Developmental Disabilities, 2008)

The AAIDD definition emphasizes limitations in both intellectual functioning and adaptive abilities, such as communication, self-care, and social skills (Turnbull et al., 2007). Functioning in both areas can improve when these students receive services designed to meet their needs.

Students with intellectual disabilities are likely to display some or all of the following characteristics:

- Lack of general knowledge about the world
- Difficulty with abstract ideas
- Poor reading and language skills
- Poorly developed learning and memory strategies
- Underdeveloped motor skills
- Immature interpersonal skills (Beirne-Smith, Ittenbach, & Patton, 2002; Hodapp & Dykens, 2006)

Some of these characteristics affect learning directly; others, such as immature interpersonal skills, are less direct but still important.

Before the 1960s, definitions of mental retardation were based primarily on below-average scores on intelligence tests, but this approach had three problems. First, tests are imprecise, so misdiagnoses sometimes occurred. Second, disproportionate numbers of minorities and non-English-speaking students were identified as mentally retarded (Hallahan & Kauffman, 2009). Third, educators found that individuals with the same intelligence test scores varied widely in their ability to cope with the real world (Heward, 2009). Because of these problems, **adaptive behavior**, the person's ability to perform the functions of everyday living, became more important (Cimera, 2006). It is in this area that teachers' input is essential.

Adaptive behavior. A person's ability to perform the functions of everyday living.

Levels of Intellectual Disability

Educators classify mental retardation in four levels that represent the amount of support needed (Turnbull et al., 2007):

- *Intermittent*: Support on an as-needed basis
- *Limited*: Support consistently needed over time
- *Extensive*: Regular, such as daily, support required
- *Pervasive*: High-intensity, potentially life-sustaining support required

This classification system replaces an earlier one based on IQ scores alone. The older system categorized people as having intellectual disability that was mild (50 to 70 IQ), moderate (35 to 50 IQ), or severe and profound (IQ below 35). The transition from the older system to the new one is not complete, so you may encounter both in your work.

Instruction for Students with Intellectual Disability

Programs for students who have intermittent (mild) intellectual disability focus on creating support systems to augment existing instruction. Schools often place these students in general education classrooms where teachers adapt instruction to meet their special needs and help them develop socially.

Research indicates that these students often fail to acquire basic learning strategies, such as maintaining attention, organizing new material, and studying for tests (Heward, 2009). Amelia, in Celina's class, is an example. Celina recognized this need and attempted to provide additional support by working with her one-on-one.

Behavior Disorders

Kyle comes in from recess sweaty and disheveled, crosses his arms, and looks at the teacher defiantly. The playground monitor has reported another scuffle, and Kyle has a history of these disturbances. He struggles with his studies but can handle them if provided with enough structure. When he becomes frustrated, he sometimes acts out, often ignoring the rights and feelings of others.

Ben, who sits next to Kyle, is so quiet that the teacher almost forgets he is there. He never causes problems; in fact, he seldom participates in class. He has few friends and walks around at recess by himself, appearing to consciously avoid other children.

Although very different, Kyle and Ben both display symptoms of **behavior disorders**, serious and persistent age-inappropriate behaviors that result in social conflict and personal unhappiness. School failure is often an outcome. The terms *serious* and *persistent* are important. Many children occasionally fight with their peers, and all children periodically want to be alone. If a child shows a pattern of these behaviors, and if the behaviors interfere with normal development and school performance, the child may have a behavior disorder.

Behavior disorders. Serious and persistent age-inappropriate behaviors that result in social conflict, personal unhappiness, and often school failure.

The term *behavior disorder* is often used interchangeably with *emotional disturbance, emotional disability*, or *emotional handicap*, and you may encounter any of these in your work (Coleman & Webber, 2002). Researchers prefer the term *behavior disorder* because it focuses on overt behaviors that can be targeted and changed (Turnbull et al., 2007).

Students with behavior disorders often have the following characteristics:

- Behaving impulsively and having difficulty interacting with others in socially acceptable ways
- Acting out and failing to follow school or classroom rules
- Displaying poor self-concepts
- Lacking awareness of the severity of their problems
- Deteriorating academic performance and frequently missing school (Hardman et al., 2008; Turnbull et al., 2007)

Students with behavior disorders often have academic problems, some of which are connected with learning disabilities. The combination of these problems results in high absentee rates, low achievement, and a dropout rate of nearly 50 percent, the highest of any group of students with special needs (U.S. Department of Education, 2004).

Estimates of the frequency of behavior disorders vary (Hardman et al., 2008). For example, some estimates suggest that about 1 or 2 percent of the total school population and close to 10 percent of the special education population have behavior disorders, but others suggest that, because of identification problems, the percentage is much higher (Hallahan & Kauffman, 2009; Hardman et al., 2008). Identification is difficult because the characteristics are elusive (Forness, Walker, & Kavale, 2005; Turnbull et al., 2007).

Kinds of Behavior Disorders

Behavior disorders can be *externalizing* or *internalizing* (Hallahan & Kauffman, 2009). Students like Kyle fall into the first category, displaying characteristics such as hyperactivity, defiance, hostility, and even cruelty. Boys are three times more likely to be labeled as having an externalizing behavior disorder than girls, and low-socioeconomic status and membership in a cultural minority increase students' chances of being given this label.

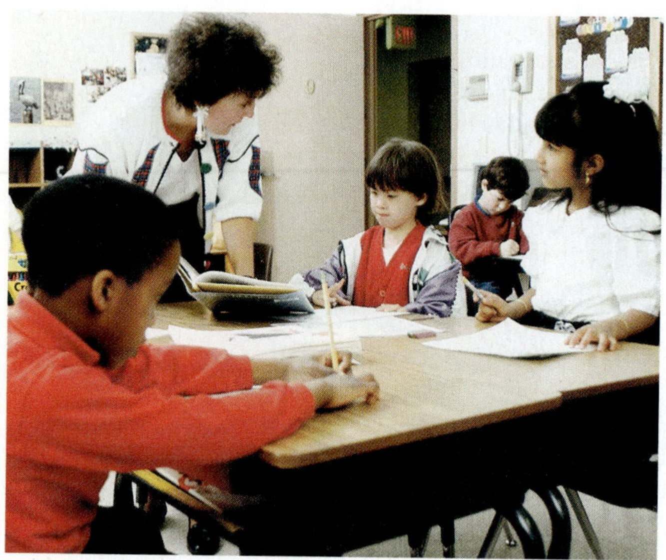

Students with internalizing behavior disorders are withdrawn and often experience anxiety.

Internalizing behavior disorders are characterized by social withdrawal, guilt, depression, and anxiety, which are problems more directed at the self than others. Like Ben, these children lack self-confidence and are often shy, timid, and depressed, sometimes suicidal. They have few friends and are isolated and withdrawn (Coleman & Webber, 2002). Because they don't have the high profile of students who act out, many go unnoticed, so a teacher's sensitivity and awareness are crucial in identifying these students.

Teaching Students with Behavior Disorders

Students with behavior disorders require a classroom environment that invites participation and success while providing structure through clearly stated and consistently enforced rules (T. Swanson, 2005).

Behavior Management Strategies. Teachers commonly use behavior management strategies to reinforce positive behaviors and eliminate negative ones (Alberto & Troutman, 2006; Warner & Lynch, 2005). These strategies include the following:

- *Positive reinforcement:* Rewarding positive behaviors, such as praising a student for behaving courteously
- *Replacement:* Teaching appropriate behaviors to substitute for inappropriate ones, such as teaching students to express personal feelings instead of fighting
- *Ignoring:* Not recognizing disruptive behaviors in an attempt to avoid reinforcing them
- *Timeout:* Isolating a child for brief periods of time
- *Overcorrection:* Requiring restitution beyond the damaging effects of the immediate behavior, such as requiring a child to return one of his own cookies in addition to the one he took from another student

We discuss the systematic use of these strategies, called *applied behavior analysis*, in detail in Chapter 6.

Teaching self-management skills can also be effective (Heward, 2009). For instance, students might be helped to identify behaviors they want to increase, such as making eye contact with the teacher, or decrease, such as snapping fingers. Over a specified period of time, students record the incidents of a behavior and graph the results, so they have a concrete record of their progress. The teacher also meets with them, frequently at first, to reinforce their efforts and set new goals. As students' self-regulation improves, teachers gradually reduce the amount of support they provide.

Teacher Sensitivity. Students with behavior disorders can be frustrating, and teachers sometimes forget that they have unique needs (Avramidis, Bayliss, & Burden, 2000). An incident with a 4-year-old boy illustrates this point. He had been referred to a school psychologist for aggressive behaviors and acting "out of control." She found him friendly, polite, and cooperative, and the session went smoothly until he announced he was done. When she urged him to continue, he became hysterical and ran out of the room.

> I assumed the testing phase of the evaluation was over and started writing a few notes. . . . A few minutes later, however, the little boy returned . . . and said that he was ready to continue. After another 10 minutes or so . . . the child again said, "I'm done now," to which I replied, "That's fine." The child calmly got out of his chair, walked around the room for a minute, and then sat down to resume testing. This pattern was repeated. . . .
>
> It was easy to see in a one-to-one testing situation that this child recognized the limits of his concentration and coped with increasing frustration by briefly removing himself. . . . It is equally easy to see, however, how this behavior created problems in the classroom. By wandering around, he would be disrupting the learning of other children. When the teacher tried to make him sit back down, she was increasing his frustration by removing from him the one method he had developed for coping. (Griffith, 1992, p. 34)

How do teachers manage behavior such as this in the general education classroom? The psychologist suggested designating an area in the back of the room where the child could go when he became frustrated. With this safety valve in place, the teacher could then work with the boy on long-term coping strategies. By attempting to understand the child as an individual, the teacher was able to work with her other students while meeting his needs.

Bipolar Disorders

Bipolar disorder is a condition characterized by alternative episodes of depressive and manic states (Heward, 2009), and the number of children treated for the disorder increased 40-fold from 20,000 in 1994 to 800,000 in 2003 (Carey, 2007). Experts believe that the incidence hasn't actually increased; rather, the numbers reflect a greater tendency to apply the diagnosis to children. The increase is also controversial, with critics claiming the label has become a catchall term applied to any child who is either depressed, the most common symptom, or explosively aggressive.

Bipolar disorder. A condition characterized by alternative episodes of depressive and manic states.

The symptoms of bipolar disorder are similar to depression or anxiety and are often linked to other issues, especially ADHD. Treatment typically includes powerful psychiatric drugs, which generally succeed in reducing or eliminating symptoms but may have negative side effects such as a gain in weight. Teachers working with children having this disorder can expect advice and assistance from special educators and school psychologists.

Autism Spectrum Disorders

Originally thought of as a single disorder under the general term *autism*, **autism spectrum disorder** is a description of a cluster of problems. They include autism and Asperger syndrome, characterized by impaired social relationships and skills, and often associated with highly unusual behavior (Hardman et al., 2008; Heward, 2009).

Autism spectrum disorder. A description of a cluster of disorders characterized by impaired social relationships and skills and often associated with highly unusual behavior.

In addition to impaired social relationships, characteristics of autism spectrum disorder include

- Communication and language deficits
- Unusual sensitivity to sensory stimuli
- Insistence on sameness and perseveration
- Ritualistic and unusual behavior patterns (Heward, 2009)

Autism spectrum disorders are thought to be caused by abnormalities in the brain. Their incidence has increased significantly in recent years, and they are four times more prevalent in boys than girls (Darden, 2007). The first symptoms are often lack of responsiveness to social stimuli and unusual, ritualistic behaviors such as rocking or repeating words or phrases. Children with the disorders span the entire range of intellectual abilities, but about three fourths also have intellectual disabilities (Heward, 2009). Many children with autism spectrum disorders are in general education classes for part or all of the school day.

Working with Students Having Autism Spectrum Disorders

Two approaches to working with these students are most common. One attempts to make the classroom environment as predictable as possible. Routines are helpful for all students; they are essential for children with autism spectrum disorder. Also, clearly outlined rules and expectations that are consistently applied provide scaffolding for these students.

A second approach focuses on social skills and attempts to help these students learn to interact with their peers and adjust to the social demands of classrooms. Students with autism spectrum disorders often lack social skills and are commonly unaware of the effects their behaviors have on others. Strategies for teaching social skills can be effective with these students and include perspective taking and social problem solving.

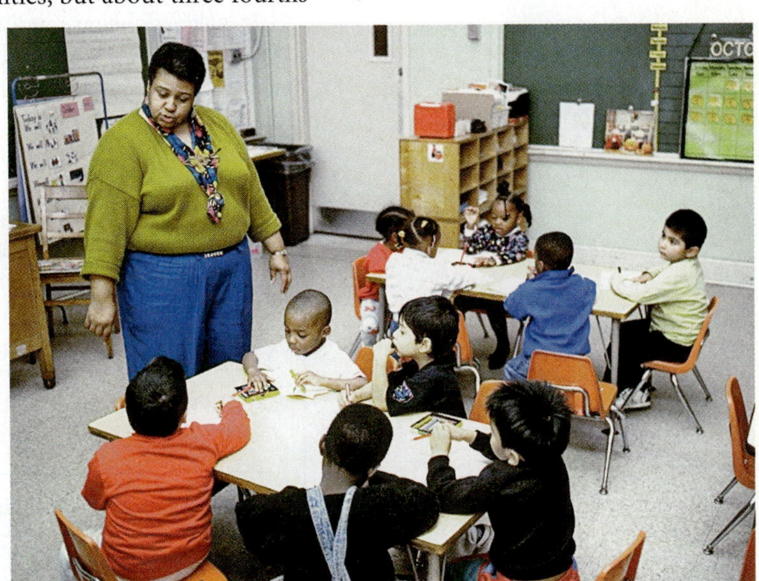

An orderly and predictable classroom is essential for children with autism spectrum disorders.

Communication Disorders

Communication disorders. Exceptionalities that interfere with students' abilities to receive and understand information from others and express their own ideas

Speech disorders *(expressive disorders)*. Problems in forming and sequencing sounds.

Language disorders *(receptive disorders)*. Problems with understanding language or using language to express ideas.

Communication disorders are exceptionalities that interfere with students' abilities to receive and understand information from others and express their own ideas. They exist in two forms (Bernstein & Tiegerman-Farber, 2002). **Speech disorders**, sometimes called *expressive disorders*, involve problems in forming and sequencing sounds. Stuttering and mispronouncing words, such as saying, "I taw it" for "I saw it," are examples. **Language disorders**, also called *receptive disorders*, include problems with understanding language or using language to express ideas. Language disorders are often connected to other problems, such as a hearing impairment, learning disability, or intellectual disability (Turnbull et al., 2007).

Specialists have identified three kinds of speech disorders (see Table 5.6). If they are chronic, a therapist is usually required, but sensitive teachers can help students cope with the emotional and social problems that are often associated with them.

Because they affect learning, language disorders are more serious than speech disorders. The vast majority of students learn to communicate quite well by the time they start school, but a small percentage—less than 1 percent—continues to experience problems expressing themselves verbally (Hardman et al., 2008; Heward, 2009). Symptoms of a language disorder include

- Seldom speaking, even during play
- Using few words or very short sentences
- Overrelying on gestures to communicate

The causes of language disorders include hearing loss, brain damage, learning disabilities, intellectual disabilities, severe emotional problems, and inadequate developmental experiences in a child's early years.

If you suspect a speech or language disorder, you should keep cultural diversity in mind. English is not the primary language for many students, and the difficulties these students encounter in learning both content and a second language should not be confused with communication disorders. English language learners will respond to an enriched language environment combined with teacher patience and understanding. Students with communication disorders require the help of a speech and language specialist.

Helping Students with Communication Disorders

Primary tasks for teachers working with students who have communication disorders include identification, acceptance, and follow-through during classroom instruction. As with other exceptionalities, teachers play an important role in identification because they are in most direct contact with students.

It isn't easy being a student who cannot communicate fluently. Modeling and encouraging acceptance are essential because teasing and social rejection can cause lasting emotional damage. In interacting with these students, a teacher should be patient and refrain from correcting their speech, which calls attention to the problem. Also, cooperative and small-

table 5.6 Kinds of Speech Disorders

Disorder	Description	Example
Articulation disorders	Difficulty in producing certain sounds, including substituting, distorting, and omitting	"Wabbit" for *rabbit* "Thit" for *sit* "Only" for *lonely*
Fluency disorders	Repetition of the first sound of a word (stuttering) and other problems in producing "smooth" speech	"Y, Y, Y, Yes"
Voice disorders	Problems with the larynx or air passageways in the nose or throat	High-pitched or nasal voice

group activities provide opportunities for students to practice language in informal and less-threatening settings.

Visual Disabilities

Approximately 20 percent of children and adults have some type of vision loss (Hardman et al., 2008). Fortunately, most problems can be corrected with glasses, surgery, or therapy. In some situations—approximately 1 child in 3,000—the impairment cannot be corrected (Batsashaw, 2003). People with this condition have a **visual disability**, an uncorrectable visual impairment that interferes with learning.

Visual disability. An uncorrectable visual impairment that interferes with learning.

Nearly two thirds of serious visual disabilities exist at birth, and most children are screened for visual problems when they enter elementary school (Hardman et al., 2008; Hunt & Marshall, 2002). Some vision problems appear during the school years as a result of growth spurts, however, and teachers should remain alert to the possibility of an undetected impairment in students. Some symptoms of these problems are outlined in Figure 5.5.

Adaptive materials, such as large-print screens and Braille, allow students with visual disabilities to work in regular classrooms.

Research on people with visual disabilities indicates that they differ from their nondisabled peers in areas ranging from understanding spatial concepts to general knowledge (Hardman et al., 2008). Word meanings may not be as rich or elaborate because of the students' lack of visual experience with the world. As a result, hands-on experiences are even more important for these students than they are for other learners.

Working with Students Who Have Visual Disabilities

Suggestions for working with students having visual disabilities include seating them near writing boards and overheads, verbalizing while writing on the board, and ensuring that duplicated handouts are dark and clear (Heward, 2009). Teachers can also supply large-print books and magnifying aids to adapt materials. Peer tutors can provide assistance in explaining and clarifying assignments and procedures.

Lowered self-esteem and learned helplessness are two possible side effects of a visual disability. Learned helplessness can result if teachers and other students overreact and do for the student what he or she, with training, can do alone. This can lead to an unhealthy dependence on others and can compound self-esteem problems (Hallahan & Kauffman, 2009).

Hearing Disabilities

Students with a hearing loss have problems perceiving sounds within the normal frequency range of human speech. The terms *deaf* and *hard of hearing* are generic terms for children with varying degrees of hearing loss and are often preferred by members of the deaf

Figure 5.5 Symptoms of potential visual problems

- Holding the head in an awkward position when reading, or holding the book too close or too far away
- Squinting and frequently rubbing the eyes
- Tuning out when information is presented on the callboard
- Constantly asking about classroom procedures, especially when information is on the board
- Complaining of headaches, dizziness, or nausea
- Having redness, crusting, or swelling of the eyes
- Losing place on the line or page and confusing letters
- Using poor spacing in writing or having difficulty in staying on the line

Source: Hallahan and Kauffman, 2006; Hardman et al., 2002.

Figure 5.6 Indicators of hearing impairment

- Favoring one ear by cocking the head toward the speaker or cupping a hand behind the ear
- Misunderstanding or not following directions, and exhibiting nonverbal cues (e.g., frowns or puzzled looks) when directions are given
- Being distracted or seeming disoriented at times
- Asking people to repeat what they have just said
- Poorly articulating words, especially consonants
- Turning the volume up loud when listening to audio recordings, radio, or television
- Showing reluctance to participate in oral activities
- Having frequent earaches or complaining of discomfort or buzzing in the ears

Source: Adapted from Tumbull et.al., 2004

Partial hearing impairment. An impairment that allows a student to use a hearing aid and to hear well enough to be taught through auditory channels.

Deaf. A hearing impairment that requires the use of other senses, usually sight, to communicate.

community (Shirin, 2007). Two major kinds of hearing disabilities exist. A **partial hearing impairment** allows a student to use a hearing aid and to hear well enough to be taught through auditory channels. For students who are **deaf**, hearing is impaired enough so that these students use other senses, usually sight, to communicate. About 1½ percent of students with exceptionalities have a hearing disability (U.S. Department of Education, 2008). Of the students with a hearing loss requiring special services, more than 60 percent receive instruction in general education classrooms for all or part of the school day, and the numbers of these students in general education classrooms have increased in recent years (Shirin, 2007).

Hearing disabilities may result from rubella (German measles) during pregnancy, heredity, complications during pregnancy or birth, meningitis, or other childhood diseases. In almost 40 percent of cases involving hearing loss, the cause is unknown; this makes prevention and remediation more difficult (Hardman et al., 2008; Heward, 2009).

Testing by a trained audiologist in a school screening program is the best method of identifying students with hearing problems, but not all schools have these programs, and problems can be overlooked if students miss the screening. When such an omission occurs, classroom teachers' sensitivity to possible hearing difficulties is essential. Some indicators of hearing impairment are outlined in Figure 5.6.

Working with Students Who Have Hearing Disabilities

Lack of proficiency in speech and in language are learning problems that can result from hearing disabilities. These problems affect learning that relies on reading, writing, and listening. Teachers should remember that these language deficits have little bearing on intelligence; learners can succeed if given appropriate help.

Effective programs for students with hearing disabilities combine general education classroom instruction with additional support. Programs for students who are deaf include lipreading, sign language, and finger spelling. Total communication, which uses the simultaneous presentation of manual approaches (signing and finger spelling) and speech (through lipreading and residual hearing), is increasing in popularity (Hardman et al., 2008).

Instructional adaptations include the following:

- Supplement auditory presentations with visual information and hands-on experiences.
- Speak clearly, and orient yourself so students can see your face.
- Minimize distracting noise.
- Frequently check for understanding. (Peterson, 2002)

It is also helpful to have nondisabled peers serve as tutors and work in cooperative groups with students who have hearing disabilities. Teaching nondisabled students elements of American Sign Language and fingerspelling provides an added dimension to their education.

check your understanding

3.1 Describe the most common learning problems that classroom teachers are likely to encounter.
3.2 Identify at least one similarity and one difference between learning disabilities and intellectual disability.
3.3 Describe the two major types of behavior disorders, and explain how they influence classroom behavior.
3.4 What are communication disorders, and how do they affect classroom performance?

To receive feedback for these questions, go to Appendix A.

Students Who Are Gifted and Talented

Although we don't typically think of students who are gifted and talented as having an exceptionality, they frequently cannot reach their full potential in general education classrooms. As you saw at the beginning of the chapter, these students are at the upper end of the ability continuum. At one time, *gifted* was the only term educators used, but now the enlarged category includes students who do well on IQ tests (typically 130 and above) and those who demonstrate talents in a range of areas, such as math, creative writing, and music (G. Davis & Rimm, 2004).

Characteristics of Students Who Are Gifted and Talented

Characteristics of students who are gifted and talented include the following:

- Ability to learn more quickly and independently than their peers
- Advanced language, reading, and vocabulary skills
- More highly developed learning and metacognitive strategies
- Higher motivation on challenging tasks and less on easy ones
- High personal standards of achievement

The challenge for teachers is to provide learning experiences rich enough to help these children develop.

The history of gifted and talented education in the United States began with a longitudinal study conducted by Louis Terman and his colleagues (Holahan & Sears, 1995; Terman, Baldwin, & Bronson, 1925; Terman & Oden, 1947, 1959). Using teacher recommendations and IQ scores, Terman identified 1,500 gifted individuals to be tracked over a lifetime (the study is projected to run until 2010). The researchers found that, in addition to being high academic achievers, these students were better adjusted as children and adults, had more hobbies, read more books, and were healthier than their peers. This study, combined with more current research, has done much to dispel the stereotype of gifted students as maladjusted and narrow "brains" (Steiner & Carr, 2003).

The current definition used by the federal government describes gifted and talented students as

> Children and youth with outstanding talent who perform or show the potential for performing at remarkably high levels of accomplishment when compared with others of their age, experience, or environment.
>
> These children and youth exhibit high performance capability in intellectual, creative, and/or artistic areas, possess an unusual leadership capacity, or excel in specific academic fields. They require services or activities not ordinarily provided by the schools.

> Outstanding talents are present in children and youth from all cultural groups, across all economic strata, and in all areas of human endeavor. (National Excellence, 1993, pp. 54–57)

Many state departments of education have incorporated components of the National Excellence description into their definitions of giftedness and talent (Stephens & Karnes, 2000).

Another popular definition uses three criteria (Renzulli & Reis, 2003):

1. Above-average ability
2. High levels of motivation and task commitment
3. High levels of creativity

Enrichment activities provide opportunities for gifted students to explore alternative areas of the curriculum.

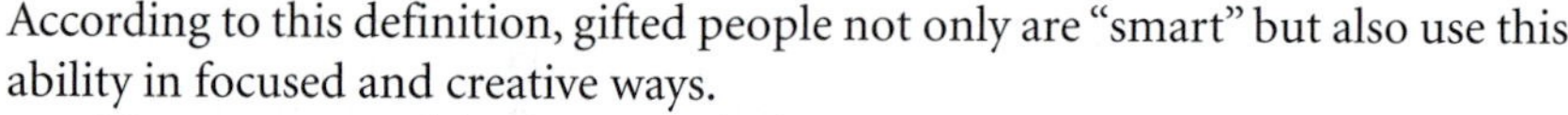

According to this definition, gifted people not only are "smart" but also use this ability in focused and creative ways.

More recent work in the area of gifted education has shifted away from the concept of giftedness as a general characteristic and toward talents in specific areas (Colangelo & Davis, 2003; G. Davis & Rimm, 2004).

Identifying Students Who Are Gifted and Talented

Meeting the needs of students who are gifted and talented requires early identification and instructional modifications. Failure to do so can result in gifted underachievers with social and emotional problems linked to boredom and lack of motivation (G. Davis & Rimm, 2004). Conventional procedures often miss students who are gifted and talented because they rely heavily on standardized test scores and teacher nominations, and females and students from cultural minorities are typically underrepresented in these programs (Castellano &

theory to practice

Teaching Students Who Are Gifted and Talented

If you have students who are gifted and talented in your classes, and they're pulled out for part of the day, you'll be expected to provide enrichment activities during the time they're with you. The following guidelines can assist you as you attempt to adapt instruction to meet these students' needs:

1. Assess frequently to identify areas where students have already mastered essential content.
2. Provide alternative activities to challenge students' abilities and interests.
3. Use technology to provide challenge.

Let's see how the guidelines assist Jared Taylor, a sixth-grade teacher, as he works with his students.

Jared has three students—Darren, Sylvia, and Gabriella—who have been identified as gifted and talented, and who meet with a teacher of the gifted twice a week in a pullout program. Jared's task is to provide a motivating menu for them while they are in his class.

To accomplish the task, Jared pretests his students before beginning a new unit, and he also closely monitors Darren's, Sylvia's, and Gabriella's homework. When he sees that they have mastered the content, he provides enrichment by first offering alternative learning activities. For instance, in a unit on plants in science, Jared arranges with the librarian to provide resources for a project, and he meets with the students to help them design its goals and scope.

Jared also creates a series of learning centers that are available to all the students. The centers focus on weather, geometry, music, and art, and students can go to them when they have free time. Each center has reading materials and projects that can be completed. When Darren, Sylvia, and Gabriella demonstrate that they have mastered the content the other students are studying, he substitutes projects from the centers for them.

Finally, Jared supplements his curriculum with technology. He works with the district's media coordinator to locate software programs and Websites that provide enrichment and acceleration.

Jared attempted to apply the guidelines by first gathering as much information as he could to assess each student's understanding of the topics he was teaching. When he found they had mastered a topic, he substituted enrichment activities (guideline 2). Acceleration has benefits, but it is difficult to implement in the general education curriculum. Jared's approach was manageable; it didn't require an inordinate amount of extra work, and it also provided enriching experiences for the students. Finally, he applied the third guideline by providing challenge through technology and by working with the district's media coordinator to supply his students with relevant materials.

exploring diversity

Pursuing Equity in Special Education

A paradox exists in special education. The very system that was created to provide fair and humane treatment for all students has resulted in one in which culturally and linguistically diverse students are both over- and underrepresented in programs for learners with exceptionalities (Harry & Klingner, 2007). For example, African American students make up less than 15 percent of the school population but account for 20 percent of students diagnosed with exceptionalities (Blanchett, 2006). In addition, minority students, especially African American and Hispanic, have been underrepresented in gifted and talented programs (Hardman et al., 2008; Heward, 2009).

These are not recent trends. As far back as 1979, the U.S. Congress recognized these disparities and asked researchers to look for possible reasons (Turnbull et al., 2007). The reasons are complex and range from problems in the students' home and neighborhood environments to factors within schools themselves (McDermott, Goldman, & Varenne, 2006; O'Connor & Fernandez, 2006). For example, poverty results in poorer prenatal care, nutrition, and health care, all of which can influence both intelligence and school performance. "Specifically, the mother's level of education (under 12 years of schooling), the mother's marital status (unmarried), prenatal care after the first three months of pregnancy (low attention to care), and the child's low birth weight (unacceptably low) all correlate with special education placement into specific learning disability programs" (Turnbull et al., 2007, p. 116). In addition, poverty can result in neighborhoods that are less nurturant, with limited access to early educational resources.

The children of poverty also attend poorer quality schools. For instance, classes in high-poverty schools are nearly 80 percent more likely to have an out-of-field teacher than those in more advantaged areas.

Critics also point to the special education placement process itself (McDermott et al., 2006; O'Connor & Fernandez, 2006). Critics ask, Are classrooms culturally responsive, and do they build on students' existing knowledge? Is the instruction sensitive to the strengths that students from diverse backgrounds possess?

The identification and placement process also depends heavily on culture and language. Tests used to identify students with exceptionalities are culturally based and depend on facility with English (Rogoff, 2003).

As a classroom teacher, you can do your part to address these issues. For example, the culturally responsive instruction that we discussed in Chapter 4 can help you build on your students' strengths and better meet the needs of students with diverse backgrounds. When learning problems exist, you will then be sure that you have done everything possible before referring students for special services. If you conclude that special services are necessary, you will be able to provide the most accurate information available for helping meet these students' needs.

Diaz, 2002; Kritt, 2004). To resolve this issue, experts recommend more flexible and less culturally dependent methods, such as creativity measures (we examine creativity in Chapter 9), tests of spatial ability, and peer and parent nominations in addition to teacher recommendations (G. Davis & Rimm, 2004; Shea, Lubinski, & Benbow, 2001).

Teachers play an essential role in identifying learners who are gifted and talented because they work with these students every day and can identify strengths that tests may miss. However, research indicates that teachers often confuse conformity, neatness, and good behavior with being gifted or talented (Colangelo & Davis, 2003).

Programs for the Gifted and Talented

Programs for students who are gifted and talented are usually based on either **acceleration**, which keeps the curriculum the same but allows students to move through it more quickly, or **enrichment**, which provides alternate instruction (Schiever & Maker, 2003). Educators disagree over which approach is better. Critics of enrichment charge that it often involves busywork and point to research suggesting that students benefit from acceleration (Feldhusen, 1998a, 1998b). Critics of acceleration counter that comparisons are unfair because the outcomes of enrichment, such as creativity and problem solving, are not easily measured. They further argue that the general education curriculum is narrow, and social development can be impaired when younger students who want accelerated content must take classes with older students. The question remains unanswered, and the debate is likely to continue.

Acceleration. Programs for students who are gifted and talented that keep the curriculum the same but allow students to move through it more quickly.

Enrichment. Programs for students who are gifted and talented that provide alternate instruction.

Programs for students who are gifted and talented are typically organized in either self-contained classes or pullout programs that occupy a portion of the school day. Self-contained classes usually include both acceleration and enrichment; pullout programs focus primarily on enrichment.

check your understanding

4.1 Identify the characteristics of students who are gifted and talented, and explain how the definition of students who are gifted and talented has changed over time.
4.2 Describe methods for identifying students who are gifted and talented. What are some advantages and disadvantages of these methods?
4.3 Describe the two most common methods for teaching students who are gifted and talented. Explain the relative advantages and disadvantages of these methods.

To receive feedback for these questions, go to Appendix A.

The Teacher's Role in Inclusive Classrooms

General education classroom teachers have three important responsibilities in working with students who have exceptionalities:

1. Assist in identifying students who may need additional help.
2. Modify instruction to best meet individuals' needs.
3. Promote social integration and student growth by encouraging acceptance of all students in the class.

In each area, general education classroom teachers are supposed to have assistance from special educators.

Collaborative Consultation: Help for the Classroom Teacher

Initially, educators viewed inclusion as additive; students with exceptionalities received additional services to help them function in general education school settings (Turnbull et al., 2007). Gradually, the concept of coordination replaced addition. Today, the intent is for special and general educators to collaborate in an attempt to ensure that experiences for students with exceptionalities are integrated.

Collaboration is essential for effective inclusion (Karten, 2005; T. Smith et al., 2004). In working with the general education classroom teacher, special educators have the following responsibilities:

- Assist in collecting assessment information.
- Maintain students' records.
- Develop special curriculum materials.
- Coordinate the efforts of team members in implementing individualized education programs.
- Work with parents.
- Assist in adapting instruction.

The special educators' most important responsibilities are perhaps to help the classroom teacher identify students needing special help and to adapt instruction, because these most directly influence academic success.

Identifying Students with Exceptionalities

Current approaches to identification are team based, and because general education classroom teachers continually work with students, they are key members of the team. Before referring a student for a special education evaluation, teachers must document the problem and the strategies they've used in attempting to solve it (Hallahan & Kauffman, 2009). Teachers in the general education classroom should describe the following:

- The nature of the problem and how it affects classroom performance
- Dates, places, and times problems have occurred
- Strategies they have tried
- Assessment of the strategies' effectiveness

Assessment is an essential part of the identification process.

Teachers use assessment to gather essential information to identify students with exceptionalities.

Curriculum-Based Assessment

In the past, special educators relied heavily on standardized intelligence tests, but as you saw earlier in the chapter, the protection against discrimination in testing provision of IDEA prevents decisions based on an intelligence test alone.

Teachers are increasingly using **curriculum-based assessments**, which measure learners' performance in specific areas of the curriculum and attempt to link assessments more closely to learning objectives (Vaughn et al., 2006). The learning objectives provide both an assessment target and a baseline against which educators gauge learning progress. The result is an identification/assessment system that connects curriculum objectives to instruction and accountability measures.

Curriculum-based assessment. Measurement of learners' performance in specific areas of the curriculum.

Adaptive Behavior

In addition to curriculum-based assessment, educators attempt to assess students' *adaptive behavior*, their ability to perform the functions of everyday living (Hardman et al., 2008). Teachers observe students to assess their abilities to perform everyday school tasks, such as initiating and completing assignments, controlling their behavior, and interacting effectively with other students (Hardman et al., 2008).

If teachers' observations indicate that a problem exists with a student's adaptive behavior, a number of instruments exist that can more systematically assess the ability to adapt (Heward, 2009). For example, the American Association on Intellectual and Developmental Disabilities Adaptive Behavior Scale—Schools contains 104 items with several questions per item (Pierangelo & Giuliani, 2006). This instrument assesses areas such as students' abilities to comprehend oral and written directions, express themselves, persist on tasks, and make friends.

Referral for Special Services

If teachers cannot solve a student's learning problem by adapting instruction, they can then initiate a referral. When considering a referral, they should check with an administrator or school psychologist to identify the school's policies.

When the data suggest that a student needs additional help, a prereferral team is formed. The team usually consists of a school psychologist, a special educator, and the classroom teacher. The team further evaluates the problem, consults with parents, and prepares the IEP.

Parents play an integral role in the process. IDEA requires parents' involvement; they can provide valuable information about the student's educational and medical history, and notifying parents is a professional courtesy, even if it weren't required by law.

MyEducationLab

To examine exceptionalities in a first-grade class, go to the *Activities and Applications* section in Chapter 5 of MyEducationLab at www.myeducationlab.com and read the case study *Analyzing Exceptionalities in a First-Grade Class.* Answer the questions following the case study.

Modifying Instruction to Meet Students' Needs

Research indicates that instruction that is effective with students in general is also effective with students having exceptionalities (Tomlinson, 2006; Vaughn et al., 2006). "In general, the classroom management and instruction approaches that are effective with special students tend to be the same ones that are effective with other students" (Good & Brophy, 2008, p. 223). (We examine effective instruction in detail in Chapter 13.)

You will need to provide additional support, however, to help students overcome a history of failure and frustration and to convince them that renewed effort will work. For instance, while the majority of the class is completing a seat-work assignment, effective teachers work with an individual student or small group. (You will find an example in Mike Sheppard's work with his students in the closing case study for this chapter, on page 158.)

Educators have also effectively used peer tutoring. Peer tutoring can benefit both the tutor and the person receiving the tutoring, and home-based tutoring programs that involve parents can also be effective (Vaughn et al., 2006).

Some additional adaptations include the following (Turnbull et al., 2007):

- Carefully model solutions to problems and other assignments.
- Teach in small steps, and provide detailed feedback on homework.
- Call on students with exceptionalities as equally as possible compared to other students in your classes.
- Provide outlines, hierarchies, charts, and other forms of organization for the content you're teaching.
- Increase the amount of time available for tests and quizzes.
- Use available technology.
- Teach learning strategies.

The last item deserves further elaboration. Strategy training is one of the most promising approaches that has been developed for helping students with learning problems. A *learning strategy* is a plan that students use to accomplish a learning objective. (We examine strategic learning in detail in Chapter 9.) For example, in applying a strategy to understand the content of a chapter, one middle school student with a learning disability in reading first looked at the chapter outline to see how the chapter was organized, and he referred back to the outline as he read the chapter. He then read the chapter to himself aloud, and stopped every few paragraphs and summarized to himself what he had just read. When he could not summarize the information, he reread the section.

Students with learning difficulties often approach tasks passively or use the same strategy for all objectives (Vaughn et al., 2006). In contrast, because he was attempting to comprehend the content of the chapter, this student used a strategy that differed from one he might use for learning to spell a list of words. Students with learning problems can use strategies, but need to be taught the strategies explicitly (Carnine et al., 2006). Teacher modeling and explanation, together with opportunities for practice and feedback, are essential.

Promote Social Integration and Student Growth

Promoting the social integration and growth of students with exceptionalities is the general education classroom teacher's third important role. Students with exceptionalities may be labeled as different, and they frequently fall behind in their academic work, often misbehave, and sometimes lack social skills (Hallahan & Kauffman, 2009). Other students develop negative attitudes toward them, and these attitudes adversely affect confidence and self-esteem. You need to make special efforts to promote the acceptance of these students in your classroom (Cook, 2004; Kliewer, et al., 2004). These efforts include developing classmates' understanding and acceptance of them, helping students with exceptionalities learn acceptable behaviors, and using strategies to promote social interaction among students (Plata, Trusty, & Glasgow, 2005).

Creative teachers design learning activities that allow students of differing abilities to interact and learn about one another.

Developing Classmates' Understanding and Acceptance

Students' negative attitudes toward their peers with exceptionalities often result from a lack of understanding (Plata et al., 2005). Open discussion and information about disabilities can help change these attitudes (Heward, 2009). Emphasizing that people with disabilities want to have friends, and want to succeed and be happy, just as everyone else does, can do much to change attitudes. These discussions can reduce stereotypes about learners with exceptionalities and break down the barriers between them and other students. Literature and videos that explore the struggles and triumphs of people with disabilities, and guests that have overcome disabilities, are also valuable sources of information.

theory to practice

Teaching Students with Exceptionalities

Almost certainly, some of your students will have exceptionalities, and you will be expected to help them reach their full potential.

Earlier in the chapter, you saw that the effective teaching strategies that work with all students also work with students having exceptionalities (Good & Brophy, 2008). For example, look at the guidelines in the "Theory to Practice" feature on page 116 of Chapter 4, and see how Diane Smith applied the guidelines in working with students having diverse backgrounds. These same guidelines apply in working with students having exceptionalities. Two additional factors are important, however. First, learners with exceptionalities will likely need additional help to keep up with their classmates, and second, they need extra support to develop effective learning strategies. The case study at the end of the chapter involving Mike Sheppard's work with his students provides a concrete example of the additional support students with exceptionalities need in order to succeed.

Having learners with exceptionalities in your classroom will increase the complexity of your work. However, helping a student with a disability adapt and even thrive can be one of the most rewarding experiences you will have as a teacher.

Helping Students Learn Acceptable Behaviors

Students with exceptionalities can help themselves by learning what constitutes acceptable behavior. Counseling and applied behavior analysis are two strategies that can help students improve their behavior (Elbaum & Vaughn, 2001). The case study at the end of the chapter includes an example of applied behavior analysis. (We also discuss applied behavior analysis in Chapter 6.)

Students with disabilities often lack the skills needed to make friends (Turnbull et al., 2007); they may avoid other students or alienate them unknowingly. Modeling and coaching can be particularly helpful for teaching social skills. To teach a student how to initiate play, for example, a teacher might say, "Barnell's over there on the playground. I think I'll say, 'Hi, Barnell! Want to play ball with me?' Now you try it, and I'll watch."

Teachers can also model social problem solving; for instance, a teacher might comment, "Mary has a toy that I want to play with. What could I do to make her want to share that toy?" Direct approaches such as these have been successful in teaching social skills such as empathy, perspective taking, negotiation, and assertiveness (Vaughn et al., 2006).

MyEducationLab

To examine ways to use peer tutoring to help students with exceptionalities, go to the *Activities and Applications* section in Chapter 5 of MyEducationLab at www.myeducationlab.com, and watch the episode *Using Peer Tutoring with Students Having Exceptionalities.* Answer the questions following the episode.

Strategies for Promoting Interaction and Cooperation

One of the most effective ways to promote acceptance of students with exceptionalities is to include them in learning activities by calling on them as often as possible. This communicates that all students are valued and are expected to participate and succeed.

Cooperative learning and peer tutoring can also be used to promote interaction among students (Mastropieri, Scruggs, & Berkeley, 2007). (We discuss cooperative learning strategies in Chapter 13.) Peer tutoring typically places students in pairs and provides them with learning activities, opportunities for practice, and feedback. For example, after introducing a new concept in math, the teacher assigns pairs to work on practice exercises, and students take turns tutoring and being tutored. Cross-age tutoring, in which older students with exceptionalities tutor younger ones, is especially promising.

check your understanding

5.1 Describe the roles that general education classroom teachers are expected to fulfill in inclusive classrooms.

5.2 What does research indicate about teaching strategies that are effective for learners with exceptionalities? What implications do these strategies have for you as a classroom teacher?

5.3 Describe at least three ways that you can promote the social integration and growth of students with exceptionalities in your classroom.

To receive feedback for these questions, go to Appendix A.

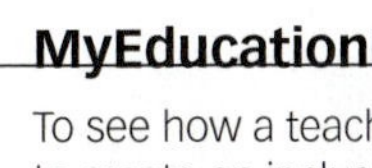

MyEducationLab

To see how a teacher attempts to create an inclusive classroom go to the *Building Teaching Skills and Dispositions* section in Chapter 5 of MyEducationLab at www.myeducationlab.com and read the case study *Creating an Inclusive Classroom.* Complete the exercises following the case study to develop your skills in creating an inclusive setting with your students.

classroom connections

Teaching Students with Exceptionalities in the General Education Classroom

1. Effective teachers adapt instruction to meet the needs and capabilities of students with exceptionalities. Provide additional instructional scaffolding to ensure success on instructional tasks.
   - **Elementary:** A third-grade teacher carefully monitors students during seat work. She often gathers students with exceptionalities in a small group to provide additional assistance at the beginning of assignments.
   - **Middle School:** A sixth-grade math teacher organizes his students in groups of four for seat-work assignments. Each student completes a problem and confers with a partner. When two students disagree, they confer with the other pair in their group. The teacher carefully monitors the groups to be sure that all four are participating and contributing.
   - **High School:** A science teacher assesses frequently and provides detailed feedback on all assessment items. She spends time in one-on-one conferences with any students having difficulty.
2. A major obstacle to social integration and growth is other students' lack of understanding. Discuss the subject of exceptionalities in an open and positive manner.
   - **Elementary:** A second-grade teacher uses role playing and modeling to illustrate problems such as teasing and taunting others. She emphasizes treating students who look or act differently with the same respect that other students receive.
   - **Middle School:** An English teacher uses literature, such as *Summer of the Swans*, by Betsy Byars (2005), as a springboard for talking about individual differences. He encourages students to reflect on their own individuality and how important this is to them.
   - **High School:** An English teacher leads a discussion of students' favorite foods, activities, movies, and music, and also discusses topics and issues that concern them. He uses the discussions as a springboard for helping create a sense of community in the classroom.
3. Students with exceptionalities often pursue learning tasks passively. Use modeling and coaching to teach effective learning strategies.
   - **Elementary:** A fourth-grade math teacher emphasizes questions such as the following in checking answers to word problems: Does the solution answer the problem? Does it make sense? Are the units correct? He reinforces this process throughout the school year.
   - **Middle School:** A math teacher teaches problem-solving strategies by thinking aloud at the chalkboard while she's working through a problem. She breaks word problems into the following steps and place these on a poster at the front of the room: (a) *Read*: What is the question? (b) *Reread*: What information do I need? (c) *Stop and think*: What do I need to do—add, subtract, multiply, or divide? (d) *Compute*: Put the correct numbers in and solve. (e) *Label and check*: What answer did I get? Does it make sense?
   - **High School:** An English teacher teaches and models step-by-step strategies. A unit on writing one-paragraph essays teaches students to use four steps: (a) Write a topic sentence, (b) write three sentences that support the topic sentence, (c) write a summary sentence, and (d) reread and edit the paragraph. The teacher models the strategy and provides positive and negative examples before asking the students to write their own.

Teaching Students Who Are Gifted and Talented in Your Classroom

4. Students who are gifted and talented need challenging learning activities to motivate them. Provide supplementary enrichment activities to challenge students who are gifted and talented.
   - **Elementary:** A fifth-grade teacher allows students who are gifted and talented to substitute projects of their choice for homework assignments once they have demonstrated that they have mastered the general education curriculum.
   - **Middle School:** A pre-algebra teacher pretests students at the beginning of each unit. Whenever a student has mastered the concepts and skills, he or she receives an honor pass to work on an alternative activity in the school media center. The activities may be extensions or applications of the concepts taught in the unit, or they may involve learning about mathematical principles or math history not usually taught in the general education curriculum.
   - **High School:** A social studies teacher caps off every unit with a hypothetical problem, such as "What would the United States be like today if Great Britain had won the Revolutionary War?" Students work in groups to address the question, and the teacher gives extra credit to those who want to pursue the topic further in a paper or project.

developmentally appropriate practice

Students with Exceptionalities at Different Ages

Development plays an important role in understanding and dealing with student exceptionalities. As you'll see in this discussion, effective practices for students with exceptionalities are influenced by the age and developmental characteristics of students.

Working with Elementary Students

Early childhood and lower elementary teachers are in a unique position to help identify learning problems. Pretesting of all students at the beginning of the school year not only provides a baseline for future growth, but can also identify potential learning problems (Reutzel & Cooter, 2008; Vaughn et al., 2006). If pretesting data cause teachers to expect learning problems, detailed records that identify the nature of the problem and records of intervention attempts can provide special educators with the tools they need to create effective interventions.

Sensitivity to the possibility of developmental lags is particularly important with young children. Research on learner development indicates that considerable variation exists in students' rates of development (Lerner, 2006).

Similarly, being aware of the role of culture and language in early school success is important. Many students grow up in homes where English isn't the first language and where newspapers, magazines, and books are not readily available. Being sure that problems cannot be traced to cultural or language differences is important before referring a child for special services.

Working with Middle School Students

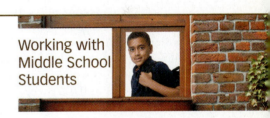

Working with Middle School Students

The middle school years present challenges to all students. These challenges take the form of physical and emotional changes, as well as the move from self-contained elementary classrooms to the less personal environments in middle schools.

Adaptive behaviors, such as keeping track of assignments and taking notes, present special challenges for students with exceptionalities (Vaughn et al., 2006). Efforts to help these students acquire learning strategies can be particularly effective.

Peers become increasingly important to middle school students. Helping students with exceptionalities learn acceptable behaviors, together with strategies for promoting interaction and cooperation, are essential. Cooperative learning and peer tutoring can be effective, but students with exceptionalities need extra support to function effectively in these settings.

Working with High School Students

High school—with large schools, less personal attention, and switching classes—can be particularly challenging for students with exceptionalities (Kincheloe, 2004; Schutz, 2004). Peer acceptance continues to be a priority for all high school students.

Making a special effort to help students with exceptionalities—who are sometimes painfully aware of their differences—feel welcome in their classrooms is very important for high school students. Teachers set the tone by modeling courtesy and respect and requiring students to treat each other the same way. Cooperative learning and small-group work provide opportunities for students with exceptionalities to interact socially and learn from their peers.

With respect to acquiring a deep understanding of the topics they're studying, helping learners with exceptionalities acquire effective learning strategies is even more effective with high school students than with younger learners.

Meeting Your Learning Objectives

1. Describe differences in the way intelligence is viewed, and explain how ability grouping can influence learning.
   - Intelligence is often defined as the ability to acquire and use knowledge, solve problems and reason in the abstract, and adapt to new situations in the environment.
   - Some theories suggest that intelligence is a single entity; others describe intelligence as existing in several dimensions.
   - Some experts believe that intelligence is largely genetically determined; others believe it is strongly influenced by experiences. Most suggest that it is determined by a combination of the two.
   - Ability grouping can influence learning through the quality of instruction that learners are provided and the expectations teachers have for students.
2. Describe the major provisions of the Individuals With Disabilities Education Act (IDEA) and the amendments to it.
   - The major provisions of the Individuals with Disabilities Education Act require instruction of students with exceptionalities in the least restrictive environment, parent involvement, protection of learners against discrimination in testing, and individualized education programs (IEPs) for each student with exceptionalities.
   - Amendments to IDEA make states responsible for locating children who need special services and have strengthened requirements for nondiscriminatory assessment, due process, parental involvement in IEPs, and the confidentiality of student records.
3. Describe the most common learning problems that classroom teachers are likely to encounter.
   - The most common learning problems that classroom teachers are likely to encounter include learning disabilities, difficulties in reading, writing, reasoning, or mathematical abilities; attention deficit/hyperactivity disorder (ADHD), an inability to concentrate on learning tasks; intellectual disability, limitations in both intellectual functioning and adaptive behavior; and behavior disorders, serious and persistent age-inappropriate behaviors.
   - Teachers may also encounter autism spectrum disorders, disabilities that affect communication and social interaction; communication disorders, exceptionalities that interfere with students' abilities to understand information and express their own ideas; as well as visual and hearing disabilities.
4. Identify characteristics of learners who are gifted and talented, and describe methods for identifying and teaching these students.
   - Students who are gifted and talented learn quickly and independently, possess advanced language and metacognitive skills, and are often highly motivated and set high personal standards for achievement.
   - Methods of identifying students who are gifted and talented include intelligence testing and teacher, parent, and peer reports of unique talents and abilities.
   - The two most common methods of teaching students who are gifted and talented include acceleration, which moves students through the general education curriculum at a faster rate, and enrichment, which provides alternative instruction to encourage student exploration.
5. Describe general education classroom teachers' roles in inclusive classrooms, and identify teaching strategies that are effective for working with students having exceptionalities.
   - Teachers' roles in inclusive classrooms include identifying learners with exceptionalities, adapting instruction to meet their needs, and promoting their social integration and growth.
   - Effective instruction for students with exceptionalities is similar to effective instruction in general. Providing additional scaffolding and helping students acquire learning strategies are also helpful.

Developing as a Professional: Preparing for Your Licensure Exam

You've examined characteristics of students with exceptionalities, and you've seen that all students can learn if instruction is adapted to meet their needs.

Let's look now at a junior high math teacher and his efforts to work with students who have exceptionalities. Read the case study, and answer the questions that follow.

> Mike Sheppard teaches math at Landrom Middle School. He has introduced his pre-algebra class to a procedure for solving word problems and assigned five problems for homework.
>
> Mike has 28 students in his second-period class, including five with exceptionalities: Herchel, Marcus, and Gwenn, who have learning problems, and Todd and Horace, who have difficulty monitoring their own behavior. Herchel, Marcus, and Gwenn each have problems with decoding words, reading comprehension, and writing.

Other teachers describe Todd as verbally abusive, aggressive, and lacking in self-discipline. He is extremely active and has a difficult time sitting through a class period. Horace is just the opposite: a very shy, withdrawn boy.

Herchel, Marcus, and Gwenn are among the first of Mike's students to file into class. As the students enter, they look at the screen in the front of the room, where one or two problems are displayed on the overhead for students to complete while Mike takes roll and finishes other beginning-of-class routines.

Mike watches as Herchel, Marcus, and Gwenn take their seats, and then he slowly reads the displayed problem:

On Saturday the Harris family drove 17 miles from Henderson to Newton, stopped for 10 minutes to get gas, and then drove 22.5 miles from Newton through Council Rock to Gildford. The trip took 1 hour and 5 minutes, including the stop. On the way back, they took the same route but stopped in Council Rock for lunch. Council Rock is 9.5 miles from Gildford. How much farther will they have to drive to get back to Henderson?

As Mike reads, he points to each displayed word. "Okay," he smiles after he finishes reading. "Do you know what the problem is asking you?"

"Could you read the last part again, Mr. Sheppard?" Gwenn asks.

"Sure," Mike nods and repeats the part of the problem that describes the return trip, again pointing to the words as he reads.

"All right, jump on it. Be ready, because I'm calling on one of you first today," he directs with another smile.

The students are in their seats, and most are studying the screen as the bell rings. Mike quickly takes roll and then walks to Todd's desk.

"Let's take a look at your chart," he says. "You've improved a lot, haven't you?"

"Yeah, look," Todd responds, proudly displaying the following chart.

	2/9–2/13	2/16–2/20	2/23–2/27
Talking out	卌 卌 卌 卌	卌 IIII 卌	卌 II
Swearing	卌 卌	卌 II	IIII
Hitting/ touching	卌 III	卌 IIII	III
Out of seat	卌 卌 卌 III	卌 卌 卌 IIII	卌 卌 卌 III
Being friendly	II	IIII	卌 II

"That's terrific," Mike whispers as he leans over the boy's desk. "You're doing much better. We need some more work on 'out-of-seat,' don't we? I don't like getting after you about it, and I know you don't like it either. . . . Stop by at the end of class. I have an idea that I think will help. Don't forget to stop. . . . Okay. Get to work on the problem." Mike gives Todd a light thump on the back and returns to the front of the room.

"Okay, everyone. How did you do on the problem?"

Amid a mix of "Okay," "Terrible," "Fine," "Too hard," some nods, and a few nonresponses, Mike begins, "Let's review for a minute. . . . What's the first thing we do whenever we have a word problem like this?"

He looks knowingly at Marcus, remembering the pledge to call on one of the five students first today. "Marcus?"

"Read it over at least twice," Marcus replies.

"Good. . . . That's what our problem-solving plan says," Mike continues, pointing to the following chart hanging on the chalkboard:

PLAN FOR SOLVING WORD PROBLEMS

1. Read the problem at least twice.
2. Ask the following questions:
   What is asked for?
   What facts are given?
   What information is needed that we don't have?
   Are unnecessary facts given? What are they?
3. Make a drawing.
4. Solve the problem.
5. Check to see whether the answer makes sense.

"Then what do we do? . . . Melissa?"

"See what the problem asks for."

"Good. What is the problem asking for? . . . Rachel?"

" . . . How much farther they'll have to drive?"

"Excellent. Now, think about this. Suppose I solved the problem and decided that they had 39½ miles left to drive. Would that make sense? Why or why not? Everybody think about it for a moment."

"Okay. What do you think? . . . Herchel?" Mike asks after a moment.

". . . I . . . I . . . don't know."

"Let's look," Mike encourages. "How far from Henderson to Gildford altogether?"

"Thir—," Rico begins until Mike puts his hand up, stopping him in mid-word. He then waits a few seconds as Herchel studies a sketch he has made on his paper:

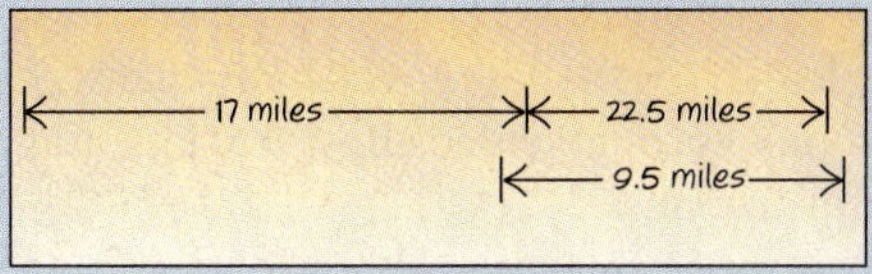

" . . . 39½," Herchel says uncertainly. "Oh! . . . The whole trip was only that far, so they couldn't still have that far to go."

"Excellent thinking, Herchel. See, you could figure it out.

"Now go ahead, Rico. How far do they still have to go?"

"Thirty miles," Rico, one of the higher achievers in the class, responds quickly.

"Okay. Not too bad for the first time through," he continues cheerfully. "Now, let's take a look at your homework."

Mike reviews each homework problem just as he did the first one, asking students to relate the parts to the steps in the problem-solving plan, drawing a sketch on the chalkboard, and calling on a variety of students to supply specific answers and describe their thinking.

With 20 minutes left in the period, he assigns five more problems for homework, and the students begin working. Once the class is working quietly, Mike gestures to Herchel, Marcus, and Gwenn to join him at a table at the back of the room.

"How'd you do on the homework?" Mike asks. "Do you think you get it?"

"Sort of," Gwenn responds, and the other two nod.

"Good," Mike smiles. "Now, let's see what we've got."

When about 5 minutes are left in the period, Mike tells the three students, "Run back to your desks now, and see whether you can get one or two problems done before the bell rings."

The bell rings, and the students begin filing out of the room. Mike catches Todd's eye, Todd stops, and Mike leads him to a small area in the back of the room where a partition has been set up. The area is partially enclosed but facing the class.

"Here's what we'll do," Mike directs. "When you have the urge to get out of your seat, quietly get up and move back here for a few minutes. Stay as long as you want, but be sure you pay attention to what we're doing. When you think you're ready to move back to your seat, go ahead. All I'm asking is that you move back and forth quietly and not bother the class. . . . What do you think?"

Todd nods, and Mike puts a hand on his shoulder. "You're doing so well on everything else; this will help, I think. You're a good student. You hang in there. . . . Now, here's a pass into Mrs. Miller's class."

Short-Answer Questions

In answering these questions, use information from the chapter and link your responses to specific information in the case.

1. Describe specifically what Mike did to create a supportive academic climate for his students.
2. How did Mike attempt to ensure success in his teaching?
3. What did Mike do to alter instruction for his students with learning disabilities? How effective were these modifications?
4. What did Mike do to meet the needs of his students with behavior disorders? How effective were these interventions?

For feedback on these responses, go to Appendix B.

Now go to Chapter 5 of MyEducationLab, loacted at www.myeducationlab.com, where you can:

- Take a quiz to test your mastery of chapter objectives. Detailed feedback is provided to explain why your responses are correct or incorrect.
- Deepen your understanding of chapter concepts with *Review, Practice, and Enrichment* exercises.
- Complete *Activities and Applications* that will help you apply what you have learned in the chapter by analyzing real classrooms through video clips, artifacts, and case studies. Your instructor will provide you with feedback for the *Activities and Applications.*
- Develop your professional knowledge and decision making in *Building Teaching Skills and Dispositions* exercises. Structured feedback will be available to you, providing you with support as you practice each skill. Your instructor will provide you with feedback on the final task that accompanies the exercise.

Important Concepts

ability grouping (p. 130)
acceleration (p. 151)
adaptive behavior (p. 142)
adaptive fit (p. 134)
attention-deficit/hyperactivity disorder (ADHD) (p. 140)
autism spectrum disorder (p. 145)
behavior disorders (p. 143)
bipolar disorder (p. 145)
communication disorders (p. 146)
crystallized intelligence (p. 127)
curriculum-based assessment (p. 153)
deaf (p. 148)
disabilities (p. 126)
discrepancy model of identification (p. 140)
disorder (p. 137)
due process (p. 135)
enrichment (p. 151)
fluid intelligence (p. 127)
gifts and talents (p. 126)
handicap (p. 137)
inclusion (p. 134)
individualized education program (IEP) (p. 135)
intellectual disability (p. 142)
intelligence (p. 126)
Joplin plan (p. 131)
language disorders (receptive disorders) (p. 146)
learners with exceptionalities (p. 126)
learning disabilities (p. 138)
learning styles (p. 131)
least restrictive environment (LRE) (p. 134)
mainstreaming (p. 133)
nature view of intelligence (p. 130)
nurture view of intelligence (p. 130)
partial hearing impairment (p. 148)
people-first language (p. 138)
response to intervention model of identification (p. 140)
special education (p. 126)
speech disorders (expressive disorders) (p. 146)
tracking (p. 130)
visual disability (p. 147)

chapter

6

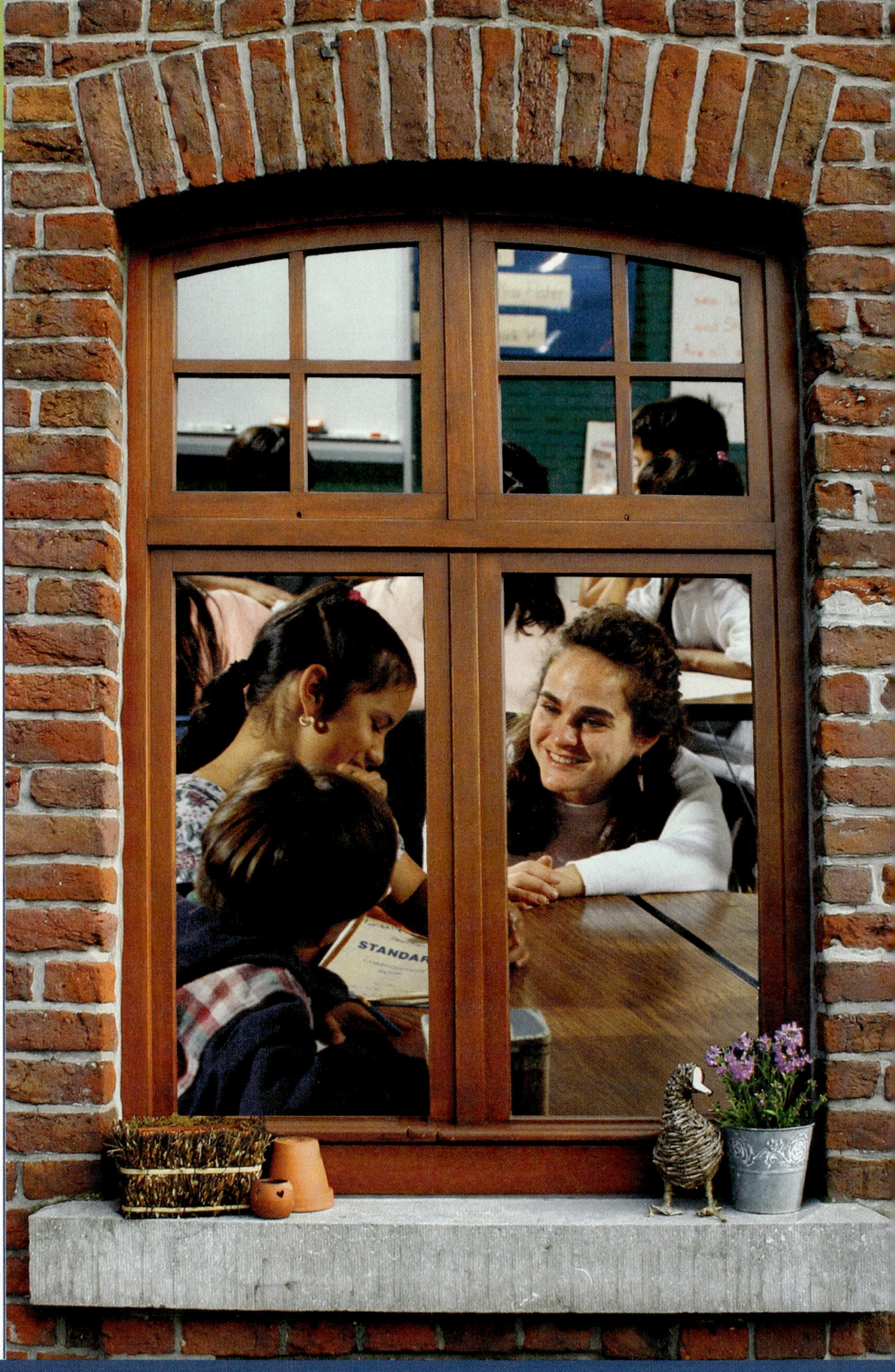

Behaviorism and Social Cognitive Theory

chapter outline

Behaviorist Views of Learning

- What Is Behaviorism?
- Classical Conditioning
- Operant Conditioning
- Applied Behavior Analysis
- Putting Behaviorism into Perspective
  - **Theory to Practice:** Using Behaviorism in Your Classroom

Social Cognitive Theory

- Comparing Behaviorism and Social Cognitive Theory
- Modeling
- Vicarious Learning
- Nonoccurrence of Expected Consequences
- The Effects of Modeling
- Processes Involved in Learning from Models
- Effectiveness of Models
- Self-Regulation
  - **Theory to Practice:** Applying Social Cognitive Theory in Your Classroom
- Putting Social Cognitive Theory into Perspective
  - **Developmentally Appropriate Practice:** Applying Behaviorism and Social Cognitive Theory with Different-Aged Learners
  - **Exploring Diversity:** Capitalizing on Behaviorism and Social Cognitive Theory with Learners from Diverse Backgrounds

learning objectives

After you have completed your study of this chapter, you should be able to:

1. Identify examples of classical conditioning in events in and outside of classrooms.
2. Identify examples of operant conditioning in classroom activities.
3. Use ideas from social cognitive theory to explain examples of people's behaviors. Include ideas such as the nonoccurrence of expected consequences, reciprocal causation, and vicarious learning.
4. Identify examples of social cognitive theory in people's behaviors. Include examples such as the types of modeling, modeling outcomes, effectiveness of models, and self-regulation.

Have you ever gotten a romantic feeling from listening to a song, tried harder after someone praised your efforts, or attempted something, like a dance, after watching others do it? If the answer is yes, you will be able to explain why after studying this chapter. Our experiences and observations of others strongly influence our behavior and our thinking. As you read the following case study involving 10th grader Tim Spencer, consider how his experiences together with his observations of his friend's behavior, influence him.

Tim has been doing well in Algebra II—getting mostly B's on the weekly quizzes. On the last quiz, however, something inexplicably went wrong. He became confused, panicked, and failed the quiz. He was devastated.

Now, on the next quiz, he's so nervous that when he starts, the first few answers he circles have wiggly lines around them from his shaking hand. "I'm not sure I can do this," he thinks. "Maybe I should drop algebra."

His hand also shakes when he takes chemistry tests, but fortunately, he isn't nervous in world history, where he is doing fine.

Tim mentions his troubles to his friend Susan, who always does well on the quizzes.

"They're tough," she comments, "so I really study for them. . . . Let's get together." Tim is skeptical but agrees, and the night before the next quiz, he goes to Susan's home to study. He sees how she selects several problems from the book and solves them completely, rather than just reading over the sample problems and explanations. As she begins working on her third problem, he asks her why she is doing another one.

"I try to do as many different kinds as I can to be sure I don't get fooled," she explains. "So, I'm more confident when I go into the quiz. . . . See, this one is different. . . . I look at the differences and then try it.

"I even make a little chart. I do at least three problems of each type and then check them off as I do them, so I can see that I'm making progress. If I get them all right, I might treat myself with a dish of ice cream."

"Good idea," Tim nods. "I usually do a couple and if I get them, I quit."

Tim sets a new goal to do three of each type, selecting the odd problems so that he can check the correct answers in the back of the book.

He does much better on the next quiz. "What a relief," he says to himself.

He's less anxious for the following week's quiz, and his efforts are paying off; he makes his highest score so far.

"Maybe I can do this after all," he says to himself.

To begin our discussion, consider these questions:

1. How can we explain Tim's nervousness on the quiz following his bad experience?
2. Why did his nervousness later decrease?
3. Why did he change his study habits and sustain his efforts?

Behaviorism and social cognitive theory can help answer these questions, and in this chapter we'll see how these theories are applied.

Behaviorist Views of Learning

Learning is at the core of any study of educational psychology, and our goal as teachers is to promote as much learning as possible for all students. This chapter is the first of four devoted to theories of learning.

We begin by examining behaviorism, a view of learning that, in spite of controversy, continues to be widely applied in schools, especially in the area of classroom management (Kazden, 2001; G. Martin & Pear, 2002).

What Is Behaviorism?

Behaviorism. A theory that explains learning in terms of observable behaviors and how they're influenced by stimuli from the environment.

Learning (behaviorism). A relatively enduring change in observable behavior that occurs as a result of experience.

Behaviorism is a theory that explains learning in terms of observable behaviors and how they're influenced by stimuli from the environment. It defines **learning** as a relatively enduring change in observable behavior that occurs as a result of experience (Schunk, 2004; B. F. Skinner, 1953). Notice that this definition doesn't include thought processes, such as expectations, beliefs, insights, or goals; temporary changes in behavior that result from illness, injury, or emotional distress; or permanent changes in behavior that result from maturation. (Later, when we study cognitive theories, you will see that cognitive theorists define learning differently.)

Tim experienced what we commonly call test *anxiety,* and we can explain it using behaviorism. Because of his experience—failing the quiz—he made wiggly lines around his problems. This behavior is observable, and it is relatively enduring; he *learned* to be nervous when he took math quizzes. We usually think of learning as acquiring some knowledge, such as knowing the causes of the War of 1812, or skill, such as finding 42 percent of 65, but emotions can also be learned. Using Tim's experience, we will describe how emotions can be learned.

Classical Conditioning

Classical conditioning. A type of learning that occurs when individuals learn to produce involuntary emotional or physiological responses similar to instinctive or reflexive responses.

At the beginning of the chapter, we asked if you have ever gotten a romantic feeling when listening to a song? Or does a certain smell, such as food cooking, cause a warm comfortable feeling? These examples, as well as Tim's nervousness, can be explained by classical conditioning.

Classical conditioning occurs when an individual *learns* to produce an involuntary emotional or physiological response similar to an instinctive or reflexive response. Tim's anxiety in response to subsequent quizzes was emotional, and it was involuntary, that is, he couldn't control the way he felt.

Classical conditioning was originally discovered by a Russian scientist named Ivan Pavlov, and to understand how it works, we focus on five concepts, together with the process of association (Baldwin & Baldwin, 2001):

Ivan Pavlov (1849–1936) was a Russian physiologist, psychologist, and physician. He was awarded the Nobel Prize in Physiology and Medicine in 1904 for his research on digestion. As a part of his research, he had his assistants feed dogs meat powder so their rates of salivation could be measured. As the research progressed, however, the dogs began to salivate at the sight of the assistants, even when they weren't carrying meat powder (Pavlov, 1927). This startling phenomenon caused a turn in Pavlov's work and opened the field of what is now known as *classical conditioning*.

Pavlov is interesting in that he was somewhat compulsive. He ate lunch at exactly noon each day, went to bed at exactly the same time each evening, and left Russia for Estonia on vacation on the same day each year.

- An **unconditioned stimulus** is an object or event that causes an instinctive or reflexive (unlearned) physiological or emotional response. In Pavlov's experiment, the unconditioned stimulus was the meat powder, and in Tim's case it was his failure.
- An **unconditioned response** is the instinctive or reflexive (unlearned) physiological or emotional response caused by the unconditioned stimulus: the dogs' salivation resulting from the meat powder, and Tim's devastation as a result of his failure.
- A **neutral stimulus** is an object or event that doesn't initially impact behavior one way or the other. The lab assistants initially had no impact on the dogs' salivation, and tests initially had no impact on Tim.
- A **conditioned stimulus** is a *formerly neutral stimulus* that becomes associated with the unconditioned stimulus. The lab assistants became associated with the meat powder, and for Tim, tests became associated with failure.
- A **conditioned response** is a *learned* physiological or emotional response that is similar to the unconditioned response. The dogs' salivation in the absence of the meat powder and Tim's anxiety in response to quizzes were conditioned responses.

Unconditioned stimulus. An object or event that causes an instinctive or reflexive (unlearned) physiological or emotional response.

Unconditioned response. The instinctive or reflexive (unlearned) physiological or emotional response caused by the unconditioned stimulus.

Neutral stimulus. An object or event that doesn't initially impact behavior one way or the other.

Conditioned stimulus. A formerly neutral stimulus that becomes associated with the unconditioned stimulus.

Conditioned response. A learned physiological or emotional response that is similar to the unconditioned response.

Association is the key to learning in classical conditioning. Pavlov's dogs associated the lab assistants with the meat powder, and Tim associated quizzes with failure. For the association to occur, the unconditioned and conditioned stimuli must be *contiguous,* that is, they must exist at the same time. Without this contiguity, an association can't be formed, and learning through classical conditioning can't take place.

Both real-world and classroom examples of classical conditioning are common (Schunk, Pintrich, & Meece, 2008). For instance, if we have a romantic encounter while a particular song is playing, hearing the song sometime later may trigger the romantic feelings; we are likely to react warmly when we smell Thanksgiving turkey; and we may be uneasy when we enter a dentist's office. Most of us have experienced test anxiety to some degree. In each of these examples, the individual learned an emotional response through classical conditioning.

Classical conditioning is also the theoretical framework for a considerable amount of contemporary research in areas ranging as widely as preschoolers' preferences for certain tastes (Lumeng & Cardinal, 2007) to couples therapy (S. D. Davis & Piercy, 2007) and the relationships between power and self-esteem (Bogdan & Struzynska-Kujalowicz, 2007).

Classical Conditioning in the Classroom

Sharon Van Horn greets Carlos, and each of her other second graders, in a warm, friendly manner every day when he comes into her classroom, and her greeting makes him feel good. Now, Carlos experiences a comfortable feeling when entering Mrs. Van Horn's room, even when she isn't there.

While Tim's failure was a negative experience, Carlos's was positive, and we can also explain it with classical conditioning. He associated Mrs. Van Horn's classroom with her inviting manner, so he learned to be comfortable when he entered her room. Some researchers suggest that students' emotional reactions resulting from their experiences in schools are among the most important outcomes of schooling (Gentile, 1996). Many examples exist. For instance, if students are anxious as they approach math, their achievement will be impeded. On the other hand, while students are often uneasy about a new school or class, if their teachers treat them with respect and encouragement, as Sharon did with Carlos, they will gradually associate their class with their teacher's manner. The class will then induce feelings of safety in them as it did with Carlos. This is an important goal, and one that can be reached with classical conditioning.

table 6.1 Classical Conditioning Examples

Example	Stimuli and Responses		
Tim	UCS *Failure*	→	UCR *Devastation and anxiety* (unlearned and involuntary)
	CS *Quizzes*	→	CR *Anxiety* (learned and involuntary)
	Quizzes associated with failure		Anxiety similar to original anxiety
Carlos	UCS *Mrs. Van Horn's manner*	→	UCR *Good feeling* (unlearned and involuntary)
	CS *The classroom*	→	CR *Comfort* (learned and involuntary)
	Classroom associated with Mrs. Van Horn's manner		Comfort similar to original good feeling

Abbreviations: CR, conditioned response; CS, conditioned stimulus; UCR, unconditioned response; UCS, unconditioned stimulus.

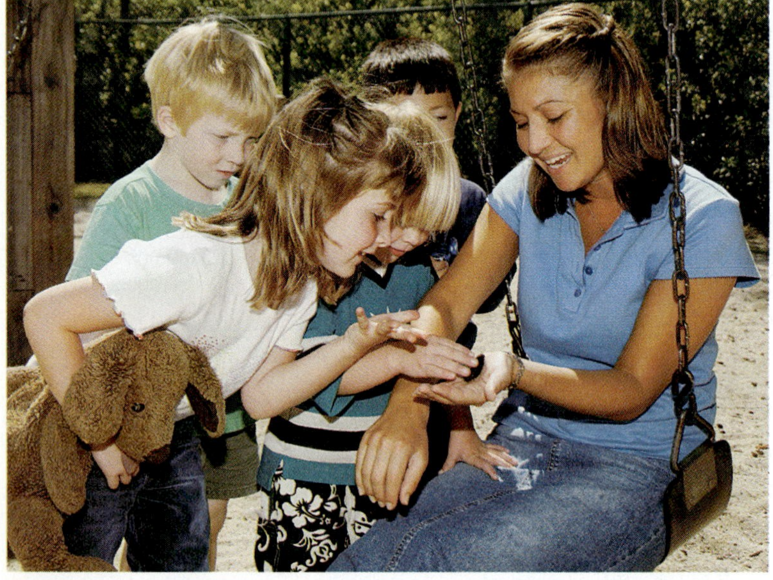

An understanding of classical conditioning helps teachers see how supportive classroom environments and warm and caring teachers result in positive feelings toward schools and learning.

The mechanisms involved in Tim's and Carlos's experiences are outlined in Table 6.1.

Generalization and Discrimination

You saw in the opening case study that Tim was also anxious in chemistry tests. His anxiety had generalized to chemistry. **Generalization** occurs when stimuli similar—but not identical—to a conditioned stimulus elicit the conditioned response by themselves (N. Jones, Kemenes, & Benjamin, 2001). Tim's chemistry tests were similar to his algebra quizzes, and they elicited the conditioned response—anxiety—by themselves.

The process can also work in a positive way. Students who associate a classroom with the warmth and respect demonstrated by one teacher may generalize their reactions to other classes, club activities, and the school in general.

The opposite of generalization is **discrimination,** which is the ability to give different responses to related but not identical stimuli (W. F. Hill, 2002). For example, Tim was nervous during chemistry tests but not those in world history. He discriminated between world history and algebra.

Extinction

After working with Susan and changing his study habits, Tim began to improve on the quizzes. As a result, he was less nervous. In time, if he continued to succeed, his nervousness would dis-

classroom connections

Applying Classical Conditioning in Your Classroom

1. Classical conditioning explains how individuals learn emotional responses through the process of association. To elicit positive emotions as conditioned stimuli in your students, create a safe and welcoming classroom environment, so your classroom elicits feelings of security.
   - **Elementary:** A first-grade teacher greets each of her students with a smile when they come into the room in the morning. She makes an attempt to periodically ask each of them about their family or some other personal part of their lives.
   - **Middle School:** A seventh-grade teacher enforces rules that forbid students from ridiculing each other in any way. He makes respect a high priority in his classroom.
   - **High School:** A geometry teacher attempts to reduce anxiety by specifying what students are accountable for on tests. She provides sample problems for practice and offers additional help sessions twice a week.

appear; that is, the conditioned response would become extinct. **Extinction** (in classical conditioning) results when the conditioned stimulus occurs often enough in the absence of the unconditioned stimulus that it no longer elicits the conditioned response (Myers & Davis, 2007). As Tim took additional quizzes (conditioned stimuli) without experiencing failure (the unconditioned stimulus), his anxiety (the conditioned response) gradually disappeared.

Generalization. The process that occurs when stimuli similar, but not identical, to a conditioned stimulus elicit the conditioned response by themselves.

Discrimination. The process that occurs when a person gives different responses to similar but not identical stimuli.

Extinction (classical conditioning). The disappearance of a conditioned response as the result of the conditioned stimulus occurring repeatedly in the absence of the unconditioned stimulus.

check your understanding

1.1 Answer the first two questions we asked at the beginning of this section: "How can we explain Tim's nervousness on the quiz following his bad experience?" and "Why did his nervousness later decrease?"

1.2 In the section entitled "Classical Conditioning in the Classroom," we said that the "class will induce feelings of safety" in students. What concept from classical conditioning is illustrated by the class, and what concept is illustrated by the safe feelings? Explain.

1.3 Think about the examples of developing an emotional feeling as a result of a romantic encounter, reacting warmly to the smell of Thanksgiving turkey, and feeling uneasy when we enter a dentist's office. Identify the unconditioned and conditioned stimuli, the unconditioned and conditioned responses, and describe the association involved in each of these examples.

1.4 Suppose the song we hear is a Latin rhythm, and later we discover that all romantic Latin music arouses the same emotion. Later, we hear some rock music and find that it doesn't have the same effect. What concepts are illustrated by our reaction to Latin music but not to rock music?

To receive feedback for these questions, go to Appendix A.

Operant Conditioning

We used classical conditioning to explain how people learn involuntary emotional and physiological responses to classroom activities and other events. However, people don't simply respond to stimuli; instead, they often "operate" on their environments by initiating behaviors. This is the source of the term **operant conditioning,** which describes learning in terms of observable responses that change in frequency or duration as the result of **consequences,** events that occur following behaviors. B. F. Skinner (1953, 1954), the most influential figure in operant conditioning, argued that behaviors are controlled more by consequences than by stimuli preceding behaviors. For example, being stopped by a highway patrol for speeding is a consequence, and it decreases the likelihood that you'll speed in the near future. A teacher's praise after a student's answer is also a consequence, and it increases the likelihood of the student trying to answer other questions. A myriad of consequences, such as high test scores, attention from peers, and reprimands for inappropriate behavior, influence behaviors in classrooms.

Operant conditioning. A form of learning in which an observable response changes in frequency or duration as a result of a consequence.

Consequence. Event (stimulus) that occurs following a behavior and that influences the probability of the behaviors recurring.

Operant and classical conditioning are often confused. To help clarify important differences, we present a comparison of the two in Table 6.2. As the table shows, learning occurs as a result of experience for both, but the type of behavior differs, and the behavior and stimulus occur in the opposite order for the two.

Earlier we said that behaviorism, although controversial, is widely used as a tool for managing student behavior in classrooms (Kazden, 2001; G. Martin & Pear, 2002). Operant conditioning, in particular, is used as a classroom management tool. (We consider classroom management in depth in Chapter 12.)

B.F. Skinner (1904–1990) originally intended to be a writer until he discovered the works of Pavlov and the behavioral psychologist, John Watson. Their influence turned his attention to psychology, which he taught at the universities of Minnesota and Indiana before joining the faculty at Harvard. He is associated with projects ranging from attempting to train pigeons to guide bombs in World War II to the development of teaching machines and programmed instruction. A considerable amount of drill-and-practice computer software is designed according to principles he originally proposed.

His influence was so great that heads of psychology departments in the late 1960s identified him as the most influential psychologist of the 20th century (M. E. Myers, 1970). Skinner continued to work on applications of operant conditioning to everyday life until his death in 1990.

table 6.2 A Comparison of Operant and Classical Conditioning

	Classical Conditioning	Operant Conditioning
Behavior	Involuntary (person does not have control of behavior) Emotional Physiological	Voluntary (person has control of behavior)
Order	Behavior follows stimulus.	Behavior precedes stimulus (consequence).
How learning occurs	Neutral stimuli become associated with unconditioned stimuli.	Consequences of behaviors influence subsequent behaviors.
Example	Learners associate classrooms (initially neutral) with the warmth of teachers, so classrooms elicit positive emotions.	Learners attempt to answer questions and are praised, so their attempts to answer increase.
Key researcher	Pavlov	Skinner

We now discuss different consequences involved in operant conditioning and how they affect behavior (see Figure 6.1).

Reinforcement

Reinforcer. A consequence that increases the likelihood of a behavior recurring.

Reinforcement. The process of applying reinforcers to increase behavior.

Suppose during a class discussion you make a comment and your instructor responds, "Very insightful idea. Good thinking." The likelihood that you'll try to make another comment in the future increases. The instructor's comment is a **reinforcer,** a consequence that increases the likelihood of a behavior recurring. **Reinforcement,** the process of applying reinforcers to increase behavior, exists in two forms: positive and negative.

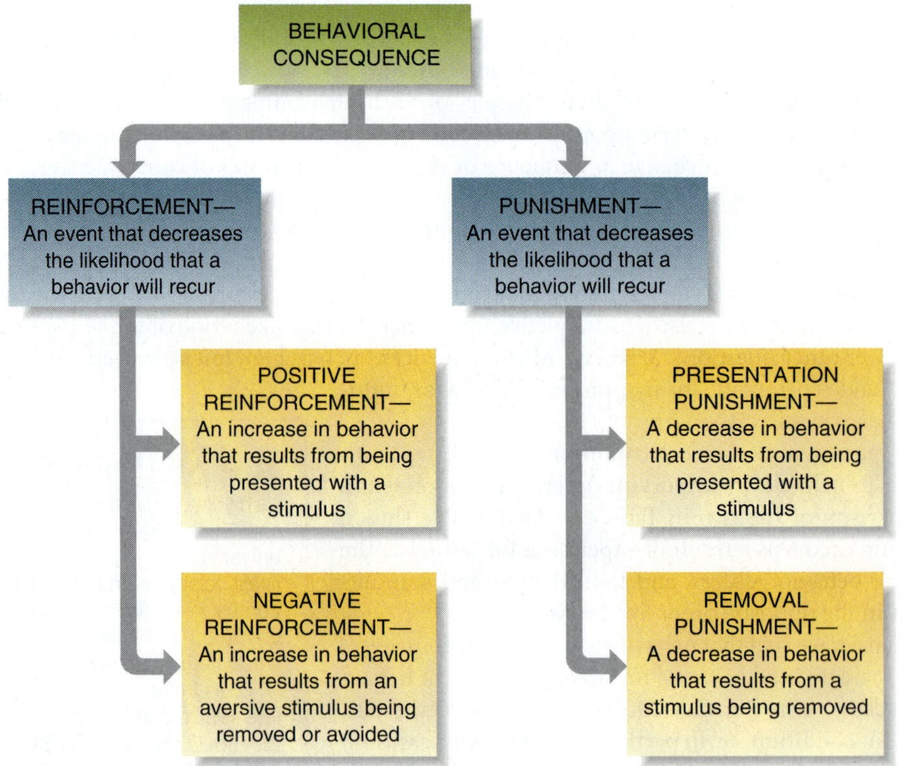

Figure 6.1 Consequences of behavior

Positive Reinforcement. **Positive reinforcement** is the process of increasing the frequency or duration of a behavior as the result of *presenting* a reinforcer. In classrooms, we typically think of a positive reinforcer as something desired or valued, such as your instructor's praise, high test scores, "happy faces," tokens that can be cashed in for privileges, and stars on the bulletin board for young children.

However, any increase in behavior as a result of being presented with a consequence is positive reinforcement, and teachers sometimes unintentionally reinforce undesirable behavior. For instance, if a student is acting out, the teacher reprimands him, and his misbehavior increases, the reprimand acts as a positive reinforcer. The student's behavior *increased* as a result of being presented with the reprimand.

Teachers also use positive reinforcement when they take advantage of the **Premack principle** (named after David Premack, who originally described it in 1965), which states that a more-desired activity can serve as a positive reinforcer for a less-desired activity. For example, suppose you say to yourself, "After I clean up the mess in my room, I'll watch a movie." The movie serves as a reinforcer for cleaning up your room.

Teachers also use the Premack principle in their work with students. For example, if a geography teacher knows her students like map work, and she says, "As soon as you've finished your summaries, you can start working on your maps," she is applying the Premack principle. The map work serves as a positive reinforcer for completing the summaries.

Positive reinforcement also occurs with teachers' behaviors. For example, students' attentive looks, nods, and raised hands are positive reinforcers and increase the likelihood of teachers' calling on them. High student test scores and compliments from students or their parents are also positive reinforcers for teachers.

Praise, high test scores, and other reinforcers can increase positive student behavior.

Negative Reinforcement. **Negative reinforcement** is the process of increasing behavior by avoiding or removing an aversive stimulus (Baldwin & Baldwin, 2001; B. F. Skinner, 1953). For example, a mother says to her teenager, "If you straighten up your room, you don't have to rake the leaves in the yard," or a teacher says, "If you're all sitting quietly when the bell rings, we'll go to lunch. If not, we'll miss 5 minutes of our lunch period." In both cases, avoiding the aversive stimulus—raking the leaves or waiting for lunch—acts as a negative reinforcer for the desired behavior—straightening the room or sitting quietly.

Positive reinforcement. The process of increasing the frequency or duration of a behavior as the result of *presenting* a reinforcer.

Premack principle. The principle stating that a more-desired activity can serve as a positive reinforcer for a less-desired activity.

Negative reinforcement. The process of increasing behavior by avoiding or removing an aversive stimulus.

Negative reinforcement can also occur unintentionally, as the following example illustrates.

> Kathy Long is discussing the skeletal system with her science students.
> "Why do you suppose the rib cage is shaped the way it is? . . . Jim?" she asks.
> He sits silently for several seconds and finally says, "I don't know."
> "Can someone help Jim out?" Kathy continues.
> "It protects our heart and other internal organs," Athenia volunteers.
> "Good, Athenia," Kathy smiles.
> Later, Kathy calls on Jim again. He hesitates briefly and says, "I don't know."

In this example, Kathy negatively reinforced Jim (unintentionally) for failing to respond by removing the potentially anxiety-provoking question after he said, "I don't know." We know he is being negatively reinforced because he said "I don't know" more quickly after being called on the second time. If students can't answer teachers' questions, being called on can be aversive, and they're likely to try and "get off the hook" as Jim did, or avoid being called on at all by not making eye contact with the teacher.

This example has important implications for instruction. We want to reinforce students *for* answering, as Kathy did with Athenia, instead of for *not answering*, as she did with Jim. Instead of turning the question to another student, Kathy should have prompted him to help him provide an acceptable answer, which she could then have positively reinforced (Good & Brophy, 2008). (We discuss teacher questioning and prompting in detail in Chapter 13.)

One way of thinking about the difference between positive and negative reinforcement is to use positive and negative numbers. Positive reinforcement means *adding* a stimulus, and negative reinforcement means *subtracting* (or avoiding) a stimulus. In our examples above,

Kathy "added" the praise when she responded to Athenia and "subtracted" the question when Jim said, "I don't know."

Shaping. Suppose you have a student who is so shy and reluctant to interact with his peers that he rarely speaks. Acquiring social skills is an important part of students' development, and you can use **shaping,** the process of reinforcing successive approximations of a behavior, as a tool. For instance, you might first reinforce the student for any interaction with others, such as a simple smile or sharing a pencil. Later, you reinforce him for greeting other students as they enter the classroom. Finally, you reinforce him only for more prolonged interactions.

Shaping. The process of reinforcing successive approximations of a desired behavior.

Shaping can also be used to develop complex learning behaviors. When students are initially struggling with difficult ideas, you can reinforce their efforts and partially correct responses. For example,

> "I start out praising every attempt," Maria Brugera comments to one of her colleagues. "Then, as they improve, I praise them only for better, more complete answers, until finally they have to give well thought-out explanations before I'll say anything."

Although Maria was obviously seeking correct answers, she considered student effort a beginning step and a partially correct response an approximation of the desired behavior. Through shaping, she hoped to eventually get complete and thoughtful answers from her students.

Reinforcement Schedules. As you saw in the example involving shaping, Maria initially praised her students for every answer, but later praised them only for answers that were better and more complete. Maria's strategic use of praise illustrates an important principle of operant conditioning: *The timing and spacing of reinforcers have different effects on learning.* These effects are illustrated in **reinforcement schedules,** descriptions of patterns in the frequency and predictability of reinforcers that have differential effects on behavior (Baldwin & Baldwin, 2001).

Reinforcement schedules. Different patterns in the frequency and predictability of reinforcers that have differential effects on behavior.

Continuous reinforcement schedule. A reinforcement schedule where every desired behavior is reinforced.

Intermittent reinforcement schedule. A reinforcement schedule where some, but not all, behaviors are reinforced.

Ratio schedule. An intermittent reinforcement schedule where specific behaviors are reinforced, either predictably (fixed) or unpredictably (variable).

Interval schedule. An intermittent reinforcement schedule in which behaviors are reinforced after a certain predictable interval (fixed) or unpredictable interval of time has passed (variable).

For example, Maria initially praised every answer, but later praised answers only some of the time. Her reinforcement schedule was initially **continuous**—every desired behavior was reinforced—but later she turned to an **intermittent schedule,** where some, but not all, of the desired behaviors are reinforced.

Two types of intermittent schedules exist, and they influence behavior differently. **Ratio schedules** depend on the number of individual behaviors, and **interval schedules** depend on time. Both can be either *fixed* or *variable.* In fixed schedules, the individual receives reinforcers predictably; in variable schedules, unpredictably. For instance, when playing slot machines, you insert a coin, pull the handle, and coins periodically drop into the tray. Receiving coins (reinforcers) depends on the number of times you pull the handle, not on how long you play, and you can't predict when you'll receive coins, so it is a *variable-ratio* schedule.

Many examples of variable-ratio schedules exist in classrooms, such as teacher praise and comments on papers. Fixed-ratio schedules are uncommon in classrooms, except for some forms of drill-and-practice computer software. For instance, a student signs on to the program, receives a personalized greeting, and solves three problems. The program then replies, "Congratulations, Antonio, you have just correctly solved three problems." If the program then gives a similar response for every three problems answered correctly, it is using a fixed-ratio schedule.

Now, suppose you're in a class that meets Mondays, Wednesdays, and Fridays; you have a quiz each Friday, and your instructor returns the quiz each Monday. You study on Sunday, Tuesday, and particularly on Thursday evenings, but you aren't reinforced for studying until the following Monday, when you receive your score. Reinforcement occurs at a predictable interval—every Monday—so it is a *fixed-interval* schedule. On the other hand, if some of your instructors give "pop" quizzes, they are using a variable-interval schedule, because you can't predict when you will be reinforced.

The relationships among the different types of reinforcement schedules are illustrated in Figure 6.2, and additional classroom examples are outlined in Table 6.3.

Reinforcement schedules affect behavior differently, and each has advantages and disadvantages. For instance, a continuous schedule yields the fastest rates of initial learning (R. Lee, Sturmey, & Fields, 2007), so it is effective when students are acquiring new skills such as solving equations in algebra. However, when teachers eliminate reinforcers, the frequency of con-

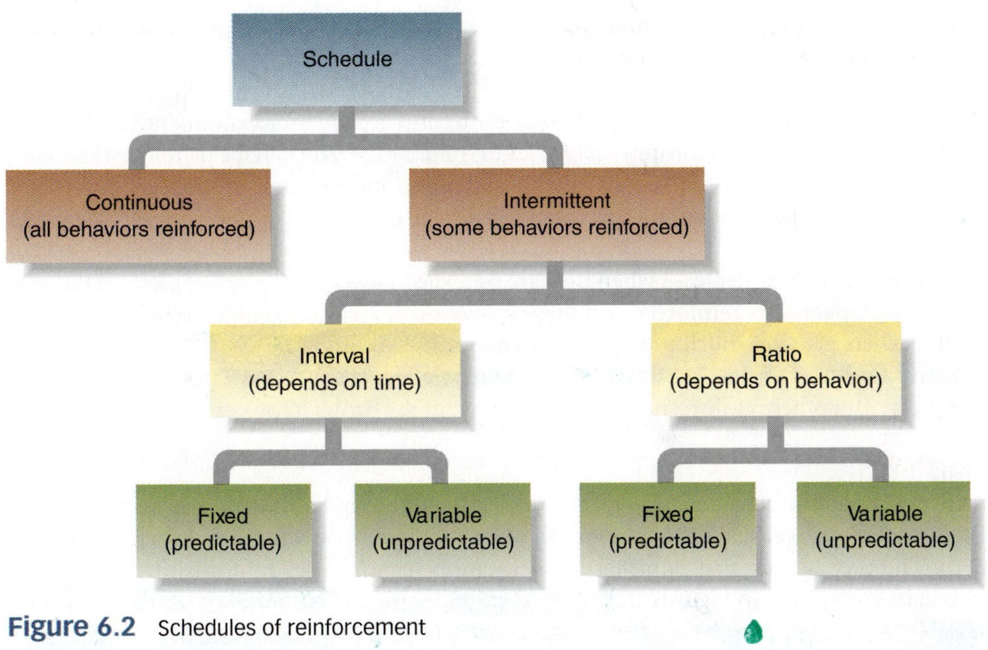

Figure 6.2 Schedules of reinforcement

tinually reinforced behaviors decreases more quickly than behaviors reinforced using intermittent schedules (Costa & Boakes, 2007).

Intermittent schedules create more persistent or enduring behaviors but also have disadvantages (R. Lee et al., 2007). With fixed schedules, behavior increases rapidly just before the reinforcer is given and then decreases rapidly and remains low until just before the next reinforcer is given. Giving Friday quizzes is an example; students often study carefully just before the quiz and then don't study again until just before the next quiz.

Extinction. **Extinction** (in operant conditioning) occurs when a behavior ceases as a result of nonreinforcement. An example follows:

Extinction (operant conditioning). The disappearance of a behavior as a result of nonreinforcement.

> Renita, a tenth-grader, enjoys school and likes to respond in her classes. She is attentive and eager to answer questions.
>
> When Mr. Frank, her world history teacher, asks a question, Renita raises her hand, but someone usually blurts out the answer before she can respond. This happens repeatedly.
>
> Now Renita rarely raises her hand and often catches herself daydreaming in class.

table 6.3 **Reinforcement Schedules and Examples**

Schedule	Example
Continuous	A teacher "walks students through" the steps for solving simultaneous equations. Students are liberally praised at each step as they first learn the solution.
Fixed-ratio	The algebra teacher announces, "As soon as you've done two problems in a row correctly, you may start on your homework assignment so that you'll be able to finish by the end of class."
Variable-ratio	Students volunteer to answer questions by raising their hands and are called on at random.
Fixed-interval	Students are given a quiz every Friday.
Variable-interval	Students are given unannounced quizzes.

For Renita, being called on reinforced both her attempts to respond and her attention. Because she wasn't called on, she wasn't reinforced, so her behaviors (raising her hand and paying attention) became extinct.

This example has important implications for teaching. Student involvement and learning are closely related (Good & Brophy, 2008), and Renita's experience helps us understand why. When students are involved, their interest and attention increase, and more learning results. When they aren't, their attention wanes, and learning decreases.

Satiation. Behaviors decrease when they are punished (we examine punishment in the next section) or inadequately reinforced, but they can also decrease when they are reinforced too often. If teachers give too much praise, for instance, **satiation,** the process of using a reinforcer so frequently that it loses its ability to strengthen behaviors, can occur. Effective teachers use their praise and other reinforcers strategically to avoid the problem of satiation.

Satiation. The process of using a reinforcer so frequently that it loses its potency—its ability to strengthen behaviors.

Punishment

Positive and negative reinforcers are consequences that increase behavior. Other consequences, called **punishers,** weaken behaviors or decrease the likelihood of them recurring (Mazur, 2006). The process of using punishers to decrease behavior is called **punishment,** and two kinds exist. As you saw in Figure 6.1, **presentation punishment** occurs when a learner's behavior decreases as a result of being presented with a punisher. For example, when a teacher puts her fingers to her lips, signaling "Shh," and students stop whispering, the students are *presented* with the teacher's signal, and their behavior—whispering—decreases.

Removal punishment occurs when a behavior decreases as a result of removing a stimulus, or the inability to get positive reinforcement. For example, if students are noisy and the teacher keeps them in the room for 5 minutes of their lunch period, she is using removal punishment. Under normal conditions, they go to lunch at the scheduled time, and the teacher takes away some of that free time.

Punishers. Consequences that weaken behaviors or decrease the likelihood of the behaviors' recurring.

Punishment. The process of using punishers to decrease behavior.

Presentation punishment. A decrease in behavior that occurs when a stimulus (punisher) is presented.

Removal punishment. A decrease in behavior that occurs when a stimulus is removed, or when an individual cannot receive positive reinforcement.

MyEducationLab

To see behaviorism operating in the world of work, go to the *Activities and Applications* section in Chapter 6 of MyEducationLab at www.myeducationlab.com, and read the vignette *Behaviorism in the Workplace.* Answer the questions following the vignette.

Using Punishment Effectively. Some critics suggest that punishment should never be used (e.g., Kohn, 1996b), and research indicates that systems based on reinforcing positive behavior are superior to those using punishment (Alberto & Troutman, 2006; Miltenberger, 2004). Punishment decreases unacceptable behaviors, but doesn't teach desirable ones, which is why reinforcement is more effective. However, punishment is sometimes necessary; when all punishers are removed, some students become more disruptive (Pfiffner, Rosen, & O'Leary, 1985; Rosen, O'Leary, Joyce, Conway, & Pfiffner, 1984). A more practical approach is to use punishment judiciously, combined with appropriate amounts of reinforcement for good behavior (Maag, 2001).

Some types of punishers that research has found to be effective include the following:

- *Desists.* **Desists** are verbal or nonverbal communications that teachers use to stop a behavior (Kounin, 1970). A simple form of presentation punishment, such as a teacher putting her fingers to her lips, signaling "Shh," as you saw earlier, is a desist. When administered immediately, briefly, and unemotionally, they can be effective (Emmer, Evertson, & Worsham, 2006; Evertson, Emmer, & Worsham, 2006).
- *Timeout.* **Timeout** involves removing a student from the class and physically isolating him or her in an area away from classmates. Typically used with young children, the isolation eliminates the student's opportunities for positive reinforcement, so it is a form of removal punishment. It is effective for a variety of disruptive behaviors (Alberto & Troutman, 2006).
- *Detention.* Similar to timeout, and typically used with older students, detention involves taking away some of the students' free time (typically a half hour or more) by keeping students in school either before or after school hours. While somewhat controversial (L. Johnson, 2004), it is widely used and generally viewed as effective (Gootman, 1998). It is most effective when students are required to sit quietly and do nothing, because the possibility of positive reinforcement is eliminated (imagine sitting doing absolutely nothing for a half hour).
- *Response cost.* **Response cost** involves the removal of reinforcers already given (L. Zhou, Goff, & Iwata, 2000). For example, some teachers design systems where students receive

Desists. Verbal or nonverbal communications that teachers use to stop a behavior.

Timeout. The process of isolating a student from his or her classmates.

Response cost. The process of removing reinforcers already given.

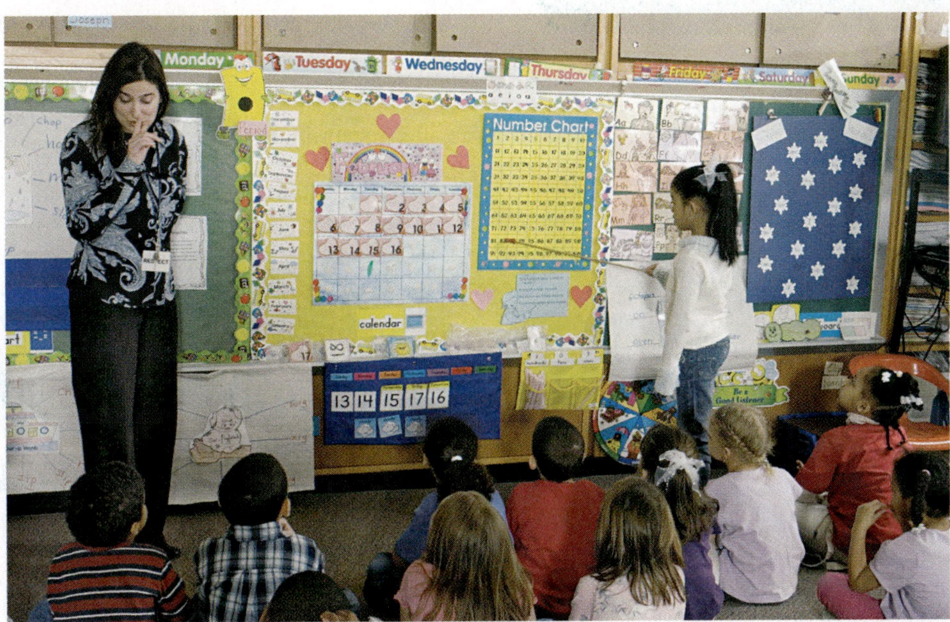

Desists are appropriate uses of punishment in classrooms.

tokens or other reinforcers for desirable behavior, which they can then use to purchase items from a school store, or redeem for free time and other privileges. Taking away some of them for inappropriate behavior is a form of response cost.

Ineffective Forms of Punishment. While judicious use of punishment can be effective, some forms are unacceptable and should never be used. They include the following:

- *Physical punishment.* Physical punishment, such as "swats" or even a slap with a ruler can result in individuals later demonstrating similar behaviors as undesirable side effects (Bandura, 1986), becoming even more defiant after receiving the punishers (Nilsson & Archer, 1989), or learning more sophisticated ways to avoid getting caught. Students avoid teachers who frequently use punishment, and a number of states forbid physically punishing students (Zirpoli & Melloy, 2001).
- *Embarrassment and humiliation.* Embarrassment and humiliation can lead to some of the same negative side effects as physical punishment (J. E. Walker, Bauer, & Shea, 2004).
- *Classwork.* Using classwork as a form of punishment can teach students that it is aversive and may, through classical conditioning, cause negative emotional reactions to it (Baldwin & Baldwin, 2001). Learners may generalize their aversion to their assignments, other teachers, and the school as well.

As with using reinforcers, the use of punishers requires sound professional judgment. For example, if teachers use desists, but students are reinforced by the attention they receive, the desists are ineffective. Similarly, if being in a class is aversive, timeout—instead of being an effective punisher—may be a negative reinforcer. If undesirable behaviors don't decrease, you must use a different strategy. We examine these issues in detail in our discussion of classroom management in Chapter 12.

The Influence of Antecedents on Behavior

To this point, we have discussed the influence of consequences—reinforcers and punishers—on behavior. But behavior is also influenced by **antecedents,** stimuli that precede and induce behaviors. Antecedents are important because they signal desired behaviors. Antecedents of behaviors that were reinforced in the past increase the likelihood of eliciting the behavior in the future, and antecedents of behaviors that were punished in the past decrease the likelihood of eliciting the behavior (Baldwin & Baldwin, 2001).

Antecedents. Stimuli that precede and induce behaviors.

Common forms of antecedents include

- Environmental conditions
- Prompts and cues
- Past reinforcers (which lead to generalization and discrimination)

Environmental Conditions. When we walk into a dark room, our first inclination is to turn on the lights. The darkness is an environmental antecedent that causes us to turn on the lights. We're reinforced for that action, because now we can see. We've been reinforced for turning on the lights in the past, so we repeat the behavior. On the other hand, a traffic light turning red is an antecedent that causes us to stop, because running the light increases the likelihood of being punished by getting a ticket or being hit by another car.

Some teachers dim the lights when students come in from recess. The dim light acts as an environmental antecedent, reminding students that they are inside and need to use inside voices and behaviors.

These examples remind us that we can use classroom environments as antecedents for desirable behaviors, which we can then reinforce.

Teacher questions can act as antecedents to elicit desired responses from students.

Prompts and Cues. Prompts and cues are specific stimuli intended to produce desirable behaviors, particularly in learning activities. For example:

Alicia Wendt wants her students to understand the concept *adverb.* She writes this sentence on the chalkboard:

> *John quickly jerked his head when he heard his name called.*
>
> She then asks, "What is the adverb in the sentence? . . . Wendy?"
> ". . ."
> "What did John do?"
> ". . . He . . . jerked his head."
> "How did he jerk it?"
> ". . . Quickly."
> "So what is the adverb?"
> ". . . Quickly."
> "Yes, . . . well done, Wendy."

Alicia's questions were prompts (antecedents) that helped Wendy make the desired response (behavior), which Alicia then reinforced.

Cues also come in other forms. When a teacher moves to the front of the class or walks among the students as they do seat work, she is cuing them to turn their attention toward her or to remain on task. In each case, the teacher can then reinforce the desired behaviors.

Generalization and Discrimination. Past reinforcers also serve as antecedents for responses to similar, but not identical, stimuli. For instance, if a child has been reinforced for identifying object 1 in Figure 6.3 as a square, that reinforcer can be an antecedent for her identifying 2, 3, and 4 as squares. However, if she labels 5 a square and is told, "No, it's a rectangle because two of the sides are longer," she is less likely to identify 6 as a square.

Identifying 2, 3, and 4 as squares illustrates *generalization,* which is the process of giving the same response to similar, but not identical, stimuli. No longer identifying 6 as a square illustrates discrimination, which is the process of giving different responses to slightly different stimuli (Hergenhahn & Olson, 2001; W. F. Hill, 2002).

Similarly, after dissecting a shark or frog, biology students can recognize the heart in each case. A shark's heart is two chambered, whereas a frog's is three chambered, but when students conclude that they are both hearts, they are generalizing. When they learn to tell them apart, they are *discriminating.*

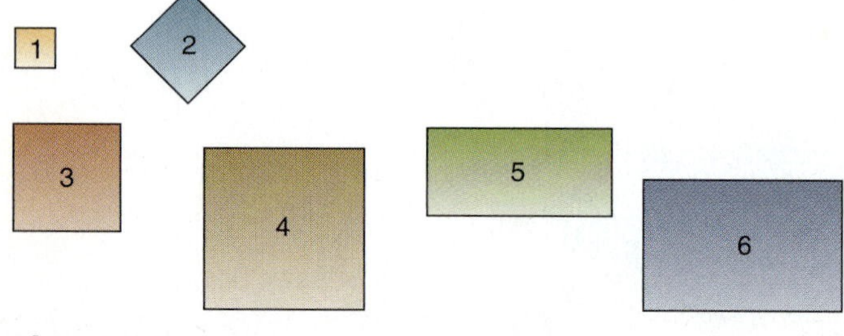

Figure 6.3 Squares and rectangles

Applied Behavior Analysis

Behaviorism is widely used as a framework for two important tasks: (1) Creating productive learning environments and (2) using applied behavior analysis. We examine productive learning environments in detail in Chapter 12. Here we look at applied behavior analysis.

Applied behavior analysis (ABA) is the process of systematically applying the principles of behaviorism to change student behavior (Baldwin & Baldwin, 2001). (It is also called *behavior modification,* but this term has a negative connotation for some people, so experts prefer the term we use here.) It has been used successfully in helping people increase their physical fitness, overcome fears and panic attacks, learn social skills, and stop smoking. It is widely used in working with students who have exceptionalities (J. B. Ryan, Katsiyannis, & Peterson, 2007).

Applied behavior analysis (ABA). The process of systematically applying the principles of behaviorism to change student behavior.

Steps in Applied Behavior Analysis

The application of behaviorist principles in ABA typically involves the following steps:

1. Identify target behaviors.
2. Establish a baseline for the target behaviors.
3. Choose reinforcers and punishers (if necessary).
4. Measure changes in the target behaviors.
5. Gradually reduce the frequency of reinforcers as behavior improves.

To see how to implement these steps, let's look back at Mike Sheppard's work with his middle school pre-algebra class in the closing case study on page 158 of Chapter 5. Todd, one of Mike's 28 students, was verbally abusive, aggressive, and lacked self-discipline. Mike saw that Todd was active and had a hard time sitting through a class period. After working with Todd to help him learn to control his behavior, Mike saw positive changes. Four of five target behaviors had improved over a 3-week period:

	2/9–2/13	2/16–2/20	2/23–2/27
Talking out	𝍸 𝍸 𝍸 𝍸	𝍸 IIII 𝍸	𝍸 II
Swearing	𝍸 𝍸	𝍸 II	IIII
Hitting/ touching	𝍸 III	𝍸 IIII	III
Out of seat	𝍸 𝍸 𝍸 III	𝍸 𝍸 𝍸 IIII	𝍸 𝍸 𝍸 III
Being friendly	II	IIII	𝍸 II

Now, let's see how Mike implemented the steps.

Identify Target Behaviors. Identifying behaviors you want to change is the first step in ABA. Mike identified five target behaviors: *talking out, swearing, hitting/touching other students, being out-of-seat,* and *being friendly.* Some experts might argue that Mike included too many target behaviors and might further suggest that "being friendly" isn't specific enough. As with most teaching–learning applications, these decisions are a matter of professional judgment.

Establish a Baseline. Establishing a baseline for the target behaviors simply means measuring their frequency to provide a reference point for later comparison. For instance, during the baseline period (the week of 2/9 to 2/13), Todd talked out in class 20 times, swore 10 times, hit or touched another student 8 times, was out of his seat 18 times, and was friendly to other students only twice. The teacher or an objective third party, typically makes observations to determine the baseline. Mike created the behavior tally for the first week.

Choose Reinforcers and Punishers. Before attempting to change behavior, you need to identify the reinforcers and punishers that are likely to work for an individual student. Ideally, an ABA system is based on reinforcers instead of punishers, and this is what Mike used with Todd. If punishers are necessary, they should also be established in advance.

Mike used personal attention and praise as his primary reinforcers, and their effectiveness is indicated by the changes in Todd's behavior. And, the fact that Todd could see his own improvement was, in itself, reinforcing. If the undesirable behaviors had not decreased, Mike would have needed to modify his system by trying some additional reinforcers and perhaps some punishers as well.

Measure Changes in Behavior. After establishing a baseline and identifying reinforcers and punishers, teachers measure the target behaviors for specified periods to see if changes occur. For example, Todd talked out six fewer times in the second week than in the first. Except for "out of seat," improvement occurred for each of the other behaviors during the 3-week period.

The first intervention produced no change in Todd's out-of-seat behavior, so Mike designed an alternative. To help Todd satisfy his need for activity, yet not disturb the class, Mike prepared a place where Todd could go when the urge to get out of his seat became overwhelming.

Reduce Frequency of Reinforcers. As Todd's behavior improved, Mike gradually reduced the frequency of reinforcers. Initially, you might use a continuous, or nearly continuous, schedule and then move to an intermittent one. Reducing the frequency of reinforcers helps maintain the desired behaviors and increases the likelihood of generalization to other classrooms and everyday activities.

Functional Analysis

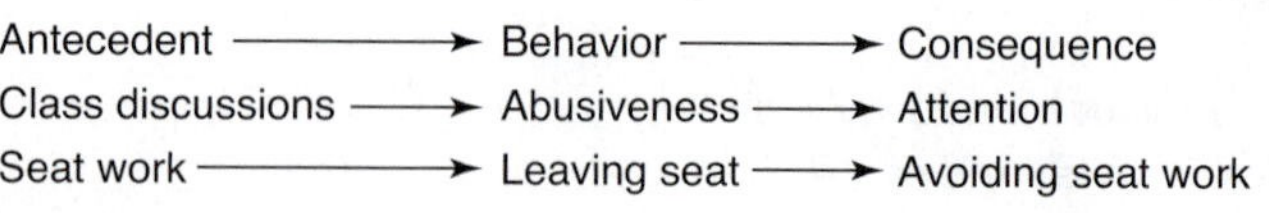

Figure 6.4 A functional analysis of Todd's behavior

The preceding sections focused on measuring changes in behavior based on the use of reinforcers and punishers when necessary. However, some researchers expand their focus to identify antecedents that trigger the inappropriate behaviors (Miltenberger, 2004). For example, Mike found that Todd's abusive behavior occurred most often during class discussions, and he believed that the attention Todd received was reinforcing. Similarly, Todd most commonly was out of his seat during seat work, because it allowed him to avoid the tasks with which he struggled. Class discussions were antecedents for abusive behavior, and seat work was an antecedent for leaving his seat. The strategy used to identify antecedents and consequences that control a behavior is called **functional analysis** (Miltenberger, 2004). These relationships in Todd's case are outlined in Figure 6.4.

Functional analysis. A strategy used to identify antecedents and consequences that control a behavior.

Functional analyses are useful for creating effective interventions, and attempts to reduce undesirable behaviors are usually coupled with reinforcing behaviors that are more appropriate (Kahng & Iwata, 1999; Lalli & Kates, 1998). For example, Mike's positively reinforcing Todd for "being friendly" was a form of attention, so it served the same purpose that being abusive had previously served. Also, Mike spent extra time with Todd to help him succeed on his seat work. Seat work was then a less-likely antecedent for being out of his seat, and Mike could also reinforce Todd for his good work.

MyEducationLab

To see how another teacher attempts to apply applied behavior analysis with her students, go to the *Building Teaching Skills and Dispositions* section in Chapter 6 of MyEducationLab at www.myeducationlab.com and read the case study *Applied Behavior Analysis in Elementary Schools*. Complete the exercises following the case study to develop your skills in using applied behavior analysis.

Like all interventions, ABA won't work magic, and teachers comment on it being labor intensive (Kaff, Zabel, & Milham, 2007). For example, you can't assume that a student will accurately measure the target behaviors, so you have to monitor them yourself. This makes managing an already busy classroom even more complex.

Also, personal attention and praise were effective reinforcers for Todd, but if they hadn't been, Mike would have needed others. Finding a reinforcer that is simple to administer yet is consistent with school procedures can be challenging.

These problems notwithstanding, ABA gives you an additional tool to use when conventional methods, such as a basic system of rules and procedures, don't work. As with all strategies, its effectiveness depends on your skill and professional judgment.

Putting Behaviorism into Perspective

Like any theory, behaviorism has both proponents and critics. Criticisms typically focus on the following areas:

- The ineffectiveness of behaviorism as a guide for instruction
- The inability of behaviorism to explain higher-order functions
- The impact of reinforcers on intrinsic motivation
- Philosophical positions on learning and teaching

Next we examine these criticisms in more detail.

theory to practice

Using Behaviorism in Your Classroom

While behaviorism isn't commonly used as a guide for instruction, it can be helpful in creating a positive classroom environment and in maintaining desired student behavior. In attempting to apply the theory in your classroom, the following guidelines can be helpful.

1. Capitalize on classical conditioning to create an emotionally safe environment.
2. Use antecedents to encourage behaviors that can be reinforced.
3. Praise students for genuine accomplishment.
4. Use appropriate reinforcement schedules to help maintain students' efforts.

To see these guidelines in practice, let's return to Sharon Van Horn's second-grade classroom, which you initially saw in the discussion of classical conditioning. Sharon has a classroom that is diverse and includes several students who are native Spanish speakers.

As Alberto enters Sharon's classroom early Tuesday morning, he hears salsa music in the background. The walls are decorated with colorful prints from Mexico, Alberto's native country, and vocabulary cards in both Spanish and English are hung around the room.

Alberto comes in for extra help each morning.

"Buenos días, Alberto. How are you today?" Sharon asks.

"Buenos días. I'm fine," Alberto responds, as he goes to his desk to take out his homework.

"I can't do it! I do not understand," Alberto says in his halting English as he attempts to do the 10 problems assigned for math homework. He has done the first two correctly, but the last eight are undone.

"Alberto, look," she says, kneeling down to eye level with him. "You did the first two just fine. Look here. . . . How is this problem different from this one?" she asks, pointing to these problems:

$$\begin{array}{r} 36 \\ -14 \\ \hline \end{array} \qquad \begin{array}{r} 45 \\ -19 \\ \hline \end{array}$$

With Sharon's guidance, Alberto recognizes that a larger number—9—is being subtracted from a smaller number—5—in the second problem.

"Very good, Alberto. It is very important to know where the bigger number is," she continues. "Now let's work this one together."

Sharon guides Alberto with prompting questions until he can perform each step of the problem and then praises him warmly when he arrives at the correct solution.

"Now try the others," she says, "and I'll be back in a few minutes to see how you're doing."

Alberto turns to his work. Sharon checks on his progress every couple minutes and provides only enough help so that he continues to make progress.

"Very good, Alberto. . . . See, you got these right," she says, pointing at three of the problems. "You're doing very well. Now, check these two. You have just enough time before we start."

Now, let's look at Sharon's attempts to apply the guidelines in her teaching. First, she created an inviting classroom with her greeting, the salsa music, and pictures from Alberto's native country. This was a conscious effort to make her classroom a conditioned stimulus that would induce positive emotions as conditioned responses. She applied the second and third guidelines by scaffolding him through each step of the problem with her questions and prompts, which provided antecedents for desired behaviors. She then reinforced him with her praise, which was effective because it reflected his genuine accomplishment.

Then, in closely monitoring Alberto's efforts to solve the other problems, she used a variable-interval reinforcement schedule to help maintain his efforts.

In applying the guidelines, Sharon not only helped Alberto feel comfortable in her classroom but also helped him learn the topic he was studying.

First, instruction based on behaviorism suggests that information should be broken down into specific items, which allows learners to display observable behaviors that can then be reinforced. For instance, most of us have completed exercises such as:

Juanita and (I, me) went to the football game.

If we identified "I" as the correct choice, we were reinforced. If we selected "me," we were given corrective feedback, so we learned to appropriately generalize and discriminate. However, most of what is taught in schools cannot be effectively learned through reinforcement of specific, decontextualized items of information. For example, we learn to write by practicing writing, not by responding to exercises such as the one above.

Also, while operant conditioning focuses on changes in behavior caused by reinforcers and punishers, learners often demonstrate misconceptions and sometimes "off-the-wall" ideas for which they haven't been reinforced. These ideas are better explained by theories that focus on learners' thought processes. (We examine these theories in detail in Chapters 7–9.)

Second, behaviorism cannot adequately explain higher-order functions, such as learning a language. For instance, Chomsky and Miller (1958) demonstrated that even people with small vocabularies would have to learn sentences at a rate faster than one per second throughout their lifetimes if their learning was based on specific behaviors and reinforcers.

Third, research suggests that offering reinforcers for engaging in intrinsically motivating activities, such as solving puzzles or playing video games, can actually decrease interest in those activities (R. Ryan & Deci, 1996).

Finally, some critics hold the philosophical position that schools should attempt to promote learning for its own sake rather than learning to gain rewards (Anderman & Maehr, 1994). Other critics argue that behaviorism is essentially a means of controlling people, instead of a way to help students learn to control their own behavior (Kohn, 1993b).

Proponents counter that behaviorism is real and it works; reinforcers and punishers can and do influence the way we behave. For example, teachers know that sincere compliments can increase both student motivation and the way students feel about themselves. Further, supporters of behaviorism ask if we would continue working if we stopped receiving paychecks, and do we lose interest in our work merely because we get paid for it (Gentile, 1996)?

MyEducationLab

To see aspects of behaviorism being applied in instruction, go to the *Activities and Applications* section in Chapter 6 of MyEducationLab at www.myeducationlab.com, and read the case study *Behaviorism in the Classroom*. Answer the questions following the case study.

Further, research indicates that reinforcing appropriate classroom behaviors, such as paying attention and treating classmates well, decreases misbehavior. And behaviorist classroom management techniques are often effective when others are not (A. Smith & Bondy, 2007).

No learning theory is complete, and this is particularly true of behaviorism. However, if judiciously applied by knowledgeable professionals, it can be a useful tool for creating environments that will maximize the opportunity to learn for all students.

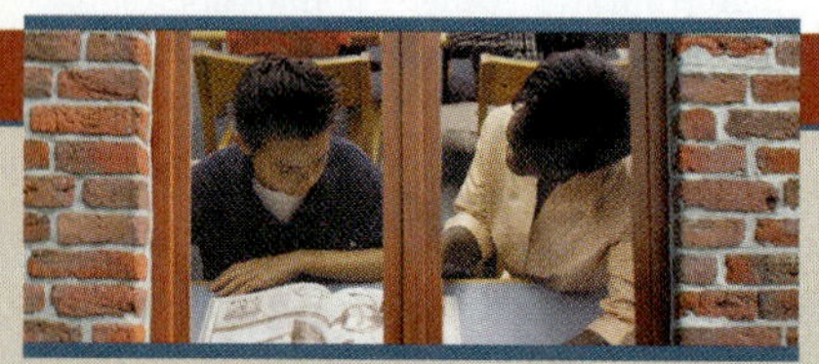

classroom connections

Applying Operant Conditioning in Your Classroom

Reinforcers and Punishers

1. Reinforcers are consequences that increase behavior, and punishers are consequences that decrease behavior. Use reinforcement if possible, and removal punishment if necessary.
   - **Elementary:** After assigning seat work, a first-grade teacher gives tickets to students who are working quietly. The students may exchange the tickets for opportunities to play games and work at learning centers.
   - **Middle School:** A seventh-grade teacher gives students "behavior points" at the beginning of the week. If students break a rule, they lose a point. At the end of the week, the students may use their remaining points to purchase special privileges such as talking with friends or listening to music with head phones.
   - **High School:** A math teacher increases the effectiveness of grades as reinforcers by awarding bonus points for quiz scores that are higher than students' personal averages.

Reinforcement Schedules

2. Reinforcement schedules influence both the acquisition of responses and their extinction. Continuous schedules increase behavior most rapidly, but intermittent schedules result in the most enduring behavior. Select the schedule that is most effective for meeting your goals.
   - **Elementary:** At the beginning of the school year, a first-grade teacher plans activities that all students can accomplish successfully. He praises liberally and rewards frequently. As students' capabilities increase, he requires more effort.
   - **Middle School:** A sixth-grade teacher only compliments students when they demonstrate thorough understanding. She also praises students when they demonstrate extra effort.
   - **High School:** A geometry teacher gives frequent announced quizzes to prevent the decline in effort that can occur after reinforcement with a fixed-interval schedule.

Shaping

3. Shaping is the process of reinforcing successive approximations of a desired behavior. Capitalize on the process to develop complex skills.
   - **Elementary:** A second-grade teacher openly praises a student whose behavior is improving. As improvement continues, longer periods of acceptable behavior are required before the student is praised.
   - **Middle School:** As a language arts teacher scores students' paragraphs, she is initially generous with positive comments, but as the students' work improves, she is more critical.
   - **High School:** An Algebra II teacher liberally praises students as they make the initial steps in solving equations. As their skills improve, he reduces the amount of reinforcement.

Antecedents

4. Antecedents are signals that induce desired behaviors, which can then be reinforced. Provide cues to elicit appropriate behaviors.
   - **Elementary:** Before students line up for lunch, a first-grade teacher reminds them to stand quietly while waiting to be dismissed. When they do so, she compliments them on their good behavior.
   - **Middle School:** After assigning seat work, a seventh-grade English teacher circulates around the room, reminding students to stay on task.
   - **High School:** When a chemistry teacher's students respond incorrectly, or fail to respond, he prompts them with additional questions that help them respond acceptably.

check your understanding

2.1 Judy is off task in your class, and you admonish her. In about 10 minutes, she's off task again, and again you admonish her. About 5 minutes later, she's off task a third time. What idea from operant conditioning does Judy's behavior illustrate? Explain.

2.2 "This test was too long," Rick's students complain as he finishes a discussion of a test he just handed back. Rick reduces the length of his next test, but halfway through the discussion, his students again grumble about the length. Rick reduces the length of his third test even more, and as he is turning the test back, his students begin, "What's going on, Mr. Kane? Is writing long tests the only thing you do?" Identify the operant conditioning idea best illustrated by Rick's reducing the length of the test, and identify the concept best illustrated by the students' complaining.

2.3 To encourage on-task behaviors, Mrs. Emerick uses a beeper. If students are on task when the beeper goes off, the class earns points toward a classroom party. What reinforcement schedule is Mrs. Emerick using? Explain.

2.4 As part of her routine, Anita Mendez has a warmup exercise displayed on the overhead each day when the students walk in her room. They immediately begin working on the exercise as she takes roll. She frequently compliments them on their conscientiousness and good behavior as they work. Identify the antecedent, the behavior, and the reinforcers in this example.

To receive feedback for these questions, go to Appendix A.

Social Cognitive Theory

"What are you doing?" Jason asks Kelly as he comes around the corner and catches her swinging her arms back and forth.

"I'm trying to swing at a ball like the pros do, but I haven't been able to quite do it," Kelly responds. "I was watching a game on TV last night, and the way those guys swing looks so easy, but they hit it so hard. I think I can do that if I work at it."

Three-year-old Jimmy crawls up on his dad's lap with a book. "I read too, Dad," he says as his father puts down his own book to help Jimmy up.

You're driving 65 miles an hour on the interstate, and you're passed by a sports car that appears to be going at least 75. The posted speed limit is 55. A moment later, you see the sports car that passed you pulled over by a highway patrol. You immediately slow down.

These events have two common features. First, each involved learning by observing the behavior of others; Kelly tried to imitate the swing of professional baseball players she had observed on TV, and Jimmy saw his dad reading and wanted to imitate him. You observed the consequences for the other driver and modified your own behavior as a result.

Second, behaviorism can't explain them. It focuses on changes in behavior that have *direct causes* outside the learner. For instance, in our opening case study, taking algebra quizzes directly caused Tim's hand to shake. And, when the sports car owner drives 55 after being fined, behaviorism suggests that the fine directly caused him to drive slower. Nothing directly happened to Kelly, Jimmy, or you; you changed your behavior simply by observing others.

Social cognitive theory, a theory of learning that focuses on changes in behavior that result from observing others, emerged from work pioneered by Albert Bandura (1925–) (Bandura, 1986, 1997, 2001). Because behaviorism and social cognitive theory both examine changes in behavior, let's look at the relationships between the two.

Social cognitive theory. A theory of learning that focuses on changes in behavior that result from observing others.

Albert Bandura was born in 1925 in a small town in northern Canada. He earned his doctorate at the University of Iowa and joined the faculty at Stanford University, where he remains today. Often described as America's greatest living psychologist, he is widely recognized as the primary developer of social cognitive theory. He has written on topics ranging from homelessness to terrorism.

A 2002 survey ranked Bandura as the third most frequently cited psychologist of all time, behind only Sigmund Freud and B. F. Skinner.

Comparing Behaviorism and Social Cognitive Theory

You might be asking yourself, "If behaviorists focus on observable behavior, and the term *cognitive* implies memory and thinking, why is a cognitive learning theory included in the same chapter with behaviorism?"

Here's why: Social cognitive theory has its historical roots in behaviorism, but, as the name implies, it has evolved over the years into a more cognitive perspective (Kim & Baylor, 2006). Even today, many authors continue to include aspects of social cognitive theory in books focusing on behavioral principles (e.g., Baldwin & Baldwin, 2001). In addition, behaviorism and social cognitive theory are similar in three ways:

- They agree that experience is an important cause of learning (as do other cognitive descriptions, e.g., those found in Piaget's and Vygotsky's work).
- They include the concepts of *reinforcement* and *punishment* in their explanations of learning.
- They agree that feedback is important in promoting learning.

However, the two theories differ in three important ways. First, they define learning differently, and second, social cognitive theory emphasizes the role of beliefs, self-perceptions, and expectations in learning. Third, social cognitive theory suggests that the environment, personal factors, and behavior are interdependent, a concept called *reciprocal causation.* Next we discuss these differences.

Definition of Learning

Learning (cognitive). A change in mental processes that creates the capacity to demonstrate different behaviors.

Behaviorists define learning as a change in observable behavior, whereas social cognitive theorists view **learning** as a change in mental processes that creates the capacity to demonstrate different behaviors (W. F. Hill, 2002). So, learning may or may not result in immediate behavioral change. The role of mental activity (cognition) in this internal process is illustrated in our examples. Kelly, for instance, didn't try to imitate the baseball swing until the next day, so her observations had to be stored in her memory or she wouldn't have been able to reproduce the behaviors. Also, neither Kelly, Jimmy, nor you were directly reinforced or punished, so you were all responding to mental processes and not directly to the environment.

The Role of Expectations

Instead of viewing reinforcers and punishers as direct causes of behavior, as is the behaviorist interpretation, social cognitive theorists believe that reinforcers and punishers create *expectations,* cognitive processes that then influence behavior. For example, students may study for an exam for several days, but they aren't reinforced until they receive their score. They sustain their efforts because they *expect* to be reinforced for studying. You slowed down when you saw the other car stopped because you expected to be punished—pulled over and fined—if you continued speeding. Behaviorists don't consider the role of expectations in learning, but they are central to social cognitive theory.

The fact that people respond to their expectations means they are aware of which behaviors will be reinforced or punished. This is important because, according to social cognitive theory, reinforcement changes behavior only when learners know what behaviors are being reinforced (Bandura, 1986). Tim expected his changed study habits to improve his math scores, so he maintained those habits. If he had expected some other strategy to be effective, he would have used it. He wasn't merely responding to reinforcers; he was actively assessing the effectiveness of his strategy.

The importance of student cognitions has two implications for you as a teacher. First, you should clearly specify the behaviors you will reinforce, so students can adapt their behavior accordingly, and second, you should provide students with clear feedback so they know what behaviors have been reinforced. If a student receives full credit for an essay item on a test, for instance, but doesn't know why she received it, she may not know how to respond correctly the next time.

Reciprocal Causation

Behaviorism suggests a one-way relationship between the environment and behavior; the environment influences behavior, but the opposite doesn't occur. Social cognitive theory's explanation is more complex, suggesting that behavior, the environment, and personal factors, such as expectations, are interdependent, meaning each influences the other two. The term **reciprocal causation** describes this interdependence.

Reciprocal causation. The interdependence of the environment, behavior, and personal factors in learning.

For instance, Tim's low score on his algebra quiz (an environmental factor) influenced his expectations (a personal factor) about future success on algebra quizzes. His expectations then influenced his behavior (he adapted his study habits), and his behavior influenced the environment (he went to Susan's home to study).

Reciprocal causation was also involved in your experience with the other driver. Seeing the other driver pulled over (an environmental factor) influenced your expectations (a personal factor), which influenced your behavior (you slowed down). Your behavior then influenced the environment; you changed the way you drove, allowing you to pass other highway patrols without incident.

We turn now to core concepts in social cognitive theory.

Modeling

Modeling is "a general term that refers to behavioral, cognitive, and affective changes deriving from observing one or more models" (Schunk, 2004, p. 88). Modeling is the central concept of social cognitive theory. Tim, for example, observed that Susan was successful in her approach to studying for exams. As a result, he imitated her behavior; direct imitation is one form of modeling.

Modeling. A general term that refers to behavioral, cognitive, and affective changes deriving from observing one or more models.

The importance of modeling in our everyday lives is difficult to overstate. Children learn acceptable ways of behaving by observing the behaviors of parents and other adults. Teenagers' hair and dress are influenced by both television and movies. Even as adults, we pick up cues from others in deciding how to dress and act.

Modeling is also important in schools. Teachers demonstrate a variety of skills, such as solutions to math problems, effective writing techniques, and critical thinking (Braaksma et al., 2004). Teachers also display courtesy and respect for others, tolerance for dissenting opinions, motivation to learn, and other attitudes and values. Coaches demonstrate techniques for correctly hitting a serve in volleyball, making a corner kick in soccer, and other skills, together with team work, a sense of fair play, humility in victory, and graciousness in defeat. Teacher educators are urged to be models for their students (Lunenberg, Korthagen, & Swennen, 2007).

When teachers or coaches display intellectual or physical skills, they are *direct* models. Videotaped examples, as well as characters in movies, television, books, and plays are *symbolic* models, and combining different portions of observed acts represents *synthesized modeling* (Bandura, 1986). Table 6.4 outlines these different forms of modeling.

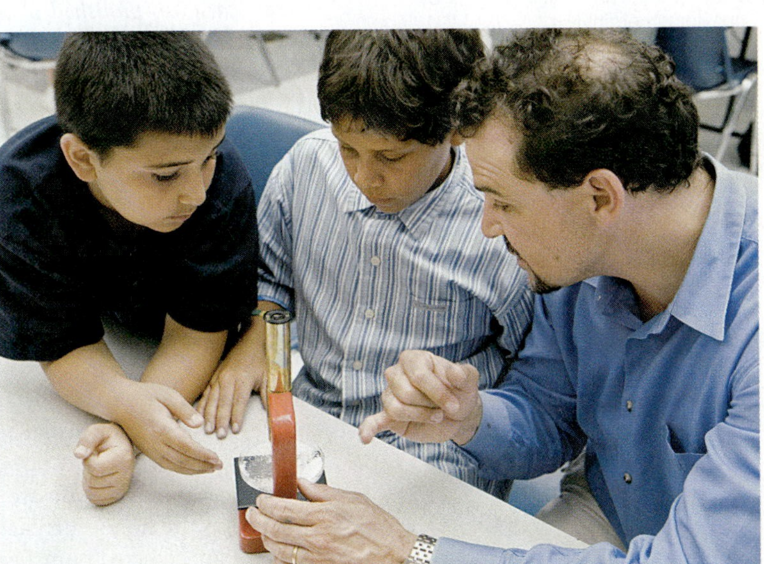

Teacher modeling can help students develop a variety of abilities.

table 6.4 Different Forms of Modeling

Type	Description	Example
Direct modeling	Simply attempting to imitate the model's behavior	Tim imitates Susan in studying for exams. A first grader forms letters in the same way a teacher forms them.
Symbolic modeling	Imitating behaviors displayed by characters in books, plays, movies, or television	Teenagers begin to dress like characters on a popular television show oriented toward teens.
Synthesized modeling	Developing behaviors by combining portions of observed acts	A child uses a chair to get up and open the cupboard door after seeing her brother use a chair to get a book from a shelf and seeing her mother open the cupboard door.

Cognitive Modeling

Cognitive modeling. The process of performing a demonstration combined with verbalizing the thinking behind the actions.

Effective teachers also use **cognitive modeling,** the process of performing a demonstration combined with verbalizing the thinking behind the actions (Schunk, 2004). An example follows:

> "Wait," Jeanna Edwards says as she sees Nicole struggling with the microscope. "Let me show you. . . . Watch closely as I adjust it. The first thing I think about is getting the slide in place. Otherwise, I might not be able to find what I'm looking for. Then, I want to be sure I don't crack the slide while I lower the lens, so I watch from the side. Finally, I slowly raise the lens until I have the object in focus. You were trying to focus as you lowered it. It's easier and safer if you try to focus as you raise it. Go ahead and try it."

As Jeanna demonstrated how to use the microscope, she also described her thoughts, such as, "The first thing I think about is getting the slide into place." When teachers put their thinking into words, or when they encourage students to verbalize their understanding, they provide learners with concrete examples of how to think about and solve problems (Braaksma et al., 2004).

Vicarious Learning

Vicarious learning. The process of people observing the consequences of other's actions and adjusting their own behavior accordingly.

In addition to modeling, people also learn by observing the consequences of other's actions and adjusting their own behavior accordingly, a process called **vicarious learning** (Gholson & Craig, 2006). For example, you saw the sports car pulled over, and you slowed down, so you were *vicariously punished,* and when a student is publicly reprimanded for leaving his seat without permission, other students in the class are vicariously punished.

On the other hand, Tim saw how well Susan did on quizzes, so he was *vicariously reinforced* through her success. When students hear a teacher say, "I really like the way Kevin is working so quietly," they are also being vicariously reinforced.

Expectations help us understand the effectiveness of vicarious learning. Tim *expected* to be reinforced for imitating Susan's behavior, and the other students expect to be reinforced for imitating Kevin's behavior. You expected to be punished if you continued speeding, so you slowed down.

Nonoccurrence of Expected Consequences

Expectations are also important because they influence behavior when they aren't met. For example, suppose your instructor gives you a homework assignment, you work hard on it, but she doesn't collect it. The nonoccurrence of the expected reinforcer (credit for the assignment) can act as a punisher; you are less likely to work hard on the next assignment.

Just as the nonoccurrence of an expected reinforcer can act as a punisher, the nonoccurrence of an expected punisher can act as a reinforcer (Bandura, 1986). For example, students expect to be reprimanded (punished) for breaking rules, so if they break rules and aren't reprimanded, they are more likely to break rules in the future. The nonoccurrence of the expected punisher (reprimand) acts as a reinforcer for the misbehavior.

The nonoccurrence of expected consequences is common in the outside world. For example, teachers are frequently asked to provide input into school policy, and it is reinforcing to have the input used. When it isn't used, they are less likely to offer input in the future. Sports fans buy season tickets to see their local team play, but if the team consistently loses, they're less likely to buy tickets in the future. Seeing the team win would be reinforcing, and its nonoccurrence decreases fans' season-ticket-buying behavior.

check your understanding

3.1 Teachers who do cooperative learning activities sometimes give all the students in the group the same grade. Research indicates that this practice is ineffective (Slavin, 1995). Using the information in this section, explain why the practice is ineffective.

3.2 Mike was taking chemistry from an instructor who only lectured and then assigned problems for practice. He found he often "drifted off" during class. Because he felt he wasn't learning, he managed (with the help of his parents) to get switched to Mr. Adams's class. "If he sees you aren't paying attention, he calls on you," Mike comments. "So, I don't sleep in his class, and I'm getting to where I really understand the stuff now." Explain how reciprocal causation is illustrated in this example.

3.3 Coach Jeffreys emphasizes hard but fair play with his soccer team. Seeing one of his players cut an opposing team member's legs out from under him, Coach Jeffreys benches the player, explaining to him (and the rest of the team) why he did so. He doesn't see another incident of this type of foul for the rest of the year. Explain why this occurred, including the role of expectations in your explanation.

3.4 Answer the third question we asked at the beginning of the chapter: "Why did he [Tim] change his study habits and sustain his efforts?"

To receive feedback for these questions, go to Appendix A.

Having introduced modeling, vicarious learning, and the nonoccurrence of expected consequences, we now examine these ideas in greater detail as we discuss:

- The effects of modeling
- The processes involved in learning from models
- The effectiveness of models
- Self-regulation

The Effects of Modeling

Modeling can result in behavioral change but it can also affect cognition and emotions. Figure 6.5 outlines these influences, and we discuss them in the sections that follow.

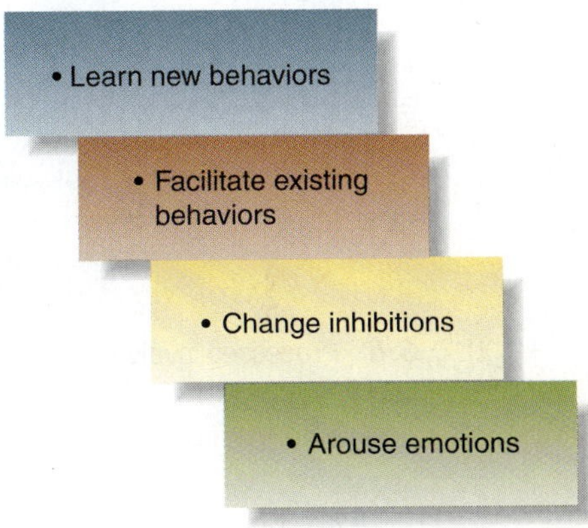

• Learn new behaviors
• Facilitate existing behaviors
• Change inhibitions
• Arouse emotions

Figure 6.5 The effects of modeling

Learning New Behaviors. Through imitation, people can acquire abilities they couldn't display before observing the model. Solving an algebra problem after seeing the teacher show a solution, making a new recipe after seeing it demonstrated on television, or learning to write a clear paragraph after seeing an exemplary one are all examples. Kelly's comment, "I'm trying to swing at a ball like the pros do, but I haven't been able to quite do it," indicates that she was attempting to learn a new behavior when she watched the players on television.

Facilitating Existing Behaviors. Suppose you're attending a concert, and at the end of one of the numbers, someone stands and begins to applaud. Others notice and join in to create a standing ovation. People already know how to stand and applaud, so new behaviors aren't learned. Instead, the observed person "facilitated" others' behaviors.

Tim also illustrated this process. He practiced solving problems before quizzes, but he admitted, "I usually do a couple, and if I'm okay on them, I quit." After observing Susan, he changed the way he studied. Her approach to preparing for quizzes facilitated Tim's studying behavior.

Changing Inhibitions. An **inhibition** is a self-imposed restriction on one's behavior, and observing a model and the consequences of the model's behavior can either strengthen or weaken it. Unlike actions that facilitate existing behaviors, changing inhibitions involves socially unacceptable behaviors, such as breaking classroom rules (Schunk et al., 2008).

Inhibition. A self-imposed restriction on one's behavior.

For example, students are less likely to break a rule if one of their peers is reprimanded; their inhibition about breaking the rule has been strengthened. Jacob Kounin (1970), one of the pioneer researchers in the area of classroom management, called this phenomenon the *ripple effect*. On the other hand, if a student speaks without permission and isn't reprimanded, other students are more likely to do the same. The inhibition is weakened.

Vicarious learning and the *nonoccurrence of expected consequences* help explain changed inhibitions. For instance, if students see a peer reprimanded for breaking a rule, they are vicariously punished; they expect the same result if they break the rule, and their inhibition about breaking the rule is strengthened. However, if the student is not reprimanded, the nonoccurrence of the expected punisher acts as a reinforcer, and both the student and the rest of the class are more likely to break the rule. Their inhibition about breaking the rule has been weakened.

Arousing Emotions. Finally, a person's emotional reactions can be changed by observing a model's display of emotions. For example, observing the uneasiness of a diver on a high board may cause an observer to become more fearful of the board. On the other hand, observing teachers genuinely enjoying themselves as they discuss a topic can help generate similar enthusiasm in students (Brophy, 2004).

Earlier, we defined modeling as "behavioral, cognitive, and affective changes deriving from observing one or more models," and these examples help us better understand the definition. For example, we see behavioral changes when behaviors are learned or facilitated, cognitive changes in strengthening or weakening inhibitions, and affective changes when emotions are aroused.

Processes Involved in Learning from Models

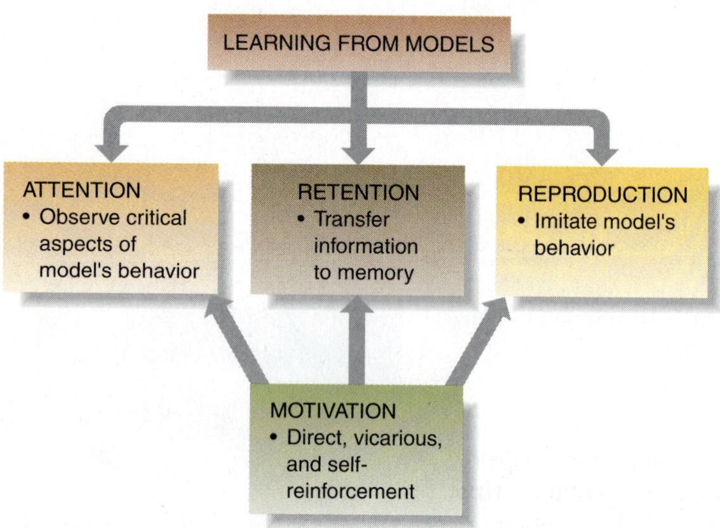

Figure 6.6 Processes involved in learning from models

Now, we'll discuss how learning and facilitating behaviors, changing inhibitions, and arousing emotions all occur. Four processes are involved: *attention, retention, reproduction,* and *motivation* (Bandura, 1986). They're illustrated in Figure 6.6 and summarized as follows:

- *Attention:* A learner's attention is drawn to the essential aspects of the modeled behavior.
- *Retention:* The modeled behaviors are transferred to memory. Storing the modeled behavior allows the learner to reproduce it later.
- *Reproduction*: Learners reproduce the behaviors that they have stored in memory.
- *Motivation:* Learners are motivated by the expectation of reinforcement for reproducing the modeled behaviors.

With respect to these processes, three factors are important for teachers. First, to learn from models, learners' attention must be drawn to the essential aspects of the modeled behavior (Bandura, 1986). For example, preservice teachers often go into schools and observe veterans in action, but if they don't know what they're looking for, the observations don't significantly influence their learning. As teachers, we need to call attention to the important aspects of the skill we're demonstrating.

Second, attending to the modeled behaviors and recording them in memory don't ensure that learners will be able to reproduce them. Additional scaffolding and practice with feedback are often required. (We examine this issue in more detail in the "Theory to Practice" feature later in the chapter.)

Third, although motivation appears as a separate component in Figure 6.6, it is integral to each of the other processes. Motivated learners are more likely to attend to a model's behavior, to record the behavior in memory, and to reproduce it. This is illustrated by the arrows from "motivation" pointing to each of the other processes.

Effectiveness of Models

The effectiveness of a model describes the likelihood that the behavioral, cognitive, or affective changes derived from observing models will occur. A model's effectiveness depends on three factors:

- Perceived similarity
- Perceived competence
- Perceived status

When we observe a model's behavior, we are more likely to imitate him or her if we perceive the model as similar to us. This helps us understand why presenting nontraditional career models and teaching students about the contributions of women and people from minority groups are important. Either gender can effectively demonstrate that engineering presents career opportunities, for example, but girls are more likely to believe that it is a viable career if they observe the work of a female rather than a male engineer. Similarly, a Hispanic student is more likely to believe he can accomplish challenging goals if he sees the accomplishments of a successful Hispanic adult than if the adult is a nonminority.

Perceived similarity is an important factor in a model's effectiveness.

Perception of a model's competence, the second factor, interacts with perceptions of similarity. People are more likely to imitate models perceived as competent than those perceived as less competent, regardless of similarity. Although Tim and Susan were similar in that they were classmates, Tim would have been unlikely to change his behavior after observing her if she had not been a successful student.

Perceived status, the third factor, is acquired when individuals distinguish themselves from others in their fields. People tend to imitate high-status individuals, such as professional athletes, popular rock stars, and world leaders, more often than others. At the school level, athletes, cheerleaders, and in some cases even gang leaders have high status for some students.

Teachers are also influential models. Despite concerns expressed by educational reformers and teachers themselves, they have been and continue to be high-status models for students.

High-status models enjoy an additional benefit. They are often tacitly credited for competence outside their own areas of expertise. This is why you see professional athletes (instead of nutritionists) endorsing breakfast cereal, and actors (instead of engineers) endorsing automobiles and motor oil.

Self-Regulation

Earlier, you saw that learners' expectations can influence both behavior and the environment. This is accomplished through **self-regulation,** the process of setting personal goals, combined with the motivation, thought processes, strategies, and behaviors that lead to reaching the goals (Zimmerman & Schunk, 2001). Self-regulated learners take responsibility for their own learning (Greene & Azevedo, 2007). Tim, for example, was motivated to improve his understanding. He went to Susan's home to study, and he modified and monitored his study strategies as a result of his experience. Behaviorists can't explain Tim's change in behavior, because he wasn't reinforced for doing so until his efforts paid off sometime later. To behave as he did, Tim had to be self-regulated (Bandura, 1986).

Self-regulation. The process of setting personal goals, combined with the motivation, thought processes, strategies, and behaviors that lead to reaching the goals.

Self-regulation includes the following components:

- Set goals.
- Monitor progress toward the goals.
- Assess the extent to which goals are met.
- Use strategies effectively. (Meichenbaum, 2000; Paris & Paris, 2001; Winne, 2001)

Setting Goals

Goals provide direction for a person's actions and benchmarks for measuring progress. Susan set the goal of working at least three of each type of algebra problem, and Tim imitated her behavior by setting goals of his own.

Goals set by students themselves, and especially goals that are challenging but realistic, are more effective than those imposed by others (Schunk et al., 2008; Stipek, 2002). Helping students create effective goals is important, but difficult, because they have a tendency to set simple and low-level goals.

theory to practice

Applying Social Cognitive Theory in Your Classroom

Social cognitive theory has a wide range of classroom applications. The following guidelines can help you apply the theory with your students.

1. Model desirable behaviors for students.
2. Place students in modeling roles, and use cognitive modeling to share their strategies.
3. Capitalize on modeling effects and processes to promote learning.
4. Use guest role models.

Let's see how Sally Campese, an eighth-grade algebra teacher, attempts to apply these guidelines with her students. Sally has a number of students in her class who are members of cultural minorities.

"We'd better get going," Arthur says to Tameka, as they approach Sally's room. "You know how she is. She thinks algebra is sooo important."

As Sally begins her class, she comments, "Just a reminder. I've invited a man named Javier Sanchez to speak on Friday. He is an engineer, and he's going to tell you how he uses math in his career.

"Okay, look here," Sally says, turning to the day's topic. "We're having a little difficulty with some of these problems, so let's go over some additional examples.

"Try this one," she says, writing the following on the board:

$$4a + 6b = 24$$
$$5a - 6b = 3$$

Sally watches the students, and seeing that Gabriela has solved the problem successfully, says, "Gabriela, come up to the board and describe your thinking for us as you solved the problem."

Gabriela explains that she added the two equations to get $9a + 0b = 27$, and as she writes the new equation on the board, Sally then asks, "What is the value of *a*? . . . Chris?"

". . . Three."

"And how did you get that?"

"Zero *b* is zero, and I divided both sides by 9, so I have 1*a* equals 3."

"Good! . . . Now, let's find the value of *b*. What should we do first? . . . Mitchell?"

Now, let's look at Sally's attempts to apply the guidelines with her students. First, Arthur's comment, "She thinks algebra is sooo important," resulted from Sally modeling her own genuine interest in the topic. Modeling won't make all students enthusiastic learners, but it can make a difference in student motivation, as we saw in Arthur's comment (Brophy, 2004).

Sally applied the second and third guidelines by having Gabriela explain her thinking (cognitive modeling) and guiding her students through the solution with questions rather than simply explaining the solution. This type of instruction made them more likely to *attend* to the demonstrated behavior, *retain* it, and *reproduce* it (N. Lambert & McCombs, 1998). And, Gabriela was an effective model because of perceived similarity.

Finally, Sally applied the last guideline by inviting Mr. Sanchez to her class. Because he was Hispanic, he would, through perceived similarity, be an effective role model for her students who were members of cultural minorities. Inviting a guest even once or twice a year can do much to capitalize on the influence of minority role models.

Monitoring Progress

Once they have established their goals, self-regulated learners monitor their progress. Susan, for example, said, "I sometimes even make a little chart. I try to do at least three problems of each type we study, and then I check them off as I do them."

Students can be taught to monitor a variety of behaviors. For example, they can keep a chart and make a check every time they catch themselves "drifting off" during an hour of study, every time they blurt out an answer in class, or every time they use a desired social skill. Research indicates that self-observation combined with appropriate goals can improve concentration, study habits, social skills, and a variety of others (Alberto & Troutman, 2006).

Self-Assessment

In schools, a person's performance is typically judged by someone else. This doesn't always have to be the case. Though teachers provide valuable feedback, students can learn to assess their own work (Stiggins, 2005). For example, students can assess the quality of their solutions to word problems by comparing their answers with estimates and asking themselves if their answers make sense. Tim's comparing his answers to those in the back of the book is a form of self-assessment.

Developing self-assessment skills takes time and requires that learners are aware of their goals and the strategies they use to reach them, a process called *metacognition*. (We discuss metacognition in Chapter 7.) Initially, students won't be good at it, and the best way to help students develop these skills is to be sure their goals are specific and measurable, as were Susan's and Tim's. Helping students make valid self-assessments based on accurate self-observations is one of the most important tasks teachers face in promoting self-regulation.

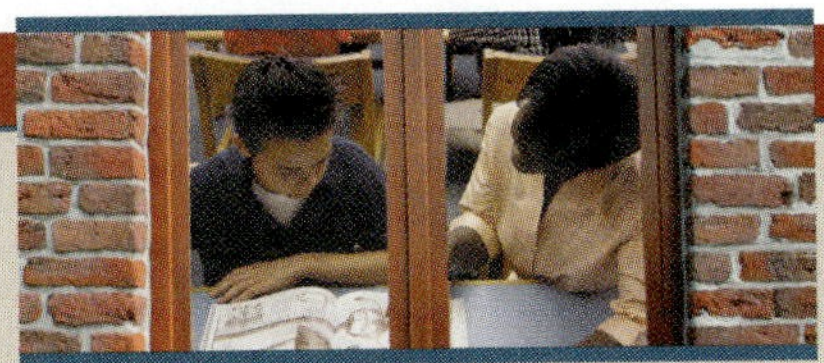

classroom connections

Applying Social Cognitive Theory in Your Classroom

1. Cognitive modeling involves verbalizing your thinking as you demonstrate skills. Use cognitive modeling in your instruction, and act as a role model for your students.
   - **Elementary:** A kindergarten teacher helps her children form letters by saying, "I start with my pencil here and make a straight line down," as she begins to form a *b*.
   - **Middle School:** A seventh-grade teacher has a large poster at the front of his room that says, "I will always treat you with courtesy and respect, you will treat me with courtesy and respect, and you will treat each other with courtesy and respect." She models, reinforces, and calls attention to this rule throughout the school year.
   - **High School:** A physics teacher solving acceleration problems writes F = ma on the board and says, " First, I know I want to find the force on the object. Then, I think about what the problem tells me. Tell us one thing we know about the problem, . . . Lisa."
2. Effective modeling requires attending to a behavior, retaining it in memory, and then reproducing it. To capitalize on these processes, provide group practice by walking students through examples before having them practice on their own.
   - **Elementary:** A fourth-grade class is adding fractions with unlike denominators. The teacher displays the problem 1/4 + 2/3 = ? and then begins, "What do we need to do first? . . . Karen?" She continues guiding the students with questioning as they solve the problem.
   - **Middle School:** After showing students how to find exact locations using longitude and latitude, a seventh-grade geography teacher says to his students, "We want to find the city closest to 85° west and 37° north. What do these numbers tell us? . . . Josh?" He continues to guide students through the example until they locate Chicago as the closest city.
   - **High School:** After demonstrating several proofs, a geometry teacher wants her students to prove that angle 1 is greater than angle 2 in the accompanying drawing. She begins by asking, "What are we given?" After the students identify the information, she asks, "What can we conclude about segments BE and BD?" and continues to guide students to a completion of the proof with her questions.

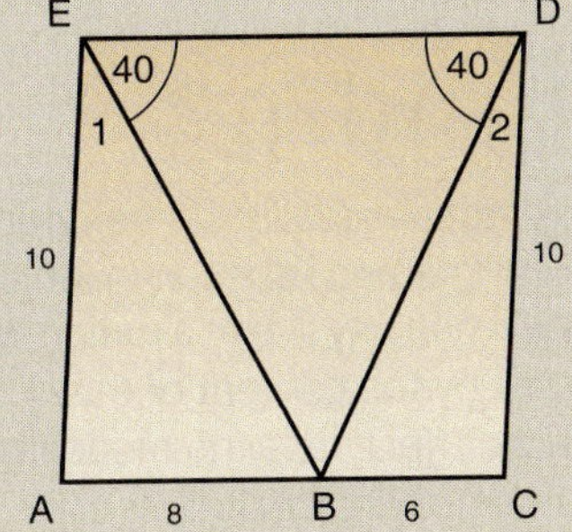

3. When learners observe a classmate being reinforced, they are vicariously reinforced. Use vicarious reinforcement to improve behavior and increase learning.
   - **Elementary:** As students in a reading group move back to their desks, a first-grade teacher comments, "I like the way this group is quietly returning to their desks. Karen, Vicki, Ali, and David each get a star."
   - **Middle School:** An eighth-grade English teacher displays examples of well-written paragraphs on the overhead and comments, "Each of these has excellent paragraph structure, and each shows some imagination. Let's look at them more closely."
   - **High School:** An art teacher displays several well-done pottery pieces and comments, "Look at these, everyone. These are excellent. Let's see why. . . . "

The English and art teachers accomplished three things. First, the students whose paragraphs or pottery were displayed were directly reinforced, but they weren't put on the spot, because the teachers didn't identify them. Second, the rest of the students in the classes were vicariously reinforced. Third, the teachers gave the classes feedback and provided models for future imitation.

4. Self-regulation is the process of students taking responsibility for their own learning. Teach self-regulation by systematically working on its components.
   - **Elementary:** A third-grade teacher helps his students design a checklist that they can use to monitor their ability to leave their seats only when given permission. The teacher initially reminds them to make a check when they are out of their seats, and later he monitors the students to see if they've given themselves checks when appropriate.
   - **Middle School:** A pre-algebra teacher helps her students create a rating scale to assess their progress on homework. For each assignment, they circle a 3 if they complete the assignment and believe they understand it, a 2 if they complete it but are uncertain about their understanding, and a 1 if they do not complete it.
   - **High School:** An English teacher helps his students set individual goals by asking each to write a study plan. He returns to the plan at the end of the unit and has each student assess his or her progress.

Strategy Use

Self-regulated learners are able to select the most effective strategies to reach their goals. For example, Tim initially worked a couple practice problems, and if he was able to do them, he quit. But, because of Susan's modeling, he selected a wider variety of problems. This seemingly simple change was a more effective strategy.

Even young children can learn to use effective strategies. For example, if a first grader is strategic in studying a list of spelling words, he will practice the words he doesn't know how to spell more than those he can already spell. (We examine strategy use in detail in Chapter 9.)

Developing self-regulation in students is powerful but difficult. For example, students need a great deal of help in setting challenging but realistic goals, and students won't initially be good at monitoring their own progress and conducting self-assessments (Yell, Robinson, & Drasgow, 2001). However, if it can be achieved, self-regulation is a capability that extends to everything in life.

Cognitive Behavior Modification

Cognitive behavior modification. A procedure that combines behavioral and cognitive learning principles to promote behavioral change in students through self-talk and self-instruction.

Self-regulation can be enhanced through **cognitive behavior modification,** a procedure that combines behavioral and cognitive learning principles to promote behavioral change in students through self-talk and self-instruction (Meichenbaum, 2000). Teachers use cognitive modeling to help students develop skills that are part of self-regulation, such as organization and time management. After observing the modeled abilities, students practice them with the teachers' support and then use self-talk as a guide when performing the skills without supervision. Cognitive behavior modification strategies are particularly effective with students having exceptionalities (Turnbull, Turnbull, & Wehmeyer, 2007).

We examine specific strategies for developing learner self-regulation in Chapter 11.

MyEducationLab

To see how another teacher attempts to use modeling to help her students develop problem solving skills, go to the *Activities and Applications* section in Chapter 6 of MyEducationLab at www.myeducationlab.com, and watch the episode *Demonstrating Problem Solving in High School Chemistry.* Answer the questions following the episode.

Putting Social Cognitive Theory into Perspective

Like all descriptions of learning, social cognitive theory has important strengths. For example, modeling is one of the most powerful factors that exists in learning. Social cognitive theory also overcomes some of the limitations of behaviorism by helping us understand the importance of learner cognition, and particularly expectations, on their actions (Schunk et al., 2008).

Like any theory, however, social cognitive theory also has limitations. For example:

- It cannot explain why learners attend to some modeled behaviors but not others.
- It can't explain why learners can reproduce some behaviors they observe but can't reproduce others.
- It doesn't account for the acquisition of complex abilities, such as learning to write (beyond mere mechanics).
- It cannot explain the role of context and social interaction in complex learning environments. For example, research indicates that student interaction in small groups facilitates learning (Fernandez-Berrocal & Santamaria, 2006). The processes involved in these settings extend beyond simple modeling and imitation.

As we said at the end of the discussion of behaviorism, every theory of learning is incomplete. This is why we discuss the prominent theories in this book; you can then apply the aspects of each that will help you maximize learning for all your students.

check your understanding

4.1 With the goal of promoting idealism in her students, a teacher shows a videotape of Martin Luther King's famous speech in which he said, "I have a dream that my four little children will one day live in a nation where they will not be judged by the color of their skin but by the content of their character." What type of modeling is being illustrated, how effective is the modeling likely to be, and what is the most likely modeling outcome? Explain.

4.2 You're in a large city waiting to cross the street. No cars are coming from either direction, so a person who is standing beside you crosses against the red light. You and the rest of the people then also cross. Explain why you cross the street. Include all relevant concepts in your explanation.

4.3 To develop a deep understanding of the topics you're studying in this text, you decide that you're going to answer and understand each of the "Check Your Understanding" questions in writing. You make a chart with the question number on it, and you make a check mark on the chart when you've answered and believe you understand the question. Then, you go to Appendix A to compare your answers to those in the feedback section. If you answer incorrectly, you reread the section and look for examples that illustrate the topic being measured by the question. Identify each of the components of self-regulation in your behavior.

To receive feedback for these questions, go to Appendix A.

developmentally appropriate practice

Applying Behaviorism and Social Cognitive Theory with Different-Aged Learners

While many applications of behaviorism and social cognitive theory apply at all grade levels, some important developmental differences exist. The following paragraphs outline some of these differences.

Working with Elementary Students

Working with Elementary Students

The emotional environment we create for our students is important at all levels but is perhaps most important for young children. This explains why kindergarten and first-grade teachers, for example, adopt practices such as giving hugs or "high fives" when children come into their classrooms.

Young children bask openly in positive reinforcement, and it is virtually impossible to satiate them with praise. On the other hand, they respond to punishment quite differently. Because their moral reasoning tends to be external, they conclude that they must be "bad" if they're punished, so punishment should be used sparingly and judiciously. Physical punishment and humiliation should never be used in classrooms, and they are particularly destructive with young children.

In the modeling process, attention is important. Because young children's attention is limited, modeling is often problematic; the children don't attend to the modeled behavior. This means that modeling must be very explicit and concrete.

Working with Middle School Students

Working with Middle School Students

A warm and supportive classroom environment continues to be important with middle school students, and, because they are going through many physical, intellectual, and emotional changes, consistent enforcement of rules and procedures is essential to help them maintain their sense of equilibrium. Middle school students become increasingly sensitive to inconsistent treatment by their teachers, and fairness is crucial to them.

Middle school students evaluate the praise they receive, and they may even react negatively to praise they view as insincere or unwarranted.

Because of their increased experience and improved language skills, cognitive modeling becomes a valuable instructional tool. They are capable of developing self-regulation, but they are unlikely to do so without extensive guidance and support.

Working with High School Students

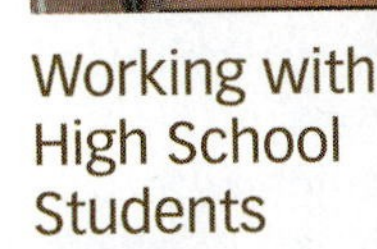

Classroom climate remains important with high school students, but the focus turns more to treating students with respect and communicating that you're genuinely committed to their learning. These students continue to be sensitive to perceptions of fairness and teachers favoring some students over others (Emmer et al., 2006).

Praise that communicates that their understanding is increasing is very effective and can increase these students' intrinsic motivation (Deci & Ryan, 2002).

High school students are increasingly self-regulated, and they're capable of setting and monitoring goals and using sophisticated learning strategies. However, they— particularly the lower achievers—are unlikely to use strategies effectively without extensive monitoring and support (Pressley & Hilden, 2006). Modeling effective strategy use becomes particularly important, and cognitive modeling can be a very effective tool for promoting their self-regulation.

exploring diversity

Capitalizing on Behaviorism and Social Cognitive Theory with Learners from Diverse Backgrounds

For some students, schools can seem cold and uninviting, and this can be particularly true for members of cultural minorities. An example follows.

Roberto, a fourth grader, shuffles into class and hides behind the big girl in front of him. If he is lucky, his teacher won't discover that he hasn't done his homework—12 problems! How can he ever do that many? Besides, he isn't good at math. Roberto hates school. It seems strange and foreign. His teacher sometimes frowns when he speaks because his English isn't as good as the other students'. And, sometimes he has trouble understanding what the teacher is saying.

Even lunch isn't much fun. If his friend Raul isn't there, he eats alone. One time when he sat with some other students, they started laughing at the way he talked and made fun of the tortillas he was eating. He can't wait to go home.

The way teachers and other students treat members of cultural minorities has a strong impact on their emotional reactions to school. School wasn't associated with positive feelings for Roberto, and he didn't feel wanted, safe, or comfortable.

It doesn't have to be this way. At the beginning of the chapter, you saw how Sharon Van Horn treated her students each morning. Let's look again.

Sharon Van Horn greets Carlos (and each of her other second graders) in a warm, friendly manner every day when he comes into her classroom, and her greeting makes him feel good. Now, Carlos experiences a comfortable feeling when entering Mrs. Van Horn's room, even when she isn't there.

Carlos had an instinctive emotional reaction to Sharon's warmth, and in time, her classroom became associated with her manner. We can explain Carlos's reaction with classical conditioning, and we can capitalize on it to help all our students feel safe in our classrooms. This is particularly important for students who are members of cultural minorities.

When students struggle, we can use antecedents in the form of prompts to encourage students, and then use praise when they succeed. While these efforts are effective with all students, they are particularly important for members of cultural minorities.

Finally, you saw that Sally Campese (in the "Theory to Practice" example on page 186) planned to bring Javier Sanchez into her class to discuss the importance of math. Mr. Sanchez's presence would provide clear evidence that a person of Hispanic background can succeed in a demanding academic field. Using role models in this way sends a powerful message to minority youth.

In their efforts to provide role models for members of cultural minorities, teachers often overlook the opportunity to use symbolic models from society at large. For example, editorial columnists, such as Walter Williams and Clarence Page—both African American—are nationally syndicated, and they frequently express opinions about prosocial values, such as the need to accept responsibility for personal behavior and success. Their pictures always appear with their columns, so teachers merely need to watch the newspapers and clip columns that are relevant to their goals. This strategy requires minimal effort, and again, minority youth receive a powerful message.

Meeting Your Learning Objectives

1. Identify examples of classical conditioning in events in and outside of classrooms.
   - Classical conditioning occurs when a formerly neutral stimulus, such as a teacher's room, becomes associated with a naturally occurring (unconditioned) stimulus, such as the teacher's warm and inviting manner, to produce a response similar to an instinctive or reflexive response, such as feelings of safety.
2. Identify examples of operant conditioning in classroom activities.
   - Operant conditioning focuses on voluntary responses that are influenced by consequences. Consequences that increase behavior are reinforcers, and consequences that decrease behavior are punishers. Teachers' praise are common reinforcers, and reprimands are common punishers. The schedule of reinforcement influences both the rate of initial learning and the persistence of the behavior.
   - Antecedents precede and induce behaviors that can then be reinforced. They exist in the form of environmental stimuli, prompts and cues, and past experiences.
3. Use ideas from social cognitive theory to explain examples of people's behaviors. Include ideas such as the nonoccurrence of expected consequences, reciprocal causation, and vicarious learning.
   - Social cognitive theory considers, in addition to behavior and the environment, learners' beliefs and expectations. According to social cognitive theory, each can influence the other in a process described as reciprocal causation.
   - The nonoccurrence of expected reinforcers can act as punishers, and the nonoccurrence of expected punishers can act as reinforcers.
   - Modeling is the core concept of social cognitive theory, and vicarious learning occurs when people observe the consequences of others' actions and adjust their own behavior accordingly.
4. Identify examples of social cognitive theory in people's behaviors. Include examples such as types of modeling, modeling outcomes, effectiveness of models, and self-regulation.
   - Modeling can be direct (from live models), symbolic (from books, movies, and television), or synthesized (combining the acts of different models).
   - The effectiveness of models describes the likelihood of an observer's imitating a model's behavior and depends

on perceived similarity, perceived status, and perceived competence.

- Social cognitive theory also helps explain events such as why teachers' describing their thought processes as they demonstrate skills is effective, and why students who set goals, monitor progress toward the goals, and assess the extent to which the goals are met achieve higher than peers who don't.

Developing as a Professional: Practicing for Your Licensure Exam

You've seen how you can use behaviorism and social cognitive theory to explain student learning. Let's look now at a teacher attempting to apply these theories in his work with his middle school students. Read the case study, and answer the questions that follow.

Warren Rose's seventh graders are working on a unit on decimals and percentages. He begins class on Thursday by saying, "Let's review what we did yesterday."

Hearing some mumbles, he notes wryly, "I realize that percentages and decimals aren't your favorite topic, and I'm not wild about them either, but they'll be on the state exam, so we might as well buckle down and learn them.

"Let's start by looking at a few examples," he continues, displaying the following problem on the overhead:

You are at the mall, shopping for a jacket. You see one that looks great, originally priced at $84, marked 25 percent off. You recently got a check for $65 from the fast-food restaurant where you work. Can you afford the jacket?

"Now, . . . when I see a problem like this, I think, 'What does the jacket cost now?' I have to figure out the price, and to do that I will take 25% of the $84. . . . That means I first convert the 25% to a decimal. I know when I see 25% that the decimal is understood to be just to the right of the 5, so I move it two places to the left. Then I can multiply 0.25 times 84."

Warren demonstrates the process as he talks, working the problem to completion. He has his students work several examples at their desks and discusses their solutions.

He then continues, "Okay, for homework, do the odd problems on page 113."

"Do we have to do all eight of them?" Robbie asks.

"Why not?" Warren responds.

"Aww, gee, Mr. Rose," Will puts in, "they're so hard."

Several other students chime in, arguing that six word problems were too many.

"Wait, people, please," Warren holds up his hands. "All right. You only have to do 1, 3, 5, 7, and 9."

"Yeah!" the class shouts.

"Yikes, Friday," Helen comments to Jenny as they walk into Warren's room Friday morning. "I, like, blanked out last week, and I felt like an idiot. Now, I get so nervous when he makes us go up to the board, and everybody's staring at us. If he calls me up today, I'll die."

Warren discusses the day's homework and then says, "Okay, let's look at this problem."

A bicycle selling for $145 is marked down 15%. What is the new selling price?

"First, let's estimate, so that we can see whether our answer makes sense. About what should the new selling price be? . . . Pamela?"

". . . I'm not sure," Pamela says.

"Callie, what do you think?"

"I think it would be about $120."

"Good thinking. Describe for everyone how you arrived at that."

"Well, 10% would be $14.50, . . . so 15% would be about another $7. That would be about $21, and $21 off would be a little over $120."

"Good," Warren nods. "Now, let's go ahead and solve it. What do we do first? . . . David?"

". . . We make the 15% into a decimal."

"Good, David. Now, what next? . . . Leslie?"

"Take the 0.15 times the 145."

"Okay. Do that everybody. . . . What did you get?"

". . . $200.17," Cris volunteers. "Whoops, that can't be right. That's more than the bicycle cost to start with. . . . Wait. . . . $21.75."

"Good," Warren smiles. "That's what we're trying to do. We are all going to make mistakes, but if we catch ourselves, we're making progress. Keep it up. You can do these problems. Now what do we do?" he continues.

"Subtract," Matt volunteers.

"All right, go ahead," Warren directs.

Warren finishes guiding students through the problem, has them do two additional problems, and then begins to assign six problems for homework. But just as he starts, several students chime in, "How about just four problems tonight, Mr. Rose. We always have so much math to do."

"Okay," Warren shrugs, "numbers 2, 6, 7, and 8 on page 114."

Warren continues monitoring students until 2 minutes are left in the period. "All right, everyone, the bell will ring in 2 minutes. Get everything cleaned up around your desks, and get ready to go."

Short-Answer Questions

In answering these questions, use information from the chapter, and link your responses to specific information in the case.

1. Describe where classical conditioning occurred in the case study. Identify the classical conditioning concepts in your description.

2. Warren's behavior was influenced by punishment in two different places in the case study. Explain where they occurred, and describe their likely impact on learning.

3. Warren inadvertently negatively reinforced the students at two points in the lesson. Identify and explain both points.

4. Warren's modeling was both effective and ineffective. Identify and explain one effective and one ineffective feature.

5. Warren capitalized on the effects of perceived similarity and vicarious learning in the case study. Explain where and how this occurred.

For feedback on these questions, go to Appendix B.

Now go to Chapter 6 of MyEducationLab, located at www.myeducationlab.com, where you can:

- Take a quiz to test your mastery of chapter objectives. Detailed feedback is provided to explain why your responses are correct or incorrect.
- Deepen your understanding of chapter concepts with *Review, Practice, Enrichment* exercises.
- Complete *Activities and Applications* that will help you apply what you have learned in the chapter by analyzing real classrooms through video clips, artifacts, and case studies. Your instructor will provide you with feedback for the *Activities and Applications.*
- Develop your professional knowledge and decision making in *Building Teaching Skills and Dispositions* exercises. Structured feedback will be available to you, providing you with support as you practice each skill. Your instructor will provide you with feedback on the final task that accompanies the exercise.

Important Concepts

antecedents (p. 173)
applied behavior analysis (ABA) (p. 175)
behaviorism (p. 164)
classical conditioning (p. 164)
cognitive behavior modification (p. 188)
cognitive modeling (p. 182)
conditioned response (p. 165)
conditioned stimulus (p. 165)
consequences (p. 167)
continuous reinforcement schedule (p. 170)
desists (p. 172)
discrimination (p. 167)
extinction (classical conditioning) (p. 167)
extinction (operant conditioning) (p. 171)
functional analysis (p. 176)
generalization (p. 167)
inhibition (p. 183)
intermittent reinforcement schedule (p. 170)
interval schedules (p. 170)
learning (behaviorism) (p. 164)
learning (cognitive) (p. 180)
modeling (p. 181)
negative reinforcement (p. 169)
neutral stimulus (p. 165)
operant conditioning (p. 167)
positive reinforcement (p. 169)
Premack principle (p. 169)
presentation punishment (p. 172)
punishers (p. 172)
punishment (p. 172)
ratio schedules (p. 170)
reciprocal causation (p. 181)
reinforcement (p. 168)
reinforcement schedules (p. 170)
reinforcer (p. 168)
removal punishment (p. 172)
response cost (p. 172)
satiation (p. 172)
self-regulation (p. 185)
shaping (p. 170)
social cognitive theory (p. 179)
timeout (p. 172)
unconditioned response (p. 165)
unconditioned stimulus (p. 165)
vicarious learning (p. 182)

chapter

7

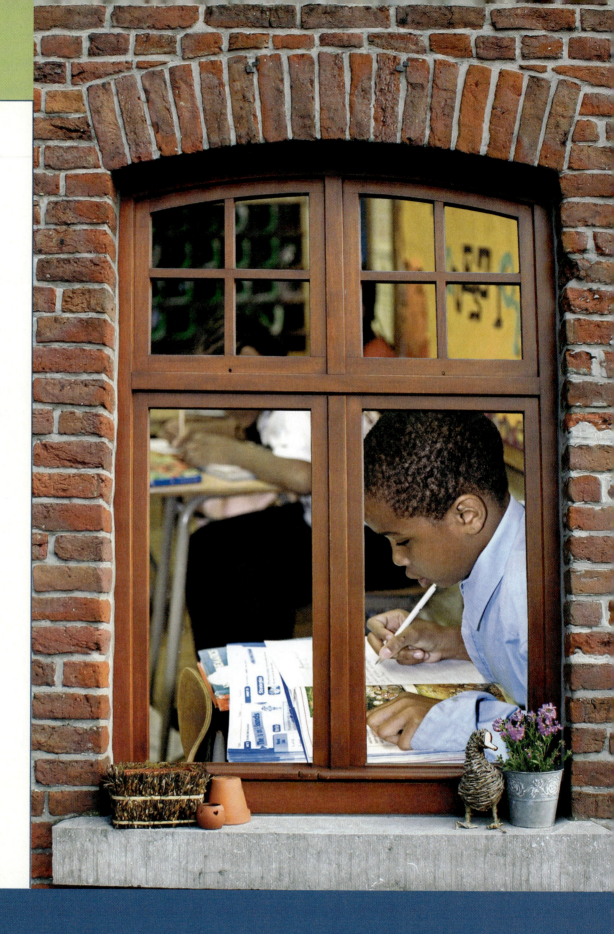

Cognitive Views of Learning

chapter outline

Cognitive Perspectives on Learning
- Principles of Cognitive Learning Theory
- A Model of Human Memory

Memory Stores
- Sensory Memory
- Working Memory
- Long-Term Memory
- Developmental Differences in the Memory Stores

Cognitive Processes
- Attention
- Perception
- Encoding
- Forgetting
  - ■ **Exploring Diversity:** The Impact of Diversity on Cognition
- Developmental Differences in Cognitive Processes

Metacognition: Knowledge and Control of Cognitive Processes
- Developmental Differences in Metacognition
  - ■ **Developmentally Appropriate Practice:** Applying the Model of Memory with Different-Aged Learners
  - ■ **Theory to Practice:** Applying an Understanding of the Human Memory Model in Your Classroom
- Putting the Memory Model into Perspective

learning objectives

After you have completed your study of this chapter, you should be able to:

1. Describe and explain the principles of cognitive learning theory.
2. Use the characteristics of the memory stores in the human memory model to explain events in and out of the classroom.
3. Describe the cognitive processes in the human memory model and identify applications in classroom activities.
4. Define *metacognition*, and explain how it can influence learning.

Have you ever commented, "I'm suffering from mental overload?" Do you make lists so you won't forget to pick up items at the store? If the answer is yes, cognitive learning theories can be used to explain your thinking. These theories help us understand our thought processes as we respond to stimuli from the environment, make sense of the information, and store it in memory. As you read the following case study, keep the students' thinking in mind, and consider how David Shelton, their teacher, supported that thinking.

David's ninth-grade earth science class is working in a unit on the solar system. He has prepared a transparency showing the sun throwing globs of gases into space and a model illustrating the planets in their orbital planes, which he has hung in the corner of the room.

David introduces the unit on Monday, displays the transparency and model, notes that they relate to one theory of how the solar system was formed, and asks the students for their interpretations of what they see. After some discussion and explanation, David assigns groups to use books and the Internet to gather information about each planet. The students spend the rest of Monday and all period Tuesday collecting and putting information into a chart.

On Wednesday, David reviews the information from Monday and Tuesday and poses some questions. The first is, Why is Pluto's orbital plane different from the planes of the planets?

The sun threw off hot spheres of gas which eventually became planets.

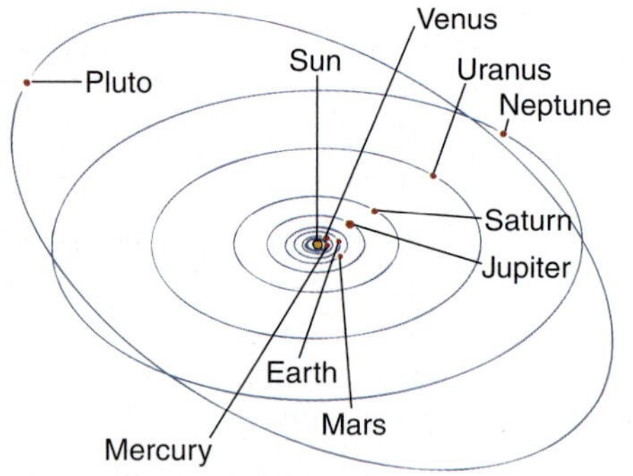

The orbital planes of the planets and Pluto.

"When I try to answer questions like these," David continues, "I first look for a relationship in the parts of the question, like what do we know about Pluto compared to the planets? . . . Be sure you write and explain each of your answers."

"I know the answer to the first question," Juan comments to Randy and Tanya in one group as the students go to work. "Pluto isn't a part of the solar system. . . . Actually, it's called a dwarf planet. It was once considered to be a planet, but it isn't anymore."

"What do you mean?" Randy wonders.

"I was watching *Nova* with my mom, and they said that Pluto was an asteroid, or some other body floating around, and the sun kind of grabbed it. . . . See," Juan continues, pointing to the model.

"What's that got to do with it?" Randy asks, still uncertain.

"Look. . . . See how Pluto is up above the rest of them," Juan says, referring to Pluto's orbit in the model.

"Gee, I didn't even notice that," Randy shrugs.

"Oh, I get it, now! . . . Pluto isn't level with the rest of them," Tanya jumps in. "I got kinda lost when Mr. Shelton was explaining all that on Monday, but now it makes sense. . . . And look there," she says, pointing to the chart. "See how small Pluto is? It's the littlest, so it would be easy to capture."

"And it's the last one," Randy adds, beginning to warm to the task. "I better write some of this stuff down, or I'll never remember it."

Now, consider some questions related to the thinking that occurred in the lesson:

1. Why was Juan able to make connections in the different items of information that Randy and Tanya were initially unable to make?
2. Why did Tanya get "kinda lost when Mr. Shelton was explaining all that on Monday?"
3. What impact will Randy's decision to "write some of this stuff down" have on his learning?

Cognitive learning theory helps answer these and other questions, and in this chapter we'll see how David applies this theory in his teaching.

Cognitive Perspectives on Learning

In Chapter 6, you saw that behaviorism explains learning in terms of observable changes in behavior that occur as a result of experience, and social cognitive theory focuses on the effects of observing others to explain learning.

Think about a time when you got an idea, essentially "out of the blue." You hadn't been reinforced for it as behaviorism would require, nor was it modeled as would be necessary according to social cognitive theory. Different explanations are required. Similarly, neither theory can explain why Juan was able to make connections in the information they were studying that neither Tanya nor Randy were able to make.

Research examining the development of complex skills, the inability of behaviorism to adequately explain how individuals learn language (Chomsky, 1959), and the development of computers all led to a search for different explanations for people's behaviors. The result was the "cognitive revolution," which marked a shift toward **cognitive learning theories,** theories that explain learning in terms of changes in the mental structures and processes involved in acquiring, organizing, and using knowledge (Royer, 2005; Sawyer, 2006). They help us explain tasks as simple as remembering a phone number and tasks as complex as understanding relationships in the solar system or solving ill-defined problems.

Cognitive learning theories. Theories that explain learning in terms of changes in the mental structures and processes involved in acquiring, organizing, and using knowledge.

The cognitive revolution occurred between the mid-1950s and early 1970s, and its influence on education has steadily increased since that time (Berliner, 2006).

Principles of Cognitive Learning Theory

Cognitive learning theories are grounded in the following principles:

- Learning and development depend on learners' experiences.
- Learners are mentally active in their attempts to make sense of those experiences.

- Learners *construct* knowledge in the process of developing an understanding of their experiences. Learners do not record knowledge.
- Knowledge that is constructed depends on knowledge that learners already possess.
- Learning is enhanced in a social environment.

Learning and Development Depend on Learners' Experiences

If you never went anywhere, met anyone, or read anything, you would have little knowledge of our world. All theories of learning and development emphasize the importance of experience, and it is illustrated in the students' discussion in the opening case. David's transparency and model, together with the information they gathered, provided experiences necessary for later learning. Understanding the solar system without these experiences would have been impossible. The influence of experience was also illustrated in Juan's and Randy's comments during group work. Because Juan had experiences (watching *Nova*) that Randy lacked, he was able to make connections beyond those Randy made.

One of our essential roles as teachers is to provide students with the experiences that become the raw material for their learning and development.

Learners Are Mentally Active in Their Attempts to Make Sense of Their Experiences

Cognitive learning theorists view students as "goal-directed agents who actively seek information" (Bransford et al., 2000, p. 10). For example, how many times have you said to yourself or to someone else, "That doesn't make any sense?" That simple statement reflects people's innate desire to understand their experiences, and it is illustrated in Tanya's comment, "Oh, I get it, now! . . . Pluto isn't level with the rest of them. . . . I got kinda lost when Mr. Shelton was explaining all that on Monday, but now it makes sense." She was cognitively active in her attempt to understand the ideas they were studying.

Learners Construct Knowledge

In attempts to understand their experiences, learners construct knowledge that makes sense to them, rather than recording information in their memories in the exact form in which it's presented (Greeno et al., 1996; R. Mayer, 2002). As a result, every student will construct and remember the ideas they are being taught a bit differently based on what makes sense to them. For instance, Tanya's comment, "See how small Pluto is? It's the littlest, so it would be easy to capture," was an original idea for her. She didn't get it from Randy or Juan, nor did David explain it. She constructed it because it made sense to her.

Knowledge That Is Constructed Depends on Learners' Prior Knowledge

People don't construct knowledge in a vacuum; their knowledge constructions depend on what they already know. For example, a child who has traveled with her parents is more likely to find geography meaningful than is someone who hasn't traveled, because she will have more experiences to which she can relate new knowledge.

Prior knowledge can also lead to misconceptions. For instance, some children mistakenly believe that a fraction with a larger denominator, such as 1/5, is greater than one with a smaller denominator, like 1/3. Knowing that 5 is greater than 3, they conclude that 1/5 should be greater than 1/3. (We examine the process of knowledge construction and the construction of misconceptions in detail in Chapter 8.)

This principle helps us answer our first question at the beginning of the chapter. As a result of watching *Nova*, Juan had prior knowledge that Tanya and Randy lacked, so he was able to make connections they were initially unable to make.

Learning Is Enhanced in a Social Environment

Vygotsky's work (1978, 1986) and increased attention from researchers (e.g., Moll & Whitmore, 1993; Rogoff, 1998) have helped educators understand that the process of knowledge construction is enhanced by social interaction. For example, Tanya and Randy both heard David explain the information demonstrated in the transparency and model, yet they didn't find the connections in the information until they discussed it. Expert teachers guide their students with questioning and use cooperative groups, as you saw in David's lesson, to help students socially construct knowledge and understanding (Fernandez-Berrocal & Santamaria, 2006).

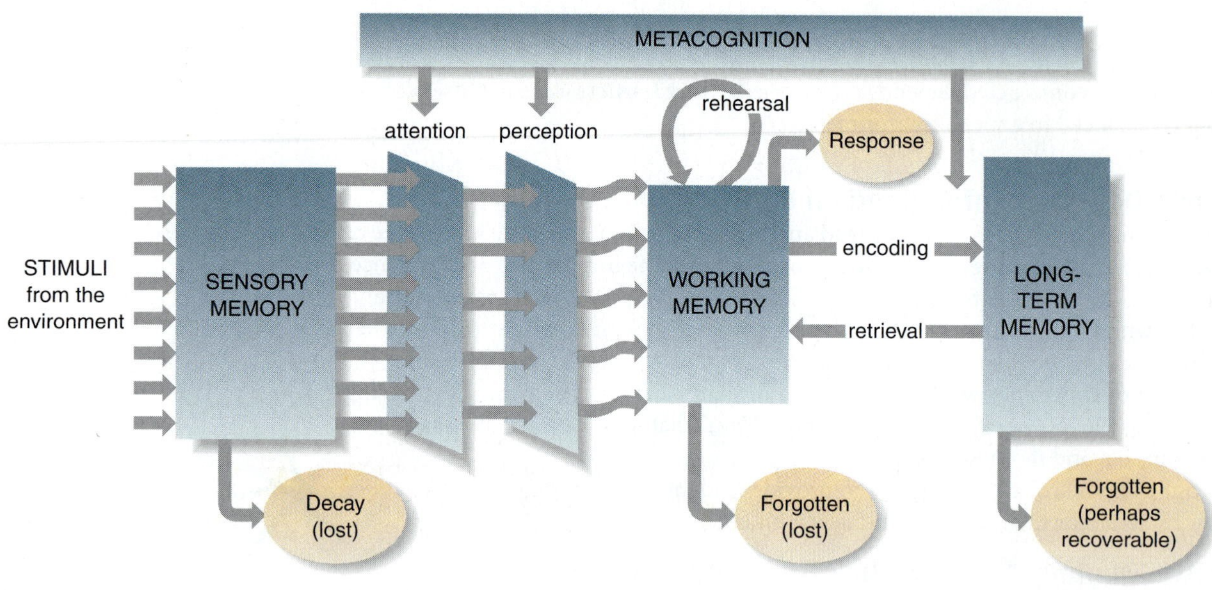

Figure 7.1 A model of human memory

These learning principles provide a foundation for helping us understand how learning occurs, but they also raise additional questions. For example, how do learners acquire the experiences they use to construct their knowledge, and how do learners combine prior knowledge with new experiences? Where is the knowledge that is constructed stored, and in what form is it stored? The answers to these and other questions are the focus of the rest of this chapter.

A Model of Human Memory

People throughout history have been fascinated by memory. While cognitive learning theorists don't totally agree on the structure of human memory, most use a model similar to what you see in Figure 7.1, which was initially proposed by R. Atkinson & Shiffrin (1968), and is often described in the framework of **information processing theory.** Since it was originally proposed, this theory has generated a great deal of research and has undergone considerable refinement. We discuss this model and modifications made to it throughout the chapter.

Information processing theory. A theory that describes how information enters our memory system, is organized, and finally stored.

The model of human memory has three major components:

- Memory stores
- Cognitive processes
- Metacognition

We examine these components in the following sections.

check your understanding

1.1 Describe the principles of cognitive learning theories.

1.2 You and a friend are trying to install a sound card in your computer, but you're a little uncertain about how to do it. You open the computer, look inside, and as you talk about how to proceed, she suggests looking to see where the speakers are attached. "Good idea," you say, and you easily install the card. Which principle of learning is best illustrated by this example?

1.3 Explain how the principles of cognitive learning theory relate to the model of human memory:

To receive feedback for these questions, go to Appendix A.

Memory Stores

Memory stores are repositories that hold information, in some cases in a raw state, and in others in organized, meaningful form. They are *sensory memory, working memory,* and *long-term memory.*

Memory stores. Repositories that hold information, in some cases in a raw state, and in others in organized, meaningful form.

Sensory Memory

Hold your finger in front of you, and rapidly wiggle it. Do you see a faint "shadow" that trails behind your finger as it moves? This shadow is the image of your finger that has been briefly stored in your visual sensory memory. Likewise, when someone says, "That's an oxymoron," you retain "Ox see moron" in your auditory sensory memory, even if it has no meaning for you.

Sensory memory is the store that briefly holds incoming stimuli from the environment until they can be processed (Neisser, 1967). Sensory memory is nearly unlimited in capacity, but if processing doesn't begin almost immediately, the memory trace quickly fades away. Sensory memory is estimated to retain information for about 1 second for vision and 2 to 4 seconds for hearing (Pashler & Carrier, 1996).

Sensory memory. The memory store that briefly holds incoming stimuli from the environment until they can be processed.

Sensory memory is the beginning point for further processing. In reading, for example, it would be impossible to obtain meaning from a sentence if you lost the first words from your visual sensory memory before you reached the end of the sentence. Sensory memory holds the information until you attach meaning to it and transfer it to working memory, the next store.

Working Memory

Working memory is the store that holds information as you process and try to make sense of it. It is the workbench of our mind where "conscious" thinking occurs (Paas et al., 2004), and it is where we construct our knowledge. We aren't aware of the contents of either sensory memory or long-term memory until they're pulled into working memory for processing.

Working memory. The store that holds information as people process and try to make sense of it. The workbench of the mind, where conscious thinking occurs and where individuals construct knowledge.

Central executive. A supervisory component of working memory that controls the flow of information to and from the other components.

Phonological loop. A short-term storage system for words and sounds in working memory.

A Model of Working Memory

Figure 7.1 represents working memory as a single unit, which is how researchers initially described it (R. Atkinson & Shiffrin, 1968). Current views of working memory, however, suggest that it is composed of three components that work together to process information (Baddeley, 1986, 2001). This model is outlined in Figure 7.2.

To illustrate the components shown in Figure 7.2, find the area of the figure you see here.

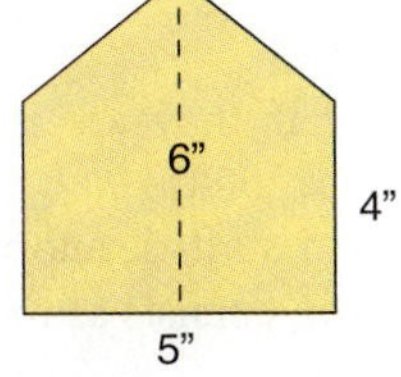

To solve the problem, you probably subtracted the 4 from the 6 to determine that the height of the triangular portion of the figure was 2 inches. You recalled that the formulas for the areas of a triangle and a rectangle are ½ (b)(h) and (l)(w) respectively, and you calculated the areas to be (½)(5)(2) = 5 sq. in. and (5)(4) = 20 sq. in. Adding the two, you found the total area to be 25 square inches.

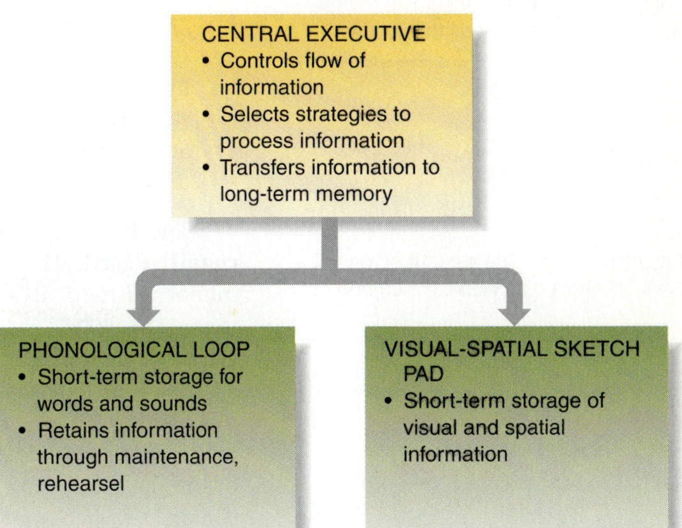

Figure 7.2 A model of working memory

Components of the Model. Let's see how the components of working memory executed the task. The **central executive,** a supervisory system, controls the flow of information to and from the other components. For instance, the decision to break the figure into a triangle and rectangle, find the area of each, and add the two was a function of the central executive.

The **phonological loop,** a short-term storage system for words and sounds, temporarily held the formulas and the dimensions of

Working memory is the "workbench" where students think about and solve problems.

Maintenance rehearsal. The process of repeating information over and over, either out loud or silently, without altering its form.

Visual-spatial sketchpad. A short-term storage system for visual and spatial information in working memory.

Short-term memory. Historically, the part of our memory system that temporarily holds information until it can be processed.

MyEducationLab

To examine student work that capitalizes on the distributed processing capabilities of working memory, go to the *Activities and Applications* section in Chapter 7 of MyEducationLab at www.myeducationlab.com, and look at the artifact *The Number 34.* Answer the questions that follow.

the figure until you could make the calculations. Information can be kept in the phonological loop indefinitely through **maintenance rehearsal,** the process of repeating information over and over, either out loud or silently, without altering its form (R. Atkinson & Shiffrin, 1968). For example, you look up a phone number, repeat it to yourself until you dial it, and then it is quickly lost. (We examine rehearsal in more detail later in the chapter.)

The **visual-spatial sketchpad,** a short-term storage system for visual and spatial information, allowed you to picture the figure and see that it could be broken into a rectangle and triangle. The visual-spatial sketchpad and the phonological loop are independent, so each can perform mental work without taxing the resources of the other (Baddeley, 1986, 2001). They serve the functions that researchers historically attributed to **short-term memory.** "Short-term memory loss" is the phrase often used to describe someone who has difficulty remembering specific events or people's names. This loss actually reflects impairment in the phonological loop or, less commonly, in the visual-spatial sketchpad.

Baddeley (1986, 2001) suggests that the phonological loop can hold about as much information as we can say to ourselves in 1½ to 2 seconds, and the visual-spatial sketchpad is also limited. We examine these limitations in the next section.

A considerable amount of research has examined the working memory model and how it impacts learning. For instance, researchers have found that learners with attention-deficit/hyperactivity disorder (ADHD) rehearse verbal and spatial information as effectively as healthy children, but their central executive is impaired (Karateken, 2004), whereas learners with reading disabilities have impaired functioning of the phonological loop (Kibby, Marks, & Morgan, 2004). Students with ADHD have trouble controlling their attention and selecting effective learning strategies, and students with reading difficulties have trouble processing verbal information.

Limitations of Working Memory

The most striking feature of working memory is the extent of its limitations (Sweller et al., 1998). Early experiments suggested that it can hold only about seven items of information at a time and can hold the items for only about 10 to 20 seconds in adults (G. Miller, 1956). (The limitations of children's working memories are even greater.) Selecting and organizing information also use working memory space, so we "are probably only able to deal with two or three items of information simultaneously when required to process rather than merely hold information" (Sweller et al., 1998, p. 252). These limitations are important because working memory is where we make conscious decisions about how to link new information from the environment to our existing knowledge (R. C. Clark & Mayer, 2003). When you said, "I'm suffering from mental overload," you were referring to your working memory.

The limited capacity of working memory has important implications for teaching and learning. Consider the following research results:

- Students' writing often improves more rapidly if they are initially allowed to ignore grammar, punctuation, and spelling (McCutchen, 2000).
- In spite of research about its ineffectiveness and staff-development efforts to promote more sophisticated forms of instruction, lecturing persists as the most common teaching strategy (Cuban, 1993).
- Students write better essays using word processors if their word processing skills are well developed. If not, handwritten essays are superior (Roblyer, 2006).

Cognitive load. The amount of mental activity imposed on working memory.

The limitations of working memory relate to these findings through the concept of **cognitive load,** which is the amount of mental activity imposed on working memory. The number of elements that you must attend to is one factor that contributes to cognitive load (Paas et al., 2004). For instance, remembering digit sequences, such as 7 9 5 3 and 3 9 2 4 6 7, can be thought of as having cognitive loads of 4 and 6, respectively.

A second factor influencing cognitive load is the extent to which the elements interact with one another (Paas et al., 2004). In the case study, for example, David's explanations imposed too heavy a cognitive load on Tanya's working memory, and she lost some of the information before she could make sense of it. This helps answer our second question (Why did Tanya get "kinda lost when Mr. Shelton was explaining all that on Monday?").

Similarly, attempting to create a well-organized essay, while at the same time using correct grammar, punctuation, and spelling, imposes a heavy cognitive load on the writer, and using sophisticated teaching strategies, such as guiding students with questioning, imposes a heavy cognitive load on teachers. The load on students is reduced if they're allowed to ignore grammar, punctuation, and spelling, and teachers reduce it by lecturing, a less cognitively demanding instructional strategy.

Reducing cognitive load in these ways is undesirable, however, because students must ultimately use correct grammar, spelling, and punctuation in their writing, and teachers are encouraged to interact with their students. We address these issues in the next section.

Reducing Cognitive Load: Accommodating the Limitations of Working Memory

We can accommodate the limitations of working memory by reducing cognitive load in three primary ways:

- Chunking
- Automaticity
- Distributed processing

Chunking. **Chunking** is the process of mentally combining separate items into larger, more meaningful units (G. Miller, 1956). For example, the sequence 9 7 4 6 3 0 1 7 5 2 is a phone number, but it isn't written as phone numbers appear. Now, as normally written, (974) 630-1752, it has been "chunked" into three larger units, which reduces cognitive load. Interestingly, working memory is sensitive only to the number of chunks and not their size. "Although the number of elements is limited, the size, complexity and sophistication of elements [are] not" (Sweller et al., 1998, p. 256).

Chunking. The process of mentally combining separate items into larger, more meaningful units.

Developing Automaticity. If you have an electric garage door opener, it is likely that you sometimes can't remember if you've put the garage door down when you left home, so you drive back to check, and you see that you have, indeed, closed it. **Automaticity** is the ability to perform mental operations with little awareness or conscious effort (Feldon, 2007a; W. Schneider & Shiffrin, 1977), and it can explain your actions. You put the garage door down without thinking about it.

Automaticity. The ability to perform mental operations with little awareness or conscious effort.

Automaticity is a second way of reducing cognitive load, and computer keyboarding skill is an example of its power and efficiency. Once our word processing capabilities become automatic, we can devote our working memory space to the composition of our writing. Until then, we must devote working memory to placing our hands on the keys, and the cognitive load becomes too great to compose quality products. This explains why students compose better essays on word processors but only if they are skilled at word processing. Also, students' grammar, punctuation, and spelling must eventually become automatic if they are to be good writers, and essential teaching skills, such as questioning, are automatic for expert teachers.

Using Distributed Processing. Earlier, you saw that the visual-spatial sketchpad and the phonological loop are independent, so each can perform mental work without taxing the resources of the other (Baddeley, 1986, 2001). This suggests that students learn more if verbal explanations are combined with visual representations (R. C. Clark & Mayer, 2003; Moreno & Duran, 2004). The visual processor supplements the verbal processor and vice versa.

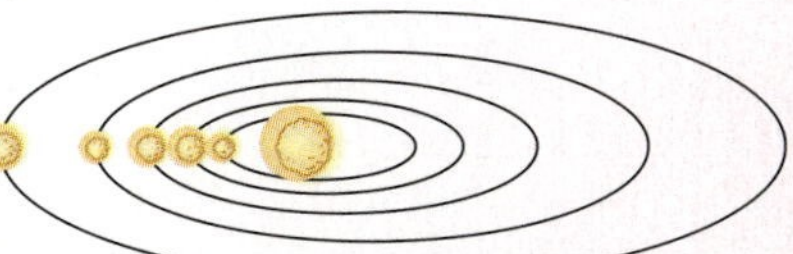

The sun threw off hot spheres of gas which eventually became planets.

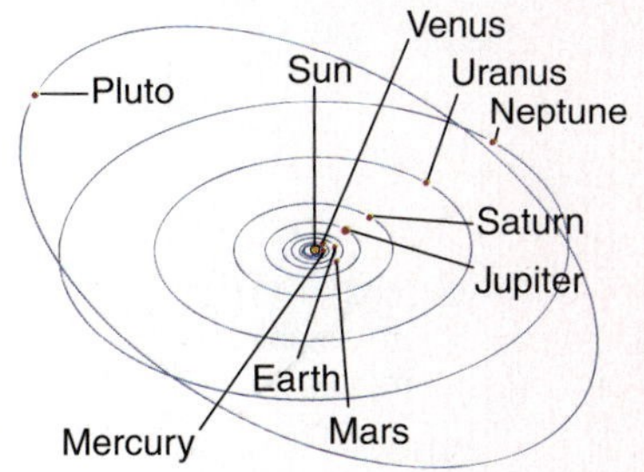

The orbital planes of the planets and Pluto.

David capitalized on the independent processing capabilities of these components by combining the visual aspects of his model and transparency with words that explained the information in them. "The integration of words and pictures is made easier by lessons that present the verbal and visual information together rather than separated" (R. C. Clark & Mayer, 2003, p. 38).

Teachers often use words, alone, to present information, which reduces learning by wasting some of working memory's processing capability and often imposing a cognitive load greater than working memory's capacity.

Long-Term Memory

Long-term memory is our permanent information store. It's like a library with millions of entries and a network that allows them to be retrieved for reference and use (Schacter, 2001;

Long-term memory. The permanent information store in the model of human memory.

Sweller, 2003). Long-term memory's capacity is vast and durable; some experts suggest that information in it remains for a lifetime.

Declarative knowledge. Knowledge of facts, definitions, procedures, and rules.

Semantic memory. Memory for concepts, principles, and the relationships among them.

Episodic memory. Memory for personal experiences.

Long-term memory contains three kinds of knowledge: *declarative knowledge, procedural knowledge,* and *conditional knowledge.* **Declarative knowledge** is knowledge of facts, concepts, procedures, and rules, and within this category, some researchers (e.g., Tulving, 2002) have distinguished between **semantic memory,** which is memory for concepts, principles, and the relationships among them, and **episodic memory,** which is memory for personal experiences.

To illustrate these ideas, let's look at some dialogue between Juan and Randy:

Juan: I know the answer to the first question. . . . Pluto isn't part of the solar system. . . . Actually, it's called a dwarf planet. It was once considered to be a planet, but it isn't anymore.

Randy: What do you mean?

Juan: I was watching *Nova* with my mom, and they said that Pluto was an asteroid, or some other body floating around, and the sun kind of grabbed it.

Juan's comments are forms of declarative knowledge; they are facts he recalled from his experience. Then, when he talked about watching *Nova* with his mom, the information came from his episodic memory; it was based on a personal experience.

The lines between episodic and semantic memory are often blurred, but one factor is significant. When people have strong emotional reactions to an event, episodic memories are more enduring. For example, you probably remember exactly where you were and what you were doing when you received word of the terrorist attacks of 9/11. Similarly, you likely recall the events surrounding your first date or kiss. These events are stored in your episodic memory. As teachers, we can capitalize on episodic memory by personalizing content or teaching it in such a way that it also has an emotional impact on our students.

Procedural knowledge. Knowledge of how to perform tasks.

Conditional knowledge. Knowledge of where and when to use declarative and procedural knowledge.

Procedural knowledge is knowledge of how to perform tasks, and **conditional knowledge** is knowledge of where and when to use declarative and procedural knowledge (J. R. Anderson, 2005; Hergenhahn & Olson, 2001). For example, consider the following problems:

$$2/7 + 4/7 =$$
$$1/4 + 2/3 =$$

You know that to add fractions you first must have like denominators. This is a form of declarative knowledge. Recognizing that you must find a common denominator in the second problem but not in the first is a form of conditional knowledge, and actually finding that the answer to the first problem is 6/7 and the answer to the second is 11/12 requires procedural knowledge.

Declarative knowledge can be determined from a person's comments, and most declarative knowledge is *explicit,* meaning, once we recall it, we are aware of what we know. On the other hand, procedural and conditional knowledge are inferred from a person's performance, and this knowledge is often *implicit,* meaning we cannot recall or explain it. For instance, when working at a computer, you can't recall the knowledge you use as you move your fingers over the keyboard, and you cannot explain exactly what you're doing. The relationships among these different forms of knowledge are outlined in Figure 7.3.

Now, let's look at how these different forms of knowledge are stored in long-term memory.

Representing Declarative Knowledge in Long-Term Memory

Schemas. Cognitive constructs that organize information into meaningful systems on long-term memory.

Acquiring declarative knowledge involves integrating new information with existing knowledge. So, people learn more effectively when they have well-developed knowledge to which new information can be related. This knowledge is organized in the form of **schemas** (also called *schemata*). Although theorists don't totally agree on a definition, schemas can be viewed as cognitive constructs that organize information into *meaningful systems* in long-term memory (J. R. Anderson, 2005; Willingham, 2004).

Meaningful Learning. Look at Figure 7.4, which helps us visualize Randy's and Juan's schemas for the solar system. Note that schemas are actually structures "in people's heads" that have been constructed; Figure 7.4 merely helps us visualize these structures. Both Randy's and Juan's schemas organize information into a system that makes sense to them. However, impor-

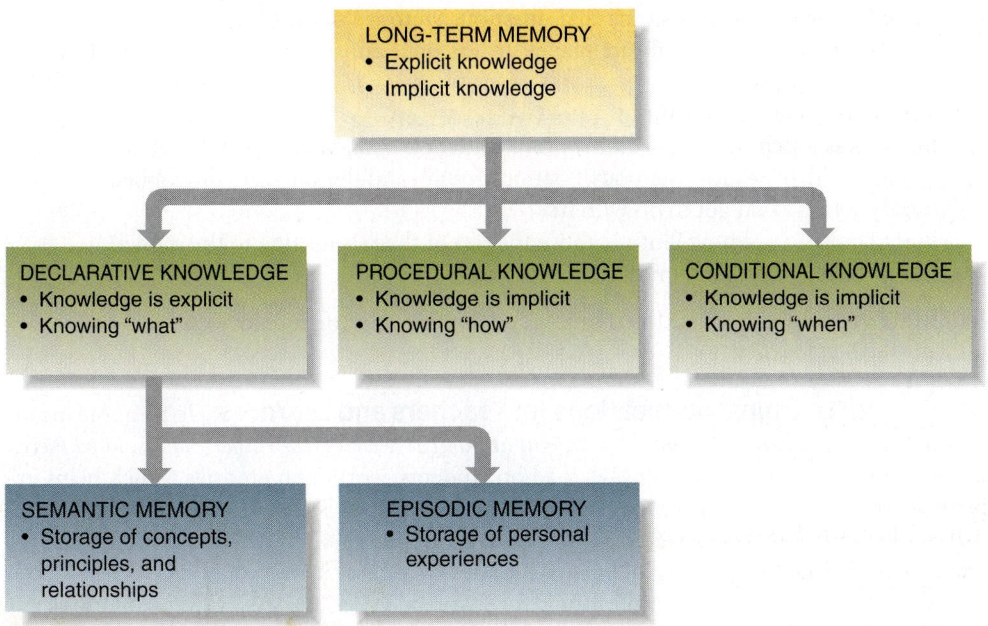

Figure 7.3 Knowledge in long-term memory

tant differences exist in the two. For instance, both contain 11 individual elements, but Randy's has only 6 "links" in it, compared to 13 in Juan's. Juan's system is more **meaningful,** which describes the extent to which individual elements of a schema are interconnected in long-term memory (Gagne et al., 1997).

Meaningfulness. The extent to which information in long-term memory is interconnected with other information.

A long history of research indicates that meaningful learning is more effective than *rote learning,* or learning that involves acquiring information in isolated pieces, most commonly through memorization (Lin, 2007; R. Mayer, 2002). We can illustrate these ideas with Juan's and Randy's schemas. You saw earlier that the number of chunks that working memory can hold is limited, but the size and complexity of the chunks are not (Sweller et al., 1998). Because Juan's schema is completely interconnected, it behaves like one chunk (Bransford et al., 2000), so it takes up only one slot when he retrieves it from long-term memory back into working memory. Because Randy's is less interconnected, it takes up five slots in working memory: one for the *smallest–farthest–Pluto–asteroid* chunk, another for the *third–Earth–Sun–solar system* chunk, and one each for *origins, globs,* and *orbital plane.* When Randy thought about the origins of our solar system, the cognitive load on his working memory was greater than the load on Juan's, making additional processing more difficult for him. Let's look again at some of their dialogue to see the impact of this extra load on Randy's working memory.

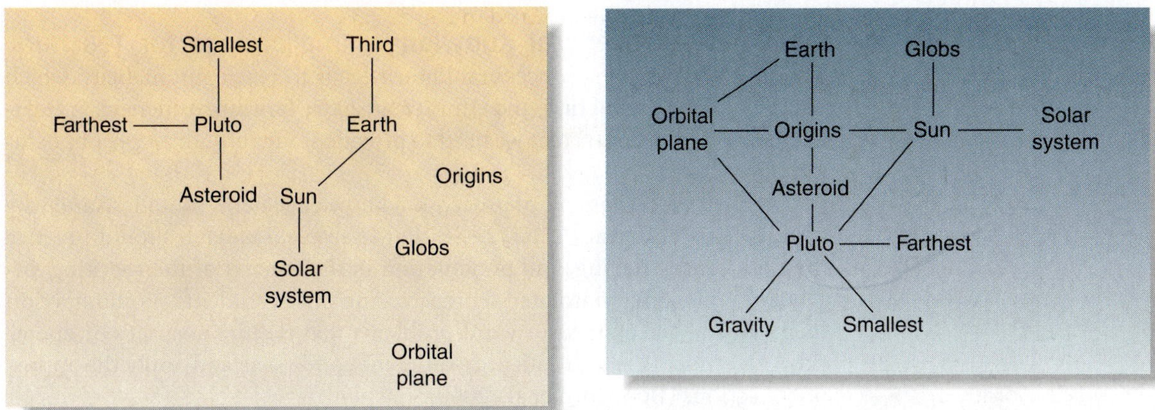

Figure 7.4 Schemas illustrating Randy's (on the left) and Juan's understanding

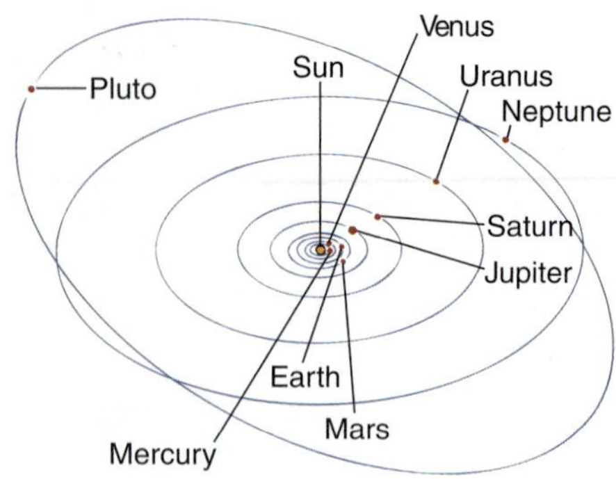

The orbital planes of the planets and Pluto.

Juan: I know the answer to the first question. Pluto isn't part of the solar system. . . . Actually, it's called a dwarf planet. It was once considered to be a planet, but it isn't anymore.

Randy: What do you mean?

Juan: I was watching *Nova* with my mom, and the person talking said that Pluto was an asteroid, or some other body floating around, and the sun kind of grabbed it.

Randy: What's that got to do with it?

Juan: Look. . . . See how Pluto is above the rest of them (pointing to the model).

Randy: Gee, I didn't even notice that.

Randy didn't "notice," because the cognitive load on his working memory was greater, making his learning less efficient.

Meaningful Learning: Implications for Teachers and Learners. To promote meaningful learning, *information should be taught as interconnected ideas rather than isolated pieces.* Isolated information imposes a heavy load on students' working memories, which helps explain why they seem to retain so little of what they're taught. Connecting ideas reduces the load, makes the information more meaningful, and increases learning by providing more places to attach new information.

Meaningfulness also has implications for learners. When we study, we should look for relationships in the content instead of studying ideas in isolation. This explains why memorizing definitions and other individual items of information is an ineffective study strategy.

Schemas as Scripts. In addition to organizing information, schemas can also guide our actions. For example, when we first enter a college class, we often ask questions such as

- What are the instructor's expectations?
- How should I prepare for quizzes and other assessments?
- How will I interact with my peers?

Scripts. Schemas for events that guide behavior in particular situations.

Answers to these questions come from **scripts,** which can be thought of as schemas for events, which are developed over years of experience and guide behavior in particular situations (Nuthall, 2000; Schank & Abelson, 1977). For example, you have a script that guides your behavior as you prepare for, attend, and participate in your classes. In this regard, scripts also contain procedural knowledge, which we consider next.

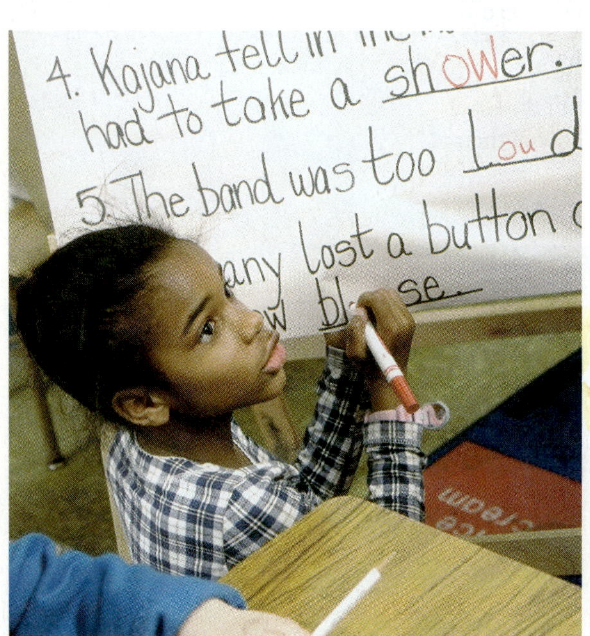

To develop procedural knowledge, learners need opportunities to practice.

Representing Procedural Knowledge in Long-Term Memory

The effectiveness of procedural knowledge depends on both declarative and conditional knowledge (J. R. Anderson, 2005; Star, 2004). For example, think back to the problems with fractions. Your ability to add them depended on your declarative knowledge of the rules for adding fractions and your conditional knowledge, so you knew when finding a common denominator was necessary and when it wasn't.

Developing Procedural Knowledge: Implications for Teachers. The goal in developing procedural knowledge is to reach automaticity, which requires a great deal of time and effort (Star, 2005; Taraban, Anderson, & DeFinis, 2007). This suggests that we need to provide students with ample opportunities to practice.

Also, the development of procedural knowledge helps us understand why context is so important (Star, 2004). For example, students should practice their grammar, spelling, and punctuation in the context of their writing, instead of practicing on isolated sentences. And, math students should develop their skills in the context of word problems that require a variety of operations, so students learn to identify different conditions and apply the appropriate actions (Bransford et al., 2000).

The development of procedural knowledge also has implications for your growth as a teacher. You will find, for example, that your questioning skills will

table 7.1 Characteristics of Different Memory Stores

Store	Characteristics
Sensory Memory	• Virtually unlimited capacity • Holds information in unorganized form • Information is quickly lost if it isn't further processed
Working Memory	• Limited capacity • Conscious component of the memory stores • The workbench where thinking and problem solving occur • A processing bottleneck • Contains a verbal processor and a visual processor that work independently
Long-Term Memory	• Virtually unlimited capacity • Permanent information store • Stores information in the form of schemas and images, encoded from working memory

improve even after years of teaching and, with experience, you will learn to recognize different learning conditions that require different strategies.

As a review of this section, look at Table 7.1, which outlines the characteristics of the memory stores.

Developmental Differences in the Memory Stores

Our description of the model of human memory might lead you to believe that people of all ages process information in essentially the same way, and to a certain extent this is true. For example, small children and adults both briefly store stimuli from the environment in their sensory memories, make sense of it in their working memories, and store it in their long-term memories.

Important developmental differences exist, however. For instance, researchers have found that older children retain sensory memory traces longer than do their younger counterparts (Nelson, Thomas, & De Haan, 2006). This means that kindergarten teachers are less likely to be successful in giving their students detailed directions, for example, than are teachers of older children.

Also, experience is essential for promoting development, and because of experience, the working memory components significantly increase in efficiency as children develop (Gathercole, Pickering, Ambridge, & Wearing, 2004). For example, more of older children's procedural knowledge becomes automatic, so they can process information more quickly and handle complex tasks more efficiently than can younger children (Luna, Garver, Urban, Lazar, & Sweeny, 2004).

Also, because of their experiences, older children have a broader and deeper store of prior knowledge, which increases their ability to make new learning meaningful. Experience can also result in developmental differences in learners who are the same age. For example, because he had experiences that Randy and Tanya lacked, Juan's understanding of the solar system was more fully developed than was theirs, so the information David presented was more meaningful to him.

Research also indicates that each of these factors is strongly language related. For example, children with language impairments lag behind their normally developing peers in working memory efficiency and processing speed (Conti-Ramsden, & Durkin, 2007; Leonard, Weismer, & Miller, 2007). This suggests that teachers should both encourage and help their students of all ages to put their understanding into words. The more children practice using language, the more efficient their learning becomes.

classroom connections

Applying an Understanding of Memory Stores in Your Classroom

Sensory Memory

1. Sensory memory briefly holds incoming stimuli from the environment until they can be processed. Therefore, to keep students from losing a sensory memory trace, allow them to attend to one stimulus before presenting a second one.
   - **Elementary:** A second-grade teacher asks one question at a time and gets an answer before asking a second question.
   - **Middle School:** A pre-algebra teacher displays two problems on the overhead and waits until students have copied them before she starts talking.
   - **High School:** A geography teacher places a map on the overhead and says, "I'll give you a minute to examine the geography of the countries on this map in the front of the room. Then we'll go on."

Working Memory

2. Working memory is where learners consciously process information, and its capacity is limited. To avoid overloading learners' working memories, conduct lessons with questioning.
   - **Elementary:** A first-grade teacher presents directions for seat work slowly and one at a time. He asks different students to repeat the directions before they begin.
   - **Middle School:** A teacher in a woodworking class begins by saying, "The hardness and density of wood from the same kind of tree vary, depending on the amount of rainfall the tree has received." Then, she waits a moment, holds up two pieces of wood, and says, "Look at these. What do you notice about the rings on them?"
   - **High School:** An Algebra II teacher "walks" students through the solutions to problems by having a different student describe each succeeding step to the solution.
3. Automaticity is the ability to perform tasks with little conscious effort, so it reduces the cognitive load on working memory. To help students develop automaticity, provide frequent practice and present information in both verbal and visual forms.
   - **Elementary:** A first-grade teacher has his students practice their writing by composing a short paragraph each day about an event of the previous evening.
   - **Middle School:** To capitalize on the distributed processing capability of the phonological loop and the visual-spatial sketchpad, an eighth-grade history teacher prepares a flowchart of the events leading to the Revolutionary War. As she questions the students, she refers to the flowchart for each point and encourages students to use the chart to organize their note taking.
   - **High School:** As a physics teacher discusses the relationship between force and acceleration, he demonstrates by pulling a cart along the desktop with a constant force so the students can see that the cart accelerates.

Long-Term Memory

4. Schemas describe the organization of information into meaningful systems in learners' long-term memories. To promote meaningfulness, encourage students to explore relationships between ideas.
   - **Elementary:** During story time, a second-grade teacher asks students to explain how the events in a story contribute to the conclusion.
   - **Middle School:** In developing the rules for solving equations by substitution, an algebra teacher asks, "How does this process compare to solving equations by addition? What do we do differently? Why?"
   - **High School:** To help his students understand cause–effect relationships, a world history teacher asks questions such as, "Why was shipping so important in ancient Greece?" "Why was Troy's location so important?" and "How does its location relate to the location of today's big cities?"

check your understanding

2.1 Use the characteristics of the memory stores to explain why Tanya, from the opening case, might have become "kinda lost when Mr. Shelton was explaining all that yesterday." What implications does this have for our teaching?

2.2 Use the characteristics of the memory stores to explain why a health club would advertise its telephone number as 2HEALTH rather than 243–2584.

2.3 Procedural knowledge exists in which of our memory stores? Identify an example in the opening case study that illustrates students' being required to demonstrate procedural knowledge. Explain.

To receive feedback for these questions, go to Appendix A.

Cognitive Processes

How does information move from sensory to working memory and from working memory to long-term memory? How do we help our students store the information most efficiently? To answer these questions, let's look again at the model of human memory first presented in Figure 7.1, focusing now on the processes (*attention, perception, encoding,* and *retrieval*) that move information from one store to another. These processes are highlighted in Figure 7.5 and discussed in the sections that follow.

Attention

Earlier in the chapter, you saw that learning and development depend on learners' experiences. They are gathered through everything we see, hear, touch, taste, or smell. This process is represented in Figure 7.5 as stimuli entering our sensory memories. However, we remain unaware of the stimuli until we consciously devote our attention to them. For instance, we likely don't "pay attention" to the whisper of an air conditioner until we are made aware of the fact that it is running. This is illustrated in the model by fewer arrows coming out of "attention" than entering it. **Attention** is the process of consciously focusing on a stimulus. Our attention acts as a screen, allowing us to filter out unimportant information.

Attention. The process of consciously focusing on a stimulus.

Two characteristics of attention are important. First, although individual differences in students exist, everyone's attention is limited, both in capacity and duration (Curtindale, Laurie-Rose, & Bennett-Murphy, 2007; Q. Zhou, Hofer, & Eisenberg, 2007). So, students are likely to pay attention to parts of teachers' explanations but miss others.

Second, our attention easily shifts from one stimulus to another; people in general are easily distracted (Q. Zhou et al., 2007). This helps us understand why students seem to derive less from teachers' explanations than they should. A myriad of distractions exist in classrooms—students whispering, noises outside the room, and people in the hallway, among others. Any one or more of these can cause students to miss parts of teachers' explanations.

Attracting and Maintaining Attention

Because attention is where learning begins, attracting and maintaining student attention are essential (Curtindale et al., 2007; Valenzeno, Alibali, & Klatzky, 2003). Effective teachers plan their lessons so students attend to what is being taught and ignore irrelevant stimuli. If a teacher pulls a live crab out of a cooler to begin a lesson on crustaceans, for example, even the most disinterested student is likely to pay attention. Similarly, if students are actively involved

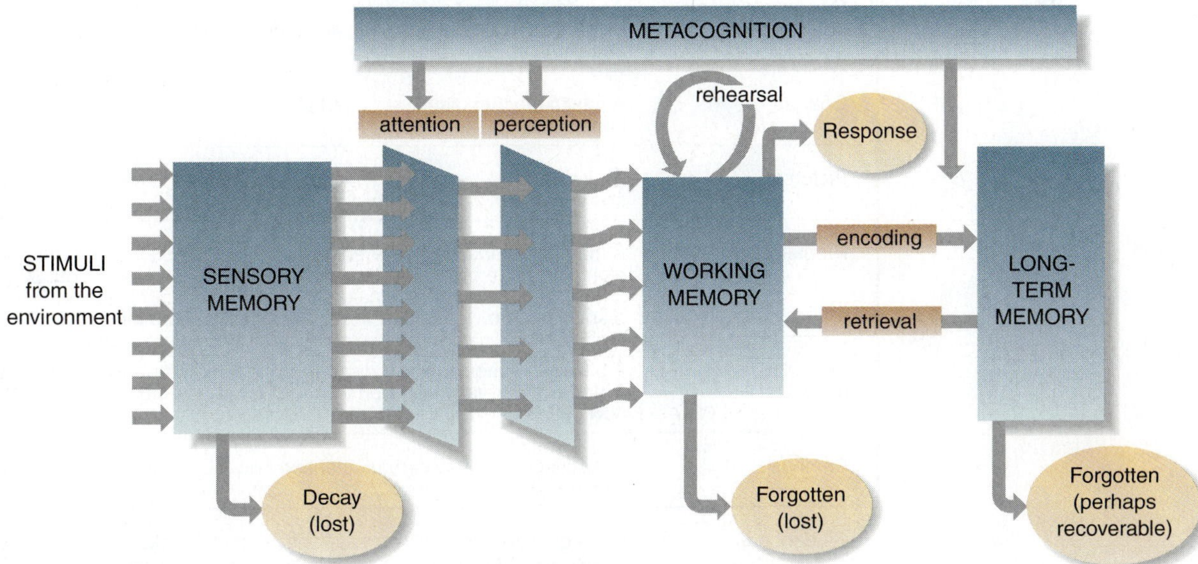

Figure 7.5 Cognitive processes in the information processing model

in learning activities, they're more attentive than if they're passively listening to a lecture (Dolezal, Welsh, Pressley, & Vincent, 2003; B. Taylor, Pearson, Peterson, & Rodriguez, 2003).

David attempted to attract and maintain his students' attention in two ways. First, his transparency and model were effective attention getters, and second, the fact that his students were involved in gathering information about the planets and answering the questions he posed helped maintain their attention.

MyEducationLab

To examine different teachers' attempts to attract their students' attention, go to the *Activities and Applications* section in Chapter 7 of MyEducationLab at www.myeducationlab.com, and watch the episode *Applying Information Processing: Attracting Students' Attention.* Answer the questions following the episode.

Additional examples of ways to attract student attention are outlined in Table 7.2. Because of its importance, one strategy deserves increased emphasis: *calling on students by name.* The use of students' names is one of the most powerful attention getters that exists, and effective teachers call on individuals instead of directing questions to the class as a whole. When this becomes a pattern, attention and achievement increase significantly (Eggen & Kauchak 2006; McDougall & Granby, 1996).

Perception

Perception. The process people use to find meaning in stimuli.

Look at the picture in the margin. Do you see a young, glamorous woman, or an old, wrinkled one? This classic example illustrates the nature of **perception,** the process people use to find meaning in stimuli.

For those of you who "saw" an old woman, this is the meaning you attached to the picture, and the same is true for those of you who "saw" a young woman. Technically, we were asking, "Do you 'perceive' a young or an old woman?"

We can also think of perception as the way we interpret objects and events. This is the way the term is commonly used in our everyday lives (Way, Reddy, & Rhodes, 2007), and it depends on factors such as learners' dispositions and expectations (Huan, Yeo, & Ang, 2006). For example, consider the following:

> "How was your interview?" Lenore, a job applicant asked her friend, Kelly, who was also applying for a job at the same school.

table 7.2 Strategies for Attracting Attention

Type	Example
Demonstrations	A science teacher pulls a student in a chair across the room to demonstrate the concepts *force* and *work*.
Discrepant events	A world history teacher who usually dresses conservatively comes to class in a sheet, makeshift sandals, and a crown to begin a discussion of ancient Greece.
Charts	A health teacher displays a chart showing the high fat content of some popular foods.
Pictures	An English teacher shows a picture of a bearded Ernest Hemingway as she introduces 20th-century American novels.
Problems	A math teacher says, We w ant to go to the rock concert on Saturday night, but we're broke. The tickets are $45, and we need about $20 for gas and something to eat.We make $5.50 an hour in our part-time jobs. How many hours do we have to work to be able to afford the concert?"
Thought-provoking questions	A history teacher begins a discussion of World War II with the question, "Suppose Germany had won the war. How might the world be different now?"
Emphasis	A teacher says, "Pay careful attention now. The next two items are very important."
Student names	In his question-and-answer sessions, a teacher asks his question, pauses briefly, and then calls on a student by name to answer.

"Terrible," Kelly responded. "He grilled me, asking me specifically how I would teach a certain topic, and what I would do in the case of two students disrupting my class. He treated me like I didn't know anything. Brenna, a friend of mine who teaches there, told me about him. . . . How was yours?"

"Gosh, I thought mine was good. He asked me the same questions, but I thought he was just trying to find out how we would think about teaching if he hired us."

Kelly and Lenore interpreted their interviews very differently. Kelly viewed it as being "grilled," but Lenore felt as if the interviewer only wanted to examine her thinking. Kelly's interpretation was influenced by her friend, Brenna, whose description created a set of expectations in her.

People's perceptions are constructed, and because they're constructed, they differ among students. The arrows emerging from "perception" in Figure 7.5 are curved to remind you that learners' perceptions will vary. And, because the knowledge learners construct depends on what they already know, learners' perceptions also depend on their prior knowledge. This also helps us understand why Randy didn't "notice" that Pluto's plane differed from those of the planets; his perception of the information in the transparency and model was affected by his lack of prior knowledge.

Accurate perceptions in classroom learning are essential, because students' perceptions of what they see, hear, touch, taste, or smell enter working memory, and if these perceptions aren't accurate, the information that students ultimately store in long-term memory will also be inaccurate.

The only way teachers can determine if students accurately perceive the information they present is to ask them. For instance, if a geography teacher is discussing the economies of different countries in the Middle East, she is checking students' perceptions when she asks, "What do we mean by the term *economy?*" Students also commonly misperceive homework and test items, which is why discussing items afterward is essential.

Encoding

After learners attend to and perceive information, and organize it in working memory, it is ready for **encoding,** which is the process of representing information in long-term memory (J. R. Anderson, 2007). This information can be represented either visually, such as Juan's forming an image of Pluto with a different orbital plane, or verbally, when students construct schemas that relate ideas to each other.

Encoding. The process of representing information in long-term memory.

Earlier in the chapter, we described *maintenance rehearsal,* which is the process we use to retain information in working memory until it is used or forgotten. However, if rehearsed enough, this information can be transferred to long-term memory, and this is the strategy learners often use to remember factual information, such as specific dates and math facts like $6 \times 9 = 54$. Teachers commonly use rehearsal, such as practicing with flash cards, to help their students learn math facts. Rehearsal is an inefficient encoding strategy, however, because the information in long-term memory exists in isolation. This was described earlier in the chapter as *rote learning.*

In contrast with rote learning, we want the information to be encoded meaningfully; we want it to be connected to other information. For example, Juan encoded the information they were studying more meaningfully than did Randy, because the schema he constructed had more connections in it.

Teachers can use several strategies to promote meaningful encoding, and we examine four of them in this section:

- Imagery
- Organization
- Schema activation
- Elaboration

The strategies are outlined in Figure 7.6, and we discuss them in the sections that follow.

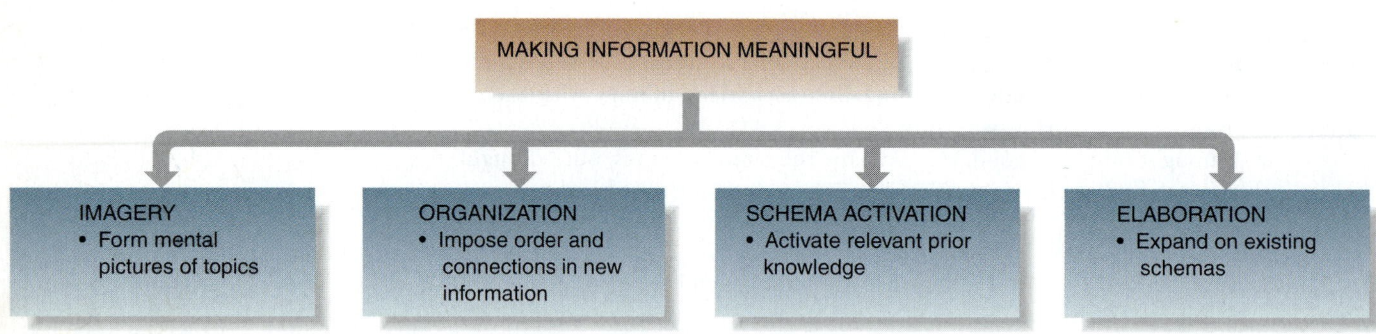

Figure 7.6 Strategies for promoting meaningful encoding

Imagery

Imagery. The process of forming mental pictures of an idea.

Dual-coding theory. A theory suggesting that long-term memory contains two distinct memory systems: one for verbal information and one that stores images.

Imagery is the process of forming mental pictures of an idea (D. Schwartz & Heiser, 2006), and its value as an encoding strategy is supported by **dual-coding theory,** which suggests that long-term memory contains two distinct memory systems: one for verbal information and one for images (Paivio 1991; Sadoski & Paivio, 2001). According to dual-coding theory, ideas that can be represented both visually and verbally, such as *ball, house,* or *dog,* are easier to remember than ideas that are more difficult to visualize, such as *value, truth,* and *ability* (Paivio, 1986).

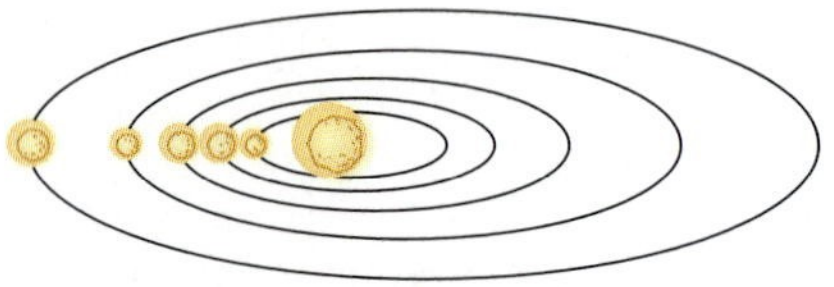

The sun threw off hot spheres of gas which eventually became planets.

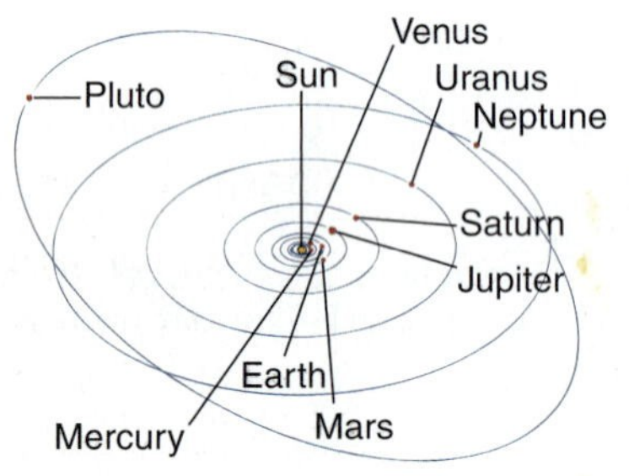

The orbital planes of the planets and Pluto.

As we study human memory, for example, the fact that we can both visualize the models in Figures 7.1 and 7.5 and read about the information in them helps us capitalize on the dual-coding capability of long-term memory. Information in the model becomes more meaningfully encoded than it would be if we had only described it verbally (J. Clark & Paivio, 1991; Willoughby, Porter, Belsito, & Yearsley, 1999). Dual-coding theory again reminds us of the importance of supplementing verbal information with visual representations (Igo, Kiewra, & Bruning, 2004). This capitalizes on both distributed processing in working memory and the dual-coding capability of long-term memory.

Teachers take advantage of imagery in many ways (D. Shwartz & Heiser, 2006). For instance, they can use pictures and diagrams, such as David's model of the solar system and transparency showing the globs of gases coming off the sun; they can ask students to form mental pictures of processes or events; and they can ask students to draw their own diagrams about ideas they are learning.

Imagery can be particularly helpful in problem solving (Kozhevnikov, Hegarty, & Mayer, 1999). It would have been harder for you to solve the area-of-the-pentagon problem, for example, if you hadn't been given the drawing as an aid.

Organization

Organization. An encoding strategy that involves the clustering of related items of content into categories that illustrate relationships.

Organization is an encoding strategy that involves the clustering of related items of content into categories that illustrate relationships. Because well-organized content illustrates connections among its elements, cognitive load is decreased, and encoding (and subsequent retrieval) is more effective (R. Mayer, 2008). Research in reading, memory, and classroom instruction confirms the value of organization in promoting learning (R. Mayer, 2008; Nuthall, 1999b). Research indicates that experts learn more efficiently than novices because their knowledge in long-term memory is better organized, allowing them to access it and connect it to new information (Bransford et al., 2000; Simon, 2001).

We can help learners organize information in several ways:

- *Charts and matrices* are useful for organizing large amounts of information into categories. David used a matrix to help his students organize their information about the planets. Table 7.3 shows the completed matrix.
- *Hierarchies* are effective when new information can be subsumed under existing ideas. We made frequent use of hierarchies in our discussion of behaviorism in Chapter 6 (e.g., Figure 6.1, "Consequences of Behavior" on page 168).
- *Models* are helpful for representing relationships that students cannot observe directly. David's model of the solar system and the model of human memory in this chapter are examples.

MyEducationLab

To examine different teachers' efforts to organize content so that it is meaningful to students, go to the *Building Teaching Skills and Dispositions* section in Chapter 7 of MyEducationLab at www.myeducationlab.com, and watch the episode *Applying Information Processing: Organizing Content.* Complete the exercises following the episode to build your skills in organizing information.

- *Outlines* are useful for representing the organizational structure in a body of written material. The detailed table of contents for this book is an example.

Other types of organization include graphs, tables, flowcharts, and maps (Merkley & Jefferies, 2001). Learners can also use these organizers as personal study aids in their attempts to make the information they're studying meaningful.

A word of caution: As you saw in the list of learning principles at the beginning of the chapter, learners construct knowledge that makes sense to them, so if the organizational structure we offer does not make sense to learners, they will (mentally) reorganize it in a way that does, whether or not it is correct. When content organization is unclear, learners often memorize snippets of it, resulting in rote learning, or they ignore it altogether.

Classroom interaction is essential to making the organization of new material meaningful to learners. David, for example, not only organized his content by using a transparency, model, and matrix, he also guided his students' developing understanding through questioning and discussion.

Teachers can capitalize on imagery with the use of aids that encourage students to form mental pictures of the topics they're studying.

table 7.3 David's Completed Planet Matrix

	Diameter (miles)	Distance from Sun (millions of miles)	Length of Year (orbit)	Length of Day (rotation)	Gravity (compared to Earth's)	Average Surface Temperature (°F)	Characteristics
Mercury	3,030	35.9	88 E.D.[a]	59 E.D. counterclockwise	.38	300 below to 800 above zero	No atmosphere; no water; many craters
Venus	7,500	67.2	225 E.D.	243 E.D. clockwise	.88	900	Thick cloud cover; high winds; no water
Earth	7,900	98.0	365½ E.D.	24 hours counterclockwise	1	57	Atmos. of 78% nitrogen, 21% oxygen; 70% water on surface
Mars	4,200	141.5	687 E.D.	24½ hours counterclockwise	.38	67 below zero	Thin carbon dioxide atmos.; white caps at poles; red rocky surface
Jupiter	88,700	483.4	12 E.Y.[b]	10 hours counterclockwise	2.34	162 below zero	No water; great red spot; atmos. of hydrogen, helium, ammonia
Saturn	75,000	914.0	30 E.Y.	11 hours counterclockwise	.92	208 below zero	Atmos. of hydrogen, helium; no water, mostly gaseous; prominent rings
Uranus	31,566	1,782.4	84 E.Y.	24 hours counterclockwise	.79	355 below zero	Atmos. of hydrogen, helium; no water
Neptune	30,200	2,792.9	165 E.Y.	17 hours counterclockwise	1.12	266 below zero	Atmos. of hydrogen, helium; no water
Pluto	1,423	3,665.0	248 E.Y.	6½ days colunterclockwise	.43	458 below zero	No atmos.; periodically orbits closer to sun than Neptune

[a] Earth days.
[b] Earth years.

Schema Activation

Think back to some of your most effective teachers. In most cases, they likely began their classes with a review of the previous class, and a long history of research supports the effectiveness of well-structured reviews in promoting student achievement (Berliner, 1986; Rutter, Maughan, Mortimore, Ousten, & Smith, 1979; Shuell, 1996).

Schema activation. An encoding strategy that involves activating relevant prior knowledge so that new knowledge can be connected to it.

Reviews capitalize on **schema activation,** which is an encoding strategy that involves activating relevant prior knowledge so that new knowledge can be connected to it (R. E. Mayer & Wittrock, 2006). Schema activation was illustrated in Juan's comment, "I know the answer to the first question. . . . Pluto isn't part of the solar system. . . . Actually, it's called a dwarf planet. It was once considered to be a planet, but it isn't anymore." He had a schema related to the formation of the solar system that was activated by the discussion. He then connected the new information—the question "Why is Pluto's orbital plane different from the planes of the planets?" to his prior knowledge. This connection resulted in his deeper understanding of the solar system.

The most effective way of activating students' prior knowledge is to ask them what they already know about a topic, which occurs in reviews, or to ask them to provide some personal experiences related to the topic. Any teaching strategy that helps students form conceptual bridges between what they already know and what they are to learn is a form of schema activation.

Elaboration

You're at a noisy party. When you miss some of a conversation, you fill in details, trying to make sense of an incomplete message. You do the same when you read a text or listen to a lecture. You expand on (and sometimes distort) information to make it fit your expectations and current understanding. In each case, you are *elaborating* on either the message or what you already know.

Elaboration. An encoding strategy that increases the meaningfulness of new information by connecting it to existing knowledge.

Elaboration is an encoding strategy that increases the meaningfulness of new information by connecting it to existing knowledge (Terry, 2006). For example, a student who remembers the location of the Atlantic ocean on the globe because it starts with an *a* and the Americas and Africa also begin with *a*, or a student who remembers $6 \times 9 = 54$ because the sum of the digits in the product of a number times 9 always equals 9 ($5 + 4 = 9$) is capitalizing on elaboration as an encoding strategy. The use of elaboration to remember factual information (e.g., the location of the Atlantic Ocean, or $6 \times 9 = 54$) is often called *elaborative rehearsal.* Research confirms the superiority of elaborative rehearsal for long-term retention of information (Craik, 1979; King-Friedrichs & Browne, 2001).

Tanya, in David's class, capitalized on elaboration when she said, "Oh, I get it now! Pluto isn't level with the rest of them." She linked Pluto to her existing knowledge of the planets, making this new information more meaningful.

In addition to elaborative rehearsal, two additional elaboration strategies can be effective. They are (1) the use of examples and analogies and (2) mnemonics.

Examples and Analogies. One of the most effective ways of promoting elaboration is through examples and other representations that illustrate the topic. This includes constructing, finding, or analyzing examples. It is arguably the most powerful elaboration strategy because it also capitalizes on schema activation (Cassady, 1999). When learners create or identify a new example of an idea, they activate their prior knowledge and then elaborate on their understanding of that idea. Our extensive use of examples throughout this book demonstrates our belief in this strategy, and we encourage you to focus on the examples when you study. You can do the same with the concepts you teach.

Analogies. Descriptions of relationships between ideas that are similar in some but not all respects.

When examples aren't available, using **analogies,** descriptions of relationships that are similar in some but not all respects, can be an effective elaboration strategy (Bulgren et al., 2000). As an example, consider the following analogy from science:

> Our circulatory system is like a pumping system that carries the blood around our bodies. The veins and arteries are the pipes, and the heart is the pump.

The veins and arteries are similar, but not identical, to pipes, and the heart is a type of pump. The analogy is an effective form of elaboration because it links new information to a pumping station, an idea learners already understand.

Using examples also helps accommodate students' lack of prior knowledge. For example, most of David's students had little prior knowledge about the formation of the solar system, and they didn't know how its formation related to the orbital planes of the planets. So, he provided it for them with his transparency and model.

Mnemonics. **Mnemonic devices** are memory strategies that create associations that don't exist naturally in the content (Terry, 2006). Mnemonics link knowledge to be learned to familiar information, and they have been proven effective in a variety of content areas (M. E. Bloom & Lamkin, 2006; Uygur & Ozdas, 2007) with learners ranging from children to older adults (Brehmer & Li, 2007).

Mnemonic devices. Memory strategies that create associations that don't exist naturally in the content.

MyEducationLab

To examine student work that represents efforts to meaningfully encode information, go to the *Activities and Applications* section in Chapter 7 of MyEducationLab at www.myeducationlab.com, and look at the artifact *Five Brain Coral.* Answer the questions that follow.

Mnemonics can take several forms. We can use acronyms, for example, such as HOMES to remember the names of the Great Lakes (Huron, Ontario, Michigan, Erie, and Superior) and phrases, such as "Every good boy does fine," to remember the names of the notes in the treble clef (E, G, B, D, and F). When learners think of the mnemonic, they link it to the information it represents, which aids the recall of information.

Learners use mnemonics to help remember vocabulary, names, rules, lists, and other kinds of factual knowledge.Table 7.4 provides some additional examples.

The Importance of Cognitive Activity

Regardless of the encoding strategy being employed, it is essential that learners are cognitively active when using the strategy. For example, suppose you and a friend are studying this book. You read and attempt to write an answer to each of the "Check Your Understanding" questions in the chapters. Then you study the feedback in Appendix A. Your friend simply reads each question and then reads the answer. Your approach is more effective because *you've placed yourself in a more cognitively active role than has your friend.* Thinking about (and writing) an answer is active, and it capitalizes on both schema activation and elaboration. You attempt to activate a relevant schema by searching long-term memory for information related to the questions, and you then use elaboration when you answer them. Merely reading the feedback is passive, resulting in fewer connections to information in long-term memory and less meaningful learning. Similarly, asking students to provide additional examples places them in cognitively active roles; providing the example doesn't encourage as much active processing (Bransford et al., 2000).

Cognitive activity is essential for meaningful encoding.

table 7.4 Types and Examples of Mnemonic Devices

Mnemonic	Description	Example
Method of loci	Learner combines imagery with specific locations in a familiar environment, such as the chair, sofa, lamp, and end table in a living room.	Student wanting to remember the first seven elements in order visualizes hydrogen at the chair, helium at the sofa, lithium at the lamp, and so on.
Peg-word method	Learner memorizes a series of "pegs"—such as a simple rhyme like "one is bun" and "two is shoe"—on which to-be-remembered information is hung.	A learner wanting to remember to get pickles and carrots at the grocery visualizes a pickle in a bun and carrot stuck in a shoe.
Link method	Learner visually links items to be remembered.	A learner visualizes *homework* stuck in a *notebook,* which is bound to her *textbook, pencil,* and *pen* with a rubber band to remember to take the (italicized) items to class.
Key-word method	Learner uses imagery and rhyming words to remember unfamiliar words.	A learner remembers that *trigo* (which rhymes with *tree*) is the Spanish word for *wheat* by visualizing a sheaf of wheat sticking out of a tree.
First-letter method	Learner creates a word from the first letter of items to be remembered.	A student creates the word *Wajmma* to remember the first six presidents in order:Washington, Adams, Jefferson, Madison, Monroe, and Adams.

One of the most effective ways of putting students in active roles is to guide their increasing understanding through questioning. To illustrate this process, let's return to David's lesson. We rejoin the class on Thursday.

> David begins by saying, "Yesterday, you were supposed to use the information we've gathered to answer a series of questions. Let's see what you've come up with."
>
> Juan, speaking for his group [as you saw earlier in the chapter], offers his explanation for the first question, which asked about Pluto's orbital plane, and David then asks, "What did you come up with for the next question? which was, 'Why is Mercury so hot on one side and so cold on the other?'"
>
> "We couldn't answer it, Mr. Shelton," several students respond.
>
> "Okay, let's see if we can figure it out. . . . Look at Mercury's length of day. What do you notice about it? . . . Marcos?"
>
> "It's really long, 59 Earth days. . . . It rotates really slow," Marcos responds after looking at the chart [in Table 7.3] for several seconds.
>
> "Good," David nods. "So, what does that tell us? . . . Serena?"
>
> "One side is . . . facing the sun for a long time," Serena answers hesitantly.
>
> "Aha, . . . I get it," LaToya blurts out. "If one side faces the sun for a long time, it gets really hot, so the other side gets really cold."
>
> "Excellent thinking, LaToya," David smiles. "That's a very good analysis."

David encouraged his students to be cognitively active with questions that asked them to identify relationships, such as the relationship between Mercury's period of rotation and its surface temperature. He also built the discussion around the information that appeared in the matrix, so he capitalized on organization as an encoding strategy. He could have simply explained these relationships, which teachers commonly do. This would have allowed the students to remain passive, however, and the learning experience would have been less meaningful for them.

David's use of group work also promoted cognitive activity, as you saw in Juan's, Randy's, and Tanya's discussion. His careful supervision, however, was an essential part of this process. Students become physically or verbally active in group work and hands-on activities but can remain cognitively passive; they're not "thinking about" what they're doing. Teachers miss this fact if the group work isn't well supervised. Group work and hands-on activities don't ensure "minds-on" activities (Ball, 1992; Brophy, 2006a).

Forgetting

Forgetting. The loss of, or inability to retrieve, information from long-term memory.

Forgetting is the loss of, or inability to retrieve, information from long-term memory, and it is both a real part of people's everyday lives and an important factor in learning.

Look again at the model first presented in Figure 7.1. There we see that information lost from both sensory memory and working memory is unrecoverable. However, information in long-term memory has been encoded. Why can't we find it?

Forgetting as Interference

Interference. The loss of information because something learned either before or after detracts from understanding.

Proactive interference. The loss of new information because of the influence of prior learning.

Retroactive interference. The loss of previously learned information because of the influence of new learning.

Some experts explain forgetting with the concept **interference,** the loss of information because something learned either before or after detracts from understanding (M. L. Howe, 2004). For example, students learn that the rule for forming singular possessives states that an apostrophe *s* is added to the singular noun. If their understanding of the rule for forming singular possessives later interferes with learning the rules for forming plural possessives and contractions, **proactive interference,** prior learning interfering with new understanding, has occurred. On the other hand, if the rules for forming plural possessives confuses their prior understanding, **retroactive interference** has occurred. Students' understanding of plural possessives and contractions can interfere with their understanding of singular possessives and vice versa.

Teaching closely related ideas together is perhaps the most effective strategy that exists for reducing interference (R. Hamilton, 1997). Examples include teaching adjectives with adverbs, longitude with latitude, and adding fractions that have similar denominators with adding those that have different denominators. In doing so, teachers help students recognize similarities and differences, and identify areas that are easily confused.

Teachers can also reduce interference by using reviews to activate prior knowledge and then compare the new topic to the closely related information that students have already studied. This helps students identify easily confused similarities, and it promotes elaboration.

Forgetting as Retrieval Failure

Retrieval is the process of pulling information from long-term memory back into working memory, and many researchers believe that "forgetting" is actually the inability to retrieve information from long-term memory (C. Williams & Zacks, 2001). We've all had the experience of realizing that we know a name, fact, or some other information, but we simply can't pull it up.

Retrieval. The process of pulling information from long-term memory into working memory.

classroom connections

Applying an Understanding of Cognitive Processes in Your Classroom

Attention

1. Attention is the process of consciously focusing on a stimulus, so it is the beginning point for learning. To capitalize on this essential process, conduct lessons to attract and maintain attention.
   - **Elementary:** A third-grade teacher calls on all his students whether or not they have their hands up. He periodically asks, "Who have I not called on lately?" to be sure all students are attending to the lesson.
   - **Middle School:** A science teacher introducing the concept *pressure* has students stand by their desks, first on both feet and then on one foot. They then discuss the force and pressure on the floor in each case.
   - **High School:** To be sure that her students attend to important points, a world history teacher emphasizes, "Everyone, listen carefully now, because we're going to look at three important reasons that World War I broke out in Europe."

Perception

2. Perception describes the meaning learners attach to the information they attend to, so accurate perceptions are essential for understanding. Check frequently to be certain that students are perceiving your examples and other representations accurately.
   - **Elementary:** A kindergarten teacher wants his students to understand living things. He picks up a large potted plant and then asks, "What do you notice about the plant?" and calls on several children for their observations.
   - **Middle School:** A geography teacher shows her class a series of colored slides of landforms. After displaying each slide, she asks students to describe the landform.
   - **High School:** An English teacher and his students are reading an essay and encounter the line, "I wouldn't impose this regimen on myself out of masochism." He stops and asks, "What does the author mean by 'masochism'?"

Encoding

3. Encoding is the process of representing information in long-term memory. To promote encoding, carefully organize the information you present to students, and place them in cognitively active roles.
   - **Elementary:** A fourth-grade teacher illustrates that heat causes expansion by placing a balloon-covered soft drink bottle in a pot of hot water and by presenting a drawing that shows the spacing and motion of the air molecules. She then guides the students with questioning to understand the relationship between heat and expansion.
   - **Middle School:** A math teacher presents a flowchart with a series of questions students are encouraged to ask themselves as they solve word problems (e.g., "What do I know? What am I trying to find out?"). As students work on the problems, he asks them to describe their thinking and tell where they are on the flowchart.
   - **High School:** A history teacher presents a matrix comparing different immigrant groups, their reasons for relocating to the United States, the difficulties they encountered, and their rates of assimilation. The students then search for patterns in the information in the chart.

4. Learners elaborate their understanding when they make new connections between the items of information they're studying. Encourage students to capitalize on elaboration and to form mental images as often as possible.
   - **Elementary:** A second-grade teacher says, "Let's see what we've found now about chemical and physical changes. Picture the differences between the two, and give me two new examples of each."
   - **Middle School:** A geography teacher encourages her students to visualize flat parallel lines on the globe as they think about latitude, and vertical lines coming together at the North and South Poles as they think about longitude. She then asks her students to compare them.
   - **High School:** An English teacher asks students to imagine the appearance of the characters in a novel by pretending they are casting them for a movie version. He then asks them to suggest a current actor or actress to play the role.

Retrieval

5. Retrieval occurs when learners pull information from long-term memory back into working memory for further processing, and interference can inhibit this process. To prevent interference and aid retrieval, teach closely related ideas together and emphasize their differences.
   - **Elementary:** To teach area and perimeter, a fifth-grade teacher has her students lay squares side by side to illustrate area, and she has them measure the distance around the pieces to illustrate perimeter. She then moves to irregular plane figures and repeats the process.
   - **Middle School:** An English teacher displays a passage on the overhead that includes both gerunds and participles. He then asks the students to compare the way the author used words in the passage to demonstrate that gerunds function as nouns and participles function as adjectives.
   - **High School:** A biology teacher begins a unit on arteries and veins by saying, "We've all heard of hardening of the arteries, but we haven't heard of 'hardening of the veins.' Why not? Are we using the term *artery* to mean both, or is there a difference? Why is hardening of the arteries bad for people?"

exploring diversity

The Impact of Diversity on Cognition

Learners' prior knowledge strongly influences their perceptions and the way they encode new information. Students come to our classes with widely varying experiences, and addressing this diversity is one of the biggest challenges teachers face (S. Veenman, 1984). For example, Juan's experiences watching *Nova* influenced his perception of Pluto's orbital pattern. Randy and Tanya lacked this knowledge, so they had a harder time understanding the significance of Pluto's orbit.

Differences in experience and prior knowledge are particularly pronounced when students come from a variety of cultural and economic backgrounds (J. R. Anderson, 2005; Huan et al., 2006). Research, however, suggests several strategies for accommodating this diversity (Brenner et al., 1997; Nuthall, 1999b). The following are some of them.

- *Assess students' prior knowledge and perceptions by asking them what they already know about a topic*. For example, because he has several recent-immigrant children in his class, a third-grade teacher begins a unit on communities by saying, "Tell us about the communities where you lived before coming to this country." He has students whose English skills are more fully developed work as interpreters for other students. He then uses the information as a framework for the study of their community.
- *Supplement students' prior experiences with rich examples*. For instance, a middle school science teacher introduces the study of refraction by having students put coins in opaque dishes and backing up until they can't see the coins. Partners pour water into the dishes until the coins become visible, and the teacher shows a model illustrating how the light rays are bent when they enter and leave the water.
- *Use students' experiences to augment the backgrounds of those lacking the experiences*. For instance, a teacher whose class is studying modern European history might say something like, "Celeena, you lived in Europe. What do people there say about the conflict in the former Yugoslavia?"

In each case, the teacher can then use the students' existing knowledge, example, or varying experiences as a launching point for the lesson. The ability to adapt lessons in this way is an important characteristic of teaching expertise.

Teachers can capitalize on learners' differing experiences to increase achievement for all students.

Retrieval depends on context and the way information is encoded (C. Williams & Zacks, 2001). For instance, you know a person at school, but you can't remember his name when you see him at a party; his name was encoded in the school context, and you're trying to retrieve it in the context of the party.

Meaningfulness is the key to retrieval. The more detailed and interconnected knowledge is in long-term memory, the easier it is to retrieve (Nuthall, 1999a). David attempted to make the information about the solar system meaningful for his students by using his transparency, model, and matrix, and by putting his students in cognitively active roles. In doing so, he increased the chance of later retrieval (J. Martin, 1993).

Practice to the point of automaticity also facilitates retrieval (Chaffen & Imreh, 2002). When students know their math facts to the point of automaticity, for example, they can easily retrieve them for use in problem solving, leaving more working memory space to focus on solutions.

Developmental Differences in Cognitive Processes

As with the memory stores, developmental differences in the cognitive processes exist (Nelson et al., 2006). One of the most important involves *attention*. Older children are better able to maintain their attention, they are less distracted by irrelevant stimuli, and their attention becomes more purposeful (Dempster & Corkill, 1999; Higgins & Turnure, 1984). For example, when Juan attempted to explain why Pluto's orbital plane differed from the planes of the planets, he immediately focused his attention on the model. A younger child would have been less purposeful with his attention, and learners with disabilities, such as ADHD, lag developmentally behind their peers (Bental & Tirosh, 2007).

Developmental differences in *perception* are related primarily to learners' experiences, and because older students have more experiences than their younger counterparts, their percep-

tions are more likely to be accurate. This suggests that checking students' perceptions is even more important for teachers of young children.

Students gradually learn to use rehearsal as an encoding strategy (Pressley & Hilden, 2006). Preschoolers rarely use it, but by the second or third grade, they begin to use maintenance rehearsal spontaneously and gradually shift to elaborative rehearsal as they become more strategic.

Encoding is similar. As learners develop, they gradually use strategies, such as imagery, organization, and elaboration, to efficiently encode information (Pressley & Hilden, 2006). We examine developmental differences in learner use of strategies later in the chapter.

check your understanding

3.1 Describe the cognitive processes in the human memory model.

3.2 A language arts teacher wants to involve her students in a discussion of plot development in a novel. She begins by asking, "What do we mean by plot development?" To which of the cognitive processes does the teacher's question most closely relate? Explain.

3.3 A second-grade teacher uses flash cards to help her students acquire math facts, such as $6 \times 8 = 48$ and $7 \times 9 = 63$, and she also has her students practice solving word problems by comparing new problems to problems that they have discussed in class. What cognitive process were the students employing when they used the flash cards? What encoding strategies did the students use when they compared and practiced solving problems?

To receive feedback for these questions, go to Appendix A.

Metacognition: Knowledge and Control of Cognitive Processes

Have you ever said to yourself, "I'm going to sit near the front of the class so I won't fall asleep," or "I'm beat today. I'd better drink a cup of coffee before I go to class." If you have, you were being metacognitive. **Metacognition,** commonly described as "knowing about knowing" is our awareness of and control over our cognitive processes, and **meta-attention,** awareness of and control over our ability to pay attention, is one type of metacognition (Meltzer et al., 2007; Pressley & Hilden, 2006). You were aware of the fact that your drowsiness might affect your ability to attend, and you exercised control over it by sitting near the front of the class or drinking the cup of coffee. Metacognition also explains why we make lists. We realize that we may forget to pick up some items at the store, and we exercise control by writing the items on a list.

Metacognition. Our awareness of and our control over our cognitive processes.

Meta-attention. Knowledge of and control over the ability to pay attention.

Students who are aware of the way they study and learn achieve more than those who are less aware (Kuhn & Dean, 2004). In other words, students who are metacognitive learn more than those who aren't (D. Anderson, & Nashon, 2007; K. S. Smith, Rook, & Smith, 2007), and at least four reasons exist for these differences.

First, students who are aware of the importance of attention are more likely to create effective personal learning environments, which can be as simple as moving to the front of the class or turning off a radio while studying.

Second, learners who are aware of the possibility of misperceptions attempt to find corroborating information or ask if their understanding is accurate.

Third, metacognition helps regulate the flow of information through working memory. Randy demonstrated **metamemory**—knowledge and control of memory strategies—when he said, "I better write some of this stuff down, or I'll never remember it," and this answers

Metamemory. Knowledge of and control over our memory strategies.

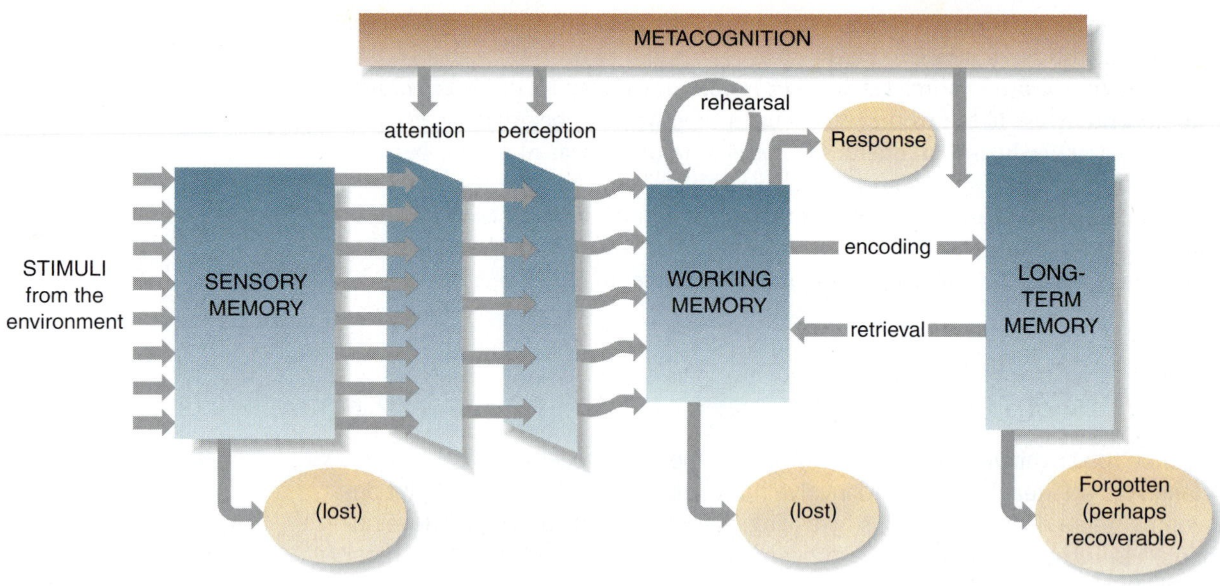

Figure 7.7 Metacognition is the model of human memory

the third question that we asked at the beginning of the chapter (What impact will Randy's decision to "write some of this stuff down" have on his learning?). His learning will increase, and the more metacognitive he becomes, the greater impact it will have on his learning. The ability to monitor the processing of information in working memory is essential because of its limited capacity.

Finally, metacognition influences the meaningfulness of encoding. For example, learners who are metacognitive about their encoding consciously look for relationships in the topics they study. This influences their study strategies, and ultimately how much they learn. The metacognitive components of the memory model are illustrated in Figure 7.7.

Developmental Differences in Metacognition

Young learners' metacognitive abilities are limited (Von der Linden, & Roebers, 2006), but they gradually become more strategic about their learning as they mature and gain experience. For example, as learners develop, they use rehearsal more strategically. However, low achievers tend to rely on rehearsal as a strategy even when they get older, and even high achievers will revert to rehearsal for material that is difficult for them to understand (Barnett, 2001).

classroom connections

Applying an Understanding of Metacognition in Your Classroom

1. Metacognition is knowledge of and control over the way we study and learn, and learners who are metacognitive achieve higher than those who aren't. To capitalize on metacognition, integrate metacognitive strategies into your instruction, and model your own metacognition.
    - **Elementary:** During a lesson, a second-grade teacher holds up a card with the sentence, "If you're paying attention, raise your hand." He then acknowledges those who are and encourages them to share their strategies for maintaining attention during class.
    - **Middle School:** A social studies teacher emphasizes metamemory by saying, "Suppose you're reading, and the book states that there are three important differences between capitalism and socialism. What should you do?"
    - **High School:** An economics teacher models metacognitive strategies by making statements such as, "Whenever I read something new, I always ask myself, 'How does this relate to what I've been studying?' For example, how is the liberal economic agenda different from the conservative agenda?"

Metacognitive skills tend to be general for older students but domain-specific in younger learners (M. V. Veenman & Spaans, 2005). For example, older children are generally aware of the importance of attention and can direct it toward important information in a learning task, whereas young children are likely to be aware of the need to pay attention only when reminded to do so by their teacher.

The process is similar for metamemory (Gaskill & Murphy, 2004). Older children will use encoding strategies, such as imagery or organization, but younger children do not. And, older learners are more aware of their memory limitations (Flavell, Miller, & Miller, 2002; Pressley & Hilden, 2006).

In spite of these developmental differences, older learners and even some college students are not as metacognitive about their learning as they should be (Peverly, Brobst, & Graham, 2003), but they can develop these skills with teacher guidance and practice. We summarize developmental differences with respect to the model of human memory in the "Developmentally Appropriate Pratice" feacture that follows.

developmentally appropriate practice

Applying the Model of Memory with Different-Aged Learners

Although many applications of cognitive learning theory and the model of human memory apply at all grade levels, important developmental differences exist. The following paragraphs outline some suggestions for responding to these differences.

Working with Elementary Students

Our attentional capacities are limited, and these limitations are even more pronounced in young children. To maintain their attention, teachers should ensure that learning activities are short and change frequently.

Teachers of elementary students must give simple and precise directions for tasks and should continually check children's perceptions of the task requirements. Teachers should break complex tasks into shorter and simpler ones and ensure that students complete each before moving to the next task.

Young children's thinking is concrete, so concrete and personalized examples are important for illustrating concepts and particularly concepts that might be abstract for young learners. Because young children's language is developing, teachers should give them extensive practice in putting their understanding into words.

Modeling metacognition and helping children develop an awareness of factors that influence their learning are particularly helpful with young students (Meltzer, Pollica, & Barzillai, 2007). Children who become aware of the fact that they are no longer paying attention, for example, have important learning advantages over those who are less aware.

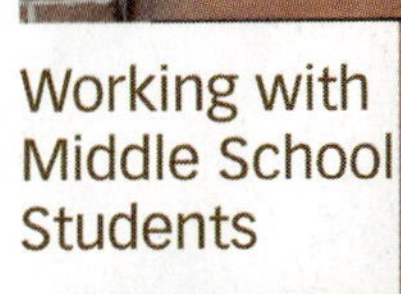

Working with Middle School Students

To capitalize on middle school students' increased ability to monitor their own learning, emphasizing metacognition and teaching learning strategies can be effective. For example, encouraging students to ask themselves questions, such as, "How is this idea similar to and different from the previous idea?" and "What would be a real-world example of this idea?" can significantly increase learning.

Much of middle school students' thinking remains concrete, however, so teachers should continue to use concrete examples to illustrate abstract concepts. And, because so much of learning is verbal, guiding students as they put their understanding into words continues to be essential.

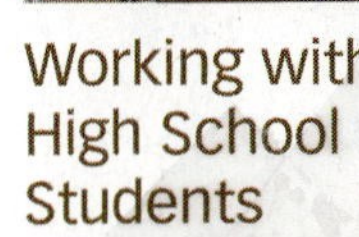

Working with High School Students

High school students can use sophisticated learning strategies, but they are unlikely to use them unless teachers model and encourage the strategies (Pressley & Hilden, 2006). Modeling and promoting the use of encoding strategies, such as organization, elaboration, and imagery are valuable. Even high school students are likely to use rehearsal as a strategy when material is difficult for them, however, so practice with other strategies is important.

High school teachers tend to rely on lecture but teaching strategies such as questioning and small-group work that put students in cognitively active roles are generally more effective. Monitoring group work to ensure that students who are physically or socially active are also cognitively active is also important.

High school students should be encouraged to examine questions in depth and to consider cause-and-effect relationships, such as the questions David asked as his students studied the solar system.

Concrete examples continue to be important for teaching abstract and unfamiliar concepts, and the use of language continues to be important as well.

theory to practice

Applying an Understanding of the Human Memory Model in Your Classroom

The human memory model has important implications for teaching. As you attempt to apply the theory in your instruction, the following guidelines can help you in your efforts:

1. Begin lessons with an activity that attracts attention.
2. Conduct frequent reviews to activate students' prior knowledge and check their perceptions.
3. Proceed in short steps, and represent content both visually and verbally to reduce the cognitive load on working memory.
4. Help students make information meaningful, and aid encoding through organization, imagery, elaboration, and cognitive activity.
5. Model and encourage metacognition.

Let's review David's lesson now to see how he applied these guidelines in his teaching. He applied the first by beginning the lesson with a display of his model and transparency. He then helped maintain the students' attention with his questioning and group work.

He checked his students' perceptions by asking them to describe their interpretations of the transparency and model, and on Wednesday he reviewed the information in Monday's and Tuesday's lesson. This applied the second guideline.

The sun threw off hot spheres of gas which eventually became planets.

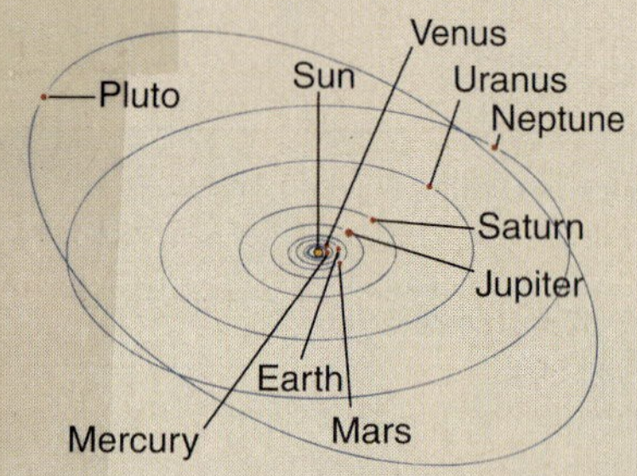

The orbital planes of the planets and Pluto

He applied the third by representing the content with his transparency and model, and, when the students struggled, he used information in the matrix combined with questioning to guide the students' developing understanding. Both reduced the cognitive load on working memory.

His transparency and model promoted the students' use of imagery, and his matrix capitalized on organization to make the information meaningful. The discussion put the students in cognitively active roles and also helped the students elaborate on their understanding. These processes applied the fourth guideline.

Finally, in saying, "When I try to answer questions like these, I first look for relationships in the parts of the question, like what do I know about Pluto compared to the planets?" he was modeling metacognition, which applied the fifth guideline.

Applying the memory model in your teaching need not take an enormous amount of extra effort. For instance, once created, David reused his materials with little or no further preparation. And, with practice, checking students' perceptions and guiding their learning with questioning can become essentially automatic. This is true for applying learning theory in general: Effective application is more a matter of clear teacher thinking than it is increased effort.

check your understanding

4.1 Define *metacognition,* and explain how it can influence learning.

4.2 As you read this book, you stop and go back to the top of a page and reread one of the sections. Is this an example of metacognition? Explain.

4.3 Note taking is a study strategy. You have a classmate, who, in an attempt to be sure that he doesn't miss anything, writes down virtually everything the instructor says. You write down only the points that you believe are most important. Which of you is more metacognitive in your approach to note taking? Explain.

To receive feedback for these questions, go to Appendix A.

MyEducationLab

To see how another middle school teacher attempts to help his students understand the solar system, go to the *Activities and Applications* section in Chapter 7 of MyEducationLab at www.myeducationlab.com, and read the case study *Teaching the Solar System.* Answer the questions following the case study.

Putting the Memory Model into Perspective

The human memory model makes an important contribution to increasing our understanding of the way we gather and organize information and store it for further use. However, the model, as initially presented in Figure 7.1 oversimplifies the nature of human memory. For example, the model presents attention as a filter between sensory memory and working memory, but some evidence indicates that the central executive in working memory governs what we pay attention to and how we perceive that information. So, attending to incoming stimuli and attaching meaning to them are not as simple as the one-way flow of information that the model suggests (Demetriou, Christou, Spanoudis, & Platsidou, 2002). In addition, some researchers question whether or not working memory and long-term memory are as distinct as the model suggests (Baddeley, 2001; Wolz, 2003).

The memory model has also been criticized for failing to adequately consider the social context in which learning occurs (Greeno & van de Sande, 2007), as well as cultural and personal factors that influence learning, such as students' emotions (Nasir, Rosebery, Warren, & Lee, 2006). Critics also argue that it doesn't adequately account for the extent to which learners construct their own knowledge, one of the principles of cognitive learning theory presented at the beginning of the chapter (Kafai, 2006). (We examine the process of knowledge construction in detail in Chapter 8.)

However, despite these criticisms, virtually all cognitive descriptions of learning, including those endorsing the principle that learners construct knowledge, accept the basic structure of the human memory model, including a limited-capacity working memory, a long-term memory that stores information in organized form, cognitive processes that move the information from one store to another, and the regulatory mechanisms of metacognition (Bransford et al., 2000; Sweller et al., 1998). These components help us explain learning events that neither behaviorism nor social cognitive theory can explain. Further, they help provide a framework for the process of constructing knowledge, which you will study in the next chapter.

Meeting Your Learning Objectives

1. Describe and explain the principles of cognitive learning theory.
   - The principles of cognitive learning theory suggest (a) learning and development depend on learners' experiences, (b) learners are mentally active in their attempts to make sense of those experiences, (c) learners construct knowledge, (d) prior knowledge influences knowledge construction, and (e) learning is enhanced in a social environment.
   - The human memory model is the cognitive architecture that one can use to describe how people gather, organize, and store their experiences. The model designates where knowledge is constructed and where prior knowledge is stored until needed for new knowledge construction.
2. Use the characteristics of the memory stores in the human memory model to explain events in and out of the classroom.
   - Sensory memory is the store that briefly holds stimuli from the environment until individuals can process the stimuli. Working memory is the conscious part of our information processing system, and its most significant feature is its limited capacity. Long-term memory is the permanent information store, and it is where individuals store declarative, procedural, and conditional knowledge.
   - When students struggle with complex tasks, such as writing or solving problems, the cause is often lack of prior knowledge stored in long-term memory or skills that haven't been developed to automaticity.
   - Development influences the memory stores. Older students can more effectively accommodate the limitations of working memory and better capitalize on their experiences to represent information in long-term memory.
3. Describe the cognitive processes in the human memory model, and identify applications in classroom activities.
   - Attention and perception move information from sensory memory to working memory. Attention is the process of consciously focusing on a stimulus, and perception is the meaning we attach to the stimulus.
   - Learners use rehearsal to retain information in the phonological loop of working memory, and intensive rehearsal can move information into long-term memory.
   - Encoding represents information in long-term memory. Learners encode information more effectively if it is represented both visually and verbally than if it is represented in only one way.
   - Retrieval is the process of pulling information from long-term memory back into working memory for problem solving or further processing.
   - Students' use of the cognitive processes improve as they develop. Older learners can better focus their attention and more effectively use strategies to promote meaningful encoding.
4. Define *metacognition,* and explain how it can influence learning.
   - *Metacognition* is individuals' knowledge of, and control over, their cognitive processes.
   - Metacognition influences learning by making learners aware of the way they study and learn and by enabling learners to develop strategies to increase learning.
   - Metacognition is developmental, with young children being less aware of their study strategies than their older counterparts.

Developing as a Professional: Practicing for Your Licensure Exam

In the opening case study, David Shelton planned and conducted his lesson to make the solar system meaningful for his ninth-grade students. In the following case, a teacher helps a group of high school students understand different characters in the novel *The Scarlet Letter*. Read the case study, and then answer the questions that follow.

Sue Southam, an English teacher, decides to use Nathaniel Hawthorne's *The Scarlet Letter* as the vehicle to help her examine timeless issues, such as moral dilemmas involving personal responsibility and emotions such as guilt, anger, loyalty, and revenge. The novel, set in Boston in the 1600s, describes a tragic and illicit love affair between the heroine (Hester Prynne) and a minister (Arthur Dimmesdale). The novel's title refers to the letter *A*, meaning "adulterer," which the Puritan community makes Hester wear as punishment for her adultery. The class has been discussing the book for several days, and they are now examining Reverend Dimmesdale's character.

To begin, Sue reads a passage from the text describing Dimmesdale and then says, "In your logs, jot down some of the important characteristics in that description. If you were going to draw a portrait of him, what would he look like? Try to be as specific as possible."

She gives the students a few minutes to write in their logs, asking them to describe what they think he looks like and who they might cast in the role of a movie adaptation of the novel.

Then she says, "Let's see if we can find out more about the Dimmesdale character through his actions. Listen carefully while I read the speech he gives in which he confronts Hester in front of the congregation and exhorts her to identify her secret lover and partner in sin."

She reads Dimmesdale's speech, then divides the class into "Dimmesdales" and "Hesters" around the room, and says, "Dimmesdales, in your logs I want you to tell me what Dimmesdale is really thinking during his speech. Hesters, I want you to tell me what Hester is thinking while she listens. Write in your logs in your own words the private thoughts of your character."

After giving the students a few minutes to write in their logs, she organizes them into groups of four, with each group composed of two Hesters and two Dimmesdales. Once students are settled, she says, "In each group, I want you to start off by having Dimmesdale tell what he is thinking during the first line of the speech. Then I'd like a Hester to respond. Then continue with Dimmesdale's next line, and then Hester's reaction. Go ahead and share your thoughts in your groups."

She gives the students 5 minutes to share their perspectives, then calls the class back together: "Okay, let's hear it. A Dimmesdale first. Just what was he thinking during his speech? . . . Mike?"

"The only thing I could think of was, 'Oh God, help me. I hope she doesn't say anything. If they find out it's me, I'll be ruined.' And then here comes Hester with her powerful speech," Mike concludes, turning to his partner in the group, Nicole.

"I wrote, 'Good man, huh. So why don't you confess then? You know you're guilty. I've admitted my love, but you haven't. Why don't you just come out and say it?'" Nicole comments.

"Interesting. . . . What else? How about another Hester? . . . Sarah?"

"I just put, 'No, I'll never tell. I still love you, and I'll keep your secret forever,' " Sarah offers.

Sue pauses for a moment, looks around the room, and comments, "Notice how different the two views of Hester are. Nicole paints her as very angry, whereas Sarah views her as still loving him." Sue again pauses to look for reactions. Karen raises her hand, and Sue nods to her.

"I think the reason Hester doesn't say anything is that people won't believe her, because he's a minister," Karen suggests. "She's getting her revenge just by being there, reminding him of his guilt."

"But if she accuses him, won't people expect him to deny it?" Brad adds.

"Maybe he knows she won't accuse him because she still loves him," Julie offers.

"Wait a minute," Jeff counters. "I don't think he's such a bad guy. I think he feels guilty about it all, but he just doesn't have the courage to admit it in front of all of those people."

"I think he's really admitting it in his speech but is asking her secretly not to tell," Caroline adds. "Maybe he's really talking to Hester and doesn't want the rest of the people to know."

The class continues, with students debating the meaning in the speech and trying to decide whether Reverend Dimmesdale is really a villain or a tragic figure. "Interesting ideas," Sue says as the end of the class nears. "Keep them in mind, and for tomorrow, I'd like you to read Chapter 4, in which we meet Hester's husband," and she then closes the lesson.

Short-Answer Questions

In answering these questions, use information from the chapter, and link your responses to specific information in the case.

1. Assess the extent to which Sue applied the principles of cognitive learning theory in her lesson. Include both strengths and weaknesses in your assessment.

2. Assess the extent to which Sue applied the human memory model in her lesson. Include both strengths and weaknesses in your assessment.

3. Which cognitive process from the memory model was most prominent in Sue's lesson? Explain.

4. Identify at least one instance in Sue's lesson in which she focused on declarative knowledge. Identify another in which she focused on procedural knowledge. Was the primary focus of Sue's lesson the acquisition of declarative knowledge or procedural knowledge?

For feedback on these responses, go to Appendix B.

Now go to Chapter 7 of MyEducationLab, located at www.myeducationlab.com, where you can:

- Take a quiz to test your mastery of chapter objectives. Detailed feedback is provided to explain why your responses are correct or incorrect.
- Deepen your understanding of chapter concepts with *Review, Practice, Enrichment* exercises.
- Complete *Activities and Applications* that will help you apply what you have learned in the chapter by analyzing real classrooms through video clips, artifacts and case studies. Your instructor will provide you with feedback for the *Activities and Applications.*
- Develop your professional knowledge and decision making in *Building Teaching Skills and Dispositions* exercises. Structured feedback will be available to you, providing you with support as you practice each skill. Your instructor will provide you with feedback on the final task that accompanies the exercise.

Important Concepts

analogies (p. 212)
attention (p. 207)
automaticity (p. 201)
central executive (p. 199)
chunking (p. 201)
cognitive learning theories (p. 196)
cognitive load (p. 200)
conditional knowledge (p. 202)
declarative knowledge (p. 202)
dual-coding theory (p. 210)
elaboration (p. 212)
encoding (p. 209)
episodic memory (p. 202)
forgetting (p. 214)
imagery (p. 210)
information processing theory (p. 198)
interference (p. 214)
long-term memory (p. 201)
maintenance rehearsal (p. 199)
meaningfulness (p. 203)
memory stores (p. 199)
meta-attention (p. 217)
metacognition (p. 217)
metamemory (p. 217)
mnemonic devices (p. 213)
organization (p. 210)
perception (p. 208)
phonological loop (p. 199)
proactive interference (p. 214)
procedural knowledge (p. 202)
retrieval (p. 215)
retroactive interference (p. 214)
schema activation (p. 212)
schemas (p. 202)
scripts (p. 204)
semantic memory (p. 202)
sensory memory (p. 199)
short-term memory (p. 200)
visual-spatial sketchpad (p. 200)
working memory (p. 199)

chapter

8

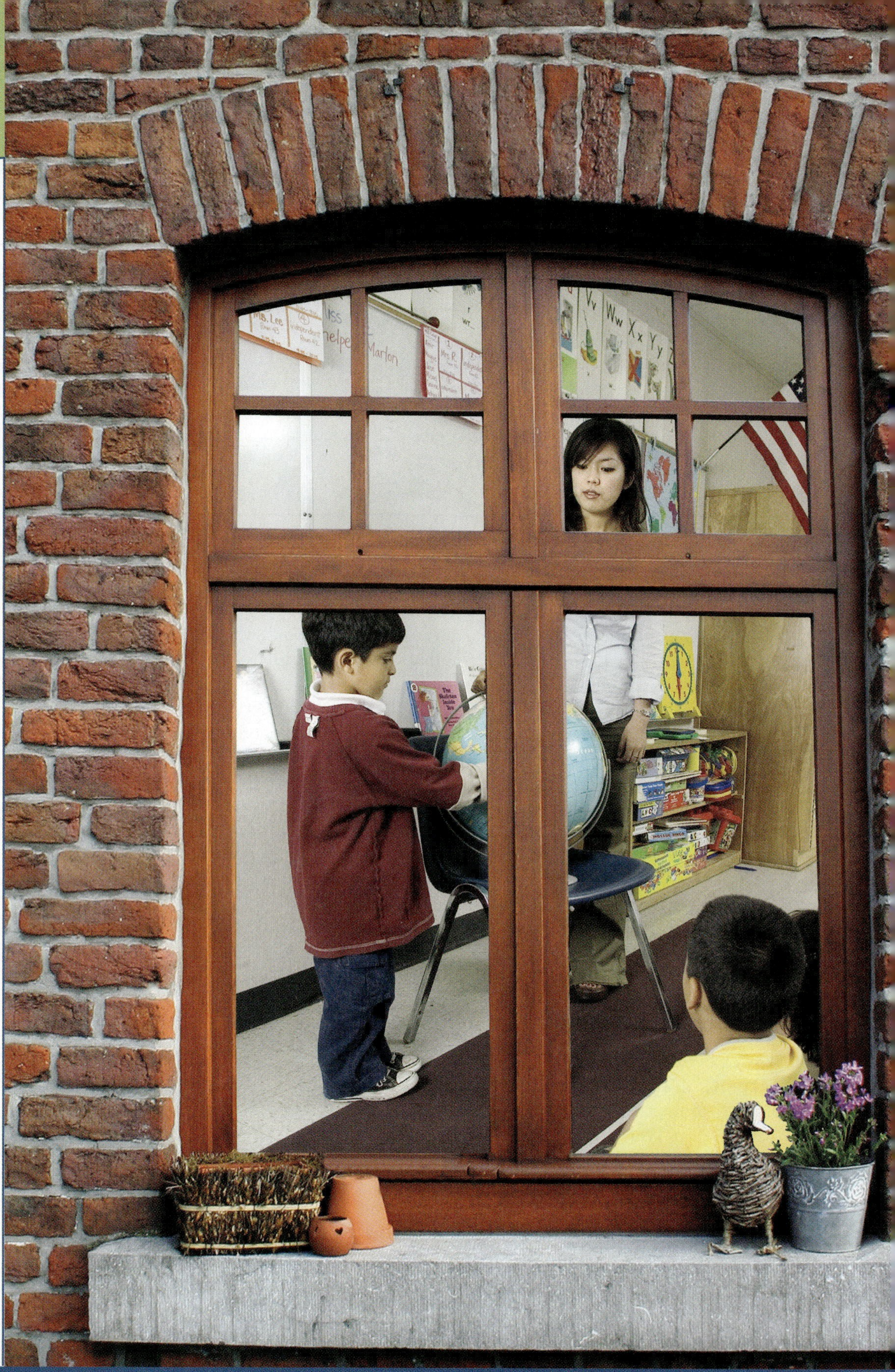

Constructing Knowledge

chapter outline

What Is Constructivist Learning Theory?

- Cognitive Constructivism
- Social Constructivism

Characteristics of Constructivist Learning Theory

- Learners Construct Understanding That Makes Sense to Them
- New Learning Depends on Current Understanding
- Social Interaction Facilitates Learning
- Meaningful Learning Occurs Within Real-World Tasks

When Learners Construct Invalid Knowledge: Misconceptions and Conceptual Change

- Misconceptions in Teaching and Learning
- The Origin of Misconceptions
- Misconceptions' Resistance to Change
- Teaching for Conceptual Change
  - **Exploring Diversity:** The Impact of Diversity on Knowledge Construction

Constructivist Learning Theory in Classrooms

- The Teacher's Role in Constructivist Classrooms
- Constructivism and Human Memory
- Suggestions for Classroom Practice
- Learning Contexts: Knowledge Construction in Urban Environments
  - **Theory to Practice:** Applying Constructivist Learning Theory in Your Classroom

Putting Constructivist Learning Theory into Perspective

- **Developmentally Appropriate Practice:** Applying Constructivist Learning Theory with Different-Aged Learners

learning objectives

After you have completed your study of this chapter, you should be able to:

1. Describe differences between cognitive and social constructivism, and give examples of each.
2. Identify characteristics and applications of constructivist learning theory.
3. Describe misconceptions and how they occur, and explain how teachers can eliminate them.
4. Describe suggestions from constructivist learning theory for your teaching.

One of the learning principles discussed in Chapter 7 states that students construct their own knowledge of the topics they study. As a result, individuals' thinking about those topics may vary widely. Keep this idea in mind as you examine the thinking of students in the following case study.

> Jenny Newhall, a fourth-grade teacher, wants her students to understand the principle behind beam balances: that they balance when the weight times the distance on one side of the fulcrum equals the weight times the distance on the other. She begins by dividing her students into groups of four and giving the groups balances with tiles on them that appear as follows:

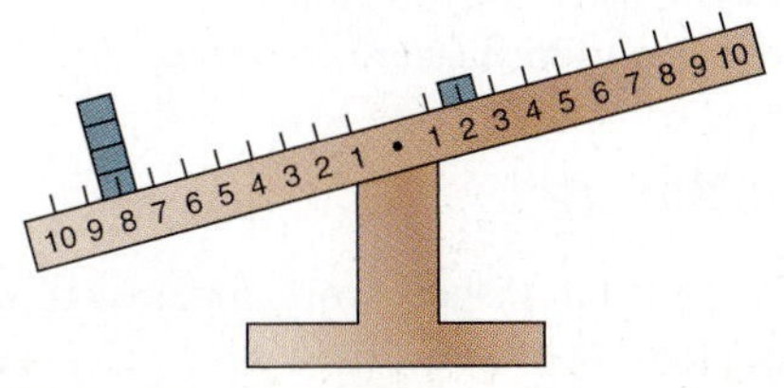

Jenny tells the students that they are to figure out how to balance the beam, but before adding tiles to the balances, they need to write down possible solutions and explain to their group mates why they think their solutions will work.

As the class begins to work, Jenny circulates around the room and then joins one of the groups—Molly, Suzanne, Tad, and Drexel—as they attempt to solve the problem.

Suzanne begins by offering, "There are 4 on the 8 and 1 on the 2. I want to put 3 on the 10 so there will be 4 on each side."

Here's the solution she proposes:

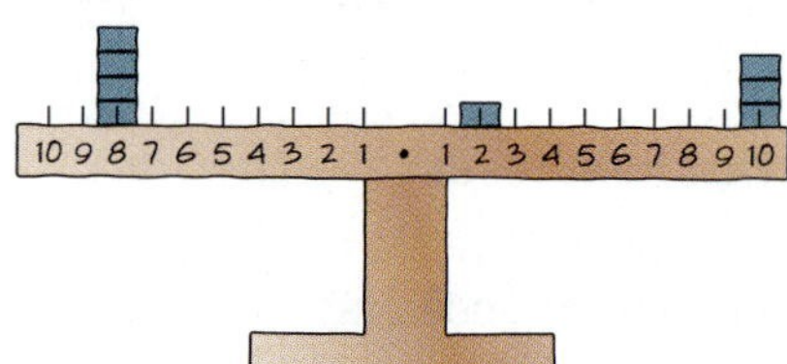

Molly agrees that Suzanne's arrangement of tiles will make the beam balance but offers a different explanation. "I think we should put 3 on 10, because 4 on the 8 is 32 on one side. And since we only have 2 on the other side, we need to make them equal. So 3 on 10 would equal 30, plus 2, and we'd have 32 on both sides."

We return to this lesson later in the chapter, but for now, let's consider three questions.

1. Where did Suzanne get the idea that the beam would balance if the numbers of tiles on each side of the fulcrum were equal?
2. How might we explain the difference in Suzanne's and Molly's thinking?
3. What implications do these differences in thinking have for our teaching?

Constructivist learning theory helps answer these and other questions, and in this chapter you will see how you can apply this theory in your teaching.

What Is Constructivist Learning Theory?

Constructivism is a term used in different ways by philosophers, educational psychologists, and teachers (Palincsar, 1998; Phillips, 2000). In this book we take the perspective of educational psychologists, who study constructivism as a theory of learning, and teachers, who consider the implications of this theory for their instruction (Andrew, 2007).

Despite differences, all who study constructivism agree with the following principle: Learners construct, rather than record, knowledge. Grounded in this principle, **constructivism** is a theory of learning suggesting that learners create their own knowledge of the topics they study rather than receiving that knowledge as transmitted to them by some other source, such as another person or something they read (Bransford, Brown, & Cocking, 2000).

Constructivism. A theory of learning suggesting that learners create their own knowledge of the topics they study rather than receiving that knowledge as transmitted to them by some other source.

This definition helps us answer our first question. Suzanne didn't get her ideas about beam balances from Jenny, another teacher, or something she read; she "constructed" them on her own. Constructivism adds to our understanding of learning, because no other theory, alone, can explain Suzanne's reasoning. Having been reinforced for this thinking isn't likely, as a behaviorist explanation would require, and it's equally unlikely that it had been modeled, so social cognitive theory can't provide an explanation either. And the model of human memory doesn't address the issue of learners' unique constructions and misconceptions.

Views of knowledge construction vary, influenced primarily by the works of Piaget (1952, 1959, 1970) and Vygotsky (1978, 1986), but also by other sources including Dewey (1938), Bruner (1966, 1973), and Gestalt psychology (Scholl, 2001). We examine the two primary perspectives, *cognitive constructivism* and *social constructivism*, in the following sections.

Cognitive Constructivism

Cognitive constructivism. A constructivist view that focuses on individual, internal constructions of knowledge.

Cognitive constructivism, grounded in Piaget's work, focuses on individual, internal constructions of knowledge (Greeno, Collins, & Resnick, 1996; Meter & Stevens, 2000; Nuthall, 1999a). It emphasizes individuals' search for meaning as they interact with the environment and test and modify existing schemas (Packer & Goicoechea, 2000). Social interaction influences the process, but primarily as a catalyst for individual cognitive conflict (Palincsar, 1998). When one child suggests an idea that causes disequilibrium in another, for example, the second child resolves the disequilibrium by individually reconstructing his or her understanding. To illustrate this idea, consider the following exchange between two life science students:

> **Devon:** (Holding a spider between his fingers and pointing at a beetle) Look at the bugs.
> **Gino:** Yech. . . . Put that thing down (gesturing to the spider). Besides, that's not a bug. It's a spider.
> **Devon:** What do you mean? A bug is a bug.
> **Gino:** Nope. Bugs have six legs. See (touching the legs of the beetle). This one has eight. . . . Look (pointing to the spider).
> **Devon:** So, . . . bugs have six legs, and spiders have eight? . . . Hmm?
> **Gino:** Yeah . . . so, what do you think this is (holding up a grasshopper)?

Cognitive constructivists would interpret this episode by saying that Devon's equilibrium was disrupted as a result of the discussion, and—individually—he resolved the problem by reconstructing his thinking to accommodate the new evidence Gino offered.

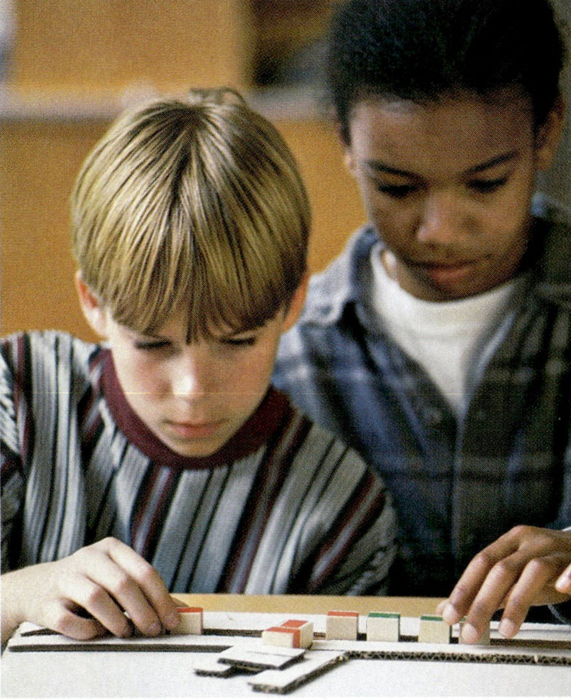

Constructivism suggests that learners construct their own knowledge rather than having it transmitted by some other source.

A literal interpretation of this position emphasizes learning activities that are experience based and discovery oriented. This view suggests, for example, that children learn math most effectively if they discover ideas while manipulating concrete objects such as blocks and sticks, rather than having them presented by a teacher or other expert.

This interpretation creates a dilemma for teachers because it "fundamentally distrust[s]. . . all attempts to instruct directly" (Resnick & Klopfer, 1989, p. 3), suggesting that teacher–student interaction is important, but that teachers need to guard against imposing their thinking on developing learners (DeVries, 1997). So, other than providing materials and a supportive learning environment, what is the teacher's role? This question hasn't been satisfactorily answered (Airasian & Walsh, 1997; Greeno et al., 1996).

Social Constructivism

Most of us have had the experience of talking to another person about an idea, with neither understanding it completely. But as the discussion continues, understanding for both increases. This experience illustrates the basic premise of **social constructivism**, which, influenced by Vygotsky's (1978) work, suggests that learners first construct knowledge in a social context and then individually internalize it. Vygotsky believed that,

Social constructivism A view of constructivism suggesting that learners first construct knowledge in a social context and then individually internalize it.

> Every function in the child's cultural development appears twice: first, on the social level, and later on the individual level; first between people . . . and then inside the child. . . . This applies equally to voluntary attention, to logical memory, and to the formation of concepts. All the higher functions originate as actual relationships between individuals. (Vygotsky, 1978, p. 57).

Social constructivism has become the view most influential in guiding the thinking of educational leaders and teachers (J. Martin, 2006).

To see how social constructivism differs from cognitive constructivism, think again about the exchange between Devon and Gino. Social constructivists would argue that Devon's understanding increased as a direct result of the exchange, and that the dialogue, itself, helped Devon more clearly understand the difference between insects and spiders.

A social constructivist interpretation helps resolve the dilemma about teachers' roles. This perspective "does not suggest that educators get out of the way so children can do their natural work, as Piagetian theory often seemed to imply" (Resnick & Klopfer, 1989, p. 4). Rather, it suggests that teachers consider all the traditional questions of instruction: how to organize and conduct learning activities, motivate students, and assess learning. The focus, however, is on facilitating students' constructions of knowledge using social interaction (Fleming & Alexander, 2001). From a social constructivist perspective, creating learning environments in which learners exchange ideas and collaborate in solving problems is an essential teacher role (R. Anderson et al., 2001; Meter & Stevens, 2000).

Sociocultural Learning Theory

Sociocultural theory A form of social constructivism that emphasizes the social dimensions of learning, but places greater emphasis on the larger cultural contexts in which learning occurs.

Just as constructivism, in general, is interpreted differently, theorists emphasize different dimensions of social constructivism. **Sociocultural theory**, while still emphasizing the social dimensions of learning, places greater emphasis on the larger cultural contexts in which learning occurs (Kozulin, 1998; Mason, 2007). Shrugging shoulders is an example. In our culture it communicates uncertainty, but in some Ethiopian cultures, it is an integral part of a courtship dance between young men and women (Issa Saleh, Personal Communication, October 14, 2007).

Culture also influences the language patterns that students bring to school (Cazden, 2002; Heath, 1989). For instance, in some homes, children are not viewed as legitimate partners in conversation, while in others, they are expected to speak openly with adults (Au, 1992; Tharp & Gallimore, 1991). When children come to our classrooms, they bring different views of acceptable behavior patterns. Also, differences exist in the cultural experiences, attitudes, and values that students bring to school, and these all influence learning (Rogoff, 2003; Rogoff, Turkanis, & Bartlett, 2001).

The Classroom as a Community of Learners

Community of learners. A learning environment in which the teacher and all the students work together to help everyone achieve.

The sociocultural view of learning shifts the emphasis from the individual to the group and from acquiring knowledge, per se, to belonging, participating, and communicating within a community of learners (Mason, 2007). This perspective reminds us that our actions create microcultures in our classrooms. Our rules and procedures and the way we interact with students can make classrooms inviting and cooperative or competitive and even frightening. A **community of learners** is a learning environment in which the teacher and all the students work together to help everyone achieve (A. Brown & Campione, 1994; Palincsar, 1998).

The characteristics of a learning community, with illustrations from Jenny's lesson, are outlined as follows (A. Brown & Campione, 1994; Palincsar, 1998):

- All students participate in learning activities. Each student in Jenny's class was involved in trying to solve the problem.
- Teachers and students work together to help one another learn; promoting learning isn't the teacher's responsibility alone. Jenny's students had to explain their proposed solutions to their group mates before actually trying them.

In a community of learners, the teacher and all students work together to help everyone achieve.

- Student–student interaction is an important part of the learning process. As they proposed alternate solutions, the interaction was mostly among the students in Jenny's activity.
- Teachers and students respect difference in interests, thinking, and progress. All the students listened patiently as their group mates offered solutions.
- The thinking involved in learning activities is as important as answers. Jenny emphasized that the students verbalize their thinking before they actually tried solutions to the problem.

Each of these characteristics is grounded in the idea that learners first socially construct knowledge before they appropriate and internalize it.

MyEducationLab

To see how a teacher attempts to develop a community of learners in her classroom, go to the *Building Teaching Skills and Dispositions* section in Chapter 8 of MyEducationLab at www.myeducationlab.com, and watch the episode *Author's Chair.* Complete the exercises following the episode to build your skills in creating a learning community.

Cognitive Apprenticeship

Historically, apprenticeships helped novices working with experts to acquire skills they couldn't learn on their own (S. Black, 2007). Apprenticeships are still common in trades such as furniture construction, weaving, or cooking, but they are also used in areas such as learning to play musical instruments or creating pieces of art.

Cognitive apprenticeships, also resulting from the influence of social constructivism on education, occur when less-skilled learners work at the side of experts in developing cognitive skills, such as reading comprehension, writing, or problem solving (A. Collins, 2006; Englert, Berry, & Dunsmore, 2001). Cognitive apprenticeships are similar to apprenticeships in general, except the focus is on developing mental abilities. They commonly include the following components:

Cognitive apprenticeship. The process of having a less-skilled learner work at the side of an expert to develop cognitive skills.

- *Modeling:* Teachers demonstrate skills, such as solutions to problems, and simultaneously model their thinking by describing it in words.
- *Scaffolding:* As students perform tasks, teachers ask questions and provide support, decreasing the amount of scaffolding as students' proficiency increases.
- *Verbalization:* Teachers encourage students to express their developing understanding in words, which allows teachers to assess both the students' skills and their thinking.
- *Increasing complexity:* As students' proficiency increases, teachers present them with more challenging problems or other tasks.
- *Exploration:* Teachers ask students to identify new applications of what they've learned.

Cognitive apprenticeships can also exist between students, and the exchange between Devon and Gino is a simple example. Gino modeled his thinking as he described the differences between bugs (insects) and spiders, and he scaffolded Devon's thinking in the process. Then in saying, "So . . . bugs have . . . six legs, and spiders have eight," Devon verbalized his increasing understanding, and Gino finally asked him to apply it by classifying a grasshopper.

Research indicates that cognitive apprenticeships are more effective than one-way transmission of information by teachers (Englert et al., 2001). *Verbalization*—students' putting their understanding into words—is the component that is most compromised with a transmission view of teaching. Students receive the information, but teachers can't assess the extent to which their thinking is advancing.

Situated Cognition

Situated cognition (or situated learning), a view suggesting that learning depends on, and cannot be separated from, the context in which it occurs, is another product of social constructivism (J. Brown, Collins, & Duguid, 1989; Lave, 1997; Mason, 2007). According to this view, a student who learns to solve subtraction and division problems while determining a car's gas mileage, for example, has a different kind of understanding than one who solves subtraction and division problems in school tasks (Rogoff, 2003). Similarly, when you apply your understanding of learning theories to the students' thinking in the balance beam problem, you acquire a different understanding than you would if you studied them without this context.

Situated cognition. A theoretical position in social constructivism suggesting that learning depends on, and cannot be separated from, the context in which it occurs.

Situated cognition, when taken to the extreme, suggests that transfer is difficult, if not impossible. **Transfer** is the ability to take understanding acquired in one context and apply it to a different context. An extreme view of situated congnition would suggest, for example, that people who learn to drive in rural areas would be unable to drive in big cities with their heavy traffic, because their driving is situated in the rural setting, and the big city context is different.

Transfer. The ability to take understanding acquired in one context and apply it to a different context.

Transfer does exist, however (R. C. Clark & Mayer, 2003; R. E. Mayer & Wittrock, 2006). For example, many people are comfortable driving in both rural areas and large cities, and they develop this expertise by practicing driving in both contexts.

Similar attempts to promote transfer can also be made in school by varying the learning context (Vosniadou, 2007). Math students, for example, should practice solving a variety of real-world problems, and language arts students should practice writing in each of their content areas (R. E. Mayer & Wittrock, 2006). While most experts don't take an extreme view of situated cognition, it reminds us that context is important, and we accommodate it by using real-world applications whenever possible.

check your understanding

1.1 Describe the primary difference between cognitive and social constructivism.

1.2 In the case study at the beginning of the chapter, is Suzanne's thinking a better example of cognitive or of social constructivism? Explain your conclusion.

1.3 A second-grade teacher wants her students to understand diphthongs (speech sounds that begin with one vowel sound and gradually change to another vowel sound within the same syllable, as "oi" in *boil*). She presents her students with the passage

> A *boy*, Jeremy, walks over by the window of his *house* one evening and *looks* at the full *moon*. It is so bright that he *could* see his shadow on the *floor*. Off in the tree, with a branch that is *bowed*, he hears an *owl* hoot.

She asks the students to make observations of the italicized words and then helps them pronounce each correctly.

Explain why this is, or is not, an example of situated cognition. Provide evidence from the example to support your assessment.

To receive feedback for these questions, go to Appendix A.

Characteristics of Constructivist Learning Theory

Though interpretations vary, most constructivists agree on four characteristics that influence learning (Bruning et al., 2004; R. Mayer, 1996). They're outlined in Figure 8.1 and discussed in the sections that follow.

Learners Construct Knowledge That Makes Sense to Them

Learners constructing their own knowledge is an accepted principle of all cognitive learning theories. Among theorists, "the view of the learner has changed from that of a recipient of knowledge to that of a constructor of knowledge" (R. Mayer, 1998, p. 359).

Suzanne's thinking is an example. For her, it made sense that an equal number of tiles on each side of the fulcrum would cause the beam to balance. She didn't receive this understanding from anyone else; she constructed this intuitively sensible, but incorrect, conclusion on her own.

- Learners construct knowledge that makes sense to them.
- New learning depends on current understanding.
- Social interaction facilitates learning.
- The most meaningful learning occurs within real-world tasks.

Figure 8.1 Characteristics of constructivism

New Learning Depends on Current Understanding

We described the role of current understanding (prior knowledge) when we discussed the importance of making information meaningful in Chapter 7. Constructivists go further, emphasizing that the ideas learners construct directly depend on the knowledge they currently possess (Bae, 2003; Shapiro,

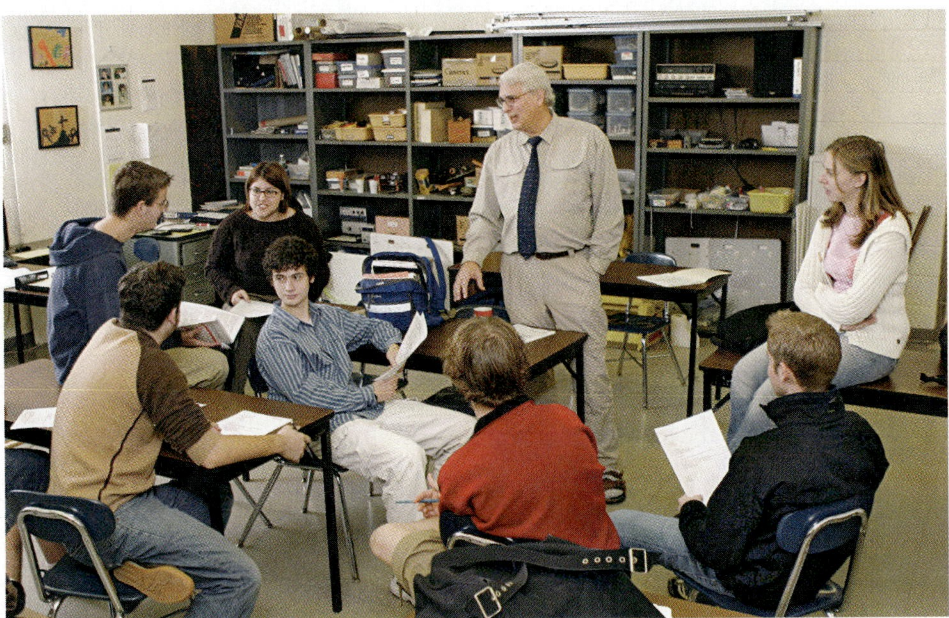

Social constructivist learning theory emphasizes the role of social interaction in knowledge construction.

2004). For instance, learners commonly conclude that summer is warmer than winter (in the Northern Hemisphere) because the Earth is closer to the Sun in summer. This makes sense. The closer we hold our hands to a candle or a hot burner, the warmer they feel, so, based on this experience, concluding that we're closer to the Sun makes more sense than the actual explanation involving the tilt of Earth's axis. We construct an understanding of the seasons in the context of previous experiences with candles and stoves.

The influence of prior knowledge helps answer our second question from the beginning of the chapter, "How might we explain the difference in Suzanne's and Molly's thinking?" The answer is that Molly had prior knowledge that Suzanne lacked. How she acquired this knowledge is uncertain; it might have been the result of more experiences, greater motivation, or higher ability. Constructivism helps us better understand why differences in prior knowledge are so important in classroom learning.

Social Interaction Facilitates Learning

Social constructivist learning theory emphasizes the role of social interaction in knowledge construction (Rogoff, 2001, 2003; Vygotsky, 1978). We will discuss the role of social interaction in detail in this section, but first we again examine Suzanne's thinking.

> After both Suzanne and Molly offer their alternate solutions and explanations, the group discusses them, and Jenny instructs the students to test their ideas on the actual balances. She then reassembles the class and asks Mavrin, who has solved the problem correctly, to come to the board and explain it, using the sketch you see here, which she has drawn on the board.

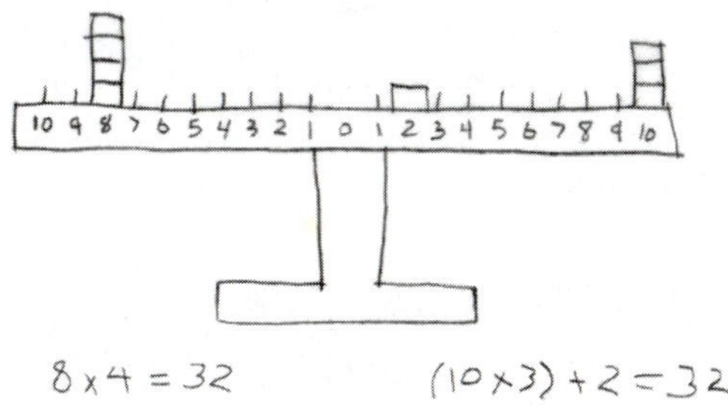

Mavrin explains that $8 \times 4 = 32$ on the left side of the fulcrum equals $(10 \times 3) + 2 = 32$ on the right side, referring to the sketch in his explanation. Jenny reviews it, carefully describes the logic of his thinking and concludes by saying, "He has an excellent number sentence here."

An interviewer from a nearby university is observing the class, and following the lesson, he talks with Suzanne, Molly, Tad, and Drexel about their understanding of beam balances. He gives them the following problem, allows them some time to think about it, and then says, "Suzanne, tell us where you would put tiles to make the beam balance."

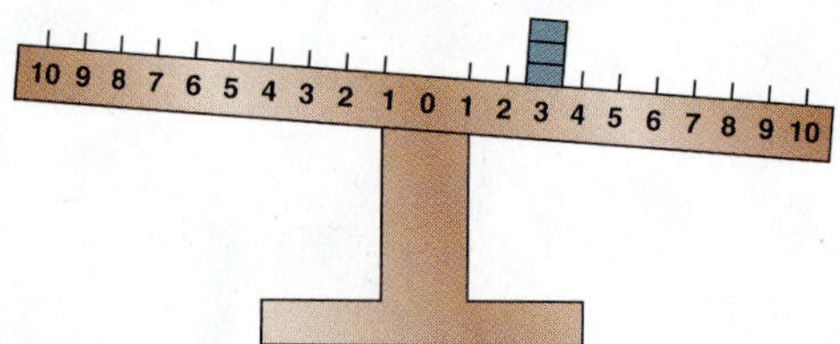

Suzanne offers the following solution:

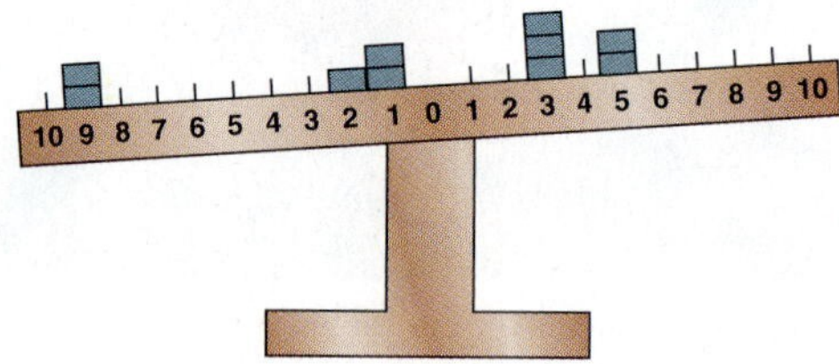

She reasons, "I put 2 here (indicating that she had added 2 tiles to the right side of the fulcrum) so that 2 plus 3 equals 5 . . . and 2 plus 1 plus 2 here, so it will be 5" (indicating that she had put 5 tiles on the left side of the fulcrum)."

This segment raises an important question. During both the small-group and whole-group discussions, Suzanne heard three correct explanations for making the beam balance: Molly's, at the end of the first segment of our case study; Mavrin's at the board; and Jenny's. Yet, her thinking didn't change at all; she continued to believe that the beam would balance if the numbers of tiles on each side of the fulcrum were equal. Why might this have been the case?

The answer lies in an essential idea in learning: *Wisdom can't be told.* Originally proposed by Charles Gragg (1940) nearly three quarters of a century ago, and emphasized repeatedly by researchers since then (Bransford et al., 2000; Bransford, Derry, Berliner, Hammerness, & Beckett, 2005), it suggests that lecturing and explaining, as strategies for promoting learning, are often ineffective. Suzanne's thinking illustrates why this is the case. Although she was part of a group, and she appeared to be interacting, *she remained cognitively passive,* and as a result, her thinking didn't change.

Now, let's return to the interview.

After Suzanne offers her solution, the interviewer asks, "Molly, what do you think of that solution?"

"It won't work. . . . It doesn't matter how many blocks there are," Molly answers. "It's where they're put."

The interviewer asks Drexel and Tad what they think. Drexel confirms Molly's thinking and provides an explanation. Tad shrugs in uncertainty.

The students try Suzanne's solution, and the beam tips to the left.

Suzanne suggests taking a block off the 9, reasoning that the blocks near the end of the beam bring it down more, indicating that her thinking is starting to change as a result of seeing the example and interacting with the others.

The interviewer nods but doesn't affirm any explanation, instead giving the students the following additional problem and asking for solutions:

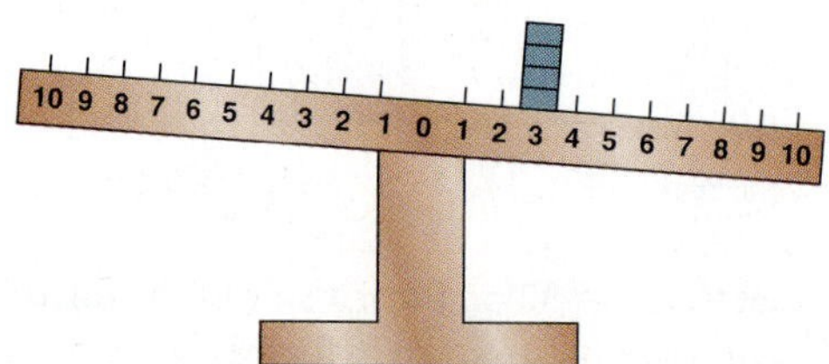

Molly offers, "Put 1 on the 8 and 4 on the 1."

"What do you think? . . . Tad?" the interviewer asks.

Tad stares at the beam for several seconds, concludes that the solution is correct, and when asked to explain his thinking, says, "Oh, okay, . . . 3 times 4 is 12, . . . and 4 times 1 is 4, . . . and 8 times 1 is 8, and 8 plus 4 is 12."

The interviewer asks for another solution, and Drexel offers, "One on the 2 and 1 on the 10."

"Okay, I want you to tell us whether or not that'll work, Suzanne."

". . . I think it will."

"Okay, explain why you think it will."

"Because, 10 times 1 equals 10, . . . and 2 times 1 equals 2, and 10 plus 2 equals 12. . . . So it'll be even."

Molly, Tad, and Drexel confirm the solution, and the interview is ended.

Why did Suzanne's thinking change during the interview when it didn't change during the lesson? In simple terms, she became cognitively active. Let's look at this process in more detail.

This interview is an application of social constructivist learning theory, and it illustrates essential characteristics of a cognitive apprenticeship. For example, when Molly and Drexel (and later, Tad) offered their explanations, they were *cognitive models*. The modeling, together with the discussion, allowed the students to share their perspectives and view ideas in different ways, which is an important function of social interaction (Greeno & Van De Sande, 2007). This process *scaffolded* Suzanne's thinking.

Then, when she said, "Because, 10 times 1 equals 10, . . . and 2 times 1 equals 2, and 10 plus 2 equals 12. . . . So it'll be even," she *verbalized* her understanding as she applied it to a new application. Verbalizing understanding helps students put their sometimes fuzzy thoughts into words and helps clarify their thinking (Kastens & Liben, 2007).

Social constructivist learning theory also emphasizes the process of *appropriating understanding*, which suggests that knowledge is first constructed in a social environment and is later internalized by individuals (Applebee, Langer, Nystrand, & Gamoran, 2003; Leont'ev, 1981; Y. Li et al., 2007). As you saw earlier in the chapter, Vygotsky (1978) believed that, "Every function in the child's cultural development appears twice: first, on the social level, and later on the individual level" (p. 57).

Tad's thinking illustrates this process. He initially had no schema for what made the beam balance. His understanding gradually developed as a direct result of the interaction with the others in his group. In the videotape from which this dialogue was taken, we could almost see "the wheels turning" in Tad's head as he hesitantly described his understanding. As he struggled to articulate his thinking, his understanding also increased.

Despite consistent evidence indicating that social interaction increases learning (Brophy, 2006c), research suggests that it is quite rare, with teachers spending most of their instructional time lecturing and explaining or having students do seat work (Pianta, Belsky, Houts, & Morrison, 2007).

Meaningful Learning Occurs Within Real-World Tasks

Situated cognition suggests that "much of what is learned is specific to the situation in which it is learned" (J. Anderson et al., 1996, p. 5). This suggests that real-world problems are more meaningful for students than are problems presented in the abstract.

Jenny's lesson illustrates this characteristic. She used concrete materials to help her students understand beam balances, which they might later apply to teeter-totters and force and resistance in everyday tools such as pliers and scissors. Her lesson used a real-world task. **Real-world tasks** are often called *authentic* tasks, and they are learning activities in which students practice thinking similar to that required in the real world (van Merriënboer, Kirschner, & Kester, 2003). Thinking is the key: "Authentic activities foster the kinds of thinking and problem-solving skills that are important in out-of-school settings, whether or not the activities themselves mirror what practitioners do" (Putnam & Borko, 2000, pp. 4–5). So when students use their math skills to find the carpeted area of their classroom, their writing skills in a letter of application, or their understanding of science to explain why they should wear a seatbelt while driving, for example, they are involved in authentic learning activities.

Real-world task (*authentic* task). A learning activity in which students practice thinking similar to that required in the real world.

MyEducationLab

To further analyze Jenny's lesson and the students' thinking, go to the *Activities and Applications* section in Chapter 8 of MyEducationLab at www.myeducationlab.com, and watch the episode *Constructing Knowledge of Balance Beams*. Answer the questions following the episode.

check your understanding

2.1 Of the four characteristics of constructivism, which is best illustrated by Suzanne's initial conclusion that the beam would balance if the number of tiles on each side of the fulcrum were the same? Explain.

2.2 For centuries, people believed that the Earth was the center of our solar system. Which of the four characteristics of constructivism is best illustrated by this historical fact? Explain.

2.3 You want your students to use grammar rules correctly in their writing. Describe a real-world context that would be most effective for helping them reach the objective.

To receive feedback for these questions, go to Appendix A.

When Learners Construct Invalid Knowledge: Misconceptions and Conceptual Change

To begin this section, look at the following example, which shows a ball in flight just after it has left the thrower's hand and just before the receiver catches it. Draw an arrow to represent the direction of the *primary force* on the ball at each of the numbered points. (For purposes of this problem, ignore the air resistance on the ball.)

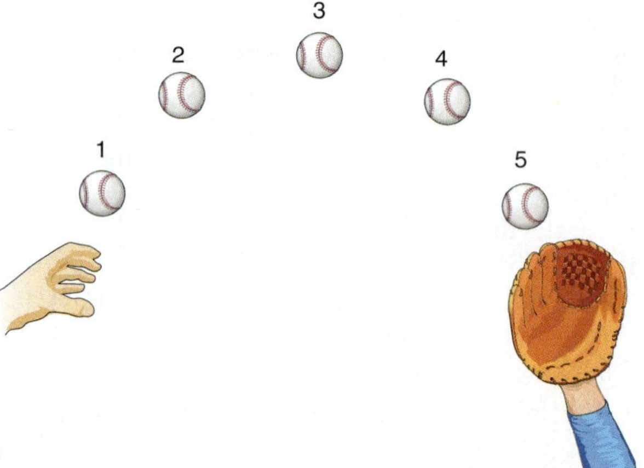

If you're typical, you will have drawn the arrows as you see here. Why did you represent the forces in this way?

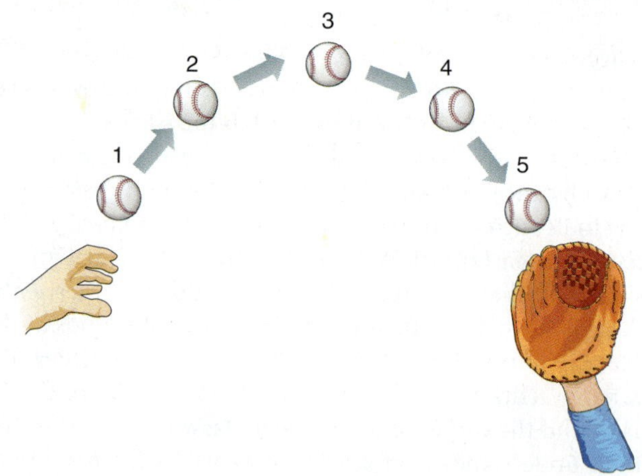

You represented the forces as you did because it *made sense* to represent them this way. Making sense of our experiences is arguably our most basic cognitive need, and it is the foundation for the learning principle: "Learners construct knowledge that makes sense to them." However, what makes sense to us is sometimes inconsistent with evidence or commonly accepted explanations. In those cases, we have constructed a **misconception**. For example, gravity is the only force on the ball at each of the points, as shown here. Suzanne had also formed a misconception about beam balances, mistakenly believing that the beam would balance if the numbers of tiles on each side of the fulcrum were equal.

Misconception. A belief that is inconsistent with evidence or commonly accepted explanations.

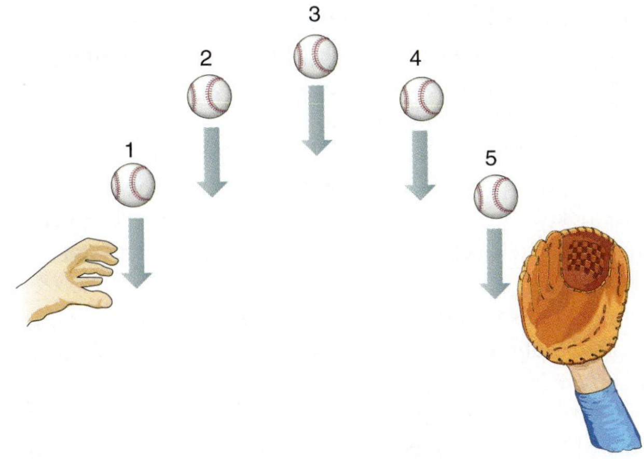

Misconceptions are most common in science, but they exist in other content areas as well. For instance, when faced with the following problems:

$$\begin{array}{r} 49 \\ -\underline{35} \end{array} \qquad \begin{array}{r} 45 \\ -\underline{39} \end{array}$$

young children often get an answer of 14 for both, believing that simply subtracting the smaller from the larger number is the correct operation in both cases. Language arts students commonly believe that an adverb is a word that ends in *ly* and adjectives always precede the nouns they modify, and many people believe that Communism and Socialism represent the same ideology. Each is a misconception.

Misconceptions in Teaching and Learning

A number of misconceptions also exist in teaching and learning. For instance, many teachers believe that the most effective way of helping students understand a topic is to explain it to them (Andrew, 2007; Cuban, 1993). As we saw in the case of Suzanne's thinking, this is a misconception. Many people, and even some educational leaders, believe that knowledge of content, such as math, English, or history, is all that is necessary to be an effective teacher (Bransford et al., 2000; R. Mayer, 2002). This is another misconception.

Teachers and school leaders have additional misconceptions about effective instruction, tending to equate it with orderly classrooms and teachers who are asking questions, and ignoring the need for clear learning objectives and learning activities that are consistent with the objectives (Eggen, 2004; Eggen & Gonzalez, 2005).

Misconceptions also exist in learning theory. The concept *negative reinforcement* is an example. It is a process that increases behavior, yet, likely because of the emotional reaction to the term *negative*, many students view it as a process that decreases behavior, inappropriately equating it with punishment. Also, many teachers believe that middle and high school students can be taught in the abstract, since their chronological age suggests that they are formal operational in their thinking. This is a common misconception about the application of Piaget's (1970, 1977) theory for instruction.

Misconceptions are important in our study of constructivism because, as you saw earlier in the chapter, constructivism is the only theory that can explain why they occur.

The Origin of Misconceptions

People's need to make sense of their experiences and the fact that people interpret new information using their prior knowledge helps us understand the origins of misconceptions (di Sessa, 2006). The misconceptions people construct are sensible to them because they are embedded in schemas that also make sense to them (Vosniadou, 2007). It made sense, for example, that the forces on the ball would be in the same direction as the ball's flight, and keeping the numbers of tiles on both sides of the fulcrum equal was simple and made sense to Suzanne.

Several factors contribute to misconceptions. Some include:

- *Prior experience.* This is perhaps the most important factor. For example, in your prior experiences, objects moving in a certain direction had forces acting on them in that direction. Rarely have you experienced an object moving in one direction but having the primary force acting on it in a different direction.
- *Appearances.* People tend to infer cause–effect relationships between two objects or events because they occur together, and one appears to cause the other (Kuhn, 2001; Reiner, Slotta, Chi, & Resnick, 2000). For example, because the beam balanced when the numbers of tiles on each side of the fulcrum were equal, Suzanne concluded that the equal number *caused* the beam to balance.
- *Society.* Commonly held societal beliefs contribute to misconceptions. For instance, many people in the United States think of Africa as a country, composed primarily of desert, and populated by people with a common culture. It is, in fact, a vast continent, with a great deal of geographic and cultural diversity.
- *Language.* Misuse of language can contribute to misconceptions. For instance, we describe the Sun and Moon as "rising" and "setting," which can lead children to believe that they revolve around the Earth; we refer to lead as a "heavy" metal, which can lead to misconceptions about the concept *density*; and we hear expressions such as, "He is on a meteoric rise in his career," or "Our company is light years ahead of the competition," which can cause misconceptions about meteors and light-years.

Misconceptions' Resistance to Change

Teachers commonly try to eliminate students' misconceptions by providing information that contradicts the misconception (Alparsian, Tekkaya, & Geban, 2004; Yip, 2004). This rarely works, as we saw with Suzanne's thinking about the balance beam.

Why are misconceptions so resistant to change? The answer lies in Piaget's concept of equilibrium. The misconception makes sense to the individual and is embedded in a larger schema, so he or she is at equilibrium (Sinatra & Pintrich, 2003). Changing thinking requires reconstruction of the schema, which is disequilibrating. Assimilating an experience into an existing schema is simpler.

Knowing that students bring misconceptions to learning experiences and realizing that these misconceptions are resistant to change, what can you do in response? The idea of conceptual change provides some answers.

Teaching for Conceptual Change

Conceptual change involves fundamentally altering students' beliefs about a topic. Teaching for conceptual change capitalizes on Piaget's concepts of *disequilibrium, accommodation,* and *assimilation* (Alparsian et al., 2004). Three conditions are required for students to change their thinking:

- The existing conception must become dissatisfying; it must cause disequilibrium.
- An alternative conception must be understandable. Students must be able to accommodate their thinking so the alternative conception makes sense.
- The new conception must be useful in the real world. It must reestablish equilibrium, and students must be able to assimilate new experiences into it.

The change in Suzanne's thinking illustrates these conditions. First, the group tried her solution during the interview, and she could see it didn't work (the beam didn't balance). So, her conception became dissatisfying. Seeing convincing evidence that an existing con-

exploring diversity

The Impact of Diversity on Knowledge Construction

The beliefs that students bring to our classrooms are among the most powerful influences that exist in determining what they take away from their learning experiences. For example, Muslim students and students who are Jewish are likely to have very different views of the Arab–Israeli conflict and the Iraq war. Also, students whose religious teachings conflict with scientists' description of the earth being about four and a half billion years old, or the idea that humans developed from more primitive species, will be unlikely to accept the basic tenets of evolution (Southerland & Sinatra, 2003). These varying beliefs can have a powerful influence on the effectiveness of our instruction.

As you saw earlier, beliefs are unlikely to change unless compelling evidence exists indicating that the belief is invalid, such as happened when Suzanne could see that her original suggestion for making the beam balance didn't work. However, in many cases, irrefutable evidence doesn't exist. For example, consider Columbus's voyage to the New World; it is interpreted by some as the beginning point in the development of the Americas and by others as plundering resources and destroying native culture.

So, what can you do? The most effective approach with your students is to emphasize that they are accountable for *understanding* an idea, theory, or interpretation, but you don't necessarily expect them to agree with or believe it (Southerland & Sinatra, 2003.) For instance, in some parts of the country, the theory of evolution is highly controversial. However, this doesn't mean that students shouldn't understand the principles of evolution. Whether or not they choose to accept the principles is up to them.

Classrooms as learning communities are important when dealing with diversity of beliefs and understandings. All students should be given the opportunity to share their beliefs, and diversity in thinking should be respected. Recognizing that their classmates have different beliefs than their own, and learning to acknowledge and respect those differences are important learning experiences.

ception is invalid is the most important factor leading to conceptual change.

Second, an alternative conception—one involving both the number of tiles and the distance from the fulcrum—was understandable, as indicated by her ability to use both to explain the solution to a different problem. And third, the alternative conception was fruitful; she could explain additional examples, and this alternate explanation could be applied to real-world cases such as teeter-totters.

Even with these conditions in place, conceptual change is not easy, as anyone who has attempted to convince someone to change their thinking will attest. Considerable cognitive inertia exists, requiring teachers to take an active role in the conceptual change process (Southerland et al., 2002; Vosniadou, 2007). Questions that challenge and reveal misconceptions and require students to apply their revised thinking to new situations are teachers' most effective tools for promoting conceptual change (Crockett, 2004; Yip, 2004).

Teachers encourage conceptual change with the examples they provide and the discussions they guide.

Conceptual change is grounded in social constructivist learning theory. Suzanne changed her thinking because the new conception made sense to her. And, it made sense because the social interaction in the interview, combined with examples that provided the needed experience, facilitated the change process.

check your understanding

3.1 What are misconceptions, and how are they related to constructivist learning theory?

3.2 Describe four common sources of misconceptions, and provide an example of each.

3.3 Explain how misconceptions can be eliminated.

To receive feedback for these questions, go to Appendix A.

classroom connections

Promoting Conceptual Change in Your Classroom

1. Students construct their own knowledge, and this knowledge is sometimes invalid. Ask questions that reveal and challenge students' existing understanding.
   - **Elementary:** When one of his second graders solves the first problem below, and gets 45, an elementary teacher presents the second problem. When the student also gets 45 for this problem, he asks, "We have two very different problems. How can we get the same answer when the numbers are different?"

     $$\begin{array}{r} 54 \\ -19 \\ \hline \end{array} \qquad \begin{array}{r} 59 \\ -14 \\ \hline \end{array}$$

   - **Middle School:** When one of her eighth graders explains that transparent objects are objects that we can see through, and opaque objects are those we can't see through, a physical science teacher asks, "If we can see through a transparent object, why can't we see through it at night?
   - **High School:** When one of his students describes all Native Americans as nomadic hunter gatherers, a history teacher shows pictures of pueblos and other permanent living structures and asks, "If they are nomadic, why would they build dwellings like these?"
2. Conceptual change requires students to apply their revised thinking to new situations. Provide students with tasks that require them to apply reconstructed knowledge to new situations.
   - **Elementary:** The second-grade teacher in suggestion 1 asks his students to solve a series of problems that require regrouping.
   - **Middle School:** The eighth-grade teacher in suggestion 1 asks her students to explain why they can't see a person they hear walking down the hall outside their classroom. She guides them to conclude that the light rays that are reflected from the person won't pass through the opaque wall of the classroom.
   - **High School:** The social studies teacher in suggestion 1 has the students describe the cultural and economic characteristics of different Native American groups, such as plains Indians and those who lived in the Northwest and Northeast.

Constructivist Learning Theory in Classrooms

What are the specific practices that constructivist learning theory suggests for classroom instruction? In this section we answer this question and examine its implications for teachers' roles.

The Teacher's Role in Constructivist Classrooms

Many of the teacher's roles are the same when instruction is grounded in constructivist learning theory as they are in traditional classrooms. These roles include specifying learning objectives, preparing learning activities, and designing assessments. The primary difference is a shift in emphasis away from the teacher merely providing information and toward the teacher promoting the interaction that makes students' thinking open and visible (Bransford et al., 2000; Donovan & Bransford, 2005). This shift results in several specific suggestions for classroom practice.

However, our understanding of human memory strongly influences how we apply constructivist learning theory in our classrooms. We now briefly revisit the model you first studied in Chapter 7 before examining the suggestions for practice.

Constructivism and Human Memory

Figure 8.2 illustrates the model of human memory as it appeared in Chapter 7. The model and constructivist learning theory are consistent and complement each other.

The following components of the model have direct implications for constructivist-influenced instruction:

- Attention
- Perception
- The limitations of working memory
- Learners' existing schemas in long-term memory
- Strategies that promote encoding, such as organization, elaboration, and schema activation
- Cognitive activity

In this section, we examine each of these components.

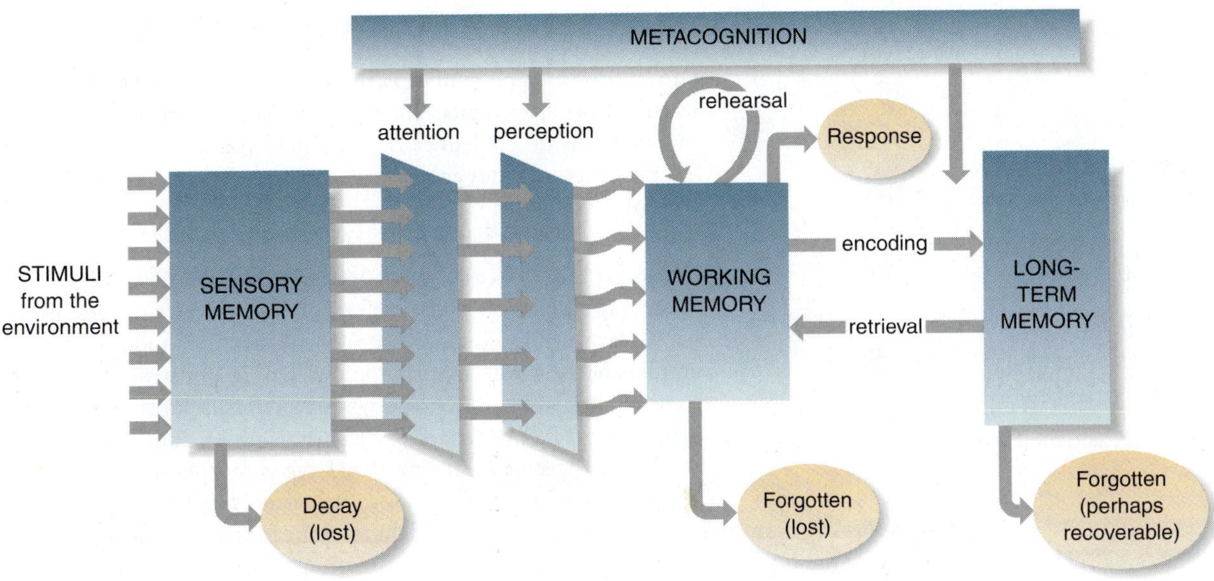

Figure 8.2 A model of human memory

Attention. All learning begins with attention, so learners will be unable to construct usable knowledge if they aren't paying attention. Though Suzanne was sitting next to Molly, she wasn't paying attention to the explanations that Molly, Mavrin, and Jenny offered.

Perception. If students misperceive aspects of the information they're studying, the knowledge they construct will be invalid. As you saw earlier, appearances can lead to misconceptions. Learners perceive information based on the way it appears, so checking learners' perceptions is essential for avoiding the construction of misconceptions.

Limitations of Working Memory. The limitations of working memory may be the most important characteristic of the human memory model. All forms of instruction can place a heavy cognitive load on students, so you should keep the limitations of working memory in mind as you guide students' knowledge constructions.

Schemas in Long-Term Memory. We have emphasized repeatedly that learners construct knowledge based on the knowledge (schemas) they already possess. If their existing schemas are inadequate or inaccurate, incomplete understanding or the construction of misconceptions is likely.

Strategies to Promote Encoding. Teachers sometimes mistakenly believe that, because learners are constructing their own knowledge, careful organization of the content is less important than it would be if the instruction were grounded in a different learning theory. This isn't true. Organization, elaboration, and other strategies for promoting encoding are as important, or are even more important, in constructivist classrooms.

Cognitive Activity. Teachers may also tacitly assume that, because their students are involved in constructivist learning activities, they are cognitively active. As you saw earlier, this isn't necessarily the case. In spite of being involved in small-group work with considerable social interaction, Suzanne remained cognitively passive throughout the lesson. This helps us understand why she retained her misconception until it was directly confronted during the interview. Students' remaining cognitively passive is a common problem, particularly in classrooms where lecturing and explaining are the most common teaching strategies.

Now, keep in mind the characteristics of the human memory model as you read about suggestions for classroom practice based on constructivist learning theory.

- Provide learners with a variety of examples and representations of content.
- Connect content to the real world.
- Promote high levels of interaction.
- Treat verbal explanations skeptically.
- Promote learning with assessment.

Figure 8.3 Suggestions for classroom practice

Suggestions for Classroom Practice

Grounding instruction in constructivist learning theory can increase learning for all students. The following suggestions for classroom practice provide guidelines that can help you apply this theory in your instruction. They are outlined in Figure 8.3 and discussed in the sections that follow.

Provide High-Quality Representations of Content

"Learning and development depend on learners' experiences" is one of the learning principles you studied in Chapter 7, and we have also emphasized the role of prior knowledge in constructing understanding. So, what can you do when students lack experiences and sufficient prior knowledge? The answer is simple (but not necessarily easy): *Supplement existing knowledge with high-quality examples and other representations of the content being taught.*

High-quality examples. Examples that include all the information learners need to understand a topic.

High-quality examples are examples that ideally include all the information learners need to understand the topic, and they serve three important functions. First, they become the experiences learners use to construct their knowledge (Eggen, 2001; J. Freeman, McPhail, & Berndt, 2002). Second, they attract and maintain learners' attention, so they also apply the model of human memory. Third, they provide the basis for conceptual change when necessary. For instance, the solution that Drexel offered during the interview helped Suzanne revise her thinking and construct a valid understanding of the principle that makes beams balance. Without this high-quality example, Suzanne would have been unlikely to change her thinking.

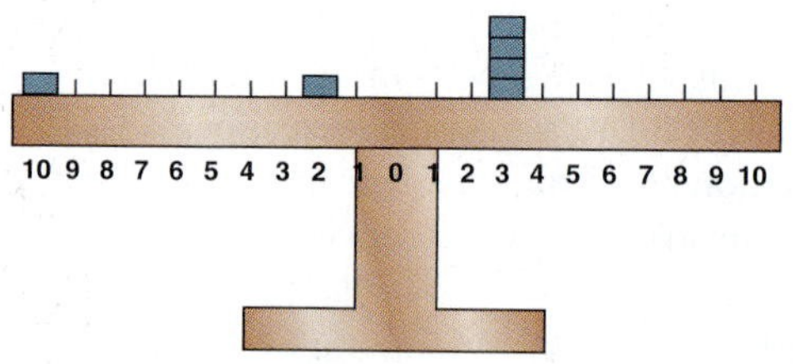

High-quality examples are important for all topics at all grade levels. They are especially important for learners first encountering a new idea (Kalyuga, Ayres, Chandler, & Sweller, 2003) and for limited-English-proficiency learners because their prior experiences may not match those of their peers (Bae, 2003; Echevarria & Graves, 2007).

Table 8.1 includes additional examples of different ways teachers that you've studied in this text have represented their topics.

High-quality examples become the experiences learners use to construct their knowledge.

Connect Content to the Real World

Social constructivist learning theory, and particularly *situated cognition*, emphasize the importance of connecting topics to real-world experiences (J. Brown et al., 1989; Lave, 1997; Lave & Wenger, 1991). When geography students connect *longitude* and *latitude* to the location of a favorite hangout, science students connect *inertia* to seatbelts in their cars, or English students write a persuasive essay for their school newspaper, for example, their learning is more meaningful than it would be if the information were studied outside of real-world contexts (van Merriënboer et al., 2003). Jenny created a real-world problem with the beam balances, and other teachers you've studied in this book have done the same. For instance, Jan Davis (on page 3 of Chapter 1) didn't teach decimals and percentages in the abstract; she used different-sized soft-drink containers and their cost to show that understanding decimals and percents is necessary to determine which product was the

table 8.1 Teachers' Representations of Content

Teacher and Chapter	Learning Objective	Representations
Jan Davis, Chapter 1 (page 3)	For students to understand decimals and percents by calculating cost per ounce to determine which product is the best buy	12-ounce soft drink and its cost 20-ounce soft drink and its cost 6-pack of soft drinks and its cost
Karen Johnson, Chapter 2 (page 36)	For students to understand the concept *density*	Cotton balls pressed into a drink cup Wooden cubes of different sizes to show that the ratio of weight to volume remains the same Equal volumes of water and vegetable oil on a balance
Jenny Newhall, Chapter 2 (page 56)	For students to understand that air takes up space	Inverted glass pushed into a fishbowl of water Air bubbles released from the cup
Diane Smith, Chapter 4 (page 116)	For students to understand comparative and superlative adjectives	Students' pencils of different lengths to show that one is "longer" and another is the "longest" Students' hair color to show that one is "darker" and another is the "darkest"

best buy in a supermarket. And Karen Johnson (on page 36 of Chapter 2) related the concept *density* to screen-door screens and population density.

Promote High Levels of Interaction

Although essential, high-quality examples by themselves won't necessarily produce learning (Moreno & Duran, 2004). Students might misperceive the examples, or they may remain cognitively passive, as Suzanne did during the lesson. Because she was passive, she retained her original conception until she was directly involved in the interaction during the interview.

Social interaction is an integral part of the social construction of knowledge. It also allows teachers to check learners' perceptions and places students in cognitively active roles. And it reduces the cognitive load on students' working memories, because the interaction will progress only as rapidly as the students can encode new information.

Teachers play an essential role in ensuring that social interaction promotes as much learning as possible (Webb, Farivar, & Mastergeorge, 2002). They guide the interaction in whole-group lessons, and they monitor small-group activities to be sure students focus on understanding, instead of simply getting the right answer (Blatchford et al., 2006). And they design assessments that evaluate understanding and hold students accountable for their learning.

Treat Verbal Explanations Skeptically

Earlier in the chapter we introduced the idea, "Wisdom can't be told"; you saw that researchers have understood it for decades (Gragg, 1940; Bransford, Derry, et al., 2005), and Jenny's lesson illustrated the concept. You saw that Suzanne heard three clear and accurate explanations for the beam balance problem—Molly's, Mavrin's, and Jenny's—yet at the beginning of the interview, she still believed that the number of tiles was the only factor determining whether or not the beam would balance. These verbal explanations didn't work, and this is true for much of the talk that occurs in classrooms. In spite of this fact, many teachers continue to believe that the best way to get students to learn is to lecture to them (Alparsian et al., 2004; Yip, 2004).

We are not saying that teachers shouldn't explain topics to students, and we're not saying that learners cannot construct knowledge from explanations. Rather, *don't conclude that your students understand an idea because you explained it to them.* Explanations need to be combined with examples and thorough discussions of how the examples illustrate ideas. This brings us to the essential role of assessment in promoting learning.

Promote Learning with Assessment

Because learners construct their own knowledge, individuals' understanding of the topics they study will vary. For example, before the interview, Mavrin and Molly understood the principle for making beams balance, whereas Suzanne and Tad did not. Making assessment an integral part of the teaching–learning process is the essence of "assessment *for* learning," and it is the only way teachers can determine whether or not students' knowledge constructions are valid (Stiggins, 2007).

Informal assessment, gathering incidental information during learning activities, is an important part of this process. In her lesson, for example, Jenny knew that Mavrin understood the principle, because she heard him explain it at the board. As teachers listen to students describe their developing understanding, they can assess the extent to which students' constructions are valid. When their understanding is inaccurate or incomplete, teachers provide feedback to help students revise their thinking (Hattie & Timperly, 2007; Shute, 2008).

Informal assessments are valuable but incomplete and potentially misleading. For instance, hearing Mavrin explain the principle, combined with the fact that she explained it, could lead Jenny to conclude that all her students understood it. In fact, her informal assessments provided little information about the rest of her students' understanding, as we saw earlier with Suzanne and Tad. Teachers can enhance the effectiveness of their informal assessments by requiring that all students respond to questions or problems with hand signals or individual chalk or writing boards (Beers, 2006). This provides immediate information about learning progress and allows teachers to adjust lessons accordingly.

However, effective teachers also supplement informal assessment with formal assessment, the process of systematically gathering information about understanding from all learners. "Effectively designed learning environments must also be assessment centered. . . . They should provide opportunities for feedback and revision and that what is assessed must be congruent with one's learning goals (Bransford et al., 2000, pp. 139–140).

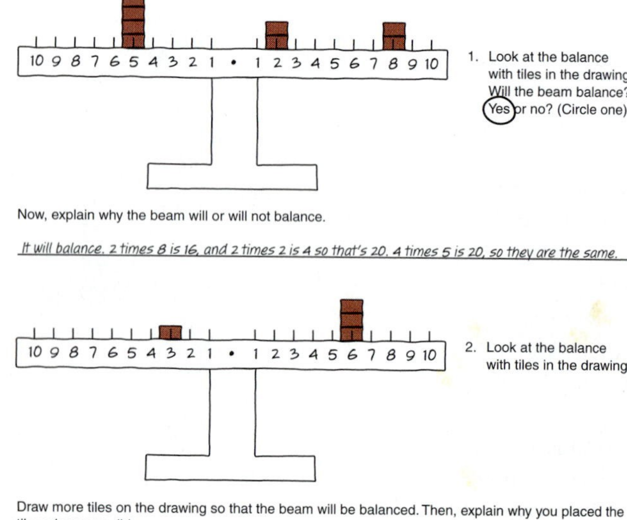

10 9 8 7 6 5 4 3 2 1 • 1 2 3 4 5 6 7 8 9 10
1. Look at the balance with tiles in the drawing. Will the beam balance? Yes or no? (Circle one).
Now, explain why the beam will or will not balance.
It will balance. 2 times 8 is 16, and 2 times 2 is 4 so that's 20. 4 times 5 is 20, so they are the same.
10 9 8 7 6 5 4 3 2 1 • 1 2 3 4 5 6 7 8 9 10
2. Look at the balance with tiles in the drawing.
Draw more tiles on the drawing so that the beam will be balanced. Then, explain why you placed the tiles where you did.
I want to place more tiles on so that it will balance.

Figure 8.4 Beam balance problems for assessment

Accessing students' *thinking* is an essential part of the process. Jenny, realizing that she didn't have insights into all of her students' thinking, formally assessed her students' understanding with two problems that she gave the class the day after the lesson.

The assessment, with Tad's responses, is shown in Figure 8.4. As we look at the figure, we see that Tad's schema for the principle was still a work in progress. He determined that the beam would balance in the first problem, but he could not draw or write a solution to the second. His experience was not unique; Jenny's assessment revealed that several other students in the class were also still uncertain about solving problems with beam balances.

This helps us understand why formal assessment should be an integral part of the teaching–learning process. In classrooms with 25 to 30 or more students, it is impossible to informally assess the thinking of all learners. Formal assessment is the only way teachers can determine the extent to which each student's construction is valid. (We examine assessment *for* learning together with informal and formal assessment in detail in Chapter 14.)

Learning Contexts: Constructing Knowledge in Urban Environments

Urban classrooms provide both opportunities and challenges for teachers attempting to facilitate knowledge construction. First, as you've seen in our discussions of urban environments in other chapters, urban students typically come from diverse backgrounds, so they bring with them widely varying degrees of school-related prior knowledge (Serafino & Cicchelli, 2003; B. Weiner, 2000). Second, because of their home and neighborhood environments, the real world of urban students can differ widely from their suburban and rural peers. Textbooks are typically written for an idealized average student, making connections to the background experiences of urban students more difficult (Manzo, 2000). Third, the interaction patterns of urban students sometimes differ from those found in suburban or rural schools. Urban students may have difficulty with the fast-paced question-and-answer patterns typical of suburban classrooms, and they may interpret direct questions as threatening rather than attempts by teachers to promote learning (Heath, 1989; T. Howard, 2001).

So, how should teachers in urban environments respond in their efforts to help students construct usable knowledge? Examples, real-world connections, and increased social interaction are three essential components of effective urban classroom instruction.

Need for Examples. The need for high-quality examples is important for all learners, regardless of context. However, because of the diversity of urban students' prior experiences, high-quality examples are critical when teaching in urban schools. In effect, examples become the students' prior knowledge, and they provide students with the experiences needed to make the concepts meaningful.

Real-World Connections. Real-world connections are important for all students, but teachers in urban environments make a special effort to link the topics they teach to their students' experiences (Charner-Laird et al., 2004). For example, a sixth-grade world history teacher in an urban middle school was discussing the rise of nationalism as an important factor in the events leading up to World War I. The students' textbooks defined nationalism as a feeling of loyalty and devotion to one's country, language, and culture. This definition is both abstract and distant from the world in which these students lived. In an attempt to personalize the concept, the teacher created a series of vignettes, which she used as analogies for *nationalism.* The vignettes included the name of the students' own school, Matthew Gilbert, as well as the name of a rival school in the same city, Mandarin Middle School. The vignettes illustrated the students' loyalty to the school, everyday language, and the school's culture, all of which were analogous to these same characteristics in *nationalism.* The following are two of the vignettes:

> The students at Matthew Gilbert love their school. "We don't want someone coming in here and changing our school," they say. "We understand each other when we talk. The rest of them are different than we are. They play funny music, and they don't do the things we do after school or on the weekends."
>
> "We're Gilbertites," they say. "We don't want to be anybody else, and we don't want anybody telling us what to do."
>
> Students at Mandarin Middle School have some similar thoughts. "I don't like the way they talk at Gilbert," some of them have been overheard saying. "They want to hang around with each other after school, and we want to go to the Mall. I don't want anybody from there to tell us how to think.
>
> "We're Mandariners, and we want to stay that way." (Eggen, 1998)

Connecting content to their day-to-day experiences is essential to motivate urban students, who sometimes question the importance of their studies for their daily lives (Brophy, 2004). Teachers can make similar adaptations for suburban and rural students and different content areas.

Social Interaction. Social interaction is essential for learning in all contexts, but it can be especially challenging in urban environments because of overcrowded classrooms and urban students' interaction patterns (Griffith, Hayes, & Pascarella, 2004). In addition, problems with lecturing are even more acute in urban contexts, because students' prior experiences vary so greatly.

Open-ended questions that allow a variety of acceptable answers are effective to promote interaction at the beginning of lessons and to develop students' confidence in their ability to respond (Eggen, 1998). They are particularly useful in urban environments because they reduce the potential threat that urban students may associate with being questioned. Regardless of perceptions, questioning is essential, not only to involve students in knowledge construction but also to monitor their learning progress. Aspects of effective questioning, such as prompting and adequate wait time, are crucial when working with urban students, and particularly those in middle and high schools, who may be sensitive about having their thinking and understanding revealed to peers.

MyEducationLab

To see how a fifth-grade teacher attempts to apply constructivist learning theory in an urban environment, go to the *Activities and Applications* section in Chapter 8 of MyEducationLab at www.myeducationlab.com, and read the case study *Constructivist Instruction in Fifth Grade.* Answer the question following the case study.

A final word of caution about introducing constructivist-based instruction in urban classrooms. Because of the current emphasis on accountability, schools are placing greater emphasis on teacher-centered instruction (Cochran-Smith & Lytle, 2006; Viadero, 2007b). This trend is especially pronounced in urban schools with high percentages of students from low socioeconomic classes and those who are members of cultural minorities (Kozol, 2006). Consequently, urban students may not know how to react when constructivist-based instruction is first introduced. As a result, you should make a special effort to clearly explain what you are attempting to do and why. For example, simply tell the students that you're going to call on them, and emphasize that

theory to practice

Applying Constructivist Learning Theory in Your Classroom

Grounding instruction in constructivist learning theory, and particularly social constructivism, can increase learning for all students. The suggestions for classroom practice that you first saw in Figure 8.3 provide the guidelines that help us apply this theory in your instruction. Again, they are:

1. Provide high-quality representations of content.
2. Connect content to the real world.
3. Promote high levels of interaction.
4. Treat verbal explanations skeptically.
5. Promote learning with assessment.

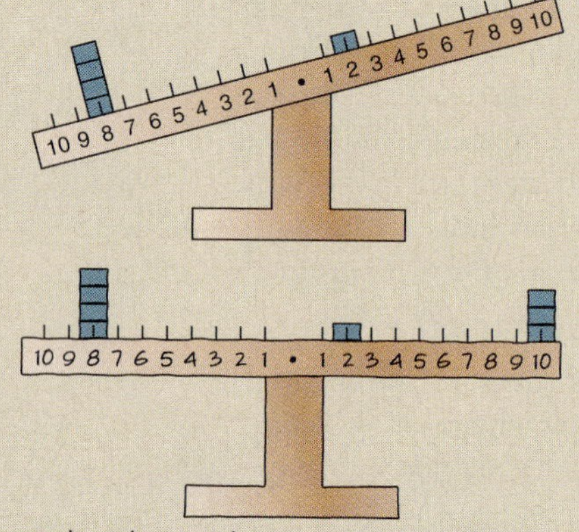

Let's review Jenny's lesson and examine the extent to which she applied the guidelines in her lesson. As with many aspects of instruction, the process isn't as simple as it appears on the surface. For instance, Jenny didn't quite apply the first. As you saw earlier in the chapter, *a high-quality example is one that includes all the information students need to understand the topic.* The balances and the problem Jenny presented were the examples she used. However, the balances with the tile arrangement that she initially presented didn't contain all the information the students needed to understand the principle for making beams balance. So, to solve the problem, the students needed prior knowledge that not all of them possessed (e.g., Suzanne and Tad). It wasn't until the students suggested putting three tiles on the 10 point on the right side of the fulcrum that the example became high quality, containing all the information the students needed.

The balances provided a real-world experience, so Jenny applied the second guideline well.

In the real world of teaching, the level of social interaction suggested by social constructivism and cognitive apprenticeships, which provide the framework for the third and fourth guidelines, is very difficult. Ideally, the interaction during teachers' lessons would be similar to the interaction in the interview that followed Jenny's lesson. However, the interviewer was working with only four students, so each could describe his or her thinking. This level of interaction is virtually impossible in a whole-group setting. And, students might remain cognitively passive even in a small group, as Suzanne did until she was directly involved in the interview.

This helps us understand why formal assessment must be an integral part of the teaching-learning process. In classrooms with 25 to 30 or more students, it is impossible to informally assess the thinking of all learners. Formal assessment is the only way teachers can determine the extent to which each student's constructions are valid. The assessment Jenny gave the next day was essential and effectively applied the fifth guideline.

Applying constructivist learning theory in classrooms is sophisticated and demanding instruction. It is not impossible, however. The combination of high-quality examples, as much interaction as possible, and carefully designed assessments can maximize learning for all students.

you genuinely want them to describe their thinking. This communication can do much to break down the barriers to interaction.

As you see from this discussion, instruction in urban environments does not differ qualitatively from instruction in general. Students in urban schools need the same factors that promote knowledge construction in all settings: high-quality examples, connections to the real world, and social interaction. And these knowledge-construction factors are simply more important and more challenging in urban environments.

check your understanding

4.1 Describe the suggestions for classroom practice that are based on constructivist learning theory. Explain how each suggestion is grounded in the theory.

4.2 A language arts teacher wants his students to understand the rules for forming possessive nouns and writes a passage about the school in which he illustrates the rules. Which of the suggestions for classroom practice is best illustrated by his use of this passage about the school to illustrate the rules?

4.3 Assessments grounded in constructivist views of learning have an essential characteristic. What is this characteristic? Explain.

To receive feedback for these questions, go to Appendix A.

MyEducationLab

To see how a high school English teacher attempts to apply constructivist learning theory in her class, go to the *Activities and Applications* section in Chapter 8 of MyEducationLab at www.myeducationlab.com, and watch the episode *The Scarlet Letter in High School English.* Answer the questions following the episode.

classroom connections

Applying Constructivist Views of Learning in Your Classroom

1. Learners construct their own knowledge, and the knowledge they construct depends on what they already know. To accommodate differences in prior knowledge, provide a variety of examples and other representations of the content you want students to understand.
   - **Elementary:** A third-grade teacher in a unit on chemical and physical change has students melt ice, crumple paper, dissolve sugar, and break toothpicks to illustrate physical change. She then has them burn paper, pour vinegar into baking soda, and chew soda crackers to illustrate chemical change.
   - **Middle School:** An English teacher presents the following excerpts to illustrate *internal conflict*:

     Kelly didn't know what to do. She was looking forward to the class trip, but if she went, she wouldn't be able to take the scholarship qualifying test.

     Calvin was caught in a dilemma. He saw Jason take Olonzo's calculator but knew that if he told Mrs. Stevens what he saw, Jason would realize that it was he who reported the theft.
   - **High School:** While teaching about the Great Depression, a social studies teacher has students read excerpts from *The Grapes of Wrath*, presents a video of people standing in bread lines, shares statistics on the rash of suicides after the stock market crash, and passes out descriptions of Franklin D. Roosevelt's back-to-work programs.
2. Knowledge construction is most effective when learners have real-world experiences. Develop learning activities around realistic problems.
   - **Elementary:** In a lesson relating geography and the way we live, a third-grade teacher has students describe the way they dress for their favorite forms of recreation. She also asks students who have moved from other parts of the country to do the same for their previous locations. She then guides them as they construct an understanding of the effect of geography on lifestyle.
   - **Middle School:** In a unit on percent increase and decrease, a math teacher asks students to look for examples of marked-down clothes while shopping. He also brings in newspaper ads. The class discusses the examples and calculates the amount saved in each case.
   - **High School:** To help her students understand the importance of persuasive writing, an English teacher brings in three examples of "Letters to the Editor" on the same topic. Students discuss the letters, determine which is most effective, and with the teacher's guidance, identify the characteristics of effective persuasive writing.
3. Social constructivist views of learning emphasize the role of social interaction in the process of knowledge construction. To capitalize on this characteristic, promote high levels of quality interaction, and avoid relying on explanations to promote learning.
   - **Elementary:** A fourth-grade teacher wants his students to understand the concept of *scale* on a map. After placing them in groups, he asks them to create a map of their desktops. Then he instructs them to draw a map of their room, and finally, they go outside and draw a map of their playground. When finished, he guides a class discussion to help them understand how the maps are similar and different.
   - **Middle School:** A sixth-grade science teacher asks his students to take 8 identical wooden cubes and make one stack of 5 and another stack of 3. He directs them to discuss the mass, volume, and densities of the two stacks. Then, with questioning, he guides them to conclude that the mass and volume of the stack of 5 are greater than the mass and volume of the stack of 3 but that the densities of the two stacks are equal.
   - **High School:** An algebra teacher "walks" students through the solutions to problems by calling on individuals to provide specific information about each step and explain why the step is necessary. When students have difficulty, the teacher asks additional questions to help them understand the step.

Putting Constructivist Learning Theory into Perspective

Constructivist theory makes an important contribution to our understanding of learning because it helps us understand why prior knowledge and interaction are so important for developing deep understanding, and it also helps us understand why monitoring student thinking is essential (Carver, 2006). Because we know that students construct their own knowledge, we better understand why they don't grasp an idea that's been discussed several times, why they seem to ignore a point that's been emphasized, and why they retain misconceptions. With this understanding, our frustration can be reduced and our patience increased. Constructivist learning theory also helps us understand why explaining, alone, is often ineffective, and why relying on worksheets fails to produce the understanding we desire.

Constructivism is often misinterpreted, however:

> A common misconception regarding "constructivist" theories of knowledge . . . is that teachers should never tell students anything directly but, instead, should always allow them to construct knowledge for themselves. This perspective confuses a theory of pedagogy (teaching) with a theory of knowing. (Bransford et al., 2000, p. 11)

developmentally appropriate practice

Applying Constructivist Learning Theory with Different-Aged Learners

Although constructivist learning theory applies to learners of all ages, a number of developmental differences exist. The following sections outline some suggestions for responding to these differences.

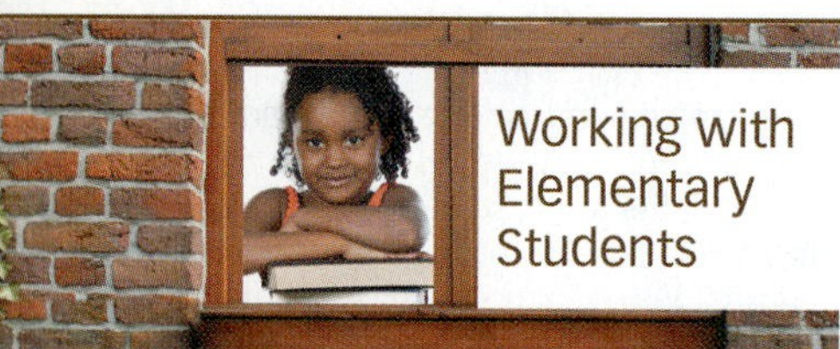

Working with Elementary Students

Young children tend to center, i. e. focus on the most perceptually obvious aspects of objects and events, and they tend to be quite literal in their thinking, which can lead to the construction of many misconceptions. For instance, young children tend to equate size with age, meaning someone who is bigger is older, and, in social studies they may think that lines of latitude and longitude actually exist on the earth.

As a result, explanations presented in the abstract are almost useless with these children. When working with young children, high-quality examples are even more important than they are with older learners. In addition, interactive classroom instruction allows teachers both to investigate the ideas students currently hold and to assist them as they construct new ones.

Working with Middle School Students

Middle school students overcome much of the tendency to interpret events literally, but often, in the process of knowledge construction, they fail to recognize relationships among objects and events. For instance, instead of recognizing that rectangles and squares are subsets of parallelograms, they see the figures as different categories.

To accommodate these tendencies, cognitive apprenticeships that include opportunities to think and talk about new ideas are effective. For instance, teachers should carefully scaffold students' efforts, and students' *verbalization* of their understanding during small-group work is essential for maximizing learning.

Middle school students are also developing interaction skills, such as perspective taking and social problem solving. This allows teachers to use cooperative learning and other small-group strategies to integrate social interaction into their instruction. Experts caution, however, that teachers should carefully structure and monitor these activities so that learning is maximized (Blatchford, et al., 2006; Ding, Li, Piccolo, & Kulm, 2007).

Working with High School Students

High school students' experiences can provide them with a rich store of prior knowledge that increases the validity of their knowledge constructions. However, they continue to construct a variety of misconceptions, particularly when working with symbols and abstract ideas. For instance, in simplifying the expression $2 + 5 \times 3 - 6$, they often get 15 ($2 + 5 = 7; 7 \times 3 = 21; 21 - 6 = 15$) instead of the correct answer: 11 ($5 \times 3 = 15; 15 + 2 = 17; 17 - 6 = 11$).

As students move to more advanced classes in high school (e.g., physics, chemistry, and calculus), high levels of interaction become even more important. And, it is in these classes that teachers tend to become more like college instructors, where lecture is the most common instructional strategy.

High school students can also participate in and benefit from classroom discussions that provide opportunities to compare and develop their thinking based on the ideas of others (Hadjioannou, 2007). As with all forms of instruction, teachers need to structure and monitor discussions closely to ensure that they are aligned with learning goals.

This distinction between a *theory of learning* and a *theory of instruction* is important. Theories of learning focus on students and help explain how they develop understanding. In comparison, theories of instruction focus on teachers, and you will decide how to implement constructivist ideas in your own classroom.

Confusing learning and instruction can lead to misconceptions about appropriate method and oversimplified suggestions for classroom practice. For example, a potential problem when using social interaction in small group work is the assumption that if the group accomplishes a task, individual members can also complete the task. Research suggests this does not occur (B. Barron, 2000; Southerland et al., 2002), and Jenny's lesson illustrated this potential problem. The group of four in Jenny's lesson was able to accomplish the task, but Suzanne and Tad were not. This finding further underscores the essential role that assessment plays in instruction grounded in constructivist views of learning.

The relationship between constructivism and teaching method is also frequently confused. For example, "Social interaction facilitates learning" is sometimes interpreted to mean that a teacher who uses cooperative learning is "constructivist," whereas one who relies on large-group activities is not. In fact, both teachers may be basing their instruction on constructivist views of learning, or neither teacher may be. Large-group instruction, effectively done, may promote knowledge construction, and cooperative learning, improperly done, may not.

Also, as with any theory, constructivism doesn't provide a complete picture of learning and its implications for teaching. For instance, research suggests that many skills must be practiced to automaticity (Feldon, 2007a; Péladeau, Forget, & Gagné, 2003). The model of human memory better explains this research than does constructivism. In fact, discussions of constructivism tend to ignore the memory model. For example, students will construct valid understandings of the topics they study only to the extent to which they pay attention, correctly perceive the information, and avoid having their working memories overloaded. Further, students who are metacognitive about their learning are more successful than their peers who are less aware (Azevedo & Cromley, 2004; Eilam & Aharon, 2003). Ignoring these elements of the human memory model leaves important parts of the learning puzzle unattended.

Table 8.2 outlines a comparison of the different learning theories you've studied to this point, aspects of learning that each theory can explain, and some of their limitations.

Fortunately, many of the controversies that historically have been associated with constructivism have been resolved. For instance, researchers now reject the philosophical position suggesting that all students' unique constructions of understanding are equally valid (Derry, 1992; Moshman, 1997; D. Phillips, 1997, 2000).

In addition, the teacher's role in classroom applications of constructivism has been clarified. These applications don't suggest that teachers' roles in promoting learning are diminished; in fact, quite the opposite is the case. As you saw earlier, traditional teaching roles, such as establishing clear objectives, creating effective learning activities, and developing valid assessments are even

table 8.2 Comparing Different Theories of Learning

Theory	Can Explain	Examples	Cannot Explain	Examples
Behaviorism	The acquisition of responses resulting from associations	Why people learn to fear water and get over the fear	Changes in behavior that don't have a direct cause	Why children stop talking when a classmate is told to stop
	Changes in behavior resulting from consequences	Why people take pain killers for headaches		
Social cognitive theory	The acquisition of behaviors that result from observing others	Why people wear fashions popularized by celebrities	Behaviors that occur regardless of the presence of someone else	How a student figures out an answer to a problem that hasn't been explained or modeled
	Changes in behavior resulting from observing the consequences of others' behaviors	Why children stop talking when a classmate is told to stop	Why people fail to imitate modeled behavior	Why a student is unable to replicate the solution to a problem that has been modeled by a teacher
The human memory model	Behaviors that occur regardless of whether or not a consequence or another person is involved	Why some students can reproduce solutions modeled by teachers but others cannot	The acquisition of misconceptions	Why people think the Earth is closer to the Sun in June than it is in December
		Why students who are aware of the way they study and learn achieve higher than those who aren't	Why people with the same sets of experiences acquire different understandings of an event	
Constructivism	Original ideas and misconceptions	Why people believe the Earth is closer to the Sun in June than it is in December	How the model of human memory influences learning	Why students write poorer essays on computers if they lack computer skills
			Behaviors that are acquired involuntarily and without awareness	How people learn to fear water if they nearly drowned
			Learning by nonhuman animals	How Pavlov's dogs learned to salivate at the sight of lab assistants

more important in applying constructivist learning theory than in applying other theories of learning (Bransford et al., 2000; Howe & Berv, 2000; D. Phillips, 1995, 2000). For instance, instead of merely presenting information (commonly described as a *transmission view* of instruction), teachers attempting to apply constructivist learning theory in their teaching must carefully listen to students as they describe their developing understanding and intervene when necessary to help students construct complete and valid schemas. Applying constructivist learning theory challenges teachers to monitor students' thinking, assist in the knowledge-construction process, and intervene soon enough to prevent misconceptions, but not so soon that students' ownership for learning is diminished. However, as you acquire expertise you will be able to master the demands of this very sophisticated instruction.

Meeting Your Learning Objectives

1. Describe differences between cognitive and social constructivism, and give examples of each.
   - Constructivism is a theory of learning suggesting that learners construct their own knowledge of the topics they study rather than having that understanding delivered to them in already organized form.
   - Cognitive constructivism focuses on individual construction of understanding. When an experience disrupts an individual's equilibrium, cognitive constructivists believe that the individual reconstructs understanding that reestablishes equilibrium. Social constructivism emphasizes that knowledge is first constructed in a social environment and is then appropriated by individuals. According to social constructivists, knowledge grows directly out of the interaction.
   - Emphasis on sociocultural theory, communities of learners, cognitive apprenticeships, and situated cognition are all outcomes of the influence of social constructivism on instruction.
2. Identify characteristics and applications of constructivist learning theory.
   - Learners construct, rather than record, knowledge. This is the basic principle of constructivist learning theory.
   - Constructivist learning theory emphasizes the importance of prior knowledge, the role of social interaction, and the value of real-world tasks in the process of constructing knowledge.
3. Describe misconceptions and how they occur, and explain how teachers can eliminate them.
   - Misconceptions are beliefs that are inconsistent with evidence or commonly accepted explanations.
   - The following factors can contribute to people's misconceptions: prior experiences, appearances that lead people to infer cause–effect relationships between two objects or events because they occur together, society, and even the misuse of language.
   - Changing misconceptions is difficult because the change disrupts individuals' equilibrium, the misconceptions are often consistent with everyday experiences, and individuals don't recognize inconsistencies between new information and their existing beliefs.
   - For conceptual change to occur, existing conceptions must become dissatisfying, an alternative conception must be understandable, and the alternative must be useful in the real world.
4. Describe suggestions from constructivist learning theory for your teaching.
   - Instruction based on constructivist learning theory emphasizes the use of high-quality examples and other representations of content, student interaction, and content connected to the real world.
   - Teachers who ground their instruction in constructivist learning theory realize that lecturing and explaining often fail to promote deep understanding in learners.
   - Basing instruction on constructivist learning theory requires teachers to use ongoing assessment as an integral part of the teaching–learning process.

Developing as a Professional: Preparing for Your Licensure Exam

At the beginning of the chapter, you saw how Jenny Newhall designed and conducted a lesson to help her students construct knowledge about balance beams. In the following case, Scott Sowell, a middle school science teacher, instructs his students to examine factors that influence the frequency of a simple pendulum. Read the case study, and answer the questions that follow.

Scott's students are struggling with the process of controlling variables, even though he has carefully explained the process and has conducted a whole-class experiment with plants. He decides to give them additional experiences by working with simple pendulums in small groups.

Scott begins by demonstrating a simple pendulum with paper clips attached to a piece of string. He explains that *frequency* means the number of swings in a certain time period and asks students what factors they think will influence the frequency. After some discussion, they suggest length, weight, and angle of release as possible hypotheses. (In reality, only the length of the pendulum determines its frequency.)

"Okay, your job as a group is to design your own experiment," Scott continues. "Think of a way to test how each affects the frequency. Use the equipment at your desk to design and carry out the experiment."

One group of four—Marina, Paige, Wensley, and Jonathan—ties a string to a ring stand and measures its length, as shown:

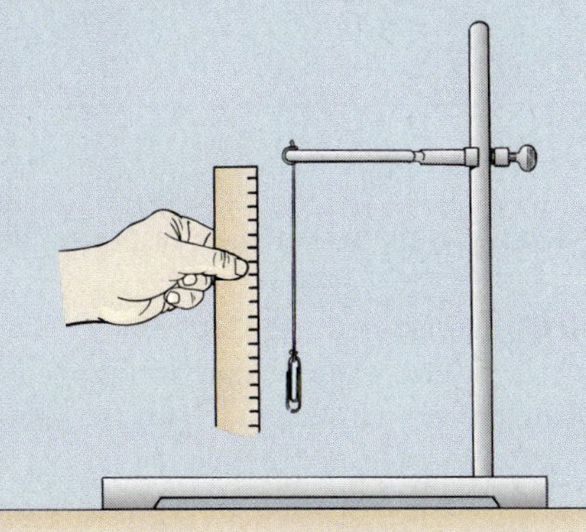

"Forty-nine centimeters," Wensley notes, measuring the length of the string.

The group agrees to use 15 seconds and then do their first test with the 49-centimeter length and one paper clip as weight. Marina counts 21 swings.

A few minutes later, Scott again walks by the group, examines their results, and says, "So you've done one test so far. . . . What are you going to do next? . . . I'm going to come back after your next test and look at it." He then moves to another group.

The group conducts their second test by shortening the string and adding a second paper clip. (This violates the principle of altering only one variable at a time.)

"Mr. Sowell, we found out that the shorter it is and the heavier it is, the faster it goes," Marina reports to Scott when he returns to the group.

Scott then asks which of the two variables was responsible for the change in the frequency.

Wensley and Jonathan say simultaneously, "They both changed."

"Think about that. You need to come up with a conclusion about length, about weight, and about angle—how each of them influences the frequency of your pendulum," Scott reminds them as he moves from group to group.

As the group investigates the three variables—length, weight, and angle of release—they continue to change two of these at the same time, confounding their results.

"What did you find out?" Scott asks as he returns to check on their progress.

Marina begins, "Okay, Mr. Sowell, we figured out that the shorter it is, the faster the frequency is, . . . and the heavier it is . . . the faster the frequency is."

Scott asks the students to explain their findings about the height.

"In the first one, the height (angle of release) was 56 and the weight was 3, and it came out to 21, and in the second one, the height was higher and the weight was lower, so it was still 21," Marina says, again concluding that the change in weight explains why the frequency was the same even though the angle of release was different.

"Let's do it out loud before you write it. . . . Tell me about length," Scott directs.

"The longer the string is, the slower the frequency is," Wensley says.

"What about weight?" Scott probes.

"The heavier it is, the faster it goes," Marina adds.

"I want to look at these again. . . . Write those down for me."

Scott gives the students a few minutes to write their conclusions, and he then walks to the front of the room and rings a bell to call the class together.

"When I call your group, I want the speaker for your group to report your findings to the class," he says to the class as a whole.

One by one, the spokesperson for each group goes to the front of the room to report their findings. In general, the groups conclude (erroneously) that each variable—length, weight, and angle—affect the frequency.

In response to this misconception, Scott tries a whole-class demonstration.

"Let's take a look at something here," Scott says, placing a ring stand onto his demonstration table. He attaches a paper clip to the pendulum, puts it in motion, and asks a student to count the swings. He adds a second paper clip and again has the students count, to demonstrate that weight doesn't affect the frequency. He has a student state this conclusion, and he writes it on the board. Then he does a second demonstration to show that angle also has no effect on the frequency and again asks a student to make a conclusion so Scott can write it on the board.

After the demonstrations, he says, "Now I want someone to make a conclusion about what we learned about designing experiments and how we use our variables when we design experiments. . . . Who wants to talk about that? . . . Wensley? Tell me what we learned about how to set up an experiment. What did we learn from this?"

"Each time, you do a different part of the experiment, only change one of the variables," Wensley explains.

"Why is that?"

"You're only checking one thing at a time. If you do two, there might be an error in the experiment."

"Okay, if you change more than one thing at one time, why would it be difficult?"

"Because, . . . if you change two different things, you can't tell which one caused the change," Wensley continues.

"Good thinking, Wensley. So, for example, if you were testing weight and length, your group had to finally decide that we can't change weight at the same time as we change length, because when we test it. . . . "

"You couldn't compare them," Marina responds.

"Right, you couldn't compare them. You couldn't tell which one was causing it, could you? . . . It might go faster, but all of a sudden you'd say, well, is it the weight or is it the length?"

Running out of time, Scott then asks if there are any questions, and hearing none, he dismisses the class.

Short-Answer Questions

In answering these questions, use information from Chapter 8, and link your responses to specific information in the case.

1. Describe the extent to which Scott applied constructivist learning theory in his lesson.
2. Scott's students had some misconceptions about controlling variables. They failed to keep length constant, for example, as they changed the weight. How effectively did Scott teach for conceptual change in responding to this misconception? Explain.
3. Assess how effectively Scott implemented the "Suggestions for Classroom Practice" (see Figure 8.3).
4. Assess the effectiveness of Scott's lesson for learners with diverse backgrounds.

For feedback on these responses, go to Appendix B.

Now go to Chapter 8 of MyEducationLab, located at www.myeducationlab.com, where you can:

- Take a quiz to test your mastery of chapter objectives. Detailed feedback is provided to explain why your responses are correct or incorrect.
- Deepen your understanding of chapter concepts with *Review, Practice, Enrichment* exercises.
- Complete *Activities and Applications* that will help you apply what you have learned in the chapter by analyzing real classrooms through video clips, artifacts and case studies. Your instructor will provide you with feedback for the *Activities and Applications.*
- Develop your professional knowledge and decision making in *Building Teaching Skills and Dispositions* exercises. Structured feedback will be available to you, providing you with support as you practice each skill. Your instructor will provide you with feedback on the final task that accompanies the exercise.

Important Concepts

cognitive apprenticeship (p. 229)
cognitive constructivism (p. 226)
community of learners (p. 228)
constructivism (p. 226)
high-quality example (p. 240)
misconception (p. 235)
real-world task (p. 233)
situated cognition (p. 229)
social constructivism (p. 227)
sociocultural theory (p. 228)
transfer (p. 229)

chapter

9

Complex Cognitive Processes

chapter outline

Concept Learning

- Theories of Concept Learning
- Learning and Teaching Concepts: The Need for Examples
  - **Theory to Practice:** Promoting Concept Learning in Your Classroom

Problem Solving

- Well-Defined and Ill-Defined Problems
- A Problem-Solving Model
- Expert–Novice Differences in Problem-Solving Ability
- Creativity in Problem Solving
- Problem-Based Learning
  - **Theory to Practice:** Helping Students Develop Their Problem-Solving Abilities

The Strategic Learner

- Metacognition: The Foundation of Strategic Learning
- Study Strategies
- Critical Thinking
  - **Theory to Practice:** Helping Students Become Strategic Learners
  - **Exploring Diversity:** Learner Differences in Complex Cognitive Processes

Transfer of Learning

- General and Specific Transfer
- Factors Affecting the Transfer of Learning
  - **Developmentally Appropriate Practice:** Developing Complex Cognitive Skills with Different-Aged Learners

learning objectives

After you have completed your study of this chapter, you should be able to:

1. Define concepts, and identify applications of concept learning theory.
2. Identify examples of ill-defined and well-defined problems, and describe applications of a general problem-solving model.
3. Identify applications of study strategies and critical thinking.
4. Identify applications of the factors that influence the transfer of learning.

Developing students' problem-solving, strategic learning, and other complex cognitive abilities are important classroom goals. As you read the following case study, think about the teacher's attempts to help her students solve a real-world problem and the extent to which the approach is effective.

In an attempt to help her students become better problem solvers, Laura Hunter, a fifth-grade teacher, decides to instruct them to find the area of the carpeted portion of their classroom. This portion has an irregular shape because the floor under the computers and the sink is covered with linoleum.

She begins the lesson on Monday by reviewing *area* and *perimeter* and then displays the diagram on the right on the overhead:

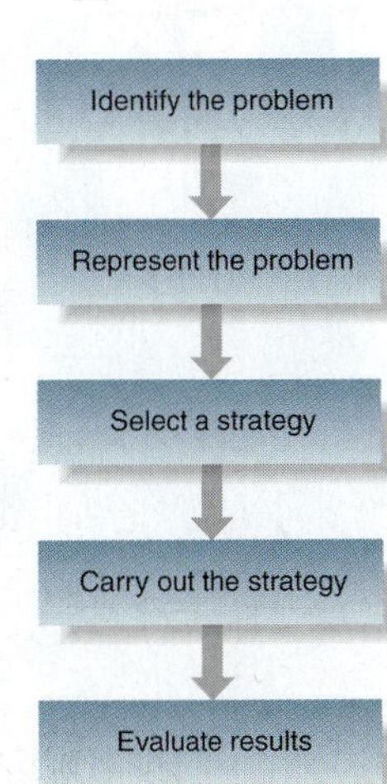

"When we try to solve a problem, we first need to identify what the problem actually is," Laura begins. "We're going to get carpeting for this room, but we don't know how much to order, and your job is to figure that out."

Having identified the problem, Laura breaks her students into groups and asks them how they will represent it. They decide that they first need to know the size of the room, so she has the groups measure the room and the different parts in it. After measuring the room, Laura gives each group

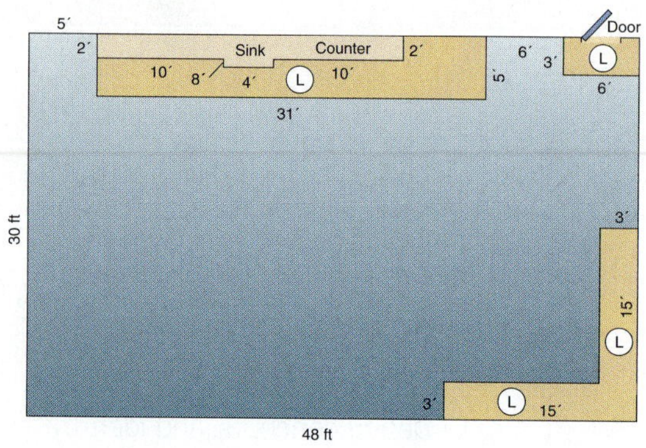

a diagram showing its dimensions and tells students that the places marked with an "L" are the parts of the floor covered with linoleum.

"Okay, look at our overhead," Laura directs. "This diagram represents our problem. . . . What's your next job?"

Nephi volunteers, "We didn't actually measure the area of the carpeted part; we just measured the perimeter. We need to figure out the area from our measurements."

Laura then tells the groups to work together to select a strategy for finding the carpeted area, and they go to work.

Different groups identify two strategies; one finding the area of the room and subtracting the areas covered with linoleum, and the other finding the area of an interior rectangle and then adding the extra areas of carpeting.

The students work in their groups, and after they're done, she has them report to the whole class. The different groups get the following areas for the carpeted portion: 1,173, 1,378, 1,347, 1,440, 1,169, and 1,600 square feet.

When asked if they are comfortable with the fact that the groups all got different answers, most of the students say no, but a few say yes.

These results and the students' reactions raise several questions, such as the following:

1. Why did the groups get such varying answers to the same problem?
2. Because no group got the correct answer, was the time spent on the activity used wisely?
3. What must Laura now do to help her students improve their problem solving?

The students' experiences and our questions help us understand why this chapter is titled "Complex Cognitive Processes." The cognitive learning theories you studied in Chapters 7 and 8 help us understand this complexity, and they also offer suggestions for what Laura must do next. We examine these processes in the sections that follow, beginning with concept learning.

Concept Learning

Concept. A mental construct or representation of a category that allows one to identify examples and nonexamples of the category.

People instinctively strive to make sense of their experiences (Marinoff, 2003), and they begin to do so as infants (Quinn, 2002). This is the foundation of the learning principle, *Learners construct knowledge that makes sense to them.* One way of making sense of our experiences is to categorize them into mental classes or sets, an idea pioneered by Jerome Bruner (1960, 1966, 1990), who argues that people interpret the world in terms of its similarities and differences.

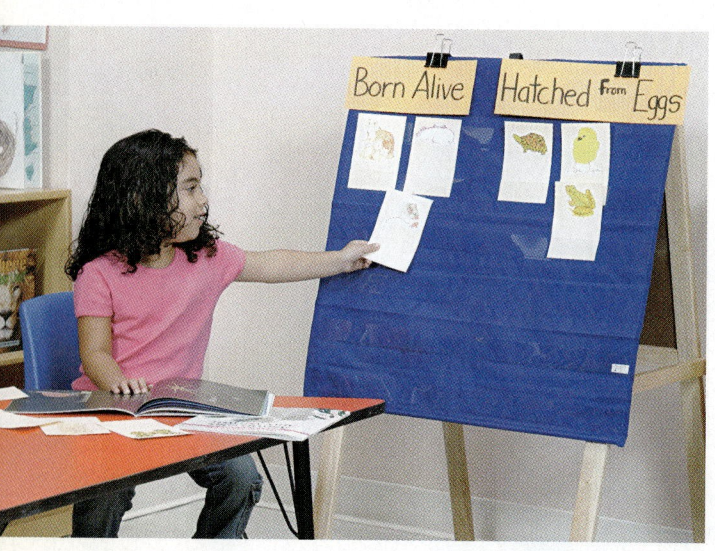

Learners simplify and make sense of their experiences by constructing concepts.

A class, or set, is a **concept,** which is, "a mental construct or representation of a category that allows one to identify examples and nonexamples of the category" (Schunk, 2004, p. 196). Concepts are constructed from our experiences and are fundamental building blocks of our thinking (Ferrari & Elik, 2003).

Constructing concepts allows us to simplify the world, and in doing so, helps reduce the cognitive load on working memory. For example, Laura's students needed to understand that the concept *area* is a physical quantity describing the size of surfaces, such as those in Figure 9.1. *Area* is a mental construct that encompasses all examples of the size of a surface regardless of dimension or orientation. The concept *area* also allows us to think and talk about sizes of surfaces as a group, instead of as specific objects. Having to remember each separately would make learning impossibly complex and unwieldy.

A great many concepts have guided your thinking as you've studied this book. For example, you learned about *equilibrium* and *zone of proximal development* in Chapter 2, *initiative* and *self-concept* in Chapter 3, and *culture* and *socioeconomic status* in Chapter 4. Each is a concept. To help you in constructing and organizing your knowledge of educational psychology, we define important concepts in the margins and list them at the end of each chapter. (We ask you to identify concepts from Chapters 5 to 8 in "Check Your Understanding" Question 1.1 at the end of this section.)

Concepts also represent a major portion of the school curriculum (Brophy & Alleman, 2003; McCleery, Twyman & Tindal, 2003). Table 9.1 includes examples in language arts, social studies, science, and math; many others exist. In addition, students study *rhythm* and *tempo* in music, *perspective* and *balance* in art, and *aerobic* and *isotonic exercises* in physical education. Other concepts such as *honesty, bias, love,* and *internal conflict* appear across the curriculum.

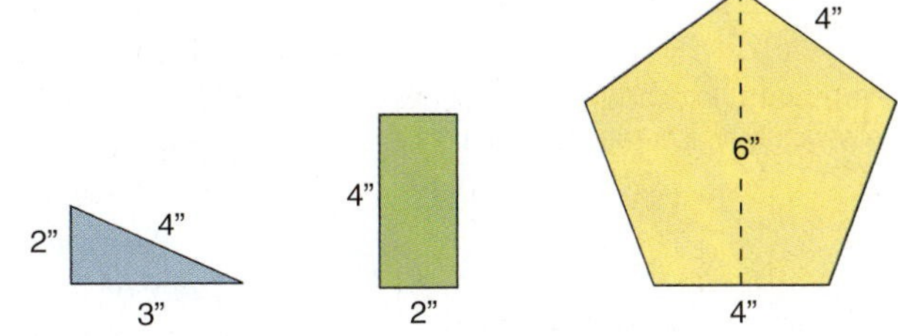

Figure 9.1 Areas of different polygons

Theories of Concept Learning

Theorists offer different explanations for how people construct concepts. In this section, we consider three theories that focus on characteristics, prototypes, and exemplars.

Rule-Driven Theories of Concept Learning

Rule-driven theories of concept learning use the characteristics of concepts to define them. Some, such as *square, longitude* or *adverb,* have well-defined **characteristics,** which are the concept's defining elements (Medin, Proffitt, & Schwartz, 2000). For instance, *closed, equal sides* and *equal angles* are the characteristics of the concept *square.* Learners can identify examples of squares based on a rule stating that squares must have these attributes. Other characteristics, such as size, color, or spatial orientation, aren't essential, so learners don't have to consider them in making their classifications. This rule-driven theory of concept learning was investigated by early researchers (e.g., Bruner, Goodenow, & Austin, 1956), who found that people differentiate concepts on the basis of the defining characteristics of each (Bourne, 1982).

Characteristics. A concept's defining elements.

Prototype Theories of Concept Learning

Many concepts don't have well-defined characteristics, however, so creating rules to help differentiate them is difficult. For instance, what are the characteristics of the concepts *Democrat* or *Republican*? Despite frequent political references to them, most people can't define *Democrat* or *Republican* with any degree of precision. Even common concepts, such as *car,* can have "fuzzy boundaries" (Terry, 2006). For instance, some people describe sport utility vehicles as cars, but others don't. How about minivans or railroad "cars"?

A second theory of concept learning suggests that people construct a **prototype,** the best representation of the category or class, for concepts such as *Democrat, Republican,* and even *car* (Hampton, 1995; Medin et al., 2000). Prominent politicians might be prototypes for the concepts *Republican* or *Democrat,* for example, and a common passenger car, like a Honda Accord, might be a prototype for *car.*

Prototype. In concept-learning theory, the best representation of a category or class.

Prototypes aren't necessarily physical examples. Rather, they can be a mental composite, constructed from examples that individuals experience (Reisberg, 2006; B. Ross & Spalding, 1994). For instance, a person who has encountered a number of different dogs might construct a prototype that doesn't look exactly like any particular breed.

table 9.1 Concepts in Different Content Areas

Language Arts	Social Studies	Science	Math
Adjective	Culture	Acid	Prime number
Verb	Longitude	Conifer	Equivalent fraction
Plot	Federalist	Element	Set
Simile	Democracy	Force	Addition
Infinitive	Immigrant	Inertia	Parabola

Exemplar Theories of Concept Learning

Exemplars. In concept-learning theory, the most highly typical examples of a concept.

A third theory of concept learning holds that learners don't construct a single prototype; rather they store **exemplars,** the most highly typical examples of a concept (Medin et al., 2000). For instance, a child may construct a concept of *dogs* by storing images of a golden retriever, cocker spaniel, collie, and German shepherd in memory as exemplars.

Each theory explains different aspects of concept learning. For instance, concepts such as *square* or *odd number* are likely constructed based on their characteristics. Others, such as *car* or *dog,* are probably represented with prototypes or exemplars.

MyEducationLab

To further examine teachers' attempts to promote concept learning in their students, go to the *Activities and Applications* section in Chapter 9 of MyEducationLab at www.myeducationlab.com, and watch the episode *Constructing Concepts: Using Concrete Examples*. Answer the questions following the episode.

Learning and Teaching Concepts: The Need for Examples

Regardless of a concept's complexity, the key to teaching a concept is giving students experiences with a carefully selected set of examples and nonexamples combined with a definition that specifies essential characteristics (Schunk, 2004; Tennyson & Cocchiarella, 1986). If concepts are constructed on the basis of a well-defined rule, such as the rules for *square* or *force,* they will illustrate all the essential characteristics. If not, the examples will help learners construct a valid prototype or set of exemplars.

theory to practice

Promoting Concept Learning in Your Classroom

Constructivist learning theory has important implications for the way we teach concepts. The following guidelines can help you in your efforts to apply this theory in your instruction:

1. Provide a variety of examples and nonexamples of the concept.
2. Present the examples in a real-world context.
3. Sequence the examples beginning with the most typical and ending with those least familiar.
4. Promote meaningful learning by linking the concept to related concepts.

Now, read about how Carol Lopez applies the guidelines as she attempts to help her fifth graders construct the concept *adjective*.

Carol begins by displaying the following vignette on the overhead:

John and Karen, with her brown hair blowing in the wind, drove together in his old car to the football game. They soon met their very best friends, Latoya and Michael, at the large gate near the entrance. The game was incredibly exciting, and because the team's running game was sparkling, the home team won by a bare margin.

Carol has the students read the vignette and then says, "We've discussed nouns, so let's see what you remember. Identify a noun in the passage. . . . Bharat?"

"John and Karen," Bharat responds.

Carol continues until the students have named each of the nouns, and she then asks, "What do we know about Karen's hair?. . . Jesse?"

"It's brown."

"And what kind of game did they attend?"

"A football game," several students say together.

Carol continues having the students describe the nouns, and she identifies each of the words that describe them as *adjectives*.

Then she says, "Now let's take a closer look. . . . What's different about *exciting* and *sparkling* compared to others like *brown* and *old*?. . . Duk?"

"They . . . don't come in front of the noun . . . like the others do?"

"Very good, Duk. Yes, adjectives don't always come before the noun. . . . Now, what is important about *running* and *football*?. . . Sharon?"

"*Running* looks like a verb . . . and *football* looks like a noun."

"Yes they do . . . . but how do we know they're adjectives?. . . Lakesha?"

"They describe nouns . . . like *football* describes *game,* and . . . *running* does too."

"Excellent," Carol smiles. "Now, take a look at the word *the*, like in *the* entrance and *the* game. How do we know that they're not adjectives?"

After several seconds, Yolanda offers, "They don't tell us anything about the noun. . . . It just says, 'the' entrance. It doesn't describe it."

"Very good, Yolanda," Carol nods.

Carol then has her students look at the words *soon*, *very*, and *incredibly* and explain why they aren't adjectives, and finally, she has them write a paragraph that includes three or more adjectives, with at least one coming after the noun.

Carol collects the paragraphs, puts three of them on transparencies (without names to avoid having the class know whose paragraphs are being analyzed), and discusses them the next day.

Now, let's examine Carol's attempts to implement the guidelines. By embedding a variety of examples and nonexamples in the context of the vignette, she applied the first guideline (provide a variety of examples and nonexamples) and the second guideline (use a real-world context). She also sequenced the examples so the most obvious ones, such as *brown* and *old* were presented first (guideline 3). And, finally, in discussing the words *soon, very* and *incredibly*, she linked *adjective* to the concept *adverb* in order to make them more meaningful (guideline 4).

Carol grounded her lesson in constructivist learning theory. Her examples provided the experiences the students needed to construct their knowledge of the concept, and she embedded them in the context of a written passage. A written passage is more "real world" than words or individual sentences. The examples in context also helped the students understand that *running*, which looks like a verb, and *football*, which looks like a noun, functioned as adjectives in this context. And finally, she developed the lesson with her questioning, which promoted high levels of social interaction. Each is an application of social constructivist learning theory, and the nuances of Carol's lesson help us understand why concept learning is a complex cognitive process.

Nonexamples are important when the concept can be confused with a closely related concept. For instance, *frog* would be an important nonexample for the concept *reptile*, because many people believe frogs are reptiles; and *simile* would be an important nonexample for the concept *metaphor*, because the two are easily confused.

Analogies can also be used to make concepts meaningful (Bulgren et al., 2000). For instance, comparing the temperature control systems of mammals (new concept) to the analogous system in a house helps students make connections to experiences stored in long-term memory. Graphic organizers that highlight similarities and differences in two concepts can also be effective instructional aids (R. C. Clark & Mayer, 2003).

In teaching concepts, some experts argue that teachers should present a sequence of examples and guide students' constructions of the concept, and this is the approach historically advocated by Bruner (1960, 1966). Others suggest that presenting a definition and then illustrating it with examples is more effective. This approach was advocated by David Ausubel (1963, 1977), a prominent psychologist who argued that people learn their knowledge primarily through reception rather than discovery. Both can be effective, and both should be used to add variety to instruction.

check your understanding

1.1 Define *concepts*, and identify three concepts each that you've studied from Chapters 5 to 8 of this text.

1.2 Of the concepts *noun* and *culture*, which should be easier to learn? Which theory of concept learning best explains how each concept is constructed? Explain, basing your answer on the information in this section.

1.3 You're teaching the concept *reptile*, and you've shown common examples, such as a lizard, alligator, snake, and turtle. Identify at least one important additional example and one important nonexample that you should provide, and explain why they are important.

To receive feedback for these questions, go to Appendix A.

classroom connections

Promoting Concept Learning in Your Classroom

1. Examples provide learners with the experiences they need to construct concepts. To provide authentic experiences, use examples that include all the information learners need to understand the concept.
   - **Elementary:** A fourth-grade teacher presents a crab and shrimp, together with pictures of a spider, beetle, and grasshopper, to illustrate the concept *arthropod*. He also includes a clam, earthworm, and the students themselves as nonexamples.
   - **Middle School:** A geometry teacher presents her students with drawings of similar triangles such as those shown below: She has the students measure the sides and angles of the two triangles. They see that the sides of one are twice as long as the sides of the other, and the angles in the two are equal. She includes additional examples of similar triangles and other pairs of triangles that are not similar.

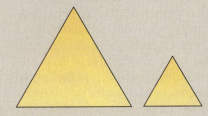

   - **High School:** A tennis coach is helping his students learn how to serve. He videotapes several people, some with good serves and others less skilled. He shows the class the videotapes and asks the students to identify the differences in the serves.
2. To help students make concepts more meaningful, link new concepts to related concepts.
   - **Elementary:** A kindergarten teacher wants her class to understand that living things exist in many different forms. She instructs the children to identify themselves, pets, and plants in their classroom as living things. They identify "the ability to grow and change" and "the need for food and water" as two characteristics the examples have in common.
   - **Middle School:** To help his students understand the relationships between descriptive and persuasive writing, an English teacher displays paragraphs illustrating each and asks the class to identify their similarities and differences.
   - **High School:** A social studies teacher instructs her students to compare cultural revolutions to other revolutions, such as the Industrial Revolution, the American Revolution, and the technological revolution, pointing out similarities and differences in each case.

Problem Solving

To begin this section, look at each of the following examples:

- You want to send a birthday card to a friend who has moved to New York, but you don't know his home address.
- You're a teacher, and your seventh graders resist thinking on their own. They expect to find all the answers specifically stated in the textbook.
- Laura asked her students to find the area of the carpeted portion of their classroom.

Problem. A state that occurs when a problem solver has a goal but lacks an obvious way of achieving the goal.

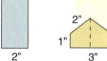

Although they look different, each describes a **problem,** which "occurs when a problem solver has a goal but lacks an obvious way of achieving the goal" (R. E. Mayer & Wittrock, 2006, p. 288). In our examples, the goals are finding the address, having students think on their own, and finding the carpeted area of the classroom. A broad definition of *problem* is helpful because it recognizes the pervasiveness of problem solving in our daily lives and allows people to apply general strategies to solve different kinds of problems (R. E. Mayer & Wittrock, 2006).

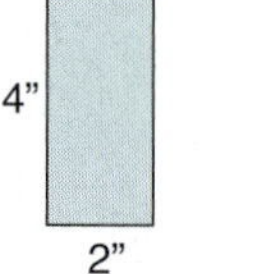

Prior knowledge is an essential component of problem solving because it helps students understand the problem and select an appropriate solution (Jitendra et al., 2007). Lack of prior knowledge was part of the reason Laura's students struggled with their problem—as revealed in an interview with four students after the lesson. The interviewer showed the students figures on the left, and then began questioning them.

Interviewer: What do we mean by *perimeter?* . . . Show us on one of these figures. . . . Yashoda?
Yashoda: It's the distance around the figure, like here (moving her finger around the rectangle and then the pentagon).
Interviewer: So, what is the perimeter here (pointing to the rectangle)? . . . Erica?
Erica: . . . 12.
Interviewer: And how did you get that?
Erica: I added 4 and 4 and 2 and 2.
Interviewer: How about the perimeter of this (pointing to the pentagon)? . . . Hasan?
Hasan: . . . 9. . . . I added 3 and 1 and 1 and 2 and 2.
Interviewer: Now, what do we mean by area? . . . Show us. . . . Daniel?
Daniel: It's like if you covered it up with dirt or paper or something (moving his hand back and forth over the rectangle). It's how much you need to cover it up.
Interviewer: So, what is the area of the rectangle?
Daniel: . . . 8. I multiplied 4 times 2 because the area is the length times the width.
Interviewer: Good. So, how would you find the area of this (pointing to the pentagon)? . . . Yashoda?
Yashoda: (After thinking for several seconds) I would multiply the 3 times the 1, which would be 3, and then I would take that times 2 (pointing at the 2 in the figure), so the area would be 6.
Interviewer: How do the rest of you feel about that?
The others nod, agreeing Yashoda's strategy makes sense.

This interview and cognitive learning theory help us answer the first question we asked at the beginning of the chapter: "Why did the groups get such varying answers to the same problem?" Part of the reason likely resulted from their misconception about calculating the area of an irregular figure, such as the pentagon. Their experience with calculating area was limited to regular shapes, like the rectangle. So, they used a similar strategy to find the area of the pentagon. They understood the concept *area,* which requires declarative knowledge, but they lacked the procedural and conditional knowledge needed to calculate the area. As the interview revealed, having declarative knowledge about area doesn't imply that they will also have the necessary procedural and conditional knowledge needed to calculate an area. This case further illustrates the complexities of problem solving.

Well-Defined and Ill-Defined Problems

Experts on problem solving find it useful to distinguish between well-defined and ill-defined problems (R. E. Mayer & Wittrock, 2006). A **well-defined problem** has only one correct solution and a certain method for finding it, whereas an **ill-defined problem** has more than one acceptable solution, an ambiguous goal, and no generally agreed-upon strategy for reaching a solution (R. E. Mayer & Wittrock, 2006). Our first example at the beginning of this section is well defined; your friend has only one home address, and a straightforward strategy for finding it exists. Many problems in math and some sciences, such as physics, are well defined.

Well-defined problem. A problem that has only one correct solution and a certain method for finding it.

Ill-defined problem. A problem that has more than one acceptable solution, an ambiguous goal, and no generally agreed-upon strategy for reaching a solution.

In contrast, the seventh graders' not wanting to think for themselves is an ill-defined problem. The goal isn't clear, because teachers often aren't sure what "thinking" means. And no agreed-upon strategy exists for improving students' thinking. The problem can be solved with several strategies, and it can have more than one "right" answer.

As teachers, we have an ill-defined problem when we attempt to improve the problem-solving abilities of our students; research indicates that they are not very good at it (R. E. Mayer, 2002; R. E. Mayer & Wittrock, 2006), and two reasons for this weakness are often cited. First, most of the problems learners solve in schools are well-defined, but the majority of life's problems are ill defined. Second, problem solving is personal and contextual (R. E. Mayer & Wittrock, 2006). A well-defined problem for one person is ill defined for another. Laura's lesson is an example. Finding the amount of carpeting necessary for the room is well defined for experienced problem solvers, but for Laura's students it was ill defined. Their understanding of the goal wasn't clear, and, as the interview revealed, in applying the same strategy to finding the area of the pentagon as they used for the rectangle, they indicated a lack of procedural and conditional knowledge. Further, some of them were willing to accept answers that indicated a lack of metacognitive knowledge; for example, they accepted the answer of 1,600 square feet, which was more than the total area of the room.

Concrete and hands-on experiences provide effective beginning points for problem solving.

Helping students become better problem solvers is one of the biggest challenges teachers face. As you attempt to meet this challenge, the following strategies can be effective:

- Help students understand a problem-solving model that they can apply in a variety of domains.
- Describe how expert problem solvers solve problems, and use them as models for novices.
- Teach a specific set of strategies to help students improve their problem-solving abilities.

A Problem-Solving Model

Since the 1950s, computer scientists and cognitive psychologists have attempted to develop a general problem-solving model that can be applied in domains varying as widely as traditional math and science, to school leadership (A. Canter, 2004), counseling in response to classroom management issues (Dwairy, 2005), and curbing excessive drinking on college campuses (Biscaro, Broer, & Taylor, 2004).

Researchers have developed a number of models (e.g., Bransford & Stein, 1984; J. R. Hayes, 1988), but most models are similar and can be summarized in the five-stage sequence that appears in Figure 9.2. We discuss these stages in the sections that follow.

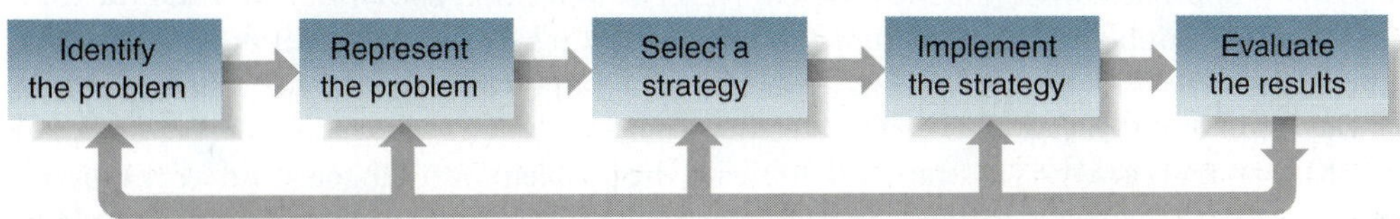

Figure 9.2 A general problem-solving model

Identifying the Problem

There are 26 sheep and 10 goats on a ship. How old is the captain?

In one study 75 percent of the second graders who were asked this question answered 36 (cited in Prawat, 1989)! Obviously, they didn't understand the problem.

While identifying a problem appears to be straightforward, it is one of the most difficult aspects of problem solving (Jitendra et al., 2007). It requires patience and a willingness to avoid committing to a solution too soon. Obstacles to identifying problems include:

- Lack of domain-specific knowledge. As in all areas of learning, prior knowledge is essential for problem solving (R. E. Mayer & Wittrock, 2006).
- Lack of experience in defining problems. As you saw earlier, most of the problems students solve in schools are well-defined (Bruning, Schraw, Norby, & Ronning, 2004).
- The tendency to rush toward a solution (Lan, Repman, & Chyung, 1998), as was illustrated by the second graders who added the sheep and goats to get the age of the captain.
- The tendency to think convergently. Novice problem solvers tend to focus on one approach to solving problems and often persist with this approach even when it isn't working (P. Alexander, 2006).

These obstacles are not limited to students. For example, scientists were asked to solve the problem of tomatoes being bruised when they were picked by machines. After a number of unsuccessful attempts to develop gentler picking machines, scientists finally changed their thinking and turned their efforts to developing tomatoes less susceptible to bruising. This explains why the ones we buy in stores sometimes feel like rocks (D. Schwartz et al., 2005).

Overcoming each of these obstacles requires a great deal of experience with problem solving.

Representing the Problem

Representing the problem, the second phase of our problem-solving model, is important because it encourages learners to conceptualize it in familiar terms (Jitendra et al., 2007). A problem can be represented by (1) restating it in more meaningful terms, (2) relating it to a familiar problem, or (3) representing it visually, such as the diagram that Laura's students used. Many problems impose a heavy cognitive load on learners' working memories, and putting problems on paper reduces this load (Lowrie & Kay, 2001).

Selecting a Strategy

After identifying and representing the problem, we must select a strategy for solving it. Algorithms and heuristics are two commonly used strategies.

Algorithm. A specific set of steps for solving a problem.

Algorithms. To understand how algorithms are used in problem solving, think back to the interview and finding the area of the rectangle. Most people know that we simply multiply the length times the width, which applies an **algorithm,** a specific set of steps for solving a problem. Algorithms vary widely in their complexity. Examples of using a simple algorithm include finding the area of a rectangle, subtracting whole numbers with regrouping, and adding fractions with unlike denominators. In contrast, computer experts use complex algorithms to solve sophisticated programming problems.

Heuristics. General, widely applicable problem-solving strategies.

Heuristics. Many problems can't be solved with algorithms, because they don't exist for ill-defined problems or for many that are well-defined. In those cases, problem solvers use **heuristics,** which are general, widely applicable problem-solving strategies (Chronicle, MacGregor, & Ormerod, 2004). The more complex and unfamiliar the task, the greater the need for a heuristic approach to solving the problem (J. Lee & Reigeluth, 2003).

A number of heuristics exist. Trial and error is one. It's inefficient, but it provides learners with experience, and many people use it as a first step in trying to solve unfamiliar problems (J. Davidson & Sternberg, 2003).

Means–ends analysis. A heuristic that breaks a problem into subgoals and works successively on each.

Means–ends analysis, a strategy that breaks the problem into subgoals and works successively on each, is a heuristic that is effective for solving ill-defined problems. For example, in the case of the seventh graders who don't want to "think," we might define thinking first as the ability to make conclusions based on evidence, and second as the inclination to do so. With these as our subgoals, we can design learning activities that give our students practice with each.

Drawing analogies, a strategy used to solve unfamiliar problems by comparing them with those already solved, is a third heuristic (R. E. Mayer, 2002). It can be difficult to implement, however, because learners often can't find problems in their memories analogous to the one they want to solve, or they may make inappropriate connections between the two problems.

Drawing analogies. A heuristic that is used to solve unfamiliar problems by comparing them with those already solved.

Some evidence indicates that teaching heuristics can improve problem-solving ability even in early elementary students (Hohn & Frey, 2002), but ultimately, prior knowledge and experience with problem solving are essential for successfully selecting a strategy, and no heuristic can replace them (Pittman & Beth-Halachmy, 1997).

Implementing the Strategy

Clearly defining and representing the problem and selecting an appropriate algorithm or heuristic are keys to successfully implementing a strategy. If these processes have been effective, implementation is routine. If learners cannot implement a strategy, they should rethink the original problem or the strategy they've selected. Laura's students, for example, lacked experience in defining problems, and they had misconceptions about finding the area of irregular shapes; their difficulties occurred well before they attempted to implement their strategies.

Evaluating the Results

Evaluating results is the final step in effective problem solving, and it requires the metacognitive knowledge that helps us reflect on our actions (R. E. Mayer & Wittrock, 2006). As illustrated in Laura's lesson, students often aren't metacognitive about the process; they accept virtually any answer they get, whether or not it makes sense.

Teachers can increase learner metacognition by requiring that students justify their thinking as they solve problems instead of focusing exclusively on answers (R. E. Mayer, 2002). Requiring estimates beforehand is also effective. Unrealistic estimates indicate a lack of understanding, so estimating can also be an effective informal assessment tool.

Keep these problem-solving steps in mind, as you read about Laura's class the next day, to see how she modifies her instruction.

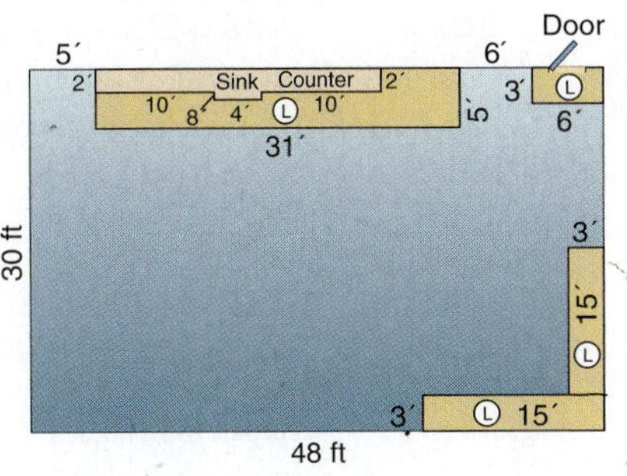

Laura begins Tuesday's lesson by saying, "Let's look at our diagram again," and she displays the diagram on the overhead.

The class agrees to try the first strategy: Find the area of the room, and subtract the parts with the linoleum (marked "L"). So, Laura first has them calculate the area of the room.

She watches to see that they get 1,440 square feet and then asks, "What do we do next?"

The students agree that they must subtract the parts marked "L," and they suggest starting at the top of the diagram.

"How will we find the area of this part? . . . Fred?" Laura asks.

". . . Multiply 31 times 5."

Laura has Fred explain his thinking, the students calculate the area, and she checks to be sure they all get 155 square feet. She then has them repeat the process with the portion by the door, where they get 18 square feet.

Laura then points to the linoleum at the lower right. She asks the students for suggestions, and finding that several are uncertain, she goes to the board and writes:

$$15 \times 3 = 45 \text{ square feet}$$
$$12 \times 3 = 36 \text{ square feet}$$
$$45 + 36 = 81 \text{ square feet}$$

She waits for several seconds and then says, "Someone explain where these numbers came from."

"The 15 is the length of that part," Nephi offers pointing to the bottom of the diagram. "And the 3 is how wide it is . . . so, the area is 45."

"Forty-five what?" Laura probes.

"Square feet," Nephi adds quickly.

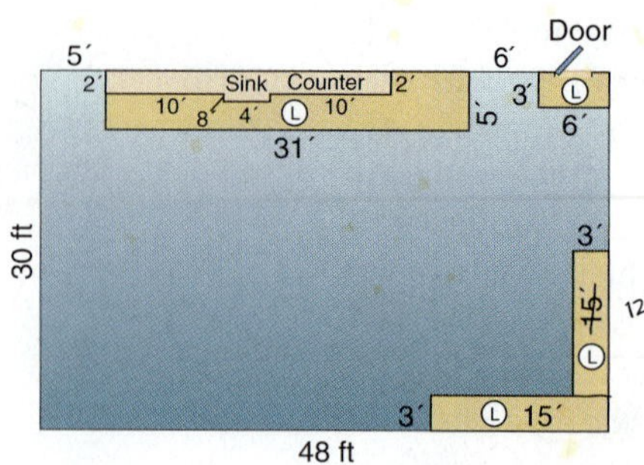

"Now, let's be good thinkers. How do we know the second statement must be 12 times 3 instead of 15 times 3?"

". . . I've got it!" Anya shouts.

"Come up and show us."

Anya goes to the overhead and alters the diagram, as shown here:

"See, we already have this," she says, pointing to the lower right corner of the drawing. "So, this length is 12, not 15. . . . So, it's 12 times 3."

Laura asks the class if Anya's thinking makes sense, they agree that it does, and she then asks them what they need to do next. They agree that they must add the 45 and 36 to get 81 square feet.

The class then adds the 115, 18, and 81, to get a total of 254 square feet, and they conclude that they must subtract the 254 from 1,440. Laura asks them to explain why, and they then find that the carpeted portion is 1,186 square feet.

She then says, "For your homework, I want you to figure out what the area of the carpeted portion is using the second strategy," she hands them another diagram showing the dimensions of the inside area, and asks, "Now, what do we always ask ourselves when we try a strategy?"

"Does it make sense?" Shayna answers after thinking for several seconds.

"Yes, exactly," Laura smiles. You'll be ready to explain how you got your answers when we start. . . . We'll look for that tomorrow."

The primary difference between the two lessons is that the instruction on Tuesday was more highly structured than it was on Monday. After the students agreed that they would use their first strategy, Laura used specific questions to scaffold them through the process of implementing the strategy. Then, she carefully monitored their work to ensure that they were making progress.

MyEducationLab

To further examine Laura's attempts to help her students develop their problem solving skills, go to the *Activities and Applications* section in Chapter 9 of MyEducationLab at www.myeducationlab.com, and watch the video episode *Using a Problem-Solving Model: Finding Area in Elementary Math*. Answer the questions following the episode.

Laura's instruction in the two lessons leaves some issues unresolved. The students floundered using her unstructured approach on Monday, so she was much more direct on Tuesday. These issues also address the second question from the beginning of the chapter: "Was the time spent on the activity [Monday's lesson] used wisely?" A clear answer doesn't exist. One of the cognitive learning principles introduced in Chapter 7 states that learning and development depend on learners' experiences. Laura's students acquired considerable experience with designing and implementing strategies and working cooperatively, all of which are valuable for promoting self-regulation. On the other hand, they spent valuable class time floundering, and Laura spent a full additional lesson helping them implement a procedure for solving the problem. The answer to the question ultimately is a matter of professional judgment.

Expert–Novice Differences in Problem-Solving Ability

Experts. Individuals who are highly skilled or knowledgeable in a given domain.

Experts are individuals who are highly skilled or knowledgeable in a specific domain, and four important differences in problem-solving ability exist between experts and novices (Bruning et al., 2004; Hatano & Oura, 2003). These differences are outlined in Table 9.2 and discussed in the paragraphs that follow. The expression "specific domain" is important; an expert in math, for example, may be a novice in history, writing, or teaching.

The pattern in Table 9.2 suggests that experts have more fully developed schemas in long-term memory, which allow them to better accommodate the limitations of working memory when they are immersed in problem solving. Experts represent problems more effectively because their complex schemas act as "chunks" that reduce cognitive load. And much of their procedural knowledge is automatic, which further reduces cognitive load and leaves more working memory space to focus on the problem. In addition, experts are metacognitive in their approach to solving unfamiliar problems. They plan carefully, try new strategies when existing ones are unproductive, and carefully monitor results.

Experts have these abilities because they possess a great deal of both domain-specific and general knowledge, which have been acquired through extensive experience (Schraw, 2006). Because of their experience, they can use heuristics, such as drawing analogies, effectively. Experts' experiences are often stored in memory as "cases," which they can index and search and can apply analogically to new problems (Bransford, 1993; R. Mayer & Wittrock, 2006).

table 9.2 Expert–Novice Differences in Problem-Solving Ability

Area	Experts	Novices
Representing problems	Search for context and relationships in problems.	See problems in isolated pieces.
Problem-solving efficiency	Solve problems rapidly and possess much knowledge that is automatic.	Solve problems slowly, and focus on mechanics.
Planning for problem solving	Plan carefully before attempting solutions to unfamiliar problems.	Plan briefly when attempting solutions to unfamiliar problems; quickly adopt and try solutions.
Monitoring problem solving	Demonstrate well-developed metacognitive abilities; abandon inefficient strategies.	Demonstrate limited metacognition; persevere with unproductive strategies.

An understanding of expertise can help you promote better problem solving in your students by involving them in deliberate practice. Let's look at this process.

Developing Expertise: The Role of Deliberate Practice

"Experts are made, not born. This is not to say that intellectual ability and talent do not exist, or are unimportant, but that effort, deliberate practice, and feedback from experts are essential to the development of high-level expertise" (Schraw, 2006, p. 255). For students to develop their problem-solving skills in math, for example, they must solve a great many problems, including those that are ill-defined. Drill-and-practice activities that require the application of memorized algorithms aren't adequate.

Recognizing this need, researchers emphasize the role of *deliberate practice* in developing expertise (Ericsson, 2003). Effective practice has four dimensions:

- Effective practice is goal directed. Individuals identify skills they want to improve and practice those skills before moving on.
- The practice is systematic. For example, learners practice every day.
- Learners practice in real-world settings.
- Learners receive extensive feedback.

Simply increasing the amount of time spent studying doesn't necessarily increase achievement or expertise, whereas using the deliberate-practice framework can increase both (Plant, Ericsson, & Hill, 2005). And, while problem solving will be easier for some students than for others, with deliberate practice most students can become competent problem solvers.

Creativity in Problem Solving

Creativity is the ability to produce original works or solutions to problems that are productive (Plucker, Beghetto, & Dow, 2004). *Original* implies that the behavior is not learned from someone else, and *productive* means that the product or solution is useful in our culture. For example, a student offered the following as an example to explain why season ticket sales go down when their sports teams don't win.

Creativity. The ability to produce original work or solutions to problems that are productive.

> People who buy season tickets expect to see their team win, and seeing the team win is reinforcing. When the team doesn't win, the nonoccurrence of the expected reinforcer acts as a punisher and reduces the likelihood of them continuing to buy season tickets. (Dawn Emerick, Personal Communication, October 4, 2004)

Dawn offered this description as an example of *the nonoccurrence of expected consequences.* It was original—she didn't get the example from anyone else—and it was productive, because it deepened our understanding of social cognitive theory with an additional, real-world example. It met the criteria for creativity.

Divergent thinking. The ability to generate a variety of original answers to questions or problems.

Divergent thinking is the ability to generate a variety of alternate, original solutions to questions or problems, and it is an important component of creativity (G. Davis & Rimm, 2004). People who think divergently have two important characteristics. First, these people possess a great deal of domain-specific knowledge. It is impossible to think creatively in the absence of knowledge, and people who are creative in one domain, such as art, may not be creative in another, such as writing or music (von Károlyi, Ramos-Ford, & Gardner, 2003). Second, divergent thinkers are strongly intrinsically motivated. They're curious and committed, and they have a passion for the task. Creativity, instead of being an innate talent, is developed through years of practice and commitment (Elder & Paul, 2007).

Measuring Creativity

Creativity is usually measured by giving students a verbal or pictorial stimulus and asking them to generate responses, such as listing as many uses for a brick as possible (e.g., doorstop, bookshelf, paperweight, weapon, building block), or suggesting ways to improve a common object such as a chair (G. Davis & Rimm, 2004). Methods of measuring creativity are controversial, with critics charging that existing tests are too narrow and fail to capture its varying aspects (Tannenbaum, 2003).

Fostering Creativity in Learners

The kind of classroom environment you create can influence the development of creativity. Research offers some suggestions:

- Help learners develop their domain-specific knowledge (Elder & Paul, 2007).
- Create a safe environment where students feel free to risk offering unique ideas and opinions (Md-Yunus, 2007; Runco, 2004).
- Communicate that creativity is valued. Express enthusiasm in response to unusual ideas, and reward students for original thinking (Runco, 2004).
- When assessing learning, avoid social comparisons, increase the number of assessments to reduce the pressure on any single one, and emphasize its role in promoting learning (VanDeWeghe, 2007).

Teachers sometimes complain that the emphasis on standards and high-stakes testing eliminates opportunities to foster creativity in students. This doesn't have to be the case. Creativity in teaching is the ability to find, or create, original examples and representations of the topics being taught, regardless of the emphasis on standards and accountability. For example, a teacher who had her students involved in a unit on cells, tissues, and organ systems, brought in a piece of bubble wrap and used the organization of the air pockets as an analogy for tissue (S. Schellenberg, Personal Communication, February 15, 2008). This example was both original and productive, so it met the criteria for creativity. Perhaps more important, it was very simple and required little effort on her part. Similarly, fostering creativity in students depends more on the kind of learning environment in which they work, than on whether or not they're expected to meet certain standards (Kaufman & Sternberg, 2007).

Problem-Based Learning

Problem-based learning. A teaching strategy that uses problems as the focus for developing content, skills, and self-regulation.

Think again about Scott Sowell's lesson at the end of Chapter 8 and Laura's lessons in this chapter. They both illustrate **problem-based learning,** a teaching strategy that uses problems as the focus for developing content, skills, and self-regulation (Hmelo-Silver, 2004; Serafino & Cicchelli, 2005). Problem-based learning activities have the following characteristics (Gijbels et al., 2005; Krajcik & Blumenfeld, 2006):

- Lessons begin with a problem, and solving it is the lesson focus.
- Students are responsible for designing strategies and finding solutions to the problem. Groups need to be small enough (typically 3 or 4) so that all students are involved in the process.
- The teacher guides students' efforts with questioning and other forms of scaffolding.

As we saw in Laura's lessons, the third characteristic is essential. Because her students floundered on Monday, she provided considerably more scaffolding the next day. Some would argue that she should have intervened sooner and more specifically, whereas others would suggest that the experience the students gained through their struggles was a worthwhile goal in itself.

Some evidence indicates that content learned in problem-based lessons is retained longer and transfers better than content learned with direct instruction approaches (Barak & Dori, 2005; Sungur & Tekkaya, 2006). Additional evidence indicates that learners are more motivated in problem-based lessons than in traditional activities (Luft, Brown, & Sutherin, 2007). Most of the research, however, has been conducted with older or advanced students, and more is needed in order to examine its implementation with learners whose problem-solving skills are less developed (Hmelo-Silver, 2004).

Problem-based learning uses problems as the focus for teaching content and developing skills, and self-regulation.

Using Technology to Promote Problem Solving

As we said earlier in this section, students get little experience in solving ill-defined problems. Most problems presented in textbooks are well-defined and routine, and only the information needed to solve the problem is typically included (Jonassen et al., 2003). Even the operation is often suggested by the wording, such as asking "how many more?" which suggests subtraction (Jitendra et al., 2007). This lack of experience helps explain why students are not better problem solvers.

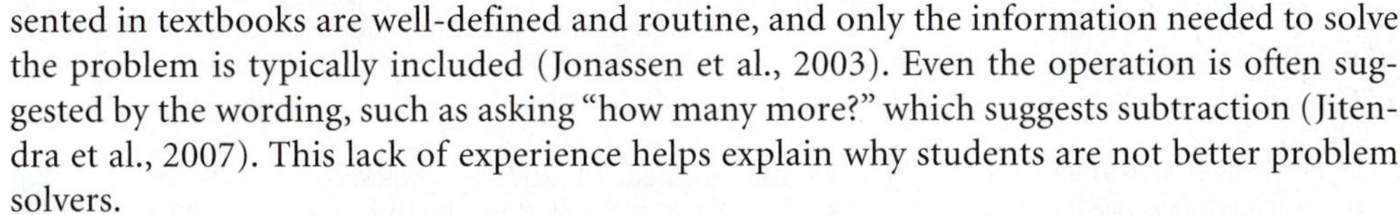

To address these issues, experts have attempted to capitalize on technology to present engaging and real-world problems (D. Schwartz et al., 2005). One of the best known efforts is the series titled *The Adventures of Jasper Woodbury* created by the Cognition and Technology group at Vanderbilt (1992). The series consists of 12 videodisc-based adventures that focus on problem finding and problem solving. To access information about the Jasper series go to http://peabody.vanderbilt.edu/projects/funded/jasper/Jasperhome.html.

The following is an abbreviated version of one of the problems called "Journey to Cedar Creek":

> Jasper has just purchased a new boat and is planning to drive it home. The boat travels 8 mph and consumes 5 gallons of gas per hour. The tank holds 12 gallons of gas. The boat is at mile marker 156, and Jasper's dock is at marker 132. There are two gas stations on the way home. One is at mile marker 140.3 and the other is at mile marker 133. They charge $1.109 and $1.25 per gallon, respectively. They don't take credit cards. Jasper started the day with $20. He bought 5 gallons of gas at $1.25 per gallon (not including a discount of 4 cents per gallon for paying cash) and paid $8.25 for repairs to his boat. It's 2:35. Sundown is at 7:52. Can Jasper make it home before sunset without running out of fuel?

The problems are purposely made complex and left ill-defined to give students practice in defining problems, and they include extraneous material, so students learn to separate relevant from irrelevant information. They also gain experience in identifying subgoals, such as finding out how much money Jasper has left for the trip home. Students work on these problems in teams over several class periods (ranging from a few days to more than a week). They share their ideas, receive feedback to refine their thinking, and present their solutions to the class.

Software designers have developed problem-solving simulations in other areas, as well (Krajcik & Blumenfeld, 2006). In geometry, programs such as *The Geometric Supposer* (http://www.cet.ac.il/math-international/software5.htm) allow students to electronically manipulate figures as they attempt to solve geometry problems. Another program, *Interactive Physics* (http://www.interactivephysics.com), provides objectives and tools to allow students to solve problems using concepts such as force, acceleration, and momentum.

Some research indicates that these simulations produce as much learning as hands-on experience with concrete materials (Triona & Klahr, 2003), but more research is needed to confirm these conclusions.

theory to practice

Helping Learners Develop Their Problem-Solving Abilities

Cognitive learning theory and problem-solving research provide a framework for helping learners develop their problem solving. The following guidelines can help you as you attempt to apply this theory and research in your teaching.

1. Present problems in real-world contexts, and take students' prior knowledge into account.
2. Capitalize on social interaction.
3. Provide scaffolding for novice problem solvers.
4. Teach general problem-solving strategies.

Now, review Laura's lessons to analyze the extent to which she implemented these guidelines.

Social constructivism, particularly situated cognition, suggests presenting problems in real-world contexts. By building her lesson around the problem of finding the carpeted area of their classroom, Laura applied this theory and implemented the first guideline.

Constructivist learning theory also emphasizes social interaction, and it was prominent in both her lessons. Her Monday lesson, however, demonstrates that not all social interaction is effective. Much of the interaction wasn't productive, as indicated by the students' answers. She was more direct on Tuesday, but she still maintained high levels of interaction, which more effectively applied the second guideline.

Laura applied the third guideline in her Tuesday lesson in three ways. First, she developed the lesson almost entirely through questioning, and she also asked the students to explain their thinking in each case. The more students practice using language—both verbal and written—to describe their understanding, the deeper their understanding becomes (Leinhardt & Steele, 2005).

Second, the diagram provided a visual representation of the problem. Third, she provided scaffolding with simple, worked examples by writing

$$15 \times 3 = 45 \text{ square feet}$$
$$12 \times 3 = 36 \text{ square feet}$$
$$45 + 36 = 81 \text{ square feet}$$

Worked examples are problems with completed solutions that provide students with one way of solving problems.

Then, she used additional questioning to help clarify the worked examples. Look again at some of the dialogue:

Laura: Someone explain where these numbers came from.
Nephi: The 15 is the length of that part (pointing to the bottom of the diagram). And the 3 is how wide it is . . . so, the area is 45.
Laura: Forty-five what?
Nephi: Square feet.
Laura: Now, let's be good thinkers. How do we know that the second statement must be 12 times 3?
Anya: . . . I've got it! . . . It's because you already have that much.
Laura: Come up and show us.

Anya then went to the overhead and altered the diagram and explained what she had done.

Research with learners ranging from lower elementary to university students indicates that worked examples can make problem solving more meaningful than traditional instruction, particularly when students are first learning a procedure (Crippen & Earl, 2007; van Gog, Paas, & van Merriënboer, 2004). And, students often prefer worked examples to traditional instruction (Renkl, Stark, Gruber, & Mandl, 1998).

Finally, Laura applied the fourth guideline by attempting to teach her students a general problem-solving strategy. General strategies in the absence of domain-specific knowledge have limited value. Within specific domains such as mathematics, however, they can be effective, because they help students become more metacognitive about their problem solving (R. Mayer & Wittrock, 2006).

This section helps answer the third question from the beginning of the chapter: "What must Laura now do to help her students improve their problem-solving abilities?" She didn't provide the students with enough scaffolding in her Monday lesson, but she adapted her instruction and provided much more on Tuesday without reverting to lecture and explaining. In doing so, her Tuesday lesson applied social constructivist learning theory and cognitive apprenticeships in helping her students develop their problem solving abilities.

Productive social interaction is an important part of problem solving.

Worked examples. Problems with completed solutions that provide students with one way of solving the problems.

A second issue involves the amount of effort required of teachers in using this technology. For instance, students who are used to straightforward, well-defined problems will struggle and likely become frustrated in attempting to solve problems such as those in the Jasper series. This makes teachers' roles demanding. They must provide enough scaffolding to help students make progress, but not so much that they rob students of experience with solving ill-defined problems. This is very sophisticated instruction.

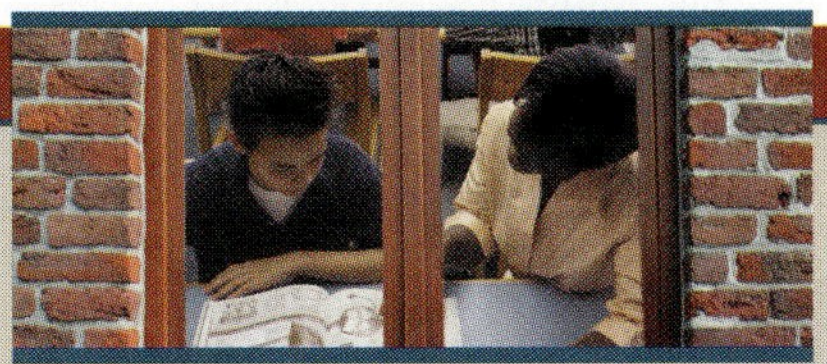

classroom connections

Developing Your Students' Problem-Solving Abilities

1. Constructivist learning theory and situated cognition suggest that real-world problems enhance students' problem-solving efforts. When you use real-world problems, promote high levels of interaction to actively engage students in analyzing problem situations.
   - **Elementary:** A fourth-grade teacher breaks her students into pairs and gives each pair a chocolate bar composed of 12 square pieces. She has the students break off certain numbers of pieces and then represent the numbers as fractions of the whole bar. She has them explain their thinking in each case.
   - **Middle School:** A middle school teacher has a "problem of the week." Each student is required to bring in at least one real-world problem each week. The teacher selects from among them, and the class solves them.
   - **High School:** An Algebra II teacher presents students with the problem of finding peak and off-peak cell phone rates as an introduction to solving simultaneous equations. She then uses questioning to "walk" her students through the process of representing the problem and implementing a strategy for solving it.
2. Cognitive apprenticeships provide opportunities for students to learn problem-solving skills from more knowledgeable others. As students practice solving problems, provide students with scaffolding and encourage them to put their understanding into words.
   - **Elementary:** A second-grade teacher begins a lesson on graphing by asking students how they might determine their classmates' favorite jelly bean flavor. She guides them as they identify the problem and how they might represent and solve it.
   - **Middle School:** A pre-algebra teacher uses categories such as "We Know" and "We Need to Know" as scaffolds for analyzing word problems. They then solve at least two word problems each day.
   - **High School:** In a unit on statistics and probability, a teacher requires her students to make estimates before solving problems. They then compare the solutions to the estimates.

check your understanding

2.1 You're involved in a relationship, but it isn't as satisfying as you would like. Is this a well-defined or an ill-defined problem? Explain. Describe a means–ends analysis that you might use to solve the problem.

2.2 Heuristics, such as means–ends analysis, or drawing analogies, are used in which stage of problem solving? Explain.

2.3 In her Monday lesson, Laura's students got a variety of answers, and some were satisfied with the fact that their answers varied. This was an ineffective application of which stage of problem solving?

To receive feedback for these questions, go to Appendix A.

The Strategic Learner

Do you take notes in your classes? Do you highlight important passages in your texts to help you remember essential ideas? If you do, you're using **strategies,** cognitive operations that exceed the normal activities required to carry out a task (Pressley & Harris, 2006). Highlighting is a strategy, for example, because it exceeds simply reading, which is the normal activity involved in trying to understand a written passage.

Strategies. Cognitive operations that exceed the normal activities required to carry out a task.

A wide variety of general learning strategies exists, including concept mapping, note taking, highlighting, summarizing, and self-questioning (P. Alexander, 2006). Each can enhance learning.

Regardless of the strategy, students' ability to use it effectively depends on their metacognition.

Metacognition: The Foundation of Strategic Learning

In Chapter 7 you saw that **metacognition** is our awareness of and control over our cognitive processes. It is the mechanism we use to match a strategy to a goal, and students who are metacognitive can even compensate for lack of native ability (M. V. Veenman & Spaans, 2005).

Metacognition. Awareness of, and control over, our cognitive processes.

Metacognitive learners, when using note taking as a strategy, for example, ask questions such as

- Am I writing down important ideas or trivial details?
- Am I taking enough notes, or am I taking too many?
- When I study, am I simply reading my notes, or do I use examples to elaborate on them?

Without this kind of metacognitive monitoring, strategies are largely worthless.

Strategy instruction has focused on reading, writing, second-language learning, and problem solving, with reading being the most common (Pressley & Harris, 2006). This research indicates that effective strategy users, in addition to being metacognitive, also have (1) extensive prior knowledge and (2) a repertoire of strategies.

Prior Knowledge

Prior knowledge is important for all learning, and it is equally true for strategy use (Coiro & Dobler, 2007; Peverly, Brobst, & Graham, 2003). Learners with extensive prior knowledge can use deep processing strategies to generate questions, create images, and use analogical thinking. Without this knowledge base, strategy use is difficult (P. Alexander, Graham, & Harris, 1998).

Prior knowledge also helps students make better decisions about what is important to study and helps them efficiently allocate their mental resources to the task (Verkoeijen, Rikers, & Schmidt, 2005).

A Repertoire of Strategies

Just as expert problem solvers draw on a wealth of experiences, effective strategy users have a variety from which to choose (P. Alexander, 2006; P. Alexander & Jetton, 2000). For instance, they take notes, skim, use outlines, generate diagrams and figures, take advantage of bold and italicized print, and capitalize on examples. They also use heuristics, such as means–ends analysis, to break ill-defined learning tasks into manageable parts. Without a repertoire, learners cannot match strategies to different tasks.

Becoming a strategic learner takes time and effort, and even after receiving strategy instruction, many students fail to use them unless prompted to do so by their teachers (Pressley & Harris, 2006). Also, most students, including those in college, tend to use primitive strategies, such as rehearsal, regardless of the difficulty of the material (Peverly et al., 2003).

Study Strategies

Study strategies. Specific techniques students use to increase their understanding of written materials and teacher presentations.

Study strategies are specific techniques students use to increase their understanding of written materials and teacher presentations. A variety of study strategies exist, and we examine several of the most widely used in this section. They include

- Note taking
- Concept mapping
- Using text signals
- Summarizing
- Elaborative questioning
- SQ3R

Note Taking

Note taking is probably the most common study strategy, and it has been examined extensively. In spite of the popularity of note taking, research indicates that many students, including those in college, are poor note takers (Austin, Lee, & Carr, 2004; Peverly et al., 2007; Titsworth, 2004). It is associated with increased achievement, however, especially when it encourages students to actively process information (Igo, Bruning, & McCrudden, 2005). Effective notes include both the main ideas presented in either lectures or texts and details that support the main ideas (Peverly et al., 2007).

The human memory model and constructivist learning theory both help us explain the positive effects of note taking. First, taking notes helps maintain attention and puts students in cognitively active roles, and second, the notes provide a form of external storage (Igo et al., 2005). Because memory is unreliable, we may fail to encode the information, or we may recon-

1. Give an example of how each of the following influences climate:

Latitude ______

Wind direction ______

Ocean currents ______

Land forms ______

2. Describe each climate, and identify at least one state that has this climate. Then identify one type of plant that lives in this climate and two different animals that are typically found in the climate.

The Mediterranean Climate ______

______ State ______

Plant ______ Animals ______

The Marine West Coast Climate ______

______ State ______

Plant ______ Animals ______

The Humid Subtropical Climate ______

______ State ______

Plant ______ Animals ______

The Humid Continental Climate ______

______ State ______

Figure 9.3 Guided note taking in U.S. geography

struct our understanding in a way that makes more sense to us but isn't valid. The notes provide a source of information against which we can check our understanding.

We can help our students improve their note-taking skills with **guided notes,** teacher-prepared handouts that "guide" students with cues and space available for writing key ideas and relationships. Using guided notes has been found to increase achievement in students ranging from those with learning disabilities (S. L. Hamilton, Seibert, Gardner, & Talbert-Johnson, 2000) to college students (Austin et al., 2004). Figure 9.3 illustrates a guided-notes form used for different climate regions of the United States by a seventh-grade geography teacher.

Guided notes. Teacher-prepared handouts that "guide" students with cues and space available for writing key ideas and relationships.

Concept mapping. A learning strategy in which learners construct visual relationships among concepts.

Guided notes also model the organization and key points of the topic, and, as students acquire experience, they gradually develop organizational skills that they can apply on their own. These skills, combined with metacognitive awareness, can significantly increase students' strategic learning abilities.

Concept Mapping

Concept mapping is a learning strategy in which learners construct visual relationships among concepts (Liu, 2004; Nesbit & Adesope, 2006). It is popular in e-learning environments (Tseng, Sue, & Su, 2007) and can also be used to measure conceptual change in learners (Hilbert & Renkl, 2008; Nesbit & Hadwin, 2006).

Concept mapping is an application of cognitive learning theory (De Simone, 2007). Constructing concept maps puts students in cognitively active roles and employs dual-coding theory and the encoding strategies you studied in Chapter 7 (Nesbit & Adesope, 2006). For example, a concept map visually represents relationships among concepts, so it capitalizes on *imagery*, and the map itself is a form of *organization*. As learners' understanding increases, the map can be modified and expanded, which is a form of *elaboration*. Research supports these applications and indicates that the strategy makes conceptual change more durable (Kakkarainen & Ahtee, 2007).

Teachers can also use concept mapping as an assessment tool (MacNeil, 2007). For example, the student who created the concept map in Figure 9.4 didn't include figures with more than four sides or

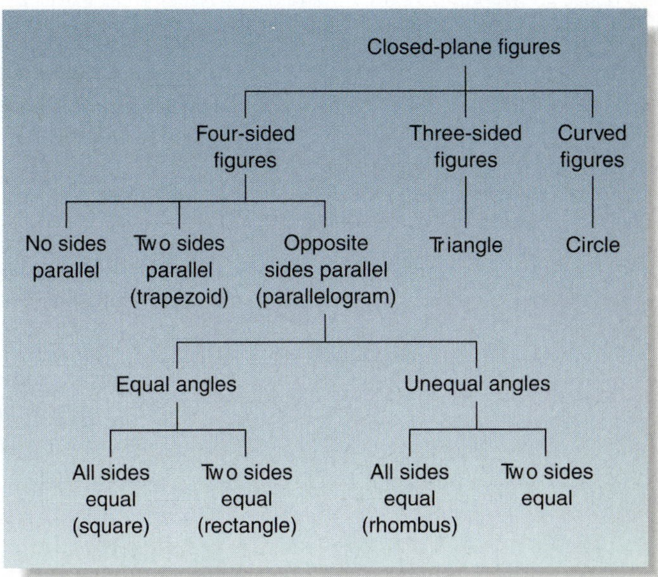

Figure 9.4 Concept map for closed-plane figures

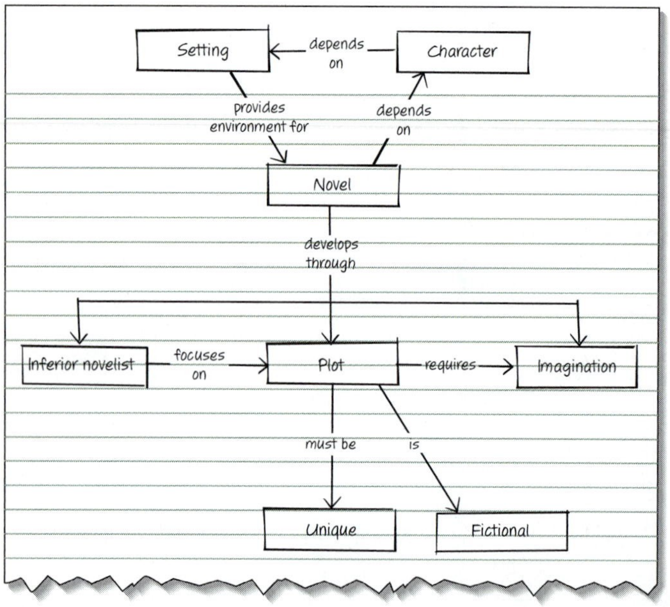

curved shapes other than circles. Seeing that the learner's understanding is incomplete, the teacher can provide examples of other figures, such as pentagons, hexagons, and ellipses.

The concepts in Figure 9.4 are organized hierarchically, but not all relationships among concepts exist this way, so other types of concept maps may be more effective (Nesbit & Adesope, 2006). For example, Figure 9.5 illustrates a student's understanding of the parts of a novel, together with the factors that influence a novel's quality, in a **network**, a concept map illustrating nonhierarchical relationships. As with the example of closed-plane figures, teachers can use information from networks to assess students' understanding and help them further develop the concept.

Figure 9.5 A learner's network for the concept *novel*

Network. A concept map illustrating nonhierarchical relationships.

Text signals. Elements included in written materials that communicate text organization and key ideas.

The type of concept map students use should be the one that best illustrates relationships among the concepts. Hierarchies often work best in math and science; in other areas, such as reading or social studies, a network may be more effective.

Using Text Signals

Text signals are elements included in written materials that communicate text organization and key ideas. Common text signals include the following:

- *Headings.* For example, in this chapter *concept mapping* and *note taking* are subheadings under the heading *study strategies*, so this organization signals that each is a study strategy.
- *Numbered and bulleted lists.* For instance, the bulleted list you're reading now identifies different text signals.
- *Underlined, bold, or italicized text.* Each of the important concepts in this text, for example, is emphasized in bold print.
- *Preview and recall sentences.* For instance, we introduced our discussion of metacognition in this chapter by saying, "In Chapter 7 you saw that metacognition is. . . ." This signal links the concept to a discussion in an earlier chapter and suggests that you reread the section if you are uncertain about the topic.

Strategic learners use these signals to develop a framework for the topic they're studying (Vacca & Vacca, 2008). Teachers can encourage the use of the strategy by discussing the organization of a topic and reminding students of other text signals that can help make the information they're studying more meaningful.

Summarizing

Summarizing. The process of preparing a concise description of verbal or written passages.

Comprehension monitoring. The process of checking to see if we understand what we have read or heard.

Summarizing is the process of preparing a concise description of verbal or written passages. It is effective for **comprehension monitoring**—checking to see if we understand what we have read or heard. If we can prepare a summary of a topic, it is one indicator that we understand it.

Learning to summarize takes time and effort, but with training, students can become skilled at it (P. Alexander, 2003, 2006). Training usually involves walking students through a passage and helping them construct general descriptions, generate statements that relate ideas to each other, and identify unimportant information (J. P. Byrnes, 2001a).

For instance, we might summarize the problem-solving section of this chapter as follows:

> *To solve problems, we must identify and represent the problem, select and implement a strategy to solve it, and check to see if the solution makes sense. We can help our students become better problem solvers by examining the thinking of experts, using real-world problems, discussing problems and solutions, and using questioning and worked examples to scaffold novice problem solvers.*

Research suggests that summarizing can increase both students' understanding of the topics they study and their metacognitive skills (Thiede & Anderson, 2003). As a modification, having students generate key terms that capture the essence of a text passage can also increase comprehension (Thiede, Anderson, & Therriault, 2003).

Elaborative Questioning

Elaborative questioning is the process of drawing inferences, identifying examples, and forming relationships. It is arguably the most effective comprehension-monitoring strategy because it encourages learners to create connections in the material they're studying (E. Wood et al., 1999). Three elaborative questions are especially effective:

Elaborative questioning. The process of drawing inferences, identifying examples, and forming relationships in the material being studied.

- What is another example of this idea?
- How is this topic similar to or different from the one in the previous section?
- How does this idea relate to other ideas I have been studying?

For example, as you were studying the section on problem solving, you could have asked questions, such as

What is another example of a well-defined problem in this class?
What is an example of an ill-defined problem?
What makes the first well-defined and the second ill-defined?
How are problem-solving and learning strategies similar? How are they different?

Questions such as these create links between new information and knowledge in long-term memory, which makes the new information more meaningful.

SQ3R

SQ3R is a complex strategy that teaches students to use a series of sequential steps to monitor comprehension while reading. Its origins go back to the 1940s, and it has earned the title "the grandfather of study strategies" (Lipson & Wixson, 2003). The steps in SQ3R are

1. **Survey:** Students survey the text they're about to read.
2. **Question:** Based on their prereading, students create elaborative questions that they expect to be answered as they read.
3. **Read:** Students read the material.
4. **Recite:** Students reflect on what they've read, try to answer their questions, and find relationships between the passage and earlier passages. (As you see here, students are doing much more than literally "reciting" in this step.)
5. **Review:** Learners summarize what they've read, reread parts of the passage about which they're uncertain, and take notes if necessary.

The effectiveness of SQ3R is not clear. Some authors support its use (e.g., R. L. Potter, 1999; Topping & McManus, 2002), but their endorsement appears to be based primarily on the strategy's long-term reputation (Spor & Schneider, 1999). Evidence indicating that SQ3R is effective is largely lacking (Huber, 2004).

On the other hand, it incorporates *using text signals* in the first step, *elaborative questioning* in the second, and *summarizing* in the final step (Thiede & Anderson, 2003). Whether or not these strategies are more effective when synthesized into a comprehensive strategy such as SQ3R than they would be alone is uncertain.

Research indicates that most students can learn study strategies, and strategy instruction is especially important for younger students and low achievers, because they have a smaller repertoire of strategies (Bruning et al., 2004; Gaskill & Murphy, 2004). The effectiveness of the strategies depends on learners' motivation, their ability to activate relevant prior knowledge, and their metacognition (Huber, 2004). If one or more of these factors is missing, no strategy is effective.

MyEducationLab

To examine learners' use of strategies at different developmental levels, go to the *Activities and Application* section in Chapter 9 of MyEducationLab at www.myeducationlab.com, and watch *Video 1: Memory and Cognition: Early and Middle Childhood* and *Video 2: Memory and Cognition: Early and Late Adolescence.* Answer the questions following the episodes.

Critical Thinking

Critical thinking is becoming increasingly important in today's world because of the large amounts of advertising, conscious distortions, and even propaganda that we must constantly sift through. **Critical thinking** has been defined in various ways, but most definitions include an individual's ability and inclination to make and assess conclusions based on evidence (van Gelder, 2005; Willingham, 2007). For example, an advertisement says, "Doctors recommend . . . more often," touting a health product. A person thinking critically

Critical thinking. An individual's ability and inclination to make and assess conclusions based on evidence.

Asking students to provide evidence for their conclusions promotes critical thinking.

is wary because the advertisement provides no evidence for its claims. Similarly, a critical thinker listens to another person's argument with skepticism because people often have unconscious biases.

The Challenge of Critical Thinking

Making and assessing conclusions based on evidence is more difficult than it appears, and most people are not good at it (Willingham, 2007). For example, when asked to justify an opinion, "to provide some evidence to back it up—more than half the population flounder. . . . The problem is that they do not have a general grasp of the notion of evidence and what would properly count as providing evidence in support of their view" (van Gelder, 2005, p. 42).

Some experts also suggest that humans are not naturally disposed to think critically, and high achievers often think no more critically than do lower achievers (Macpherson & Stanovich, 2007). We want experiences to make sense, and if we find an account that seems valid, we rarely pursue the matter further (Shermer, 2002).

Belief preservation. The tendency to make evidence subservient to belief, rather than the other way around.

Belief preservation, the tendency to make evidence subservient to belief, rather than the other way around, poses an additional challenge (Douglas, 2000). When we strongly believe an idea, or desire it to be true, we tend to seek evidence that supports the belief and avoid or ignore evidence that disputes it, or we retain beliefs in the face of overwhelming contrary evidence if we can find some minimal support for the belief.

Constructivist learning theory and Piaget's work help us understand these tendencies. People construct knowledge that makes sense to them. When experiences make sense, even if they're illusory or distorted, we are at equilibrium, so we have no need to pursue a matter further.

In addition, people sometimes have a personal investment in existing beliefs. They feel that changing the beliefs negatively reflects on their intelligence or their resolve, so the change threatens their sense of self-worth (Linnenbrink & Pintrich, 2003). Also, beliefs are sometimes integral to their culture or religion (Southerland & Sinatra, 2003). Meeting these challenges is at the heart of instruction that promotes critical thinking, and experts believe that critical thinking should be integrated into the regular curriculum (Burke, Williams, & Skinner, 2007; Kuhn, 1999; Willingham, 2007).

Promoting Critical Thinking

With awareness and planning, teachers can make critical thinking an integral part of instruction (Burke et al., 2007; Macpherson, & Stanovich, 2007). The following guidelines can be helpful in this process:

- Make questions such as, "Why do you say that?" and "How do you know?" a part of your questioning repertoire. These questions require students to provide evidence for their conclusions, and, in many cases, they follow naturally from other questions.
- Promote metacognition by helping students become aware of their own thinking.
- Model thinking dispositions, such as the use of evidence in making conclusions, a sense of curiosity and a desire to be informed, and a willingness to respect opinions different from your own.

As an illustration of these guidelines, let's go back to Laura's Tuesday lesson. She had written the following on the board:

$15 \times 3 = 45$ square feet
$12 \times 3 = 36$ square feet
$45 + 36 = 81$ square feet

theory to practice

Helping Students Become Strategic Learners

Cognitive learning theory offers suggestions for helping your students become better strategy users. The following guidelines can help you in your efforts (Pressley & Harris, 2006):

1. Describe the strategy, and explain why it is useful.
2. Explicitly teach the strategy by modeling both its use and metacognitive awareness.
3. Provide opportunities for students to practice the strategy in a variety of contexts.
4. Provide feedback as students practice.

Let's see how Donna Evans, a middle school geography teacher, attempts to apply the guidelines.

Donna begins her geography class by giving each of her students a blank transparency and a marking pen.

She directs them to the section of her text that describes the low-, middle-, and high-latitude climates, and says, "One way to become more effective readers is to summarize the information we read in a few short statements that capture its meaning. This makes the information easier to remember, and it will help us compare one climate region with another. You can do the same thing when you study different classes of animals in biology or parts of the court system in government. . . . Now read the section on page 237, and see if you can identify the features of a low-latitude climate."

The class reads the section, and Donna continues, "As I was reading, here's how I thought about it, and she then displays the following information on a transparency and describes her thinking.

Low latitudes can be hot and wet or hot and dry. Close to the equator, the humid tropical climate is hot and wet all year. Farther away, it has wet summers and dry winters. In the dry tropical climate, high-pressure zones cause deserts, like the Sahara."

She then says "Now, let's all give it a try with the section on the middle-latitude climates. Go ahead and read the section, and try to summarize it the way I did. . . . Write your summaries on your transparencies, and we'll share what you've written."

After they finish, Donna asks a student to volunteer a summary.

Kari volunteers, displays her summary, and Donna and other students add information and comments to what Kari has written. Donna then has two other students display their summaries, and the class practices again with the section on the high-latitude climates.

Throughout the school year, Donna continues to have her students practice summarizing once or twice a week.

Now let's look at Donna's efforts to apply the guidelines. She began by describing the process of summarizing and explaining why it is useful. For instance, she said, "One way to become more effective readers is to summarize the information we read in a few short statements that capture its meaning. This makes information easier to remember. . . ."

She then applied the second guideline by modeling both the skill and metacognition when she commented, "As I was reading, here's how I thought about it. . . ." Research indicates that young children's metacognitive awareness can be increased with explicit instruction such as this (J. M. Alexander, Johnson, & Leibham, 2005; G. M. Jacobs, 2004).

Donna then had students practice by having them read a passage, prepare a summary, and provide feedback. She had them display their summaries on the overhead, so everyone would be responding to the same information. And, she continued the process throughout the school year.

Continued practice is essential. As with all forms of complex learning, it requires a great deal of experience and deliberate practice.

Now, look again at some of the dialogue.

Laura: Someone explain where these numbers came from.
Nephi: The 15 is the length of that part (pointing to the bottom of the diagram). And the 3 is how wide it is . . . so, the area is 45.
Laura: Forty-five what?
Nephi: Square feet.
Laura: Now, let's be good thinkers. How do we know that the second statement must be 12 times 3?
Anya: . . . I've got it!
Laura: Come up and show us.
Anya: See, we already have this (pointing to the lower right corner of the drawing). So, this length is 12, not 15. . . . So, it's 12 times 3.

Laura then completes the activity and assigns homework.

Laura: Now, what do we always ask ourselves when we try a strategy?
Shayna: Does it make sense?
Laura: Yes, exactly. You'll need to be ready to explain how you got your answers.

In this exchange, Laura asked students to justify their thinking, and she promoted metacognition in asking, "What do we always do when we try a strategy?" With practice, students improve, and it takes a minimum of additional effort from teachers.

exploring diversity

Learner Differences in Complex Cognitive Processes

The basic processes involved in concept learning, problem solving, and strategic learning are essentially the same for all students. However, their cultural knowledge, approaches to problem solving, and attitudes and beliefs will vary. For example, as you first saw in Chapter 2, the Yu'pik people living in the Bering Sea just west of Alaska have 99 different concepts for ice (Block, 2007). This is cultural knowledge important to them as they travel and hunt, but it's alien to most of us living in warmer climates.

Cultural differences also exist in the way people approach concept learning. For example, adults in western cultures tend to classify items *taxonomically,* such as putting animals in one group, food items in another, and tools in a third. However, adults in some other cultures classify items into *functional groups*, such as putting a shovel and potato together, because a shovel is used to dig up a potato (Luria, 1976).

Attitudes and beliefs are also influenced by cultural differences. For instance, learning-related attitudes and beliefs are offered as an explanation for the impressive problem-solving achievements of Japanese students. "Attitudes toward achievement emphasize that success comes from hard work (not from innate ability). . . . Teachers examined a few problems in depth rather than covering many problems superficially; children's errors were used as learning tools for the group" (Rogoff, 2003, pp. 264–265). Believing in hard work and accepting errors as a normal part of the learning process are important achievement-oriented values (J. Li & Fischer, 2004).

In view of their impressive academic achievements, the fact that early childhood education in Japan focuses on social development instead of academics may be surprising (Abe & Izzard, 1999; C. C. Lewis, 1995). Some experts believe this emphasis helps children feel part of a group and responsible to it, which results in greater attention to the topics being taught and fewer classroom-management problems (Rogoff, 2003).

Culture also influences strategic learning. For example, students use more effective comprehension-monitoring strategies when exposed to written materials consistent with their cultural experiences (Pritchard, 1990).

Interestingly, few cultural differences in memory performance are found when tasks are embedded in real-world contexts. For example, when people, such as vendors, carpenters, or dieters, use math for practical purposes, they rarely get answers that don't make sense. "However, calculations in the context of schooling regularly produce some absurd errors, with results that are impossible if the meaning of the problem is being considered" (Rogoff, 2003, p. 262). This was illustrated in Laura's lesson. Even though finding the carpeted area of the classroom was a real-world task for her students, some were willing to accept widely varying answers to the problem, even answers that didn't make sense. This demonstrates the need to promote metacognition and provide a great deal of scaffolding for all learners, regardless of their cultural backgrounds.

Experiences and cultural and religious beliefs can also influence critical thinking. Learners whose early school experiences involve a great deal of memory-level tasks are more likely to use primitive study strategies, such as rehearsal, and they are less equipped to be critical thinkers than are their peers with different experiences. Memory-level tasks are common in urban schools, and urban schools typically have large numbers of minorities (Kozol, 2005). Also, members of cultures who have been taught to respect elders, and learners with strong authoritarian religious beliefs, may be less disposed to critical thinking (Kuhn & Park, 2005; Qian & Pan, 2002).

These differences all point to the need to embed learning experiences in real-world contexts, promote high levels of interaction, and provide the scaffolding that will help students make sense of those experiences. This is true for all students, regardless of their cultural backgrounds.

MyEducationLab

To examine a teacher's attempt to help students with diverse learning backgrounds learn to find the areas of irregular figures, go to the *Activities and Applications* section in Chapter 9 of MyEducationLab at www.myeducationlab.com, and read the case study *Finding Areas of Irregular Figures.* Answer the questions following the case study.

check your understanding

3.1 Three students are discussing the use of highlighting as a study strategy.

"I highlight the first sentence of nearly every paragraph, because that's supposed to be the topic sentence," Alexie comments. "Sometimes I highlight other sentences if they seem to be the topic sentence."

"I highlight passages that I think are important," Ruiz adds. "I look for key terms and lists and examples."

"I highlight practically whole chapters," Will offers. "I read along with it as I'm highlighting."

Which student is using the most effective strategy? Whose strategy is least effective? Explain.

3.2 You read this chapter carefully in an effort to understand the content. Does your effort illustrate strategic learning? Explain why or why not.

3.3 Mrs. Solis's students are analyzing a table illustrating the average global temperature for the years 1960 to 2000. They conclude that the table shows a general increase. "What have we done here?" Mrs. Solis asks.

"We've found a pattern in the data," Francisco responds.

What important aspect of critical thinking is Mrs. Solis promoting with her question? Explain.

To receive feedback for these questions, go to Appendix A.

classroom connections

Promoting Strategic Learning and Critical Thinking in Your Classroom

Study Strategies

1. Study strategies are techniques learners use to increase their understanding of written materials and teacher presentations. Teach study strategies across the curriculum to make them most effective.
   - **Elementary:** A second-grade teacher models elaborative questioning and encourages her children to ask themselves what each lesson was about and what they learned from it.
   - **Middle School:** A sixth-grade teacher introduces note taking as a study skill. He then provides note-taking practice in his social studies class by using skeletal outlines to organize his presentations and by having his students use them as a guide for their note taking.
   - **High School:** A biology teacher closes each lesson by having her students provide summaries of the most important parts of the lesson. She adds material to summaries that are incomplete.

Critical Thinking

2. Helping students learn to make and assess conclusions based on evidence promotes critical thinking. Integrate critical thinking into the regular curriculum.
   - **Elementary:** A fourth-grade teacher makes it a point to ask questions, such as (1) What do you observe? (2) How are these alike or different? (3) Why is A different from B? (4) What would happen if . . . ? (5) How do you know?
   - **Middle School:** A seventh-grade geography teacher develops her topics with examples, charts, graphs, and tables. She develops lessons around students' observations, comparisons, and conclusions related to the information they see, and she requires students to provide evidence for their conclusions.
   - **High School:** An English teacher helps his students analyze literature by asking questions such as, "How do you know that?" and, "What in the story supports your idea?"

Transfer of Learning

Consider the following situation:

> *You get into your car, put the key in the ignition, and the seat-belt buzzer goes off. You quickly buckle the belt. Or, anticipating the buzzer, you buckle the belt before you insert the key. How might we explain your behavior?*

If you explained your behavior—buckling the seat belt—as the result of negative reinforcement, you have demonstrated **transfer**, the ability to take understanding acquired in one context and apply it to a different context (R. Mayer & Wittrock, 2006). Because schools cannot teach students everything they need to know, the ability to transfer is essential. Transfer is the ability to recognize or provide a new example of a concept, solve a unique problem, or apply a learning strategy to a new situation (De Corte, 2007). One way to think of transfer is as "preparation for future learning" (D. Schwartz et al., 2005, p. 5).

Transfer. The ability to take understanding acquired in one context and apply it to a different context.

Recalling information doesn't involve transfer. If, for example, your instructor has previously discussed buckling the seat belt as an example of negative reinforcement, you merely remembered the information.

Transfer can be either positive or negative. Positive transfer occurs when learning in one context facilitates learning in another, whereas negative transfer occurs when learning in one situation hinders performance in another (R. Mayer & Wittrock, 2006). For instance, positive transfer occurs if students know that a mammal nurses its young and breathes through lungs and then conclude that a whale is a mammal. On the other hand, if they believe that a fish is an animal that lives in the sea and conclude that a whale is a fish, negative transfer has occurred.

General and Specific Transfer

At one time, educators advocated taking courses such as Latin or mathematics to "discipline" the mind. If they had accomplished this goal, **general transfer**, the ability to apply knowledge or skills learned in one context to a wide variety of different contexts, would have occurred (Phye, 2005). For example, if playing chess would help a person learn math, because both require logic, general transfer would occur. **Specific transfer** is the ability to apply information in a context similar to the one in which it was originally learned. For example, when students know that the Greek prefix *photos* means "light" and it helps them better understand the concept *photosynthesis*, specific transfer has occurred.

General transfer. The ability to apply knowledge or skills learned in one context in a variety of different contexts.

Specific transfer. The ability to apply information in a context similar to the one in which it was originally learned.

Research over many years has consistently confirmed that general transfer is rare (Driscoll, 2005; E. Thorndike, 1924). Studying Latin, for example, results in specific transfer to the Latin roots of English words; it does little to improve thinking in general.

Factors Affecting the Transfer of Learning

Several factors affect students' ability to transfer:

- Similarity between learning situations
- Depth of learners' original understanding
- Quality and variety of examples and other learning experiences
- Learning context
- Emphasis on metacognition

Similarity Between Learning Situations

The more closely two learning situations are related, the more likely transfer is to occur (L. S. Fuchs et al., 2003; Phye, 2001). For instance, when first graders are given this problem,

> *Angi has two pieces of candy. Kim gives her three more pieces of candy. How many pieces does Angi have now?*

they do well on this one:

> *Bruce had three pencils. His friend Orlando gave him two more. How many pencils does Bruce have now?*

However, when they're given the problem with Angi and Kim followed by this problem,

> *Sophie has three cookies. Flavio has four cookies. How many do they have together?*

they perform less well (Riley, Greeno, & Heller, 1982). The first two are more closely related than the first and third, and transfer is more likely to occur between the first two.

Similarly, if children understand that a dog, horse, mouse, and deer are mammals, they're more likely to conclude that a cow is a mammal than to conclude that a seal is one, because a cow is more similar to the other examples than is a seal. These results further demonstrate that transfer is specific.

Depth of Original Understanding

Transfer requires a high level of original understanding, and research indicates that students often fail to transfer because they don't understand the topic in the first place (Bereiter & Scardamalia, 2006; DeCorte, 2003).

The more practice and feedback learners have with the topics they study, the greater the likelihood that transfer will occur (Moreno & Mayer, 2005). And, the value of guided experiences even applies to infants and young children (Barrett, Davis, & Needham, 2007; Tunteler, & Resing, 2007).

So, what do teachers do when students' original understanding lacks depth? Provide learners with a variety of high-quality examples, and embed them in meaningful contexts.

Quality of Examples

In Chapter 8, we emphasized the importance of high-quality examples and other representations of content in helping learners construct their knowledge. You may want to reread this section, beginning on page 240, and also look again at Table 8.1 on page 241, which outlines the ways several teachers you've studied in this book represented their topics.

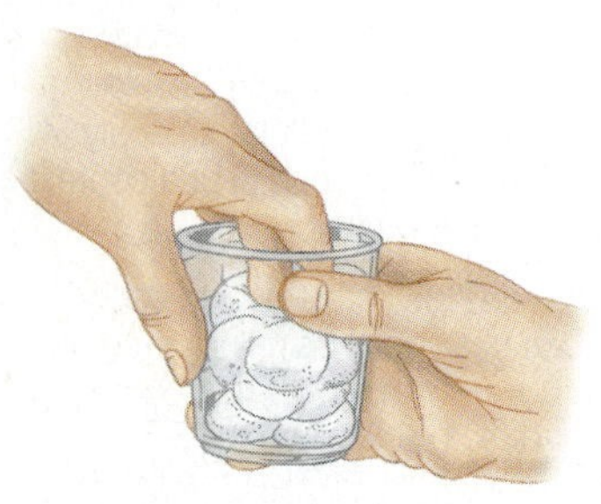

Karen Johnson's compressed cotton example in the case on page 32 of Chapter 2 is a good illustration of a high-quality example for the concept *density*. Students can *see* that no cotton balls were added or removed, so the mass of cotton hasn't changed. They can also *see* that the compressed cotton takes up less space, so compressing the cotton increases its density. These kinds of experiences are important for all students but are particularly important for those who lack school-related prior knowledge.

classroom connections

Promoting Transfer in Your Classroom

1. Transfer occurs when knowledge learned in one context is applied in a different context. To promote transfer, provide examples and applications of the content you teach in a variety of different contexts.
   - **Elementary:** A fourth-grade teacher selects samples of student writing to teach grammar and punctuation rules. She displays samples on overheads and uses the samples as the basis for her instruction.
   - **Middle School:** A science teacher begins a discussion of light refraction by asking students why they can see better with their glasses on than they can without them. He then illustrates refraction by putting a pencil in a glass of water, so the pencil appears differently above and below the water line and asks the students to look at objects through magnifying lenses.
   - **High School:** A geometry teacher illustrates applications of course content with examples from architecture. She also uses photographs from magazines and slides to illustrate how math concepts relate to the real world.
2. High-quality examples provide the experiences learners need to construct knowledge and promote transfer. Use high-quality examples and representations to promote transfer in the topics you are teaching.
   - **Elementary:** A fifth-grade teacher illustrates the concept *volume* by putting 1-cm cubes in a box 4 cm long, 3 cm wide, and 2 cm high. He instructs the students to count the cubes until the box is filled with 24 cubes. Then he relates the activity to the formula for finding volume.
   - **Middle School:** A history teacher writes short cases to illustrate hard-to-understand concepts, such as *mercantilism*. She guides students' analyses of the cases, helping them identify the essential characteristics of the concepts.
   - **High School:** An English teacher prepares a matrix illustrating the characters, setting, and themes for several of Shakespeare's plays. Students use the information to summarize and draw conclusions about Shakespeare's works.

Variety of Examples

To see how variety influences transfer, let's look again at the vignette Carol Lopez used to help her students understand the concept *adjective* in the "Theory to Practice" feature as part of our discussion of concept learning. Here it is again.

> *John and Karen, with her brown hair blowing in the wind, drove together in his old car to the football game. They soon met their very best friends, Latoya and Michael, at the large gate near the entrance. The game was incredibly exciting, and because the team's running game was sparkling, the home team won by a bare margin.*

In the vignette, *brown, old, football, best, large, exciting, running, sparkling, home,* and *bare* are all adjectives. An array of examples is provided, illustrating the idea of multiple knowledge representations, which research indicates is valuable for constructing knowledge and promoting transfer (D. Schwartz et al., 2005; Spiro et al., 1992). For instance, two of the examples—*exciting* and *sparkling*—follow the nouns they modify, so students won't conclude that adjectives always precede nouns, a common misconception in grammar. Each example adds perspectives that others may miss and increases the likelihood of learners experiencing examples that are individually meaningful to them.

In another case, a sea turtle would be an important example for a lesson on *reptiles,* just as a bat would be an important example for *mammals.* A sea turtle would help learners understand that reptiles can live in water, and the bat would help them realize that some mammals fly.

Transfer is facilitated by quality learning experiences in a variety of contexts.

Learning Context

Social constructivist learning theory and situated cognition help us understand why context is so important. As an illustration, look again at the vignette illustrating the concept *adjective.* In it *football, home,* and *running* are all adjectives. If the examples were presented as isolated words rather than in the context of the vignette, students would conclude that *football* and *home* are nouns and *running* is a verb.

developmentally appropriate practice

Developing Complex Cognitive Skills with Different-Aged Learners

While learners of all ages can develop higher-level cognitive skills, important developmental differences exist. The following paragraphs outline some of them.

Working with Elementary Students

The concepts young children construct are generally concrete and best explained by rule-driven theories of concept learning. This explains why we see concepts such as *triangle, circle, pets*, and *farm animals* taught to kindergarten children. Young learners often overgeneralize, classifying spiders as insects, for example, or they undergeneralize, such as limiting adverbs to any words that end in *ly*. Because of this tendency, providing a variety of high-quality examples and discussing them thoroughly are important with young learners.

Their tendencies to center also impact their problem solving. For example, young children tend to use superficial strategies in solving word problems, such as, looking for key words like *altogether*, which suggests that they add, or *how many more*, which suggests subtraction. These strategies can bypass understanding completely but are often quite successful (Schoenfeld, 1991, 2006). To accommodate these patterns, asking young students to put their thinking into words is essential. They need a great deal of scaffolding, so patience and effort are required.

Young children also tend to be "strategically inert," either not using learning strategies at all, or employing primitive strategies such as rehearsal. While their lack of prior knowledge is often a factor, with effort and patience, they can learn to use strategies quite effectively (Kato & Manning, 2007).

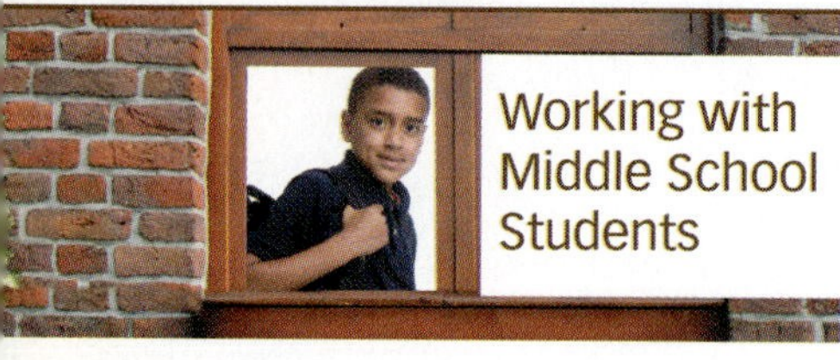

Working with Middle School Students

Middle school students' maturation makes them capable of constructing abstract concepts, such as *culture* and *justice*, the learning of which are better explained by prototype and exemplar theories. However, many older students lack the experiences needed to make abstract concepts meaningful, so they are best represented as concretely as possible. For example, Suzanne Schellenberg, a 7th-grade teacher, used vignettes, such as the following, to illustrate the concept *anaphylactic shock* (a body's overreaction to a minor stimulus) for her students:

> Chet is walking through some tall grass on property he has just purchased. He hears a buzzing sound and suddenly feels a sharp sting on his leg. Within minutes Chet feels his throat swelling up, and it becomes very difficult for him to breathe. Beginning to panic, he calls 911 on his cell phone.
>
> Twelve-year-old Amiel recently moved from Alaska to Florida. It's her first day of school, and Amiel, who is sitting with Janine, a classmate, at lunch, unwraps her tuna sandwich as Janine munches on her peanut butter and jelly sandwich. Amiel smells something she has never smelled before and asks Janine what she is eating. Before Janine can answer Amiel falls off her chair and is curled up on the floor gasping for breath. The students at Amiel's table yell for help. One of the lunchroom workers calls 911. (S. Schellenberg, personal communication, May 10, 2008).

Concrete representations of topics such as these are much more meaningful for middle school students than attempts to describe them.

Middle school students also tend to lack the metacognition needed to monitor their problem solving. For example, 13-year-olds were given the following problem:

An army bus holds 36 soldiers. If 1,128 soldiers are being bused to their training site, how many buses are needed?

Fewer than one fourth of the 13-year-olds answered it correctly; most of the other students either dropped the remainder or reported 31 1/3 buses, ignoring the fact that a third of a bus is meaningless (T. O'Brien, 1999). With middle school students, teachers need to emphasize evaluating the results of problem solving to ensure that the results make sense (Shoenfeld, 2006).

Middle school students can use sophisticated learning strategies but rarely do so unless their teachers model and encourage the strategies (Pressley & Harris, 2006). Efforts such as Donna Evans made can be very effective (see "Theory to Practice" on page 273 at the end of our discussion of strategic learning).

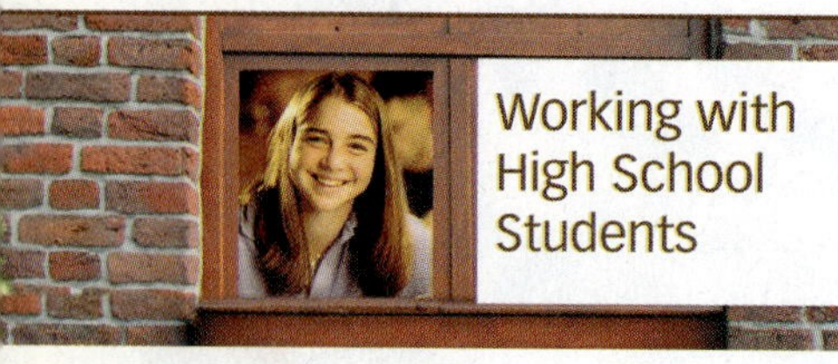

Working with High School Students

Though Piaget described high-school aged students as formal operational, most are not. This suggests that using analogies, role playing, simulations, and vignettes, such as the one illustrating *anaphylactic shock*, continues to be important for making abstract concepts meaningful to these students.

With respect to problem solving, authentic activities and real-world applications are particularly important for older students who want to see the utility of their experiences.

Many older students use strategies, such as highlighting, passively instead of making decisions about what is most important to highlight (Pressley & Harris, 2006). Often, they fail to monitor their comprehension as well as they should, which leads them to overestimate how well they understand the topics they study (W. Schneider & Lockl, 2002). For this reason, encouraging study strategies across the curriculum and emphasizing metacognition are important with these students.

Also, students are more likely to transfer their understanding of the law of inertia if the law is applied to seatbelts and headrests in cars or other real-world applications than if the ideas are not applied to everyday examples (D. Schwartz et al., 2005). Similarly, to promote transfer of problem solving, students need to solve a variety of real-world problems, and transfer of strategies requires that students use the strategies in a variety of contexts.

MyEducationLab

To examine a teacher's attempt to promote problem solving and transfer in his students, go to the *Building Teaching Skills and Dispositions* section in Chapter 9 of MyEducationLab at www.myeducationlab.com, and watch the video episode *Designing Experiments*. Complete the exercises following the episodes to build your skills in promoting problem solving and transfer in your students.

Emphasis on Metacognition

Metacognition also increases transfer, and in some cases, even general transfer (Donovan & Bransford, 2005; Pressley & Harris, 2006). For example, remaining open-minded, reserving judgment, searching for facts to support conclusions, and taking personal responsibility for learning are general dispositions, all grounded in metacognition. Teachers can encourage transfer of these dispositions through modeling across disciplines and by communicating that learning is a meaningful activity that is facilitated by awareness of their own thinking.

check your understanding

4.1 You have shown your students pictures of a *dog, cat, horse*, and *deer* in an effort to help them understand the concept *mammal*. Which of the following—*cow, mouse, dolphin*, or *squirrel*—are they *least likely* to identify as a mammal? Which factor influencing transfer is best illustrated in this case? Explain.

4.2. Using the factors that affect transfer as a basis for answering, how effective were your efforts when you used the pictures of a dog, cat, horse, and deer in 4.1? Explain.

4.3 You want to teach your students the concept of *internal conflict* in literature. Which of the following is the highest quality example: (1) a picture of a girl with a thoughtful look on her face, and a caption saying, "The girl is experiencing internal conflict"; (2) the statement, "Shelly didn't know what to do. She was looking forward to the class trip, but if she went, she wouldn't be able to take the scholarship qualifying test," displayed on the overhead; or (3) the statement, "Internal conflict represents a dilemma of a person caught between two unpleasant alternatives," displayed on the overhead? Explain.

To receive feedback for these questions, go to Appendix A.

Meeting Your Learning Objectives

1. Define concepts, and identify applications of concept learning theory.
   - A concept is a mental construct or representation of a category that allows us to identify examples and nonexamples of the category.
   - Rule-driven theories of concept learning are applied when people learn well-defined concepts such as *perimeter, adjective*, and *latitude*.
   - Prototype theories of concept learning are applied when learners construct concepts on the basis of a prototype, which is the best representation of its class.
   - Exemplar theories are applied when learners construct concepts on the basis of the most highly typical examples of a class or category.
2. Identify examples of ill-defined and well-defined problems, and describe applications of a general problem-solving model.
   - A problem occurs when a person has a goal but lacks an obvious way of achieving the goal.
   - A well-defined problem, such as finding the solution for $3x + 4 = 13$, has only one correct solution and a certain method for finding it.
   - An ill-defined problem, such as students' failing to accept personal responsibility for their own learning, has an ambiguous goal, more than one acceptable solution, and no generally agreed-upon strategy for reaching a solution.
   - A general problem-solving model includes identifying the problem, representing the problem, selecting a strategy, implementing the strategy, and evaluating the results as stages in the problem-solving process.
   - Deliberate practice involves purposeful and systematic practice combined with detailed feedback.
3. Identify applications of study strategies and critical thinking.
   - Strategies are cognitive operations that exceed the normal activities required to carry out a task. Taking notes

is a strategy, for example, because it is a cognitive operation used to help learners remember more of what they hear or read.

- Learners who use strategies effectively are metacognitive about their approaches to learning. They also possess a repertoire of strategies and prior knowledge about the topics they're studying. Ineffective strategy users are less metacognitive, and they lack prior knowledge and possess fewer strategies.
- Critical thinking is the process of making and assessing conclusions based on evidence. Teachers promote critical thinking when they ask students to justify their thinking and provide evidence for their conclusions.

4. Identify applications of the factors that influence the transfer of learning.
   - Transfer occurs when learners can apply previously learned information in a new context. Specific transfer involves an application in a situation closely related to the original; general transfer occurs when two learning situations are quite different.
   - Teachers apply the factors that influence the transfer of learning when they provide students with a variety of high-quality examples embedded in a real-world context. These examples provide the experiences learners need to construct their knowledge and apply it in new settings.
   - Transfer tends to be specific, but metacognitive and self-regulatory skills may transfer across domains.

Developing as a Professional: Practicing for Your Licensure Exam

In our discussion of problem solving, you saw how Laura Hunter planned and conducted a lesson in an effort to promote thinking and problem solving in her students. Finding that her efforts were ineffective, she provided more scaffolding in a second lesson. Now, look at a teacher with a group of second graders involved in a lesson on graphing. Read the case study, and answer the questions that follow.

Sue Brush has her second graders involved in a unit on graphing. She introduces the day's lesson by saying that she is planning a party for the class but has a problem because she doesn't know the class's favorite flavor of jelly bean.

Students offer suggestions for solving the problem, and they finally settle on having students taste a variety of jelly beans and indicate their favorite.

Anticipating the idea of tasting the jelly beans, Sue has prepared plastic bags with seven different-flavored jelly beans. She gives each student a bag, and after students taste each one, she says, "Okay, I need your help. . . . How can we organize our information so that we can look at it as a whole group?"

Students offer some additional suggestions, and Sue then says, "Here's what we're going to do. Stacey mentioned earlier that we could graph the information, and we have an empty graph up in the front of the room." She moves to the front of the room and displays the outline of a graph:

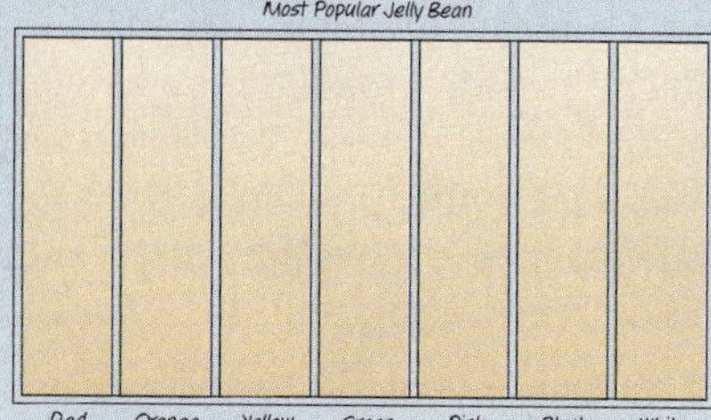

She then asks students to come to the front of the room and paste colored pieces that represent their favorite jelly beans on the graph.

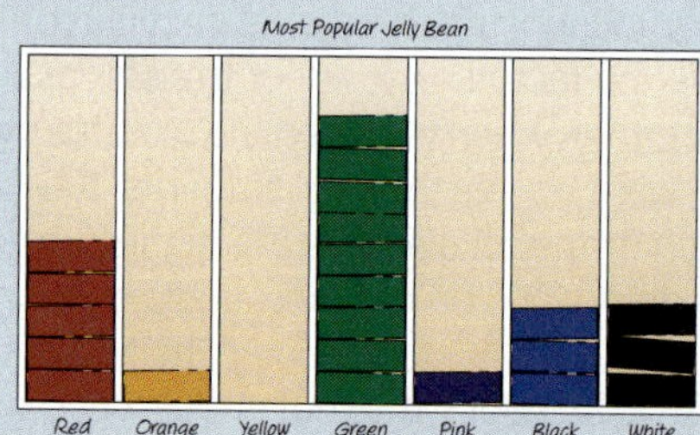

"Now, look up here," she smiles. "We collected and organized the information, so now we want to analyze it. I need you to tell me what we know by looking at the graph. . . . Candice?"

"People like green," Candice answers.

"How many people like green?"

". . . Nine."

"Nine people like green. . . . And how did you find that out? Come up here and show us how you read the graph."

Candice goes up to the graph and moves her hand up from the bottom, counting the nine green squares as she goes.

Sue continues asking students to interpret the graph, and then changes the direction of the lesson by saying, "Okay, here we go. . . . How many more people liked green than red? . . . Look up at the graph, and set up the problem on your paper."

She watches as students look at the graph and set up the problem, and when they're finished, she says, "I'm looking for a volunteer to share an answer with us. . . . Dominique?"

"Nine plus 5 is 14," Dominique answers.

"Dominique says 9 plus 5 is 14. Let's test it out," Sue responds, asking Dominique to go up to the graph and show the class how she arrived at her answer.

As Dominique walks to the front of the room, Sue says, "We want to know the difference. . . . How many more people liked green than red, and you say 14 people, . . . 14 more people liked green. Does that work?"

Dominique looks at the graph for a moment and then says, "I mean 9 take away 5."

"She got up here and she changed her mind," Sue says with a smile to the rest of the class. "Tell them."

"Nine take away 5 is 4," Dominique says.

"Nine take away 5 is 4," Sue continues, "so how many more people liked green than red? . . . Carlos?"

"Four," Carlos responds.

"Four, good, four," she smiles at him warmly. "The key was, you had to find the difference between the two numbers."

Sue has students offer additional problems, they solve and explain them, and she then continues, "I have one more question, and then we'll switch gears. How many people took part in this voting?"

Sue watches as students consider the problem for a few minutes, and then says, "Matt? . . . How many people?"

"Twenty-four."

"Matt said 24. Did anyone get a different answer? So we'll compare. . . . Robert?"

"Twenty-two."

"How did you solve the problem?" she asks Robert.

"Nine plus 5 plus 3 plus 3 plus 1 plus 1 equals 22," he answers, adding up all the squares on the graph.

"Where'd you get all those numbers?"

"There," he says, pointing to the graph. "He went from the highest to the lowest, added them, and the answer was 22."

Sue then breaks the children into groups and has them work at centers where they gather and summarize information in bar graphs. They tally and graph the number of students who have birthdays each month, interview classmates about their favorite soft drinks, and call pizza delivery places to compare the cost of comparable pizzas.

As time for lunch nears, Sue calls the groups back together, and after they're settled, says, "Raise your hand if you can tell me what you learned this morning in math."

"How to bar graph," Jenny responds.

"So, a graph is a way of organizing information, so we can look at it and talk about it. Later we'll look at some additional ways of organizing information," and she ends the lesson.

Short-Answer Questions

In answering these questions, use information from the chapter, and link your responses to specific information in the case.

1. How effectively did Suzanne teach problem solving in her lesson? Explain.
2. To what extent did Sue encourage critical thinking in her lesson? What could she have done to give students more practice in developing critical-thinking abilities?
3. How effective would Sue's lesson have been for promoting transfer? What could Sue have done to increase the likelihood of transfer in her students?

For feedback on these responses, go to Appendix B.

Now go to Chapter 9 of MyEducationLab, located at www.myeducationlab.com, where you can:

- Take a quiz to test your mastery of chapter objectives. Detailed feedback is provided to explain why your responses are correct or incorrect.
- Deepen your understanding of chapter concepts with *Review, Practice, Enrichment* exercises.
- Complete *Activities and Applications* that will help you apply what you have learned in the chapter by analyzing real classrooms through video clips, artifacts, and case studies. Your instructor will provide you with feedback for the *Activities and Applications.*
- Develop your professional knowledge and decision making in *Building Teaching Skills and Dispositions* exercises. Structured feedback will be available to you, providing you with support as you practice each skill. Your instructor will provide you with feedback on the final task that accompanies the exercise.

Important Concepts

algorithm (p. 260)
belief preservation (p. 272)
characteristics (p. 255)
comprehension monitoring (p. 270)
concept (p. 254)
concept mapping (p. 269)
creativity (p. 263)
critical thinking (p. 271)
divergent thinking (p. 264)
drawing analogies (p. 261)
elaborative questioning (p. 271)
exemplar (p. 256)
experts (p. 262)
general transfer (p. 275)
guided notes (p. 269)
heuristics (p. 260)
ill-defined problem (p. 259)
means–ends analysis (p. 260)
network (p. 270)
problem (p. 258)
problem-based learning (p. 264)
prototype (p. 255)
specific transfer (p. 275)
strategies (p. 267)
summarizing (p. 270)
study strategies (p. 268)
text signals (p. 270)
transfer (p. 275)
well-defined problem (p. 259)
worked examples (p. 266)

chapter

10

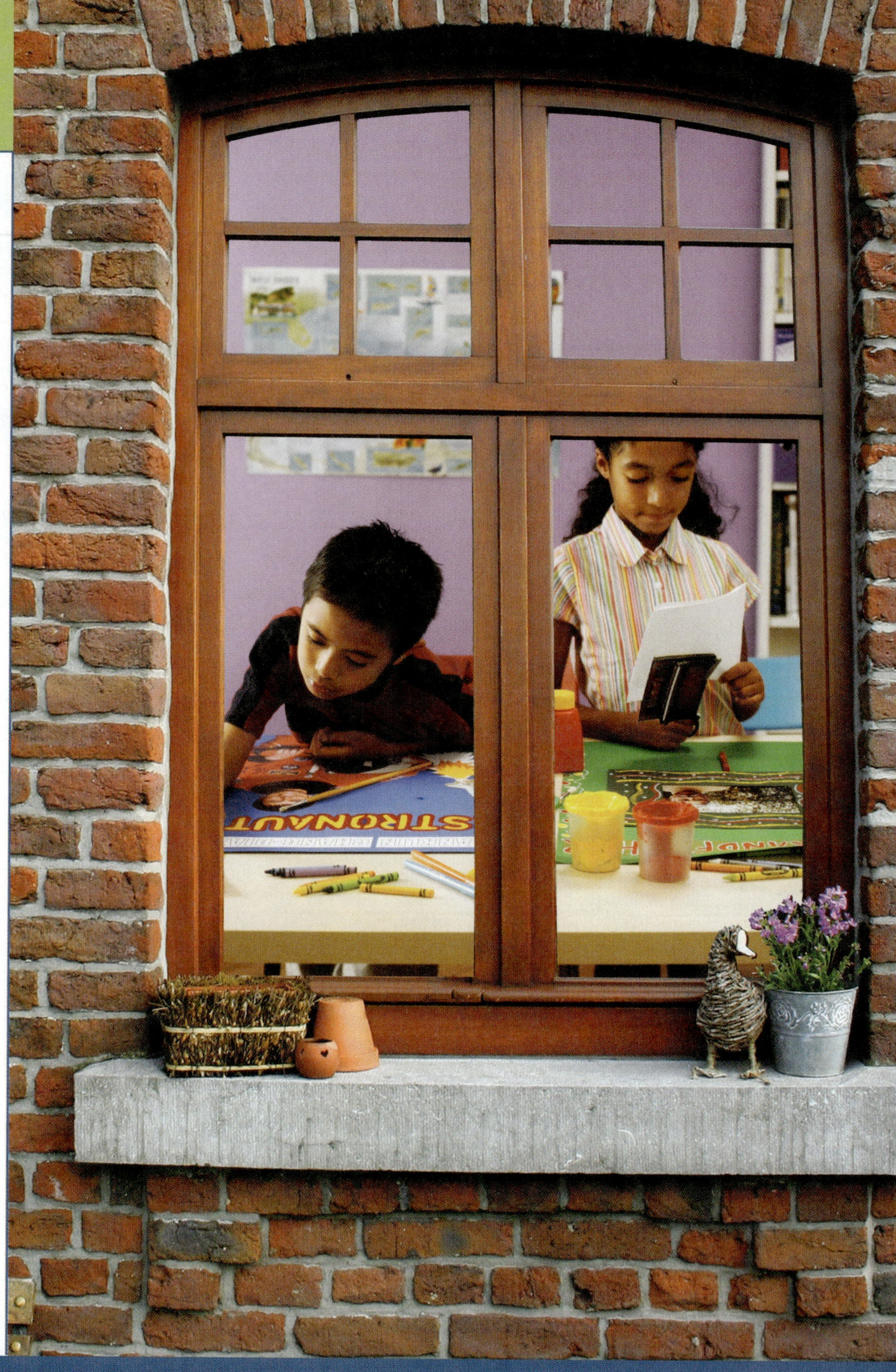

Theories of Motivation

chapter outline

What Is Motivation?

- Extrinsic and Intrinsic Motivation
- Motivation to Learn
- Theoretical Views of Motivation

The Influence of Needs on Motivation to Learn

- Maslow's Hierarchy of Needs
- The Need for Self-Determination
- The Need to Preserve Self-Worth
  - **Theory to Practice:** Capitalizing on Learners' Needs to Increase Motivation to Learn

The Influence of Beliefs on Motivation to Learn

- Expectations: Beliefs About Future Outcomes
- Beliefs About Intelligence
- Self-Efficacy: Beliefs About Capability
- Beliefs About Value
- Attributions: Beliefs About Causes of Performance

The Influence of Goals on Motivation to Learn

- Mastery and Performance Goals
- Social Goals
- Work-Avoidance Goals
- Goals, Motivation, and Achievement
- Using Goals Effectively
  - **Exploring Diversity:** Learner Differences in Motivation to Learn

The Influence of Interest and Emotion on Motivation to Learn

- The Influence of Interest on Motivation to Learn
- The Influence of Emotion on Motivation to Learn
  - **Theory to Practice:** Capitalizing on Students' Beliefs, Goals, and Interests to Increase Motivation to Learn
  - **Developmentally Appropriate Practice:** Motivation to Learn at Different Ages

learning objectives

After you have completed your study of this chapter, you should be able to:

1. Define motivation, and describe different theoretical explanations for learner motivation.
2. Explain how learners' needs influence their motivation to learn.
3. Explain how learners' beliefs can influence their motivation to learn.
4. Explain how learners' goals can influence their motivation to learn.
5. Explain how teachers can capitalize on learners' interests and emotions to increase motivation to learn.

Why do you like some of your classes more than others? Why do you enjoy certain activities, such as reading, games, or sports? The answers to these questions involve *motivation*, which is at the heart of all learning. As you read the following case study involving a high school history class in a unit on the Crusades, think about the students' motivation and their teacher's influence on it.

"We'd better get moving," Susan urges Jim as they approach the door of Kathy Brewster's classroom. "The bell is gonna ring, and you know how Brewster is about this class. She thinks it's sooo important."

"Did you finish your homework?" Jim asks and then stops himself. "What am I talking about? You always do your homework."

"Actually, I've always liked history and knowing about the past, . . . and I'm pretty good at it. My dad helps me. He says he wants to keep up with the world," Susan laughs.

"In some classes, I just do enough to get a decent grade, but not in here," Jim responds. "I used to hate history, but I sometimes even read ahead a little, because Brewster makes you think. She's so gung ho, and it's kind of interesting the way she's always telling us about the way we are because of something that happened a zillion years ago—I never thought about this stuff in that way before."

"Gee, Mrs. Brewster, that assignment was impossible," Harvey grumbles as he comes in the room.

"That's good for you," Kathy smiles. "I know it was a tough assignment, but you need to be challenged. It's hard for me, too, when I'm studying and trying to put together new ideas, but if I hang in, I always feel like I can get it."

"Aw, c'mon, Mrs. Brewster. You know everything."

"I wish. I study every night to keep up with you people, and the harder I study, the smarter I get. . . . And I feel good about it when I do."

"But you make us work so hard," Harvey continues.

"Yes, but look how good you're getting at writing," Kathy smiles again. "I think you hit a personal best on your last paper. You're becoming a very good writer."

"Yeah, yeah, I know," Harvey replies on his way to his desk, "and being good writers will help us in everything we do in life," echoing a rationale the students often hear from Kathy.

"Stop by and see me after class," Kathy quietly says to Jenny as she comes in the room. "I'd like to talk to you for a minute."

"Just a reminder," Kathy says after the students are settled in their desks, "group presentations on the Renaissance are on Thursday and Friday. You decide what groups will present on each day. Remember, we're all doing our best; we're not competing with each other. . . . Also, for those who chose to write the paper on the Middle Ages, we agreed that they're due on Friday."

We'll return to Kathy's lesson later in the chapter, but for now we pose three questions:

1. How does Susan's general orientation toward school differ from Jim's?
2. How does Jim's motivation in Kathy's class differ from his other classes?
3. How has Kathy influenced Jim's motivation?

Theories of motivation help us answer these and other questions, and we examine applications of these theories in this chapter.

What Is Motivation?

Motivation. A process whereby goal-directed activity is instigated and sustained.

"**Motivation** is the process whereby goal-directed activity is instigated and sustained" (Schunk, Pintrich & Meece, 2008, p. 4). For example, if we work hard to solve a math problem or attempt to perfect a golf swing, we say we are motivated in each case. Solving the problem and perfecting the swing are the goals, and we are maintaining and sustaining our efforts to reach them.

Learners' motivation is the primary factor influencing both test performance and success in school (N. E. Perry, Turner, & Meyer, 2006; K. E. Ryan, Ryan, Arbuthnot, & Samuels, 2007). Also, given rapid technological advances, an ever-expanding knowledge base, and shifting workplace needs, a continuing motivation to learn is essential for success in life (Eisenman, 2007; Horst, Finney, & Barron, 2007). In general, motivated students

- Have positive attitudes toward school and describe school as satisfying.
- Persist on difficult tasks and cause few management problems.
- Process information in depth and excel in classroom learning experiences. (Stipek, 1996, 2002)

Not surprisingly, motivated students are a primary source of job satisfaction for teachers.

Extrinsic and Intrinsic Motivation

Extrinsic motivation. Motivation to engage in an activity as a means to an end.

Intrinsic motivation. Motivation to be involved in an activity for its own sake.

Motivation is often classified into two broad categories. **Extrinsic motivation** is motivation to engage in an activity as a means to an end, whereas **intrinsic motivation** is motivation to be involved in an activity for its own sake (Schunk et al., 2008). Extrinsically motivated learners may study for a test because they believe studying will lead to a good grade, for example; intrinsically motivated learners study because they want to understand the content and they view learning as worthwhile in itself. This helps answer our first question (How does Susan's general orientation toward school differ from Jim's?). Jim's comment, "In some classes, I just do enough to get a decent grade," reflects extrinsic motivation, whereas Susan's comment, "I've always liked history and knowing about the past" suggests intrinsic motivation. These relationships are illustrated in Figure 10.1.

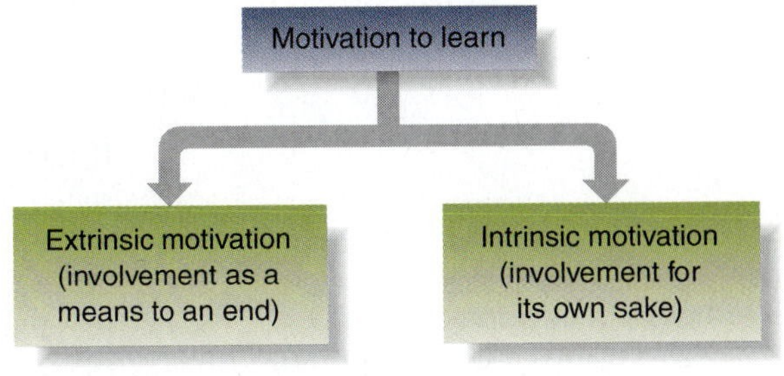

Figure 10.1 Extrinsic and intrinsic motivation

Although people often think of extrinsic and intrinsic motivation as two ends of a continuum (meaning the higher the extrinsic motivation, the lower the intrinsic motivation and vice versa), they are actually on separate continua (Covington, 2000; Schunk et al., 2008). For example, students might study both because a topic is interesting and because they want good grades. Others might study only to receive the good grades. The first group is high in both extrinsic and intrinsic motivation; the second is high in extrinsic motivation but low in intrinsic motivation. As you would expect, research indicates that intrinsic motivation is preferable because of its focus on learning and understanding (Brophy, 2004).

Motivation is also contextual and can change over time (Wigfield et al., 2004). For example, Jim's comment, "In some classes I just do enough to get a decent grade," suggests that he is extrinsically motivated in other classes, but saying, "I sometimes even read ahead a little," and "it's kind of interesting . . ." indicates that he is intrinsically motivated in Kathy's. Kathy's class is different enough to influence his intrinsic motivation. This helps answer our second question (How does Jim's motivation in Kathy's class differ from his other classes?).

We can also begin to answer the third question (How has Kathy influenced Jim's motivation?) by examining intrinsic motivation in more detail. Researchers have found that learners are intrinsically motivated by experiences that achieve the following:

- *Present a challenge.* Challenge occurs when goals are moderately difficult, and success isn't guaranteed. Meeting challenges is also emotionally satisfying (R. Ryan & Deci, 2000; Stipek, 2002).
- *Promote learners' feelings of autonomy.* Learners are more motivated when they feel that they have influence over their own learning (N. Perry, 1998; R. Ryan & Deci, 2000).
- *Evoke curiosity.* Novel, surprising, or discrepant experiences can trigger intrinsic motivation (Brophy, 2004).
- *Involve creativity and fantasy.* Creative learning tasks allow learners to personalize content by using their imagination (Lepper & Hodell, 1989).

In addition, some researchers suggest that aesthetic experiences (those associated with beauty and evoke emotional reactions) may be intrinsically motivating as well (Ryan & Deci, 2000).

Jim's comments suggest that Kathy capitalized on two of these factors. "Brewster really makes you think," suggests he was reacting to the challenge in her class, and "It's kind of interesting the way she's always telling us about the way we are because of something that happened a zillion years ago," suggests her teaching aroused his curiosity.

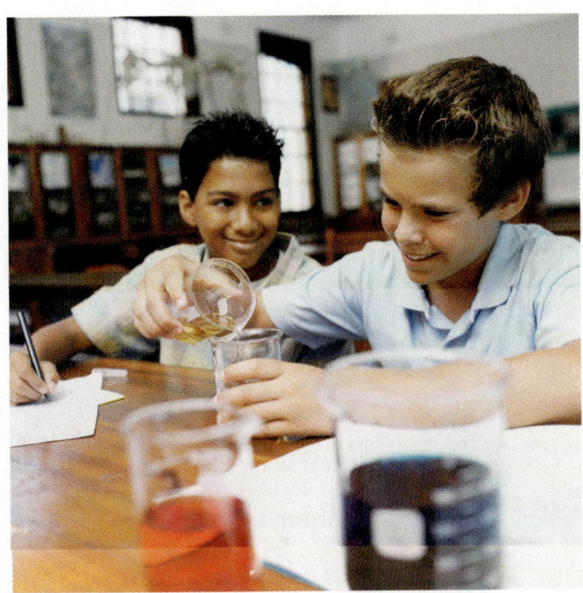

Learning tasks that evoke curiosity increase learners' intrinsic motivation.

Motivation to Learn

All teachers want their students to be intrinsically motivated, and teachers sometimes (mistakenly) believe that their instruction should be so stimulating that students will always be intrinsically motivated. This is a worthwhile ideal, but it isn't realistic for all, or even most, learning activities. The following are some reasons (Brophy, 2004):

- School attendance is compulsory, and content reflects what society believes students should learn, not what students would choose for themselves.
- Teachers work with large numbers of students and cannot always meet their individual needs.
- Students' performances are evaluated and reported to parents and other caregivers, so students focus on meeting external demands instead of on personal benefits they might derive from the experiences.

Jere Brophy (2004) offers a reasonable alternative.

> If intrinsic motivation is ideal but unattainable as an all-day, everyday motivational state for teachers to seek to develop in their students, what might be a more feasible goal? I believe that it is realistic for you to seek to develop and sustain your students' **motivation to learn** from academic activities: their tendencies to find academic activities meaningful and worthwhile and to try to get the intended learning benefits from them. (p. 15)

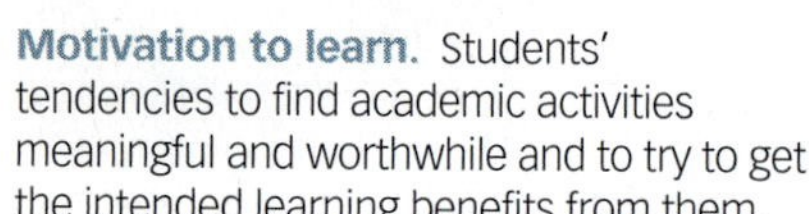

Motivation to learn. Students' tendencies to find academic activities meaningful and worthwhile and to try to get the intended learning benefits from them.

Students with a motivation-to-learn orientation make an effort to understand topics whether or not they find studying them intrinsically interesting or enjoyable. They maintain this effort because they believe that the understanding that results is valuable and worthwhile. In this chapter we will focus on motivation to learn, and if students' intrinsic motivation also increases in the process, then their potential for learning increases that much more.

Theoretical Views of Motivation

As with learning, different theoretical orientations provide frameworks for understanding students' motivation to learn (Brophy, 2004; Schunk et al., 2008). They are outlined in Figure 10.2 and discussed in the sections that follow.

Behaviorist Views of Motivation

Behaviorism views learning as a change in behavior that occurs as a result of experience, and it treats motivation the same way. An increase in the amount of time spent studying, for example, is viewed as evidence of motivation, so reinforcers, such as praise, comments on homework, and good grades are motivators (Schunk et al., 2008).

Critics argue that using rewards sends students the wrong message about learning (Anderman & Maehr, 1994; Kohn, 1996a), and they cite research suggesting that rewards actually decrease interest in intrinsically motivating tasks (Kohn, 1996b; R. Ryan & Deci, 1996; Sansone & Harackiewicz, 2000).

Critics also suggest that behaviorism cannot adequately explain motivation. For instance, if a student believes he can't complete a difficult assignment, he will be unlikely to work hard on it despite being reinforced for completing past assignments. His motivation is influenced by

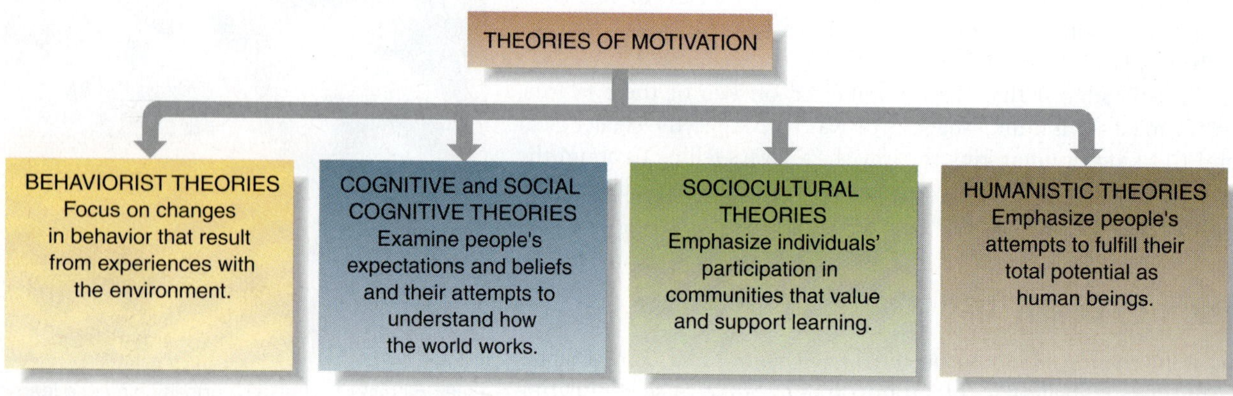

Figure 10.2 Theoretical views of motivation

his belief, which is a cognitive factor. "Most motivation researchers find purely behaviorist approaches to the study of human learning and motivation unsatisfactory . . ." (N. E. Perry et al., 2006, p. 329).

In spite of these criticisms, teachers commonly use rewards as motivators in classrooms (N. E. Perry et al., 2006). For example, teachers in elementary schools use praise, candy, and entertainment such as computer games as rewards. Middle and secondary teachers attempt to increase motivation with high test scores, comments on written work, free time to talk to classmates, and quiet compliments as rewards.

Also, research indicates that rewards, judiciously used, can be effective. For instance, praise for genuine achievement (Cameron, Pierce, & Banko, 2005) and rewards that recognize increasing competence can increase intrinsic motivation (Covington, 2000; Gehlbach & Roeser, 2002). We revisit the use of rewards used in these contexts later in the chapter.

Effective teachers judiciously use rewards to increase students' motivation.

Cognitive and Social Cognitive Theories of Motivation

"C'mon, let's go," Melanie urges her friend Yelena as they're finishing a series of homework problems.

"Just a sec," Yelena mutters. "I'm not quite getting this one."

"Let's work on it tonight. Everybody's leaving," Melanie urges.

"Go ahead, I'll catch up to you in a minute. I know that I can figure this out. . . . I just don't get it right now."

How might we explain Yelena's persistence in the face of her uncertainty? Behaviorism doesn't provide much help. Although getting the right answer would be reinforcing, it doesn't account for her attempt to understand why the problem made sense but still came out wrong. Also, because behaviorism doesn't consider beliefs or expectations, it can't explain her saying, "I know that I can figure this out," which indicates that she believes she can resolve the discrepancy and expects to do so.

People instinctively want to make sense of their experiences, and this idea is at the heart of cognitive motivation theory: "Children are seen as naturally motivated to learn when their experience is inconsistent with their current understanding" (Greeno, Collins, & Resnick, 1996, p. 25). For example, why do young children so eagerly explore their environments? Why was Yelena unable to leave until she solved the problem? Cognitive theorists suggest that each is motivated by the need to understand and make sense of their experiences.

Piaget (1977) described the need for understanding with his concept of equilibrium. When people cannot explain experiences using their existing schemes, they are motivated to modify the schemes to reestablish equilibrium. Ultimately, the new understanding leads to advanced development.

Cognitive theories of motivation help explain a variety of human behaviors, such as why people

- Are intrigued by brain teasers and other problems with no practical application
- Are curious when something occurs unexpectedly
- Persevere on challenging activities and then quit after they've mastered the tasks
- Want feedback about their performance

These tendencies all indicate an innate desire to understand and make sense of our experiences.

Social cognitive theories extend the cognitive views by emphasizing learners' beliefs and expectations and the influence of observing others on our motivation (Schunk & Pajares, 2004; Zimmerman & Schunk, 2004). They help explain Jim's comment, "She's so gung ho, and it's kind of interesting the way she's always telling us about the way we are because of something that happened a zillion years ago." His motivation in Kathy's class was the result of observing her model her enthusiasm and interest in the topic she was teaching.

MyEducationLab

To examine what an elementary student's written report suggests about the factors that influence learner motivation, go the *Activities and Applications* section in Chapter 10 of MyEducationLab at www.myeducationlab.com, and look at the artifact *Pig Dissection*. Answer the questions that follow.

Sociocultural views of motivation suggest that participating in communities of learners can increase students' motivation to learn.

Sociocultural Views of Motivation

Sociocultural views of motivation focus on participation in a learning community (Hickey & Zuiker, 2005), and some experts argue for a *motivational* zone of proximal development that is analogous to Vygotsky's original description of the cognitive zone of proximal development (Brophy, 1999b). This suggests that a learning environment can provide a form of motivational scaffolding that results in learners' engaging in activities that they would not do on their own. A learning community is one in which all students participate in learning activities, differences in interests and thinking are respected, and the teacher and all the students work together to help everyone learn. Sociocultural views of motivation suggest that individuals in communities of learners are more motivated than they would be in a classroom environment that is competitive or provides less support.

Humanistic Views of Motivation

In the mid-1950s when the "cognitive revolution" in learning was emerging, a parallel movement called humanistic psychology also began. It focuses on the "whole person" and views motivation as people's attempts to become "self-actualized," or to fulfill their total potential as human beings (Schunk et al., 2008). According to this view, understanding individuals' motivation requires an understanding of their behaviors, thoughts, and feelings (Schunk & Zimmerman, 2006). This perspective remains popular both in schools and in the workplace.

Carl Rogers, a psychologist who founded "person-centered" therapy, and Abraham Maslow, famous for his hierarchy of needs (we discuss his hierarchy in the next section of the chapter), were the two most prominent leaders in the humanistic movement, and both emphasized people's attempts to become self-actualized (Maslow, 1968, 1970; Rogers, 1963).

According to Rogers, the actualizing tendency is oriented toward competence, autonomy, and freedom from control by external forces. The tendency is innate, but experiences with others can foster or hinder growth and the development of autonomy (Rogers, 1959; Rogers & Freiberg, 1994). Of those experiences, **unconditional positive regard,** the belief that someone is innately worthy regardless of their behavior, is one of the most essential.

Unconditional positive regard. The belief that someone is innately worthy regardless of their behavior.

Unconditional positive regard isn't as simple as it appears. Parents usually feel it for their small children, but as they get older, parents' regard may become "conditional" and depend on factors such as high grades or choosing the right partner or career (Kohn, 2005a). In the outside world, regard is almost always conditional, because society rarely separates people from their actions. In schools, high achievers and students who are well-behaved are regarded more positively than their lower-achieving peers, as are students who excel in extracurricular activities such as music and sports. According to Rogers (1959, 1963), conditional regard hinders personal growth, and he recommended treating all students as developing individuals with potential.

More recent work corroborates his views (Cornelius-White, 2007; Kohn, 2005b). "Students who felt unconditionally accepted by their teachers were more likely to be interested in learning and to enjoy challenging academic tasks, instead of just doing schoolwork because they had to and preferring easier assignments at which they knew they would succeed" (Kohn, 2005b, p. 21).

To see these views applied in classrooms, let's return to Kathy's work with her students.

As the students are leaving the room, Jenny stops at Kathy's desk. "You wanted to see me, Mrs. Brewster?"

"I've been watching you for a few days, and you don't seem to be yourself. . . . Is everything okay?"

"Yes, . . . no, . . . not really," Jenny says, her eyes starting to fill with tears. "My mom and dad are having trouble, and I'm really scared. I'm afraid they're going to break up."

"Do you want to talk?"

". . . No, . . . not right now."

Kathy touches Jenny on the shoulder, and says, "I realize that there isn't anything specific that I can do, but I'm here if you want to talk about it, . . . or anything else . . . anytime."

"Thanks," Jenny nods weakly as she turns to go.

As Kathy is working after school, Harvey pokes his head into the room.

"Come in," she smiles. "How's our developing writer?"

"I just came by to say I hope you're not upset with me, complaining so much about all the work."

"Not at all. . . . I haven't given it a second thought."

"You already know how much you've done for me. . . . You believed in me when the rest of the world wrote me off. . . . My drug conviction is off my record now, and I'm okay. I couldn't have made it without you. You made me work, and you put in all kinds of extra time with me. You wouldn't let me give up on myself. I was headed for trouble, and now . . . I'm headed for college."

"We all need a nudge now and then," Kathy smiles. "That's what I'm here for. I appreciate it, but I didn't do it; you did. . . . Now, scoot. I'm working on a rough assignment for you tomorrow."

"Mrs. Brewster, you're relentless," Harvey waves as he heads out the door.

Caring teachers who are committed to their students both as people and as learners are essential for motivation and learning.

Caring teachers who are committed to their students both as people and as learners are essential for motivation and learning (Cornelius-White, 2007). Kathy was concerned because Jenny wasn't herself, so she asked Jenny to stop by after class. And, in separating Harvey's drug conviction from his innate worth as a human being, she demonstrated the unconditional positive regard that Rogers (1963) emphasized.

At the same time, she demonstrated that she cared about her students as learners by maintaining high expectations. As you saw in her conversation with Harvey in the chapter-opening case study, she pushed him (and all her students), offered evidence of his progress, and emphasized the value of what they were studying.

In the real world, unfortunately, you won't be able to "save" every troubled student. You can make a difference with many, however, and for those students, you will have made an immeasurable contribution to their lives.

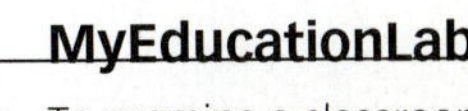

MyEducationLab

To examine a classroom incident and its impact on student motivation, go to the *Activities and Applications* section in Chapter 10 of MyEducationLab at www.myeducationlab.com, and read the case study *Classroom Environments and Motivation.* Answer the questions following the case study.

check your understanding

1.1 Define motivation, and explain how it influences learning.
1.2 Describe how behaviorism explains learner motivation.
1.3 How do cognitive and social cognitive views of motivation explain people's motivation to learn?
1.4 How do sociocultural views of motivation explain people's motivation to learn?
1.5 How do humanistic views of motivation explain students' motivation to learn?

To receive feedback for these questions, go to Appendix A.

The Influence of Needs on Motivation to Learn

Need. An internal force or drive to attain a certain state or object

Survival is the most basic *need* that exists in all species, and food, water, and sex are commonly described as essential for ensuring that survival. In motivation theory, a **need** is an internal force or drive to attain or to avoid a certain state or object (Schunk et al., 2008). For instance, the need for food is an internal force, with food being the object the individual is attempting to attain.

In this section we examine three theories based on needs:

- Maslow's hierarchy of needs
- The need for self-determination
- The need to preserve self-worth

Maslow's Hierarchy of Needs

Growth needs. Needs in intellectual achievement and aesthetic appreciation that increase as people have experiences with them.

Abraham Maslow (1968, 1970, 1987), often viewed as the father of the humanistic movement in psychology, developed a hierarchy reflecting the needs of the "whole person" (see Figure 10.3). For instance, we see the physical person in survival and safety needs, the social person in belonging needs, the emotional person in self-esteem needs, and the self-actualized person in growth needs. These **growth needs** are needs in intellectual achievement and aesthetic appreciation that increase as people have experiences with them. Next, we'll discuss these needs in more detail.

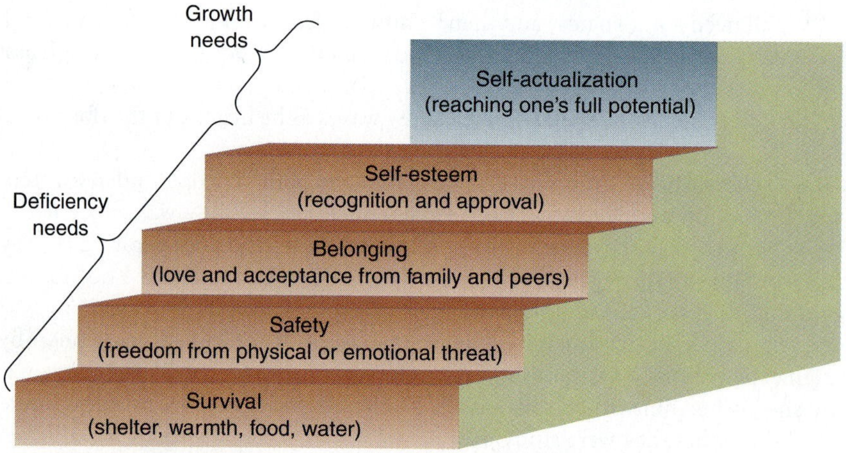

Figure 10.3 Maslow's hierarchy of needs

Source: Adapted from *Motivation and Personality* 3rd Edition by Abraham H. Maslow. Copyright 1954, 1987 by Harper & Row, Publishers, Inc. Copyright © 1970 by Abraham H. Maslow. Reprinted by permission of Addison Wesley Educational Publishers Inc.

Deficiency and Growth Needs

Maslow (1968, 1970) described human needs as existing in two groups. The first, **deficiency needs,** energize people to meet them if they're unfulfilled. They occupy the bottom of the hierarchy in Figure 10.3. According to Maslow, people won't move to the growth needs unless our deficiency needs—survival, safety, belonging, and self-esteem—have all been met.

Deficiency needs. Needs that, if unfulfilled, energize people to meet them.

Once deficiency needs are met, an individual can focus on the growth needs that can lead to **self-actualization,** the need to reach our full potential and be all that we are capable of being. In contrast with deficiency needs, the need for self-actualization is never completely satisfied. For instance, as people develop a greater understanding of literature, their interest in it actually increases rather than decreases. This can explain why some people seem to have an insatiable desire for learning or why individuals never tire of fine art or music. Continuing to engage in these activities responds to their need for personal growth, gives them pleasure, and can lead to *peak experiences*, a concept that originated with Maslow.

Self-actualization. The need to reach our full potential and be all that we are capable of being.

Putting Maslow's Work Into Perspective

Maslow's work is intuitively sensible and appealing. For example, when you meet with your instructors, it's likely that your first reaction is to how "nice" they are and how they treat you, not how intelligent or competent they seem to be. The same applies to people in general. We react more positively to people who are warm and inviting than to those who appear cold and distant. Emotionally supportive people help us meet our needs for safety and belonging. Maslow's work reminds us that we're all initially social and emotional beings and that these factors influence our motivation.

Applications of Maslow's work in schools also seem to support its validity. Schools provide free or reduced-cost breakfasts and lunches because it makes sense that motivation to learn will decrease if children are hungry. Schools also strive to make students feel safe—both physically and emotionally—because those who don't will also be less motivated to learn (N. Lambert & McCombs, 1998; B. L. McCombs, 2001). Ignoring the human side of teaching excludes an essential domain.

On the other hand, Maslow's work has been criticized because research evidence supporting his description of needs is largely lacking (Schunk et al., 2008). The hierarchy's inconsistency and lack of predictive ability is a second criticism. For instance, we've all heard about people who have serious illnesses or disabling conditions—which suggests that their deficiency needs are not being met—who accomplish significant intellectual or aesthetic achievements and who seek order, truth, and beauty in their experiences. Maslow's work would predict that this could not happen.

Finally, Maslow's belonging and self-esteem needs are very similar to needs described in more contemporary theories of motivation, discussed in the following sections.

The Need for Self-Determination

Self-determination is the need to act on and control one's environment (R. Ryan & Deci, 2000). According to self-determination theory, having choices and making decisions are intrinsically motivating, and people aren't content if all their needs are satisfied without opportunities for decision making. Self-determination theory assumes that people have three innate psychological needs: *competence, autonomy,* and *relatedness* (Levesque et al., 2004; R. Ryan & Deci, 2000).

Self-determination. The motivational need to act on and control one's environment.

The Need for Competence

We all want to look "smart." As you interact with people, think about the number of times they attempt to demonstrate how much they know about a topic or how good they are at some skill. Self-determination theory explains these efforts by saying that they are attempting to meet their need for **competence,** the ability to function effectively in the environment.

Competence. The ability to function effectively in the environment.

This need can be described at several levels. At an anthropological level, for instance, if an organism can't function effectively in its environment, it isn't likely to survive (Schunk et al., 2008). At another level, competent people succeed and grow in their careers, whereas those less competent languish and stagnate. Competent students are successful learners, and they find school satisfying and rewarding (Morgan & Fuchs, 2007).

Meeting challenges provides evidence that competence is increasing and helps meet students' need for self-determination.

The need for competence helps explain why challenging activities and those that evoke curiosity are intrinsically motivating. Meeting challenges and resolving novel and discrepant experiences provide evidence that competence is increasing. In contrast, completing trivial tasks or solving predictable problems provides little evidence about competence, so they are rarely motivating.

The need for competence is similar to the need for mastery of the environment described by R. White (1959) in a paper that has become a classic. He suggested that people acquire proficiency and skill "because it satisfies an intrinsic need to deal with the environment" (p. 318). The need for competence is also consistent with historical descriptions of achievement motivation theory, which emphasizes the need to master and do well in a particular domain (J. Atkinson, 1958).

The most important factor influencing students' perception of competence is evidence that their knowledge and skills are increasing. This helps us understand why praise for genuine achievement can increase intrinsic motivation (Cameron et al., 2005). The praise communicates that competence is increasing and helps meet this innate need.

Teachers can also influence their students' perceptions of competence in subtle and unintended ways with

- Attributional statements about performance
- Praise and criticism
- Emotional reactions
- Offers of help

Attributional statements Comments teachers make about the causes of students' performance.

Attributional Statements. **Attributional statements** are comments teachers make about the causes of students' performance. For instance, if a teacher says to a student struggling with a problem, "Keep trying. I know these problems are hard for you," she is implying that lack of ability is the reason the student is struggling, which undermines beliefs about competence (Stipek, 1996). In contrast, the statement, "Keep trying. I know you can solve this problem," suggests that with increased effort competence can be achieved.

Praise and Criticism. Praise and criticism can also influence students' perceptions of competence. Older students may perceive praise for performance on easy tasks as an indication that the teacher believes they are not competent (Larrivee, 2002; Stipek, 1996). By comparison, a statement such as, "You can do better work than this," communicates that the teacher believes the student is capable of achieving competence. So, while we're not suggesting that teachers make a habit of criticizing students, inappropriate praise can detract from motivation to learn, whereas timely criticism can actually increase it.

Emotional Reactions. Teachers' emotional reactions to learners' successes and failures can also affect learners' beliefs about competence. For example, teachers expressing annoyance in response to learner failure implies increased effort can lead to competence. In comparison, expressions of sympathy imply that students lack the ability to become competent (Stipek, 1996, 2002).

Offers of Help. Offering students unsolicited help can also be problematic and lead to decreased feelings of competence. Researchers have found that children as young as six rated a student offered unsolicited help lower in ability than another not offered help (Graham & Barker, 1990). Also, learners who are offered unsolicited help may feel incompetent, angry, or anxious, and feelings of incompetence are a primary reason that children who need help fail to ask for it (Marchand & Skinner, 2007).

To put this section into perspective, we're not suggesting that teachers should avoid praising students, expressing sympathy, or offering help. Rather, it reminds us that we must be aware of how learners can interpret, or misinterpret, our actions. As always, the way we respond to students requires sensitivity and careful professional judgment.

Autonomy. Independence and an individual's ability to alter the environment when necessary.

The Need for Autonomy

The need for **autonomy** is the need for independence and the ability to alter the environment when necessary, and it is the second innate need described by self-determination theory. The need for autonomy is also a source of intrinsic motivation (Lepper & Hodell, 1989). Conversely, lack of autonomy reduces intrinsic motivation and causes stress. For instance, it is widely believed that the stress of assembly line work comes from workers' having little control over their environments (Lundberg, Granqvist, Hansson, Magnusson, & Wallin, 1989).

Autonomy as described by self-determination theorists is similar to other historical discussions of the topic, such as *locus of control* (Rotter, 1966) and *personal causation* (deCharms, 1968, 1984). Also, autonomy and competence are strongly related. As learners' competence increases, so do their perceptions of autonomy (A. Black & Deci, 2000; Bruning et al., 2004).

The most obvious way that teachers can increase students' perceptions of autonomy is to give them choices. For example, Kathy gave her students the choice of making a presentation on the Renaissance or writing a paper on the Middle Ages. She also let them decide the order of their presentations. However, because providing choices often isn't possible, teachers can enhance perceptions of autonomy in other ways, such as the following:

- Solicit student input in creating classroom rules and procedures.
- Encourage students to set and monitor their own learning goals.
- Create high levels of student participation in classroom activities.
- Emphasize the impact of effort and strategy use, and deemphasize the influence of ability on achievement.
- Use assessments that provide feedback and focus on learning progress.

Each can increase perceptions of autonomy, and as this perception increases, so does motivation to learn.

The Need for Relatedness

We all want to feel like we belong. **Relatedness**, the feeling of being connected to others in one's social environment and feeling worthy of love and respect, is the third innate need described by self-determination theory. Some researchers treat belonging, as described by Maslow (1968, 1970), and relatedness in the same way. "Terms such as *belongingness, relatedness*, and *connectedness* are used interchangeably" (Juvonen, 2006, p. 654). The need for relatedness is also similar to the need for *affiliation* as described by other early motivational researchers (e.g., Exline, 1962; Terhune, 1968).

Relatedness. The feeling of being connected to others in one's social environment and feeling worthy of love and respect.

The need for relatedness can result in students' developing a strong **need for approval**, the desire to be accepted and judged positively by others (Urdan & Maehr, 1995). Children in elementary schools generally seek the approval of their teachers, but older students with a strong need for approval often have low self-esteem, and they engage in activities primarily to get praise from their teachers (H. A. Davis, 2003). When the need for approval becomes excessive, students with a fear of rejection easily submit to peer pressure. These efforts can be counterproductive, however, because these students are often relatively unpopular with their peers (Rudolph, Caldwell, & Conley, 2005; Wentzel & Wigfield, 1998).

Need for approval. The desire to be accepted and judged positively by others.

Teachers can help meet students' needs for relatedness and approval by communicating unconditional positive regard and a genuine commitment to students and their learning (Cornelius-White, 2007). Students are more engaged—behaviorally, cognitively, and emotionally—in classroom activities when they believe their teachers like, understand, and empathize with them (H. A. Davis, 2006; Furrer & Skinner, 2003). They also report more interest in their class work, behave in more socially responsible ways, and are more likely to seek help when they need it (Cornelius-White, 2007; Marchand & Skinner, 2007; Wentzel, 1996).

Formal attempts to increase learners' perceptions of self-determination are linked to increased intrinsic motivation and school engagement, a greater likelihood of school completion (Eisenman, 2007; Vansteenkiste, Lens, & Deci, 2006), improved literacy (Crow, 2007), and even a more active lifestyle (Bryan & Solmon, 2007; Gillison, Standage, & Skevington, 2006).

Assessment and Learning: The Role of Assessment in Self-Determination

As we have emphasized throughout this book, assessment is an essential part of the learning–teaching process. This raises an issue, however, because some research suggests that evaluation can detract from self-determination and intrinsic motivation (Deci & Ryan, 1987).

As with most aspects of learning and teaching, the issue isn't simply a matter of assess or don't assess; it depends on how the process is handled. For instance, assessments that students view as punitive or controlling detract from intrinsic motivation, whereas those that provide information about increasing competence enhance it (Deci & Ryan, 1987).

Some suggestions for using assessments to increase self-determination include the following:

- Provide clear expectations for students, and align assessments with these expectations (Schunk et al., 2008). (We discuss instructional alignment in detail in Chapter 13.)
- Assess frequently and thoroughly, and emphasize the learning benefits of assessment (Dochy & McDowell, 1997).
- Provide detailed feedback about responses to assessments, and emphasize the reasons for answers as much as the answers themselves (Deci & Ryan, 1987; Schunk et al., 2008).
- Avoid social comparisons in communicating assessment results (H. Patrick, Anderman, Ryan, Edelin, & Midgley, 1999; Stipek, 1996, 2002).
- Allow students to drop one or more of their lowest test or quiz scores for purposes of grading.

Establishing a climate that focuses on learning and increased competence should be our goal in assessing student achievement (Stiggins, 2007). Clear expectations and alignment make assessments predictable, which increases perceptions of autonomy, as does dropping one or more quiz scores for purposes of grading. Frequent assessment provides students with information about their increasing competence. Detailed feedback that includes reasons for answers, and avoiding social comparisons, emphasizes that promoting learning is the purpose of assessment. Some teachers write students' scores on the back page of tests and quizzes and encourage them to avoid sharing their scores with each other. Although they will still share scores, the practice is symbolic, communicating that assessments are private and designed to increase learning, not to see who is the "smartest."

The Need to Preserve Self-Worth

> "I'm a genius; I'm a genius," Andrew, an eighth grader enthusiastically shouts to his mom as he bounces into the house after school. "I got a 97 on my history test, and I didn't study a lick. I'm a genius; I'm a genius."

How might we explain Andrew's reaction to his score?

Self-worth. An emotional reaction to or an evaluation of the self.

Self-worth (or self-esteem, as it is more commonly called) is an emotional reaction to or an evaluation of the self (Schunk et al., 2008). Self-worth theorists suggest that people have an innate need to protect their sense of self-worth and achieve self-acceptance (Covington, 1992). They further suggest that our society so strongly values ability that people will go to great lengths to protect perceptions of high ability (Covington, 1992; Graham & Weiner, 1996).

This helps us understand Andrew's comment. By emphasizing that he didn't study, he was communicating that he had high ability, which enhanced his feelings of self-worth.

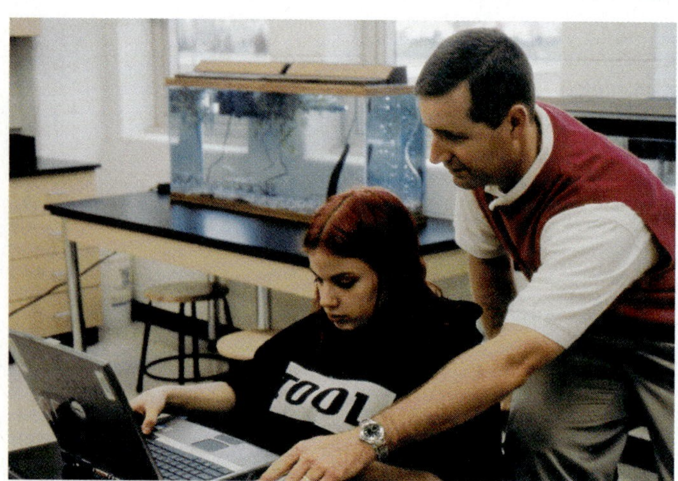

Teachers who emphasize learning over performance and deemphasize social comparisons can increase students' motivation to learn.

Research reveals some interesting developmental patterns in learners' perceptions of effort and ability. For instance, when asked, most kindergarten children say they're smart. And young children assume that people who try hard are smart, and people who are smart try hard (Stipek, 2002). As students move through school, their views change. Their need to be perceived as having high ability increases, and they view expending effort as an indicator of low ability. Social comparisons, such as displaying scores on tests, are the most significant factors in this process (Brophy, 2004). Children as young as second or third grade begin to judge their ability and competence based on their performance compared to others (Stipek, 2002).

Because of their need to be perceived as having high ability, older students may hide the fact that they've studied hard for a test, so if they do well, they can, at least in the eyes of their peers, attribute their success to high ability. Others engage in "self-handicapping" strategies to protect their self-worth, such as procrastinating ("I could have done a

theory to practice

Capitalizing on Learners' Needs to Increase Motivation to Learn

An understanding of learners' needs has important implications for teachers attempting to increase students' motivation to learn. As you apply this understanding in your classroom, the following guidelines can help you in your efforts.

1. To meet students' needs for belonging and relatedness, treat them as people first.
2. Help meet students' needs for competence by maintaining high expectations and providing evidence that their competence is increasing.
3. Address students' needs for autonomy by giving them input into decisions and offering them choices when possible.
4. Emphasize the relationship between effort and increased ability, and avoid social comparisons among students.

Let's review Kathy's work with her students to see how she applied the guidelines. She applied the first in the way she interacted with Jenny and Harvey before her class. When she saw that Jenny hadn't been herself, she called her in and talked with her. She also treated Harvey with the unconditional positive regard that humanistic motivation theory suggests is important. Both actions helped meet her students' needs for belonging and relatedness.

Second, in commenting to Harvey, "Look how good you're getting at writing. . . . You're becoming a very good writer," she provided evidence that his competence was increasing. Evidence of increasing competence also addresses the growth needs in Maslow's hierarchy. This evidence is even more significant because Harvey viewed the assignment as difficult. Success on trivial tasks does little to increase learners' perceptions of competence or self-actualization.

Third, as you saw in our discussion of people's need for self-determination, increasing competence contributes to individuals' perceptions of autonomy. And Kathy also helped students meet their need for autonomy by giving them choices to either write a paper or make a group presentation and to decide the order of the presentations.

Finally, in our discussion of self-worth theory, you saw that self-worth is associated with perceptions of high ability. Kathy's comments, "It's hard for me, too, when I'm studying and trying to put together new ideas, but if I hang in, I always feel like I can get it," modeled the belief that ability can be increased with effort, as did the comment, "I study every night to keep up with you people, and the harder I study, the smarter I get." If students adopt this belief, both motivation and learning increase.

As with theories in general, these guidelines won't work all the time or with all students. However, the applications can make a difference, which increases the likelihood of increased motivation and learning for many.

lot better, but I didn't start studying until after midnight"), making excuses (such as suggesting that the teacher was poor or the tests were tricky), anxiety ("I understand the stuff, but I get nervous in tests"), or making a point of not trying. In these cases, students believe that failure doesn't indicate low ability if they didn't try (Covington, 1998; Wolters, 2003). Self-handicapping behaviors have been found in a range of academic areas, and have been observed in physical education as well (Standage, Treasure, Hooper, & Kuczka, 2007). They are most common in low achievers, who often choose to not seek help when it's needed (Marchand & Skinner, 2007; Middleton & Midgley, 1997).

Although teachers cannot eliminate all social comparisons, they can model effort and emphasize beliefs about the role of effort in increasing competence. Teachers are powerful models, and modeling the belief that effort can increase ability is important. We examine the influence of beliefs on motivation to learn in the next section of the chapter.

check your understanding

2.1 Explain how learners' needs, as described in Maslow's hierarchy, can influence their motivation to learn.

2.2 Explain how learners' needs for competence, autonomy, and relatedness can influence their motivation to learn.

2.3 Explain how learners' need to preserve their sense of self-worth can influence their motivation to learn.

To receive feedback for these questions, go to Appendix A.

classroom connections

Applying an Understanding of Learners' Needs in Your Classroom

Maslow's Hierarchy of Needs

1. Maslow described people's needs in a hierarchy with deficiency needs (survival, safety, belonging, and self-esteem) preceding the growth need for self-actualization. Address students' deficiency and growth needs both in instruction and in the way you interact with students.
   - **Elementary:** A fourth-grade teacher calls on all students to promote a sense of belonging in the classroom community. He makes them feel safe by helping them respond correctly when they are unable to answer.
   - **Middle School:** To help meet learners' belonging needs, a seventh-grade teacher asks two of the more popular girls in her class to introduce a new girl to some of the other students and to take her under their wings until she gets acquainted.
   - **High School:** To address learners' growth needs, an American government teacher brings in a newspaper columnist's political opinion piece, comments that it was interesting to her, and asks students for their opinions on the issue.

Learners' Needs for Self-Determination

2. Self-determination theory suggests that people have innate needs for competence, autonomy, and relatedness. Design challenging tasks that, when completed, can provide evidence for increasing competence, and emphasize these accomplishments when students succeed.
   - **Elementary:** A fifth-grade teacher drops one ice cube into a cup of water and a second cube into a cup of alcohol (which the students initially think is water). The teacher then guides the students with questioning to explain why the cube floats in one and sinks in the other. When they solve the problem, she praises them for their thinking.
   - **Middle School:** A math teacher has a problem of the week that requires the students to bring in a challenging, everyday problem for the class to solve. When they solve the problem, she comments on how good they are getting at solving difficult problems.
   - **High School:** A biology teacher beginning a unit on the skeletal system says, "Our skull is nearly solid and very hard. But when we were infants, it was flexible and there were even gaps in it. Why might this be the case?" He then guides them to an understanding of the relationship between body structure and function.
3. Learners' perceptions of autonomy increase when teachers ask them to provide input into classroom procedures, involve them in learning activities, and give them informative feedback on assessments. Create a classroom environment that helps meet learners' needs for autonomy.
   - **Elementary:** A fourth-grade teacher holds periodic class meetings in which they discuss issues such as students' treatment of each other. She encourages students to offer suggestions for improving the classroom environment.
   - **Middle School:** A pre-algebra teacher returns all tests and quizzes the following day and discusses frequently missed problems in detail. She frequently comments on students' continually improving skills.
   - **High School:** A world history teacher asks students to identify specific archeological evidence for sites that represent Old Stone Age compared to New Stone Age civilizations. He comments that the students' ability to link evidence to conclusions in their reports has improved significantly.
4. Learners' needs for relatedness are met when teachers communicate a commitment to students both as individuals and as learners.
   - **Elementary:** A first-grade teacher greets her students each morning at the door with a hug, "high five," or handshake. She tells them what a good day they're going to have.
   - **Middle School:** A seventh-grade teacher calls a parent to express concern about a student whose behavior seems to have changed quite markedly. He asks if she has gone through some trying experience.
   - **High School:** A 10th-grade math teacher in an urban school conducts help sessions after school on Mondays through Thursdays. She also encourages students to talk about their personal lives and hopes for the future.

Learners' Needs to Preserve Self-Worth

5. Self-worth theory suggests that people instinctively attempt to preserve their sense of self-worth. Emphasize that self-worth is an outcome of effort and that ability can be increased with effort.
   - **Elementary:** When her second graders succeed with word problems during their seat work, a teacher comments "You're really understanding what we're doing. Your hard work is paying off, isn't it?"
   - **Middle School:** A life-science teacher comments, "You're really seeing the connections between these animals' body structures and their ability to adapt to their environments. I'm so pleased with the progress you're making, and I'm sure you're feeling good about yourselves."
   - **High School:** As students' understanding of balancing equations increases, a chemistry teacher comments, "You people are doing great. You've really gotten good at this stuff."

The Influence of Beliefs on Motivation to Learn

To begin this section, look at the following statements and try to decide what they tell us about each person's motivation to learn:

1. "If I study hard for the next test, I'm going to do well."
2. "Learning a foreign language doesn't come naturally for me, but with some more work, I'm going to be good at it by the end of the year."
3. "I'm a good cross-country runner; I've got to do well in this race."

4. "I'm not that crazy about algebra, but I need to get good at it. I want to major in engineering in college, and I'll need it."
5. "I'm not going to play in the jazz band this year. I'm just too busy, and I don't have the time to commit to it."

Each of the statements describes a **belief**, a cognitive idea we accept as true without necessarily having definitive evidence to support it. In this section, we look at different ways in which our beliefs can influence our motivation to learn, as we examine the following:

Belief. A cognitive idea we accept as true without necessarily having definitive evidence to support it.

- Beliefs about future outcomes
- Beliefs about intelligence
- Beliefs about capability
- Beliefs about value
- Beliefs about causes of performance

Expectations: Beliefs About Future Outcomes

Look again at the first statement: "If I study hard for the next test, I'm going to do well." It describes an **expectation**, a belief about a future outcome (Schunk & Zimmerman, 2006). The influence of expectations on motivation is often described using **expectancy × value theory**, a theory that explains learner motivation using the extent to which learners *expect* to succeed on a learning task *times* the value they place on succeeding at the task as a framework (Wigfield & Eccles, 1992, 2000). (We examine the influence of values on motivation later in this section.) The × is important, because anything times zero is zero: so, if learners don't expect to succeed, they will not be motivated to learn, regardless of how valuable the activity is to them (Tollefson, 2000). For example, as a young man, one of your authors toyed with the idea of a career in music. However, his lack of ability was obvious, resulting in low expectation for success. This resulted in low motivation for pursuing a career in music and a fortunate turn to a rewarding one studying teaching and learning.

Expectation. A belief about a future outcome.

Expectancy × value theory. A theory that explains learner motivation by saying that learners will be motivated to engage in a task to the extent that they *expect* to succeed on the task *times* the value they place on the success.

Students with high success expectations persist longer on tasks, choose more challenging activities, and achieve higher than those whose expectations are lower (Eccles et al., 1998; Wigfield, 1994).

Past experience is the primary factor influencing expectations. Students who usually succeed expect to succeed in the future, and the opposite is true for students who don't succeed. This helps us understand why promoting motivation to learn is such a challenge when working with low achievers. They typically have a long history of failure, so their motivation to learn is low as a result of low expectations for success. This, combined with learners' needs to preserve their sense of self-worth, creates a problem that is doubly difficult for teachers.

The only way teachers can increase motivation to learn in students whose expectations for success are low is to design learning experiences that are in the students' zones of proximal development and then provide the scaffolding necessary to ensure success. It is very challenging, but in time, and with effort, teachers can increase motivation to learn in low-expectation students.

Beliefs About Intelligence

To begin this section, look at the words of an eighth-grader, Sarah, as she explains her beliefs about her ability in math:

> My brother, I, and my mom aren't good at math at all, we inherited the "not good at math gene" from my mom and I am good at English, but I am not good at math. (K. E. Ryan, Ryan, Arbuthnot, & Samuels, 2007, p. 5)

Sarah is describing an **entity view of intelligence**, the belief that intelligence is essentially fixed and stable over time (Dweck, 1999; Dweck & Leggett, 1988). She believes that her ability is fixed and there is little she can do about it.

Entity view of intelligence. The belief that intelligence is essentially fixed and stable over time.

In contrast, look again at our second statement from the beginning of this section: "Learning a foreign language doesn't come naturally for me, but with some more work, I'm going to be good at it by the end of the year." This statement reflects an **incremental view of intelligence**, the belief that intelligence, or ability, is not stable and can be increased with effort. "If there is an upper limit

Incremental view of intelligence. The belief that intelligence is not stable and can be increased with effort.

on ability, it is very high and should not prevent one from working harder to improve" (Schunk & Zimmerman, 2006, p. 358).

Beliefs about intelligence help us understand why learners sometimes engage in self-handicapping behaviors. People's self-worth is often connected to perceptions of high ability, so if they believe that ability is fixed, experiencing difficulty and failure are troublesome, because both suggest lack of ability. To protect their sense of self-worth, learners may avoid situations that can reflect negatively on their intelligence. As a result, their motivation and learning both decrease.

On the other hand, if learners believe that ability can be increased with effort, difficulty and failure merely suggest that more effort is needed. They believe they will succeed if they work harder or use more effective strategies, and their success is evidence that their ability is increasing (Burhans & Dweck, 1995). Because they believe that effort can increase ability, their motivation and learning are both likely to increase. Modeling incremental views of intelligence is one of the most effective strategies teachers can use to overcome students' tendencies to view intelligence as fixed. For example, in the opening case study, Kathy commented to Harvey, "I wish. I study every night to keep up with you people, and the harder I study, the smarter I get."

Self-Efficacy: Beliefs About Capability

To begin this section, let's look again at the conversation between Melanie and Yelena, which introduced the discussion of cognitive theories of motivation.

> "C'mon, let's go," Melanie urges her friend Yelena as they're finishing a series of homework problems in math.
>
> "Just a sec," Yelena mutters. "I'm not quite getting this one."
>
> "Let's work on it tonight. Everybody's leaving," Melanie urges.
>
> "Go ahead, I'll catch up to you in a minute. I know that I can figure this out. . . . I just don't get it right now."

Self-efficacy. The belief that one is capable of accomplishing a specific task.

Yelena's statement illustrates **self-efficacy**, the belief that one is capable of accomplishing a specific task (Bandura, 1986, 1997, 2004). She believes she is capable of solving the problem if she perseveres. Self-efficacy, self-concept, and expectation for success are closely related, but they aren't synonymous (Bong & Skaalvik, 2003; R. Pajares & Schunk, 2002; Schunk, 2004). For example, if Yelena believes she is generally competent in math, we would say that she has a positive *self-concept* with respect to math. Self-efficacy is more specific. She believes she can solve this particular math problem. However, Yelena likely believes that she will not succeed on the next math quiz if she doesn't do her homework (low expectation for success).

Research indicates that self-efficacy is domain specific (P. Smith & Fouad, 1999). For instance, a person might have high self-efficacy for writing quality essays but have low self-efficacy for balancing chemical equations.

Factors Influencing Self-Efficacy

Research suggests that self-efficacy depends on four factors, which are outlined in Figure 10.4 and discussed in the following paragraphs (Bandura, 1986).

Past performance on similar tasks is the most important. A history of success in giving oral reports, for example, increases a person's self-efficacy for giving future reports. Observing the modeling of others, such as those delivering excellent reports, increases self-efficacy by raising expectations and providing information about the way a skill should be performed (Bandura, 1986, 1997; Kitsantas, Zimmerman, & Cleary, 2000).

Although limited in its effectiveness, verbal persuasion, such as a teacher's commenting, "I know you will give a fine report," can also increase self-efficacy. It probably does so indirectly by encouraging students to try challenging tasks, and if they succeed, efficacy increases.

Finally, anxiety can reduce efficacy by filling working memory with thoughts of failure, and physiological factors, such as fatigue or hunger, can also temporarily reduce self-efficacy.

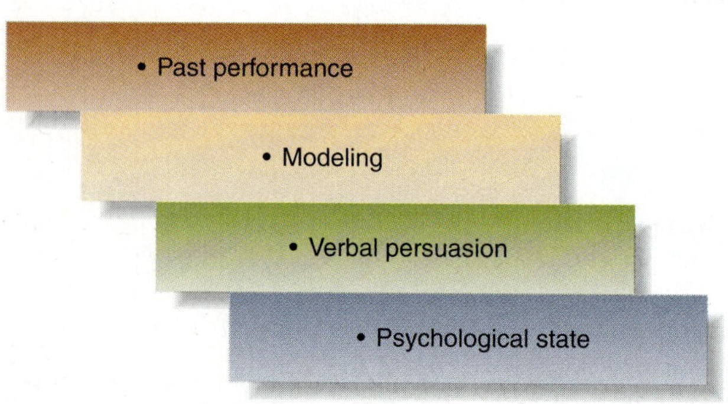

Figure 10.4 Factors influencing self-efficacy

table 10.1 The Influence of Self-Efficacy on Motivation

	High Self-Efficacy Learners	Low Self-Efficacy Learners
Task orientation	Accept challenging tasks	Avoid challenging tasks
Effort	Expend high effort when faced with challenging tasks	Expend low effort when faced with challenging tasks
Persistence	Persist when goals arent initi ally reached	Give up when goals aren't initially reached
Beliefs	Believe they will succeed Control stress and anxiety when goals aren't met Believe they're in control of their environment	Focus on feelings of incompetence Experience anxiety and depression when goals aren't met Believe they're not in control of their environment
Strategy use	Discard unproductive strategies	Persist with unproductive strategies
Performance	Perform higher than low-efficacy students of equal ability	Perform lower than high-efficacy students of equal ability

The Influence of Self-Efficacy on Motivation

Self-efficacy strongly influences motivation to learn. For instance, compared to low-efficacy students, high-efficacy learners accept more challenging tasks, exert more effort, persist longer, use more effective strategies, and generally perform better (Bandura, 1997; Eccles et al., 1998; Schunk & Ertmer, 2000). These characteristics are outlined in Table 10.1.

Developmental Differences in Self-Efficacy

Self-efficacy often changes as students move through school. For instance, young children generally have high self-efficacy, sometimes unrealistically so (Eccles et al., 1998). As they move through school, they become less confident, which may reflect more realistic beliefs. They also become more aware of, and are more concerned with, their performance compared to their peers (A. Elliot & McGregor, 2000).

Promoting high self-efficacy should be an important goal for teachers. Experts suggest that "increases in self-efficacy perceptions, in task effort and persistence, and in ultimate performance levels can be achieved by . . . encouraging students to set specific and challenging, but attainable goals" (Brophy, 2004, p. 65). (We discuss the influence of goals on motivation to learn later in the chapter.)

Beliefs About Value

Value refers to the benefits, rewards, or advantages that individuals believe may result from participating in an activity, and it is the second component of expectancy × value theory. "The perceived value of a task is a strong determinant of why an individual would want to become or stay engaged in an academic activity or task" (Anderman & Wolters, 2006, p. 373).

Value. The benefits, rewards, or advantages that individuals believe may result from participating in a task or activity.

Researchers have identified three types of values that influence learner motivation (Wigfield & Eccles, 2000, 2002):

- Attainment value
- Utility value
- Cost

Attainment Value. **Attainment value** refers to the importance an individual attaches to doing well on a task (Wigfield & Eccles, 2000, 2002). For instance, the third statement at the beginning of this section, "I'm a good cross-country runner; I've got to do well in this race." Doing well in the race has high attainment value for this person because she believes she is a good runner. It helps her validate a belief she has about herself (Anderman & Wolters, 2006). However, for a person who

Attainment value. The importance that an individual attaches to doing well on a task.

doesn't view herself as a good writer, for example, being able to produce a high-quality written product won't have high attainment value. Our self-concepts, beliefs, and other information we store about ourselves are often described as *self-schemas* (Schunk et al., 2008).

Utility value. The belief that a topic, activity, or course of study will be useful for meeting future goals, including career goals.

Utility Value. Now, let's look again at the fourth example that introduced our discussion of beliefs, "I'm not that crazy about algebra, but I need to get good at it. I want to major in engineering in college, and I know I'll need it." This statement describes **utility value**, the belief that a topic, activity, or course of study will be useful for meeting future goals, including career goals (Wigfield & Eccles, 1992).

For the individual, studying algebra has high utility value. He isn't intrinsically interested in algebra, and may not believe that he is particularly good at it, but he believes it will be valuable to him in the future. At this point, his motivation is primarily extrinsic, but as his competence increases, so will his intrinsic motivation. This example demonstrates how motivation to learn can lead to intrinsic motivation.

Cost. A consideration of what an individual must give up to engage in the task.

Cost. Now, let's look at the example, "I'm not going to play in the jazz band this year. I'm just too busy, and I don't have the time to commit to it." This individual is referring to **cost**, the consideration of what an individual must give up to engage in a task (Wigfield & Eccles, 2002).

In this case the cost is too high, so the person is not motivated to engage in the activity. As another example, you may decide not to take a demanding course at this point in your program because you already have a heavy load.

Beliefs about future outcomes (expectations), intelligence, capability (self-efficacy), and value help us understand why learners are, or are not, likely to engage in and persevere on tasks. Their beliefs about the outcomes of their engagement also can influence their continued motivation. This leads us to a discussion of attributions.

Attributions: Beliefs About Causes of Performance

Why do you succeed on some academic tasks and not others? When you don't succeed, what is the reason? To see how our explanations for successes and failures affect our motivation to learn, let's look at four students' responses to the results of a test.

"How'd you do, Bob?" Anne asks.

"Terrible," Bob answers sheepishly. "I just can't do this stuff. I'm no good at essay tests. . . . I'll never get it."

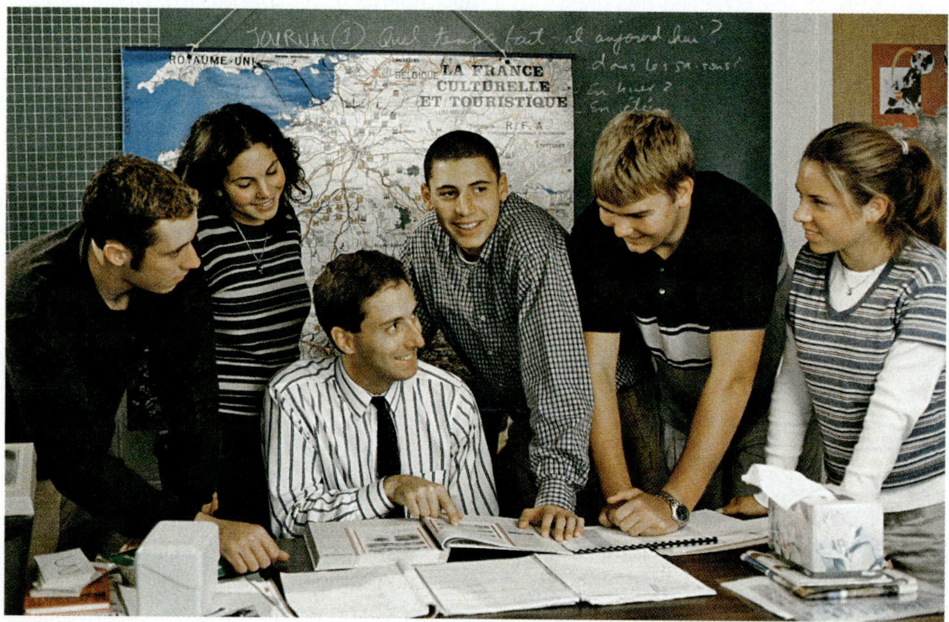

Believing that a topic, activity, or course of study will be useful for meeting future goals can increase motivation to learn.

"I didn't do so good either," Anne replies, "but I knew I wouldn't. I just didn't study hard enough. I won't let that happen again."

"Unbelievable!" Armondo adds. "I didn't know what the heck was going on, and I got a B. I don't think she read mine."

"I think the test was too tough," Ashley shakes her head. "I looked at the test, and just went blank. All I could think of was, 'I've never seen this stuff before. Where did it come from?' I thought I was going to throw up."

Each of the students is offering an **attribution**, a belief about the cause of their performance. Bob, for example, believes that his poor performance resulted from lack of ability, whereas Ann believes that lack of effort caused hers. Armondo believed he was successful because he was lucky, and Ashley thought the test was too difficult.

Attribution. A belief about the cause of performance.

Research indicates that *ability, effort, luck,* and *task difficulty* are the attributions learners most commonly offer for school success and failure, but others, such as effective or ineffective strategies, lack of help, interest, unfair teacher practices, or clarity of instruction are also cited (B. Weiner, 1992, 2001).

Attribution theory attempts to systematically describe learners' beliefs about the causes of their successes and failures and how these beliefs influence motivation to learn. Attributions occur on three dimensions (B. Weiner, 1992, 2000, 2001). The first is *locus,* the location of the cause, which is either within or outside the learner. Ability and effort are within the learner, for example, whereas luck and task difficulty are outside. The second is *stability,* whether or not the cause can change. Effort and luck are unstable because they can change, whereas ability is considered stable in attribution theory. The third is *control,* the extent to which students accept responsibility for their successes or failures. Learners control their effort, for example, but they cannot control luck or task difficulty. These relationships are outlined in Table 10.2.

Attribution theory. A cognitive theory of motivation that attempts to systematically describe learners' beliefs about the causes of their successes and failures and how these beliefs influence motivation to learn.

Impact of Attributions on Learners

Attributions influence learners in four ways:

- Emotional reactions to success and failure
- Expectations for future success
- Future effort
- Achievement

To see how these influences work, let's look at Anne's and Bob's attributions again. Anne attributed her poor score to lack of effort. Because she was responsible for her effort, guilt was her emotional reaction. She can expect to succeed in the future because effort is alterable. Her comment "I won't let that happen again" suggests that she will increase her effort, and improved achievement is likely (B. Weiner, 2000, 2001).

Bob attributed his failure to lack of ability. So, instead of guilt, his emotional reaction was embarrassment and shame, because he viewed ability as uncontrollable. Because he attributed his failure to lack of ability, he doesn't expect future success, as indicated by his statement, "I'll never get it." His effort is likely to decrease, with lower achievement the

table 10.2 Relationships Among the Dimensions of Attributions

Attributions	Locus (location of cause)	Stability (of cause)	Control (of learning situation)
Ability	Inside the learner	Stable (cannot change)	Learner out of control
Effort	Inside the learner	Unstable (can change)	Learner in control
Luck	Outside the learner	Unstable (can change)	Learner out of control
Task difficulty	Outside the learner	Stable (cannot change)	Learner out of control

Attributing success to effort can increase students' motivation to learn.

probable result (B. Weiner, 1994). (We ask you to analyze Armondo's and Ashley's reactions in "Check Your Understanding" question 3.4 at the end of this section.)

Motivation tends to increase when students attribute failure to lack of effort, as Anne did, because effort can be controlled. It tends to decrease when students attribute failure to uncontrollable causes (e. g., luck, or ability if it is viewed as stable), as Bob did (B. Weiner, 2000, 2001; Weinstock, 2007).

Research indicates that people tend to attribute success to internal causes, such as hard work or high ability, and failures to external causes, such as bad luck or the behaviors of others (Marsh, 1990). When students do poorly, for example, they commonly attribute their failure to poor teaching, boring topics, tricky tests, or some other external cause.

Attributions also influence teachers. For instance, if they believe students are succeeding because of their teaching, they're likely to continue making the effort (Shahid, 2001). On the other hand, if they believe that learners are doing poorly because of students' lack of prior knowledge, poor home lives, or some other cause beyond their control, their efforts decrease.

classroom connections

Applying an Understanding of Learners' Beliefs in Your Classroom

1. Expectations are beliefs about future outcomes, and self-efficacy describes beliefs about our capability of accomplishing specific tasks. Develop expectations for success and self-efficacy by providing enough scaffolding to ensure that students make progress on challenging tasks.
   - **Elementary:** After displaying a problem, a fourth-grade teacher asks students to suggest different ways of solving it. The class discusses each strategy, and the teacher points out areas in which the students' problem solving is improving.
   - **Middle School:** A seventh-grade English teacher instructs his students to write paragraphs on transparencies. He displays and discusses students' products and makes suggestions for improvement. He emphasizes how much the quality of the paragraphs is increasing.
   - **High School:** An art teacher has students keep a portfolio of their work. She periodically asks them to review their products to demonstrate their progress.
2. Learners with incremental views of intelligence believe that ability can increase with effort. Emphasize incremental views of intelligence with your students.
   - **Elementary:** After her students have solved a series of word problems in math, a second-grade teacher comments, "We're all getting so smart. I guess I'll have to give you harder problems next time."
   - **Middle School:** A seventh-grade geography history teacher says, "Your understanding of how the geography of the Middle East has influenced their economies and politics has become really good. I tell the other teachers what geography experts I have in my class."
   - **High School:** A chemistry teacher emphasizes that he studies every night. "The harder I work, the smarter I get," he smiles. "And, you can do the same thing.
3. Utility value is the perception that a topic or activity will be useful for meeting future goals. Emphasize the utility value of the topics students study.
   - **Elementary:** A fifth-grade teacher has his students feel the different bones in their bodies and guides a discussion of the function of each. He emphasizes the importance of understanding our bodies so they can make good decisions about keeping their bodies healthy.
   - **Middle School:** A seventh-grade math teacher working on percentage problems brings in newspaper advertisements for marked-down products. The class determines the actual reduction in cost, and the teacher then emphasizes the value of understanding how much people save in promotions.
   - **High School:** An English teacher displays examples of well-written (and not so well-written) attempts to make and defend an argument. She uses the examples to emphasize the value of being able to express oneself clearly in writing as well as in interactions with others.
4. Attributions describe beliefs about causes of performance. Model and encourage students to attribute success to increasing competence and failure to lack of effort or ineffective strategies.
   - **Elementary:** As his students initially work on word problems, a second-grade teacher carefully monitors student effort during seat work. When he sees assignments that indicate effort, he makes comments to individual students, such as "Your work is improving all the time."
   - **Middle School:** A sixth-grade English teacher comments, "I wasn't good at grammar for a long time. But I kept trying, and I found that I could do it. I'm good at grammar and writing now. You can become good too, but you have to work at it."
   - **High School:** A chemistry teacher comments, "The way we're attacking balancing equations is working much better, isn't it? You tried to memorize the steps before, and now you're understanding what you're doing. And you're getting better and better at it."

Learned Helplessness

If attributing failure to lack of ability becomes a pattern, **learned helplessness**, the debilitating belief that one is incapable of accomplishing tasks and has little control of the environment, can result. Bob's comment, "I just can't do this stuff. . . . I'll never get it," suggests that he is a potential case. Concluding, "I'll never get it," can result in overwhelming feelings of shame and self-doubt and giving up without trying.

Learned helplessness. The debilitating belief that one is incapable of accomplishing tasks and has little control of the environment.

Learned helplessness has both an affective and a cognitive component. Students with learned helplessness have low self-esteem and often suffer from anxiety and depression (Graham & Weiner, 1996). Cognitively, they expect to fail, so they exert little effort and use ineffective strategies, which result in less success and an even greater expectation for failure (Dweck, 2000). Fortunately, efforts to intervene have been successful.

Attribution Training

Learners can improve the effectiveness of their attributions through training (Robertson, 2000). In a pioneering study, Dweck (1975) provided students who demonstrated learned helplessness with both successful and unsuccessful experiences. When the students were unsuccessful, the experimenter specifically stated that the failure was caused by lack of effort or ineffective strategies. Comparable students were given similar experiences but no training. After 25 sessions, the learners who were counseled about their effort and strategies responded more appropriately to failure by persisting longer and adapting their strategies more effectively. Additional research has corroborated Dweck's findings (Schunk et al., 2008). Strategy instruction was most effective for students who believed that they were already trying hard. This research suggests that teachers can increase students' motivation to learn by teaching them learning strategies and encouraging them to attribute successes to effort.

check your understanding

3.1 Explain how learners' beliefs can influence their motivation to learn.

3.2 Explain differences in the ways learners with entity views of intelligence and those with incremental views of intelligence will respond to difficult tasks and the possibility of failure.

3.3 Using Kathy Brewster's conversation with Harvey on page 284, cite a specific example where she emphasized utility value in learning.

3.4 Look again at the conversation among the four students at the beginning of our discussion of attribution theory. Explain Armondo's emotional reactions, expectations for future success, future effort, and achievement, based on attributing his success to luck. Then, explain Ashley's reactions based on attributing her failure to task difficulty. (See Table 10.2 to review these factors.)

To receive feedback for these questions, go to Appendix A.

The Influence of Goals on Motivation to Learn

Do you think about what you're trying to accomplish when you begin an activity—other than merely completing it? These thoughts can have an important influence on your motivation and achievement. To see how, examine what some of Kathy's students are thinking as they prepare their group presentations on the Renaissance.

Susan: This should be interesting. I don't know much about the Renaissance, and it began a whole new emphasis on learning all over the world. Mrs. Brewster has given us a lot of responsibility, so we need to come through. We need to make a presentation she'll like.

Damien: I'll get my Dad to help us. He's really up on history. Our presentation will be the best one of the bunch, and the class will be impressed.

Sylvia: Yikes! Everyone in my group is so smart. What can I do? They'll think I'm the dumbest one. I'm going to just stay quiet when we're working together.

Charlotte: This should be fun. We can get together to work on this at one of our houses. If we can get the project out of the way quickly, I might have time to get to know Damien better.

Antonio: I don't know anything about this. I'd better do some studying so my group will think I'm pulling my weight.

Patrick: I like group activities. They're usually easy. Somebody is always gung ho and does most of the work.

Goal. An outcome an individual hopes to attain.

Each of the students' thinking reflects a **goal**, an outcome an individual hopes to attain (Anderman & Wolters, 2006; Schunk et al., 2008). As you see, significant differences exist in students' goals. For instance, Susan's goal was to understand the Renaissance and please Mrs. Brewster, Charlotte wanted to socialize, and Patrick simply wanted to do as little work as possible. Let's see how these goals influence motivation and learning.

Mastery and Performance Goals

Mastery goal. A goal that focuses on accomplishing a task, improvement, and increased understanding. Sometimes called a *learning goal*.

Performance goal. A goal that focuses on a learner's ability and competence in comparison to others.

Performance-approach goal. A goal that emphasizes looking competent and receiving favorable judgments from others.

Performance-avoidance goal. A goal that focuses on avoiding looking incompetent and being judged unfavorably.

Much of the research examining goals and their influence on motivation has focused on differences between *mastery* and *performance* goals (Schunk et al., 2008; K. E. Ryan et al., 2007). For instance, Susan's desire to understand the Renaissance is a **mastery goal** (sometimes called a learning goal), a goal that focuses on accomplishing a task, improvement, and increased understanding (Midgley, 2001; Pintrich, 2000). In comparison, **performance goals** focus on ability and competence and how they compare to others (A. Elliot & McGregor, 2000; A. Elliot & Thrash, 2001; Midgley, 2001).

Performance goals exist in two forms: **Performance-approach goals** emphasize looking competent and receiving favorable judgments from others. Damien's wanting to make the best presentation and impress the class is an example. In contrast, Sylvia's thinking, "They'll think I'm the dumbest one. I'm going to just stay quiet when we're working together," reflects a **performance-avoidance goal**, an attempt to avoid looking incompetent and being judged unfavorably (K. E. Ryan et al., 2007).

Some researchers also use the labels *task-involved* and *ego-involved* (Nicholls, 1984), or *task-focused* and *ability-focused* (Maehr & Midgley, 1991), for mastery and performance goals, respectively, so you may also encounter these terms when you study goal theory (Schunk et al., 2008).

Mastery and performance goals are not mutually exclusive, and students may have more than one simultaneous goal (Boekaerts & Koning, 2006; Pintrich, 2000). For example, a student might want to understand the Renaissance, make an impressive presentation, and avoid looking uninformed, which would include mastery and both types of performance goals (Covington & Müeller, 2001).

Students with mastery goals focus on accomplishment, improvement, and increased understanding.

Adopting mastery goals is the most effective approach for both motivation and learning. Students who adopt mastery goals have high efficacy and persist in the face of difficulty; they attribute success to effort; they accept academic challenges; and they use effective strategies, such as self-questioning and summarizing (Kumar et al., 2002; Wolters, 2003). Mastery goals lead to sustained interest and effort even after formal instruction is finished. Teachers can increase students' mastery orientation by using instructional strategies that emphasize understanding and higher-order thinking (Morrone, Harkness, D'Ambrosio, & Caulfield, 2003).

The influence of performance goals on motivation to learn is more complex. Initially, many students adopt both mastery and performance goals; they want to both understand the topic and score near the top of their classes, for example (Covington & Müeller, 2001; Harackiewicz, Barron, Taurer, Carter, & Elliot, 2000). Also, students with a performance-approach orientation tend to be confident and have high self-efficacy (Middleton & Midgley, 1997). Even so, performance-approach goals are less desirable than mastery goals. To reach them, students may use superficial strategies, such as memorization; exert only enough effort to meet them; engage in self-handicapping behaviors, such as not trying when they're not sure they can meet the goals; or even cheat in order to reach them (Brophy, 2004; Midgley, Kaplan, & Middleton, 2001).

In addition, mastery goals have at least two other advantages over performance-approach goals. First, learners are in control of mastery goals, but less so for performance goals. For instance, Damien's group may not make the best presentation even if they prepare carefully.

Second, failure on a mastery goal can lead to increased effort or a change in strategies. Failure on a performance goal can lead to anxiety and a performance-avoidance orientation (Midgley et al., 2001).

Performance-avoidance goals are the most detrimental for motivation and achievement (Midgley & Urdan, 2001). Students who attempt to avoid looking incompetent tend to have low self-efficacy, lack self-confidence, and experience anxiety about tests and other tasks (Midgley et al., 2001). They often try to avoid the tasks that will help them master new skills. For example, Sylvia's only goal was to avoid looking "dumb" to the other students. As a result, her motivation to learn was low, and ultimately, her achievement will decrease.

Unfortunately, as students progress through school, their performance orientation tends to increase while their mastery orientation decreases (A. Elliot & McGregor, 2000). Parents and teachers both influence this developmental trend. Children are more likely to adopt a mastery orientation if parents and teachers emphasize that the purpose of school is to promote achievement and an increase in understanding, and deemphasize grades and performance compared to others (Friedel, Cortina, & Turner, 2007). Teachers contribute to the development of a performance orientation by emphasizing that students need to get good grades if they want to go to college, by displaying grades, or by discussing differences in the way students are performing.

Goals and Theories About the Nature of Intelligence

Earlier in this section we discussed beliefs about the nature of intelligence, and some researchers (e.g., Dweck, 1999; Dweck & Leggett, 1988) believe that the tendency to adopt mastery or performance goals is related to these beliefs. For example, people with *entity views* of intelligence are likely to adopt performance goals, whereas those with *incremental views* are more apt to adopt mastery goals (Dweck, 1999; Quihuis et al., 2002).

Let's see how individuals' beliefs about intelligence can affect their choice of goals. Making the best presentation in the class, for example, could be interpreted as an indicator of high ability, and evidence of high ability is important for individuals who view intelligence as fixed. This isn't a problem if individuals' confidence in their intelligence is high; they will seek challenging tasks and persist in the face of difficulty. However, if they aren't confident about their intelligence, they're likely to avoid challenge, because failure suggests low ability.

In contrast, individuals with an incremental view are more likely to seek challenge and persist even if they aren't confident about their ability, because failure merely indicates that more work is required, and, as competence increases, so does intelligence.

Social Goals

In addition to mastery and performance goals, students also have **social goals,** goals to achieve particular social outcomes or interactions (Wentzel, 2002). Charlotte, for example, thought, "If we can get the project out of the way quickly, I might have time to get to know Damien better," and Antonio decided, "I don't know anything about this. I'd better do some studying so my group will think I'm pulling my weight." Both had social goals, and more specifically, Antonio had a *social-responsibility* goal. Other social goals include

Social goals. Goals to achieve particular social outcomes or interactions.

- Forming friendships
- Gaining teacher or peer approval
- Meeting social obligations
- Assisting and supporting others
- Underachieving to make others feel better (H. A. Davis, 2003; Wentzel, 1999b, 2000; P. White et al., 2002)

Social goals can both increase and decrease motivation to learn (Horst et al., 2007). For instance, Charlotte's wanting to "get the project out of the way quickly," so she could get to know Damien detracted from her motivation to learn. As would be expected, low achievers report

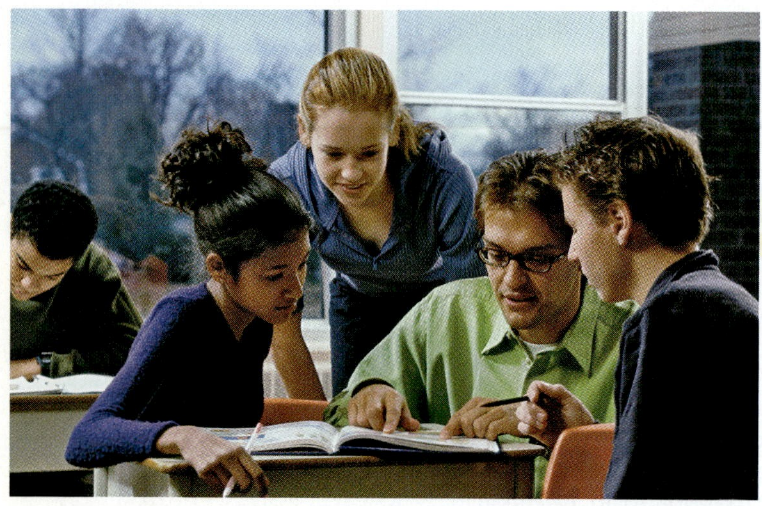

Combining social-responsibility goals with mastery goals can have a powerful impact on motivation to learn.

this orientation more often than do high achievers (Wentzel, 1999a; Wentzel & Wigfield, 1998). On the other hand, *social-responsibility goals* such as Antonio's are associated with both high motivation to learn and achievement (Wentzel, 1996).

When social-responsibility goals are combined with mastery goals, motivation to learn and achievement can be even higher (Wentzel, 1999b, 2000). This is illustrated in Susan's thinking: "This should be interesting. I don't know much about the Renaissance" (a mastery goal) and "Mrs. Brewster has given us a lot of responsibility, so we need to come through. We need to make a presentation she'll like" (a social-responsibility goal).

Work-Avoidance Goals

Patrick's comment, "I like group activities. They're usually easy. Somebody is always gung ho and does most of the work," indicates a work-avoidance goal. Students with these goals feel successful when tasks are easy or can be completed with little effort (Dowson & McInerney, 2001; Gallini, 2000). They also tend to use ineffective learning strategies, make minimal contributions to group activities, ask for help even when they don't need it, and complain about challenging activities. Not surprisingly, students like Patrick are a source of challenge and frustration for teachers.

Most of the research on students with work-avoidance goals has been done at the middle school level, and more is needed to determine how those goals originate (Dowson & McInerney, 2001; Gallini, 2000).

Table 10.3 summarizes the different types of goals and their influence on motivation and achievement.

Goals, Motivation, and Achievement

Teachers obviously can't adapt to each student's goal orientation. However, by varying instruction, such as combining small-group work, which can help meet students' social goals, with whole-class instruction, which is often preferred by students with a performance-approach orientation, teachers can help a range of students meet their goals (Bong, 2001). Students who set mastery goals flourish with any well-organized instruction. Although difficult, encouraging

table 10.3 Goals, Motivation, and Achievement

Type of Goal	Example	Influence on Motivation and Achievement
Mastery goals	Understand the influence of the Renaissance on American history.	Leads to sustained effort, high self-efficacy, willingness to accept challenges, and high achievement.
Performance-approach goals	Produce one of the best essays on the Renaissance in the class.	Can lead to sustained effort and high self-efficacy for confident learners. Can increase achievement. Can detract from willingness to accept challenging tasks, which decreases achievement.
Performance-avoidance goals	Avoid the appearance of low ability in front of peers and teachers.	Detracts from motivation and achievement, particularly for learners lacking confidence.
Social goals	Be perceived as reliable and responsible. Make friends and socialize.	Can either increase or decrease motivation and achievement. *Social-responsibility goals* enhance motivation and achievement, particularly when combined with mastery goals. Can detract from motivation and achievement if social goals compete for time with mastery goals.
Work-avoidance goals	Complete assignments with as little effort as possible.	Detracts from effort and self-efficacy. Strongly detracts from achievement.

students with a performance-avoidance or work-avoidance orientation to set and monitor appropriately challenging goals can increase motivation to learn. Let's see how teachers can help students set effective goals.

Using Goals Effectively

Goal setting has been widely used to increase motivation and performance in the business world, and educators are increasingly recognizing the effectiveness of goals for promoting motivation and learning (P. K. Murphy & Alexander, 2000). When students set goals they believe they can meet, their self-efficacy and motivation to learn both increase.

Unfortunately, many learners, including university students, study without clear goals in mind (Urdan, 2001). Students copy and reorganize their notes, for instance, but don't ask themselves if doing so contributes to their understanding. They seem to think that spending time equals learning.

Using goals effectively involves four processes that are outlined in Figure 10.5 and discussed in the paragraphs that follow.

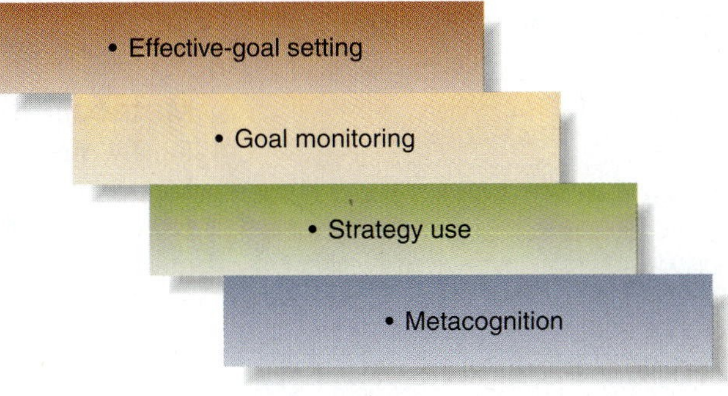

Figure 10.5 Effective use of goals

Goal Setting

As would be expected, the process begins with setting goals. Look at these four goals, and decide which is most effective:

- Learn more in my classes.
- Get into better shape.
- Lose 20 pounds by the end of this year.
- Answer and understand all the "Check Your Understanding" questions for each chapter of this text.

The last goal is the most effective. The first two are general, and as a result, monitoring progress on them and identifying strategies to achieve them is difficult. What, specifically, will you do to learn more, or to get into better shape, for instance? The third goal is distant. Losing 20 pounds is likely a worthwhile goal, but the end of the year is too far into the future. Goals that are close at hand increase self-efficacy more than distant ones, because meeting them is more easily observed. The fourth goal is specific, moderately challenging, and can be attacked immediately. It can also be readily monitored, and it lends itself to strategy use.

To summarize, effective goals have three characteristics. They are

- Specific (versus broad and general)
- Immediate or close at hand (versus distant)
- Moderately challenging

The appropriate degree of challenge isn't easy to specify, but it's important. Goals that are too easily reached don't increase self-efficacy as much as those that are more challenging. On the other hand, goals that are too challenging may reduce expectations for success so much that motivation is decreased.

For goals to be motivating, people must be committed to them (Schunk et al., 2008). The best way to increase goal commitment is to guide learners in setting their own goals, rather than imposing goals on them (Ridley, McCombs, & Taylor, 1994).

Goal Monitoring

Once people have committed to a set of goals, monitoring them leads to a sense of accomplishment, promotes self-efficacy, and can be a pleasant emotional experience. For instance, there are 18 "Check Your Understanding" questions in this chapter, so, suppose this is Monday, and you set the goal of answering all of these questions by the following Sunday. If by Wednesday evening you've answered the first 10, and you believe you understand them, you feel good about your progress; you've answered more than half of them in 3 days. You have evidence of your progress, and your self-efficacy increases. In addition, you've taken responsibility for your own learning, which further increases your sense of accomplishment.

Strategy Use

Use of appropriate strategies is the third component of effective goal use. For example, simply reading the "Check Your Understanding" questions and then reading the answers in Appendix A is an ineffective strategy, because you are studying passively. Writing an answer to each question and then checking the feedback is more effective. Also, waiting until Saturday to start answering the questions doesn't work as well as answering three or four each day.

MyEducationLab

To examine applications of factors that influence motivation, go to the *Building Teaching Skills and Dispositions* section in Chapter 10 of MyEducationLab at www.myeducationlab.com, and watch the video episode *Applying Cognitive Motivation Theory: Writing Paragraphs in Fifth Grade.* Complete the exercises following the episode to build your skills in applying motivation theory in your classroom.

Metacognition

Finally, metacognition enhances the entire process of using goals (Paris & Paris, 2001). Metacognition involves being aware of your goals and monitoring your efforts to reach them. For instance, if you're writing definitions of concepts on note cards, but your instructor's tests measure application, you'll realize that you're using an ineffective strategy and you'll change it.

Teachers can help learners become more metacognitive by modeling their own metacognition and by explaining specific examples of effective and ineffective strategies (Paris & Paris, 2001). The message that teachers want to communicate is that learning is conscious, intentional, and requires effort.

check your understanding

4.1 Explain how learners' goals can influence their motivation to learn.

4.2 Which combination of goal orientations is likely to result in the highest level of motivation and achievement? Explain.

4.3 In our discussion of goal theory, we identified the following goals as being ineffective:
Learn more in my classes.
Get into better shape.
Lose 20 pounds by the end of this year.
Rewrite each to make them more effective.

To receive feedback for these questions, go to Appendix A.

classroom connections

Capitalizing on Goals to Increase Motivation to Learn in Your Classroom

1. Goals are outcomes learners hope to achieve. Promote learner responsibility with goal setting and self-monitoring. Emphasize mastery goals.
   - **Elementary:** A fifth-grade teacher confers with students as they begin a writing project. He instructs them to write a schedule for completing the project, and he periodically meets with each to assess their progress.
   - **Middle School:** An eighth-grade history teacher promotes metacognition by saying to her students, "It's very important to think about and be aware of the way you study. If you have your stereo on, ask yourself, 'Am I really learning what I'm studying, or am I distracted by the stereo?'" She emphasizes that learning is always the goal and that being aware of the way they study will increase their understanding.
   - **High School:** A biology teacher promotes strategy use by saying, "Let's read the next section in our books. After we've read it, we're going to stop and make a one-sentence summary of the passage. This is something each of you can do as you read on your own. If you do, your understanding of what you're reading will increase."
2. A combination of mastery goals and social responsibility goals can lead to the highest levels of motivation to learn. Emphasize social responsibility with your students.
   - **Elementary:** A third-grade teacher instructs her students to work in pairs to solve a series of math problems. "Work hard to solve the problems," she emphasizes, "so you can help out your partner if he or she needs it."
   - **Middle School:** An eighth-grade English teacher is discussing *To Kill a Mockingbird* with her students. "In order for us to get the most out of the book, we're all responsible for making a contribution to the class discussions. I expect you all to come to class prepared and to participate," she emphasizes.
   - **High School:** An American history teacher asks her students to work in groups of four to prepare a project comparing the American, French, and Russian revolutions. Each member is given a specific responsibility. "Remember, the quality of your project depends on all of you doing your parts to contribute to the final product," she emphasizes.

exploring diversity

Learner Differences in Motivation to Learn

The theory and research we've examined in this chapter describe general patterns in motivation to learn, and, in many ways they are true for most students. For instance, all students, regardless of culture, gender, or socioeconomic status have needs for competence, autonomy, and relatedness; they all set goals; and they all offer attributions for their successes and failures.

How these factors influence motivation to learn can vary among groups and individuals, however (d'Ailly, 2003; Rogoff, 2003). For instance, research indicates that some Native American groups give young children more autonomy in decision making than do parents in mainstream Western culture (Deyhle & LeCompte, 1999), whereas African American parents give their students less autonomy, possibly to protect them in potentially dangerous environments (McLoyd, 1998). Also, while being allowed to make choices increases learner autonomy, Asian students may prefer letting people they trust, such as parents or teachers, make choices for them (Vansteenkist, Zhou, Lens, & Soenens, 2005).

Differences in learners' need for relatedness also exist. Some Asian students, for example, meet this need by excelling in school and gaining the approval of their parents and teachers (J. Li, 2005), whereas members of other minorities meet the need for relatedness by *not* achieving. "Indeed, many students from minority groups experience peer pressure discouraging them from adopting attitudes and behaviors associated with achieving good grades" (Rubinson, 2004, p. 58).

Many students from Native American, Asian, and Hispanic groups also have strong family ties, and they help meet their needs for relatedness by succeeding in school to meet their responsibilities to their communities (Dien, 1998).

Differences also exist in the types of goals learners set. For instance, some research indicates that both Asian American and African American students tend to focus on mastery goals, whereas European American students focus more on performance goals (K. E. Freeman, Gutman, & Midgley, 2002; Qian & Pan, 2002). Asian American students are also more likely to attribute their successes to effort and their failures to lack of effort than are Caucasian students (Lillard, 1997; Steinberg, 1996). And, African American students may have a greater tendency to develop learned helplessness than other groups, probably because of perceived prejudice (R. A. Goldstein, 2004).

Gender differences also exist. For example, the stereotypical belief that some domains, such as English, are more nearly suited for girls, whereas others, such as math and science, are for boys, still exists (M. E. Pajares & Valiante, 1999), so motivation to learn in these domains can vary because of different perceptions of utility value (J. E. Jacobs et al., 2002). Further, boys' self-efficacy tends to remain higher than girls' in spite of the fact that girls get higher grades (Eccles et al., 1998; Middleton, 1999), and girls are more easily discouraged by failure than are boys (Dweck, 2000). Research suggests that these gender differences may be due to attributions; boys tend to attribute success to high ability and failure to lack of effort, whereas girls show a reverse pattern (Vermeer, Boekaerts, & Seegers, 2000).

As teachers apply this information in their classes, it is also important to remember that individuals within groups may vary significantly. For instance, many European American students set mastery goals, and many Asian American students set performance goals. Many girls have high efficacy, and the self-efficacy of some boys is low. As teachers, we want to avoid thinking that can result in stereotyping any group.

The Influence of Interest and Emotion on Motivation to Learn

"Because it's interesting" is an intuitively sensible answer to why a learner would be motivated to engage in a task. Students are obviously more motivated to study topics they find interesting, and teachers often attempt to capitalize on student interest in their instruction (Anderman & Wolters, 2006; Brophy, 2004).

In this section we examine factors that can increase interest in learning activities.

The Influence of Interest on Motivation to Learn

To begin this section, let's return to our chapter-opening case study. As they headed to Kathy's class, Susan commented, "I've always liked history and knowing about the past, . . . and I'm pretty good at it," to which Jim replied, "In some classes I just do enough to get a decent grade, but not in here. I used to hate history, but I sometimes even read ahead a little, because Brewster makes you think. . . . It's kind of interesting the way she's always telling us about the way we are because of something that happened a zillion years ago."

Both students expressed interest in Kathy's class, but the nature of their interest differed. Susan expressed **personal interest**, "a person's ongoing affinity, attraction, or liking for a domain, subject area, topic, or activity" (Anderman & Wolters, 2006, p. 374), whereas Jim demonstrated **situational interest**, a person's current enjoyment, pleasure, or satisfaction generated by the immediate context (Schraw & Lehman, 2001).

Personal interest. A person's ongoing affinity, attraction, or liking for a domain, subject area, topic, or activity.

Situational interest. A person's current enjoyment, pleasure, or satisfaction generated by the immediate context.

Expert teachers capitalize on situational interest to increase students' motivation to learn.

Personal interest is relatively stable, and a well-developed level of prior knowledge is necessary for true personal interest (Renninger, 2000). This stability and knowledge are illustrated in Susan's comment, "I've always liked history. . . . and I'm pretty good at it." Situational interest, in contrast, can change quickly and depends on the current situation. As an individual's expertise in an area develops, however, situational interest can lead to personal interest.

Researchers tend to focus more on situational interest, because teachers have more control over it (Schraw, Flowerday, & Lehman, 2001; Shraw & Lehman, 2001). Some topics, such as *death, danger, power, money, romance*, and *sex*, seem to be universally interesting, as evidenced by both popular movies and television programs (Hidi, 2001). For younger students, scary stories, humor, and animals also seem to generate situational interest (Worthy, Moorman, & Turner, 1999).

While we can't build a curriculum around danger, money, or romance, we can increase situational interest through employing several strategies (Schraw et al., 2001; Schraw & Lehman, 2001). Some include:

MyEducationLab

To see students of different ages describe what interests them, go to *Activities and Applications* section in Chapter 10 of MyEducationLab at www.myeducationlab.com, and watch the video episode *Motivation*. Answer the questions following the episode.

- Develop learning activities that focus on real-world applications.
- Personalize content by linking topics to students' lives.
- Promote high levels of student involvement.
- Provide concrete examples.
- Make logical and coherent presentations.
- Give students choices when the opportunity arises.

In addition, teachers modeling their own interest in the topics they teach can also increase students' interest (Brophy, 2004), and modeling mastery goals can be particularly effective for increasing situational interest (Shen, Chen, & Guan, 2007). It won't increase motivation to learn in all situations or for all students, but teachers have nothing to lose by modeling enthusiasm and a mastery goal orientation about the topics they teach (Schweinle, Meyer, & Turner, 2006).

We examine strategies for increasing student interest in more detail in Chapter 11.

The Influence of Emotion on Motivation to Learn

How would you personally react to the following experiences?

- You've just solved a challenging math problem.
- Your instructor brings a newspaper clipping to class that graphically describes atrocities occurring on the African continent.
- You've studied carefully for a test in one of your classes, and you still didn't do well.

In each case, the experience likely aroused an emotion. In the first, you felt a sense of accomplishment, pleasure, and pride, and your motivation increased (Linnenbrink & Pintrich, 2004). The second may have caused feelings of outrage, increased your attention and interest, and left you thinking about it for an extended period (Zeelenber, Wadenmakers, & Rotteveel, 2006). The third likely left you feeling discouraged and frustrated, because you didn't expect to do poorly, and decreased motivation may result (Sheppard & McNulty, 2002).

These examples illustrate the relationship between emotion, or affect, and motivation to learn. This relationship is complex, because emotions can range from guilt, shame, and anxiety, to more positive feelings such as pride, joy, and relief. Each can influence motivation to learn (Do & Schallert, 2004; Pekrun, Goetz, Titz, & Perry, 2002). For instance, in our discussion of attributions, you saw that attributing failure to lack of effort leads to feelings of guilt and increased motivation to learn, whereas attributing failure to lack of ability can lead to feelings of shame and decreased motivation. In contrast, attributing success to either effort or ability can lead to feelings of pride and increased effort.

Anxiety is one of the most studied emotions in teaching and learning. We examine it next in more detail.

The Impact of Anxiety on Motivation to Learn

In the conversation that introduced our discussion of attributions, Ashley commented,

> "I looked at the test, and just went blank. All I could think of was, 'I've never seen this stuff before. Where did it come from?' I thought I was going to throw up."

Ashley experienced **anxiety**, a general uneasiness and feeling of tension relating to a situation with an uncertain outcome. At one time or another, it's likely that we've all experienced anxiety when anticipating a test or presentation.

Anxiety. A general uneasiness and feeling of tension, relating to a situation with an uncertain outcome.

The relationship between anxiety, motivation, and achievement is curvilinear; some is good, but too much can be damaging (Cassady & Johnson, 2002). For example, some anxiety makes us study hard and develop competence. Relatively high anxiety improves performance on tasks where our expertise is well developed (Covington & Omelich, 1987). Too much anxiety, however, can decrease motivation and achievement; classrooms where the evaluation threat is high are particularly anxiety producing (Hancock, 2001). Its main source is fear of failure and, with it, the loss of self-worth (K. Hill & Wigfield, 1984). Low achievers and students who are concerned with performance versus mastery are particularly vulnerable to these feelings (K. E. Ryan et al., 2007).

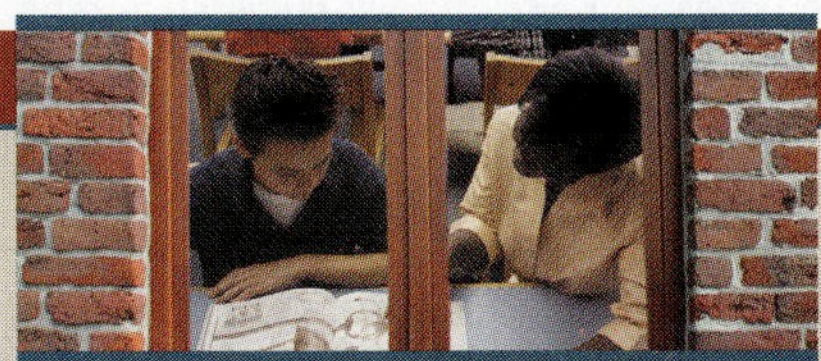

classroom connections

Capitalizing on Interest and Emotion to Promote Motivation to Learn in Your Classroom

1. Promote interest in your learning activities by using concrete and personalized examples and promoting high levels of student involvement.
   - **Elementary:** A fourth-grade teacher puts his students' names into word problems in math, and has different students explain the solutions to each. He is careful to be sure that all students' names are used over a 3-day period.
   - **Middle School:** A geography teacher draws lines of latitude and longitude on a globe, and pinpoints the location of their city. She asks students to work in pairs to identify similarities and differences in the lines, and they arrive at definitions for each and the exact location of their city.
   - **High School:** A physics teacher creates problems using the velocity and momentum of soccer balls after they've been kicked, and she asks students to determine the acceleration and speed players must run to intercept the kicks. The students then describe solutions for each.
2. To reduce anxiety, emphasize understanding the content of tests instead of grades, provide opportunities for practice, and give students ample time to finish assessments.
   - **Elementary:** A second-grade teacher monitors his students as they work on a quiz. When he sees their attention wander, he reminds them of the work they have done on the topic and to concentrate on their work.
   - **Middle School:** An eighth-grade algebra teacher gives her students extensive practice with the types of problems they'll be expected to solve on their tests.
   - **High School:** At the beginning of a unit test, a physics teacher suggests, "Go immediately to the first problem you're sure you know how to solve. Force any thoughts not related to physics out of your heads, and don't let them back in."

theory to practice

Capitalizing on Students' Beliefs, Goals, and Interests to Increase Motivation to Learn

An understanding of learners' beliefs, goals, and interests has important implications for the way we work with our students. As you attempt to apply these ideas in your teaching, the following guidelines can help you in your efforts:

1. Increase learner self-efficacy by providing students with evidence of accomplishment and modeling your own self-efficacy.
2. Encourage internal attributions for successes and controllable attributions for failures.
3. Emphasize the utility value of increased skills.
4. Promote student interest by modeling your own interest, personalizing content, providing concrete examples, involving students, and offering choices.
5. Emphasize mastery and social responsibility goals, effective strategies, and metacognition.

Now we return once again to Kathy's classroom and her work with her students to see how she attempts to apply the guidelines. She is in the second day of her unit on the Crusades.

"We began our discussion of the Crusades yesterday. . . . How did we start?" Kathy asks.

"We imagined that Lincoln High School was taken over by people who believed that extracurricular activities should be eliminated," Carnisha volunteers.

"Good," Kathy smiles. "Then what?"

"We decided we'd talk to them. . . . We'd be on a 'crusade' to change their minds and save our school."

"Very good. . . . Now, what were the actual Crusades all about?. . . Selena?"

"The Christians wanted to get the Holy Land back from the Muslims."

"And why? . . . Becky?"

"The holy lands were important to the Christians."

The class then discusses reasons for the actual Crusades, such as religion, economics, the military threat posed by the Muslim world, and the amount of territory they held.

"Excellent analysis. . . . In fact, we'll see that these factors influenced Columbus's voyage to the New World and its exploration. . . . Think about that. The Crusades nearly 1,000 years ago have had an influence on us here today," she continues energetically.

"Now, for today's assignment, you were asked to write an analysis answering the question, 'Were the Crusades a success or a failure?' and we emphasized the importance of providing evidence for your position, not the position itself. Remember, the ability to make and defend an argument is a skill that goes way beyond a specific topic.

"So, let's see how we did. Go ahead. . . . Nikki?"

Kathy asks several students to present their positions and then closes the discussion by saying, "See how interesting this is? Again, we see ourselves influenced by people who lived hundreds of years ago. . . . That's what history is all about."

"Brewster loves this stuff," David whispers to Kelly.

Kathy then tells the students to revise their analyses based on their discussion. "Remember," she emphasizes, "when you make your revisions, ask yourself, 'Do I have evidence here, or is it simply an opinion?' . . . The more aware you are when you write, the better your work will be. When you're done, switch with a partner and critique each other's paper. We made a commitment at the beginning of the year to help each other when we give feedback on our writing. . . . So, I know that you'll come through."

Now, let's look at Kathy's attempts to apply the guidelines. Her interaction with Harvey in the case study at the beginning of the chapter illustrates the first three. She applied the first (increase learner self-efficacy) when she said, "Yes, but look how good you're getting at writing. I think you hit a personal best on your last paper." She also commented, "It's hard for me, too, when I'm studying and trying to put together new ideas, but if I hang in, I always feel like I can get it." Her first comment provided Harvey with evidence of his accomplishment, and the second modeled her own developing self-efficacy.

She applied the second guideline (encourage internal attributions for successes) when she responded to Harvey's comment, "But you make us work so hard," by saying, "Yes, but look how good you're getting at writing." Her response encouraged him to attribute his success to effort and increased ability, both of which are internal attributions. His comment, "Yeah, yeah, I know, and being good writers will help us in everything we do in life," reflected her emphasis on the utility value of what they were learning, an application of the third guideline.

Kathy attempted to apply the fourth guideline (promote student interest) in three ways. First, she modeled her own interest in saying, "Think about that. The Muslims and the Crusades nearly a 1,000 years ago have had an influence on us here today," and "See how interesting this is. . . ." Her statements' impact on students was reflected in David's comment, "Brewster loves this stuff."

She also attempted to increase students' interest by personalizing the topic with the analogy of "crusading" to prevent the school from eliminating extracurricular activities, using the analogy as a concrete example of a crusade, and involving students throughout the activity.

Finally, as you saw in the case study at the beginning of the chapter, Kathy allowed the students to choose either a presentation on the Renaissance or a paper on the Middle Ages, to decide which groups would present on certain days, and to negotiate the due date for the papers ("Remember . . . we agreed that they're due on Friday").

Kathy attempted to apply the last guideline (emphasize mastery and social responsibility goals, effective strategies, and metacognition) by encouraging students to be metacognitive about their writing, "Remember, . . . Ask yourself, 'Do I actually have evidence here, or is it simply an opinion?' . . . The more aware you are when you write, the better your work will be," and she emphasized social responsibility goals when she said, "We made a commitment . . . to help each other when we give feedback on our writing. . . . So, I know that you'll come through." The combination of social responsibility goals and mastery goals increases motivation and achievement more than either alone.

At the beginning of the chapter, we said that with effort teachers can increase the motivation to learn in many of their students. This is what Kathy tried to do as she worked with hers.

developmentally appropriate practice

Motivation to Learn at Different Ages

Many applications of motivation theory apply to learners at all grade levels, such as using high-quality and personalized examples, involving students, and creating safe and orderly learning environments. Developmental differences exist, however. The following paragraphs outline some suggestions for responding to these differences.

Working with Elementary Students

In contrast with older students, young children bask openly in praise, and they rarely evaluate whether or not the praise is justified. They also tend to have incremental views of intelligence and set mastery goals. Because of these factors, emphasizing that all students can learn, avoiding social comparisons, praising students for their effort, and reminding them that hard work "makes us smart" can increase motivation to learn.

Working with Middle School Students

As learners grow older, their mastery orientation tends to decrease while their performance orientation increases. Modeling the belief that intelligence is incremental, and emphasizing the relationship between effort and increased competence and ability are important. Middle school students increasingly meet their needs for belonging and relatedness with peer experiences, so social goals tend to increase in importance. Combining whole-group with small-group activities can help students meet these needs and goals.

Middle school students' need for autonomy also increases, so involving them in activities that increase their sense of autonomy, such as asking them to provide input into classroom rules, can be effective.

Working with High School Students

High school students are beginning to think about their futures, so emphasizing the utility value of the topics they study and the skills they develop can increase their motivation to learn.

Because of the myriad of experiences that high school students can access, such as video games and the Internet, generating interest in school topics can be a challenge. However, using concrete and personalized examples and promoting high levels of interaction remain effective.

Evidence that their competence is increasing is important to high school students, so sincere praise and other indicators of genuine accomplishment can increase motivation to learn.

The model of human memory helps us understand the debilitating effects of anxiety (Cassady & Johnson, 2002). First, anxious students have difficulty concentrating, so attention suffers. Second, because they worry about—and even expect—failure, they often misperceive the information they see and hear. Third, test-anxious students often use superficial strategies, such as memorizing definitions, instead of strategies that are more productive, such as summarizing and self-questioning.

Research suggests that the primary problem with highly test-anxious students is they don't learn the content very well in the first place, which further increases their anxiety when they're required to perform on tests (Wolf, Smith, & Birnbaum, 1997; Zeidner, 1998). Finally, during assessments, test-anxious students often waste working memory space on thoughts such as Ashley's thinking, "I've never seen this stuff before. Where did it come from?" leaving less memory space available for focusing on the task.

Instruction that emphasizes understanding can be more effective than any other strategy to help students cope with anxiety. Such instruction includes providing high-quality examples, promoting student involvement, providing specific feedback on assessments, and providing outside help. When understanding increases, poor performance decreases. In time, fear of failure and the anxiety it produces will also decrease.

Remember, our descriptions of learner anxiety represent general patterns, and individuals will vary. For instance, some high achievers continue to experience anxiety in spite of a long history of success. In all cases, remember that we teach individuals and not groups, and we want to treat our students in the same way.

check your understanding

5.1 Identify four ways in which teachers can increase interest in their learning activities.
5.2 Explain how teachers can capitalize on emotions to increase students' motivation to learn.
5.3 Describe three ways teachers can reduce anxiety in their students.

To receive feedback for these questions, go to Appendix A.

Meeting Your Learning Objectives

1. Define motivation, and describe different theoretical explanations for learner motivation.
   - Motivation is a process whereby goal-directed activity is instigated and sustained.
   - Extrinsic motivation is motivation to engage in an activity as a means to an end; intrinsic motivation is motivation to be involved in an activity for its own sake. Challenge, autonomy, curiosity, fantasy, and aesthetic value all promote intrinsic motivation.
   - Behaviorism describes motivation and learning in the same way; an increase in behavior is evidence of both learning and motivation.
   - Cognitive and social cognitive theories of motivation focus on learners' beliefs, expectations, and needs for order and understanding.
   - Sociocultural views of motivation focus on individuals' participating in the practices of a learning community. Through communities of practice and a motivational zone of proximal development, students' motivation to learn is increased.
   - Humanistic views of motivation are grounded in the premise that people are motivated to fulfill their total potential as human beings.
2. Explain how learners' needs influence their motivation to learn.
   - In motivation theory, a need is an internal force or drive to attain or avoid certain states or objects.
   - According to Maslow, all people have needs for survival, safety, belonging, and self-esteem. If these needs are not met, people are motivated to meet them. Once these needs are met, people are motivated to fulfill their potential as human beings.
   - According to self-determination theory, all people have needs for competence, autonomy, and relatedness. If these needs are met, motivation increases.
   - Self-worth theory suggests that all people have the need to protect their sense of self-worth. Since our culture values high ability, people are motivated to protect the perception that they have high ability.
3. Explain how learners' beliefs can influence their motivation to learn.
   - A belief is a cognitive idea we accept as true without necessarily having definitive evidence to support it.
   - Learners' motivation increases when they expect to succeed and believe that a future outcome will be positive.
   - Learners who believe that intelligence can be increased with effort have an incremental view of intelligence. They tend to have higher motivation to learn than learners who believe intelligence is fixed, who have an entity view.
   - Students who believe they are capable of accomplishing specific tasks have high self-efficacy and are more motivated to learn than students whose self-efficacy is lower.
   - Believing that increased understanding has utility value and will help them meet future goals increases students' motivation to learn.
   - Students who believe that effort and ability are the causes of their success, or that lack of effort is the cause of failure, are likely to be motivated to learn. Believing that lack of ability is the reason for failure is likely to decrease motivation to learn.
4. Explain how learners' goals can influence their motivation to learn.
   - A goal is an outcome an individual hopes to attain.
   - Learners whose goals focus on mastery of tasks, improvement, and increased understanding have higher motivation to learn than do learners whose goals focus on social comparisons.
   - Social goals can decrease motivation to learn if they focus exclusively on social factors. Social responsibility goals, however, and particularly social responsibility goals combined with mastery goals, can lead to sustained motivation and achievement.
   - Goals that are specific, close at hand, and moderately challenging are effective for increasing motivation to learn.
5. Explain how teachers can capitalize on learners' interests and emotions to increase motivation to learn.

- Teachers can increase students' interest in the topics they study by using concrete and personalized examples, emphasizing real-world applications, and promoting high levels of student involvement in learning activities.
- Teachers can capitalize on emotions to increase motivation to learn by emphasizing the emotional component of topics when opportunities present themselves.
- Teachers can decrease learner anxiety by making expectations about learning and how students will be assessed clear and specific, using teaching strategies that promote understanding, and providing students with opportunities to receive outside help.

Developing as a Professional: Preparing for Your Licensure Exam

You saw in this chapter how Kathy Brewster applied an understanding of theories of motivation in her teaching. We now present a case study involving another world history teacher who is also teaching the Crusades. Read the case study, and then answer the questions that follow. As you read, compare this teacher's approach to Kathy Brewster's.

Damon Marcus watches as his students take their seats, and then announces, "Listen, everyone, I have your tests here from last Friday. Liora, Ivan, Lynn, and Segundo, super job on the test. Unfortunately, they were the only A's in the class."

After handing back the tests, Damon writes the following on the chalkboard:

A 4 D 4
B 7 F 3
C 11

"You people down here better get moving," Damon comments, pointing to the D's and F's on the chalkboard. "This wasn't that hard a test. Remember, we have another one in 2 weeks. We need to see some improvement. C'mon, now. I know you can do better. Let's give these sharp ones with the A's a run for their money.

"Now let's get going. We have a lot to cover today.... As you'll recall from yesterday, the Crusades were an attempt by the Christian powers of Western Europe to wrestle control of the traditional holy lands of Christianity away from the Muslims. Now, when was the First Crusade?"

"About 1500, I think," Clifton volunteers.

"No, no," Damon shakes his head. "Remember that Columbus sailed in 1492, which was before 1500, so that doesn't make sense.... Liora?"

"It was about 1100, I think."

"Excellent, Liora. Now, remember, everyone, you need to know these dates, or otherwise you'll get confused. I know that learning dates and places isn't the most pleasant stuff, but you might as well get used to it, because that's what history is about. Plus, they'll be on the next test."

He continues, "The First Crusade was in 1095, and it was called the 'People's Crusade.' There were actually seven in all, starting in 1095 and continuing until enthusiasm for them ended in 1300.

"They weren't just religiously motivated," he goes on. "The Muslim world was getting stronger and stronger, and it was posing a threat to Europe. For example, it had control of much of northern Africa, had expanded into southern Spain, and even was moving into other parts of southern Europe. So it was an economic and military threat as well."

Damon continues presenting information about the Crusades, and then, seeing that about 20 minutes were left in the period, he says, "Now, I want you to write a summary of the Crusades that outlines the major people and events and tells why they were important. You should be able to finish by the end of the period, but if you don't, turn your papers in at the beginning of class tomorrow. You may use your notes. Go ahead and get started."

As he monitors students, he sees that Jeremy has written only a few words on his paper. "Are you having trouble getting started?" Damon asks quietly.

"Yeah, ... I don't quite know how to get started," Jeremy mumbles.

"I know you have a tough time with written assignments. Let me help you," Damon nods.

He takes a blank piece of paper and starts writing as Jeremy watches. He writes several sentences on the paper and then says, "See how easy that was? That's the kind of thing I want you to do. Go ahead—that's a start. Keep that so you can see what I'm looking for. Go back to your desk, and give it another try."

Short-Answer Questions

In answering these questions, use information from Chapter 10, and link your responses to specific information in the case.

1. With respect to humanistic views of motivation, assess the extent to which Damon helped students meet the deficiency needs and contributed to the growth needs in Maslow's hierarchy.
2. Assess Damon's effectiveness in meeting his students' self-determination needs.
3. Assess Damon's effectiveness in accommodating students' needs to preserve feelings of self-worth.
4. How effectively did Damon promote interest in the topic?

To receive feedback for these questions, go to Appendix B.

Now go to Chapter 10 of MyEducationLab, located at www.myeducationlab.com, where you can:

- Take a quiz to test your mastery of chapter objectives. Detailed feedback is provided to explain why your responses are correct or incorrect.
- Deepen your understanding of chapter concepts with *Review, Practice, and Enrichment* exercises.
- Complete *Activities and Applications* that will help you apply what you have learned in the chapter by analyzing real classrooms through video clips, artifacts and case studies. Your instructor will provide you with feedback for the *Activities and Applications.*
- Develop your professional knowledge and decision making in *Building Teaching Skills and Dispositions* exercises. Structured feedback will be available to you, providing you with support as you practice each skill. Your instructor will provide you with feedback on the final task that accompanies the exercises.

Important Concepts

anxiety (p. 311)
attainment value (p. 299)
attribution (p. 301)
attribution theory (p. 301)
attributional statements (p. 292)
autonomy (p. 292)
belief (p. 297)
competence (p. 291)
cost (p. 300)
deficiency needs (p. 291)
entity view of intelligence (p. 297)
expectancy × value theory (p. 297)
expectation (p. 297)
extrinsic motivation (p. 285)
goal (p. 304)
growth needs (p. 290)
incremental view of intelligence (p. 297)
intrinsic motivation (p. 285)
learned helplessness (p. 303)
mastery goal (p. 304)
motivation (p. 284)
motivation to learn (p. 286)
need (p. 290)
need for approval (p. 293)
performance-approach goal (p. 304)
performance-avoidance goal (p. 304)
performance goal (p. 304)
personal interest (p. 309)
relatedness (p. 293)
self-actualization (p. 291)
self-determination (p. 291)
self-efficacy (p. 298)
self-worth (p. 294)
situational interest (p. 309)
social goals (p. 305)
unconditional positive regard (p. 288)
utility value (p. 300)
value (p. 299)

chapter

11

Motivation in the Classroom

chapter outline

Class Structure: Creating a Mastery-Focused Environment

Self-Regulated Learners: Developing Student Responsibility

- Developing Self-Regulation: Applying Learners' Needs for Self-Determination

Teacher Characteristics: Personal Qualities That Increase Motivation to Learn

- Personal Teaching Efficacy: Beliefs About Teaching and Learning
- Modeling and Enthusiasm: Communicating Genuine Interest
- Caring: Meeting Needs for Belonging and Relatedness
- Teacher Expectations: Increasing Perceptions of Competence
  - **Theory to Practice:** Personal Qualities That Increase Motivation to Learn

Climate Variables: Creating a Motivating Environment

- Order and Safety: Classrooms as Secure Places to Learn
- Success: Developing Learner Self-Efficacy
- Challenge: Increasing Perceptions of Competence
- Task Comprehension: Increasing Feelings of Autonomy and Value
- The TARGET program: Applying Goal Theory in Classrooms

Instructional Variables: Developing Interest in Learning Activities

- Introductory Focus: Attracting Students' Attention
- Personalization: Links to Students' Lives
  - **Exploring Diversity:** Personalizing Content to Increase Interest in Students with Diverse Backgrounds
- Involvement: Increasing Intrinsic Interest
- Feedback: Meeting the Need to Understand
  - **Theory to Practice:** Capitalizing on Climate and Instruction Variables to Increase Student Motivation to Learn
- Assessment and Learning: Using Feedback to Increase Interest and Self-Efficacy
- Learning Contexts: Increasing Motivation in Urban Classrooms
  - **Developmentally Appropriate Practice:** Applying the Model for Promoting Motivation with Learners at Different Ages

learning objectives

After you have completed your study of this chapter, you should be able to:

1. Describe differences between a mastery-focused and a performance-focused classroom.
2. Identify strategies that teachers can use to develop learner self-regulation.
3. Describe teachers' personal characteristics that can increase students' motivation to learn.
4. Identify classroom environment variables that can increase students' motivation to learn.
5. Describe instructional strategies that can increase students' motivation to learn.

Think about some of your favorite teachers. How did they treat you, and what did they do that made their classes interesting and worthwhile? These questions relate to motivation in classrooms. Teachers' personal characteristics, the classroom environments they create, and the way they teach all have important influences on students' motivation to learn. Consider the extent to which these factors are applied in the following case study:

> DeVonne Lampkin, a fifth-grade teacher, begins her day's science lesson by reaching into a cooler and taking out a live lobster.
>
> The students "ooh" and "aah" at the wriggling animal, and DeVonne asks Stephanie to carry it around the room and let students look at and touch it.
>
> She then says, "Observe carefully, because I'm going to ask you to tell us what you see. . . . Okay, what did you notice?"

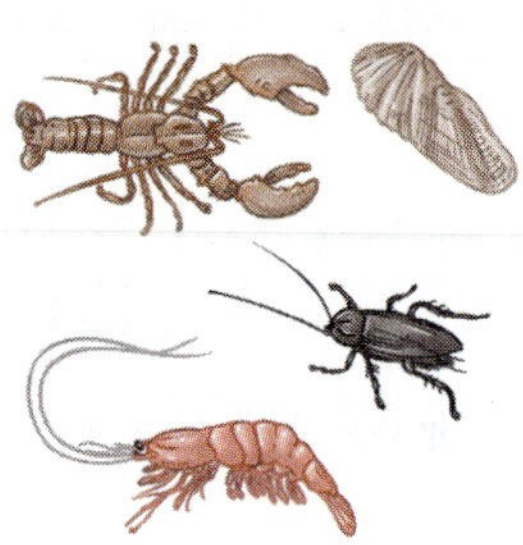

"Hard," Tu observes.

"Pink and green," Saleina comments.

"Wet," Kevin adds.

The students make additional observations. DeVonne lists them on the board, and prompts the students to conclude that the lobster has a hard outer covering, which she labels an *exoskeleton;* three body parts; and segmented legs. She identifies these as essential characteristics of *arthropods.*

Reaching into her bag again, DeVonne pulls out a cockroach. Amid more squeals, she walks around the class holding it with tweezers, and then asks, "Is this an arthropod?"

After some discussion to resolve uncertainty about whether or not the cockroach has an exoskeleton, the class concludes that it is.

DeVonne next takes a clam out of her cooler, and asks, "Is this an arthropod?"

Some students conclude that it is, reasoning that it has a hard shell.

A.J. comments, "It doesn't have any legs," and, following some additional discussion, the class decides that it isn't an arthropod.

"Now," DeVonne asks, "Do you think Mrs. Sapp [the school principal] is an arthropod? . . . Tell us why or why not."

Amid more giggles, some of the students conclude that she is, because she has segmented legs. Others disagree because she doesn't look like a lobster or a roach. After some discussion, Tu observes, "She doesn't have an exoskeleton," and the class finally agrees that she is not an arthropod.

DeVonne then instructs the students to form pairs, passes out shrimp for examination, calms the excited students, and asks them to observe the shrimp carefully and decide if they're arthropods.

During the whole-group discussion that follows, she discovers that some of the students are still uncertain about the idea of an exoskeleton, so she has them peel the shrimp and feel the head and outer covering. After seeing the peeled covering, they conclude that the shrimp does indeed have an exoskeleton.

DeVonne then reviews the activities and closes the lesson.

As you think about this case study, consider these questions:

1. What did DeVonne do that stimulated students' high intrinsic interest?
2. How did DeVonne's personal characteristics, the characteristics of the classroom, and her instruction contribute to her students' motivation to learn?

Classroom applications of the motivation theories you studied in Chapter 10 help answer these and other questions about student motivation. We examine these applications in this chapter.

Class Structure: Creating a Mastery-Focused Environment

Mastery-focused environment. A classroom environment that emphasizes effort, continuous improvement, and understanding.

Performance-focused environment. A classroom environment that emphasizes high grades, public displays of ability, and performance compared to others.

We begin to answer our questions by considering two types of classroom environments. A **mastery-focused environment** emphasizes effort, continuous improvement, and understanding, as compared to a **performance-focused environment,** which makes high grades, public displays of ability, and performance compared to others the priorities (Anderman & Wolters, 2006).

DeVonne attempted to create a mastery-focused environment for her students in three ways: (1) She created high levels of interest by using real animals—the lobster, cockroach, and shrimp—to teach the concept *arthropod,* (2) she emphasized understanding, and (3) she promoted cooperation versus competition as they studied the topic. Differences in mastery- and performance-focused environments are summarized in Table 11.1 (Covington, 2000; Pintrich, 2000; Urdan, 2001).

Within this mastery-oriented framework, this chapter describes a model for promoting student motivation to learn that synthesizes and applies the theory and research you

table 11.1 Comparisons of Mastery-Focused and Performance-Focused Classrooms

	Mastery Focused	Performance Focused
Success defined as . . .	Mastery, improvement	High grades, doing better than others
Value placed on . . .	Effort, improvement	High grades, demonstration of high ability
Reasons for satisfaction . . .	Meeting challenges, hard work	Doing better than others, success with minimum effort
Teacher oriented toward . . .	Student learning	Student performance
View of errors . . .	A normal part of learning	A basis for concern and anxiety
Reasons for effort . . .	Increased understanding	High grades, doing better than others
Ability viewed as . . .	Incremental, alterable	An entity, fixed
Reasons for assessment . . .	Measure progress toward preset criteria, provide feedback	Determine grades, compare students to one another

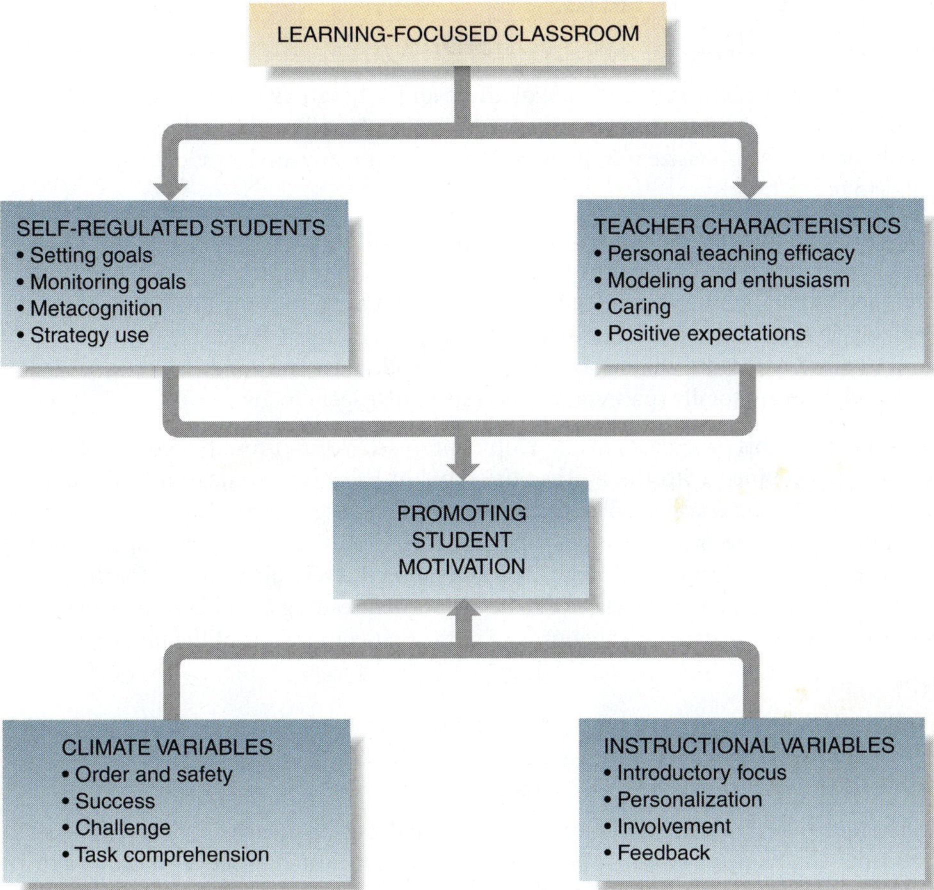

Figure 11.1 A model for promoting student motivation to learn

studied in Chapter 10 (Eggen & Kauchak, 2002). It is outlined in Figure 11.1 and has four components:

1. Self-regulated learners: Developing student responsibility
2. Teacher characteristics: Personal qualities that increase student motivation

3. Climate variables: Creating a motivating environment
4. Instructional variables: Developing interest in learning activities

Four *variables* exist within each *component*. The components and variables in the model are interdependent; a single variable cannot be effectively applied if the others are missing. Keep this in mind as you study the following sections.

check your understanding

1.1 Describe the differences between a mastery-focused and a performance-focused classroom.

1.2 A teacher says, "Excellent job on the last test, everyone. More than half the class got an A or a B." Based on descriptions of mastery-focused versus performance-focused classrooms, how effective is this comment for promoting motivation? Explain.

To receive feedback for these questions, go to Appendix A.

Self-Regulated Learners: Developing Student Responsibility

Teachers commonly lament students' lack of effort and willingness to take responsibility for their own learning (J. Cooper, Horn, Strahan, & Miller, 2003). All teachers want students to be responsible, and they emphasize it in their classrooms, but many are less successful than they would like to be:

> "My kids are so irresponsible," Kathy Hughes, a seventh-grade teacher grumbles in a conversation at lunch. "They don't bring their books, they forget their notebooks in their lockers, they come without pencils. . . . I can't get them to come to class prepared, let alone get them to read their assignments."
>
> "I know," Mercedes Blount, one of Kathy's colleagues, responds, smiling wryly. "Some of them are totally spacey, and others just don't seem to give a rip."

Self-regulation. The process of setting personal goals, combined with the motivation, thought processes, strategies, and behaviors that lead to reaching the goals.

The solution to this problem is the development of **self-regulation,** the process of setting personal goals, combined with the motivation, thought processes, strategies, and behaviors that lead to reaching the goals. Ideally, students who are self-regulated set and monitor goals, they are motivated to reach the goals, and they are metacognitive in their attempts to match strategies to goals. For example, a self-regulated student takes a very different approach to reading a novel assigned in his English class than he does when reading about atomic structure in his chemistry class. These variables are outlined in the first component of the model as

- Setting goals
- Monitoring goals
- Metacognition
- Strategy use

Reaching the ideal of self-regulation is a major challenge for teachers, however, because many students don't know how to create goals and aren't motivated to set or commit to them (Schunk, 2005; Zimmerman, 2005).

In the following sections, we look at ways to try to solve these problems.

Developing Self-Regulation: Applying Learners' Needs for Self-Determination

Self-determination is an important need for people, and teachers can capitalize on this need to help students set, commit to, and monitor goals. Let's see how.

Though its focus is on intrinsic motivation, self-determination theory acknowledges that not all behaviors are initially intrinsically motivated (R. Ryan & Deci, 2000; Schunk, Pintrich, & Meece, 2008). For instance, students first attempt to meet goals to receive rewards and avoid punishers (R. Ryan & Deci, 2000). As their self-regulation develops, they gradually learn to become responsible for meeting mastery goals because, for example, they believe that meeting the goal helps them get better grades. Although this behavior is still extrinsically motivated, it represents increasing self-regulation. As students further develop, they attempt to meet goals because doing so is consistent with beliefs about the kind of people they are. For instance, if a student monitors goal achievement because she begins to view herself as responsible, she has made further progress toward self-determination.

Eventually (and ideally) learners set and monitor goals for their own sake, which is behavior that is intrinsically motivated and self-determined (Schunk et al., 2008). In the real world, many students never reach this point; however, for those who do, the probability of long-term achievement and success are greatly enhanced. As a teacher, you play a crucial role in helping self-determination develop (Friedel, Cortina, & Turner, 2007; N. E. Perry, Turner, & Meyer, 2006).

Because self-regulation is developmental, you will need to initially scaffold students' efforts and then gradually turn more responsibility over to them (Bohn, Roehrig, & Pressley, 2004). Suggestions for providing this scaffolding are outlined in Figure 11.2 and illustrated in the case study and suggestions that follow

Let's see how Sam Cook, a seventh-grade geography teacher, attempts to apply the suggestions in Figure 11.2 with his students.

- Emphasize the relationship between responsibility and learning.
- Solicit student input into class procedures that include responsibility.
- Teach responsibility as a concept, and link consequences to action.
- Model responsibility and a mastery focus, and guide students' goal setting.
- Provide a concrete mechanism to help students monitor goal achievement.

Figure 11.2 Suggestions for developing learner self-regulation

Sam begins the first day of school by welcoming the students, having them introduce themselves, and then says, "To learn as much as possible, we need to work together. For instance, I need to think about what we're trying to accomplish, and I need to bring the examples that will help you understand our topics. . . . That's my part. . . . So, what is your part?"

With some guidance from Sam, the students conclude that they should bring their books and other materials to class each day, that they need to be in their seats when the bell rings, and they need to understand their homework instead of merely getting it done.

"Now, who is responsible for all this?" Sam asks.

"We are," several students respond.

"Yes. . . . I'm responsible for my part, and you're responsible for your parts.

"Now, let's see what happens when people aren't responsible," and he displays the following on the overhead:

Josh brings all his materials to school every day, and he carefully does his homework. He has a list that he checks off to be sure that he has each of the items and that he understands his homework. If he's uncertain about any part, he asks the next day.

Josh is learning a lot, and he says his classes are interesting. His teachers respect his effort.

Andy gets in trouble with his teachers because he often forgets to bring his book, notebook, or pencil to class. He sometimes forgets his homework, so he doesn't get credit for the assignment, and he isn't learning very much. Andy's teacher called his mom to discuss his lack of responsibility, and now Andy can't watch TV for a week.

"What are some differences you notice between Josh and Andy?" Sam asks after giving students a minute to read the vignettes.

The students make several comments, and in the process, Ronise concludes, "It's his own fault," in response to someone pointing out that Andy isn't learning very much.

"Yes," Sam nods, "if we don't take responsibility for ourselves, whose fault is it if we don't learn?"

"Our own," several students respond.

"Yes," Sam emphasizes. "We're all responsible for ourselves."

Week of ____________		Name________________			
Responsibility Goals	**Monday**	**Tuesday**	**Wednesday**	**Thursday**	**Friday**
Bring sharpened pencil	✓	✓			
Bring notebook					
Bring textbook					
In seat when bell rings					
Learning Goals	**Monday**	**Tuesday**	**Wednesday**	**Thursday**	**Friday**
Finish homework					
Understand homework					

Figure 11.3 Monitoring sheet

With Sam's guidance, the students set goals that will help them take responsibility, and the next day, he distributes a monitoring sheet (see Figure 11.3), which he has prepared based on the discussion. He has them put the sheet in the front of their notebooks and check off the items the first thing each morning. As the sheets accumulate, the students have a "responsibility portfolio" that gives them a record of their progress.

Sam then asks the students how they will determine whether or not they understand their homework, and they agree that they will either explain it in class or to their parents.

Finally, they decide that each week the students who get 18 or more checks for the responsibility goals and 8 or more for the learning goals will have free time on Fridays. Those with fewer than 15 checks on the responsibility goals will spend "quiet time" alone during that period, and those with fewer than 8 checks for the learning goals will work with Sam on areas that need improvement.

Now, we'll examine how Sam attempted to apply the suggestions in Figure 11.2. First, he emphasized from the beginning of the year that they were there to learn and that accepting responsibility was necessary if they were to learn as much as possible. This began the process of establishing a mastery-focused environment.

Second, he asked for students' input into class procedures. Being asked for input contributes to students' feelings of autonomy, a basic need according to self-determination theory (R. Ryan & Deci, 2000). It also increases the likelihood that students will commit to the goals they create.

Third, Sam treated responsibility as a concept and illustrated it with an example and a nonexample. Students sometimes fail to take responsibility because they don't clearly understand what responsibility is and the relationship between their actions and the consequences of those actions. By using examples to illustrate the consequences of behaving either responsibly or irresponsibly, Sam used an informational rather than a controlling strategy for promoting self-regulation. This strategy can contribute to intrinsic motivation (Charles & Senter, 2005; Emmer & Stough, 2001).

Fourth, in saying, "I need to think about what we're trying to accomplish, and I need to bring the examples that will help you understand our topics. . . . That's my part," he personally modeled responsibility and a mastery focus. He also guided students as they set goals, which were specific, immediate, and, for Sam's students, moderately challenging.

Finally, Sam prepared a concrete structure (the sheet) to help students monitor their goals. Accumulating checks on the sheets can increase self-efficacy, even though the process is as basic as bringing required materials to class. Gradually, they may increasingly accept responsibility for following these procedures and also learn to make decisions that will increase their own learning. This marks progress on the path to self-regulation.

Sam's students initially met goals to receive rewards (free time) and avoid punishers (quiet time alone during the free period). As self-regulation develops, his students hopefully will be-

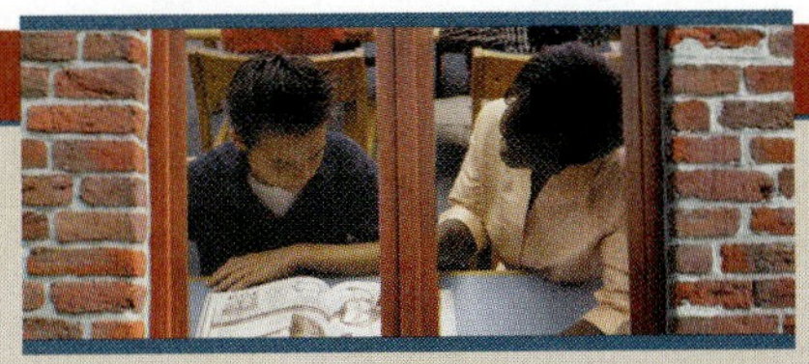

classroom connections

Promoting Self-Regulation in Your Classroom

Self-regulation is the process of setting and reaching personal goals. Promote learner responsibility with goal setting, self-monitoring, and metacognition.

- **Elementary:** A fourth-grade teacher presents a "problem of the week" each Monday in math. Students set the goal of solving the problem, and when they've completed the solution, they put it in their math portfolios and put a check on the first page of the portfolio. When they've explained it to a parent, other adult, or sibling, they make a second check on the sheet. They then discuss solutions on Fridays.
- **Middle School:** A seventh-grade history teacher provides a study guide for her students. The students set the goal of answering and understanding all the study guide questions each week. They check off each question when they've answered and believe they understand it.
- **High School:** Physics students set the goal of creating one real-world application of each of the topics they study. When they believe they have a good application, they offer it to the class for analysis and discussion.

gin setting their own goals because they see that setting and monitoring goals increase learning (R. Ryan & Deci, 2000).

This example focused on middle school students, but self-regulation can also be a goal for young children. To account for developmental differences, the process must be adapted. The case study on page 360 of Chapter 12 describes how Martha Oakes teaches her first graders to put away their worksheets. Martha incorporated several of the suggestions you saw Sam use. She taught the procedure using examples, she modeled it, and she expected her students to accept responsibility for following it. And Martha believed that her first graders could make productive contributions in classroom meetings. These are all part of the development of self-regulation.

Regardless of how hard you try, some of your students may fail to accept responsibility, just as, in spite of your best efforts, not all students will be motivated to learn. However, for students who do become self-regulated, you will have made a lifelong contribution to their learning and overall well-being.

check your understanding

2.1 Identify strategies that teachers can use to increase learner self-regulation, and explain how Sam Cook implemented these strategies with his students.

2.2 Sam's students initially attempted to meet goals to receive rewards and avoid punishers. Offer an example that would illustrate a move toward greater self-regulation (and ultimately self-determination).

2.3 We said in this section that Sam used an informational rather than a controlling strategy for promoting self-regulation. This is demonstrated by his use of examples to illustrate behaving responsibly versus irresponsibly. Explain how the two approaches are different, using information from the case study.

To receive feedback for these questions, go to Appendix A.

Teacher Characteristics: Personal Qualities That Increase Motivation to Learn

Teachers make a difference in student learning, and it is true for motivation as well. Teachers create learning environments, implement instruction, and establish mastery-oriented or performance-oriented classrooms. None of the other components of the model are effective if the teacher characteristics highlighted in Figure 11.4 are lacking.

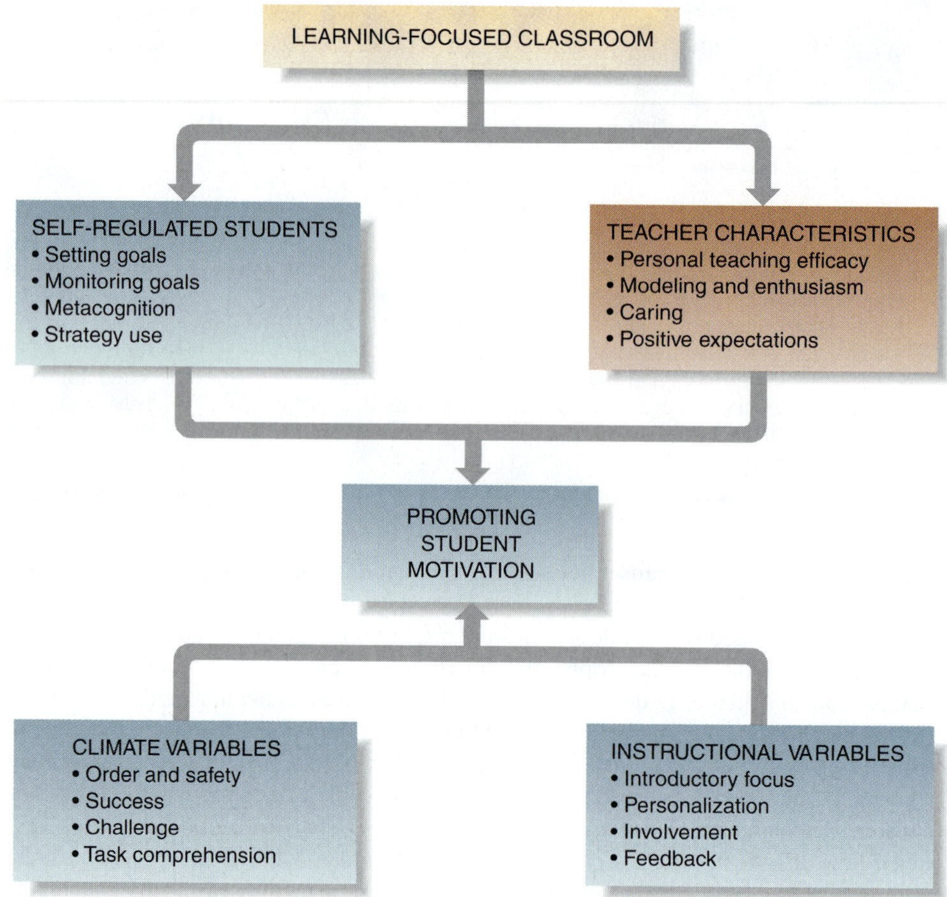

Figure 11.4 Teacher characteristics in the model for promoting student motivation to learn

Personal Teaching Efficacy: Beliefs About Teaching and Learning

Personal teaching efficacy. A teacher's belief that he or she can cause all students to learn regardless of their prior knowledge or ability.

In Chapter 10, you saw that self-efficacy is individuals' beliefs about their capability of accomplishing specific tasks. **Personal teaching efficacy,** a teacher's belief that he or she can cause all students to learn regardless of their prior knowledge or ability, is an extension of this concept (Woolfolk Hoy, Davis, & Pape, 2006; Yeh, 2006).

Teachers who are high in personal teaching efficacy take responsibility for the success or failure of their instruction. They are fair but demanding. They maximize the time available for instruction, praise students for their increasing competence, avoid the use of rewards to control behavior, and persevere with low achievers (Roeser, Marachi, & Gehlbach, 2002; Ware & Kitsantas, 2007). Low-efficacy teachers, in contrast, are more likely to blame low achievement on lack of intelligence, poor home environments, uncooperative administrators, or other external causes. They have lower expectations, spend less time on learning activities, "give up" on low achievers, and are more critical when students fail (Brouwers & Tomic, 2001; Henson, Kogan, & VachaHaase, 2001). Low-efficacy teachers are also more controlling and value student autonomy less than do high-efficacy teachers (Henson et al., 2001).

Not surprisingly, students taught by high-efficacy teachers learn more and are more motivated than those taught by teachers with lower efficacy (Tschannen-Moran, Woolfolk Hoy, & Hoy, 1998). Teacher efficacy is also related to commitment to teaching and job satisfaction (Caprara, Barbaranelli, Borgogni, & Steca, 2003).

Collective efficacy. Beliefs that the faculty as a whole can have a positive effect on students.

The entire student body benefits from **collective efficacy,** beliefs that the faculty as a whole can have a positive effect on students (Goddard, Hoy & Woolfolk Hoy, 2004; Hoy, Tarter, & Hoy, 2006). Such schools are notable for their positive effects on the achievement levels of students from diverse backgrounds. The correlation between low socioeconomic status (SES) and low achievement is well-documented. In schools where collective efficacy is high, however, low-SES students have achievement gains nearly as high as those of high-SES students from schools with low collective efficacy (V. Lee, 2000; Tschannen-Moran & Barr, 2004). Also, differences in achievement gains among low-, middle-, and high-SES students are smaller when collective efficacy is high (V. Lee, 2000). In other words, these schools reduce achievement differences between groups who typically benefit differently from schooling.

What can you do to promote collective efficacy? The best you can do is to remain positive when colleagues are cynical or pessimistic, and you can remind your fellow teachers of the research that confirms how important teachers are in promoting motivation to learn for all students.

Modeling and Enthusiasm: Communicating Genuine Interest

Teacher modeling can have a powerful impact on students' interests. Increasing student motivation to learn is virtually impossible if teachers model distaste or disinterest with statements such as, "I know this stuff is boring, but we have to learn it," or "This isn't my favorite topic, either."

Enthusiastic teachers increase motivation by modeling their own interest in the subjects they teach.

In contrast, the likelihood that students will be more motivated to learn increases significantly if teachers model their own interest in the topics they study (Brophy, 2006c). For example, when Kathy Brewster, in her lesson on the Crusades in Chapter 10, said, "See how interesting this is. . . . Again, we see ourselves influenced by people who lived hundreds of years ago . . ." her obvious interest in the topic increased the students' interest. The same kind of impact can exist if a geography teacher says, for example, "Geography has an enormous impact on our lives. For example, New York, Chicago, and San Francisco didn't become major cities for no reason. Their success is related to their geography." Unlike pep talks, theatrics, or efforts to entertain students, genuine interest can induce in students the feeling that the information is valuable and worth learning (Brophy, 2004). Research indicates that students taught by enthusiastic teachers achieve higher than those whose teachers are less enthusiastic, and their perceptions of autonomy and self-efficacy are higher (B. C. Patrick, Hisley, & Kempler, 2000).

Teachers can also influence student motivation by modeling effort attributions and incremental views of intelligence. A teacher who says, "The harder I study, the smarter I get," communicates that effort is desirable and leads to higher ability. In doing so, he or she is increasing the likelihood that students will imitate these beliefs in their own thinking (Bruning, Schraw, Norby, & Ronning, 2004).

Caring: Meeting Needs for Belonging and Relatedness

- A first-grade teacher greets each of her children every morning with a hug or a "high five."
- A fifth-grade teacher immediately calls parents if one of his students fails to turn in a homework assignment or misses more than 2 days of school in a row.
- An algebra teacher learns the name of each student in all five of her classes by the end of the first week of school, and she stays in her room during her lunch hour to help students who are struggling.

Each of these teachers is demonstrating **caring,** which refers to a teacher's empathy and investment in the protection and development of young people (Noddings, 2001; N. E. Perry et al., 2006; Roeser, Peck, & Nasir, 2006). Caring teachers help meet a student's need for *belonging,* a need preceded only by safety and survival in Maslow's hierarchy (Maslow 1968, 1970), and *relatedness,* which is central to self-determination theory (R. Ryan & Deci, 2000).

Caring. A teacher's empathy and investment in the protection and development of young people.

> Research supports the importance of caring.
>
> Students who perceived that teachers cared about them reported positive motivational outcomes such as more prosocial and social responsibility goals, academic effort, and greater internal control beliefs. It appears that students want teachers to care for them both as learners and as people. (N. E. Perry et al., 2006, p. 341)

Additional research also indicates that students are more engaged in classroom activities when they perceive their teachers as liking them and being responsive to their needs (Osterman, 2000).

Communicating Caring

How do teachers communicate that they care about their students? Some ways include the following (Alder, 2002; Osterman, 2000; Wilder, 2000):

- Learn students' names quickly, and call on students by their first name.
- Greet them each day, and get to know them as individuals.
- Make eye contact, smile, lean toward them when talking, and demonstrate relaxed body language.
- Use "we" and "our" in reference to class activities and assignments.
- Spend time with students.
- Demonstrate respect for students as individuals.

The last two items deserve special emphasis. We all have exactly 24 hours in our days, and the way we choose to allocate our time is the truest measure of our priorities. Choosing to allocate some of our time to an individual student communicates caring better than any other single factor. Helping students who have problems with an assignment or calling a parent after school hours communicates that teachers care about student learning. Spending personal time to ask a question about a baby brother or compliment a new hairstyle communicates caring about a student as a human being.

Showing respect is also essential. Teachers can show respect in a variety of ways, but maintaining standards is one of the most important:

> One of the best ways to show respect for students is to hold them to high standards—by not accepting sloppy, thoughtless, or incomplete work, by pressing them to clarify vague comments, by encouraging them not to give up, and by not praising work that does not reflect genuine effort. Ironically, reactions that are often intended to protect students' self-esteem—such as accepting low quality work—convey a lack of interest, patience, or caring. (Stipek, 2002, p. 157)

Research corroborates this view. When researchers asked junior high students, "How do you know when a teacher cares about you?" they responded that paying attention to them as human beings was important, but more striking was their belief that teachers who care are committed to their learning and hold them to high standards (B. L. Wilson & Corbett, 2001).

Respect, of course, is a two-way street. Teachers should model respect for students, and in turn they have the right to expect students to respect them and one another. "Treat everyone with respect" is a rule that should be universally enforced. An occasional minor incident of rudeness can be overlooked, but teachers should clearly communicate that chronic disrespect will not be tolerated.

Teacher Expectations: Increasing Perceptions of Competence

Positive expectations is the last of the four teacher characteristics in our model for promoting student motivation (Figure 11.4). Positive teacher expectations have been consistently linked to increased achievement in a long history of classroom research (Brophy, 2006c; Stipek, 2002).

> Teacher expectations about students' learning can have profound implications for what students actually learn. Expectations affect the content and pace of the curriculum, the organization of instruction, evaluation, instructional interactions with individual students, and many subtle and not-so-subtle behaviors that affect students' own expectations for learning and thus their behavior. (Stipek, 2002, p. 210)

To increase student motivation to learn, teachers must strive to make all students feel competent, an innate need according to self-determination theory. However, teachers' expectations sometimes lead them to make statements to students that instead communicate perceptions of incompetence (R. Weinstein, 2002). For example, compare the following two comments:

> "This is a new idea, and it will be challenging, but if you work hard I know you can get it. Start right in while the ideas are still fresh in your mind. I'll be coming around, so if you have any questions, just raise your hand."

> "This material is hard, but we've got to learn it. Some of you will probably have trouble with this, and I'll be around as soon as I can to straighten things out. No messing around until I get there."

The first teacher acknowledged that the assignment was difficult but communicated confidence in students' competence by saying that she expected them to succeed. In saying, "Some of you will probably have trouble with this," the second suggested that they were not competent. These seemingly innocuous comments can have a strong impact on students' motivation to learn.

Most commonly, teachers' expectations influence their interactions with individual students. Specifically, they treat students they perceive to be high achievers differently from those they perceive to be low achievers (R. Weinstein, 2002). This differential treatment typically takes four different forms (Good, 1987a, 1987b; Good & Brophy, 2008):

- *Emotional support:* Teachers interact more with perceived high achievers; their interactions are more positive; they make more eye contact, stand closer, and orient their bodies more directly toward the students; and they seat these students closer to the front of the class.
- *Teacher effort and demands:* Teachers give perceived high achievers more thorough explanations, their instruction is more enthusiastic, they ask more follow-up questions, and they require more complete and accurate student answers.
- *Questioning:* Teachers call on perceived high achievers more often, they allow the students more time to answer, and they provide high achievers with more prompts and cues when they're unable to answer.
- *Feedback and evaluation:* Teachers praise perceived high achievers more and criticize them less. They offer perceived high achievers more complete and lengthier feedback and more conceptual evaluations.

Self-fulfilling prophecy. A phenomenon that occurs when a person's performance results from and confirms beliefs about his or her capabilities.

At an extreme, teachers' expectations for a student—either high or low—can become a **self-fulfilling prophecy**, a phenomenon that occurs when a person's performance results

Teachers communicate positive expectations by calling on all their students as equally as possible.

theory to practice

Personal Qualities That Increase Motivation to Learn

Personal qualities that promote motivation to learn can be applied in a number of ways. The following guidelines can help you in your efforts:

1. Strive to maintain high personal teaching efficacy.
2. Maintain appropriately high expectations for all students.
3. Model responsibility, effort, and interest in the topics you're teaching.
4. Demonstrate caring and commitment to your students' learning by spending time outside of class with them.

Let's see how the guidelines for demonstrating personal qualities that increase motivation to learn guide DeVonne as she continues to work with her fifth graders.

"Wow, you're here early," Karla Utley, another teacher in the school, says to DeVonne at 7:15 one morning.

"I've got kids coming in," DeVonne replies. "I did a writing lesson yesterday, and we evaluated some of their paragraphs as a whole class." (DeVonne's writing lesson is the case study at the end of this chapter.) "Several of the kids, like Tu and Saleina, did really well . . . but some are behind. So, Justin, Picey, and Rosa are coming in before school this morning, and we're going to practice some more. They aren't my highest achievers, but I know I can get more out of them than I am right now. They're good kids; they're just a little behind."

At 7:30 DeVonne is waiting as Justin, Picey, and Rosa come in the door. She smiles at them and says, "We're going to practice a little more on our writing. I know that you can all be good writers. It's the same thing for me. I've practiced and practiced, and now I'm good at it. You can do the same thing. . . . Let's look at your paragraphs again."

She displays Justin's paragraph on the overhead again (his was one of the papers evaluated in class the day before) and asks, "What did we suggest that you might do to improve this?"

There was a boy named Josh. He lives in a house with the roof falling in and the windows were broke. He had holes in the wall and the ceiling leaked when it rained. But then again it always rained and thunder over his house. Noone every goes to his gate because he was so Weird. They say he is a vampire.

"He needs to stay on either the boy or the house," Rosa offers.

"Good," DeVonne nods. "Staying focused on your topic sentence is important." Together, the group looks at each of the students' original paragraphs and makes specific suggestions for improvement.

DeVonne then says, "Okay, now each of you rewrite your paragraphs based on our suggestions. When we're finished, we'll look at them again."

The students rewrite their paragraphs, and the four of them again discuss the products.

"Much improvement," DeVonne says after they've finished. "If we keep at it, we're going to get there. . . . I'll see you again tomorrow at 7:30."

Now, let's look at DeVonne's efforts to apply the guidelines. First, in saying to Karla, "I know I can get more out of them than I am right now," and "They're good kids," she applied the first guideline, demonstrating high personal teaching efficacy.

In commenting, "I know I can get more out of them than I am right now. They're good kids; they're just a little behind," she also communicated positive expectations, applying the second guideline. Her comment indicates that she expects all students to learn, not just high achievers like Tu and Saleina.

As she worked with the small group, she applied the third guideline by modeling responsibility and effort with her comment, "I have practiced and practiced, and now I'm good at it. You can do the same thing. . . . Let's look at your paragraphs again."

Finally, and perhaps most significantly, DeVonne demonstrated caring and commitment by arriving at school 45 minutes early to devote extra time to helping students who needed additional support. She kept the study session upbeat and displayed the respect for the students that is essential for promoting motivation to learn.

Demonstrating these personal characteristics won't turn all your students into motivated learners, but you can impact many, and for those, you will have provided an invaluable service to their education.

from and confirms beliefs about his or her capabilities (R. Weinstein, 2002). We can explain this using self-efficacy beliefs. Communicating positive expectations suggests to students that they will be successful. When they are, their self-efficacy increases, and a positive relationship between motivation and achievement is created. The reverse can also occur. Communicating low expectations can lead children to confirm predictions about their abilities by exerting less effort and ultimately performing less well.

Children of all ages are aware of the different expectations teachers hold for students (Stipek, 2002). In one study, researchers concluded, "After ten seconds of seeing and/or hearing a teacher, even very young students could detect whether the teacher talked about or to an excellent or a weak student and could determine the extent to which that student was loved by the teacher" (Babad, Bernieri, & Rosenthal, 1991, p. 230).

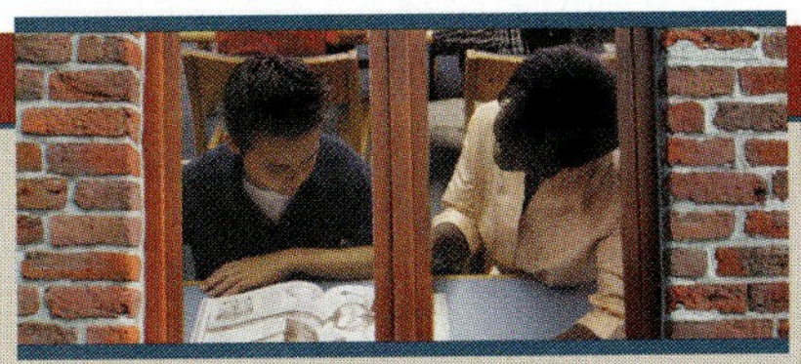

classroom connections

Demonstrating Personal Characteristics in the Model for Promoting Student Motivation in Your Classroom

Caring

1. Caring teachers promote a sense of belonging and relatedness in their classrooms and commit to the protection and development of students both as people and as learners. Demonstrate caring by respecting students and giving them your personal time.
   - **Elementary:** A first-grade teacher greets each of her students every day as they come into the classroom. She makes it a point to talk to each student about something personal several times a week.
   - **Middle School:** A geography teacher calls parents as soon as he sees a student having even minor academic or personal problems. He solicits parents' help in monitoring and supporting the student and offers his assistance in solving problems.
   - **High School:** An Algebra II teacher conducts help sessions after school three nights a week. Students are invited to attend to get help with homework or to discuss any other personal concerns about the class or school.

Modeling and Enthusiasm

2. Teachers best demonstrate enthusiasm by modeling their own interest in the content of their classes. Model interest in the topics you're teaching.
   - **Elementary:** During individual reading time, a fourth-grade teacher comments on a book she's interested in and also reads while the students are reading.
   - **Middle School:** A life science teacher brings science-related clippings from the local newspaper to class and asks students to do the same. He discusses them and pins them on a bulletin board for students to read.
   - **High School:** A world history teacher frequently describes connections between classroom topics and their impact on today's world.

Positive Expectations

3. Teachers communicate their expectations through the demands they place on students, the emotional support they give, and in the way they interact with students. Maintain appropriately high expectations for all students.
   - **Elementary:** A second-grade teacher makes a conscious attempt to call on all her students equally and asks high-level questions whenever possible.
   - **Middle School:** When his students complain about word problems, a seventh-grade pre-algebra teacher reminds them of how important problem solving is for their lives and tells them that the only way to become good at solving the problems is to practice. Each day, he guides a detailed discussion of at least two challenging word problems.
   - **High School:** When her American history students turn in sloppily written essays, the teacher displays a well-written example on the overhead and then requires a second, higher quality product from the rest. She continues this process throughout the year.

One of our goals in writing this section is to make you aware of the influence of expectations on motivation and achievement. Expectations are usually unconscious, and teachers often don't realize that they have different expectations for their students. With awareness and effort, they are more likely to maintain appropriately high expectations for all students. The experience of Elaine Lawless, a first-grade teacher, is an example. When she began calling on her students as equally as possible, she saw immediate benefits: "Joseph made my day. He said to one of the other kids, 'Put your hand down. Mrs. Lawless calls on all of us. She thinks we're all smart' " (Elaine Lawless, personal communication, February 19, 2002).

check your understanding

3.1 Describe the personal characteristics of teachers who increase students' motivation to learn.

3.2 Research indicates that high-efficacy teachers adopt new curriculum materials and change strategies more readily than do low-efficacy teachers (Roeser et al., 2002). Using the characteristics of personal teaching efficacy as a basis, explain why this is likely to be the case.

3.3 Based on the information in this section, what is the most effective way to communicate your enthusiasm to students? Explain.

3.4 Explain why *not* being called on by a teacher communicates to students that the teacher has low expectations for them.

To receive feedback for these questions, go to Appendix A.

Climate Variables: Creating a Motivating Environment

Positive classroom climate. A classroom environment where the teacher and students work together as a community of learners, to help everyone achieve.

As students spend time in school, they sense whether or not the classroom is a safe and positive place to learn. These feelings reflect the classroom climate. In a **positive classroom climate,** the teacher and students work together as a community of learners, to help everyone achieve (Palincsar, 1998; Rogoff, 1998). The goal is to promote students' feelings of safety and security, together with a sense of success, challenge, and understanding (see Figure 11.5).

Let's see how teachers can create a positive classroom climate.

Order and Safety: Classrooms as Secure Places to Learn

Order and safety. A climate variable that creates a predictable learning environment and supports learner autonomy together with a sense of physical and emotional security.

Order and safety is a climate variable that creates a predictable learning environment and supports learner autonomy together with a sense of physical and emotional security. It is grounded in both Piaget's (1970, 1977) work and self-determination theory. Safe, orderly classrooms help meet students' needs for equilibrium, and sharing authority with students in making classroom decisions contributes to students' feelings of autonomy (Brophy, 2006b; Roeser et al., 2006), an essential need according to self-determination theory (R. Ryan & Deci, 2000). Some examples of shared authority include soliciting student input into classroom rules and procedures and encouraging students to set and monitor their own learning goals. It can also include giving students choices in selecting the order and kinds of learning activities and establishing due dates for assignments when appropriate.

Humanistic views of motivation, additional aspects of self-determination theory, and the human memory model also help us understand the need for a safe learning environment. For instance, safety is a deficiency need preceded only by survival in Maslow's (1970) hierarchy. Also, being in a safe classroom environment allows students to meet their needs for related-

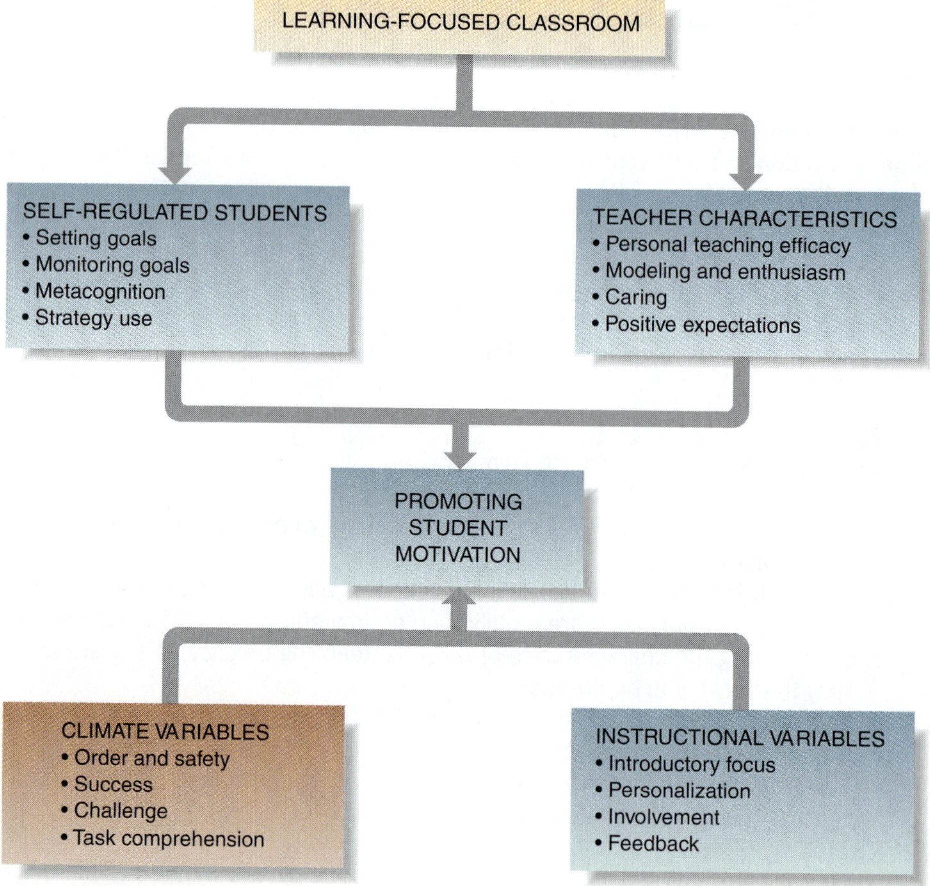

Figure 11.5 Climate variables in the model for promoting student motivation to learn

ness, another essential need in self-determination theory (Deci & Ryan, 2000). Finally, the human memory model suggests that thinking about being criticized or ridiculed occupies working memory space that could otherwise be devoted to the learning task. The American Psychological Association Board of Educational Affairs (1995) believes emotional safety is so important that it is specifically addressed in its Learner-Centered Psychological Principles.

Teachers set the tone for this essential variable by modeling respect and courtesy and expecting students to treat everyone else in the classroom in the same way (Barth, 2002; Blum, 2005).

Success: Developing Learner Self-Efficacy

Once teachers have established a safe and orderly environment, student success becomes the most important climate variable. Success doesn't simply mean getting high scores on tests or other assignments, however. Success is indicated by learning progress and accomplishing tasks, not high grades and performing better than others. Praise and other rewards should communicate that competence is increasing. Mistakes don't indicate that students aren't successful; rather, they're a normal part of the learning process.

Teachers can promote success in several ways:

- Begin lessons with open-ended questions that assess learners' current understanding and promote involvement.
- Use a variety of high-quality examples that develop background knowledge and promote understanding.
- Develop lessons with questioning, together with prompting students when they have difficulty answering.
- Provide scaffolded practice before expecting students to work on their own.
- Make assessment an integral part of the teaching–learning process, and provide detailed feedback about learning progress.

However, even with continuous progress, success won't increase motivation to learn if the learning tasks aren't challenging, another component of effective classroom climate.

Challenge: Increasing Perceptions of Competence

Success, alone, doesn't increase perceptions of self-efficacy and competence; they also depend on the challenge involved in the learning task (Dolezal, Welsh, Pressley, & Vincent, 2003). For instance, with enough rehearsal, students can succeed in memorizing a list of meaningless facts. This success, however, does little to increase perceptions of competence. Only when learners succeed on tasks they perceive as challenging will perceptions of competence develop.

A long line of theory and research confirms the need for challenge. It is one characteristic of intrinsically motivating activities, and both self-determination theory and beliefs about value help us understand why. Succeeding on challenging tasks helps meet students' needs for competence and autonomy, which are innate according to self-determination theory (Deci & Ryan, 2000). Further, learners value success on challenging tasks more than success on trivial tasks (Lam & Law, 2007). Value and feelings of competence and autonomy then lead to increased effort and persistence. This helps explain why children persevere in learning to ride a bicycle, for example, even though they fall repeatedly, and why they lose interest in a skill after it has been mastered.

Learners' self-efficacy increases when they succeed on challenging tasks.

Teachers capitalize on the motivating characteristics of challenge by encouraging students to identify relationships in the topics they study and the implications of these relationships for new learning (Brophy, 2004; B. Taylor, Pearson, Peterson, & Rodriguez, 2003). Limiting discussions to isolated, meaningless facts has the opposite effect. When students complain about the difficulty of their tasks, effective teachers don't decrease the challenge; they provide scaffolding to ensure that students can meet it.

Task Comprehension: Increasing Feelings of Autonomy and Value

As with success, a challenging task won't increase motivation to learn if students don't perceive it as meaningful and worth understanding (Vavilis & Vavilis, 2004). For instance, a world history teacher gives the following reading assignment:

> Read Chapter 20 carefully because most of the test will be on it. In particular, be sure you know the dates of the Crusades. And, what was the "Children's Crusade"? All this information will be on your test.

Now, compare this assignment with dialogue from Kathy Brewster's lesson on the Crusades in Chapter 10.

> Now, what were the actual Crusades all about? . . . Selena?"
> "The Christians wanted to get the Holy Land back from the Muslims."
> "And why? . . . Becky?"
> "The holy lands were important to the Christians."
> The class then discusses reasons for the Crusades, such as religion, economics, the military threat posed by the Muslim world, and the amount of territory they held. "Excellent analysis. . . . In fact, we'll see that these factors also influenced Columbus's voyage to the New World. . . . Think about that. The Muslims and the Crusades nearly 1,000 years ago have had an influence on us here today."

Realistically, not all students will be interested in the Crusades, regardless of what a teacher does. However, the likelihood of students' being motivated to learn in Kathy's class is much greater than in the first teacher's class.

Task comprehension. Learners' awareness of what they are supposed to be learning and an understanding of why the task is important and worthwhile.

These differences reflect **task comprehension,** which is learners' awareness of what they are supposed to be learning and an understanding of why the task is important and worthwhile (Eggen & Kauchak, 2002). Task comprehension also includes decisions about time allocated to tasks, pace of instruction, and provisions for extra help if needed. The first teacher communicated that the reason we study the Crusades is to know dates and labels and perform well on the chapter test. Instead, Kathy suggested that we study the Crusades because they have an effect on us today.

The need for task comprehension can be explained with both beliefs about value and the need for self-determination. First, task comprehension contributes to perceptions of utility value, the belief that understanding is useful for meeting future goals. Second, understanding what they're learning and why they're learning it increases students' feelings of autonomy, an essential need in self-determination theory.

As with teacher characteristics, climate variables are interdependent. A challenging assignment can be motivating, for example, if students feel safe. If they're worried about the consequences of making mistakes, the motivating effects of challenge are lost. Similarly, if students don't understand the point in an activity, neither success nor challenge will increase motivation to learn. And each of the climate variables depends on the extent to which teachers care about students and hold them to high standards.

The TARGET Program: Applying Goal Theory in Classrooms

Carol Ames (1990, 1992) developed a program grounded in goal theory that is consistent with the climate variables in the model for promoting student motivation. TARGET is the program acronym, and it refers to *task, authority, recognition, grouping, evaluation,* and *time.* Classroom environments in which mastery goals are emphasized result in higher levels of motivation to learn than do performance goals, some social goals, and work-avoidance goals. TARGET is grounded in research on family structures that influence students' motivation to learn in the home, and it has been expanded to applications in schools. Table 11.2 outlines the TARGET categories and the related variables in the model for promoting student motivation.

table 11.2 The TARGET Program for Motivation and Related Variables in the Model for Promoting Student Motivation

TARGET Category	Description	Related Variable(s) in the Model for Promoting Student Motivation
Task	Tasks are designed to be optimally challenging, so that students see their relevance and meaning.	Challenge Task comprehension
Authority	Authority is shared, and student autonomy is supported.	Order and safety
Recognition	Recognition is provided for all students who make learning progress.	Success
Grouping	Grouping is designed to foster a "community of learners."	Classroom climate variables
Evaluation	Evaluation is used to promote learning.	Success
Time	Time encompasses the workload, pace of instruction, and the amount allocated for completing work.	Task comprehension

classroom connections

Applying the Climate Variables in Your Classroom

Order and Safety

1. Order and safety create a predictable learning environment and support learner autonomy, together with a sense of physical and emotional security. Attempt to create a safe and orderly learning environment.
   - **Elementary:** A first-grade teacher establishes and practices daily routines until they're predictable and automatic for students.
   - **Middle School:** An eighth-grade American history teacher leads a beginning-of-the-year discussion examining the kind of environment the students want to work in. They conclude that all "digs" and discourteous remarks should be forbidden. The teacher consistently enforces the agreement.
   - **High School:** An English teacher reminds her students that all relevant comments about a topic are welcome, and she models acceptance of every idea. She requires students to listen courteously when a classmate is talking.

Success and Challenge

2. Succeeding on challenging tasks promotes learner self-efficacy and helps them develop a sense of competence. Structure instruction so students succeed on challenging tasks.
   - **Elementary:** A fourth-grade teacher comments, "We're really getting good at fractions. Now I have a problem that is going to make us all think. It will be a little tough, but I know that we'll be able to do it." After students attempt the solution, he guides a discussion of the problem and different ways to solve it.
   - **Middle School:** A sixth-grade English teacher has the class practice three or four homework exercises as a whole group each day and discusses them before students begin to work independently.
   - **High School:** As she returns their homework, a physics teacher gives her students worked solutions to the most frequently missed problems. She has students put the homework and the worked examples in their portfolios to study for the biweekly quizzes.

Task Comprehension

3. Task comprehension reflects students' awareness of what they are supposed to be learning and an understanding of why the task is important and worthwhile. Promote task comprehension by describing rationales for your learning activities and assignments.
   - **Elementary:** As he gives students their daily math homework, a third-grade teacher says, "We know that understanding math is really important, so that's why we practice word problems every day."
   - **Middle School:** A seventh-grade English teacher carefully describes her assignments and due dates and writes them on the board. Each time, she explains why the assignment is important.
   - **High School:** A biology teacher displays the following on an overhead:

     We don't just study flatworms because we're interested in flatworms. As we look at how they've adapted to their environments, we'll gain additional insights into ourselves.

     He then says, "We'll return to this idea again and again to remind ourselves why we study each organism."

check your understanding

4.1 Identify classroom climate variables that can increase students' motivation to learn.

4.2 "I try to keep my assignments basic," a seventh-grade life science teacher comments. "So, in one activity, I give them a drawing of a skeleton, and they can look up the names in their books. They need to succeed, and they do succeed on this activity." Analyze this teacher's approach for promoting her students' motivation to learn. Explain using the climate variables in the model for promoting student motivation as a basis for your explanation. Also, assess the approach based on the TARGET categories.

4.3 "I have an inviolable rule in my classroom management system," a middle school teacher comments. "They may make no sarcastic or demeaning comments of any kind when one of their classmates is trying to answer a question. I explained why this is so important, and they agreed. They slip now and then, but mostly they're quite good."

Which two climate variables in the model for promoting student motivation is this teacher attempting to address? Explain.

4.4 Look at Table 11.2. Describe specifically how each of the variables identified in the table relates to the corresponding TARGET category. For example, explain how challenge and task comprehension relate to the TARGET category *task*. Then, describe the relationship for each of the other TARGET categories and variables in the model for promoting student motivation.

To receive feedback for these questions, go to Appendix A.

Instructional Variables: Developing Interest in Learning Activities

Teacher and climate variables form a general framework for motivation. Within this context, teachers can do much through their learning activities to enhance motivation to learn. From an instructional perspective, a motivated student is someone who is actively engaged in the learning process (Brophy, 2004; Stipek, 2002). To promote motivation, we must initially capture—and then maintain—students' attention and engagement throughout a learning activity. Some ways of doing so are outlined in Figure 11.6.

Introductory Focus: Attracting Students' Attention

Introductory focus. A lesson beginning that attracts attention and provides a conceptual framework for the lesson.

Introductory focus is a lesson beginning that attracts student attention and provides a conceptual framework for the lesson (Marzano, 2003b). It attempts to capitalize on the effects of curiosity and novelty, which are characteristics of intrinsically motivating activities (Brophy, 2004). For example, DeVonne began her lesson on arthropods by bringing a live lobster to class, and the study of arthropods was its conceptual framework. The squeals and "oohs" and "aahs" clearly indicated that she had attracted their attention. Let's look at another example.

> As an introduction to studying cities and their locations, Marissa Allen, a social studies teacher, hands out a map of a fictitious island. On it are physical features such as lakes, rivers, and mountains. Information about altitude, rainfall, and average seasonal temperature is also included. Marissa begins, "The name of this activity is Survival. Our class has just been sent to this island to settle it. We have information about its climate and physical features. Where should we make our first settlement?"

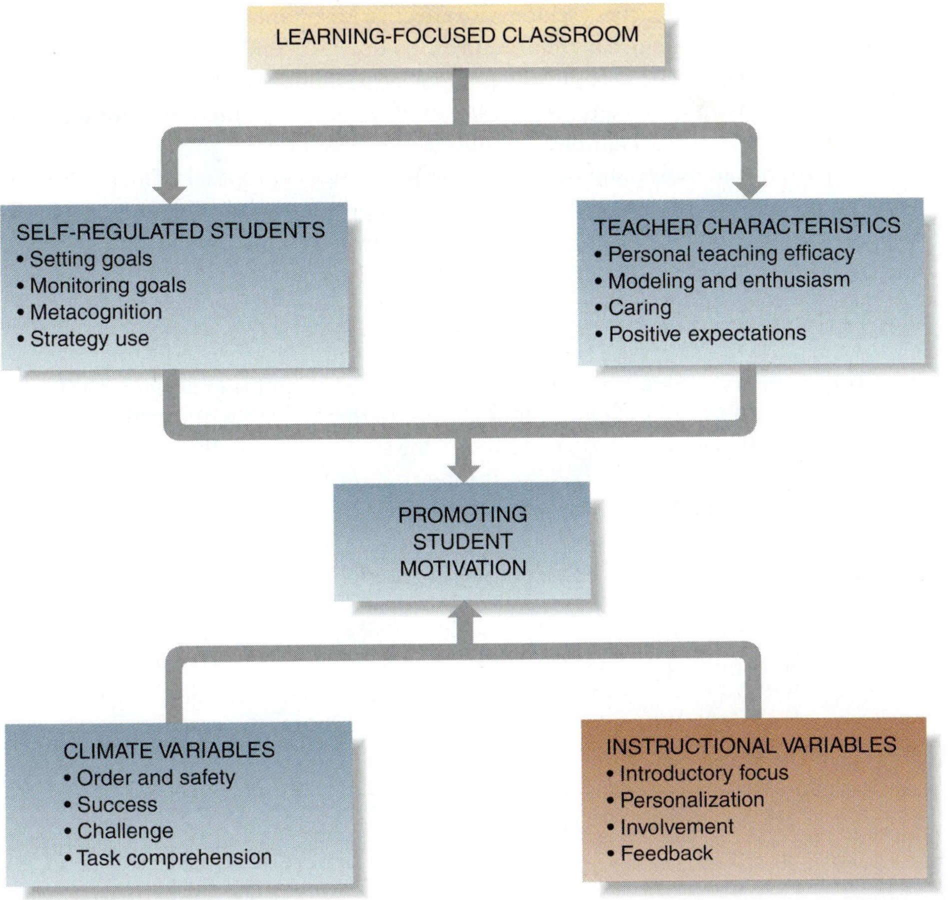

Figure 11.6 Instructional variables in the model for promoting student motivation to learn

Teachers can attract attention with unique problems, such as Marissa's survival task; by asking paradoxical questions ("If Rome was such a powerful and advanced civilization, why did it collapse?"); by using demonstrations with seemingly contradictory results (e.g., dropping two balls of different weights and seeing that they hit the floor at the same time); or with eye-catching examples, such as DeVonne's lobster (Hidi & Renninger, 2006).

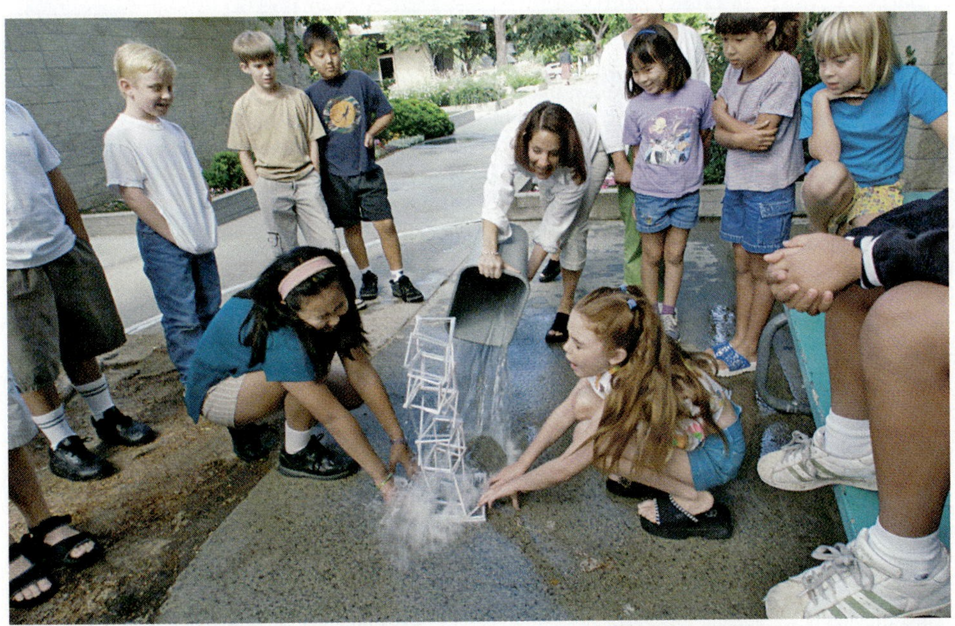

Effective teachers use introductory focus to capture student's attention and draw them into the lesson.

MyEducationLab

To examine teachers' attempts to capitalize on introductory focus in their lessons, go to the *Activities and Applications* section in Chapter 11 of MyEducationLab at www.myeducationlab.com, and watch the video episode *Introductory Focus: Attracting Students' Attention.* Answer the questions following the episode.

Research indicates that teachers seldom use effective lesson introductions; when teachers do use introductions, they are usually short and fail to draw students into the lesson (Brophy, 2004, 2006c). Providing for effective introductory focus need not be difficult, however. All that is required is conscious effort to connect the content of the lesson to students' prior knowledge and interests. Some additional examples are outlined in Table 11.3.

Once learners are attending and the teacher has provided a conceptual framework, the lesson has to maintain their attention and provide information about learning progress. Personalization, involvement, and feedback can help meet this goal.

Personalization: Links to Students' Lives

Sue Crompton, a second-grade math teacher, introduces the topic of graphing by measuring her students' heights. She continues by giving them a length of construction paper and has them place their strip of paper on the spot on a graph that corresponds to their height. After discussing the results, she does a similar activity with hair color to reinforce the idea of graphing.

Chris Emery, a science teacher, begins a unit on genetics by saying, "Reanne, what color are your eyes?"

"Blue," Reanne responds.

"And how about yours, Eddie?"

"Green."

table 11.3 Tools and Techniques for Providing Introductory Focus

Tool/Technique	Example
Problems and questions	• A literature teacher shows a picture of Ernest Hemingway and says, "Here we see 'Papa in all his splendor. He seemed to have everything—fame, adventure, romance. Yet he took his own life. Why would this happen?" • A science teacher asks the students to explain why two pieces of paper come together at the bottom (rather than move apart) when students blow between them. • An educational psychology instructor introducing social cognitive theory displays the following vignette: *You're driving 75 mph on the interstate—with a posted speed limit of 65—when another car blazes past you. A minute later, you see the car stopped by the highway patrol. You immediately slow down. How would behaviorism explain your slowing down?*
Inductive sequences	• An English teacher displays the following: *I had a ton of homework last night! I was upset because I had a date with the most gorgeous girl in the world! I guess it was okay, because she had on the ugliest outfit ever!* The students find a pattern in the examples and develop the concept *hyperbole.* • An educational psychology instructor begins a discussion of development with these questions: Are you bothered when something doesn't make sense? Do you want the world to be predictable? Are you more comfortable in classes when the instructor specifies the requirements, schedules the classes, and outlines the grading practices? Does your life in general follow patterns more than random experiences? The class looks at the pattern and arrives at the concept of *equilibrium.*
Concrete examples	• An elementary teacher begins a unit on amphibians by bringing in a live frog. • A geography teacher draws lines on a beach ball to demonstrate that longitude lines intersect at the poles and latitude lines are parallel to each other. • An educational psychology instructor introduces the concept *negative reinforcement* by describing his inclination to take a pain killer to reduce his discomfort after a demanding workout.
Objectives and rationales	• A math teacher begins, "Today we want to learn about unit pricing. This will help us decide which product is a better buy. It will help us all save money and be better consumers." • A world history teacher says, "Today we're going to look at the concept of *mercantilism.* It will help us understand why, throughout history, Europe came to the New World and went into South Asia and Africa." • An educational psychology instructor says, "We know that learners construct, rather than record, understanding. Today we want to see what that principle suggests about the way we should teach most effectively."

"Interesting," Chris smiles. "When we're done with this unit, we'll be able to figure out why Reanne's are blue and Eddie's are green, and a whole bunch of other things related to the way we look."

Sue and Chris both attempted to increase their students' interest through **personalization,** the process of using intellectually and/or emotionally relevant examples to illustrate a topic.

Personalization. The process of using intellectually and/or emotionally relevant examples to illustrate a topic.

Personalization is a valuable motivation strategy for several reasons (Strong, Silver, Perini, & Tuculescu, 2003; Wortham, 2004). First, it is widely applicable and intuitively sensible. Experienced teachers describe it as one of the most important ways to promote student interest in learning activities, and its value is confirmed by research (Schraw & Lehman, 2001; Zahorik, 1996). Second, personalized content is meaningful because it encourages students to connect new information to structures already in long-term memory (Moreno & Mayer, 2000). Third, students feel a sense of autonomy when they study topics to which they can personally relate (Iyengar & Lepper, 1999). Teachers in several of the case studies you've already studied in this book used personalization to increase their students' motivation to learn. The teachers and the way they personalized their topics are outlined in Table 11.4.

Involvement: Increasing Intrinsic Interest

Think about your experience at lunch with friends or a party. When you're talking and actively listening, you pay more attention to the conversation than you do when you're on its fringes. The same applies in classrooms. **Involvement,** the extent to which students are actively participating in a learning activity, results in increased interest and learning (Hidi, 2002; Lutz, Guthrie, & Davis, 2006). Cognitive activity is essential for meaningful learning, and involvement is important for putting students in cognitively active roles (Blumenfeld, Kempler, & Krajcik, 2006). Some researchers also suggest that putting students in active roles is one way to personalize instruction (Schraw & Lehman, 2001).

Involvement. The extent to which students are actively participating in a learning activity.

Next, we'll discuss two strategies for increasing student involvement: open-ended questioning and hands-on activities.

Using Open-Ended Questioning to Promote Involvement

Questioning is the most generally applicable tool teachers have for maintaining involvement. Students' attention is high when they're being asked questions but drops during teacher monologues. Although we discuss questioning in detail in Chapter 13, we introduce open-ended questioning here because it is particularly effective for promoting involvement

table 11.4 Teachers' Attempts to Personalize Topics

Teacher and Chapter	Attempt at Personalization
Karen Johnson (Chapter 2) (page 36)	Used population density and the density of window screens to illustrate the concept *density*.
Diane Smith (Chapter 4) (pages 116–117)	Used differences in the lengths of students' pencils and differences in students' hair color to illustrate comparative and superlative adjectives.
Mike Sheppard (Chapter 5) (pages 158–160)	Used distances from the students' hometown to neighboring towns as the basis for word problems in math.
Laura Hunter (Chapter 9) (pages 253–254)	Used finding the area of the classroom as a basis for developing skills in finding the areas of irregularly shaped figures.
Sue Brush (Chapter 9) (pages 280–281)	Used students' favorite flavor of jelly beans, their favorite soft drinks, and the cost of pizzas at local restaurants as a basis for a lesson on bar graphing.
Kathy Brewster (Chapter 10) (page 312)	Used the class's "crusade" to prevent extracurricular activities from being eliminated at the school as an analogy for the Crusades in history.

Open-ended questions. Questions for which a variety of answers is acceptable.

(Brophy, 2006c). **Open-ended questions** are questions for which a variety of answers is acceptable.

One type of open-ended question asks students to make observations. For instance, DeVonne asked her students to examine the lobster:

> **DeVonne:** Okay, who can tell me one thing that you noticed?
> **Tu:** Hard.
> **Saleina:** Pink and green.
> **Kevin:** Wet.

Virtually any answer to her question would have been acceptable. As another example, a teacher in a lesson on Shakespeare's Julius Caesar might ask questions, such as:

> "What has happened so far in the play?"
> "What are some of the major events?"
> "What is one thing you remember about the play?"

Like DeVonne's question, these are easy to answer, activate prior knowledge, and draw students into the lesson.

A second type of open-ended question asks for comparisons. For instance, a teacher in a lesson on amphibians and reptiles might ask the following questions:

> "How is a frog similar to a lizard?"
> "How are the frog and a toad similar to or different from each other?"

In the lesson on Julius Caesar, the teacher might ask:

> "How are Brutus and Marc Antony similar? How are they different?"
> "How does the setting for Act I compare with that for Act II?"

Because many answers are acceptable, open-ended questions are safe and ensure success—two of the climate variables we discussed earlier. By combining safety and success, a teacher can encourage even the most reluctant student to respond without risk or fear of embarrassment. Also, because they can be asked and answered quickly, open-ended questions can help involve

exploring diversity

Personalizing Content to Increase Motivation to Learn in Students with Diverse Backgrounds

Jack Seltzer, a high school biology teacher on the Navajo Nation Reservation uses his students' background experiences to illustrate hard to understand science concepts. He uses Churro sheep, a local breed that Navajos use for food and wool, to illustrate genetic principles. When they study plants, he focuses on local varieties of squash and corn that have been grown by students' ancestors for centuries. Geologic formations in nearby Monument Valley are used to illustrate igneous, sedimentary and metamorphic rocks. (D. Baker, 2006)

In Chapter 10 you saw that *belonging* and *relatedness* are needs that have a strong influence on students' motivation to learn. A growing body of research indicates that threats to belonging detract from both motivation and learning (R. F. Baumeister & DeWall, 2005). In addition, research indicates that students drop out of school when they don't participate in academic or extracurricular activities because they don't feel a sense of belonging and don't identify with their schools (Juvonen, 2006, 2007). This problem is particularly acute among students who are disadvantaged or are members of cultural minorities (Becker & Luther, 2002; Wentzel & Wigfield, 2007). Further, minority students' disengagement is often exacerbated by the school curriculum, much of which is oriented toward mainstream, middle-class, nonminority students (P. M. Anderson & Summerfield, 2004). Because students who are members of cultural minorities don't personally identify with the topics being taught, their interest and motivation to learn decrease.

Research suggests that gender differences in interest also exist (Buck, Kostin, & Morgan, 2002). For instance, males tend to be more interested in topics such as war, politics, hard science, and business, whereas females are more interested in human relationships, arts, literature, marginalized groups, and social reform. Some researchers link these differences to differences in performance on standardized exams, such as advanced placement tests in high school (Halpern, 2006).

Now, let's look back to Jack Seltzer and his work with his Navajo students. He attempted to create a sense of belonging and interest in his class by capitalizing on the motivating effects of personalization. This variable is important for all students, but it can be particularly effective with members of cultural minorities, who commonly say they don't belong, or don't feel welcome in school (Rubinson, 2004). When these students are presented with examples and experiences that directly relate to their lives, as Jack did, their interest and sense of belonging can significantly increase. When teachers combine personalization with active participation in learning activities, motivation to learn can also increase.

a large number of students during a single lesson. A final advantage of open-ended questions is that they provide teachers with insights into students' thinking and allows them to build on students' prior knowledge (Powell & Caseau, 2004).

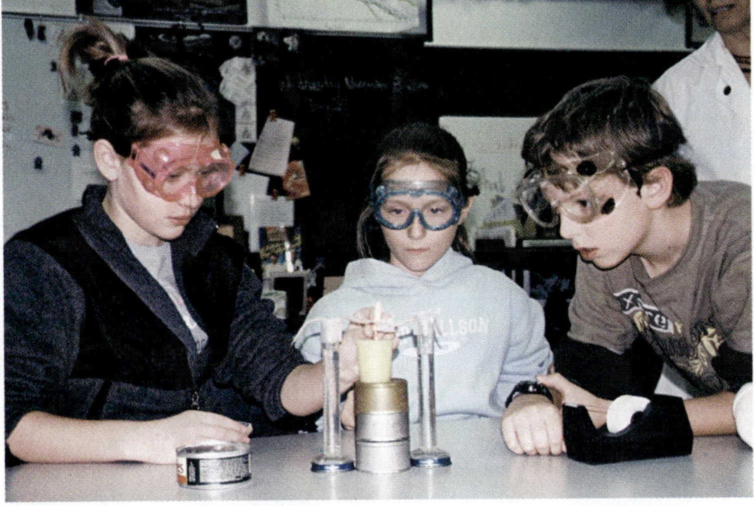

Hands-on activities can be effective for promoting involvement and student interest.

Using Hands-On Activities to Promote Involvement

Hands-on activities are another way of promoting involvement and student interest (Zahorik, 1996). For example, when students are working with manipulatives in math, concrete materials in science, maps and globes in geography, or computers in language arts, their level of interest increases significantly. The involvement in DeVonne's lesson, for example, was at its highest when students in groups worked with the shrimp. In addition, hands-on activities add variety to learning activities, which increases learner interest (M. E. Perry et al., 2006).

Additional strategies for promoting involvement and interest are outlined in Table 11.5.

Each of the activities in Table 11.5 promotes cognitive engagement. Improvement drills add an element of game-like novelty to otherwise routine activities, and personal improvement increases self-efficacy. Having students use chalkboards in individual work spaces is similar to having them solve problems on paper at their desks, but the chalkboards allow sharing and discussion, and students often will use them to attempt problems they wouldn't try on paper.

Group work, in which students work together toward common learning goals, can also increase involvement (D. W. Johnson & Johnson, 2006; Marzano, 2003b). Group work provides opportunities for students to interact and compare their ideas with others. All the teachers in the cognitive learning chapters (David Shelton and Sue Southam in Chapter 7, Jenny Newhall and Scott Sowell in Chapter 8, and Laura Hunter and Sue Brush in Chapter 9) used group work to promote involvement and interest. DeVonne also used group work when she had students examine the shrimp.

MyEducationLab

To examine a second-grade teacher's attempts to personalize her content and involve her students, go to the *Activities and Applications* section in Chapter 11 of MyEducationLab at www.myeducationlab.com, and watch the episode: *Guiding Students' Problem Solving: Graphing in Second Grade.* Answer the questions following the episode.

Feedback: Meeting the Need to Understand

Feedback also contributes to learner motivation, and its value can be explained with cognitive motivation theory (Hattie & Timperley, 2007). For instance, feedback indicating that competence is increasing contributes to self-efficacy and self-determination. In addition, feedback helps us understand why we perform the way we do, which attribution theory considers an important need. Feedback also contributes to self-regulation. It gives us information about progress toward goals, and when they're met, our self-efficacy increases. If they're not met, we can then increase our effort or change strategies.

table 11.5 Strategies for Promoting Involvement

Technique	Example
Improvement drills	Students are given a list of 10 multiplication facts on a sheet. Students are scored on speed and accuracy, and points are given for individual improvement.
Games	The class is divided equally according to ability, and the two groups respond in a game format to teacher questions.
Individual work spaces	Students are given their own chalkboards on which they solve math problems and identify examples of concepts. They hold the chalkboards up when they've solved the problem or when they think an example illustrates a concept. They also write or draw their own examples on the chalkboards.
Student group work	Student pairs observe a science demonstration and write down as many observations of it as they can.

theory to practice

Capitalizing on Climate and Instruction Variables to Increase Student Motivation to Learn

Throughout the chapter, we've emphasized that the variables in the model for promoting student motivation are interdependent. This is particularly true for the climate and instructional variables. The following guidelines can help you capitalize on this interdependence as you attempt to apply the model in your classroom:

1. Establish rules and procedures that maintain a safe, orderly learning environment.
2. Create links between topics and students' personal lives.
3. Describe the reasons for studying particular topics, and provide evidence for increasing competence.
4. Establish and maintain high levels of student involvement in learning activities.
5. Provide specific and detailed feedback on student work.

Let's see how David Crawford, a world history teacher at Baker County High School, attempts to apply these guidelines as he works with his students.

As the bell rings, the students are in their seats and have their notebooks on their desks. David moves to the front of the room and begins, "Okay, everyone, let's think about some of the technology that we have in today's world. Go ahead. . . . Brenda?"

The students offer examples such as computers, cell phones, and iPods, and then David continues, "Good examples. . . . Now, we tend to think of technology as something recent, but it's existed throughout history, and we can tell a great deal about a civilization by looking at its artifacts.

He clarifies the term *artifact* and then says, "Today we're going to examine some artifacts to see what they might tell us about the people who left them behind. This will give us the thinking tools to understand the civilizations we study as we look at the history of the world."

David reaches into a box, pulls out two animal skulls, a piece of woven fabric, and a stone spear point that is ground to a fine edge, and puts them on the table at the front of the room. Then, he puts another stone spear point that is also sharp but chipped, two small animal bones, and a fragment from an animal skin on the table next to the first group.

"We'll call this Civilization A, and this one Civilization B," he says, pointing to the sets of materials.

The class observes the artifacts and with David's guidance concludes that the two skulls are from a cow and a sheep and the bones are leg and rib bones from an antelope or deer.

"Now," David smiles, "We're archeological teams, and we found these sites. . . . I want you to work with your partners and write down as many conclusions as you can about the people from each, and any comparisons between the two, such as which one you believe was more advanced. In each case, provide evidence for your conclusions."

At the end of their allotted time, David says, "Okay, what did you come up with?"

"We think those are newer," Lori says, pointing at the chipped spear points.

"No way," Rodney interjects.

"Rod," David says firmly, "remember that we can disagree, but we extend the courtesy of listening to what others have to say."

"Sorry."

"Go ahead, Lori."

"The points are sharp, and they're sort of like art."

"Okay, Rod, go ahead," David says after Lori finishes.

"Those look like they're ground," Rodney responds, referring to the points with fine edges. "Grinding would be a more advanced technology than chipping."

The class continues discussing the artifacts, and from the cow and sheep skulls and the cloth, the students conclude that Civilization A had domesticated animals and the ability to weave. And, they decide that the antelope bones and skin indicate that Civilization B probably consisted of hunter-gatherers.

After completing the discussion, David says, "Okay, for tonight, I want you to read about the Old, Middle, and New Stone Ages on pages 35 to 44 of your books and decide what ages these artifacts probably belonged to. . . . You did a great job today. You made some excellent conclusions and supported them in each case.

Now, let's look at David's attempts to apply the guidelines. First, his classroom was safe and orderly. For instance, all the students were in their desks with their notebooks out when the bell rang, indicating a well-established routine. In addition, David admonished Rodney for interrupting Lori, which suggests he was attempting to create an emotionally safe environment. These were all applications of the first guideline.

He attempted to personalize the activity, applying the second guideline, by beginning the lesson with examples of today's technology and by placing students in the role of archeologists.

Then, in displaying the artifacts and saying, "This will give us the thinking tools to better understand the civilizations we study, . . ." he provided a rationale for the activity and capitalized on introductory focus and task comprehension. Also, his comment, "You did a great job today. You made some excellent conclusions and supported them in each case," provided further evidence of their increasing competence. Each of these factors helped apply the third guideline.

Finally, David's students were highly involved in the lesson, and success was enhanced because the task—making conclusions—was open-ended and challenging. Any conclusion that the students could support was acceptable.

Next, we'll discuss the topic of assessment, feedback, and motivation to learn—the fifth guideline.

The type of feedback is important (Hattie & Timperley, 2007). When it provides information about learning progress, motivation increases. On the other hand, feedback that involves social comparisons or has a performance orientation can detract from motivation to learn (Brophy, 2004; Schunk et al., 2008). Performance-oriented feedback has a particularly detrimental effect on less-able students and detracts from intrinsic motivation for both low and high achievers.

MyEducationLab

To further examine DeVonne's attempts to apply the model for promoting student motivation with her students, go to the *Building Teaching Skills and Dispositions* section in Chapter 11 of MyEducationLab at www.myeducationlab.com, and watch the episode *Applying the Motivation Model: Studying Arthropods in Fifth Grade.* Complete the exercises following the episode to build your skills in applying the model for promoting student motivation in your teaching.

Assessment and Learning: Using Feedback to Increase Interest and Self-Efficacy

To examine the role of assessment and its influence on learning and motivation, let's look at David Crawford's work with his students in the feature you just read, "Theory to Practice."

> The day after his lesson, David begins by saying, "One of our goals for yesterday and throughout the year is to be able to provide evidence for the conclusions we make. . . . You did a good job on this, but we need a little more practice in some cases. . . . I'm going to display the conclusions and evidence that some of you offered. . . . Now, remember the spirit we're doing this in. It's strictly for the sake of learning and improvement. It's not intended to criticize any of you.
>
> "I've put what you wrote on transparencies, so everyone can remain anonymous. . . . Let's take a look at what two groups wrote," and he displays the following:
>
> **Conclusion:** *The people had cloth.*
> **Evidence:** *There is cloth from Civilization A.*
> **Conclusion:** *The people in Civilization A were more likely to survive.*
> **Evidence:** *They had cows and sheep, so they didn't have to find wild animals. The cloth piece suggests that they wove cloth, so they didn't have to use animal skins.*
>
> "What comments can you make about the two sets of conclusions?"
>
> "The first one isn't really a conclusion," Shantae offers. "You can see the cloth, so it really doesn't say anything."
>
> "Good observation, Shantae. . . .Yes, a conclusion is a statement based on a fact; it isn't the fact itself."
>
> The class then discusses the second example and agrees that the conclusion is based on evidence.
>
> "This is the kind of thing we're looking for," David comments. "I know that you're all capable of this kind of thinking, so let's see it in your next writing sample."
>
> He then brings out a can of soup and asks students to make conclusions about the civilization that might have produced such an artifact and to give evidence that supports each conclusion.
>
> The class, beginning to understand the process, makes a number of comments, and David writes the students' conclusions and evidence on the board.

Detailed feedback that results from assessment is essential for learning. Some of David's students had little experience in making and defending conclusions. Collecting and reading their papers was a form of assessment, and without it—combined with feedback—they were unlikely to understand the difference between good and poor conclusions. Likewise, language arts students won't construct an understanding of what makes a good essay without having their work assessed and being provided feedback on that work.

Feedback is important for motivation to learn because it helps students improve the quality of their work. As they see that the quality is increasing, their perceptions of competence, self-determination, and intrinsic motivation also increase. None of this is possible without ongoing assessment and feedback based on the assessment.

Learning Contexts: Increasing Motivation in Urban Classrooms

Student motivation to learn is one of the areas in which urban contexts play a particularly prominent role. Motivation has been and continues to be one of the thorniest problems urban teachers face (N. E. Perry et al., 2006; Rubinson, 2004). While the causes are complex, three patterns emerge: (1) the impersonal nature of many urban schools, (2) the emphasis placed on control, and (3) the consistently low expectations teachers have for urban students.

Because urban schools tend to be large, teachers often have difficulty establishing the personal connections that helps meet students' needs for relatedness (Rubinson, 2004), a basic component of intrinsic motivation according to self-determination theory (R. Ryan & Deci, 2000). The tendency of many urban teachers to view delivering content as their only job, instead of also considering students' personal, social, and emotional needs, contributes to this problem (Charner-Laird et al., 2004).

The impersonal nature of urban environments is further exacerbated by teachers' tendencies to focus on the control of behavior, instead of developing student self-regulation, in attempting to create safe and orderly classrooms (Charner-Laird et al., 2004; Rimm-Kaufman & Sawyer, 2004; L. Weiner, 2002).

And, perhaps most pernicious of the three, consistently low expectations for student achievement is prominent (Ferguson, 2003; Landsman, 2004). Academic focus tends to be on low-level, routine tasks (L. Weiner, 2002, 2006), and students spend a disproportionate amount of time completing worksheets and written exercises (Manouchehri, 2004). Over time, these factors can have a strong impact on students' beliefs. "Children treated with low regard come to believe it and often fulfill low expectations" (Rubinson, 2004, p. 59).

Research indicates that threats to belonging detract from both motivation and learning (R. F. Baumeister & DeWall, 2005). In addition, research indicates that students are more likely to drop out of school when they don't participate in school-related activities because they don't feel a sense of belonging and don't identify with the school (Juvonen, 2006, 2007). "African American students and students enrolled in urban school settings are particularly vulnerable to an emotional detachment from school" (Honora, 2003, p. 59).

While easy solutions to these problems don't exist, research provides some answers.

The Impact of Teachers

Teachers influence motivation and learning for all students, and their role is even more essential in urban environments. "When we pressed students to explain why they regarded a particular experience in a positive or negative light, they laid the praise or blame at teachers' feet. Being a hero or a scapegoat was an unavoidable part of being a teacher in these inner-city schools" (B. L. Wilson & Corbett, 2001, p. 32). This leads to the following question: What factors that are under teachers' control can influence urban students' motivation to learn? The following variables in the model for promoting student motivation are particularly important:

- Caring
- Order and safety
- Involvement
- Challenge

Caring. We emphasized the need for caring teachers in our discussion of urban environments in earlier chapters, and it is particularly important for promoting urban students' motivation to learn (T. Howard, 2001; Noddings, 2001). "Students said caring teachers made class interesting, talked and listened to students, were fair, and asked if they needed help. In contrast, uncaring teachers went off topic, did not explain when students were confused, embarrassed or yelled at students, and demeaned them by forgetting their names" (Perry et al., 2006, p. 341).

Let's see what urban students, themselves, have to say about caring.

> "I like the ones that don't allow excuses.... I need to have someone to tell me when I'm tired and don't feel like doing the work that I should do it anyway. If they don't keep after you, you'll slide and never do the work. You just won't learn anything if they don't stay on you." (Corbett & Wilson, 2002, p. 19)

Caring teachers go beyond "not allowing excuses" and "staying on you," however. They are also helpful. "If they help us with our work, help us understand, they care" (Alder, 2002, p. 257).

Order and Safety. Effective teachers in urban schools also create safe and orderly learning environments. Teachers who aren't able to maintain order create conditions that interfere with both learning and motivation. One student comments, "The kids don't do the work. The

classroom connections

Applying the Instructional Variables in the Model for Promoting Student Motivation in Your Classroom

Introductory Focus

1. Introductory focus is a motivational variable that attracts students' attention and provides a conceptual umbrella for the lesson. Plan lesson introductions to capitalize on this variable.
   - **Elementary:** A fifth-grade teacher introduces a lesson on measuring by bringing in a cake recipe and ingredients that have to be modified if everyone in the class is going to get a piece of cake. He says, "We want to make enough cake so we can all get a piece. This is what we're going to figure out today." He concludes the lesson by baking the cake in the school cafeteria and sharing it with his students.
   - **Middle School:** A physical science teacher begins her lessons with a simple demonstration, such as whirling a cup of water suspended on the end of a string around her head. "Why doesn't the water fly out of the cup?. . . Let's see what we need to figure this out," she says in beginning the lesson.
   - **High School:** An English teacher introduces *A Raisin in the Sun* (Hansberry, 1959) by saying, "Think about a Muslim family in Detroit. What do you think they talk about? What is important to them? How do you think they felt after the events of 9/11? Keep those questions in mind as we read *A Raisin in the Sun*."

Personalization

2. Personalization is the process of using intellectually or emotionally relevant examples to illustrate a topic. Personalize content to create links between content and students' lives.
   - **Elementary:** A fourth-grade teacher begins a lesson comparing animals with exoskeletons and those with endoskeletons by having students squeeze their legs to demonstrate that their bones are inside. He then passes out a number of crayfish and has the students compare the crayfish to themselves.
   - **Middle School:** A seventh-grade teacher begins a lesson on percentages by bringing in an ad for computer games and products from a local newspaper. The ad says "10% to 25% off marked prices." The class works problems to see how much they might save on popular computer games.
   - **High School:** As her class studies the Vietnam War, a history teacher asks students to interview someone who served in the military at the time. The class uses the results of the interviews to remind themselves of the "human" dimension of the war.

Involvement

3. Involvement describes the extent to which students are actively participating in a lesson. Promote high levels of involvement in all learning activities.
   - **Elementary:** Each day a second-grade teacher passes out a sheet with 20 math facts on it. The students quickly write the answers and then score the sheets. Students who improve their scores from the previous day or get all 20 facts correct receive a bonus point on their math averages.
   - **Middle School:** A seventh-grade pre-algebra teacher assigns students to work in pairs to complete seat-work assignments. He requires them to work each problem individually, check with each other, and ask for help if they can't agree on the solution.
   - **High School:** An English teacher randomly calls on all students as equally as possible, whether or not they raise their hands. At the beginning of the year, he explains that this is his practice, that his intent is to encourage participation, and that students will soon get over any uneasiness about being "put on the spot." He prompts students who are unable to answer until they give an acceptable response.

Feedback

4. Feedback provides students with information about their learning progress. Provide prompt and informative feedback about learning progress.
   - **Elementary:** A fourth-grade teacher discusses the most frequently missed items on each of her quizzes, providing detailed information about each of the items.
   - **Middle School:** A seventh-grade teacher writes on a student paper, "You have some very good ideas. Now you need to rework your essay so that it is grammatically correct. Look at the notes I've made on your paper."
   - **High School:** A world history teacher displays an "ideal answer" on the overhead for each of the items on his homework assignments and essay items on his tests. Students compare their answers to the ideal and take notes with suggestions for improving their responses.

teacher is hollering and screaming, 'Do your work and sit down.' This makes the ones that want to learn go slower. . . . It just messes you up" (Corbett & Wilson, 2002, p. 19).

Research indicates that teachers who are effective in promoting orderly and safe urban classrooms empathize with their students but don't expect less of them (Benner & Mistry, 2007). And they are "warm demanders," teachers who maintain high expectations combined with the care and support that helps students feel as if they belong in school (Milner, 2006).

Involvement. Involvement is essential for motivation to learn in all students. Ironically, urban students, for whom involvement is even more important, tend to be taught less actively than their suburban or rural counterparts. Effective teachers of urban students ask more questions, distribute the questions more equitably, and respond more positively to student answers and student questions than do their

Student involvement is important in all environments, but it is essential in urban classrooms.

less-effective counterparts (Manouchehri, 2004). Involving urban students in learning activities is particularly challenging because they often have a long history of being placed in passive roles. Developing their willingness to take academic risks and engage in learning activities takes time and effort but, when finally achieved, it can be very rewarding (Kincheloe, 2004).

Challenge. Urban students are commonly treated as though they're unintelligent and unable to do cognitively demanding work (Conchas & Noguera, 2006). This is a double whammy. While they may lack the school-related prior knowledge that contributes to school success, they are often "street smart" in ways that even their teachers don't understand. They fully understand the way they're being treated, which exacerbates their resentment and disengagement (R. A. Goldstein, 2004). Effective teachers provide background knowledge by using a variety of high-quality examples, and they don't simply "give" students answers and solutions to problems. Instead, they provide the scaffolding needed to help students do their own thinking and arrive at their own understanding. The result is the development of self-efficacy and competence that is essential for self-determination (Manouchehri, 2004).

Unquestionably, the development of urban students' motivation to learn is one of the most daunting challenges that educators face. However, many rise to the challenge. "I am humbled,

developmentally appropriate practice

Applying the Model for Promoting Student Motivation with Learners at Different Ages

The variables in the Model for Promoting Student Motivation apply to learners at all grade levels. For example, caring teachers, a safe and orderly environment, success, and high levels of student involvement are essential for all students. Developmental differences exist, however. We outline some of these differences in this section.

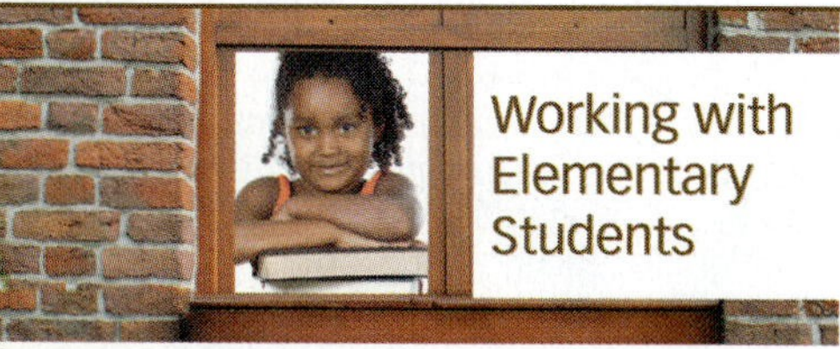

Working with Elementary Students

Elementary students enter school wide-eyed and optimistic, with only vague ideas about what they will do or learn. However, school is often the first time they are separated from their homes and parents, and anxiety about the unfamiliar may result. Taking extra time to make classrooms inviting places to learn are important with these children.

Interest can be a powerful motivating factor for elementary students (Hidi, Renninger, & Krapp, 2004). Topics such as animals, cartoon characters, sports, dinosaurs, and fantasy seem to be interesting for most children. Incorporating these topics into reading, writing, and math assignments can be effective.

Elementary students' ability to set goals and use learning strategies are largely undeveloped, but the beginnings of self-regulation can be established with conscious efforts to model and teach metacognition (Paris, Morrison, & Miller, 2006).

Working with Middle School Students

Middle school students have become savvy about rules and procedures and the schooling "game." However, the transition to middle school can be challenging for adolescents, and both motivation and learning often suffer (Wigfield, Byrnes & Eccles, 2006). Classes are usually larger and less personal, and students leave the security of one teacher for a schedule that sends them to different classes. Caring teachers who take the time to form personal relationships with their students are essential at this age.

Peers become increasingly important during the middle school years, and cooperative learning and group work become effective vehicles for increasing involvement and motivation. However, the growing influence of peers can result in off-task behavior during group work, so structuring it carefully, monitoring student behavior during the activities, and holding students accountable for a product are important.

Variables such as *challenge* and *task comprehension* become more important than they were with elementary students. Middle schoolers also begin to assess the relevance and value of what they're studying, so *personalization* also becomes an increasingly important variable.

Working with High School Students

While more mature, many high school students still have not reached a high level of self-regulation. Modeling self-regulation and conscious efforts to teach more sophisticated learning strategies can help these students meet their needs for self-determination (Pressley & Hilden, 2006).

High school students are also self-aware and are thinking about their futures after high school, so they assess the value of the topics they study. In addition, high school students' needs for competence and autonomy are prominent. As a result, climate variables, such as *challenge* and *task comprehension*, and instructional variables, such as *personalization* and *feedback* become increasingly important.

amazed, and inspired by gifted urban teachers who motivate and support resilient urban students in their efforts to avoid the pitfalls of growing up in urban poverty. They are some of the most heroic figures of our era, working their magic in the most difficult of circumstances" (Kincheloe, 2004, p. 269). This is the ideal that we strive for when teaching in urban environments.

MyEducationLab

To analyze a teacher's attempt to apply the model for promoting student motivation with urban students, go to the *Activities and Applications* section in Chapter 11 of MyEducationLab at www.myeducationlab.com, and read the case study *Instruction and Motivation to Learn.* Answer the questions following the case study.

check your understanding

5.1 Describe instructional strategies that can increase students' motivation to learn.

5.2 Look back at Kathy Brewster's lesson in Chapter 10 on page 312. Describe how she applied introductory focus in her lesson.

5.3 Identify where DeVonne used personalization in her lesson.

5.4 Provide an example of "mastery-oriented" and another example of "performance-oriented" feedback, using the topic of writing an effective paragraph. Explain the difference between the two.

To receive feedback for these questions, go to Appendix A.

Meeting Your Learning Objectives

1. Describe differences between a mastery-focused and a performance-focused classroom.
   - Mastery-focused classrooms focus on learning goals, which emphasize increased understanding and mastery of tasks. Performance-focused classrooms emphasize performance goals, which focus on demonstrating high ability, and particularly ability compared to others.
   - Mastery-focused environments increase student motivation to learn, whereas performance-focused environments can detract from motivation to learn for all but the highest achievers.
2. Identify strategies that teachers can use to develop learner self-regulation.
   - Teachers can increase learners' responsibility by emphasizing the relationships between accepting responsibility for one's own learning and the increased achievement that can result.
   - Strategies that can help students develop self-regulation include soliciting student input in establishing procedures that include student responsibility, treating responsibility as a concept by illustrating the consequences of taking and not taking responsibility, modeling responsibility, and providing concrete mechanisms that allow students to monitor and assess goal achievement.
3. Describe teachers' personal characteristics that can increase students' motivation to learn.
   - Personal teaching efficacy, modeling, caring, and high expectations are personal characteristics that can increase student motivation to learn.
   - Teachers who are high in personal teaching efficacy believe they can help students learn, regardless of students' prior knowledge or other factors.
   - Modeling courtesy and respect is essential for motivation, and demonstrating genuine interest in the topics they teach is the essence of teacher enthusiasm.
   - Teachers demonstrate that they care about their students by being willing to spend personal time with them and demonstrating respect for each individual. One of the most effective ways to demonstrate respect is to hold students to high standards. Holding students to high standards also communicates that teachers expect all students to succeed.
4. Identify classroom environment variables that can increase students' motivation to learn.
   - Motivating environments are safe, secure, and orderly places that focus on learning.
   - Success on tasks students perceive as challenging increases motivation to learn. Meeting challenges provides evidence that competence is increasing, which also leads to feelings of autonomy. Both factors increase intrinsic motivation.
   - In motivating environments, students understand what they're expected to learn and why they're expected to do so. Understanding what they're learning and why also increases perceptions of autonomy and contributes to task value.
   - The climate variables in the model for promoting student motivation correspond to the categories in the TARGET program with relationships between *challenge* and *task comprehension* and the TARGET category task; *order and safety* and authority; *success* and recognition; each of the *climate variables* and grouping; *success* and evaluation; and *task comprehension* and time.
5. Describe instructional strategies that can increase students' motivation to learn.

- Teachers can increase motivation to learn by beginning lessons with examples, activities, or questions that attract students' attention and provide frameworks for information that follows.
- Students maintain their attention and interest when teachers make content personally relevant to them and keep them highly involved in learning activities.
- Teachers can increase student motivation to learn by providing feedback about learning progress. When feedback indicates that competence is increasing, self-efficacy and self-determination both improve, and intrinsic motivation increases.

Developing as a Professional: Preparing for Your Licensure Exam

You saw at the beginning of the chapter how DeVonne Lampkin taught the concept *arthropod*. Now read about a language arts lesson on the construction of paragraphs that DeVonne taught later that same day. Read the case study, and answer the questions that follow.

DeVonne is working with her fifth graders on their writing skills. She plans to have them practice writing paragraphs and conduct self-assessments using criteria given in a 3-point rubric. She hands each student a blank transparency and pen, and then begins, "Today, we're going to practice some more on composing good paragraphs. . . . Now, we know the characteristics of a good paragraph, but let's review for a moment. . . . What do we look for in a well-composed paragraph?"

"Topic sentence," several students say immediately.

"Okay, what else?"

"Sentences that go with the topic," others add.

"Yes, 'go with the topic' means that the sentences support your topic sentence. You need to have at least four supporting sentences."

DeVonne reminds students that they also need to use correct grammar and spelling, and then displays the following paragraphs:

Computers come in all shapes and sizes. One of the first computers, named UNIVAC, filled a room. Today, some large computers are as big as refrigerators. Others are as small as books. A few are even tiny enough to fit in a person's pocket.

Ann's family bought a new color television. It had a 54-inch screen. There were controls for color and brightness. Ann likes police stories. There were also controls for sound and tone.

After some discussion, the class concludes that the first example meets the criteria for an acceptable paragraph, but the second one does not, because the topic sentence doesn't have four supporting sentences and the information "Ann likes police stories" doesn't pertain to the topic.

She then says, "Now, you're going to write a paragraph on any topic on the transparencies I gave you at the beginning of class, and then the class is going to grade your paper." DeVonne smiles as she hears several calls of "Woo, woo" from the students.

The students go to work, and when they've finished, DeVonne says, "Okay, now we're going to grade the paragraphs." She reviews the criteria from the 3-point rubric, and then says, "Okay, who wants to go first?"

"Me!" several of the students shout.

"I should have known that," DeVonne smiles. "Okay, Tu, come on up."

Tu displays his paragraph and reads it aloud:

Quidditch is a wizard sport that is famous in the wizard world. There is 7 people allowed on each team. On the field there are 4 balls. The Quaffle is a red soccerball. The two bludgers try to knoch players of their brooms. Finally, the Golden Snitch is very small and when caught the team gets 150 points. And that team mostly always win. Therefore, Quidditch is very exciting.

The class discusses his paragraph, agrees that it deserves a 3, and then several students call out, "I want to go next! I want to go next!"

DeVonne asks Justin to display his paragraph:

There was a boy named Josh. He lives in a house with the roof falling in and the windows were broke. He had holes in the wall and the ceiling leaked when it rained. But then again it always rained and thunder over his house. Noone every goes to his gate because he was so weird. They say he is a vampire.

She asks students to raise their hands to vote on the score for this paragraph. About half give it a 2, and the remainder give it a 1.

"Samantha, why did you give it a 2?" DeVonne asks, beginning the discussion.

"He didn't stay on his topic. . . . He needs to stay on either the boy or the house," Samantha notes.

"Haajar? . . . You gave him a 1. . . . Go ahead."

"There was a boy named Josh, and then he started talking about the house. And then the weather and then the boy again," Haajar responds.

A few more students offered comments, and the class agrees that Justin's paragraph deserves a 1.5. Justin takes his seat.

"Me, me! I want to do mine!" several students exclaim with their hands raised. DeVonne calls on Saleina to display her paragraph, the students agree that it deserves a 3, and DeVonne then says, "I am so impressed with you guys. . . . Your work is excellent."

"Okay, let's do one more," DeVonne continues. "Joshua."

"No! No!" the students protest, wanting to continue the activity and have theirs read.

"Okay, one more after Joshua," DeVonne relents with a smile. The class assesses Joshua's paragraph and one more, and just before the end of the lesson, several students ask, "Are we going to get to do ours tomorrow?"

DeVonne smiles and assures them that they will get to look at the rest of the paragraphs the next day.

Short-Answer Questions

In answering these questions, use information from Chapter 11, and link your responses to specific information in the case.

1. Feeling safe is essential for student motivation to learn. Assess the extent to which DeVonne's students felt safe in her classroom.

2. Assess DeVonne's application of the instructional variables in her classroom.

3. In spite of the fact that they were having their paragraphs publicly evaluated, DeVonne's students were enthusiastic about displaying their work. Offer an explanation for their enthusiasm, including as many of the variables in the model for promoting student motivation as apply.

4. DeVonne's students' backgrounds are very diverse, and she teaches in an urban school. Assess her classroom environment for learners from urban contexts.

For feedback on these responses, go to Appendix B.

Now go to Chapter 11 of MyEducationLab, located at www.myeducationlab.com, where you can:

- Take a quiz to test your mastery of chapter objectives. Detailed feedback is provided to explain why your responses are correct or incorrect.
- Deepen your understanding of chapter concepts with *Review, Practice, Enrichment* exercises.
- Complete *Activities and Applications* that will help you apply what you have learned in the chapter by analyzing real classrooms through video clips, artifacts and case studies. Your instructor will provide you with feedback for the *Activities and Applications.*
- Develop your professional knowledge and decision making in *Building Teaching Skills and Dispositions* exercises. Structured feedback will be available to you, providing you with support as you practice each skill. Your instructor will provide you with feedback on the final task that accompanies the exercise.

Important Concepts

caring (p. 327)
collective efficacy (p. 326)
introductory focus (p. 336)
involvement (p. 339)
mastery-focused environment (p. 320)
open-ended questions (p. 340)
order and safety (p. 332)
performance-focused environment (p. 320)
personal teaching efficacy (p. 326)
personalization (p. 339)
positive classroom climate (p. 332)
self-fulfilling prophecy (p. 329)
self-regulation (p. 322)
task comprehension (p. 334)

chapter

12

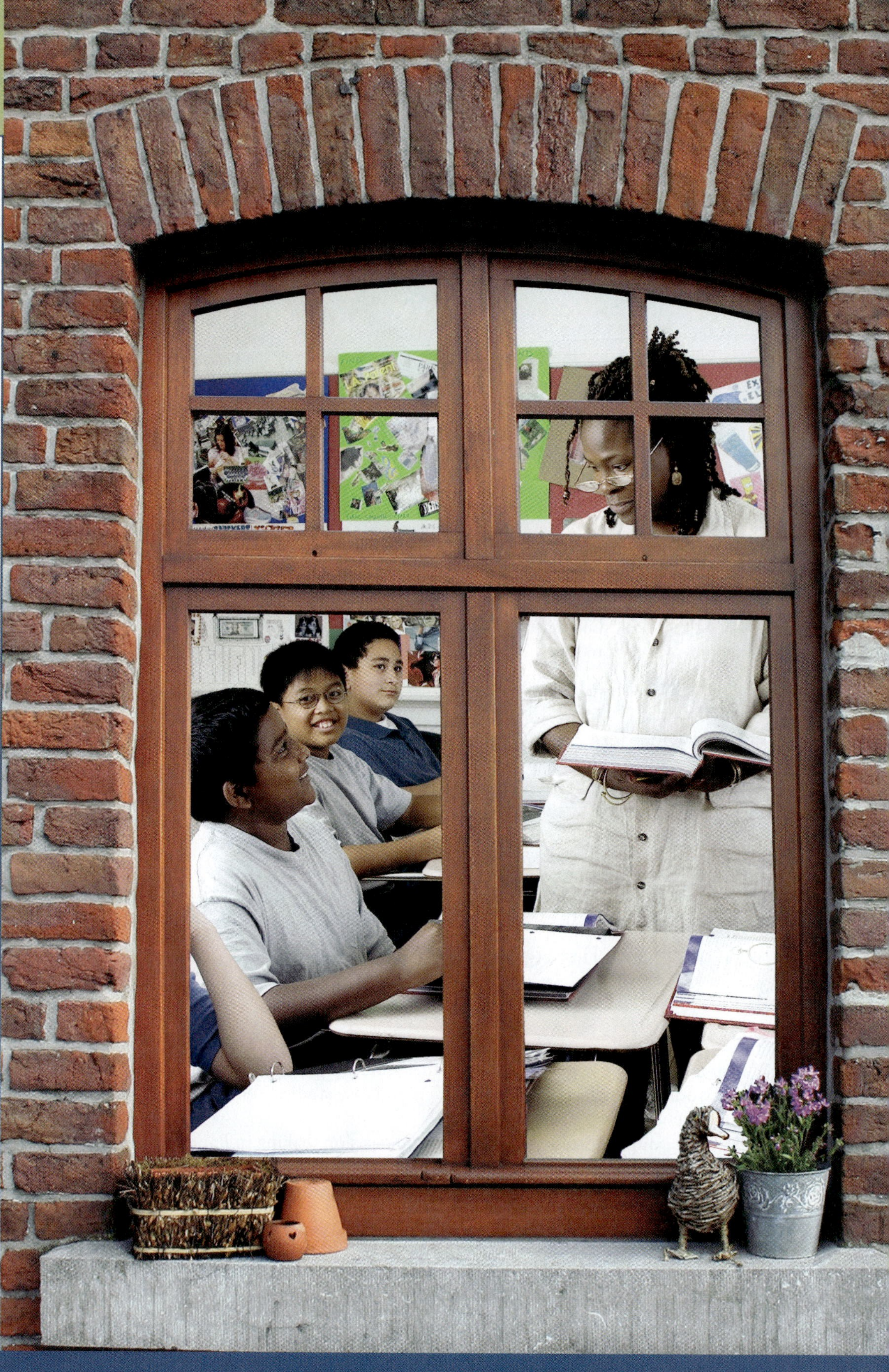

Creating Productive Learning Environments: Classroom Management

chapter outline

The Importance of Well-Managed Classrooms

- Public and Professional Concerns
- The Complexities of Classrooms
- Influence on Motivation and Learning
- Goals of Classroom Management

Planning for Effective Classroom Management

- Principles of Planning for Classroom Management
- Planning for Effective Classroom Management in Elementary Schools
- Planning for Effective Classroom Management in Middle and Secondary Schools
- Learning Contexts: Classroom Management in Urban Environments
  - **Theory to Practice:** Creating and Teaching Classroom Rules

Communicating Effectively with Parents

- Benefits of Communication
- Strategies for Involving Parents

Intervening When Misbehavior Occurs

- Principles of Successful Interventions
- Cognitive Interventions
- Behavioral Interventions
- An Intervention Continuum
  - **Exploring Diversity:** Classroom Management in Diverse Environments
  - **Theory to Practice:** Responding Effectively to Misbehavior

Serious Management Problems: Violence and Aggression

- School Violence and Aggression
- Long-Term Solutions to Violence and Aggression
  - **Developmentally Appropriate Practice:** Classroom Management with Different-Aged Learners

learning objectives

After you have completed your study of this chapter, you should be able to:

1. Explain why effective classroom management is important.
2. Identify characteristics of elementary, middle, and secondary students and how they influence planning for classroom management.
3. Describe characteristics of effective communication with parents.
4. Use cognitive and behavioral learning theories to explain effective interventions.
5. Describe teachers' professional and legal responsibilities in cases of aggressive acts and effective steps for responding to school violence and aggression.

As you anticipate your first teaching position, what is your greatest concern? If you're typical, the answer is "classroom management." As you read the following case study, think about the management incidents that occur in it and how Judy Harris, a middle school teacher, handles them.

Judy's seventh-grade geography class is involved in a cultural unit on the Middle East.

As the students enter the room, they see a large map, together with the following directions.

Identify the longitude and latitude of Cairo and Damascus.

Judy's students begin each class by completing a review exercise while she takes roll and hands back papers. They also pass their homework forward, each putting his or her paper on top of the stack.

Judy waits for the students to finish, and then begins, "About what latitude is Damascus. . . . Bernice?" as she walks down one of the rows.

". . . About 34 degrees north, I think," Bernice replies.

As Judy walks past him, Darren reaches across the aisle and pokes Kendra with his pencil. Her 32 students are in a room designed for 24, so the aisles are narrow. Darren watches Judy's back from the corner of his eye.

"Stop it, Darren," Kendra mutters loudly.

Judy turns, comes back up the aisle, stands near Darren, and continues, "Good, Bernice. It's close to 34 degrees.

"So, would it be warmer or colder than here in the summer? . . . Darren?" she asks, looking directly at him.

". . . Warmer, I think," Darren responds after Judy repeats the question for him, since he didn't initially hear it.

"Okay. Good. And why might that be the case? . . . Jim?"

As she waits for Jim to answer, Judy leans over Rachel's desk and points to the rules displayed on a poster and says quietly but firmly, "We agreed that it was important to listen when other people are talking, and you have been whispering and passing notes to Deborah.

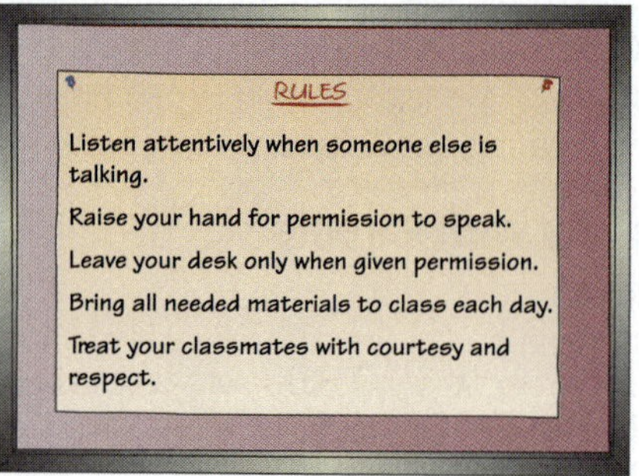
RULES
Listen attentively when someone else is talking.
Raise your hand for permission to speak.
Leave your desk only when given permission.
Bring all needed materials to class each day.
Treat your classmates with courtesy and respect.

"We can't learn when people aren't paying attention, and I'm uncomfortable when my class isn't learning. Please move quickly now," Judy says evenly, looking Rachel in the eye and directing her to an empty desk at the front of the room.

"Damascus is south of us and also in a desert," Jim responds.

"Good, Jim. Now let's look at Cairo," she continues as she watches Rachel move to the new desk.

Productive learning environment. A classroom that is orderly and focused on learning.

A **productive learning environment** is a classroom that is orderly and focused on learning. In it students feel physically and emotionally safe, and the daily routines, learning activities, and standards for appropriate behavior are all designed to promote learning.

As you read this chapter, consider two questions:

1. What did Judy do to create a productive learning environment?
2. How can you establish and maintain a similar environment in your own classroom?

The learning and motivation theories you've studied in earlier chapters, together with a large body of classroom-based research, will help you answer these questions. We examine applications of the theories and research in this chapter.

The Importance of Well-Managed Classrooms

Classroom management is one of the most challenging tasks teachers face. Three factors contribute to its importance:

- Public and professional concerns about classroom management
- The complexities of classroom life
- The influence of orderly classrooms on learning and motivation

Public and Professional Concerns

We introduced the chapter by asking you to describe your greatest concern about teaching, and we said that *classroom management* would most likely be your answer. Research corroborates your concern.

> Classroom management is a topic of enduring concern for teachers, administrators, and the public. Beginning teachers consistently perceive student discipline as their most serious challenge, management problems continue to be a major cause of teacher burnout and job dissatisfaction, and the public repeatedly ranks discipline as the first or second most serious problem facing the schools. (Evertson & Weinstein, 2006, p. 3)

From the 1960s until 2004, polls identified classroom management as one of teachers' most challenging problems, and from 2004 to the present it ranked second, only behind school funding as the most important problem schools face (L. C. Rose & Gallup, 2007).

Though the ability to manage classrooms can be a challenge, it isn't impossible, and with careful planning and effective instruction, it can be readily accomplished. Our goal in writing this chapter is to help you acquire the knowledge and skills that will allow you to do so.

The Complexities of Classrooms

The complexities of classrooms are a second reason classroom management is so important. Researchers have identified several characteristics of classrooms that make them complex and demanding (Doyle, 1986, 2006):

- *Multidimensional and simultaneous*: Judy, for example, had to deal with Darren's and Rachel's misbehavior, while simultaneously maintaining the attention of the rest of the class.
- *Immediate*: To avoid having events escalate, Judy needed to immediately react to Darren, and she needed to immediately decide whether or not to intervene in the case of Rachel's whispering.
- *Unpredictable*: Judy couldn't predict Kendra's reaction to Darren's horseplay. For example, instead of muttering, she might have hit him, or she might have blurted out a response that would have attracted the attention of the rest of the class.
- *Public*: If Judy had reprimanded Kendra instead of responding to Darren—the original perpetrator of the incident—it might communicate that she didn't know what was going on in her class.

Also, classrooms meet 5 days a week over the course of a school year, so they develop a set of norms and routines. If the norms are oriented toward safety, order, and learning, the classroom environment will promote both motivation and achievement. Establishing these positive norms will be one of your goals (Doyle, 2006).

The complexities of classrooms make classroom management challenging and important.

Influence on Motivation and Learning

Perhaps the most significant reason for the importance of classroom management is that students learn more and are more motivated to learn in orderly environments (Brophy, 2006b).

The relationship between classroom management and learning is well documented (Good & Brophy, 2008). Effective classroom management increases student engagement, decreases disruptive behaviors, and increases instructional time, all of which increase student achievement (Emmer, Evertson, & Worsham, 2006; Evertson, Emmer, & Worsham, 2006).

A long line of research indicates that students need to feel physically and emotionally safe in order to be motivated to learn, and orderly classrooms contribute to these feelings of safety (Brophy, 2006b; Watson & Ecken, 2003; Wessler, 2003).

Goals of Classroom Management

Classroom management. Actions teachers take to create an environment that supports and facilitates both academic and social–emotional learning.

Discipline. Teachers' responses to student misbehavior.

Some of the earliest research in this area was conducted by Jacob Kounin (1970), who helped teachers understand the difference between *classroom management* and *discipline.* **Classroom management** consists of "actions teachers take to create an environment that supports and facilitates both academic and social–emotional learning" (Evertson & Weinstein, 2006, p. 4). **Discipline** consists of teachers' responses to student misbehavior. Kounin (1970) found that the key to orderly classrooms is the teacher's ability to *prevent* management problems, rather than handling misbehavior once it occurs. His findings have been consistently corroborated over the years (Emmer & Stough, 2001; Freiberg, 1999a). For example, experts estimate that anticipation and prevention are 80 percent of an effective management system (Freiberg, 1999b).

Classroom management is more than simply creating an orderly environment. It is a process that contributes to learners' academic, personal, and social development. Effective managers have three primary goals:

- Create a community of caring and trust.
- Develop learner responsibility.
- Maximize time and opportunity for learning.

Creating a Community of Caring and Trust

Community of caring and trust. A classroom environment where learners feel physically and emotionally safe and their needs for belonging and relatedness are met.

The definition of classroom management emphasizes both academic and *social–emotional* learning. Helping our students develop socially and emotionally creates a **community of caring and trust,** a classroom environment where learners feel physically and emotionally safe and their needs for belonging and relatedness are met (Watson & Battistich, 2006; Watson & Ecken, 2003). "This requires a school and classroom climate in which students can afford to be emotionally vulnerable, and in which that vulnerability extends to the student's willingness to risk engagement in acts of kindness and concern for others" (Nucci, 2006, p. 716). In addition, students feel emotionally connected to their teacher and other students, and they feel worthy of love and respect.

Communities of caring and trust are grounded in social constructivist learning theory (Chapter 8), which underscores the social nature of learning (Watson & Battistich, 2006), as well as self-determination theory (Chapter 10), which emphasize relatedness as a basic need (R. Ryan & Deci, 2000).

Caring teachers are at the core of communities of caring and trust. They emphasize prosocial behaviors and moral development. They model courtesy and respect, expect the same in return, and systematically teach personal responsibility (H. A. Davis, 2003; Watson & Ecken, 2003).

Developing Learner Responsibility

In the cognitive learning chapters (Chapters 7 to 9) we emphasized the importance of learner metacognition and learners' need to make sense of their experiences. These ideas are the foundation for developing learner responsibility (Elias & Schwab, 2006; Emmer & Stough, 2001). As learners develop socially and emotionally, they recognize that they are also responsible for helping to create a productive learning environment. They obey rules because the rules make sense instead of obeying rules because of the threat of punishment for breaking them. Teachers promote this orientation by explicitly teaching responsibility and emphasizing the reasons for rules and procedures. Students understand that order is important for learning and understand the need for rules to promote that order.

Developing student responsibility is both sensible and practical. Learners are more likely to obey rules when the rules make sense and when they recognize that rules exist to protect their rights and the rights of others (Good & Brophy, 2008). This responsibility orientation can also contribute to ethical thinking and character development (Nucci, 2006). Children don't call their classmates nasty names, for example, because they recognize that name calling hurts other people's feelings. By promoting student responsibility and understanding, teachers promote social–emotional development and make their own jobs easier. This takes time, and some classrooms will be more challenging than others. Research indicates, however, that even students who display aggressiveness and other conduct disorders can be taught to accept responsibility for their own behavior (Singh et al., 2007).

Maximizing Time and Opportunity for Learning

While social–emotional development is an important goal, promoting academic learning is at the core of any effective classroom management system. Academic learning depends on two factors: (1) Time available for learning, and (2) effective instruction (we focus on effective instruction in Chapter 13). To maximize time for learning, some reform efforts have suggested lengthening the school year, school day, and even the amount of time devoted to certain subjects. Increasing time isn't as simple as it appears on the surface, however (C. S. Weinstein & Mignano, 2007). As suggested in Table 12.1, different types of classroom time influence learning in different ways.

Progressing from allocated time to academic learning time as shown in Table 12.1, represents a stronger correlation with learning (Nystrand & Gamoran, 1989). In classrooms where students are engaged and successful, achievement is high, learners feel a sense of competence and self-efficacy, and interest in the topics increases (Bransford et al., 2000; Wigfield & Eccles, 2000).

The ideal in classroom management is to maximize instructional, engaged, and academic learning time so that teachers use the amount allocated to a topic or content area as efficiently as possible. Expert teachers more nearly reach this ideal than do novices (Bohn et al., 2004). For example, Judy gave her students a review exercise to complete while she took roll and handed back papers. The exercise activated students' prior knowledge, focused their attention on the day's topic, and eliminated noninstructional time when disruptions are most common. This begins to answer the first question at the beginning of the chapter: "What did Judy do to create a productive learning environment?" She maximized the time available for learning.

Less-effective teachers waste opportunities for learning and create vacuums where management problems can occur. Some teachers seem unaware of the importance of time, viewing it as something to be filled—or even "killed"—instead of a valuable resource that increases learning (Brophy, 2006a; Wiley & Harnischfeger, 1974).

Maximizing learning time also promotes responsibility. Because Judy had taught her students the importance of going to work as soon as they entered the classroom, she didn't have to spend time explaining what they were supposed to do and reminding them to get started;

table 12.1 Types of Classroom Time

Type	Description
Allocated time	The amount of time a teacher or school designates for a content area or topic
Instructional time	The amount left for teaching after routine management and administrative tasks are complete
Engaged time	The amount of time students are actively involved in learning activities
Academic learning time	The amount of time students are actively involved in learning activities during which they're successful

they took responsibility for doing it on their own. And, because the students acted responsibly, more time was available for learning.

The general approach to meeting each of these goals should be a management style that parallels the authoritative parenting style you studied in Chapter 3 (Baumrind, 1991). Authoritative teachers have high expectations for their students, they're firm but caring, they provide reasons for rules, and they enforce the rules consistently. They contribute to both students' intellectual and social–emotional growth (D. Brown, 2004).

Now, we turn to our second question: How can you create a productive learning environment in your own classroom? The first step is careful planning, which we discuss in the next section.

check your understanding

1.1 Explain why effective classroom management is so important.

1.2 Which characteristic of classroom complexity did Judy most directly address by having an exercise waiting for the students when they entered the room?

1.3 A teacher tries to call on all students in her classes as equally as possible. To which component of time—allocated time, instructional time, engaged time, or academic learning time—is this suggestion most closely related? Explain.

To receive feedback for these questions, go to Appendix A.

Planning for Effective Classroom Management

Creating productive learning environments begins with planning, and beginning teachers often underestimate the amount of time and energy it takes. Let's see how expert teachers plan for classroom management.

Principles of Planning for Classroom Management

As with many aspects of teaching and learning, basic principles can guide you as you plan for a productive learning environment. These include the following:

- Developmental differences influence classroom management.
- Management and instruction are interdependent.
- Organization is essential for effective classroom management.
- Rules and procedures are the cornerstone of an effective management system.
- The first days of school set the tone for the year.

Developmental Differences Influence Classroom Management

Your students' development will influence how you manage your classroom. To illustrate this idea, let's look at two teachers' experiences.

> Sam Cramer, an elementary education major, is beginning his internship in a first-grade classroom. It is a disaster. Students get up from their seats and wander around the room. They begin playing with materials at their desks while he is trying to explain a topic. They get into arguments about their roles in cooperative learning activities. Reminders to pay attention have no effect. They are not destructive or intentionally misbehaving. They are little kids. Observations of his directing teacher suggest that she has a rather laissez faire approach to classroom management, and the lack of focus in her classroom doesn't seem to bother her.
>
> Laurie Jacobs' experience is completely different. She is in a high school American History honors class, and except for a few rough spots, everything is going well. The students are interested and responsive, she feels successful, and classroom management doesn't seem to be an issue.

The developmental characteristics of students influence planning for classroom management.

After reading these vignettes, you might conclude that elementary classrooms are harder to manage than those in middle or high schools. This isn't necessarily the case, and Sam's observations of his directing teacher were telling. The apparent lack of order in the class was largely a function of the teacher and how she responded to the developmental needs of her students.

Planning to create a productive elementary classroom environment is not the same as planning for middle and secondary classrooms (Carter & Doyle, 2006; Emmer & Gerwels, 2006). You know from your study of Chapters 2 and 3 that students think, act, and feel differently at different stages of development, and teachers need to respond to these differences when they plan (Emmer et al., 2006; Evertson et al., 2006). It is likely that Sam's directing teacher didn't take her students' developmental characteristics into consideration when she planned for classroom management.

Management and Instruction Are Interdependent

Think about Judy's work with her students. It would have been virtually impossible for her to maintain a productive learning environment if her instruction had been ineffective. This historically overlooked relationship is corroborated by research (G. Gay, 2006; Kaff, Zabel, & Milham, 2007), and it is true regardless of the developmental level of your students. As you plan for classroom management, you must simultaneously plan for effective instruction (Good & Brophy, 2008).

Classroom Organization Is Essential for Classroom Management

Classroom organization is essential for creating orderly learning environments at every developmental level. **Organization** is a professional skill that includes:

- Preparing materials in advance
- Starting classes and activities on time
- Making transitions quickly and smoothly
- Creating well-established routines

Organization. A professional skill that includes preparing materials in advance, starting classes and activities on time, making transitions quickly and smoothly, and creating well-established routines.

Judy was well organized. For example, she had an exercise prepared and waiting for the students as they entered the room, so instruction began the instant the bell rang. When teachers prepare materials in advance and begin classes immediately, they eliminate "dead" time, when disruptions can occur.

Transitions from one activity to another, such as from whole-class instruction to group work and back again, are also times when disruptions can occur. Providing clear and precise directions for group work helps make transitions quick and smooth and reduces the opportunities for disruptions.

Well-established routines, such as procedures for turning in papers, going to the bathroom, and lining up for lunch, are important for three reasons. First, they increase instructional time, and second, they reduce the likelihood of management problems. Third, they reduce the cognitive load on both teachers and students; when students learn to perform routines, such as turning in papers, automatically, teachers don't have to spend cognitive energy explaining or reminding students of what to do.

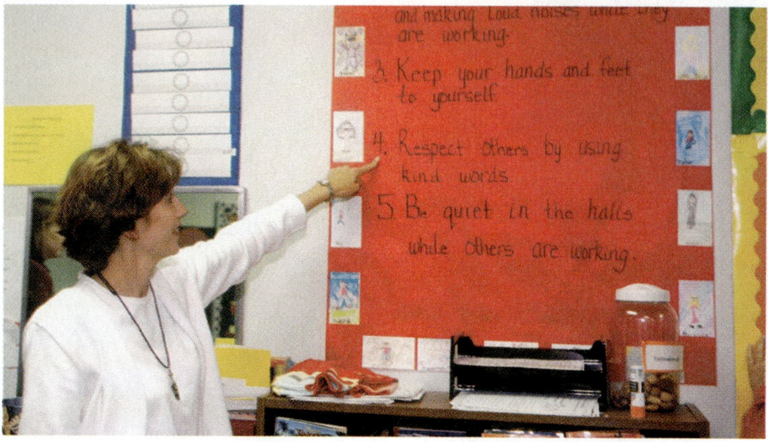

Effectively designed rules and procedures can facilitate both academic and social–emotional learning.

Rules and Procedures Are the Cornerstone of an Effective Management System

Regardless of your students' developmental level, the cornerstone of an effective management system is a clearly understood and consistently monitored set of rules and procedures. These **rules** are descriptions of standards for acceptable behavior, and the **procedures** are guidelines for accomplishing recurring tasks, such as sharpening pencils and making transitions from one activity to another (Carter & Doyle, 2006; Good & Brophy, 2008).

Rules. Descriptions of standards for acceptable behavior.

Procedures. Guidelines for accomplishing recurring tasks, such as sharpening pencils and making transitions from one activity to another.

Earlier in the chapter, you saw that classroom management facilitates both academic and social–emotional learning, and evidence indicates that effective use of rules and procedures supports both (Emmer et al., 2006; Evertson et al., 2006; J. C. Murphy, 2007). For example, researchers found that implementing a rule that did not allow kindergarteners to exclude classmates promoted social acceptance to a greater extent than did individual efforts to help excluded or isolated children (Harriet & Bradly, 2003).

Similar evidence exists at the middle school level. For example, social responsibility increases when rules are established that discourage students from laughing, snickering, or insulting classmates during instruction (Emmer & Gerwels, 2006). Additional evidence indicates that clear, reasonable rules, fairly and consistently enforced, promote feelings of pride and responsibility in the entire school (Marzano, 2003a), and students view clear standards of behavior as evidence that the teacher cares about them (Brophy, 2004).

The First Days of School Set the Tone for the Year

Research consistently confirms that patterns of behavior for the entire year are established in the first few days of school (Gettinger & Kohler, 2006; V. F. Jones & Jones, 2004). Let's see how two teachers handle the first day.

> Donnell Alexander is waiting at the door for her eighth graders with prepared handouts as students come in the room. As she distributes them, she says, "Take your seats quickly, please. You'll find your name on the desk. The bell is going to ring in less than a minute, and everyone needs to be at his or her desk and quiet when it does. Please read the handout while you're waiting." She is standing at the front of the room, surveying the class as the bell rings. When it stops, she begins, "Good morning, everyone."
>
> Vicki Williams, who also teaches eighth graders across the hall from Donnell, is organizing her handouts as the students come in the room. Some take their seats while others mill around, talking in small groups. As the bell rings, she looks up and says over the hum of the students, "Everyone take your seats, please. We'll begin in a couple minutes," and she turns back to organizing her materials.

In these first few minutes, Donnell's students learned that they were expected to be in their seats and ready to start at the beginning of class, whereas Vicki's learned just the opposite. Students quickly understand these differences, and unless Vicki changes this pattern, she will soon have problems, perhaps not dramatic, but chronic and low grade, like nagging sniffles that won't go away. Problems such as these cause more teacher stress and fatigue than any other (Friedman, 2006; L. Weiner, 2002).

Guidelines for beginning the first few days of school are summarized in Table 12.2.

table 12.2 **Guidelines for Beginning the School Year**

Guideline	Examples
Establish expectations	• Explain requirements and grading systems, particularly with older students. • Emphasize that learning and classroom order are interdependent.
Plan structured instruction	• Plan with extra care during this period. • Conduct eye-catching and motivating activities. • Use the first few days to assess learners' skills and background knowledge. • Use large- rather than small-group instruction. • Minimize transitions from one activity to another.
Teach rules and procedures	• Begin teaching rules and procedures the first day. • Frequently discuss and practice rules and procedures during the first few days. • Intervene and discuss every infraction of rules.
Begin communication with parents	• Send a letter to parents that states positive expectations for the year. • Call parents after the first or second day to nip potential problems in the bud.

Planning for Effective Classroom Management in Elementary Schools

Earlier in the chapter, we said that developmental differences exist in our classrooms, and effective teachers take those differences into account when they plan. Next, you'll see how effective elementary teachers plan to manage their classrooms.

Characteristics of Elementary Students

As you know from your study of Chapter 2, young children's thinking is concrete, and their attention spans are short (Piaget, 1970, 1977). Socially and emotionally, they are eager to please their teachers and are vulnerable to criticism and harsh treatment (Carter & Doyle, 2006).

One of the most important tasks for young children is to develop a sense of personal autonomy as they move from their family to the school setting. An orderly and predictable school environment is important, because it mirrors the stability they—hopefully—experience in the home. In cases where constancy and predictability are not part of the home, an orderly classroom can be a stabilizing force that helps build a sense of trust and security (Watson & Ecken, 2003).

Young children need enough freedom to develop initiative but sufficient structure to maintain their sense of equilibrium. As they progress through the elementary grades, they continue to need acceptance and the recognition that helps them develop a sense of industry and self-assurance. This is a challenge. "It is difficult to meet the misbehaving child's needs for autonomy, belonging, and competence, and also maintain a safe and productive classroom" (Watson & Ecken, 2003, p. 3).

Effective elementary teachers attempt to meet this challenge by creating a system of rules and procedures that make sense to children, are concretely taught and practiced, and are monitored and discussed in attempts to develop individual responsibility. Let's look at them.

Rules and Procedures in Elementary Classrooms

Rules and procedures are especially important for young children (Emmer et al., 2006; Evertson et al., 2006). One first-grade classroom had these rules:

- We raise our hands before speaking.
- We leave our seats only when given permission by the teacher.

Orderly elementary classrooms create feelings of safety and equilibrium for young children.

- We stand politely in line at all times.
- We keep our hands to ourselves.
- We listen when someone else is talking.

Another elementary teacher stated her rules more broadly.

- We treat everyone with respect.
- We listen politely.
- We wait our turn to speak.
- We leave our seats only when given permission.

Three features were consistent for the two teachers. First, the number of rules was small, which made them easy to remember. Second, the teachers began the process of teaching the rules on the first day of school. They stated the rules, explained carefully why they are important, provided clear examples to illustrate each, and answered questions, a process supported by research (Emmer, Evertson, & Anderson, 1980).

Third, both teachers continued to teach the rules over time. Establishing an effective set of rules doesn't end after the first day of school. Students construct knowledge of rules and procedures just as they construct knowledge of any idea. Expert teachers therefore capitalize on examples that occur during the natural course of classroom activities, explain how an incident relates to one of the rules, and provide specific feedback to their students (Carter & Doyle, 2006). Over the first few weeks of school, children gradually construct an understanding of the rules' meanings and how they are expected to behave (J. C. Murphy, 2007).

Providing rules that make sense, and providing clear reasons for them, is an essential part of the classroom management process, even with young children. People want their experiences to make sense, and this applies as much to classroom management as to any other form of learning. Explaining the reasons for rules helps students make sense of their classroom environment.

Some experts suggest that teachers should involve students in rule setting, because (1) the process is consistent with democratic and constructivist teaching philosophy, (2) rules and procedures make more sense to the students if they have input into forming them, and (3) the process contributes to moral development (DeVries & Zan, 2003; A. Lewis, 2001). However, no clear evidence suggests that student input is essential for rules and procedures to be effective; this aspect of classroom management therefore is a professional decision (Carter & Doyle, 2006).

Evidence does indicate that young children need explicit instruction and even rehearsal for rules and procedures (Evertson et al., 2006). Let's see how Martha Oakes, a first-grade teacher, helps her students understand how to put away worksheets.

> "I put each of their names, and my own, on cubby holes on the wall of my room. Then, while they were watching, I did a short worksheet myself and walked over and put it in my storage spot, while saying out loud, 'I'm finished with my worksheet. . . . What do I do now? . . . I need to put it in my cubby hole. If I don't put it there, my teacher can't check it, so it's very important. . . . Now, I start on the next assignment.'
>
> "Then I gave my students the same worksheet, directing them to take it to their cubbies, quietly and individually, as soon as they were finished. After they had done that, we spent a few minutes discussing the reasons for taking the finished work to the cubbies immediately, not touching or talking to anyone as they move to the cubbies and back to their desks, and starting right back to work. Then I gave them another worksheet, asked them what they were going to do and why, and had them do it. We then spent a few more minutes talking about what might happen if we didn't put papers where they belong.
>
> "We have a class meeting nearly every day just before we leave for the day. We discuss classroom life and offer suggestions for improvement. Some people might be skeptical about whether or not first graders can handle meetings like this, but they can. This is also one way I help them keep our rules and procedures fresh in their minds."

Martha's approach is grounded in cognitive learning theory. She modeled the process for taking worksheets to the cubbies, and she used cognitive modeling in verbalizing what she was doing. Then, she had students practice taking their worksheets to their cubbies. Each of these actions provided the concrete examples they needed to construct their understanding of the process. Being specific and concrete was essential for Martha's students because they were first graders; simply explaining how they were to deposit their papers wouldn't have worked. In time, and with practice, the procedure will become automatic, which will reduce the cognitive load on both Martha and the children.

MyEducationLab

To examine a second-grade teacher's attempts to create and teach classroom rules, go to the *Activities and Applications* section in Chapter 12 of MyEducationLab at www.myeducationlab.com, and watch the video episode *Establishing and Practicing Classroom Rules.* Answer the questions following the episode.

Arranging the Physical Environment in Elementary Classrooms

Experts emphasize the importance of the physical environment in elementary classrooms (e.g., Weinstein & Mignano, 2007). Effective classrooms are flexible and adaptable settings that include tables, chairs, cubbies, carpeted areas, plants, easels, building blocks, and shelves. They physically accommodate whole-group, small-group, and individual study.

Although the actual arrangement of your classroom will depend on professional judgment, some guidelines can be helpful (Evertson et al., 2006):

- Be sure that all students can see the writing board, overhead projector, or other displays. If students have to move, or crane their necks to see, disruptions are more likely.
- Design your room so you can see all your students. Monitoring students' reactions to instruction is important for both learning and classroom management.
- Make sure that students can easily access commonly used materials without disrupting their classmates.
- Keep high-traffic areas free from obstructions, and provide ample space for student movement.

Figure 12.1 illustrates the physical arrangement of one elementary classroom. Note how it is designed to maximize these guidelines. This is merely an example, and you may choose to arrange your classroom differently.

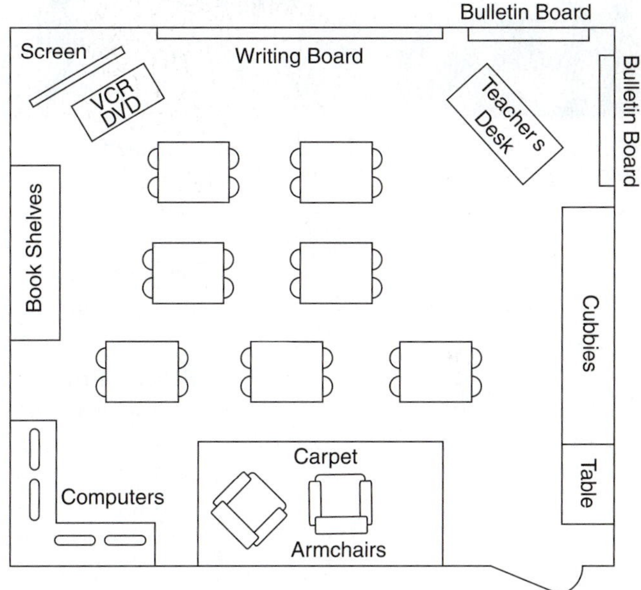

Figure 12.1 The physical arrangement of an elementary classroom

Planning for Effective Classroom Management in Middle and Secondary Schools

Two important differences exist between elementary, middle, and secondary classrooms, both of which influence how teachers plan for classroom management. First, these classes are divided into separate periods, and students have different teachers for each of the periods. Second, middle, and secondary classes are populated by adolescents, who have unique developmental characteristics.

Characteristics of Middle and Secondary Students

As students move through school, several developmental trends become significant:

- The influence of peers increases.
- Needs for belonging and social acceptance increase.
- Search for a sense of identity begins.
- Desire for autonomy and independence increases.

The theories you've studied in earlier chapters help us understand the implications of these developmental changes for classroom management. First, social cognitive theory explains the impact of increasing peer influence. Peers become important models, and students tend to imitate peers who are accomplished in academics, athletics, or even delinquency. The peer group, for example, has a strong influence on adolescent smoking, drinking, and sexual behavior (Kidron & Fleischman, 2006). Vicarious reinforcement and punishment can also be effective if peers believe that the reinforcers and punishers are fairly administered. Judy's interventions with Darren and

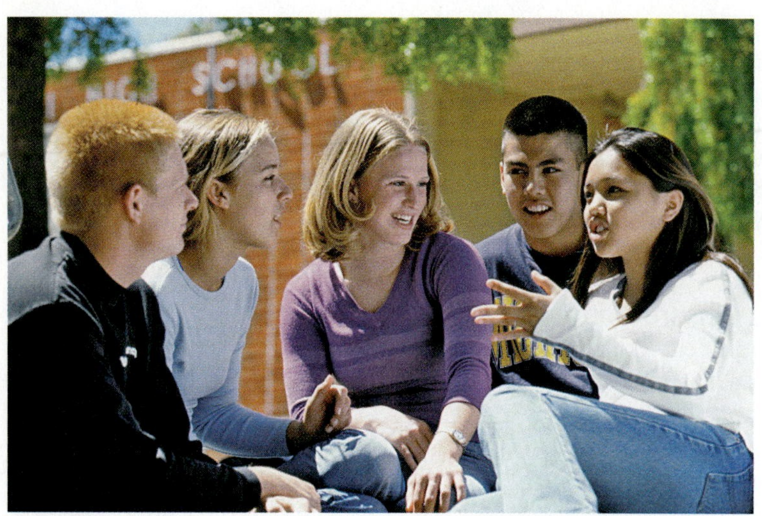
As students move through school, the influence of peers and the need for belonging and social acceptance increase.

Rachel in our chapter opening case study are examples. Their classmates could see that they were breaking rules that the class had agreed upon and that Judy was enforcing the rules fairly.

Second, as you saw in Chapters 10 and 11, theory and research in motivation demonstrate the importance of belonging and relatedness, and the need to be accepted by peer groups increases as students move into adolescence. This explains why they are so conforming in their speech, behavior, and dress, even when they seem bizarre by adult standards. Peer rejection can lead to academic, personal, and social problems, which can then result in disruptive student behavior (Wentzel, 2003). Teachers can promote feelings of belonging and relatedness by communicating a genuine commitment to students, both as people and as learners, calling on all students equally, and enforcing rules forbidding students from mistreating each other.

Third, adolescents are beginning their search for identity, and their need for autonomy and independence increases. This can result in attempts at rebellious and seemingly capricious behavior, which can be frustrating for teachers. However, while attempting to exercise their newfound independence, adolescents need the stability and equilibrium that results from the firm hand of a caring teacher who sets clear limits for acceptable behavior.

Rules and Procedures in Middle and Secondary Classrooms

As students move into middle school, perceptions of fairness, inequitable treatment, and teachers having "favorites" increase. As a result, clear rationales for rules are essential, and students must perceive the rules as fair and consistently enforced. Allowing students to provide input into the rules is more important than it is with elementary students. Does it work? Let's see what one middle school teacher had to say.

> I began with my first-period class. We started slowly, with my asking them about what it would take for the class to work for them. I then told them what it would take for the class to work for me. I was amazed at the overlap. . . . We talked about respect and the need to respect ideas and each other, to listen to and be willing to be an active participant without [verbally] running over other people in the class or being run over. . . . Well, this was five months ago and I was amazed at the level of cooperation. I am well ahead of last year in the curriculum; we have class meetings once a week to see how things are going and adjust as needed. We created a classroom constitution and had a constitutional convention when we felt it needed to be changed. I didn't believe it would make a difference; the students really surprised me with their level of maturity and responsibility and I surprised myself with my own willingness to change. This has been a great year and I am sorry to see it end. (Freiberg, 1999c, p. 169)

Although involving students in management decisions won't solve all problems, it is an important first step in gaining students' cooperation.

The following are sample rules from one seventh-grade class.

- Be in your seat and quiet when the bell rings.
- Follow directions the first time they're given.
- Bring covered textbooks, notebook, pen, pencils, and planner to class every day.
- Raise your hand for permission to speak or leave your seat.
- Keep hands, feet, and objects to yourself.
- Leave class only when dismissed by the teacher.

As with elementary classrooms, the specific rules you create will depend on your professional judgment. For example, some teachers suggest that the third rule is too specific, but this teacher noted that the specifics were necessary to ensure that her students actually brought the materials to class (J. A. Holmquist, Personal Communication, January 14, 2008).

As students move into high school, their behavior tends to stabilize, and they are less capricious than middle school students. They communicate more effectively at an adult level, and they respond generally well to clear rationales.

The following are rules taken from a tenth-grade class:

- Do all grooming outside of class.
- Be in your seat before the bell rings.
- Stay in your seat at all times.
- Bring all materials daily. This includes your book, notebook, pen/pencil, and paper.
- Give your full attention to others in discussions, and wait your turn to speak.
- Leave when I dismiss you, not when the bell rings.

The rules at each level vary in specificity, but none of the teachers created more than six, they provided clear rationales for the rules, and they applied the rules consistently throughout the school year. (We discuss applying rules later in the chapter.)

MyEducationLab

To examine a seventh-grade teacher's attempts to create rules and procedures, go to the *Activities and Applications* section in Chapter 12 of MyEducationLab at www.myeducationlab.com, and watch the video episode *Establishing Rules and Procedures at the Beginning of the School Year.* Answer the questions following the episode.

Arranging the Physical Environment in Middle and Secondary Classrooms

The physical environment in middle and secondary classrooms tends to be the more nearly traditional arrangement of desks in rows or in a semicircle facing the front of the room. Figures 12.2 and 12.3 illustrate these arrangements.

Where teachers use a combination of whole-group and small-group instruction, they arrange the room to make transitions back and forth simple and easy. Students are seated with their group mates so they don't have to move to get into their groups. Then, when the learning activity moves from small to whole group, students merely have to turn their heads to see the teacher, board, and overhead. Figure 12.4 illustrates this type of arrangement.

Research indicates that no single room arrangement works for all situations. For example, one study found that behavior improved when learners were seated in rows (N. Bennett & Blundel, 1983), but another found that a semicircle was most effective (Rosenfield, Lambert, & Black, 1985). You should experiment and use the arrangement that works best for you.

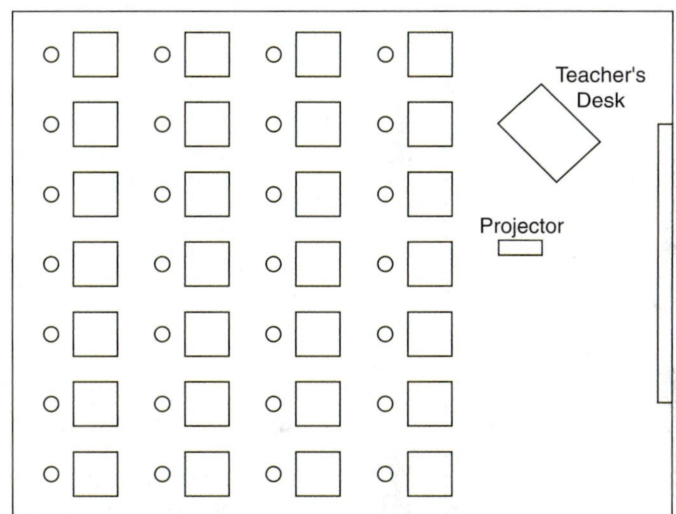

Figure 12.2 Classroom arrangement in traditional rows

Personalizing Your Classroom

In Chapter 11, you saw that personalization increases student motivation to learn. There, we discussed personalization in the context of learning activities, but it applies to the physical environment as well. Many classrooms, and particularly classrooms in middle and secondary schools, are quite impersonal, and they reveal little about the people who spend time in them (Emmer et al., 2006).

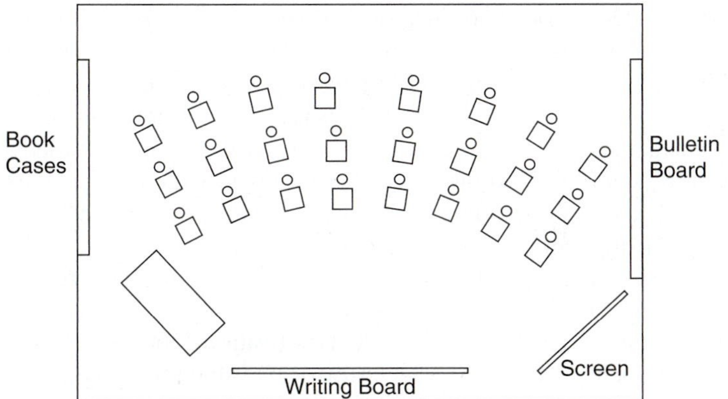

Figure 12.3 Classroom arrangement in a semicircle

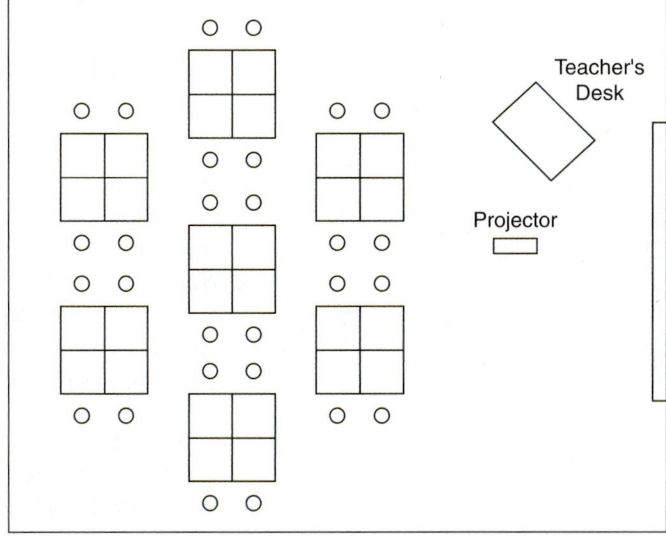

Figure 12.4 Sample seating arrangement for group work

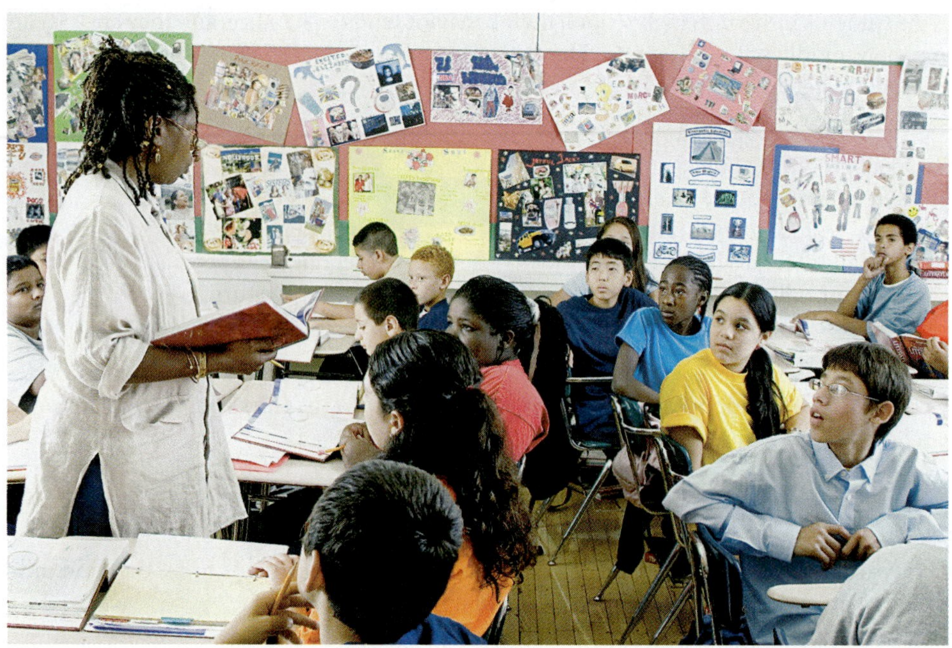

Classrooms decorated with personal items and student work create inviting learning environments.

Your classroom will be more inviting if you post personal items such as individual or class pictures, artwork, poetry, and other products prepared by students on bulletin boards or posters. A section of a bulletin board can be used for names of students who improved from one test to another or some other form of recognition where all students have an equal chance of being honored.

You can also personalize the physical environment by involving students in decisions about its arrangement. If students know that the goal is promoting learning, and if responsibility is stressed, their input can be worthwhile.

Learning Contexts: Classroom Management in Urban Environments

Three themes have emerged from our discussions of teaching in urban contexts. First, students in urban environments come from diverse backgrounds. As an example, let's look at Mary Gregg, a first-grade teacher in an urban school in the San Francisco Bay Area.

> Mary's room, a small portable with a low ceiling and very loud air fans, has one teacher table and six rectangular student tables with six chairs at each. Mary has thirty-two first graders (fourteen girls and 18 boys). Twenty-five of the children are children of color; a majority are recent immigrants from Southeast Asia, with some African Americans and Latinos, and seven European Americans. (LePage et al., 2005, p. 328)

As a result of this diversity, students' prior knowledge and experiences vary, so their views of acceptable behavior also vary. Second, urban schools are large; Mary had 32 first graders in a room built for 25. Third, and perhaps most pernicious, negative stereotypes about urban environments create the perception that working in these contexts is difficult if not impossible. With respect to classroom management, two of the most common stereotypes are, "Students can't control themselves," and "Students don't know how to behave because the parents don't care" (R. A. Goldstein, 2004, p. 43). In response to this stereotype, urban teachers often "teach defensively" (McNeil, 2000), "choosing methods of presentation and evaluation that simplify content and reduce demands on students in return for classroom order and minimal student compliance on assignments" (LePage et al., 2005, p. 331).

The results are lowered expectations and decreased student motivation. Students who are not motivated to learn are then more likely to be disruptive because they don't see the point in what they're being asked to do, a downward spiral of motivation and learning occurs, and management issues become increasingly troublesome.

It doesn't have to be this way. In spite of the diversity and large number of students in a small classroom, Mary Gregg created an active and orderly learning environment. Let's look at her classroom management during a lesson on buoyancy.

> Once into the science activity, management appears to be invisible. There is, of course, some splashing and throwing things into the water, but as the lesson progresses, the teacher engages in on-the-spot logistical management decisions. For instance, everyone is supposed to get a chance to go to the table to choose objects to be placed in cups. After choosing the first one to go, Mary sets them to the task. Very quickly, it is the second person's turn and the students do not know how to choose who should get the next turn. At first she says "you choose," then foresees an "It's my turn. No it's my turn" problem and redirects them with a counterclockwise motion to go around the table. (LePage et al., 2005, pp. 328–329)

This example demonstrates that classroom management in an urban environment doesn't have to be overly restrictive, harsh, or punitive. How is this accomplished? Research suggests four factors:

- Caring
- Clear standards for acceptable behavior
- High structure
- Effective instruction

Caring

We have emphasized the need for caring and supportive teachers in all our discussions of teaching in urban contexts. And, as we discussed earlier in the chapter, creating a community of caring and trust begins with a caring teacher (Watson & Battistich, 2006; Watson & Ecken, 2003). Teachers who care are important in all schools but are essential in urban environments (Milner, 2006). When students perceive their teachers as uncaring, disengagement from school often occurs, and disengaged students are much more likely act out than their more-engaged peers (Charles & Senter, 2005; V. F. Jones & Jones, 2004).

Clear Standards for Acceptable Behavior

Because their prior knowledge and experiences are diverse, urban students' views of acceptable behaviors often vary. As a result, being clear about what behaviors are and are not acceptable is essential in urban contexts (D. Brown, 2004). Interestingly, a strong relationship exists between standards for behavior and the perception that teachers care. As we saw earlier in the chapter, students see setting clear standards of behavior as evidence that the teacher cares about them (Brophy, 2006b). One urban student had this to say:

> She's probably the strictest teacher I've ever had because she doesn't let you slide by if you've made a mistake. She is going to let you know. If you've made a mistake, she's going to let you know it. And, if you're getting bad marks, she's going to let you know it. She's one of my strictest teachers, and that's what makes me think she cares about us the most. (Alder, 2002, pp. 251–252)

The line between clear standards for behavior and an overemphasis on control is not cut and dried. Alder (2002) describes the difference as order being created through "the ethical use of power" (p. 245). Effective teachers are demanding but also helpful; they model and emphasize personal responsibility, respect, and cooperation; and they are willing to take the time to ensure that students understand the reasons for rules (C. S. Weinstein & Mignano, 2007). Further, in responding to minor problems such as the inevitable incidents of students' failing to bring needed materials to class, talking, or otherwise being disruptive, effective teachers in urban schools consistently enforce rules. However, they also provide rationales for the rules and remind students that completing assigned tasks is essential because it helps develop the skills needed for more advanced work (D. Brown, 2004). In contrast, less-effective urban teachers tend to focus on negative consequences, such as, "If you don't finish this work, you won't pass the class" (Manouchehri, 2004).

High Structure

As you saw in Chapter 2, being at equilibrium is important for all people, and students in urban schools sometimes come from environments that lack the stability needed to create a sense of equilibrium. This makes order, structure, and predictability even more important in urban environments than in other classrooms. Procedures that lead to well-established routines are important, and predictable consequences for behaviors are essential. A predictable environment leads to an atmosphere of safety, which is crucial for developing the sense of attachment to school that increases learning and motivation.

Effective Instruction

As you saw earlier in the chapter, classroom management and instruction are interdependent, but teachers often use low-level activities and excessive amounts of seat work with urban students (Milner, 2006). This type of instruction detracts from motivation and feelings of engagement, which increases the likelihood of management problems. We discuss instructional strategies that promote involvement and avoid disengagement in Chapter 13.

theory to practice

Creating and Teaching Classroom Rules

You have seen that rules are essential for creating a productive learning environment. The ways that teachers create and teach rules are important in this process. The following guidelines can help you in your efforts:

1. State rules positively.
2. Minimize the number.
3. Solicit student input.
4. Emphasize rationales.
5. Use concrete examples to illustrate rules and procedures.

(We focus on rules in this section, but the guidelines apply equally well to procedures.)

Let's flash back to the beginning of the year to see how Judy Harris created and taught her rules:

Judy begins by introducing herself and having students introduce themselves, including any personal items they would like to share.

When she is finished, she says, "Our goal for this class is to learn as much as possible about the geography of our world and how it impacts the way we live.

In order to learn as much as possible, we need some rules that will guide the way we operate. So, think about some rules that make sense and are fair to all of us. . . . Go ahead Jonique."

". . . We should listen," Jonique offers after pausing for several seconds.

The class agrees that the rule makes sense, Judy writes it on the board, and then asks, "Why is this rule so important?"

". . . It's rude if we don't listen to each other or if we interrupt when someone is talking," Enita offers.

"Of course," Judy smiles. "What's the very most important reason?"

"To learn," Antonio responds, remembering what Judy said at the beginning of the discussion.

"Absolutely, that's what school is all about. We learn less if we don't listen. . . . And, we're all responsible for our own behavior, so this will also help us learn to be responsible. . . . And listening attentively is a part of treating everyone with courtesy and respect."

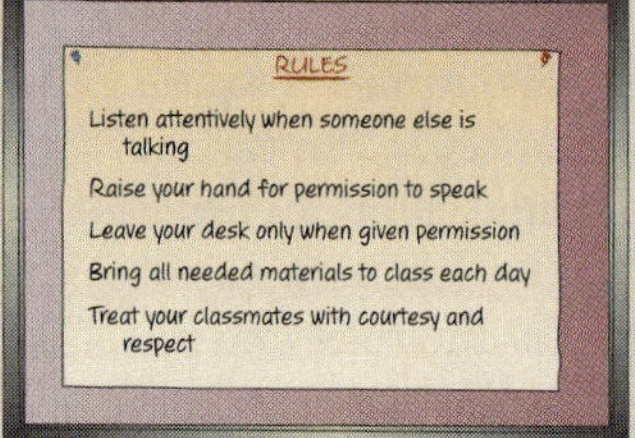

RULES
Listen attentively when someone else is talking
Raise your hand for permission to speak
Leave your desk only when given permission
Bring all needed materials to class each day
Treat your classmates with courtesy and respect

The students agree that they all want to be treated courteously, Judy writes it on the board, and she continues to lead the discussion until the rules you see here appear on the list.

In each case she emphasizes why the rule is important, how it will increase learning, and their ability to take responsibility for their own behavior.

Throughout the year, and particularly during the first few weeks of school, when an incident occurs, such as one student's interrupting another, Judy stops what they are doing, reminds the class of the rule, and again asks the students why the rule is important. The students gradually adapt to the rules and become acclimated to the classroom environment.

Let's look now at Judy's attempts to apply the guidelines. The first two are illustrated in the rules themselves: She stated the rules positively, and created only five. Positively stated rules specify desired behavior and help promote a positive emotional climate. Keeping the number small reduces the amount students must remember. Students most commonly break rules—particularly in elementary schools—because they simply forget!

Judy applied the third guideline, soliciting student input, when she said, "In order to learn as much as possible, we need some rules that will guide . . . us. . . . Go ahead, Jonique." Being asked for input creates social contracts that can increase moral development, increase students' feelings of autonomy, and contribute to motivation to learn (Brophy, 2004; R. Ryan & Deci, 2000).

Applying the fourth, and perhaps most important, guideline, Judy provided a careful rationale for each rule. Students are more likely to accept a rule, even when they disagree with it, if they understand why it's important.

Finally, Judy applied the fifth guideline by using incidents as concrete examples during the normal course of learning activities to illustrate the rules. Earlier, you saw how Martha Oakes had her first graders practice the procedure for putting worksheets in their cubbies. Concrete examples such as these help students construct their understanding of the rules, just as they construct understanding of any concept.

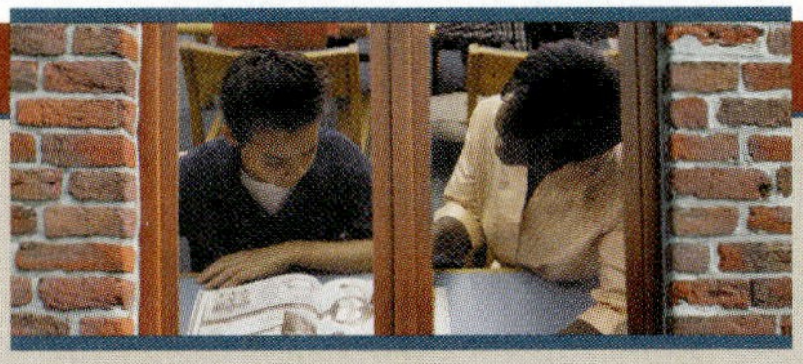

classroom connections

Planning for Effective Classroom Management

1. Effective classroom management begins with planning. Carefully plan your rules and procedures before you meet your first class.
   - **Elementary:** A third-grade teacher prepares a handout for his students and their parents, which he gives students the first day of school. The students take the handout home and have their parents sign it. It describes homework procedures, how grades are determined, and how work is made up when a student is absent.
   - **Middle School:** A pre-algebra teacher prepares a short written list of rules before she starts class on the first day. She plans to ask her students to suggest additional rules that will increase everyone's opportunity to learn.
   - **High School:** An English teacher prepares a description of his procedures for the way writing drafts will be handled and how his class will use peer comments to improve essays. He displays and discusses the procedure the first day of class.

Teaching Rules and Procedures

2. The developmental characteristics of elementary, middle, and secondary levels influence teachers' management strategies. Consider the developmental level of your students when teaching rules and procedures.
   - **Elementary:** At the beginning of the school year, a first-grade teacher takes a few minutes each day to have her students practice procedures such as turning in materials, lining up for lunch, and going to the bathroom. She continues having them practice until students can follow the procedures without being reminded.
   - **Middle School:** A sixth-grade teacher has a rule that says, "Treat everyone with respect." She offers specific examples, and asks students to decide whether the example illustrates treating everyone with respect. They discuss cases where differences of opinion exist.
   - **High School:** A chemistry teacher takes a full class period to teach safe lab procedures. She models correct procedures, explains the reasons for them, and gives students a handout describing them. She monitors students as they work in the lab, reminding them about the importance of safety.

check your understanding

2.1 Identify the characteristics of elementary, middle, and secondary students and how they influence planning for classroom management.

2.2 We see the rule "We keep our hands to ourselves" in the first-grade list and we see a similar rule in the seventh-grade list, but not in the tenth-grade list. How would you explain this difference?

2.3 Using your understanding of cognitive learning theory as a basis, explain why using examples to teach rules and procedures is so important.

To receive feedback for these questions, go to Appendix A.

Communicating Effectively with Parents

Students' home environments can have a powerful effect on both learning and classroom management, so you need to involve parents in their children's academic life as much as possible. Strategies for involving parents should go beyond traditional, once-a-year parent–teacher conferences and should include, for example, encouraging parents to help with homework, read to their young children, and monitor television viewing (Allen, 2007).

Classrooms with large numbers of students from diverse backgrounds present unique communication challenges (J. M. Walker & Hoover-Dempsey, 2006). Lower parent participation in school activities is often associated with families who are members of cultural minorities, lower in socioeconomic status, or have a child enrolled in either special education or English-as-a-second-language programs (Hong & Ho, 2005). Teachers often need to make special efforts to initiate and maintain home–school communication (Zaragoza, 2005). These might include sending communications home in parents' native languages and issuing special invitations to school events.

Students benefit from home–school cooperation in a number of ways, including higher achievement and increased motivation to learn.

Benefits of Communication

Students benefit from home–school cooperation in several ways:

- Higher long-term achievement
- Greater willingness to do homework
- More positive attitudes and behaviors
- Better attendance and graduation rates
- Higher levels of responsibility and self-regulation
- Increased enrollment in postsecondary education (C. L. Green, Walker, Hoover-Dempsey, & Sandler, 2007; Hong & Ho, 2005; Sheldon, 2007)

These outcomes likely result from parents' increased participation in school activities, higher expectations for their children's achievement, and teachers' increased understanding of learners' home environments. Deciding how to respond to a student's disruptive behavior is easier, for example, when his teacher knows that his mother or father has lost a job, his parents are going through a divorce, or there's an illness in the family.

Parent–teacher collaboration can have long-term benefits for teachers. For example, teachers who encourage parental involvement report more positive feelings about teaching and their school. They also have higher expectations for parents and rate them higher in helpfulness and follow-through (C. S. Weinstein & Mignano, 2007).

Strategies for Involving Parents

Virtually all schools have formal communication channels, such as open houses (usually occurring within the first 2 weeks of the year, when teachers introduce themselves and describe general guidelines); interim progress reports, which tell parents about their youngsters' achievements at the midpoint of each grading period; parent–teacher conferences; and, of course, report cards. Although these processes are school-wide and necessary, you can enhance existing communication processes. Let's see how Jacinta Escobar attempts to increase communication with her students' parents.

> Every year Jacinta prepares a letter to parents, which states that she expects to have a productive and exciting year, outlines her expectations and procedures, and solicits parents' support. She shares it with her students the first day of class, discusses it, and explains why having their parents involved is so important. She also asks for their suggestions on rules and procedures to include in the letter. She then takes the letter home, revises it, and brings a final copy to school the next day. She sends the letters home with her students, reminding them that the letters must be signed and returned. She follows up on those that aren't returned with e-mails and phone calls. Her letter appears in Figure 12.5.
>
> Every 3 weeks throughout the year, Jacinta sends assignments and graded homework home to be read and signed. She encourages parents to contact her if they have any questions about the packets.
>
> During the evening, Jacinta periodically calls parents to let them know about their children's progress. If students miss more than one assignment, she calls immediately and expresses her concern. She also makes a point of e-mailing parents to report positive news, such as a student's exceeding requirements, overcoming an obstacle, or showing kindness to a classmate.

Jacinta attempted to establish and maintain communication with parents in three ways. First, she sent her letter home. (Her letter is obviously only intended as an example. You will tailor your letter to best meet your students' needs.)

The letter is important for several reasons:

- It begins the communication process.
- It expresses positive expectations and reminds parents that they are essential for their child's learning.

August 22, 2009

Dear Parents,

I am looking forward to a productive and exciting year, and I am writing this letter to encourage your involvement and support. You always have been and still are the most important people in your youngster's education. We cannot do the job without you.

For us to work together most effectively, some guidelines are necessary. With the students' help, we prepared the ones listed here. Please read this information carefully, and sign where indicated. If you have any questions, please call me at Southside Middle School (441-5935) or at home (221-8403) in the evenings.

Sincerely,

Jacinta Escobar

AS A PARENT, I WILL TRY MY BEST TO DO THE FOLLOWING:

1. I will ask my youngsters about school every day. (Evening meal is a good time.) I will ask them about what they're studying and try to learn about it.
2. I will provide a quiet time and place each evening for homework. I will set an example by also working at that time or reading while my youngsters are working.
3. Instead of asking if their homework is finished, I will ask to see it. I will have them explain some of the information to see if they understand it.

Parent's Signature ______________________________

STUDENT SURVIVAL GUIDELINES:

1. I will be in class and seated when the bell rings.
2. I will follow directions the first time they are given.
3. I will bring covered textbook, notebook, paper, and two sharpened pencils to class each day.
4. I will raise my hand for permission to speak or leave my seat.
5. I will keep my hands, feet, and objects to myself.

HOMEWORK GUIDELINES:

1. Our motto is I WILL ALWAYS TRY. I WILL NEVER GIVE UP.
2. I will complete all assignments. If an assignment is not finished or ready when called for, I understand that I get no credit for it.
3. If I miss work because of an absence, it is my responsibility to come in before school (8:15–8:45) to make it up.
4. I know that I get one day to make up a test or turn in my work for each day I'm absent.
5. I understand that extra credit work is not given. If I do all the required work, extra credit isn't necessary.

Student's Signature ______________________________

Figure 12.5 Letter to parents

- It specifies class rules (described as "guidelines") and outlines procedures for homework, absences, and extra credit.
- It asks parents to sign the letter, which commits them to the support of their child's education, and asks her students to sign a contract committing them to follow the guidelines.

Signatures aren't guarantees, but they symbolize a commitment and increase the likelihood that the parents and students will attempt to honor it. Also, because students have input into the content of the letter, they feel ownership of the process and are more likely to ask parents for help on their homework.

Notice also that the letter is free from grammar, punctuation, and spelling errors. Teachers sometimes send communications home with errors in them. Don't. First impressions are important and lasting. Your first letter creates a perception of your competence, and errors detract from your credibility.

Second, Jacinta enhanced communication by sending packets of students' work home every 3 weeks and asking parents to sign and return them. In addition to creating a link between home and school, these packets give parents an ongoing record of their child's progress.

Third, she periodically called and e-mailed parents. Contacting parents in this way is one of the most effective ways to maintain communication and enlist cooperation (K. Anderson & Minke, 2007). By allocating some of your personal time to call, you communicate caring better than any other way. Also, talking to a parent allows you to be specific in describing a student's needs and gives you a chance to again solicit support. If a student is missing assignments, for example, you can ask for an explanation and can encourage parents to more closely monitor their child's study habits.

When we talk to parents, we need to establish a positive, cooperative tone that lays the foundation for joint efforts. Consider the following:

> "Hello, Mrs. Hansen? This is Jacinta Escobar, Jared's geography teacher."
>
> "Oh, uh, is something wrong?"
>
> "Not really. I just wanted to call to share with you some information about your son. He's a bright, energetic boy, and I enjoy seeing him in class every day. But he's missing some homework assignments."
>
> "I didn't know he had geography homework. He never brings any home."
>
> "That might be part of the problem. He just might forget that he has any to do. I have a suggestion. I have the students write their homework assignments in their folders each day. Please ask Jared to share his folder with you every night, and make sure that his homework is done. Then, please initial it so I know you and he talked. I think that will help a lot. How does that sound?"
>
> "Sure. I'll try that."
>
> "Good. We don't want him to fall behind. If he has problems with the homework, have him come to my room before or after school, and I'll help him. Is there anything else I can do? . . . If not, I look forward to meeting you soon."

This conversation was positive, created a partnership between home and school, and offered a specific plan of action.

Decisions about calling parents regarding management issues are matters of professional judgment. The question, "To what extent does this issue influence learning?" is a good guideline. For instance, a middle school student slipping and using inappropriate language in class is probably best handled by the teacher. On the other hand, if the student's language or other behaviors are disrupting learning activities, a call to parents may be called for.

Finally, emphasizing accomplishments should be uppermost in all types of communication with parents. When you call parents about a problem, first try to describe accomplishments and progress if possible. You can also initiate communication for the sole purpose of reporting good news, as Jacinta did in her e-mails. All parents want reasons to feel proud of their children, and sharing accomplishments can further improve the home–school partnership.

As it continues to expand, technology provides an additional channel for improving communication. For example, as they become more accessible, both voice mail and e-mail are useful to connect with busy parents. In many schools, newsletters and other communications are offered in digital and paper formats.

MyEducationLab

To examine teachers' attempts to communicate effectively with parents, go to the *Building Teaching Skills and Dispositions* section in Chapter 12 of MyEducationLab at www.myeducationlab.com, and watch the episode *Communicating Effectively with Parents.* Complete the exercises following the episodes to build your skills in working with parents.

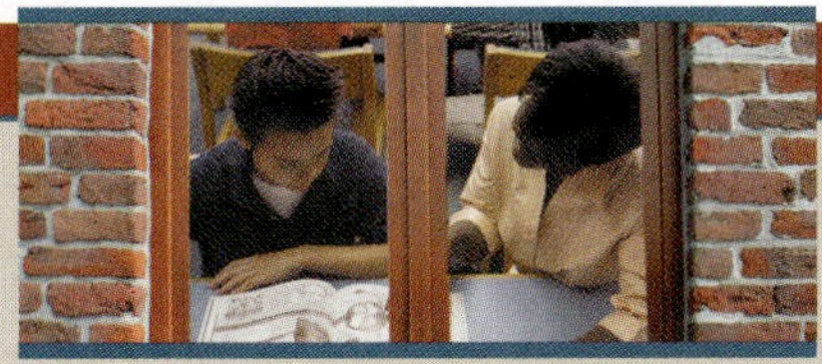

classroom connections

Communicating Effectively with Parents

1. Communication with parents is an essential part of effective classroom management. Begin communication during the first few days of school, and maintain it throughout the year.
   - **Elementary:** A kindergarten teacher calls each of her students' parents during the first week of school, tells them how happy she is to have their children in her class, finds out a little about each child, and encourages them to contact her at any time.
   - **Middle School:** Each month, a sixth-grade social studies teacher sends home a "class communicator" describing the topics his students will be studying, and giving suggestions parents might follow in helping their children. Students write notes to their parents on the communicator, describing their efforts and progress.
   - **High School:** A geometry teacher sends a letter home at the beginning of the school year describing his homework and assessment policy. He calls parents when more than one homework assignment is missing.
2. Effective communication with parents is positive, clear, and concise. Communicate in nontechnical language, and make specific suggestions to parents for working with their children.
   - **Elementary:** A third-grade teacher asks all her parents to sign a contract agreeing that they will: (a) designate at least 1 hour an evening when the television is shut off and children do homework, (b) ask their children to show them their homework assignments each day, (c) attend the school's open house, and (d) look at, ask their children about, and sign the packet of papers that is sent home every other week.
   - **Middle School:** A sixth-grade teacher discusses a letter to parents with his students. He has them explain what each part of the letter says and then asks the students to read and explain the letter to their parents.
   - **High School:** A ninth-grade basic math teacher makes a special effort at the beginning of the school year to explain to parents of students with exceptionalities how she'll modify her class to meet their children's needs. She strongly encourages parents to monitor homework and assist if they can.
3. Take extra steps to communicate with the parents of minority children.
   - **Elementary:** A second-grade teacher in an urban school enlists the aid of several teachers skilled in various languages. When he sends messages home, he asks these teachers' help in translating the notes for parents.
   - **Middle School:** At the beginning of each grading period, a sixth-grade teacher sends a letter home, in each student's native language, describing the topics that will be covered, the tests and the approximate times they will be given, and any special projects that are required.
   - **High School:** A biology teacher, who has many students with parents who speak little English, holds student-led conferences in which the students report on their progress. She participates in each conference and has students serve as translators.

check your understanding

3.1 Describe the essential components of effective communication with parents.

3.2 Explain how Jacinta's letter home helped to meet the classroom management goals discussed earlier in the chapter.

3.3 In this section, we said that calling parents communicates caring better than any other way. Explain how calling parents communicates caring. (Hint: Think about your study of time earlier in the chapter.)

To receive feedback for these questions, go to Appendix A.

Intervening When Misbehavior Occurs

Our focus to this point has been on preventing management problems. We emphasized the interdependence of instruction and classroom management, the importance of planning, and the central role of rules and procedures. Despite teachers' best efforts, however, they still need to intervene in cases of disruptive behavior or chronic inattention. Judy, in our opening case study, for example, had carefully planned her rules and procedures, was well organized, and she promoted high levels of student involvement in her teaching. In spite of these efforts, she still had to intervene with Darren and Rachel. This is more common than not.

In the following sections, we discuss interventions as we consider

- Principles of successful interventions
- Cognitive approaches to intervention
- Behavioral approaches to intervention

Principles of Successful Interventions

Intervening when problems occur is never easy. If it were, management wouldn't remain an ongoing issue for teachers. As you work with your students, we recommend a cognitive management system, but a behavioral approach may be necessary in some cases.

Regardless of the theoretical orientation, several principles increase the likelihood that your interventions will be effective:

- Demonstrate withitness.
- Preserve student dignity.
- Be consistent.
- Follow through.
- Keep interventions brief.
- Avoid arguments.

Withitness. A teacher's awareness of what is going on in all parts of the classroom at all times and communicating this awareness to students.

Demonstrate Withitness. **Withitness,** a teacher's awareness of what is going on in all parts of the classroom at all times and communicating this awareness to students, is an essential component of successful interventions (Kounin, 1970). Expert teachers describe withitness as "having eyes in the back of your head." Let's compare the withitness of two teachers.

> Ron Ziers is explaining the process for finding percentages to his seventh graders. While Ron illustrates the procedure, Steve, in the second desk from the front of the room, is periodically poking Katilya, who sits across from him. She retaliates by kicking him in the leg. Bill, sitting behind Katilya, pokes her in the arm with his pencil. Ron doesn't respond to the students' actions. After a second poke, Katilya swings her arm back and catches Bill on the shoulder. "Katilya!" Ron says sternly. "We keep our hands to ourselves! . . . Now, where were we?"
>
> Karl Wickes has the same group of students in life science. He puts a transparency displaying a flowering plant on the overhead. As the class discusses the information, he notices Barry whispering something to Julie, and he sees Steve poke Katilya, who kicks him and loudly whispers, "Stop it." As Karl asks, "What is the part of the plant that produces fruit?" he moves to Steve's desk, leans over, and says quietly but firmly, "We keep our hands to ourselves in here." He then moves to the front of the room, watches Steve out of the corner of his eye, and says, "Barry, what other plant part do you see in the diagram?"

Karl, in contrast with Ron, demonstrated withitness in three ways:

- He identified the misbehavior immediately, and quickly responded by moving near Steve. Ron did nothing until the mischief had spread to other students.
- He correctly identified Steve as the original cause of the incident. In contrast, Ron reprimanded Katilya, leaving students with a sense that he didn't know what was going on.
- He responded to the more serious infraction first. Steve's poking was more disruptive than Barry's whispering, so Karl first responded to Steve and then called on Barry, which drew him back into the activity, making further intervention unnecessary.

Withitness involves more than dealing with misbehavior after it happens (Hogan et al., 2003). Teachers who are withit also watch for evidence of inattention or confusion; they approach or call on inattentive students to bring them back into lessons; and they respond to signs of confusion with questions such as "Some of you look puzzled. Do you want me to rephrase that question?" They are sensitive to students and make adjustments to ensure that they are as involved and successful as possible.

Research indicates that lack of withitness can be a problem for beginning teachers (Wubbels, Brekeimans, den Brok, & van Tartwijk, 2006). This is likely because the cognitive load on beginning teachers is so high that their working memories are overloaded, making the process of continually monitoring student behavior difficult. Beginning teachers can best resolve this congnitive overload with well-established routines and carefully planned instruction that reduce the load on their working memories.

Effective teachers stop undesirable behavior while simultaneously maintaining the flow of their lessons.

Preserve Student Dignity. No one likes to look stupid in front of their peers, and preserving a student's dignity is essential for any intervention. As you saw in Chapters 10 and 11, safety is essential for motivation, and the emotional tone of your interactions with students influences both the likelihood of their compliance and their attitudes toward you and the class. Loud public reprimands, criticism, and sarcasm reduce students' sense of safety, create resentment, and detract from classroom climate. When students break rules, simply reminding them of the rule and why it's important, as Judy did with Rachel, and requiring compliance are as far as a minor incident should go.

Be Consistent. "Be consistent" is recommended so often that it has become a cliché. But the need for consistency is central to cognitive learning theory—people want their experiences to make sense. If one student is reprimanded for breaking a rule and another is not, students are unable to make sense of the inconsistency. They are likely to conclude that the teacher doesn't know what's going on or has "pets," either of which detracts from classroom climate.

Although consistency is important, achieving complete consistency in the real world is virtually impossible. Experts recommend that our interventions be adapted to the student and context (Doyle, 1986). For example, most classrooms have a rule about speaking only when recognized by the teacher, and as you're monitoring seat work, one student asks another a question about the assignment and then goes back to work. Failing to remind the student that talking is not allowed during seat work is technically inconsistent, but an intervention in this case is both unnecessary and counterproductive. On the other hand, a student who repeatedly turns around and whispers becomes a disruption, and intervention is necessary. Students understand the difference, and the "inconsistency" is appropriate and effective.

Follow Through. Following through means doing what you've said you'll do. Without follow-through, a management system breaks down because students learn that teachers aren't fully committed to maintaining an orderly environment. This is confusing and leaves them with a sense of uncertainty. Once again, the first few days of the school year are important. If you follow through consistently during this period, enforcing rules and reinforcing procedures will be much easier during the rest of the year.

Keep Interventions Brief. Keep all interventions as brief as possible. A negative relationship exists between time spent on discipline and student achievement; extended interventions break the flow of a lesson and take time away from instruction (Good & Brophy, 2008).

Judy applied this idea in her work with her seventh graders. She communicated her withitness and resolve with Darren by moving near him and calling on him. She spoke briefly to Rachel, and maintained the flow of the lesson in both cases.

Avoid Arguments. Finally, avoid arguing with students. Teachers never "win" arguments. They can exert their authority, but resentment is often a side effect, and the encounter may expand into a major incident.

Consider the following example that occurred after a teacher directed a chronically misbehaving student to move:

Student: I wasn't doing anything.
Teacher: You were whispering, and the rule says listen when someone else is talking.
Student: It doesn't say no whispering.
Teacher: You know what the rule means. We've been over it again and again.

Student: Well, it's not fair. You don't make other students move when they whisper.
Teacher: You weren't listening when someone else was talking, so move.

The student knew what the rule meant and was simply playing a game with the teacher, who allowed herself to be drawn into an argument. Let's look at an alternative course of action.

Teacher: Please move up here (pointing to an empty desk in the first row).
Student: I wasn't doing anything.
Teacher: One of our rules says that we listen when someone else is talking. If you would like to discuss this, come in and see me after school. Please move now (turning back to the lesson as soon as the student moves).

This teacher maintained an even demeanor and didn't allow herself to be pulled into an argument or even a brief discussion. She handled the event quickly, offered to discuss it with the student, and immediately turned back to the lesson.

With these general principles in mind, let's turn now to cognitive interventions, the foundation for all teacher actions.

Cognitive Interventions

Understanding is at the core of cognitive approaches to management; rules and interventions must make sense to students if the students are to accept them. In this section, we examine three factors, each intended to help students make sense of the intervention:

- Verbal–nonverbal congruence
- I-messages
- Logical consequences

Verbal–Nonverbal Congruence

For teachers' communications to make sense to students, their verbal and nonverbal behaviors must be congruent (Doyle, 2006). Compare the following interventions.

Karen Wilson's eighth graders are working on their homework as she circulates among them. She is helping Jasmine when Jeff and Mike begin whispering loudly behind her.

"Jeff. Mike. Stop talking, and get started on your homework," she says, glancing over her shoulder.

The two slow their whispering, and Karen turns back to Jasmine. Soon, the boys are whispering as loudly as ever.

"I thought I told you to stop talking," Karen says over her shoulder again, this time with irritation in her voice.

The boys glance at her and quickly resume whispering.

Isabel Rodriguez is in a similar situation with her pre-algebra students. As she is helping Vicki, Ken and Lance begin horseplay at the back of the room.

Isabel excuses herself, turns, and walks directly to the boys. Looking Lance in the eye, she says evenly and firmly, "Lance, we have plenty to do before lunch, and noise disrupts others' work. Begin your homework now." Then, looking directly at Ken, she continues, "Ken, you, too. Quickly now. We have only so much time, and we don't want to waste it." She waits briefly until they are working quietly and then returns to Vicki.

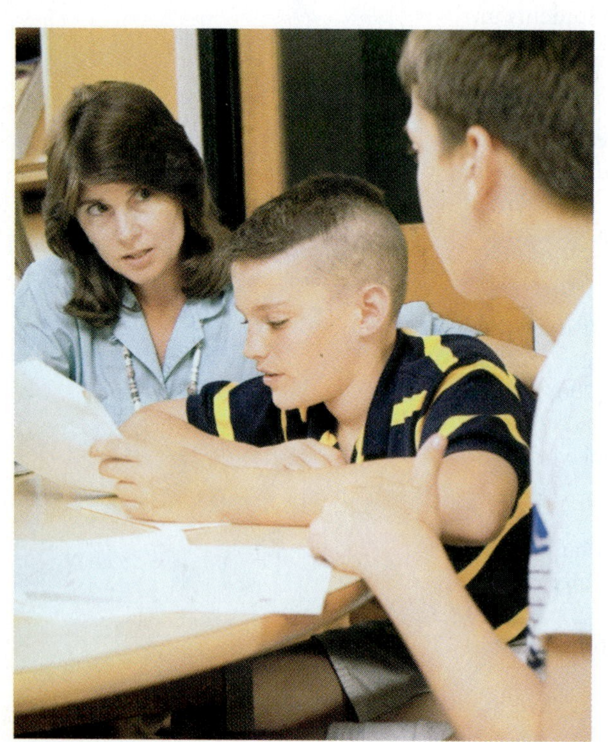

Cognitive interventions require congruent verbal and nonverbal communication.

The teachers had similar intents, but their impact on the students was very different. When Karen glanced over her shoulder as she told the boys to stop whispering and then failed to follow through, her communication was confusing; her words said one thing, but her body language said another. When messages are inconsistent, people attribute more credibility to tone of voice and body language than to spoken words (Aronson et al., 2005).

table 12.3 Characteristics of Effective Nonverbal Communication

Nonverbal Behavior	Example
Proximity	A teacher moves close to an inattentive student.
Eye contact	A teacher looks an off-task student directly in the eye when issuing a directive.
Body orientation	A teacher directs himself squarely to the learner, rather than over the shoulder or sideways.
Facial expression	A teacher frowns slightly at a disruption, brightens her face at a humorous incident, and smiles approvingly at a student's effort to help a classmate.
Gestures	A teacher puts her palm out (Stop!) to a student who interjects as another student is talking.
Vocal variation	A teacher varies the tone, pitch, and loudness of his voice for emphasis and displays energy and enthusiasm.

In contrast, Isabel's communication was clear and consistent. She responded immediately, faced her students directly, emphasized the relationship between order and learning, and made sure her students were on-task before she went back to Vicki. Her verbal and nonverbal behaviors were consistent, so her message made sense. Characteristics of effective nonverbal communication are outlined in Table 12.3.

I-Messages

Successful cognitive interventions should both focus on the inappropriate behavior and help students understand the effects of their actions on others. To illustrate, let's look again at Judy's encounter with Rachel in the case study at the beginning of the chapter. She pointed to the rule and then said:

> We agreed that it was important to listen when other people are talking. . . . We can't learn when people aren't paying attention, and I'm uncomfortable when my class isn't learning.

In this encounter, Judy sent an **I-message,** a nonaccusatory communication that addresses a behavior, describes the effects on the sender, and the feelings it generates in the sender (Gordon, 1974, 1981).

I-message. A nonaccusatory communication that addresses a behavior, describes the effects on the sender, and the feelings it generates in the sender.

In using an I-message, Judy addressed Rachel's behavior, which communicated that she was valued as a person but that her behavior was unacceptable. Judy also described the behavior's effect on the sender—herself—and the feelings it generated: "We can't learn when people aren't paying attention, and I'm uncomfortable when my class isn't learning." The intent of an I-message is to promote understanding, as it always is in cognitive interventions. Judy wanted Rachel to understand the effects of her actions on others, and if successful, this becomes a step toward responsible behavior.

Judy was also assertive in her directive to Rachel. Lee and Marlene Canter (1992; L. Canter, 1996), founders of **assertive discipline,** an approach to classroom management that promotes a clear and firm response style, suggest that teachers are often ineffective because their responses to students are either passive or hostile. For example, a passive response to Rachel might be, "Please. How many times do I have to remind you of our rule about paying attention?" A hostile response would be, "Your whispering is driving me up the wall," which implies a weakness in students' characters and detracts from the emotional climate in the classroom.

Assertive discipline. An approach to classroom management that promotes a clear and firm response style with students.

Logical Consequences

Logical consequences. Consequences that are conceptually related to the misbehavior.

Logical consequences are outcomes that are conceptually related to the misbehavior; they help learners make sense of an intervention by creating a link between their actions and the consequences that follow. For example:

> Allen, a rambunctious sixth grader, is running down the hall toward the lunchroom. As he rounds the corner, he bumps Alyssia, causing her to drop her books.
>
> "Oops," he replies, continuing his race to the lunchroom.
>
> "Hold it, Allen," Doug Ramsay, who is monitoring the hall, says. "Go back and help her pick up her books and apologize."
>
> Allen walks back to Alyssia, helps her pick up her books, mumbles an apology, and then returns. As he approaches, Doug again stops him.
>
> "Now, why did I make you do that?" Doug asks.
>
> "Cuz we're not supposed to run."
>
> "Sure," Doug says evenly, "but more important, if people run in the halls, they might crash into someone, and somebody might get hurt. . . . Remember that you're responsible for your actions. Think about not wanting to hurt yourself or anybody else, and the next time you'll walk whether a teacher is here or not. . . . Now, go on to lunch."

In this incident, Doug applied a logical consequence. It made sense to Allen that he should have to pick up Alyssia's books after he bumped her and caused her to drop them. Logical consequences help children understand the effects of their actions on others and promote a community of caring and trust (Watson & Battistich, 2006).

Behavioral Interventions

While learner understanding and personal responsibility are the ideals we strive for in classrooms, in the real world some students seem either unable or unwilling to accept responsibility for their behavior. In these cases, behavioral interventions can be effective. These are interventions that apply the concepts of reinforcement and punishment, which you studied in Chapter 6 (Fabiano, Pelham, & Gnagy, 2007; J. B. Ryan, Katsiyannis, & Peterson, 2007). Experts recommend using behavioral interventions as short-term solutions to specific problems, with development of responsibility remaining the long-term goal (Freiberg, 1999a; Gottfredson, 2001).

Let's see how Cindy Daines, a first-grade teacher, uses a behavioral intervention with her students:

> Cindy has a problem with her students' making smooth and orderly transitions from one activity to another. In an attempt to improve the situation, she makes "tickets" from construction paper, gets local businesses to donate small items to be used as prizes, and displays the items in a fishbowl on her desk. She then explains, "We're going to play a little game to see how quiet we can be when we change lessons. . . . Whenever we change, I'm going to give you 2 minutes, and then I'm going to ring this bell." She rings the bell to demonstrate. "Students who have their books out and are waiting quietly when I ring the bell will get one of these tickets. On Friday afternoon, you can turn them in for prizes you see in this fishbowl. The more tickets you have, the better the prize will be."
>
> During the next few days, Cindy moves around the room, handing out tickets and making comments such as "I really like the way Merry is ready to work," "Ted already has his books out and is quiet," and "Thank you for moving to math so quickly."
>
> She realizes her strategy is starting to work when she hears "Shh" and "Be quiet!" from the students, so she is gradually able to space out the rewards as the students become more responsible.

Cindy used concepts from both behaviorism and social cognitive theory in her system. Her tickets and prizes were positive reinforcers for making quick and quiet transitions, and her comments, such as, "I really like the way Merry is ready to work" and "Ted already has his books out and is quiet" were vicarious reinforcers for the other children.

As you saw in Chapter 6, reinforcement is more effective for changing behavior than is punishment, and this principle applies when using behavioral interventions (Landrum & Kaufman, 2006). However, as you also saw in Chapter 6, punishment may be necessary in some cases. Desists, timeout, detention, and response cost can be effective punishers. However, physical punishment, embarrassment or humiliation, and class work are ineffective, and teachers should not use them. Guidelines for using punishment as management alternatives are outlined in Figure 12.6.

- Use punishment as infrequently as possible.
- Apply punishment immediately and directly to the behavior.
- Apply punishment only severe enough to eliminate the behavior.
- Apply punishment dispassionately instead of angrily.
- Explain and model alternative positive behaviors.

Figure 12.6 Guidelines for using punishment in classrooms

Designing and Maintaining a Behavioral Management System

Clear rules and expectations followed by consistently applied consequences are the foundation of a behavioral management system. Designing a management system based on behaviorism involves the following steps:

- Prepare a list of specific rules, such as "Leave your desk only when given permission."
- Specify reinforcers for obeying each rule and punishers for breaking the rules, such as the consequences in Table 12.4.
- Display the rules, and explain the consequences.
- Consistently apply consequences.

A behavioral system doesn't preclude providing rationales or creating the rules with learner input. The primary focus, however, is on clearly specifying behavioral guidelines and applying consequences, in contrast with a cognitive approach, which emphasizes learner understanding and responsibility.

In designing a comprehensive management system, teachers usually combine elements of both cognitive and behavioral approaches. Behavioral systems have the advantage of being immediately applicable; they're effective for initiating desired behaviors, particularly with young students; and they're useful for reducing chronic misbehavior. Cognitive systems take longer to produce results but are more likely to develop learner responsibility.

Despite the most thorough planning and implementation, the need for periodic teacher intervention is inevitable. Keeping both cognitive and behavioral approaches in mind, we next consider intervention options.

MyEducatonLab

To see how one teacher implements a behavioral management system, go to the *Activities and Applications* section in Chapter 12 of MyEducationLab at www.myeducationlab.com, and read the case study *Using a Behavioral Management System.* Answer the questions following the case study.

An Intervention Continuum

Disruptions vary from isolated incidents, such as a student briefly whispering to a neighbor, to chronic infractions, such as someone repeatedly poking and kicking other students or even fighting. Because infractions vary, teachers' reactions should also vary. To maximize instructional

table 12.4 Sample Consequences for Following or Breaking Rules

Consequences for Breaking Rules	
First infraction	Name on list
Second infraction	Check by name
Third infraction	Second check by name
Fourth infraction	Half-hour detention
Fifth infraction	Call to parents

Consequences for Following Rules

A check is removed for each day that no infractions occur. If only a name remains, and no infractions occur, the name is removed.

All students without names on the list are given 45 minutes of free time Friday afternoon to do as they choose. The only restrictions are that they must stay in the classroom, and they must not disrupt the students who didn't earn the free time.

Minor infractions				Serious infractions
Praising desired behavior	Ignoring inappropriate behavior	Using indirect cues	Using desists	Applying consequences

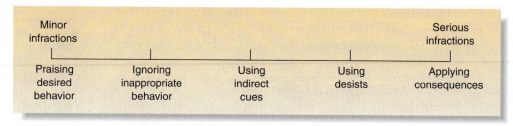

Figure 12.7 An intervention continuum

time, interventions should be as unobtrusive as possible. A continuum of interventions is shown in Figure 12.7 and discussed in the following sections.

Praising Desired Behavior

Because promoting desired behaviors is an important goal, praising students for displaying them is a sensible first intervention. Praise occurs less often than might be expected, so efforts to "catch 'em being good" are worthwhile, especially as a method of prevention. Elementary teachers can praise openly and freely, and middle and secondary teachers can make private comments such as "I'm extremely pleased with your work this week—keep it up." Making an effort to acknowledge desired behavior and good work contributes to a positive classroom climate.

Reinforcing behaviors that are incompatible with misbehavior is an extension of this idea (Alberto & Troutman, 2006). For instance, participating in a learning activity is incompatible with daydreaming, so calling on a student and reinforcing any attempt to respond are more effective than reprimanding a student for not paying attention.

Ignoring Inappropriate Behavior

Behaviors that aren't reinforced become extinct. The attention students receive when they're admonished for minor misbehaviors is often reinforcing, so ignoring the behavior can eliminate the reinforcers teachers might be inadvertently providing (Baldwin & Baldwin, 2001; Landrum & Kaufman, 2006). This is effective, for example, when two students are whispering but soon stop. A combination of praising desired behaviors, reinforcing incompatible behaviors, and ignoring misbehavior can be effective with minor disruptions.

Using Indirect Cues

Effective teachers use indirect cues—such as proximity, methods of redirecting attention, and vicarious reinforcers—when students are displaying behaviors that can't be ignored but can be stopped or diverted without addressing them directly (Babad, AvniBabad, & Rosenthal, 2003; V. F. Jones & Jones, 2004). For example, Judy moved near Darren and called on him after she heard Kendra mutter. Her proximity stopped his misbehavior, and calling on him directed his attention back to the lesson.

Vicarious reinforcement can also be effective. Teachers, especially in the lower grades, can use students as models and vicariously reinforce the rest of the students with statements such as, "I really like the way Row 1 is working quietly" or "Elisa has already started the assignment."

Desist. A verbal or nonverbal communication a teacher uses to stop a behavior.

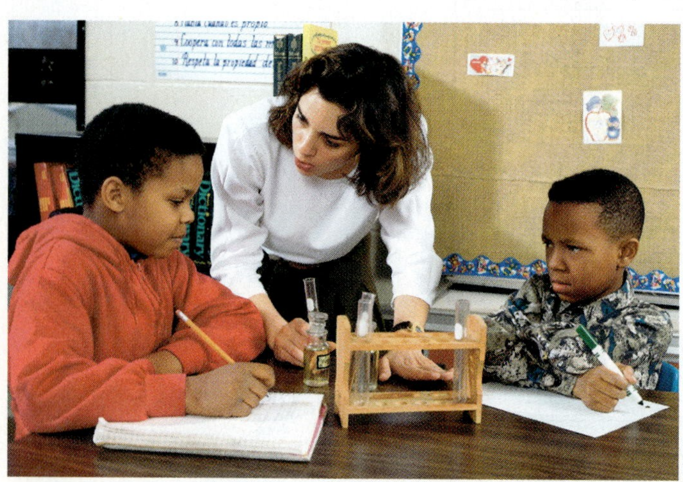

Desists can be used to stop undesirable behavior.

Using Desists

A **desist** is a verbal or nonverbal communication a teacher uses to stop a behavior (Kounin, 1970). "Glenys, we leave our seats only when given permission," "Glenys!" and a finger to the lips, or a stern facial expression are all desists. They are the most common teacher reactions to misbehavior.

classroom connections

Using Interventions Successfully in Your Classroom

1. Cognitive interventions are grounded in learners' needs to make sense of their experiences. Use logical consequences to help students develop responsibility. Hold discussions regarding fairness or equity after class and in private.
   - **Elementary:** During weekly classroom chores, two first graders begin a tug-of-war over a cleaning rag and knock over a potted plant. The teacher talks to the students, they agree to clean up the mess, and they write a note to their parents explaining that they will be working in the classroom before school the next week to pay for a new pot.
   - **Middle School:** A social studies teacher tries to make her interventions learning experiences, identifying rules that were broken and explaining why the rules exist. In cases of uncertainty, she talks privately to students to clear up misunderstanding.
   - **High School:** After having been asked to stop whispering for the second time in 10 minutes, a ninth grader protests that he was asking about the assigned seat work. The teacher reminds him of the incidents, points out that his behavior is disruptive, and reprimands him without further discussion. After class, the teacher talks to him, explaining why rules exist, and reminding him that he is expected to accept responsibility for his behavior.
2. Positive reinforcement can be used to increase appropriate behavior. Use positive reinforcers to initiate and teach desirable behaviors.
   - **Elementary:** A first-grade teacher, knowing that the times after recess and lunch are difficult for many students, institutes a system in which the class has 1 minute after a timer rings to settle down and get out their materials. When the class meets the requirement, they earn points toward free time.
   - **Middle School:** To encourage students to clean up quickly after labs, a science teacher offers 5 minutes of free time to talk in their seats if the lab is cleaned up in time. Students who don't clean up in time are required to finish in silence.
   - **High School:** A ninth-grade basic math teacher is encountering problems getting his students to work quietly in small groups. He discusses the problem with the class and then closely monitors the groups, circulating and offering praise and reinforcement when they are working smoothly.
3. Linking consequences to behaviors helps students see the connection between their actions and their effects on others. To help students see the logical connection between behaviors and consequences, follow through consistently in cases of disruptive behavior.
   - **Elementary:** A second-grade teacher finds that transitions to and from recess, lunch, and bathroom breaks are noisy and disruptive. She talks with the class about the problem, initiates a "no-talking" rule during these transitions, and carefully enforces the rule.
   - **Middle School:** A teacher separates two seventh graders who disrupt lessons with their talking, telling them the new seat assignments are theirs until further notice. The next day, they sit in their old seats as the bell is about to ring. "Do you know why I moved you two yesterday?" the teacher says immediately. After a momentary pause, both students nod. "Then move quickly now, and be certain you're in your new seats tomorrow. You can come and talk with me when you believe you're ready to accept responsibility for your talking."
   - **High School:** An eleventh-grade history teacher reminds students about being seated when the bell rings. As it rings the next day, two girls remain standing and talking. The teacher turns to them and says, "I'm sorry, but you must not have understood me yesterday. To be counted on time, you need to be in your seats when the bell rings. Please go to the office and get a late-admit pass."

Clarity and tone are important for the effectiveness of desists. For example, "Randy, what is the rule about touching other students?" or "Randy, how do you think that makes Willy feel?" are more effective than "Randy, stop that," because they link the behavior to a rule or to the behavior's effects. Students react to these subtle differences and prefer rule and consequence reminders to teacher commands (Nucci, 1987).

The tone of desists should be firm but not angry. Kounin (1970) found that kindergarten students managed with rough desists actually became more disruptive, and older students are uncomfortable in classes where harsh desists are used. In contrast, firm but pleasant reprimands, the suggestion of alternative behaviors, and questioning that maintains student involvement in learning activities can reduce off-task time in most classrooms.

Clear communication, including congruence between verbal and nonverbal behavior, an awareness of what is happening in the classroom (withitness), and effective instruction are essential in using desists. However, even when these elements exist, desists sometimes aren't enough.

Applying Consequences

Careful planning and effective instruction often eliminate most misbehavior before it starts. Some minor incidents can be ignored, and simple desists will stop others. When these strategies don't work, however, teachers must apply consequences. Logical consequences are preferred because they treat misbehaviors as problems and create a conceptual link between

exploring diversity

Classroom Management in Diverse Environments

Learner diversity presents a unique set of challenges for classroom teachers. A long history of research suggests that discrepancies exist in disciplinary referrals and punishment for students who are members of cultural minorities (G. Gay, 2006). For example, African American boys are referred for behavior problems at a much higher rate than their peers, and they also receive harsher punishments (Skiba, Michael, Nardo, & Peterson, 2002).

Further, research indicates that European American students are disciplined for infractions that could be described as *objective,* such as smoking, leaving school without permission, or profanity. By comparison African American students are more commonly disciplined for infractions that require a teacher's interpretation, such as disrespect, defiance, or class disruptions. And, subsequent punishments for African American students were more severe (Skiba et al., 2002; Townsend, 2000).

Research suggests that miscommunication often occurs between teachers and students who are members of cultural minorities, because most teachers are middle class, female, and White. For example,

> "Fear may . . . contribute to overreferral [among students of color]. Teachers who are prone to accepting stereotypes of adolescent African American males as threatening or dangerous may overreact to relatively minor threats to authority, especially if their anxiety is paired with a misunderstanding of cultural norms of interaction (Skiba et al., 2002, p. 336)

Experts suggest that **culturally responsive classroom management,** which combines cultural knowledge with teachers' awareness of possible personal biases, can help overcome some of these problems. A culturally responsive classroom management model designed to address this problem has five elements:

- Become personally aware of cultural biases.
- Acquire knowledge about students' cultural heritage.
- Become knowledgeable about the sociopolitical and economic contexts of schools.
- Create caring learning environments.
- Develop culturally responsive classroom management strategies. (C. S. Weinstein, Curran, & Tomlinson-Clark, 2003; C. S. Weinstein, Tomlinson-Clark, & Curran, 2004)

As teachers become more aware of their own possible fears and biases and acquire cultural knowledge about their students' interaction patterns, they may come to realize that student responses that appear threatening or disrespectful are not intended that way. Increased awareness and knowledge, combined with culturally responsive classroom management strategies, can contribute a great deal toward overcoming the racial disproportionality in classroom discipline issues (McCurdy, Kunsch, & Reibstein, 2007). These strategies include creating a community of caring and trust, establishing clear expectations for behavior, carefully teaching rules and procedures, conducting highly interactive lessons, and providing students with specific and nonjudgmental feedback about their learning progress. As with any set of strategies, these efforts won't solve every problem, but they can contribute to creating a productive learning environment for all your students.

Culturally responsive classroom management. Classroom management that combines teachers' awareness of possible personal biases with cultural knowledge.

behaviors and outcomes. However, because classrooms are complex and busy, it isn't always possible to solve problems with logical consequences. In these instances, behavioral consequences offer an acceptable alternative. Behavioral consequences are solely intended to change a behavior quickly and efficiently (Kaff et al., 2007; J. C. Murphy, 2007). Let's see how one teacher uses consequences:

> Jason is an intelligent and active fifth grader. He loves to talk and seems to know just how far he can go before Mrs. Aguilar becomes exasperated with him. He understands the rules and the reasons for them, but his interest in talking seems to take precedence. Ignoring him isn't working. A call to his parents helped for a while, but soon he's back to his usual behavior—never quite enough to require a drastic response, but always a thorn in Mrs. Aguilar's side.
>
> Finally, she decides to give him only one warning. At a second disruption, he's placed in timeout from regular instructional activities. She meets with him and explains the rules. The next day, he begins to misbehave almost immediately.
>
> "Jason," she warns, "you can't work while you're talking, and you're keeping others from finishing their work. Please get busy."
>
> He stops, but a few minutes later, he's at it again.
>
> "Jason," Mrs. Aguilar says quietly as she moves back to his desk, "Please go back to the timeout area."
>
> Now, a week later, Jason is working quietly with the rest of the class.

Behavior such as Jason's is common, particularly in elementary and middle schools, and it causes teacher stress more often than do highly publicized threats of violence and bodily harm (V. F. Jones & Jones, 2004). The behavior is disruptive, so it can't be ignored; praise for good work helps to a certain extent, but students get much of their reinforcement from friends; desists work briefly, but teachers tire of constant monitoring. Mrs. Aguilar had little choice but to apply behavioral consequences with Jason.

theory to practice

Responding Effectively to Misbehavior

Incidents of misbehavior will inevitably occur in your classroom. The following guidelines can help you intervene effectively.

1. Maintain the flow of instruction while intervening in cases of misbehavior.
2. Apply the principles for intervening successfully.
3. Use cognitive interventions when possible; revert to behavioral interventions when necessary.
4. Move along the intervention continuum only as far as necessary.

Let's look again at Judy's work with her students to see how she applied these guidelines.

First, she maintained the flow of the lesson while intervening in each case. Let's review some of the dialogue:

Judy: About what latitude is Damascus. . . . Bernice?
Bernice: It's about 34 degrees north latitude, I think.
Judy: Good, Bernice. It's close to 34 degrees. . . . So, would it be warmer or colder than here in the summer? . . . Darren? (seeing that Darren has poked Kendra with his pencil, and walking near him)
Judy: And, why might that be the case? . . . Jim? (moving over to Rachel and telling her to move to a different desk)

In this brief episode Judy intervened with both Darren and Rachel without disrupting the flow of her lesson, an ability called **overlapping** (Kounin, 1970).

Second, Judy applied each of the principles for intervening successfully. She displayed *withitness* by recognizing that Darren was the perpetrator of the incident with Kendra; her interventions were not harsh or critical, so she *preserved her students' dignity;* she was *consistent* and *followed through* to be sure Rachel complied; she *kept her interventions brief* and didn't allow herself to be drawn into an *argument* with Rachel.

Third, she used cognitive interventions by keeping her verbal and nonverbal behavior consistent (e.g., looking directly at Darren when she called on him, and leaning over Rachel's desk when she told Rachel to move); responded to Rachel with an I-message; and applied the logical consequence of moving Rachel when she was whispering and passing notes to Deborah.

Finally, she only had to go as far along the intervention continuum as using indirect cues with both Darren and Rachel. She simply moved over near Darren and called on him, and she referred Rachel to the class rule and had her move to an empty desk. Neither teacher action disrupted the flow of her lesson.

Careful planning for classroom management combined with creating an environment of caring and trust can prevent many management problems from occurring in the first place, and applying the guidelines can quickly eliminate most others.

Once in a great while, however, serious problems occur. We discuss them in the next section of the chapter.

Consistency is the key to promoting change in students like Jason. He understood what he was doing, and he was capable of controlling himself. When he could, with certainty, predict the consequences of his behavior, he quit. He knew that his second infraction would result in a timeout, and when it did, he quickly changed his behavior. There was no argument, little time was used, and the class wasn't disrupted.

Overlapping. The ability to intervene without disrupting the flow of a lesson.

check your understanding

4.1 What is the framework on which all cognitive interventions are based? Use cognitive learning theory to explain why verbal–nonverbal congruence, I-messages, and logical consequences are effective interventions.

4.2 Use behaviorism and/or social cognitive theory to explain why each of the points on the intervention continuum (Figure 12.7) is an effective intervention.

4.3 One of your students is talking without permission. Describe an I-message that would be appropriate as a response.

4.4 A teacher sees a seventh-grader spit on the door to the classroom. According to the information in this section, which is the more appropriate response: putting the student in after-school detention (which is part of the school's management policy) or having the student wash the door? Explain.

To receive feedback for these questions, go to Appendix A.

Serious Management Problems: Violence and Aggression

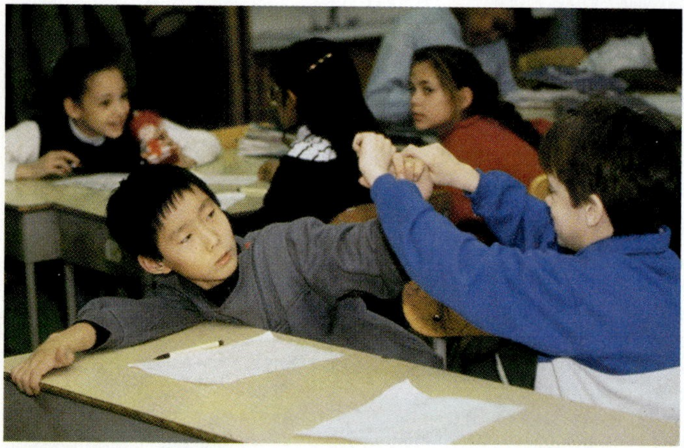

Serious management problems require both short- and long-term strategies.

As you work with a small group of your fourth graders, a fight suddenly breaks out between Trey and Neil, who are supposed to be working on a group project together. You hear sounds of shouting and see Trey flailing at Neil, who is attempting to fend off Trey's blows. Trey is often verbally aggressive and sometimes threatens other students.

What do you do?

Matt, one of your seventh graders, is shy and a bit small for his age. As he comes into your class this morning, he appears disheveled and depressed. Concerned, you take him aside and ask if anything is wrong. With some prodding he tells you that he repeatedly gets shoved around on the school grounds before school, and two boys have been taunting him and calling him gay. "I hate school," he comments.

How do you respond?

Tyrone, one of your students, has difficulty maintaining his attention and staying on task. He frequently makes loud and inappropriate comments in class and disrupts learning activities. You warn him, reminding him that being disruptive is unacceptable, and blurting out another comment will result in timeout.

Within a minute, Tyrone blurts out again.

"Please go to the timeout area," you say evenly.

"I'm not going and you can't make me," he says defiantly. He remains seated at his desk.

How do you react?

We discuss situations such as these in this section.

School Violence and Aggression

As you saw in Chapter 3, violence is a problem in the United States. Since 1993, this country has had the highest rates of childhood homicides, suicides, and firearm-related deaths of any of the world's 26 wealthiest nations (Aspy et al., 2004). More than a third of students report being involved in a physical fight, and nearly 10 percent of youth have carried a weapon to school (Kodjo, Auinger, & Ryan, 2003). You may have to respond to student fighting or some other act of violence at some point in your teaching career.

Responding to Aggression Against Peers

Negligence. The failure to exercise sufficient care in protecting students from injury.

Aggressive students must not be allowed to hurt or intimidate peers or damage property. In the situation between Trey and Neil, you are required by law to intervene. If you don't, you and the school can be sued for **negligence,** the failure to exercise sufficient care in protecting students from injury (L. Fischer, Schimmel, & Stellman, 2006). However, the law doesn't require you to physically break up the fight; immediately reporting it to administrators is acceptable.

An effective response to violence involves three steps: (1) Stop the incident (if possible), (2) protect the victim, and (3) get help. For instance, in the case of the classroom scuffle, a loud noise, such as shouting, clapping, or slamming a chair against the floor, will often surprise the students enough so they'll stop (Evertson et al., 2006). At that point, you can begin to talk to them, check to see if the victim is all right, and then take the students to the main office, where you can get help. If your interventions don't stop the fight, you should immediately send an uninvolved student for help. Unless you're sure that you can separate the students without danger to yourself, or them, attempting to do so is unwise. As a guideline in these situations, teachers are first responsible for the safety of the other students and themselves, second for the involved students, and then to property (Good & Brophy, 2008).

Responding to Bullying

As you also saw in Chapter 3, bullying, a more subtle form of school violence, is receiving increased attention (Hyman et al., 2006). Educators now recognize its damaging effects on students, as well as possible links to suicide and other forms of school violence (Nansel et al., 2001). In most cases of school shooting incidents, the perpetrators had been victims of bullying (Aspy et al., 2004).

Teachers should respond to bullying in the same way as they react to other aggressive acts (Pellegrini, 2002). Those committing the acts must be stopped, and victims should be protected. Attempts can then be made to help the bullies understand the consequences of their actions, both for the victims and for themselves. (We examine long-term efforts later in this section.)

Responding to Defiant Students

Most teachers find the possibility of dealing with a student like Tyrone frightening. What do you do when he says, "I'm not going, and you can't make me?" Experts offer two suggestions (Henricsson & Rydell, 2004; A. Smith & Bondy, 2007). First, remain calm to avoid a power struggle. A teacher's natural tendency is to become angry and display a show of force to demonstrate to students that they "can't get away with it." Remaining calm gives you time to control your temper, and the student's mood when facing a calm teacher is likely to change from anger and bravado to fear and contrition (Good & Brophy, 2008).

Second, if possible, give the rest of the class an assignment, and then tell the student calmly but decisively to please step outside the classroom so you can talk. Communicate a serious and concerned, but not threatening tone.

Defiance is often the result of a negative student–teacher relationship (Gregory & Weinstein, 2004). These negative relationships occur most often with students who display externalizing behavior problems, such as aggression, temper tantrums, or impulsive and hyperactive behavior (Henricsson & Rydell, 2004). When a problem occurs with such a student, it is important to let the student say everything that is on his or her mind in a private conference before responding. Finally, arrange to meet with the student before or after school, focus on the defiance as a problem, and attempt to generate solutions that are acceptable to both of you.

In the case of a student who refuses to step outside the classroom, or one who becomes physically threatening, immediately send someone to the front office for help. Defiance at this level likely requires help from a mental health professional.

Long-Term Solutions to Violence and Aggression

Long-term, students must be helped to understand that aggression will not be permitted and that they're accountable for their behavior (Burstyn & Stevens, 2001). Trey, for example, must understand that his aggressive actions are unacceptable and that they won't be tolerated. Then, teaching students broadly applicable personal and social competencies can reduce aggressive behaviors and improve social adjustment. These competencies include self-control, perspective taking, and constructive assertiveness. For example, one program taught students to express anger verbally instead of physically and to solve conflicts through communication and negotiation instead of fighting (D. Johnson & Johnson, 2004, 2006). Learning to make and defend a position, to argue effectively, is one approach. Students taught to make effective arguments, and who learn that arguing and verbal aggression are very different, become less combative when encountering others with whom they disagree (Burstyn & Stevens, 1999). Learning to argue also has incidental benefits: Those skilled in this area are seen by their peers as intelligent and credible.

To decrease aggressive incidents, experts also recommend the involvement of parents and other school personnel (Burstyn & Stevens, 2001). Not surprisingly, research indicates that students who communicate openly with their families are less likely to be involved in aggressive acts or to behave as bullies (Aspy et al., 2004). In addition, school counselors and psychologists, social workers, and principals have all been trained to deal with these problems and can provide advice and assistance (Greenberg et al., 2003). Experienced teachers can also provide a wealth of information about how they've handled similar problems. No teacher should face serious problems of violence or aggression alone.

In conclusion, we want to put violence and aggression into perspective. Although they are possibilities, and you should understand your options for dealing with them, the majority of your management problems will involve issues of cooperation and motivation. Many problems can be prevented; others can be dealt with quickly, while some require individual attention. We have all heard about students carrying guns to school and incidents of assault on teachers. Statistically, however, considering the huge numbers of students who pass through schools each day, these incidents remain very infrequent.

check your understanding

5.1 Describe your legal responsibilities in the event of a fight or other aggressive act in your classroom.

5.2 If you encounter two students fighting, or you see a smaller student being bullied by one or more other students, what steps you should take?

5.3 Describe the focus of a long-term cognitive approach to bullying and other acts of aggression.

To receive feedback for these questions, go to Appendix A.

developmentally appropriate practice

Classroom Management with Different-Aged Learners

While many aspects of classroom management, such as creating a caring classroom community, developing learner responsibility, and careful planning apply across the P–12 continuum, development differences exist. The following paragraphs outline some suggestions for responding to these differences.

Working with Elementary Students

Earlier in the chapter we discussed the importance of teaching rules and procedures to elementary students. These children are often unaware of rules and procedures and may not understand how they contribute to learning. Because their cognitive development is likely to be preoperational, special efforts to explain the importance of rules and their connection to personal responsibility and learning can be helpful.

Young children are trusting and vulnerable, so criticism and harsh reprimands and desists are particularly destructive with them (Carter & Doyle, 2006). They respond well to praise, but ignoring inappropriate behavior and using indirect cues are likely to be less effective with them than with older students. Behavioral interventions, such as timeout for chronic interruptions can be effective if they are not overdone. Developing personal responsibility for behavior is an important long-term goal.

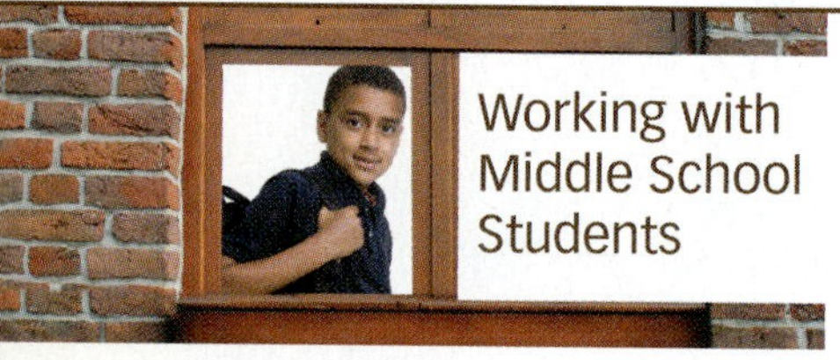

Working with Middle School Students

As students develop, they become more cognitively, personally, and socially aware. As a result, consistency and logical consequences become increasingly important and effective. Middle school students continue to need a caring teacher; clear boundaries for acceptable behavior and consistently enforced boundaries are indicators of caring for these students. Timely and judicious praise continues to be important, but ignoring inappropriate behavior and using indirect cues can also be effective for minor rule infractions.

The increasing importance of peers can present both challenges and opportunities in middle schools. Whispering, note passing, and general attempts to socialize can be problems, and clear, consistently applied rules become essential. Middle school students appreciate being involved in rule setting, and periodic class meetings are effective in enlisting student commitment to and cooperation with classroom rules and procedures.

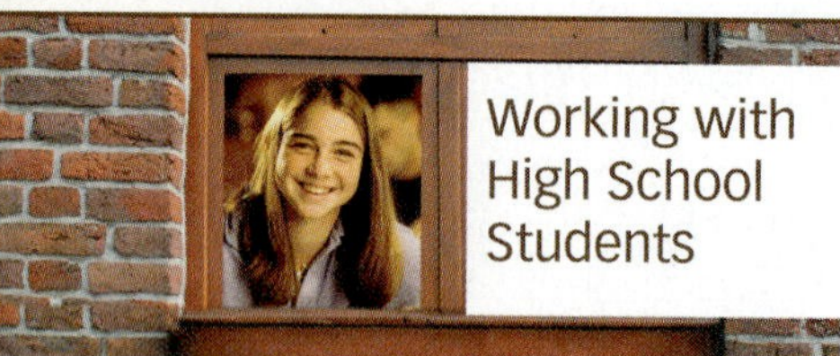

Working with High School Students

High school students react well to being treated as adults. Developing personal responsibility is important, and private conferences that appeal to their sense of responsibility can be effective. Peers continue to exert a powerful influence on behavior, so avoiding embarrassing students in front of their peers is important. Often, a simple request to turn around or get busy is all the intervention that is necessary.

High school students are also becoming increasingly skilled at reading social and nonverbal cues, so congruence between verbal and nonverbal channels is important. Honest interventions that directly address the problem, leave students' dignity intact, but still communicate commitment and resolve are very effective.

A positive teacher–student relationship remains the foundation of an effective management system, and high school students react well to personal comments, such as a compliment about a new outfit or hairstyle, or questions, such as asking about an ill parent's progress or how a new brother or sister is doing.

Meeting Your Learning Objectives

1. Explain why effective classroom management is important.
   - Classroom management is beginning teachers' greatest concern and is also a source of stress and burnout for veteran teachers. Public opinion polls rate it as one of the most important problems that schools face.
   - Classroom management is also important because it helps teachers cope with the multidimensional, immediate, unpredictable, and public aspects of teaching.
   - Students in well-managed classrooms are more motivated to learn and achieve higher than those in environments that are less orderly.
2. Identify characteristics of elementary, middle, and secondary school students and how they influence planning for classroom management.
   - Young children's thinking is perceptual and concrete; they are eager to please their teachers and are vulnerable to criticism and harsh treatment.
   - Effective teachers in elementary schools develop rules and procedures that they teach and practice concretely in order to create an orderly and predictable school environment that builds a sense of trust and develops autonomy.
   - Middle school students experience increasing peer influence, needs for belonging and social acceptance, and desire for independence.
   - Effective teachers in middle schools treat students with unconditional positive regard and provide the firm hand of a caring teacher who sets clear limits for acceptable behavior.
   - As students move into high school, they communicate more effectively at an adult level, and they respond well to clear rationales and rules and procedures that make sense to them.
3. Describe characteristics of effective communication with parents.
   - Effective communication with parents begins with early communication and maintains links throughout the school year.
   - Home–school cooperation increases students' achievement, willingness to do homework, improves attitudes and behaviors, and increases attendance and graduation rates.
4. Use cognitive and behavioral learning theories to explain effective interventions.
   - Cognitive learning theory is grounded in the premise that people want their experiences to make sense.
   - The following are consistent with cognitive learning theory: verbal and nonverbal messages that are congruent, I-messages that identify a behavior as unacceptable but communicate the student is intrinsically worthy, and logical consequences that make sense to students.
   - Praising desired behavior, ignoring inappropriate behavior, using desists, and applying consequences all capitalize on behavioral concepts, such as reinforcement, extinction, and punishment to maintain an orderly classroom.
5. Describe teachers' professional and legal responsibilities in cases of aggressive acts, and effective steps for responding to school violence and aggression.
   - Teachers are required by law to intervene in cases of violence or aggression.
   - The first steps involved in responding to fighting or bullying are to stop the incident, protect the victim, and seek assistance.
   - Long-term responses to violence and aggression include attempts to help aggressive students understand the impact of their behavior on others and the development of skills to act in socially acceptable ways.

Developing as a Professional: Preparing for Your Licensure Exam

In the opening case study, you saw how instruction and classroom management converged in Judy Harris's classroom. In the following case study, Janelle Powers, another seventh-grade geography teacher, also has her students working on a lesson about the Middle East. As you read the case study, compare the two teachers' approaches to classroom management, and answer the questions that follow.

> In homeroom this morning, Shiana comes through the classroom doorway just as the tardy bell rings.
>
> "Take your seat quickly, Shiana," Janelle directs. "You're just about late. All right. Listen up, everyone," she continues. "Ali?"
>
> "Here."
>
> "Gaelen?"
>
> "Here."
>
> "Chu?"
>
> "Here."
>
> When Janelle finishes taking the roll, she walks around the room, handing back a set of papers.
>
> "You did quite well on the assignment," she comments. "Let's keep up the good work. . . . Howard and Manny, please stop talking while I'm returning papers. Can't you just sit quietly for 1 minute?"
>
> The boys, who were whispering, turn back to the front of the room.

"Now," Janelle continues, returning to the front of the room, "we've been studying the Middle East, so let's review for a moment. . . . Look at the map and identify the longitude and latitude of Cairo. Take a minute, and figure it out right now."

The students begin as Janelle goes to her file cabinet to get out some transparencies.

"Stop it, Damon," she hears Leila blurt out behind her.

"Leila," Janelle responds sternly, "we don't talk out like that in class."

"He's poking me, Mrs. Powers."

"Are you poking her, Damon?"

". . ."

"Well?"

"Not really."

"You did, too," Leila complains.

"Both of you stop it," Janelle warns. "Another outburst like that, Leila, and your name goes on the board."

As the students are finishing the problem, Janelle looks up from the materials on her desk to check an example on the overhead. She hears Howard and Manny talking and laughing at the back of the room.

"Are you boys finished?"

"Yes," Manny answers.

"Well, be quiet then until everyone is done," Janelle directs and goes back to rearranging her materials.

"Quiet, everyone," she again directs, looking up in response to a hum of voices around the room. "Is everyone finished? . . . Good. Pass your papers forward. . . . Remember, put your paper on the top of the stack. . . . Roberto, wait until the papers come from behind you before you pass yours forward."

Janelle collects the papers, puts them on her desk, and then begins, "We've talked about the geography of the Middle East, and now we want to look at the climate a bit more. It varies somewhat. For example, Syria is extremely hot in the summer but is actually quite cool in the winter. In fact, it snows in some parts.

"Now, what did we find for the latitude of Cairo?"

"Thirty," Miguel volunteers.

"North or south, Miguel? . . . Wait a minute. Howard? . . . Manny? . . . This is the third time this period that I've had to say something to you about talking, and the period isn't even 20 minutes old yet. Get out your rules and read me the rule about talking without permission. . . . Howard?"

". . ."

"It's supposed to be in the front of your notebook."

". . ."

"Manny?"

"'No speaking without permission of the teacher,'" Manny reads from the front page of his notebook.

"Howard, where are your rules?"

"I don't know."

"Move up here," Janelle directs, pointing to an empty desk at the front of the room. "You've been bothering me all week. If you can't learn to be quiet, you will be up here for the rest of the year."

Howard gets up and slowly moves to the desk Janelle has pointed out. After Howard is seated, Janelle begins again, "Where were we before we were rudely interrupted? . . . Oh, yes. What did you get for the latitude of Cairo?"

"Thirty North," Miguel responds.

"Okay, good. . . . Now, Egypt also has a hot climate in the summer—in fact, very hot. The summer temperature often goes over 100 degrees Fahrenheit. Egypt is also mostly desert, so the people have trouble making a living. Their primary source of subsistence is the Nile River, which floods frequently. Most of the agriculture of the country is near the river."

Janelle continues presenting information to the students for the next several minutes.

"Andrew, are you listening to this?" Janelle interjects when she sees Andrew poke Jacinta with a ruler.

"Yes," he responds, turning to the front.

"I get frustrated when I see people not paying attention. When you don't pay attention, you can't learn, and that frustrates me because I'm here to help you learn." Janelle continues with her presentation.

Short-Answer Questions

In answering these questions, use information from the chapter, and link your responses to specific information in the case.

1. Analyze Janelle's planning for classroom management.
2. Evaluate the effectiveness of Janelle's management interventions.
3. The chapter stressed the interdependence of management and instruction. Analyze the relationship between management and instruction in Janelle's class. Include both strengths and weaknesses in your analysis.

To receive feedback for these questions, go to Appendix B.

Now go to Chapter 12 of MyEducationLab, located at www.myeducationlab.com, where you can:

- Take a quiz to test your mastery of chapter objectives. Detailed feedback is provided to explain why your responses are correct or incorrect.
- Deepen your understanding of chapter concepts with *Review, Practice, Enrichment* exercises.
- Complete *Activities and Applications* that will help you apply what you have learned in the chapter by analyzing real classrooms through video clips, artifacts, and case studies. Your instructor will provide you with feedback for the *Activities and Applications.*
- Develop your professional knowledge and decision making in *Building Teaching Skills and Dispositions* exercises. Structured feedback will be available to you, providing you with support as you practice each skill. Your instructor will provide you with feedback on the final task that accompanies the exercise.

Important Concepts

assertive discipline (p. 375)
classroom management (p. 354)
community of caring and trust (p. 354)
culturally responsive classroom management (p. 380)
desist (p. 378)
discipline (p. 354)
I-message (p. 375)
logical consequences (p. 376)
negligence (p. 382)
organization (p. 357)
overlapping (p. 381)
procedures (p. 358)
productive learning environment (p. 352)
rules (p. 358)
withitness (p. 372)

chapter

13

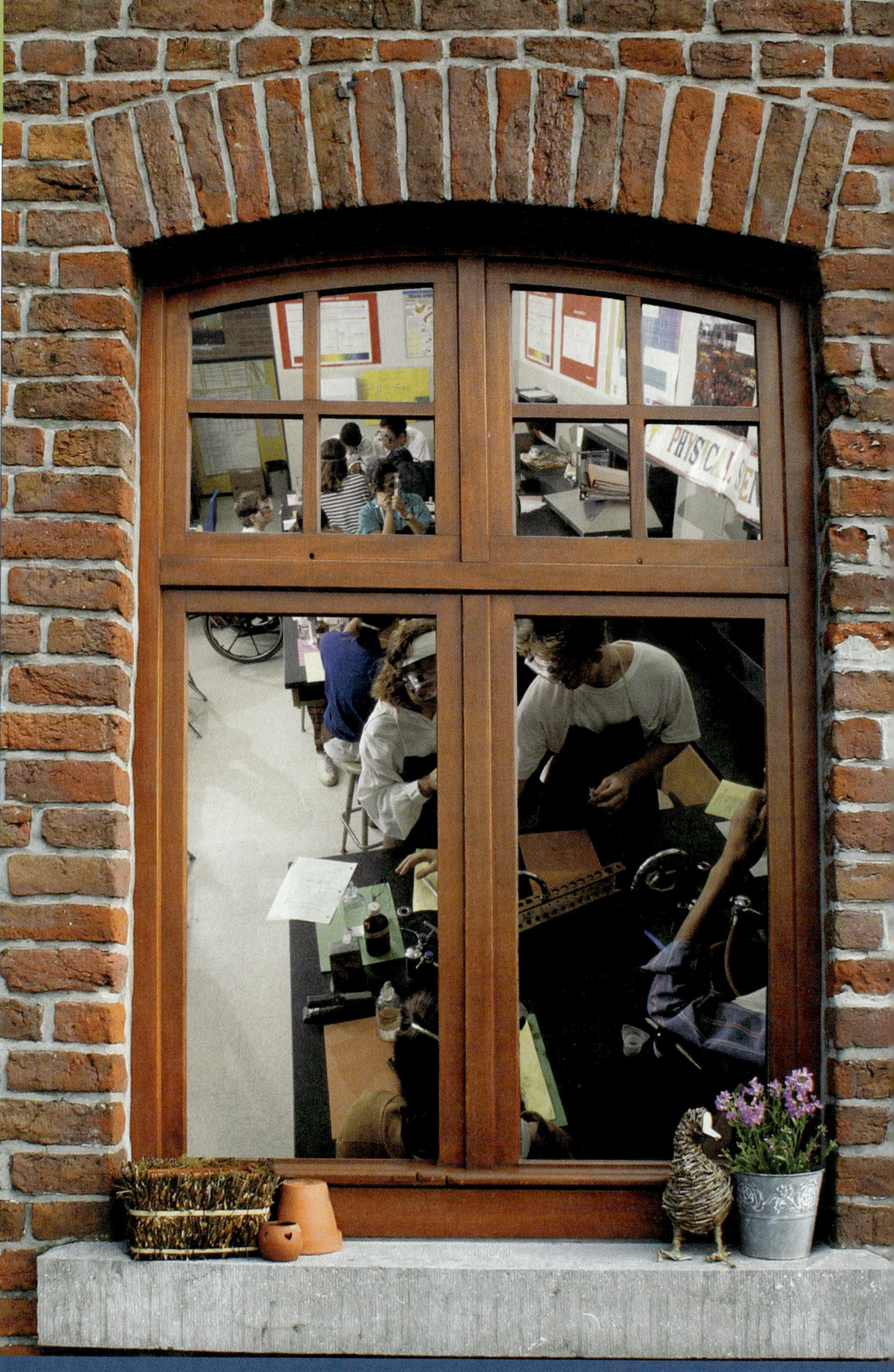

Creating Productive Learning Environments:

Principles and Models of Instruction

chapter outline

Planning for Instruction

- Selecting Topics
- Preparing Learning Objectives
- Preparing and Organizing Learning Activities
- Planning for Assessment
- Instructional Alignment
- Planning in a Standards-Based Environment

Implementing Instruction: Essential Teaching Skills

- Attitudes
- Organization
- Communication
- Focus
- Feedback
- Questioning
- Review and Closure
- Learning Contexts: Effective Instruction in Urban Classrooms
  - **Theory to Practice**: The Theoretical Framework for Essential Teaching Skills

Models of Instruction

- Direct Instruction
- Lecture Discussion
- Guided Discovery
- Cooperative Learning
  - **Exploring Diversity: Using Cooperative Learning to Capitalize on Diversity in Your Classroom**
  - **Developmentally Appropriate Practice:** Using Models of Instruction with Different-Aged Learners

Assessment and Learning: Using Assessment as a Learning Tool

learning objectives

After you have completed your study of this chapter, you should be able to:

1. Describe essential components of planning for instruction.
2. Describe essential teaching skills, and explain why they are important.
3. Explain the relationships between essential teaching skills and models of instruction, and analyze the components of different models.
4. Identify the essential characteristics of effective assessments.

What is "good" or "effective" teaching? If you walked into a classroom and observed a teacher, would you be able to tell if he or she was "effective"? How would you know? Keep these questions in mind as you follow the work of Scott Sowell, a seventh-grade science teacher, through this chapter.

As Scott is working on a Saturday afternoon to plan his next week, he looks at his textbook and his state's standards for middle school science. One standard says:

The student knows that if more than one force acts on an object, then the forces can reinforce or cancel each other, depending on their direction and magnitude. (Florida Department of Education, 2007, p. 2 [italics added])

As he plans, he also thinks about his past experience with the topic and decides that he will incorporate the standard into lessons on Bernoulli's principle, the law that helps explain how different forces enable airplanes to fly. "The kids like it," he remembers, "because it's both interesting and has a lot of real-world applications."

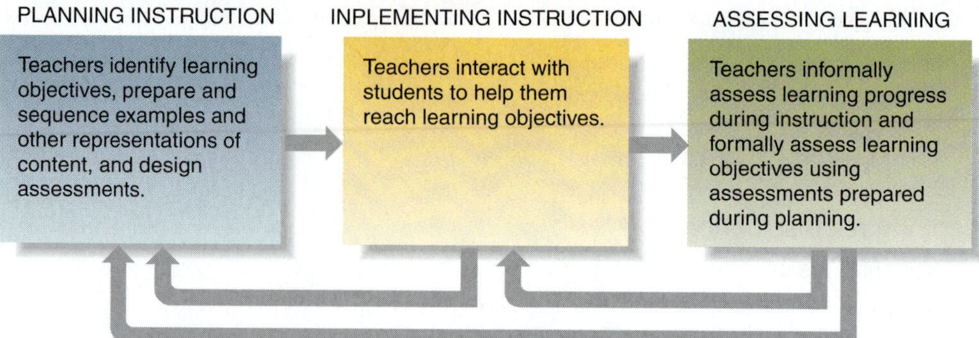

Figure 13.1 Phases of instruction

He first decides that he wants his students to understand that a force is a push or a pull, and he thinks about examples he can use, such as pulling a student's chair across the floor, pushing on the chalk board, and having the students lift their books off their desks. Then, he thinks, "I'll demonstrate that objects move in the direction of the greater force, which will help them understand the part of the standard that says, 'forces can reinforce or cancel each other, depending on their direction and magnitude.' I'll do a little tug of war with one of the kids," he smiles to himself, "and I'll let him pull me to show that since his force is greater, we'll move that way."

Finally, he decides to teach Bernoulli's principle on Tuesday and Wednesday with a review Thursday and a quiz on Friday.

Effective teaching. Teaching that maximizes student learning.

Effective teaching is teaching that maximizes student learning. Our purpose in writing this chapter is to help you recognize the actions of effective teachers, see how they relate to the theories of learning you studied earlier, and teach effectively in your own classroom. We will use Scott's work with his students as the framework for our discussion.

The process of instruction can be summarized in three essential phases, which are outlined in Figure 13.1. As you see in the figure, the phases are interconnected and cyclical. The process begins with planning.

Planning for Instruction

You saw in Chapter 12 that effective teachers carefully plan for classroom management, and it is equally important for instruction. As they plan for instruction, expert teachers make a series of sequential decisions:

- Select topics that are important for students to learn.
- Specify learning objectives related to the topics.
- Prepare and organize learning activities to help students reach the learning objectives.
- Design assessments to measure the amount students have learned.
- Ensure that instruction and assessments are aligned with the learning objectives. (L. Anderson & Krathwohl, 2001; Jalongo, Rieg, & Hellerbran, 2007)

Next we'll examine these decisions in more detail.

Selecting Topics

"What is important to learn?" is one of the first questions that teachers address when they plan (L. Anderson & Krathwohl, 2001). They rely on textbooks, curriculum guides, and standards, such as the one Scott used, to help answer this question (Reys, Reys, & Chavez, 2004). Their personal philosophies, students' interests in the topic, and real-world applications are other sources. Scott, for example, believed that Bernoulli's principle was important, because it's related to *force,* a basic science concept, and because it helps students understand a number of real-world phenomena such as how airplanes can fly.

Some teachers tacitly avoid making decisions about what is important to study by simply teaching topics as they appear in their textbooks or curriculum guides (Marzano, 2003b). This can be a problem, however, because more content appears in textbooks than can be learned in depth. Teachers' knowledge of content, such as Scott's understanding of physical science, is particularly important in helping decide if a topic is important enough to teach (Bereiter & Scardamalia, 2006; Darling-Hammond & Bransford, 2005).

Preparing Learning Objectives

After identifying a topic, teachers specify **learning objectives,** what they want students to know or be able to do with respect to the topic. Clear learning objectives are essential because they guide the rest of teachers' planning decisions. Without clear objectives, teachers don't know how to design their learning activities, and they can't create accurate assessments. Learning objectives also guide teachers as they implement their learning activities. Unsuccessful lessons are often the result of teachers' not being clear about their objectives.

Learning objective. A statement that specifies what students should know or be able to do with respect to a topic or course of study.

Having "clear" learning objectives doesn't imply that they must be written. It means that teachers are clear in their thinking about the objectives. For example, Scott didn't have the objectives for his lessons written on paper. However, he was very clear about what he wanted his students to understand, as you'll see when he implements his lesson.

Objectives in the Cognitive Domain

Scott wanted his students to understand the concept of *force,* the relationships among forces, and how to apply Bernoulli's principle to real-world examples. These describe learning objectives in the **cognitive domain,** the area of learning that focuses on knowledge and higher cognitive processes such as applying and analyzing. Next we'll take a brief historical look at objectives in this domain.

Cognitive domain. The area of learning that focuses on memory and higher cognitive processes such as applying and analyzing.

In his classic work, *Basic Principles of Curriculum and Instruction,* Ralph Tyler (1950) suggested that the most useful form for stating objectives is "to express them in terms which identify both the kind of behavior to be developed in the student and the content or area of life in which this behavior is to operate" (p. 46). Applications of his ideas, such as management-by-objectives in the business world, became popular in the 1950s and 1960s. Some approaches, such as Robert Mager's in his highly readable book *Preparing Instructional Objectives* (1962), expanded Tyler's original conception to include the conditions under which learners would demonstrate the behavior and the criteria for acceptable performance. Mager's work also strongly influenced teaching and remains popular today (Mager, 1998). Examples of objectives using Mager's approach are outlined in Table 13.1.

Norman Gronlund (2004) offered a popular alternative to Mager's approach, suggesting that teachers state a general objective, such as *know, understand,* or *apply,* followed by specific

table 13.1 Objectives Using Mager's Approach

Objective	Condition	Performance	Criteria
Given 3 examples of *force* in a real-world problem, students will identify each.	Given 3 examples of force in a real-world problem	Identify	Each
Given 10 problems involving subtraction with regrouping, students will correctly solve 7.	Given 10 problems involving subtraction with regrouping	Solve	7 of 10
Using a topic of their choice, students will write a paragraph that includes at least two examples each of metaphors, similes, and personification.	Using a topic of their choice	Write	A paragraph including 2 examples each of metaphors, similes, and personification

table 13.2 Objectives Using Gronlund's Approach

General Objective	Specific Learning Outcome
Understands *force*	1. Identifies examples of force in problems 2. Gives examples of forces
Understands fractions with grouping	1. Recognizes need for regrouping 2. Performs operations 3. Solves problems
Uses figurative language in writing	1. Gives written examples 2. Puts examples into written context

learning outcomes that operationally define these terms. Table 13.2 includes examples of objectives written according to Gronlund's guidelines.

These approaches to preparing objectives were influenced by behaviorism. Tyler used *behavior* and content in his description of objectives, Mager also used the term *behavior* in his, and Gronlund emphasized that each specific learning outcome, "starts with an action verb that indicates observable student responses; that is, responses that can be seen by an outside observer" (Gronlund, 2004, p. 23).

More recent thinking about objectives reflects the influence of cognitive learning theory on teaching and avoids the use of both behavior and content (L. Anderson & Krathwohl, 2001). Leaders today recommend that objective statements should address students' cognitive processes rather than behaviors. In addition, educators use the term *knowledge* to reflect what students should know or acquire (L. Anderson & Krathwohl, 2001). For example, one of Scott's objectives was "Students will understand that a force is a push or a pull." *Force* is the knowledge, and *understand* is the cognitive process; it specifies what the students will do with that knowledge.

A Taxonomy for Cognitive Objectives

While one of Scott's objectives was for his students to "understand that a force is a push or a pull," other objectives involving the same knowledge exist. For example, possibilities include

- Students will state the definition of *force* in their own words.
- Students will solve a problem requiring them to determine the net effect of two forces on the same object.

All three objectives involve the concept *force,* but each requires different cognitive processes. In response to these differences, researchers developed a system to classify different objectives (L. Anderson & Krathwohl, 2001). A revision of the famous "Bloom's taxonomy" first published in 1956 (Bloom, Englehart, Furst, Hill, & Krathwohl, 1956), the system is a matrix with 24 cells that represent the intersection of four types of knowledge with six cognitive processes. The revision reflects the increase in researchers' understanding of learning and teaching since the middle of the 20th century, when the original taxonomy was created, and it now more nearly reflects the influence of cognitive learning theory on education (L. Anderson & Krathwohl, 2001). The revised taxonomy appears in Figure 13.2.

To understand this objectives classification matrix, let's analyze the three objectives. *Force* is a concept, so the objective "understand that a force is a push or a pull" would be placed in the cell where *conceptual knowledge* intersects with *understand.* The second objective, being able to state a definition of force, would be classified into the cell where *conceptual knowledge* intersects with *remember.* The third objective, solving a problem, belongs in the cell where *procedural knowledge* intersects with *apply,* because solving a problem requires the application of procedural knowledge.

The taxonomy reminds us that learning is complex, with many possible outcomes. It also reminds us that we want our students to do more than remember factual knowledge. Unfortu-

The Knowledge Dimension	The Cognitive Process Dimension 1. Remember	2. Understand	3. Apply	4. Analyze	5. Evaluate	6. Create
A. Factual knowledge						
B. Conceptual knowledge						
C. Procedural knowledge						
D. Metacognitive knowledge						

Figure 13.2 A taxonomy for learning, teaching, and assessing
Source: From Lorin W. Anderson & David R. Krathwohl, *A Taxonomy for Learning, Teaching, and Assessing; A Revision of Bloom's Taxonomy of Educational Objectives,* © 2001. Published by Allyn and Bacon, Boston, MA. Copyright © 2001 by Pearson Education. Reprinted by permission of the publisher.

nately, schooling often focuses more on this most basic type of learning than it does on the other 23 cells combined. These other forms of knowledge and more advanced cognitive processes are even more important now in the 21st century, as student thinking, decision making, and problem solving are increasingly emphasized.

Preparing and Organizing Learning Activities

Once Scott had specified his learning objectives, he then prepared and organized his learning activities. This process involves four steps:

1. Identify the components of the topic—the concepts, principles, and relationships among them that students should understand.
2. Sequence the components.
3. Prepare examples that students can use to construct their knowledge of each component.
4. Order the examples with the most concrete and obvious presented first.

Scott used *task analysis* to accomplish these steps. Next we'll examine task analysis as a planning tool.

Task Analysis: A Planning Tool

Task analysis. The process of breaking content into component parts and sequencing the parts.

Task analysis is the process of breaking content into component parts and sequencing the parts. While different forms of task analysis exist, a *subject matter analysis* is most common in classrooms (Alberto & Troutman, 2006).

During task analysis, the teacher first identifies the specific concepts and principles included in the general topic, then sequences them in a way that will be most understandable to students, and finally identifies examples to illustrate each.

Scott knew that his students needed to understand the concept *force* and the principle relating forces and movement in order to understand Bernoulli's principle. So, he sequenced these topics and prepared examples of each. He then planned to teach *force* and *movement* on Monday and Bernoulli's principle on Tuesday and Wednesday. Scott's task analysis is outlined in Table 13.3.

In Chapter 1, we identified *knowledge of content, pedagogical content knowledge, general pedagogical knowledge,* and *knowledge of learners and learning* as types of professional knowledge that expert teachers possess. Scott's planning in general, and his task analysis in particular, required each of these forms of knowledge (Lajoie, 2003). For example, his knowledge of content helped him decide that the relationships among forces and Bernoulli's

table 13.3 A Task Analysis for Teaching *Force* and Bernoulli's Principle

Task Analysis Step	Example
1. Identify components of the topic.	Scott identified the concept *force,* the principle *objects move in the direction of the greater force,* and *Bernoulli's principle* as different components of the topic.
2. Sequence the components.	Scott planned to teach the (1) concept *force;* (2) the principle stating that *objects move in the direction of the greater force*; and (3) *Bernoulli's principle*, in that order.
3. Prepare examples of each.	Scott prepared examples of each, such as pulling a student in a chair, pushing on the chalkboard, and having students lift their books.
4. Order the examples.	Scott first planned to pull a student in his chair because it was the best attention getter, then push on the chalkboard, and finally have the students lift their books.

principle were important topics to study, and his decisions about what examples to use reflected his pedagogical content knowledge. Deciding to first illustrate force by pulling a student in a chair because it was an attention getter was based on his knowledge of learners and learning. Each form of professional knowledge was essential. (His general pedagogical knowledge will be demonstrated in the way he conducted the lesson, which you will see later in the chapter.)

Planning for Assessment

Because formal assessments, such as quizzes and tests, are given after students complete a learning activity, you might assume that thinking about assessment also occurs after learning activities are conducted. This isn't true; effective teachers think about assessment as they plan (Jalongo et al., 2007). Effective assessments answer the questions, "How can I determine if my students have reached the learning objectives?" and "How can I use assessment to facilitate learning?" Assessment decisions are essential during planning because they help teachers align their instruction. (We examine Scott's assessment in greater detail later in the chapter.)

Instructional Alignment

Thinking about assessment during planning served an additional function for Scott. It helped him answer the question, "How do I know that my instruction and assessments are logically connected to my objectives?"

Instructional alignment. The match between learning objectives, learning activities, and assessments.

Instructional alignment is the match between learning objectives, learning activities, and assessments, and it is essential for promoting learning (L. Anderson & Krathwohl, 2001; Bransford, Brown, & Cocking, 2000; Brophy, 2006c).

> Without this alignment, it is difficult to know what is being learned. Students may be learning valuable information, but one cannot tell unless there is alignment between what they are learning and the assessment of that learning. Similarly, students may be learning things that others don't value unless curricula and assessments are aligned with . . . learning goals. (Bransford et al., 2000, pp. 151–152)

Maintaining alignment isn't as easy as it appears. For instance, if a teacher's objective is for students to be able to write effectively, yet learning activities focus on isolated grammar skills, the instruction is out of alignment. It is similarly out of alignment if the objective is for students to apply math concepts to the real world, but learning activities have students practicing computation problems.

Scott's instruction was aligned. His objectives were for students to understand the concept *force,* the principle relating force and movement, and Bernoulli's principle; his learning activity focused on those objectives, and his assessment measured the extent to which students understood these ideas.

MyEducationLab

To examine the extent to which a fifth-grade teacher's instruction is aligned, go to the *Activities and Applications* section in Chapter 13 of MyEducationLab at www.myeducationlab.com, and watch the video episode *Analyzing Instructional Alignment.* Answer the questions following the episode.

Planning in a Standards-Based Environment

A great deal has been written about American students' lack of knowledge about history. For example, one survey found that more than half of high school students identified Germany, Japan, or Italy, instead of the Soviet Union, as America's World War II ally, another indicated that two thirds of high school seniors couldn't explain an old photo of a sign over a theater door reading "COLORED ENTRANCE" (Bauerlein, 2007), and a survery of college students indicated that more than 4 in 10 college seniors couldn't place the Civil War in the correct half-century (Bertman, 2000).

Similar concerns have been raised about math and science, where international comparisons indicate that American students lag behind many of their counterparts in other countries (Gonzales et al., 2004; Lemke et al., 2004).

In response to concerns about students' lack of knowledge, educators have established academic **standards,** statements that describe what students should know or be able to do at the end of a prescribed period of study (J. McCombs, 2005). While the "standards movement" is controversial among educational leaders, all states and the District of Columbia have established standards, and your planning decisions will be influenced by them. It is likely that your school will be held accountable for helping students meet standards, so you need to be able to design learning activities to reach them.

Standards. Statements that describe what students should know or be able to do at the end of a prescribed period of study.

Standards are essentially statements of objectives. However, because standards vary in their specificity, you often will first need to interpret the meaning of the standard, and then you must construct your own specific learning objectives based on your interpretation.

For instance, the standard that Scott used as a basis for planning his lesson said:

> The student knows that if more than one force acts on an object, then the forces can reinforce or cancel each other, depending on their direction and magnitude. (Florida Department of Education, 2008)

Based on this standard, he established the following objectives:

1. Students will understand that a force is a push or a pull.
2. Students will understand that an object moves in the direction of the greater force.
3. Students will understand that where the speed of air over a surface increases, the force it exerts on the surface decreases (Bernoulli's principle).

He then prepared his learning activity and assessment based on his objectives. Scott's complete lesson plan appears in Figure 13.3.

Scott's lesson was in middle school science. Let's look at another standard from the state of Texas in third-grade math.

> (3.2) **Number, operation, and quantitative reasoning.** The student uses fraction names and symbols to describe fractional parts of whole objects or sets of objects. The student is expected to:
>
> (A) construct concrete models of fractions;
> (B) compare fractional parts of whole objects or sets of objects in a problem situation using concrete models;
> (C) use fraction names and symbols to describe fractional parts of whole objects or sets of objects with denominators of 12 or less (Texas Education Agency, 2008)

Topic: Bernoulli's Principle

Learning Objective:

Students will understand that force decreases where the speed of air over a surface increases (Bernoulli's principle).

Content:

Bernoulli's principle states that when the speed of a fluid (most commonly air) increases over a surface, the force and pressure that it exerts on the surface decreases.

Learning Activity:

1. Show examples of forces to review the concept *force*.
2. Tug objects back and forth to review the principle: "objects move in the direction of the greater force."
3. Have students blow over a piece of paper, ask for observations, and use questioning to lead them to observe that the paper rises.
4. Have students blow between two pieces of paper and observe that the papers come together.
5. Have students blow through the neck of a funnel with a ping-pong ball in the mouth and observe that the ball stays in the mouth of the funnel.
6. Sketch the examples on the board and have them identify where the force was greater in each case. Guide them to conclude that the force under the paper, on the outside of the two papers, and in front of the ball was greater than the force on top of the paper, between the papers, and behind the ball.
7. Have students identify where the speed of the air was greater in each case.
8. Guide students to conclude that where the speed of the air was greater, the force was less (the force is greater on the opposite side). Label this relationship "Bernoulli's principle."

Assessment:

1. Have students sketch the flow of the air over the surface for each of the examples and prepare a written description of the relationship between the speed and force.
2. Ask students to use Bernoulli's principle to explain how airplanes are able to fly.

Figure 13.3 Scott's lesson plan in middle school science

Frequently, states provide sample assessment items to help guide teachers as they prepare their objectives and their own assessments. For instance, the following item is similar to one that appears on the 2006 *Texas Assessment of Knowledge and Skills* for third grade (Texas State Education Agency, 2006).

Carlos found these bird eggs in a nest.

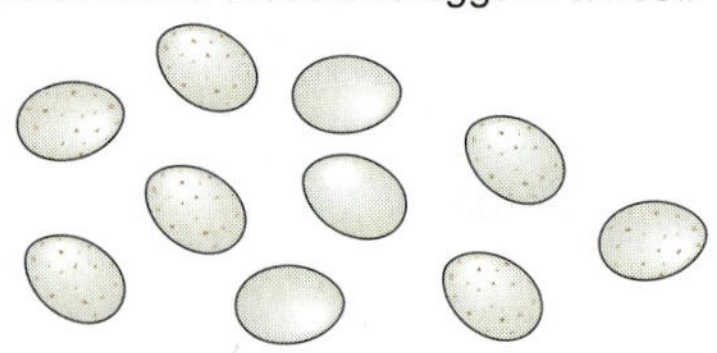

What fraction of the eggs have spots?
Mark your answer.

○ $\frac{3}{7}$

○ $\frac{7}{3}$

○ $\frac{3}{10}$

○ $\frac{7}{10}$

Based on this sample assessment item, an objective related to the standard might be:

Students will identify fractional parts in sets of objects.

This objective is an interpretation of the portion of the standard that says, "(B) compare fractional parts of whole objects or sets of objects in a problem situation using concrete models."

A lesson plan that could be used to help students reach this objective appears in Figure 13.4.

Finally, let's look at an example in 10th-grade World History in the state of California.

Students analyze the effects of the Industrial Revolution in England, France, Germany, Japan, and the United States.

1. Analyze why England was the first country to industrialize. (California State Board of Education, 2008)

Topic: Fractions

Learning Objective:

Students will identify fractional parts in sets of objects.

Learning Activity:

1. Give each student a candy bar composed of 12 equal pieces.
2. Have them unwrap the bar and make observations, and then, using questioning, guide them to identify 12 pieces as the total.
3. Guide the students to notice that all the pieces are equal in size.
4. Have them break off 3 of the pieces, and ask them to compare the number they broke off to the total number.
5. Write the fraction 3/12 on the board. Ask students what the 12 means in the fraction. When they say that it is the total number of pieces, ask them again what they know about each. Guide them to observe that each of the 12 is the same size.
6. Ask what the 3 means in the fraction, and guide them to identify it as the number broken off. Help them put their understanding into words whenever necessary.
7. Have them break off 2 more pieces, and ask them to write the fraction on their individual chalkboards that will now represent how many are broken off. Ask them to hold up their chalkboards when finished.
8. Write the fraction 6/12 on the board, and ask them to represent this fraction with their candy pieces.
9. Repeat the process with additional examples.
10. Write the fraction 12/12 on the board, and ask them to describe what this fraction means.

Assessment:

Give students a drawing with a set of same-sized squares, with some colored black and some colored red. Have them identify the fraction of the total that are black and the fraction that are red.

Have them write a description of the fraction in each case.

Figure 13.4 Lesson plan for elementary math

An objective based on this standard might appear as follows:

Students will identify the economic and political factors existing in England and in other countries that contributed to its being the first country to industrialize.

A lesson plan that could be used to help students reach this objective appears in Figure 13.5.

Keep in mind that these objectives and lesson plans are merely examples based on individual teachers' interpretations. For example, Scott included a description of the content in his lesson plan, but neither the elementary nor the high school examples did. However, a *learning objective, learning activity,* and *assessment* are essential features of all lesson plans. Based on your knowledge of content and your students, your interpretation of the standard might differ from Scott's and your lesson plan may differ from the examples you see here.

Becoming comfortable with the idea that you can—and should—use your professional judgment in interpreting standards and constructing lessons is important. As you acquire teaching experience, you will put less information on paper as you plan, but you will be no less clear about your learning objectives, how you will help your students reach them (learning activities), and how you will determine the extent to which they have been reached (assessments).

As you see, the thinking involved in planning for standards-based instruction is similar to the thinking involved in other kinds of planning. The standard begins the decision-making process, and you then are responsible for interpreting the standard and making decisions about learning activities and assessments.

Topic: The Industrial Revolution

Learning Objective:

Students will identify the economic and political factors existing in England and in other countries that contributed to it being the first country to industrialize.

Learning Activity:

1. Prepare a large skeleton matrix with England, France, China, and the United States on one axis and government, social climate, economy, technology, natural resources, and agriculture on the other.
2. Organize the class into groups of four, and assign each group to one of the 24 cells. Have the students use the Internet, their textbooks, and other books to gather information for each of the cells.
3. Monitor the groups to be sure that they include essential information, such as the invention of the steam engine, access to coal, the end of feudalism, and a ready market in the appropriate cells. Give the students 2 days to gather the information.
4. Display the completed matrix, and ask students to look for similarities and differences in the rows and columns.
5. Guide the students to identify factors in the patterns that led to England's leadership in the Industrial Revolution.

Assessment:

Have students write a short paragraph that relates industrialization to government.

Have them repeat the process, comparing industrialization to social climate, economy, technology, natural resources, and agriculture, respectively.

Figure 13.5 Lesson plan in secondary social studies

classroom connections

Applying an Understanding of Expert Planning in Your Classroom

1. Knowledge can range in levels from *factual* to *metacognitive,* and cognitive processes range from *remembering* to *creating*. Consider the level of your instruction, and prepare objectives that require students to do more than remember factual knowledge.
   - **Elementary:** A fourth-grade teacher wants her students to understand the different functions of the human skeleton, such as why the skull is solid, the ribs are curved, and the femur is the largest bone in the body. "This is better than simply having them label the different bones," she thinks.
   - **Middle School:** A seventh-grade geography teacher wants his students to understand how climate is influenced by the interaction of a number of variables. To reach his objective, he gives students a map of a fictitious island, together with longitude, latitude, topography, and wind direction. He then has students make and defend conclusions about the climate of the island.
   - **High School:** A biology teacher wants her students to understand the relationships between an organism's body structure and its adaptation to its environment. She has her students identify the characteristics of parasitic and nonparasitic worms and the differences between them. The students then link the differences to the organisms' abilities to adapt to their environments.
2. Instructional alignment ensures that learning activities are congruent with learning objectives, and assessments are consistent with both. Prepare assessments during planning, and keep the need for alignment in mind as you plan.
   - **Elementary:** The fourth-grade teacher in her unit on the skeletal system prepares the following as an assessment: "Suppose humans walked on all fours, as chimpanzees and gorillas do. Describe how our skeletons would be different from our skeletons now."
   - **Middle School:** To assess his students' developing knowledge, the geography teacher gives them another map of a fictitious island with different mountain ranges, wind directions, ocean currents, and latitude and longitude. He then asks them to identify and explain where the largest city on the island most likely would be.
   - **High School:** The biology teacher describes two organisms, one with radial symmetry and the other with bilateral symmetry. She asks her students to identify the one that is most advanced with respect to evolution and to explain their choices.

check your understanding

1.1 Describe the five essential components involved in planning for instruction.

1.2 Planning in a standards-based environment involves one additional component beyond the planning components described in this section of the chapter. Identify this additional step.

1.3 Classify the following learning objective into one of the cells of the taxonomy matrix (Figure 13.2, on page 393), and explain your classification: Students will learn to search for relevant and irrelevant information in applications of all the topics they study.

To receive feedback for these questions, go to Appendix A.

Implementing Instruction: Essential Teaching Skills

In the first section of the chapter, you saw how Scott thought about his planning. Now you'll examine the skills he demonstrated as he implemented his plans. Scott taught the concept of *force* and the principle stating that objects move in the direction of the greater force on Monday. We join him as he begins class Tuesday:

> "Let's go over what we did yesterday," he begins just as the bell stops ringing. "What is a force? . . . Shantae?"
>
> ". . . A push or a pull," she responds after thinking for a second.
>
> "Good, Shantae," Scott smiles and then reviews the concept of *force* by pushing on the board, blowing on an object sitting on his desk, and asking students to explain why they are forces.
>
> He continues by holding a stapler and having Damien pull it away from him to review the idea that objects move in the direction of the greater force.
>
> He reminds students to keep these ideas in mind, gives each student two pieces of paper, picks up one of the pieces, and blows over it as you see here.
>
> 
>
> He directs students to do the same, and then asks, "What did you notice when we blew over the top? . . . David?"
>
> "The paper moved."
>
> "How did the paper move? . . . Do it again."
>
> David again blows over the surface of the paper, and Scott repeats, "What did the paper do?"
>
> ". . . It came up."
>
> "Yes," Scott waves energetically. "When you blow over it, it comes up."
>
> He then has students pick up both pieces of paper and demonstrates how to blow between them, as shown here.
>
> 
>
> "What did you notice here? . . . Sharon?" Scott asks after they've completed the demonstration.
>
> ". . . The papers came together."
>
> "Okay, good. Remember that, and we'll talk about it in a minute," Scott smiles. "Now, Let's look at one more. . . . I have a funnel and a ping-pong ball. . . . I'm going to shoot Tristan in the head when I blow," he jokes, pointing to one of the students.
>
> He blows through the funnel's stem, and to students' surprise, the ball stays in the funnel.
>
> Scott has students repeat the demonstration and make observations, and he then draws sketches of the three examples on the board and says, "Let's look at these."
>
> 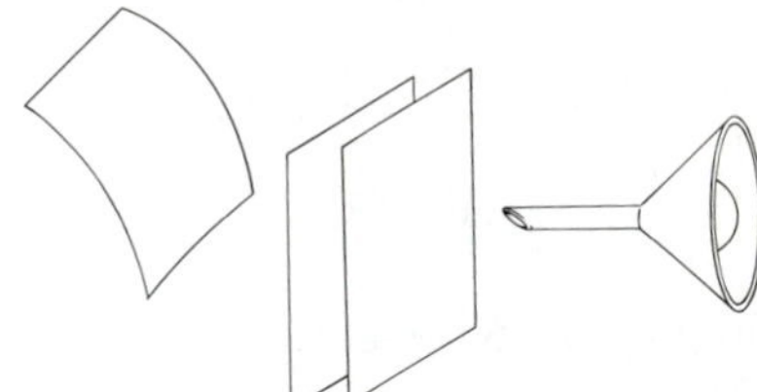
>
> Referring to the first sketch, Scott asks, "Was I blowing on the top or the bottom? . . . Rachel?"

"The top."

"And what happened there? . . . Heather?"

"The paper rose up."

Referring to the second sketch he asks, "What did we do here . . . Shantae?"

"We blew in between them."

"And what happened there? . . . Ricky?"

"They came together."

Scott does a similar analysis with the ball and funnel and then says, "Let's think about the forces here. . . . What forces are acting on the paper? . . . Colin?"

"Gravity."

"And which direction is gravity pulling?"

"Down."

Scott draws an arrow pointing downward, indicating the force of gravity, and labels it "A."

"What other force is acting on the paper? . . . William?" he continues.

"Air," William says, pointing up.

"How do you know it's pushing up?"

"The paper moved up."

"Exactly. You know there's a force pushing up, because objects move in the direction of the greater force, and the paper moved up." Scott then draws an arrow pointing up and labels it "B."

Scott guides the students through a similar analysis of the second and third examples, leading them to conclude that the forces pushing the two papers together were greater than the forces pushing them apart, and the force pushing the ball into the funnel was greater than the force pushing the ball out.

"Now let's look again at the forces and where we blew," Scott continues, as he moves back to the first sketch. "Study the drawings carefully, and see what kind of relationship exists between the two."

After several seconds Heather concludes, "It seems like wherever you blew, the force was stronger on the opposite side."

Seeing that the bell is going to ring in a minute, Scott continues, "Yes, excellent, Heather. . . . A person named Bernoulli discovered that every time you increase the speed of the air over a surface, the force goes down. . . . So, when I speed up the air over the top of the paper (holding up the single sheet of paper), the force goes down and this force takes over (motioning underneath the paper to illustrate a force pushing up).

He summarizes the other two examples in the same way, finishing just as the bell ending the period begins to ring.

Essential teaching skills. Basic abilities that all teachers, including those in their first year of teaching, should possess to maximize student learning.

During this lesson, Scott demonstrated a number of **essential teaching skills,** basic abilities that all teachers, including those in their first year of teaching, should possess to maximize student learning. Effective teachers demonstrate essential teaching skills regardless of the content area, grade level, or specific teaching strategy, and these skills reflect teachers' general pedagogical knowledge.

Derived from a long line of research (Brophy, 2006c; Good & Brophy 2008), essential teaching skills are outlined in Figure 13.6 and discussed in the sections that follow. We describe them separately for the sake of clarity, but they are interdependent; none is as effective alone as in combination with the others.

Figure 13.6 Essential teaching skills

Attitudes

Admittedly, attitudes are not skills, but positive teacher attitudes are fundamental to effective teaching. As you saw in Chapter 11, teacher characteristics such as *personal teaching efficacy, modeling and enthusiasm, caring,* and *high expectations* increase learner motivation. They also lead to increased student achievement, which makes sense, because motivation and learning are so strongly linked (Brophy, 2004; Bruning, Schraw, Norby, & Ronning, 2004).

Scott displayed several positive attitudes during his instruction. He was energetic and enthusiastic, he demonstrated the respect for students that indicates caring, and his questioning suggested that he expected all students to participate and learn. These are attitudes we hope to see in all teachers.

Effective teachers have their materials prepared and ready to use when class begins.

Organization

The need for organization demonstrates the interdependence of classroom management and effective teaching. In Chapter 12 you saw that classroom organization included *starting instruction on time, having materials ready,* and *developing classroom routines.* These components help prevent management problems, and they also maximize instructional time, which correlates with student learning (Bohn, Roehrig, & Pressley, 2004).

Scott was well organized. He began his lesson as soon as the bell finished ringing, he had sheets of paper, balls, and funnels ready to be handed out, and he made the transition from his review to the learning activity quickly and smoothly. This organization was the result of clear thinking and decision making as he planned his lesson.

Communication

The link between effective communication, student achievement, and student satisfaction with instruction is well documented (Good & Brophy, 2008; I. Weiss & Pasley, 2004). Four aspects of effective communication are important for learning and motivation:

- Precise language
- Connected discourse
- Transition signals
- Emphasis

Precise language omits vague terms (e.g., *perhaps, maybe, might, and so on,* and *usually*) from explanations and responses to students' questions. For example, if you ask, "What do high-efficacy teachers do that promotes learning?" and your instructor responds, "Usually, they use their time somewhat better and so on," you're left with a sense of uncertainty about the idea. In contrast, if the instructor responds, "They believe they can increase learning, and one of their characteristics is the effective use of time," you're given a clear picture, and this clarity leads to increased achievement.

Precise language. Teacher talk that omits vague terms from explanations and responses to students' questions.

Connected discourse refers to instruction that is thematic and leads to a point. If the point of the lesson isn't clear, if it is sequenced inappropriately, or if incidental information is interjected without indicating how it relates to the topic, classroom discourse becomes *disconnected* or *scrambled.* Expert teachers keep their lessons on track and minimize time spent on matters unrelated to the topic (Burbules & Bruce, 2001; Leinhardt, 2001).

Connected discourse. Instruction that is thematic and leads to a point.

Transition signals are verbal statements indicating that one idea is ending and another is beginning. For example, an American government teacher might signal a transition by saying, "We've been talking about the Senate, which is one house of Congress. Now we'll turn to the House of Representatives." Because not all students are cognitively at the same place, a transition signal alerts them that the lesson is making a conceptual shift—moving to a new topic—and allows them to prepare for it.

Transition signals. Verbal statements indicating that one idea is ending and another is beginning.

Emphasis consists of verbal and vocal cues that alert students to important information in a lesson (Jetton & Alexander, 1997). For example, Scott used a form of vocal emphasis, raising his voice when he said, "Keep those ideas in mind," as he moved from his review to the lesson itself. When teachers say, "Now remember, everyone, this is very important" or "Listen carefully now," they're using verbal emphasis.

Emphasis. Verbal and vocal cues that alert students to important information in a lesson.

Repeating a point is also a form of emphasis. Asking students, "What did we say these problems have in common?" stresses an important feature in the problems and helps students link new to past information. Redundancy is particularly important when reviewing abstract rules, principles, and concepts (Brophy & Good, 1986; Shuell, 1996).

Knowledge of content is essential for clear communication, because teachers who clearly understand the topics they teach use clearer language, their lessons are more thematic, and their discourse is more connected than those whose background is weaker (Brophy, 2006c;

Sensory focus helps maintain students' attention throughout a lesson.

Cruickshank, 1985). Knowledge of content allows teachers to remain focused on learning objectives while still being responsive to student ideas (Staples, 2007). This suggests that you should carefully study any topics about which you're uncertain as you plan.

Focus: Attracting and Maintaining Attention

You saw in Chapter 11 that *introductory focus* attracts students' attention and provides a framework for a lesson. Scott provided introductory focus for his students by beginning his lesson with his demonstrations. They attracted students' attention and also provided a context for the rest of the lesson.

Scott's demonstrations and drawings also acted as a form of **sensory focus,** which is created by stimuli that teachers use to maintain attention during learning activities. These stimuli can include concrete objects, pictures, models, materials displayed on the overhead, or even information written on the chalkboard.

Additional examples of sensory focus stimuli that teachers in case studies in earlier chapters used include:

- Jenny Newhall's demonstration with the empty glass and water in Chapter 2 (page 57)
- David Shelton's model and transparency in Chapter 7 (page 196)
- Jenny Newhall's balances in Chapter 8 (page 225)
- Laura Hunter's classroom diagram (page 253) and Sue Brush's graph in Chapter 9 (page 280)
- DeVonne Lampkin's paragraphs on the overhead in Chapter 11 (page 348)

Examples and other representations of content are an effective way to provide sensory focus. Building lessons around high-quality examples both provides the information students need to construct their knowledge and also helps maintain attention.

Sensory focus. The result of stimuli that teachers use to maintain attention during learning activities.

Feedback. Information learners receive about the accuracy or appropriateness of their verbal responses and written work.

Feedback

Feedback is information learners receive about the accuracy or appropriateness of their verbal responses and written work, and the importance of feedback is consistently confirmed by research (Hattie & Timperley, 2007; Marzano, 2003b). It is also supported by every learning theory you've studied in this text. Feedback allows learners to assess the accuracy of their prior knowledge, gives them information about the validity of their knowledge constructions, and helps them elaborate on existing understanding. It is also important for motivation because it provides students with information about their increasing competence and helps satisfy their need to understand how they're progressing (Brophy, 2004). The purpose of feedback is to narrow the gap between existing understanding and the learning objective (Brosvic, Epstein, Dihoff, & Cook, 2006; Hattie & Timperley, 2007).

Effective feedback has four characteristics:

- It is immediate or given soon after a learner response.
- It is specific.
- It provides corrective information for the learner.
- It has a positive emotional tone (Brophy & Good, 1986; Moreno, 2004).

To illustrate these characteristics, let's look at three examples.

Mr. Dole: What kind of figure is shown on the overhead, Jo?
Jo: A square.
Mr. Dole: Not quite. Help her out, . . . Steve?

Ms. West: What kind of figure is shown on the overhead, Jo?
Jo: A square.
Ms. West: No, it's a rectangle. What is the next figure, . . . Albert?

Ms. Baker: What kind of figure is shown on the overhead, Jo?
Jo: A square.
Ms. Baker: No, remember, we said that all sides have the same length in a square. What do you notice about the lengths of the sides in this figure?

In each case, the teacher gave immediate feedback. However, neither Mr. Dole nor Ms. West gave Jo any corrective information. Ms. Baker, in contrast, provided Jo with specific information that helped her understand the concept, which is the most important feature of effective feedback (Hattie & Timperly, 2007).

Although the examples don't illustrate the emotional tone of the teachers' responses, it is important. Harsh, critical, or sarcastic feedback detracts from students' feelings of safety and relatedness, which decreases both motivation and learning (Schunk, Pintrich & Meece, 2008).

Praise

Praise is probably the most common and adaptable form of teacher feedback. Research reveals some interesting patterns in its use:

- Praise is used less often than most teachers believe—less than five times per class.
- Praise for good behavior is quite rare; it occurs once every 2 or more hours in the elementary grades and even less as students get older.
- Praise tends to depend as much on the type of student (e.g., high achieving, well behaved, and attentive) as on the quality of the student's response.
- Teachers praise students based on the answers they expect to receive as much as on those they actually hear. (Brophy, 1981; Good & Brophy, 2008)

Praising effectively is more complex than it appears. For instance, young children tend to accept praise at face value even when overdone, whereas older students assess the validity of the praise and what they believe it communicates about their ability. Young children bask in praise given openly in front of a class, whereas adolescents often react better if it's given quietly and individually (Stipek, 2002). Experts suggest that praise delivered to older students should reflect genuine accomplishment and be delivered simply and directly using a natural voice (Good & Brophy, 2008). Highly anxious students and those from low socioeconomic status backgrounds tend to react more positively to praise than students who are confident and those from more advantaged backgrounds (Brophy, 1981; Good & Brophy, 2008).

Finally, although research indicates that specific is more effective than general praise, if every desired answer is praised specifically, it can sound stilted and artificial and can disrupt the flow of a lesson. Experts suggest that praise for student answers that are correct but tentative should provide additional, affirming information, whereas praise for answers delivered with confidence should be simple and general (Rosenshine, 1987).

Praise given quietly and individually is effective with adolescents.

Written Feedback

Much of the feedback students receive occurs during lessons, but teachers also provide valuable feedback through notes and comments on student work. Because writing detailed comments is time-consuming, written feedback is often brief and sketchy and provides students little useful information.

One solution to this problem is to provide model responses to written assignments. For instance, to help students evaluate their answers to essay items, effective teachers often write ideal answers, display them, and encourage students to compare their answers with the model. The model, combined with discussion and time available for individual help, provides informative feedback that is manageable for the teacher.

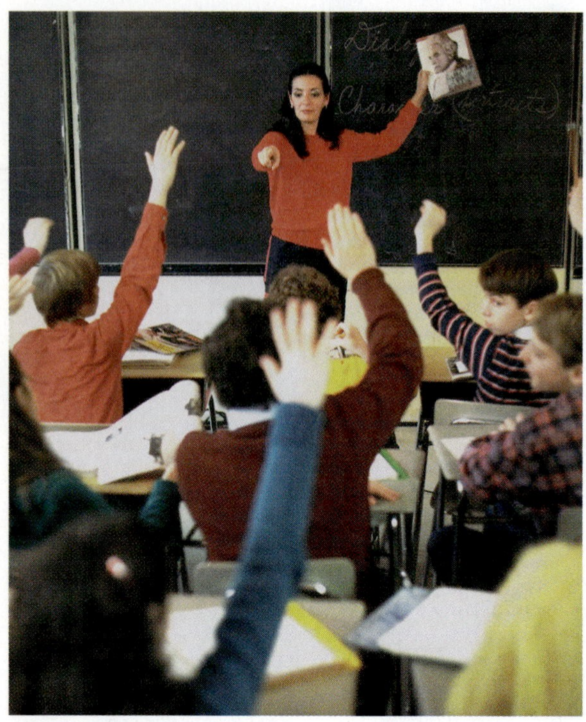

Questioning allows teachers to guide student learning while also gauging learning progress.

Questioning

One of the most replicated findings in research on teaching suggests that the most effective teachers actively instruct their students (Brophy, 2006c; Odom, Stoddard, & LaNasa, 2007; Opdenakker & Van Damme, 2006).

> Teachers who elicit greater achievement gains spend a great deal of time actively instructing their students. Their classrooms feature more time spent in interactive lessons featuring teacher–student discourse and less time spent in independent seatwork. . . . Most of their instruction occurs during interactive discourse with students rather than during extended lecture-presentations. (Brophy, 2006c, p. 764)

Questioning is the most widely applicable and effective tool teachers have for promoting this interaction (Leinhardt & Steele, 2005; J. Olson & Clough, 2004). Skilled questioning is very sophisticated, but with practice, effort, and experience, teachers can and do become expert at it (Kauchak & Eggen, 2007; I. Weiss & Pasley, 2004). To avoid overloading their own working memories, teachers need to practice questioning strategies to the point of automaticity, which leaves working memory space available to monitor students' thinking and assess learning progress (Feldon, 2007a).

The characteristics of effective questioning are outlined in Figure 13.7 and discussed in the sections that follow.

Questioning Frequency

Questioning frequency. The number of questions a teacher asks during a learning activity.

Questioning frequency refers to the number of questions a teacher asks during a learning activity, and you saw this illustrated in Scott's work where he developed his entire lesson with questioning. Questioning increases student involvement, which raises achievement (J. Finn, Pannozzo, & Achilles, 2003; Leinhardt & Steele, 2005), and greater involvement also increases a learner's sense of control and autonomy, which are essential for intrinsic motivation (R. Ryan & Deci, 2000). Effective teachers ask many more questions than do less effective teachers, and their questions remain focused on their learning objectives (Leinhardt & Steele, 2005).

Equitable Distribution

Equitable distribution. The process of calling on all the students in a class as equally as possible.

Who usually is called on in classrooms? Most commonly, they are high achievers or students who are assertive. **Equitable distribution** is the process of calling on all the students in a class as equally as possible (Kerman, 1979). To illustrate, let's return to some dialogue from Scott's lesson:

Scott: (Referring to the sketch of the single piece of paper) Was I blowing on the top or the bottom? . . . Rachel?
Rachel: The top.
Scott: And what happened there? . . . Heather?
Heather: The paper rose up.
Scott: (Referring to sketch of the two pieces of paper) What did we do here . . . Shantae?
Shantae: We blew in between them.

Figure 13.7 Characteristics of effective questioning

Scott: And what happened there . . . Ricky?
Ricky: They came together.

In this short episode, Scott directed questions to four different students, and he *first asked the question* and *then identified the student.* This sequence makes everyone responsible for generating an answer and creates the expectation that everyone is capable of responding and should be paying attention (Good & Brophy, 2008; McDougall & Granby, 1996).

> Students benefit from opportunities to practice oral communication skills, and distributing response opportunities helps keep them attentive and accountable. Also, teachers who interact primarily with a small group of active (and usually high-achieving) students are likely to communicate undesirable expectations and be generally less aware and less effective. (Good & Brophy, 2008, p. 322)

Equitable distribution is a simple idea but demanding because it requires careful monitoring of students and a great deal of teacher energy. This is another reason why you should practice questioning to the point of automaticity to reduce the cognitive load imposed by equitable distribution (Feldon, 2007a).

Prompting

In attempting to equitably distribute your questions, you might wonder: What do I do when the student I call on doesn't answer or answers incorrectly? One answer is **prompting,** an additional question or statement teachers use to elicit an appropriate student response after a student fails to answer correctly. Its value to both learning and motivation is well documented (Brophy, 2006c; Brophy & Good, 1986; Shuell, 1996).

Prompting. An additional question or statement teachers use to elicit an appropriate student response after a student fails to answer correctly.

To illustrate, let's look again at dialogue from Scott's lesson.

Scott: What did you notice when we blew over the top? . . . David?
David: The paper moved.
Scott: How did the paper move? Do it again.
(David again blew over the surface of the paper.)
Scott: What did the paper do?
David: It came up.

David didn't initially give the answer necessary to help him understand the relationship between force and the movement of the paper, so having him repeat the demonstration was a form of prompting.

As another example, Ken Duran, a language arts teacher, displays the following on an overhead:

The girl was very athletic.

Let's look at some brief dialogue:

Ken: Can you identify an adjective in the sentence . . . Chandra?
Chandra: . . .
Ken: What do we know about the girl?
Chandra: She was athletic.

Ken's prompt, which elicited an acceptable response from Chandra, kept her involved in the activity and provided a successful experience. She hadn't arrived at the answer Ken wanted, but the question kept the process in her zone of proximal development, so she continued to make learning progress.

You should be strategic as you prompt. For instance, if the question calls for factual knowledge, such as "What is 7 times 8?" or "Who was our president during the Civil War?" and the student can't answer, prompting isn't useful; students either know the fact or they don't. It is effective, however, when studying conceptual, procedural, and metacognitive knowledge, and when using cognitive processes beyond remembering (L. Anderson & Krathwohl, 2001).

Wait-Time

For questions to be effective, teachers need to give students time to think. After asking a question, effective teachers wait a few seconds before selecting an individual to answer. These few seconds alert all students that they may be called on. After calling on a student, teachers then

Wait-time. The period of silence that occurs both before and after calling on a student

wait a few more seconds to give the student time to think. This period of silence, both before and after calling on a student, is called **wait-time,** and in most classrooms, it is too short, often less than 1 second (Rowe, 1974, 1986; R. Stahl et al., 2005).

A more descriptive label for wait-time might be "think-time," because waiting gives all students—both the one called on and others in the class—time to think. Increasing wait-time, ideally to about 3 to 5 seconds, communicates that all students are expected to answer, results in longer and better answers, and contributes to a positive classroom climate (Kastens & Liben, 2007; Rowe 1974, 1986; R. Stahl et al., 2005).

As with prompting, teachers should implement wait-time strategically. For example, if students are practicing basic skills, such as multiplication facts, quick answers are desirable, and wait-times should be short (Good & Brophy, 2008; Rosenshine & Stevens, 1986). Also, if a student appears uneasy, you may choose to intervene earlier. However, if you expect students to use cognitive processes such as apply, analyze, or evaluate, wait-times should be longer, sometimes exceeding the 3- to 5-second rule of thumb.

Cognitive Levels of Questions

The kinds of questions teachers ask also influence learning, and the relative merits of low- and high-level questions have been widely researched. The results are mixed, however. Both low-level questions (e.g., remember the taxonomy in Figure 13.2) and high-level questions (e.g., *apply* or *analyze* on the taxonomy) correlate positively with achievement, depending on the teaching situation (Good & Brophy, 2008).

The appropriate level for a question depends on your learning objective, and you should think about asking sequences of questions instead of single questions in isolation. You saw this illustrated in Scott's lesson. After completing the demonstrations, Scott first asked the students to remember how the papers and the ball acted, which he followed with questions asking them to identify the relationship between the speed of the air and the forces it exerted on the objects.

In your classroom, you should focus on your learning objectives and not on the level of questions you choose to ask. When your objectives are clear, the levels of questions will take care of themselves.

Review and Closure

Review. A summary that helps students link what they have already learned to what will follow in the next learning activity.

Review is a summary that helps students link what they have already learned to what will follow in the next learning activity. It can occur at any point in a lesson, although it is most common at the beginning and end.

Beginning reviews help students activate the prior knowledge needed to understand the content of the current lesson. Scott's beginning review on Tuesday was one of the most effective aspects of his lesson. He didn't just ask the students to recall the definition of force and the principle relating opposing forces and movement; he provided examples. Though it may seem redundant to use additional examples because he had shown examples on Monday, it is often necessary. Providing students with concrete examples during the review increases its effectiveness by providing additional links in long-term memory.

Scott's review was also important because students had to understand force and the principle relating the direction of movement to the stronger force in order to understand Bernoulli's principle. His review was essential if the lesson was to be meaningful.

Closure. A form of review occurring at the end of a lesson.

Closure is a form of review occurring at the end of a lesson. The purpose of closure is to help students organize what they've learned into a meaningful schema; it pulls the different aspects of the topic together and signals the end of a lesson. When students are involved in higher-level learning, an effective form of closure is to have them identify additional examples of a concept, or apply a principle, generalization, or rule to a new situation. When teaching problem solving, summarizing the thinking involved in solving the problem can be another effective form of closure.

Learning Contexts: Effective Instruction in Urban Classrooms

Essential teaching skills improve learning for all students regardless of teaching context, but they are even more essential for instruction with urban students. Three skills are especially important in urban environments:

classroom connections

Demonstrating Essential Teaching Skills in Your Classroom

Attitudes

1. Personal teaching efficacy, high expectations, modeling and enthusiasm, and caring are teacher attitudes and beliefs associated with increased student achievement. Demonstrate positive attitudes to increase student motivation and achievement.
   - **Elementary:** A third-grade teacher communicates her personal efficacy and caring by calling a student's parents and soliciting their help as soon as the student fails to turn in an assignment or receives an unsatisfactory grade on a quiz or test.
   - **Middle School:** A seventh-grade teacher commits himself to being a role model by displaying the statement, "I will always behave in the way I expect you to behave in this class," on the bulletin board. He uses the statement as a guiding principle in his class.
   - **High School:** A geometry teacher, knowing that her students initially have problems with proofs, conducts help sessions twice a week after school. "I would much rather help them than lower my expectations," she comments.

Organization and Communication

2. Effective organization helps teachers begin classes on time, have materials prepared, and maintain well-established routines. Carefully plan and organize materials and communicate clearly to maximize instructional time.
   - **Elementary:** A first-grade teacher has several boxes filled with frequently used science materials, such as soft drink bottles, balloons, matches, baking soda, vinegar, funnels, and a hot plate. The night before a science demonstration, he spends a few minutes selecting his materials from the boxes and sets them on a shelf near his desk so that he'll have everything ready at the beginning of the lesson.
   - **Middle School:** An eighth-grade American history teacher asks a member of her team to visit her class to provide feedback about her instruction. She also asks her colleague to check if she clearly emphasizes the important points in the lesson, sequences the presentation logically, and communicates changes in topics.
   - **High School:** A biology teacher begins each class with an outline of the day's topics and activities on the board. As she makes transitions from one activity to the other, she calls students' attention to the outline so students can understand where they've been and where they're going.

Focus and Feedback

3. Lesson focus helps maintain student attention, and feedback provides students with information about their learning progress. Use problems, demonstrations, and displays to provide focus during lessons. Provide feedback throughout all learning experiences.
   - **Elementary:** A fourth-grade teacher beginning a study of different groups of animals brings a live lobster, a spider, and a grasshopper to class and builds a lesson on arthropods around these animals. After making a list of arthropods' characteristics on the board, she asks students if a clam is an arthropod. When some say it is, she provides feedback by referring them to the list and asking them to identify each in the clam. After a short discussion, they conclude that the clam isn't an arthropod.
   - **Middle School:** A science teacher dealing with the concept of kindling temperature soaks a cloth in a water–alcohol mix, ignites it, and asks, "Why isn't the cloth burning?" He provides feedback during the class discussion by asking guiding questions to help students develop their understanding.
   - **High School:** A physical education teacher shows students a videotape of a professional tennis player executing a nearly perfect backhand. She then videotapes the students as they practice backhands, and they attempt to modify their swings to more nearly imitate the pro's.

Questioning and Review

4. Reviews help activate and consolidate students' prior knowledge, and questioning puts them in cognitively active roles. Begin and end each class with a short review. Guide the review with questioning.
   - **Elementary:** A fifth-grade teacher whose class is studying different types of boundaries says, "We've looked at three kinds of boundaries between the states so far today. What are these three, and where do they occur?"
   - **Middle School:** An English teacher begins, "We studied pronoun–antecedent agreement yesterday. Give me an example that illustrates this idea, and explain why your example is correct."
   - **High School:** An art teacher says, "Today we've found that many artists use color to create different moods. Let's summarize some of the features that we've learned about. Go ahead, offer one, someone."

- Attitudes
- Questioning
- Feedback

Attitudes

Teacher attitudes influence the way they treat students, and negative stereotypes about the learning capabilities of urban students can be particularly damaging. "Such stereotypes are not only dehumanizing, they are also hard to fight against, because they have become the image that comes to people's minds the moment they think about all people, things, and places urban" (R. A. Goldstein, 2004, p. 45). The effects of stereotyping can be devastating, which is why teachers' attitudes, such as personal teaching efficacy, modeling, caring, and positive expectations are so important.

Some researchers suggest that a sense of belonging generated by caring teachers is the most important factor in promoting resilience in urban students (Judson, 2004; Valenzuela, 1999). The

theory to practice

The Theoretical Framework for Essential Teaching Skills

In addition to being well-established by research, the essential teaching skills are also supported by theory. Let's look at their theoretical foundations.

Attitudes. Social cognitive theory supports the importance of modeling, and you saw in your study of self-determination theory in Chapter 10 that people have an innate need for relatedness, which explains the importance of caring. Maintaining high expectations for students also communicates that you're committed to their learning.

Organization. The need to maximize time for learning is obvious, and creating well-established routines helps learners achieve a sense of equilibrium. The model of human memory also supports the need for routines; they reduce cognitive load for both teachers and students. The need for order and predictability is even more important for learners whose homes don't provide it.

Communication. To make sense of their experiences is arguably learners' most basic cognitive need. Clear communication makes information clear and helps learners make sense of it.

Focus. As described in the human memory model, attention is the beginning point for processing information, and focus provides a mechanism for attracting and maintaining attention.

Feedback. According to attribution theory, people have an intrinsic need to understand their successes and failures, and feedback helps meet this need.

Questioning. To promote learning, students must be in cognitively active roles, and questioning is the most widely applicable tool teachers have for promoting cognitive activity. Questioning is also one of the most important forms of scaffolding for helping students move through their zones of proximal development.

Review and Closure. To make sense of new information, learners must connect it to information that already exists in long-term memory. Reviews pull information from long-term memory back into working memory for further processing. Closure helps in the process of schema production and aids meaningful encoding.

need for belonging can be explained with self-determination theory (see Chapter 10), which suggests that relatedness (belonging) is a basic need for everyone. Caring teachers who get to know their students as human beings can do much to help their students feel like they belong.

Positive teacher attitudes don't mean that teachers are naively optimistic; urban contexts do present additional challenges. "Believing in students does not automatically mean that urban students will miraculously become 'A' students and score well on all standardized tests. That takes hard work and an intricate understanding of other aspects of students' lives" (R. A. Goldstein, 2004, p. 46). To succeed in urban classrooms, teachers need to care, and this caring must be translated into teaching that encourages and even requires student success.

Questioning

When working in challenging environments, teachers have a tendency to revert to instructional strategies that afford them the most control. This often results in an inordinate amount of passive learning activities such as lecture and seat work (Duke, 2000; Eggen, 1998). Exactly the opposite is needed.

> A great deal of classroom research suggests that students need active instruction from their teachers, not solitary work with instructional materials, in order to make good achievement progress. (Brophy, 2004, p. 155)

This quote, describing students in general, is even more important for urban students. Questioning encourages students to put their understanding into words, and responding to questions is the most effective way for them to develop this ability.

A common lament is, "I tried calling on students, but they either couldn't or wouldn't answer." This is why open-ended questions and prompting are so important. Initially, your students may encounter difficulties, because they may have limited experience with using school-related language. With scaffolding and encouragement, however, they will improve over time, and improved motivation and increased learning will result.

Finally, careful implementation of equitable distribution is essential in urban classrooms. Making equitable distribution the prevailing pattern in your classroom can do more than anything else to communicate that you believe all students can learn and you expect them to do so.

Feedback

As with attitudes and questioning, feedback is even more important when working with urban students. The knowledge constructions of these students likely vary because of the diversity of their experience and prior knowledge. This means that detailed discussions of seat work, homework, and quiz results are essential when working with urban students. Time spent providing feedback provides a link between you and your students and assists them in the knowledge-construction process.

check your understanding

2.1 Describe essential teaching skills, and explain why they are important.

2.2 We try to model with our writing the content that we're discussing in each chapter. What are we doing to provide introductory focus for each chapter's contents?

2.3 Identify at least two other essential teaching skills that we utilize in each of the chapters of this book.

To receive feedback for these questions, go to Appendix A.

MyEducationLab

To further examine Scott Sowell's attempts to implement the essential teaching skills, go to the *Building Teaching Skills and Dispositions* section in Chapter 13 of MyEducationLab at www.myeducationlab.com, and watch the episode *Essential Teaching Skills in an Urban Classroom.* Complete the exercises following the episodes to build your skills in applying essential teaching skills with your students.

Models of Instruction

As you saw in the previous section, effective teachers apply essential teaching skills in all their learning activities. By comparison, **models of instruction** are prescriptive approaches to teaching designed to help students acquire a deep understanding of specific forms of knowledge. They are grounded in learning theory, supported by research, and they include sequential steps designed to help students reach specified learning objectives.

Models of instruction. Prescriptive approaches to teaching designed to help students acquire a deep understanding of specific forms of knowledge.

Direct instruction. An instructional model designed to teach well-defined knowledge and skills needed for later learning.

Essential teaching skills support all instructional models. For instance, just as students use reading in all their content areas, organization, clear communication, and the other essential teaching skills are important regardless of the model being used.

Research indicates that no single instructional model is most effective for all students or for helping students reach all learning objectives (Knight, 2002; Kroesbergen & van Luit, 2002; Marzano, 2003b). In this section we examine four of the more widely used models:

- Direct instruction
- Lecture discussion
- Guided discovery
- Cooperative learning

Direct Instruction

Direct instruction is an instructional model designed to teach well-defined knowledge and skills needed for later learning (Eggen & Kauchak, 2006; Kuhn, 2007; Rosenshine & Stevens, 1986). Examples of these skills include young students' using basic operations to solve math problems, students' using grammar and punctuation in writing, and chemistry students' balancing equations. Direct instruction is useful when skills include specific steps, and it is particularly effective in working with low achievers and students with exceptionalities (M. M. Flores & Kaylor, 2007; Leno & Dougherty, 2007; Turnbull et al., 2004).

Effective teachers use different models of instruction to help students reach their learning objectives.

Direct instruction ranges from a highly structured, nearly scripted, and somewhat behaviorist approach (Carnine, Silbert, Kame'enui, Tarver, Jongjohann, 2006) to one that is more flexible and cognitive (Eggen & Kauchak, 2006; Rosenshine & Stevens, 1986). We discuss the latter here, which typically occurs in four phases:

- Introduction and review
- Developing understanding

- Guided practice
- Independent practice

The cognitive approach to direct instruction is grounded in the model of human memory, together with modeling and Vygotsky's (1978) concept of scaffolding. Table 13.4 outlines the phases in cognitive-based direct instruction and their relationships to cognitive learning theory.

Let's look at these phases in a second-grade math lesson taught by Sam Barnett, a teacher in a large elementary school in Illinois. The standard Sam is addressing in his lesson follows:

> *6.B.1 Solve one- and two-step problems with whole numbers using addition, subtraction, multiplication and division. (Illinois State Board of Education, 2008)*

Sam begins his lesson on the addition of two-digit numbers by saying, "Today we are going to go a step further with our work in addition so that we'll be able to solve problems like this," and he displays the following on the overhead:

Jana and Patti are friends. They were saving special soda cans to get a free CD. They can get the CD if they save 35 cans. Jana had 15 cans and Patti had 12. How many did they have together?

He gives students a few seconds to read the problem, asks what the problem calls for, and why it's important.

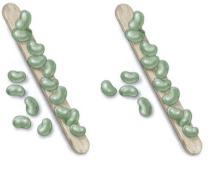

Sam's students have boxes on their desks that contain craft sticks with 10 beans glued on each as well as a number of individual beans. Sam reviews single-digit addition by having students demonstrate their answers to problems like 8 + 7 and 9 + 5, with their sticks and beans.

He then turns back to the problem on the overhead, has the students demonstrate 15 and 12 with their beans, and writes the following on the board:

$$\begin{array}{r} 15 \\ \underline{+12} \end{array}$$

"Now, watch what I do here," he continues. "When I add 5 and 2, what do I get? Let me think about that. . . . 5 and 2 are 7. Let's put a 7 on the board," he says as he walks to the board and adds a 7.

"Now show me that with your beans." He watches as students combine 5 beans and 2 beans on their desks.

table 13.4 The Relationships Between Phases and Cognitive Learning Components in Cognitive-Based Direct Instruction

Phase	Cognitive Learning Component
Introduction and Review: Teachers begin with a form of introductory focus and review previous work.	• Attract attention. • Access prior knowledge from long-term memory.
Developing Understanding: Teachers describe and model the skill or explain and present examples of the concept. Teachers emphasize understanding.	• Acquire declarative knowledge about the skill or concept. • Encode declarative knowledge into long-term memory.
Guided Practice: Students practice the skill or identify additional examples of the concept, and the teacher provides scaffolding.	• Move through the associative stage of developing procedural knowledge.
Independent Practice: Students practice on their own.	• Develop automaticity with the skill or concept.

"Now, we still have to add the tens. What do we get when we add two tens? . . .

Let's see. One ten and one ten is two tens. Now, look where I've put the 2. It is under the tens column because the 2 means two tens." With that, he writes the following on the chalkboard:

$$\begin{array}{r} 15 \\ +12 \\ \hline 27 \end{array}$$

"So, how many cans did Jana and Patti have together? . . . Alesha?"

After a short pause, Alesha offers 27.

"Good. They have 27 altogether."

Sam has students explain and demonstrate with their beans what the 7 and the 2 in 27 mean, and then asks, "Now, we saw that I added the 5 and the 2 before I added the two tens. Why do you suppose I did that? . . . Anyone?"

". . . You have to find out how many ones you have to see if we can make a 10," Callie offers.

"Good, Callie."

"So let's look again," he continues. "There's an important difference between this 2," he says, pointing to the 2 in 27, "and this 2," pointing to the 2 in the 12. "What is this difference? . . . Katrina?"

"That 2 . . . is two groups of 10, . . . and that one is just 2 by itself."

"Good, Katrina. Good work, everyone. . . . Show me this 2," Sam directs, pointing to the 2 in 27.

Students hold up two sticks with 10 beans glued on each.

"Good, and show me this 2." He points to the 2 in the 12, and the students hold up two beans.

"Great," Sam smiles. He has the students demonstrate their answers to three additional problems, discusses each in detail, and then says, "When we've had enough practice with our sticks and beans to be sure that we understand these problems, we'll start practicing with the numbers by themselves. We're going to get so good at these problems that we'll be able to do them without even thinking about it."

He assigns 5 more problems and watches carefully as the students work at their desks.

Now, let's look at Sam's use of direct instruction with his students. As you read the following sections, keep the model of human memory that you first saw in Figure 7.1 (page 198) in mind to see how each of the direct instruction phases relates to different aspects of the model.

Introduction and Review. Learning begins with attention, and Sam used the attention-getting characteristics of a real-world problem to begin his lesson. He then checked students' perceptions by having them describe what the problem asked and reviewed what they had already done to retrieve prior knowledge from long-term memory. The value of this process is well established by research (Brophy, 2006c; Evertson, Anderson, Anderson, & Brophy, 1980), and it is supported by cognitive learning theory (Kirschner, Sweller, & Clark, 2006). Although its importance seems obvious, the majority of teacher lessons begin with little or no attempt to attract attention or activate relevant prior knowledge (Brophy, 2004).

Developing Understanding. An essential part of encoding procedural knowledge into long-term memory involves recognizing when and how to use a skill. The second phase addresses this need when the teacher models the skill and explains when and how it will be used. Sam modeled the skill when he said, "Now, watch what I do here," and he used cognitive modeling when he said, "When I add 5 and 2, what do I get? Let me think about that. . . . 5 and 2 are 7. Let's put a 7 on the board." His cognitive modeling was an important part of developing students' understanding (Braaksma et al., 2004).

During this phase, students acquire the declarative and conditional knowledge that allows them to adapt when applying their procedural knowledge in different conditions. When they fail to connect procedural knowledge to declarative and conditional knowledge, students apply

The developing understanding phase of direct instruction is highly interactive.

procedures mechanically or use superficial strategies, such as subtracting when they see the words "how many more" in a math problem (Jitendra et al., 2007; R. Mayer, 2008).

To see how Sam emphasized understanding, let's look at some dialogue from his lesson:

> **Sam:** So let's look again. There's an important difference between this 2 (pointing to the 2 in 27) and this 2 (pointing to the 2 in the 12). What is this difference? . . . Katrina?
>
> **Katrina:** That 2 . . . is two groups of 10, . . . and that one is just 2 by itself.
>
> **Sam:** Good, Katrina. Good work, everyone. . . . Show me this 2 (pointing to the 2 in 27).
>
> The students held up two sticks with the beans glued on them.
>
> **Sam:** Good, and show me this 2 (pointing to the 2 in the 12).

The students then held up two beans.

Sam used questioning and concrete examples throughout this phase, both of which are essential. Questioning puts students in cognitively active roles, helps break up an explanation to reduce the cognitive load on students' working memories, and promotes encoding. Concrete examples also take advantage of working memory's distributed processing capabilities.

Teachers often fail to fully develop understanding in this phase when they emphasize memorization, fail to ask enough questions, or move too quickly to practice (Rittle-Johnson & Alibali, 1999). Or, they may involve learners in hands-on activities but then fail to establish the connection between the materials, such as the sticks and beans, and the abstractions they represent (the numbers on the board) (Ball, 1992).

Guided Practice. Once students have developed an understanding of the procedure, they begin practicing with teacher assistance, which helps them begin to acquire procedural knowledge. Initially, the teacher uses questioning to provide enough scaffolding to ensure success, but not so much that challenge is reduced (Gersten, Taylor, & Graves, 1999; Rosenshine & Meister, 1992). Practice improves both long-term retention and motivation in students (Brophy, 2004). As students practice, they develop automaticity and become more confident with the new content (Péladeau, Forget, & Gagné, 2003). Sam had his students work a problem, and they discussed it carefully while he assessed their understanding. He continued with guided practice until he believed that all students were ready to work on their own.

Independent Practice. In this final phase of direct instruction, the teacher helps students gradually make the transition from consciously thinking about the skill to performing it automatically. The teacher reduces scaffolding and shifts responsibility to students. The goal is automaticity, so working memory space can be devoted to higher-level applications (Feldon, 2007a).

Teacher monitoring continues to be important. Effective teachers carefully monitor students to assess their developing understanding (Brophy, 2006c; Safer & Fleischman, 2005); less-effective teachers are more likely to merely check to see that students are on task.

Homework. Homework is a common form of independent practice, and, perhaps surprisingly, it is somewhat controversial. Some authors argue that it is ineffective and even destructive (Kohn, 2006a; 2006b). Others note that American students are assigned more homework than students in other developed countries, yet score lower in comparisons of international achievement (Baines, 2007).

However, research consistently indicates that homework, properly designed and implemented, increases both achievement and the development of self-regulation, because learners must take responsibility for completing it (H. Cooper, Robinson, & Patall, 2006; Marzano & Pickering, 2007). The feature *properly designed and used* is essential. Simply assigning homework doesn't increase achievement, and more isn't necessarily better. Increasing the amount of homework in the name of raising expectations or increasing academic requirements is ineffective at best and, at worst, can be destructive for both motivation and achievement (D. Baker & Letendre, 2005; Marzano & Pickering, 2007).

table 13.5 Characteristics of Effective Homework at the Elementary, Middle, and Secondary Levels

Level	Characteristic
All Levels	• Aligned with learning objectives and learning activities • Clear directions • High success rates • Feedback provided • Parental involvement
Elementary	• A quiet place, free from distractions, to do homework • Part of the regular class routine
Middle and Secondary	• Clear reasons for the importance of the homework • Credit, such as points toward an overall grade

The amount of effort students expend in completing homework is the primary factor influencing its effectiveness (Trautwein & Ludtke, 2007), and cognitive motivation theory helps us understand what influences effort (Trautwein, Ludtke, & Schnyder, 2006). At least three factors are involved. The first is value. As you saw in Chapter 10, "The perceived value of a task is a strong determinant of why an individual would want to become or stay engaged in an academic activity or task" (Anderman & Wolters, 2006, p. 373). If students believe that homework is valuable for increasing their understanding, they are likely to make a conscientious effort to complete it. Homework perceived as busywork or unnecessary detracts from motivation and does little to promote learning. This is particularly true for older students.

Second, students must be generally successful on the homework assignments. Success increases their perceptions of competence and self-efficacy. Third, students are much more likely to do homework if their parents expect it and monitor the extent to which it is done. Parents should also provide a quiet place to do homework that is free from distractions.

Research identifies several characteristics of effective homework (Brophy, 2006c; H. Cooper et al., 2006; Marzano & Pickering, 2007; Mulholland & Cepello, 2006). These characteristics are outlined in Table 13.5, together with developmental differences between elementary and middle/secondary students.

As you see in Table 13.5, all students need to be generally successful on homework and receive feedback on their efforts, and the homework must be clear and aligned with learning objectives. Parental support is essential at all levels. The strategies for involving parents that you studied in Chapter 12 can be effective for soliciting parental support for homework.

The study and attention skills of young children are not usually well developed, however, so a quiet place that is free from distractions is particularly important for them. Also, if the homework is part of the regular class routine, they are less likely to forget to do it. Older students are more likely to question the value of homework, and they are unlikely to complete assignments for which they receive no credit.

Finally, teachers should carefully judge the amount of homework they assign. Assigning more exercises than necessary for maximizing learning can be counterproductive and actually decrease both motivation and learning (Marzano & Pickering, 2007).

Lecture Discussion

Lecture-discussion is an instructional model designed to help students acquire organized bodies of knowledge. **Organized bodies of knowledge** are topics that connect facts, concepts, and principles, and make the relationships among them explicit (Eggen & Kauchak, 2006; Rosenshine, 1987). For example, students are acquiring organized bodies of knowledge when they engage in the following: examine relationships among plot, character, and symbolism in a novel such as *Moby Dick* in literature;, study landforms, climate, and economy in different

Lecture-discussion. An instructional model designed to help students acquire organized bodies of knowledge.

Organized bodies of knowledge. Topics that connect facts, concepts, and principles, and make the relationships among them explicit.

countries in geography; or compare parasitic and nonparasitic worms and how differences between them are reflected in their body structures in biology.

Because lecture-discussions are modifications of traditional lectures, and because lecturing is the most common teaching method, we briefly examine lectures next before turning to a discussion of lecture-discussions.

Lectures

The prevalence of the lecture as a teaching method is paradoxical. Although the most criticized of all teaching methods, it continues to be the most commonly used (Cuban, 1993). Its popularity is due in part to the following advantages:

- Lectures help students acquire information not readily accessible in other ways; lectures can be effective if the goal is to provide students with information that would take them hours to find on their own (Ausubel, 1968).
- Lectures assist students in integrating information from a variety of sources.
- Lectures expose students to different points of view.

If the teacher is trying to accomplish one or more of these goals, lectures can be effective.

Lectures have three other advantages. First, because planning time is limited to organizing content, they're efficient. Second, they're flexible—they can be applied to virtually any content area. Third, they're simple. The teacher's cognitive load is low, and all of teachers' working memory space can be devoted to organizing and presenting content. Even novice teachers can learn to deliver acceptable lectures.

Despite their ease, efficiency, and widespread use, lectures have several disadvantages:

- Lectures put learners in cognitively passive roles. This is inconsistent with cognitive views of learning and is arguably their primary disadvantage.
- Lectures don't effectively attract and maintain students' attention. We have all sat through mind-numbing lectures with a goal of simply getting the time to pass more quickly.
- Lectures don't allow teachers to check students' perceptions and developing understanding; teachers can't determine whether students are interpreting information accurately.
- While lowering the cognitive load for teachers, lectures impose a heavy cognitive load on learners, so information is often lost from working memory before it can be encoded into long-term memory.

Lectures are especially problematic for young students because of their short attention spans and limited vocabularies, and they're also ineffective if higher-order thinking is a goal. In seven studies comparing lecture to discussion, discussion was superior in all seven on measures of retention and higher-order thinking. In addition, discussion was superior in seven of nine studies on measures of student attitude and motivation (McKeachie & Kulik, 1975).

Overcoming the Weaknesses of Lectures: Lecture-Discussions

Lecture-discussions help overcome the weaknesses of lectures by interspersing systematic teacher questioning between short presentations of information.

Lecture-discussions exist in four phases:

- Introduction and review
- Presenting information
- Comprehension monitoring
- Integration

Lecture-discussion is grounded in cognitive learning theory—both the human memory model and constructivism. Table 13.6 outlines the phases of lecture-discussion and how they relate to learning theory.

Let's see how a 10th-grade American history teacher attempts to implement these phases with her students.

> Diane Anderson is discussing the events leading up to the American Revolutionary War. She begins with a review. "Where are we now?" she asks, pointing to a timeline above the chalkboard.

table 13.6 The Relationships Between Phases and Cognitive Learning Components in Lecture-Discussions

Phase	Cognitive Learning Component
Introduction and Review: The teacher begins with a form of introductory focus and reviews previous work.	• Attract attention. • Access prior knowledge from long-term memory.
Presenting Information: The teacher presents information. The teacher keeps presentations short to prevent overloading learners' working memories.	• Acquire declarative knowledge about the topic.
Comprehension Monitoring: The teacher asks a series of questions to check learners' understanding.	• Check students' perceptions. • Put students in cognitively active roles. • Begin schema construction.
Integration: The teacher asks additional questions to help learners integrate new and prior knowledge.	• Construct integrated schemas that organize information and reduce cognitive load.

"About there," Adam responds, pointing to the middle of the 1700s.

"Good," Diane smiles. "We're almost to the Revolutionary War. However, we want to understand what happened before that time, so we're going to go back to the early 1600s. When we're finished today, we'll see that the Revolutionary War didn't just happen; there were events that led up to it that made it almost inevitable.

"For instance, the conflicts between the British and the French in America became so costly for the British that they began policies in the colonies that ultimately led to the Revolution. That's what we want to look at today."

She then begins, "We know that the British established Jamestown in 1607, but we haven't really looked at French expansion into the New World. Let's look again at the map. Here we see Jamestown, but at about the same time, a French explorer named Champlain came down the St. Lawrence River and formed Quebec City, here. . . . Over the years, at least 35 of the 50 states were discovered or mapped by the French, and they founded several of our big cities, such as Detroit, St. Louis, New Orleans, and Des Moines," she continues pointing to a series of locations she had marked on the map.

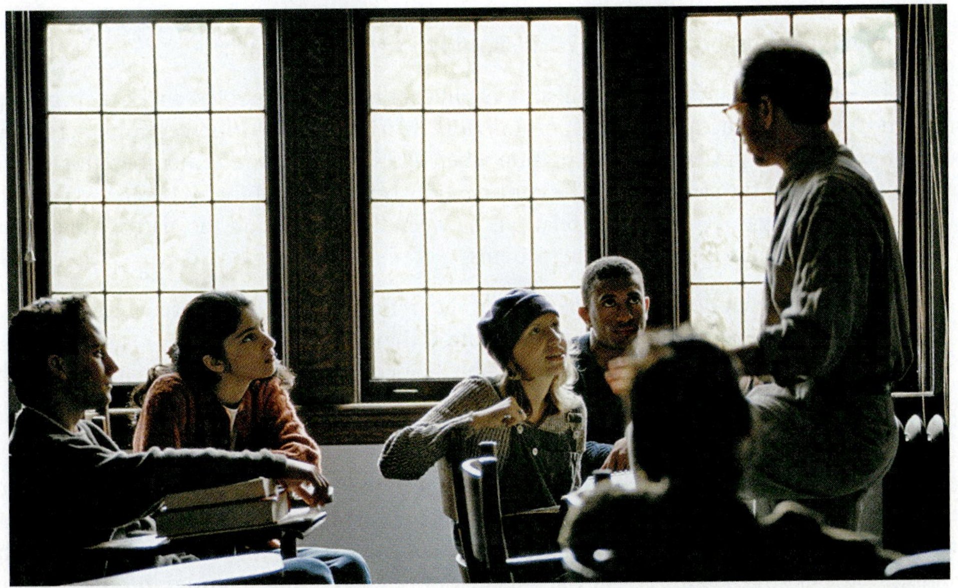

Lecture-discussions help overcome the weaknesses of lectures by promoting social interaction.

"Now, what do you notice about the location of the two groups?"

". . . The French had a lot of Canada, . . . and it looks like this country, too," Alfredo offers as he points to the north and west on the map.

"It looks like the east was British, and the west was French," Troy adds.

"Yes, and remember, this was all happening at about the same time," Diane continues. "Also, the French were more friendly with the Native Americans than the British. The French had what they called a seigniorial system, where the settlers were given land if they would serve in the military. So, . . . what does this suggest about the military power of the French?"

"Probably powerful," Josh suggests. "The people got land if they went in the army."

"And the Native Americans probably helped, because they were friendly with the French," Tenisha adds.

"Now, what else do you notice here?" Diane asks, moving her hand up and down the width of the map.

"Mountains?" Danielle answers uncertainly.

"Yes, exactly. . . . Why are they important?"

". . . The British were sort of fenced in, and the French could do as they pleased."

"Good. And now the plot thickens. The British needed land and wanted to expand. So they headed west over the mountains and guess who they ran into? . . . Sarah?"

"The French?" Sarah responds.

"Right! And conflict broke out. Now, when the French and British were fighting, why do you suppose the French were initially more successful than the British?. . . Dan?"

"Well, they had that sig . . . seigniorial system, so they were more eager to fight, because of the land and everything."

"Other thoughts? . . . Bette?"

"I think that the Native Americans were part of it. The French got along better with them, so they helped the French."

"Okay, good, now let's think about some of the advantages of the British."

Let's look now at Diane's use of lecture-discussion. She introduced the lesson with a review and attempted to capture students' attention by creating a link between the French and Indian war and the Revolutionary war. Then, she presented information about Jamestown, Quebec, and French settlements in the present-day United States. After this brief presentation, she used questioning to involve her students in the comprehension-monitoring phase. To illustrate, let's review a brief portion of the lesson.

Diane: Now, what do you notice about the location of the two groups?
Alfredo: The French had a lot of Canada, . . . and it looks like this country, too (pointing to the north and west on the map).
Troy: It looks like the east was . . . British, and the west was French.

Diane's questions were intended to put students in cognitively active roles, check their perceptions, and begin the process of schema production. Satisfied that their perceptions were accurate, she returned to presenting information when she said, "Yes, and remember, this was all happening at about the same time." She continued by briefly describing the French seignorial system and pointing out the friendly relations between the French and the Native Americans.

Then she again turned back to the students.

Diane: So, . . . what does this suggest about the military power of the French?
Josh: Probably powerful. The people got land if they went in the army.
Tenisha: And the Native Americans probably helped, because they were friendly with the French.

The two segments appear similar, but there is an important distinction. In the first, Diane was monitoring comprehension; students' responses to the question, "Now, what do you notice about the location of the two groups?" helped her assess their perceptions of what she had presented in the first segment. In the second, she attempted to promote schema production by helping students integrate the seignorial system with French military power and the relationship between the French and the Native Americans.

After completing this cycle of presenting information, monitoring comprehension, and integration, she would repeat the process, with the second integration being broader than the first. Diane's goal for the entire lesson was the development of complex schemas that would represent the students' understanding of the cause–effect relationships between the French and Indian Wars and the American Revolutionary War.

The effectiveness of lecture-discussions depends on the quality of the discussions during the lesson. Because students construct their own knowledge, the schemas they construct won't necessarily mirror the teacher's organization of the body of knowledge. Brief discussions allow the teacher to assess the process of schema construction and help students reconstruct their understanding when necessary. This is a primary reason lecture-discussion is more effective than traditional lecture.

Guided Discovery

Guided discovery is a model of instruction that involves teachers' scaffolding students' constructions of concepts and the relationships among them (Eggen & Kauchak, 2006; R. Mayer, 2008). When using the model, a teacher identifies learning objectives, arranges information so that patterns can be found, and guides students to the objectives (R. C. Clark & Mayer, 2003; Moreno, 2004).

Guided discovery. A model of instruction that involves teachers' scaffolding students' construction of concepts and the relationships among them.

Guided discovery is sometimes misunderstood, leaving teachers with the belief that students should be essentially on their own to "discover" the ideas being taught (Kirschner et al., 2006). This isn't true. Guided discovery (and other forms of learner-centered instruction, e.g., inquiry and problem-based learning) is highly scaffolded, and the teacher plays an essential role in guiding the students' learning progress (Hmelo-Silver, Duncan, & Chinn, 2007; Schmidt, Loyens, van Gog, & Paas, 2007).

Unstructured discovery consists of learning activities in which students receive limited scaffolding. Research indicates that giving students minimal guidance during learning activities often leaves students frustrated, allows them to form misconceptions, and wastes time (R. C. Clark & Mayer, 2003; Kirschner et al., 2006; R. Mayer, 2002, 2004). As a result, unstructured discovery is rarely seen in today's classrooms, except in student projects and investigations.

When done well, research supports guided discovery's effectiveness (R. Mayer, 2008; R. E. Mayer & Wittrock, 2006). "Guided discovery may take more or less time than expository instruction, depending on the task, but tends to result in better long-term retention and transfer than expository instruction" (R. Mayer, 2002, p. 68).

When using guided discovery, teachers spend less time explaining and more time asking questions, so students have more opportunities to share thinking and place their developing understanding into words (Dean & Kuhn, 2007; Moreno & Duran, 2004). Also, because guided discovery promotes high levels of student involvement, it also tends to increase students' intrinsic interest in the topics they study (Lutz, Guthrie, & Davis, 2006).

Guided discovery occurs in five phases:

- Introduction and review
- The open-ended phase
- The convergent phase
- Closure
- Application

Guided discovery is grounded in cognitive theories of learning, including the human memory model and social constructivism. Table 13.7 outlines the phases of guided discovery and their related learning components.

Scott's lesson on Bernoulli's principle on pages 399 and 400 is an application of guided discovery. You might want to read it again before studying the following sections. Let's look now at Scott's application of the phases.

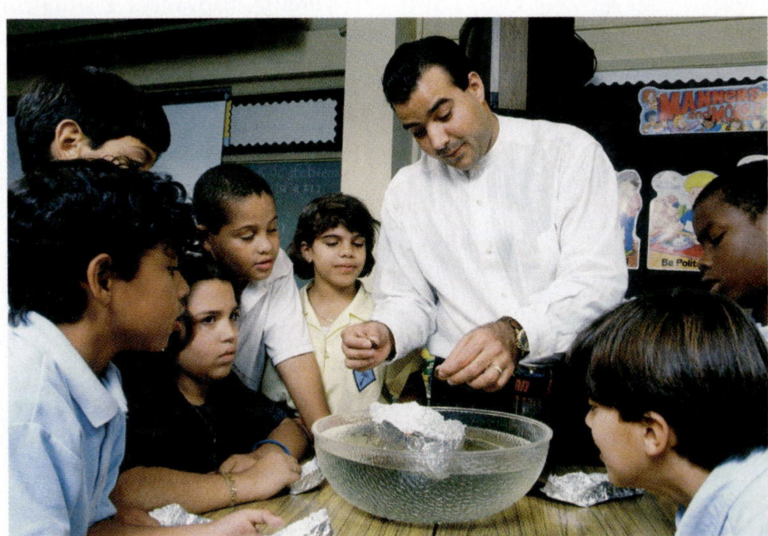

Guided discovery can increase students' intrinsic interest in the topics being studied.

table 13.7 The Relationships Between Phases and Cognitive Learning Components in Guided Discovery

Phase	Cognitive Learning Component
Introduction and Review: The teacher begins with a form of introductory focus and reviews previous work.	• Attract attention. • Activate prior knowledge.
The Open-Ended Phase: The teacher provides examples and asks for observations and comparisons.	• Provide experiences from which learners will construct knowledge. • Promote social interaction.
The Convergent Phase: The teacher guides students as they search for patterns in the examples.	• Begin schema production. • Promote social interaction.
Closure: With the teacher's guidance, students state a definition of the concept or a description of the relationship among concepts.	• Complete schema production.
Application: The teacher has students use the concept or principle to explain another (ideally) real-world example.	• Promote transfer.

Introduction and Review. Scott began his lesson by reviewing the concept of force and the principle "Objects move in the direction of a greater force." The review activated students' prior knowledge, and the examples he used in his review, such as pushing on the board, and tugging on the stapler, attracted students' attention.

The Open-Ended Phase. Scott implemented the open-ended phase when he had students blow over the pieces of paper, between the papers, and through the necks of the funnels. Each was an example that illustrated Bernoulli's principle. After his students worked with each example, Scott asked for observations, such as, "What did you notice when we blew over the top? . . . David?" and "What did you notice here? . . . Sharon?" The open-ended questions promoted active involvement and helped students begin the process of schema production.

The Convergent Phase. The convergent phase continues to capitalize on social interaction and advances schema construction. Scott began the transition to the convergent phase when he drew the sketches on the board and had students restate the observations and conclusions. Let's look again at some dialogue that illustrates this process.

Scott: Was I blowing on the top or the bottom? . . . Rachel? (Referring to the first sketch)
Rachel: The top.
Scott: And what happened there?. . . Heather?
Heather: The paper rose up.

Scott did a similar analysis with the second and third example and then guided the students as they formed conclusions.

Scott: Let's think about the forces acting on these (turning back to the first sketch). What forces are acting on the paper?. . . Colin?
Colin: Gravity.
Scott: And which direction is gravity pulling?
Colin: Down.
Scott: What other force is acting on the paper?. . . William?
William: Air (pointing up).
Scott: How do you know it's pushing up?
William: The paper moved up.

Scott guided a similar analysis of the second and third example, and the lesson then moved to closure. Teacher guidance in the form of questions and prompts is essential if students are to reach the learning objectives (Moreno, 2004; Moreno & Duran, 2004).

Closure. Closure completes the process of schema production by identifying the content objective. Scott moved toward closure when he said, "Now let's look at the forces and where we blew. Study the drawings carefully, and see what kind of relationship exists between the two." Students are then scaffolded as they attempt to put their understanding into words. Language is a learning and development tool, and practice in articulating understanding during closure is an essential part of the process.

Closure is particularly important when using guided discovery because the instruction is less explicit and the direction the lesson is taking is less obvious than it is with either direct instruction or lecture discussion. Articulating the definition of a concept or stating the principle, as was the case in Scott's lesson, helps eliminate uncertainty that may remain in students' thinking.

Several of the lessons you've already studied used guided discovery to varying degrees, such as Jenny Newhall's in Chapter 2 (page 56), and Diane Smith's (page 116) and Teri Hall's (page 121), both in Chapter 4. You may want to refer again to these case studies as additional examples of guided discovery.

MyEducationLab

To analyze a fifth-grade teacher's attempt to use the guided-discovery model with her students, go to the *Activities and Applications* section in Chapter 13 of MyEducationLab at www.myeducationlab.com, and watch the video episode *Guided Discovery in an Elementary Classroom.* Answer the questions following the episode.

Application. Application is essential for promoting transfer. Scott, for example, attempted to promote transfer by having students use Bernoulli's principle to explain how airplanes are able to fly. He showed his students the following drawing, and then guided the class to conclude that the curvature of the wing made the air flow more rapidly over the top, so the pressure above the wing was lower than the pressure below the wing, enabling planes to fly.

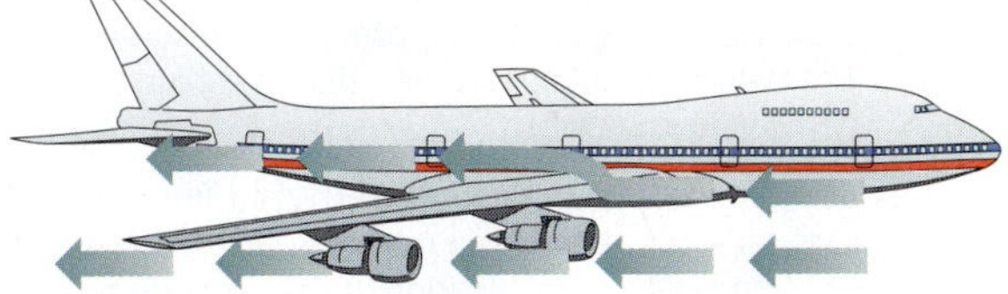

Cooperative Learning

Cooperative learning is a set of instructional models in which students work in mixed-ability groups to reach specific learning and social interaction objectives. Cooperative learning is grounded in Vygotsky's (1978, 1986) work, with its emphasis on social interaction as a mechanism for promoting cognitive development. Research suggests that groups of learners co-construct more powerful understanding than individuals do alone (R. Anderson et al., 2001; Hadjioannou, 2007; Y. Li et al., 2007). This co-constructed knowledge can then be appropriated and internalized by individuals.

Cooperative learning. A set of instructional models in which students work in mixed-ability groups to reach specific learning and social interaction objectives.

Cooperative learning can also increase motivation. When implemented effectively, it involves all students, which can be difficult in large groups. Less confident students may have few chances to participate in whole-class discussions, so they often drift off.

Several of the teachers in cases you've already studied used cooperative learning as part of their instruction: for example, Jan Davis in Chapter 1 (page 3), David Shelton (page 196) and Sue Southam (page 222) in Chapter 7, and Jenny Newhall (page 225) and Scott Sowell (page 249) in Chapter 8. It has become one of the most widely used approaches to instruction in schools today; one study found that over 90 percent of elementary teachers used some form of cooperative learning in their classrooms (Antil, Jenkins, Wayne, & Vadasy, 1998). However, many teachers equate any form of getting students into groups with cooperative learning, and they tend to ignore research about essential components that promote learning (E. Cohen, 1994; D. W. Johnson & Johnson, 2006).

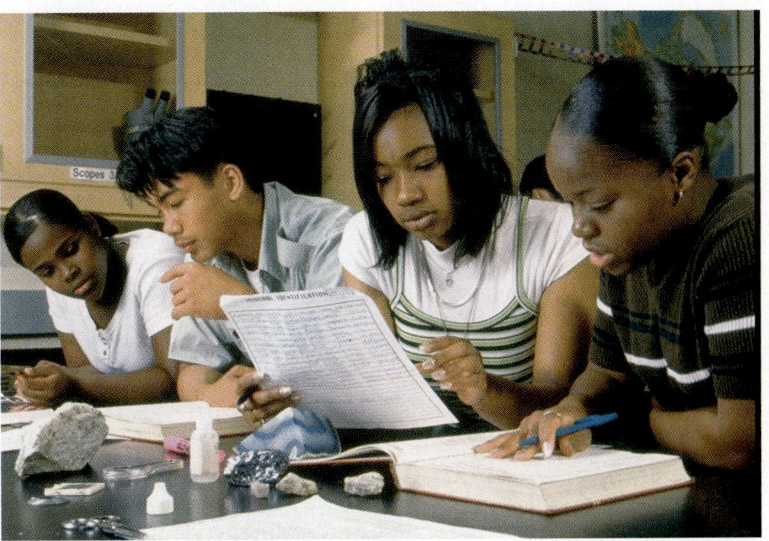

Cooperative learning activities encourage knowledge construction through social interaction.

Although a single view doesn't exist, most researchers agree that cooperative learning consists of students working together in groups small enough (typically two to five) so

exploring diversity

Using Cooperative Learning to Capitalize on Diversity in Your Classroom

Although important for constructing knowledge, social interaction doesn't always occur naturally and comfortably; people tend to be wary of those different from themselves. Common in social settings, this tendency also occurs in classrooms. Students of specific ethnic groups tend to spend most of their time together, so they don't learn that all of us are much more alike than we are different (Juvonen, 2006; Okagaki, 2006).

Teachers can't mandate tolerance, trust, and friendship among students from different backgrounds; they need additional tools, and cooperative learning can be one of them. Students working in cooperative groups improve their social skills, accept students with exceptionalities, and develop friendships and positive attitudes toward others who differ in achievement, ethnicity, and gender (D. W. Johnson & Johnson, 2006; Vaughn & Bos, 2006).

The benefits of student cooperation stem from four factors:

- Students with different backgrounds work together.
- Group members have equal status.
- Students learn about each other as individuals.
- The teacher emphasizes the value of cooperation among all students. (Slavin, 1995)

As learners work together, they frequently find that they have much in common. Let's see how Olivia Costa, an eighth-grade math teacher, attempts to improve communication in her classroom.

As Olivia watches her students work, she is both pleased and uneasy. They've improved a great deal in their math, but there is little mixing among her minority and nonminority students—and among other groups as well. She worries about six children from Central and South America who are struggling with English and four students with exceptionalities who leave her class every day for extra help.

To promote a more cohesive atmosphere, Olivia spends time over the weekend, organizing students into groups of four, with equal numbers of high- and low-ability students in each group. She also mixes students by ethnicity and gender, and she makes sure that no group has more than one student for whom English is a second language or more than one student with an exceptionality.

On Monday she explains how they are to work together. To introduce the process, she sits with one group and models cooperation and support for the others. After she finishes a lesson on problem solving, she sends the groups to different parts of the room for seat work. Each student in each group solves a problem and then shares his or her answer with groupmates. If they cannot solve the problem, or resolve differences, Olivia intervenes. She carefully monitors the groups to be sure that each student first attempts the problems before conferring with others.

Monitoring the groups is demanding, but her first session is fairly successful. "Phew," she thinks to herself at the end of the day. "This isn't any easier, but it already seems better."

Let's look at Olivia's efforts in more detail. First, because her objective was to promote interpersonal relationships, she organized the groups so that high- and low-ability students, boys and girls, members of minorities and nonminorities, and students with and without exceptionalities were represented equally. One of the most common mistakes that beginning teachers make is to let students form their own groups.

Second, knowing that effective interaction must be planned and taught, she modeled desired behaviors, such as being supportive, listening, asking questions, and staying on task. Teachers can also directly teach interaction strategies or use role-plays and videotapes of effective groups to help students learn cooperation skills (Blatchford et al., 2006; Vaughn, Bos, Candace, & Schumm, 2006). These skills are especially important for students from minority groups, who are often hesitant about seeking and giving help.

Third, she used an adaptation of the cooperative learning model *Student Teams Achievement Divisions* to promote cooperation and communication, and finally, she carefully monitored the students while they worked. Initial training, alone, won't ensure cooperation. Groups need constant monitoring and support, particularly with young children and when cooperative learning is first introduced (Blatchford et al., 2006; Vaughn et al., 2006). If problems persist, teachers may need to reconvene the class for additional training.

MyEducationLab

To analyze another teacher's application of models of instruction, go to the *Activities and Applications* section in Chapter 13 of MyEducationLab at www.myeducationlab.com, and read the case study *Models of Instruction.* Answer the questions following the case study.

that everyone can participate in a clearly assigned task (E. Cohen, 1994; D. W. Johnson & Johnson, 2006; Slavin, 1995). Cooperative learning also shares four other features:

- Learning objectives direct the groups' activities.
- Learning activities require social interaction.
- Teachers hold students individually accountable for their understanding.
- Learners depend on one another to reach objectives.

The last characteristic, called *positive interdependence* (D. W. Johnson & Johnson, 2006) or *reciprocal interdependence* (E. Cohen, 1994), is important because it emphasizes the role of peer cooperation in learning. Accountability is also essential because it keeps students focused on the objectives and reminds them that learning is the purpose of the activity (Antil et al., 1998; Slavin, 1995).

Unlike the first three models we discussed, cooperative learning activities don't follow a specific set of steps. However, successful implementation of cooperative learning activities requires careful thought and planning. We examine factors influencing its success in the following sections.

Introducing Cooperative Learning

Introducing students to cooperative learning requires careful planning (Blatchford, Baines, Rubie-Davies, Bassett, & Chowne, 2006; Saleh, Lazonder, & Jong, 2007). Poorly organized activities can result in less learning than whole-group lessons.

Suggestions for initially planning and organizing cooperative learning activities include the following:

- Seat group members together, so they can move back and forth from group work to whole-class activities with little disruption.
- Have materials ready for easy distribution to each group.
- Introduce students to cooperative learning with short, simple tasks, and make objectives and directions clear.
- Specify the amount of time available to accomplish the task (and keep it relatively short).
- Monitor groups while they work.
- Require that students produce a product, such as written answers to specific questions, as an outcome of the activity.

Each of the teachers' lessons mentioned earlier illustrated these characteristics. In all cases, the teachers seated the groups together, the task was clear and specific, the teachers required students to write conclusions, and the teachers carefully monitored group progress.

Cooperative Learning Models

Social constructivism provides the framework for all forms of cooperative learning, but each accomplishes different objectives. Some of the more widely used cooperative learning models are outlined in Table 13.8.

Other cooperative learning strategies exist, and although they differ in format, all incorporate the suggestions described earlier. As with all instruction, no single cooperative learning model can reach all learning objectives, and cooperative learning should not be overused.

Putting Cooperative Learning into Perspective

Research examining cooperative learning suggests that it can increase student achievement, improve problem-solving abilities and attitude toward their coursework, and improve communication and interpersonal skills (Gao, Losh, Shen, Turner, & Yuan, 2007; Keefer et al., 2000; Roseth et al., 2007).

table 13.8 Cooperative Learning Models

Model	Description	Example
Reciprocal Questioning	Pairs work together to ask and answer questions about a lesson or text.	Teacher provides question stems, such as "Summarize . . ." or "Why was . . . important?" and students use the stems to create specific questions about the topic.
Scripted Cooperation	Pairs work together to elaborate on each other's thinking.	Math: First member of a pair offers a problem solution. The second member then elaborates, and the process is repeated. Reading: Pairs read a passage, and the first member offers a summary. The second elaborates, and the process continues.
Jigsaw II	Individuals become expert on subsections of a topic and teach it to others in their group.	One student studies the geography of a region, another the economy, a third the climate. Each attends "expert" meetings, and the "experts" then teach the content to others in their group.
Student Teams Achievement Divisions (STAD)	Social interaction helps students learn facts, concepts, and skills.	The independent practice phase of direct instruction is replaced with team study, during which team members check and compare their answers. Team study is followed by quizzes, and individual improvement points lead to team awards.

classroom connections

Using Models of Instruction Effectively in Your Classroom

Direct Instruction

1. Direct instruction includes an introduction and review, a phase for developing understanding, and guided and independent practice. Emphasize understanding, and provide practice to develop automaticity.
   - **Elementary:** A fourth-grade teacher, in a lesson on possessives, first explains the difference between singular and plural possessives, and then asks students to punctuate the following sentences.

     The students books were lost when he forgot them on the bus.

     The students books were lost when they left them on the playground.

     Who can describe the boys adventure when he went to the zoo?

     Who can describe the boys adventure when they swam in the river?

     He then has students write paragraphs that incorporate both singular and plural possessives.
   - **Middle School:** In a unit on percentages and decimals, a math teacher comments that the star quarterback for the state university completed 14 of 21 passes in the last game. "What does that mean? Is that good or bad? Was it better than the 12 of 17 passes completed by the opposing quarterback?" she asks. She then explains how to calculate the percentages with the class and then has the students practice finding percentages in other real-world problems.
   - **High School:** A ninth-grade geography teacher helps his students locate the longitude and latitude of their city by "walking them through" the process, using a map and a series of specific questions. He then has them practice finding the longitude and latitude of other cities, as well as finding the major city nearest sets of longitude and latitude locations.

Lecture Discussion

2. Lecture discussions include an introduction and review, a phase where information is presented, a comprehension check and integration. Keep presentations short and use high levels of interaction to maintain students' attention and promote schema production.
   - **Elementary:** A first-grade teacher wants her students to know similarities and differences between farm animals and pets. To do this, she constructs a large chart with pictures of both. As they discuss the two groups of animals, she continually asks students to identify similarities and differences between the two groups.
   - **Middle School:** An American history teacher discussing immigration in the 19th and early 20th centuries compares immigrant groups of the past with today's Cuban population in Miami, Florida, and Mexican immigrants in San Antonio, Texas. He asks students to summarize similarities and differences between the two groups with respect to the difficulties they encounter and the rates of assimilation into the American way of life.
   - **High School:** A biology teacher is presenting information related to transport of liquids in and out of cells, identifying and illustrating several of the concepts in the process. After about 3 minutes, she stops presenting information and asks, "Suppose a cell is in a hypotonic solution in one case and a hypertonic solution in another. What's the difference between the two? What would happen to the cell in each case?"

Guided Discovery

3. When teachers use guided discovery, they present students with examples and guide students' knowledge construction. Provide examples that include all the information students need to understand the topic, and guide student interaction.
   - **Elementary:** A fifth-grade teacher begins a unit on reptiles by bringing a snake and turtle to class. He includes colored pictures of lizards, alligators, and sea turtles. He has students describe the animals and pictures and then guides them to an understanding of the essential characteristics of reptiles.
   - **Middle School:** A seventh-grade English teacher embeds examples of singular and plural possessive nouns in the context of a paragraph. She then guides the discussion as students develop explanations for why particular sentences are punctuated the way they are, for example, "The girls' and boys' accomplishments in the middle school were noteworthy, as were the children's efforts in the elementary school."
   - **High School:** A world history teacher presents students with vignettes such as

     You're part of an archeological team, and at one site you've found some spear points. In spite of their ages, the points are still quite sharp, having been chipped precisely from hard stone. You also see several cattle and sheep skulls and some threads that appear to be the remains of coarsely woven fabric.

     He then guides the students to conclude that the artifacts best represent a New Stone Age society.

Cooperative Learning

4. Cooperative learning requires that students work together to reach learning objectives. Provide clear directions for groups, and carefully monitor students as they work.
   - **Elementary:** A second-grade teacher begins the school year by having groups work together on short word problems in math. When students fail to cooperate, she stops the groups and immediately discusses the issues with the class.
   - **Middle School:** A life-science teacher has students create and answer questions about the characteristics, organelles, and environments of one-celled animals. He periodically offers suggestions to the pairs to help them ask more meaningful questions.
   - **High School:** A geometry teacher has pairs use scripted cooperation to solve proofs. When they struggle, she offers hints to help them continue to make progress.

5. Because of its emphasis on group interdependence, cooperative learning can promote healthy interactions between students from different backgrounds. Use cooperative learning groups to capitalize on the richness that learner diversity brings to classrooms, and design tasks that require group cooperation.
   - **Elementary:** A second-grade teacher waits until the third week of the school year to form cooperative learning groups. During that time, she observes her students and gathers information about their interests, talents, and friendships. She then uses the information in making decisions about group membership.
   - **Middle School:** A sixth-grade math teacher uses cooperative learning groups to practice word problems. He organizes the class into pairs, forming, whenever possible, pairs that are composed of a minority and nonminority student, a student with and a student without an exceptionality, and a boy and a girl.
   - **High School:** An English teacher has students work in groups of four to provide feedback on one another's writing. The teacher organizes all groups so that they're composed of equal numbers of boys, girls, minorities and nonminorities, and students who do and do not have exceptionalities.

developmentally appropriate practice

Using Models of Instruction with Different-Aged Learners

While the models of instruction discussed in this section can be used at all levels, adaptations are necessary to accommodate developmental differences in students. The following paragraphs outline some suggestions for responding to these developmental differences.

Working with Elementary Students

Because it is effective for teaching basic skills, direct instruction is probably the most widely used instructional model in the lower elementary grades. When using direct instruction with young children, the *developing understanding* and *guided practice* phases are crucial because they lay a foundation for independent practice. Monitoring learner progress during guided practice and spending extra time with lower achievers while the majority of the students are practicing independently is an effective adaptation with young children.

Lecture-discussions should be used sparingly with young children because of their short attention spans and lack of prior knowledge. Periods of explaining must be kept short and combined with frequent episodes of comprehension monitoring for young children. Models other than lecture-discussion are often more effective with these students.

Guided discovery can be particularly effective with young children if the goal is for them to understand topics that teachers can illustrate with concrete examples, such as *crustaceans, fractions,* or *parts of speech*. When using guided discovery with young children, teachers should verbally link examples to the concept being taught and emphasize new terms.

Young children need a great deal of scaffolding and practice to work effectively in groups. Clearly describing procedures for turning in materials and participating in the activities is also crucial.

Working with Middle School Students

In middle schools, direct instruction is an effective model for learning procedural skills that require practice, such as in pre-algebra, algebra, and language arts. As with younger students, the *developing understanding,* and *guided practice* phases are essential for the success of the activity.

Guided discovery is one of the most effective models with middle school students, but rules about treating each other with courtesy and respect during the activities is important with these students. If teachers use high-quality examples, middle school students are capable of learning more abstract concepts such as *symmetric and asymmetric body structures* in life science or *culture* in social students. Guided discovery continues to be an effective model for teaching concepts that can be represented with concrete examples.

Cooperative learning can be effectively used to complement direct instruction, as Olivia Costa did with her eighth graders. Cooperative learning can also help middle school students meet social goals and develop communication skills, perspective taking, and collaboration.

Lecture-discussion can be effective for teaching organized bodies of knowledge in science, literature, and social studies.

Working with High School Students

High school students typically pose fewer management challenges than younger students, but their greater willingness to sit passively can be a problem. Using lecture-discussions as an alternative to pure lectures is desirable.

Each of the other models can also be effective as instructional alternatives, depending on the teacher's goals. High school students are often familiar with the other models, as they've encountered them in earlier grades. Frequent monitoring is still needed to keep lessons on track and aligned with learning objectives.

On the other hand, simply putting students into groups doesn't ensure either increased achievement or improved motivation. For instance, when students are organized into mixed-ability groups, those with higher ability often feel they are being exploited by slackers and, in fact, frequently prefer to work alone instead of in groups (Su, 2007). Further, average-ability students often do not take advantage of learning in mixed-ability groups because high-ability students tend to dominate the group interaction (Saleh et al., 2007).

These results have two implications for teachers. First, careful planning is as important for cooperative learning as it is for any other model. For instance, when teachers give students explicit instructions for collaboration, such as ensuring that they solicit comments from everyone in the groups, interaction improves (Saleh et al., 2007). Second, group grading (grading in which all students in groups receive the same grade) should be avoided; individual accountability is essential (Su, 2007).

As with any model, when well done, cooperative learning can be effective for reaching a variety of goals, and careful planning and implementation are essential to ensure that it is effective.

check your understanding

3.1 Using the essential teaching skills as a basis, explain why the introduction phase is important in direct instruction, lecture-discussion, and guided discovery.

3.2 Which phase of direct instruction is most important for ensuring successful independent practice? Explain.

3.3 We said, "When done well, guided discovery's effectiveness is supported by research." What is necessary for instruction to be "done well"? Explain.

3.4 A teacher places her third graders in groups of three, gives each group magnets and a packet including a dime, spoon, aluminum foil, rubber band, wooden pencil, paper clip, and nails. She tells the groups to experiment with the magnets and items for 10 minutes and write three differences between objects that are and are not attracted to magnets. As they work, she answers questions and makes comments. The class as a whole group discusses the results. How effectively did the teacher introduce cooperative learning to her students? Cite evidence from the example to support your conclusion.

To receive feedback for these questions, go to Appendix A.

Assessment and Learning: Using Assessment as a Learning Tool

Assessment is the third point in the planning–implementing–assessing cycle. Let's see how Scott's assessment contributed to learning for his students. The following is an item on his Friday quiz and the students' responses to it.

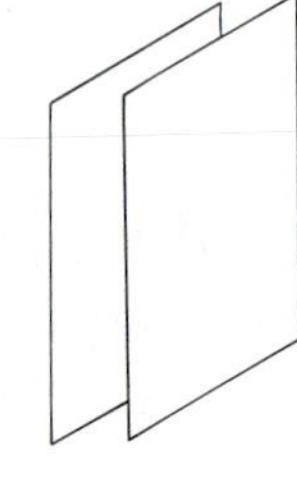

> Look at the drawing that represents the two pieces of paper that we used in the lesson. Explain what made the papers move together. Make a drawing that shows how the air flowed as you blew between the papers. Label the forces in the drawing as we did during the lesson.
>
> Shown here are two students' sketches of the flow of air between the papers:

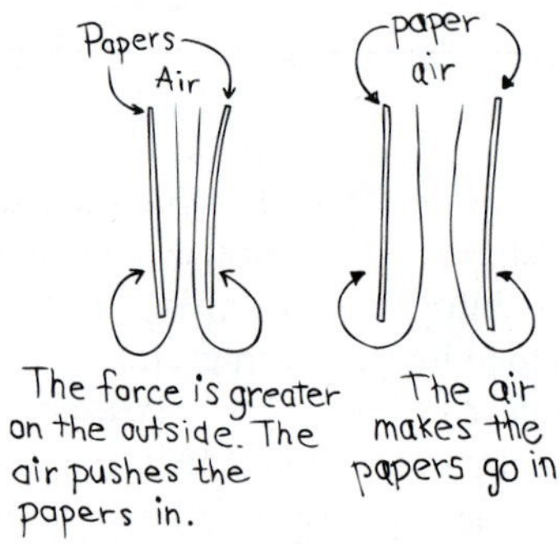

The students' responses illustrate an essential characteristic of effective assessments: *Assessments must provide information about students' thinking* (Stiggins, 2007). For instance, the responses pictured here show that two students correctly concluded that the force (pressure)

on the outside of the papers pushing in was greater than the force (pressure) between the papers pushing out. This doesn't provide a great deal of evidence about their understanding, however, because the lesson emphasized this conclusion.

The students' drawings of the air flow combined with their explanations are more revealing. They concluded that the moving air curled around the bottoms of the papers and pushed the papers together, which indicates a misconception. (The papers moved together because increasing the speed of the air over a surface [in this case over the surface of the papers] decreases the pressure the air exerts on the surface [the papers], and the still air on the outside of the papers pushes them together, as illustrated in the sketch here. This is an application of Bernoulli's principle.)

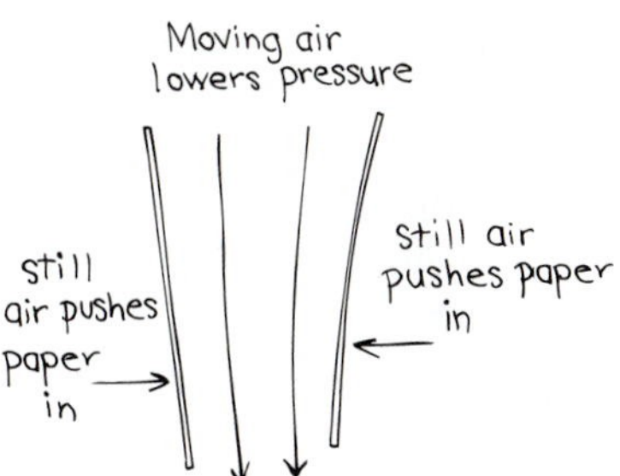

If Scott's assessment hadn't asked for both an explanation and a drawing, he might not have learned that his students left the lesson with misconceptions.

Assessments such as these provide opportunities for teachers to directly address student misconceptions. For instance, a detailed discussion of these responses together with additional examples (demonstrating that air exerts pressure in all directions and that all objects, including air particles, move in a straight line unless a force acts on them) would greatly expand the students' understanding of basic principles in science. In fact, teaching these principles after the assessment likely produces more learning than trying to teach them beforehand, because the students' responses to the assessment provide both motivation and context for learning. Ideally, all assessments provide similar opportunities to extend learning. We examine these ideas in detail in the next chapter.

check your understanding

4.1 Identify two essential characteristics of effective assessments.

4.2 Identify the essential teaching skill that teachers must use in conjunction with assessments in order for the assessments to increase student learning.

4.3 An English teacher wants his students to use figurative language, such as similes, metaphors, and personification in their writing. He gives them several examples of each, and then he gives them a quiz on which they must identify additional examples of figurative language. Evaluate his assessment with respect to its effectiveness.

To receive feedback for these questions, go to Appendix A.

Meeting Your Learning Objectives

1. Describe essential components of planning for instruction.
   - When planning for instruction, teachers must identify topics that are important for students to learn, specify learning objectives, prepare and organize learning activities, and design assessments.
   - When planning for instruction based on standards, teachers first need to interpret the standard and then design learning activities to help students meet the standard and assessments to determine whether the standard has been met.
2. Describe essential teaching skills, and explain why they are important.
   - Essential teaching skills are the abilities and attitudes that all effective teachers possess. These attitudes include high personal teaching efficacy—the belief that they are responsible for student learning and can increase it. The attitudes also include caring, modeling, enthusiasm, and high expectations for student achievement and behavior.
   - Essential abilities include the ability to organize efficiently, communicate clearly, attract and maintain student attention, provide informative feedback, and deliver succinct reviews.
   - Questioning is one of the most important essential teaching skills. Characteristics of effective questioning include high frequency and equitable distribution of questions, prompts when students can't answer, and sufficient time for students to think about their answers.
3. Explain the relationships between essential teaching skills and models of instruction, and analyze the components of different models.
   - *Essential teaching skills* support and are incorporated in all models of instruction.

- *Direct instruction* is an instructional model designed to teach knowledge and essential skills that students need for later learning. Teachers conduct direct instruction in four phases: (a) introduction and review, to attract students' attention and activate prior knowledge; (b) developing understanding, to acquire declarative knowledge about the skill; (c) guided practice, to begin the development of procedural knowledge; and (d) independent practice, to further develop the skill to automaticity.
- *Lecture-discussion* is an instructional model designed to help students acquire organized bodies of knowledge. It consists of (a) an introduction and review, to attract attention and activate prior knowledge; (b) presenting information, to provide knowledge; (c) comprehension monitoring, to check students' perceptions; and (d) integration, to promote schema production.
- *Guided discovery* is an instructional model that helps students learn concepts and the relationships among them. It consists of (a) an introduction and review, to attract students' attention and activate prior knowledge; (b) an open-ended phase in which students make observations of examples; (c) a convergent phase in which teachers identify patterns and begin schema production; (d) closure, when teachers complete schema production and clarify the learning objective; and (e) application, which helps promote transfer.
- *Cooperative learning* is a set of instructional models that uses group interaction to reach specified learning objectives. Teachers hold learners individually accountable for understanding, and learners must depend on each other to reach the objectives.

4. Identify the essential characteristics of effective assessments.
   - Productive learning environments are assessment centered. This means that assessment is an integral part of the learning–teaching process and that assessments are aligned with objectives and learning activities.
   - Effective assessments provide teachers with information about students' thinking and aren't limited to determining whether or not students get answers correct.
   - Effective assessments provide opportunities for increasing students' understanding through detailed feedback and discussion. Discussion following assessments often increases understanding as much or more than the learning activity itself.

Developing as a Professional: Preparing for Your Licensure Exam

In this chapter, you saw how Scott Sowell planned his lesson, demonstrated essential teaching skills, and assessed his students' learning. Let's look now at a teacher working with a class of ninth-grade geography students. As you read the case study, consider the extent to which the teacher applied the information you've studied in this chapter in her lesson. Read the case study, and answer the questions that follow.

Judy Holmquist, a ninth-grade geography teacher, has her students involved in a unit on climate regions of the United States. The class has worked in groups to gather information about the geography, economy, ethnic groups, and future issues in Florida, California, New York, and Alaska, and the students have entered the information on a matrix. The first two columns of the matrix are shown on the next page.

In today's lesson, Judy wants her students to understand how the geography of each region influenced its economy.

As the bell signaling the beginning of the class stops ringing, Judy refers students to the matrix, which she has hung at the front of the classroom. She reminds them they will be looking for similarities and differences in the information about the states, organizes the students into pairs, and begins, "I want you to get with your partner and write down three differences and three similarities that you see in the geography portion of the chart."

As groups begin their work, Judy moves around the classroom, answering questions and making brief suggestions.

A few minutes later, she calls the students back together. "You look like you're doing a good job. . . . Okay, I think we're ready."

"Okay, go ahead Jackie," Judy begins, pointing to the chart.

"Mmm, they all have mountains except for Florida."

"Okay, they all have mountains except for Florida," Judy repeats and writes the information under "Similarities" on the chalkboard.

"Something else. . . . Jeff?"

"They all touch the oceans in places."

"What else? . . . Missy?"

"New York and Florida both have coastal plains."

The class continues identifying similarities for a few more minutes, and Judy then says, "How about some differences? . . . Chris?"

"The temperature ranges a lot."

"All right. . . . John?"

"Different climate zones."

"Alaska is the only one that has an average low temperature below zero," Kiki puts in.

"Carnisha, do you have anything to add?"

"All except Alaska have less than 4 inches of moisture in the winter," Carnisha adds.

	Geography	Temp.	Moisture	Economy
	Coastal plain			Citrus industry
F	Florida uplands			Tourism
L	Hurricane season			Fishing
O	Warm ocean currents			Forestry
R		Temp.	Moisture	Cattle
I	Dec.	69	1.8	
D	March	72	2.4	
A	June	81	9.3	
	Sept	82	7.6	
C	Coastal ranges			Citrus industry
A	Cascades			Wine/vineyards
L	Sierra Nevadas			Fishing
I	Central Valley			Lumber
F	Desert			Television/Hollywood
O		Temp.	Moisture	Tourism
R	Dec.	54	2.5	Computers
N	March	57	2.8	
I	June	66	T	
A	Sept.	69	.3	
N	Atlantic Coastal Plain			Vegetables
E	New England uplands			Fishing
W	Appalachian Plateau			Apples
	Adirondack Mts.			Forestry
Y		Temp.	Moisture	Light manufacturing
O	Dec.	37	3.9	Entertainment/TV
R	March	42	4.1	
K	June	72	3.7	
	Sept.	68	3.9	
	Rocky Mountains			Mining
	Brooks Range			Fishing
A	Panhandle area			Trapping
L	Plateaus between mountains			Lumbering/forestry
A	Islands/treeless			Oil/pipeline
S	Warm ocean currents			Tourism
K		Temp.	Moisture	
A	Dec	–7	.9	
	March	11	.4	
	June	60	1.4	
	Sept.	46	1.0	

After students offer several more differences, Judy asks, "Okay, have we exhausted your lists? Anyone else have anything more to add?"

Judy waits a couple seconds and then says, "Okay, now I want you to look at the economy, and I want you to do the same thing; write down three similarities and three differences in the economy column. You have 3 minutes."

The students again return to their groups, and Judy monitors them as she had earlier.

After they finish, she again calls for and receives a number of similarities and differences based on the information in the economy column.

She then shifts the direction of the lesson, saying, "Okay, great. . . . Now, let's see if we can link geography and economics. For example, why do they all have fishing?" she asks, waving her hand across the class as she walks toward the back of the room. "John?"

"They're all near the coast."

"And, why do they all have forestry? . . . Okay, Jeremy?"

"They all have lots of trees," Jeremy replies as the rest of the class smiles at this obvious conclusion.

"So, what does this tell you about their climate?"

"They all have the right temperature . . . and soil . . . and enough rain for trees."

"Good, Jeremy," Judy smiles, and then says, "Now, let's look again at our chart. We have the citrus industry in California and Florida. Why do they have the citrus industry there?"

" . . . It's the climate," Jackie answers hesitantly.

"All right, what kind of climate allows the citrus industry? . . . Tim?"

" . . . Humid subtropical."

"Humid subtropical means that we have what? . . . Go ahead."

" . . . Long humid summers. . . . Short mild winters," he replies after thinking for a few seconds.

"Now let's look at tourism. Why does each area have tourism?" Judy continues. "Okay, Lance?"

"Because they're all spread out. They're each at four corners, and they have different seasons that they're popular in."

"Good, Lance," Judy nods, and then seeing that they are near the end of the period, Judy says, "Okay, I want you to describe in a short summary statement what effect climate has on the economy of those regions."

She gives the class a couple minutes to work again in their pairs, and then says, "Let's see what you've come up with. "Braden, go ahead."

"If you have mountains in the area, you can't have farmland," he responds.

"Okay, what else? . . . Becky?"

"The climate affects what's grown and what's done in that area."

"Okay, great. Climate affects what's grown, and what was the last part of that?"

With Judy's guidance, the class makes a summarizing statement indicating that the climate of a region is a major influence determining the economy of the region, and she then dismisses the class.

Short-Answer Questions

In answering these questions, use information from the chapter, and link your responses to specific information in the case.

1. Describe Judy's thinking as she planned the lesson. Identify at least three decisions that she made as she planned.
2. Analyze Judy's instructional alignment. Offer any suggestions that you might have that would have increased the alignment of the lesson.
3. Analyze Judy's application of the essential teaching skills in her lesson. Which did she demonstrate most effectively? Which did she demonstrate least effectively?

To receive feedback for these questions, go to Appendix B.

Now go to Chapter 13 of MyEducationLab, located at www.myeducationlab.com, where you can:

- Take a quiz to test your mastery of chapter objectives. Detailed feedback is provided to explain why your responses are correct or incorrect.
- Deepen your understanding of chapter concepts with *Review, Practice, Enrichment* exercises.
- Complete *Activities and Applications* that will help you apply what you have learned in the chapter by analyzing real classrooms through video clips, artifacts and case studies. Your instructor will provide you with feedback for the *Activities and Applications.*
- Develop your professional knowledge and decision making in *Building Teaching Skills and Dispositions* exercises. Structured feedback will be available to you, providing you with support as you practice each skill. Your instructor will provide you with feedback on the final task that accompanies the exercise.

Important Concepts

closure (p. 406)
cognitive domain (p. 391)
connected discourse (p. 401)
cooperative learning (p. 419)
direct instruction (p. 409)
effective teaching (p. 390)
emphasis (p. 401)
equitable distribution (p. 404)
essential teaching skills (p. 400)
feedback (p. 402)
guided discovery (p. 417)
instructional alignment (p. 394)
learning objective (p. 391)
lecture-discussion (p. 413)
models of instruction (p. 409)
organized bodies of knowledge (p. 413)
precise language (p. 401)
prompting (p. 405)
questioning frequency (p. 404)
review (p. 406)
sensory focus (p. 402)
standards (p. 395)
task analysis (p. 393)
transition signals (p. 401)
wait-time (p. 406)

chapter

14

Assessing Classroom Learning

chapter outline

Classroom Assessment

- Assessment *for* Student Learning
- Validity: Making Appropriate Assessment Decisions
- Reliability: Consistency in Assessment

Informal Assessment

- Informal Assessment During Learning Activities
- Informal Assessment in the Larger School Context
- Reliability of Informal Assessments

Formal Assessment

- Paper-and-Pencil Items
- Commercially Prepared Test Items
- Performance Assessments
- Portfolio Assessment: Involving Students in the Assessment Process
- Putting Formal Assessment Formats into Perspective

Effective Assessment Practices

- Planning for Assessment
- Preparing Students for Assessments
- Administering Assessments
- Analyzing Results
  - **Theory to Practice:** Increasing the Quality of Your Assessments

Grading and Reporting: The Total Assessment System

- Formative and Summative Assessment
- Designing a Grading System
- Assigning Grades: Increasing Learning and Motivation
  - **Exploring Diversity:** Effective Assessment Practices with Students from Diverse Backgrounds
  - **Developmentally Appropriate Practice:** Assessment of Learning with Different-Aged Students

learning objectives

After you have completed your study of this chapter, you should be able to:

1. Explain assessment *for* learning and how validity and reliability are related to it.
2. Describe informal assessment, and explain why it is an important part of assessment *for* learning.
3. Describe formal assessment, and evaluate the quality of formal assessment items.
4. Describe effective assessment practices, and explain how they increase student learning.
5. Describe the components and decisions involved in designing a total assessment system.

You've taught and planned a lesson. How do you know if your kids "got it"? This is one of the most basic questions that exist in teaching and learning, and this is why *assessment* is so important. As you read the following case study, consider how DeVonne Lampkin, a fifth-grade teacher (and the teacher in the case studies in Chapters 11) uses assessment to measure her students' understanding, and more importantly, how does she use it to increase her students' learning?

DeVonne is beginning a unit on fractions. She knows that they were introduced in the fourth grade, but she isn't sure how much her students remember, so she gives them a pretest. When she scores it, she finds responses such as the following:

Draw a figure that will illustrate each of the fractions.

¾ **3/8** **1/3**

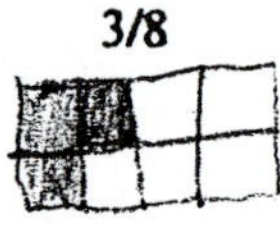

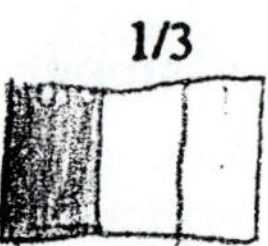

You need 3 pieces of ribbon for a project. The pieces should measure 2 5/16, 4 2/16, and 1 3/16 inches. How much ribbon do you need in all?

7 10/16

So, they seem to understand the concept *fraction* and adding fractions with like denominators. But the following responses suggest they struggle with adding fractions when the denominators are different:

Latoya made a punch recipe for a party.

Punch Recipe

¾ gallon ginger ale	**½ gallon grapefruit juice**
1 2/3 gallon orange juice	**2/3 gallon pineapple juice**

a. Will the punch she made fit into one 3-gallon punch bowl? Explain why or why not.

No because when added correctly it is more.

b. How much punch, if any, is left over?

None

On Saturday, Justin rode his bicycle 12 ½ miles. On Sunday, he rode 8 3/5 miles.

a. How many miles did he ride altogether?

21

b. How many more miles did Justin ride on Saturday than on Sunday?

4 miles more.

Based on these results, DeVonne plans to focus on *equivalent fractions* in her first lesson, because her students must understand this concept to be able to add fractions with unlike denominators.

She starts by passing out chocolate bars divided into 12 equal pieces, and with her guidance the students show how 3/12 is the same as 1/4, 6/12 is equal to 1/2, and 8/12 equals 2/3. In each case, she has them explain what they are doing.

DeVonne then goes to the board and demonstrates how to create equivalent fractions using numbers. At the end of the lesson, she gives a homework assignment that includes the following problems:

Write two equivalent fractions for each shaded part.

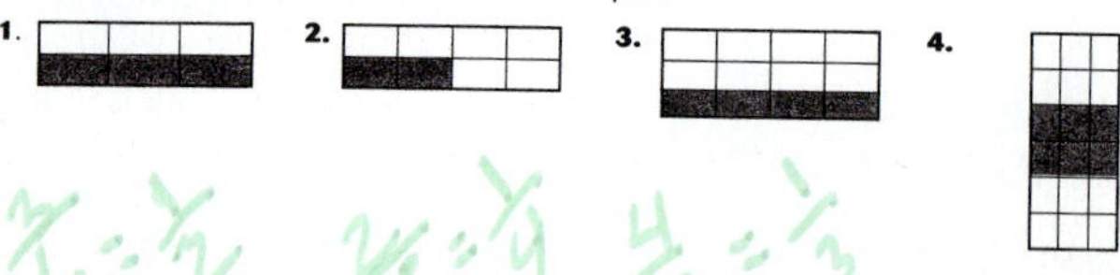

When she scores the homework, she sees that some students are still having difficulties.

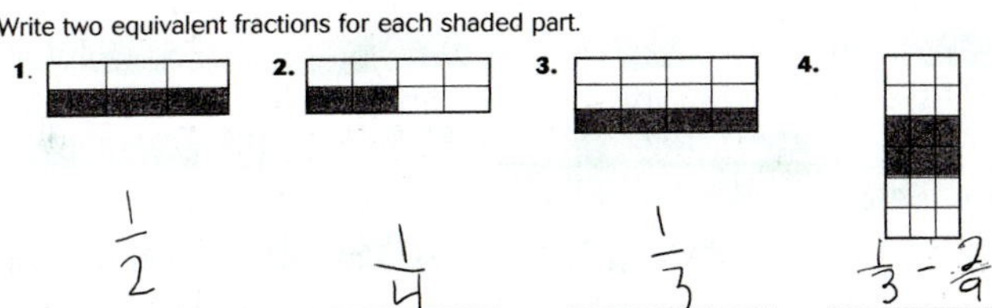

So, she designs another activity for the next day to further illustrate equivalent fractions. She begins the activity by having students construct a model fraction city with equivalent-length streets divided into different parts:

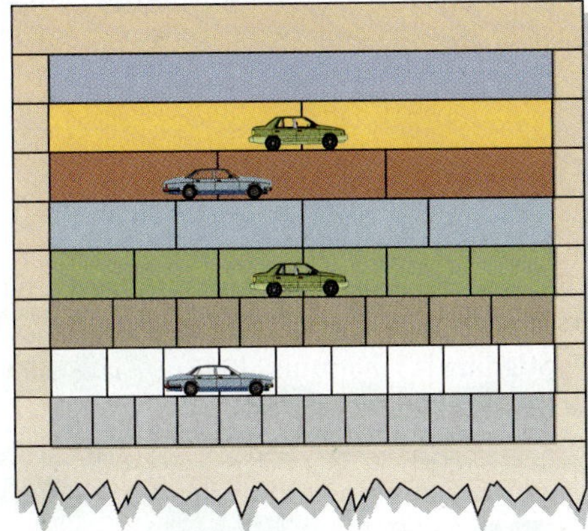

When the students are finished making their strips, she has them move cars along the different streets to illustrate equivalent fractions such as 1/2 = 3/6 and 1/3 = 3/9. Then, she illustrates adding fractions with like denominators, using the cars and strips as concrete examples. She uses the same cars and strips to illustrate adding fractions with unlike denominators.

Finally, DeVonne goes to the board, shows how to perform the same operations using numbers, and gives her students a homework assignment on adding fractions with unlike denominators. (We will return to DeVonne's lesson later in the chapter.)

Several days later, she gives a cumulative test on fractions. Her students' answers suggest that they seem to understand equivalent fractions and how to add fractions with unlike denominators:

Write the equivalent fraction.

$\frac{2}{3} = \frac{8}{12}$ $\frac{3}{8} = \frac{6}{16}$ $\frac{4}{5} = \frac{16}{20}$ $\frac{5}{6} = \frac{50}{60}$

Write each fraction in simplest terms.

$\frac{5}{10} = \frac{1}{2}$ $\frac{8}{12} = \frac{2}{3}$ $\frac{4}{20} = \frac{1}{5}$ $\frac{9}{27} = \frac{1}{3}$

$\frac{24}{30} = \frac{4}{5}$ $\frac{16}{18} = \frac{8}{9}$ $\frac{35}{49} = \frac{5}{7}$ $\frac{32}{40} = \frac{4}{5}$

An alien from a far-off planet landed her spacecraft on Earth. She had left her planet with a full tank of super interplanetary fuel. She knew that she'd need at least 3/8 of that fuel to return home from Earth. She used half a tank of fuel to get here. How much fuel did she use all together?

$\frac{3}{8} + \frac{1}{2} =$

$\frac{3}{8} + \frac{4}{8} = \frac{7}{8}$

To begin your study of this chapter, consider these questions:

1. What is classroom assessment, and how does it contribute to learning?
2. What was the primary purpose of DeVonne's assessments?
3. What forms of assessment did DeVonne use in her teaching?

Research on classroom assessment helps us answer these and other questions. In this chapter, we examine ways that you can apply this research with your students.

Classroom Assessment

Classroom assessment. All the processes involved in making decisions about students' learning progress.

Classroom assessment includes all the processes involved in making decisions about students' learning progress (Nitko, 2004; J. McMillan, 2007), and it helps answer our first question. It includes observations of students' written work, their answers to questions in class, and performance on teacher-made and standardized tests. It also includes performance assessments, such as watching first graders print or observing art students create a piece of pottery. In addition, it involves decisions such as reteaching a topic or assigning grades. In DeVonne's case, deciding to begin her unit with a lesson on equivalent fractions was part of the assessment process, as were the decisions to teach a second lesson on the topic and when to give her unit test.

Assessment is an integral part of the teaching–learning process. Despite its importance and the amount of time it requires—experts estimate up to a third of teachers' professional time—teachers often feel ill-prepared to deal with its demands (Stiggins, 2004, 2005). Our goal in writing this chapter is to help you become better prepared for this essential instructional process.

Assessment *for* Student Learning

Assessment *for* learning. Assessment that is a process designed to support and increase learning.

Historically, assessment has been used at the end of a unit or course of study to determine the amount that students have learned, essentially assessment *of* learning. In contrast, **assessment *for* learning** turns assessment into a process designed to support and increase student learning (Beers, 2006; Stiggins, 2007; Stiggins & Chappuis, 2006). Assessment *for* learning becomes an integral part of the total teaching–learning process.

All the decisions we make as teachers should increase student learning, and this definition answers the second question at the beginning of the chapter: "What was the primary purpose of DeVonne's assessments?" The purpose was to promote learning.

In order to make good decisions, we need information about our students. We need to know their existing understanding, their motivation to learn, the extent to which they are taking responsibility for their own learning, and whether or not they have reached our learning objectives. Assessment *for* learning helps provide that information (Santi & Vaughn, 2007).

Diagnostic Assessment: Measuring Current Understanding

When should we assess our students? To begin answering this question, let's look again at DeVonne's work with hers. Before she began her unit, she gave a pretest to determine her students' current level of understanding. She found that they understood the concept *fraction* and could add fractions with like denominators, but they had misconceptions about adding fractions when the denominators were different. As a result, her first learning objective was for students to understand the concept *equivalent fraction,* and her second was for them to be able to add fractions with unlike denominators.

Diagnostic assessment. A form of assessment designed to provide teachers with information about students' prior knowledge and misconceptions before beginning a learning activity.

DeVonne's pretest was a form of **diagnostic assessment,** a form of assessment designed to provide teachers with information about students' prior knowledge and misconceptions before beginning a learning activity (Burns, 2005). Diagnostic assessment helps teachers identify students' zones of proximal development and enables them to provide the scaffolding that helps move students through their zones.

DeVonne's homework assignment was also a form of diagnostic assessment. For example, she saw that the students gave the following responses to her first four items:

Write two equivalent fractions for each shaded part.

1. $\frac{1}{2}$ 2. $\frac{1}{4}$ 3. $\frac{1}{3}$ 4. $\frac{1}{3}$ - $\frac{2}{9}$

This suggested that her students retained some misconceptions about the concept *equivalent fraction,* because they wrote only one fraction for the first three problems and answered the fourth problem incorrectly. As a result, she designed a second learning activity to teach *equivalent fractions*. DeVonne's use of diagnostic assessment demonstrates its role in assessment *for* learning.

Increasing Motivation to Learn

Think about some of your own experiences in classes. For which do you study the hardest and learn the most? Almost certainly it is those in which you're thoroughly assessed and given informative feedback about your developing understanding. Research confirms your reaction. Well-designed assessments increase both learning and motivation to learn (Brookhart, 2007/2008; Stiggins, 2005).

Assessments that increase motivation to learn have several characteristics (Brookhart, Walsh, & Zientarski, 2006; Schunk, Pintrich, & Meece, 2008):

- They are aligned with learning objectives.
- They focus on mastery goals and improvement.
- They avoid social comparisons.
- They measure higher-level learning.

Assessments aligned with learning objectives provide students with the information they need to focus their efforts and increase the likelihood of success. When students succeed and attribute their success to effort, their motivation to learn and self-efficacy increase. Focusing on mastery goals and improvement, eliminating social comparisons, and measuring higher-level outcomes also promote feelings of autonomy and competence, both of which increase motivation to learn. "Setting high standards for student achievement and holding students accountable for reaching them can motivate students to excel" (Schunk et al., 2008, p. 371).

Developing Self-Regulation

Monitoring progress toward goals is an important part of self-regulation. Assessment contributes to this process by providing feedback about learning progress. High-quality assessments also contribute to self-regulation by providing students with information that can help them focus their efforts. For example, if assessments require that students do more than memorize factual information, they quickly adapt their study habits and focus on deeper understanding. Some experts believe that assessment has more influence on the way students study and learn than any other aspect of the teaching–learning process (Crooks, 1988; Stiggins, 2007).

Teachers contribute to learner self-regulation by making expectations clear, emphasizing that assessments are designed to increase learning, aligning assessments with learning objectives and learning activities, and providing detailed feedback on all assessments (Stiggins, 2007; Stiggins & Chappuis, 2006).

Measuring Achievement

Finally, assessment provides students and their parents, teachers, and school leaders with information about learner achievement (J. McMillan, 2007). This has historically been the role of assessment, but as you've seen in this section, assessment *for* learning expands its role to also include diagnosis as well as promoting motivation to learn and self-regulation. The relationships among these processes are outlined in Figure 14.1.

Validity. The degree to which an assessment actually measures what it is supposed to measure.

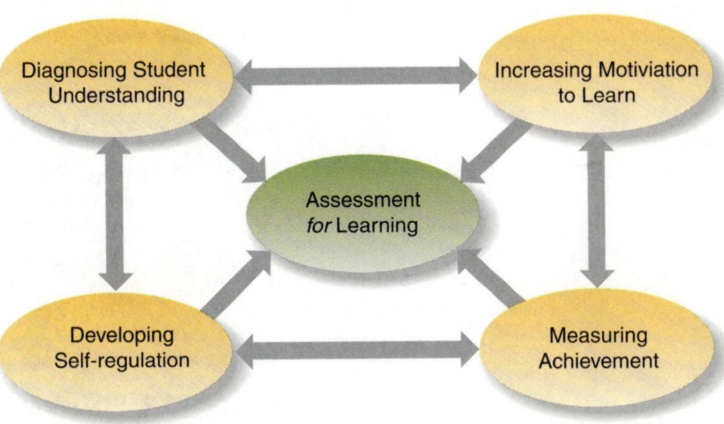

Figure 14.1 Assessment *for* learning

Validity: Making Appropriate Assessment Decisions

Validity is the degree to which an assessment actually measures what it is supposed to measure (Miller, Linn, & Gronlund, 2009). In the teaching–learning process, assessments are valid if they are aligned with learning objectives. For example, if a teacher's objective is for students to understand the causes of the Civil War, but a quiz asks them to recall names, dates, and places, it would be invalid. Based on the quiz results, the teacher might conclude the students had met the objective, when in fact she had gathered little information about their understanding of the causes of the war.

Assessment decisions are also invalid if they're based on personality, appearance, or other factors unrelated to learning objectives, such as giving lower scores on essay items because of messy handwriting (Lambating & Allen, 2002). These actions are usually unconscious; without realizing it, teachers base their assessments on appearance rather than substance.

Creating valid assessments is challenging but not impossible. If you continually look for ways to improve your tests, quizzes, and other assessments; analyze trends and patterns in student responses; and conscientiously revise your assessments, validity will improve. Creating valid assessments is part of being a professional.

Reliability: Consistency in Assessment

Reliability. The extent to which assessments are consistent and free from errors of measurement.

Reliability, an intuitively sensible concept, describes the extent to which assessments are consistent and free from errors of measurement (Miller et al., 2009). For instance, if your bathroom scale is reliable, and your weight doesn't change, the readings shouldn't vary from one day to the next. Hypothetically, if we could repeatedly give a student the same reliable test, and if no additional learning or forgetting occurred, the scores would all be the same. Unreliable assessments cannot be valid, even if they are aligned with teachers' learning objectives, because they give inconsistent information.

Ambiguous items on tests and quizzes, directions that aren't clear, and inconsistent scoring, which is common on essay items, are three factors that detract from reliability. For example, research indicates that different instructors with similar backgrounds, ostensibly using the same criteria, have awarded grades ranging from excellent to failure on the same essay (Gronlund, 2003). If scoring is inconsistent, lack of reliability makes the process invalid.

Some ways to increase reliability include the following:

- Use a sufficient number of items or tasks in an instrument. For instance, a quiz of 15 items is likely to be more reliable than a quiz that has only 5 items.
- Clearly explain requirements for responding to the assessment items.
- Specify criteria in advance for scoring students' essay items. Score all students' responses to a particular item before moving to a second one.
- To avoid being influenced by your expectations of students, score assessments anonymously, particularly if you're scoring essay items or solutions to problems where partial credit is given. Have students put their names on the last page of the quiz, for example, so you won't know whose quiz you're scoring until you're finished.

Visualizing a target is one way to think about the relationship between validity and reliability (Miller et al., 2009). A valid and reliable shooter consistently clusters shots in the target's bull's-eye. A reliable but invalid shooter clusters shots, but the cluster is not in the bull's-eye. And a shooter that scatters shots randomly over the target is analogous to an assessment instrument that is neither valid nor reliable. These relationships between validity and reliability are illustrated in Figure 14.2.

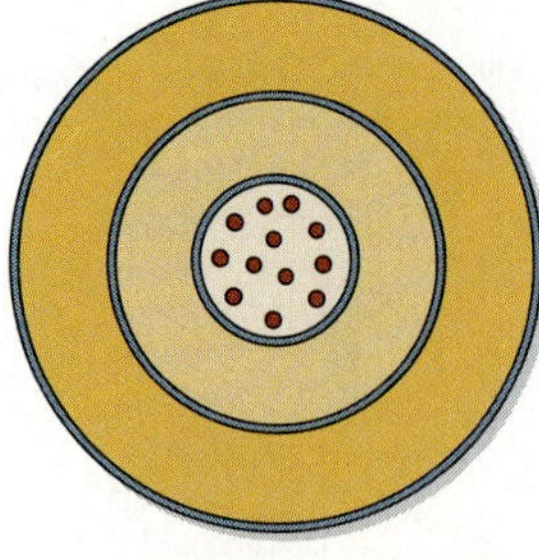
Target 1
(reliable and valid shooting)

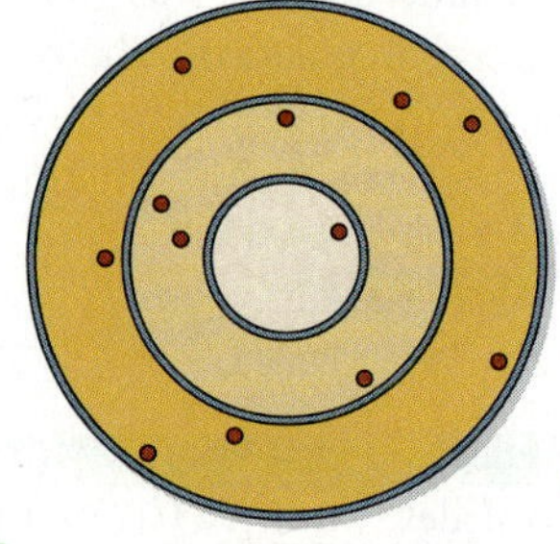
Target 2
(unreliable and invalid shooting)

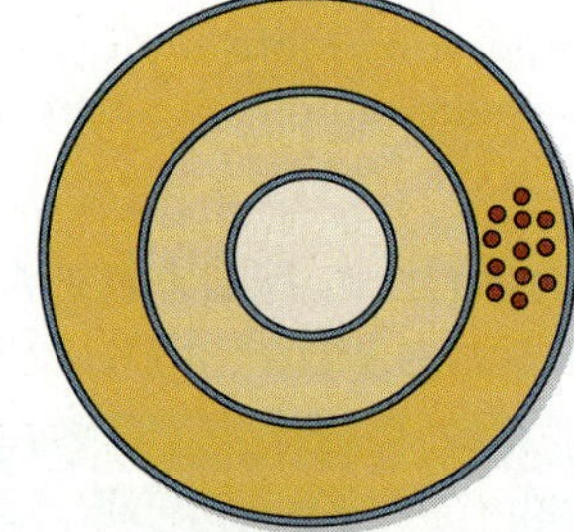
Target 3
(reliable but invalid shooting)

Figure 14.2 The relationships between validity and reliability
Source: Adapted from MEASUREMENT AND ASSESSMENT IN TEACHING 10/E by M. D. Miller, R. L. Linn, & N. E. Gronlund, p. 72, © 2009. Reprinted by permission of Pearson Education, Inc., Upper Saddle River, NJ.

check your understanding

1.1 What is assessment *for* student learning, and how are validity and reliability related to it?

1.2 An eighth-grade history teacher reminds his students that correct grammar and punctuation are important parts of expression, and he gives his students two scores on their history essay items: one for the history content and a second for grammar and punctuation. Is his assessment valid? Explain why or why not.

1.3 A high school science teacher wants her students to be able to design effective experiments. After discussing the process with them, she has them complete a lab assignment in which they are required to design an experiment. On Friday she gives a quiz that requires students to list the steps, in order, for designing an experiment. Is her assessment valid? Explain why or why not. Is her quiz likely to be reliable? Explain why or why not.

To receive feedback for these questions, go to Appendix A.

Informal Assessment

To begin this section, consider the following incidents:

- You're supervising your students as they work on a seat-work assignment in math, and you see that one of them has made the same error on three consecutive problems.
- You're teaching a lesson, and you see one of your students drifting off.
- You're watching your students on the playground, and you see a large boy push a smaller one down.

Your observations combined with the related decisions are part of **informal assessment,** the process of gathering incidental information about learning progress or other aspects of students' behavior, and making decisions based on that information. In each of the examples, you didn't plan to gather the information in advance, and you didn't get the same information from each of your students. One of your students making a consistent error, for instance, doesn't imply that other students have made the same error.

Informal assessment. The process of gathering incidental information about learning progress or other aspects of students' behavior, and making decisions based on that information.

Teachers use informal assessment when they gather incidental information about learning progress and make decisions based on that information.

Informal assessment is an essential part of the total assessment process, because it helps teachers make the many decisions required every day (P. Black, Harrison, Lee, Marshall, & William, 2004). Next, we'll look at this process in more detail.

Informal Assessment During Learning Activities

Expert teachers use informal assessments to make ongoing instructional decisions. To see how, we return to DeVonne's work with her students. The class has added fractions with unlike denominators using their fraction city, and she now wants them to add fractions with unlike denominators without the support of the concrete example.

> "Let's review what we've done," she begins. "Look at your fraction city again, and move one of your cars to First Street on Fourth Avenue and your other car to First Street on Eighth Avenue. . . . How far have your two cars moved altogether? . . . Write the problem on your paper using fractions."
>
> 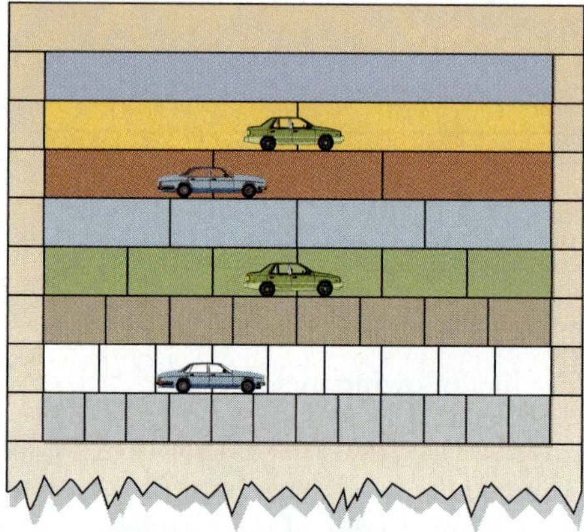
>
> She sees that Jeremy has written the following on his paper:
>
> $$\frac{1}{4} + \frac{1}{8} = \frac{2}{8}$$
>
> She also sees that Juanita, Michael, and Cassie have written 1/4 + 1/8 = 2/12 on their papers.
>
> $$\frac{1}{4} + \frac{1}{8} = \frac{2}{12} \qquad \frac{1}{4} + \frac{1}{8} = \frac{2}{12} \qquad \frac{1}{4} + \frac{1}{8} = \frac{2}{12}$$
>
> "I'll work with them when I assign seat work," she thinks to herself.
>
> She waits for the students to finish and then, seeing that Nikki has a clear solution, says, "Nikki, please come up and show us how you solved the problem."

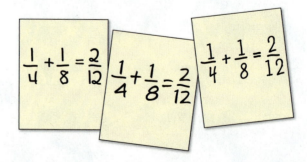

Nikki goes to the board and writes:

$$\frac{2}{2} \times \frac{1}{4} = \frac{2}{8}$$

"Explain why Nikki could write 2/2 times 1/4 to get 2/8. . . . Amir."

". . ."

"What does 2/2 equal?"

". . . One," Amir responds.

"Good, . . . and whenever we multiply something by one, we don't change the value. . . . So, now what can Nikki do? . . . Thelicia?"

". . . Add the 2/8 and 1/8 to get 3/8."

"Good, Thelicia," DeVonne smiles. "Now, let's try this one," and she gives the students another problem, again watches as they attempt to solve it, and discusses it as they discussed the first one. She does two more problems, gives a seat-work assignment, and then calls Jeremy, Juanita, Michael, and Cassie to a table at the back of the room to provide additional scaffolding.

In this brief episode, DeVonne used informal assessment in at least three ways. For example:

- She observed that Jeremy, Juanita, Michael, and Cassie had misconceptions about adding fractions with unlike denominators, and she decided to give them some extra help while the rest of the class did seat work.
- She decided to use Nikki as a peer model to demonstrate the solution. She could, for example, have demonstrated the solution herself.
- Instead of asking Nikki to explain why she could multiply ¼ by 2/2, she decided to call on Amir, and decided to prompt him when he was unable to answer, instead of turning the question to another student.

DeVonne designed each of her decisions to promote learning. They were all a part of informal assessment, and without it, making these decisions would have been impossible (K. Rose, Williams, Gomez, & Gearon, 2002).

Student artifacts are also an important part of informal assessment. For example, seeing the errors that Jeremy, Juanita, Michael, and Cassie made on their papers was important for helping DeVonne decide to provide them with additional scaffolding.

Informal Assessment in the Larger School Context

Informal assessment is an essential part of the teaching–learning process, but it's also important in the larger school context. Seeing one of your students push another down is an example. Personal, social, and moral growth are important parts of students' overall development, and virtually all the decisions teachers make in these contexts are instances of informal assessment. Examples of informal assessment include deciding to intervene in the case of a group not working well together, concluding that one of your students should be referred for counseling, or asking a student to see you after school because you believe she has a personal problem. Informal assessment is an important part of your role as a teacher.

Reliability of Informal Assessments

While informal assessments are essential in the day-to-day functioning of classrooms and schools, they provide an incomplete picture of learning, and reliability can be a problem (S. Green & Mantz, 2002). For example, concluding that all students understand an idea on the basis of responses from only a few (who usually have their hands up) is a mistake that teachers often make. And, they sometimes make decisions as important as assigning grades on the basis of informal assessment. Students who readily respond, have engaging personalities, and are physically attractive are often awarded higher grades than their less-fortunate peers (Ritts, Patterson, & Tubbs, 1992).

Similarly, concluding that a student is a bully on the basis of one playground incident is unreliable, and accusing the student of bullying could be emotionally damaging. Teachers

classroom connections

Capitalizing on Informal Assessment in Your Classroom

1. Informal assessment is the process of gathering information during learning activities and other school events and making decisions to promote learning on the basis of that information. Attempt to make your informal assessments as systematic as possible.
   - **Elementary:** A first-grade teacher notices that one of her students appears listless and sometimes falls asleep during learning activities. She watches the student for several days and then contacts the school counselor.
   - **Middle School:** A sixth-grade math teacher sees that one of her students has incorrectly solved a word problem involving decimals. He tells the student to recheck his answer, and then checks several other students' answers to see if the class appears to have a misconception.
   - **High School:** An American history teacher wants his students to understand the relationships among Marco Polo's visit to the far east, the Portuguese explorers, and Columbus's trip to the New World. A few students respond to open-ended questions, but most sit silently. Adapting, he changes the direction of the lesson and provides a short presentation on the main idea, followed by a discussion in which he asks students to describe the facts involved in each individual case and examine the relationships among the ideas.

should remember that informal assessments are always potentially unreliable and should avoid making important or damaging decisions on the basis of insufficient evidence. This leads us to a discussion of formal assessment, the topic of our next section.

check your understanding

2.1 Describe informal assessment, and explain why it is an important part of assessment *for* learning.

2.2 Which aspects of students' learning and development depend almost totally on informal assessment? Explain why this is the case.

2.3 Identify a weakness that often exists with informal assessment. Why is it important that teachers are aware of this weakness?

To receive feedback for these questions, go to Appendix A.

Formal Assessment

In the previous section, you saw how DeVonne used informal assessment as an integral part of her instruction. This is only one aspect of assessment, however. For instance, DeVonne also used:

- A diagnostic pretest, which gave her information about her students' understanding of fractions and how to add them
- Homework assignments that measured their understanding of *equivalent fractions* and adding fractions with unlike denominators
- A unit test that covered all aspects of adding fractions

Formal assessment. The process of systematically gathering the same kind of information from every student.

Each was a type of **formal assessment,** the process of systematically gathering the same kind of information from every student, and this answers the third question we asked at the beginning of the chapter: "What forms of assessment did DeVonne use in her teaching?" In addition to informal assessment, formal assessment was an essential part of her instruction. For instance, when DeVonne gave the students the following items for homework, every student responded to the same problems. Formal assessment is designed to overcome the reliability issues that often accompany informal assessment, so the combination of the two increases the likelihood of gathering accurate information for instructional decision making.

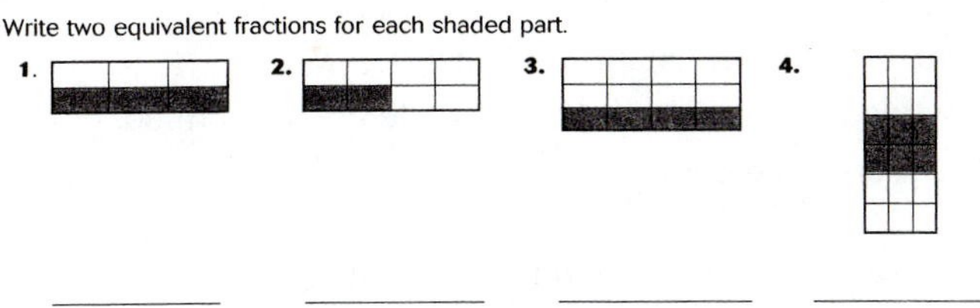

Formal assessment most commonly occurs in three forms:

- Paper-and-pencil items, such as multiple-choice and essay
- Performance assessments, such as observing students making a presentation
- Portfolios, collections of students' work that measure progress over time

We discuss each in this section.

Paper-and-Pencil Items

Educators commonly classify paper-and-pencil items as *selected-response formats* or *supply formats.* Selected-response formats include multiple-choice, true–false, and matching, because they require learners to select the correct answer from a list of alternatives. Supply formats include completion or essay, because they require learners to supply their answers (Stiggins, 2005). Other paper-and-pencil classifications are *objective* and *subjective.* Selected-response formats, such as multiple-choice, are objective, because scorers don't have to make decisions about the quality of an answer. Supply formats, and particularly essay items, are subjective, because scorer judgment is a factor (Miller et al., 2009).

Regardless of whether the format is selected-response or supply, objective or subjective, two factors are important for making the items valid and reliable. First, to be valid, the items must be aligned with learning objectives and standards. The best way to ensure alignment is to write the items during planning. Second, the teacher should analyze students' responses to the items and should modify items when necessary to make them more effective.

Next we'll look at common paper-and-pencil formats.

Multiple-Choice Items

Multiple-choice is an assessment format that consists of a question or statement, called a *stem,* and a series of answer choices called ***distracters*** because they are designed to distract students who don't understand the content the item is measuring (Miller et al., 2009). The stem should pose one question or problem to be considered, and distracters should address students' likely misconceptions so they can be identified and discussed when students receive feedback (Ciofalo & Wylie, 2006).

Multiple-choice. A paper-and-pencil format that consists of a question or statement, called a *stem,* and a series of answer choices called *distracters*.

Distracters. Incorrect choices in multiple-choice items used to identify common student misconceptions about the topic being assessed.

Multiple-choice is an effective format for preparing items at different levels of thinking; most standardized tests use it, and it is also popular with teachers (Gronlund, 2003; Kahn, 2000). Guidelines for preparing multiple-choice items are summarized in Figure 14.3.

Items may be written so that only one choice is correct, or they may be in a best-answer form, in which two or more choices are partially correct but one is clearly better than the others. The best-answer form is more demanding, promotes higher-level thinking, and measures more complex achievement. Many of the multiple-choice questions that assess your understanding of the material in this text use the best-answer form.

Many problems with faulty multiple-choice items involve clues in distracters that allow students to answer the question correctly without knowing the content. "Check Your Understanding" item 3.2 at the end of this section asks you to identify features of test items that are inconsistent with the guidelines outlined in Figure 14.3.

Assessing Higher-Level Learning. Teachers write many of their multiple-choice items at the factual knowledge–remember level of the taxonomy table you studied in Chapters 13 (see Figure 13.2 on page 393). However, the multiple-choice format can also be effective for assessing higher-order thinking (Braun & Mislevy, 2005). In an "interpretive exercise," students encounter information covered in class in a different context, and the distracters represent

1. Present one clear problem in the stem of the item.
2. Make all distracters plausible and attractive to the uninformed.
3. Vary the position of the correct choice randomly. Be careful to avoid overusing choice *c.*
4. Avoid similar wording in the stem and the correct choice.
5. Avoid phrasing the correct choice in more technical terms than distracters.
6. Keep the correct answer and the distracters similar in length. A longer or shorter answer should usually be used as an incorrect choice.
7. Avoid using absolute terms (e.g., *always, never*) in the incorrect choices.
8. Keep the stem and distracters grammatically consistent.
9. Avoid using two distracters with the same meaning.
10. Emphasize *negative wording* by underlining if it is used.
11. Use "none of the above" with care, and avoid "all of the above" as a choice.

Figure 14.3 Guidelines for preparing multiple-choice items
Source: *How to Construct Achievement Tests.* 4th ed., by N. Gronlund, © 1988, Needham Heights, MA: Allyn & Bacon. Adapted by permission of Allyn & Bacon.

different "interpretations" of it (Gronlund, 2003). The material may be a graph, chart, table, map, picture, or written vignette.

Most of the higher-level items that appear on the quizzes that you take for this class are interpretive exercises. Figure 14.4 is an example of an interpretive exercise in science. In this case, the teacher's goal is for students to apply information about heat, expansion, mass, volume, and density to a unique situation. This type of exercise promotes transfer, helps develop critical thinking, and can increase learner motivation.

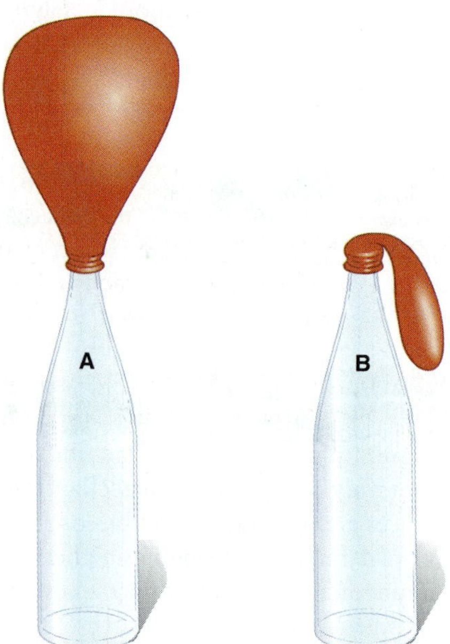

Look at the drawings above. They represent two identical soft drink bottles covered with identical balloons sitting side-by-side on a table. Bottle A was then heated. Which of the following is the most accurate statement?

a. The density of the air in Bottle A is greater than the density of the air in Bottle B.
*b. The density of the air in Bottle A is less than the density of the air in Bottle B.
c. The density of the air in Bottle A is equal to the density of the air in Bottle B.
d. We don't have enough information to compare the density of the air in Bottle A to the density of the air in Bottle B.

Figure 14.4 Interpretive exercise used with the multiple-choice format

Matching Items

The multiple-choice format can be inefficient if all of the items require the same set of answer choices, as in the following (asterisk indicates correct answer):

1. The statement "Understanding is like a light bulb coming on in your head" is an example of:
   *a. simile.
   b. metaphor.
   c. hyperbole.
   d. personification.

2. "That's the most brilliant comment ever made" is a statement of:
   a. simile.
   b. metaphor.
   *c. hyperbole.
   d. personification.

The assessment can be made more efficient by using a **matching format,** a format that requires learners to classify a series of examples using the same alternatives. The following is an example based on the preceding multiple-choice items.

Matching format. A paper-and-pencil format that requires learners to classify a series of examples using the same alternatives.

Match the following statements with the figures of speech by writing the letter of the appropriate figure of speech in the blank next to each statement. You may use each figure of speech once, more than once, or not at all.

_____	1. Understanding is like a light bulb coming on in your head.	a. alliteration
_____	2. That's the most brilliant comment ever made.	b. hyperbole
_____	3. His oratory was a bellow from the bowels of his soul.	c. metaphor
_____	4. Appropriate attitudes are always advantageous.	d. personification
_____	5. Her eyes are limpid pools of longing.	e. simile
_____	6. He stood as straight as a rod.	
_____	7. I'll never get this stuff, no matter what I do.	
_____	8. The colors of his shirt described the world in which he lived.	

The example illustrates four characteristics of effective matching items. First, the content is homogeneous; all the statements are figures of speech, and only figures of speech appear as the alternatives. Other topics appropriate for the matching format include people and their achievements, historical events and dates, terms and definitions, and authors and their works (Miller et al., 2009). Second, the item includes more statements than possible alternatives (to prevent getting the right answer by process of elimination). Third, students may use the alternatives more than once or not at all, as specified in the directions. Finally, the entire item fits on a single page. If the matching item involves more than 10 statements, you should create two separate items to prevent overloading learners' working memories.

True–False Items

True–false is an assessment format that includes statements of varying complexity that learners judge as being correct or incorrect. Because true–false items usually measure lower-level outcomes, and because students have a 50–50 chance of guessing the correct answer, teachers should use this format sparingly (Miller et al., 2009). The following are some guidelines for improving the effectiveness of these items:

True–false. A paper-and-pencil format that includes statements of varying complexity that learners judge as being correct or incorrect.

- Write more false than true items. Teachers tend to do the reverse, and students tend to mark items they're unsure of as "true."
- Make each item one clear statement.
- Avoid clues that allow students to answer correctly without fully understanding the content. Examples of clues include the term *most,* which usually indicates a true statement, or *never,* typically suggesting a false statement.

Completion Items

Completion. A paper-and-pencil format that includes a question or an incomplete statement that requires the learner to supply appropriate words, numbers, or symbols.

Completion is an assessment format that includes a question or an incomplete statement that requires the learner to supply appropriate words, numbers, or symbols.

The following are two examples.

1. What is an opinion? _____
2. _____ is the capital of Canada.

Items that consist of questions, such as the first example, are sometimes called short-answer items. This format is popular with teachers, probably because the questions seem easy to construct. This is misleading, however, because completion items have two important disadvantages. First, it is difficult to phrase a question so that only one possible answer is correct. A number of defensible responses could be given to item 1, for example. Overuse of completion items can put students in the position of trying to guess the answer the teacher wants instead of giving the one they think is correct.

Essay. A paper-and-pencil format that requires students to make extended written responses to questions or problems.

Second, unless the item requires solving a problem, completion items usually measure recall of factual information, as in item 2. Because of these weaknesses, teachers should use completion formats sparingly (Gronlund, 2003). Table 14.1 presents guidelines for preparing completion items.

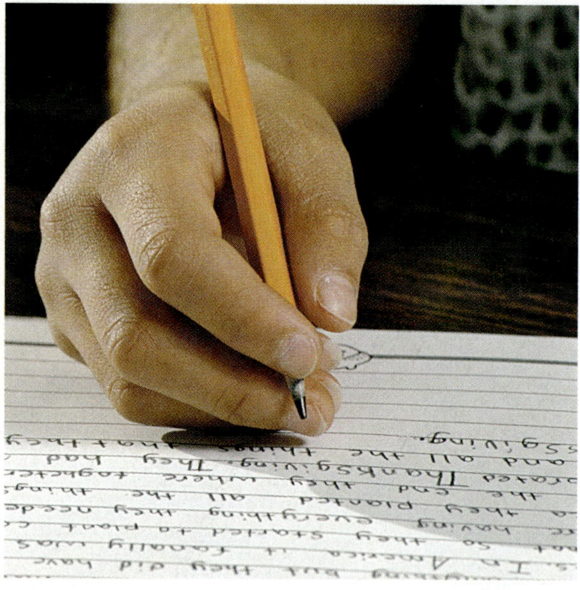

Teachers use essay items to assess complex outcomes that other formats can't assess.

Essay Items: Measuring Complex Outcomes

Essay is an assessment format that requires students to make extended written responses to questions or problems. Essay items are valuable for three reasons. First, they can assess dimensions of learning that can't be measured with other formats, including creative and critical thinking. Second, the developing ability to organize ideas, make and defend an argument, and describe understanding in writing is an important goal throughout the curriculum, and the essay format is the primary way by which teachers measure progress toward this goal (Stiggins, 2005). Third, essay items can improve the way students study. For example, if students know a test will use an essay format, they are more likely to look for relationships in what they study and to organize information in a meaningful way (Shepard, 2001).

Essay items also have disadvantages. Because essay tests require extensive writing time, it isn't possible to assess learning across as broad a spectrum, so breadth of coverage can be a problem. In addition, scoring essays is time-consuming and, as discussed earlier, sometimes unreliable. Scores on essay items are also influenced by writing skill, including grammar, spelling, and handwriting (Haladyna & Ryan, 2001; Nitko, 2004).

table 14.1 Guidelines for Preparing Completion Items

Guideline	Rationale
1. Use only one blank, and relate it to the main point of the statement.	Several blanks are confusing, and one answer may depend on another.
2. Use complete sentences followed by a question mark or period.	Complete sentences allow students to more nearly grasp the full meaning of the statement.
3. Keep blanks the same length. Use "a(an)" at the end of the statement or eliminate indefinite articles.	A long blank for a long word or a particular indefinite article commonly provides clues to the answer.
4. For numerical answers, indicate the degree of precision and the units desired.	Degree of precision and units clarify the task for students and prevent them from spending more time than necessary on an item.

1. Elicit higher-order thinking by using such terms as *explain* and *compare.* Have students defend their responses with facts.
2. Write a model answer for each item. You can use this both for scoring and for providing feedback.
3. Require all students to answer all items. Allowing students to select particular items prevents comparisons and detracts from reliability.
4. Prepare criteria for scoring in advance.
5. Score all students' answers to a single item before moving to the next item.
6. Score all responses to a single item in one sitting if possible. This increases reliability.
7. Score answers without knowing the identity of the student. This helps reduce the influence of past performance and expectations.
8. Develop a model answer complete with points, and compare a few students' responses to it, to see if any adjustments are needed in the scoring criteria.

Figure 14.5 Guidelines for preparing and scoring essay items

Essay items appear easy to write, but they can be ambiguous, leaving students uncertain about how to respond. As a result, students' ability to interpret the teacher's question is often the outcome measured. Figure 14.5 presents guidelines for preparing and scoring essay items (Stiggins, 2005). In addition to these suggestions, rubrics can help improve the reliability of scoring essays. We look at them next.

Using Rubrics

A **rubric** is a scoring scale that describes criteria for grading (Andrade, 2007/2008; Stiggins, 2005). Originally created to help teachers with the complex task of scoring essays, rubrics are also useful for assessing performances, such as a student speech or presentation, or products other than essays, such as a science lab report.

Rubric. A scoring scale that describes criteria for grading.

Rubrics provide guidance for teachers while planning; they can be useful during learning activities and are essential for assessment. During planning, the process of constructing a rubric guides teachers' thinking by providing specific targets to focus on during instruction. Experts recommend the following steps (Huba & Freed, 2000):

- Establish criteria based on elements that must exist in students' work.
- Decide on the number of levels of achievement for each criterion.
- Develop clear descriptors for each level.
- Determine a rating scale for the entire rubric.

Figure 14.6 is a rubric used for assessing paragraph structure. In it, we see that the teacher believes a topic sentence, supporting sentences, and summarizing sentence must be present in an effective paragraph. These elements appear in a column along the left side of the matrix. Next, the rubric clearly describes levels of achievement for each element. Clear descriptors guide students as they write and also provide concrete reference points for teachers when they score the products. As a final step during planning, teachers make decisions about grading criteria. For example, they might decide that 9 points would be an A, 7–8 points a B, and 5–6 points would be a C. So, a student would be required to be at a level of achievement of 3 on all three criteria to earn an A, for example, and would have to be at level 2 on two of the three elements and at level 3 on the third to earn a B.

During learning activities, teachers can use rubrics to communicate their objectives for the lesson. For example, they might display the rubric in Figure 14.6, which could help focus students' attention on essential aspects of their writing (Andrade, 2007/2008; Saddler & Andrade, 2004).

When assessing students' work, rubrics are essential for increasing reliability. As a teacher scores her student's paragraphs, for example, the descriptions of the dimensions and levels of achievement in Figure 14.6 can help her maintain consistency in evaluating

Criteria	Levels of Achievement 1	2	3
Topic Sentence	Not present; reader has no idea of what paragraph is about	Present but does not give the reader a clear idea of what the paragraph is about	Provides a clearly stated overview of the paragraph
Supporting Sentences	Rambling and unrelated to topic sentence	Provides additional information but not all focused on topic sentence	Provides supporting detail relating to the topic sentence
Summarizing Sentence	Nonexistent or unrelated to preceding sentences	Relates to topic sentence but doesn't summarize information in paragraph	Accurately summarizes information in paragraph and is related to topic sentence
Overall Score (9 Possible)			

Figure 14.6 Sample rubric for paragraph structure

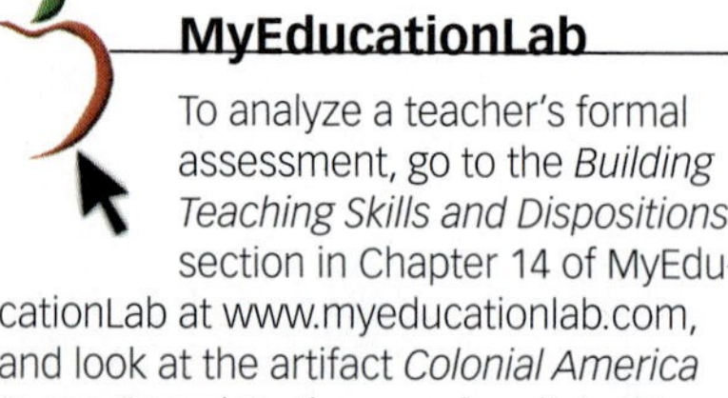

MyEducationLab

To analyze a teacher's formal assessment, go to the *Building Teaching Skills and Dispositions* section in Chapter 14 of MyEducationLab at www.myeducationlab.com, and look at the artifact *Colonial America Exam.* Complete the exercises linked to the artifact to build your skills in creating effective paper-and-pencil assessments.

each student's work. Without the rubric as a guide, the likelihood of inconsistent scoring is much higher.

Commercially Prepared Test Items

Because they are very busy, many teachers depend on the tests included in textbooks, teachers' guides, and other commercially prepared materials. Although these materials save time, teachers should use them with caution for three reasons (Nitko, 2004; Popham, 2007):

1. *Compatibility of learning objectives:* The learning objectives of the curriculum developers may not be the same as yours. If items don't reflect the objectives in your course, they are invalid.
2. *Uneven quality:* Many commercially prepared tests are low in quality.
3. *Emphasis on lower-level items:* Commercially prepared items typically measure at a knowledge-recall level.

The time and labor saved using commercially prepared items are important advantages, however. The following guidelines can help you capitalize on these benefits:

- Select items that are consistent with your learning objectives, and put them in a file in your computer for editing.
- Using feedback from students and analysis of test results, revise ineffective items.
- Create additional items that help you accurately assess your students' understanding.

Only you know what your objectives are, and you are the best judge of the extent to which commercially prepared items assess them.

Performance Assessments

Performance assessments. Direct examinations of student performance on tasks that are relevant to life outside of school.

Critics have argued that traditional paper-and-pencil assessments, most commonly in the form of multiple-choice tests, lack validity (Corcoran et al., 2004; D. French, 2003). In response to these criticisms, educators are emphasizing the use of **performance assessments,** direct examinations of student performance on tasks relevant to life outside of school, especially in the language arts (Frey & Schmitt, 2005; Popham, 2005). Let's look at two examples.

> A high school English teacher wants her students to be able to write persuasive essays. She shows an example of an exemplary essay and another example of an essay that is flawed. The students discuss the differences between the two, arrive at criteria for high-quality persuasive essays and then write essays of their own. (Stiggins, 2007)

> A health teacher reads in a professional journal that the biggest problem people have in applying first aid is not the mechanics per se, but knowing what to do and when. In an

attempt to address this problem, the teacher periodically plans "catastrophe" days. Students entering the classroom encounter a catastrophe victim with an unspecified injury. In each case, they have to first diagnose the problem and then apply first aid. The teacher observes them as they work and uses the information she gathers in discussions and assessments.

The term *performance assessment* originated in content areas such as science and the performing arts, where students are required to demonstrate an ability in a real-world situation, such as a laboratory demonstration or recital.

Designing performance assessments involves three steps, each designed to make them valid and reliable (Miller et al., 2009; Marion & Pellegrino, 2006).

1. Specify the type of performance you are trying to assess.
2. Structure the evaluation setting, balancing realism with safety and other issues.
3. Design evaluation procedures with clearly identified criteria.

Teachers use performance assessments to measure abilities similar to those required of students in the real world.

Specifying the Performance Components

Specifying the components you're attempting to measure is the first step in designing any assessment. A clear description of the performance helps students understand their requirements and assists you in designing appropriate instruction. An example of component specification in the area of persuasive writing is outlined in Figure 14.7.

In some cases the performance components will be processes, and in others they will be products. The initial focus is often on processes, with the emphasis shifting to products after procedures are mastered (Gronlund, 2003). Examples of processes and products as components of performance assessments are shown in Table 14.2.

Persuasive essay
1. Specifies purpose of the essay
2. Provides evidence supporting the purpose
3. Identifies audience
4. Specifies likely counterarguments
5. Presents evidence dispelling counterarguments

Figure 14.7 Performance outcomes in persuasive writing

table 14.2 Processes and Products as Components of Performance

Content Area	Product	Process
Math	Correct answer	Problem-solving steps leading to the correct solution
Music	Performance of a work on an instrument	Correct fingering and breathing that produce the performance
English Composition	Essay, term paper, or composition	Preparation of drafts and thought processes that produce the product
Word Processing	Letter or copy of final draft	Proper stroking and techniques for presenting the paper
Science	Explanation for the outcomes of a demonstration	Thought processes involved in preparing the explanation

Structuring the Evaluation Setting

Performance assessments are valuable because of their emphasis on real-world tasks. However, time, expense, or safety may prevent performance in the real world, so intermediate steps might be necessary. For example, in driver education, the goal is to produce safe drivers. However, putting beginning drivers in heavy traffic is both unrealistic and dangerous. So, teachers might begin by having students respond to written case studies, progress to using a simulator, then to driving on roads with little traffic, and finally driving in all kinds of conditions. As students' driving skills develop, they progress to higher degrees of realism.

Simulations provide opportunities for teachers to measure performance in cases where high realism is not feasible, and a driving simulator is an example. As another example, a geography teacher wanting to measure students' understanding of the impact of climate and geography on the location of cities might display the information shown in Figure 14.8. The simulation asks students to identify the best location for a city on the island and the criteria they use in determining the location. Their criteria provide the teacher with insights into students' thinking.

Designing Evaluation Procedures

Designing evaluation procedures is the final step in creating effective performance assessments. Scoring rubrics, similar to those used with essay items, can increase both reliability and validity (Mabry, 1999; Stiggins, 2005).

Let's look at three different strategies to evaluate learner performance: (a) systematic observation, (b) checklists, and (c) rating scales.

Systematic observation. The process of specifying criteria for acceptable performance in an activity and taking notes based on the criteria.

Systematic Observation. Teachers routinely observe students in classroom settings, but these observations usually are not systematic, and records are rarely kept. **Systematic observation** is an attempt to solve these problems; it is the process of specifying criteria for acceptable performance in an activity and taking notes based on the criteria. For example, a science teacher attempting to assess her students' ability to use the scientific method might establish the following:

1. States problem or question
2. States hypotheses
3. Specifies independent, dependent, and controlled variables

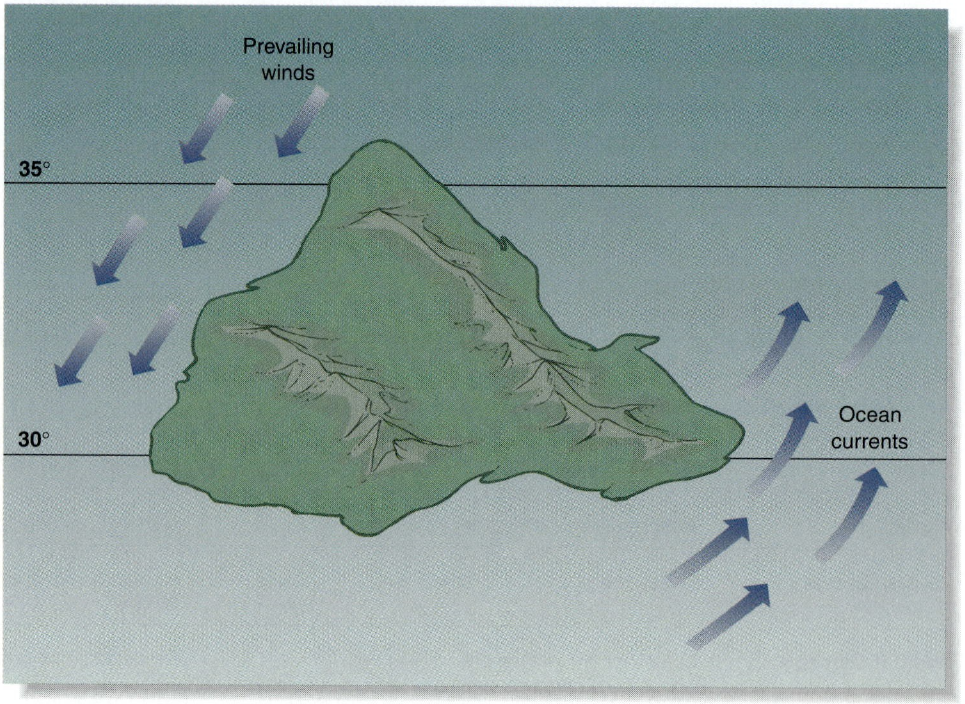

Figure 14.8 Simulation in geography

4. Gathers and displays data
5. Evaluates hypotheses based on the data

The teacher's notes then refer directly to the criteria, making them consistent for all groups. The teacher can also use these notes to give learners feedback and obtain information for use in future planning.

Checklists. Written descriptions of dimensions that must be present in an acceptable performance of an activity.

Rating scales. Written descriptions of the dimensions of an acceptable performance and scales of values on which each dimension is rated.

Portfolio assessment. The process of selecting collections of student work that both students and teachers evaluate using preset criteria.

Checklists. **Checklists** are written descriptions of dimensions that must be present in an acceptable performance, and they extend systematic observation by specifying important aspects of performance and by sharing them with students. During the assessment, teachers check off the desired dimensions rather than describing them in notes, as in systematic observation. For instance, the science teacher in the preceding example would check off each of the five criteria if they appeared in the report.

Checklists are useful when a teacher can determine whether a student did or did not meet a criterion, such as "States hypotheses." In other cases, however, such as "Evaluates hypotheses based on the data," the results aren't cut-and-dried; some evaluations will be more thorough and precise than others. Rating scales address this problem.

Rating Scales. **Rating scales** are written descriptions of the dimensions of an acceptable performance and scales of values on which each dimension is rated. Teachers can construct rating scales in numerical, graphic, or descriptive formats, such as illustrated in Figure 14.9.

As you see in the figure, rating scales are similar to the scoring rubrics we discussed earlier in the chapter. They allow more precise information to be gathered and allow more specific feedback than is possible with checklists.

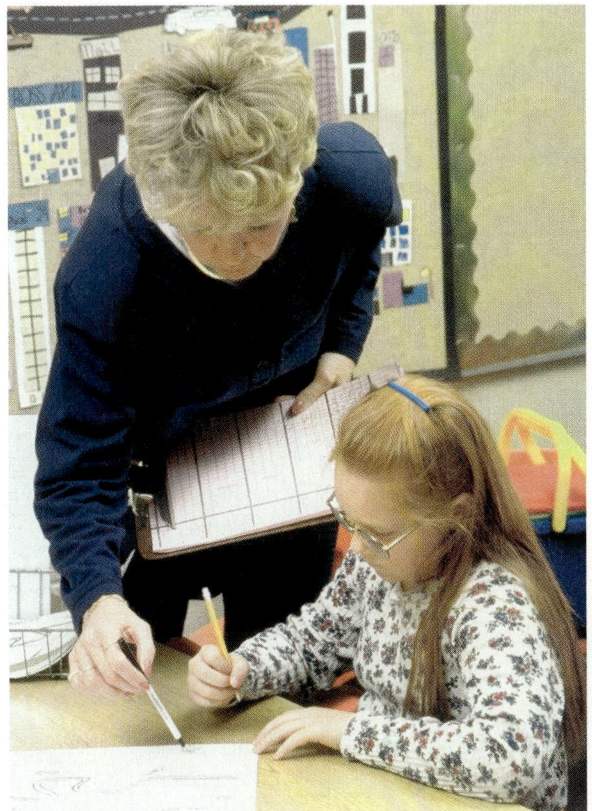

Systematic observations, checklists, and rating scales help increase the reliability of performance assessments.

Portfolio Assessment: Involving Students in the Assessment Process

Portfolio assessment is the process of selecting collections of student work that both students and teachers evaluate using preset criteria (Popham, 2005; Stiggins, 2005). The portfolio is the actual collection of works, such as essays, quizzes, projects, samples of poetry, lab reports, and videotaped performances. The use of portfolios is popular and appears in areas varying as widely as measuring readiness in children at risk for school failure (J. Smith, Brewer, & Heffner, 2003) to assessing biology students' understanding of complex life forms (Dickson, 2004). As the use of technology advances, electronic portfolios are becoming more popular (C. Lambert, DePaepe, & Lambert, 2007). Table 14.3 contains examples of portfolio assessments in different content areas.

table 14.3 Portfolio Samples in Different Content Areas

Content Area	Example
Elementary Math	Homework, quizzes, tests, and projects completed over time.
Writing	Drafts of narrative, descriptive, and persuasive essays in various stages of development. Samples of poetry.
Art	Projects over the course of the year collected to show growth in an area perspective or in a medium painting.
Science	Lab reports, projects, classroom notes, quizzes, and tests compiled to provide an overview of learning progress.

Effectiveness Concept	1	3	5
Lesson scope	No learning objective is apparent. The focus and scope of the lesson are uncertain.	Learning objective is unclear. The lesson covers too much or too little content.	A clear learning objective is apparent. The scope of the lesson is effective for reaching the objective.
Organization	Materials are not prepared and ready prior to the lesson. Routines are not apparent. Instructional time is wasted.	Some materials are prepared in advance, and some routines are apparent. Instructional time used reasonably well.	Instructional time is maximized with materials prepared in advance and well-established routines apparent.
Quality of examples/non-examples	Examples/non-examples are not used.	Examples/non-examples are used, but are inadequate to accurately represent the topic.	A variety of high-quality examples in context are used to represent the topic.
Review	No review of previous work is conducted.	A brief and superficial review of previous work is present.	A thorough review of ideas necessary to understand the present topic is conducted.
Questioning frequency	Teacher lectured. Few questions were asked.	Some questions were asked. Much of the content was delivered through lecture.	The lesson was developed with questioning throughout.
Equitable distribution of questions	Questions were not directed to specific students.	Some questions were directed to individual students. Volunteers were called on most frequently.	All students in the class were called on as equally as possible, and questions were directed to students by name.
Wait-time and prompting	Little wait-time was given. Unanswered questions were directed to other students.	Intermittent assistance was provided as well as adequate wait time in some cases.	Students were consistently given wait time and were prompted when they were unable to answer correctly.
Closure	Lesson lacked closure.	The teacher offered a summary and closure of the lesson.	The teacher guided students as they stated the main ideas of the lesson.
Instructional alignment	Learning objectives, learning activities, and assessment are out of alignment.	Objectives, learning activities, and assessment are partially aligned.	Learning objectives, the learning activity, and assessment are clearly aligned.

Figure 14.9 Rating scale for teaching effectiveness
Source: Adapted with permission from Eggen, P., & Gonzalez, C. (2007, April). *An examination of the relationships between elementary teachers' understanding of education psychology and their pedagogical practice.* Paper presented at the annual meeting of the American Education Research Association, Chicago.

Portfolio assessment has two valuable features. First, it involves the collection of work samples, so it reflects learning progress. For instance, writing samples can document improved skills that occur over a specified time period.

Second, portfolio assessment involves students in the design, collection, and evaluation of the materials to be included in the portfolio. Involving students in evaluating their own work encourages them to be more metacognitive about their approaches to studying and can increase self-regulation (Juniewicz, 2003). Further, evidence indicates that learners, both with and without learning disabilities, feel a greater sense of autonomy with portfolio assessment (Ezell & Klein, 2003).

The following are some guidelines to make portfolios effective learning tools:

- Integrate portfolios into your instruction, and refer to them as you teach.
- Provide examples of portfolios when introducing them to students.
- Involve students in the selection and evaluation of their work.
- Require students to provide an overview of each portfolio, a rationale for the inclusion of individual works, criteria they use to evaluate individual pieces, and a summary of progress.
- Provide students with frequent and detailed feedback about their decisions.

Portfolio assessment involves students in the collection and evaluation of materials to be included for examination.

Student-led conferences can be an effective way to communicate with parents about portfolio achievements (Juniewicz, 2003). Researchers have found that these conferences increase students' sense of responsibility and pride and improve both home–school cooperation and student–parent relationships (Stiggins, 2005). Time constraints and logistics are obstacles to full-scale implementation of student-led conferences, but the educational benefits of learner involvement and initiative help balance these limitations.

MyEducationLab

To analyze an elementary student's portfolio entry in science, go to the *Activities and Applications* section in Chapter 14 of MyEducationLab at www.myeducation.lab.com, and look at the artifact *Pig Lungs Dissection*. Answer the questions that follow.

Putting Formal Assessment Formats into Perspective

In this section we have discussed three types of formal assessments: paper-and-pencil items, performance assessments, and portfolios. All are controversial in different ways. For instance, critics of paper-and-pencil items argue that they focus on low-level knowledge and skills, fail to measure learners' ability to apply understanding in the real world, and measure only outcomes, so these assessments provide no insight into students' thinking (Bandalos, 2004; D. French, 2003; Popham, 2004c; Solley, 2007). Advocates of performance and portfolio assessment contend that these formats tap higher-level thinking and problem-solving skills, emphasize real-world applications, and focus on the processes learners use to produce their products (Cizek, 1997; D. French, 2003; Paris & Paris, 2001).

On the other hand, evidence doesn't support the claim that performance assessments do a better job of measuring higher-order thinking than do paper-and-pencil measures (Terwilliger, 1997). Further, education is in an era of accountability and high-stakes testing, and high-stakes tests most commonly use multiple-choice, sometimes combined with writing, as their primary format. Teachers, faced with the demands of standards-based accountability, feel pressured to prepare their students for the more traditional high-stakes tests they are required to take (Blocher et al., 2002).

Establishing reliable criteria for evaluating portfolios is another issue (E.S. Johnson & Arnold, 2007; Tillema & Smith, 2007). Obtaining acceptable levels of reliability with portfolios and performance assessments is possible if care is taken (Barnes, Torrens, & George, 2007; M. Wilson, Hoskens, & Draney, 2001), but in practice this has been a problem (Haertel, 1999; Shepard, 2001). In response to these issues, several states have reduced their use of portfolios, particularly for English Language Learners (Zehr, 2006).

At the classroom level, allowing students to determine portfolio content creates additional problems. For example, when students choose different items to place in their portfolios, cross-student comparisons are difficult, which decreases reliability. To address this issue, experts suggest supplementing portfolios with traditional measures to obtain the best of both processes (Stiggins, 2005).

MyEducationLab

To further analyze DeVonne Lampkin's assessment practices, go to the *Activities and Applications* section in Chapter 14 of MyEducationLab at www.myeducationlab.com, and watch the video episode: *Using Assessment in Decision Making.* Answer the questions following the episode.

As with all aspects of learning and teaching, assessment is complex and again illustrates the need for knowledgeable and skilled teachers. Only they can combine paper-and-pencil measures, performance assessments, and portfolios to create assessments that will maximize learning in their students.

check your understanding

3.1 Describe formal assessment, and explain how it is different from informal assessment.

3.2 Each of the following items has flaws in the distracters that might allow students to identify the correct answer without fully understanding the content. Identify the flaw in each case.

1. Which of the following is a function of the circulatory system?
   a. to support the vital organs of the body
   *b. to circulate the blood throughout the body
   c. to transfer nerve impulses from the brain to the muscles
   d. to provide for the movement of the body's large muscles
2. Of the following, the definition of *population density* is:
   a. the number of people who live in your city or town.
   b. the number of people who voted in the last presidential election.
   *c. the number of people per square mile in a country.
   d. the number of people in cities compared to small towns.
3. Of the following, the most significant cause of World War II was:
   a. American aid to Great Britain.
   b. Italy's conquering of Ethiopia.
   c. Japan's war on China.
   *d. the devastation of the German economy as a result of the Treaty of Versailles.
4. Which of the following is the best description of an insect?
   a. It always has one pair of antennae on its head.
   *b. It has three body parts.
   c. None lives in water.
   d. It breathes through lungs.
5. The one of the following that is not a reptile is a:
   a. alligator.
   b. lizard.
   *c. frog.
   d. turtle.
6. Which of the following illustrates a verb form used as a participle?
   a. Running is good exercise.
   *b. I saw a jumping frog contest on TV yesterday.
   c. Thinking is hard for many of us.
   d. All of the above.

3.3 Describe how you would create a rating scale that would allow you to assess someone's performance in creating high-quality multiple-choice test items. Provide an example.

3.4 Are essay items performance assessments? Defend your answer using the information from this section.

To receive feedback for these questions, go to Appendix A.

classroom connections

Creating Valid and Reliable Assessments in Your Classroom

1. *Validity* describes the extent to which an assessment measures what it is supposed to measure. Increase validity through careful planning before assessment.
   - **Elementary:** A third-grade teacher compares items on her quizzes, tests, and graded homework to the objectives in the curriculum guide and her unit plan to be sure all the appropriate objectives are covered.
   - **Middle School:** A social studies teacher writes a draft of one test item at the end of each day to be certain the emphasis on his tests is consistent with his instruction. When he develops the test, he checks to be sure that it covers all content areas and difficulty levels.
   - **High School:** After composing a test, a biology teacher rereads the items to eliminate wording that might be confusing or too advanced for her students.
2. Performance assessments directly examine students' ability to perform tasks similar to those they will be expected to perform in life outside of school. Increase the validity of your assessments by using performance assessment when appropriate.
   - **Elementary:** A first-grade teacher uses a rating scale to assess his students' oral reading ability. While he listens to each student read, he uses additional notes to help him remember each student's strengths and weaknesses.
   - **Middle School:** A math teacher working on decimals and percentages assigns her students the task of going to three supermarkets and comparing prices on a list of five household items. Students must determine which store provided the best bargains and the percentage difference between the stores on each item.
   - **High School:** A teacher in business technology has students write letters in response to job notices in the newspaper. The class then critiques the letters in terms of format, grammar, punctuation, and clarity.
3. Portfolio assessments involve students in the assessment process. Use portfolios to develop learner self-regulation.
   - **Elementary:** A fourth-grade teacher uses portfolios as an organizing theme for his language arts curriculum. Students collect pieces of work during the year and evaluate and share them with other members of their writing teams.
   - **Middle School:** A math teacher asks each student to compile a portfolio of work and present it at parent–teacher conferences. Before the conference, the teacher meets with students and helps them identify their strengths and weaknesses.
   - **High School:** An auto mechanics teacher makes each student responsible for keeping track of the competencies and skills each has mastered. The teacher gives each student a folder, where they must document the completion of different shop tasks.

Effective Assessment Practices

To this point, we have examined basic assessment concepts such as validity and reliability as well as informal and formal assessment in different formats. To maximize learning, however, teachers need to combine individual items into tests; plan performance assessments and the use of portfolios where appropriate; and administer, score, analyze, and discuss assessments. We consider these factors in this section as we discuss

- Planning for assessment
- Preparing students
- Administering assessments
- Analyzing results

Planning for Assessment

To ensure that assessments align with learning objectives, expert teachers prepare their assessments when they plan for instruction. This process seems obvious, but teachers usually prepare tests some time after completing instruction, so alignment is a common problem. For example, a teacher might give little emphasis to a topic in class but have several items on a quiz related to it, or emphasize a topic in class but give it minimal coverage on a quiz. Also, a teacher might discuss a topic at the applied level in class, but write the test items at a recall of factual information level. And, an objective may call for performance of some skill, but the assessment consists of multiple-choice questions. Each of these situations reduces the validity of an assessment.

Table of specifications. A matrix that helps teachers organize learning objectives by cognitive level or content area.

Tables of Specifications: Increasing Validity Through Planning

One way to ensure that learning objectives align with assessments is to prepare a **table of specifications,** a matrix that helps teachers organize learning objectives by cognitive level or content area and link both instruction and assessment to standards (Guskey, 2005; Notar, Zuelke, Wilson, & Yunker, 2004). For example, a geography teacher based her instruction in a unit on the Middle East on the following list of objectives:

Understands location of cities
1. States location
2. Identifies historical factors in settlement

Understands climate
1. Identifies major climate regions
2. Explains reasons for existing climates

Understands factors influencing economy
1. Describes economies of countries in the region
2. Identifies characteristics of each economy
3. Explains how economies relate to climate and physical features

Understands influence of physical features
1. Describes topography
2. Relates physical features to climate
3. Explains impact of physical features on location of cities
4. Analyzes impact of physical features on economy

Table 14.4 presents a table of specifications for a content-level matrix based on these objectives. The teacher had a mix of items, with greater emphasis on physical features than other topics. This emphasis reflects the teacher's objectives, which stressed the influence of physical features on the location of cities, the climate, and the economy of the region. It also reflects the time and effort spent on each area. Increasing validity of assessments by ensuring this match between objectives, instruction, and assessment is the primary function of a table of specifications.

For performance assessments, establishing criteria serves a function similar to that of a table of specifications. The criteria identify performance, determine emphasis, and attempt to ensure congruence between learning objectives and assessments.

Preparing Students for Assessments

To begin this section, let's look again at DeVonne's work with her students on Wednesday, the day before she gives her unit test.

table 14.4 Sample Table of Specifications

	Outcomes			
Content	**Knowledge**	**Comprehension**	**Higher Order Thinking and Problem Solving**	**Total Items in Each Content Area**
Cities	4	2	2	8
Climate	4	2	2	8
Economy	2	2	—	4
Physical features	4	9	7	20
Total items	14	15	11	—

"Get out your chalkboards," she directs, referring to individual chalkboards she has made for each of them at the beginning of the year.

"We're having a test tomorrow on finding equivalent fractions and adding fractions, and the test will go in your math portfolios. . . . I have some problems on the test that are going to make you think. . . . But you've all been working hard, and you're getting good at this, so you'll be able to do it. You're my team, and I know you'll come through," she smiles.

"To be sure we're okay, I have a few problems that are just like ones on the test, so let's see how we do. Write these on your chalkboards."

$$\frac{1}{3} + \frac{1}{4} = ? \qquad \frac{2}{7} + \frac{4}{7} = ?$$

DeVonne watches as they work on the problems and hold up their chalkboards when they finish. Seeing that three students miss the first problem, she reviews it with the class, and then displays the following three:

$$\frac{2}{3} + \frac{1}{6} = ? \qquad \frac{4}{9} + \frac{1}{6} = ? \qquad \frac{2}{9} + \frac{4}{9} = ?$$

Two students miss the second one, so again she reviews it carefully.

"Now, let's try one more," she continues, displaying the following problem on the overhead:

You are at a pizza party with 5 other people, and you order 2 pizzas. The 2 pizzas are the same size, but one is cut into 4 pieces and the other is cut into 8 pieces. You eat 1 piece from each pizza. How much pizza did you eat in all?

Again, she watches the students work and reviews the solution with them when they finish, asking questions such as, "What information in the problem is important?" "What do we see in the problem that's irrelevant?" and "What should we do first in solving it?" in the process.

After displaying two more word problems, she tells the students, "The problems on the test are like the ones we practiced here today." She then asks if they have any additional questions, and finishes her review by saying, "All right, when we take a test, what do we always do?"

"We read the directions carefully!" they shout in unison.

"Okay, good," DeVonne smiles. "Now, remember, what will you do if you get stuck on a problem?"

"Go on to the next one, so we don't run out of time."

"And what will we be sure not to do?"

"We won't forget to go back to the one we skipped."

In preparing students for tests, we have both long- and short-term goals. Long term, you want your students to understand test-taking strategies and enter testing situations with confidence. Short term, you want them to understand the format and the content being tested. By preparing students, you help reach both goals.

Teaching Test-Taking Strategies

You can help students improve their test-taking skills by teaching strategies such as these:

- Use time efficiently and pace themselves.
- Read directions carefully.
- Identify the important information in questions.
- Understand the demands of different testing formats.
- Determine how questions will be scored.

To be most effective, you should illustrate these strategies with concrete examples. Students also need practice with a variety of formats and testing situations. Research indicates that strategy instruction improves performance, and that young, low-ability, and minority students who have limited test-taking experience benefit the most (Pressley & Hilden, 2006).

Reducing Test Anxiety

"Listen my children and you shall hear. . . . Listen my children and you shall hear. . . . Rats! I knew it this morning in front of Mom."

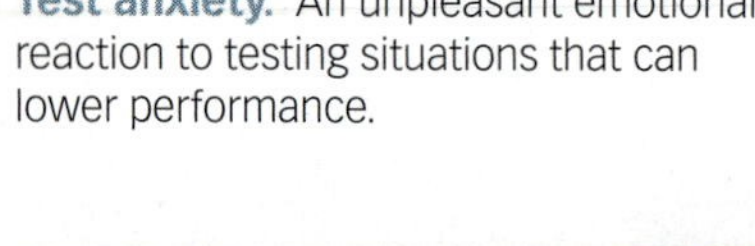

Test anxiety. An unpleasant emotional reaction to testing situations that can lower performance.

Like this student, most of us have experienced **test anxiety,** an unpleasant emotional reaction to testing situations that can lower performance. Usually, it is momentary and minor, but for a portion of the school population (estimates run as high as 10 percent), it is a serious problem (Cassady & Johnson, 2002).

Teachers can reduce test anxiety by increasing the number of assessments and by providing clear explanations of content.

Research suggests that test anxiety consists of both an emotional and a cognitive component (Schunk et al., 2008). Its emotional component can include physiological symptoms, such as increased pulse rate, dry mouth, and headache, as well as feelings of dread and helplessness and sometimes "going blank." Its cognitive, or worry, component involves preoccupation with test difficulty, thoughts of failure and other issues, such as parental concern about a low score. These thoughts take working memory space, which leaves less to analyze specific items.

Test anxiety is triggered by testing situations that (1) involve pressure to succeed, (2) students perceive as difficult, (3) impose time limits, and (4) contain unfamiliar items or formats (Cassady & Johnson, 2002). Unannounced tests are particularly significant in causing anxiety.

Teachers can do much to minimize test anxiety, and the most successful efforts focus on the worry component (Schunk et al., 2008). Suggestions include the following:

- Use criterion measures to minimize the competitive aspects of tests, and avoid social comparisons, such as public displays of test scores. (We discuss criterion referencing in the next section.)
- Give more, rather than fewer, quizzes and tests.
- Discuss test content and procedures before testing, and give clear directions for responding to test items.
- Teach test-taking skills, and give students ample time to take tests.
- Use a variety of assessments to measure students' understanding and skills.

Specific Test-Preparation Procedures

Before any test, teachers want to ensure that learners understand test content and procedures and expect to succeed on the exam. Teachers can

- Specify what will be on the test.
- Give students a chance to practice similar items under test-like conditions.
- Establish positive expectations and encourage students to link success and effort.

Teachers' clarifying test formats and content establishes structure for students, which reduces test anxiety. And students' knowing what will be on the test and how items will be formatted leads to higher achievement for all students, particularly those of low ability.

Specifying the content often isn't enough, however, particularly with young learners. So it's important to give students practice exercises and present them in a format that parallels their appearance on the test. In learning math skills, for instance, DeVonne's students first practiced adding fractions with like denominators, then learned to find equivalent fractions, and finally added fractions with unlike denominators, each in separate lessons. On the test, however, the problems were mixed, so DeVonne gave students a chance to practice integrating these skills before the test.

Finally, DeVonne communicated that she expected students to do well on the test. The motivational benefits of establishing positive expectations have been confirmed by decades of research (Schunk et al., 2008; Stipek, 2002). She also emphasized effort and modeled an incremental view of ability by saying, "But you've all been working hard, and you're getting good at this, so you'll be able to do it." As you recall from your study of motivation in Chapters 10 and 11, encouraging the belief that ability is incremental and can be improved through effort benefits both immediate performance and long-term motivation.

Administering Assessments

When teachers administer assessments, they want to create conditions to ensure that results reflect what students know and can do. To see how this is done, let's return to DeVonne's classroom.

> At 10:00 Thursday morning, she shuts a classroom window because of noise from delivery trucks outside. She considers rearranging the desks in the room but decides to wait until after the test.
>
> "Okay, everyone, let's get ready for our math test," she directs, as students put their books under their desks.
>
> She waits a moment, sees that everyone's desk is clear, and says, "When you're finished, turn the test over, and I'll come and get it. Now look up at the board. After you're done, work on the assignment listed there until everyone is finished. Then we'll start reading." As she hands out the tests, she says, "If you get too warm, raise your hand, and I'll turn on the air conditioner. I shut the window because of the noise outside.
>
> "Work carefully," she says after everyone has a copy. "You've all been working hard, and I know you will do well. You have as much time as you need." As students begin working, DeVonne stands at the side of the room, watching them.
>
> After several minutes, she notices Anthony doodling at the top of his paper and glancing around the room. She goes over and says, "It looks like you're doing fine on these problems," pointing to some near the top of the paper. "Now concentrate a little harder. I'll bet you can do most of the others." She smiles reassuringly and again moves to the side of the room.
>
> DeVonne goes over to Hajar in response to her raised hand. "The lead on my pencil broke, Mrs. Lampkin," she whispers.
>
> "Take this one," DeVonne responds, handing her another. "Come and get yours after the test."
>
> As students finish, DeVonne picks up their papers, and they begin the assignment on the board.

Now let's look at DeVonne's actions in administering the test. First, she arranged the environment to be comfortable, free from distractions, and similar to the way it was when students learned the content. Distractions can depress test performance, particularly in young or low-ability students.

Second, she gave precise directions for taking the test, turning in the papers, and spending time afterward. These directions helped maintain order and prevented distractions for late-finishing students.

Finally, she carefully monitored the students as they worked on the test. This not only allowed her to encourage those who were distracted but also discouraged cheating. In the real world, some students will cheat if given the opportunity (Bracey, 2005). However, an emphasis on mastery versus performance and efforts to create the feeling that students are part of a learning community decrease the likelihood of cheating (K. Finn & Frone, 2004; Murdock, Hale, & Weber, 2001). In addition, external factors, such as the teacher leaving the room, influence cheating more than whether or not students are inclined to do so (Blackburn & Miller, 1999; Newstead, Franklyn-Stokes, & Armstead, 1996).

In DeVonne's case, monitoring was more a form of support than of being a watchdog. For example, when she saw that Anthony was distracted, she quickly intervened, encouraged him, and urged him to increase his concentration. This encouragement is particularly important for underachieving and test-anxious students (J. Elliott & Thurlow, 2000).

Analyzing Results

> "Do you have our tests finished, Mrs. Lampkin?" students ask Friday morning.
>
> "Of course!" she smiles, returning their papers.
>
> "Overall, you did well, and I'm proud of you. I knew all that hard work would pay off. . . . There are a few items I want to go over, though. We had a little trouble with number 13, and you all made nearly the same mistake, so let's take a look at it."

theory to practice

Increasing the Quality of Your Assessments

Assessment is one of the most important components of the teaching–learning process, but creating quality assessments is a demanding process. The following guidelines can help you increase the quality of your assessments and make the assessment process more efficient.

1. Create an item file of paper-and-pencil items, store it in your computer, and create tests and quizzes from the item file.
2. Provide students with detailed feedback about frequently missed paper-and-pencil items and results of performance measures.
3. Collect assessments, and keep them on file for students.
4. Revise both paper-and-pencil and performance items to increase their quality.

Teachers' workloads help us understand why most teachers use the assessment items included with textbook series, even though they are often low quality and not aligned with teachers' learning objectives.

It is virtually impossible to continually create new assessment items at levels above recall of factual information from scratch; you simply won't have the time. However, you can gradually develop an item file of high-quality items and then create your individual assessments from the item file. Doing so saves you time, contributes to quality assessments, and helps ensure alignment. This applies the first guideline.

You can apply the second guideline by thoroughly discussing items after assessments are returned. For example, if your items measure learning at the levels of application, analysis, and evaluation of conceptual and procedural knowledge (see Figure 13.2 on page 393), your students will often learn more from the discussion of assessment items and feedback than they will from any other aspect of the teaching–learning process (Crooks, 1988). This is the essence of assessment *for* learning, and the instructional time spent on it is very worthwhile (Stiggins, 2007).

Third, after giving tests and quizzes, collect them and put them on file for students, so you can reuse the items. Again, it is impossible to continually create new high-quality test items. Keeping them on file allows students to come in and review them.

Finally, items written above the level of recall of factual information often will need to be interpretive exercises, and some students are likely to misinterpret the items. Discussion and feedback will help you identify wording in your items that can be misinterpreted, and you can then revise the items to make them clearer. The revised items can be reused, and the quality of your items continually improves. This process takes time and effort, but once you have created a file of high-quality items, your assessments truly will be designed *for* learning.

She waits a moment while students read the problem and then asks, "Now, what are we given in the problem?. . . Saleina?"

"Mr. El had two dozen candy bars."

"Okay. Good. And how many is that? . . . Kevin?"

"Umm . . . two dozen is 24."

"Fine. And what else do we know? . . . Hajar?"

DeVonne continues the discussion of the problem and then goes over two other frequently missed problems. In the process, she makes notes at the top of her copy, identifying the problems that were difficult. She writes "Ambiguous" by one and underlines some of the wording in it. By another, she writes, "Teach them how to draw diagrams of the problem." She then puts her copy of the test in a folder, lays it on her desk to be filed, and turns back to the class.

DeVonne's efforts didn't end with administering the test. She scored and returned it the next day, discussed the results, and gave students feedback as quickly as possible. Feedback helps learners correct misconceptions, and knowledge of results promotes student motivation (Brookhart, 2007/2008). Because student attention is high during discussions of missed items, many teachers believe that students learn more in these sessions than they do in original instruction (Haertel, 1986).

In addition, DeVonne made positive comments about students' performance on the test. In a study examining this factor, students who were told they did well performed better on a subsequent measure than those who were told they did poorly, even though the two groups did equally well on the first test (Bridgeman, 1974). Research also supports the benefits of encouraging comments; students who see notes such as "Excellent! Keep it up!" and "Good work!" do better on subsequent measures (Page, 1992).

Finally, DeVonne made notes on her copy of the test before filing it. Her notes reminded her that the wording on one of her problems was misleading, so she could revise it.

Classroom connections

Conducting Effective Assessment Practices in Your Classroom

1. Preparing assessments during planning for instruction helps ensure that you align assessments with learning objectives. Prepare your assessments during planning.
   - **Elementary:** As part of an extended unit on reading comprehension, a third-grade teacher is planning lessons focusing on authors' purposes and cause-and-effect relationships. As he plans, he identifies passages that he will use for practice and as the basis for assessing his students' abilities in these two areas.
   - **Middle School:** A middle school social studies teacher is planning a unit focusing on the relationships between technological events, such as the Industrial Revolution, and changes in societies. As he plans, he writes a series of short essay questions that he will use to assess the students' understanding of the relationships.
   - **High School:** A geometry teacher is planning a unit on the construction of segments and angles, angle bisectors, and parallel and perpendicular lines. As he plans, he creates problems that he will use to assess his students' understanding of these processes.
2. Providing students with specific test-preparation procedures both increases achievement and decreases test anxiety. Provide students with practice on items similar to those that will appear on the assessment, and state positive expectations about their performance.
   - **Elementary:** The third-grade teacher gives his students reading passages, and has them identify the authors' purposes in each case, as well as having them identify cause-and-effect relationships in the passages.
   - **Middle School:** The middle school social studies teacher presents examples of responses to essay questions similar to those he plans to use for his assessment. With his guidance, students identify both well-written and poorly written responses, and explain differences between the two.
   - **High School:** The geometry teacher has her students practice creating constructions similar to those that they will prepare on the assessment.
3. Feedback and discussion of assessment items increases students' understanding of the topics they are studying. Provide detailed feedback on frequently missed items.
   - **Elementary:** The third-grade teacher returns students' papers and discusses each of the items in detail.
   - **Middle School:** The social studies teacher creates ideal responses to the essay items and helps the students identify the characteristics that made them good responses.
   - **High School:** The geometry teacher demonstrates how each of the constructions of the items on the test could be created. He guides a discussion of alternate ways the constructions could be accomplished.

This, plus other information taken from the test, would assist her in future planning for both instruction and assessment.

MyEducationLab

To analyze a middle school teacher's assessment practices, go to the *Activities and Applications* section in Chapter 14 of MyEducationLab at www.myeducationlab.com, and read the case study *Assessment in Middle School Math.* Answer the questions following the case study.

check your understanding

4.1 Describe effective assessment practices, and explain how they can increase student learning.

4.2 Creating tables of specifications for assessments is considered to be an effective assessment practice. Explain the primary purpose of a table of specifications. When should it be created?

4.3 Effective assessment practices suggest that students should be taught test-taking strategies. Identify three test-taking strategies that DeVonne emphasized with her students as she prepared them for their test.

To receive feedback for these questions, go to Appendix A.

Grading and Reporting: The Total Assessment System

To this point, we have discussed formal and informal assessment and the assessment process itself, which includes preparing students, administering assessments, and analyzing results. Designing a total assessment system requires some additional decisions, such as

- How should I use formative and summative assessments?
- How many tests and quizzes should I give?

- How will I use performance assessments?
- How will I count homework?
- How will I assess and report affective dimensions, such as cooperation and effort?

These decisions will be your responsibility, a prospect that may seem daunting, because you have little experience to fall back on. However, knowing that the decisions are yours removes some of this uncertainty. We discuss these issues in this section.

Formative and Summative Assessment

Although we often think that the purpose of giving tests and quizzes is to assign grades, its most important function is to provide information about learning progress (Stiggins, 2007). Assessment *for* learning includes diagnosing students' existing understanding, assessing their learning progress, and providing feedback. Frequently, teachers use assessments to increase learning, but do not use these for grading purposes, a process called **formative assessment** (Chappuis & Chappuis, 2007/2008; Guskey, 2007/2008).

Formative assessment. The process of using both informal and formal assessments to provide students with feedback about learning progress, but not using the assessment information to make decisions about grading.

Virtually all forms of informal assessment are formative. For example, when a teacher uses students' responses to questions as a basis for deciding to move forward in a learning activity, she isn't using the information to grade students. Pretests, work samples, and writing assignments that can be rewritten are other common forms of formative assessment. Providing students with feedback, which is essential for increasing motivation and helping students learn to monitor their own progress, is its primary purpose (Frey & Schmitt, 2005; Stiggins, 2007). In this respect, formative assessment is a form of instructional scaffolding that assists students during learning (Shepard, 2005). Despite its positive effects, research suggests that teachers use formative assessment infrequently (Frey & Schmitt, 2005).

Summative assessment. The process of assessing after instruction and using the results for making grading decisions.

Summative assessment is the process of assessing after instruction and using the results for grading decisions. Although used for grading, feedback on summative assessments is also essential, and summative assessments can also be effective for promoting learning. In public schools, most assessments are used for summative purposes; however, used properly, both formative and summative assessments can be useful for making instructional decisions and increasing student motivation to learn.

Designing a Grading System

An effective grading system provides feedback to students, helps them develop self-regulation, and can increase motivation to learn. It also aids communication between teachers and parents (Guskey, 2002). The following are some guidelines that can help you in designing your system:

- Create a system that is clear, understandable, and consistent with school and district policies.
- Design your system to support learning and instruction by gathering frequent and systematic information from each student.
- Base grades on observable data.
- Assign grades consistently regardless of gender, class, race, or socioeconomic status.

You should be able to confidently defend your system to a parent or administrator if necessary (Miller et al., 2009).

Norm-Referenced and Criterion-Referenced Grading Systems

Assigning value to students' work is an integral part of assessment. Norm-referenced and criterion-referenced systems are two ways to assign value to student performance. In **norm-referenced grading,** teachers base assessment decisions about an individual's work on comparisons with the work of peers. This type of grading gets its name from the normal curve (see Figure 15.4 on page 483 in Chapters 15), and teachers using it might establish a grading system such as the following:

Norm-referenced grading. A grading system in which teachers base assessment decisions about an individual's work on comparisons with the work of peers.

A	Top 15% of students
B	Next 20% of students
C	Next 30% of students
D	Next 20% of students
F	Last 15% of students

When using **criterion-referenced grading,** teachers make assessment decisions according to a predetermined standard, such as 100–90 for an A, 89–80 for a B, and so on. The specific standards will vary among school districts, and even schools. They are often established by the school or district, but in many cases the decision will be yours.

Criterion-referenced grading. A grading system in which teachers make assessment decisions according to a predetermined standard.

Criterion-referenced systems have two important advantages over those that are norm referenced (Haladyna, 2002; Stiggins, 2005). First, because they reflect the extent to which learning objectives are met, they more nearly describe content mastery. Second, they deemphasize competition. Competitive grading systems can discourage students from helping each other, threaten peer relationships, and decrease motivation to learn (P. Black & William, 1998a; Stipek, 1996). While norm-referencing is important for standardized testing, it is rarely used in classroom assessment systems.

Paper-and-Pencil and Performance Assessments

For teachers in upper elementary, middle, and high schools, paper-and-pencil assessments are the cornerstones of most grading systems. Some add tests and quizzes together and count them as a certain percentage of the overall grade; others weigh them differently in assigning grades.

If you're using performance assessments or portfolios as part of your assessment system, you should include them in determining grades. To do otherwise communicates that they are less important than the paper-and-pencil measures you're using. If you rate student performance on the basis of well-defined criteria, scoring will have acceptable reliability, and performance assessments and/or portfolios can then be an integral part of your total assessment system.

Homework

As you saw in Chapter 13, properly designed homework contributes to learning. To be most effective, teachers should collect, score, and include homework in their grading system (Cooper et al., 2006; Marzano, 2007). Beyond this point, however, research provides little guidance as to how teachers should manage homework. Accountability, feedback, and your own workload will all influence this decision. Table 14.5 outlines some options for homework assessment.

table 14.5 Homework-assessment Options

Option	Advantages	Disadvantages
Grade it yourself	Promotes learning. Allows diagnosis of students. Increases student effort.	Is very demanding for the teacher.
Grade samples	Reduces teacher work, compared with first option.	Doesn't give the teacher a total picture of student performance.
Collect at random intervals	Reduces teacher workload.	Reduces student effort unless homework is frequently collected.
Change papers, students grade	Provides feedback with minimal teacher effort.	Consumes class time. Doesn't give students feedback on their own work.
Students score own papers	Also provides feedback with minimum teacher effort. Lets students see their own mistakes.	Is inaccurate for purposes of evaluation. Lets students not do the work and copy in class as it's being discussed.
Students get credit for completing assignment	Gives students feedback on their work when it's discussed in class.	Reduces effort of unmotivated students.
No graded homework, frequent short quizzes	Is effective with older and motivated students.	Reduces effort of unmotivated students.

As you can see in Table 14.5, each homework-assessment option has advantages and disadvantages. The best strategy is one that results in learners making the most consistent and conscientious effort on their homework without costing you an inordinate amount of time and effort.

Effective teachers use grades to provide students with information about their learning progress.

Assigning Grades: Increasing Learning and Motivation

Having made decisions about paper-and-pencil and performance assessments, portfolios, and homework, you are now ready to design your total grading system. At this point, you need to make two decisions: (1) what to include and (2) the weight to assign each component.

In addition to paper-and-pencil assessments, performance measures, and homework, some teachers build in additional factors, such as effort, class participation, and attitude. Assessment experts discourage this practice, although it is common in classrooms (Miller et al., 2009). Gathering systematic information about affective variables is difficult, and assessing them is highly subjective. In addition, a high grade based on effort suggests to both students and parents that important content was learned when it may not have been. Factors such as effort, cooperation, and class attendance should be reflected in a separate section of the report card.

Learners with exceptionalities pose special grading challenges; research indicates that large numbers of these students receive below-average grades in their general education classes (Munk, 2003). The effects of these low grades can be devastating to students who already experience frustration in attempting to keep up with their peers.

To address this problem, teachers often adapt their grading systems by grading on improvement, assigning separate grades for process and for products, and basing a grade on meeting the objectives of an individualized education program (IEP) (Venn, 2000). The dilemma for teachers is how to increase motivation to learn while providing an accurate indicator of learning progress (Tomlinson, 2005).

Let's look at two teachers' systems for assigning grades:

Kim Sook (Middle School Science)		**Lea DeLong (High School Algebra)**	
Tests and quizzes	50%	Tests	45%
Homework	20%	Quizzes	45%
Performance assessment	20%	Homework	10%
Projects	10%		

Alternative assessments. Assessment measures that include projects and performance assessment.

We see that they are quite different. Kim, an eighth-grade physical science teacher, emphasizes both homework and **alternative assessments,** which include projects and performance assessments. Traditional tests and quizzes count only 50 percent in his system. Lea emphasizes tests and quizzes more heavily; they count 90 percent in her system. The rationale in each case is simple. Kim believes that homework is important to student learning, and he believes that unless it is emphasized, students won't do it. He also includes projects as an important part of his system, believing they involve his students in the study of science. He uses performance assessments to chart students' progress as they work on experiments and other lab activities. Lea, a secondary Algebra II teacher, believes that students understand the need to do their homework in order to succeed on tests and quizzes, so she deemphasizes this component in her grading system. Instead, she gives a weekly quiz and three tests during a 9-week grading period.

To promote learning, students must understand your assessment system. Even young students can understand the relationship between effort and grades if they are assessed frequently and if their homework is scored and returned promptly. Conversely, even high school students can have problems understanding a grading system if it is too complex (E. Evans & Engelberg, 1988).

Parents must also understand your assessment system if they are to be involved in their children's learning (Guskey, 2002). Parents view parent–teacher conferences and graded exam-

exploring diversity

Effective Assessment Practices with Students from Diverse Backgrounds

As you've seen in earlier chapters, learner diversity influences teaching and learning in a number of ways. The process of assessment is one of the most important.

The current reform movement, with its emphasis on standards, has heightened awareness of the seemingly ubiquitous problem of educating students from diverse backgrounds. The problem is particularly acute in urban settings, where diversity is the most pronounced (Armour-Thomas, 2004).

Student diversity influences classroom assessment in at least three ways. First, learners with diverse backgrounds may lack experience with general testing procedures, different test formats, and test-taking strategies. Second, they may not fully understand that assessments promote learning and instead view them as punitive. Third, because most assessments are strongly language based, language may be an obstacle (E. Garcia, 2005).

The following recommendations respond to these issues (Heubert & Hausser, 1999; Popham, 2005):

- Attempt to create a mastery-focused classroom environment, such as you saw in our discussion in Chapter 11. Emphasize that assessments promote learning, provide feedback, and measure learning progress.
- Deemphasize grades, and keep all assessment results private. Establish a rule that students may not share their scores and grades with each other. (This is difficult to enforce, but it is a symbolic gesture and an attempt to protect students who want to succeed but face peer pressure not to.)
- Increase the number of assessments, and provide detailed and corrective feedback for all items. Encourage students to ask questions about test items, and when they answer incorrectly, ask them to explain their answers. Emphasize that mistakes are part of learning, and present students with evidence of their learning progress.
- Drop one or two quizzes a marking period for purposes of grading. This practice reduces test anxiety and communicates to students that you are "on their side" and want them to succeed. It also contributes to a positive classroom climate.
- Make provisions for non-native English speakers by allowing extra time and providing extra help with language aspects of your assessments.

Of these suggestions, feedback and discussion are the most important. While important in all environments, they are essential for effective assessment with learners having diverse backgrounds. First, students' explanations for their answers might reveal misconceptions, which you can then address. Second, feedback can help you identify content bias in your questions (Popham, 2005). For example, some students may have limited experiences with electric appliances such as an iron or vacuum cleaner, summertime activities such as camping and hiking, musical instruments such as a banjo, or transportation such as cable cars (Cheng, 1987). If assessment items require knowledge or experiences with these ideas, you are measuring both the intended topic and students' general knowledge, which detracts from validity. The only way you can identify these potential sources of bias is to discuss assessment items afterward. Then, you can revise and more carefully word your assessments to help eliminate bias.

Increasing the number of assessments and providing detailed feedback can increase the effectiveness of assessment for students from diverse backgrounds.

The possibility of content bias is even more likely if you have non-native English speakers in your classes. Some suggestions for supporting these students include the following (Abedi, Hofstetter & Lord, 2004):

- Provide extra time to take tests.
- Allow students to use a translation glossary or dictionary during the test.
- Read directions aloud. (It is even better if you can read the students the directions in their native languages.)
- Allow them to take the test at a different time, and read it to them, clarifying misunderstandings where possible.

The primary function of assessment in general, and with learners having diverse backgrounds in particular, is to provide evidence of increasing competence. And, evidence of learning progress can then be an important source of motivation to learn.

ples of their child's work together with report cards as valuable sources of information about their children's learning progress.

Points or Percentages?

In assigning scores to assessments, teachers have two options. In a percentage system, they convert each score to a percentage and then average the percentages as the marking period progresses. In the other system, teachers accumulate raw points and convert them to a percentage only at the end of the marking period.

A percentage-based system has an important weakness. For example, if a student misses one item on a 10-item quiz, the student's score is a 90 percent. If the teacher gives another short

classroom connections

Designing an Effective Assessment System in Your Classroom

1. Formative assessment is used primarily to provide feedback to students, summative assessments are used for grading, and both are consistent with assessment *for* learning. Use both formative and summative measures in your assessment system.
   - **Elementary:** A second-grade teacher discusses math problems that several students missed on their homework, and then asks them to rework the problems. If students are still having problems with the content, she reteaches it before she gives them a graded assessment.
   - **Middle School:** A sixth-grade science teacher has created an item pool which he has stored on his computer. He uses some of the items to create a "practice test" which the class discusses immediately after they've taken it. He then uses additional items on a summative assessment.
   - **High School:** A tenth-grade English teacher provides extensive individual comments on students' papers. In addition, he identifies problem areas common to the whole class and uses anonymous selections from students' papers to provide feedback to the whole class.
2. Frequent and thorough assessments, combined with feedback, promote learning. Design your assessment system so that gathering systematic information from each student is part of your routines.
   - **Elementary:** A second-grade teacher has his students solve two problems each morning that focus on the previous day's math topic. The class discusses the solutions before he moves to the topic for the day.
   - **Middle School:** A geography teacher gives a weekly quiz and three tests during each 9-week grading period with the majority of the items written above the level of recall of factual information. She provides detailed feedback on each of the items, and then collects the quizzes and tests, so she can reuse the items.
   - **High School:** A history teacher gives at least one quiz a week in which students must respond to items such as, "Before the Civil War the South was primarily agricultural rather than industrial. Explain how this might have influenced the outcome of the Civil War." The day after each quiz, she displays an ideal answer to the item, and a second, lower-quality response, and the class discusses the differences between the two.
3. Effective grading systems are understandable to both students and their parents. Create a grading system that is understandable and consistent with school policies.
   - **Elementary:** A fourth-grade teacher's school uses a 70–79, 80–89, and 90–100 grading system for a C, B, and A, respectively. She explains the system in a letter to her students' parents, and routinely sends home packets of student papers that indicate the students' learning progress.
   - **Middle School:** A math teacher displays his grading system on a wall chart. He explains the system and what it requires of students. He emphasizes that it is designed to promote learning and returns to the chart periodically to remind students of their learning progress.
   - **High School:** A history teacher in a school with high percentages of minority students takes extra time and effort during parent–teacher conferences to explain how she arrives at grades for her students. She saves students' work samples and shares them with parents during conferences.

quiz, and the student gets 3 of 5 items correct, the student's score on the second quiz is 60 percent, and the average of the two quizzes is 75 percent. This process gives the two quizzes equal weight, even though the first had twice as many items. If the teacher used a point system, the student got 12 of 15 items correct, which is 80 percent.

If averaging percentages is flawed, why is it so common? The primary reason is simplicity. It is both simpler for teachers to manage and easier to communicate to students and parents. Many teachers, and particularly those in elementary and middle schools, have attempted point systems and later returned to percentages because of pressure from students.

As with most aspects of teaching, the choice of a grading system is a matter of professional judgment. A percentage system is fair if assignments are similar in length, tests are also similar in length, and tests receive more weight than quizzes and assignments. On the other hand, a point system can work if students keep a running total of their points and you tell them the number required for an A, a B, and so on at frequent points in the marking period.

check your understanding

5.1 Describe the components and the decisions involved in designing a total assessment system.

5.2 Describe differences between formative and summative assessment.

5.3 Describe the advantages and disadvantages of a percentage compared to a point system for grading.

To receive feedback for these questions, go to Appendix A.

developmentally appropriate practice

Assessment of Learning with Different-Aged Students

While many aspects of assessment—such as aligning assessments with learning objectives, making them valid and reliable, and using them to promote learning at all grade levels—apply at all developmental levels, important differences exist. The following paragraphs outline some suggestions for responding to these differences.

Working with Elementary Students

In the lower elementary grades, teachers strongly emphasize reading and math, and performance assessments are more prominent than they are with older students. For example, first graders identify sounds of vowels and consonant digraphs in printed words, decode words, and print letters. In math, they write numbers, order whole numbers up to 100 or more, and represent numbers on a number line. Each task involves performance assessment.

Informal assessment and assessment of affective outcomes, such as "Gets along well with others" are also more prominent in elementary schools than with older students.

Because of these emphases, being aware of the possibility that assessments may be unreliable or invalid is important. Attempting to gather the same information from all students and increasing the frequency of assessments can be helpful when assessing young children's knowledge and skills.

Working with Middle School Students

The cognitive demands on middle school students increase significantly, and teachers use paper-and-pencil assessments to a much greater degree than do elementary teachers. For example, in social studies, eighth graders should understand ideas such as the ways in which architecture, language, and beliefs have been transmitted from one society to another; in science they should understand the difference between weight and mass, and the relationships between the temperature and the motion of particles; in math they solve systems of linear equations; and in language arts they should understand literary devices, such as meter and figurative language.

These are all abstract ideas, and instructional alignment is the key to effective assessment of these topics. If teachers' instruction of these topics is abstract, the topics won't be meaningful to students, and the students will memorize what they can in order to perform acceptably on the assessments. Instruction that includes high-quality examples and a great deal of discussion is necessary to make the topics meaningful. Then, assessments that also employ examples, such as the interpretive exercise in Figure 14.4 on page 442, can be effective for promoting learning.

Standards for high school students typically require a great deal of abstract thinking. For instance, in language arts they should understand how writers use strategies such as hyperbole, rhetorical questioning, and using glittering generalities as persuasive techniques; in science they should understand atomic theory; and in social studies they should understand why ancient civilizations such as those in Mesopotamia, Egypt, and the Indus Valley evolved and succeeded. As with middle school students, in the absence of meaningful instruction, students will try memorizing enough information to survive the assessments, and then promptly forget the information. To make the information meaningful, teachers must represent the topics in a variety of ways, such as vignettes, time lines, and artifacts in history and well-designed models in science. If the topics are meaningfully taught, and assessments are aligned with the instruction, teachers can accomplish assessment *for* learning.

Meeting Your Learning Objectives

1. Explain assessment *for* learning and how validity and reliability are related to it.
   - Assessment *for* learning makes assessment an integral part of the teaching–learning process, designed to support and increase learning.
   - All forms of assessment must be valid, meaning that they measure what they're supposed to measure.
   - All forms of assessment must be as reliable as possible, meaning they are consistently interpreted. Assessments that are unreliable cannot be valid.
2. Describe informal assessment, and explain why it is an important part of assessment *for* learning.
   - Informal assessment is the process of gathering information and making decisions during learning activities and other classroom activities.
   - Informal assessment is essential for the many instructional decisions that teachers make each day, such as how quickly to move a learning activity, who to call on, what questions to ask, how long students should be given to

respond, and many others. Without informal assessment, making these decisions would be impossible.

3. Describe formal assessment, and evaluate the quality of formal assessment items.
   - Formal assessment is the process of systematically gathering the same kind of information from each student.
   - Paper-and-pencil items, performance assessments, and portfolios are all useful as formal assessments.
   - Teachers can analzye formal assessments using specific criteria that exist for each assessment format.
4. Describe effective assessment practices, and explain how they increase student learning.
   - Teachers use effective assessment practices when they (1) design assessments that are congruent with learning objectives and instruction, that communicate assessment content, and that allow students to practice on items similar to those that will appear on tests; (2) teach test-taking skills; and (3) express positive expectations for student performance.
   - Effective assessment practices also include attempts to reduce test anxiety, such as increasing testing frequency, using criterion referencing, providing clear information about tests, and giving students ample time.
   - All effective assessment practices increase learning by making expectations clear, providing students with opportunities to practice, and providing detailed feedback.
5. Describe the components and decisions involved in designing a total assessment system.
   - A total assessment system includes creating traditional and alternative assessments, preparing students, administering assessments, analyzing results, and assigning grades.
   - Some of the decisions involved in designing a total assessment system include the number of tests and quizzes; the uses of alternative assessments; the level of assessment items, such as knowledge, application, or analysis; the role of homework in assigning grades; and the assessment and reporting of affective dimensions, such as cooperation and effort.

Developing as a Professional: Preparing for Your Licensure Exam

At the beginning of the chapter, you saw how DeVonne Lampkin used her understanding of assessment to help increase her students' achievement and align her instruction with her students' learning needs.

Now we'll see how Ron Hawkins, an urban middle school English teacher, assesses his students' understanding of pronoun cases. Read the case study, and answer the questions that follow.

> "Today we're going to begin studying pronoun cases," he begins. "Everybody turn to page 484 in your text. . . . This is important in our writing because we want to be able to write and use standard English correctly, and this is one of the places where people get mixed up. So, when we're finished, you'll all be able to use pronouns correctly in your writing."
>
> He then writes the following on the board:
>
> *Pronouns use the nominative case when they're subjects and predicate nominatives. Pronouns use the objective case when they're direct objects, indirect objects, or objects of prepositions.*
>
> "Let's review," Ron continues, briefly discussing direct and indirect objects, predicate nominatives, and objects of prepositions.
>
> "Now let's look at some additional examples," he continues, as he displays the following sentences on the overhead:
>
> 1. Did you get the card from Esteban and (I, me)?
> 2. Will Meg and (she, her) run the concession stand?
> 3. They treat (whoever, whomever) they hire very well.
> 4. I looked for someone (who, whom) could give me directions to the theater.
>
> "Okay, look at the first one. Which is correct? . . . Omar?"
>
> "Me."
>
> "Good, Omar. How about the second one?. . . Lonnie?"
>
> "Her."
>
> "Not quite, Lonnie. . . . Suppose I turn the sentence around and say, 'Meg and her will run the concession stand.' That doesn't sound right, does it? 'Meg and she' is a compound subject, and when we have a subject, we use the nominative case. . . . Okay?"
>
> Lonnie nods and Ron continues, "Look at the third one. . . . Cheny?"
>
> "I'm not sure . . . whoever, I guess."
>
> "This one is a little tricky," Ron nods. "When we use *whoever* and *whomever, whoever* is the nominative case, and *whomever* is the objective case. In this sentence, *whomever* is a direct object, so it is the correct form."
>
> After he finishes, Ron gives students another list of sentences in which they are to select the correct form of the pronoun.
>
> On Tuesday, Ron reviews the exercises the students completed for homework and gives some additional examples that use *who, whom, whoever,* and *whomever.* He then discusses the rules for pronoun–antecedent agreement (pronouns must agree with their antecedents in gender and number). He again has students work examples as he did with pronoun cases.
>
> He continues with pronouns and their antecedents on Wednesday and begins a discussion of indefinite pronouns as antecedents for personal pronouns—anybody,

either, each, one, someone—and has students work examples as before.

Near the end of class on Thursday, Ron announces, "Tomorrow, we're going to have a test on this material: pronoun cases, pronouns and their antecedents, and indefinite pronouns. You have your notes, so study hard. . . . Are there any questions? . . . Good. I expect you all to do well. I'll see you tomorrow."

On Friday morning as students file into class and the bell rings, Ron picks up a stack of tests from his desk. The test consists of 30 sentences, 10 of which deal with case, 10 with antecedents, and 10 with indefinite pronouns. The final part of the test directs students to write a paragraph. The following are some sample items from the test:

Part I. For each of the items below, mark A on your answer sheet if the pronoun case is correct in the sentence, and mark B if it is incorrect. If it is incorrect, supply the correct pronoun.

1. Be careful who you tell.
2. Will Rennee and I be in the outfield?
3. My brother and me like water skiing.

Part II. Write the pronoun that correctly completes the sentence.

1. Arlene told us about _____ visit to the dentist to have braces put on.
2. The Wilsons planted a garden in _____ backyard.
3. Cal read the recipe and put _____ in the file.
4. Each of the girls on the team wore _____ school sweater to the game.
5. None of the brass has lost _____ shine yet.
6. Few of the boys on the team have taken _____ physicals yet.

The directions for the final part of the test were as follows:

Part III. Write a short paragraph that contains at least two examples of pronouns in the nominative case and two examples of pronouns in the objective case. (Circle and label these.) Include also at least two examples of pronouns that agree with their antecedents. Remember!! The paragraph must make sense. It cannot be just a series of sentences.

Ron watches as his students work, and seeing that 15 minutes remain in the period and that some students are only starting on their paragraphs, he announces, "You only have 15 minutes left. Watch your time and work quickly. You need to be finished by the end of the period."

He continues monitoring students, again reminding them to work quickly when 10 minutes are left and again when 5 minutes are left.

Luis, Simao, Moy, and Rudy are hastily finishing the last few words of their tests as the bell rings. Luis finally turns in his paper as Ron's fourth-period students are filing into the room.

"Here," Ron says. "This pass will get you into Mrs. Washington's class if you're late. . . . How did you do?"

"Okay, I think," Luis says over his shoulder as he scurries out of the room, "except for the last part. It was hard. I couldn't get started."

"I'll look at it," Ron says. "Scoot now."

On Monday, Ron returns the tests, saying, "Here are your papers. You did fine on the sentences, but your paragraphs need a lot of work. Why did you have so much trouble with them, when we had so much practice?"

"It was hard, Mr. Hawkins."

"Not enough time."

"I hate to write."

Ron listens patiently and then says, "Be sure you write your scores in your notebooks. . . . Okay, you have them all written down?. . . Are there any questions?"

"Number 3," Enrique requests.

"Okay, let's look at 3. It says, 'My brother and me like water skiing.' There, the pronoun is part of the subject, so it should be I and not me."

"Any others?"

A sprinkling of questions comes from around the room, and Ron responds, "We don't have time to go over all of them. I'll discuss three more."

He responds to the three students who seem to be most urgent in waving their hands. He then collects the tests and begins a discussion of adjective and adverb clauses.

Short-Answer Questions

In answering these questions, use information from the chapter, and link your responses to specific information in the case.

1. How well were Ron's curriculum and assessment aligned? Explain specifically. What could he have done to increase curricular alignment?
2. In the section on effective assessment practices, we discussed preparing students for assessments, administering them, and analyzing results. How effectively did Ron perform each task? Describe specifically what he might have done to be more effective in these areas.
3. Ron teaches in an urban environment, so his students likely had diverse backgrounds. How effective were his teaching and assessment for urban students?
4. What were the primary strengths of Ron's teaching and assessment? What were the primary weaknesses? If you think Ron's teaching and assessment could have been improved on the basis of information in this chapter, what suggestions would you make? Be specific.

To receive feedback for these questions, go to Appendix B.

Now go to Chapter 14 of MyEducationLab, located at www.myeducationlab.com, where you can:

- Take a quiz to test your mastery of chapter objectives. Detailed feedback is provided to explain why your responses are correct or incorrect.
- Deepen your understanding of chapter concepts with *Review, Practice, Enrichment* exercises.
- Complete *Activities and Applications* that will help you apply what you have learned in the chapter by analyzing real classrooms through video clips, artifacts, and case studies. Your instructor will provide you with feedback for the *Activities and Applications.*
- Develop you professional knowledge and decision making in *Building Teaching Skills and Dispositions* exercises. Structured feedback will be available to you, providing you with support as you practice each skill. Your instructor will provide you with feedback on the final task that accompanies the exercise.

Important Concepts

alternative assessment (p. 462)
assessment *for* learning (p. 434)
checklists (p. 449)
classroom assessment (p. 434)
completion (p. 444)
criterion-referenced grading (p. 461)
diagnostic assessment (p. 434)
distracters (p. 441)
essay (p. 444)
formal assessment (p. 440)
formative assessment (p. 460)
informal assessment (p. 437)
matching format (p. 443)
multiple-choice (p. 441)
norm-referenced grading (p. 460)
performance assessment (p. 446)
portfolio assessment (p. 449)
rating scales (p. 449)
reliability (p. 436)
rubric (p. 445)
summative assessment (p. 460)
systematic observation (p. 448)
table of specifications (p. 454)
test anxiety (p. 456)
true–false (p. 443)
validity (p. 435)

chapter

15

Assessment Through Standardized Testing

chapter outline

Standardized Tests

- Functions of Standardized Tests
- Types of Standardized Tests
- Evaluating Standardized Tests: Validity Revisited

Understanding and Interpreting Standardized Test Scores

- Descriptive Statistics
- Interpreting Standardized Test Results

Accountability Issues in Standardized Testing

- Standards-Based Education and Accountability
- Testing Teachers
- Accountability Issues in Standardized Testing: Implications for Teachers

Diversity and Standardized Testing

- Student Diversity and Assessment Bias
- Standardized Testing and English Language Learners
  - **Theory to Practice**: The Teacher's Role in Standardized Testing
  - **Developmentally Appropriate Practice**: Standardized Testing with Different-Aged Learners

learning objectives

After you have completed your study of this chapter, you should be able to:

1. Describe the functions of standardized tests in the total assessment process.
2. Interpret standardized test results using statistics and standard scores.
3. Describe the relationships between standards-based education, accountability, and standardized testing.
4. Explain how learner diversity can influence the validity of standardized tests.

With the current emphasis on accountability, standardized testing has become an increasingly important part of teachers' lives. As you read the following case study, think about how standardized testing impacts your role as a teacher.

"Hello, Mrs. Palmer. I'm glad you could come in," Mike Chavez, a fourth-grade teacher, says, offering his hand in greeting.

"Thank you," Doris Palmer responds. "I'm anxious to see how David's doing. His sister always did so well."

"Well, let's take a look," Mike says as he offers Mrs. Palmer a seat next to his desk.

"Here are the results from the Stanford Achievement Test David took earlier this spring, pointing to a printout (see Figure 15.1). "Let me walk you through it."

After giving Mrs. Palmer a chance to look at the report, Mike begins, "Let's take a look at reading first. . . . Here we have vocabulary, reading comprehension, and total reading. David is strong in reading comprehension . . . 80th percentile locally."

"What does this 5.6 mean?" Mrs. Palmer asks, pointing to the "Grade Equiv." column. "Should he be in the fifth grade?"

"No," Mike smiles. "It says his score on this part of the test was about the same as that of the average fifth grader in the sixth month of school. It means that he did well in reading, but these tests don't tell us where kids should be placed.

"You already know he's in our top reading group," Mike continues. "This test confirms that he's properly placed. . . . I have some other materials from his portfolio that give us some more information."

"So what's the point in the tests if we already know that he's good at reading? They seem to make him nervous."

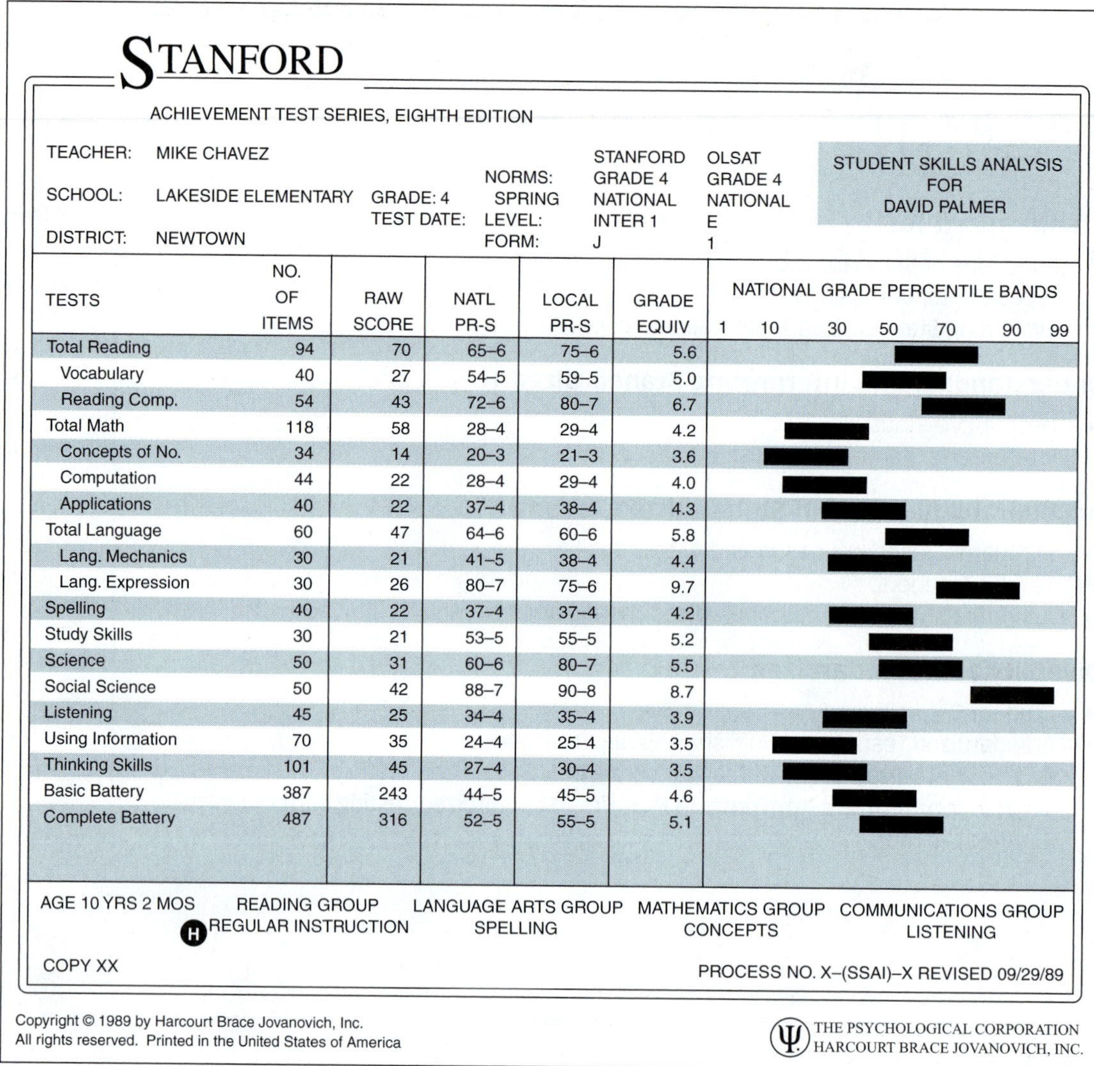

STANFORD

ACHIEVEMENT TEST SERIES, EIGHTH EDITION

TEACHER: MIKE CHAVEZ
SCHOOL: LAKESIDE ELEMENTARY GRADE: 4 TEST DATE:
DISTRICT: NEWTOWN

	STANFORD	OLSAT
NORMS:	GRADE 4	GRADE 4
SPRING	NATIONAL	NATIONAL
LEVEL:	INTER 1	E
FORM:	J	1

STUDENT SKILLS ANALYSIS FOR DAVID PALMER

TESTS	NO. OF ITEMS	RAW SCORE	NATL PR-S	LOCAL PR-S	GRADE EQUIV	NATIONAL GRADE PERCENTILE BANDS 1 10 30 50 70 90 99
Total Reading	94	70	65–6	75–6	5.6	
Vocabulary	40	27	54–5	59–5	5.0	
Reading Comp.	54	43	72–6	80–7	6.7	
Total Math	118	58	28–4	29–4	4.2	
Concepts of No.	34	14	20–3	21–3	3.6	
Computation	44	22	28–4	29–4	4.0	
Applications	40	22	37–4	38–4	4.3	
Total Language	60	47	64–6	60–6	5.8	
Lang. Mechanics	30	21	41–5	38–4	4.4	
Lang. Expression	30	26	80–7	75–6	9.7	
Spelling	40	22	37–4	37–4	4.2	
Study Skills	30	21	53–5	55–5	5.2	
Science	50	31	60–6	80–7	5.5	
Social Science	50	42	88–7	90–8	8.7	
Listening	45	25	34–4	35–4	3.9	
Using Information	70	35	24–4	25–4	3.5	
Thinking Skills	101	45	27–4	30–4	3.5	
Basic Battery	387	243	44–5	45–5	4.6	
Complete Battery	487	316	52–5	55–5	5.1	

AGE 10 YRS 2 MOS READING GROUP H REGULAR INSTRUCTION LANGUAGE ARTS GROUP SPELLING MATHEMATICS GROUP CONCEPTS COMMUNICATIONS GROUP LISTENING

COPY XX PROCESS NO. X–(SSAI)–X REVISED 09/29/89

THE PSYCHOLOGICAL CORPORATION HARCOURT BRACE JOVANOVICH, INC.

Figure 15.1 David Palmer's achievement test report
Source: Standard Achievement Test Report from the *Stanford Achievement Test: Eighth Edition.* copyright © 1988, 1992 by NCS Pearson, Inc. Reproduced with Permission. All Rights reserved.

"Good question. We actually use the tests for several reasons. They give us an objective, outside measure that helps us understand how our students are doing compared to others around the country. And, they can help us pinpoint some problem areas like in math. . . . For example, David isn't quite as strong there."

"He says he doesn't like math."

"That's what he says," Mike smiles, "but I'm not sure that's the whole picture. Look here. Notice how his lowest math score is on Concepts of Numbers. His percentile rank is 21 locally. . . . And look over here," he notes, pointing to the percentile bands column. "See how this band is lower than most of his others. This could suggest that he has a bit of difficulty understanding math concepts."

"You're telling me. He complains about all the problems you have him do. He says he knows the answer but you keep asking him 'why.'"

"That's interesting, because the test is telling us something that I can see in his work. It suggests that in his earlier math classes he may have relied on memorizing instead of developing a real understanding of the topics. Now that he's in fourth grade I'm trying to help him understand *why* he's doing what he's doing. I really believe it will pay off if he sticks with it . . . and if you and I encourage him."

"Well," she responds uncertainly, "if you're sure, we'll hang in there."

"Overall, Mrs. Palmer, I'm pleased with David's performance," Mike interjects, sensing her uncertainty. "If he can keep his reading scores up and work to get those math scores up some by next year, he will be making excellent progress."

As you begin your study of this chapter, think about two questions:

1. What is the purpose of standardized testing?
2. How can teachers use standardized test results to increase their students' learning?

Research examining standardized testing helps us answer these and other questions. We examine this research as the chapter unfolds.

Standardized Tests

Standardized tests are assessment instruments given to large samples of students (nationwide in many cases) under uniform conditions and scored and reported according to uniform procedures. We're all familiar with them. We took achievement tests as we moved through elementary school, and the SAT or ACT (Scholastic Aptitude Test or American College Test) is a rite of passage from high school to college. And, with increased emphasis on accountability, standardized testing has become an even more important part of teachers' and students' lives.

Standardized tests. Assessment instruments given to large samples of students under uniform conditions and scored and reported according to uniform procedures.

Standardized tests are designed to answer questions that are difficult to answer with teacher-made assessments alone, including:

- How do the students in my class compare with others across the country?
- How well is our curriculum preparing students for college or future training?
- How does a particular student compare to those of similar ability? (Haladyna, 2002; Nitko & Brookhart, 2007).

To answer these questions, individuals' scores are compared to the scores of a **norming group,** the representative sample whose scores are compiled for the purpose of national comparisons. The norming group typically includes students from different geographical regions, private and public schools, boys and girls, and different cultural and ethnic groups (Miller, Linn, & Gronlund, 2009). **National norms** are scores on standardized tests earned by representative groups from around the nation. Individuals' scores are then compared to the national norms.

Norming group. The representative group of individuals whose standardized test scores are compiled for the purpose of national comparisons.

National norms. Scores on standardized tests earned by representative groups of students from around the nation to which an individual's score is compared.

The influence of standardized testing can hardly be overstated. The fact that students in other industrialized countries, such as Japan and Germany, score higher than American students on some of these tests has alarmed many in this country (Hoff, 2003). Reform movements that began in the early 1980s and continue today are largely due to concerns about low scores on standardized tests. The results of a morning's testing often influence decisions about the future of individual students.

Standardized testing is also controversial (D. D. Johnson, Johnson, Farenga & Ness, 2008; Phelps, 2005). In a given year, millions of students take state-mandated tests at a cost of more than a billion dollars annually. Many teachers and parents feel that standardized testing is overemphasized, arguing that they detract from a balanced curriculum (Hoffman et al., 2001; G. Jones, Jones, & Hargrove, 2003). In addition, research suggests that beginning teachers are inadequately prepared to deal with the new assessment roles required of them by the accountability movement (Lawson & Childs, 2001). To put these concerns into perspective, we'll look at some of the ways that educators use standardized tests.

Functions of Standardized Tests

Standardized tests serve three primary functions (Aiken, 2003; Stiggins, 2005):

- Assessment and diagnosis of learning
- Selection and placement
- Program evaluation and accountability

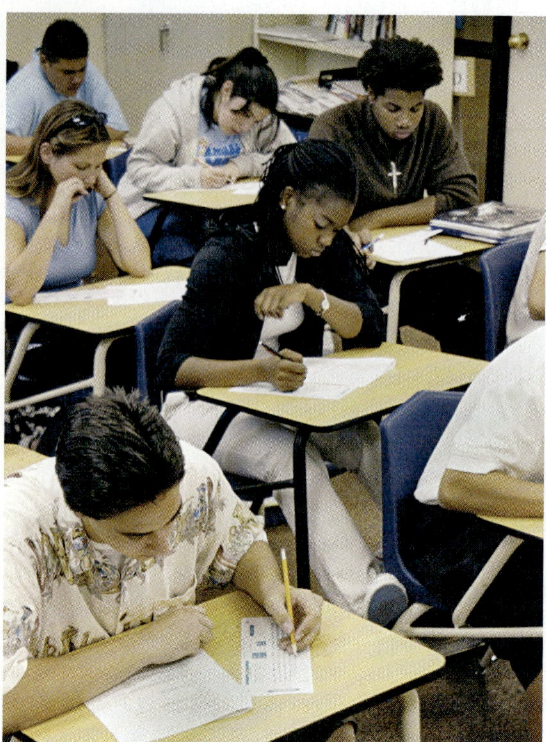

Educators use standardized tests to assess and diagnose learning, to assist in placement decisions, and to help in program evaluation.

Assessment and Diagnosis of Learning

From a teacher's perspective, the most important function of standardized testing is to provide an external, objective picture of student progress. In Mike's class, for example, David consistently receives A's in reading, but this doesn't tell his parents, teachers, or school administrators how he compares to other children at his grade level across the nation. Were his A's due to high achievement or generous grading? Standardized tests help provide a complete picture of student progress.

Standardized tests also help diagnose student strengths and weaknesses (Popham, 2005). For example, after learning that David scored low in math, Mike might schedule a standardized diagnostic test. Educators usually administer these tests individually, with the goal of obtaining information about a student's achievement in particular aspects of a content area.

Selection and Placement

Selecting and placing students in specialized or limited enrollment programs is another function of standardized tests. For instance, students entering a high school may come from "feeder" middle schools, private schools, and schools outside the district, many with different academic programs. Scores from the math section of a standardized test, for example, can help the math faculty place students in classes that will best match the students' backgrounds and capabilities.

Educators also use standardized test results to make decisions about admission to college or placement in advanced programs, such as programs for the gifted. As most college students know, their scores on the SAT or ACT are important in determining whether or not they they're accepted by the college of their choice. And standardized test scores are one criterion usually considered in recommending students for placement in programs for the gifted.

Program Evaluation and Accountability

Standardized tests also provide information about the quality of instructional programs. For example, if an elementary school moves from a reading program based on writing and children's literature to one that emphasizes phonics and basic skills, the faculty can use standardized test results to assess the effectiveness of this change.

As an extension of program evaluation, schools and teachers are increasingly being held accountable for student learning (Miller et al., 2009). Parents, school board members, state officials, and decision makers at the federal level are demanding evidence that schools are using tax dollars efficiently. Standardized test scores provide one indicator of this effectiveness. (We examine accountability issues in more detail later in the chapter.)

Norm- Versus Criterion-Referenced Standardized Tests

Norm-referenced standardized tests. Standardized tests that compare (reference) a student's performance with the performance of others.

Criterion-referenced standardized tests. Standardized tests that compare performance against a set performance standard.

In Chapter 14, you saw that norm-referenced grading compares a student's performance to that of others in a class, while criterion-referenced systems assign grades in terms of predetermined standards (e.g., 90+ = A, 80–90 = B, etc.). In a similar way, **norm-referenced standardized tests** compare (reference) a student's performance with the performance of others. **Criterion-referenced standardized tests** are sometimes called *standards-referenced, content-referenced,* or *domain-referenced* tests; they compare performance against a set standard. Criterion-referenced standardized tests may even be called *objectives-based* tests when the standards are in the form of learning objectives (Mertler, 2007).

The major difference between norm- and criterion-referenced tests is the way scores are reported. For example, percentile rank is a common way of reporting students' performance on norm-referenced standardized tests. (We discuss percentile rank later in the chapter.) This type of information is helpful when comparing local students to students around the nation.

The comparisons that norm-referenced standardized test results provide don't tell teachers what students actually know, however. This is where criterion-referenced tests are helpful, because they provide information about mastery of specific learning objectives, such as the ability to add two-digit numbers, or identify the main idea in a paragraph. Reports of criterion-referenced scores typically show the number or percent of items correct or use more general terms such as *pass–fail,* or *basic, proficient,* or *advanced.*

With the current interest in standards and accountability, decision makers are placing increased emphasis on criterion-referenced tests, especially at the state and district levels. Nationally, norm-referenced tests are still popular, because they allow location-to-location comparisons and the general nature of test content allows them to be used in a wide variety of situations.

Both are useful and depend on assessment goals. Norm-referenced tests allow wide-ranging comparisons, whereas criterion-referenced tests provide information about the attainment of specific objectives.

Types of Standardized Tests

Five kinds of standardized tests are common in educational settings:

- Achievement tests
- Diagnostic tests
- Intelligence tests
- Aptitude tests
- Readiness tests

Achievement Tests

Achievement tests, the most widely used type of standardized test, assess how much students have learned in specific content areas, most commonly reading, language arts, and math, but also in areas such as science, social studies, computer literacy, and critical thinking (Hogan, 2007; Mertler, 2007). These areas are then usually broken down into descriptions of more specific skills. For example, David's test results included, in addition to a Total Math score, a score for Concepts of Number, Computation, and Applications (see Figure 15.1). Popular achievement tests include the Iowa Test of Basic Skills, the California Achievement Test, the Stanford Achievement Test, the Comprehensive Test of Basic Skills, and the Metropolitan Achievement Test, as well as individual statewide assessments (Nitko & Brookhart, 2007; Stiggins, 2005).

Achievement tests. Standardized tests designed to assess how much students have learned in specified content areas.

Standardized achievement tests typically include batteries of subtests administered over several days. They reflect a curriculum common to most schools, which means they will assess some, but not all, of the goals of an individual school. This is both a strength and a weakness. Because they are designed for a range of schools, they can be used in a variety of locations, but this "one size fits all" approach may not accurately measure achievement for a specific curriculum. For example, one study found that less than half of the math content measured on commonly used standardized achievement batteries was the same as content covered in popular elementary math textbooks (Berliner, 1984).

Diagnostic Tests

Whereas achievement tests measure students' progress in a range of curriculum areas, **diagnostic tests** provide a detailed description of learners' strengths and weaknesses in specific skill areas. They are common in the primary grades, where instruction is designed to match the developmental level of the child. Diagnostic tests are usually administered individually, and, compared to achievement tests, they include a larger number of items, use more subtests, and provide scores in more specific areas (Thorndike, 2005). A diagnostic test in reading, for example, might measure letter recognition, word analysis skills, sight vocabulary, vocabulary in context, and reading comprehension. The Detroit Test of Learning Aptitude, the Durrell Analysis of Reading Difficulty, and the Stanford Diagnostic Reading Test are popular diagnostic tests.

Diagnostic tests. Standardized tests designed to provide a detailed description of learners' strengths and weaknesses in specific skill areas.

Intelligence Tests

Intelligence tests are standardized tests designed to measure an individual's capacity to acquire and use knowledge, to solve problems, and to accomplish new tasks. The two most widely used intelligence tests in the United States are the Stanford-Binet and the Wechsler Scales (Salvia & Ysseldyke, 2004).

Intelligence tests. Standardized tests designed to measure an individual's capacity to acquire and use knowledge, to solve problems, and to accomplish new tasks.

The Stanford-Binet. The Stanford-Binet is an individually administered intelligence test composed of several subtests. It comes in a kit that includes testing materials, such as manipulatives and pictures, along with a test manual. Earlier versions heavily emphasized verbal tasks, but the most recent edition is more diverse, targeting five factors: fluid reasoning, knowledge,

table 15.1 Sample Subtests from the Revised (5th ed.) Stanford-Binet

Subtest	Example Description
Nonverbal Knowledge	Students are shown picture absurdities (e.g., a man in a bathing suit in the snow) and asked to explain.
Verbal Knowledge	Students are asked to explain the meaning of common vocabulary words.
Nonverbal Working Memory	Students are shown block patterns and asked to describe or reproduce after a brief delay.
Verbal Working Memory	Students are given sentences and asked to provide key words after a brief delay.

Source: Riverside Publishing, 2003.

quantitative reasoning, visual-spatial processing, and working memory, each of which contains a verbal and nonverbal subtest. Table 15.1 contains descriptions of some sample subtests in the latest revision of the Stanford-Binet.

The Stanford-Binet 5th edition (Roid, 2003) is a technically sound instrument that is second only to the Wechsler scales (described in the next section) in popularity. It has been revised and renormed a number of times over the years, most recently in 2003, using 4,800 schoolchildren, stratified by economic status, geographic region, and community size. The test's developers used the 2000 U.S. Census to ensure proportional representation of White, African American, Hispanic, Asian, and Asian/Pacific Islander subcultures.

The Wechsler Scales. Developed by David Wechsler over a period of 40 years, the Wechsler scales are the most popular intelligence tests in use today (Salvia & Ysseldyke, 2004). The three Wechsler tests, aimed at preschool–primary, elementary, and adult populations, have two main parts: verbal and performance.

The Wechsler Intelligence Scale for Children—Fourth Edition (Wechsler, 2003) is an individually administered intelligence test with 13 subtests, of which 6 are verbal and 7 are performance. (Table 15.2 outlines some sample subtests.) The developers added performance sections because of dissatisfaction with the strong verbal emphasis of earlier intelligence tests. Like the Stanford-Binet, the Wechsler scales are considered technically sound by testing experts (Kaufman & Lictenberger, 2002; Salvia & Ysseldyke, 2004).

The Wechsler's two scales, yielding separate verbal and performance scores, are assets. For example, a substantially higher score on the performance compared with the verbal scale could indicate a language problem related to poor reading or language-based cultural differences. Because performance subtests demand a minimum of verbal ability, these tasks are helpful in studying learners with disabilities, persons with limited education, or students who resist school-like tasks.

Aptitude Tests

Although *aptitude* and *intelligence* are often used synonymously, aptitude—the ability to acquire knowledge—is only one characteristic of intelligence. The concept of *aptitude* is intuitively sensible; for example, people will say, "I just don't have any aptitude for math," implying that their potential for learning math is limited.

Aptitude tests. Standardized tests designed to predict the potential for future learning and measure general abilities developed over long periods of time.

Aptitude tests are standardized tests designed to predict the potential for future learning and measure general abilities developed over long periods of time. Educators commonly use aptitude tests in selection and placement decisions, and these tests correlate highly with achievement tests (Miller et al., 2009; Popham, 2005).

The two most common aptitude tests at the high school level are the SAT and ACT, designed to measure a student's potential for success in college. Experience is important, however; classroom-related knowledge, particularly in language and mathematics, is essential

table 15.2 Sample Items from the Wechsler Intelligence Scale for Children

Verbal Section

Subtest	Description/Examples
Information	This subtest taps general knowledge common to American Culture: 1. How many wings does a bird have? 2. How many nickels make a dime? 3. What is steam made of? 4. Who wrote "Tom Sawyer"? 5. What is *pepper?*
Arithmetic	This subtest is a test of basic mathematical knowledge and skills, including counting and addition through division: 1. Sam had three pieces of candy and Joe gave him four more. How many pieces of candy did Sam have altogether? 2. Three women divided eighteen golf balls equally among themselves. How many golf balls did each person receive? 3. If two buttons cost 15¢, what will be the cost of a dozen buttons?
Similarities	This subtest is designed to measure abstract and logical thinking through use of analogies: 1. In what way are a lion and a tiger alike? 2. In what way are a saw and a hammer alike? 3. In what way are an hour and a week alike? 4. In what way are a circle and a triangle alike?

Performance Section

Subtest	Description/Examples
Picture completion	Students are shown a picture with elements missing, which they are required to identify. This subtest measures general knowledge as well as visual comprehension.
Block design	This subtest focuses on a number of abstract figures. Designed to measure visual-motor coordination, it requires students to match patterns displayed by the examiner.

Picture Completion

Block Design

Source: Items similar to those found on the Wechsler *Intelligence Scale for children – Third Edition.*

for success on the tests. But, because they are reliable, the tests eliminate teacher bias and differences in teachers' grading practices. In this regard, they add valuable information in predicting future college success.

The class of 2006 was the first to write a timed essay as part of the SAT. Developers added this component to the traditional verbal and math sections, which were also revamped. The ACT also made an essay an optional part of its exam. Both changes occurred with tests taken in the spring of 2005. From that time a perfect SAT score rose from 1600 to 2400, with the writing test worth up to 800 points.

The SAT is the oldest college admission exam in the United States. Developers revised it in an attempt to more closely align it with today's high school curriculum and to address concerns among employers and university professors suggesting that the quality of student writing has declined.

Readiness Tests

Readiness tests. Standardized tests that assess the degree to which children are prepared for an academic or pre-academic program.

Readiness tests are standardized tests that assess the degree to which children are prepared for an academic or pre-academic program (Gullo, 2005). Educators most often use readiness tests to assess children's readiness for academic work in kindergarten or first grade. In this regard, they have characteristics of both aptitude and achievement tests. They are similar to aptitude tests in that they assess a student's potential for future learning. However, most readiness tests measure the extent to which students have mastered basic concepts, such as *up* and *down, left* and *right,* or *big* and *small,* which form the foundation for reading and math. This is what makes them similar to achievement tests.

Standardized readiness tests have become controversial for at least two reasons. First, poor performance on a readiness test is likely to delay a child's entry into kindergarten or first grade. This delay is a form of grade retention, a practice that can have negative effects on children's later development (Alexander, Entwisle, Dauber, & Kabboni, 2004; Beebe-Fankenberger, Bocian, MacMillan, & Gresham, 2004). Critics also argue that they assess only cognitive factors and ignore important characteristics that influence school success such as motivation and self-regulation (Stipek, 2002).

Readiness tests, like other standardized tests, can provide valuable information for educational decision making. They should not, however, be the only criterion for assessing a child's readiness for future schooling. Virtually every 5- or 6-year-old can benefit from school experiences, and observations of a child's ability to function in a school setting should also be a part of the assessment process (Stipek, 2002).

Evaluating Standardized Tests: Validity Revisited

The validity of standardized tests is important because teachers are major consumers of standardized test results. Let's look at how validity can influence teachers' lives.

> Mike Smith has been asked to serve on a district-wide committee to select a new standardized achievement battery for the elementary grades. His job is to get feedback from the faculty at his school about two options, the Stanford Achievement Test and the California Achievement Test.
>
> After providing a brief overview of the tests during a faculty meeting, Mike asks if people have questions.
>
> "How much do the two tests cover problem solving?" a fifth-grade teacher asks.
>
> "We're moving our language arts curriculum more in the direction of writing. What about it?" a first-grade teacher also asks.
>
> As the discussion continues, a confused colleague wonders, "Which is better? That's really what we're here for. How about a simple answer?"

Mike couldn't offer a simple answer, not because he was unprepared, but instead because he was asked to make judgments about validity, which, as you saw in Chapter 14, is the degree to which an assessment actually measures what it is supposed to measure (Miller et al., 2009). When creating their own tests, teachers ensure validity by considering the extent to which a test is congruent with their learning objectives. Standardized tests are already constructed, so teachers must judge only the suitability of a test for a specific purpose.* Validity, in this case, involves the appropriate use of a test, not the design of the test itself.

Experts describe three kinds of validity—*content, predictive,* and *construct*—and each provides a different perspective on the issue of appropriate use.

---

*A complete review of more than 1,400 standardized tests of achievement, aptitude, diagnosis, and personality can be found in the *Mental Measurements Yearbook* (Plake, Impara, & Spies, 2003). Originally edited by Oscar Buros, the yearbook provides accurate and critical reviews of all major standardized tests and is an important source of information for selecting and using these tests.

Content Validity

Content validity refers to a test's ability to accurately sample the content taught and measure the extent to which learners understand it (Kane, 2006; Webb, 2006). It is determined by comparing test content with curriculum objectives, and it is a primary concern when considering standardized achievement tests (Hogan, 2007). The question Mike was asked about which test was "better" addresses content validity. The "better" test is the one with the closer match between a school's learning objectives and the content of the test.

Content validity. A test's ability to accurately sample the content taught and measure the extent to which learners understand it.

Predictive Validity

Predictive validity is the measure of a test's ability to gauge future performance (Miller et al., 2009). It is central to the SAT and ACT, which are designed to measure a student's potential for doing college work, and it is also the focus of tests that gauge students' readiness for academic tasks in the early elementary grades.

Predictive validity. The measure of a test's ability to gauge future performance.

Predictive validity is usually quantified by correlating two variables, such as a standardized test score and student grades. For example, a correlation of .47 exists between the SAT and freshman college grades (Fair Test, 2008). High school grades are the only predictor that is better (a correlation of .54).

Why isn't the correlation between standardized tests and college performance higher? The primary reason is that the SAT and ACT are designed to predict "general readiness"; other factors such as motivation, study habits, and prior knowledge also affect performance (Popham, 2007).

Construct Validity

Construct validity is an indicator of the logical connection between a test and what it is designed to measure (Miller et al, 2009). The concept of construct validity is somewhat abstract, but it is important in understanding the total concept of validity (Gronlund, 2003). It answers the question, "Do these items actually assess the ideas the test is designed to measure?" For instance, many of the items on the SAT are designed to tap the ability to do abstract thinking about words and numbers, tasks that students are likely to face in their college experience. Because of this, the test has construct validity.

Construct validity. An indicator of the logical connection between a test and what it is designed to measure.

check your understanding

1.1 Describe the function of standardized tests in the total assessment process.

1.2 As a school district's officials examine different standardized math tests, they find that some provide broad coverage of math concepts and skills, whereas others provide more detailed information about individual student's strengths and weaknesses in math. What two types of standardized tests is the district considering?

1.3 In a committee meeting, teachers express different views about what they want in a test. One comments, "I want to make sure that the test matches our philosophy." "But it also should match the concepts and skills we're supposed to teach," a second adds. A third replies "That's all fine, but it also needs to tell us if our students will succeed in college math." Which of the different forms of validity are the teachers addressing?

To receive feedback for these questions, go to Appendix A.

MyEducationLab

To further examine different types of validity in standardized testing, go to the *Activities and Applications* section in Chapter 15 of MyEducationLab at www.myeducationlab.com, and read the case study *Validity in Standardized Testing.* Answer the questions following the case study.

Understanding and Interpreting Standardized Test Scores

The fact that standardized tests are given to thousands of students, which allow comparisons with samples across the United States and around the world, is one of their advantages. But these large samples result in unwieldy data. To process the vast amounts of information and to allow users to compare individuals' performances, test publishers use statistical methods to summarize results.

Descriptive Statistics

As an introduction to the use of statistics in summarizing information, take a look at Table 15.3, which contains scores made by two classes of 31 students on a 50-item test. (As you examine this information, keep in mind that a standardized test would have a sample much larger than 31 students and would contain a larger number of items. We are using a class-size example here for the sake of illustration.)

The scores for each class are ranked from highest to lowest, and the mean, median, and mode are labeled. (We discuss these concepts in the sections that follow.) As you can see in the table, a simple array of scores can be cumbersome and not very informative, even when the scores are ranked. We need more efficient ways of summarizing the information.

Frequency Distributions

Frequency distribution. A distribution of test scores that shows a count of the number of people who obtained each score.

A **frequency distribution** is a distribution of test scores that shows a simple count of the number of people who obtained each score. It can be represented in several ways, one of which is a graph with the possible scores on the horizontal (x) axis and the frequency, or the number of students who got each score, on the vertical (y) axis.

table 15.3 Scores of Two Classes on a 50-item Test

Class #1		Class #2	
50		48	
49		47	
49		46	
48		46	
47		45	
47		45	
46		44	mode
46		44	mode
45		44	mode
45		44	mode
45		44	mode
44	mode	43	
44	mode	43	
44	mode	43	
44	mode	43	
43	median	42	median & mean
42	mean	42	
41		42	
41		42	
40		41	
40		41	
39		41	
39		40	
38		40	
37		39	
37		39	
36		38	
35		38	
34		37	
34		36	
33		35	

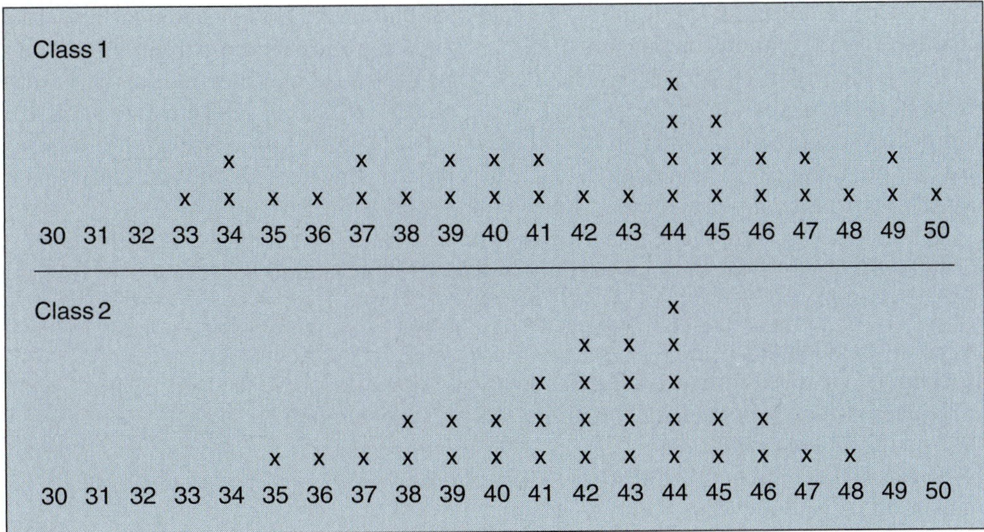

Figure 15.2 Frequency distributions for two classes on a 50-item test

The frequency distributions for our two classes are shown in Figure 15.2. Although this information is still in rough form, we already begin to see differences between the two classes. For instance, a wider range of scores occurs in the first class than in the second, and the scores are more nearly grouped near the middle of the second distribution. Beyond this qualitative description, however, the distributions aren't particularly helpful. We need a better way to summarize the information. Measures of central tendency do this.

Measures of Central Tendency

Measures of central tendency are quantitative descriptions of a group's performance as a whole and comprise the mean, median, and mode scores. In a distribution of scores, the **mean** is the average score, the **median** is the middle score in the distribution, and the **mode** is the most frequent score.

Measures of central tendency. Quantitative descriptions of a group's performance as a whole.

Mean. The average score in the distribution of a group of scores.

Median. The middle score in the distribution of a group of scores.

Mode. The most frequent score in the distribution of a group of scores.

To obtain a mean, we simply add the scores and divide by the number of scores. As it turns out, both distributions have a mean of 42 (1, 302/31). A mean of 42 is one indicator of how each group performed as a whole.

The median for the first distribution is 43, because half the scores (15) fall equal to or above 43, and the other half are equal to or below 43. Using the same process, we find that the median for the second distribution is 42.

The median is useful when extremely high or low scores skew the mean and give a false picture of the sample. For example, you commonly hear or read demographic statistics such as "The median income for families of four in this country went from . . . in 2000 to . . . in 2008." The *median* income is reported because a few multimillion-dollar incomes would make the mean quite high and would give an artificial picture of typical families' standards of living. The median, in contrast, is not affected by these extremes and provides a more realistic picture. The median serves the same function when used with test scores.

Looking once more at the two samples, you can see that the most frequent score for each is 44, which is the mode. Small samples, such as those here, often have more than one mode, resulting in "bimodal" or even "trimodal" distributions.

Using our measures of central tendency, you can see that the two groups of scores are much alike: They have the same mean, nearly the same median, and the same mode. As you saw from examining the frequency distribution, however, this doesn't give us a complete picture. We also need a measure of their variability, or "spread."

Measures of Variability

To get a more accurate picture of the samples, we need to see how the scores vary. **Variability** is the degree of difference or deviation from the mean. One measure of variability is the **range,** the distance between the top and bottom score in a distribution. The range in the first class is

Variability. The degree of difference or deviation from the mean.

Range. The distance between the top and bottom score in a distribution of scores.

Standard deviation. A statistical measure of the spread of scores.

17, and in the second it's 13, confirming the wider distribution of scores we saw in the first class. Although easy to compute, the range is overly influenced by one or more extreme scores.

The **standard deviation,** a statistical measure of the spread of scores, reduces this problem, because a few scores at the outer margins don't overly influence it, and it makes sense. For example, if we were to administer an achievement test to an entire high school grade, the standard deviation would be larger than if we administered the same test to an advanced placement class. The variability of scores for the whole grade would be greater.

With the use of computers, teachers rarely have to calculate a standard deviation manually, but we'll briefly describe the procedure to help you understand the concept. To find the standard deviation:

1. Calculate the mean.
2. Subtract the mean from each of the individual scores.
3. Square each of these values. (This eliminates negative numbers.)
4. Add the squared values.
5. Divide by the total number of scores (31 in our samples).
6. Take the square root.

In our samples, the standard deviations are 4.8 and 3.1, respectively. We saw from merely observing the two distributions that the first was more spread out, and the standard deviation provides a quantitative measure of that spread.

The Normal Distribution

Standardized tests are administered to large (in the hundreds of thousands) samples of students, and the scores often approximate a *normal distribution.* To understand this concept, look again at our two distributions and then focus specifically on the second one. If we drew a line over the top of the frequency distribution, it would appear as shown in Figure 15.3.

Normal distribution. A distribution of scores in which the mean, median, and mode are equal and the scores distribute themselves symmetrically in a bell-shaped curve.

Now imagine a very large sample of scores, such as we would find from a typical standardized test. The curve would approximate the one shown in Figure 15.4. This is a **normal distribution,** a distribution of scores in which the mean, median, and mode are equal and the scores distribute themselves symmetrically in a bell-shaped curve. Many large samples of human characteristics, such as height and weight, tend to distribute themselves this way, as do the large samples of most standardized tests.

The sample of scores in Figure 15.3 has both a mean and median of 42, but a mode of 44, so its measures of central tendency don't quite fit the normal curve. Also, as we see from Figure 15.4, 68 percent of all the scores fall within 1 standard deviation from the mean, but in our sample distribution, about 71 percent of the scores are within 1 standard deviation above and below the mean. Our samples aren't normal distributions, which is typical of the smaller samples found in most classrooms.

Interpreting Standardized Test Results

Using our two small samples, we have illustrated techniques that statisticians use to summarize standardized test scores. Again, keep in mind that data gathered from standardized tests come from hundreds of thousands of students instead of the small number in our illustrations. When standardized tests are used, comparing students from different schools, districts, states,

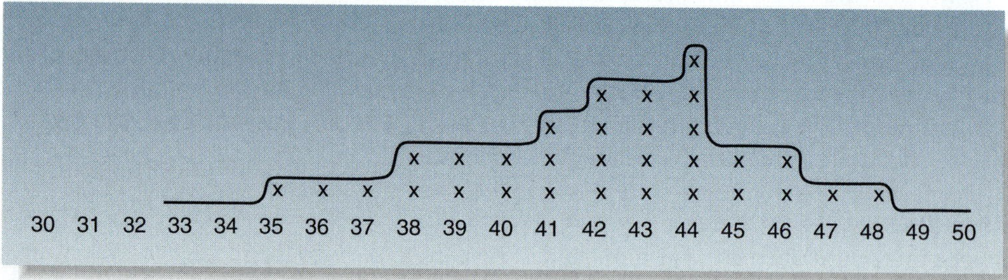

Figure 15.3 Frequency distribution for the second class

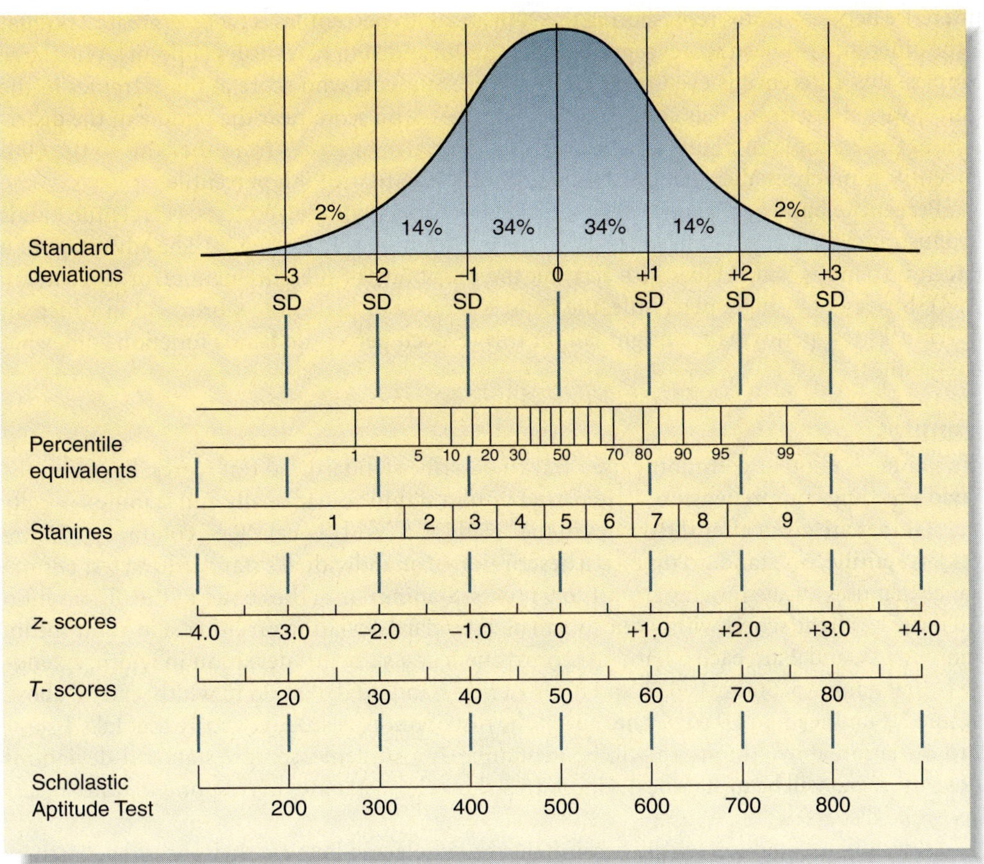

Figure 15.4 Normal distribution

and even countries is an important goal. To make these comparisons, test makers use *raw scores, percentiles, stanines, grade equivalents,* and *standard scores.* Some of these scores are illustrated in Figure 15.1 on David Palmer's report from the Stanford Achievement Test.

Raw Scores

All standardized tests are based on **raw scores,** simply the number of items an individual answered correctly on a standardized test or subtest. For example, we see in Figure 15.1 that David's raw score for reading comprehension was 43; he answered 43 out of 54 items correctly. But what does this mean? Was the test easy or hard? How did he do compared to others taking the test? This raw score doesn't tell us much until we compare it to others. Percentiles, stanines, grade equivalents, and standard scores help us do that.

Raw score. The number of items an individual answered correctly on a standardized test or subtest.

Percentiles

The percentile is one of the most commonly reported scores on standardized tests. The **percentile** (sometimes called **percentile rank** [**PR**]) shows the percentage of students in the norming sample that scored at or below a particular raw score. For instance, David's raw score of 43 in reading comprehension placed him in the 72nd percentile nationally and the 80th percentile locally (Figure 15.1). That means his score was as high or higher than 72 percent of the scores of people who took the test across the nation and 80 percent of the scores of people who took the test in his district.

Percentile, or **percentile rank (PR).** The percentage of students in the norming sample who scored at or below a particular raw score.

Parents and students often confuse percentiles with *percentages.* Percentages reflect the number of correct items compared to the total number possible. Percentile rank, in contrast, is a description that indicates how a student did in comparison to other students taking the test.

Percentiles are used because they are simple and straightforward. However, they are *rankings,* and the differences between the ranks are not equal (Miller et al., 2009). For instance, in our first distribution of 31 students, a score of 48 would be in the 90th percentile, 46 would be in the 80th, 44 would be in the 60th, and 43 would be the 50th percentile. In this sample, the difference between scores representing the 90th and 80th percentiles is twice as great (2 points) as the difference between scores representing the 60th and 50th percentiles (1 point). With large samples, this difference is even more pronounced. Students who score at the extremes in the sample vary more from their counterparts than those who score near the middle of the distribution. For example in Figure 15.4 we see that the range of scores from the 50th to the 60th percentile is much smaller than the range from the 90th to the 99th percentile.

Percentile bands. Ranges of percentile scores on standardized tests.

Percentile bands are ranges of percentile scores on standardized tests. (Percentile bands are illustrated for David Palmer's results in the last column of Figure 15.1.) The advantage of a percentile band is that it takes into account the possibility of measurement error (McMillan, 2004). Instead of a single percentile, the band is a range of percentile scores within which an individual's test performance might fall. In this respect, percentile bands function somewhat like stanines.

Stanines

Stanine. A description of an individual's standardized test performance that uses a scale ranging from 1 to 9 points.

The stanine is another commonly used way to describe standardized test scores. For example, David's reading comprehension score placed him in stanine 6 nationally and stanine 7 locally (the stanines are given after the dashes in the "Natl PR-S" and "Local PR-S" columns in Figure 15.1). A **stanine,** or "standard nine," is a description of an individual's standardized test performance that uses a scale ranging from 1 to 9 points. Stanine 5 is in the center of the distribution and includes all the scores within one fourth of a standard deviation on either side of the mean. Stanines 4, 3, and 2 are each a band of scores, one half a standard deviation in width, extending below stanine 5. Stanines 6, 7, and 8, also a half standard deviation in width, extend above stanine 5. Stanines 1 and 9 cover the tails of the distribution. A student's score that falls 1 standard deviation above the mean will be in stanine 7; a student's score 2 standard deviations above the mean will be in stanine 9. Figure 15.4 shows how stanines correspond to other measures we've discussed.

Educators use stanines widely because they're simple and because they encourage teachers and parents to interpret scores based on a possible range instead of fine distinctions that may be artificial (McMillan, 2004). For instance, a score in the 57th percentile may be the result of 1 or 2 extra points on a subtest compared to a score in the 52nd percentile, and the student may have guessed the answer correctly, so the difference between the two wouldn't be meaningful. Both scores fall in stanine 5, however. Because it describes performance as a range of possible scores, the stanine is probably a more realistic indicator of performance. Reducing the scores to a 9-point band sacrifices information, however, so it is important to keep the advantages and disadvantages of stanines in mind as you help parents and students interpret standardized test scores.

Grade Equivalents

Grade-equivalent score. A score that is determined by comparing an individual's score on a standardized test to the scores of students in a particular age group.

A third commonly reported score is the **grade equivalent,** a score that educators determine by comparing an individual's score to the scores of students in a particular age group. The first digit represents the grade, and the second, the month of the school year. For example, David's grade equivalent for total reading is 5.6. This means that he scored as well on the test as the average score for those students taking the test who are in the sixth month of the fifth grade.

As you saw when David's mother asked, "Should David be in the fifth grade?" grade equivalents can be misleading because they oversimplify results and suggest comparisons that aren't necessarily valid (Hogan, 2007). A grade equivalent of 5.6 tells us that David is somewhat advanced in reading. It doesn't suggest that he should be promoted to fifth grade, nor does it necessarily suggest that he should be reading with fifth graders. Other factors such as social development, motivation, classroom behavior, and performance on teacher-made assessments should be considered in making decisions about students. Because of these limitations and the possibility of misinterpretation, some standardized tests no longer use grade equivalents. Teachers should use them with caution when communicating with students and parents, and they should always be used in combination with other measures (Miller et al., 2009; Salvia & Ysseldyke, 2004).

Standard Scores

As you saw in our discussion of percentiles, differences in raw scores don't result in comparable differences in the percentile rank. For instance, you saw that it took only a 1-point differ-

classroom connections

Using Standardized Tests Effectively in Your Classroom

1. The validity of a standardized achievement test depends on the match between learning objectives and test content. Carefully analyze results to increase instructional alignment.
   - **Elementary:** A fourth-grade teaching team goes over the previous year's test scores to identify areas in the curriculum that need greater attention.
   - **Middle School:** The math teachers in a middle school go over standardized results item by item. Seeing that a large numbers of students missed a particular item, the teachers plan to place more emphasis on this topic in their instruction.
   - **High School:** English teachers in an urban high school use a scoring rubric to analyze student scores on a statewide writing assessment. They share the rubric with their students and use it to help students improve their writing skills.
2. The value of standardized test scores to consumers depends, in large part, on the extent to which they understand the results. Communicate test results clearly to both students and their caregivers.
   - **Elementary:** Third-grade teachers in an urban elementary school prepare a handout that explains standardized test scores including examples and answers to frequently asked questions. They use the handout in parent–teacher conferences.
   - **Middle School:** A middle school team integrates standardized test scores into a comprehensive packet of assessment materials. When they meet with students and their caregivers, they use the information to identify individual student's areas of strength and areas that need improvement.
   - **High School:** During an orientation meeting with parents, members of an English Department first give an overview of tests that students will encounter in high school and describe score reports. During individual meetings with parents, teachers provide specific information about individuals' scores.

ence 43 compared with 42 to move from the 50th to the 60th percentile, but it took a 2-point difference (48 compared with 46) to move from the 80th to the 90th percentile in our distribution in Figure 15.2. To deal with this type of discrepancy, educators developed standard scores. A **standard score** is a description of performance on a standardized test that uses the standard deviation as the basic unit (Miller et al., 2009; McMillan, 2004). Standardized test makers use the mean and standard deviation to report standard scores.

Standard score. A description of performance on a standardized test that uses the standard deviation as the basic unit.

One type of standard score is the ***z*-score,** which is the number of standard deviation units from the mean. A *z*-score of 2 is two standard deviations above the mean, for example, and a *z*-score of -1 is one standard deviation below the mean. The ***T*-score** is a standard score that defines the mean as 50 and the standard deviation as 10. A *T*-score of 70 would be two standard deviations above the mean and would correspond to a *z*-score of 2.

***z*-score.** The number of standard deviation units from the mean.

***T*-score.** A standard score that defines the mean as 50 and the standard deviation as 10.

Standard scores such as *z*-scores and *T*-scores are useful because they make comparisons convenient. Because they are based on equal units of measurement throughout the distribution, inter-group and inter-test comparisons are possible.

Standard Error of Measurement

Although standardized tests are technically sophisticated, they contain measurement error; scores represent only an approximation of a student's "true" score. Hypothetically, if we could give a student the same test over and over, for example, and the student neither gained nor lost any knowledge, we would find that the scores would vary. If we averaged those scores, we would have an estimate of the student's "true" score. A **true score** is the hypothetical average of an individual's scores if repeated testing under ideal conditions were possible. An estimate of the true score is obtained using the **standard error of measurement,** the range of scores within which an individual's true score is likely to fall. This range is sometimes termed the *confidence interval, score band,* or *profile band.* For example, suppose Ben has a raw score of 46 and Kim has a raw score of 52 on a test with a standard error of 4. This means that Ben's true score is between 42 and 50, and Kim's is between 48 and 56. At first glance, Kim appears to have scored significantly higher than Ben, but considering the standard error, their scores may be equal, or Ben's true score may even be higher than Kim's. Understanding standard error is important when we make decisions based on standardized tests. For instance, it would be unwise to place Ben and Kim in different ability groups based solely on the results illustrated here.

True score. The hypothetical average of an individual's scores if repeated testing under ideal conditions were possible.

Standard error of measurement. The range of scores within which an individual's true score is likely to fall.

MyEducationLab

To further examine standardized test results and what they mean, go to the *Building Teaching Skills and Dispositions* section in Chapter 15 of MyEducationLab at www.myeducationlab.com, and read the case study *Interpreting Standardized Test Results.* Complete the exercises following the case study to build your skills in interpreting standardized test results for students, parents, and other caregivers.

check your understanding

2.1 Carol is at the 96th percentile rank in number concepts; her friends Marsha and Lenore are at the 86th and 76th, respectively. Is the difference between Carol's and Marsha's scores greater than the difference between Marsha's and Lenore's, or vice versa? Explain.

2.2 A student in our first class (illustrated in Table 15.3 and Figure 15.2) scored 47 on the test. In what stanine is this score? In what stanine would a score of 47 be for the second class?

2.3 A fourth grader in your class has taken a standardized test, and the summary gives his grade-equivalent score as 6.7. Explain what this means. What implications does this have for your teaching?

To receive feedback for these questions, go to Appendix A.

Accountability Issues in Standardized Testing

Standardized testing is at the center of two areas that have become prominent in recent years, both in professional publications and in the popular media. They are: (1) standards-based education and accountability, and (2) the testing of teachers.

Standards-Based Education and Accountability

As you saw in Chapter 13, Americans perform poorly when polled about their world knowledge. Other studies lead to doubts about our science, reading, writing, and math knowledge as well. For example, results from the National Assessment of Educational Progress indicate that only 38 percent of U.S. eighth graders can calculate a 15 percent tip on a meal, even when given five choices from which to select (Stigler & Hiebert, 2000). Educators have responded to these inadequacies by promoting **standards-based education,** the process of focusing curricula and instruction on predetermined goals or standards. Standards specify what students at different ages and in particular content areas should know and be able to do. (As examples of standards in science, math, and history, look again on pages 395 and 396 of Chapter 13.)

Standards-based education. The process of focusing curricula and instruction on predetermined goals or standards.

Accountability. The process of requiring students to demonstrate that they have met specified standards and holding teachers responsible for students' performance.

Accountability is the process of requiring students to demonstrate that they have met specified standards and holding teachers responsible for students' performance. Standardized testing is used to determine whether or not students have met the standards.

Calls for accountability have resulted from evidence suggesting that students are being promoted from one grade to the next without mastering essential content and are graduating from high school with inadequate skills in reading, writing, and mathematics.

Schools have historically been called on to address societal problems, and the emphasis on standards and accountability is part of a recurrent cycle of reform dating all the way back to colonial times (Pulliam & Van Patten, 2007). Then, the issue was religious education, or lack of it. In the 19th and 20th centuries, reform targeted immigrants, asking schools to help them more quickly assimilate into U. S. society. In the late 20th century, with the publication of the book *A Nation at Risk* (National Commission on Excellence in Education, 1983), the aim of reform was to make our schools more academically rigorous so the United States could compete economically in global markets. This effort to make schools more academically competitive continues today with additional calls for reform using catchy titles like *Tough Choices or Tough Times* and *A New Day for Learning* (Lewis, 2007; Tucker, 2007).

Current Accountability Movements

As you first saw in Chapter 1, the accountability movement received a boost with the implementation of the No Child Left Behind Act (NCLB) of 2001, which was passed by the administration of George W. Bush. A reauthorization of the Elementary and Secondary Education Act, which began in 1965 and resulted in billions of dollars being spent on compensatory education programs for disadvantaged students, NCLB was contentious and politically charged almost as soon as it was passed. Some experts suggest that it has been, "the most significant change in federal regulation of public schools in three decades" (Hardy, 2002, p. 201), whereas critics contend that it has been ineffective and even destructive (Berliner, 2005).

Standards-based education and accountability are generally controversial, but they are likely here to stay. As you saw in Chapter 13, every state in the nation has developed standards, and the states are not going to simply discard them. In addition, and as a result of the accountability movement, standardized testing using high-stakes tests has also become a part of teachers' lives.

High-Stakes Tests

High-stakes tests are standardized tests that educators use to make important decisions that affect students, teachers, schools, and school districts (Au, 2007; Miller et al., 2009). High-stakes testing, also called *minimum competency testing*, has three components: (1) established standards for acceptable performance; (2) a requirement that all students of designated grades (e.g., 5th, 8th, and 10th) take the tests; and (3) the use of test results for decisions about promotion and graduation. When students cannot move to the next grade level or graduate from high school because they fail a test, for example, the "stakes" are very high, thus the term "high-stakes tests."

High-stakes tests. Standardized tests that educators use to make important decisions that affect students, teachers, schools, and school districts.

High-stakes tests and accountability place new pressures on both teachers and their students.

As you would expect, high-stakes testing is also controversial. Advocates claim the process helps clarify the goals of school systems, sends clear messages to students about what they should be learning, and provides the public with hard evidence about school effectiveness (Hirsch, 2000, 2006; Phelps, 2005). While conceding that teacher preparation, materials, and the tests themselves need to be improved, advocates also argue that the tests are the fairest and most effective means of providing a quality education for all students. Hirsch (2000) summarized the testing advocates' position: "They [standards and tests that measure achievement of the standards] are the most promising educational development in half a century" (p. 64).

Critics counter that teachers spend too much class time helping students practice for the tests, the tests don't reflect the curriculum being taught, and they don't accurately assess student learning (Amrein & Berliner, 2003; Behuniak, 2002; Berliner, 2004). They also contend that the cutoff scores are arbitrary, and the instruments are too crude to be used in making crucial decisions about students, teachers, and schools (Popham, 2004b). In addition, the tests have had a disproportionately adverse impact on minority students, particularly those with limited proficiency in English (Neill, 2003; Popham, 2003).

In spite of the criticisms, standards-based education and high-stakes testing are widespread. For example:

- All states have testing programs designed to measure the extent to which students meet preset standards.
- All states are required to issue overall ratings of their schools based on their students' performance on the tests.
- States must close or overhaul schools that are identified as failing (Jennings & Rentner, 2006; Swanson, 2008).

Testing Teachers

Increasingly, teachers are also being asked to pass competency tests that measure their background in academic areas, such as chemistry, history, or English, their understanding of learning and teaching, and their ability to perform basic skills. For example, a report by the National Academy of Education called for a national teacher test with results incorporated into state licensing requirements (Darling-Hammond & Baratz-Snowdon, 2005). Many states already require teachers to pass basic skills tests as well as tests of subject matter knowledge before they're licensed (Wayne & Youngs, 2003).

The Praxis™ Series

The Praxis test series from the Educational Testing Service, which you first saw discussed in Chapter 1, is the most commonly used teacher test; 70 percent of the states that test teachers use this series (Educational Testing Service, 2008a). The Praxis series consists of three components:

- ***Praxis* I®:** Academic Skills Assessments. Measures basic or "enabling" skills in reading, writing, and math that all teachers need.
- ***Praxis* II®:** Subject Assessments. Measures teachers' knowledge of the subjects they will teach. In addition to 70 content-specific tests, Praxis II® also includes the Principles of Learning and Teaching (PLT) grade-level specific tests, which measures teachers' understanding of basic principles of learning and teaching.
- ***Praxis* III®:** Classroom Performance Assessments. Using classroom observations and work samples, these tests assess teachers' ability to plan, instruct, manage, and understand professional responsibilities. In addition, Praxis III® assesses the teacher's sensitivity to learners' developmental and cultural differences.

You are most likely to encounter Praxis I® during your teacher preparation, Praxis II® after its completion, and Praxis III® during your first year of teaching.

Teacher testing has also sparked controversy in two areas. First, critics argue that teachers' classroom performance depends on factors other than teachers' knowledge (as measured on the tests), the most powerful being teachers' capacities to manage the complexities of classroom life and their ability to work with students (Cochran-Smith, 2005). Second, a disproportionate number of teacher candidates who fail the tests are members of cultural minorities (McIntosh & Norwood, 2004). Despite the controversies, the use of these tests, when properly developed and validated, has been upheld in courts (L. Fischer, Schimmel, & Stellman, 2006). The American Federation of Teachers, the second largest professional organization for educators in the United States, now proposes that prospective teachers pass tests that measure understanding of content, such as math and English, and knowledge of teaching principles (Blair, 2000). This proposal signals a change in policy from the past and suggests that teacher testing is not only here to stay but also likely to increase.

Accountability Issues in Standardized Testing: Implications for Teachers

How do the issues involved in standardized testing affect you as a teacher? At least three implications exist. First, although standardized testing is controversial, it is an integral part of educational assessment and almost certainly will remain so. As you saw earlier in the chapter, you will be expected to interpret standards, align your instruction with them, and prepare students for testing. In addition, you are likely to be held accountable for your students' performance on tests.

Second, you will be expected to know and do more (Cochran-Smith, 2005). You will likely be required to take more courses in English, math, and science than have been required of teachers in the past. You will also be expected to understand learners and learning and how content can be presented so it's understandable to students. It is likely that you will be required to pass a professional exit exam before you're licensed. Standardized testing and accountability have become facts of life for both teachers and students.

Third, and perhaps most important, you must be well informed about the strengths and limitations of standardized tests. Knowing that test bias may exist can help you avoid inappropriately lowering your expectations or stereotyping students based on the results of a single test. Other than students' caregivers, you are the person most important in determining the quality of students' education, and the better informed you are, the more capable you will be to make the best professional decisions possible.

check your understanding

3.1 Describe the relationship between standards-based education, accountability, and standardized testing.
3.2 Describe at least two arguments for and two arguments against high-stakes testing.
3.3 Identify the three main areas in which teachers are being tested, and explain how they relate to instruction.

To receive feedback for these questions, go to Appendix A.

Diversity and Standardized Testing

One of the most volatile controversies in standardized testing involves critics' claims that the tests are biased against members of cultural minorities (Platt, 2004). This is particularly true for Hispanic and African American students who, on average, consistently score lower on standardized tests than do White and Asian students (McIntosh & Norwood, 2004). The issue has become increasingly inflammatory, because scoring below established minimums on high-stakes standardized tests can result in grade retention or failure to graduate from high school (D. D. Johnson et al., 2008; Walpole, McDonough, & Bauer, 2005). A number of cases have actually gone to the courts, and the validity of tests for cultural minorities and the extent to which students have had the opportunity to learn test content have been key issues (Geisinger, 2005). The essential question is: As standardized tests are increasingly used to measure and improve student performance, will members of cultural minorities be treated fairly?

Advocates and critics, of course, disagree, and three important issues related to standardized testing with minority students remain unresolved. One is whether the tests are valid enough to justify using results to make decisions about students' academic lives (D. D. Johnson et al., 2008; G. Jones et al., 2003). A second relates to technical problems involved in testing members of minorities and particularly students who speak English as a second language (Geisinger, 2005). The question of whether test scores reflect differences in achievement or simply cultural or language differences remains controversial. Third, experts and professional organizations including the American Educational Research Association, the American Psychological Association, and the National Council on Measurement in Education are increasingly critical of making decisions about promotion or graduation on the basis of one test score (American Educational Research Association, American Psychological Association, & National Council on Measurement in Education, 1999).

Student Diversity and Assessment Bias

Because of the controversies surrounding standardized testing, educators and policy makers are focusing increased attention on the question of whether or not assessment bias exists. **Assessment bias** is a form of discrimination that occurs when a test or other assessment instrument unfairly penalizes a group of students because of their gender, ethnicity, race, or socioeconomic status (SES).

Assessment bias. A form of discrimination that occurs when a test or other assessment instrument unfairly penalizes a group of students because of their gender, ethnicity, race, or socioeconomic status.

Measurement experts have identified three types of assessment bias that detract from validity (Miller et al., 2009):

- Bias in content
- Bias in testing procedures
- Bias in test interpretation and use

As you study these topics, remember that mean differences between groups do not necessarily indicate bias. The differences may result from underlying causes, such as poverty or inadequate educational opportunities (Nitko & Brookhart, 2007).

Bias in Content

Critics contend that the content of standardized tests is geared to White, middle-class American students, and members of cultural minorities are disadvantaged by this content. For example, the following item is drawn from a standardized science test to measure the knowledge of sixth graders:

> *If you wanted to find out if a distant planet had mountains or rivers on it, which of the following tools should you use?*
>
> *a. binoculars*
> *b. microscope*
> *c. telescope*
> *d. camera (Popham, 2004b, p. 48)*

Performance on this item is likely to be influenced by SES and a student's exposure to high-cost items such as microscopes and telescopes (Popham, 2004b).

Bias can also occur in word problems (Miller et al., 2009). For example:

> *Alex Rodriguez is batting .310 after 100 trips to the plate. In his next three times at bat, he gets a single, double, and home run. What is his batting average now?*

Teachers should continually guard against bias in test content, procedures, and uses.

This item requires that students know how batting averages are computed and whether or not doubles and home runs count more than singles. Word problems can also be biased if students have trouble reading the item because of limited skills with English.

Mismatches between test content and the cultural backgrounds of students can also result in content bias. For example, students from a remote Eskimo community were asked the following question on a standardized vocabulary test: "Which of the following would most likely take you to the hospital if you got hurt?" The "correct" answer was *ambulance*, but Eskimo students replied *airplane* because that is how people in their village receive emergency medical aid (Platt, 2004).

Bias in Testing Procedures

Because students from different cultures respond differently to testing situations, bias can also occur in testing procedures. For example, in one study researchers found that Navajo students were unaware of the consequences of poor test performance, instead treating tests as game-like events (Deyhle, 1987). Other research has found that some minority students *believe* tests will be biased, and as a result they don't try to do well on them (Morgan & Mehta, 2004; Ryan & Ryan, 2005).

Bias in Test Interpretation and Use

Bias can also occur in the use and interpretation of test results. Experts are concerned about the adverse effects of testing on minority students' progress through public schools and entrance into college (D. D. Johnson et al., 2008; G. Jones et al., 2003). Evidence suggests that test results are sometimes used in ways that discriminate against members of cultural minorities and those who do not speak English as a first language. For example, a historic study of 812 students classified as being mentally retarded found 300 percent more Mexican Americans and 50 percent more African Americans than would be expected from their numbers in the general population, and, the study population had 40 percent fewer Anglo Americans than would be expected. Further, people in lower income brackets were overrepresented, whereas people in the upper brackets were underrepresented (Mercer, 1973). More recent research suggests this issue still exists (Blanchett, 2006).

Standardized Testing and English Language Learners

Standardized testing poses special challenges for English Language Learners (ELLs) and their teachers. Research shows that ELL students consistently score lower than other students on both standardized achievement and intelligence tests (Abedi & Gandara 2006; Blanchett, 2006). Though disturbing, these results are not surprising to many testing experts, because most standardized tests are developed for native English speakers and depend heavily on English language skills (Geisinger, 2005; Jones, et al., 2003). This presents a problem for teachers who are asked to use standardized test scores in their work with ELL students, because "Students must be able to read English if a test written in English is to measure performance accurately" (Peregoy & Boyle, 2001, p. 98).

The problem of standardized testing with limited-English speakers is not new, but its importance has increased with the emphasis on accountability. In the 19th century, immigrants to the United States were routinely tested on Ellis Island with English language tests that discriminated against non-English–speaking immigrant groups (Geisinger, 2005). And, the No Child Left Behind legislation has required that all ELL students who have been in this country for three consecutive years be tested in reading and language arts using a test written in English (Northwest Regional Laboratory, 2003).

Language is not the only reason for the poor performance of ELL students on standardized tests. These students tend to come from lower-SES families, and research consistently demonstrates the adverse affects of poverty on achievement (Macionis, 2006). In addition, ELL students typically attend poorer schools, with fewer resources and greater numbers of unqualified or inexperienced teachers (Kozol, 2005).

Researchers have identified additional factors influencing ELL students' performance on standardized tests, all related to the linguistic complexity of the tests (Abedi, Hofstetter, & Lord, 2004). In addition to the fact that the tests are administered in English, the tests contain many technical terms that aren't commonly used in conversation, such as *ion, colonization,* and *simile* (Echevarria & Graves, 2007). This puts ELL students at a disadvantage, because they acquire language proficiency through everyday conversation. And standardized tests are timed, placing an additional cognitive burden on ELL test-takers.

Testing Accommodations for ELL Students

Accommodations to address these problems focus on either the test itself or testing procedures (see Table 15.4). Efforts to modify the test have attempted either to translate the test into ELL students' first language or to simplify vocabulary or sentence structures, such as shortening sentences or converting from passive to active voice (Abedi, 2006). Technical and logistical problems exist with these efforts, however. Technically, testing experts question whether or not the modified and original forms of the test are comparable, which raise questions of validity (Geisinger, 2005). Logistically, it isn't economically feasible to translate tests into all the native languages that exist in some urban districts. Even when students speak a common language, cultural differences, such as variations in Spanish dialects spoken in Spain, Mexico, Cuba, and Puerto Rico, make it difficult to construct a test that is culturally and linguistically meaningful (Geisinger, 2005; Solano-Flores, & Li, 2006).

Attempts to increase validity through modifications of testing procedures, such as providing regular and bilingual dictionaries and allowing ELL students more time, appear more promising (Abedi & Gandara, 2006). Providing more time, especially when combined with test-specific glossaries, appears to be the most feasible accommodation (Abedi & Gandara, 2006).

MyEducationLab

To further examine standardized tests, their uses, and the extent to which they're valid with members of cultural minorities, go to the *Activities and Applications* section in Chapter 15 of My EducationLab at www.myeducationlab.com, and read the case study *Analyzing Standardized Testing.* Answer the questions following the case study.

table 15.4 Standardized Test Accommodations for ELL Students

Accommodations to the Test
Translating the test
Simplifying vocabulary
Simplifying sentence structure
Accommodations to Testing Procedures
General dictionaries
Bilingual dictionaries
Customized dictionaries and glossaries
Additional time

theory to practice

The Teacher's Role in Standardized Testing

You will play an important role in ensuring that standardized test scores reflect what your students have actually learned. Given current demographic trends in the United States, you almost certainly will have members of cultural minorities in your classes, and some of them will speak a native language other than English. In addition, you will communicate test results to students and their caregivers, and you will use the results to improve your instruction. The following guidelines can assist you in performing these essential functions:

1. Prepare students so that test results accurately reflect what they know and can do.
2. Make accommodations, if possible, for members of cultural minorities and students who are not native English speakers.
3. Administer tests in ways that maximize student performance.
4. Communicate results to students and their caregivers.
5. Use sources of data in addition to standardized test results in making educational decisions.

Let's see how these guidelines operate in classrooms.

Preparing Students. As you saw earlier in the chapter, the validity of standardized tests depends on the match between the test and the purpose for using it. With the present emphasis on district-, state-, and even nationally mandated tests, it has become teachers' responsibilities to ensure that students have learned the content covered on the tests (Miller et al., 2009; Popham, 2004a).

Ensuring that students are prepared depends on the effectiveness of instruction. They should have studied in detail the content covered on the test, and they should have opportunities to practice the skills measured on the test using a format similar to the test format (Mertler, 2007). For example, teachers commonly assess spelling by giving quizzes that require students to correctly spell lists of words. However, in spelling assessment on standardized tests, students encounter a list of four closely matched words and must select the one spelled correctly. To do well on these items, students need practice with this format.

Students should also be taught general test-taking strategies, which are similar to those you studied in Chapter 14. These strategies are particularly important for members of cultural minorities, ELL students, and students from low SES backgrounds. Strategies for preparing students for standardized tests include the following:

- Read and follow all directions.
- Determine how questions will be scored, such as whether or not penalties exist for errors in spelling or grammar in written responses, or for guessing on multiple-choice items.
- Eliminate options on multiple-choice items, and make informed guesses with remaining items (if guessing isn't penalized).
- Pace themselves so they have enough time to answer all the questions.
- Answer easier questions first, and go back to check answers if time permits.

check your understanding

4.1 Explain how learner diversity can influence the validity of standardized tests.

4.2 Describe the most effective strategy teachers can use to minimize content bias in the use of standardized tests with their students.

To receive feedback for these questions, go to Appendix A.

- Check to be sure that responses on the answer sheet match the numbers in the test booklet (Miller et al., 2009; Nitko & Brookhart, 2007;).

Accommodating Members of Minorities and ELL Students. As you saw in earlier sections, standardized tests often use technical language that is infrequently used in everyday conversation. Providing concrete examples of technical terms, such as *ion* and *simile,* and emphasizing the essential characteristics of the concepts can help accommodate differences in background knowledge. This is particularly important for members of cultural minorities and non-native English speakers.

Also, providing dictionaries and allowing extra time for these students are effective accommodations if the testing procedures allow it.

Administering Tests. To ensure that standardized tests yield valid results, they must be uniformly administered to all populations. Developers typically explain in detail how to administer their tests (McMillan, 2004; Nitko & Brookhart, 2007). Manuals specify the allotted time for each test and subtest; teachers should write that information on the board for students. Test manuals also provide scripts for introducing and describing the subtests. If the test administrators do not follow scripts and time frames precisely, the results can be invalid.

Interpreting Results. Once students receive their results, you are responsible for explaining the results to students and their caregivers and using them to improve your instruction. To identify areas that may need improvement, teachers commonly compare the scores of one year's class with those in earlier years (Nichols & Singer, 2000).

You should combine standardized test scores with other information about students when communicating results, and you should emphasize that the scores are only approximations of student capabilities. And, to the extent possible, avoid technical language in discussing results.

Use Additional Data Sources. Testing experts are clear on the following point: No single test should be used as the basis for educational decisions about individual students (Miller et al., 2009). At the school level, you can help ensure that the school staff use alternate data sources such as grades, work samples, and classroom observations in making decisions about individual students. At the policy level, you can become an advocate for the use of comprehensive assessment data in making these decisions.

Teachers are responsible for explaining standardized test results to parents and other caregivers and using the results to improve their instruction.

Finally, when making decisions about students, use a variety of sources of data, such as your own quizzes, tests, homework, and informal observations, in addition to standardized test results. This is important for all students, and even more so when working with members of cultural minorities and ELLs. These sources can be your most valuable forms of information for making decisions.

classroom connections

Eliminating Test Bias in Your Classroom

1. Test validity can be compromised when cultural factors unfairly affect test performance. Attempt to understand the potential effects of learner diversity on assessment performance.
   - **Elementary:** Before any of her non-native English-speaking students are referred for special education testing, a first-grade teacher talks with a school psychologist and describes the child's background and language patterns.
   - **Middle School:** Before administering a statewide exam, an eighth grade math teacher explains the purpose and format of the test and gives students practice with the content covered on the test. He reads the directions for taking the test slowly and clearly and writes the amount of time remaining on the board.
   - **High School:** A high school English teacher holds sessions after school to help her students with limited English proficiency prepare for a high-stakes test. She explains test purposes and formats and provides the students with timed practice on similar items.
2. Testing procedures can influence student performance and ultimately test validity. Adapt testing procedures to meet the needs of all students.
   - **Elementary:** An urban third-grade teacher states positive expectations for all students as they prepare for a standardized test and carefully monitors them to be sure they stay on task during the test.
   - **Middle School:** Before standardized tests are given each year, a middle school language arts teacher takes time to teach test-taking strategies (some examples are on page 455 of Chapter 14.). She models the strategies, discusses them with her students, and provides opportunities to practice them under test-like conditions.
   - **High School:** An algebra teacher makes a special effort to ensure that students understand the vocabulary on the state standardized test. Before the test, he carefully reviews important concepts the class has learned during the school year.

developmentally appropriate practice

Standardized Testing with Different-Aged Learners

Effective assessment with standardized tests requires that teachers take learner development into account. The following sections outline some suggestions for accommodating the developmental levels of your students.

Working with Elementary Students

The developmental characteristics of young children can impact the validity of standardized tests. Their short attention spans and limited language skills will influence their performance, and they don't understand that the tests are important, so they don't make efforts to perform well. For many young children, a standardized test is just one more worksheet to be completed (Gullo, 2005). They also lack experience with timed tests and multiple-choice formats, which are commonly used on standardized tests. They may not follow directions, and because they tend to be impulsive, they often select the first choice that seems plausible or may rush through the test so they can return to activities they find more enjoyable (Stipek, 2002).

Because of mismatches between testing requirements and students' developmental limitations, teachers of young children should treat standardized test results skeptically, particularly when they're not consistent with children's classroom performance. Most importantly, teachers should avoid making long-term predictions about student potential on the basis of standardized test results, and particularly on the basis of these results alone.

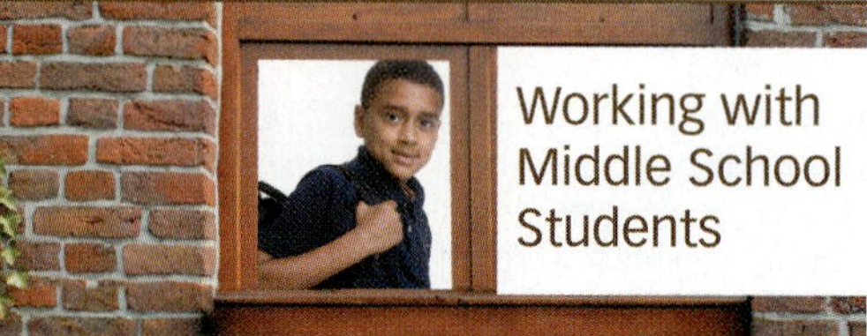

Working with Middle School Students

Middle school students generally understand the importance of standardized tests, which can have both positive and negative effects; it can increase their motivation to perform well, but it can also result in test anxiety that can decrease their performance.

While generally more fully developed than younger children in their ability to respond to standardized tests, their development varies a great deal. Some have acquired the study habits, self-regulatory abilities, and test-taking strategies needed to navigate through timed, standardized test formats successfully, whereas others haven't (Schunk, 2005; Zimmerman, 2005).

To accommodate these differences, middle school teachers should emphasize self-regulation and personal responsibility, teach test-taking strategies, and provide ample practice with formats similar to those students will encounter on standardized tests. Other strategies that can also be helpful with middle school students include emphasizing that the tests can give them valuable information about their strengths and areas that need more work, stating positive expectations about their performance, and encouraging them to do their best.

Working with High School Students

By the time they reach high school, students have had a considerable amount of experience with standardized testing. As a result, they are familiar with test formats and procedures, but for students who have had negative experiences with standardized testing, motivation can be a problem (Ryan, Ryan, Arbuthnot, & Samuels, 2007). Motivation can be a special problem for low-performing students, and it often prevents them from performing up to the limits of their capabilities. One adolescent facing challenging problems on a test commented, "I figured I would get them wrong . . . Yeah, because if I know I'm going to get them wrong I just kind of think why bother trying" (Ryan et al., 2007, p. 9).

Teachers of high school students should emphasize that standardized test results exist to provide students with information, and the results don't say anything about their intrinsic worth as human beings, nor do they determine whether or not students will be successful in life. Doing as well as possible is important, however, because the results then provide the most useful information.

High school students also need help interpreting standardized test scores and how they can be used to make career decisions. Test results can be confusing, and both students and their parents need help understanding and translating them into useful information (Carr, 2008). Caring and understanding teachers are often the people in the best position to help students understand test results, and, because they are familiar with students' classroom performance, the students' teachers are also in the best position help students make important decisions about their futures.

Meeting Your Learning Objectives

1. Describe the functions of standardized tests in the total assessment process.
   - Assessing student academic progress, diagnosing strengths and weaknesses, and providing information to place students in appropriate programs are important functions of standardized tests. Providing information for program evaluation and improvement is also an important function.
   - Achievement tests provide information about student learning; diagnostic tests provide in-depth analysis of specific student strengths and weaknesses; intelligence tests measure students' ability to acquire and use knowledge, to solve problems, and to accomplish new tasks; and aptitude tests predict potential for future learning.
   - Validity measures the appropriateness of a test for a specific purpose and includes content, predictive, and construct validity.
2. Interpret standardized test results using statistics and standard scores.
   - Educators interpret standardized test scores by using descriptive statistics to compare an individual's performance to the performance of a norming group.
   - The mean, median, and mode are measures of central tendency, and the range and standard deviation are measures of variability.
   - Percentiles, stanines, grade equivalents, and standard scores all allow comparison of a student's score with the scores of comparable students in a norming group.
3. Describe the relationships between standards-based education, accountability, and standardized testing.
   - Standards-based education is the process of focusing curricula and instruction on predetermined goals or standards, and accountability is the process of requiring students to demonstrate that they have met the standards and holding teachers responsible for students' performance. Educators use standardized testing in the form of high-stakes tests to determine whether or not students have met the standards.
   - Advocates of accountability argue that standardized tests efficiently assess the educational achievements of large numbers of students. Critics counter that misuse of standardized tests discourages innovation and encourages teaching to the test.
   - The accountability movement is also targeting teachers. Prospective teachers are now expected to demonstrate competency in basic skills, content area knowledge, and pedagogy.
4. Explain how learner diversity can influence the validity of standardized tests.
   - Learner diversity can influence the validity of standardized tests if being a member of a cultural minority or a non-native English speaker results in test bias.
   - Content bias occurs when incidental information in items discriminates against certain cultural groups.
   - Bias in testing procedures occurs when groups don't fully understand testing procedures and the implications of time limits.
   - Bias in the use of test results occurs when educators use tests in isolation to make important decisions about students.

Developing as a Professional: Preparing for Your Licensure Exam

At the beginning of the chapter, we saw how Mike Chavez interpreted standardized test scores for a parent. Let's look now at another situation in which using standardized tests can help answer questions about learning and teaching. Read the case study, and answer the questions that follow.

> Peggy Barret looks up from the stack of algebra tests that she is grading as her colleague, Stan Witzel, walks into the teacher's lounge.
>
> "How's it going?" Stan asks.
>
> "Fine, . . . I think. I'm scoring tests from my Algebra I class. That's the one where I'm trying to put more emphasis on problem solving. Quite a few kids are actually getting into the applications now, and they like the problem solving when they do small-group work. The trouble is, some of the others are really struggling. . . . So, I'm not so sure about it all."
>
> "I wish I had your problems. It sounds like your kids are learning, and at least some of them like it," Stan replies.
>
> "Yeah, I know," Peggy nods. "Getting these kids to like any kind of math is an accomplishment, but still I wonder. . . . It's just that I'm not sure if they're getting all that they should. I don't know whether this class is *really* doing better than last year's class, or even than my other classes this year, for that matter. The tests I give are pretty different in the different classes. I think the kids are doing better on problem solving, but to be honest about it, I see quite a few of them struggling with mechanics. I work on the mechanics, but not as much as in other classes. I'm not sure if I've drawn the line in the right place as far as the emphasis I'm putting on each part of the class."
>
> "Good point," Stan shrugs. "I always wonder when I make changes. By emphasizing something more, I wonder if they are they missing out on something?"

"As important," Peggy continues, "I wonder how they'll do when they go off to college. Quite a few of them in this class will be going. . . . Got any ideas?"

"Good questions, Peggy. I wish I knew, but . . . I guess that's part of teaching."

"Yeah," she replies with her voice trailing off, "it seems as if we should be able to get some better information. I can see that some of the kids just don't seem to get it. I would say their background is weak; they seem to be trying. On the other hand, I checked out some of their old standardized test results, and their math scores weren't that bad. Maybe it's not background. Maybe they just don't belong in my class."

"Tell me about the kids who are struggling," Stan suggests.

"Well, Jacinta tries really hard. Quan is a whiz at computation but struggles when I ask him to think. Carlos actually seems to do fairly well with mechanics but has a hard time with word problems. For example, I tried to motivate the class the other day with several word problems involving statistics from our basketball team. Most of the class liked them and got them right. Not these three."

"Maybe you ought to talk to Yolanda," Stan suggests. "She's been in this game for a while and might know about some tests that are available that can help you answer some of your questions."

Short-Answer Questions

In answering these questions, use information from the chapter, and link your responses to specific information in the case.

1. What type of standardized test would help Peggy determine "whether this class is *really* doing better than last year, or even than my other classes this year"?

2. What type of validity would be the primary concern with this test? Explain.

3. One of Peggy's concerns was the prior knowledge of her students. What type of standardized test might Peggy use to gather data related to this concern?

4. In investigating the problems that her students were having in math, Peggy checked out their overall test scores from past standardized tests. What else might she have done?

To receive feedback for these questions, go to Appendix B.

Now go to Chapter 15 of MyEducationLab, located at www.myeducationlab.com, where you can:

- Take a quiz to test your mastery of chapter objectives. Detailed feedback is provided to explain why your responses are correct or incorrect.
- Deepen your understanding of chapter concepts with *Review, Practice, Enrichment* exercises.
- Complete *Activities and Applications* that will help you apply what you have learned in the chapter by analyzing real classrooms through video clips, artifacts and case studies. Your instructor will provide you with feedback for the *Activities and Applications.*
- Develop your professional knowledge and decision making in *Building Teaching Skills and Dispositions* exercises. Structured feedback will be available to you, providing you with support as you practice each skill. Your instructor will provide you with feedback on the final task that accompanies the exercise.

Important Concepts

accountability (p. 486)
achievement tests (p. 475)
aptitude tests (p. 476)
assessment bias (p. 489)
construct validity (p. 479)
content validity (p. 479)
criterion-referenced standardized tests (p. 474)
diagnostic tests (p. 475)
frequency distribution (p. 480)
grade-equivalent score (p. 484)
high-stakes tests (p. 487)
intelligence tests (p. 475)
mean (p. 481)
measures of central tendency (p. 481)
median (p. 481)
mode (p. 481)
national norms (p. 473)
normal distribution (p. 482)
norming group (p. 473)
norm-referenced standardized tests (p. 474)
percentile (percentile rank, PR) (p. 483)
percentile bands (p. 484)
predictive validity (p. 479)
range (p. 481)
raw score (p. 483)
readiness tests (p. 478)
standard deviation (p. 482)
standard error of measurement (p. 485)
standardized tests (p. 473)
standards-based education (p. 486)
standard score (p. 485)
stanine (p. 484)
true score (p. 485)
T-score (p. 485)
variability (p. 481)
z-score (p. 485)

appendix A

Feedback for "Check Your Understanding" Questions

Chapter 1

1.1 The characteristics of professionalism are:

- Commitment to learners. Professional educators are committed to helping their students grow, both as learners and as people. This commitment is also reflected in a code of ethics that guides their professional practice.
- Decision making. Teaching is a complex and ill-defined practice. Professionals are able to make decisions that are designed to increase learning for all students in these ill-defined situations.
- Reflective practice. Professionals continually question their classroom performance and assess their practice with the goal of continual improvement.
- A body of specialized knowledge. Professionals base their decisions and self-assessments on a deep and thorough understanding of a professional body of specialized knowledge.

1.2 First, Keith was committed to his students and their learning, as indicated by his expressions of concern about their dislike of word problems and about Kelly's behavior. Second, his discussion with Jan indicates that he reflected on his work. Third, he made a series of decisions in his attempt to work with Kelly.

1.3 Jan demonstrated commitment to her students, as indicated by her efforts to make her learning activities more meaningful for them. Second, she reflected on her work, as indicated by her concerns about sometimes intervening too soon and at other times letting her students stumble around too long. Third, she made a number of decisions that led to the way she designed and conducted her learning activity. Finally, and most significantly, she based her decisions on a thorough understanding of professional knowledge. This understanding is the foundation of professionalism.

1.4 The primary difference between Keith's and Jan's level of professional behavior is in the depth of their professional knowledge. Because Jan was more knowledgeable, she made decisions that Keith's professional development didn't yet allow him to make.

2.1 Knowledge of content, pedagogical content knowledge, general pedagogical knowledge, and knowledge of learners and learning are four types of knowledge professional teachers possess. Knowledge of content describes teachers' understanding of math, reading, geography, or whatever topic is being taught. Pedagogical content knowledge is the ability to represent the topic in ways that are understandable, such as the folded pieces of paper discussed in Chapter 1 as a way of representing the multiplication of fractions. General pedagogical knowledge refers to the professional abilities necessary to teach in all situations, such as questioning skills, or the ability to organize classrooms. Knowledge of learners and learning refers to factors such as an understanding of how students learn, and how students' motivation influences learning.

2.2 Keith's statement that best indicates that he lacks pedagogical content knowledge is, "I explain the stuff so carefully, but some of the kids just sit with blank looks on their faces." As Chapter 1 shows, when teachers lack pedagogical content knowledge, they commonly revert to abstract explanations that aren't meaningful to students. We're not implying that teachers shouldn't try to explain topics; rather we're suggesting that relying on explanations alone often fails to increase learners' understanding as much as a teacher might expect.

2.3 The teacher in this case is using the pieces of bubble wrap to help students visualize the way that cells form tissues. The ability to create this representation is an indicator of the teacher's pedagogical content knowledge. (In this case, the bubble wrap is a model for the formation of tissue; it helps students visualize what they can't observe directly.)

3.1 The major types of research discussed in the chapter are:

- Descriptive research. Descriptive research uses interviews, observations, and surveys to describe events. Descriptive research does not imply relationships between variables and should not be used to predict future events.
- Correlational research. Correlational research describes a relationship between two or more variables. Correlational research does not imply that changes in one variable cause changes in the other.
- Experimental research. Experimental research systematically manipulates variables in an attempt to identify cause-and-effect relationships. Comparability of groups, control of extraneous variables, the size of the sample groups, and clear descriptions of how the independent variable is being manipulated are all important when conducting experimental research.
- Qualitative research. Qualitative research attempts to describe complex educational phenomena in holistic terms. It typically uses narratives to provide the reader with a fine-grained analysis of some situation or event.
- Action research. Action research is a form of applied research designed to answer specific school- or classroom-related questions. Action research can be descriptive, correlational, or experimental.

3.2 This finding is the result of correlational research. A relationship exists between the variables personal teaching efficacy and student achievement. However, the researchers didn't consciously manipulate one of the variables; that is, they didn't train some of the teachers to be high in efficacy. They merely observed the relationship between teaching efficacy and achievement.

3.3 Concluding that doing homework caused achievement to increase would not be valid. Tyra's research found a correlation between homework and achievement; correlational research does not imply that one variable causes the other.

4.1 Many of the ideas in educational psychology are quite abstract. Because they're abstract, they're difficult to understand and apply to teaching. The use of case studies provides concrete reference points that make the abstract ideas of educational psychology more meaningful and applicable to the real world that you will face when you begin your career.

4.2 Video case studies have the advantage of being more authentic and real than written case studies. They allow viewers to see, for example, differences between a confident and a hesitant student answer and why the difference might exist, or differences in room arrangements that might influence student behavior.

Chapter 2

1.1 Development refers to the changes that occur in human beings as they grow from infancy to adulthood. An understanding of development is important for three reasons. First, if provides insights into the developing thoughts and behaviors of the students we teach. Second, it helps us guide and direct that development. Third, it reminds us that students may be at different developmental levels when they enter our classrooms and we should adjust our expectations accordingly.

1.2 All development is based on three principles. First, development depends upon both heredity and environments. While heredity provides the raw materials for development, environmental influences play a major role in shaping development. Teachers play a major role in providing these experiences and shaping development.

A second basic principle of development is that development proceeds in a relatively orderly and predictable pattern. When teachers understand these patterns, they can better address these developmental strengths and limitations in their instruction.

A third principle of development is that children develop at different rates. Though we typically group children by their chronological age, this does not ensure that they are all at the same stage of development. Understanding this developmental variability makes teachers more sensitive to individual differences and helps them accommodate these differences in their teaching.

1.3 As the brain develops, synaptic connections between neurons are both strengthened and eliminated (synaptic pruning). The direction of these connections influences our cognitive development. Healthy cognitive development is dependent upon a nurturant environment which provides for both physical needs and stimulation from the environment.

The cerebral cortex is the part of the brain involved with higher cognitive processes, such as language and thinking as well as impulse control. The development of the cerebral cortex allows us to plan, problem solve, and make informed and thoughtful decisions.

2.1 Hands-on activities provide the direct experiences that Piaget believed are necessary for development. Experience also helps us understand the statement made in this section, "Although approximate chronological ages are attached to the stages, children pass through them at different rates." Differences in experience, together with differences in maturation, are the two most important reasons why children pass through the stages at different rates.

2.2 First, the children tend to center on the length of the row in the case of the coins and the length of the clay in the case of the flattened piece of clay. The length of the row and of the longer, flatter clay are more perceptually obvious than are the number of coins or the amount of clay. The children therefore conclude that more coins are in the bottom row, and more clay is in the flattened piece. Second, because young children lack transformation, they don't mentally record the process of spreading the coins apart in the bottom row, or flattening the clay, so they see each as new and different. Third, because they lack reversibility, they're unable to mentally trace the process of re-forming the length of the row to its original state, or to mentally trace the process of re-forming the flattened clay back into a ball. When lack of transformation and reversibility are combined with their tendency to center, we can see why young children conclude that the bottom row has more coins, even though no coins were added or removed, and conclude that the amount of clay differs even though no clay was added or removed.

2.3 You have had a variety of experiences with using your Mac, and you have organized those experiences into a "word processing" scheme. Your scheme has helped you to achieve equilibrium. However, when you encountered Windows your equilibrium was disrupted, and you were forced to accommodate your scheme. You modified your original scheme and constructed a new "processing-with-Windows" scheme, and your equilibrium was reestablished, allowing you to assimilate new word processing tasks.

3.1 The section "Language and Development" suggests that you should encourage your students to talk about their developing understanding of mathematics. Language is a cognitive tool that allows learners to think about the world and solve problems, and the more practice students get putting their understanding into words, the better their understanding will be, and the more their development will be advanced.

3.2 Language is a cognitive tool kit, embedded within each culture. In our culture, *ice* is a simple idea. In the Yu'pik culture, however, *ice* is a more complex concept, and they have more terms and more ways of describing it. Their language reflects the fact that *ice* is a more complex idea in their culture than it is in ours. Because of the cultural influence, their concept of *ice* is more fully developed than is ours.

3.3 The zone of proximal development is the point in your development where you can benefit from instructional support. So, being able to perform word processing skills with support represents your zone of proximal development. Your friend's zone is somewhere beyond your zone, and it might involve sophisticated presentation skills beyond mere word processing. This would be the point where she would need support to advance her development. The differences suggest that her word processing skills are more fully developed than are yours.

4.1 Nativist theory, which asserts that children have a language acquisition device that allows them to produce sentences they haven't heard before, provides the best explanation.

Neither behaviorism nor social cognitive theory can adequately explain this particular misuse of language, because it is unlikely that anyone reinforced the child for using the adjective form, "gooder," and it is also unlikely that anyone has modeled it for the child.

Sociocultural theory, which stresses the learning of language in functional settings, also is not useful for explaining this adjective form, because it isn't viewed as culturally acceptable usage.

4.2 Using "gooder" is an example of overgeneralization. The child is overgeneralizing the rule, "To make a comparative adjective, add *er* to it."

4.3 Vocabulary development involves the acquisition of new word meanings. Syntax, by contrast, involves learning the grammatical rules for combining words into sentences that make sense. Both are essential for successful school learning. Without vocabulary development, the meaning of new terms and ideas suffers; without syntax, students have problems expressing ideas and understanding the ideas of others.

Chapter 3

1.1 The components of the model include the individual, the microsystem, mesosystem, exosystem, macrosystem, and chronosystem. Each influences personal, social, and moral development. The microsystem includes immediate influences, such as parents and peers. Parents influence development through their parenting styles, and peers influence development with their attitudes and values, friendships, and emotional support. The mesosystem involves the extent to which the elements of the microsystem interact effectively, such as home–school collaboration. The ecosystem includes societal forces, such as parents' jobs, which can influence the amount of time parents have to spend with their children. The macrosystem is the larger culture in which the individual lives, and it influences development through the values it communicates and the resources it provides to promote development. The chronosystem involves the influence of temporal changes, such as people aging, changing personal relationships, and the increasing impact of technology.

1.2 The microsystem includes a child's family, peers, neighborhood, and school. These elements are the most powerful influences on development, because individuals are in most direct contact with them.

1.3 Educational influences on development are reflected in Bronfenbrenner's theory at several levels. First, at the microsystem level, schools and classrooms exert immediate influences on development. School success plays a major role in shaping who we are and how we develop. The mesosystem level reflects interactions between elements of the microsystem. For example, teachers and schools can influence how families raise their children, and the families, in turn, influence what goes on in classrooms. At the macrosystem level, broader cultural and societal influences can affect the trajectory of development by their influences on schools and schooling. For example, the current national emphasis on testing and accountability has had a major impact on schools, and these changes influence each child's experiences in the classroom.

2.1 Based on Erikson's theory, we would explain the student's behavior by saying that he hasn't positively resolved the initiative-guilt crisis. This doesn't imply that his industry-inferiority or identity-confusion crises cannot be resolved somewhat satisfactorily, however, as indicated by the fact that "he does a good job on his required work," and he "seems to be quite happy." Erikson's work would suggest that this student simply has a personality "glitch" with respect to initiative. It may never have a significant effect on his personal functioning unless he finds himself in a job in which initiative is needed and valued.

A teacher might respond by encouraging him to take initiative and then reinforcing any initiative that he takes. In addition, creating a classroom environment that deemphasizes competition can also encourage student initiative.

2.2 Based on their comments in the conversation, it appears that Taylor is in the state of identity achievement. He stated, "I'm going into nursing," and he appeared to have few doubts about his decision.

Sandy's comments suggest that she is at the state of identity diffusion. She has considered veterinary medicine, and she has also given some thought to teaching, but her thinking is somewhat haphazard.

Ramon is at the state of identity foreclosure. His parents want him to be a lawyer, and he has acquiesced to their wishes.

Nancy's comments, "I'm not willing to decide yet," and "I'm going to think about it a while," indicate that she is at the state of identity moratorium.

2.3 The student's comments reflect his self-concept, which is a cognitive appraisal of one's physical, social, and academic competence. Self-esteem, by contrast, is our emotional evaluation of the self, and we see no evidence of either high or low self-esteem in the comments. Self-concept is more closely related to academic achievement than is self-esteem.

3.1 Perspective taking and social problem solving are the two major components of advancing social development. Perspective taking is the ability to understand the thoughts and feelings of others, and teachers can promote it by encouraging students to consider the way others might think or feel. Social problem solving is the ability to resolve conflicts in ways that are beneficial to all involved. Like perspective taking, developing this social skill takes time and practice.

3.2 The teacher in this case is trying to develop social problem solving. By asking, "What could we do to make both of you happy?" she was attempting to help the children learn to resolve a conflict in ways that would be beneficial to both.

3.3 School violence and aggression are closely related to underdeveloped social skills. For example, aggressive students rarely consider others' perspectives, and they have trouble maintaining friendships. They are also more likely to react to social problems with aggressive or hostile behaviors instead of using social problem-solving skills. The same three factors that influence personal development—genetics, parents, and peers—also influence the development of aggression in children.

4.1 A driver reasoning at Stage 3 would be likely to say that everybody else is going 65, so it's okay for me to do the same. At Stage 4, a person would be more likely to say that the law says 55, so I'm slowing down. I don't care what everyone else is doing.

4.2 Gilligan's work would suggest that a woman would be more likely than a man to interpret this incident from an interpersonal perspective. For example, a woman might reason that whispering is justified because we're helping Gary, whereas a man might be more likely to reason that the assignment was given, and Gary, as with everyone else, should know it. According to Gilligan, the major difference between women and men involves the relative emphasis placed on caring and social problem solving (for women) versus abstract justice (for men).

4.3 Empathy and prosocial behaviors are most closely related to Kohlberg's Stage 3. People reasoning at this stage make moral decisions based on their concern for others, which is similar to empathy.

Chapter 4

1.1 *Culture* refers to differences in the knowledge, attitudes, values, customs, and ways of acting that characterize different social groups. *Ethnicity* is a part of cultural diversity, and refers to differences in people's ancestry, the way they identify themselves with the nation from which they or their ancestors come. *Culture* is the broader of the two terms, describing differences in the total sets of attitudes, values, and customs of different groups. Ethnicity is narrower, referring specifically to differences in people's ancestral heritage.

Culture and ethnicity Influence learning through the attitudes, values, patterns of interaction that students bring to school, which are characteristic of their culture.

1.2 A resistance culture is a culture that some members of minorities bring to school characterized by the tendency of its members to reject the attitudes, values, and ways of acting characteristics of the majority culture.

To deal with resistance cultures, experts recommend that teachers help members of cultural minorities adapt to the requirements of schools without losing their cultural identities, a process Ogbu (2002) calls "accommodation without assimilation."

1.3 Competition on classrooms is one way in which classroom organization can clash with the values of cultural minorities. Competition poses challenges for some cultural minority students because it clashes with values of cooperation that are taught at home. Teachers can deal with this problem by deemphasizing student–student comparison and by using instructional strategies, such as cooperative learning, that emphasize students working together to help each other.

2.1 Federal legislation, which ended quotas based on national origin, resulted in more immigrants coming to the United States from a wider variety of places. This resulted in much more cultural, ethnic, and linguistic diversity.

Teachers can accommodate this diversity by first communicating that they value and respect all cultures, such as Gary Nolan did with his students. Second, teachers should involve all students—regardless of cultural background or language skills—in learning activities. Involving students communicates that you believe each student is important and that you expect all students to participate and learn. Third, represent the topics you teach as concretely as possible. Actual objects are most effective, and when they are unavailable, pictures are an acceptable alternative. Finally, maximize opportunities for students to practice language, placing extra emphasis on important vocabulary. When students struggle with particular terms, or with putting their understanding into words, provide prompts and cues to scaffold their efforts.

2.2 English dialects are variations of standard English that are distinct in vocabulary, grammar, or punctuation. Teachers sometimes misinterpret students' dialects as sub-standard English, which can lead to lowered evaluations of student work and lowered expectations for student achievement. Effective teachers accept and build on students' dialects and develop bidialecticism in their students.

2.3 The major approaches to helping English language learners (ELLs) are maintenance, transitional, English as a second language (ESL) pullout, sheltered English, and immersion programs. They are similar in that they all have the goal of teaching English. They differ in the extent to which they emphasize maintaining and building on students' native languages, and the amount of structure and support they provide in academic content. For example, maintenance programs have the dual goals of maintaining and developing literacy in the native language and also teaching English literacy skills. Transition programs use the first language as an aid to learning English. Pullout and sheltered English programs adapt instruction in content areas by providing scaffolds that assist content acquisition. Immersion programs place ELLs in English-only classrooms.

3.1 Gender can influence learning if either girls or boys adopt gender-stereotyped beliefs, such as believing that math or computer science are male domains, or believing that girls are inherently better at English and writing than are boys.

Teachers can attempt to eliminate gender bias by openly discussing gender issues, expecting the same academic behaviors from both boys and girls, and inviting nonstereotypical role models to their classes to discuss gender issues.

3.2 Gender-role identity describes beliefs about appropriate characteristics and behaviors of the two sexes. It is important to teachers because a student's gender-role identity can influence how a student approaches different subjects. For example, when girls believe that math and science are male domains, or when boys believe that nursing is a female domain, they are less likely to take related courses or attempt to excel in them.

3.3 Treating boys and girls as equally as possible in learning activities is an important factor that you should attempt to apply as you conduct these activities. This means calling on boys and girls as equally as possible, keeping the level of questions similar for both, providing similar detail in feedback, and putting them in leadership and other roles on as equal a basis as possible.

4.1 Socioeconomic status (SES) is defined as an individual's relative standing in society resulting from a combination of family income, parents' occupations, and the level of education parents attain. High-income parents, and parents who are in fields such as medicine, law, education, or engineering and architecture, and level of education, such as earning college degrees, are considered to be high in SES.

SES affects learning in at least three ways. The first is in the way students' basic needs are met and the quality of their experiences. Poverty can influence a family's ability to provide adequate housing, nutrition, and medical care. SES can also affect the quality of background experiences that adults offer to children. A second way that SES affects learning is by influencing the level of parental involvement; lower-SES parents tend to be less involved in their children's education. A third way SES influences learning is through attitudes and values. For example, many high-SES parents encourage autonomy, individual responsibility, and self-control, whereas lower-SES parents tend to value obedience and conformity. High-SES parents also have positive expectations for their children and to encourage them to graduate from high school and attend college; low-SES parents tend to have lower aspirations for academic advancement.

4.2 When considering a student's SES, you should be careful about stereotyping students based on their SES. You should remember that the research describes group patterns, which may or may not apply to individuals. Many lower-SES families provide rich learning environments for their children and have positive attitudes and values that promote learning.

4.3 Schools that promote resilience have high and uncompromising standards, promote strong personal bonds between teachers and students, have high order and structure, and encourage student participation in after-school activities.

Teachers who are effective in promoting resilience in students placed at risk form strong personal bonds with their students, interacting with them to get to know their families and lives. They maintain high expectations, use interactive teaching strategies, and emphasize success and mastery of content. They also motivate students through personal contacts and instructional support, and they attempt to link school to students' lives.

Effective teachers promote resilience in their students by creating and maintaining productive learning environments. They also combine high expectations with frequent feedback about learning progress. They use interactive teaching strategies that use high-quality examples; both of these help ensure student success. Finally, they stress student self-regulation and the acquisition of learning strategies.

Chapter 5

1.1 One definition of intelligence suggests that it is the ability to acquire and use knowledge, solve problems and reason in the abstract, and adapt to new situations in the environment. A second perspective simply suggests that intelligence is the characteristic or set of characteristics that intelligence tests measure.

Historical views of intelligence suggest that it is a single trait that influences performance across a myriad of tasks. Gardner (1983) and Sternberg, (2004), in contrast, argue that it is composed of several dimensions. Gardner suggests that the dimensions are relatively independent. Sternberg believes that the ability to adapt to one's environment is an indicator of intelligence.

1.2 Ability grouping is the process of placing students with similar academic abilities in the same learning environments. Research indicates that, while well-intentioned, ability grouping has potential drawbacks that can decrease achievement, such as lowered teacher expectations and poorer instruction for those in lower-ability groups (Good & Brophy, 2008; McDermott et al., 2006). Experts recommend that teachers minimize its use in classrooms and constantly be aware of potentials for adverse effects (Castle et al., 2005).

1.3 The nature view of intelligence asserts that it is essentially determined by genetics; the nurture view of intelligence emphasizes the influence of the environment. Evidence indicates that it is influenced by both (Ackerman & Lohman, 2006). For example, children exposed to enriched learning experiences, both in preschool and in later schooling, score higher on intelligence tests than those lacking the experiences.

2.1 The Individuals with Disabilities Education Act (IDEA) was passed in 1975 to ensure a free and appropriate public education for all students with disabilities. Its provisions stipulate education in a least restrictive environment (LRE) and protection against discrimination in testing. The provisions further guarantee parental involvement in the development of each child's individualized education program (IEP).

2.2 Recent amendments to IDEA make states responsible for locating children who need special services and have strengthened requirements for nondiscriminatory assessment, due process, parents' involvement in IEPs, and the confidentiality of school records.

2.3 The FAPE provision of IDEA asserts that every student can learn and is entitled to a free and appropriate public education. Mainstreaming—the practice of moving students with exceptionalities from segregated settings into general education classrooms—was the first attempt to meet the requirements of FAPE. Over time, mainstreaming evolved into inclusion, a comprehensive approach to educating students with exceptionalities that advocates a total, systematic, and coordinated web of services.

3.1 The most common learning problems that teachers in general education classrooms are likely to encounter include learning disabilities, which represent difficulties in specific areas, such as reading; attention-deficit/hyperactivity disorders, indicated by problems with maintaining attention; mild mental retardation, characterized by limitations in intellectual functioning and adaptive behavior; and behavior disorders, characterized by persistent, age-inappropriate behaviors. Communication disorders and visual and hearing disabilities also may exist.

3.2 Learning disabilities and mental retardation are similar in that both are disabilities that interfere with learning. In addition, both can result from a variety of causes, and they are related to some type of central nervous system dysfunction. They are different in that learning disabilities usually involve students with average intelligence or above and are often limited to a specific area such as math or reading, whereas intellectual handicaps involve a broad range of intellectual functioning.

3.3 Students with behavior disorders display serious and persistent age-inappropriate behaviors that result in social conflict, personal unhappiness, and often school failure. Externalizing behavior disorders are characterized by hyperactivity, defiance, hostility, and failure to respond to typical rules and consequences. Internalizing behavior disorders, by contrast, are characterized by social withdrawal, guilt, depression, and anxiety problems.

3.4 Communication disorders are exceptionalities that interfere with students' abilities to receive and to understand information from others and to express their own ideas or questions. Because much of the information and interactions in classrooms are verbal, communication disorders can disrupt the flow of communication and information.

4.1 Characteristics of students who are gifted and talented commonly include the ability to learn quickly and independently, advanced language and reading skills, effective learning and metacognitive strategies, and high motivation and achievement. Educators have broadened the definition of students who are gifted and talented to encompass not only students who score well on intelligence tests but also students who may have unique talents in specific areas such as art, music, or writing. The broadening of this definition means that teachers play a crucial role in helping to identify these students, whose talents may not show up on standardized tests.

4.2 Gifted and talented students are commonly identified through performance on standardized tests and nominations from teachers. However, because tests depend heavily on language, these scores are not always valid, particularly for cultural minorities. And teachers sometimes confuse conformity, neatness, and good behavior with being gifted and talented. In addition to test scores and teacher recommendations, experts recommend the inclusion of more flexible and less culturally dependent methods, such as creativity measures, tests of spatial ability, and peer and parent nominations, when attempting to identify gifted and talented students.

4.3 Acceleration and enrichment are the two most common methods used for teaching gifted and talented students. Acceleration keeps the curriculum the same but allows students to move through it more quickly. Because acceleration curriculum is the same, it is easier to implement, but it maintains a narrow focus on the general education curriculum and may cause developmental problems when younger students are mixed with older ones.

Enrichment, by contrast, alters curriculum and instruction by providing varied instruction. Though harder to implement, enrichment provides students with more choice and flexibility.

5.1 Teachers are expected to fulfill the following roles when working with students having exceptionalities: First, they help identify students who may have exceptionalities. Experts now emphasize a shift away from the sole use of standardized tests toward the use of more ecologically valid measures, such as performance on classroom tasks and teacher observations. This makes teachers even more important in the process of identifying students with exceptionalities, because they are most familiar with students' classroom behavior and performance. Second, teachers adapt instruction to best meet individuals' needs. Third, teachers encourage acceptance of all students in their classes.

5.2 Research indicates that the teaching strategies that are effective for all students are also effective for learners with exceptionalities. This means that you teach in the same way that you teach all students, but you make an even greater effort with your students having exceptionalities. In addition, you should provide additional instructional scaffolding, such as working with these students one-on-one, to ensure their success. Homework, seat-work assignments, and reading may need to be adapted. You also should teach these students learning strategies, such as how to monitor their attention, take notes, summarize important points, and organize their time.

5.3 You can promote the social integration and growth of students with exceptionalities in the following ways: First, try to help all students understand and appreciate different forms of diversity, including exceptionalities. Second, help students with exceptionalities learn acceptable behaviors through direct instruction and modeling. Third, use interactive teaching strategies and peer interaction strategies such as peer tutoring and cooperative learning to promote social interaction.

Chapter 6

1.1 We can explain Tim's nervousness following his bad experience in the following way. Tim failed the algebra quiz and was devastated as a result. The failure was an unconditioned stimulus and the devastation was an unconditioned response. He associated subsequent quizzes with the initial failure, so they became conditioned stimuli, which caused nervousness as conditioned responses. He learned to be nervous in those quizzes. Notice that the conditioned response is similar to the unconditioned response, and both were out of Tim's control, i.e., they were involuntary.

Tim's nervousness later decreased because he took additional quizzes (conditioned stimuli) without experiencing failure (the unconditioned stimulus), so his anxiety (the conditioned response) became extinct. (Similarly, and unfortunately, if you continue to hear a song that triggers a romantic feeling, but you don't have a romantic encounter with which the song was originally associated, the song will eventually stop triggering the romantic feeling.)

1.2 The class is a conditioned stimulus. It has become associated with the warmth and support of the teacher. The safe feeling is a conditioned response. It is a learned and involuntary response that is caused by the conditioned stimulus. These concepts were illustrated in the example with Carlos and Mrs. Van Horn. Note also in this example that the conditioned response is similar to the unconditioned response.

1.3 In the example of developing an emotional feeling, the unconditioned stimulus is the romantic encounter. It is an event that aroused an emotion as an unconditioned response, which is unlearned (instinctive) and involuntary. The song *became associated* with the romantic encounter, so it is a conditioned stimulus that causes the emotion similar to the emotion you initially experienced. The conditioned response is also involuntary, but learned.

In the example with the warm feeling when smelling Thanksgiving turkey, the warm feeling is the conditioned response, and the smell is the conditioned stimulus. The unconditioned stimulus is past experience at Thanksgiving, such as being in the company of loving family members, and the unconditioned response is the warm feeling that results from being around family. The smell of turkey is associated with the company of loving family.

In the case of the uneasy feeling in a dentist's office, the office is the conditioned stimulus, and the uneasy feeling is the conditioned response. Having dental work done is the unconditioned stimulus, and the discomfort that results is the conditioned response. The dentist's office is associated with having dental work done.

1.4 Our reaction to Latin music illustrates the concept *generalization*. Other forms of Latin music are stimuli similar to the initial conditioned stimulus (the song we heard when we had the romantic encounter), so our emotion has generalized to all forms of romantic Latin music. We *discriminate*, however, between Latin and rock music.

2.1 The idea illustrated is positive reinforcement. You are presenting her with your admonishment, and her behavior is increasing (she goes off task sooner).

2.2 Rick's behavior can be explained with the concept of presentation punishment. His behavior is decreasing—he is decreasing the length of his tests—as a result of being presented with the students' complaints.

The students' behavior can be explained with the concept of negative reinforcement. Their complaining is increasing—they complained sooner each time—as a result of Rick removing an aversive stimulus—some of the test material.

2.3 Because the beeper going off depends on time, it is an interval schedule, and because it is unpredictable, it is a variable-interval schedule.

2.4 The displayed exercise is the antecedent; it induces the desired behavior. The students' conscientious work is the behavior, and Anita's compliments are the reinforcers.

3.1 The ineffectiveness of this practice can be explained using the *nonoccurrence of expected consequences.* In cooperative learning groups, some students make a greater contribution than do others. Those who make the greater contribution expect to be reinforced by receiving a higher grade than those who contributed less. When all members of the group receive the same grade, the expectation isn't met, so the nonoccurrence of the expected reinforcer can act as a punisher, making a similar contribution in the next cooperative learning activity less likely. The nonoccurrence of the expected reinforcer can also lead to resentment, a problem in some cooperative learning activities (E. Cohen, 1994).

3.2 Reciprocal causation describes the interdependence of the environment, personal factors (e.g., beliefs and expectations), and behavior. In Mike's case, the environment (the first instructor's class) influenced his behavior (he often drifted off), and his behavior influenced his expectations (he believed he wasn't learning). In turn, his behavior influenced the environment (he switched to Mr. Adams's class); the environment influenced a personal factor (he expected to be called on); and the personal factor influenced his behavior (he paid attention as a result of his expectation).

3.3 The benched player was punished, and being punished explains why that player didn't commit the foul again. The rest of the team was vicariously punished through the benching of the player who committed the foul. They expected to be benched for committing a similar foul, so they avoided doing so.

3.4 Tim was vicariously reinforced through Susan's success, and she was a model for him. He observed the consequences of her study habits, and he changed his behavior accordingly. He sustained his efforts because he *expected* to be reinforced for imitating Susan's behavior.

4.1 Because the speech was seen on videotape, it is a form of *symbolic modeling.* The modeling is likely to be effective because Martin Luther King, Jr., is a high-status model. For African American students, the modeling would also be effective because of *perceived similarity.* Assuming that students knew how to be idealistic, the modeling outcome most likely would *facilitate existing behaviors.* If we assume that the students didn't know how to be idealistic, the outcome could involve *learning new behaviors. Emotional arousal* is also likely, because of the powerful way he delivered his speech.

4.2 The person who first crossed the street is a *direct model.* You imitated the behavior of a live person instead of someone you saw on TV, in the movies, or in a book. The model's behavior weakened your inhibition about crossing the street against the red light. The modeling outcome is *changing inhibitions* instead of facilitating an existing behavior because crossing the street against a red light is socially unacceptable.

4.3 Your self-regulation began with a *goal:* to answer and understand each of the "Check Your Understanding" questions in the chapter. You *monitored your progress* by checking off each question that you answered and understood. You completed a *self-assessment* by checking your answers against the feedback that appears in the appendix, and you modified your strategy use if you answered incorrectly.

Chapter 7

1.1 The principles on which cognitive learning theory is based follow:

- *Learning and development depend on learners' experiences.* This principle is evident in our everyday life. Learning to drive is a simple example. If our only experience with driving involves vehicles with automatic transmissions, our ability to drive is less fully developed than it would be if we have experiences driving cars with automatic transmissions and those with stick shifts.
- *People are mentally active in their attempts to make sense of their experiences.* People instinctively strive to understand their experiences. They want the world to make sense, and as a result, they attempt to create understanding that makes sense to them.
- *Learners construct knowledge in the processs of developing an understanding of their experiences. Learners do not record knowledge.* Learners don't behave like tape recorders, keeping an exact copy of what they hear or read in their memories. Instead, they mentally modify the experiences so they make sense. This is consistent with their instinctive drive to understand their world, which was explained in the description of the second principle.
- *Knowledge that is constructed depends on knowledge that learners already possess.* People construct understanding based on what they already know. For example, many people believe that summers in the northern hemisphere are warmer than winters because we are closer to the sun in the summer. (We, in fact, are slightly farther away, but the sun's rays are more direct.) This idea is based on knowing that as we move closer to an open fire or a hot stove burner, we get warmer.
- *Learning is enhanced in a social environment.* As people discuss ideas, they construct understanding that they wouldn't have acquired on their own. This is consistent with the old adage, "Two heads are better than one."

1.2 This illustrates the principle: *Learning is enhanced in a social environment.* You have a problem, discuss it, and solve it during the course of the discussion.

1.3 The human memory model is the cognitive architecture that can be used to describe how people gather, organize, and store their experiences. It is where knowledge is constructed and where prior knowledge is stored until needed for new knowledge construction.

2.1 We can explain why Tanya might have become "kinda lost when Mr. Shelton was explaining all that yesterday," with the characteristics of working memory. It is likely that the cognitive load imposed by the information David presented exceeded Tanya's working memory capacity, so she was unable to process it, and as a result, it was lost. The implication for teaching is that we should present only small amounts of information at a time and intersperse our presentations with questioning to encourage elaboration and reduce the cognitive load.

2.2 We can also use the characteristics of working memory to explain why a health club would advertise its telephone number as 2HEALTH rather than 243-2584. 2HEALTH has been chunked into two units, so 2HEALTH imposes a lighter load on working memory than do the numbers 243-2584. Because the load is lighter, the information is easier to encode and remember.

2.3 Procedural knowledge, as with declarative knowledge, is stored in long-term memory. An example in the opening case that illustrates students' being required to demonstrate procedural knowledge occurred when David said, "Be sure you write and explain each of your answers," after he presented the students with the questions. Being required to write the answers required students to demonstrate procedural knowledge.

Developing procedural knowledge requires a great deal of practice and also strongly depends on declarative knowledge. In this case, declarative knowledge about the particular aspect of the solar system that they were examining would be required.

3.1 The cognitive processes in the human memory model follow:

- *Attention* is the process of focusing on a particular stimulus or group of stimuli and ignoring the myriad of other stimuli that exist. The idea of "white noise" relates to the concept of attention. We are often not aware of "white noise" such as the whisper of an air conditioner until we're made aware of its existence; that is, until we attend to it.
- *Perception* is the meaning we attach to stimuli. It is illustrated by the fact that we commonly see two people have the same experience but interpret it very differently.
- *Rehearsal* is the process of repeating information over and over without altering its form, such as memorizing names, dates, and other facts, such as $8 \times 7 = 56$. *Elaborative rehearsal* is the process of linking information to be learned to existing information, and it is much more effective than is maintenance rehearsal. When rehearsal moves information to long-term memory, it is a form of encoding.
- *Encoding* is the process of representing information in long-term memory. The goal in encoding is to make the information as meaningful as possible by connecting it to knowledge already in long-term memory.
- *Retrieval* is the process of pulling information from long-term memory back into working memory for further processing. Retrieval is an essential process, because constructing new knowledge depends on the knowledge that already exists in long-term memory.

3.2 When a teacher asks, "What do we mean by plot development?" she is checking her students' perceptions, because she is attempting to determine what the idea means to them. The most effective way of checking students' perceptions is to simply ask them—ask them what they see or notice, or ask them what the information means to them in a picture, term, map, or whatever is displayed.

3.3 The students used *maintenance rehearsal* when they practiced with the flash cards. We see no evidence in the description that the students were relating the facts in the flash cards to other information, which is what *elaborative rehearsal* would involve.

When the students compared the problems to problems they had solved in class, they were using *schema activation* and *elaboration* as encoding strategies.

4.1 Metacognition, commonly described as "thinking about thinking," is our awareness of, and control over, our cognitive processes. Metacognition regulates the way we process information. For instance, if an individual is aware that she is not fully comprehending the information she is reading, and if she stops periodically to summarize what she has read, she is demonstrating metacognition. Because she is metacognitive, she will process the information she is reading more efficiently, and learning will increase. Learners who are metacognitive recognize when they are using an ineffective strategy and they then modify the strategy, or select a new strategy, in order to increase their understanding. The result is higher achievement.

4.2 Yes, stopping and going back to the top of the page and rereading one of the sections is an example of metacognition. You realize that you haven't understood the section (which is knowledge [awareness] of your memory strategy), and you go back and reread (which is exercising control over your memory strategy).

4.3 You are more metacognitive about your note taking than is your friend. You are continually making decisions about what information is most important to write down, which demonstrates knowledge of, and control over, your thinking about note taking. And, because you're constantly making decisions, you are more cognitively active than your friend.

Chapter 8

1.1 Cognitive constructivism is based on the view that knowledge construction is an internal, individual process, whereas social constructivism is grounded in the position that knowledge construction first occurs in the social environment and then is appropriated and internalized by individuals.

1.2 Suzanne's thinking better illustrates cognitive constructivism. She had a clear (to her) schema that guided her thinking (her belief that keeping the number of tiles equal on each side of the fulcrum would make the beam balance), and she brought this view to the learning activity. It didn't result from her interaction with her peers.

1.3 This is an example of situated cognition. The teacher presented several examples of diphthongs—*oy, ou, oo,* and *ow.* However, ou was used in two different ways—*house and could*; *oo* is used in three different ways—*looks, moon,* and *floor*; and *ow* is used in two different ways—*bowed* and *owl.* The children would have been unable to determine the differences if the examples had not been embedded (situated) in the context of the passage.

2.1 Suzanne's initial conclusion best illustrates the following characteristic of constructivism: "Learners construct knowledge that makes sense to them." We are virtually certain that she didn't get the conclusion from a teacher or something she read; she constructed it on her own. We don't have evidence about her prior knowledge, and we don't know about her prior social interaction or real-world experiences.

2.2 "New learning depends on current understanding" is the characteristic that is best illustrated. When people saw the Sun rise in the morning and move across the sky, they assumed they were stationary and the Sun was moving. This was similar to most of their experiences observing moving objects, so they used these experiences as the basis for their belief.

2.3 Analyzing written passages is one effective context for learning the rules of grammar. Written passages are more nearly real-world examples than are sentences or words in isolation. Having students actually use the rules of grammar in their own writing would be even more effective.

3.1 A misconception is a belief that is inconsistent with evidence or commonly accepted explanations. Constructivism is the only learning theory that is able to explain the origin of misconceptions. It states that learners' prior experiences, beliefs, expectations, and emotions result in the construction of knowledge that may be invalid.

3.2 People's prior experiences are the most common source of misconceptions, and many examples exist. For instance, because 5 is greater than 3, some children believe that 1/5 is greater than 1/3.

Appearances are a second source of misconceptions. For example, because oil appears thick, many people believe that it is more dense than water, whereas it is less dense; oil floats on water.

Society is a third source. For instance, minority youth are often led to believe that a career in professional sports is a realistic goal as an adult, but statistics indicate that the vast majority of student athletes never make it to the pro ranks.

Finally, language can contribute to misconceptions. The news media will periodically refer to the danger of "heavy metals" such as lead and mercury, when, in fact, any metal can be "heavy," depending on the amount.

3.3 First, the original misconception must become dissatisfying. This means that students need convincing evidence that the misconception is invalid, such as Suzanne saw when they tried her solution and it didn't work.

Second, an alternative explanation must become satisfying. When Suzanne could see that the beam would balance if she took both the number of tiles and the distance from the fulcrum into account, the alternative conception become more satisfying.

Third, the new conception must be useful. Suzanne was able to explain the solution to additional problems using the new conception.

4.1 The suggestions for classroom practice and their connection to constructivist learning theory are outlined as follows:

Provide learners with a variety of high-quality examples and other representations of content. Examples and other representations are the experiences learners use to construct their knowledge. These experiences provide the background knowledge learners need to construct their knowledge, because the new knowledge they construct depends on the knowledge that learners already possess.

Connect content to the real world. Situated cognition suggests that the knowledge learners construct depends on the context in which it is constructed. Real-world contexts make knowledge construction more meaningful than it would be if the content were not connected to the real world.

Promote high levels of social interaction. Social constructivist learning theory suggests that learners first construct knowledge in a social environment and later appropriate knowledge.

Treat verbal explanations skeptically. Learners construct their own knowledge, and "wisdom can't be told." Explaining tries to "tell" wisdom, instead of guiding students in the knowledge construction process.

Promote learning with assessment. Because learners construct their own knowledge, the knowledge they construct may vary considerably. Ongoing assessment is the only way to determine if their constructions are valid.

4.2 "Connect content to the real world" is the suggestion best illustrated. Studying the rules in the context of a written passage is a more nearly real-world task than studying the rules in the context of isolated sentences. Having the students write their own essays using possessives would also be effective.

4.3 Effective assessments give teachers insights into students' thinking. This means that the reasoning students use to arrive at their answers is as important as the answers themselves.

Chapter 9

1.1 A *concept* is a mental class or category constructed in such a way that an individual can identify examples and nonexamples of the category. While many examples exist for each chapter, some include *inclusion, learning disabilities,* and *attention-deficit/hyperactivity disorder* in Chapter 5; *conditioned response, negative reinforcement,* and *vicarious learning* in Chapter 6; *working memory, encoding,* and *metacognition* in Chapter 7; and *social constructivism, cognitive apprenticeship,* and *conceptual change* in Chapter 8.

1.2 The concept *noun* is easier to learn than the concept *culture* because it obeys a well-defined rule; it is the name of a person, place, or thing. And the characteristics are more concrete than are the characteristics of the concept *culture.* The rule-driven theory best explains how people learn the concept *noun.* The concept *culture* most likely is constructed from a set of exemplars.

1.3 An additional example you would want to show for the concept *reptile* is a reptile such as a sea turtle or a water snake, so that students learn that some reptiles live in water. A frog would be an important nonexample, because, although it's an amphibian, students often think it's a reptile.

2.1 This is an ill-defined problem. You are probably not completely clear as to what a "satisfying relationship" should be, and it's unlikely that you have a clear idea of how to achieve it, even if you did know what it meant.

A means–ends analysis would first define a "satisfying relationship." Improved communication would likely be one aspect. Then, a strategy for improving communication could be devised, such as making it a point to always actively listen to what your partner is saying. Strategies for reaching goals when problems are ill-defined can vary greatly.

2.2 Heuristics are general strategies that are used to solve problems, so they are part of the *select a strategy* stage of problem solving.

2.3 In being satisfied with the fact that their answers varied, the students ineffectively applied the *evaluate the results* stage of problem solving. This tendency illustrates a common problem in problem-solving activities. Students tend to be satisfied with their answers whether or not they make sense. Requiring students to justify their thinking by providing reasons for their answers and asking for estimates can increase their metacognition about their problem solving.

3.1 Ruiz's strategy is the most effective, because he is demonstrating the highest level of metacognition in his approach. He is making conscious decisions about what information is most important to highlight. Will's strategy is the least effective, because passive highlighting requires little cognitive effort and is the least metacognitive. (Even though he is physically "active" in highlighting whole chapters, he is cognitively passive, because he isn't thinking about the process.)

3.2 No, reading the chapter carefully is not strategic learning. Strategic learning is the application of cognitive operations that go beyond the normal activities required to carry out a task. While you are attempting to read carefully and understand the content, you are not applying any technique that goes beyond the normal activity—reading—required to carry out the task.

3.3 Francisco's comment, "We found a pattern in the data," best illustrates metacognition. He recognized that they had previously found a pattern. Students being aware of their thinking is an essential component of critical thinking.

4.1 With respect to transfer, the students are least likely to identify a dolphin as a mammal, because it is least similar to the other examples. Similarity between the two learning situations is the factor that is best illustrated in this case.

4.2 Based on the factors that affect transfer, your efforts were not effective. First, pictures of the mammals, while better than written words, are not as high quality as a live mammal, such as a student's hamster, would be. A combination of one or two live mammals, such as the hamster and the students themselves, combined with pictures, would be much higher quality. Second, the variety of examples is inadequate. Better variety would include a bat, so they see that some mammals fly; a whale, porpoise, or some other aquatic mammal, so the students don't conclude that only fish live in water; and perhaps an egg-laying mammal, such as a duck-billed platypus. Finally, we have no evidence of whether or not the examples were presented in any realistic context.

4.3 Choice 2 is the most effective example. It is the only one that actually illustrates the concept. Choice 1 only illustrates a thoughtful look, and the words, "The girl is experiencing internal conflict," provide little critical information. It could even lead to the misconception that whenever a person looks thoughtful, they're experiencing internal conflict. Choice 3 is only a definition. Definitions are abstract, and many students can't do much more than memorize definitions. Definitions, alone, lead to superficial learning.

Chapter 10

1.1 Motivation is defined by prominent theorists as a process whereby goal-directed activity is instigated and sustained. Motivation is one of the most powerful influences on learning.

1.2 Behaviorism describes motivation in the same way that it describes learning. For example, an increase in behavior is viewed as evidence of learning, and it is also viewed as evidence of motivation.

1.3 Cognitive views of motivation describe motivation as people's need to understand and make sense of their experiences. Social cognitive views emphasize the role of beliefs, expectations, and observing the actions of others in their explanations of motivation.

1.4 Sociocultural views of motivation focus on individuals' participating in a learning community. Through participating in a community in which all members help each other learn, individuals' motivation to learn is increased.

1.5 Humanistic views of motivation describe motivation as people's attempts to fulfill their total potential as human beings and to become self-actualized.

2.1 According to Maslow, deficiency needs—survival, safety, belonging, and self-esteem—must be met before students will be motivated to move to growth needs. This suggests, for example, that students must feel safe (both physically and emotionally) in classrooms if they are going to be motivated to learn.

2.2 As learners receive given evidence that their competence is increasing, their motivation to learn also increases. This explains why praise for genuine accomplishment can increase intrinsic motivation. Similarly, as students' perceptions of autonomy increase, so does their motivation to learn. And when students believe that their teachers are committed to them both as learners and as people, they are motivated to learn because these teachers help students meet their need for relatedness.

2.3 High ability is strongly valued in our society, so self-worth is linked to perceptions of high ability. Students' motivation to learn often depends on maintaining perceptions of high ability to maintain their sense of self-worth. Teachers can help reduce this inclination by deemphasizing social comparisons and emphasizing the belief that ability can be increased with effort.

3.1 Beliefs are cognitive ideas we accept as true without necessarily having definitive evidence to support them. Expectations, for example, are beliefs about future outcomes. If learners believe that they're going to succeed, their motivation to learn is likely to increase. The opposite is true if they don't believe they're going to succeed.

Similarly, if learners believe they can accomplish a specific task (high self-efficacy), they are more likely to persevere on the task than if they don't believe they can. And, if learners believe that accomplishing a task has high attainment or utility value, they are also more likely to persevere.

3.2 Learners with an entity view of intelligence may avoid difficult tasks because failure could indicate lack of ability. And, because ability is fixed, experiences that reflect negatively on ability can detract from their sense of self-worth. If they avoid difficult tasks or engage in self-handicapping behaviors, motivation to learn decreases.

Learners with an incremental view of intelligence view difficulty and the potential for failure differently. Failure merely means that more effort is needed, and with effort, ability can increase. As a result, both motivation and learning are likely to increase.

3.3 In their conversation, Kathy said, "Yes, but look how good you're getting at writing. I think you hit a personal best on your last paper. You're becoming a very good writer." Harvey then responded, "Yeh, yeh, I know, . . . and being good writers will help us in everything we do in life," suggesting that Kathy had emphasized the utility value of writing as an important skill in the world outside of school.

3.4 Because Armondo attributed his success to luck, his emotional reaction is likely to be neutral. Because luck is external, he won't feel the pride that attributing his success to either ability or effort would cause. (Because he succeeded, he also won't feel the shame that results from failure that is attributed to lack of ability, or guilt that people feel when they attribute failure to lack of effort.) Because his success resulted from luck, he won't expect similar results in the future, his future effort is likely to decrease, and, as a result, his achievement is also likely to decrease.

Ashley's emotional reaction is likely to be frustration or something similar to it, because task difficulty is not controllable. Because she is out of control, she is not likely to expect success in the future, and her motivation and learning will decrease.

4.1 Learners' goals can influence their motivation to learn in several ways. For example, students with mastery goals persist on challenging tasks, accept challenges, and use effective strategies. Students with performance-approach goals may use superficial learning strategies, exert only enough effort to perform on the task, and engage in self-handicapping strategies. Students with performance-avoidance goals emphasize avoiding looking incompetent and being judged unfavorably by others, and to do so, they may avoid the very tasks that can lead to competence. Social goals can either increase or decrease motivation to learn (see the feedback for item 4.2), and work-avoidance goals strongly detract from both motivation and learning.

4.2 The combination of mastery goals and social-responsibility goals results in the highest level of motivation and achievement. Mastery goals focus on understanding and mastery of tasks, and social-responsibility goals emphasize avoiding disappointing others. The combination of the two leads to sustained effort, and with it, increased achievement.

4.3 A number of possibilities exist for each goal. The essential features of effective goals are that they're specific, immediate (close at hand), and moderately challenging.

Given these characteristics, a modification for the first goal might be, "Answer and understand all the items on all of the practice quizzes for each chapter" (in this class, for instance).

For getting in shape, a more effective goal would be, "Jog a minimum of 9 miles a week" (e.g., jogging 3 miles, 3 times a week).

For losing weight, a better goal would be, "Limit calorie consumption to 1,500 calories a day."

5.1 Connecting topics to the real world, personalizing content, involving students, using concrete examples, and making clear and logical presentations can all increase learner interest. Teachers can also increase interest by giving students choices when opportunities exist.

5.2 The most effective way of capitalizing on emotions to increase motivation to learn is by attempting to increase learner interest, because interesting activities arouse positive emotions. Teachers can also capitalize on emotions to increase motivation to learn by raising questions about moral issues and personal characteristics related to the topics they teach. For instance, beginning a study of the American Revolution by posing questions about the fairness of taxes levied by the British, the rationale they had in imposing them, and the colonists' reactions, can provoke emotional reactions, and with them, increased interest.

5.3 Teachers can reduce anxiety in students in several ways. Some of them include the following:

- Make clear and specific your expectations about learning and how you will assess students.
- Use instructional strategies that promote understanding, such as providing high-quality examples, promoting student involvement, and providing specific feedback on assessments.
- Provide outside help for students who request it.
- Drop one or two quizzes during a grading period for purposes of assigning grades.

These strategies won't eliminate anxiety in all cases or for all students, but they can be important factors in reducing anxiety for many students.

Chapter 11

1.1 A mastery-focused classroom emphasizes effort, improvement, and deep understanding of the topics being studied. A performance-focused classroom emphasizes high grades, public displays of ability, and performance compared to others.

1.2 Based on the descriptions of mastery-focused and performance-focused classrooms, this is an ineffective comment. The statement, "Excellent job on the last test, everyone. More than half the class got an A or a B," emphasizes high grades and performance instead of effort, improvement, and understanding.

2.1 Strategies for promoting learning self-regulation typically involve setting and monitoring goals. Getting students to commit to the goals is an essential aspect of the process. Sam promoted commitment to goals by emphasizing the relationship between personal responsibility and learning, soliciting student input into class procedures, providing examples of responsible and irresponsible behavior, modeling responsibility, and providing a chart that allowed students to monitor progress toward their goals.

2.2 Sam recognized that his students would initially be externally regulated, which meant that they would behave responsibly to receive rewards for meeting their responsibility and learning goals and avoid being punished (e.g., spending "quiet time" alone) if they failed to meet their social responsibility goals.

His students would demonstrate an advance in self-regulation if, at a later point in the year, they decided to set and meet social responsibility and learning goals because they believed that meeting the goals would help them get better grades. This would still illustrate extrinsic motivation, but it would be an advance in self-regulation.

2.3 A controlling strategy for promoting self-regulation would involve the immediate use of punishers for failing to behave responsibly, such as being punished for failing to be in their seats when the bell rang. Instead, Sam gave examples of logical consequences that Josh and Andy, the students in his vignettes, experienced as a result of behaving responsibly compared to behaving irresponsibly.

3.1 Teachers who increase students' motivation to learn believe they can increase student learning regardless of their teaching conditions or students' backgrounds (high personal teaching efficacy). They care about their students as people, and they are committed to their students' learning. They model desirable characteristics, demonstrate enthusiasm by communicating their own genuine interest in the topics they teach, and create positive expectations for their students.

3.2 High-efficacy teachers believe that their efforts to help students learn make a difference, whereas low-efficacy teachers believe that their efforts are largely in vain. Because low-efficacy teachers don't believe that they make a difference anyway, trying something new—according to their beliefs—is not likely to matter. As a result, they are not inclined to try new curriculum materials or strategies.

3.3 The most effective way to communicate your enthusiasm to students is to model your own genuine interest in the topics you're teaching. Because people tend to imitate behaviors they observe in others, if students see that you are truly interested in the topics you're teaching, the likelihood that they also will be interested increases.

3.4 Teachers call on students who, they expect, will be able to answer their questions. If they don't believe that a student can answer, they are less likely to call on the student.

Two factors come into play. First, a student's answering the question is reinforcing for the teacher. Second, if a student can't answer, the teacher should provide prompts or cues that will help the student give an acceptable answer. Thinking of these prompts and cues during the course of a lesson presents a heavy cognitive load for the teacher.

4.1 Classrooms that increase motivation to learn are *orderly* and *safe*, students experience *success* on *challenging* tasks, and they understand what they're supposed to be learning and why the topic is important *(task comprehension)*.

4.2 Based on the discussion of the climate variables in the model for promoting student motivation, the teacher's approach would be unlikely to increase students' motivation to learn, even if they succeed. First, the task presents a minimal level of challenge, and no rationale for the task is evident. So, based on the task category in the TARGET model together with the challenge and task comprehension categories in the model for promoting student motivation, the teacher's approach is unlikely to increase students' motivation to learn.

4.3 The two variables in the model for promoting student motivation that the teacher is attempting to address are *order and safety* and *task comprehension.* Enforcing a rule that prevents students from making sarcastic or demeaning comments promotes a sense of emotional security, and providing a rationale is consistent with task comprehension.

4.4 The TARGET model describes ideal tasks as optimally challenging, so this relates directly to the *challenge* variable in the model for promoting student motivation. The TARGET model also describes tasks so that students see their relevance and meaning, and part of the definition of task attraction is that students understand why the task is important and worthwhile.

The TARGET model describes authority as shared, and the model supports autonomy. The model for promoting student motivation defines order and safety as a climate variable that creates a predictable learning environment and supports learner autonomy together with a sense of physical and emotional security. Both models therefore emphasize autonomy.

The TARGET model emphasizes recognition for all students who make learning progress, and in the model for promoting student motivation, success means continuous learning progress. Praise and other rewards should communicate that competence is increasing. Mistakes don't mean that students aren't successful; rather, they're a normal part of the learning process.

In the TARGET model, grouping fosters a community of learners, and the introduction to the classroom climate variables defines a positive classroom climate as follows: The teacher and students work together as a community of learners, a learning environment in which the teacher and all the students work together to help everyone achieve.

The TARGET model describes evaluation as a mechanism to promote learning, and suggestions for promoting success in the model for promoting student motivation include making assessment an integral part of the teaching–learning process, and providing detailed feedback about learning progress.

The TARGET model describes time as encompassing the workload, pace of instruction, and amount allocated for completing work. The description of task comprehension in the model for promoting student motivation includes the statement, "Task comprehension also includes decisions about time allocated to tasks, pace of instruction, and provisions for extra help if it is needed."

5.1 Teachers can increase students' motivation to learn when they consciously plan to attract students' attention and provide a conceptual umbrella for the lesson *(introductory focus), personalize* content, promote high levels of *involvement* in learning activities, and provide informative *feedback* about learning progress.

5.2 Kathy applied introductory focus in her lesson on the Crusades by having the students imagine that they had left Lincoln High School and that it was taken over by people who believed that extracurricular activities should be eliminated. She then used the suggestion of them being on a "crusade" to change the school officials' minds as an analogy for the actual Crusades.

5.3 The best example of the way DeVonne personalized her lesson was by asking the students if Mrs. Sapp (the school principal) was an arthropod.

5.4 Mastery-oriented feedback provides information about existing understanding or information that teachers can use to increase understanding. For instance, "Your paragraph needs to include at least two supporting details for your conclusion. Your second sentence is the only supporting detail in your paragraph" is an example of mastery-oriented feedback about the quality of written paragraphs.

Performance-oriented feedback describes grades or comparisons among students. Examples include statements such as, "Well done. You got all the points on your essay," or "There were five A's and four B's on the last quiz."

Chapter 12

1.1 Classroom management is important because, first, it is the primary factor that causes teacher stress and burnout, and it can destroy a teacher's career.

Second, classrooms are complex, with many unpredictable events occurring at the same time, and teachers must respond to them immediately and in public view. Well-managed classrooms make accommodating the complexities of classrooms easier.

Third, classroom management and learning and motivation are strongly linked. Students are more motivated to learn and learn more in well-managed classrooms.

1.2 Although Judy addressed aspects of each of the characteristics with her beginning-of-class exercise, she addressed the multidimensional and simultaneous characteristics of classrooms most directly. Doing routine activities, such as taking roll and handing back papers, and conducting learning activities are two different classroom events, and Judy conducted them simultaneously. Being able to conduct them simultaneously reduced the opportunity for off-task behavior. She also simultaneously maintained the flow of instruction while responding to Darren's and Rachel's misbehavior.

1.3 The suggestion to call on all students as equally as possible most closely relates to engaged time. Teachers call on students to involve them in learning activities, or in other words, to engage them. Being called on doesn't ensure that students will succeed, so academic learning time isn't as directly addressed.

2.1 Because their thinking is concrete, children in elementary schools need rules that are clear and concrete. Rules and procedures must be explicitly taught as Martha Oakes did with her first graders. The number of rules should be kept small, since one of the most common reasons for breaking rules in elementary schools is that the children simply forget them.

The influence of peers increases in middle schools, and their needs for belonging, social acceptance, autonomy, and independence increase. Providing reasons for rules, and enforcing rules fairly and consistently, become increasingly important with these students.

High school students' behavior tends to stabilize, they communicate more effectively at an adult level, and they respond well to clear rationales for rules and the need to accept personal responsibility.

2.2 As students mature, they are less likely to hit, poke, and otherwise put their hands on other students. As a result, a rule requiring them to keep their hands to themselves is less necessary with older students.

2.3 As you saw in Chapter 8, examples provide the experiences learners use to construct their understanding of the topics they study. They construct their understanding of rules and procedures in the same way that they construct understanding of any other topic.

3.1 Formal communication with parents includes open houses, interim progress reports, and report cards. Teachers can enhance communication with a beginning-of-school letter to parents expressing a commitment to learning, optimism about the school year, and a general description of class procedures. In addition, some teachers send packets of work home to parents, which are to be signed and returned. Finally, calling or e-mailing parents about both positive and negative events is an important part of the overall communication process.

3.2 First, the letter contributed to the creation of a positive classroom climate by making all students in her class feel welcome and important. Second, she helped develop learner responsibility by involving students in preparing the letter home. Eventually, reaching the first two goals would contribute to reaching the third—maximizing time and opportunity for learning.

3.3 Time is a unique resource in that everyone has the same amount of it. So, the way people choose to allocate their time is a direct indicator of their priorities. When teachers choose to allocate some of their time to calling parents, it communicates to parents that the child is important.

4.1 People's need to make sense of their experiences is the framework on which all cognitive interventions are based. For example, when teachers' verbal and nonverbal behaviors are congruent, the communication makes sense. Also, when a person describes a behavior combined with the impact that the behavior has on others, as is the case with I-Messages, the communication also makes sense. And, logical consequences make sense. For example, it made more sense to Allen to have to pick up Alyssia's books when he knocked them out of her hands than serving detention would have.

4.2 First, *praising desired behavior* is a form of positive reinforcement. The next point, *ignoring inappropriate behavior,* is an application of extinction, which is the process of not reinforcing a behavior. The next point, *using indirect cues* capitalizes on vicarious reinforcement. *Desists* are mild punishers, and *applying consequences,* such as time-out, is another form of punishment.

4.3 An appropriate I-message that a teacher could use in responding to a student's talking might be: "Talking interrupts my teaching, this makes me lose my train of thought, and I get annoyed when my train of thought is disrupted." It addressed the behavior (talking), describes the effect on the sender (makes me lose my train of thought), and describes the feelings generated in the sender (annoyance when my train of thought is disrupted).

4.4 Having the student wash the door is the preferred consequence. It is logical; if you spit on the door and make it dirty, you should wash it. Being put in detention is a punishment, but no logical connection exists between the behavior and the consequence.

5.1 You are required by law to intervene in the case of a fight or other aggressive act. Failure to do so can result in being sued for negligence. You are not legally required to break up the fight; immediately reporting it to administrators is acceptable.

5.1 First, you must attempt to stop the fighting or bullying if possible. If a loud noise, such as shouting or slamming a chair on the floor, doesn't stop it, immediately send an uninvolved student for help. Second, you must protect the victim, and third, you should get help if you have not already done so.

5.3 Long-term cognitive approaches to bullying focus on helping students develop social skills, such as self-control, perspective taking, expressing anger verbally instead of physically, and learning to make and defend arguments.

Chapter 13

1.1 The five essential steps involved in planning for instruction consist of the following:

1. Select topics. Standards, curriculum guides, textbooks, and the teacher's professional knowledge are sources that help make this decision.
2. Specify learning objectives. Though the format for preparing learning objectives varies, the important aspect of preparing learning objectives is clarity about desired learning outcomes.
3. Prepare and organize learning activities. A task analysis can be helpful in this process: identify the components of the topic, sequence them, and prepare and order examples.
4. Prepare assessments. This means that assessments are created during planning instead of after learning activities have been completed.
5. Ensure that instruction and assessment are aligned with the learning objectives.

1.2 When teachers' planning involves standards, interpreting the standard is an additional step, and it precedes the other steps. Descriptions of standards vary; some are very specific, whereas others are quite general. When working with a standard described in general terms, teachers must first make a decision about what the standard means, then follow the rest of the planning steps, that is, plan learning activities and assessments.

1.3 This objective is best classified into the cell where metacognitive knowledge intersects with analysis. The tendency to look for relevant and irrelevant information in all the topics suggests metacognition, and determining what is relevant and irrelevant involves analysis.

2.1 Essential teaching skills are the abilities that all teachers should possess. They are analogous to the basic skills of reading, writing, and math that all people need to function effectively in our world. Essential teaching skills are the abilities that all teachers, regardless of content area, topic, or grade level, should have in order to function effectively in classrooms. They are important because they help promote learning in students.

2.2 The case studies that introduce each chapter are our attempts to provide introductory focus for the chapters. They are intended to attract your attention by beginning the chapter with a realistic look at classrooms. Then, the cases provide an umbrella under which the content of the chapter is developed.

2.3 The two essential teaching skills that are best illustrated in each chapter are *feedback* and *review and closure.* For example, here, in Appendix A, you receive feedback for all of the "Check Your Understanding" questions. When you go to Appendix B, you receive feedback for all of the "Preparing for Your Licensure Exam" questions that appear at the end of each chapter.

In the "Meeting Your Learning Objectives" section of each chapter, you receive a review of the chapter's contents, which are aligned with the learning objectives.

We also attempt to model effective clear communication in our writing. We try to use clear language; to emphasize important points with figures, tables, bulleted lists, and margin definitions; and to develop the chapters in thematic ways that represent connected discourse.

3.1 The introduction phase of direct instruction, lecture-discussion, and guided discovery is important because it capitalizes on *introductory focus.* Introductory focus attracts students' attention and provides a conceptual umbrella for the lesson.

We can also explain the need for the introduction phase using the human memory model. Attention is where processing begins. If learners don't attend to the information, it is lost, so attracting and maintaining attention are essential. The introduction phase helps meet this need.

3.2 The presentation phase of direct instruction is most important for ensuring successful independent practice, and it is in this phase that we see the most difference between effective and ineffective teachers. If the presentation phase is ineffective, both guided practice and independent practice will be difficult and confusing. Remember, independent practice strengthens earlier understanding; it does not teach the skill. If teachers have to provide a great deal of explanation during independent practice, error rates increase and student achievement decreases.

3.3 Effective instruction requires that the teacher's objectives are clear and the learning activity is aligned with the objectives. Also, the teacher should carefully monitor students' thinking throughout and intervene soon enough to prevent misconceptions, but not so soon that opportunities for constructing understanding are reduced.

3.4 She introduced cooperative learning quite effectively. Her task was short and simple, it was clear and specific (write three differences on paper), these written differences provided a product, and she monitored students' work. We have no evidence about them moving into and out of the groups.

4.1 First, effective assessments are aligned with a teacher's objectives and learning activity. Second, effective assessments give teachers information about students' thinking, as you saw with Scott's item that asked students to explain what made the papers go together.

4.2 Feedback is the essential teaching skill that teachers must use in conjunction with assessments if the assessments are to increase student learning. This means that teachers should always thoroughly discuss assessment items after scoring and returning them to students, which allows students to revise and elaborate on their thinking.

4.3 The primary problem with the assessment (and the learning activity) is that it is not aligned with his learning objective. His objective was for them to use figurative language in their writing. But we saw no evidence that they practiced writing. Giving them examples, and having them identify examples is an effective first step, but if the assessment is aligned with the objective, his assessment must require them to write.

Chapter 14

1.1 Assessment *for* learning makes assessment an integral part of the teaching–learning process and is designed to support and increase learning. It includes diagnosing students' current understanding, attempting to increase students' motivation to learn and self-regulation, and it measures student achievement.

To promote learning, all forms of assessment must be valid and reliable. Assessments that are invalid or unreliable don't provide teachers with the kind of information they need to make decisions that will promote learning.

1.2 Assuming that the assessment is consistent with his learning objectives, it is valid. Specifying that grammar and punctuation are important and then giving students a score for this component of the essay is a valid procedure.

1.3 Her assessment is not valid. Her learning objective is for students to be able to design experiments, but she assesses their recall of the steps involved. Her assessment isn't aligned with her learning objective, so it is invalid. It is likely that her assessment is reliable, because she will be able to score it consistently.

2.1 Informal assessment is the process of gathering incidental information about learning progress or other aspects of students' behavior and making decisions based on that information. To maximize learning, teachers must make an enormous number of decisions every day, ranging from which students to call on and when, whether or not to intervene in a classroom incident, or when to modify a lesson if students seem to be struggling. None of these decisions would be possible without informal assessment.

2.2 Teachers' ability to promote learners' personal, social, and moral development depend largely on informal assessment. When teachers make decisions about students' perspective taking or social problem-solving abilities—both important parts of social development—the decisions are part of informal assessment. Similarly, when teachers make decisions affecting moral development by promoting prosocial behaviors, their decisions are also part of informal assessment.

2.3 Because obtaining consistent information is difficult with informal assessments, they can be unreliable. Teachers need to be aware of the possibility of unreliable information, so they don't make decisions that can decrease learning or damage students emotionally.

3.1 Formal assessment is the process of gathering the same kind of systematic information from each student. Quizzes, tests, performance assessments, and homework are all forms of formal assessment.

Formal assessment differs from informal assessment in its systematic nature. Informal assessments don't gather the same information from each student.

3.2 In item 1, forms of the term circulate appear in both the stem and the correct answer. In item 2, the correct choice is written in more technical terms than are the distracters. Teachers fall into this trap when they take the correct choice directly from the text and then make up the distracters. Their informal language appears in the distracters, whereas text language appears in the correct answer.

In item 3, the correct choice is significantly longer than the incorrect choices; the teacher gives a similar clue when the correct choice is shorter than the distracters. If one choice is significantly longer or shorter than others, it should be a distracter.

In item 4, choices *a* and *c* are stated in absolute terms, which alerts test-wise students. Absolute terms, such as *all, always, none,* and *never,* are usually associated with incorrect answers. If used, they should be in the correct answer, such as "All algae contain chlorophyll."

The stem in item 5 is stated in negative terms without this fact being emphasized: the word *not* should be underlined. Also, choice *a* is grammatically inconsistent with the stem. One solution to the problem is to end the stem with "a(n)," so grammatical consistency is preserved.

In item 6, choices *a* and *c* are automatically eliminated, because both are gerunds, and only one answer can be correct. Also, item 6 uses "all of the above" as a choice; it can't be correct if *a* and *c* are eliminated. That makes *b* the only possible choice. A student could get the item right and have no idea what a participle is.

Preparing valid multiple-choice items requires both thought and care. With effort and practice, however, you can become skilled at it, and when you do, you have a powerful learning and assessment tool.

3.3 You would create a rating scale by first identifying the criteria for effective multiple-choice items. You would then describe each of these criteria in a single statement, which could be rated.

An example might appear as follows:

DIRECTIONS: Assess each of the test items using the following dimensions. For each dimension, circle a 5 for an excellent performance, 4 for a very good performance, 3 for good performance, 2 for fair, and 1 for poor.

5 4 3 2 1	States one clear problem in the stem.
5 4 3 2 1	Each distracter is plausible.
5 4 3 2 1	Wording in the stem and in the correct choice are dissimilar.
5 4 3 2 1	Phrasing in the correct choice and in the distracters are similar.
5 4 3 2 1	The correct choice and distracters are similar in length.
5 4 3 2 1	Negative wording is appropriately emphasized.
5 4 3 2 1	All distracters have different meanings.

3.4 Essay items can be performance assessments to the extent that they tap higher-level thinking in real-life situations. For example, asking students to write an essay on a topic of their choice, using available resources, would be closer to the idea of a performance assessment than a closed-book, timed test, with the teacher specifying the topic.

4.1 Effective assessment practices include careful planning for assessment, preparing students for assessments, creating a positive environment for administering assessments, and analyzing results.

Effective assessment practices increase student learning in the following ways: First, creating assessments during the planning process helps ensure instructional alignment. Second, preparing students for assessments provides them with practice responding to items similar to those that will be on the actual assessment, and also allows you to teach test-taking strategies. Both increase learning. Third, creating an environment similar to the one in which the students studied the topics covered on the assessment and eliminating distractions also increase performance. Finally, analyzing results and providing students with feedback help develop a more accurate and deeper understanding of the topics measured on the assessment.

4.2 The primary purpose of a table of specifications is to ensure that assessments are valid by aligning them with learning objectives. A table of specifications increases validity in two ways: First, by systematically identifying important information, it helps guarantee content coverage. Second, by focusing on the level of the items, it helps ensure that the level of each item on the test matches the level of the objectives and instruction.

Tables of specifications should be created during the process of planning for instruction.

4.3 First, DeVonne emphasized reading the directions carefully. Second, she told them to skip a problem if they got stuck. Third, she reminded them not to forget to go back to any problem that they had skipped.

5.1 The components of a total assessment system include preparing specific items such as paper-and-pencil, performance assessment, and portfolio assessments in some cases. The components also include preparing students, administering assessments, analyzing results, and assigning grades.

Some of the decisions involved in designing a total assessment system include the following:

- The number of tests and quizzes to be given
- Whether to use performance assessments and/or portfolios and how they will be used
- The level at which assessment items will be written, such as recall of factual knowledge, or application of conceptual knowledge
- How homework will be included in the process of assigning grades
- The assessment and reporting of affective dimensions, such as cooperation and effort

5.2 Formative assessment is an ongoing process that uses informal assessments, homework, and ungraded quizzes and tests to provide students with feedback and to allow teachers to diagnose learning problems. Summative assessment occurs after instruction, and teachers use it for grading purposes. Providing students with detailed feedback about their performance on the assessments is an essential component of both.

5.3 A grading system based on percentages is easier to manage and easier to communicate to students and parents. However, it can provide a distorted picture of learning progress, because percentages for different assignments are usually averaged, which attaches equal weight to assignments that differ in length. A point system may be harder to communicate to students and parents but provides a more accurate picture of learning progress.

Chapter 15

1.1 Standardized tests serve three primary functions: (1) assessment and diagnosis of learning, such as how students' achievement compares to the achievement of other students around the nation (or even the world); (2) selection and placement, such as placing students new to a school in a certain class level, a program for the gifted and talented, or admission to college; and (3) program evaluation and accountability, such as assessing a new curriculum and the extent to which a school or district meets state-mandated accountability measures.

1.2 The district is considering both achievement and diagnostic tests. Standardized achievement tests are designed to provide comprehensive coverage of different content areas. Diagnostic tests, in comparison, are designed to provide more specific, detailed information about an individual student's strengths and weaknesses.

1.3 The first teacher is addressing construct validity, a description of the extent to which an assessment accurately measures a characteristic that is not directly observable. The second is addressing content validity, the match between a test's contents and the content of the math curriculum. The third teacher is looking for predictive validity, the test's ability to gauge future performance in college.

2.1 A greater difference exists between the performances of Carol and Marsha than between Marsha and Lenore. Students' percentile ranks at the extremes of a distribution vary more from their counterparts than those who score near the middle of the distribution.

2.2 In the first class, with a standard deviation of 4.8, a score of 47 would be in stanine 7 (slightly more than 1 standard deviation above the mean). In the second distribution, with a standard deviation of 3.1, a score of 47 would be in stanine 8 (more than 1.5 standard deviations above the mean).

2.3 A grade equivalent score of 6.7 means that he scored as well as the average sixth grader in the seventh month of the sixth grade. It means that the fourth grader is somewhat advanced. (It does not mean that the student should be in the sixth grade, nor does it mean that the student is generally capable of doing sixth-grade work.)

3.1 Standards-based education is the process of focusing curricula and instruction on predetermined goals or standards. Accountability is the process of requiring students to demonstrate that they have met the standards and holding teachers responsible for students' performance. Schools use standardized testing in the form of high-stakes tests to determine whether or not students have met the standards.

3.2 Arguments for high-stakes testing include the following: The process identifies important learning outcomes, communicates them to both students and the public, and provides evidence about whether or not students are acquiring essential knowledge. Advocates also claim that this process improves learning for all students.

Arguments against high-stakes testing suggest that it narrows the curriculum; in essence, what is tested becomes the curriculum. This encourages teachers to ignore areas that aren't tested, such as art and music. Critics also argue that minimum-competency testing stifles teacher creativity because teachers are essentially teaching to the test.

3.3 The areas in which teachers are being tested include basic skills such as reading, writing, and math; content area knowledge; and principles of learning and teaching. Proponents of teacher testing argue that teachers must be skilled and knowledgeable in these areas in order to teach effectively. For example, basic skills are required in order to communicate effectively; knowledge of content is essential, because teachers can't teach what they don't understand themselves; and teachers must understand both the instructional process and the characteristics of their students in order to teach effectively.

4.1 Learner diversity can influence the validity of standardized tests if bias exists in the content of the tests, testing procedures, or test use. Content bias exists if performance on a test requires knowledge that is not relevant to the concept or skill being tested and is knowledge that learners from diverse backgrounds may not possess. Bias in testing procedures exists if students are not familiar with aspects of the testing process, (e.g., time limits or testing formats), which places a burden on the students that detracts from their performance. Tests can also be biased with respect to use if educators make decisions about students based on the results of a single test.

4.2 Teachers' most effective strategy for minimizing content bias is to prepare students as fully as possible for the tests. This includes providing concrete reference points for technical vocabulary, carefully teaching and emphasizing test-taking strategies, aligning instruction with prescribed standards, and providing students with ample practice with formats similar to the formats they will face on the tests. This strategy is important for all students, and it is even more essential for members of cultural minorities and students who are not native English speakers.

appendix B

Feedback for "Preparing for Your Licensure Exam" Questions

Chapter 1

1. Rebecca most explicitly demonstrated general pedagogical knowledge in her lesson. The class was orderly, and she used questioning to involve a number of the children in the lesson.

2. Richard demonstrated each of the forms of knowledge, but pedagogical content knowledge and knowledge of learners and learning were most prominent. Using concrete examples such as a starfish and Jason to illustrate different types of symmetry demonstrated his pedagogical content knowledge (his ability to represent abstract concepts in ways that make sense to learners).

   Richard demonstrated knowledge of learners and learning by having Jason go to the front of the room. He understood, for instance, that using a personalized example, such as Jason, increases motivation to learn, and that concrete examples, such as the sponge, starfish, and Jason are more effective than abstract examples.

3. Didi primarily demonstrated pedagogical content knowledge in her lesson. Her ability to represent the relationship between temperature and pressure in a way that made sense to students demonstrated her ability to illustrate an abstract idea (Charles's law) with concrete examples (the balloons).

4. Bob Duchaine primarily demonstrated knowledge of content. He obviously understood the factors surrounding the Vietnam War. However, the fact that he only used lecture as a way of teaching the content suggests that he might not be as knowledgeable about other types of teacher knowledge.

Chapter 2

1. Jenny's students demonstrated characteristics of preoperational learners. For instance, Jessica's reason for the towel staying dry was, "Cause it's inside and the water is outside," and Anthony concluded that "A water seal," had kept the towel dry. This is perceptually based reasoning, which is characteristic of preoperational learners.

   Jenny's instruction was quite effective, because she provided direct and concrete experiences for her students. For example, to demonstrate that air was in the glass, she tipped it sideways to allow a bubble to escape. She also allowed her students to experiment with the materials in a follow-up hands-on activity, which provided even more direct experience.

2. The water was concrete and perceptual. Without the water, for example, the students wouldn't have been able to see air bubbles escape from the glass, so they wouldn't have had any direct experience with air being in the glass. Preoperational students need direct experiences to provide a foundation for logical thought, which marks the next step in development.

3. Jenny described the disagreement as a problem to be solved by the class. This is a desirable approach from a developmental perspective because it places responsibility for making sense of the world on students.

   She could simply have told the students that the inside of the glass was dry. She could also have asked other students to come up and check on the glass. The disadvantage of telling the students is that it wouldn't be convincing for those who believed that it was wet. The disadvantage of having other students come up is simply time and management. The advantage in having others check the glass is that more students would have directly experienced feeling the inside of the glass.

4. While we don't have enough evidence to determine if the lesson was conducted in all the students' zones of proximal development, the comments of several indicated that, with Jenny's guidance, they understood the topic. This suggests that the lesson was conducted in their zones.

   Jenny provided effective scaffolding in the form of questions, prompts, and altering materials (e.g., tipping the glass to allow the air bubbles to escape, and having the students try the activities themselves).

Chapter 3

1. Based on Erikson's work, we might conclude that Karl hasn't positively resolved the industry/inferiority crisis with respect to English. He says, "I'm no good at English," for example. On the other hand, he presumably feels a sense of accomplishment with respect to basketball, since Helen described him as "poetry in motion."

2. Research indicates that the strongest correlations exist between specific academic self-concepts and achievement. This is corroborated in Karl's case. His self-concept in English is low, but in math and science, it appears to be better. Also, his physical self-concept is probably quite high, since, according to Helen, he's very good at basketball.

3. Helen's handling of the cheating problem was ineffective. First, her classroom structure promoted a form of external morality; for example, her comment to Nathan was, "Nathan, remember my first rule?" instead of, "Nathan, why is it important to raise your hand when you want to speak?"

Second, her comment, "If I catch anyone cheating on Thursday, I'll tear up your quiz and give you a failing grade," was again consistent with external morality. A more effective approach would have been to try to promote autonomous morality by discussing the issue of cheating, and by describing teaching and learning as social contracts. When students take tests, they are in a contract that requires them to do the work on their own. While this orientation won't stop all cheating, it creates a more effective climate for promoting moral development.

4. Several things in Helen's approach to her classroom and her instruction could have been improved. In addition to the emotional climate, as indicated by her response to Nathan and her threat to tear up papers if others were caught cheating, her expectations for students were negative. For example, she commented to them, "You did so poorly on the quiz, and I explained everything so carefully. You must not have studied very hard." Although we can't be completely sure, her instruction appears to be very teacher centered and built around abstract rules. She did not address the rules in the context of written work, and she did not provide a setting where students could develop an understanding of the rules based on social interaction between the teacher and the students as well as between the students. When students don't have opportunities to interact with each other, valuable opportunities for social development are lost.

Chapter 4

1. The most prominent strategy Teri used to eliminate gender bias was to call on all students—both male and female—equally. Other strategies she might have employed include: strategically assigning girls to key roles in small groups, openly talking about the problem in class, and bringing female role models into her class.

2. The overheads that Teri used to illustrate *mercantilism* minimized the role of previous background knowledge by containing all of the essential characteristics.

3. Teri provided challenge by asking her students to find commonalities between the two examples of *mercantilism*. She encouraged success by structuring her questioning strategies so that students were able to construct the concept from the examples.

4. She actively involved her students in two ways. She had them work in groups, and she used questioning to involve them in the whole-group portion of the lesson.

Chapter 5

1. Mike helped create a supportive climate in several ways. Some seem minor, but they were all significant. For example, he smiled at his students, willingly repeated part of the problem for Gwenn, and offered encouragement by telling them in a positive tone that he was going to call on them first in the lesson. He also provided support for other students, such as whispering, "That's terrific," to Todd and giving him a light "thump" on the back and encouraging Herchel when he said, "I . . . I . . . don't know." Each of these behaviors—alone—is relatively minor; when combined, they result in a climate of support and positive expectations.

2. First, Mike was consistently positive with the students, and he stated positive expectations throughout the lesson. Second, he taught the lesson in small steps and prompted students, such as Herchel, whenever they were unable to answer.

3. First, he had the three students with learning disabilities come to class a few minutes early, so he could carefully read his warm-up problem to them and be sure they understood what was asked for in the problem before the rest of the students began. Then he worked with them in a small group while the rest of the students were doing seat work to give them the extra scaffolding they needed to help get them to the point where they could work on their own.

4. He helped Todd develop a system in which Todd would chart his own behavior, with the goal being the development of self-management. He also provided Todd with the emotional support and reinforcement needed to help make the system work.

   We don't have evidence in the case study about support for Horace. This can be a problem, because Horace is shy and withdrawn, and he can become "lost in the shuffle." A relatively simple way to provide support would be to include him in the question-and-answer activity and prompt him if necessary to ensure that he can answer successfully before turning to another student. In this way, he can involve Horace, and hopefully, in time, make significant progress with him.

Chapter 6

1. Helen's nervousness, as indicated in her comment to Jenny, in reaction to having to go to the chalkboard is a conditioned response. Having to go to the board became associated with "blanking out." Blanking out was the unconditioned stimulus, and through the association, going to the board is the conditioned stimulus. Blanking out resulted in Helen feeling like an idiot as the unconditioned stimulus.

   Warren could help Helen's nervousness become extinct by ensuring that she succeeded as she worked at the board. This might require some extra scaffolding and emotional support as she worked through the problems.

2. The first example of punishment occurred when Warren reduced his first homework assignment from 6 to 5 word problems. The students' complaints were presentation punishers. They presented him with their complaints, and he reduced the length of the assignment.

   The second example occurred when students complained again and he reduced the assignment from 6 to 4 problems. While longer homework assignments don't necessarily result in more learning, students need to practice the problem-solving skills Warren was trying to teach. Reducing the homework assignments too much is likely to decrease learning.

3. Warren negatively reinforced students by reducing the length of the homework assignments when they complained. Their behavior increased, as indicated by the fact that they complained about the homework assignment sooner on Friday than they did on Thursday. Taking away some of the homework assignment was the negative reinforcer.

   Warren also negatively reinforced Pamela for not answering his question by removing the question and turning it to Callie. This is likely to result in Pamela saying she doesn't know more quickly the next time she is called on and is uncertain about the answer. A more effective move would be to prompt Pamela and then positively reinforce her for her efforts. We want to reinforce students *for answering* instead of *for not answering.*

4. Warren's modeling was effective in two ways. First, he demonstrated the solution to a problem, and second, he capitalized on cognitive modeling as he articulated his thinking during the demonstration in saying, "Now, . . . the first thing I think about when I see a problem like this one is, 'What does the jacket cost now?' I have to figure out the price, and to do that I will take 25% of the $84. . . ."

   Warren's modeling was ineffective when he said, "I realize that percentages and decimals aren't your favorite topic, and I'm not wild about them either, but we have no choice, so we might as well buckle down and learn them." Because people tend to imitate behaviors they observe in others, modeling distaste for a topic increases the likelihood that students will decide that the topic is boring.

5. When Cris caught his error and corrected himself, Warren commented, "Good, . . . that's what we're trying to do. We are all going to make mistakes, but if we catch ourselves, we're making progress. Keep it up." His comment reinforced Cris and simultaneously vicariously reinforced the other students. He also used Cris as a model, and, because everyone in the class is similar in that they are all students, Cris was likely to be an effective model because of perceived similarity. (Warren's praise suggested that Cris was also competent, which would further increase his effectiveness as a model.)

Chapter 7

1. Five principles of cognitive learning theory were outlined in the chapter. The following identifies the principle and offers an assessment of Sue's implementation of each.

   Learning and development depend on learners' experiences. The students acquired experience through their reading of the novel together with the class discussion of it. They developed their understanding of the themes of the novel through these experiences.

   Learners are cognitively active. Sue put the students in active roles with her questioning and by having them write in their journals.

   Learners construct knowledge. The fact that the students offered different interpretations of Hester's reaction to Dimmesdale's speech is evidence that they construct their own understanding. For instance, Nicole viewed Hester as angry, whereas Sarah saw her as devoted. Because one of Sue's goals was for students to understand Dimmesdale's character, she might have been more focused in her questioning, helping students to form a more complete picture of his character. This might have been accomplished by referring the students to specific passages in the novel that would give the students insights into his character.

   Knowledge that is constructed depends on learners' prior knowledge. Sue helped her students build on their prior knowledge by encouraging them to think about their discussion of Hester's character from previous lessons.

   Learning is enhanced in a social environment. This is the principle Sue perhaps implemented most effectively. She had students work in groups, and she conducted much of the whole-group portion of the lesson through her questioning. Social interaction was prominent throughout the lesson.

2. Applying the memory model requires that teachers consciously attempt to attract and maintain students' attention, check their perceptions, and promote meaningful encoding without imposing a cognitive load that exceeds their working memory capacities. Sue's lesson was an effective application of the memory model. She helped attract and maintain students' attention by challenging them to find evidence in the book that Dimmesdale was the illicit lover and by using the passage from the book describing Dimmesdale's speech. She also used class discussion as a mechanism to maintain attention. In each instance, she used student responses to check their perceptions. Sue avoided imposing too heavy a cognitive load by asking one question at a time and giving them time to consider their answers. She promoted meaningful encoding by encouraging her students to use imagery to gain more insights into Dimmesdale's character. When they wrote in their journals and discussed Hester's reaction to Dimmesdale's speech, they were cognitively active, linking the information in the novel to their background knowledge. Through the discussion, they elaborated on each other's understanding. Imagery, activity, and elaboration are all processes that make information meaningful.

3. Encoding was the cognitive process most prominent in her lesson. As we saw in item 2, Sue promoted encoding by encouraging students to use imagery to gain more insights into Dimmesdale's character, by putting them in active roles with their journal writing and class discussion, and promoting elaboration in the class discussion.

While encoding was most significant, perception was prominent as well. For instance, when the students offered different views of Hester's reaction to Dimmesdale's speech, they were presenting their perceptions

4. Declarative knowledge is knowledge of facts, definitions, procedures, and rules; procedural knowledge involves knowing how to perform tasks. Sue focused on declarative knowledge when she reviewed the novel's plot at the beginning of the lesson. The primary focus of the lesson was on declarative knowledge—helping the students develop an understanding of the characters in the novel. When the students wrote in their journals, they were demonstrating procedural knowledge.

Chapter 8

1. Scott's lesson clearly demonstrated the characteristics of constructivism. For example, the students' tendency to try and solve the problem by changing more than one variable at a time illustrated the characteristic *learners construct knowledge that makes sense to them.* Changing two—or even all three—variables made sense to the students.

   The students' tendency to change more than one variable at a time illustrated a second characteristic, *new learning depends on current understanding.* The students knew that they had to manipulate the variables, but they didn't have sufficient background experiences to help them understand that the variables had to be changed systematically, varying only one at a time.

   The lessson also demonstrated a third characteristic, *social interaction facilitates learning.* First, Scott's questions helped them reconsider their procedures, and talking to each other provided different perspectives on ways to identify and isolate key variables.

   The final characteristic, *meaningful learning occurs within real-world tasks,* was perhaps the strongest aspect of Scott's lesson. By actually handling the equipment, students could see how the abstract variables they were considering related to the real world.

2. When students said, "Mr. Sowell, we figured out that the shorter it is . . . and the heavier it is, the faster it goes," this indicated that they had changed both variables and revealed a misconception about controlling variables. Scott then asked which of the two variables was responsible for the change in the frequency.

   When Wensley and Jonathan said simultaneously, "They both changed," Scott responded, "Think about that. You need to come up with a conclusion about length, about weight, and about angle—how each of them influences the frequency of your pendulum." This question challenged their thinking, but probably not directly enough to result in conceptual change. Scott later demonstrated and explained the need to control variables, but whether or not the explanation would have been effective for promoting conceptual change is uncertain, because we don't know about the results of his subsequent assessments.

3. We will consider these suggestions one at a time, starting with the strengths of the lesson:

   Promote high levels of interaction. Scott effectively accomplished this through his group work (which allowed students to discuss the process in detail) and through his strategic questions during the lesson.

   Treat verbal explanations skeptically. Scott also effectively implemented this suggestion. He didn't lecture about controlling variables; instead, he provided experiences and asked questions, guiding students in their knowledge construction.

   Connect content to the real world. Scott effectively implemented this suggestion by providing the students a real-world experience with controlling variables. The students also acquired real-world experience with working cooperatively and making decisions.

   Provide learners with a variety of examples and representations of content. This suggestion was probably the least well demonstrated in the lesson. While Scott presented students with a concrete, hands-on problem, they likely will need a number of additional problems where they will be required to control variables in order to develop a deep understanding of the process.

   The suggestion: *Promote learning with assessment.* By carefully monitoring the groups as they worked, Scott informally assessed the students' understanding. No evidence of formal assessment exists in the case study.

4. Scott's lesson was quite effective for learners with diverse backgrounds. First, the group that was showcased in his lesson consisted of an Asian American, an African American, and two Caucasians, one a recent immigrant from Russia. Scott used group work for a part of his lesson, which is effective for students from diverse backgrounds. Group work provides opportunities for students from different backgrounds to share their different perspectives about the content being learned. In addition it provides opportunities for students to learn to work together. The task required that they work together to solve a common problem, and, as was evident in the videotaped episode from which the transcript was taken, the students worked together very cooperatively.

   In addition, his task provided concrete experiences for the students, which is also effective for learners with backgrounds that are diverse.

Chapter 9

1. Sue did a generally good job of teaching problem solving with young children. She introduced the situation and asked the children how they would solve the problem. In this way she provided some practice in identifying the problem and selecting a strategy for solving it. The learning-center work gave the students experience in applying their understanding of graphing to other problems.

   Sue did a very good job of presenting her problem in a meaningful context, and she provided considerable scaffolding for the children who had difficulty with the process and the applications.

2. Sue did quite well at promoting critical thinking in her lesson. For example, she asked students to make observations of the information in the graphs, and she asked students to confirm their conclusions with observations (e.g., "How did you solve the problem?" and "Does that work?").

   She could have increased the emphasis on critical thinking by giving her students the chance to practice critical thinking in other contexts. For instance, she might have posed questions, such as, "Suppose we went around the school and asked people what their favorite flavor of jelly bean is. What do you think they would say?" After the students predicted, she could ask them for the basis for their prediction (such as the information in their graph).

3. Promoting transfer was one of the strengths of Sue's lesson. After she conducted the whole-group activity, she had students work at a series of centers, each of which focused on gathering information and preparing bar graphs in different contexts. In this way, the students had a variety of high-quality experiences, all of which were in realistic contexts.

Chapter 10

1. Damon's instruction was less than effective for meeting the needs described in Maslow's hierarchy. For example, his comment, "so that doesn't make sense," is not likely to make students feel safe in their attempts to answer. And, safety is preceded only by survival in Maslow's deficiency needs. Further, he lectured, and the content of his lecture was mostly a list of facts, which would not appeal to students' intellectual achievement needs.

2. Self-determination theory is grounded in the belief that learners have innate needs for *competence, autonomy,* and *relatedness.* Learners' needs for competence are met when they receive evidence that their competence is increasing. Damon's comment to Clifton, "No, no, remember that Columbus sailed in 1492, which was before 1500, so that doesn't make sense," communicates that Clifton lacked competence. Also, he praised Liora for her performance (identifying the correct date) but made no comment about her understanding, which also gave her no feedback about her competence in this important area.

   Learners' perceptions of autonomy are enhanced when the teacher promotes high levels of student participation in learning activities, emphasizing effort and de-emphasizing ability in promoting success, and using assessments that emphasize deep understanding of content. Damon primarily lectured, so student participation was low; he focused on ability with statements such as, "Let's give these sharp ones with the A's a run for their money"; and his assessments focused on factual information. Each detracts from students' self determination.

3. According to self-worth theory, people try to preserve perceptions of high ability, because ability is so strongly valued in our society. By displaying the grades on the board, and making comments such as, "Let's give these sharp ones with the A's a run for their money," he made demonstrations of ability a priority. In addition, his comment, "This wasn't that hard a test," would tend to detract even further from the self-worth of the students who didn't do well.

   A more effective approach would be to de-emphasize students' performance, instead emphasizing and modeling effort attributions as Kathy Brewster did in her interactions with her students.

4. Personalizing content, using concrete examples, and promoting high levels of involvement increase intrinsic interest. In contrast with Kathy Brewster, who personalized the topic with the "crusade" to prevent the school from eliminating extracurricular activities, Damon presented facts about the Crusades in a lecture. The lecture was delivered in the abstract, and the students were generally uninvolved. Further, his comment, "I know that learning dates and places isn't the most pleasant stuff, but you might as well get used to it because that's what history is about," would also be likely to detract from intrinsic interest.

Chapter 11

1. It appears that DeVonne's students felt very safe in her class. This conclusion is based on the fact that they knew that their paragraphs were going to be openly evaluated by their peers, yet they were eager to have them displayed, as indicated by comments such as "I want to go next! I want to go next!" and "Are we going to get to do ours tomorrow?" Further, they were eager to have their paragraphs displayed and evaluated in spite of the fact that Justin was given a fairly low rating on his paragraph.

2. DeVonne provided *introductory focus* by saying that they were going to practice composing good paragraphs and reviewing the characteristics of paragraphs that were well-written. She enhanced introductory focus by her example with computers and television displayed on the overhead. She *personalized* the task by emphasizing that their paragraphs could be about any topic. The students were actively *involved* as they constructed their paragraphs and when they assessed those that were displayed. The assessments provided *feedback* for both the student whose paragraph was being displayed and the class as a whole. The lesson demonstrated each of the instructional variables.

3. The students' enthusiasm can be explained with both teacher characteristics and climate variables. DeVonne was *enthusiastic, caring,* and *had positive expectations* for her students. With respect to the climate variables, her class was orderly, and, as we saw in item 1, the students felt very *safe.* In addition, she explained the writing task clearly, which increased *task comprehension,* and the assignment provided opportunities for both *challenge* and *success.*

4. Research suggests that teachers who are successful with urban learners are enthusiastic, supportive, and have high expectations. They also create lessons that connect to students' lives and have high rates of involvement. DeVonne

possessed each of these teacher characteristics, her lesson connected to students' lives by allowing them to write on a topic of their choice, and they were actively involved throughout the lesson.

Chapter 12

1. Janelle's planning for classroom management was quite ineffective. For example, in contrast with Judy Harris at the beginning of the chapter, Janelle's students were expected to sit quietly while she called the roll, went to the file cabinet to get out her transparencies, and finished arranging her materials. The result was "dead" time for students, during which disruptions occurred and lost instructional time for Janelle.

2. Several problems existed in Janelle's management interventions. First, she demonstrated lack of withitness when she admonished Leila for blurting out "Stop it Damon." Janelle initially 'caught' the wrong one and allowed the incident to disrupt the learning activity to a greater extent than did Judy. Janelle also allowed her encounter with Howard and Manny to disrupt the momentum of her lesson. Janelle's nonverbal behavior also didn't communicate that she was "in charge," or that she meant it when she intervened. For example, she glanced up from her papers to admonish Howard and Manfred, and she again "looked up" in response to a hum of voices around the classroom. Also, requiring Manfred to read the rule aloud in front of the class was a form of power play that did nothing to improve the classroom climate, and her comment, "You've been bugging me all week . . . " was inconsistent with recommendations of experts to criticize the behavior and not the student.

3. Janelle's instruction would have been more effective if it had been more interactive and developed with more supporting materials such as maps and globes. This would have allowed her to involve students more, which usually results in fewer management problems. Janelle's management was also less effective than it might have been. She wasn't well-organized and she didn't communicate as clearly and assertively as she might have to be effective. In addition, she was slightly less "withit" than what would have been desirable and she allowed her interventions with the students to disrupt the momentum and smoothness of her lesson, resulting in more problems with management.

   Some suggestions for improvement include the following: First, Janelle would have been more effective if she had been better organized. A beginning-of-class warm-up activity would have helped her better use her time and would also have eliminated "dead" time at the beginning of the lesson during which management problems can occur. Also, her materials should have been ready and waiting, so she didn't have to spend time arranging them while students were supposed to sit quietly. Ensuring that her verbal and nonverbal communications were congruent would have made her admonishments of the students more credible. Using an I-message with Howard would have been a more effective intervention than saying, "You've been bothering me all week." Finally, keeping her intervention with Howard and Manny brief would have allowed her to maintain the flow of her lesson.

Chapter 13

1. Planning typically involves several decisions. First, Judy had to decide that the topic—identifying relationships between geography and economy of different geographical regions—was an important topic to study. Second, Judy decided that her learning objective would be for students to describe the effect of geography on the economy of a region. Third, she had to make a decision about how the learning activity would be prepared. She decided that she would have the students gather information about the regions, organize the information in a matrix, and then analyze the information. She also decided that she would use a combination of group work and whole-class discussion in her learning activity.

2. *Alignment* refers to the connections between learning objectives, instructional activities, and assessment. Judy's learning objective was for students to understand the relationships between geography and the economy of different regions in the country. Because her learning activity focused on these relationships, her objective and learning activity were aligned.

3. Judy demonstrated several of the essential teaching skills in her lesson. First, she demonstrated a positive approach to the lesson with appropriately high expectations. She was well organized. She began the lesson immediately after the bell rang, she had the chart already displayed on the wall of her room, and students moved back and forth from small-group to whole-group activities quickly and smoothly.
   - Judy's communication was clear. She used clear language, and the lesson was thematic and led to a point (connected discourse). We didn't see explicit transition signals in the lesson, nor was emphasis apparent.
   - The chart that Judy and the students had prepared provided a good form of sensory focus. Introductory focus wasn't evident in the lesson.
   - Judy's questioning was quite good. She called on a variety of students, called on girls and boys about equally, called on students by name, and ensured success with open-ended questions and prompting.
   - Because of the way the lesson was organized, much of Judy's feedback was a simple acknowledgment of students' observations, and her closure was quite brief, because the period was nearing an end. She would need to do a careful review the next day to ensure that the students had encoded the information clearly into long-term memory.

Chapter 14

1. Ron's curriculum was out of alignment. His stated learning objective was, ". . . you'll all be able to use pronouns

correctly in your writing." This goal was congruent with the second part of his assessment, which asked the students to write a passage in which they use pronoun cases correctly. However, his learning activity was behaviorist; it focused on the sentences in isolation rather than on writing, so it was not congruent with his goal and with the second part of his assessment. To make his instruction congruent with his goal, Ron needs to provide students with practice using pronouns correctly in their writing.

2. Effective preparation for testing involves giving students the opportunity to practice on test-like items that are similar to those they will encounter on the test itself. Ron's students only responded to the specific and isolated sentences, and they didn't practice using pronouns in their writing.

   The only problem that existed with his administration of the test was the fact that students were pressed for time, and he may have increased the anxiety of test-anxious students by his repeated reminders of the amount of time remaining. Giving students more time to finish the exam would remedy this problem.

   In discussing the test results, Ron again de-emphasized their writing in favor of the specific items, and his feedback was somewhat vague. Unquestionably, providing feedback for every student is very demanding, but he could have written a model response to which the students could have compared their own paragraphs.

3. Ron's instruction for urban learners would have been more effective if he had made his instruction more concrete. For example, he could have prepared a personalized written passage that included examples of pronoun cases, and in this way his content would have been more meaningful for his students.

   Research indicates that learners with diverse backgrounds benefit from explicit test-preparation procedures. Had Ron provided more test-preparation practice, particularly with writing, his assessment would have been more effective and valid.

4. Ron used his time well, his instruction was interactive, he had a clear learning objective for his students, and he provided practice for his students with respect to properly placing the pronoun in specific sentences. These were the strengths of his instruction and assessment.

   His primary weaknesses were the fact that his learning objective, learning activity, and assessment were out of alignment, he didn't provide as much practice for his students as he might have, especially with using pronouns in their writing, and he didn't discuss the test results as thoroughly as he might have.

Chapter 15

1. Standardized achievement tests are specifically designed to provide information about how much students learn in various content areas. To be useful in answering her question, the standardized achievement test would have to be carefully aligned with her curriculum.

2. The primary concern with a standardized achievement test would be content validity, or the extent to which the test actually covers important content. This is essentially an issue of alignment.

3. Because of their focus on specific content, standardized diagnostic tests would be most useful here. Diagnostic tests assess more narrowly, but do so more thoroughly, thus providing the teacher with more in-depth information about specific topics.

4. The more information that teachers gather in their decision making, the better their decisions. Other possible sources of information include specific subtests within the standardized tests, previous grades in math classes, and observations and evaluations from previous teachers.

appendix C

Using This Text to Practice for the Praxis™ *Principles of Learning and Teaching* Exam

In the United States, 44 states plus the District of Columbia, Guam, and the U.S. Virgin Islands use Praxis™ exams as part of their teacher licensing requirement. Four Principles of Learning and Teaching (PLT) tests, one each for teachers seeking licensure in Early Childhood, or grades K–6, 5–9, and 7–12, are among the Praxis exams. *Educational Psychology: Windows on Classrooms* addresses virtually all of the topics covered in the PLT tests.

The Principles of Learning and Teaching exam has two parts (Educational Testing Service, 2008b). One consists of 24 multiple-choice questions organized into two sections of 12 questions each. The multiple-choice questions are similar to those in the test bank that accompanies *Educational Psychology: Windows on Classrooms.* The second part is based on "case histories" (case studies), which you will be asked to read and analyze. The case histories are very similar to the case studies that appear throughout this text.

The case-based part of the Praxis Principles of Learning and Teaching exam consists of four case histories followed by three short-answer questions each. The short-answer questions cover all of the topics identified in the column under "Topics Covered on the Praxis Exam" in the table below. Each short-answer question will be scored on a scale of 0–2. Questions require you to "demonstrate understanding of the importance of an aspect of teaching, demonstrate understanding of the principles of learning and teaching underlying an aspect of teaching, or recognize when and how to apply the principles of learning and teaching underlying an aspect of teaching" (Educational Testing Service, 2008b, p 1). We designed this text to help you succeed on the Praxis Principles of Learning and Teaching exam by including case studies at the end of each chapter, which are followed by short-answer questions. The case studies and questions provide you with practice responding to questions similar to those that will appear on the exam. We provide feedback for the short-answer questions in Appendix B of this text.

Topics Covered on the Praxis™ Exam	Chapter Content Aligned With Praxis™ Topics
I. Students as Learners (approximately 33% of total test)	
A. Student Development and the Learning Process	
1. Theoretical foundations about how learning occurs: how students construct knowledge, acquire skills, and develop habits of mind	Chapter 2: The Development of Cognition and Language • The human brain and cognitive development (pp. 31–33) • Piaget's theory of intellectual development (pp. 34–43) • A sociocultural view of development: The work of Lev Vygotsky (pp. 45–49) Chapter 6: Behaviorism and Social Cognitive Theory (Entire chapter) Chapter 7: Cognitive Views of Learning (Entire chapter) Chapter 8: Constructing Knowledge (Entire chapter) Chapter 9: Complex Cognitive Processes (Entire chapter)
2. Human development in the physical, social, emotional, moral, speech/language, and cognitive domains	Chapter 2: The Development of Cognition and Language (Entire chapter) Chapter 3: Personal, Social, and Moral Development (Entire chapter) Chapter 6: Behaviorism and Social Cognitive Theory • Self-regulation (pp. 185–186) Chapter 7: Cognitive Views of Learning • Metacognition: Knowledge and control of cognitive processes (pp. 217–219) Chapter 9: Complex Cognitive Processes • The strategic learner (pp. 267–275) Chapter 11: Motivation in the Classroom • Self-regulated learners: Developing student responsibility (pp. 322–325)

B. Students as Diverse Learners	
1. Differences in the ways students learn and perform	Chapter 2: The Development of Cognition and Language • Stages of development (pp. 37–42) • Language development (pp. 50–55) Chapter 4: Learner Diversity • Culture and classrooms (pp. 97–101) • Linguistic diversity (pp. 101–107) • Theory to practice: Teaching culturally and linguistically diverse students in your classroom (p. 106) • Gender differences in classroom behavior (p. 109) • Theory to practice: Responding to gender differences in your classroom (p. 110) • How SES influences learning (pp. 112–113) Chapter 5: Learners with Exceptionalities • Gardner's theory of multiple intelligences (pp. 127–128) • Learning styles (pp. 131–133)
2. Areas of exceptionality in students' learning	Chapter 5: Learners with Exceptionalities • Learning disabilities (pp. 138–140) • Attention deficit/hyperactivity disorder (pp. 140–141) • Intellectual disability (pp. 141–143) • Behavior disorders (pp. 143–145) • Autism spectrum disorder (p. 145) • Communication disorders (pp. 146–147) • Visual disabilities (p. 147) • Hearing disabilities (pp. 147–148)
3. Legislation and institutional responsibilities relating to exceptional students	Chapter 5: Learners with Exceptionalities • Individuals with Disabilities Education Act (pp. 133–137) • Amendments to the Individuals with Disabilities Education Act (pp. 137–138)
4. Approaches for accommodating various learning styles, intelligences, or exceptionalities	Chapter 5: Learners with Exceptionalities • Gardner's theory of multiple intelligences (pp. 127–128) • Ability grouping (pp. 130–131) • Learning styles (pp. 131–133) • Identifying students with exceptionalities (pp. 152–153) • Modifying instruction to meet students' needs (pp. 153–154) • Theory to practice: Teaching students with exceptionalities (p. 155) • Students with exceptionalities at different ages: Developmentally appropriate practice (p. 157) Chapter 14: Assessing Classroom Learning • Performance assessments (pp. 446–449) • Exploring diversity: Effective assessment with learners from diverse backgrounds (p. 463)
5. Process of second language acquisition and strategies to support the learning of students for whom English is not a first language	Chapter 4: Learner Diversity • English dialects (pp. 101–102) • English language learners (pp. 103–105) • Theory to practice: Teaching culturally and linguistically diverse students in your classroom (pp. 106–107)
6. Understanding the influence of individual experiences, talents, and prior learning, as well as language, culture, family, and community values on students' learning	Chapter 2: The Development of Cognition and Language (Entire chapter) Chapter 3: Personal, Social, and Moral Development • Bronfenbrenner's bioecological theory of development (pp. 62–66) • Social development (pp. 75–79) Chapter 4: Learner Diversity • Culture and classrooms (pp. 97–101) • Linguistic diversity (pp. 101–107) • How SES influences learning (pp. 112–113) Chapter 7: Cognitive Views of Learning • Exploring diversity: The impact of diversity on cognition (p. 216) Chapter 8: Constructing Knowledge • Exploring diversity: The impact of diversity on knowledge construction (p. 237)

C. Student Motivation and the Learning Environment	
1. Theoretical foundations of human motivation and behavior	Chapter 10: Theories of Motivation • Behaviorist views of motivation (p. 286) • Cognitive and social cognitive views of motivation (p. 287) • Sociocultural views of motivation (p. 288) • Humanistic views of motivation (p. 288)
2. How knowledge of human motivation and behavior should influence strategies for organizing and supporting individual and group work in the classroom	Chapter 10: Theories of Motivation • Theory to practice: Capitalizing on learners' needs to increase motivation to learn (p. 295) • Theory to practice: Capitalizing on students' beliefs, goals, and interests to increase motivation to learn (p. 312) • Developmentally appropriate practice: Motivation to learn at different ages (p. 313) Chapter 11: Motivation in the Classroom • Class structure: Creating a mastery-focused environment (pp. 320–322) • Self-regulated learners: Developing student responsibility (pp. 322–325) • Theory to practice: Personal qualities that increase motivation to learn (p. 330) • Climate variables: Creating a motivating environment (pp. 332–336) • Instructional variables: Developing interest in learning activities (pp. 336–347) • Theory to practice: Capitalizing on the climate and instructional variables to increase student motivation to learn (p. 342)
3. Factors and situations that are likely to promote or diminish students' motivation to learn, and how to help students become self-motivated	Chapter 3: Personal, Social, and Moral Development • Exploring diversity: Ethnic identity and pride (p. 73) Chapter 6: Behaviorism and Social Cognitive Theory • Self-regulation (pp. 185–186) Chapter 10: Theories of Motivation • Theory to practice: Capitalizing on learners' needs to increase motivation to learn (p. 295) • Theory to practice: Capitalizing on students' beliefs, goals, and interests to increase motivation to learn (p. 312) Chapter 11: Motivation in the Classroom • Self-regulated learners: Developing student responsibility (pp. 322–325) • Climate variables: Creating a motivating environment (pp. 332–336) • Instructional variables: Developing interest in learning activities (pp. 336–347) • Exploring diversity: Motivation to learn in urban classrooms (pp. 343–347) Chapter 13: Creating Productive Learning Environments: Principles and Models of Instruction • Focus: Attracting and maintaining attention (p. 402)
4. Principles of effective classroom management and strategies to promote positive relationships, cooperation, and purposeful learning	Chapter 11: Motivation in the Classroom • Class structure: Creating a mastery-focused environment (pp. 320–322) • Order and safety: Classrooms as secure places to learn (pp. 332–333) Chapter 12: Creating Productive Learning Environments: Classroom Management (Entire chapter) Chapter 13: Creating Productive Learning Environments: Principles and Models of Instruction • Implementing instruction: Essential teaching skills (pp. 399–409)

II. Instruction and Assessment (approximately 33% of total test)	
A. Instructional Strategies	
1. Major cognitive processes associated with student learning	Chapter 2: The Development of Cognition and Language • Theory to practice: Applying Piaget's work in your classroom (p. 48) • Theory to practice: Applying Vygotsky's work in your classroom (p. 50) Chapter 6: Behaviorism and Social Cognitive Theory • Social cognitive theory (pp. 179–190) Chapter 7: Cognitive Views of Learning (Entire chapter) Chapter 8: Constructing Knowledge (Entire chapter) Chapter 9: Complex Cognitive Processes • Problem solving (pp. 258–267) • The strategic learner (pp. 267–275) • Critical thinking (pp. 271–273)
2. Major categories, advantages, and appropriate uses of instructional strategies	Chapter 7: Cognitive Views of Learning • Theory to practice: Applying an understanding of the human memory model in your classroom (p. 220) Chapter 8: Constructing Knowledge • Theory to practice: Applying constructivist learning theory in your classroom (p. 225) Chapter 9: Complex Cognitive Processes • Theory to practice: Helping students become strategic learners (p. 273) Chapter 13: Creating Productive Learning Environments: Principles and Models of Instruction • Implementing instruction: Essential teaching skills (pp. 399–409) • Models of instruction (pp. 409–424)
3. Principles, techniques, and methods associated with major instructional strategies	Chapter 13: Creating Productive Learning Environments: Principles and Models of Instruction • Direct instruction (pp. 408–413) • Lecture discussion (pp. 413–417) • Guided discovery (pp. 417–419) • Cooperative learning (pp. 419–424)
4. Methods for enhancing student learning through the use of a variety of resources and materials	Chapter 2: The Development of Cognition and Language • Theory to practice: Applying Piaget's work in your classroom (p. 48) • Theory to practice: Applying Vygotsky's work in your classroom (p. 50) Chapter 7: Cognitive Views of Learning • Theory to practice: Applying an understanding of the human memory model in your classroom (p. 220) Chapter 8: Constructing Knowledge • Theory to practice: Applying constructivist learning theory in your classroom (p. 244) Chapter 9: Complex Cognitive Processes • Using technology to promote problem solving (pp. 265–266) • Theory to Practice: Helping learners develop their problem-solving abilities (p. 267) • Theory to practice: Helping students become strategic learners (p. 273) Chapter 13: Creating Productive Learning Environments: Principles and Models of Instruction • Implementing instruction: Essential teaching skills (pp. 399–409) • Direct instruction (pp. 409–413) • Lecture discussion (pp. 413–417) • Guided discovery (pp. 417–419) • Cooperative learning (pp. 419–424)

B. Planning Instruction	
1. Techniques for planning instruction, including addressing curriculum goals, selecting content topics, incorporating learning theory, subject matter, curriculum development, and student development and interests	Chapter 13: Creating Productive Learning Environments: Principles and Models of Instruction • Selecting topics (pp. 390–391) • Preparing learning objectives (pp. 391–393) • Preparing and organizing learning activities (pp. 393–394) • Planning for assessment (p. 394) • Instructional alignment (pp. 394–395) • Planning in a standards-based environment (pp. 395–399)
2. Techniques for creating effective bridges between curriculum goals and students' experiences	Chapter 6: Behaviorism and Social Cognitive Theory • Modeling (pp. 181–182) Chapter 7: Cognitive Views of Learning • Imagery (p. 210) • Organization (pp. 210–211) • Schema activation (p. 212) • Elaboration (p. 212) Chapter 8: Constructing Knowledge • The origin of misconceptions (p. 236) • Teaching for conceptual change (pp. 236–237) Chapter 9: Complex Cognitive Processes • Theory to practice: Helping students develop their problem-solving abilities (p. 266) • Theory to practice: Helping students become strategic learners (p. 273) Chapter 13: Creating Productive Learning Environments: Principles and Models of Instruction • Guided practice (p. 412) • Independent practice (p. 412) • Homework (pp. 412–413)
C. Assessment Strategies	
1. Types of assessments	Chapter 10: Theories of Motivation • Assessment and learning: The role of assessment in self-determination (pp. 293–294) Chapter 11: Motivation in the Classroom • Assessment and learning: Using feedback to increase interest and self-efficacy (p. 346) Chapter 13: Creating Productive Learning Environments: Principles and Models of Instruction • Assessment and learning: Using assessment as a learning tool (pp. 424–425) Chapter 14: Assessing Classroom Learning • Informal assessment (pp. 437–440) • Paper-and-pencil items (pp. 441–446) • Performance assessments (pp. 446–449) • Portfolio assessment: Involving students in the assessment process (pp. 449–451) Chapter 15: Assessment Through Standardized Testing • Types of standardized tests (pp. 475–478)
2. Characteristics of assessments	Chapter 14: Assessing Classroom Learning • Validity: Making appropriate assessment decisions (pp. 435–436) • Reliability: Consistency in assessment (pp. 436–437) • Paper-and-pencil items (pp. 441–446) • Performance assessments (pp. 446–449) • Portfolio assessment: Involving students in the assessment process (pp. 449–451) Chapter 15: Assessment Through Standardized Testing • Evaluating standardized tests: Validity revisited (pp. 478–479)

3. Scoring assessments	Chapter 14: Assessing Classroom Learning • Using rubrics (pp. 445–446) • Performance assessments (pp. 446–449) • Portfolio assessment: Involving students in alternative assessment (pp. 449–451) • Analyzing results (pp. 457–459) Chapter 15: Assessment Through Standardized Testing • Understanding and interpreting standardized test scores (pp. 479–486)
4. Uses of assessments	Chapter 13: Creating Productive Learning Environments: Principles and Models of Instruction • Planning for assessment (p. 394) • Assessment and learning: Using assessment as a learning tool (pp. 424–425) Chapter 14: Assessing Classroom Learning • Effective assessment practices (pp. 453–459) • Grading and reporting: The total assessment system (pp. 459–464) Chapter 15: Assessment Through Standardized Testing • Functions of standardized tests (pp. 473–475) • Interpreting standardized test results (pp. 482–486) • Standards-based education and accountability (pp. 486–487) • Diversity and standardized testing (pp. 489–494)
5. Understanding of measurement theory and assessment-related issues	Chapter 14: Assessing Classroom Learning • Assessment *for* student learning (pp. 434–435) • Commercially prepared test items (p. 446) • Planning for assessment (pp. 453–454) • Preparing students for assessments (pp. 454–456) • Administering assessments (p. 457) • Designing a grading system (pp. 460–462) • Assigning grades: Increasing learning and motivation (pp. 462–464) Chapter 15: Assessment Through Standardized Testing • Accountability issues in standardized testing (pp. 486–489) • Student diversity and assessment bias (pp. 489–490) • Standardized testing and English language learners (pp. 490–493)
6. Interpreting and communicating results of assessments	Chapter 14: Assessment of Classroom Learning • Designing a grading system (pp. 460–462) • Assigning grades: Increasing learning and motivation (pp. 462–464) Chapter 15: Assessment Through Standardized Testing • Understanding and interpreting standardized test scores (pp. 479–486) • Accountability issues in standardized testing (pp. 486–489) • Diversity and standardized testing (pp. 489–494)
III. Communication Techniques (approximately 11% of total test)	
A. Basic, Effective Verbal and Nonverbal Communication Techniques	
	Chapter 2: The Development of Cognition and Language • Language development (pp. 50–55) • Developmentally appropriate practice: Promoting cognitive and linguistic development with different-aged learners (p. 55) Chapter 3: Personal, Social, and Moral Development • Social development (pp. 75–79) Chapter 8: Constructing Knowledge • Social interaction facilitates learning (pp. 231–233) Chapter 12: Creating Productive Learning Environments: Classroom Management • Benefits of communication (p. 368) • Strategies for involving parents (pp. 368–371) • Verbal–nonverbal congruence (pp. 374–375) Chapter 13: Creating Productive Learning Environments: Principles and Models of Instruction • Communication (pp. 401–402)

B. Effect of Cultural and Gender Differences on Communications in the Classroom	
	Chapter 4: Learner Diversity • Culture and classrooms (pp. 97–101) • Languistic diversity (pp. 101–107) • Theory to practice: Teaching culturally and linguistically diverse students in your classroom (p. 106) • Gender differences in classroom behavior (p. 109) • Gender stereotypes and perceptions (pp. 109–111) Chapter 11: Motivation in the Classroom • Learning contexts: Increasing motivation in urban classrooms (pp. 343–346) Chapter 13: Creating Productive Learning Environments: Principles and Models of Instruction • Exploring diversity: Using cooperative learning as a tool for capitalizing on diversity in your classroom (p. 420)
C. Types of Communications and Interactions That Can Stimulate Discussion in Different Ways for Particular Purposes	
	Chapter 2: The Development of Cognition and Language • Theory to practice: Applying Piaget's work in your classroom (p. 48) • Theory to practice: Applying Vygotsky's work in your classroom (p. 50) Chapter 7: Cognitive Views of Learning • Theory to practice: Applying an understanding of the human memory model in your classroom (p. 220) Chapter 8: Constructing Knowledge • Theory to practice: Applying constructivist learning theory in your classroom (p. 244) Chapter 9: Complex Cognitive Processes • Creativity in problem solving (pp. 263–264) • Theory to practice: Helping students develop their problem-solving abilities (p. 266) Chapter 11: Motivation in the Classroom • Instructional variables: Developing interest in learning activities (pp. 336–347) Chapter 12: Creating Productive Learning Environments: Classroom Management • Creating a community of caring and trust (p. 354) Chapter 13: Creating Productive Learning Environments: Principles and Models of Instruction • Questioning (pp. 404–406) • Direct instruction (pp. 409–413) • Lecture and lecture–discussion (pp. 413–417) • Guided discovery (pp. 417–419) • Cooperative learning (pp. 419–424)
IV. Teacher Professionalism (Profession and Community) (approximately 22% of total test)	
A. The Reflective Practitioner	
1. Types of resources available for professional development and learning	Chapter 1: Educational Psychology: Developing a Professional Knowledge Base • Educational psychology and becoming a professional (pp. 4–6) • Professional knowledge and learning to teach (pp. 6–13)
2. Ability to read, understand, and apply articles and books about current research, views, ideas, and debates regarding best teaching practices	Chapter 1: Educational Psychology: Developing a Professional Knowledge Base • Educational psychology and becoming a professional (pp. 4–6) • Professional knowledge and learning to teach (pp. 6–13) • The role of research in acquiring professional knowledge (pp. 14–22)
3. Ongoing personal reflection on teaching and learning practices as a basis for making professional decisions	Chapter 1: Educational Psychology: Developing a Professional Knowledge Base • Characteristics of professionalism (pp. 4–6) • Professional knowledge and learning to teach (pp. 6–13) • Theory to practice: Conducting research in classrooms (p. 21)

B. The Larger Community	
1. The role of the school as a resource to the larger community	Chapter 3: Personal, Social, and Moral Development • Theory to practice: Promoting identity and self-concept development in the classroom (p. 72) • Theory to practice: Promoting social development in the classroom (p. 77) Chapter 12: Creating Productive Learning Environments: Classroom Management • Communicating effectively with parents (pp. 367–371)
2. Factors in the students' environment outside of school (family circumstances, community environments, health and economic conditions) that may influence students' life and learning	Chapter 3: Personal, Social, and Moral Development • Bronfenbrenner's bioecological theory of development (pp. 62–66) Chapter 4: Learner Diversity • Culture and classrooms (pp. 97–101) • How SES influences learning (pp. 112–113)
3. Develop and utilize active partnerships among teachers, parents/guardians, and leaders in the community to support the educational process	Chapter 3: Personal, Social, and Moral Development • Violence and aggression (pp. 76–79) Chapter 12: Creating Productive Learning Environments: Classroom Management • Benefits of communication (p. 368) • Strategies for involving parents (pp. 368–371)
4. Major laws related to students' rights and teacher responsibilities	Chapter 5: Learners with Exceptionalities • Individuals with Disabilities Education Act (IDEA) (pp. 133–137) • Amendments to the Individuals with Disabilities Education Act (p. 137) Chapter 12: Creating Productive Learning Environments: Classroom Management • Responding to aggression against peers (p. 382) • Responding to bullying (p. 383) • Responding to defiant students (p. 383)

glossary

Ability grouping. The process of placing students of similar abilities into groups and attempting to match instruction to the needs of these groups.
Academic language proficiency. A level of proficiency in English that allows students to handle demanding learning tasks with abstract concepts.
Acceleration. Programs for students who are gifted and talented that keep the curriculum the same but allow students to move through it more quickly.
Accommodation. A form of adaptation during which individuals modify an existing scheme and create a new one in response to experience.
Accountability. The process of requiring learners to demonstrate that they possess specified knowledge and skills as demonstrated by standardized measures, and making teachers responsible for student performance.
Accountability. The process of requiring students to demonstrate that they have met specified standards and holding teachers responsible for students' performance.
Achievement tests. Standardized tests designed to assess how much students have learned in specified content areas.
Action research. A form of applied research designed to answer a specific school- or classroom-related question.
Adaptation. The process of adjusting schemes and experiences to each other to maintain equilibrium.
Adaptive behavior. A person's ability to perform the functions of everyday living.
Adaptive fit. The degree to which a school environment accommodates the student's needs and the degree to which a student can meet the requirements of a particular school setting.
Algorithm. A specific set of steps for solving a problem.
Alternative assessments. Assessment measures that include projects and performance assessment.
Analogies. Descriptions of relationships between ideas that are similar in some but not all respects.
Antecedents. Stimuli that precede and induce behaviors.
Anxiety. A general uneasiness and feeling of tension, relating to a situation with an uncertain outcome.
Applied behavior analysis (ABA). The process of systematically applying the principles of behaviorism to change student behavior.
Aptitude tests. Standardized tests designed to predict the potential for future learning and measure general abilities developed over long periods of time.
Assertive discipline. An approach to classroom management that promotes a clear and firm response style with students.
Assessment bias. A form of discrimination that occurs when a test or other assessment instrument unfairly penalizes a group of students because of their gender, ethnicity, race, or socioeconomic status.
Assessment *for* learning. Assessment that is a process designed to support and increase learning.
Assimilation. A form of adaptation during which individuals incorporate an experience in the environment into an existing scheme.
Attainment value. The importance that an individual attaches to doing well on a task.
Attention. The process of consciously focusing on a stimulus.
Attention-deficit/hyperactivity disorder (ADHD). A learning problem characterized by difficulties in maintaining attention.
Attribution theory. A cognitive theory of motivation that attempts to systematically describe learners' beliefs about the causes of their successes and failures and how these beliefs influence motivation to learn.
Attribution. A belief about the cause of performance.
Attributional statements Comments teachers make about the causes of students' performance.
Autism spectrum disorder. A description of a cluster of disorders characterized by impaired social relationships and skills and often associated with highly unusual behavior.
Automaticity. The ability to perform mental operations with little awareness or conscious effort.
Autonomous morality. A stage of moral development characterized by the belief that fairness and justice is the reciprocal process of treating others as they would want to be treated.
Autonomy. Independence and an individual's ability to alter the environment when necessary.
Axons. Components of neurons that transmit outgoing messages to other neurons.
Basic interpersonal communication skills. A level of proficiency in English that allows students to interact conversationally with their peers.
Behavior disorders. Serious and persistent age-inappropriate behaviors that result in social conflict, personal unhappiness, and often school failure.
Behaviorism. A theory that explains learning in terms of observable behaviors and how they're influenced by stimuli from the environment.
Belief preservation. The tendency to make evidence subservient to belief, rather than the other way around.
Belief. A cognitive idea we accept as true without necessarily having definitive evidence to support it.
Bidialecticism. The ability to switch back and forth between a dialect and standard English.
Bilingualism. The ability to speak, read, and write in two languages.
Bipolar disorder. A condition characterized by alternative episodes of depressive and manic states.
Bully. A student who frequently threatens, harasses, or causes injury to peers.

Caring. A teacher's empathy and investment in the protection and development of young people.
Case studies (cases). Authentic stories of teaching and learning events in classrooms.
Central executive. A supervisory component of working memory that controls the flow of information to and from the other components.
Centration (centering). The tendency to focus on the most perceptually obvious aspect of an object or event, neglecting other important aspects.
Characteristics. A concept's defining elements.
Checklists. Written descriptions of dimensions that must be present in an acceptable performance of an activity.
Chronosystem. The final level in bioecological theory that includes temporal, or time-dependent, influences on development.
Chunking. The process of mentally combining separate items into larger, more meaningful units.
Classical conditioning. A type of learning that occurs when individuals learn to produce involuntary emotional or physiological

responses similar to instinctive or reflexive responses.

Classification. The process of grouping objects on the basis of common characteristics.

Classroom assessment. All the processes involved in making decisions about students' learning progress.

Classroom management. Actions teachers take to create an environment that supports and facilitates both academic and social-emotional learning.

Clique. A small group of peers who act as friends, providing support and temporary identities.

Closure. A form of review occurring at the end of a lesson.

Cognitive apprenticeship. The process of having a less-skilled learner work at the side of an expert to develop cognitive skills.

Cognitive behavior modification. A procedure that combines behavioral and cognitive learning principles to promote behavioral change in students through self-talk and self-instruction.

Cognitive constructivism. A constructivist view that focuses on individual, internal constructions of knowledge.

Cognitive development. Changes in our thinking that occur as a result of learning, maturation, and experience.

Cognitive domain. The area of learning that focuses on memory and higher cognitive processes such as applying and analyzing.

Cognitive learning theories. Theories that explain learning in terms of changes in the mental structures and processes involved in acquiring, organizing, and using knowledge.

Cognitive load. The amount of mental activity imposed on working memory.

Cognitive modeling. The process of performing a demonstration combined with verbalizing the thinking behind the actions.

Cognitive tools. The concepts and symbols (numbers and language) together with the real tools that allow people to think, solve problems, and function in a culture.

Collective efficacy. Beliefs that the faculty as a whole can have a positive effect on students.

Collective self-esteem. Individuals' perceptions of the relative worth of the groups to which they belong.

Colorblindness. The belief that students' culture of ethnicity should not be a consideration in teaching.

Communication disorders. Exceptionalities that interfere with students' abilities to receive and understand information from others and express their own ideas.

Community of caring and trust. A classroom environment where learners feel physically and emotionally safe and their needs for belonging and relatedness are met.

Community of learners. A learning environment in which the teacher and all the students work together to help everyone achieve.

Competence. The ability to function effectively in the environment.

Completion. A paper-and-pencil format that includes a question or an incomplete statement that requires the learner to supply appropriate words, numbers, or symbols.

Comprehension monitoring. The process of checking to see if we understand what we have read or heard.

Concept mapping. A learning strategy in which learners construct visual relationships among concepts.

Concept. A mental construct or representation of a category that allows one to identify examples and nonexamples of the category.

Conditional knowledge. Knowledge of where and when to use declarative and procedural knowledge.

Conditioned response. A learned physiological or emotional response that is similar to the unconditioned response.

Conditioned stimulus. A formerly neutral stimulus that becomes associated with the unconditioned stimulus.

Connected discourse. Instruction that is thematic and leads to a point.

Consequence. Event (stimulus) that occurs following a behavior and that influences the probability of the behaviors recurring.

Conservation. The idea that the "amount" of some substance stays the same regardless of its shape or the number of pieces into which it is divided.

Construct validity. An indicator of the logical connection between a test and what it is designed to measure.

Constructivism. A theory of learning suggesting that learners create their own knowledge of the topics they study rather than receiving that knowledge as transmitted to them by some other source.

Content validity. A test's ability to accurately sample the content taught and measure the extent to which learners understand it.

Continuous reinforcement schedule. A reinforcement schedule where every desired behavior is reinforced.

Conventional morality. A moral orientation linked to uncritical acceptance of society's conventions about right and wrong.

Cooperative learning. A set of instructional models in which students work in mixed-ability groups to reach specific learning and social interaction objectives.

Correlation. A relationship, either positive or negative, between two or more variables.

Correlational research. The process of looking for relationships between variables that enables researchers to predict changes in one variable on the basis of changes in another without implying a cause-effect relationship between them.

Cost. A consideration of what an individual must give up to engage in the task.

Creativity. The ability to produce original work or solutions to problems that are productive.

Crisis. A psychosocial challenge that presents opportunities for development.

Criterion-referenced grading. A grading system in which teachers make assessment decisions according to a predetermined standard.

Criterion-referenced standardized tests. Standardized tests that compare performance against a set performance standard.

Critical thinking. An individual's ability and inclination to make and assess conclusions based on evidence.

Crystallized intelligence. Culture-specific mental ability, heavily dependent on experience and schooling.

Cultural mismatch. A cultural clash that occurs when a child's home culture and the culture of the school create conflicting expectations for a student's behavior.

Culturally responsive classroom management. Classroom management that combines teachers' awareness of possible personal biases with cultural knowledge.

Culture. The knowledge, attitudes, values, and customs that characterize a social group.

Curriculum-based assessment. Measurement of learners' performance in specific areas of the curriculum.

Deaf. A hearing impairment that requires the use of other senses, usually sight, to communicate.

Declarative knowledge. Knowledge of facts, definitions, procedures, and rules.

Deficiency needs. Needs that, if unfulfilled, energize people to meet them.

Dendrites. Branchlike structures in neurons that extend from the cell body and receive messages from other neurons.

Descriptive research. Research that uses tests, surveys, interviews, and observations to describe the status or characteristics of a situation or phenomenon.

Desist. A verbal or nonverbal communication a teacher uses to stop a behavior.

Desists. Verbal or nonverbal communications that teachers use to stop a behavior.

Development. The changes that occur in human beings as we grow from infancy to adulthood.

Diagnostic assessment. A form of assessment designed to provide teachers with information about students' prior knowledge and misconceptions before beginning a learning activity.
Diagnostic tests. Standardized tests designed to provide a detailed description of learners' strengths and weaknesses in specific skill areas.
Dialect. A variation of standard English that is associated with a particular regional or social group and is distinct in vocabulary, grammar, or pronunciation.
Direct instruction. An instructional model designed to teach well-defined knowledge and skills needed for later learning.
Disabilities. Functional limitations or an inability to perform a certain act.
Discipline. Teachers' responses to student misbehavior.
Discrepancy model of identification. One method of identifying students with learning disabilities that focuses on differences between achievement and intelligence tests or subtests within either.
Discrimination. The process that occurs when a person gives different responses to similar but not identical stimuli.
Disorder. A general malfunction of mental, physical, or psychological processes.
Distracters. Incorrect choices in multiple-choice items used to identify common student misconceptions about the topic being assessed.
Divergent thinking. The ability to generate a variety of original answers to questions or problems.
Drawing analogies. A heuristic that is used to solve unfamiliar problems by comparing them with those already solved.
Dual-coding theory. A theory suggesting that long-term memory contains two distinct memory systems: one for verbal information and one that stores images.
Due process. The guarantee of parents' rights to be involved in identifying and placing their children in special programs, to access school records, and to obtain an independent evaluation if they're not satisfied with the school's evaluation.

Educational psychology. The academic discipline that focuses on human teaching and learning.
Effective teaching. Teaching that maximizes student learning.
Egocentrism. The tendency to believe that other people look at the world as the individual does.
Elaboration. An encoding strategy that increases the meaningfulness of new information by connecting it to existing knowledge.
Elaborative questioning. The process of drawing inferences, identifying examples, and forming relationships in the material being studied.
Emotional intelligence. The ability to understand emotions in ourselves and others.
Empathy. The ability to experience the same emotion someone else is feeling.
Emphasis. Verbal and vocal cues that alert students to important information in a lesson.
Encoding. The process of representing information in long-term memory.
English Language Learners. Students for whom English is not their first or home language.
Enrichment. Programs for students who are gifted and talented that provide alternate instruction.
Entity view of intelligence. The belief that intelligence is essentially fixed and stable over time.
Episodic memory. Memory for personal experiences.
Equilibrium. A cognitive state in which we can explain new experiences by using existing understanding.
Equitable distribution. The process of calling on all the students in a class as equally as possible.
ESL pullout programs. Programs for English language learner (ELL) students who receive most of their instruction in regular classrooms but are also pulled out for extra help.
Essay. A paper-and-pencil format that requires students to make extended written responses to questions or problems.
Essential teaching skills. Basic abilities that all teachers, including those in their first year of teaching, should possess to maximize student learning.
Ethnic identity. An awareness of ethnic group membership and a commitment to the attitudes, values, and behaviors of that group.
Ethnicity. A person's ancestry and the way individuals identify with the nation from which they or their ancestors came.
Exemplars. In concept-learning theory, the most highly typical examples of a concept.
Exosystem. In bioecological theory, societal influences that affect both the micro- and mesosystems.
Expectancy [multi] value theory. A theory that explains learner motivation by saying that learners will be motivated to engage in a task to the extent that they *expect* to succeed on the task *times* the value they place on the success.
Expectation. A belief about a future outcome.
Experimental research. Research that systematically manipulates variables in attempts to determine cause and effect.
Experts. Individuals who are highly skilled or knowledgeable in a given domain.
External morality. A stage of moral development in which individuals view rules as fixed and permanent and enforced by authority figures.
Extinction (classical conditioning). The disappearance of a conditioned response as the result of the conditioned stimulus occurring repeatedly in the absence of the unconditioned stimulus.
Extinction (operant conditioning). The disappearance of a behavior as a result of nonreinforcement.
Extrinsic motivation. Motivation to engage in an activity as a means to an end.

Feedback. Information learners receive about the accuracy or appropriateness of their verbal responses and written work.
Fluid intelligence. The flexible, culture-free mental ability to adapt to new situations.
Forgetting. The loss of, or inability to retrieve, information from long-term memory.
Formal assessment. The process of systematically gathering the same kind of information from every student.
Formative assessment. The process of using both informal and formal assessments to provide students with feedback about learning progress, but not using the assessment information to make decisions about grading.
Frequency distribution. A distribution of test scores that shows a count of the number of people who obtained each score.
Functional analysis. A strategy used to identify antecedents and consequences that control a behavior.

Gender-role identity. Beliefs about appropriate characteristics and behaviors of the two sexes.
General pedagogical knowledge. An understanding of essential principles of instruction and classroom management that transcends individual topics or subject matter areas.
General transfer. The ability to apply knowledge or skills learned in one context in a variety of different contexts.
Generalization. The process that occurs when stimuli similar, but not identical, to a conditioned stimulus elicit the conditioned response by themselves.
Gifts and talents. Abilities at the upper end of the continuum that require additional support to reach full potential.
Goal. An outcome an individual hopes to attain.
Grade-equivalent score. A score that is determined by comparing an individual's

score on a standardized test to the scores of students in a particular age group.
Growth needs. Needs in intellectual achievement and aesthetic appreciation that increase as people have experiences with them.
Guided discovery. A model of instruction that involves teachers' scaffolding students' construction of concepts and the relationships among them.
Guided notes. Teacher-prepared handouts that "guide" students with cues and space available for writing key ideas and relationships.
Guilt. The uncomfortable feeling people get when they know they've caused distress for someone else.

Handicap. A condition imposed on a person's functioning that restricts the individual's abilities.
Heuristics. General, widely applicable problem-solving strategies.
High-quality examples. Examples that include all the information learners need to understand a topic.
High-stakes tests. Standardized tests that educators use to make important decisions that affect students, teachers, schools, and school districts.
Hostile attributional bias. A tendency to view others' behaviors as hostile or aggressive.

Identity. Individuals' sense of self, what their existence means, and what they want in life.
Ill-defined problem. A problem that has more than one acceptable solution, an ambiguous goal, and no generally agreed-upon strategy for reaching a solution.
Imagery. The process of forming mental pictures of an idea.
I-message. A nonaccusatory communication that addresses a behavior, describes the effects on the sender, and the feelings it generates in the sender.
Immersion programs. English language programs that place ELLs in regular classrooms without additional assistance to help them learn both English and academic content at the same time.
Inclusion. A comprehensive approach to educating students with exceptionalities that advocates a total, systematic, and coordinated web of services.
Incremental view of intelligence. The belief that intelligence is not stable and can be increased with effort.
Individualized education program (IEP). An individually prescribed instructional plan devised by special education and general education teachers, resource professionals, and parents (and sometimes the student).
Informal assessment. The process of gathering incidental information about learning progress or other aspects of students' behavior, and making decisions based on that information.
Information processing theory. A theory that describes how information enters our memory system, is organized, and finally stored.
Information processing theory. A theory that explains development in terms of the increasingly sophisticated strategies that learners use to complete cognitive tasks, such as remembering and solving problems.
Inhibition. A self-imposed restriction on one's behavior.
Instructional alignment. The match between learning objectives, learning activities, and assessments.
Intellectual disability. A disability characterized by significant limitations both in intellectual functioning and in adaptive behavior.
Intelligence tests. Standardized tests designed to measure an individual's capacity to acquire and use knowledge, to solve problems, and to accomplish new tasks.
Intelligence. The ability to acquire and use knowledge, solve problems and reason in the abstract, and adapt to new situations in the environment.
Interference. The loss of information because something learned either before or after detracts from understanding.
Intermittent reinforcement schedule. A reinforcement schedule where some, but not all, behaviors are reinforced.
Internalization. The process through which learners incorporate external, society-based activities into internal cognitive processes.
Interpersonal harmony. A stage of moral reasoning in which conclusions are based on loyalty, living up to the expectations of others, and social conventions.
Interval schedule. An intermittent reinforcement schedule in which behaviors are reinforced after a certain predictable interval (fixed) or unpredictable interval of time has passed (variable).
Intrinsic motivation. Motivation to be involved in an activity for its own sake.
Introductory focus. A lesson beginning that attracts attention and provides a conceptual framework for the lesson.
Involvement. The extent to which students are actively participating in a learning activity.

Joplin plan. Homogeneous grouping in reading, combined with heterogeneous grouping in other areas.

Language acquisition device (LAD). A genetically controlled set of processing skills that enables children to understand and use the rules governing language.
Language disorders *(receptive disorders)*. Problems with understanding language or using language to express ideas.
Law and order. A stage of moral reasoning in which conclusions are based on following laws and rules for their own sake.
Learned helplessness. The debilitating belief that one is incapable of accomplishing tasks and has little control of the environment.
Learner diversity. The group and individual differences that we see in our students.
Learners with exceptionalities. Students who need special help and resources to reach their full potential.
Learning (behaviorism). A relatively enduring change in observable behavior that occurs as a result of experience.
Learning (cognitive). A change in mental processes that creates the capacity to demonstrate different behaviors.
Learning disabilities. Difficulty in acquiring and using reading, writing, reasoning, listening, or mathematical abilities.
Learning objective. A statement that specifies what students should know or be able to do with respect to a topic or course of study.
Learning styles. Students' personal approaches to learning, problem solving, and processing information.
Least restrictive environment (LRE). A policy that places students in as typical an educational setting as possible while still meeting the students' special needs.
Lecture-discussion. An instructional model designed to help students acquire organized bodies of knowledge.
Logical consequences. Consequences that are conceptually related to the misbehavior.
Long-term memory. The permanent information store in the model of human memory.

Macrosystem. Bronfenbrenner's fourth level of influences on developing children, which includes cultural influences on development.
Mainstreaming. The practice of moving students with exceptionalities from segregated settings into general education classrooms.
Maintenance ELL programs. Programs for English language learner (ELL) students that build on students' native languages by teaching in both English and the native languages.
Maintenance rehearsal. The process of repeating information over and over, either out loud or silently, without altering its form.
Market exchange. A stage of moral reasoning in which conclusions are based on an act of reciprocity on someone else's part.

Mastery goal. A goal that focuses on accomplishing a task, improvement, and increased understanding. Sometimes called a *learning goal.*
Mastery-focused environment. A classroom environment that emphasizes effort, continuous improvement, and understanding.
Matching format. A paper-and-pencil format that requires learners to classify a series of examples using the same alternatives.
Maturation. Genetically controlled, age-related changes in individuals.
Mean. The average score in the distribution of a group of scores.
Meaningfulness. The extent to which information in long-term memory is interconnected with other information.
Means-ends analysis. A heuristic that breaks a problem into subgoals and works successively on each.
Measures of central tendency. Quantitative descriptions of a group's performance as a whole.
Median. The middle score in the distribution of a group of scores.
Memory stores. Repositories that hold information, in some cases in a raw state, and in others in organized, meaningful form.
Mesosystem. In Bronfenbrenner's bioecological theory, the interactions and connections between the different elements of children's immediate settings.
Meta-attention. Knowledge of and control over the ability to pay attention.
Metacognition. Awareness of, and control over, our cognitive processes.
Metacognition. Our awareness of and our control over our cognitive processes.
Metamemory. Knowledge of and control over our memory strategies.
Microsystem. In Bronfenbrenner's bioecological theory, the people and activities in a child's immediate surroundings.
Misconception. A belief that is inconsistent with evidence or commonly accepted explanations.
Mnemonic devices. Memory strategies that create associations that don't exist naturally in the content.
Mode. The most frequent score in the distribution of a group of scores.
Modeling. A general term that refers to behavioral, cognitive, and affective changes deriving from observing one or more models.
Models of instruction. Prescriptive approaches to teaching designed to help students acquire a deep understanding of specific forms of knowledge.
Moral development. The development of prosocial behaviors and traits such as honesty, fairness, and respect for others.
Moral dilemma. An ambiguous, conflicting situation that requires a person to make a moral decision.
Motivation to learn. Students' tendencies to find academic activities meaningful and worthwhile and to try to get the intended learning benefits from them.
Motivation. A process whereby goal-directed activity is instigated and sustained.
Multiple-choice. A paper-and-pencil format that consists of a question or statement, called a *stem,* and a series of answer choices called *distracters.*

National norms. Scores on standardized tests earned by representative groups of students from around the nation to which an individual's score is compared.
Nativist theory. A theory of language development that focuses on heredity and asserts that all humans are genetically "wired" to learn language.
Nature view of intelligence. The assertion that intelligence is essentially determined by genetics.
Need for approval. The desire to be accepted and judged positively by others.
Need. An internal force or drive to attain a certain state or object
Negative reinforcement. The process of increasing behavior by avoiding or removing an aversive stimulus.
Negligence. The failure to exercise sufficient care in protecting students from injury.
Neo-Piagetian theory. A theory of cognitive development that accepts Piaget's stages but explains developmental changes in terms of information processing efficiency and capacity.
Network. A concept map illustrating nonhierarchical relationships.
Neurons. Nerve cells composed of cell bodies, dendrites, and axons, which make up the learning capability of the brain.
Neutral stimulus. An object or event that doesn't initially impact behavior one way or the other.
Normal distribution. A distribution of scores in which the mean, median, and mode are equal and the scores distribute themselves symmetrically in a bell-shaped curve.
Norming group. The representative group of individuals whose standardized test scores are compiled for the purpose of national comparisons.
Norm-referenced grading. A grading system in which teachers base assessment decisions about an individual's work on comparisons with the work of peers.
Norm-referenced standardized tests. Standardized tests that compare (reference) a student's performance with the performance of others.
Nurture view of intelligence. The assertion that emphasizes the influence of the environment on intelligence.

Object permanence. The understanding that objects exist separate from the self.
Open-ended questions. Questions for which a variety of answers are acceptable.
Operant conditioning. A form of learning in which an observable response changes in frequency or duration as a result of a consequence.
Order and safety. A climate variable that creates a predictable learning environment and supports learner autonomy together with a sense of physical and emotional security.
Organization. A professional skill that includes preparing materials in advance, starting classes and activities on time, making transitions quickly and smoothly, and creating well-established routines.
Organization. An encoding strategy that involves the clustering of related items of content into categories that illustrate relationships.
Organization. The process of creating and using schemes to make sense of experiences.
Organized bodies of knowledge. Topics that connect facts, concepts, and principles, and make the relationships among them explicit.
Overgeneralization. A language pattern that occurs when a child uses a word to refer to a broader class of objects than is appropriate.
Overlapping. The ability to intervene without disrupting the flow of a lesson.

Parenting style. General patterns of interacting with and disciplining children.
Partial hearing impairment. An impairment that allows a student to use a hearing aid and to hear well enough to be taught through auditory channels.
Pedagogical content knowledge. An understanding of how to represent topics in ways that make them understandable to learners, as well as an understanding of what makes specific topics easy or hard to learn.
People-first language. Language in which a student's disability is identified after the student is named.
Percentile bands. Ranges of percentile scores on standardized tests.
Percentile, or percentile rank (PR). The percentage of students in the norming sample who scored at or below a particular raw score.
Perception. The process people use to find meaning in stimuli.
Performance assessments. Direct examinations of student performance on tasks that are relevant to life outside of school.

Performance goal. A goal that focuses on a learner's ability and competence in comparison to others.
Performance-approach goal. A goal that emphasizes looking competent and receiving favorable judgments from others.
Performance-avoidance goal. A goal that focuses on avoiding looking incompetent and being judged unfavorably.
Performance-focused environment. A classroom environment that emphasizes high grades, public displays of ability, and performance compared to others.
Personal development. Age-related changes in personality and the ways that individuals react to their environment.
Personal interest. A person's ongoing affinity, attraction, or liking for a domain, subject area, topic, or activity.
Personal teaching efficacy. A teacher's belief that he or she can cause all students to learn regardless of their prior knowledge or ability.
Personal, social, and emotional development. Changes in our personality, the ways we interact with others, and our ability to manage our feelings.
Personalization. The process of using intellectually and/or emotionally relevant examples to illustrate a topic
Perspective taking. The ability to understand the thoughts and feelings of others.
Phonological loop. A short-term storage system for words and sounds in working memory.
Physical development. Changes in the size, shape, and functioning of our bodies.
Portfolio assessment. The process of selecting collections of student work that both students and teachers evaluate using preset criteria.
Positive classroom climate. A classroom environment where the teacher and students work together as a community of learners, to help everyone achieve.
Positive reinforcement. The process of increasing the frequency or duration of a behavior as the result of *presenting* a reinforcer.
Postconventional morality. A moral orientation that views moral issues in terms of abstract and self-developed principles of right and wrong.
Precise language. Teacher talk that omits vague terms from explanations and responses to students' questions.
Preconventional morality. An egocentric orientation lacking any internalized standards for right and wrong.
Predictive validity. The measure of a test's ability to gauge future performance.
Premack principle. The principle stating that a more-desired activity can serve as a positive reinforcer for a less-desired activity.
Presentation punishment. A decrease in behavior that occurs when a stimulus (punisher) is presented.
Private speech. Self-talk that guides thinking and action.
Proactive interference. The loss of new information because of the influence of prior learning.
Problem. A state that occurs when a problem solver has a goal but lacks an obvious way of achieving the goal.
Problem-based learning. A teaching strategy that uses problems as the focus for developing content, skills, and self-regulation.
Procedural knowledge. Knowledge of how to perform tasks.
Procedures. Guidelines for accomplishing recurring tasks, such as sharpening pencils and making transitions from one activity to another.
Productive learning environment. A classroom that is orderly and focused on learning.
Prompting. An additional question or statement teachers use to elicit an appropriate student response after a student fails to answer correctly.
Prototype. In concept-learning theory, the best representation of a category or class.
Punishers. Consequences that weaken behaviors or decrease the likelihood of the behaviors' recurring.
Punishment. The process of using punishers to decrease behavior.
Punishment-obedience. A stage of moral reasoning in which conclusions are based on the chances of getting caught and being punished.

Qualitative research. Research that attempts to describe a complex educational phenomenon in a holistic fashion using nonnumerical data, such as words and pictures.
Questioning frequency. The number of questions a teacher asks during a learning activity.

Random assignment. A process used to ensure that an individual has an equal likelihood of being assigned to either group within a study.
Range. The distance between the top and bottom score in a distribution of scores.
Rating scales. Written descriptions of the dimensions of an acceptable performance and scales of values on which each dimension is rated.
Ratio schedule. An intermittent reinforcement schedule where specific behaviors are reinforced, either predictably (fixed) or unpredictably (variable).
Raw score. The number of items an individual answered correctly on a standardized test or subtest.
Readiness tests. Standardized tests that assess the degree to which children are prepared for an academic or pre-academic program.
Real-world task (*authentic* task). A learning activity in which students practice thinking similar to that required in the real world.
Reciprocal causation. The interdependence of the environment, behavior, and personal factors in learning.
Reflective practice. The process of conducting a critical self-examination of one's teaching.
Reforms. Suggested changes in teaching and teacher preparation intended to increase student learning.
Reinforcement schedules. Different patterns in the frequency and predictability of reinforcers that have differential effects on behavior.
Reinforcement. The process of applying reinforcers to increase behavior.
Reinforcer. A consequence that increases the likelihood of a behavior recurring.
Relatedness. The feeling of being connected to others in one's social environment and feeling worthy of love and respect.
Reliability. The extent to which assessments are consistent and free from errors of measurement.
Removal punishment. A decrease in behavior that occurs when a stimulus is removed, or when an individual cannot receive positive reinforcement.
Research. The process of systematically gathering information in an attempt to answer professional questions.
Resilience. A learner characteristic that, despite adversity, raises the likelihood of success in school and later life.
Resistance cultures. Cultures with beliefs, values, and behaviors that reject the values of mainstream culture.
Response cost. The process of removing reinforcers already given.
Response to intervention model of identification. A method of identifying a learning disability that focuses on the specific classroom instructional adaptations that teachers use and their success.
Retrieval. The process of pulling information from long-term memory into working memory.
Retroactive interference. The loss of previously learned information because of the influence of new learning.
Reversibility. The ability to mentally trace the process of moving from an existing state back to a previous state.

Review. A summary that helps students link what they have already learned to what will follow in the next learning activity.
Rubric. A scoring scale that describes criteria for grading.
Rules. Descriptions of standards for acceptable behavior.

Satiation. The process of using a reinforcer so frequently that it loses its potency-its ability to strengthen behaviors.
Scaffolding. Assistance that helps children complete tasks they cannot complete independently.
Schema activation. An encoding strategy that involves activating relevant prior knowledge so that new knowledge can be connected to it.
Schemas. Cognitive constructs that organize information into meaningful systems on long-term memory.
Schemes. Mental operations that represent our constructed understanding of the world.
Scientifically based research. Research that emphasizes experimental research using classic techniques of the scientific method instead of descriptive or qualitative approaches.
Scripts. Schemas for events that guide behavior in particular situations.
Self-actualization. The need to reach our full potential and be all that we are capable of being.
Self-concept. A cognitive assessment of one's physical, social, and academic competence.
Self-determination. The motivational need to act on and control one's environment.
Self-efficacy. The belief that one is capable of accomplishing a specific task.
Self-esteem or self-worth. An emotional reaction to, or an evaluation of, the self.
Self-fulfilling prophecy. A phenomenon that occurs when a person's performance results from and confirms beliefs about his or her capabilities.
Self-regulation. The process of setting personal goals, combined with the motivation, thought processes, strategies, and behaviors that lead to reaching the goals.
Self-regulation. The process of setting personal goals, combined with the motivation, thought processes, strategies, and behaviors that lead to reaching the goals.
Self-worth. An emotional reaction to or an evaluation of the self.
Semantic memory. Memory for concepts, principles, and the relationships among them.
Semantics. The study of the meanings of words and word combinations.
Sensory focus. The result of stimuli that teachers use to maintain attention during learning activities.
Sensory memory. The memory store that briefly holds incoming stimuli from the environment until they can be processed.
Seriation. The ability to order objects according to increasing or decreasing length, weight, or volume.
Sexual identity. Students' self-constructed definition of who they are with respect to gender orientation.
Sexual orientation. The gender to which an individual is romantically and sexually attracted.
Shame. The painful emotion aroused when people recognize that they have failed to act or think in ways they believe are good.
Shaping. The process of reinforcing successive approximations of a desired behavior.
Sheltered English. An approach to teaching ELL students in academic classrooms that modifies instruction to assist students in learning content.
Short-term memory. Historically, the part of our memory system that temporarily holds information until it can be processed.
Situated cognition. A theoretical position in social constructivism suggesting that learning depends on, and cannot be separated from, the context in which it occurs.
Situational interest. A person's current enjoyment, pleasure, or satisfaction generated by the immediate context.
Social cognitive theory. A theory of learning that focuses on changes in behavior that result from observing others.
Social constructivism A view of constructivism suggesting that learners first construct knowledge in a social context and then individually internalize it.
Social contract. A stage of moral reasoning in which conclusions are based on socially agreed-upon principles.
Social conventions. Societal norms and ways of behaving in specific situations.
Social development. The advances people make in their ability to interact and get along with others.
Social experience. The process of interacting with others.
Social goals. Goals to achieve particular social outcomes or interactions.
Social problem solving. The ability to resolve conflicts in ways that are beneficial to all involved.
Sociocultural theory of development. A theory of cognitive development that emphasizes the influence of social interactions and language, embedded within a cultural context, on cognitive development.
Sociocultural theory A form of social constructivism that emphasizes the social dimensions of learning, but places greater emphasis on the larger cultural contexts in which learning occurs.
Socioeconomic status (SES). The combination of parents' income, occupation, and level of education that describes the relative standing in society of a family or individual.
Special education. Instruction designed to meet the unique needs of students with exceptionalities.
Specific transfer. The ability to apply information in a context similar to the one in which it was originally learned.
Speech disorders (*expressive disorders*). Problems in forming and sequencing sounds.
Standard deviation. A statistical measure of the spread of scores.
Standard error of measurement. The range of scores within which an individual's true score is likely to fall.
Standard score. A description of performance on a standardized test that uses the standard deviation as the basic unit.
Standardized tests. Assessment instruments given to large samples of students under uniform conditions and scored and reported according to uniform procedures.
Standards. Statements that describe what students should know or be able to do at the end of a prescribed period of study.
Standards-based education. The process of focusing curricula and instruction on predetermined goals or standards.
Stanine. A description of an individual's standardized test performance that uses a scale ranging from 1 to 9 points.
Stereotype threat. The anxiety experienced by members of a group resulting from concern that their behavior might confirm a stereotype.
Strategies. Cognitive operations that exceed the normal activities required to carry out a task.
Structured immersion. A type of immersion program that attempts to assist ELLs by teaching both English and academic subjects at a slower pace.
Students placed at risk. Learners in danger of failing to complete their education with the skills necessary to succeed in today's society.
Study strategies. Specific techniques students use to increase their understanding of written materials and teacher presentations.
Summarizing. The process of preparing a concise description of verbal or written passages.
Summative assessment. The process of assessing after instruction and using the results for making grading decisions.
Synapses. The tiny spaces between neurons that allow messages to be transmitted from one neuron to another.

Syntax. The set of rules that we use to put words together into meaningful sentences.
Systematic observation. The process of specifying criteria for acceptable performance in an activity and taking notes based on the criteria.

Table of specifications. A matrix that helps teachers organize learning objectives by cognitive level or content area.
Task analysis. The process of breaking content into component parts and sequencing the parts.
Task comprehension. Learners' awareness of what they are supposed to be learning and an understanding of why the task is important and worthwhile.
Temperament. The relatively stable inherited characteristics that influence the way we respond to social and physical stimuli.
Test anxiety. An unpleasant emotional reaction to testing situations that can lower performance.
Text signals. Elements included in written materials that communicate text organization and key ideas.
Theory of mind. An understanding that other people have distinctive perceptions, feelings, desires, and beliefs.
Theory. A set of related principles derived from observations that are used to explain events in the world and make predictions.
Timeout. The process of isolating a student from his or her classmates.
Tracking. Placing students in different classes or curricula on the basis of achievement.
Transfer. The ability to take understanding acquired in one context and apply it to a different context.
Transfer. The ability to take understanding acquired in one context and apply it to a different context.
Transformation. The ability to mentally record the process of moving from one state to another.
Transition signals. Verbal statements indicating that one idea is ending and another is beginning.
Transitional ELL programs. English language learner (ELL) programs that attempt to use the native language as an instructional aid until English becomes proficient.
Transitivity. The ability to infer a relationship between two objects based on knowledge of their relationship with a third object.
True score. The hypothetical average of an individual's scores if repeated testing under ideal conditions were possible.
True-false. A paper-and-pencil format that includes statements of varying complexity that learners judge as being correct or incorrect.
***T*-score.** A standard score that defines the mean as 50 and the standard deviation as 10.

Unconditional positive regard. The belief that someone is innately worthy regardless of their behavior.
Unconditioned response. The instinctive or reflexive (unlearned) physiological or emotional response caused by the unconditioned stimulus.
Unconditioned stimulus. An object or event that causes an instinctive or reflexive (unlearned) physiological or emotional response.
Undergeneralization. A language pattern that occurs when a child uses a word too narrowly.
Universal principles. A stage of moral reasoning in which conclusions are based on abstract and general principles that transcend society's laws.
Utility value. The belief that a topic, activity, or course of study will be useful for meeting future goals, including career goals.
Validity. The degree to which an assessment actually measures what it is supposed to measure.
Value. The benefits, rewards, or advantages that individuals believe may result from participating in a task or activity.
Variability. The degree of difference or deviation from the mean.
Vicarious learning. The process of people observing the consequences of other's actions and adjusting their own behavior accordingly.
Visual disability. An uncorrectable visual impairment that interferes with learning.
Visual-spatial sketchpad. A short-term storage system for visual and spatial information in working memory.

Wait-time. The period of silence that occurs both before and after calling on a student
Well-defined problem. A problem that has only one correct solution and a certain method for finding it.
Withitness. A teacher's awareness of what is going on in all parts of the classroom at all times and communicating this awareness to students.
Worked examples. Problems with completed solutions that provide students with one way of solving the problems.
Working memory. The store that holds information as people process and try to make sense of it. The workbench of the mind, where conscious thinking occurs and where individuals construct knowledge.

Zone of proximal development. A range of tasks that an individual cannot yet do alone but can accomplish when assisted by the guidance of others.
***z*-score.** The number of standard deviation units from the mean.

references

Abe, J. A., & Izzard, C. E. (1999). Compliance, noncompliance strategies, and the correlates of compliance in 5-year-old Japanese and American children. *Social Development, 8,* 1–20.

Abedi, J. (2006). Language issues in item development. In S. Downing, & T. Haladyna (Eds.), *Handbook of test development* (pp. 377–398). Mahwah, NJ: Erlbaum.

Abedi, J., & Gandara, P. (2006). Performance of English language learners as a subgroup in large-scale assessment: Interaction of research and policy. *Educational Measurement: Issues and Practice, 25*(4), 36–46.

Abedi, J., Hofstetter, C., & Lord, C. (2004). Assessment accommodations for English language learners: Implications for policy-based empirical research. *Review of Educational Research, 74*(1), 1–28.

Aboud, F., & Skerry, S. (1984). The development of ethnic identity: A critical review. *Journal of Cross-Cultural Psychology, 15,* 3–34.

Ackerman, P., & Lohman, D. (2006). Individual differences in cognitive function. In P. A. Alexander & P. H. Winne (Eds.), *Handbook of educational psychology* (2nd ed., pp. 139–162). Mahwah, NJ: Lawrence Erlbaum Associates.

Aiken, L. R. (2003). *Psychological testing and assessment* (11th ed.). Boston: Allyn & Bacon.

Airasian, P., & Walsh, M. (1997). Constructivist cautions. *Phi Delta Kappan, 78*(6), 444–449.

Alberto, P., & Troutman, A. (2006). *Applied behavior analysis for teachers* (7th ed.). Upper Saddle River, NJ: Merrill/Pearson.

Alder, N. (2002). Interpretations of the meaning of care: Creating caring relationships in urban middle school classrooms. *Urban Education, 37*(2), 241–266.

Alexander, J. M., Johnson, K. E., & Leibham, M. E. (2005). Constructing domain-specific knowledge in kindergarten: Relations among knowledge, intelligence, and strategic performance. *Learning and Individual Differences, 15,* 35–52.

Alexander, K., Entwisle, D., Dauber, S., & Kabboni, N. (2004). Dropout in relation to grade retention: An accounting of the Beginning School Study. In H. Walberg, A. Reynolds, & M. Wang (Eds.), *Can unlike students learn together? Grade retention, tracking, and crowding* (pp. 5–34). Greenwich, CT: Information Age Publishing.

Alexander, P. (2003). The development of expertise: The journey from acclimation to proficiency. *Educational Researcher, 32*(8), 10–14.

Alexander, P. (2006). *Psychology in learning and instruction.* Upper Saddle River, NJ: Merrill/Pearson.

Alexander, P., Graham, S., & Harris, K. (1998). A perspective on strategy research: Progress and prospects. *Educational Psychology Review, 10*(2), 129–153.

Alexander, P., & Jetton, T. (2000). Learning from text: A multidimensional and developmental perspective. In M. Kamil, P. Mosenthal, P. D. Pearson, & R. Barr (Eds.), *Handbook of reading research* (Vol. 3, pp. 285–310). Mahwah, NJ: Erlbaum.

Allen, J. (2007). *Creating a welcoming school: A practical guide to home–school partnerships with diverse families.* New York: Teachers College Press.

Allington, R. L., & McGill-Franzen, A. (2003). The impact of summer setback on the reading achievement gap. *Phi Delta Kappan, 85*(1), 68–71.

Alparsian, C., Tekkaya, C., & Geban, Ö. (2004). Using the conceptual change instruction to improve learning. *Journal of Biological Education, 37,* 133–137.

Alperstein, J. F. (2005). Commentary on girls, boys, test scores and more. *Teachers College Record.* Retrieved June 21, 2005, from http://tcrecord.org/Content.asp?ContentID=11874

Altermatt, E., Jovanovic, J., & Perry, M. (1998). Bias or responsivity? Sex and achievement-level effects on teachers' classroom questioning practices. *Journal of Educational Psychology, 90*(3), 516–527.

American Association of University Women. (1998). *Gender gaps: Where schools still fail our children.* Annapolis Junction, MD: Author.

American Association on Mental Retardation. (2002). *Mental retardation: definition, classification, and systems of supports* (10th ed.). Washington, DC: Author.

American Educational Research Association, American Psychological Association, & National Council on Measurement in Education. (1999). *Standards for educational and psychological testing* (2nd ed.). Washington, DC: Author.

American Psychiatric Association. (2000). *Warning signs.* Retrieved December 16, 2007, from http://apahelpcenter.org/featuredtopics/feature.php?id=38

American Psychological Association Board of Educational Affairs. (1995). *Learner-centered psychological principles: A framework for school redesign and reform.* Retrieved October 1, 2002, from http://www.apa.org/ed/lcp.html

Ames, C. (1990). Motivation: What teachers need to know. *Teachers College Record, 91,* 409–421.

Ames, C. (1992). Classrooms: Goals, structures, and student motivation. *Journal of Educational Psychology, 84*(3), 261–271.

Amrein, A., & Berliner, D. (2003). The effects of high-stakes testing on student motivation and learning. *Educational Leadership, 60*(5), 32–38.

Anderman, E. M., & Maehr, M. (1994). Motivation and schooling in the middle grades. *Review of Educational Research, 64,* 287–309.

Anderman, E. M., & Wolters, C. A. (2006). Goals, values, and affect: Influences on motivation. In P. A. Alexander & P. H. Winne (Eds.), *Handbook of educational psychology* (2nd ed., pp. 369–389). Mahwah, NJ: Erlbaum.

Anderson, D., & Nashon, S. (2007). Predators of knowledge construction: Interpreting students' metacognition in an amusement park physics program. *Science Education, 91,* 298–320.

Anderson, J., Reder, L., & Simon, H. (1996). Situated learning and education. *Educational Researcher, 25*(4), 5–10.

Anderson, J. R. (2005). *Cognitive psychology and its implications* (6th ed.). New York: Worth.

Anderson, J. R. (2007). Information-processing modules and their relative modality specificity. *Cognitive Psychology, 54*(3), 185–217.

Anderson, K., & Minke, K. (2007). Parent involvement in education: Toward an understanding of parents' decision making. *Journal of Educational Research, 199*(5), 311–323.

Anderson, L., Evertson, C., & Brophy, J. (1979). An experimental study of effective teaching in first-grade reading groups. *Elementary School Journal, 79,* 193–223.

Anderson, L., & Krathwohl, D. (Eds.). (2001). *A taxonomy for learning, teaching, and assessing: A revision of Bloom's taxonomy of educational objectives.* New York: Addison Wesley Longman.

Anderson, P. M., & Summerfield, J. P. (2004). Why is urban education different from suburban and rural education? In S. R. Steinberg & J. L. Kinchloe (Eds.), *19 urban questions: Teaching in the city* (pp. 29–39). New York: Peter Lang.

Anderson, R., Nguyen-Jahiel, K., McNurlen, B., Archodidou, A., Kim, S., Reznitskaya, A., Tillmanns, M., & Gilbert, L. (2001). The snowball phenomenon: Spread of ways of talking and ways of thinking across groups of children. *Cognition and Instruction, 19*(1), 1–46.

Andrade, H. (2007/2008). Self-assessment through rubrics. *Educational Leadership, 65*(4), 60–63.

Andrew, L. (2007). Comparison of teacher educators' instructional methods with the constructivist ideal. *The Teacher Educator, 42,* 157–184.

Antil, L., Jenkins, J., Wayne, S., & Vadasy, P. (1998). Cooperative learning: Prevalence, conceptualizations, and the relation between research and practice. *American Educational Research Journal, 35*(3), 419–454.

Applebee, A., Langer, J., Nystrand, M., & Gamoran, A. (2003). Discussion-based approaches to developing understanding: Classroom instruction and student performance in middle and high school English. *American Educational Research Journal, 40*(3), 685–730.

Armour-Thomas, E. (2004). What is the nature of evaluation and assessment in an urban context? In S. R. Steinberg & J. L. Kincheloe (Eds.), *19 Urban questions: Teaching in the city* (pp. 109–118). New York: Peter Lang.

Arnett, J. J. (2002). High hopes in a grim world: Emerging adults' views of their futures and of "Generation X." *Youth and Society, 31,* 267–286.

Aronson, E., Wilson, T., & Akert, R. (2005). *Social psychology.* (5th ed.). Upper Saddle River, NJ: Pearson.

Aronson, J. Fried, C., & Good, C. (2002). Reducing the effects of stereotype threat on African American college students: The role of theories of intelligence. *Journal of Experimental Social Psychology, 33,* 113–125.

Aronson, J., & Inzlicht, M. (2004). The ups and downs of attributional ambiguity: Stereotype vulnerability and the academic self-knowledge of African American college students. *Psychological Science, 15,* 829–836.

Asian-Nation. (2005). Retrieved February 17, 2005, http://www.asian-nation.org/model-minority.shtml

Aspy, C. B., Oman, R. F., Vesely, S. K., McLeroy, K., Rodine, S., & Marshall, L. (2004). Adolescent violence: The protective effects of youth assets. *Journal of Counseling and Development, 82,* 268–276.

Atkinson, J. (1958). *Motives in fantasy, action, and society.* Princeton, NJ: Van Nostrand.

Atkinson, R., & Shiffrin, R. (1968). Human memory: A proposed system and its control processes. In K. Spence & J. Spence (Eds.), *The psychology of learning and motivation: Advances in research and theory* (Vol. 2). San Diego, CA: Academic Press.

Atkinson, R. K., Renkl, A., & Merril, M. M. (2003). Transitioning from studying examples to solving problems: Effects of self-explanation prompts and fading worked-out steps. *Journal of Educational Psychology, 95,* 774–783.

Au, K. (1992, April). *"There's almost a lesson here": Teacher and students' purposes in constructing the theme of a story.* Paper presented at the annual meeting of the American Educational Research Association, San Francisco.

Au, W. (2007). High-stakes testing and curricular control: A qualitative metasynthesis. *Educational Researcher, 36*(5), 258–267.

Austin, J. L., Lee, M., & Carr, J. P. (2004). The effects of guided notes on undergraduate students' recording of lecture content. *Journal of Instructional Psychology, 31,* 314–320.

Ausubel, D. P. (1963). *The psychology of meaningful verbal learning.* New York: Grune & Stratton.

Ausubel, D. P. (1968). *Educational psychology: A cognitive view.* New York: Holt, Rinehart & Winston.

Ausubel, D. P. (1977). The facilitation of meaningful verbal learning in the classroom. *Educational Psychologist, 12,* 162–178.

Avramidis, E., Bayliss, P., & Burden, R. (2000). Student teachers' attitudes toward the inclusion of children with special education needs in the ordinary school. *Teaching and Teacher Education, 16,* 277–293.

Azevedo, R., & Cromley, J. (2004). Does training on self-regulated learning facilitate students' learning with hypermedia? *Journal of Educational Psychology, 96*(3), 523–535.

Babad, E., Avni-Babad, D., & Rosenthal, R. (2003). Teachers' brief nonverbal behaviors in defined instructional situations can predict students' evaluations. *Journal of Educational Psychology, 95,* 553–562.

Babad, E., Bernieri, F., & Rosenthal, R. (1991). Students as judges of teachers' verbal and nonverbal behavior. *American Educational Research Journal, 28*(1), 211–234.

Baddeley, A. (2001). Is working memory still working? *American Psychologist, 56,* 851–864.

Baddeley, A. D. (1986). *Working memory: Theory and practice.* London, UK: Oxford University Press.

Bae, G. (2003, April). *Rethinking constructivism in multicultural contexts: Does constructivism in education take the issue of diversity into consideration?* Paper presented at the annual meeting of the American Educational Research Association, Chicago.

Bailey, S. (1993). The current status of gender equity research in American Schools. *Educational psychologist, 28,* 321–339.

Baines, L. (2007). Learning from the world: Achieving more by doing less. *Phi Delta Kappan, 89,* 98–100.

Baker, D. (2006). For Navajo, science and tradition intertwine. *Salt Lake Tribune,* pp. D1, D5.

Baker, D., & Letendre, G. (2005). *National differences, global similarities: World culture and the future of schooling.* Sanford, CA: Stanford University Press.

Baker, S., Gersten, R., Haager, D., & Dingle, M. (2006). Teaching practice and the reading growth of first-grade English learners: Validation of an observation instrument. *Elementary School Journal, 107*(2), 199–220.

Baldwin, J. D., & Baldwin, J. I. (2001). *Behavior principles in everyday life* (4th ed.). Upper Saddle River, NJ: Prentice Hall.

Ball, D. (1992, Summer). Magical hopes: Manipulatives and the reform of math education. *American Educator,* pp. 28–33.

Ball, D., & Forzine, F. (2007). What makes education research "educational"? *Educational Researcher, 36*(9), 529–540.

Bandalos, D. L. (2004). Introduction to the special issue on Nebraska's alternative approach to statewide assessment. *Educational Measurement, 23*(2), 6–8.

Bandura, A. (1986). *Social foundations of thought and action: A social cognitive theory.* Upper Saddle River, NJ: Prentice Hall.

Bandura, A. (1989). Social cognitive theory. In R. Vasta (Ed.), *Annals of child development* (Vol. 6, pp. 1–60). Greenwich, CT: JAI Press.

Bandura, A. (1997). *Self-efficacy: The exercise of control.* New York: Freeman.

Bandura, A. (2001). Social cognitive theory. In *Annual Review of Psychology.* Palo Alto, CA: Annual Review.

Bandura, A. (2004, May). *Toward a psychology of human agency.* Paper presented at the meeting of the American Psychological Society, Chicago.

Banks, J. (2008). *An introduction to multicultural education* (4th ed.). Boston: Allyn & Bacon.

Barak, M., & Dori, Y. J. (2005). Enhancing undergraduate students' chemistry understanding through project-based learning in an IT environment. *Science Education, 89,* 117–139.

Baringa, M. (1997). New insights into how babies learn language. *Science, 277,* 641.

Barnes, S. P., Torrens, A., & George, V. (2007). The use of portfolios in coordinated school health programs: Benefits and challenges to implementation. *The Journal of School Health, 77,* 171–179.

Barnett, J. E. (2001, April). *Study strategies and preparing for exams: A survey of middle and high school students.* Paper presented at the annual meeting of the American Educational Research Association, Seattle.

Barone, M. (2000). In plain English: Bilingual education flunks out of schools in California. *U.S. News and World Report, 128*(21), 37.

Barr, R., D., & Parrett, W. H. (2001). *Hope fulfilled for at-risk and violent youth* (2nd ed.). Boston: Allyn & Bacon.

Barrett, T. M., Davis, E. F., & Needham, A. (2007). Learning about tools in infancy. *Developmental Psychology, 43,* 352–368.

Barron, B. (2000). Problem solving in video-based microworlds: Collaborative and individual outcomes of high-achieving sixth-grade students. *Journal of Educational Psychology, 92*(2), 391–398.

Barry, C., & Wentzel, K. (2006). Friend influence on prosocial behavior: The role of motivational factors and friendship characteristics. *Developmental Psychology, 42*(1), 153–163.

Barth, R. (2002). The culture builder. *Educational Leadership, 59*(8), 6–12.

Barton, P. (2004). Why does the gap persist? *Educational Leadership, 62*(3), 9–13.

Batsashaw, M. L. (2003). Children with disabilities (5th ed.). Baltimore, MD: Paul H. Brookes.

Bauerlein, M. (2008). *The dumbest generation: How the digital age stupefies young Americans and jeopardizes our future (or, don't trust anyone under 30).* New York: Tarcher/Penguin.

Baumeister, R., Campbell, J., Krueger, J., & Vohs, K. (2005). Exploding the self-esteem myth. *Scientific American, 292*(1), 84–92.

Baumeister, R. F., & DeWall, C. N. (2005). The inner dimension of social exclusion: Intelligent thought and self-regulation among rejected persons. In K. D. Williams, J. P. Forgas, & W. von Hippel (Eds.), *The social outcast: Ostracism, social exclusion, rejection, and bullying* (pp. 53–73). New York: Psychology Press.

Baumrind, D. (1991). The influence of parenting style on adolescent competence and substance use. *Journal of Early Adolecence, 11,* 56–95.

Becker, B. E., & Luther, S. S. (2002). Social-emotional factors affecting achievement outcomes among disadvantaged students: Closing the achievement gap. *Educational Psychologist, 37,* 197–214.

Beebe-Fankenberger, M., Bocian, K., MacMillan, D., & Gresham, F. (2004). Sorting second grade students with academic deficiencies: Characteristics differentiating those retained in grade from those promoted to third grade. *Journal of Educational Psychology, 96,* 204–215.

Beers, B. (2006). *Learning-driven schools: A practical guide for teachers and principals.* Alexandria, VA: Association for Supervision and Curriculum Development.

Behuniak, P. (2002). Consumer-referenced testing. *Phi Delta Kappan, 84,* 199–206.

Beirne-Smith, M., Ittenbach, R. F., & Patton, J. R. (2002). *Mental retardation* (6th ed.). Upper Saddle River, NJ: Merrill/Pearson.

Benner, A., & Mistry, R. (2007). Congruence of mother and teacher educational expectations and low-income youth's academic competence. *Journal of Educational Psychology, 99*(1), 140–153.

Bennett, C. (2007). *Multicultural education* (6th ed.). Boston: Allyn & Bacon.

Bennett, N., & Blundel, D. (1983). Quantity and quality of work in rows of classroom groups. *Educational Psychology, 3,* 93–105.

Benson, P., Scales, P., Hamilton, S., & Sesma, A. (2006). Positive youth development: Theory, research, and applications. In R. Lerner (Vol. Ed.), *Handbook of child psychology: Vol. 1. Theoretical models of human development* (6th ed., pp. 894–941). Hoboken, NJ: John Wiley & Sons, Inc.

Bental, B., & Tirosh, E. (2007). The relationship between attention, executive functions and reading domain abilities in attention deficit hyperactivity disorder and reading disorder: A comparative study. *The Journal of Child Psychology and Psychiatry and Allied Disciplines, 48,* 455–463.

Bereiter, C., & Scardamalia, M. (2006). Education for the knowledge age: Design-centered models of teaching and instruction. In P. A. Alexander & P. H. Winne (Eds.), *Handbook of educational psychology* (2nd ed., pp. 695–714). Mahwah, NJ: Lawrence Erlbaum Associates.

Berger, K. (2007). Update on bullying at school: Science forgotten? *Developmental Review,* 90–126.

Berk, L. (2003). *Child development* (6th ed.). Boston: Allyn & Bacon.

Berk, L. (2008). *Infants & children* (6th ed.). Boston: Allyn & Bacon.

Berliner, D. (1984). *Making our schools more effective: Proceedings of three state conferences.* San Francisco: Far West Laboratory.

Berliner, D. (1994). Expertise: The wonder of exemplary performances. In J. Mangieri & C. Collins (Eds.), *Creating powerful thinking in teachers and students* (pp. 161–186). Fort Worth, TX: Harcourt Brace.

Berliner, D. (2004). If the underlying premise for No Child Left Behind is false, how can that act solve our problems? In K. Goodman, P. Shannon, Y. Goodman, & R. Rapoport (Eds.), *Saving our schools.* Berkeley, CA: RDR Books.

Berliner, D. C. (1986). In pursuit of the expert pedagogue. *Educational Researcher, 15,* 5–13.

Berliner, D. C. (2000). A personal response to those who bash education. *Journal of Teacher Education, 51,* 358–371.

Berliner, D. C. (2005). Our impovershed view of educational reform. *Teachers College Record,* August 2. ID Number: 12106. Retrieved January 12, 2006, from http://www.tcrecord.org

Berliner, D. C. (2006). Educational psychology: Searching for essence throughout a century of influence. In P. A. Alexander & P. H. Winne (Eds.), *Handbook of educational psychology* (2nd ed., pp. 3–42). Mahwah, NJ: Erlbaum.

Berndt, T. (2002). Friendship quality and social development. *Current Directions in Psychological Science, 11,* 7–10.

Berninger, V. (2006). A developmental approach to learning disabilities. In K. A. Renninger, & I. Sigel (Vol. Eds.), *Handbook of child psychology: Vol. 4. Child psychology in practice* (6th ed., pp. 420–452). Hoboken, NJ: John Wiley & Sons, Inc.

Berninger, V., & Richards, T. (2002). *Brain literacy for educators and psychologists.* San Diego, CA: Academic Press.

Bernstein, D. K., & Tiegerman-Farber, E. (2002). *Language and communication disorders in children* (5th ed.). Boston: Allyn & Bacon.

Berrill, D., & Whalen, C. (2007). "Where are the children?" Personal integrity and reflective teaching portfolios. *Teaching and Teacher Education, 23,* 868–884.

Bertman, S. (2000). *Cultural amnesia: America's future and the crisis of memory.* Westport, CT: Praeger.

Berzonsky, M. D., & Kuk, L. S. (2000). Identity status, identity processing style, and the transition to university. *Journal of Adolescent Research, 15,* 81–98.

Bettis, P., & Adams, N. (Eds.) (2005). *Geographies of girlhood: Identities in-between.* Mahwah, NJ: Lawrence Erlbaum.

Bialystok, E. (2001). *Bilingualism in development: Language, literacy, and cognition.* Cambridge, England: Cambridge University Press.

Biddle, B. J. (2001). Poverty, ethnicity, and achievement in American Schools. In B. J. Biddle (Ed.), *Social class, poverty, and education* (pp. 1–30). New York: Routlege Falmer.

Biddle, B., & Berliner, D. (2002). Unequal school: Funding in the United States. *Education Leadership, 59*(8), 48–59.

Bielenberg, B., & Fillmore, L. W. (2005). The English they need for the test. *Educational Leadership, 62*(4), 45–49.

Biemiller, A. (2005). Addressing developmental patterns in vocabulary. In E. H. Hiebert, & M. L. Kamil (Eds.), *Teaching and learning vocabulary.* Mahwah, NJ: Erlbaum.

Biscaro, M., Broer, K., & Taylor, N. (2004). Self-efficacy, alcohol expectancy and problem-solving appraisal as predictors of alcohol use in college students. *College Student Journal, 38,* 541–555.

Black, A., & Deci, E. (2000). The effects of instructors' autonomy support and students' autonomous motivation on learning organic chemistry: A self-determination theory perspective. *Science Education, 84,* 740–756.

Black, P., Harrison, C., Lee, C., Marshall, B., & William, D. (2004). Working inside the black box: Assessment for learning in the classroom. *Phi Delta Kappan, 86*(1), 9–21.

Black, P., & William, D. (1998a). Assessment and classroom learning. *Assessment in Education: Principles, Policy and Practice, 5*(1), 7–75.

Black, P., & William, D. (1998b). Inside the black box. *Phi Delta Kappan, 80*(2), 139–148.

Black, S. (2007). Apprenticeships: A tradition that works. *American School Board Journal, 194*(2), 38–40.

Blackburn, M., & Miller, R. (1999, April). *Intrinsic motivation for cheating and optimal challenge: Some sources and some consequences.* Paper presented at the annual meeting of the American Educational Research Association, Montreal, Canada.

Blair, J. (2000). AFT urges new tests, expanded training for teachers. *Education Week, 19*(32), 11.

Blanchett, W. (2006). Disproportionate representation of African American students in special education: Acknowledging the role of white privilege and racism. *Educational Researcher, 35*(6), 24–28.

Blatchford, P, Baines, E., Rubie-Davies, Ch, Bassett, P., & Chowne, A. (2006). The effect of a new approach to group work on pupil–pupil and teacher–pupil interactions. *Journal of Educational Psychology, 98*(4), 750–765.

Bleeker, M. M., & Jacobs, J. E. (2004). Achievement in math and science: Do mothers' beliefs matter 12 years later? *Journal of Educational Psychology, 96*(1), 97–109.

Blocher, M., Echols, J., Tucker, G., de Montes, L., & Willis, E. (2002, April). *Re-thinking the validity of assessment: A classroom teacher's dilemma.* Paper presented at the annual meeting of the American Educational Research Association, New Orleans.

Block, M. (2007). Climate changes lives of whalers in Alaska. All Things Considered. National Public Radio. Retrieved September 17, 2007, from http://www.npr.org/templates/story/story.php?storyId=14428086

Bloom, B., Englehart, M., Furst, E., Hill, W., & Krathwohl, O. (1956). *Taxonomy of educational objectives: The classification of educational goals: Handbook 1. The cognitive domain.* White Plains, NY: Longman.

Bloom, C. M., & Lamkin, D. M. (2006). The Olympian struggle to remember the cranial nerves: Mnemonics and student success. *Teaching of Psychology, 33,* 128–129.

Bloom, L. (1998). The intentionality model of language development: How to learn a word, any word. In R. Golinkoff, K. Hirsh-Pasek, M. Akhtar, L. Bloom, G. Hollich, L. Smith, M. Tomasello, & A. Woodward (Eds.), *Becoming a word learner: A debate on lexical acquisition.* New York: Oxford University Press.

Blum, R. (2005). A case for school connectedness. *Educational Leadership, 62*(8), 16–19.

Blumenfeld, P., Kempler, T., & Krajcik, J. (2006). Motivation and cognitive engagement in learning environments. In R. K. Sawyer (Ed.), *Cambridge handbook of the learning sciences* (pp. 475–488). Cambridge, MA: Cambridge University Press.

Blumenreich, M., & Falk, B., (2006). Trying on a new pair of shoes: Urban teacher–learners conduct research and construct knowledge in their own classrooms. *Teaching and Teacher Education, 22,* 864–873.

Boekaerts, M., & Koning, E. (2006). Goal-directed behavior and contextual factors in the classroom: An innovative approach to the study of multiple goals. *Educational Psychologist, 41,* 33–51.

Bogdan W., & Struzynska-Kujalowicz, A. (2007). Power influences self-esteem. *Social Cognition, 25,* 472–494.

Bohn, C. M., Roehrig, A. D., & Pressley, M. (2004). The first days of school in the classrooms of two more effective and four less effective primary-grades teachers. *Elementary School Journal, 104*(4), 269–288.

Bong, M. (2001). Between- and within-domain relations of academic motivation among middle and high school students: Self-efficacy, task-value, and achievement goals. *Journal of Educational Psychology, 93,* 23–34.

Bong, M., & Skaalvik, E. (2003). Academic self-concept and self-efficacy: How different are they really? *Educational Psychology Review, 15,* 1–40.

Borko, H., & Putnam, R. (1996). Learning to teach. In D. Berliner & R. Calfee (Eds.), *Handbook of educational psychology* (pp. 673–708). New York: Macmillan.

Borman, G. D., & Overman, L. R. (2004). Academic resilience in mathematics among poor and minority students. *Elementary School Journal, 104*(3), 177–196.

Bortfeld, H., & Whitehurst, G. (2001). Sensitive periods in first language acquisition, In D. Bailey, Jr., J. Bruer, F. Symons, & J Lichtman (Eds.), *Critical thinking about critical periods* (pp. 173–192). Baltimore: Brookes.

Bourne, L. (1982). Typicality effects in logically defined categories. *Memory & Cognition, 10,* 3–9.

Braaksma, M., Rijlaarsdam, G., van den Bergh, H., & van Hout-Wolters, B. (2004). Observational learning and its effects on the orchestration of writing processes. *Cognition & Instruction, 22*(1), 1–36.

Bracey, G. (2005). A nation of cheats. *Phi Delta Kappan, 86*(5), 412–413.

Brainerd, C. (2003). Jean Piaget, learning research, and American education. In B. Zimmerman, & D. Schunk (Eds.), *Educational psychology: A century of contributions* (pp. 251–287). Mahwah, NJ: Erlbaum.

Bransford, J. (1993). Who ya gonna call? Thoughts about teaching problem solving. In P. Hallinger, K. Leithwood, & J. Murphy (Eds.), *Cognitive perspectives on educational leadership* (pp. 2–30). New York: Teachers College Press.

Bransford, J., Brown, A., & Cocking, R. (Eds.). (2000). *How people learn: Brain, mind, experience, and school.* Washington, DC: National Academy Press.

Bransford, J., Darling-Hammond, L., & LePage, P. (2005). Introduction. In L. Darling-Hammond & J. Bransford (Eds.), *Preparing teachers for a changing world: What teachers should learn and be able to do* (pp. 1–39). San Francisco: Jossey-Bass/Wiley.

Bransford, J., Derry, S., Berliner, D., Hammerness, K, & Beckett, K. L. (2005). Theories of learning and their roles in teaching. In L. Darling-Hammond & J. Bransford (Eds.), *Preparing teachers for a changing world: What teachers should learn and be able to do* (pp. 40–87). San Francisco: John Wiley & Sons.

Bransford, J., & Stein, B. (1984). *The IDEAL problem solver.* New York: Freeman.

Bransford, J. D., & Johnson, M. K. (1972). Contextual prerequisites for understanding: Some investigations of comprehension and recall. *Journal of Verbal Learning and Verbal Behavior, 11,* 717–726.

Braun, H., & Mislevy, R. (2005). Intuitive test theory. *Phi Delta Kappan, 86*(7), 489–497.

Brehmer, Y., & Li, S-C. (2007). Memory plasticity across the life span: Uncovering children's latent potential. *Developmental Psychology, 43,* 465–478.

Brendgen, M., Vitar, F., Boivin, M., Dionne, G., & Perusse, D. (2006). Examining genetic and environmental effects on reactive versus proactive aggression. *Developmental Psychology, 42*(6), 1299–1312.

Brenner, M., Mayer, R., Moseley, B., Brar, T., Durán, R., Reed, B., & Webb, D. (1997). Learning by understanding: The role of multiple representations in learning algebra. *American Educational Research Journal, 34*(4), 663–689.

Bridgeman, B. (1974). Effects of test score feedback on immediately subsequent test performance. *Journal of Educational Psychology, 66,* 62–66.

Bronfenbrenner, U., & Morris, P. (2006). The bioecological model of human development. In R. Lerner (Ed.), *Handbook of child psychology: Vol. 1 Theoretical models of human development* (6th ed., pp. 793–828). Hoboken, NJ: John Wiley & Sons, Inc.

Brookhart, S. (2007/2008). Feedback that fits. *Educational Leadership, 65*(4), 54–59.

Brookhart, S. M., Walsh, J. M., & Zientarski, W. A. (2006). The dynamics of motivation and effort for classroom assessments in middle school science and social studies. *Applied Measurement in Education, 19,* 151–184.

Brophy, J. (1981). On praising effectively. *Elementary School Journal, 81,* 269–278.

Brophy, J. (1999a). Perspectives of classroom management. In J. Freiberg (Ed.), *Beyond behaviorism: Changing the classroom management paradigm* (pp. 43–56). Boston: Allyn & Bacon.

Brophy, J. (1999b). Research on motivation in education: Past, present, and future. In M. L. Maehr & P. R. Pintrich (Series Eds.) & T. C. Urdan (Vol. Ed.), *Advances in motivation and achievement: Vol. 11. The role of context* (pp. 1–44). Stamford, CT: JAI.

Brophy, J. (2004). *Motivating students to learn* (2nd ed.). Boston: McGraw-Hill.

Brophy, J. (2006a) Graham Nuttall and social constructivist teaching; Research-based cautions and qualifications. *Teaching and Teacher Education, 22,* 529–537.

Brophy, J. (2006b). History of research on classroom management. In C. M. Evertson & C. S. Weinstein (Eds.), *Handbook of classroom management: Research, practice, and contemporary issues* (pp. 17–43). Mahwah, NJ: Erlbaum.

Brophy, J. (2006c).Observational research on generic aspects of classroom teaching. In P. A. Alexander & P. H. Winne (Eds.), *Handbook of educational psychology* (2nd ed., pp. 755–780). Mahwah, NJ: Erlbaum.

Brophy, J., & Alleman, J. (2003). Primary-grade students' knowledge and thinking about the supply of utilities (water, heat, and light) to modern homes. *Cognition & Instruction, 21*(1), 79–112.

Brophy, J., & Good, T. (1986). Teacher behavior and student achievement. In M. Wittrock (Ed.), *Handbook of research on teaching* (3rd ed., pp. 328–375). New York: Macmillan

Brosvic, G. M., Epstein, M. L., Dihoff, R. E., & Cook, M. J. (2006). Feedback facilitates the acquisition and retention of numerical fact series by elementary school students with mathematics learning disabilities. *The Psychological Record, 56,* 35–54.

Brouwers, A., & Tomic, W. (2001). The factorial validity of the Teacher Interpersonal Self-Efficacy Scale. *Educational and Psychological Measurement, 61,* 433–445.

Brown, A., Bransford, J., Ferrara, R., & Campione, J. (1983). Learning, remembering, and understanding. In J. Flavell & E. Markman (Eds.), *Handbook of child psychology: Vol. 3. Cognitive development* (4th ed., pp. 77–166). New York: Wiley.

Brown, A., & Campione, J. (1994). Guided discovery in a community of learners. In K. McGilly (Ed.), *Classroom lessons: Integrating cognitive theory and classroom practice* (pp. 229–270). Cambridge, MA: MIT Press.

Brown, D. (2004). Urban teachers' professed classroom management strategies: Reflections of culturally responsive teaching. *Urban Education, 39*(3), 266–289.

Brown, J., Collins, A., & Duguid, P. (1989). Situated cognition and the culture of learning. *Educational Researcher, 18,* 32–42.

Brown, K., Anfara, V., & Roney, K. (2004). Student achievement in high performing, suburban middle schools and low performing, urban middle schools: Plausible explanations for the differences. *Education and Urban Society, 36*(4), 428–456.

Brown, R., & Evans, W. (2002). Extracurricular activity and ethnicity: Creating greater school connections among diverse student populations. *Urban Education, 37*(1), 41–58.

Brown-Chidsey, R. (2007). No more "waiting to fail." *Educational Leadership, 62*(2), 40–46.

Bruer, J. T. & Greenough, W. T. (2001). The subtle science of how experience affects the brain. In D. B. Bailey, Jr., J. T. Bruer, F. J. Symons, & J. W. Lichtman (Eds.), *Critical thinking about critical periods* (pp. 209–232). Baltimore: Brookes.

Bruner, J. (1973). *Beyond the information given: Studies in the psychology of knowing.* New York: Norton.

Bruner, J. (1990). *Acts of meaning.* Cambridge, MA: Harvard University Press.

Bruner, J., Goodenow, J., & Austin, G. (1956). *A study of thinking.* New York: Wiley.

Bruner, J. S. (1960). *The process of education.* Cambridge, MA: Harvard University Press.

Bruner, J. S. (1966). *Toward a theory of instruction.* New York: Norton.

Bruning, R. H., Schraw, G. J., Norby, M. M., & Ronning, R. R. (2004). *Cognitive psychology and instruction* (4th ed.). Upper Saddle River, NJ: Prentice Hall.

Bryan, C. L., & Solmon, M. A. (2007). Self-determination in physical education: Designing class environments to promote active lifestyles. *Journal of Teaching in Physical Education, 26,* 260–278.

Buck, G., Kostin, I., & Morgan, R. (2002). *Examining the relationship of content to gender-based performance difference in advanced placement exams.* (Research Report No. 2002-12). New York: College Board.

Bulgren, J., Deshler, D., Schumaker, J., & Lenz, B. K. (2000). The use and effectiveness of analogical instruction in diverse secondary content classrooms. *Journal of Educational Psychology, 92*(3), 426–441.

Bullough, R., Jr. (1989). *First-year teacher: A case study.* New York: Teachers College Press.

Burack, J., Flanagan, T., Peled, T., Sutton, J., Zygmuntowicz, C., & Manley, J. (2006). Social perspective-taking skills in maltreated children and adolescents. *Developmental Psychology, 42,* 207–217.

Burbules, N., & Bruce, B. (2001). Theory and research on teaching as dialogue. In V. Richardson (Ed.), *Handbook of research on teaching* (4th ed., pp. 1102–1121). Washington, DC: America Educational Research Association.

Burhans, K., & Dweck, C. S. (1995). Helplessness in early childhood: The role of contingent worth. *Child Development, 66,* 1719–1738.

Burke, L. A., Williams, J. M., & Skinner, D. (2007). Teachers' perceptions of thinking skills in the primary curriculum. *Research in Education, 77,* 1–13.

Burns, M. (2005). Looking at how students reason. *Educational Leadership, 63*(3), 26–31.

Burstyn, J., & Stevens, R. (1999, April). *Education in conflict resolution: Creating a whole school approach.* Paper presented at the annual meeting of the American Educational Research Association, Montreal, Canada.

Burstyn, J., & Stevens, R. (2001). Involving the whole school in violence prevention. In J. Burstyn, G. Bender, R. Casella, H. Gordon, D. Guerra, K. Luschen, R. Stevens, & K. Williams (Eds.), *Preventing violence in schools: A challenge to American democracy* (pp. 139–158). Mahwah, NJ: Erlbaum.

Byrnes, J. P. (2001a). *Cognitive development and learning in instructional contexts* (2nd ed.). Boston: Allyn & Bacon.

Byrnes, J. P. (2001b). *Minds, brains, and learning: Understanding the psychological and educational relevance of neuroscientific research.* New York: Guilford Press.

Byrnes, J. P. (2003). Factors predictive of mathematics achievement in White, Black, and Hispanic 12th graders. *Journal of Educational Psychology, 95,* 316–326.

Byrnes, J., & Fox, N. (1998). The educational relevance of research in cognitive neuroscience. *Educational Psychology Review, 10,* 297–342.

California State Board of Education. (2008). *Grade Ten. History-Social Science Content Standards.* Retrieved January 25, 2008, from http://www.cde.ca.gov/be/st/ss/hstgrade10.asp

Cameron, J., Pierce, W. D., & Banko, K. M. (2005). Achievement-based rewards and intrinsic motivation: A test of cognitive mediators. *Journal of Educational Psychology, 97,* 641–655.

Campbell, F. A., Pungello, E. P., Miller-Johnson, S., Burchinal, M., & Ramey, C. T. (2001). The development of cognitive and academic abilities: Growth curves from an early childhood educational experiment. *Developmental Psychology, 37,* 231–243.

Canter, A. (2004). A problem-solving model for improving student achievement. *Principal Leadership, 5,* 11–15.

Canter, L. (1996). First the rapport—then the rules. *Learning, 24,* 12–13.

Canter, L., & Canter, M. (1992). *Assertive discipline: Positive behavior management for today's classrooms.* Santa Monica, CA: Lee Canter and Associates.

Caplan, N., Choy, M., & Whitmore, J. (1992). Indochinese refugee families and academic achievement. *Scientific American, 266*(2), 36–42.

Caprara, G. V., Barbaranelli, C., Borgogni, L., & Steca, P. (2003). Efficacy beliefs as determinants of teachers' job satisfaction. *Journal of Educational Psychology, 95,* 821–832.

Carey, B. (2007, September 4). Bipolar illness soars as a diagnosis for the young. *New York Times,* pp. A1, A15.

Carlson, C., Uppal, S., & Prosser, E. (2000). Ethnic differences in processes contributing to self-esteem of early adolescent girls. *Journal of Early Adolescence, 20,* 44–67.

Carlson, N. (1999). *Foundations of physiological psychology.* Boston: Allyn & Bacon.

Carnine, D., Silbert, J., Kameenui, E., Tarver, S., & Jongjohann, K. (2006). *Teaching struggling and at-risk readers: A direct instruction approach.* Upper Saddle River, NJ: Merrill/Pearson.

Carpendale, J. (2000). Kohlberg and Piaget on stages and moral reasoning. *Developmental Review, 20,* 181–205.

Carr, N. (2008). Talking about test scores. *American School Board Journal, 195(1),* 38–39.

Carrier, D. (2007). Double jeopardy: Repeat births to teens: One in five teens giving birth are already mothers. *Child Trends* [Online]. Retrieved from http://www.childtrends.org/_pressrelease_page.cfm?LID=F9DF71F0-B45F-4396-9F537D6C0577B220

Carter, K., & Doyle, W. (2006). Classroom management in early childhood and elementary classrooms. In C. M. Evertson & C. S. Weinstein (Eds.), *Handbook of classroom management: Research, practice, and contemporary issues* (pp. 373–406). Mahwah, NJ: Erlbaum.

Carver, S. (2006). Assessing for deep understanding. In R. K. Sawyer (Ed.), *Cambridge handbook of the learning sciences* (pp. 205–224). Cambridge, MA: Cambridge University Press.

Case, R. (1992). *The mind's staircase: Exploring the conceptual underpinnings of children's thought and knowledge.* Hillsdale, NJ: Erlbaum.

Case, R. (1998). The development of central conceptual structures. In D., Kuhn, & R. Siegler (Eds.), *Handbook of child psychology: Vol. 2. Cognition, perception, and language* (5th ed., pp. 745–800). New York: Wiley.

Cassady, J. (1999, April). *The effects of examples as elaboration in text on memory and learning.* Paper presented at the annual meeting of the American Educational Research Association, Montreal, Canada.

Cassady, J. C., & Johnson, R. E. (2002). Cognitive anxiety and academic performance. *Contemporary Educational Psychology, 27,* 270–295.

Castellano, J. A., & Diaz, E. (Eds.). (2002). *Reaching new horizons: Gifted and talented education for culturally and linguistically diverse students.* Boston: Allyn & Bacon.

Castle, S., Deniz, C., & Tortora, M. (2005). Flexible grouping and student performance. *Contemporary Educational Psychology, 27,* 270–295.

Cattel, R., (1963). Theory of fluid and crystallized intelligence: A critical experiment. *Journal of Educational Psychology, 54,* 1–22.

Cattel, R., (1987). *Intelligence: Its structure, growth, and action.* Amsterdam: North-Holland.

Cazden, C. B. (2002). *Classroom discourse: The language of teaching and learning* (2nd ed.). Portsmouth, NH: Heineman.

Ceci, S., & Williams, W. (1997). Schooling, intelligence, and income. *American Psychologist, 53,* 185–204.

Chaffen, R., & Imreh, G. (2002). Practicing perfection: Piano performance and expert memory. *Psychological Science, 13,* 342–349.

Chao, R. (1994). Beyond parental control and authoritarian parenting style: Understanding Chinese parenting through the cultural notion of training. *Child Development, 65,* 1111–1119.

Chao, R. (2001). Extending research on the consequences of parenting style for Chinese American and European Americans. *Child Development, 72,* 1832–1843.

Chapman, J. W., Tunmer, W. E., & Prochnow, J. E. (2000). Early reading-related skills and performance, reading self-concept, and the development of academic self-concept: A longitudinal study. *Journal of Educational Psychology, 92,* 703–708.

Chappuis, S., & Chappuis, J. (2007/2008). The best value in formative assessment. *Educational Leadership, 65*(4), 14–18.

Charles, C. M. (2002). *Essential elements of effective discipline.* Boston: Allyn & Bacon.

Charles, C. M., & Senter, G. W. (2005). *Building classroom discipline* (8th ed.). Boston: Allyn & Bacon.

Charner-Laird, M., Watson, D., Szczesuil, S., Kirkpatrick C., & Gordon, P. (2004, April). *Navigating the "Culture Gap:" New teachers experience the urban context.* Paper presented at the annual meeting of the American Educational Research Association, San Diego.

Chatterji, M., (2008). Synthesizing evidence from impact evaluations in education to inform action. *Educational Researcher, 37*(1), 23–26.

Chavous, T. M., Bernat, D. H. Schmeelk-Cone, K., Caldwell, C. H., Kohn-Wood, L., & Zimmerman, M. A. (2003). Racial identity and academic attainment among African American Adolescents. *Child Development, 74,* 1076–1090.

Chekley, K. (1997). The first seven . . . and the eighth. *Educational Leadership, 55,* 8–13.

Chen, J. (2004). Theory of multiple intelligences: Is it a scientific theory: *Teachers College Record, 106,* 17–23.

Chen, Z., & Siegler, R. (2000). Intellectual development in childhood. In R. J. Sternberg (Ed.), *Handbook of intelligence* (pp. 92–116). New York: Cambridge University Press.

Cheng, L. R. (1987). *Assessing Asian language performance.* Rockville, MD: Aspen.

Children's Defense Fund. (2004). *The state of America's children yearbook 2004.* Washington, DC: Author.

Choi, N. (2005). Self-efficacy and self-concept as predictors of college students' academic perfor-mance. *Psychology in the Schools, 42*(2), 197–205.

Chomsky, N. (1959). A review of Skinner's verbal behavior. *Language, 35,* 25–58.

Chomsky, N. (1972). *Language and mind* (2nd ed.). Orlando, FL: Harcourt Brace.

Chomsky, N. (1976). *Reflections on language.* London: Temple Smith.

Chomsky, N., & Miller, G. (1958). Finite-state languages. *Information and Control, 1,* 91–112.

Chorzempa, B., & Graham, S. (2006). Primary-grade teachers' use of within-class ability grouping in reading. *Journal of Educational Pyschology, 98*(3), 529–541.

Christenson, S., & Havsy, L. (2004). Family–school–peer relationships: Significance for social, emotional, and academic learning. In J. Zins, R. Weissberg, M. Wang, & H. Walberg (Eds.), *Building academic success on social and emotional learning* (pp. 59–75). New York: Teachers College Press.

Christian, K., Bachnan, H. J., & Morrison, F. J. (2001). Schooling and cognitive development. In R. J. Sternberg & E. L. Grigorenko (Eds.), *Environmental effects on cognitive abilities.* Mahwah, NJ: Erlbaum.

Chronicle, E., MacGregor, J., & Ormerod, T. (2004). What makes an insight problem? The roles of heuristics, goal conception, and solution recoding in knowledge-learn problems. *Journal of Experimental Psychology: Learning, Memory, and Cognition, 30*(1), 14–217.

Chumlea, W., Schubert, C., Roche, A., Kulin, H., Lee, P., Himes, J., & Sun, S. (2003). Age at menarche and racial comparisons in U.S. girls. *Pediatrics, 111*(1), 110–113.

Cimera, R. (2006). *Mental retardation doesn't mean "stupid"! A guide for parents and teachers.* New York: Rowman & Littlefield, Lanham.

Ciofalo, J. F., & Wylie, E. G. (2006, January 10). Using diagnostic classroom assessment: One question at a time. *Teachers College Record,* Retrieved June 20, 2007, from http://www.tcrecord.org/Content.asp.?ContentID=12285

Cizek, G. (1997). Learning, achievement, and assessment: Constructs at a crossroads. In G. Phye (Ed.), *Handbook of classroom assessment* (pp. 1–31). San Diego, CA: Academic Press.

Clark, J., & Paivio, A. (1991). Dual coding theory and education. *Educational Psychology Review, 3,* 149–210.

Clark, K., & Clark, M. (1939). The development of consciousness of self and the emergence of racial identification in Negro preschool children. *Journal of Social Psychology, 10,* 591–599.

Clark, R. C., & Mayer, R. E. (2003). *e-learning and the science of instruction: Proven guidelines for consumers and designers of multimedia learning.* San Francisco: Pfeiffer/Wiley.

Clarke, A. (2006). The nature and substance of cooperating teacher reflection. *Teaching and Teacher Education, 22,* 910–921.

Cochran-Smith, M. (2005). The new teacher education: For better or for worse? *Educational Researcher, 34(6),* 1–17.

Cochran-Smith, M., & Lytle, S. (2006). Troubling images of teaching in No Child Left Behind. *Harvard Educational Review, 76*(4), 668–697.

Coffield, F., Moseley, D., Hall, E., & Ecclestone, K. (2004). *Learning styles and pedagogy in post-16 learning: A systematic and critical review.* London: Learning and Skills Research Centre/University of Newcastle upon Tyne.

Cohen, E. (1994). Restructuring the classroom: Conditions for productive small groups. *Review of Educational Research, 64,* 1–35.

Cohen, J., Collins, R., Darkes, J., & Gwartney, D. (2007). A league of their own: Demographics, motivations and patterns of use of 1,955 male adult non-medical anabolic steroid users in the United States. *Journal of the International Society of Sports Nutrition* [Online]. Retrieved from http://www.jissn.com/imedia/1374735248154681_article.pdf?random=454689

Coiro, J., & Dobler, E. (2007). Exploring the online reading comprehension strategies used by sixth-grade skilled readers to search for and locate information on the Internet. *Reading Research Quarterly, 42,* 214–257.

Colangelo, N., & Davis, G. (Eds.). (2003). *Handbook of gifted education* (3rd ed.). Boston: Allyn & Bacon.

Cole, D. A., Maxwell, S. E., Martin, J. M., Peeke, L. G., Seroczynski, A. D., Tram, J. M., Hoffman, K. B., Ruiz, M. D., Jacquiz, F., & Maschman, T. (2001). The development of multiple domains of child and adolescent self-concept: A cohort sequential longitudinal design. *Child Development, 72,* 1723–1746.

Cole, M. (1996). *Cultural psychology: A once and future discipline.* Cambridge, MA: Harvard University Press.

Cole, M., Cole, S. R., & Lightfoot, C. (2005). *The development of children* (5th ed.). New York: W. H. Freeman.

Coleman, M. C., & Webber, J. (2002). *Emotional and behavioral disorders: Theory and practice* (4th ed.). Boston: Allyn & Bacon.

Coles, G. (2004). Danger in the classroom: "Brain glitch" research and learning to read. *Phi Delta Kappan, 85*(5), 344–351.

Coll, C., Bearer, E., & Lerner, R. (Eds.). (2004). *Nature and nurture: The complex interplay of genetic and environmental influences on human behavior and development.* Mahwah, NJ: Erlbaum.

College Entrance Examination Board. (2003). *School AP grade distributions, national totals.* Princeton, NJ: Author.

Collins, A. (2006). Cognitive apprenticeship. In R. K. Sawyer (Ed.), *Cambridge handbook of the learning sciences* (pp. 47–60). Cambridge, MA: Cambridge University Press.

Collins, W. A., Maccoby, E. E., Steinberg, L., Hetherington, E.M., & Bornstein, M. H. (2000). Contemporary research on parenting: The case for nature and nurture. *American Psychologist, 55,* 218–232.

Collins, W. A., & Steinberg, L. (2006). Adolescent development in interpersonal context. In N. Eisenberg (Vol. Ed.,), *Handbook of child psychology, Vol. 3. Social, emotional, and personality development* (6th ed., pp. 1003–1068). Hoboken, NJ: John Wiley & Sons, Inc.

Comer, J., Joyner, E., & Ben-Avie, M. (Eds.). (2004). *Six pathways to healthy child development and academic success.* Thousand Oaks, CA: Corwin Press.

Comstock, G., & Scharrer, E. (2006). Media and popular culture. In K. Renninger, & I. Sigel (Vol. Eds.), *Handbook of child psychology: Vol. IV. Child psychology in practice* (6th ed., pp. 817–863). Hoboken, NJ: John Wiley & Sons.

Comunian, A. L., & Gielan, U. P. (2000). Sociomoral reflection & prosocial & antisocial behavior: Two Italian studies. *Psychological Reports, 87,* 161–175.

Conchas, G., & Noguera, P. (2006). *The color of success: Race and high achieving urban youth.* New York: Teachers College Press.

Conti-Ramsden, G., & Durkin, K. (2007). Phonological short-term memory, language and literacy: Developmental relationships in early adolescence in young people with SLI. *The Journal of Child Psychology and Psychiatry and Allied Disciplines, 48,* 147–156.

Cook, B. G. (2001). A comparison of teachers' attitudes toward their included students with mild and severe disabilities. *Journal of Special Education, 34*(4), 203–213.

Cook, B. G. (2004). Inclusive teachers' attitudes toward their students with disabilities: A replication and extension. *Elementary School Journal, 104*(4), 307–320.

Cooper, D., & Snell, J. (2003). Bullying—not just a kid thing. *Educational Leadership, 60*(6), 22–25.

Cooper, H. (2006). Research questions and research designs. In P. Alexander & P. Winne (Eds.), *Handbook of educational psychology* (2nd ed., pp. 849–879). Mahwah, NJ: Lawrence Erlbaum Associates.

Cooper, H., Robinson, J. C., & Patall, E. A. (2006). Does homework improve academic achievement? A synthesis of research, 1987–2003. *Review of Educational Research, 76,* 1–62.

Cooper, J., Horn, S., Strahan, D., & Miller, S. (2003, April). *"If only they would do their homework:" Promoting self-regulation in high school English classes.* Paper presented at the annual meeting of the American Educational Research Association, Chicago.

Corbett, D., & Wilson, B. (2002). What urban students say about good teaching. *Educational Leadership, 60*(1), 18–22.

Corcoran, C. A., Dershimer, E. L., & Tichenor, M. S. (2004). A teacher's guide to alternative assessment: Taking the first steps. *The Clearing House, 77*(5), 213–216.

Cornelius-White, J. (2007). Learner-centered teacher-student relationships are effective: A meta-analysis. *Review of Educational Research, 77,* 113–143.

Corno, L., Cronbach, L. J., Kupermintz, H., Lohman, D. F., Mandinach, E. B., Porteu, A. W., & Talbert, J. E. (2002). *Remaking the concept of aptitude: Extending the legacy of Richard E. Snow.* Mahwah, NJ: Erlbaum.

Costa, D. S. J., & Boakes, R. A. (2007). Maintenance of responding when reinforcement becomes delayed. *Learning & Behavior, 35,* 95–105.

Council for Exceptional Children (2005). Retrieved May 17, 2005, from http://www.CEC.sped.org.IDEALaw&resources

Covington, M. (1992). *Making the grade: A self-worth perspective on motivation and school reform.* Cambridge, MA: Harvard University Press.

Covington, M. (1998). *The will to learn: A guide for motivating young people.* New York: Cambridge University Press.

Covington, M. (2000). Intrinsic versus extrinsic motivation in schools: A reconciliation. *Current Directions in Psychological Science, 9,* 22–25.

Covington, M. V., & Müeller, K. J. (2001). Intrinsic versus extrinsic motivation: An approach/avoidance reformulation. *Educational Psychology Review, 13,* 157–176.

Covington, M., & Omelich, C. (1987). "I knew it cold before the exam": A test of the anxiety blockage hypothesis. *Journal of Educational Psychology, 79,* 393–400.

Craig, D. (2003). Brain-compatible learning: Principles and applications in athletic training. *Journal of Athletic Training, 38*(4), 342–350.

Craik, F. I. M. (1979). Human memory. *Annual Review of Psychology, 30,* 63–102.

Craik, F. I. M., & Lockhart, R. S. (1986). CHARM is not enough: Comments on Eich's model of cued recall. *Psychological Review, 93,* 360–364.

Crick, N. R., Grotpeter, J. K., & Bigbee, M. A. (2002). Relationally and physically aggressive children's intent attributions and feelings of distress for relational and instructional peer provocation. *Child Development, 73,* 1134–1142.

Crippen, K. J., & Earl, B. L. (2007). The impact of web-based worked examples and self-explanation on performance, problem solving, and self-efficacy. *Computers & Education, 49,* 809–821.

Crockett, C. (2004). What do kids know—and misunderstand—about science? *Educational Leadership, 61*(5), 34–37.

Crooks, T. (1988). The impact of classroom evaluation practices on students. *Review of Educational Research, 58,* 438–481.

Crosnoe, R. (2005). Double disadvantage or signs of resilience? The elementary school contexts of children from Mexican immigrant families. *American Educational Research Journal, 42*(2), 269–303.

Cross, T. L., (2001). Gifted children and Erikson's theory of psychosocial development. *Gifted Child Today, 24*(1), 54–55, 61.

Crow, S., R., (2007). Information literacy: What's motivation got to do with it? *Knowledge Quest, 35,* 48–52

Cruickshank, D. (1985). Applying research on teacher clarity. *Journal of Teacher Education, 35*(2), 44–48.

Cuban, L. (1993). *How teachers taught: Constancy and change in American classrooms*: 1890–1990 (2nd ed). New York: Teachers College Press, Teachers College, Columbia University.

Cuban, L. (2001). *Computers in the classroom: Oversold and underused.* Cambridge, MA: Harvard University Press.

Cuban, L. (2004). Assessing the 20-year impact of multiple intelligences on schooling. *Teachers College Record, 106*(1), 140–146.

Cummins, J. (2000). *Language, power, and pedagogy: Bilingual children in the crossfire.* Clevedon, UK: Multilingual Matters.

Curtindale, L., Laurie-Rose, C., & Bennett-Murphy, L. (2007). Sensory modality, temperament, and the development of sustained attention: A vigilance study in children and adults. *Developmental Psychology, 43*(3), 576–589.

Cushman, K. (2003). *Fires in the bathroom: Advice for teachers from high school students.* New York: The New Press.

d'Ailly, H. (2003). Children's autonomy and perceived control in learning: A model of motivation and achievement in Taiwan. *Journal of Educational Psychology, 95,* 84–96.

D'Arcangelo, M. (2000). How does the brain develop? *Educational Leadership, 58*(3), 68–71.

Darden, E. (2007). Autism, the law, and you. *American School Board Journal, 194*(9), 60–61.

Darling-Hammond, L., & Baratz-Snowdon, J. (Eds.). (2005). *A good teacher in every classroom: Preparing the highly qualified teachers our children deserve.* San Francisco: Jossey-Bass/Wiley.

Darling-Hammond, L., & Bransford, J. (Eds.) (2005). *Preparing teachers for a changing world: What teachers should learn and be able to do.* San Francisco: Jossey-Bass.

Davidson, B., Dell, G., & Walker, H. (2001, April). *In-school clubs: Impacting teaching and learning for at-risk students.* Paper presented at the annual meeting of the American Educational Research Association, Seattle.

Davidson, J., & Sternberg, R. (Eds.). (2003). *The psychology of problem solving.* Cambridge: Cambridge University.

Davis, A. (2004). The credentials of brain-based learning. *Journal of Philosophy of Education, 38*(1), 21–35.

Davis, G. (2003). Identifying creative students, teaching for creative growth. In N. Colangelo, & G. Davis (Eds.), *Handbook of gifted education* (3rd ed., pp. 311–324). Boston: Allyn & Bacon.

Davis, G., & Rimm, S. (2004). *Education of the gifted and talented* (5th ed.). Boston: Allyn & Bacon.

Davis, H. A. (2003). Conceptualizing the role and influence of student–teacher relationships on children's social and cognitive development. *Educational Psychologist, 38,* 207–234.

Davis, H. A. (2006). Conceptualizing the role and influence of student–teacher relationships on children's social and cognitive development. *Educational Psychologist, 38,* 207–234.

Davis, S. D., & Piercy, F. P. (2007). What clients of couple therapy model developers and their former students say about change, part I: Model-dependent common factors across three models. *Journal of Marital and Family Therapy, 33,* 318–343.

Davis-Kean, P. E., & Sandler, H. M. (2001). A meta-analysis of measures of self-esteem for young children: A framework for future measurers. *Child Development, 72,* 887–906.

DeCorte, E. (2003). Transfer as the productive use of acquired knowledge, skills, and motivations. *Current Directions in Psychological Science, 12,* 142–146.

De Corte, E. (2007). Learning from instruction: the case of mathematics. *Learning Inquiry, 1,* 19–30.

De Lisi, R., & Straudt, J. (1980). Individual differences in college students' performance on formal operations tasks. *Journal of Applied Developmental Psychology, 1,* 201–208.

De Simone, C. (2007). Applications of concept mapping. *College Teaching, 55,* 33–36.

Dean, D. Jr., & Kuhn, D. (2007). Direct instruction vs. discovery: The long view. *Science Education, 91,* 384–397.

deCharms, R. (1968). *Personal causation.* San Diego: Academic Press.

deCharms, R. (1984). Motivation enhancement in education settings. In R. Ames & C. Ames (Eds.), *Research on motivation in education* (Vol. 1, pp. 275–310). New York: Academic Press.

Deci, E., & Ryan, R. (1987). The support of autonomy and the control of behavior. *Journal of Personality and Social Psychology, 53,* 1024–1037.

Deci, E., & Ryan, R. (2000). The "what" and "why" of goal pursuits: Human needs and the self-determination of behavior. *Psychological Inquiry, 11,* 227–268.

Deci, E., & Ryan, R. (Eds.). (2002). *Handbook of self-determination research.* Rochester, NY: University of Rochester Press.

Delpit, L. (1995). *Other people's children: Cultural conflict in the classroom.* New York: The New Press.

Demetriou, A., Christou, C., Spanoudis, G., & Platsidou, M. (2002). The development of mental processing: Efficiency, working memory, and thinking. *Monographs of the Society for Research in Child Development* (Serial No. 268, Vol. 67, No. 1). Boston: Blackwell Publishing.

DeMeulenaere, E. (2001, April). *Constructing reinventions: Black and Latino students negotiating the transformation of their academic identities and school performance.* Paper presented at the annual meeting of the American Educational Research Association, Seattle.

Dempster, R., & Corkill, A. (1999). Interference and inhibition in cognition and behavior: Unifying themes for educational psychology. *Educational Psychology Review, 11,* 1–88.

Denig, S. J. (2003, April). *A proposed relationship between multiple intelligences and learning styles.* Paper presented at the annual meeting of the American Educational Research Association, Chicago.

Dennis, T. A., Cole, P. M., Zahn-Waxler, C., & Mizuta, I. (2002). Self in context: Autonomy and relatedness in Japanese and U. S. mother–preschooler dyads. *Child Development, 73,* 1803–1817.

Denzin, N., & Lincoln, Y. (2007). *The landscape of qualitative research* (3rd ed.). Thousand Oaks, CA: Sage.

Derry, S. (1992). Beyond symbolic processing: Expanding horizons for educational psychology. *Journal of Educational Psychology, 84,* 413–419.

Deutsch, N., & Hirsch, B. (2001, April). *A place to call home: Youth organizations in the lives of inner city adolescents.* Paper presented at the biennial meeting of the Society for Research in Child Development, Minneapolis, MN.

DeVries, R. (1997). Piaget's social theory. *Educational Researcher, 26*(2), 4–18.

DeVries, R., & Zan, B. (2003). When children make rules. *Educational Leadership, 61,* 64–67.

Dewey, J. (1938). *Experience and education.* New York: Macmillan.

Deyhle, D. (1987). Learning failure: Tests as gatekeepers and the culturally different child. In H. Trueba (Ed.), *Success or failure?* (pp. 85–108). Cambridge, MA: Newbury House.

Deyhle, D., & LeCompte, M. (1999). Cultural differences in child development: Navajo adolescents in middle schools. In R. H. Sheets & E. R. Holins (Eds.), *Racial and ethnic identity in school practices: Aspects of human development* (pp. 123–139). Mahwah, NJ: Erlbaum.

Diamond, J., & Gomez, K. (2004). African American parents' educational orientations: The importance of social class and parents' perceptions of schools. *Education and Urban Society, 36*(4), 383–427.

Dickson, S. M. (2004). Tracking concept mastery using a biology portfolio. *The American Biology Teacher, 66*(9), 628–634.

Dien, T. (1998). Language and literacy in Vietnamese American communities. In B. Pérez (Ed.), *Sociocultural contexts of language and literacy.* Mahwah, NJ: Erlbaum.

Ding, M., Li, X., Piccolo, D., & Kulm, G. (2007). Teacher interventions in cooperative-learning mathematics classes. *Journal of Educational Research, 100*(3), 162–176.

diSessa, A. (2006). A history of conceptual change research: Threads and fault lines. In R. K. Sawyer (Ed.), *Cambridge handbook of the learning sciences* (pp. 265–282). Cambridge, MA: Cambridge University Press.

Do, S. L., & Schallert, D. L. (2004). Emotions and classroom talk: Toward a model of the role of affect in students' experiences of classroom discussions. *Journal of Educational Psychology, 96,* 619–634.

Dochy, F., & McDowell, L. (1997). Introduction: Assessment as a tool for learning. *Studies in Educational Evaluation, 23*(4), 279–298.

Dodge, K., Coie, J., & Lynam, D. (2006). Aggression and antisocial behavior in youth. In N. Eisenberg (Ed.,), *Handbook of child psychology: Vol. 3. Social, emotional, and personality development* (6th ed., pp. 719–788). Hoboken, NJ: John Wiley & Sons.

Dodge, K. A., Lansford, J. E., Burks, V. S., Bates, J. E., Pettit, G. S., Fontaine, R., & Price, J. M. (2003). Peer rejection and social information-processing factors in the development of aggressive behavior problems in children. *Child Development, 74,* 374–393.

Dolezal, S., Welsh, L., Pressley, M., & Vincent, M. (2003). How nine third-grade teachers motivate student academic engagement. *Elementary School Journal, 103,* 239–268.

Doll, B., Zucker, S., & Brehm, K. (2004). *Resilient classrooms: Creating healthy environments for learning.* New York: Guilford Press.

Donovan, M. S., & Bransford, J. D. (2005). Introduction. In M. S. Donovan & J. D. Bransford (Eds.), *How students learn: History, mathematics, and science in the classroom* (pp. 1–26). Washington, DC: National Academies Press.

Douglas, N. L. (2000). Enemies of critical thinking: Lessons from social psychology research. *Reading Psychology, 21,* 129–144.

Downey, J. (2003, April). *Listening to students: Perspectives of educational resilience from children who face adversity.* Paper presented at the annual meeting of the American Educational Research Association, Chicago.

Dowson, M., & McInerney, D. (2001). Psychological parameters of students' social and work avoidance goals: A qualitative investigation. *Journal of Educational Psychology, 93,* 35–42.

Doyle, W. (1986). Classroom organization and management. In M. Wittrock (Ed.), *Handbook of research on teaching* (3rd ed., pp. 392–431). New York: Macmillan.

Doyle, W. (2006). Ecological approaches to classroom management. In C. M. Evertson & C. S. Weinstein (Eds.), *Handbook of classroom management: Research, practice, and contemporary issues* (pp. 97–125). Mahwah, NJ: Erlbaum.

Driscoll, M. (2005). *Psychology of learning for instruction* (3rd ed.). Needham Heights, MA: Allyn & Bacon.

Dubois, D. L. (2001). Family disadvantage, the self, and academic achievement. In B. J. Biddle (Ed.), *Social class, poverty, and education* (pp. 133–174). New York: Routledge Falmer.

Duke, N. (2000). For the rich it's richer: Print experience and environments offered to children in very low- and very high-socioeconomic status first-grade classrooms. *American Educational Research Journal, 37,* 441–478.

Dwairy, M. (2005). Using problem-solving conversation with children. *Intervention in School and Clinic, 40,* 144–150.

Dweck, C. (1975). The role of expectations and attributions in the alleviation of learned helplessness. *Journal of Personality and Social Psychology, 31,* 674–685.

Dweck, C. (1999). Self-theories and goals: Their role in motivation, personality, and development. In R. Dienstbier (Ed.), *Perspectives on motivation: Nebraska Symposium on Motivation 1990* (Vol. 38, pp. 199–325). Lincoln: University of Nebraska Press.

Dweck, C. (2000). *Self-theories: Their role in motivation, personality, and development.* Philadelphia, PA: Psychology Press.

Dweck, C., & Leggett, E. (1988). A social-cognitive approach to motivation and personality. *Psychological Review, 95,* 256–273.

Dwyer, K., & Osher, D. (2000). *Safeguarding our children: An action guide.* Washington, DC: U.S. Department of Education and Justice, American Institutes for Research. Retrieved June 13, 2005, from http://www.ed.gov/pubs/edpubs.html

Dynarski, M., & Gleason, P. (1999, April). *How can we help? What we have learned from evaluations of federal dropout-prevention programs.* Paper presented at the annual meeting of the American Educational Research Association, Montreal, Canada.

Eccles, J., Templeton, J., Barber, B., & Stone, M. (2003). Adolescence and emerging adulthood: The critical passage ways to adulthood. In M. Bornstein, L. Davidson, C. Keyes, K. Moore, & The Center for Child Well-Being (Eds.), *Well-being: Positive development across the life course* (pp. 383–406).

Eccles, J., Wigfield, A., Flanagan, C., Miller, C., Reuman, D., & Yee, D. (1989). Self-concepts, domain values, and self-esteem: Relations and changes at early adolescence. *Journal of Personality, 57,* 283–310.

Eccles, J. S., Wigfield, A., & Schiefele, U. (1998). Motivation to succeed. In W. Damon (Series Ed.) & N. Eisenberg (Vol. Ed.), *Handbook of child psychology: Vol. 3. Social, emotional, and personality development* (5th ed., pp. 1017–1095). New York: Wiley.

Echevarria, J., & Graves, A. (2007). *Sheltered content instruction* (3rd ed.). Boston: Allyn & Bacon.

Echevarria, J., Vogt, M., & Short, D. (2004). *Making content comprehensible to English learners: The SIOP model.* Boston: Allyn & Bacon.

Eckardt, N. (2007, November 8). The prevalence of qualitative methodology at AERA's annual meeting and the potential consequences. *Teachers College Record,* ID Number 14741. Retrieved March 21, 2008, from http//:www.tcrecord.org

Edens, K. M., & Potter, E. F. (2001). Promoting conceptual understanding through pictorial representation. *Studies in Art Education, 42,* 214–233.

Education Vital Signs. (2005). Poverty. *American School Board Journal, February,* 22–23.

Educational Testing Service. (2008a). *The Praxis Series™ 2007–2008: Information Bulletin.* Retrieved from http://www.etsliteracy.org/Media/Tests/PRAXIS/pdf/01361.pdf

Educational Testing Service. (2008b). *The Praxis Series™: Principles of Learning and Teaching: Grades 7–12 (0524).* Retrieved from http://www.ets.org/Media/Tests/PRAXIS/pdf/0524.pdf

Eggen, P. (1997, March). *The impact of frequent assessment on achievement, satisfaction with instruction, and intrinsic motivation of undergraduate university students.* Paper presented at the annual meeting of the American Educational Research Association, Chicago.

Eggen, P. (1998, April). *A comparison of urban middle school teachers' classroom practices and their expressed beliefs about learning and effective instruction.* Paper presented at the annual meeting of the American Educational Research Association, San Diego.

Eggen, P. (2001, April). *Constructivism and the architecture of cognition: Implications for instruction.* Paper presented at the annual meeting of the American Educational Research Association, Seattle.

Eggen, P. (2004, April). *A longitudinal study of teachers' and educational leaders' conceptions of classroom interaction.* Paper presented at the annual meeting of the American Educational Research Association, San Diego.

Eggen, P., & Gonzales, C. (2005, April). *A cross-cultural study of teachers' and educational leaders' conceptions of classroom interaction.* Paper presented at the annual meeting of the American Educational Research Association, Montreal.

Eggen, P., & Gonzalez, C. (2007, April). *An examination of the relationships between elementary teachers' understanding of educational psychology and their pedagogical practice.* Paper presented at the annual meeting of the American Educational Research Association, Chicago.

Eggen, P., & Kauchak, D. (2002, April). *Synthesizing the literature of motivation: Implications for instruction.* Paper presented at the annual meeting of the American Educational Research Association, New Orleans, LA.

Eggen, P., & Kauchak, D. (2006). *Strategies and models for teachers: Teaching content and thinking skills* (5th ed.). Boston: Allyn & Bacon.

Eilam, B., & Aharon, I. (2003). Students' planning in the process of self-regulated learning. *Contemporary Educational Psychology, 28,* 304–334.

Eisenberg, N., Fabes, R., & Spinrad, T. (2006). Prosocial development. In N. Eisenberg (Vol. Ed,), *Handbook of child psychology: Vol. 3. Social, emotional, and personality development* (6th ed., pp. 646–718). Hoboken, NJ: John Wiley & Sons.

Eisenman, L. T. (2007). Self-determination interventions: Building a foundation for school completion. *Remedial and Special Education, 28,* 2–8.

Elbaum, B., & Vaughn, S. (2001). School-based interventions to enhance the self-concept of students with learning disabilities: A meta-analysis. *Elementary School Journal, 101*(3), 303–330.

Elder, L., & Paul, R. (2007). Critical thinking: The nature of critical and creative thought: Part II. *Journal of Developmental Education, 30*, 36–37.

Elias, M. (2004). Strategies to infuse social and emotional learning into academics. In J. Zins, R. Weissberg, M. Wang, & H. Walberg (Eds.), *Building academic success on social and emotional learning* (pp. 113–134). New York: Teachers College Press.

Elias, M. J., & Schwab, Y. (2006). From compliance to responsibility: Social and emotional learning and classroom management. In C. M. Evertson & C. S. Weinstein (Eds.), *Handbook of classroom management: Research, practice, and contemporary issues* (pp. 309–341). Mahwah, NJ: Erlbaum.

Elliot, A., & McGregor, H. (2000, April). Approach and avoidance goals and autonomous-controlled regulation: Empirical and conceptual relations. In A. Assor (Chair), *Self-determination theory and achievement goal theory: Convergences, divergences, and educational implications.* Symposium conducted at the annual meeting of the American Educational Research Association, New Orleans.

Elliot, A., & Thrash, T. (2001). Achievement goals and the hierarchical model of achievement motivation. *Educational Psychology Review, 13*, 139–156.

Elliott, J., & Thurlow, M. (2000). *Improving test performance of students with disabilities.* Thousand Oaks, CA: Corwin Press.

Emerson, M. J., & Miyake, A. (2003). The role of inner speech in task switching: A dual-task investigation. *Journal of Memory and Language, 48*, 148–168.

Emmer, E. T., Evertson, C. M., & Anderson, L. (1980). Effective classroom management at the beginning of the school year. *Elementary School Journal, 18*, 219–231.

Emmer, E. T., Evertson, C. M., & Worsham, M. E. (2006). *Classroom management for middle and high school teachers* (7th ed.). Boston: Allyn & Bacon.

Emmer, E. T., & Gerwels, M. C. (2006). Classroom management in middle and high school classrooms. In C. M. Evertson & C. S. Weinstein (Eds.), *Handbook of classroom management: Research, practice, and contemporary issues* (pp. 407–437). Mahwah, NJ: Erlbaum.

Emmer, E. T., & Stough, L. M. (2001). Classroom management: A critical part of educational psychology with implications for teacher education. *Educational Psychologist, 36*, 103–112.

Englert, C., Berry, R., & Dunsmoore, K. (2001). A case study of the apprenticeship process. *Journal of Learning Disabilities, 34*, 152–171.

Epstein, J. (2001, April). *School, family, and community partnerships: Preparing educators and improving schools.* Paper presented at the annual meeting of the American Educational Research Association, Seattle.

Ericsson, K. A. (2003). The acquisition of expert performance as problem solving: Construction and modification of mediating mechanisms through deliberate practice. In J. E. Davidson and R. J. Sternberg (Eds.), *The psychology of problem solving* (pp. 31–83). Cambridge, UK: Cambridge University Press.

Erikson, E. (1968). *Identity: Youth and crisis.* New York: Norton.

Erikson, E. (1980). *Identity and the life cycle* (2nd ed.). New York: Norton.

Evans, C., Kirby, U., & Fabrigar, L. (2003). Approaches to learning, need for cognition, and strategic flexibility among university students. *The British Journal of Educational Psychology, 73*, 507–528.

Evans, E., & Engelberg, R. (1988). Student perceptions of school grading. *Journal of Research and Development in Education, 21*(2), 45–54.

Evans, G. W., & English, K. (2002). The environment of poverty: Multiple stressor exposure, psychophysiological stress, and socioemotional adjustment. *Child Development, 73*, 1238–1248.

Evans, L., & Davies, K. (2000). No sissy boys here: A content analysis of the representation of masculinity in elementary school reading texts. *Sex Roles, 42*, 255–270.

Everson, H., & Tobias, S. (1998). The ability to estimate knowledge and performance in college: A metacognitive analysis. *Instructional Science, 26*(1–2), 65–79.

Evertson, C., Anderson, C., Anderson, L., & Brophy, J. (1980). Relationships between classroom behaviors and student outcomes in junior high mathematics and English classes. *American Educational Research Journal, 17*, 43–60.

Evertson, C. M., Emmer, E. T., & Worsham, M. E. (2006). *Classroom management for elementary teachers* (7th ed.). Boston: Allyn & Bacon.

Evertson, C. M., & Weinstein, C. S. (2006). Classroom management as a field of inquiry. In C. M. Evertson & C. S. Weinstein (Eds.), *Handbook of classroom management: Research, practice, and contemporary issues* (pp. 3–15). Mahwah, NJ: Erlbaum.

Exline, R. (1962). Need affiliation and initial communication behavior in problem solving groups characterized by low interpersonal visibility. *Psychological Reports, 10*, 405–411.

Ezell, D., & Klein, C. (2003). Impact of portfolio assessment on locus of control of students with and without disabilities. *Education and Training in Developmental Disabilities, 38*(2), 220–228.

Fabiano, G. A., Pelham, W. E., Jr., & Gnagy, E. M. (2007). The single and combined effects of multiple intensities of behavior modification and methylphenidate for children with attention deficit hyperactivity disorder in a classroom setting. *The School Psychology Review, 36*, 195–216.

Faiman-Silva, S. (2002). Students and a "culture of resistance" in Provincetown's schools. *Anthropology & Education Quarterly, 33*(2), 189–212.

Fair Test. (2008). SAT I: *A faulty instrument for predicting college success.* Fair Test: The National Center for Fair and Open Testing. Retrieved January 9, 2008, from http://www.fairtest.org

Farkas, R. (2003). Effects of traditional versus learning-styles instructional methods on middle school students. *Journal of Educational Research, 97*(1), 42–51.

Fauth, R., Roth, J., & Brooks-Gunn, J. (2007). Does the neighborhood context alter the link between youth's after-school time activities and developmental outcomes? A Multilevel analysis. *Developmental Psychology, 43*(3), 760–777.

Feiman-Nemser, S. (2001). From preparation to practice: Designing a continuum to strengthen and sustain teaching. *Teachers College Record, 103*, 1013–1055.

Feldhusen, J. (1998a). Programs and service at the elementary level. In J. VanTassel-Baska (Ed.), *Excellence in educating gifted and talented learners* (3rd ed., pp. 211–223). Denver: Love.

Feldhusen, J. (1998b). Programs and services at the secondary level. In J. VanTassel-Baska (Ed.), *Excellence in educating gifted and talented learners* (3rd ed., pp. 225–240). Denver: Love.

Feldon, D. F. (2007a). Cognitive load and classroom teaching: The double-edged sword of automaticity. *Educational Psychologist, 42*, 123–137.

Feldon, D. F. (2007b). The implications of research on expertise for curriculum and pedagogy. *Educational Psychology Review, 19*(2), 91–110.

Ferguson, R. (2003). Teachers' perceptions and expectations and the black–white test score gap. *Urban Education, 38*(4), 460–507.

Fernandez-Berrocal, P., & Santamaria, C. (2006). Mental models in social interaction. *The Journal of Experimental Education, 74*(3), 229–248.

Ferrari, M., & Elik, N. (2003). Influences on intentional conceptual change. In G. M. Sinatra & P. R. Pintrich (Eds.), *Intentional conceptual change* (pp. 21–54). Mahwah, NJ: Erlbaum.

Finn, J., Gerber, S., & Boyd-Zaharias, J. (2005). Small classes in the early grades, academic achievement, and graduating from high school. *Journal of Educational Psychology, 97*(2), 214–223.

Finn, J., Pannozzo, G., & Achilles, C. (2003). The "why's" of class size: Student behavior in small classes. *Review of Educational Research, 72*(3), 321–368.

Finn, K., & Frone, M. (2004). Academic performance and cheating: Moderating role of school identification and self-efficacy. *Journal of Educational Research, 97*(3), 115–122.

Fischer, K., & Bidell, T. (2006). Dynamic development of action and thought. In R. Lerner (Vol. Ed.), *Handbook of child psychology: Vol. 1. Theoretical models of human development* (6th ed., pp. 313–399). Hoboken, NJ: John Wiley & Sons.

Fischer, L., Schimmel, D., & Stellman, L. (2006). *Teachers and the law.* New York: Longman.

Fishman, B., & Davis, E., (2006). Teacher learning research and the learning sciences. In R. K. Sawyer (Ed.), *Cambridge handbook of the learning sciences* (pp. 535–550). New York: Cambridge University Press.

Flavell, J., Miller, P., & Miller, S. (2002). *Cognitive development* (4th ed.). Upper Saddle River, NJ: Prentice Hall.

Fleming, V., & Alexander, J. (2001). The benefits of peer collaboration: A replication with a delayed posttest. *Contemporary Educational Psychology, 26*, 588–601.

Flores, E., Cicchetti, D., & Rogosch, F. A. (2005). Predictors of resilience in maltreated and nonmaltreated Latino children. *Developmental Psychology, 41*(2), 338, 351.

Flores, M. M., & Kaylor, M. (2007). The effects of a direct instruction program on the fraction performance of middle school students at-risk for failure in mathematics. *Journal of Instructional Psychology, 34*, 84–94.

Florida Department of Education. (2007). *Grade level expectations for the Sunshine State Standards: Science Grades 6–8*. Retrieved January 25, 2008, from http://etc.usf.edu/flstandards/sss/pdf/science6.pdf

Forness, S., Walker, H., & Kavale, K. (2005). Psychiatric disorders and treatments: A primer for teachers. In K. Freiberg (Ed.), *Educating exceptional children 05/06* (7th ed., pp. 107–115). Dubuque, IA: McGraw-Hill/Dushkin.

Fowler, R. (1994, April). *Piagetian versus Vygotskian perspectives on development and education.* Paper presented at the annual meeting of the American Educational Research Association, New Orleans, LA.

Fredericks, J. A., & Eccles, J. S. (2006). Is extracurricular participation associated with beneficial outcomes? Concurrent and longitudinal relations. *Developmental Psychology, 42*(4), 698–713.

Freeman, J., McPhail, J., & Berndt, J. (2002). Sixth graders' views of activities that do and do not help them learn. *Elementary School Journal, 102*(4), 335–347.

Freeman, K. E., Gutman, L. M., & Midgley, C. (2002). Can achievement goal theory enhance our understanding of the motivation and performance of African American young adolescents? In C. Midgely (Ed.), *Goals, goal structures and patterns of adaptive learning* (pp. 175–204). Mahwah, NJ: Erlbaum.

Freiberg, J. (Ed.). (1999a). *Beyond behaviorism: Changing the classroom management paradigm.* Boston: Allyn & Bacon.

Freiberg, J. (1999b). Consistency management and cooperative discipline. In J. Freiberg (Ed.), *Beyond behaviorism: Changing the classroom management paradigm* (pp. 75–97). Boston: Allyn & Bacon.

Freiberg, J. (1999c). Sustaining the paradigm. In J. Freiberg (Ed.), *Beyond behaviorism: Changing the classroom management paradigm* (pp. 164–173). Boston: Allyn & Bacon.

French, D. (2003). A new vision of authentic assessment to overcome the flaws in high-stakes testing. *Middle School Journal, 35*(1), 14–23.

French, S., Seidman, E., Allen, L., & Aber, J. (2006). The development of ethnic identity during adolescence. *Developmental Psychology, 42,* 1–10.

Frey, B., & Schmitt, V. (2005, April). *Teachers' classroom assessment practices.* Paper presented at the annual meeting of the American Educational Research Association, Montreal, Canada.

Friedel, J. M., Cortina, K. S., & Turner, J. C. (2007). Achievement goals, efficacy beliefs and coping strategies in mathematics: The roles of perceived parent and teacher goal emphases. *Contemporary Educational Psychology, 32,* 434–458.

Friedman, I. A. (2006). Classroom management and teacher stress and burnout. In C. M. Evertson & C. S. Weinstein (Eds.), *Handbook of classroom management: Research, practice, and contemporary issues* (pp. 925–944). Mahwah, NJ: Erlbaum.

Fry, R. (2007). The changing racial and ethnic composition of U.S. public schools. *Pew Hispanic Center.* Retrieved November 16, 2007, from http://www.pewhispanic.org/reports/report.php?ReportID=79

Fuchs, D. (2006). Cognitive profiling of children with genetic disorders and the search for a scientific basis of differentiated education. In P. Alexander & P. Winne (Eds.), *Handbook of educational psychology* (2nd ed., pp. 187–206). Mahwah, NJ: Erlbaum .

Fuchs, L. S., Fuchs., D., Prentice, K., Burch, M., Hamlett, C. L., Owen, R., Hosp, M., & Jancek, D. (2003). Explicitly teaching for transfer: Effects on third-grade students' mathematical problem solving. *Journal of Educational Psychology, 95,* 295–305.

Fujimura, N. (2001). Facilitating children's proportional reasoning: A model of reasoning processes and effects of intervention on strategy change. *Journal of Educational Psychology, 93,* 589–603.

Furrer, C., & Skinner, E. (2003). Sense of relatedness as a factor in children's academic engagement and performance. *Journal of Educational Psychology, 95,* 148–162.

Gagne, E. D., Yekovich, F. R., & Yekovich, C. W. (1997). *The cognitive psychology of school learning* (2nd ed.). Boston: Allyn & Bacon.

Gall, M., Gall, J., & Borg, W. (2007). *Educational research: An introduction* (8th ed.). Boston: Allyn & Bacon.

Gallini, J. (2000, April). *An investigation of self-regulation developments in early adolescence: A comparison between non at-risk and at-risk students.* Paper presented at the annual meeting of the American Educational Research Association, New Orleans.

Gao, H., Losh, S. C., Shen, E., Turner, J. E., & Yuan, R. (2007, April). *The effect of collaborative concept mapping on learning, problem solving, and learner attitude.* Paper presented at the annual meeting of the American Educational Research Association, Chicago.

Garcia, E. (2005, April). *A test in English is a test of English: Assessment's new role in educational equity.* Paper presented at the annual meeting of the American Educational Research Association, Montreal, Canada.

Gardner, H. (1983). *Frames of mind: The theory of multiple intelligences.* New York: Basic Books.

Gardner, H. (1993). *Creating minds: An anatomy of creativity seen through the lives of Freud, Einstein, Picasso, Stravinsky, Elliot, Graham, and Gandhi.* New York: Basic Books.

Gardner, H. (1995). Reflections on multiple intelligences: Myths and messages. *Phi Delta Kappan, 77,* 200–209.

Gardner, H., & Hatch, T. (1989). Multiple intelligences go to school. *Educational Researcher, 18*(8), 4–10.

Gardner, H., & Moran, S. (2006). The science of multiple intelligences theory: A response to Lynn Waterhouse. *Educational Psychologist, 41*(4), 227–232.

Garrahy, D. (2001). Three third-grade teachers' gender-related beliefs and behavior. *Elementary School Journal, 102,* 81–94.

Gaskill, P. J., & Murphy, P. K. (2004). Effects of a memory strategy on second-graders' performance and self efficacy. *Contemporary Educational Psychology, 29,* 27–49.

Gathercole, S. E., Pickering, S. J., Ambridge, B., & Wearing, H. (2004). The structure of working memory from 4 to 15 years of age. *Developmental Psychology, 49*(2), 177–190.

Gay, B. (2000). Educational equality for students of color. In J. Banks & C. Banks (Eds.), *Multicultural education: Issues and perspectives* (4th ed., pp. 195–228). Boston: Allyn & Bacon.

Gay, G. (2005). Politics of multicultural teacher education. *Journal of Teacher Education, 56*(3), 221–228.

Gay, G. (2006). Connections between classroom management and culturally responsive teaching. In C. Evertson, & C. Weinsten (Eds.), *Handbook of classroom management: Research, practice, and contemporary issues* (pp. 343–370). Mahwah, NJ: Erlbaum.

Gay, L., Mills, G., & Airasian, P. (2006). *Educational research* (8th ed.). Upper Saddle River, NJ: Merrill/Pearson.

Gehlbach, H., & Roeser, R. (2002). The middle way to motivating middle school students: Avoiding false dichotomies. *Middle School Journal, 33,* 39–46.

Geisinger, K. (2005). The testing industry, ethnic minorities, and individuals with disabilities. In R. Phelps (Ed.), *Defending standardized testing* (pp. 187–204). Mahwah, NJ: Erlbaum.

Gelman, S., & Kalish, C. (2006). Conceptual development. In W. Damon & R. Lerner (Series Eds.), D. Kuhn & R. Siegler (Vol. Eds.), *Handbook of child psychology: Vol. II. Cognition, perception, and language* (pp. 687–733, 6th ed.). New York: Wiley.

Genessee, F. (2004). What do we know about bilingual education for majority-language students? In T. Bhatia & W. Ritchie (Eds.), *The handbook of bilingualism.* Oxford, UK: Blackwell.

Gentile, J. (1996). Setbacks in the advancement of learning *Educational Researcher, 25,* 37–39.

Gersten, R., Taylor, R., & Graves, A. (1999). Direct instruction and diversity. In R. Stevens (Ed.), *Teaching in American schools* (pp. 81–106). Upper Saddle River, NJ: Merrill/Pearson.

Gettinger, M., & Kohler, K. M. (2006). Process–outcome approaches to classroom management and effective teaching. In C. M. Evertson & C. S. Weinstein (Eds.), *Handbook of classroom management: Research, practice, and contemporary issues* (pp. 73–95). Mahwah, NJ: Erlbaum.

Gholson, B., & Craig, S. D. (2006). Promoting constructive activities that support vicarious learning during computer-based instruction. *Educational Psychology Review, 18,* 119–139.

Gijbels, D., Dochy, F., Van den Bossche, P., & Segers, M. (2005). Effects of problem-based learning: A meta-analysis from the angle of assessment. *Review of Educational Research, 75*(1), 27–61.

Gillies, R. M. (2003). The behaviors, interactions, and perceptions of junior high school students during small-group learning. *Journal of Educational Psychology, 95,* 137–147.

Gilligan, C. (1977). In a different voice: Women's conceptions of the self and of morality. *Harvard Educational Review, 47,* 481–517.

Gilligan, C. (1982). *In a different voice: Psychological theory and women's development.* Cambridge, MA: Harvard University Press.

Gilligan, C. (1998). *Minding women: Reshaping the education realm.* Cambridge, MA: Harvard University Press.

Gilligan, C., & Attanucci, J. (1988). Two moral orientations: Gender differences and similarities. *Merrill-Palmer Quarterly, 34,* 223–237.

Gillison, F. B., Standage, M., & Skevington, S. M. (2006). Relationships among adolescents' weight perceptions, exercise goals, exercise motivation, quality of life and leisure-time exercise behavior: A self-determination theory approach. *Health Education Research, 21,* 836–847.

Gimbel, P. (2008). Helping new teachers reflect. *Principal Leadership (High School Ed.), 8,* 6–8.

Ginsberg, A. E., Shapiro, J. P., & Brown, S. P. (2004). *Gender in urban education: Strategies for student achievement.* Portsmouth, NH: Heinemann.

Glassman, M. (2001). Dewey and Vygotsky: Society, experience, and inquiry in educational practice. *Educational Researcher, 30*(4), 3–14.

Glassman, M., & Wang, Y. (2004). On the interconnected nature of interpreting Vygotsky: Rejoinder to Gredler and Shields *Does no one read Vygotsky's words? Educational Researcher, 33*(6), 19–22.

Goddard, R. D. (2001). Collective efficacy: A neglected construct in the study of schools and student achievement. *Journal of Educational Psychology, 93,* 467–476.

Goddard, R. D., Hoy, W. K., & Woolfolk Hoy, A. (2004). Collective efficacy beliefs: Theoretical developments, empirical evidence and future directions. *Educational Researcher, 33,* 3–13.

Godley, A., Sweetland, J., Wheeler, R., Minnici, A., & Carpenter, B. (2006). Preparing teachers for dialectally diverse classrooms. *Educational Researcher, 35*(8), 30–37.

Goldstein, R. A. (2004). Who are our urban students and what makes them so different? In S. R. Steinberg & J. L. Kincheloe (Eds.), *19 Urban questions: Teaching in the city* (pp. 41–51). New York: Peter Lang.

Goleman, D. (2006). *Social intelligence.* New York: Westlake Books.

Gollnick, D., & Chinn, P. (2006). *Multicultural education in a pluralistic society* (7th ed.). Upper Saddle River, NJ: Merrill/Pearson.

Gomes, H., Sussman, E., & Ritter, W. (1999). Electrophysiological evidence of developmental changes in the duration of auditory sensory memory. *Developmental Psychology, 35*(1), 294–302.

Gonzales, P., Guzman, J. C., Partelow, L., Pahlke, E., Jocelyn, L., Kastberg, D., & Williams, T. (2004). *Highlights from the trends in international mathematics and science study (TIMSS) 2003 (NCES 2005–2005).* U.S. Department of Education. Washington, DC: National Center for Educational Statistics.

Good, T. (1987a). Teacher expectations. In D. Berliner & B. Rosenshine (Eds.), *Talks to teachers* (pp. 159–200). New York: Random House.

Good, T. (1987b). Two decades of research on teacher expectations: Findings and future directions. *Journal of Teacher Education, 37*(4), 32–47.

Good, T., & Brophy, J. (1986). School effects. In M. Wittrock (Ed.), *Handbook of research on teaching* (3rd ed, pp. 570–604). New York: Macmillan.

Good, T. L., & Brophy, J E. (2008). *Looking in classrooms* (10th ed.). Boston: Allyn & Bacon.

Goodman, J. (2005). How bad is cheating? *Education Week, 24*(16), 32, 35.

Goodman, J., & Balamore, U. (2003). *Teaching goodness: Engaging the moral and academic promise of young children.* Boston: Allyn & Bacon.

Gootman, M. E. (1998). Effective in-house suspension. *Educational Leadership, 56*(1), 39–41.

Gordon, T. (1974). *Teacher effectiveness training.* New York: Wyden.

Gordon, T. (1981). Crippling our children with disruption. *Journal of Education, 163,* 228–243.

Gottfredson, P. (2001). *Schools and delinquency.* Cambridge, England: Cambridge University Press.

Gragg, C. I. (1940). Because wisdom can't be told. *Harvard Alumni Bulletin* (October 19), 78–84.

Graham, S. (2006). Writing. In P. Alexander, & P. Winne (Eds.), *Handbook of educational psychology* (2nd ed., pp. 457–478). Mahwah, NJ: Erlbaum.

Graham, S., & Barker, G. (1990). The downside of help: An attributional–developmental analysis of helping behavior as a low ability cue. *Journal of Educational Psychology, 82,* 7–14.

Graham, S., Berninger, V., Weintraub, N., & Schafer, W. (1998). Development of handwriting speed and legibility in grades 1–9. *Journal of Educational Research, 92,* 42–49.

Graham, S., & Weiner, B. (1996). Theories and principles of motivation. In D. Berliner & R. Calfee (Eds.), *Handbook of educational psychology* (pp. 63–84). New York: Macmillan.

Grant, L. W. (2006). Persistence and self-efficacy: A key to understanding teacher turnover. *The Delta Kappa Gamma Bulletin,* 72(2), 50–54.

Gray, T., & Fleischman, S. (2005). Successful strategies for English language learners. *Educational Leadership, 62*(4), 84–85.

Gray-Little, B., & Hafdahl, A. R. (2000). Factors influencing racial comparisons of self-esteem: A quantitative review. *Psychological Bulletin, 126,* 26–54.

Gredler, M., & Shields, C. (2004). Does no one read Vygotsky's words? Commentary on Glassman. *Educational Researcher, 33*(2), 21–25.

Green, C. L., Walker, J. M., Hoover-Dempsey, K. V., & Sandler, H. M. (2007). Parents' motivations for involvement in children's education: An empirical test of a theoretical model of parental involvement. *Journal of Educational Psychology, 99,* 532–544.

Green, S., & Mantz, M. (2002, April). *Classroom assessment practices: Examining impact on student learning.* Paper presented at the annual meeting of the American Educational Research Association, New Orleans.

Greenberg, M., Weissberg, R., O'Brien, M., Zins, J., Fredericks, L., Resnik, H., & Elias, M. (2003). Enhancing school-based prevention and youth development through coordinated social, emotional, and academic learning. *American Psychologist, 58,* 466–474.

Greene, J. A., & Azevedo, R. (2007). A theoretical review of Winne and Hadwin's model of self-regulated learning: New perspectives and directions. *Review of Educational Research, 77,* 334–372.

Greenfield, P., Trumbull, E., Keller, H., Rothstein-Fisch, C., Suzuki, L., & Quiroz, B. (2006). Cultural conceptions of learning and development. In P. Alexander & P. Winner (Eds.), *Handbook of educational psychology* (2nd ed., pp. 675–692). Mahwah, NJ: Erlbaum.

Greeno, J., Collins, A., & Resnick, L. (1996). Cognition and learning. In D. Berliner & R. Calfee (Eds.), *Handbook of educational psychology* (pp. 15–46). New York: Macmillan.

Greeno, J., & van de Sande, C. (2007). Perspectival understanding of conceptions and conceptual growth in interaction. *Educational Psychologist, 42*(1), 9–24.

Gregory, A., & Weinstein, R. (2004, April). *Toward narrowing the discipline gap: Cooperation or defiance in the high school classroom.* Paper presented at the annual meeting of the American Educational Research Association, San Diego.

Griffith, D. (1992, April). Prenatal exposure to cocaine and other drugs: Developmental and educational prognoses. *Phi Delta Kappan, 74,* 30–34.

Griffith, D., Hayes, K., & Pascarella, J. (2004). Why teach in urban settings? In S. Steinberg & J. Kincheloe (Eds.), *19 Urban questions: Teaching in the city* (pp. 267–280). New York: Peter Lang.

Gronlund, N. (2003). *Assessing student achievement* (7th ed.). Needham Heights, MA: Allyn & Bacon.

Gronlund, N. (2004). *Writing instructional objectives for teaching and assessment* (7th ed.). Upper Saddle River, NJ: Merrill/Pearson.

Gschwend, L., & Dembo, M. (2001, April). *How do high-efficacy teachers persist in low-achieving, culturally diverse schools?* Paper presented at the annual meeting of the American Educational Research Association, Seattle.

Gullo, D. (2005). *Understanding assessment and evaluation in early childhood education* (2nd ed.). New York: Teachers College Press.

Gurian, M., & Stevens, K. (2005). What is happening with boys in school? *Teachers College Record.* Retrieved June 21, 2005, from http://www.tcrecord. org/Content.asp?ContentID=11854

Guskey, T. (2002, April). *Perspectives on grading and reporting: Differences among teachers, students, and parents.* Paper presented at the annual meeting of the American Educational Research Association, New Orleans.

Guskey, T. (2005). Mapping the road to proficiency. *Educational Leadership, 63*(3), 32–38.

Guskey, T. (2007/2008). The rest of the story. *Educational Leadership, 65*(4), 28–35.

Gutiérrez, K., Asato, J., Pacheco, M., Moll, L., Olson, K., Horng, E., Ruiz, R., García, E., & McCarty, T. (2002). "Sounding American": The consequences of new reforms on English language learners. *Reading Research Quarterly, 37*(2), 328–343.

Hacker, D., Bol, L., Horgan, D., & Rakow, E. (2000). Test prediction and performance in a classroom context. *Journal of Education Psychology, 92,* 160–170.

Hadjioannou, X. (2007). Bringing the background to the foreground: What do classroom environments that support authentic discussions look like? *American Educational Research Journal, 44*(2), 370–399.

Haertel, E. (1986, April). *Choosing and using classroom tests: Teachers' perspectives on assessment.* Paper presented at the annual meeting of the American Educational Research Association, San Francisco.

Haertel, E. (1999). Performance assessment and education reform. *Phi Delta Kappan, 80*(9), 662–666.

Hakuta, K. (1999). The debate on bilingual education. *Developmental & Behavioral Pediatrics, 20,* 36–37.

Hakuta, K., Bialystok, E., & Wiley, E. (2003). Critical evidence: A test of the critical-period hypothesis for second-language acquisition. *Psychological Science, 14,* 31–38.

Haladyna, T. H. (2002). *Essentials of standardized achievement testing: Validity and accountability.* Boston: Allyn & Bacon.

Haladyna, T., & Ryan, J. (2001, April). *The influence of rater severity on whether a student passes or fails a performance assessment.* Paper presented at the annual meeting of the American Educational Research Association, Seattle.

Halford, G., & Andrews, G. (2006). Reasoning and problem solving. In D. Kuhn, & R. Siegler (Vol. Eds.), *Handbook of child psychology: Vol. 2. Cognition, perception, and language* (6th ed., pp. 557–608). Hoboken, NJ: John Wiley & Sons.

Hallahan, D., & Kauffman, J. (2009). *Exceptional children* (11th ed.). Needham Heights, MA: Allyn & Bacon.

Halpern, D. F. (2006). Assessing gender gaps in learning and academic achievement. In P. A. Alexander & P. H. Winne (Eds.), *Handbook of educational psychology* (2nd ed., pp. 635–653). Mahwah, NJ: Erlbaum.

Halpern, D., & LaMay, M. (2000). The smarter sex: A critical review of sex differences in intelligence. *Educational Psychology Review, 12*(2), 229–245.

Halpern, S. (2008). *Can't remember what I forgot: The good news from the front lines of memory research.* Chatsworth, CA: Harmony Books.

Hamilton, R. (1997). Effects of three types of elaboration on learning concepts from text. *Contemporary Education Psychology, 22,* 299–318.

Hamilton, S. L., Seibert, M. A., Gardner, III, R., & Talbert-Johnson, C. (2000). Using guided notes to improve the academic achievement of incarcerated adolescents with learning and behavior problems. *Remedial and Special Education, 21,* 133–140.

Hamm, J., & Coleman, H. (1997, March). *Adolescent strategies for coping with cultural diversity: Variability and youth outcomes.* Paper presented at the annual meeting of the American Educational Research Association, Chicago.

Hampton, J. (1995). Testing the prototype theory of concepts. *Journal of Memory and Language, 32,* 686–708.

Hancock, D. R. (2001). Effects of test anxiety and evaluative threat on students' achievement and motivation. *The Journal of Educational Research, 94,* 284–290.

Hanich, L., Jordan, N., Kaplan, D., & Dick, J. (2001). Performance across different areas of mathematical cognition in children with learning difficulties. *Journal of Educational Psychology, 93*(3), 615–626.

Hansbery, L. (1959). *A raisin in the sun.* New York: Random House.

Harackiewicz, J., Barron, K., Taurer, J., Carter, S., & Elliot, A. (2000). Short-term and long-term consequences of achievement goals: Predicting interest and performance over time. *Journal of Educational Psychology, 92,* 316–330.

Hardman, M., Drew, C., & Egan, W. (2008). *Human exceptionality* (9th ed.). Needham Heights, MA: Allyn & Bacon.

Hardre, P. L., & Reeve, J. (2003). A motivational model of rural students' intentions to persist in, versus drop out of, high school. *Journal of Education Psychology, 95,* 347–356.

Hardy, L. (2002). A new federal role. *American School Board Journal, 18*(9), 20–24.

Harriet, A. W., & Bradley, K. D. (2003). "You can't say you can't play:" Intervening in the process of social exclusion in the kindergarten classroom. *Early Childhood Research Quarterly, 18,* 185–205.

Harry, B. (1992). An ethnographic study of cross-cultural communication with Puerto Rican American families in the special education system. *American Educational Research Journal, 29*(3), 471–488.

Harry, B., & Klingner, J. (2007). Discarding the deficit model. *Educational Leadership, 64*(5), 16–21.

Hatano, G., & Oura, Y. (2003). Commentary: Reconceptualizing school learning using insight from expertise research. *Educational Researcher, 32*(8), 26–29.

Hattie, J., & Timperley, H. (2007). The power of feedback. *Review of Educational Research, 77*(1), 81–112.

Hawkins, M. (2004). Researching English language and literacy development in schools. *Educational Researcher, 33*(3), 14–25.

Haycock, K. (2001). Closing the achievement gap. *Educational Leadership, 58*(6), 6–11.

Hayes, J. R. (1988). *The complete problem solver* (2nd ed.). Mahwah, NJ: Erlbaum.

Hayes, K., & Salazar, J. (2001, April). *Evaluation of the Structured English Immersion Program, final report: Year 1.* Paper presented at the annual meeting of the American Educational Research Association, Seattle.

Hayes, S., Rosenfarb, I., Wulfert, E., Munt, E., Korn, Z., & Zettle, R. (1985). Self-reinforcement effects: An artifact of social standard setting? *Journal of Applied Behavior Analysis, 18,* 201–214.

Heath, S. B. (1982). Questioning at home and at school: A comparative study. In G. Spindler (Ed.), *The ethnography of schooling: Educational anthropology in action.* New York: Holt, Rinehart & Winston.

Heath, S. B. (1983). *Ways with words: Language, life, and work in communities and classrooms.* Cambridge, England: Cambridge University Press.

Heath, S. B. (1989). Oral and literate traditions among Black Americans living in poverty. *American Psychologist, 44,* 367–373.

Helsing, D. (2007). Regarding uncertainty in teachers and teaching. *Teaching and Teacher Education, 23,* 1317–1333.

Henricsson, L., & Rydell, A. M. (2004). Elementary school children with behavior problems: Teacher–child relations and self-perception. A prospective study. *Merrill-Palmer Quarterly, 50,* 111–138.

Henson, R. K., Kogan, L. R., & Vacha-Haase, T. (2001). A reliability generalization study of the Teacher Efficacy Scale and related instruments. *Educational and Psychological Measurement, 61,* 404–420.

Herbert, J., & Stipek, D. (2005). The emergence of gender differences in children's perceptions of their academic competence. *Journal of Applied Developmental Psychology, 26,* 276–295.

Hergenhahn, B. R., & Olson, M. H. (2001). *An introduction to theories of learning* (6th ed.). Upper Saddle River, NJ: Merrill/Pearson.

Herzig, A. (2004). Becoming mathematicians: Women and students of color choosing and leaving doctoral mathematics. *Review of Educational Research, 74*(2), 171–214.

Heubert, J., & Hauser, R. (Eds.). (1999). *High stakes testing for tracking, promotion, and graduation.* Washington, DC: National Academy Press.

Heward, W. (2009). *Exceptional children* (9th ed.). Upper Saddle River, NJ: Merrill/Pearson.

Hickey, D. T., & Zuiker, S. J. (2005). Engaged participation: A sociocultural model of motivation with implications for educational assessment. *Educational Assessment, 10,* 277–305.

Hidi, S. (2001). Interest, reading, and learning: Theoretical and practical considerations. *Educational Psychology Review, 13,* 191–209.

Hidi, S. (2002). An interest researcher's perspective: The effects of extrinsic and intrinsic factors on motivation. In C. Sansone & J. Harackiewicz (Eds.), *Intrinsic and extrinsic motivation: The search for optimal motivation and performance* (pp. 309–339). San Diego: Academic Press.

Hidi, S., & Renninger, K. A. (2006). The four-phase model of interest development. *Educational Psychologist, 41*(2), 111–127.

Hidi, S., Renninger, K. A., & Krapp, A. (2004). Interest, a motivational variable that combines affecting and cognitive functioning. In D. Dai & R. Sternberg (Eds.), *Motivation, emotion, and cognition: Integrative perspectives on intellectual functioning and development* (pp. 89–155). Mahwah, NJ: Erlbaum.

Hiebert, E. H., & Kamil, M. L. (Eds.). (2005). *Teaching and learning vocabulary.* Mahwah, NJ: Erlbaum.

Hiebert, J., Gallimore, R., & Stigler, J. (2002). A knowledge base for the teaching profession: What would it look like and how can we get one? *Educational Researcher, 31*(5), 3–15.

Higgins, A. T., & Turnure, J. E. (1984). Distractibility and concentration of attention in children's development. *Child Development, 55,* 1799–1810.

Hilbert, T. S., & Renkl, A. (2008). Concept mapping as a follow-up strategy to learning from texts: What characterizes good and poor mappers? *Instructional Science, 36,* 53–73.

Hill, K., & Wigfield, A. (1984). Test anxiety: A major educational problem and what can be done about it. *Elementary School Journal, 85,* 105–126.

Hill, W. F. (2002). *Learning: A survey of psychological interpretations* (7th ed.). Boston: Allyn & Bacon.

Hirsch, E. (2000). The tests we need and why we don't quite have them. *Education Week, 19*(21), 40–41.

Hirsch, E. (2006). Knowledge deficit: Closing the shocking education gap for American children. Boston: Hougton Mifflin.

Hmelo-Silver, C. E. (2004). Problem-based learning: What and how do students learn? *Educational Psychology Review, 16*, 236–266.

Hmelo-Silver, C. E., Duncan, R. G., & Chinn, C. A. (2007). Scaffolding and achievement in problem-based and inquiry learning: A response to Kirschner, Sweller, and Clark (2006). *Educational Psychologist, 42*, 99–107.

Hodapp, R., & Dykens, E. (2006). Mental retardation. In K. A. Renninger, & I. Sigel (Vol. Eds.), *Handbook of child psychology: Vol. 4. Child psychology in practice* (6th ed., pp. 453–496). Hoboken, NJ: John Wiley & Sons.

Hoff, D. (2003). Adding it all up. *Education Week, 22*(23), 28–31.

Hoffman, J., Assaf, L., & Paris, S. (2001). High-stakes testing in reading: Today in Texas, tomorrow? *Reading Teacher, 54*(5), 482–491.

Hoffman, L. (2002). Promoting girls' interest and achievement in physics classes for beginners. *Learning and Instruction, 12*, 447–465.

Hoffman, L. (2003). *Overview of public elementary and secondary schools and districts: School year 2001–02* (NCES 2003-411). U.S. Department of Education, National Center for Education Statistics. Washington, DC: U.S. Government Printing Office.

Hogan, T. (2007). *Educational assessment: A practical introduction.* Hoboken, NJ: John Wiley & Sons.

Hogan, T., Rabinowitz, M., & Craven, J. (2003). Representation in teaching: Inference from research on expert and novice teachers. *Educational Psychologist, 38*, 235–247.

Hohn, R. L., & Frey, B. (2002). Heuristic training and performance in elementary mathematical problem solving. *The Journal of Educational Research, 95*, 374–390.

Holahan, C., & Sears, R. (1995). *The gifted group in later maturity.* Stanford, CA: Stanford University Press.

Holliday, D. (2002, April). *Using cooperative learning to improve the academic achievements of inner-city middle school students.* Paper presented at the annual meeting of the American Educational Research Association, New Orleans.

Holloway, J. (2001). Inclusion and students with learning disabilities. *Educational Leadership, 58*(6), 86–88.

Holloway, J. (2004). Family literacy. *Education Leadership, 61*(6), 88–89.

Hong, S., & Ho, H. (2005). Direct and indirect longitudinal effects of parental involvement on student achievement: Second-order latent growth modeling across ethnic groups. *Journal of Educational Psychology, 97*(1), 32–42.

Honora, D. (2003). Urban African American adolescents and school identification. *Urban Education, 38*(1), 58–76.

Horst, S. J., Finney, S. J., & Barron, K. E. (2007). Moving beyond academic achievement goal measures: A study of social achievement goals. *Contemporary Educational Psychology, 32*, 667–698.

Howard, P. (2000). The owner's manual for the brain: Everyday applications from mid-brain research (2nd ed.). Atlanta, GA: Bard Press.

Howard, T. (2001). Powerful pedagogy for African American Students: A case of four teachers. *Urban Education, 36*(2), 179–202.

Howe, K., & Berv, J. (2000). Constructing constructivism, epistemological and pedagogical. In D. Phillips (Ed.), *Constructivism in education: Opinions and second opinions on controversial issues* (pp. 19–40). Chicago: National Society for the Study of Education.

Howe, M. L. (2004). The role of conceptual recoding in reducing children's retroactive interference. *Developmental Psychology, 40*, 131–139.

Hoy, W., Tarter, C. J., & Hoy, A. (2006). Academic optimism of schools: A force for student achievement. *American Educational Research Journal, 43*(3), 425–446.

Huan, V. S., Yeo, L. S., & Ang, R. P. (2006). The influence of dispositional optimism and gender on adolescents' perception of academic stress. *Adolescence, 41*, 533–546.

Huba, M., & Freed, J. (2000). *Learner-centered assessment on college campuses.* Boston: Allyn & Bacon.

Huber, J. A. (2004). A closer look at SQ3R. *Reading Improvement, 41*, 108–112.

Hughes, D., Rodriguez, J., Smith, E., Johnson, D., Stevenson, H., & Spicer, P. (2006). Parents' ethnic-racial socialization practices: A review of research and directions for future study. *Developmental Psychology, 42*(5), 747–770.

Hughes, T. L., & McIntosh, D. E. (2002). Differential ability scales: Profiles of preschoolers with cognitive delay. *Psychology in the Schools, 39*, 19–29.

Hulse, C. (2006, May 16). Senate passes a bill that favors English. *New York Times*, p. A19.

Hunt, N., & Marshall, K. (2002). *Exceptional children and youth: An introduction to special education* (3rd ed.). Boston: Houghton Mifflin.

Huntsinger, C. S., Jose, P. E., Larsen, S. L. (1998). Do parent practices to encourage academic competence influence the social adjustment of young European American and Chinese American children? *Developmental Psychology, 34*, 747–756.

Hvitfeldt, C. (1986). Traditional culture, perceptual style, and learning: The classroom behavior of Hmong adults. *Adult Education Quarterly, 36(2)*, 65–77.

Hyman, I., Kay, B., Tabori, A., Weber, M., Mahon, M., & Cohen, I. (2006). Bullying: Theory, research, and interventions. In C. M. Evertson & C. S. Weinstein (Eds.), *Handbook of classroom management: Research, practice, and contemporary issues* (pp. 855–884). Mahwah, NJ: Erlbaum.

Igo, L. B., Bruning, R., & McCrudden, M. (2005). Exploring differences in students' copy-and-paste decision making and processing: A mixed-methods study. *Journal of Educational Psychology, 97*(1), 103–116.

Igo, L. B., Kiewra, K., & Bruning, R. (2004). Removing the snare from the pair: Using pictures to learn confusing word pairs. *Journal of Experimental Education, 72*(3), 165–178.

Ilg, T., & Massucci, J. (2003). Comprehensive urban high school: Are there better options for poor and minority children. *Education and Urban Society, 36*(1), 63–78.

Illinois State Board of Education. (2008). *Illinois learning standards: Mathematics, State Goal 6: Number sense.* Retrieved from http://www.isbe.net/ils/math/pdf/goal6.pdf

Ingersoll, R. (2003). *Who controls teachers' work?* Cambridge, MA: Harvard University Press.

Ingersoll, R., & Smith, T. (2004). What are the effects of induction and mentoring on beginning teacher turnover? *American Educational Research Journal, 41*(3), 681–714.

Inhelder, B., & Piaget, J. (1958). *The growth of logical thinking from childhood to adolescence* (A. Parsons & S. Milgram, Trans.). New York: Basic Books.

Iyengar, S., & Lepper, M. (1999). Rethinking the role of choice: A cultural perspective on intrinsic motivation. *Journal of Personality and Social Psychology, 76*, 349–366.

Jackson, P. (1968). *Life in classrooms.* New York: Holt, Rinehart & Winston.

Jacobs, G. M. (2004). A classroom investigation of the growth of metacognitive awareness in kindergarten children through the writing process. *Early Childhood Journal, 32*, 17–23.

Jacobs, J. E., Lanza, S., Osgood, D. W., Eccles, J. S., & Wigfield, A. (2002). Changes in children's self-competence and values: Gender and domain differences across grades one through twelve. *Child Development, 73*, 509–527.

Jalongo, R., Rieg, S., & Hellerbran, V. (2007). *Planning for learning.* New York: Teachers College Press.

Jenkins, H., Bailey, J., & Fraser, B. (2004, April). *Predictors of mathematics skills in boys with and without attention deficit hyperactivity disorder (ADHD).* Paper presented at the annual meeting of the American Educational Research Association, San Diego.

Jennings, J., & Rentner, D. (2006). Ten big effects of the No Child Left Behind Act on public schools. *Phi Delta Kappan, 88(2)*, 110–113.

Jesse, D., & Pokorny, N. (2001, April). *Understanding high achieving middle schools for Latino students in poverty.* Paper presented at the annual meeting of the American Educational Research Association, Seattle.

Jetton, T., & Alexander, P. (1997). Instruction importance: What teachers value and what students learn. *Reading Research Quarterly, 32*, 290–308.

Jitendra, A., Haria, P., Griffin, C., Leh, J., Adams, A., & Kaduvettoor, A. (2007). A comparison of single and multiple strategy instruction on third-grade students' mathematical problem solving. *Journal of Educational Psychology, 99*(1), 115–127.

Johnson, A. P. (2005). *A short guide to action research* (2nd ed.). Boston: Pearson.

Johnson, B., & Christensen, L. (2008). *Educational research: Quantitative, qualitative and mixed approaches* (3rd ed.). Los Angeles: Sage.

Johnson, D. D., Johnson, B., Farenga, S., & Ness, D. (2008). *Stop high-stakes testing: An appeal to American's conscience.* Lanham, MD: Rowan & Littlefield.

Johnson, D. W., & Johnson, R. (2004). The three Cs of promoting social and emotional learning. In J. Zins, R. Weissberg, M. Wang, & H. Walberg (Eds.), *Building academic success on social and emotional learning* (pp. 40–58). New York: Teachers College Press.

Johnson, D. W., & Johnson, R. (2006). *Learning together and alone: Cooperation, competition, and individualization* (8th ed.). Needham Heights, MA: Allyn & Bacon.

Johnson, E. S., & Arnold, N. (2007). Examining an alternate assessment. *Journal of Disability Policy Studies, 18,* 23–31.

Johnson, J. (2002). Will parents of special-needs children endorse reform in special ed? *Phi Delta Kappan, 84*(2), 160–163.

Johnson, J., & Duffett, A. (2002). *When it's your own child: A report on special education and the families who use it.* New York: The Public Agenda.

Johnson, L. (2002). "My eyes have been opened": White teachers and racial awareness. *Journal of Teacher Education, 53*(2), 153–167.

Johnson, L. (2004). Down with detention. *Education Week, 24*(14), 39–40.

Johnson, S., & Birkeland, S. (2003, April). *Pursuing a "sense of success:" New teachers explain their career decisions.* Paper presented at the annual meeting of the American Educational Research Association, New Orleans, LA.

Johnson, W., & Bouchard, T. (2005). The structure of human intelligence: It is verbal, perceptual, and image rotation (VPR), not fluid and crystallized. *Intelligence, 33,* 393–416.

Jonassen, D., Howland, J., Moore, J., & Marra, R. (2003). *Learning to solve problems with technology* (2nd ed.). Upper Saddle River, NJ: Merrill/Pearson.

Jones, G., Jones, B., & Hargrove, T. (2003). *The unintended consequences of high-stakes testing.* Lanham, MD: Rowman & Littlefield.

Jones, M. (1999). *Identity as strategy: Rethinking how African American students negotiate desegregated schooling.* Paper presented at the annual meeting of the American Educational Research Association, Montreal, Canada.

Jones, N., Kemenes, G., & Benjamin, P. (2001). Selective expression of electrical correlates of differential appetitive classical conditioning in a feedback network. *Journal of Neurophysiology, 85,* 89–97.

Jones, S. M., & Dindia, K. (2004). A meta-analytic perspective on sex equity in the classroom. *Review of Educational Research, 74*(4), 443–471.

Jones, V. F., & Jones, L. S. (2004). *Comprehensive classroom management: Creating communities of support and solving problems* (7th ed.). Boston: Allyn & Bacon.

Jordan, W. (2001). Black high school students' participation in school-sponsored sports activities: Effects on school engagement and achievement. *Journal of Negro Education, 68*(1), 54–71.

Jorgenson, O. (2003). Brain scam? Why educators should be careful about embracing "brain research." *The Educational Forum, 67,* 364–369.

Judson, M. (2004, April). *Smaller learning communities in urban high schools: Increasing communication among teachers and students.* Paper presented at the annual meeting of the American Educational Research Association, San Diego.

Juniewicz, K. (2003). Student portfolios with a purpose. *The Clearing House, 77*(2), 73–77.

Juvonen, J. (2006). Sense of belonging, social bonds, and school functioning. In P. A. Alexander & P. H. Winne (Eds.), *Handbook of educational psychology* (2nd ed., pp. 655–674). Mahwah, NJ: Erlbaum.

Juvonen, J. (2007). Reforming middle schools: Focus on continuity, social connectedness, and engagement. *Educational Psychologist, 42,* 197–208.

Kafai, Y. (2006). Constructionism. In R. K. Sawyer (Ed.), *The Cambridge handbook of the learning sciences* (pp. 35–46). New York: Cambridge University Press.

Kaff, M. S., Zabel, R. H., & Milham, M. (2007). Revisiting cost–benefit relationships of behavior management strategies: What special educators say about usefulness, intensity, and effectiveness. *Preventing School Failure, 51,* 35–45.

Kahlenberg, R. (2006). Integration by income. *American School Board Journal, 193*(4), 51–52.

Kahn, E. (2000). A case study of assessment in a grade 10 English course. *Journal of Educational Research, 93*(5), 276–286.

Kahng, S. W., & Iwata, B. A. (1999). Correspondence between outcomes of brief and extended functional analyses. *Journal of Applied Behavior Analysis, 32,* 149–159.

Kakkarainen, O., & Ahtee, M. (2007). The durability of conceptual change in learning the concept of weight in the case of a pulley in balance. *International Journal of Science and Mathematics Education, 5,* 461–482.

Kalyuga, S., Ayres, P., Chandler, P., & Sweller, J. (2003). The expertise reversal effect. *Educational Psychologist, 38*(1), 23–31.

Kamil, M., & Walberg, H. (2005). The scientific teaching of reading. *Education Week, 24*(20), 38, 40.

Kane, M. (2006). Content-related validity evidence in test development. In S. Dowing & T. Haladyna (Eds.), *Handbook of test development* (pp. 131–154). Mahwah, NJ: Erlbaum Associates.

Karateken, C. (2004). A test of the integrity of the components of Baddeley's model of working memory in attention-deficit/hyperactivity disorder (ADHD). *The Journal of Child Psychology and Psychiatry and Allied Disciplines, 45*(5), 912–926.

Karten, T. (2005). *Inclusion strategies that work: Research-based methods for the classroom.* Thousand Oaks, CA: Corwin Press.

Kastens, K., & Liben, L. (2007). Eliciting self-explanations improves children's performance on a field-based map skills task. *Cognition and Instruction, 25*(1), 45–74.

Kato, T., & Manning, M. (2007). Content knowledge—The real reading crisis. *Childhood Education, 83,* 238–239.

Kauchak, D., & Eggen, P. (2007). *Learning and teaching: Research-based methods* (5th ed.). Needham Heights, MA: Allyn & Bacon.

Kauffman, J., McGee, K., & Brigham, M. (2004). Enabling or disabling? Observations on changes in special education. *Phi Delta Kappan, 85*(8), 613–620.

Kaufman, A. S., & Lictenberger, E. O. (2002). *Assessing adolescent and adult intelligence* (2nd ed.). Boston: Allyn & Bacon.

Kaufman, J. C., & Sternberg, R. J. (2007). Creativity. *Change, 39,* 55–58.

Kavale, K. A., & Forness, S. R. (2000). History, rhetoric, and reality. *Remedial and Special Education, 21*(5), 279–296.

Kazden, A. (2001). *Behavior modification in applied settings* (6th ed.). Belmont, CA: Wadsworth.

Keating, D. P. (2004). Cognitive and brain development. In R. Lerner & L. Steinberg (Eds.), *Handbook of adolescent psychology* (2nd ed.). New York: Wiley.

Keefer, M., Zeitz, C., & Resnick, L. (2000). Judging the quality of peer-led student dialogues. *Cognition and Instruction, 18*(1), 53–81.

Kerman, S. (1979). Teacher expectations and student achievement. *Phi Delta Kappan, 60,* 70–72.

Kibby, M. Y., Marks, W., & Morgan, S. (2004). Specific impairment in developmental reading disabilities: A working memory approach. *Journal of Learning Disabilities, 37*(4), 349–363.

Kidron, Y., & Fleischman, S. (2006). Promoting adolescents' prosocial behavior. *Educational Leadership, 63*(7), 90–91.

Kim, Y., & Baylor, A. L. (2006). A social-cognitive framework for pedagogical agents as learning companions. *Educational Technology Research and Development, 54,* 569–596.

Kincheloe, J. (2004). Why a book on urban education? In S. Steinberg & J. Kincheloe (Eds.), *19 Urban questions: Teaching in the city* (pp. 1–27). New York: Peter Lange.

Kindler, A. L. (2002). *Survey of the states' limited English proficient students and available educational programs and services, 2000–2001 Summary Report.* Washington, DC: National Clearinghouse for English Language Acquisition and Language Instruction Educational Programs.

King-Friedrichs, J., & Browne, D. (2001). Learning to remember. *The Science Teacher, 68,* 44–46.

Kirschner, P. A., Sweller, J., & Clark, R. E. (2006). Why minimal guidance during instruction does not work: An analysis of the failure of constructivist, discovery, problem-based, experiential, and inquiry-based teaching. *Educational Psychologist, 41,* 75–86.

Kitsantas, A., Zimmerman, B., & Cleary, T. (2000). The role of observation and emulation in the development of athletic self-regulation. *Journal of Educational Psychology, 92*(4), 811–817.

Kliewer, C., Fitzgerald, L., Meyer-Mork, J., Hartman, P., English-Sand, P., & Raschke, D. (2004). Citizenship for all in the literate community: An ethnography of young children with significant disabilities in inclusive early childhood settings. *Harvard Educational Review, 74*(4), 373–403.

Kluth, P., Villa, R., & Thousand, J. (2002). "Our school doesn't offer inclusion" and other legal blunders. *Educational Leadership, 83*(4), 24–27.

Knapp, M. S. (2001). Policy, poverty, and capable teaching: Assumptions and issues in policy design. In B. J. Biddle (Ed.), *Social class, poverty, and education* (pp. 175–212). New York: Routlege Falmer.

Knight, J. (2002). Crossing the boundaries: What constructivists can teach intensive-explicit instructors and vice versa. *Focus on Exceptional Children, 35,* 1–14, 16.

Kober, N. (2006). *A public education primer: Basic (and sometimes surprising) facts about the U.S. education system.* Washington, DC: Center on Education Policy.

Koc, K., & Buzzelli, C. A. (2004). The moral of the story is . . . Using children's literature in moral education. *Young Children, 59*(1), 92–97.

Kodjo, C. M., Auinger, P., & Ryan, S. (2003). Demographic, intrinsic, and extrinsic factors associated with weapon carrying at school. *Archives of Pediatrics & Adolescent Medicine, 157*, 96–103.

Kohlberg, L. (1963). The development of children's orientation toward moral order: Sequence in the development of human thought. *Vita Humana, 6*, 11–33.

Kohlberg, L. (1969). Stage and sequence: The cognitive-developmental approach to socialization. In D. Goslin (Ed.), *Handbook of socialization theory and research.* Chicago: Rand McNally.

Kohlberg, L. (1975). The cognitive development approach to moral education. *Phi Delta Kappan, 56*, 670–677.

Kohlberg, L. (1981). *Philosophy of moral development.* New York: Harper & Row.

Kohlberg, L. (1984). *Essays on moral development: Vol. 2. The psychology of moral development.* New York: Harper & Row.

Kohn, A. (1993). *Punished by rewards: The trouble with gold stars, incentive plans, A's, praise, and other bribes.* Boston: Houghton Mifflin.

Kohn, A. (1996a). *Beyond discipline: From compliance to community.* Alexandria, VA: Association for Supervision and Curriculum Development.

Kohn, A. (1996b). By all available means: Cameron and Pierce's defense of extrinsic motivators. *Review of Educational Research, 66*, 1–4.

Kohn, A. (2004). Challenging students—and how to have more of them. *Phi Delta Kappan, 86*(3), 184–194.

Kohn, A. (2005a). *Unconditional parenting: Moving from rewards and punishments to love and reason.* New York: Atria Books.

Kohn, A. (2005b). Unconditional teaching. *Educational Leadership, 63*(1), 20–24.

Kohn, A. (2006a). *The homework myth: Why our kids get too much of a bad thing.* Cambridge, MA: Da Capo Press.

Kohn, A. (2006b). Abusing research: The study of homework and other examples. *Phi Delta Kappan, 88*, 9–22.

Kornhaber, M., Fierros, E., & Veenema, S. (2004). *Multiple intelligences: Best ideas from research and practice.* Boston: Allyn & Bacon.

Kounin, J. (1970). *Discipline and group management in classrooms.* New York: Holt, Rinehart & Winston.

Kozhevnikov, M., Hegarty, M., & Mayer, R. (1999, April). *Students' use of imagery in solving qualitative problems in kinematics.* Paper presented at the annual meeting of the American Educational Research Association, Montreal, Canada.

Kozol, J. (2005). *The shame of the nation: The restoration of apartheid schooling in America.* New York: Crown.

Kozol, J. (2006). Success for all: Trying to make an end run around inequality and segregation. *Phi Delta Kappan, 87*(8), 624–626.

Kozulin, A. (1998). *Psychological tools: A sociocultural approach to education.* Cambridge: Harvard University Press.

Kozulin, A. (Ed.). (2003). *Vygotsky's educational theory in cultural context.* Cambridge, UK: Cambridge University Press.

Krajcik, J., & Blumenfeld, P. (2006). Project-based learning. In R. K. Sawyer, (Ed.), *Cambridge handbook of the learning sciences* (pp. 317–334). Cambridge, MA: Cambridge University Press.

Kramer, P. A. (2003). The ABC's of professionalism. *Kappa Delta Pi Record, 40*(1), 22–25.

Krashen, S. (2005). Skyrocketing scores: An urban legend. *Educational Leadership, 62*(4), 37–39.

Kratzig, G., & Arbuthnott, K. (2006). Perceptual learning style and learning proficiency: A test of the hypothesis. *Journal of Educational Psychology, 98*(1), 238–246.

Krebs, D., & Denton, K. (2005). *A guide for establishing prosocial communities.* New York: Springer.

Kress, J., & Elias, M. (2006). School-based social and emotional learning programs. In K. A. Renninger & I. Sigel (Vol. Eds,), *Handbook of child psychology: Vol. 4. Child psychology in practice* (6th ed., pp. 592–618). Hoboken, NJ: John Wiley & Sons.

Kritt, D. (2004). Strengths and weaknesses of bright urban children: A critique of standardized testing in kindergarten. *Education and Urban Society, 36*(4), 466–467.

Kroesbergen, E. H., & van Luit, E. H. (2002). Teaching multiplication to low math performers: Guided versus structured instruction. *Instructional Science, 30*, 361–378.

Kroger, J. (2000). *Identity development: Adolescence through adulthood.* Thousand Oaks, CA: Sage.

Kuhn, D. (1999). A developmental model of critical thinking. *Educational Researcher, 28*(2), 16–26, 46.

Kuhn, D. (2001). Why development does (and does not) occur: Evidence from the domain of inductive reasoning. In J. L. McClelland & R. S. Seigler (Eds.), *Mechanisms of cognitive development: Behavioral and neural perspectives* (pp. 221–249). Mahwah, NJ: Erlbaum.

Kuhn, D. (2007). Is direct instruction the right answer to the right question? *Educational Psychologist, 42*, 109–113.

Kuhn, D., & Dean, D., Jr. (2004). Metacognition: A bridge between cognitive psychology and educational practice. *Theory Into Practice, 43*(4), 268–273.

Kuhn, D., & Franklin, S. (2006). The second decade: What develops (and how). In D. Kuhn & R. Siegler (Vol. Eds.), *Handbook of child psychology: Vol. 2. Cognition, perception, and language* (6th ed., pp. 953–994). Hoboken, NJ: John Wiley & Sons.

Kuhn, D., & Park, S.-H. (2005). Epistemological understanding and the development of intellectual values. *International Journal of Educational Research, 43*, 111–124.

Kumar, R., Gheen, M. H., & Kaplan, A. (2002). Goal structures in the learning environment and students' disaffection from learning and schooling. In C. Midgely (Ed.), *Goals, goal structures and patterns of adaptive learning* (pp. 143–173). Mahwah, NJ: Erlbaum.

Kuther, T., & Higgins-D'Alessandra, M. (1997, March). *Effects of a just community on moral development and adolescent engagement in risk.* Paper presented at the annual meeting of the American Educational Research Association, Chicago.

Labov, W. (1972). *Language in the inner city: Studies in the "Black" English vernacular.* Philadelphia: University of Pennsylvania Press.

Lajoie, S. P. (2003). Transitions and trajectories for studies of expertise. *Educational Researcher, 32*, 21–25.

Lalli, J. S., & Kates, K. (1998). The effects of reinforcer preference on functional analysis outcomes. *Journal of Applied Behavior Analysis, 31*, 79–90.

Lam, S-F., & Law, Y-K. (2007). The roles of instructional practices and motivation in writing performance. *The Journal of Experimental Education, 75*, 145–164.

Lambating, J., & Allen, J. (2002, April). *How the multiple functions of grades influence their validity and value as measures of academic achievement.* Paper presented at the annual meeting of the American Educational Research Association, New Orleans.

Lambert, C., DePaepe, J., & Lambert, L. (2007). e-portfolios in action. *Kappa Delta Pi Record, 43*, 76–81.

Lambert, N., & McCombs, B. (1998). Introduction: Learner-centered schools and classrooms as a direction for school reform. In N. Lambert & B. McCombs (Eds.), *How students learn: Reforming schools through learner-centered education* (pp. 1–22). Washington, DC: American Psychological Association.

Lan, W., Repman, J., & Chyung, S. (1998). Effects of practicing self-monitoring of mathematical problem-solving heuristics on impulsive and reflective college students' heuristics knowledge and problem-solving ability. *Journal of Experimental Education, 67*(1), 32–52.

Landrum, T. J., & Kaufman, J. M. (2006). Behavioral approaches to classroom management. In C. M. Evertson & C. S. Weinstein (Eds.), *Handbook of classroom management: Research, practice, and contemporary issues* (pp. 47–71). Mahwah, NJ: Erlbaum.

Landry, S., Smith, K., & Swank, P. (2006). Responsive parenting: Establishing early foundations for social, communication, and independent problem-solving skills. *Developmental Psychology, 42*(4), 627–642.

Landsman, J. (2004). Confronting the racism of low expectations. *Educational Leadership, 62*(3), 28–32.

Lareau, A. (2003). *Unequal childhoods: Class, race, and family life.* Berkeley, CA: University of California Press.

Larrivee, B. (2002). The potential perils of praise in a democratic interactive classroom. *Action in Teacher Education, 23*(4), 77–88.

Lave, J. (1997). The culture of acquisition and the culture of understanding. In D. Kirshner & J. A. Whitson (Eds.), *Situated cognition: Social, semiotic, and psychological perspectives* (pp. 17–35). Mahwah, NJ: Erlbaum.

Lave, J., & Wenger, E. (1991). *Situated learning: Legitimate peripheral participation.* Cambridge, UK: Cambridge University Press.

Lawson, A., & Childs, R. (2001, April). *Making sense of large-scale assessments: Communicating with teachers.* Paper presented at the annual meeting of the American Educational Research Association, Seattle.

Lee, J., & Reigeluth, C. M. (2003). Formative research on the heuristic task analysis process. *Educational Technology Research and Development, 51*, 5–24.

Lee, J. D. (2002). More than ability: Gender and personal relationships influence science and technology involvement. *Sociology of Education, 75,* 349–373.

Lee, R., Sturmey, P., & Fields, L. (2007). Schedule-induced and operant mechanisms that influence response variability: A review and implications for future investigations. *The Psychological Record, 57,* 429–465.

Lee, V. (2000). Using hierarchical linear modeling to study social contexts: The case of school effects. *Educational Psychologist, 35,* 125–141.

Lee, V. E., & Burkam, D. T. (2002). *Inequality at the starting gate: Social background differences in achievement as children begin school.* Washington, DC: Economic Policy Institute.

Lee, V. E., & Burkam, D. T. (2003). Dropping out of high school: The role of school organization and structure. *American Educational Research Journal, 40*(2), 353–393.

Lei, J. L. (2003). (Un)necessary toughness? Those "loud Black girls" and those "quiet Asian boys." *Anthropology & Education Quarterly, 34*(2), 158–181.

Leinhardt, G. (2001). Instructional explanations: A commonplace for teaching and location for contrast. In V. Richardson (Ed.), *Handbook of research on teaching* (4th ed., pp. 333–357). Washington, DC: American Educational Research Association.

Leinhardt, G., & Steele, M. (2005). Seeing the complexity of standing to the side: Instructional dialogues. *Cognition and Instruction, 23*(1), 87–163.

Lemke, M., Sen A., Pahlke, E., Partelow, L., Miller D., Williams, T., Kastberg, D., & Jocelyn, L. (2004). *International outcomes of learning in mathematics literacy and problem solving: PISA 2003 results from the U.S. perspective (NCES 2005-003).* U.S. Department of Education. Washington, DC: National Center for Education Statistics.

Leno, L. C., & Dougherty, L. A. (2007). Using direct instruction to teach content vocabulary. *Science Scope, 31,* 63–66.

Leonard, L. B., Weismer, S. E., & Miller, C. A. (2007). Speed of processing, working memory, and language impairment in children. *Journal of Speech, Language, and Hearing Research, 50,* 408–428.

Leont'ev, A. (1981). The problem of activity in psychology. In J. Wertsch (Ed.), *The concept of activity in Soviet psychology* (pp. 37–71). Armonk, NY: Sharpe.

LePage, P., Darling-Hammond, L., & Akar, H., with Gutierrez, C., Jenkins-Gunn, E., & Rosebrock, K. (2005). Classroom management. In L. Darling-Hammond & J. Bransford (Eds.), *Preparing teachers for a changing world: What teachers should learn and be able to do* (pp. 327–357). San Francisco: Jossey-Bass/Wiley.

Lepper, M., & Hodell, M. (1989). Intrinsic motivation in the classroom. In C. Ames & R. Ames (Eds.), *Research on motivation in education* (Vol. 3, pp. 73–105). San Diego: Academic Press.

Lerner, R. (2002). *Adolescence: Development, diversity, context, and application.* Upper Saddle River, NJ: Prentice Hall.

Lerner, R. (2006). Developmental science, developmental systems, and contemporary theories of human development. In W. Damon & R. Lerner (Series Eds.), R. Lerner (Vol. Ed.), *Handbook of child psychology: Vol. I. Theoretical models of human development* (6th ed., 1–17). New York: Wiley.

Levesque, C., Stanek, L., Zuehlke, A. N., & Ryan, R. (2004). Autonomy and competence in German and American university students: A comparative study based on self-determination theory. *Journal of Educational Psychology, 96*(1), 68–84.

Lew, J. (2004). The "other" story of model minorities: Korean American high school dropouts in an urban context. *Anthropology and Education Quarterly, 35*(3), 303–323.

Lewis, A. (2001). There is no "race" in the schoolyard: Colorblind ideology in an (almost) all White school. *American Educational Research Journal, 38*(4), 781–811.

Lewis, A. (2007). Looking beyond NCLB. *Phi Delta Kappan, 88*(7), 483–484.

Lewis, C. C. (1995). *Educating hearts and minds: Reflections on Japanese preschool and elementary education.* Cambridge, UK: Cambridge University Press.

Lewis, J. L., & Kim, E. (2008). A desire to learn: African American children's positive attitudes toward learning within school cultures of low expectations. *Teachers College Record, 110,* 1304–1329. Retrieved June 4, 2008, from http://tcrecord:org/Content.asp?ContentID=14749

Lewis, R. (2001). Classroom discipline & student responsibility: The students' view. *Teaching and Teacher Education, 17,* 307–319.

Lewis, V. (2002). *Development and disability* (2nd ed.). Malden, MA: Blackwell.

Li, J. (2004). High abilities and excellence: A cultural perspective. In L. V. Shavininina & M. Ferrari (Eds.), *Beyond knowledge: Extracognitive aspects of developing high ability* (pp. 187–208). Mahwah, NJ: Erlbaum.

Li, J. (2005). Mind or virtue: Western and Chinese beliefs about learning. *Current Directions in Psychological Science, 14,* 190–194.

Li, J., & Fischer, K. W. (2004). Thought and affect in American and Chinese learners' beliefs abut learning. In D. Y. Dai & R. J. Sternberg (Eds.), *Motivation, emotion, and cognition: Integrative perspectives in intellectual functioning and development* (pp. 385–418). Mahwah, NJ: Erlbaum.

Li, Y., Anderson, R., Nguyen-Jahiel, K., Dong, T., Archodidou, A., Kim, I., Kuo, L., Clark, A., Wu, X., Jadallah, M., & Miller, B. (2007). Emergent leadership in children's discussion groups. *Cognition and Instruction, 25,* 75–111.

Lillard, A. S. (1997). Other folks' theories of mind and behavior. *Psychological Science, 8,* 268–274.

Lin, J-R. (2007). Responses to anomalous data obtained from repeatable experiments in the laboratory. *Journal of Research in Science Teaching, 44*(3), 506–528.

Linnenbrink, E. A., & Pintrich, P. R. (2003). Achievement goals and intentional conceptual change. In G. M. Sinatra & P. R. Pintrich (Eds.), *Intentional conceptual change* (pp. 347–374). Mahwah, NJ: Erlbaum.

Linnenbrink, E. A., & Pintrich, P. R. (2004). Role of affect in cognitive processing in academic contexts. In D. Y. Dai & R. J. Sternberg (Eds.), *Motivation, emotion, and cognition: Integrative perspectives on intellectual functioning and development* (pp. 57–87). Mahwah, NJ: Erlbaum.

Lippa, R. A. (2002). *Gender, nature, and nurture.* Mahwah, NJ: Erlbaum.

Lipson, M. Y., & Wixson, K. K. (2003). *Assessment and instruction of reading and writing disability* (3rd ed.). New York: Longman.

Liston, D., Whitcomb, J., & Borko, H. (2007). NCLB and scientifically-based research: Opportunities lost and found. *Journal of Teacher Education, 58*(2), 99–107.

Liu, X. (2004). Using concept mapping for assessing and promoting relational conceptual change in science. *Science Education, 88,* 373–396.

Lohman, D. (2001, April). *Fluid intelligence, inductive reasoning, and working memory: Where the theory of multiple intelligences falls short.* Paper presented at the annual meeting of the American Educational Research Association, Seattle.

Lopes, P., & Salovey, P. (2004). Toward a broader education: Social, emotional, and practical skills. In J. Zins, R. Weissberg, M. Wang, & H. Walberg (Eds.), *Building academic success on social and emotional learning* (pp. 76–93). New York: Teachers College Press.

Lopez, N. (2003). *Hopeful girls, troubled boys: Race and gender disparity in urban education.* New York: Routledge.

Lopez del Bosque, R. (2003). Sticks and stones: What words are to self-esteem. *Intercultural Development Research Association Newsletter, 27*(5), 4–7, 16.

Loughran, J., Mulhall, P., & Berry, A. (2004). In search of pedagogical content knowledge in science: Developing ways of articulating and documenting professional practice. *Journal of Research in Science Teaching, 41,* 370–391.

Lovelace, M. (2005). Meta-analysis of experimental research based on the Dunn and Dunn Model. *Journal of Educational Research, 98*(3), 176–183.

Lowrie, T., & Kay, R. (2001). Relationship between visual and nonvisual solution methods and difficulty in elementary mathematics. *Journal of Educational Research, 94*(4), 248–255.

Luft, P., Brown, C. M., & Sutherin, L. J. (2007). Are you and your students bored with the benchmarks? Sinking under the standards? *Teaching Exceptional Children, 39,* 39–46.

Lumeng, J. C., & Cardinal, T. M. (2007). Providing information about a flavor to preschoolers: Effects on liking and memory for having tasted it. *Chemical Senses, 32,* 505–513.

Luna, B., Garver, K. E., Urban, T. A., Lazar, N. A., & Sweeny, J. A. (2004). Maturation of cognitive processes from late childhood to adulthood. *Child Development, 75,* 1357–1372.

Lundberg, U., Granqvist, M., Hansson, T., Magnusson, M., & Wallin, L. (1989). Psychological and physiological stress responses during repetitive work at an assembly line. *Work & Stress, 3,* 143–153.

Lunenberg, M., Korthagen, F., & Swennen, A. (2007). The teacher educator as a role model. *Teaching and Teacher Education, 23,* 586–601.

Luria, A. R. (1976). *Cognitive development: Its cultural and social foundations.* Cambridge, MA: Harvard University Press.

Lutz, S., Guthrie, J., & Davis, M. (2006). Scaffolding for engagement in elementary school reading instruction. *Journal of Educational Research, 100*(1), 3–20.

Luyckx, K., Goossens, L., & Soenens, B. (2006). A developmental contextual perspective on identity construction in emerging adulthood: Change dynamics in commitment formation and commitment evaluation. *Developmental Psychology, 42*(2), 366–380.

Lynch, M. (2001). *Fostering creativity in children, K–8: Theory and practice.* Boston: Allyn & Bacon.

Ma, X. (2001). Bullying and being bullied: To what extent are bullies also victims? *American Educational Research Journal, 38*(2), 351–370.

Maag, J. (2001). Rewarded by punishment: Reflections on the disuse of positive reinforcement in schools. *Exceptional Children, 67,* 173–186.

Mabry, L. (1999). Writing to the rubrics: Lingering effects of traditional standardized testing on direct writing assessment. *Phi Delta Kappan, 80,* 673–679.

Macionis, J. (2006). *Society: The basics* (8th ed.). Upper Saddle River, NJ: Prentice Hall.

Macionis, J., & Parillo, V. (2007). *Cities and urban life* (4th ed.). Upper Saddle River, NJ: Prentice Hall.

MacNeil, M. S. (2007). Concept mapping as a means of course evaluation. *Journal of Nursing Education, 46,* 232–234.

Macpherson, R., & Stanovich, K. E. (2007). Cognitive ability, thinking dispositions, and instructional set as predictors of critical thinking. *Learning and Individual Differences, 17,* 115–127.

Maehr, M., & Midgley, C. (1991). Enhancing student motivation: A schoolwide approach. *Educational Psychologist, 26,* 399–427.

Mager, R. (1962). *Preparing instructional objectives.* Palo Alto, CA: Featon.

Mager, R. (1998). *Preparing instructional objectives: A critical tool in the development of effective instruction* (3rd ed.). Atlanta, GA: Center for Effective Performance.

Mahoney, J., Larson, R., & Eccles, J. (2005). *Organized activities as contexts of development: Extracurricular activities.* New York: Routledge.

Mainela-Arnold, E., & Evans, J. L. (2005). Beyond capacity limitations: Determinants of word recall performance on verbal working memory span tasks in children with SLI. *Journal of Speech, Language, and Hearing Research, 48,* 897–909.

Manouchehri, A. (2004). Implementing mathematics reform in urban schools: A study of the effect of teachers' motivation style. *Urban Education, 38,* 472–508.

Manzo, K. (2000). Book binds. *Education Week, 19*(17), 29–33.

Manzo, K. (2008). Researchers propose NAEP look beyond academic measures. *Education Week, 27*(25), 8.

Marchand, G., & Skinner, E. A. (2007). Motivational dynamics of children's academic help-seeking and concealment. *Journal of Educational Psychology, 99,* 65–82.

Marcia, J. (1980). Identity in adolescence. In J. Adelson (Ed.), *Handbook of adolescent psychology.* New York: Wiley.

Marcia, J. (1987). The identity status approach to the study of ego identity development. In T. Honess & K. Yardley (Eds.), *Self and identity: Perspectives across the life span.* London: Routledge & Kegan Paul.

Marcia, J. (1999). Representational thought in ego identity, psychotherapy, and psychosocial development. In I. E. Sigel (Ed.), *Development of mental representation: Theories and applications.* Mahwah, NJ: Lawrence Erlbaum.

Marinoff, L. (2003). *The big questions: How philosophy can change your life.* New York: Bloomsbury.

Marion, S., & Pellegrino, J. (2006). A validity framework for evaluating the technical quality of alternate assessments. *Educational Measurement: Issues and Practices, 25*(4), 47–57.

Marsh, H. (1990). Causal ordering of academic self-concept and academic achievement: A multiwave, longitudinal panel analysis. *Journal of Educational Psychology, 82,* 646–656.

Marsh, H., & Ayotte, V. (2003). Do multiple dimensions of self-concept become more differentiated with age? The differential distinctiveness hypothesis. *Journal of Educational Psychology, 95,* 687–706.

Marsh, H., Kong, C., & Hau, K. (2001). Extension of the internal/external frame of reference model of self-concept formation: Importance of native and non-native languages for Chinese students. *Journal of Educational Psychology, 93*(3), 543–553.

Martin, G., & Pear, J. (2002). *Behavior modification* (7th ed.). Upper Saddle River, NJ: Merrill/Pearson.

Martin, J. (1993). Episodic memory: A neglected phenomenon in the psychology of education. *Educational Psychologist, 28*(2), 169–183.

Martin, J. (2006). Social cultural perspectives in educational psychology. In P. A. Alexander & P. H. Winne (Eds.), *Handbook of educational psychology* (2nd ed., pp. 595–614). Mahwah, NJ: Erlbaum.

Marzano. R. J. (2003a). *Classroom management that works: Research-based strategies for every teacher.* Alexandria, VA: Association for Supervision and Curriculum Development.

Marzano, R. J. (2003b). *What works in schools: Translating research into action.* Alexandria VA: Association for Supervision and Curriculum Development.

Marzano, R. J. (2007). *Classroom assessment and grading that work.* Alexandria VA: Association for Supervision and Curriculum Development.

Marzano, R. J., & Pickering, D. J. (2007). Errors and allegations about research on homework. *Phi Delta Kappan, 88,* 507–513.

Maslow, A. (1968). *Toward a psychology of being* (2nd ed.). New York: Van Nostrand.

Maslow, A. (1970). *Motivation and personality* (2nd ed.). New York: Harper & Row. (Original work published 1954)

Maslow, A. H. (1987). *Motivation and personality* (3rd ed.). New York: Harper & Row.

Mason, L. (2007). Introduction: Bridging the cognitive and sociocultural approaches in research on conceptual change: Is it feasible? *Educational Psychologist, 42*(1), 1–8.

Mastropieri, M., Scruggs, T., & Berkeley, S. (2007). Peers helping peers. *Educational Leadership, 64*(5), 54–58.

Maughan, A., & Ciccetti, D. (2002). Impact of child maltreatment and interadult violence on children's emotion regulation abilities and socioemotional adjustment. *Child Development, 73,* 1525–1542.

Mawhinney, T., & Sagan, L. (2007). The power of personal relationships. *Phi Delta Kappan, 88*(6), 460–464.

Mayer, R. (1996). Learners as information processors: Legacies and limitations of educational psychology's second metaphor. *Educational Psychologist, 31*(4), 151–161.

Mayer, R. (1997). Multimedia learning: Are we asking the right questions? *Educational Psychologist, 32*(1), 1–19.

Mayer, R. (1998). Cognitive theory for education: What teachers need to know. In N. Lambert & B. McCombs (Eds.), *How students learn: Reforming schools through learner-centered instruction* (pp. 353–378). Washington, DC: American Psychological Association.

Mayer, R. (1999). *The promise of educational psychology: Learning in the content areas.* Upper Saddle River, NJ: Merrill/Pearson.

Mayer, R. (2002). *The promise of educational psychology: Volume II. Teaching for meaningful learning.* Upper Saddle River, NJ: Merrilll/Pearson.

Mayer, R. (2008). *Learning and instruction* (2nd ed.). Upper Saddle River, NJ: Pearson.

Mayer, R. E. (2004). Should there be a three-strikes rule against pure discovery learning? *American Psychologist, 59,* 14–19.

Mayer, R. E., & Wittrock, M. C. (2006). Problem solving. In P. A. Alexander & P. H. Winne (Eds.), *Handbook of educational psychology* (2nd ed., pp. 287–303). Mahwah, NJ: Erlbaum.

Mazur, J. E. (2006). *Learning and behavior* (6th ed.). Upper Saddle River, NJ: Merrill/Pearson.

McAllister, G., & Ervine, J. J. (2002). The role of empathy in teaching culturally diverse students: A qualitative study of teachers' beliefs. *Journal of Teacher Education 53,* 433–443.

McCaughtry, N. (2004). The emotional dimensions of a teacher's pedagogical content knowledge: Influences on content, curriculum, and pedagogy. *Journal of Teaching in Physical Education, 23,* 30–47.

McCleery, J., Twyman, T., & Tindal, G. (2003, April). *Using concepts to frame history content with explicit instruction.* Paper presented at the annual meeting of the American Educational Research Association, Chicago.

McCoach, D. B., O'Connell, A., & Levitt, H. (2006). Ability grouping across kindergarten using an early childhood longitudinal study. *Journal of Educational Research, 99*(6), 339–346.

McCombs, B. L. (2001, April). *What do we know about learners and learning? The learner-centered framework.* Paper presented at the annual meeting of the American Educational Research Association, Seattle.

McCombs, B., & Miller, L. (2007). *Learner-centered classroom practices and assessment.* Thousand Oaks, CA: Corwin.

McCombs, J. (2005, March). *Progress in implementing standards, assessment for highly qualified teacher provisions of NCLB: Initial finding from California, Georgia, and Pennsylvania.* Paper presented at the annual meeting of the American Educational Research Association, Montreal.

McCurdy, B. L., Kunsch, C., & Reibstein, S. (2007). Secondary prevention in the urban school: Implementing the behavior education program. *Preventing School Failure, 51,* 12–19.

McCutchen, D. (2000). Knowledge, processing, and working memory: Implications for a theory of writing. *Educational Psychologist, 35*(1), 13–23.

McDermott, R., Goldman, S., & Varenne, H. (2006). The cultural work of learning disabilities. *Educational Researcher, 35*(6), 12–17.

McDevitt, T., Spivey, N., Sheehan, E., Lennon, R., & Story, R. (1990). Children's beliefs about listening: Is it enough to be still and quiet? *Child Development, 61,* 713–721.

McDougall, D., & Granby, C. (1996). How expectation of questioning method affects undergraduates' preparation for class. *Journal of Experimental Education, 65,* 43–54.

McIntosh, S., & Norwood, P. (2004). The power of testing: Inverstigating minority teachers' responses to certification examination questions. *Urban Education, 39*(1), 33–51.

McKeachie, W., & Kulik, J. (1975). Effective college teaching. In F. Kerlinger (Ed.), *Review of research in education: Vol. 3* (pp. 24–39). Washington, DC: American Educational Research Association.

McLeod, J., & Yates, L. (2006). *Making modern lives: Subjectivity, schooling, and social change.* Albany, NY: State University of New York Press.

McLoyd, V. C. (1998). Socioeconomic disadvantage and child development. *American Psychologist, 53,* 185–204.

McMahon, S., Rose, D., & Parks, M. (2004). Multiple intelligences and reading achievement; An examination of the Teele Inventory of Multiple Intelligences. *Journal of Experimental Education, 73*(1), 41–52.

McMillan, J. (2004). *Classroom assessment* (3rd ed.). Boston: Allyn & Bacon.

McMillan, J. (2007). *Classroom assessment: Principles and practices for effective standards-based instruction* (4th ed.). Boston: Allyn & Bacon.

McMillan, J. H. (2008). *Educational research: Fundamentals for the consumer* (5th ed.). Boston: Allyn & Bacon.

McNeil, L. (2000). *Contradictions of school reform: Educational costs of standardized testing.* New York: Routledge.

Md-Yunus, S. (2007). How parents can encourage creativity in children. *Childhood Education, 83,* 236–237.

Medin, D., Proffitt, J., & Schwartz. H. (2000). Concepts: An overview. In A. Kazdin (Ed.), *Encyclopedia of psychology* (Vol. 2, pp. 242–245). New York: Oxford University Press.

Meece, J. L. (2002). *Child and adolescent development for educators* (2nd ed.). New York: McGraw-Hill.

Meek, C. (2006). From the inside out: A look at testing special education students. *Phi Delta Kappan, 88*(4), 293–297.

Meichenbaum, D. (2000). *Cognitive behavior modification: An integrative approach.* Dordrecht, Netherlands: Kluwer Academic Publishers.

Meltzer, L., Pollica, L., & Barzillai, M. (2007). Executive function in the classroom: Embedding strategy instruction into daily teaching practices. In L. Meltzer, (Ed.), *Executive function in education: From theory to practice* (pp. 165–193). New York: Guilford Press.

Mercer, J. (1973). *Labeling the mentally retarded.* Berkeley: University of California Press.

Merisuo-Storm, T. (2007). Pupils' attitudes towards foreign-language learning and the development of literacy skills in bilingual education. *Teacher & Teacher Education, 23,* 226–235.

Merkley, D., & Jefferies, D. (2001). Guidelines for implementing a graphic organizer. *Reading Teacher, 54*(4), 350–357.

Mertler, C. (2007). *Interpreting standardized test scores: strategies for data-driven instructional decision making.* Los Angeles: Sage Publications.

Merzenich, M. M. (2001). Cortical plasticity contributing to child development. In J. L. McClelland & R. S. Siegler (Eds.), *Mechanisms of cognitive development: Behavioral and neural perspectives* (pp. 67–95). Mahwah, NJ: Erlbaum.

Meter, P., & Stevens, R. (2000). The role of theory in the study of peer collaboration. *Journal of Experimental Education, 69*(1), 113–127.

Middleton, M. J. (1999). *Classroom effects on the gender gap in middle school students' math self-efficacy.* Paper presented at the annual meeting of the American Educational Research Association, Montreal, Canada.

Middleton, M., & Midgley, C. (1997). Avoiding the demonstration of lack of ability: An underexplored aspect of goal theory. *Journal of Educational Psychology, 89,* 710–718.

Midgley, C. (2001). A goal theory perspective on the current status of middle level schools. In T. Urdan & F. Pajares (Eds.), *Adolescence and education* (Vol. I, pp. 33–59). Greenwich, CT: Information Age Publishing.

Midgley, C., Kaplan, A., & Middleton, M. (2001). Performance-approach goals. Good for what, for whom, under what circumstances, and at what cost? *Journal of Educational Psychology, 93,* 77–86.

Midgley, C., & Urdan, T. (2001). Academic self-handicapping and achievement goals: A further examination. *Contemporary Educational Psychology, 26,* 61–75.

Miller, G. (1956). The magical number seven, plus or minus two: Some limits on our capacity for processing information. *Psychological Review, 63,* 81–97.

Miller, M. D., Linn, R. L., & Gronlund, N. E. (2009). *Measurement and assessment in teaching* (10th ed.). Upper Saddle River, NJ: Merrill/Pearson.

Miller, P. (2002). *Theories of developmental psychology* (4th ed.). New York: Worth.

Mills, G. (2002, April). *Teaching and learning action research.* Paper presented at the annual meeting of the American Educational Research Association, New Orleans.

Milner, H. R. (2006). Classroom management in urban classrooms. In C. M. Evertson & C. S. Weinstein (Eds.), *Handbook of classroom management: Research, practice, and contemporary issues* (pp. 491–522). Mahwah, NJ: Erlbaum.

Miltenberger, R. (2004). *Behavior modification: Principles and procedures* (3rd ed.). Belmont, CA: Wadsworth.

Moll, L. C., & Whitmore, K. (1993). Vygotsky in classroom practice: Moving from individual transmission to social transaction. In E. Forman, N. Minick, & C. Stone (Eds.), *Contexts for learning* (pp. 19–42). New York: Oxford University Press.

Moreno, R. (2004). Decreasing cognitive load for novice students: Effects of explanatory versus corrective feedback in discovery-based multimedia. *Instructional Science, 32,* 99–113.

Moreno, R., & Duran, R. (2004). Do multiple representations need explanations: The role of verbal guidance and individual differences in multimedia mathematics learning. *Journal of Educational Psychology, 96,* 492–503.

Moreno, R., & Mayer, R. (2000). Engaging students in active learning: The case for personalized multimedia messages. *Journal of Educational Psychology, 92*(4), 724–733.

Moreno, R., & Mayer, R. (2005). Role of guidance, reflection, and interactivity in an agent-based multimedia game. *Journal of Educational Psychology, 97*(1), 117–128.

Moreno, R., & Valdez, A. (2007). Immediate and delayed effects of using a classroom case exemplar in teacher education: The role of presentation format. *Journal of Educational Psychology, 99*(1), 194–206.

Morgan, P. L., & Fuchs, D. (2007). Is there a bidirectional relationship between children's reading skills and reading motivation? *Exceptional Children, 73,* 165–183.

Morgan, S. L., & Mehta, J. D. (204). Beyond the laboratory: Evaluating the survey evidence for the disidentification explanation of black–white differences in achievement. *Sociology of Education, 77*(1), 82–101.

Morrone, A., Harkness, S., D'Ambrosio, B., & Caulfield, R. (2003, April). *Patterns of instructional discourse that promote the perception of mastery goals in a social constructivist mathematics course.* Paper presented at the annual meeting of the American Educational Research Association, Chicago.

Moshman, D. (1997). Pluralist rational constructivism. *Issues in Education: Contributions From Educational Psychology, 3,* 229–234.

Mulholland, R., & Cepello, M. (2006). What teacher candidates need to know about academic learning time. *International Journal of Special Education, 21,* 63–73.

Munakata, Y. (2006). Information processing approaches to development. In D. Kuhn & R. Siegler (Vol. Eds.), *Handbook of child psychology: Vol. 2. Cognition, perception, and language* (6th ed., pp. 426–463). Hoboken, NJ: John Wiley & Sons.

Munby, H., Russel, T., & Martin, A. (2001). Teachers' knowledge and how it develops. In V. Richardson (Ed.), *Handbook of research on teaching* (4th ed., pp. 877–904). Washington, DC: American Educational Research Association.

Munk, D. (2003). Grading students with disabilities. *Educational Leadership, 61*(2), 38–43.

Murdock, T., Hale, N., & Weber, M. (2001). Predictors of cheating among early adolescents: Academic and social motivations. *Contemporary Educational Psychology, 26*(2), 96–115.

Murdock, T. B., & Anderman, E. A. (2006). Motivational perspectives on student cheating: Toward an integrated model of academic dishonesty. *Educational Psychologist, 41,* 129–145.

Murdock, T. B., Miller, A., & Kohlhardt, J. (2004). Effects of classroom context variables in high school students' judgments of the acceptability and likelihood of cheating. *Journal of Educational Psychology, 96*(4), 765–777.

Murphy, J. C. (2007). Hey, Ms. A! One student teacher's success story. *Kappa Delta Pi Record, 43,* 52–55.

Murphy, P. K., & Alexander, P. (2000). A motivated exploration of motivation terminology. *Contemporary Educational Psychology, 25,* 3–53.

Myers, C. (1970). Journal citations and scientific eminence in contemporary psychology. *American Psychologist, 25,* 1041–1048.

Myers, K. M., & Davis, M. (2007). Mechanisms of fear extinction. *Molecular Psychiatry, 12,* 120–150.

Nagy, W., & Scott, J. (2000). Vocabulary processes. In M. L. Kamil, & P. B. Mosenthal (Eds.), *Handbook of reading research* (Vol. 3, pp. 269–284). Mahwah, NJ: Erlbaum.

Nansel, T. R., Overpeck, M., Pilla, R. S., Ruan, W. J., Simmons-Morton, B., & Scheift, P. (2001). Bullying behaviors among U.S. young: Prevalence and association with psychosocial adjustment. *Journal of the American Medical Association, 285,* 2094–2100.

Nasir, N., Rosebery, A., Warren, B., & Lee, C. (2006). Learning as a cultural process: Achieving equity through diversity. In R. K. Sawyer (Ed.), *The Cambridge handbook of the learning sciences* (pp. 489–504). New York: Cambridge University Press.

National Assessment of Educational Progress. (2001). *National report: 2000.* Washington, DC: National Center for Educational Statistics.

National Center for Education Statistics. (2007). *The condition of education 2007.* Washington, DC: U.S. Department of Education.

National Center for Research on Teacher Learning. (1993). *Findings on learning to teach.* East Lansing: Michigan State University.

National Commission on Excellence in Education. (1983). *A nation at risk: The imperative for educational reform.* Washington, DC: Government Printing Office.

National Council on Disability (2000, January). *Achieving independence: The challenge for the 21st century.* Washington, DC: Author.

National Education Association. (2007). *Status of the American school teacher, 2006–2007.* Washington, DC: Author.

National excellence: A case for developing America's talent. (1993). Washington, DC: U.S. Department of Education, Office of Educational Research and Improvement.

National Joint Committee on Learning Disabilities. (1994). Learning disabilities: Issues on definition. A position paper of the National Joint Committee in Learning Disabilities. In *Collective perspectives on issues affecting learning disability: Position papers and statements.* Austin, TX: Pro-Ed.

National Law Center on Homelessness and Poverty. (2007). *2007 Annual Report.* Retrieved August 9, 2008, from http://www.nlchp.org/content/pubs/2007_Annual_Report1.pdf

Neill, M. (2003). High stakes, high risk. *American School Board Journal, 190*(2), 18–21.

Neisser, U. (1967). *Cognitive psychology.* New York: Appleton-Century-Crofts.

Neisser, U., Boodoo, G., Bouchard, A., Boykin, W., Brody, N., Ceci, S., Halpern, D., Loehlin, J., Perloff, R., Sternberg, R., & Urbina, S. (1996). Intelligence: Knowns and unknowns. *American Psychologist, 51,* 77–101.

Nelson, C., Thomas, K., & de Haan, M. (2006). Neural bases of cognitive development. In D. Kuhn, & R. Siegler (Vol. Eds.), *Handbook of child psychology: Vol. 2. Cognition, perception, and language* (6th ed., pp. 3–57). Hoboken, NJ: John Wiley & Sons.

Nesbit, J., & Adesope, O. (2006). Learning with concept and knowledge maps: A meta-analysis. *Review of Educational Research, 76*(3), 413–448.

Nesbit, J., & Hadwin, A. (2006). Methodological issues in educational psychology. In P. A. Alexander & P. H. Winne (Eds.), *Handbook of educational psychology* (2nd ed., pp. 825–848). Mahwah, NJ: Erlbaum.

New Commission on the Skills of the American Workforce. (2007). *Tough choices or tough time.* Retrieved December 9, 2007, from: http://www.skillscommission.org/executive.htm

Newman, R., & Murray, B. (2005). How students and teachers view the seriousness of peer harassment: When is it appropriate to seek help? *Journal of Educational Psychology, 97,* 347–365.

Newstead, J., Franklyn-Stokes, A., & Armstead, P. (1996). Individual differences in student cheating. *Journal of Educational Psychology, 88*(2), 229–241.

Niaz, M. (1997). How early can children understand some form of "scientific reasoning"? *Perceptual and Motor Skills, 85,* 1272–1274.

Nicholls, J. (1984). Achievement motivation: Conceptions of ability, subjective experience, task choice, and performance. *Psychological Review, 91,* 328–346.

Nichols, B., & Singer, K. (2000). Developing data mentors. *Educational Leadership, 57*(5), 34–37.

Nichols, S., & Berliner, D. (2005). *The inevitable corruption of indicators and educators through high-stakes testing.* Tempe, AZ: Education Policy Studies Laboratory.

Nilsson, L., & Archer, T. (1989). Aversively motivated behavior: Which are the perspectives? In T. Archer & L. Nilsson (Eds.), *Aversion, avoidance and anxiety.* Hillsdale, NJ: Erlbaum.

Nitko, A. (2004). *Educational assessment of students* (4th ed.). Upper Saddle River, NJ: Pearson.

Nitko, A., & Brookhart, S. (2007). *Educational assessment of students* (5th ed.). Upper Saddle River, NJ: Merrill/Pearson.

No Child Left Behind Act of 2001. *Public Law 107–110* (8 January 2002). Washington, DC: U.S. Government Printing Office.

Noddings, N. (1992). *The challenge to care in schools: An alternative approach to education.* New York: Teachers College Press.

Noddings, N. (2001). The caring teacher. In V. Richardson (Ed.), *Handbook of research on teaching* (4th ed., pp. 99–105). Washington, DC: American Educational Research Association.

Noddings, N. (2002). *Educating moral people: A caring alternative approach to education.* New York: Teachers College Press.

Noguera, P. (2003a). *City schools and the American dream: Reclaiming the promise of public education.* New York: Teachers College Press.

Noguera, P. (2003b). The trouble with black boys: The role and influence of environmental and cultural factors on the academic performance of African American males. *Urban Education, 38*(4), 431–459.

Nokelainen, P., & Flint, J. (2002). Genetic effects on human cognition: Lessons from the study of mental retardation syndromes. *Journal of Neurology, Neurosurgery, and Psychiatry, 43,* 287–296.

Northwest Regional Laboratory. (2003). *In context: English language learners and NO Child Left Behind.* Retrieved January, 13, 2007, from http://www.NWREL.org/request/2003May/incontext.html Accessed 1/13/07.

Nosek, B., Banaji, M., & Greenwald, A. (2002). Math = male, me = female, therefore math [not equal to] me. *Journal of Personality and Social Psychology, 83,* 44–59.

Notar, C. E., Zuelke, D. C., Wilson, J. D., & Yunker, B. D. (2004). The table of specifications: Ensuring accountability in teacher made tests. *Journal of Instructional Psychology, 31*(2), 115–129.

Nucci, L. (1987). Synthesis of research on moral development. *Educational Leadership, 44*(5), 86–92.

Nucci, L. (2001). *Education in the moral domain.* Cambridge, England: Cambridge University Press.

Nucci, L. (2006). Classroom management for moral and social development. In C. Evertson & C. Weinstein (Eds.), *Handbook of classroom management: Research, practice, and contemporary issues* (pp. 711–731). Mahwah, NJ: Erlbaum.

Nuthall, G. (1999a). Learning how to learn: The evolution of students' minds through the social processes and culture of the classroom. *International Journal of Educational Research, 31*(3), 141–256.

Nuthall, G. (1999b). The way students learn: Acquiring knowledge from an integrated science and social studies unit. *Elementary School Journal, 99*(4), 303–342.

Nuthall, G. A. (2000). The role of memory in the acquisition and retention of knowledge in science and social studies units. *Cognition and Instruction, 18*(1), 83–139.

Nystrand, M., & Gamoran, A. (1989, March). *Instructional discourse and student engagement.* Paper presented at the annual meeting of the American Educational Research Association, San Francisco.

Oakes, J. (2005). *Keeping track: How schools structure inequality* (2nd ed.). New Haven, CT: Yale University Press.

O'Brien, L., & Crandall, C. (2003). Stereotype threat and arousal: Effects on women's math performance. *Personality and Social Psychology Bulletin, 29,* 782–789.

O'Brien, T. (1999). Parrot math. *Phi Delta Kappan, 80*, 434–438.

O'Conner, C., & Fernandez, S. (2006). Race, class, and disproportionality: Reevaluating the relationship between poverty and special education placement. *Educational Researcher, 35*(6), 6–11.

O'Connor, E., & McCartney, K. (2007). Examining teacher–child relationships and achievement as part of an ecological model of development. *American Educational Research Journal, 44*(2), 340–369.

Odom, A. L., Stoddard, E. R., & LaNasa, S. M. (2007). Teacher practices and middle-school science achievements. *International Journal of Science Education, 29*, 1329–1346.

O'Donnell, A. (2006). The role of peers and group learning. In P. Alexander & P. Winne (Eds.), *Handbook of educational psychology* (2nd ed., pp. 781–802). Mahwah, NJ: Erlbaum.

Ogbu, J. (1992). Understanding cultural diversity and learning. *Educational Researcher, 21*(8), 5–14.

Ogbu, J. (1999a). Beyond language: Ebonics, proper English, and identity in a Black-American speech community. *American Educational Research Journal, 36*(2), 147–184.

Ogbu, J. (1999b, April). *The significance of minority status.* Paper presented at the annual meeting of the American Educational Research Association, Montreal, Canada.

Ogbu, J. (2002). *Black American students in an affluent suburb: A study of academic disengagement.* Mahwah, NJ: Erlbaum.

Ogbu, J. U. (2003). *Black American students in an affluent suburb: A study of academic disengagement.* Mahwah, NJ: Erlbaum.

Ogbu, J., & Simons, H. (1998). Voluntary and involuntary minorities: A cultural-ecological theory of school performance with some implications for education. *Anthropology & Education Quarterly, 29*(2), 155–188.

Okagaki, L. (2006). Ethnicity, learning. In P. A. Alexander & P. H. Winne (Eds.), *Handbook of educational psychology* (2nd ed., pp. 615–634). Mahwah, NJ: Erlbaum.

Olson, J., & Clough, M. (2004). *What questions do you have? In defense of general questions: A response to Croom.* ID=11366. Retrieved August 20, 2004, from http://www.tcrecord.org/content.asp?content

O'Mara, A., Marsh, H., Craven, R., & Debus, R. (2006). Do self-concept interventions make a difference? A synergistic blend of construct validation and meta-analysis. *Educational Psychologist, 41*(3), 181–206.

Opdenakker, M. C., & Van Damme, J. (2006). Teacher characteristics and teaching styles as effectiveness enhancing factors of classroom practice. *Teaching and Teacher Education, 22*, 1–21.

O'Reilly, T., Symons, S., & MacLatchy-Gaudet, H. (1998). A comparison of self-explanation and elaborative interrogation. *Contemporary Educational Psychology, 23*, 434–445.

Orr, A. (2003). Black–white differences in achievement: The importance of wealth. *Sociology of Education, 76*(October), 281–304.

Osterman, K. F. (2000). Students' need for belonging in the school community. *Review of Educational Research, 70*, 323–367.

Owens, R. E., Jr. (2005). *Language development* (6th ed.). Boston: Allyn & Bacon.

Paas, F., Renkl, A., & Sweller, J. (2004). Cognitive load theory: Instructional implications of the interaction between information structures and cognitive architecture. *Instructional Science, 32*(1), 1–8.

Packer, M., & Goicoechea, J. (2000). Sociocultural and constructivist theories of learning: Ontology, not just epistemology. *Educational Psychologist, 35*(4), 227–241.

Padilla, A. (2006). Second language learning: Issues in research and teaching. In P. Alexander & P. Winne (Eds.), *Handbook of educational psychology* (2nd ed., pp. 571–592). Mahwah, NJ: Erlbaum.

Page, E. (1992). Is the world an orderly place? A review of teacher comments and student achievement. *Journal of Experimental Education, 60*(2), 161–181.

Paivio, A. (1986). *Mental representations: A dual-coding approach.* New York: Oxford University.

Paivio, A. (1991). Dual coding theory: Retrospect and current status. *Canadian Journal of Psychology, 45*, 255–287.

Pajares, F., & Valiante, G. (1999, April). *Writing self-efficacy of middle school students: Relation to motivation constructs, achievement, gender, and gender orientation.* Paper presented at the annual meeting of the American Educational Research Association, Montreal, Canada.

Pajares, R., & Schunk, D. H. (2002). Self and self-belief in psychology and education: A historical perspective. In J. Aronson & D. Cordova (Eds.), *Improving academic achievement: Impact of psychological factors on education* (pp. 3–21). New York: Academic Press.

Palincsar, A. (1998). Social constructivist perspectives on teaching and learning. *Annual Review of Psychology, 49*, 345–375.

Paris, S. G., Morrison, F. J., & Miller, K. F. (2006). Academic pathways from preschool through elementary school. In P. A. Alexander & P. H. Winne (Eds.), *Handbook of educational psychology* (2nd ed., pp. 61–85). Mahwah, NJ: Erlbaum.

Paris, S. G., & Paris, A. H. (2001). Classroom application of research on self-regulated learning. *Educational Psychologist, 36*, 89–101.

Parish, J., Parish, T., & Batt, S. (2001, April). *Academic achievement and school climate—interventions that work.* Paper presented at the annual meeting of the American Educational Research Association, Seattle.

Pashler, H., & Carrier, M. (1996). Structures, processes, and the flow of information. In E. Bjork & R. Bjork (Eds.), *Memory* (pp. 3–29). San Diego, CA: Academic Press.

Patrick, B. C., Hisley, J., & Kempler, T. (2000). "What's everybody so excited about?:" The effects of teacher enthusiasm on student intrinsic motivation and vitality. *The Journal of Experimental Education, 68*, 217–236.

Patrick, H., Anderman, L., Ryan, A., Edelin, K., & Midgley, C. (1999, April). *Messages teachers send: Communicating goal orientations in the classroom.* Paper presented at the annual meeting of the American Educational Research Association, Montreal, Canada.

Patrick, H., Anderman, L. H., & Ryan, A. M. (2002). Social motivation and the classroom social environment. In C. Midgley (Ed.), *Goals, goal structures, and patterns of adaptive learning* (pp. 85–108). Mahwah, NJ: Erlbaum.

Pavlov, I. P. (1927). *Conditioned reflexes* (G. V. Anrep, Trans.). London: Oxford University Press.

Peevely, G., Hedges, L., & Nye, B. A. (2005). The relationship of class size effects and teacher salary. *Journal of Education Finance*, 31(1), 101–109.

Pekrun, R., Goetz, T., Titz, W., & Perry, R. (2002). Academic emotions in students' self-regulated learning and achievement: A program of qualitative and quantitative research. *Educational Psychologist, 37*, 91–105.

Péladeau, N., Forget, J., & Gagné, F. (2003). Effect of paced and unpaced practice on skill application and retention: How much is enough? *American Educational Research Journal, 40*(3), 769–801.

Pellegrini, A. D. (2002). Bullying, victimization, and sexual harassment during the transition to middle school. *Educational Psychologist, 37*, 151–163.

Peregoy, S., & Boyle, O. (2001). *Reading, writing, and learning in ESL* (3rd ed.). New York: Longman.

Peregoy, S., & Boyle, O. (2005). *Reading, writing, and learning in ESL* (4th ed.). New York: Longman.

Perkins-Gough, D. (2004). A two-tiered education system. *Educational Leadership, 62*(3), 87–88.

Perkins-Gough, D. (2006). Do we really have a "boy crisis"? *Educational Leadership, 64*(1), 93–94.

Perry, N. (1998). Young children's self-regulated learning and contexts that support it. *Journal of Educational Psychology, 90*(4), 715–729.

Perry, N. E., Turner, J. C., & Meyer, D. K. (2006). Classrooms as contexts for motivating learning. In P. A. Alexander & P. H. Winne (Eds.), *Handbook of educational psychology* (2nd ed., pp. 327–348). Mahwah, NJ: Erlbaum.

Perry T., Steele, C., & Hilliard, A. (2003). *Young, gifted, and Black: Promoting high achievement among African American students.* Boston: Beacon Press.

Peterson, C. C. (2002). Drawing insight from pictures: The development of concepts of false drawing and false belief in children with deafness, normal hearing, and autism. *Child Development, 73*, 1442–1459.

Peverly, S. P., Brobst, K. E., & Graham, M. (2003). College adults are not good at self-regulation: A study on the relationship of self-regulation, note taking, and test taking. *Journal of Educational Psychology, 95*, 335–346.

Peverly, S., Ramaswamy, V., Brown, C., Sumowski, J., Alidoost, M., & Garner, J. (2007). What predicts skill in lecture note taking? *Journal of Educational Psychology, 99*(1), 167–180.

Pfiffner, L., Rosen, L., & O'Leary, S. (1985). The efficacy of an all-positive approach to classroom management. *Journal of Applied Behavior Analysis, 18*, 257–261.

Phelps, L., McGrew, K., Knopik, S., & Ford, L. (2005). The general (g), broad, and narrow CHC stratum characteristics of the WJ III and WISC-III tests: A confirmatory cross-battery investigation. *School Psychology Quarterly, 20*, 66–88.

Phelps, R. (Ed.) (2005). *Defending standardized testing.* Mahwah, NJ: Erlbaum.

Phillips, D. (1995). The good, the bad and the ugly: The many faces of constructivism. *Educational Researcher, 24*(7), 5–12.

Phillips, D. (1997). How, why, what, when, and where: Perspectives on constructivism in psychology and education. *Issues in Education, 3,* 151–194.

Phillips, D. (2000). An opinionated account of the constructivist landscape. In D. Phillips (Ed.), *Constructivism in education: Opinions and second opinions on controversial issues* (pp. 1–16). Chicago: National Society for the Study of Education.

Phye, G. D. (2001). Problem-solving instruction and problem-solving transfer: The correspondence issue. *Journal of Educational Psychology, 93,* 571–578.

Phye, G. (2005). Transfer and problem solving: A psychological integration of models, metaphors, and methods. In J. Royer (Ed.), *The cognitive revolution in educational psychology* (pp. 249–292). Greenwich, CT: Information Age Publishing.

Piaget, J. (1926). *The language and thought of the child.* New York: Harcourt, Brace & World.

Piaget, J. (1952). *Origins of intelligence in children.* New York: International Universities Press.

Piaget, J. (1959). *Language and thought of the child* (M. Grabain, Trans.). New York: Humanities Press.

Piaget, J. (1965). The *moral judgment of the child.* New York: Free Press. (Original work published 1932)

Piaget, J. (1970). *The science of education and the psychology of the child.* New York: Orion Press.

Piaget, J. (1977). Problems in equilibration. In M. Appel & L. Goldberg (Eds.), *Topics in cognitive development: Vol. 1. Equilibration: Theory, research, and application* (pp. 3–13). New York: Plenum Press.

Piaget, J. (1980). *Adaptation and intelligence: Organic selection and phenocopy* (S. Eames, Trans.). Chicago: University of Chicago Press.

Piaget, J., & Inhelder, B. (1956). *The child's conception of space.* Boston: Routledge and Kegan-Paul.

Pianta, R., Belsky, J., Houts, R., Morrison, F., & NICHD Early Child Care Research Network. (2007). Opportunities to learn in America's elementary classrooms. *Science, 315,* 1795–1796.

Pierangelo, R., & Guiliani, G. (2006). *Assessment in special education* (2nd ed.). Boston: Allyn & Bacon.

Pintrich, P. (2000). Multiple goals, multiple pathways: The role of goal orientation in learning and achievement. *Journal of Educational Psychology, 92,* 544–555.

Pittman, K., & Beth-Halachmy, S. (1997, March). *The role of prior knowledge in analogy use.* Paper presented at the annual meeting of the American Educational Research Association, Chicago.

Plake, B., Impara, J., & Spies, R. A. (Eds.). (2003). *The fifteenth mental measurements yearbook.* Lincoln: University of Nebraska Press.

Plant, E. A., Ericsson, K. A., & Hill, L. (2005). Why study time does not predict grade point average across college students: Implications of deliberate practice for academic performance. *Contemporary Educational Psychology, 30,* 96–116.

Plata, M., Trusty, J., & Glasgow, D. (2005). Adolescents with learning disabilities: Are they allowed to participate in activities? *Journal of Educational Research, 98*(3), 136–143.

Platt, R. (2004). Standardized tests: Whose standards are we talking about? *Phi Delta Kappan, 85*(5), 381–382.

Plucker, J. A., Beghetto, R. A., & Dow, G. T. (2004). Why isn't creativity more important to educational psychologists? Potentials, pitfalls, and future directions in creativity research. *Educational Psychologist, 39,* 83–96.

Pomerantz, E., & Dong, W. (2006). Effects of mothers' perceptions of children's competence: The moderating role of mothers' theories of competence. *Developmental Psychology, 42*(5), 950–961.

Popham, W. (2003). The seductive lure of data. *Educational Leadership, 60*(5), 48–51.

Popham, W. J. (2004a). A game without winners. *Educational Leadership, 62*(3), 46–50.

Popham, W. J. (2004b). *American's failing schools: How parents and teachers can cope with No Child Left Behind.* New York: Routledge Falmer.

Popham, W. J. (2004c). "Teaching to the test:" An expression to eliminate. *Educational Leadership, 62*(3), 82–83.

Popham, W. J. (2005). *Classroom assessment: What teachers need to know* (4th ed.). Boston: Pearson.

Popham, W. J. (2007). Who should make the test? *Educational Leadership, 65*(1), 80–82.

Potter, R. L. (1999). Technical reading in the middle school. *Phi Delta Kappa Fastbacks, 456,* 7–56.

Powell, R., & Caseau, D. (2004). *Classroom communication and diversity.* Mahwah, NJ: Erlbaum.

Prawat, R. (1989). Promoting access to knowledge, strategy, and disposition in students: A research synthesis. *Review of Educational Research, 59,* 1–41.

Premack, D. (1965). Reinforcement theory. In D. Levine (Ed.), *Nebraska Symposium on Motivation* (Vol. 13, pp. 3–41). Lincoln: University of Nebraska Press.

Pressley, M., & Harris, K. R. (2006). Cognitive strategies instruction: From basic research to classroom instruction. In P. A. Alexander & P. H. Winne (Eds.), *Handbook of educational psychology* (2nd ed., pp. 265–286). Mahwah, NJ: Erlbaum.

Pressley, M., & Hilden, K. (2006). Cognitive strategies. In D. Kuhn & R. Siegler (Eds.), *Handbook of child psychology* (6th ed., Vol. 2, pp. 511–556). Hoboken, NJ: John Wiley & Sons.

Pressley, M., Raphael, L., & Gallagher, J. G. (2004). Prodience-St. Mel School: How a school that works for African American students works. *Journal of Educational Psychology, 96*(2), 216–235.

Pritchard, R. (1990). The effects of cultural schemata on reading processing strategies. *Reading Research Quarterly, 25,* 273–295.

Pulliam, J., & Van Patten, J. (2007). *History of education in America* (9th ed.). Upper Saddle River, NJ: Merrill/Pearson.

Puntambekar, S., & Hübscher, R. (2005). Tools for scaffolding students in a complex learning environment: What have we gained and what have we missed? *Educational Psychologist, 40*(1), 1–12.

Purdie, N., Hattie, J., & Carroll, A. (2002). A review of the research on interventions for attention deficit hyperactivity disorder: What works best? *Review of Educational Research, 72*(1), 61–100.

Putnam, R., & Borko, H. (2000). What do new views of knowledge and thinking have to say about research on teacher learning? *Educational Researcher, 29*(1), 4–15.

Pyryt, M., & Mendaglio, S. (2001, April). *Intelligence and moral development: A meta-analytic review.* Paper presented at the annual meeting of the American Educational Research Association, Seattle.

Qian, G., & Pan, J. (2002). A comparison of epistemological beliefs and learning from science text between American and Chinese high school students. In B. K Hofer & P. R. Pintrich (Eds). *Personal epistemology: The psychology of beliefs about knowledge and knowing* (pp. 365–385). Mahwah: NJ; Erlbaum.

Quihuis, G., Bempechat, J., Jiminez, N., & Boulay, P. (2002). Implicit theories of intelligence across academic domains: A study of meaning making in adolescents of Mexican descent. In J. Bempechat, & J. Elliott (Eds.), *Learning in culture and context: Approaching the complexities of achievement motivation in student learning* (pp. 87–100). San Francisco: Jossey-Bass.

Quinn, P. C. (2002). Category representation in your infants. *Current Directions in Psychological Science, 11,* 66–70.

Quiocho, A., & Ulanoff, S. (2002, April). *Teacher research in preservice teacher education: Asking burning questions.* Paper presented at the annual meeting of the American Educational Research Association, New Orleans.

Rainwater, L., & Smeedings, T. (2003). *Poor kids in a rich country.* New York: Russell Sage Foundation.

Ramey, C. T., Ramey, S. L., & Lanzi, R. G. (2001). Intelligence and experience. In R. J. Sternberg & E. L. Grigorenko (Eds.), *Environmental effects on cognitive abilities.* Mahwah, NJ: Erlbaum.

Raskauskas, J., & Stoltz, A. (2007). Involvement in traditional and electronic bullying among adolescents. *Developmental Psychology, 43*(3), 564–575.

Reiner, M., Slotta, J. D., Chi, M. T. H., & Resnick, L. B. (2000). Naïve physics reasoning: A commitment to substance-based conceptions. *Cognition and Instruction, 18,* 1–34.

Reis, S. M., Colbert, R. D., & Hébert, T. P. (2005). Understanding resilience in diverse, talented students in an urban high school. *Roeper Review, 27*(2), 110–120.

Reisberg, D. (2006). *Cognition: Exploring the science of the mind* (3rd ed.). New York: Norton.

Renkl, A., Stark, R., Gruber, H., & Mandl, H. (1998). Learning from worked-out examples: The effects of example variability and elicited self-explanations. *Contemporary Educational Psychology, 23,* 90–108.

Renninger, K. A. (2000). Individual interest and its implications for understanding intrinsic motivation. In J. M. Harackiewicz & C. Sansone (Eds.), *Intrinsic and extrinsic motivation: The search for optimal motivation and performance* (pp. 373–404). San Diego, CA: Academic Press.

Renzulli, J., & Reis, S. (2003). The schoolwide enrichment model: Developing creative and productive giftedness. In N. Colangelo, & G. Davis (Eds.), *Handbook of gifted education* (3rd ed., pp. 184–203). Boston: Allyn & Bacon.

Resnick, L., & Klopfer, L. (1989). Toward the thinking curriculum: An overview. In L. Resnick & L. Klopfer (Eds.), *Toward the thinking curriculum: Current cognitive research* (pp. 1–18).

Rest, J., Narvaez, D., Bebeau, M., & Thoma, S. (1999). A neo-Kohlbergian approach: The DIT and schema theory. *Educational Psychology Review, 11*, 291–324.

Reutzel, D., & Cooter, R. (2008). *Teaching children to read: The teacher makes the difference* (5th ed.). Upper Saddle River, NJ: Merrill/Pearson.

Reys, B., Reys, R., & Chávez, O. (2004). Why mathematics textbooks matter. *Educational Leadership, 62*(5), 61–66.

Richardson, V., & Placier, P. (2001). Teacher change. In V. Richardson (Ed.), *Handbook of research on teaching* (4th ed., pp. 905–950). Washington, DC: American Educational Research Association.

Ridley, D., McCombs, B., & Taylor, K. (1994). Walking the talk: Fostering self-regulated learning in the classroom. *Middle School Journal, 26*(2), 52–57.

Riehl, C. (2006). Feeling better: A comparison of medical and education research. *Educational Researcher, 35*(5), 24–29.

Riley, M., Greeno, J., & Heller, J. (1982). The development of children's problem-solving ability in arithmetic. In H. Ginsburg (Ed.), *Development of mathematical thinking.* San Diego, CA: Academic Press.

Rimm-Kaufman, S. E., & Sawyer, B. E. (2004). Primary-grade teachers' self-efficacy beliefs, attitudes toward teaching, and discipline and teaching practice priorities in relation to the Responsive Classroom approach. *Elementary School Journal, 104*(4), 321–341.

Rittle-Johnson, B., & Alibali, M. (1999). Conceptual and procedural knowledge of mathematics: Does one lead to the other? *Journal of Educational Psychology, 91*(1), 175–189.

Ritts, V., Patterson, M., & Tubbs, M. (1992). Expectations, impressions, and judgments of physically attractive students: A review. *Review of Educational Research, 62*, 413–426.

Roberts, S. (2007). In name count, Garcias are catching up to Joneses. *New York Times.* Retrieved November 17, 2007, from http://www.nytimes.com/2007/11/17/us/17surnames.html?th&emc=th

Robertson, J. (2000). Is attribution training a worthwhile classroom intervention for K–12 students with learning difficulties? *Educational Psychology Review, 12*(1), 111–134.

Roblyer, M. (2006). *Integrating educational technology into teaching* (4th ed.). Upper Saddle River, NJ: Merrill/Pearson.

Roeser, R. W., Mariachi, R., & Gehlbach, H. (2002). A goal theory perspective on teachers' professional identities and the contexts of teaching. In C. Midgley (Ed.), *Goals, goal structure, and patterns of adaptive learning* (pp. 205–241). Mahwah, NJ: Erlbaum.

Roeser, R. W., Peck, S. C., & Nasir, N. S. (2006). Self and identity processes in school motivation, learning and achievement.). In P. A. Alexander & P. H. Winne (Eds.), *Handbook of educational psychology* (2nd ed., pp. 391–424). Mahwah, NJ: Erlbaum.

Rogers, C. (1959). A theory of therapy, personality, and interpersonal relationships, as developed in the client-centered framework. In S. Koch (Ed.), *Psychology: A study of a science* (Vol. 3, pp. 184–256). New York: McGraw-Hill.

Rogers, C. (1963). Actualizing tendency in relation to motives and to consciousness. In M. Jones (Ed.), *Nebraska Symposium on Motivation* (Vol. 11, pp. 1–24). Lincoln: University of Nebraska Press.

Rogers, C., & Freiberg, H. J. (1994). *Freedom to learn* (3rd ed.). Upper Saddle River, NJ: Merrill/Pearson.

Rogoff, B. (1998). Cognition as a collaborative process. In W. Damon (Series Ed.), D. Kuhn, & R. S. Siegler (Vol. Eds.), *Handbook of child psychology: Vol. 2* (5th ed., pp. 679–744). New York: Wiley.

Rogoff, B. (2001). *Everyday cognition: Its development in social context.* New York: Replica Books.

Rogoff, B. (2003). *The cultural context of human development.* Oxford, England: Oxford University Press.

Rogoff, B., Turkanis, C., & Bartlett, L. (Eds.). (2001). *Learning together: Children and adults in a school community.* New York: Oxford University Press.

Roid, G. (2003). *Stanford-Binet Intelligence Scales, Fifth Edition.* Itasca, IL: Riverside Publishing.

Romboy, D., & Kinkead, L. (2005). Surviving in America. *Deseret Morning News, 155*(303), *April 14*, pp. 1, 11, 12.

Rose, K., Williams, K., Gomez, L., & Gearon, J. (2002, April). *Building a case for what our students know and can do: How trustworthy are our judgments?* Paper presented at the annual meeting of the American Educational Research Association, New Orleans.

Rose, L., & Gallup, A. (2000). The 32nd annual Phi Delta Kappa/Gallup Poll of the public's attitudes toward the public schools. *Phi Delta Kappan, 82*, 41–58.

Rose, L. C., & Gallup, A. M. (2007). The 39th annual Phi Delta Kappa/Gallup poll of the public's attitudes toward the public schools. *Phi Delta Kappan, 89*, 33–48.

Rosen, L., O'Leary, S., Joyce, S., Conway, G., & Pfiffner, L. (1984). The importance of prudent negative consequences for maintaining the appropriate behavior of hyperactive students. *Journal of Abnormal Child Psychology, 12*, 581–604.

Rosenfield, P., Lambert, S., & Black, R. (1985). Desk arrangement effects on pupil classroom behavior. *Journal of Educational Psychology, 77*, 101–108.

Rosenshine, B. (1987). Explicit teaching. In D. Berliner & B. Rosenshine (Eds.), *Talks to teachers.* New York: Random House.

Rosenshine, B. (2006). The struggles of the lower-scoring students. *Teaching and Teacher Education, 22*, 555–562.

Rosenshine, B., & Meister, C. (1992, April). *The use of scaffolds for teaching less structured academic tasks.* Paper presented at the annual meeting of the American Educational Research Association, San Francisco.

Rosenshine, B., & Stevens, R. (1986). Teaching functions. In M. Wittrock (Ed.), *Handbook of research on teaching* (3rd ed., pp. 376–391). New York: Macmillan.

Roseth, C. J., Johnson, D. W., Johnson, R. T., Fang, F., Hilk, C. L., & Fleming, M. A. (2007, April). *Effects of cooperative learning on elementary school students' achievement: A meta-analysis.* Paper presented at the annual meeting of the American Educational Research Association, Chicago.

Ross, B., & Spalding, T. (1994). Concepts and categories. In R. Sternberg (Ed.), *Handbook of perception and cognition* (Vol. 12). New York: Academic Press.

Roth, W., & Lee, Y. (2007). "Vygotsky's neglected legacy:" Cultural-historical activity theory. *Review of Educational Research, 77*(2), 186–232.

Rothstein, R. (2004a). *Class and schools: Using social, economic, and educational reform to close the black–white achievement gap.* New York: Teachers College Press.

Rothstein, R. (2004b). The achievement gap. *Educational Leadership, 62*(3), 40–43.

Rotter, J. (1966). Generalized expectancies for internal versus external control of reinforcement. *Psychological Monographs, 80*(1, Whole No. 609).

Rowe, M. (1974). Wait-time and rewards as instructional variables, their influence on language, logic, and fate control: Part I. Wait-time. *Journal of Research in Science Teaching, 11*, 81–94.

Rowe, M. (1986). Wait-time: Slowing down may be a way of speeding up. *Journal of Teacher Education, 37*(1), 43–50.

Royer, J. (Ed.) (2005). *The cognitive revolution in educational psychology.* Greenwich, CT: Information Age Publishing.

Rubin, K., Bukowski, W., & Parker, J. (2006). Peer interactions, relationships, and groups. In N. Eisenberg (Vol. Ed,), *Handbook of child psychology: Vol. 3. Social, emotional, and personality development* (6th ed., pp. 571–645). Hoboken, NJ: John Wiley & Sons.

Rubinson, F. (2004). Urban dropouts: Why so many and what can be done? In S. R. Steinberg & J. L. Kincheloe (Eds.), *19 Urban questions: Teaching in the city* (pp. 53–67). New York: Peter Lang.

Ruble, D., Martin, C., & Berenbaum, S. (2006). Gender development. In W. Damon & R. Lerner (Series Eds.), N. Eisenberg (Vol. Ed.), *Handbook of child psychology: Vol. III. Social, emotional, and personality development* (6th ed., pp. 858–932). New York: Wiley.

Rudolph, K. D., Caldwell, M. S., & Conley, C. S. (2005). Need for approval and children's well-being. *Child Development, 72, 309–323.*

Rudolph, K. D., Lambert, S. F., Clark, A. G., & Kurlakowsky, K. D. (2001). Negotiating the transition to middle school: The role of self-regulatory processes. *Child Development, 72*, 926–946.

Runco, M. A. (2004). Creativity as an extracognitive phenomenon. In L. V. Shavinina & M. Ferrari (Eds.), *Beyond knowledge: Extracognitive aspects of developing high ability* (pp. 17–25). Mahwah, NJ: Erlbaum.

Rutter, M., Maughan, B., Mortimore, P., Ousten, J., & Smith, A. (l979). *Fifteen thousand hours. Secondary schools and their effects on children.* Cambridge, MA: Harvard University Press.

Ruzic, R. (2001, April). *Lessons for everyone: How students with reading-related learning disabilities survive and excel in college courses with heavy reading requirements.* Paper presented at the annual meeting of the American Educational Research Association, Seattle.

Ryan, J. B., Katsiyannis, A., & Peterson, R. (2007). IDEA 2004 and disciplining students with disabilities. *NASSP Bulletin, 91,* 130–140.

Ryan, K. E., & Ryan, A. M. (2005). Psychological processes of stereotype threat and standardized math test performance. *Educational Psychologist, 40*(1), 53–63.

Ryan, K. E., Ryan, A. M., Arbuthnot, K., & Samuels, M. (2007). Students' motivation for standardized math exams. *Educational Researcher, 36*(1), 5–13.

Ryan, R., & Deci, E. (1996). When paradigms clash: Comments on Cameron and Pierce's claim that rewards do not undermine intrinsic motivation. *Review of Educational Research, 66,* 33–38.

Ryan, R., & Deci, E. (2000). Intrinsic and extrinsic motivations: Classic definitions and new directions. *Contemporary Educational Psychology, 25,* 54–67.

Saarni, C., Campos, J., Camras, L., & Witherington, D. (2006). Emotional development: Action, communication, and understanding. In N. Eisenberg (Vol. Ed,), *Handbook of child psychology: Vol. 3. Social, emotional, and personality development* (6th ed., pp. 226–299). Hoboken, NJ: John Wiley & Sons.

Sack-Min, J. (2007). The issues of IDEA. *American School Board Journal, 194*(3), 20–25.

Saddler, B., & Andrade, H. (2004). The writing rubric. *Educational Leadership, 62*(2), 48–52.

Sadoski, M., & Paivio, A. (2001). *Imagery and text: A dual coding theory of reading and writing.* Mahwah, NJ: Erlbaum.

Safer, N., & Fleischman, S. (2005). How student progress monitoring improves instruction. *Educational Leadership, 62*(5), 81–83.

Sailor, W., & Roger, B. (2005). Rethinking inclusion: Schoolwide applications. *Phi Delta Kappan, 86*(7), 503–509.

Saleh, M., Lazonder, A. W., & Jong, Ton de. (2007). Structuring collaboration in mixed-ability groups to promote verbal interaction, learning, and motivation of average-ability students. *Contemporary Educational Psychology, 32,* 314–331.

Salend, S., & Salinas, A. (2003). Language differences or learning difficulties. In K. Freiberg (Ed.), *Educating exceptional children 05/06* (7th ed., pp. 70–77). Dubuque, IA: McGraw-Hill/Dushkin.

Salvia, J., & Ysseldyke, J. (2004). *Assessment in special and remedial education* (9th ed.). Boston: Houghton Mifflin.

San Antonio, D., & Salzfass, E. (2007). How we treat one another in school. *Educational Leadership, 64*(8), 32–38.

Sand, B. (2004, April). *Toward a definition of creativity: Construct validation the cognitive components of creativity.* Paper presented at the annual meeting of the American Educational Research Association, San Diego.

Sanders, J., & Nelson, S. C. (2004). Closing gender gaps in science. *Educational Leadership, 62*(3), 74–77.

Sansone, C., & Harackiewicz, J. (Eds.). (2000). *Intrinsic and extrinsic motivation: The search for optimal motivation and performance.* San Diego: Academic Press.

Santi, K., & Vaughn, S. (2007). Progress monitoring: An integral part of instruction, *Reading and Writing, 20,* 535–537.

Sapon-Shevin, M. (2007). *Widening the circle: The power of inclusive classrooms.* Boston: Beacon Press.

Sattler, J. M. (2001). *Assessment of children: Cognitive applications* (4th ed.). San Diego, CA: Jerome M. Sattler.

Sawyer, R, K. (2006). Introduction: The new science of learning. In R. K. Sawyer (Ed.), *The Cambridge handbook of the learning sciences* (pp. 1–18). New York: Cambridge University Press.

Schacter, D. (2001). *The seven deadly sins of memory.* Boston: Houghton Mifflin.

Schank, R. C., & Abelson, R. (1977). *Scripts, plans, goals, and understanding.* Mahwah, NJ: Erlbaum.

Schellenberg, S., & Eggen, P. (2008, March). *Educational psychology students' awareness of moral issues in classroom instruction: A developmental analysis.* Paper presented at the annual meeting of the American Educational Research Association, New York.

Schiever, S., & Maker, C. J. (2003). New directions in enrichment and acceleration. In N. Colangelo, & G. Davis (Eds.), *Handbook of gifted education* (3rd ed., pp. 163–173). Boston: Allyn & Bacon.

Schlesinger, A. (1992). *The disuniting of America: Reflections on a multicultural society.* New York: Norton.

Schlozman, S., & Schlozman, V. (2000). Chaos in the classroom: Looking at ADHD. *Educational Leadership, 58*(3), 28–33.

Schmidt, H. G., Loyens, S. M., van Gog, T., & Paas, F. (2007). Problem-based learning is compatible with human cognitive architecture: Commentary on Kirschner, Sweller, and Clark (2006). *Educational Psychologist, 42,* 91–97.

Schneider, B. (2002). Social capital: A ubiquitous emerging conception. In D. L. Levinson, P. W. Cookson, Jr., & A. R. Sadovnik (Eds.), *Education and sociology: An encyclopedia* (pp. 545–550). New York: Routledge Falmer.

Schneider, W., & Lockl, K. (2002). The development of metacognitive knowledge in children and adolescents. In T. J. Perfect & B. L. Schwartz (Eds.), *Applied metacognition* (pp. 224–257). Cambridge, UK: Cambridge University Press.

Schneider, W., & Shiffrin, R. (1977). Controlled and automatic human information processing: Detection, search, and attention. *Psychological Review, 84,* 1–66.

Schoenfeld, A. H. (1991). On mathematics as sense making: An informal attack on the unfortunate divorce of formal and informal mathematics. In J. Voss, D. Perkins, & J. Segal (Eds.), *Informal reasoning and education* (pp. 311–343). Hillsdale, NJ: Erlbaum.

Schoenfeld, A. H. (2006). Mathematics teaching and learning. In P. A. Alexander & P. H. Winne (Eds.), *Handbook of educational psychology* (2nd ed., pp. 479–510). Mahwah, NJ: Erlbaum.

Scholl, B. J. (2001). Objects and attention: The state of the art. *Cognition, 80,* 1–46.

Schommer, M. (1994). An emerging conceptualization of epistemological beliefs and their role in learning. In R. Garner & P. Alexander (Eds.), *Beliefs about text and instruction with text* (pp. 211–243). Hillsdale, NJ: Erlbaum.

Schraw, G. (2006). Knowledge structures and processes. In P. A. Alexander & P. H. Winne (Eds.), *Handbook of educational psychology* (2nd ed., pp. 245–263). Mahwah, NJ: Erlbaum.

Schraw, G., Flowerday, T., & Lehman, S. (2001). Increasing situational interest in the classroom. *Educational Psychology Review, 13*(3), 211–224.

Schraw, G., & Lehman, S. (2001). Situational interest: A review of the literature and directions for future research. *Educational Psychology Review, 13*(1), 23–52.

Schraw, G., & Moshman, D. (1995). Metacognitive theories. *Educational Psychology Review, 7,* 351–371.

Schult, C. A. (2002). Children's understanding of the distinction between intentions and desires. *Child Development, 73,* 1737–1747.

Schulz, L., & Bonawitz, E. (2007). Serious fun: Preschoolers engage in more exploratory play when evidence is confounded. *Developmental Psychology, 43*(4), 1045–1050.

Schunk, D. (2004). *Learning theories: An educational perspective* (4th ed.). Upper Saddle River, NJ: Merrill/Pearson.

Schunk, D. (2005). Self-regulated learning: The educational legacy of Paul R. Pintrich. *Educational Psychologist, 40*(2), 85–94.

Schunk, D. & Ertmer, P. (2000). Self-regulation and academic learning: Self-efficacy enhancing interventions. In M. Boekaerts, P. Pintrich, & M. Zeidner (Eds.), *Handbook of self-regulation* (pp. 631–649). San Diego: Academic Press.

Schunk, D. H., & Pajares, F. (2004). Self-efficacy in education revisited: Empirical and applied evidence. In D. M. McInerney & S. Van Etten (Eds.), *Sociocultural influences on motivation and learning: Vol. 4. Big theories revisited* (pp. 115–138). Greenwich, CT: Information Age.

Schunk, D. H., Pintrich, P. R, & Meece, J. L. (2008). *Motivation in education: Theory, research, and applications* (3rd ed.). Upper Saddle River, NJ: Merrill/Pearson.

Schunk, D. H., & Zimmerman, B. J. (2006). Competence and control beliefs: Distinguishing the means and the ends. In P. A. Alexander & P. H. Winne (Eds.), *Handbook of educational psychology* (2nd ed., pp. 349–367). Mahwah, NJ: Erlbaum.

Schutz, A. (2004, April). *Home is a prison in the global city: A critical review of urban school–community relationships.* Paper presented at the annual meeting of the American Educational Research Association, San Diego.

Schwartz, D., Bransford, J., & Sears, D. (2005). Efficiency and innovation in transfer. In J. Mestre (Ed.), *Transfer of learning from a modern multidisciplinary perspective* (pp. 1–51). Greenwich, CT: Information Age Publishing.

Schwartz, D., & Heiser, J. (2006). Spatial representations and imagery in learning. In R. K. Sawyer (Ed.), *The Cambridge handbook of the learning sciences* (pp. 283–298). New York: Cambridge University Press.

Schwartz, N., Ellsworth, L., Graham, L., & Knight, B. (1998). Accessing prior knowledge to remember text: A comparison of advance organizers and maps. *Contemporary Educational Psychology, 23,* 65–89.

Schweinle, A., Meyer, D. K., & Turner, J. C. (2006). Striking the right balance: Students' motivation and affect in elementary mathematics. *The Journal of Educational Research, 99,* 271–293.

Segall, A. (2004). Revising pedagogical content knowledge: The pedagogy of content/the content of pedagogy. *Teaching and Teacher Education, 20,* 489–504.

Selingo, J. (2004). The cheating culture. *ASEE Prism, 14*(1), 24–30.

Selwyn, D. (2007). Highly quantified teachers: NCLB and teacher education. *Journal of Teacher Education, 58*(2), 124–137.

Serafino, K., & Cicchelli, T. (2003). Cognitive theories, prior knowledge, and anchored instruction on mathematical problem solving and transfer. *Education and Urban Society, 36*(1), 79–93.

Serafino, K., & Cicchelli, T. (2005, April). *Mathematical problem-based learning: Theories, models for problem solving and transfer.* Paper presented at the annual meeting of the American Educational Research Association, Montreal, Canada.

Shahid, J. (2001, April). *Teacher efficacy: A research synthesis.* Paper presented at the annual meeting of the American Educational Research Association, Seattle.

Shapiro, A. (2004). How including prior knowledge as a subject variable may change outcomes of learning research. *American Educational Research Journal, 41*(1), 159–189.

Shaw, P., & Rapoport, J. (2007). Attention-deficit/hyperactivity disorder is characterized by a delay in cortical maturation. *Proceedings of the National Academy of Sciences,* 104(49), 19649–19654.

Shaywitz, S. E., & Shaywitz, B. A. (2004). Reading disability and the brain. *Educational Leadership, 61*(6), 7–11.

Shea, D., Lubinski, D., & Benbow, C. (2001). Importance of assessing spatial ability in intellectually talented young adolescents: A 20-year longitudinal study. *Journal of Educational Psychology, 93*(3), 604–614.

Sheets, R. (2005). *Diversity pedagogy: Examining the role of culture in the teaching–learning process.* Boston: Allyn & Bacon.

Sheldon, S. (2007). Improving student attendance with school, family, and community partnerships. *Journal of Educational Research, 199*(5), 267–275.

Shen, B., Chen, A., & Guan, J. (2007). Using achievement goals and interest to predict learning in physical education. *The Journal of Experimental Education, 75,* 89–108.

Shepard, L. (2001). The role of classroom assessment in teaching and learning. In V. Richardson (Ed.), *Handbook of research on learning* (4th ed., pp. 1066–1101). Washington, DC: American Educational Research Association.

Shepard, L. (2005). Linking formative assessing to scaffolding. *Educational Leadership, 63*(3), 66–71.

Sheppard, J. A., & McNulty, J. K. (2002). The affective consequences of expected and unexpected outcomes. *Psychological Science, 13,* 85–88.

Shermer, M. (2002). *Why people believe weird things: Pseudoscience, superstition, and other confusions of our time.* New York: Freeman.

Shields, P., & Shaver, D. (1990, April). The *mismatch between the school and home cultures of academically at-risk students.* Paper presented at the annual meeting of the American Educational Research Association, Boston.

Shirin, A. (2007). *Can deaf and hard of hearing students be successful in general education classes?* Retrieved May 21, 2007, from http://www.tcrecord.org/Content.asp?ContentID=13461

Short, D., & Echevarria, J. (2004/2005). Promoting academic literacy for English language learners. *Educational Leadership, 62*(4), 8–13.

Short, E., Schatschneider, C., & Friebert, S. (1993). Relationship between memory and metamemory performance: A comparison of specific and general strategy knowledge. *Journal of Educational Psychology, 85*(3), 412–423.

Shuell, T. (1996). Teaching and learning in a classroom context. In D. Berliner & R. Calfee (Eds.), *Handbook of educational psychology* (pp. 726–764). New York: Macmillan.

Shulman, L. (1986). Those who understand: Knowledge growth in teaching. *Educational Researcher, 15*(2), 4–14.

Shulman, L. (1987). Knowledge and teaching: Foundations of the new reform. *Harvard Educational Review, 57,* 1–22. *Teachers College Record, 110,* 1304–1329. Retrieved June 4, 2008, from http://www.tcrecord.org/Content.asp?ContentID=14749

Shute, V. J. (2008). Focus on formative feedback. *Review of Educational Research, 78,* 153–189.

Siegel, M. (2002, April). *Models of teacher learning: A study of case analyses by preservice teachers.* Paper presented at the annual meeting of the American Educational Research Association, New Orleans.

Siegler, R. (2006). Microgenetic analyses of learning. In D. Kuhn, & R. Siegler (Vol. Eds.), *Handbook of child psychology: Vol. 2. Cognition, perception, and language* (6th ed., pp. 464–510). Hoboken, NJ: John Wiley & Sons.

Simon, H. (2001). Learning to research about learning. In S. M. Carver & D. Klake (Eds.), *Cognition and instruction.* Mahwah, NJ: Erlbaum.

Simonton, D. K. (2000). Creativity: Cognitive, personal, developmental, and social aspects. *American Psychologist, 55,* 151–158.

Sinatra, G. M., & Pintrich, P. R. (2003). The role of intentions in conceptual change learning. In G. M. Sinatra & P. R. Pintrich (Eds.), *Intentional conceptual change* (pp. 1–18). Mahwah, NJ: Erlbaum.

Singh, N. N., Lancioni, G. E., Joy, S. D. S., Winton, A. S. W., Sabaawi, M., Wahler, R. G., & Singh, J. (2007). Adolescents with conduct disorder can be mindful of their aggressive behavior. *Journal of Emotional and Behavioral Disorders, 15,* 56–63.

Skiba, R. J., Michael, R. S., Nardo, A. C., & Peterson, R. L. (2002). The color of discipline: Sources of racial and gender disproportionality in school punishment. *The Urban Review, 34,* 317–342.

Skiba, R. J., Peterson, R. L., & Williams, T. (1997). Office referrals and suspensions: Disciplinary intervention in middle schools. *Education and Treatment of Children, 20,* 295–315.

Skinner, B. F. (1953). *Science and human behavior.* New York: Macmillan.

Skinner, B. F. (1954). The science of learning and the art of teaching. *Harvard Educational Review, 24,* 86–97.

Skinner, B. F. (1957). *Verbal behavior.* Upper Saddle River, NJ: Prentice Hall.

Slavin, R. (1987). Ability grouping and student achievement in elementary schools: A best-evidence synthesis. *Review of Educational Research, 57,* 293–336.

Slavin, R. (1995). *Cooperative learning: Theory, research, and practice* (2nd ed.). Needham Heights, MA: Allyn & Bacon.

Slavin, R. (2008). What works? Issues in synthesizing educational program evaluations. *Educational Researcher, 37*(1), 5–14.

Slavin, R., & Cheung, A. (2004). *Effective reading programs for English language learners: A best-evidence synthesis.* Baltimore: Center for Research on the Education of Students Placed At Risk, Johns Hopkins University. Retrieved January 12, 2008, from www.csos.jhu.edu/crespar/techReports/Report66.pdf

Sloane, F. (2008). Through the looking glass: Experiments, quasi-experiments, and the medical model. *Educational Researcher, 37*(1), 41–46.

Smith, A., & Bondy, E. (2007). "No! I won't!" Understanding and responding to defiance. *Childhood Education, 83,* 151–157.

Smith, F. (2005). Intensive care. *Edutopia, 1*(9), 47–49.

Smith, J., Brewer, D. M., & Heffner, T. (2003). Using portfolio assessments with young children who are at risk for school failure. *Preventing School Failure, 48*(1), 38–40.

Smith, K. S., Rook, J. E., & Smith, T. W. (2007). Increasing student engagement using effective and metacognitive writing strategies in content areas. *Preventing School Failure, 51,* 43–48.

Smith, P., & Fouad, N. (1999). Subject-matter specificity of self-efficacy, outcome expectancies, interest, and goals: Implications for the social-cognitive model. *Journal of Counseling Psychology, 46,* 461–471.

Smith, T., Polloway, E., Patton, J., & Dowdy, C. (2004). *Teaching students with special needs in inclusive settings* (4th ed.). Boston: Allyn & Bacon.

Smokowski, P. (1997, April). *What personal essays tell us about resiliency and protective factors in adolescence.* Paper presented at the annual meeting of the American Educational Research Association, Chicago.

Snary, J. (1995). In a communitarian voice: The sociological expansion of Kohlbergian theory, research, and practice. In W. Kurtines & J. Gewirtz (Eds.), *Moral development: An introduction.* Boston: Allyn & Bacon.

Snow, C., Griffin, P., & Burns, M. S. (2005). *Knowledge to support the teaching of reading: Preparing teachers for a changing world.* San Francisco: Jossey-Bass.

Snow, C., & Kang, J. (2006). Becoming bilingual, biliterate, and bicultural. In K. A. Renninger &

I. Sigel (Vol. Eds.), *Handbook of child psychology: Vol. 4. Social, emotional, and personality development* (6th ed., pp. 75–102). Hoboken, NJ: John Wiley & Sons.

Snow, R., Corno, L., & Jackson, D. (1996). Individual differences in affective and cognitive functions. In D. Berliner & R. Calfee (Eds.), *Handbook of educational psychology* (pp. 243–310). New York: Macmillan.

Soenens, B., Vansteenkiste, M., Lens, W., Luyckx, K., Goossens, L., Beyers, W., & Ryan, R. (2007). Conceptualizing parental autonomy support: Adolescent perceptions of promotion of independence versus promotion of volitional functioning. *Developmental Psychology, 43*(1), 633–646.

Solano-Flores, G., & Li, M. (2006). The use of generalizability (G) theory in the testing of linguistic minorities. *Educational Measurement: Issues and Practices, 25*(1), 13–22.

Solley, B. A. (2007). On standardized testing. *Childhood Education, 84*, 31–37.

Son, L. (2004). Spacing one's study: Evidence for a metacognitive control strategy. *Journal of Experimental Psychology: Learning, Memory, and Cognition, 3*(3), 601–604.

Southerland, S., Kittleson, J., & Settlage, J. (2002, April). *The intersection of personal and group knowledge construction: Red fog, cold cans, and seeping vapor or children talking and thinking about condensation in a third grade classroom.* Paper presented at the annual meeting of the National Association for Science Teaching, New Orleans.

Southerland, S. A., & Sinatra, G. M. (2003). Learning about biological evolution: A special case of intentional conceptual change. In G. M. Sinatra & P. R. Pintrich (Eds.), *Intentional conceptual change* (pp. 317–345). Mahwah, NJ: Erlbaum.

Spearman, C. (1927). *The abilities of man: Their nature and measurement.* New York: Macmillan.

Spencer, M. B., Noll, E., Stoltzfus, J., & Harpalani, V. (2001). Identity and school adjustment: Revisiting the "acting White" phenomenon. *Educational Psychologist, 36*, 21–30.

Spiro, R., Feltovich, P., Jacobson, M., & Coulson, R. (1992). Knowledge representation, content specification, and the development of skill in situation-specific knowledge assembly: Some constructivist issues as they relate to cognitive flexibility theory and hypertext. In T. Duffy & D. Jonassen (Eds.), *Constructivism and the technology of instruction: A conversation* (pp. 121–127). Hillsdale, NJ: Erlbaum.

Spor, M., & Schneider, B. (1999). Content reading strategies: What teachers know, use, and want to learn. *Reading Research and Instruction, 38*, 221–231.

Stahl, R., DeMasi, K., Gehrke, R., Guy, C., & Scown, J. (2005, April). *Perceptions, conceptions and misconceptions of wait time and wait time behaviors among pre-service and in-service teachers.* Paper presented at the annual meeting of the American Educational Research Association, Montreal, Canada.

Stahl, S. (2002). Different strokes for different folks? In L. Abbeduto (Ed.), *Taking sides: Clashing on controversial issues in educational psychology* (pp. 98–107). Guilford, CT: McGraw-Hill/Duskin.

Standage, M., Treasure, D. C., Hooper, K., & Kuczka, K. (2007). Self-handicapping in school physical education: The influence of the motivational climate. *The British Journal of Educational Psychology, 77*, 81–99.

Stanovich, K. (1998). Cognitive neuroscience and educational psychology: What season is it? *Educational Psychology Review, 10*, 419–426.

Stanton-Salazar, R. D., & Spina, S. U. (2003). Informal mentors and role models in the lives of urban Mexican-origin adolescents. *Anthropology & Education Quarterly, 34*(3), 231–254.

Staples, M. (2007). Supporting whole-class collaborative inquiry in a secondary mathematics classroom. *Cognition and Instruction, 25*, 161–217.

Star, J. (2004, April). *The development of flexible procedural knowledge in equation solving.* Paper presented at the annual meeting of the American Educational Research Association, San Diego.

Star, J. R. (2005). Reconceptualizing Procedural Knowledge. *Journal for Research in Mathematics Education, 36*(5), 404–411.

Steinberg, L. (1996). *Beyond the classroom: Why school reform has failed and what parents need to do.* New York: Touchstone.

Steiner, H. H., & Carr, M. (2003). Cognitive development in gifted children: Toward a more precise understanding of emerging differences in intelligence. *Educational Psychology Review, 15*, 215–246.

Stengel, B., & Tom, A. (2006). *Moral matters.* New York: Teachers College Press.

Stephens, K., & Karnes, F. (2000). State definitions for the gifted and talented revisited. *Exceptional Children, 66*(2), 219–238.

Sternberg, R. (1998a). Applying the triarchic theory of human intelligence in the classroom. In R. Sternberg & W. Williams (Eds.), *Intelligence, instruction, and assessment* (pp. 1–16). Mahwah, NJ: Erlbaum.

Sternberg, R. (1998b). Metacognition, abilities, and developing expertise: What makes an expert student? *Instructional Science, 26*(1–2), 127–140.

Sternberg, R. (2003a). *Cognitive psychology* (3rd ed.). Belmont, CA: Wadsworth.

Sternberg, R. (2003b). *Wisdom, intelligence, and creativity synthesized.* Cambridge: Cambridge University Press.

Sternberg, R. (2004). Culture and intelligence. *American Psychologist, 59*, 325–338.

Sternberg, R. (2006). Recognizing neglected strengths. *Educational Leadership, 64*(1), 30–35.

Sternberg, R. (2007). Who are bright children? The cultural context of being and acting intelligent. *Educational Researcher, 36*(3), 148–155.

Sternberg, R., & Grigorenko, E. (2001). Learning disabilities, schooling, and society. *Phi Delta Kappan, 83*(4), 335–338.

Stevenson, H., & Fantuzzo, J. (1986). The generality and social validity of a competency-based self-control training intervention for underachieving students. *Journal of Applied Behavior Analysis, 19*, 269–276.

Stevenson, H., Lee, S., & Stigler, J. (1986). Mathematics achievement of Chinese, Japanese, and American children. *Science, 231*, 693–699.

Stewart, E., Stewart, E., & Simons, R. (2007). The effect of neighborhood context on the college aspirations of African American adolescents. *American Educational Research Journal, 44*(4), 896–919.

Stiggins, R. (2004). New assessment beliefs for a new school mission. *Phi Delta Kappan, 86*(1), 22–27.

Stiggins, R. (2005). *Student-centered classroom assessment* (4th ed.). Upper Saddle River, NJ: Merrill/Pearson.

Stiggins, R. (2007). Assessment through the student's eyes. *Educational Leadership, 64*(8), 22–26.

Stiggins, R. J., & Chappuis, J. (2006). What a difference a word makes: Assessment FOR learning rather than assessment OF learning helps students succeed. *Journal of Staff Development, 27*, 10–14.

Stigler, J., & Hiebert, J. (2000). *The teaching gap.* New York: Free Press.

Stipek, D. (1996). Motivation and instruction. In D. Berliner & R. Calfee (Eds.), *Handbook of educational psychology* (pp. 85–113). New York: Macmillan.

Stipek, D. (2002). *Motivation to learn* (4th ed.). Boston: Allyn & Bacon.

Strickland, B. B., & Turnbull, A. P. (1990). *Developing and implementing individualized education programs* (3rd ed.). Upper Saddle River, NJ: Merrill/Pearson.

Stright, A., Neitzel, C., Sears, K., & Hoke-Sinex, L. (2001). Instruction begins in the home: Relations between parental instruction and children's self-regulation in the classroom. *Journal of Educational Psychology, 93*(3), 456–466.

Strong, R., Silver, H., Perini, M., & Tuculescu, G. (2003). Boredom and its opposite. *Educational Leadership, 61*(1), 24–29.

Stuebing, K., Fletcher, J., LeDoux, J., Lyon, G., Shaywitz, S., & Shaywitz, B. (2002). Validity of IQ-discrepancy classifications of reading disabilities: A meta-analysis. *American Educational Research Journal, 39*(2), 469–518.

Su, A. Y-L. (2007). The impact of individual ability, favorable team member scores, and student perception of course importance on student preference of team-based learning and grading methods. *Adolescence, 42*, 805–826.

Sungur, S., & Tekkaya, C. (2006). Effects of problem-based learning and traditional instruction on self-regulated learning. *Journal of Educational Research, 99*(5), 307–318.

Swanson, C. (2008). Grading the states. *Education Week, 27*(18), 36–38.

Swanson, J. M., & Volkow, N. D. (2002). Pharmacokinetic and pharmacodynamic properties of stimulants: Implications of the design of new treatments for ADHD. *Behavior and Brain Research, 130*, 73–80.

Swanson, T. (2005). Providing structure for children with learning and behavior problems. *Intervention in School and Clinic, 40*, 182–187.

Sweller, J. (2003). Evolution of Human Cognitive Architecture. *The Psychology of Learning and Motivation, 43*, 215–266.

Sweller, J., van Merrienboer, J., & Paas, F. (1998). Cognitive architecture and instructional design. *Educational Psychology Review, 10*, 251–296.

Tamis-LeMonda, C. S., Bornstein, M. H., & Baumwell, L. (2001). Maternal responsiveness and children's achievement of language milestones. *Child Development, 72*, 748–767.

Tannenbaum, A. (2003). Nature and nurture of giftedness. In N. Colangelo, & G. Davis (Eds.), *Handbook of gifted education* (3rd ed., pp. 45–59). Boston: Allyn & Bacon.

Tanner, D., & Tanner, L. (2007). *Curriculum development: Theory into practice* (4th ed.). Upper Saddle River, NJ: Merrill/Prentice Hall.

Tannock, R., & Martinussen, R. (2001). Reconceptualizing ADHD. *Educational Leadership, 59*(3), 20–25.

Taraban, R., Anderson, E. E., & DeFinis, A. (2007). First steps in understanding engineering students' growth of conceptual and procedural knowledge in an interactive learning context. *Journal of Engineering Education, 96,* 57–68.

Taylor, B., Pearson, P. D., Peterson, D., & Rodriguez, M. (2003). Reading growth in high-poverty classrooms: The influence of teacher practices that encourage cognitive engagement in literacy learning. *Elementary School Journal, 104*(1), 3–28.

Tenenbaum, H., & Leaper, C. (2003). Parent–child conversations about science: The socialization of gender inequities? *Developmental Psychology, 39,* 34–47.

Tennyson, R., & Cocchiarella, M. (1986). An empirically based instructional design theory for teaching concepts. *Review of Educational Research, 56,* 40–71.

Terhune, K. (1968). Studies of motives, cooperation, and conflict within laboratory microcosms. In G. Snyder (Ed.), *Studies in international conflict* (Vol. 4, pp. 29–58). Buffalo, NY: SUNY Buffalo Council on International Studies.

Terman, L., Baldwin, B., & Bronson, E. (1925). Mental and physical traits of a thousand gifted children. In L. Terman (Ed.), *Genetic studies of genius* (Vol. 1). Stanford, CA: Stanford University Press.

Terman, L., & Oden, M. (1947). The gifted child grows up. In L. Terman (Ed.), *Genetic studies of genius* (Vol. 4). Stanford, CA: Stanford University Press.

Terman, L., & Oden, M. (1959). The gifted group in mid-life. In L. Terman (Ed.), *Genetic studies of genius* (Vol. 5). Stanford, CA: Stanford University Press.

Terry, S. (2006). *Learning and memory: Basic principles, process, and procedures* (3rd ed.). Boston: Allyn & Bacon.

Terwilliger, J. (1997). Semantics, psychometrics, and assessment reform: A close look at "authentic assessments." *Educational Researcher, 26,* 24–27.

Texas Education Agency. (2006). *Texas Assessment of Knowledge and Skills (TAKS)—Spring 2006.* Retrieved January 26, 2008, from http://scotthochberg.com/files/taas/math3.pdf

Texas Education Agency. (2008). *Chapter 111. Texas essential knowledge and skills for mathematics. Grade 3.* Retrieved January 25, 2008, from http://www.tea.state.tx.us/rules/tac/ch111.html#s11111

Tharp, R., & Gallimore, R. (1991). *The instructional conversation: Teaching and learning in social activity.* Washington, DC: National Center for Research on Cultural Diversity and Second Language Learning.

Thiede, K. W., & Anderson, M. C. M. (2003). Summarizing can improve metacomprehension accuracy. *Contemporary Educational Psychology, 28,* 129–160.

Thiede, K. W., Anderson, M. C. M., & Therriault, D. (2003). Accuracy of metacognitive monitoring affects learning of texts. *Journal of Educational Psychology, 95,* 66–73.

Thirunarayanan, M. O. (2004). The "significantly worse" phenomenon: A study of student achievement in different content areas by school location. *Education and Urban Society, 36*(4), 467–481.

Thompson, G. (2007). *Up where we belong: Helping African American and Latino students rise in school and in life.* San Francisco: Jossey-Bass.

Thorndike, E. (1924). Mental discipline in high school studies. *Journal of Educational Psychology, 15,* 1–2, 83–98.

Thorndike, R. M. (2005). *Measurement and evaluation in psychology and education* (7th ed.). Upper Saddle River, NJ: Merrill/Pearson.

Tillema, H., & Smith, K. (2007). Portfolio appraisal: In search of criteria. *Teaching and Teacher Education, 23,* 442–456.

Titsworth, S. (2004). Students' notetaking: The effects of teacher immediacy and clarity. *Communication Education, 53,* 305–320.

Tollefson, N. (2000). Classroom applications of cognitive theories of motivation. *Educational Psychology Review, 12,* 63–83.

Tomasello, M. (2006). Acquiring linguistic constructions. In D. Kuhn, & R. Siegler (Vol. Eds.), *Handbook of child psychology: Vol. 2. Cognition, perception, and language* (6th ed., pp. 255–298). Hoboken, NJ: John Wiley & Sons.

Tomlinson, C. (2005). *How to differentiate instruction in mixed-ability classroom* (2nd ed.). Upper Saddle River, NJ: Pearson.

Tomlinson, C. A. (2006). *Fulfilling the promise of the differentiated classroom: Strategies and tools for responsive teaching.* Alexandria, VA: Association for Supervision and Curriculum Development.

Tompkins, G. (2006). *Literacy for the 21st century: A balanced approach* (4th ed.). Upper Saddle River, NJ: Merrill/Pearson.

Topping, D. H., & McManus, R. A. (2002). A culture of literacy in science. *Educational Leadership, 60,* 30–33.

Townsend, B. L. (2000). The disproportionate discipline of African American learners: Reducing school suspension and expulsions. *Exceptional Children, 66,* 381–391.

Trautwein, U., & Ludtke, O. (2007). Students' self-reported effort and time on homework in six school subjects: Between-student differences and within-student variation. *Journal of Educational Psychology, 99,* 432–444.

Trautwein, U., Ludtke, O., & Schnyder, I. (2006). Predicting homework effort: Support for a domain-specific, multilevel homework model. *Journal of Educational Psychology, 98,* 438–456.

Trawick-Smith, J. (2003). *Early childhood development: A multicultural perspective* (3rd ed.). Upper Saddle River, NJ: Merrill/Pearson.

Triona, L., & Klahr, D. (2003). Point and click or grab and heft: Comparing the influence of physical and virtual instructional materials on elementary school students' ability to design experiments. *Cognition and Instruction, 2*(2), 149–173.

Trotter, A. (2005). Tool helps Washington teachers write learning plans. *Education Week, 24*(23), 6.

Trzesniewski, K., Donnellan, M., Moffitt, T., Robins, R., Poulton, R., & Caspi, A. (2006). Low self-esteem during adolescence predicts poor health, criminal behavior, and limited economic prospects during adulthood. *Developmental Psychology, 42*(2), 381–390.

Tschannen-Moran, M., & Barr, M. (2004). Fostering student achievement: The relationship between collective teacher efficacy and student achievement. *Leadership and Policy in Schools, 3,* 187–207.

Tschannen-Moran, M., Woolfolk-Hoy, A., & Hoy, W. (1998). Teacher efficacy: Its meaning and measure. *Review of Educational Research, 68*(2), 202–248.

Tseng, S-S., Sue, P-C., & Su, J.-M. (2007). A new approach for constructing the concept map. *Computers and Education, 49,* 691–707.

Tucker, M. (2007). Charting a new course for schools. *Educational Leadership, 64*(7), 48–52.

Tulving, E. (2002). Episodic memory: From mind to brain. *Annual Review of Psychology, 53,* 1–25.

Tunteler, E., & Resing, W. C. (2007). Effects of prior assistance in using analogies on young children's unprompted analogical problem solving over time: A microgenetic study. *The British Journal of Educational Psychology, 77,* 43–68.

Turiel, E. (2006). The development of morality. In N. Eisenberg (Vol. Ed,), *Handbook of child psychology: Vol. 3. Social, emotional, and personality development* (6th ed., pp. 789–857). Hoboken, NJ: John Wiley & Sons.

Turnbull, A., Turnbull, R., Shank, M., Smith, S., & Leal, D. (2004). *Exceptional lives: Special education in today's schools* (4th ed.). Upper Saddle River, NJ: Merrill.

Turnbull, A., Turnbull, R. &. Wehmeyer, M. L. (2007). *Exceptional lives: Special education in today's schools* (5th ed.). Upper Saddle River, NJ: Merrill/Pearson.

Twenge, J. M., & Campbell, W. K. (2001). Age and birth cohort differences in self-esteem: A cross temporal meta-analysis. *Journal of Personality and Social Psychology Review, 5,* 321–344.

Tyler, R. (1950). *Basic principles of curriculum and instruction.* Chicago: University of Chicago Press.

Urdan, T. (2001). Contextual influences on motivation and performance: An examination of achievement goal structures. In F. Salili, C. Chiu, & Y. Hong (Eds.), *Student motivation: The culture and context of learning* (pp. 171–201). New York: Kluer/Plenum.

Urdan, T. C., & Maehr, M. L. (1995). Beyond a two-goal theory of motivation and achievement: A case for social goals. *Review of Educational Research, 65,* 213–243.

U.S. Bureau of Census. (2003). *Statistical abstract of the United States* (123rd ed.). Washington, DC: U.S. Government Printing Office.

U.S. Bureau of Census. (2004). *The foreign-born population in the United States: 2003.* Washington, DC: U.S. Government Printing Office.

U.S. Bureau of Census. (2007). *Income, earnings, and poverty estimates released in American Fact Finder, 8/28/07.* Retrieved December 19, 2007, from http://factfinder.census.gov/home/saff/main.html?_lang=en

U.S. Department of Agriculture. (2007). *Healthy food: Healthy communities.* Retrieved December 9, 2007, from http://www.csrees.usda.gov/newsroom/news/2007news/cfp_report.pdf

U.S. Department of Education. (1999). *34 Federal Code of Regulation 300.7 9(c)(6).* Retrieved December 16, 2007, from http://www.nectac.org/idea/300regs.asp

U. S. Department of Education. (2004). *Twenty-sixth annual report to Congress on the implementation of the Individuals With Disabilities Education Act.* Washington, DC: U.S. Government Printing Office.

U.S. Department of Education. (2005). *Education for homeless children and youth.* Washington, DC: U.S. Printing Office. Retrieved July, 12, 2006, from www.ed.gov//programs/homeless/index.html

U.S. Department of Education. (2008a). *Provisions related to children with disabilities enrolled by their parents in private schools.* Retrieved August 9, 2008, from http.//www.rrfcnetwork.org/images/stories/FRC/IDEA/idea.pdf

U.S. Department of Education. (2008b). *Thirtieth annual report to Congress on the implementation of the Individuals With Disabilities Education Act.* Washington, DC: U.S. Government Printing Office.

U. S. English. (2005). Retrieved March 5, 2008, from http://www.usenglish.org

U.S. English, Inc. (2007). Official English still overwhelmingly popular despite divided nation. Retrieved September 13, 2007, from http://www.us-english.org

Uygur, T., & Ozdas, A. (2007). The effect of arrow diagrams on achievement in applying the chain rule. *Primus, 17,* 131–147.

Vacca, R., & Vacca, J. (2008). *Content area reading* (9th ed). Boston: Allyn & Bacon.

Valenzeno, L., Alibali, M., & Klatsky, R. (2003). Teachers' gestures facilitate students' learning: A lesson in symmetry. *Contemporary Educational Psychology, 28,* 187–204.

Valenzuela, A. (1999). *Subtractive schooling: U.S.-Mexican youth and the politics of caring.* Albany: State University of New York Press.

van Gelder, T. (2005). Teaching critical thinking: Some lessons from cognitive science. *College Teaching, 53,* 41–46.

VanDeWeghe, R. (2007). How does assessment affect creativity? *English Journal, 96,* 91–93.

van Gog, T., Paas, F., & van Merriënboer, J. (2004). Process-oriented worked examples: Improving transfer performance through enhanced understanding. *Instructional Science, 32*(1–2), 83–98.

Van Horn, R. (2008). *Bridging the chasm between research and practice.* Lanham, MD: Rowman & Littlefield.

van Merriënboer, J., Kirschner, P., & Kester, L. (2003). Taking the load off a learner's mind: Instructional design for complex learning. *Educational Psychologist, 38*(1), 5–13.

van Meter, P. (2001). Drawing construction as a strategy for learning from text. *Journal of Educational Psychology, 93*(1), 129–140.

Vang, C. T., (2003). Learning more about Hmong students. *Multicultural Education, 11*(2), 10–14.

VanLeuvan, P. (2004). Young women's science/mathematics career goals from seventh grade to high school graduation. *Journal of Educational Research, 97*(5), 248–262.

Vansteenkiste, M., Lens, W., & Deci, E. L. (2006). Intrinsic versus extrinsic goal contents in self-determination theory: Another look at the quality of academic motivation. *Educational Psychologist, 41,* 19–31.

Vansteenkiste, M., Zhou, M., Lens, W., & Soenens, B. (2005). Experiences of autonomy and control among Chinese learners: Vitalizing or immobilizing. *Journal of Educational Psychology, 97,* 468–483.

Vaughn, S., & Bos, C. S. (2006). *Strategies for teaching students with learning and behavior problems* (6th ed.). Boston: Allyn & Bacon.

Vaughn, S., Bos, C., Candace, S., & Schumm, J. (2006). *Teaching exceptional, diverse, and at-risk students in the general education classroom* (3rd ed.). Boston: Allyn & Bacon.

Vaughn, S., & Fuchs, L. (2003). Redefining learning disabilities as inadequate response to instruction: The promise of potential problems. *Learning Disabilities Research and Practice, 18*(3), 137–146.

Vavilis, B., & Vavilis, S. (2004). Why are we learning this? What is this stuff good for, anyway?: The importance of conversation in the classroom. *Phi Delta Kappan, 86*(4), 282–287.

Veenman, M. V., & Spaans, M. A. (2005). Relation between intellectual and matacognitive skills: Age and task differences. *Learning and Individual Differences, 15,* 159–176.

Veenman, S. (1984). Perceived problems of beginning teachers. *Review of Educational Research, 54,* 143–178.

Venn, J. J. (2000). *Assessing students with special needs* (2nd ed.). Upper Saddle River, NJ: Merrill/Pearson.

Verkoeijen, P. P., Rikers, R. M., & Schmidt, H. G. (2005). The effects of prior knowledge on study-time allocation and free recall: Investigating the discrepancy reduction model. *The Journal of Psychology, 139,* 67–79.

Vermeer, H. J., Boekaerts, M., & Seegers, G. (2000). Motivational and gender differences: Sixth-grade students' mathematical problem-solving behavior. *Journal of Educational Psychology, 92,* 308–315.

Viadero, D. (2003). Two studies highlight links between violence, bullying by students. *Education Week, 22*(36), 6.

Viadero, D. (2007a). ADHD experts fear brain-growth study being misconstrued. *Education Week, 27*(14), 1, 14.

Viadero, D. (2007b). Teachers say NCLB has changed classroom practice. *Education Week, 26*(42), 6, 22.

Villegas, A. (1991). *Culturally responsive pedagogy for the 1990s and beyond.* Princeton, NJ: Educational Testing Service.

Von der Linden, N., & Roebers, C. M. (2006). Developmental changes in uncertainty monitoring during an event recall task. *Metacognition and Learning, 1,* 213–228.

von Károlyi, C., Ramos-Ford, V., & Gardner, H. (2003). Multiple intelligences: A perspective on giftedness. In N. Colangelo & G. Davis (Eds.), *Handbook of gifted education* (3rd ed., pp. 100–112). Boston: Allyn & Bacon.

Vosniadou, S. (2007). The cognitive-situative divide and the problem of conceptual change. *Educational Psychologist, 42*(1), 55–66.

Vygotsky, L. (1978). *Mind in society: The development of higher psychological processes* (M. Cole, V. John-Steiner, S. Scribner, & E. Souberman, Eds. & Trans.). Cambridge, MA: Harvard University Press.

Vygotsky, L. (1986). *Thought and language.* Cambridge, MA: MIT Press.

Wadsworth, B. J. (2004). *Piaget's theory of cognitive and affective development* (5th ed.). Boston: Pearson Education.

Walker, J. E., Bauer, A. M., & Shea, T. M. (2004). *Behavior management: A practical approach for educators* (8th ed.). Upper Saddle River, NJ: Merrill/Pearson.

Walker, J. M., & Hoover-Dempsey, K. V. (2006). Why research on parents' involvement is important to classroom management. In C. M. Evertson & C. S. Weinstein (Eds.), *Handbook of classroom management: Research, practice, and contemporary issues* (pp. 665–684). Mahwah, NJ: Erlbaum.

Walpole, M., McDonough, P. M., & Bauer, C. J. (2005). This test is unfair: Urban African American and Latino high school students' perceptions of standardized college admissions tests. *Urban Education, 40*(3), 321–349.

Walsh, D., & Bennett, N. (2004). *Why do they act that way?: A survival guide to the adolescent brain for you and your teen.* New York: Free Press.

Ware, H., & Kitsantas, A. (2007). Teacher and collective efficacy beliefs as predictors of professional commitment. *Journal of Educational Research, 100*(5), 303–310.

Warner, L., & Lynch, S. (2005). Classroom problems that don't go away. In K. Freiberg (Ed.), *Educating exceptional children 05/06* (7th ed., pp. 128–131). Dubuque, IA: McGraw-Hill/Dushkin.

Waterhouse, L. (2006). Multiple intelligences, the Mozart effect, and emotional intelligence: A critical review. *Educational Psychologist, 41*(4), 217–225.

Watson, M., & Battistich, V. (2006). Building and sustaining caring communities. In C. M. Evertson & C. S. Weinstein (Eds.), *Handbook of classroom management: Research, practice, and contemporary issues* (pp. 253–279). Mahwah, NJ: Erlbaum.

Watson, M., & Ecken, L. (2003). *Learning to trust: Transforming difficult elementary classrooms through developmental discipline.* San Francisco: Jossey-Bass.

Waxman, H., Huang, S., Anderson, L., & Weinstein, T. (1997). Classroom process differences in inner-city elementary schools. *Journal of Educational Research, 91*(1), 49–59.

Waxman, S., & Lidz, J. (2006). Early word learning. In W. Damon & R. Lerner (Series Eds.), D. Kuhn & R. Siegler (Vol. Eds.), *Handbook of child psychology: Vol. II. Cognition, perception, and language* (6th ed., pp. 299–335). New York: Wiley.

Way, N., Reddy, R., & Rhodes, J. (2007). Students' perceptions of school climate during the middle school years: Associations with trajectories of psychological and behavioral adjustment. *American Journal of Community Psychology, 40,* 194–213.

Wayne, A., & Youngs, P. (2003). Teacher characteristics and student achievement gains: A review. *Review of Educational Research, 73,* 89–122.

Webb, N. (2006). Indentifying content for student achievement tests. In S. Downing & T. Haladyna (Eds.), *Handbook of test development* (pp. 155–180). Mahwah, NJ: Erlbaum.

Webb, N., Farivar, S., & Mastergeorge, A. (2002). Productive helping in cooperative groups. *Theory Into Practice, 41*(1).

Wechsler, D. (2003). *Wechsler Intelligence Scale for Children* (4th ed.) San Antonio, TX: Psychological Corporation.

Weigel, D., Martin, S., & Bennett, K. (2005). Ecological influences of the home and the child-care center on preschool-age children's literacy development. *Reading Research Quarterly, 40*(2), 204–228.

Weiland, A., & Coughlin, R. (1979). Self-identification and preferences: A comparison of White and Mexican American first and third graders. *Journal of Social Psychology, 10,* 356–365.

Weiler, B. (1998). *Children's misconceptions about science: A list compiled by the AIP Operation Physics Project* [Online]. Retrieved from www.amasci.com/miscon/opphys.html

Weiner, B. (1992). *Human motivation: Metaphors, theories, and research.* Newbury Park, CA: Sage.

Weiner, B. (1994). Ability versus effort revisited: The moral determinants of achievement evaluation and achievement as a moral system. *Educational Psychologist, 29,* 163–172.

Weiner, B. (2000). Interpersonal and intrapersonal theories of motivation from an attributional perspective. *Educational Psychology Review, 12,* 1–14.

Weiner, B. (2001). Intrapersonal and interpersonal theories of motivation from an attribution perspective. In F. Salili, C. Chiu, & Y. Hong (Eds.), *Student motivation: The culture and context of learning* (pp. 17–30). New York: Kluer Academic/Plenum.

Weiner, L. (2002, April). *Why is classroom management so vexing to urban teachers? New Directions in theory and research about classroom management in urban schools.* Paper presented at the annual meeting of the American Educational Research Association, New Orleans.

Weiner, L. (2006). *Urban teaching: The essentials* (2nd ed.). New York: Teachers College Press.

Weinstein, C. S., Curran, M., & Tomlinson-Clarke, S. (2003). Culturally responsive classroom management: Awareness into action. *Theory Into Practice, 42,* 269–276.

Weinstein, C. S., & Mignano, A. J., Jr. (2007). *Elementary classroom management: Lessons from research and practice* (4th ed.). New York: McGraw-Hill.

Weinstein, C. S., Tomlinson-Clarke, S. & Curran, M. (2004). Toward a conception of culturally responsive classroom management. *Journal of Teacher Education, 55,* 25–38.

Weinstein, R. (2002). *Reaching higher: The power of expectations in schooling.* Cambridge, MA: Harvard University Press.

Weinstock, J. (2007). Don't call my kid smart. *T.H.E. Journal, 34,* 6.

Weiss, H., Mayer, E., Kreider, H., Vaughan, M., Dearing, E., Hencke, R., & Pinto, K. (2003). Making it work: Low-income working mothers' involvement in their children's education. *American Educational Research Journal, 40*(4), 879–901.

Weiss, I., & Pasley, J. (2004). What is high-quality instruction? *Educational Leadership, 61*(5), 24–28.

Weissglass, S. (1998). *Ripples of hope: Building relationships for educational change.* Santa Barbara, CA: Center for Educational Change in Mathematics & Science, University of California.

Wenner, G. (2003). Comparing poor, minority elementary students' interest and background in science with that of their white, affluent peers. *Urban Education, 38*(2), 153–172.

Wentzel, K. (1996). Social goals and social relationships as motivators of school adjustment. In J. Juvonen & K. Wentzel (Eds.), *Social motivation: Understanding children's school adjustment* (pp. 226–247). Cambridge, England: Cambridge University Press.

Wentzel, K. (1999a). Social influences on school adjustment: Commentary. *Educational Psychologist, 34*(1), 59–69.

Wentzel, K. (1999b). Social-motivational processes and interpersonal relationships: Implications for understanding students' academic success. *Journal of Educational Psychology, 91,* 76–97.

Wentzel, K. (2000). What is it that I'm trying to achieve? Classroom goals from a content perspective. *Contemporary Educational Psychology, 25,* 105–115.

Wentzel, K. R. (2002). The contribution of social goal setting to children's school adjustment. In A. Wigfield & J. S. Eccles (Eds.), *Development of achievement motivation* (pp. 221–246). New York: Academic Press.

Wentzel, K. R. (2003). Sociometric status and adjustment in middle school: A longitudinal study. *Journal of Early Adolescence, 23,* 5–28.

Wentzel, K. R., & Wigfield, A. (1998). Academic and social motivational influences on students' academic performance. *Educational Psychology Review, 10,* 155–175.

Wentzel, K. R., & Wigfield, A. (2007). Motivational interventions that work: Themes and remaining issues. *Educational Psychologist, 42,* 261–271.

Wertsch, J. (1991). *Voices of the mind: A sociocultural approach to mediated action.* Cambridge, MA: Harvard University Press.

Wessler, S. (2003). It's hard to learn when you're scared. *Educational Leadership, 61*(1), 40–43.

Whalen, C. K., Jamner, L. D., Henker, B., Delfino, R. J., & Lozano, J. M. (2002). The ADHD spectrum and everyday life: Experience sampling of adolescent moods, activities, smoking, and drinking. *Child Development, 73,* 209–227.

Whitcomb, J., Borko, H., & Liston, D. (2006). Living in the tension—Living with the heat. *Journal of Teacher Education, 57*(5), 447–453.

White, P., Sanbonmatsu, D., Croyle, R., & Smittipatana, S. (2002). Test of socially motivated underachievement: "Letting up" for others. *Journal of Experimental Social Psychology, 38,* 162–169.

White, R. (1959). Motivation reconsidered: The concept of competence. *Psychological Review, 66,* 297–333.

Wigfield, A. (1994). Expectancy-value theory of achievement motivation: A developmental perspective. *Educational Psychology Review, 6,* 49–78.

Wigfield, A., Byrnes, J., & Eccles, J. (2006). Development during early and middle adolescence. In P. Alexander & P. Winne (Eds.), *Handbook of educational psychology* (2nd ed., pp. 87–114). Mahwah, NJ: Erlbaum.

Wigfield, A., & Eccles, J. (1992). The development of achievement task values: A theoretical analysis. *Developmental Review, 12,* 265–310.

Wigfield, A., Eccles, J., & Pintrich, P. (1996). Development between the ages of 11 and 25. In D. Berliner & R. Calfee (Eds.), *Handbook of educational psychology* (pp. 148–185). New York: Macmillan.

Wigfield, A., & Eccles, J. (2000). Expectancy-value theory of achievement motivation. *Contemporary Educational Psychology, 25,* 68–81.

Wigfield, A., & Eccles, J. S. (2002). The development of competence beliefs, expectancies for success, and achievement values from childhood through adolescence. In. A. Wigfield & J. S. Eccles (Eds.), *Development of achievement motivation. A volume in the educational psychology series* (pp. 91–120). San Diego, CA: Academic Press.

Wigfield, A., Guthrie, J., Tonks, S., & Perencevich, K. (2004). Children's motivation for reading: Domain specificity and instructional influences. *Journal of Educational Research, 97*(6), 299–310.

Wilder, M. (2000). Increasing African American teachers' presence in American schools: Voices of students who care. *Urban Education, 35*(2), 205–220.

Wiley, D., & Harnischfeger, A. (1974). Explosion of a myth: Quantity of schooling and exposure to instruction, major education vehicles. *Education Researcher, 3,* 7–12.

Williams, C., & Zacks, R. (2001). Is retrieval-induced forgetting an inhibitory process? *American Journal of Psychology, 114,* 329–354.

Willingham, D. T. (2004). *Cognition: The thinking animal* (2nd ed.). Upper Saddle River, NJ: Merrill/Pearson.

Willingham, D. T. (2006). "Brain-based" learning: More fiction than fact. *American Educator, 30*(3), 27–30, 40–41.

Willingham, D. T. (2007). Critical thinking: Why is it so hard to teach? *American Educator, 31,* 8–19.

Willis, J. (2006). *Research-based strategies to ignite student learning: Insights from a neurologist and classroom teacher.* Alexandria, VA: ASCD.

Willis, J. (2007). Which brain research can educators trust? *Phi Delta Kappan, 88*(9), 697–699.

Willoughby, T., Porter, L., Belsito, L., & Yearsley, T. (1999). Use of elaboration strategies by students in grades two, four, and six. *Elementary School Journal, 99*(3), 221–232.

Wilson, B. L., & Corbett, H. D. (2001). *Listening to urban kids: School reform and the teachers they want.* Albany, NY: State University of New York Press.

Wilson, K., & Swanson, H. (1999, April). *Individual and age-related differences in working memory and mathematics computation.* Paper presented at the annual conference of the American Educational Research Association, Montreal, Canada.

Wilson, M., Hoskens, M., & Draney, K. (2001, April). *Rater effects: Some issues, some solutions.* Paper presented at the annual meeting of the American Educational Research Association, Seattle.

Winitzky, N. (1994). Multicultural and mainstreamed classrooms. In R. Arends (Ed.), *Learning to teach* (3rd ed., pp. 132–170). New York: McGraw-Hill.

Winne, P. (2001). Self-regulated learning viewed from models of information processing. In B. J. Zimmerman & D. H. Schunk (Eds.), *Self-regulated learning and academic achievement: Theoretical perspectives* (2nd ed.). Mahwah, NJ: Erlbaum.

Winsler, A., & Naglieri, J. (2003). Overt and covert verbal problem-solving strategies: Developmental trends in use, awareness, and relations with task performance in children aged 5 to 17. *Child Development, 74,* 659–678.

Wolf, L., Smith, J., & Birnbaum, M. (1997, March). *Measure-specific assessment of motivation and anxiety.* Paper presented at the annual meeting of the American Educational Research Association, Chicago.

Wolters, C. (2003). Understanding procrastination from a self-regulated learning perspective. *Journal of Educational Psychology, 95,* 179–187.

Wolz, D. J. (2003). Implicit cognitive processes as aptitudes for learning. *Educational Psychologist, 38,* 95–104.

Wood, D., Bruner, J., & Ross, S. (1976). The role of tutoring in problem solving. *British Journal of Psychology, 66,* 181–196.

Wood, E., Willoughby, T., McDermott, C., Motz, M., Kaspar, V., & Ducharme, M. (1999). Developmental differences in study behavior. *Journal of Educational Psychology, 91*(3), 527–536.

Wood, M. (2005). *High school counselors say they lack skills to assist gay, lesbian students.* Retrieved July 14, 2006, from www.bsu.edu/news

Woolfolk Hoy, A., Davis, H., & Pape, S. J. (2006). Teacher knowledge and beliefs. In P. A. Alexander & P. H. Winne (Eds.), *Handbook of educational psychology* (2nd ed., pp. 715–737). Mahwah, NJ: Erlbaum.

Wortham, S. (2004). The interdependence of social identification and learning. *American Educational Research Journal, 41*(3), 715–750.

Worthy, J., Moorman, M., & Turner, M. (1999). What Johnny likes to read is hard to find in school. *Reading Research Quarterly, 34,* 12–27.

Wright, S., & Taylor, D. (1995). Identity and the language of the classroom: Investigating the impact of heritage versus second-language instruction on personal and collective self-esteem. *Journal of Educational Psychology, 87*(2), 241–252.

Wubbels, T., Brekeimans, M., den Brok, P., & van Tartwijk, J. (2006). An interpersonal perspective on classroom management in secondary classrooms in the Netherlands. In C. M. Evertson & C. S. Weinstein (Eds.), *Handbook of classroom management: Research, practice, and contemporary issues* (pp. 1161–1191). Mahwah, NJ: Erlbaum.

Yeager, M. (2007). *Understanding NAEP: Inside the nation's education report card.* Retrieved March 8, 2008, from http://www. educationsector.org/analysis/analysis_show.htm?doc_id=560606

Yeh, Y.-C. (2006). The interactive effects of personal traits and guided practices on preservice teachers' changes in personal teaching efficacy. *British Journal of Educational Technology, 37,* 513–526.

Yell, M. L., Robinson, T. R., & Drasgow, E. (2001). Cognitive behavior modification. In T. J. Zirpoli & K. J. Melloy, *Behavior management: Applications for teachers* (3rd ed., pp. 200–246). Upper Saddle River, NJ: Merrill/Pearson.

Yeung, A. S., McInerney, D. M., Russell-Bowie, D., Suliman, R., Chui, H., & Lau, I. C. (2000). Where is the hierarchy of academic self-concept? *Journal of Educational Psychology, 92,* 556–567.

Yip, D. Y. (2004). Questioning skills for conceptual change in science instruction. *Journal of Biological Education, 38,* 76–83.

York-Barr, J., Sommers, W. A., Ghere, G. S., & Montie, J. (2001). *Reflective practice to improve schools: An action guide for educators.* Thousand Oaks, CA: Corwin Press.

Young, B., & Smith, T. (1999). *The condition of education, 1996: Issues in focus: The social context of education.* Washington, DC: U.S. Department of Education. Retrieved October 1, 2002, from http://nces.ed.gov/pubs99/condition99

Young, M., & Scribner, J. (1997, March). *The synergy of parental involvement and student engagement at the secondary level: Relationships of consequence in Mexican-American communities.* Paper presented at the annual meeting of the American Educational Research Association, Chicago.

Yussen, S., & Levy, V. (1975). Developmental changes in predicting one's own span of short-term memory. *Journal of Experimental Child Psychology, 19,* 502–508.

Zahorik, J. (1996). Elementary and secondary teachers' reports of how they make learning interesting. *The Elementary School Journal, 96*(5), 551–564.

Zambo, D. (2003). *Uncovering the conceptual representations of students with learning disabilities.* Unpublished doctoral dissertation, Arizona State University, Tempe.

Zaragoza, N. (2005). Including families in the teaching and learning process. In J. Kincheloe (Ed.), *Classroom teaching: An introduction.* New York: Peter Lang.

Zeelenberg, R., Wadenmakers, E.-J., & Rotteveel, M. (2006). The impact of emotion on perception: Bias or enhanced processing. *Psychological Science, 17,* 287–291.

Zehr, M. A. (2006). Reacting to reviews, states cut portfolio assessments for ELL students. *Education Week, 26*(12), 7.

Zeidner, M. (1998). *Test anxiety: The state of the art.* New York: Plenum Press.

Zhou, L., Goff, G., & Iwata, B. (2000). Effects of increased response effort on self-injury and objective manipulation as competing responses. *Journal of Applied Behavioral Analysis, 33,* 29–40.

Zhou, Q., Hofer, C., & Eisenberg, N. (2007). The developmental trajectories of attention focusing, attentional and behavioral persistence, and externalizing problems during school-age years. *Developmental Psychology, (43),* 369–385.

Zimmerman, B. (2005, April). *Integrating cognition, motivation and emotion: A social cognitive perspective.* Paper presented at the annual meeting of the American Educational Research Association, Montreal, Canada.

Zimmerman, B., & Schunk, D. (Eds.). (2001). *Self-regulated learning and academic achievement: Theoretical perspectives* (2nd ed.). Mahwah, NJ: Erlbaum.

Zimmerman, B. J., & Schunk, D. H. (2004). Self-regulating intellectual process and outcomes: A social cognitive perspective. In D. Y. Dai & R. J. Sternberg (Eds.), *Motivation, emotion, and cognition: Integrative perspectives on intellectual functioning and development* (pp. 323–349). Mahwah, NJ: Erlbaum.

Zins, J., Bloodworth, M., Weissberg, R., & Walberg, H. (2004). The scientific base linking social and emotional learning to school success. In J. Zins, R. Weissberg, M. Wang, & H. Walberg (Eds.), *Building academic success on social and emotional learning* (pp. 3–22). New York: Teachers College Press.

Zirkel, S. (2008). The influence of multicultural educational practices on student outcomes and intergroup relations. *Teachers College Record, 110,* 1147–1181. Retrieved June 4, 2008, from http://tcrecord.org/Content.asp?ContentID=14711

Zirpoli, T. J., & Melloy, K. J. (2001). *Behavior management: Applications for teachers.* Upper Saddle River, NJ: Merrill/Pearson.

Zook, K. (1991). Effects of analogical processes on learning and misrepresentation. *Educational Psychology Review, 3,* 41–72.

Zull, J. E. (2004). The art of changing the brain. *Educational Leadership, 62*(1), 68–72.

Zwiers, J. (2005). The third language of academic English. *Educational Leadership, 62*(4), 60–63.

name index

Abe, J. A., 274
Abedi, J., 101, 103, 463, 490, 491
Abelson, R., 204
Aber, J., 73
Aboud, F., 73
Achilles, C., 404
Ackerman, P., 126, 127
Adams, N., 69
Adesope, O., 269, 270
Aharon, I., 247
Ahtee, M., 269
Aiken, L. R., 473
Airasian, P., 18, 227
Akert, R., 100
Alberto, P., 144, 172, 186, 378, 393
Alder, N., 328, 344, 365
Alexander, J., 228
Alexander, J. M., 273
Alexander, K., 478
Alexander, P., 7, 41, 42, 260, 267, 268, 270, 307, 401
Alibali, M., 207, 412
Alleman, J., 255
Allen, J., 367, 436
Allen, L., 73
Allington, R. L., 111
Alparsian, C., 236, 241
Alperstein, J. F., 108, 110
Altermatt, E., 109
Ambridge, B., 205
American Association of University Women, 110
American Association on Mental Retardation, 142
American Educational Research Association, 489
American Psychiatric Association, 141
American Psychological Association, 489
American Psychological Association, Board of Educational Affairs, 333
Ames, C., 334
Amrein, A., 487
Anderman, E. A., 79
Anderman, E. M., 178, 286, 299, 304, 309, 320, 413
Anderman, L., 294
Anderman, L. H., 76
Anderson, C., 411
Anderson, D., 217
Anderson, E. E., 204
Anderson, J., 233
Anderson, J. R., 202, 204, 209, 216
Anderson, K., 370
Anderson, L., 17, 120, 360, 390, 392, 394, 405, 411
Anderson, L. W., 393
Anderson, M. C. M., 270, 271
Anderson, P. M., 340
Anderson, R., 228, 419
Andrade, H., 445
Andrew, L., 226, 235
Andrews, G., 42
Ang, R. P., 208
Antil, L., 419, 420
Applebee, A., 233
Arbuthnot, K., 284, 297, 494
Arbuthnott, K., 132
Archer, T., 173
Armour-Thomas, E., 14, 463
Armstead, P., 457
Arnett, J. J., 70
Arnold, N., 451
Aronson, E., 100, 374
Aronson, J., 99
Asian-Nation, 101
Aspy, C. B., 76, 382, 383
Atkinson, J., 292
Atkinson, R., 198, 199–200
Attanucci, J., 85
Au, K., 228
Au, W., 487
Auinger, P., 382
Austin, G., 255
Austin, J. L., 268, 269
Ausubel, D. P., 257, 414
Avni-Bada, D., 378
Avramidis, E., 144
Ayotte, V., 71
Ayres, P., 240
Azevedo, R., 185, 247

Babad, E., 330, 378
Bachnan, H. J., 130
Baddeley, A., 221
Baddeley, A. D., 199, 200, 201
Bae, G., 230, 240
Bailey, S., 70
Baines, E., 421
Baines, L., 412
Baker, D., 340, 412
Baker, S., 107
Balamore, U., 87
Baldwin, B., 149
Baldwin, J. D., 21, 165, 169, 170, 173, 175, 180, 378
Baldwin, J. I., 21, 165, 169, 170, 173, 175, 180, 378
Ball, D., 19, 214, 412
Banaji, M., 109
Bandalos, D. L., 451
Bandura, A., 51, 173, 179, 180, 181, 182, 184, 185, 298, 299
Banko, K. M., 287
Banks, J., 96, 107
Barak, M., 265
Baratz-Snowdon, J., 4, 8, 9, 13, 487
Barbaranelli, C., 326
Baringa, M., 51
Barker, G., 292
Barnes, S. P., 451
Barnett, J. E., 218
Barone, M., 106
Barr, M., 327
Barr, R. D., 114, 115, 117, 120
Barrett, T. M., 276
Barron, B., 246
Barron, K., 304
Barron, K. E., 284
Barry, C., 77
Barth, R., 333
Bartlett, L., 228
Barton, P., 113, 114
Barzillai, M., 219
Bassett, P., 421
Batsashaw, M. L., 147
Batt, S., 115
Battistich, V., 354, 365, 376
Bauer, A. M., 173
Bauer, C. J., 489
Bauerlein, M., 395
Baumeister, R., 70, 72
Baumeister, R. F., 340, 344
Baumrind, D., 63, 356
Baumwell, L., 51
Bayliss, P., 144
Baylor, A. L., 180
Bearer, E., 130
Becker, B. E., 340
Beckett, K. L., 232
Beebe-Frankenberger, M., 478
Beers, B., 242, 434
Beghetto, R. A., 263
Behuniak, P., 487
Beirne-Smith, M., 142
Belsito, L., 210
Belsky, J., 233
Ben-Avie, M., 65
Benbow, C., 151
Benjamin, P., 166
Benner, A., 345
Bennett, K., 63, 99
Bennett, N., 33, 363
Bennett-Murphy, L., 207
Benson, P., 65
Bental, B., 216
Bereiter, C., 276, 391
Berenbaum, S., 70, 119
Berger, K., 77
Berk, L., 32, 112, 113
Berkeley, S., 155
Berliner, D., 15, 65, 232, 475, 487
Berliner, D. C., 4, 5, 14, 196, 212, 487
Berndt, J., 240
Bernieri, F., 330
Berninger, V., 31, 32, 139
Bernstein, D. K., 146
Berrill, D., 6
Berry, A., 9
Berry, R., 229
Bertman, S., 395
Berv, J., 248
Berzonsky, M. D., 69
Beth-Halachmy, S., 261
Bettis, P., 69
Biddle, B., 65
Biddle, B. J., 111–112, 114
Bidell, T., 42
Bielenberg, B., 103, 114
Biemiller, A., 50, 52
Bigbee, M. A., 75
Birkeland, S., 8
Birnbaum, M., 313
Biscaro, M., 259
Black, A., 293
Black, P., 438, 461
Black, R., 363
Black, S., 229
Blackburn, M., 457
Blair, J., 488
Blanchett, W., 151, 490
Blatchford, P., 241, 246, 420, 421
Bleeker, M. M., 108, 109, 110
Blocher, M., 451
Block, M., 46, 274
Bloodworth, M., 75
Bloom, B., 392
Bloom, C. M., 213
Blum, R., 333
Blumenfeld, P., 264, 265, 339
Blumenreich, M., 20
Blundel, D., 363
Boakes, R. A., 171
Bocian, K., 478
Boekaerts, M., 304, 309
Bogdan, W., 165
Bohn, C. M., 323, 355, 401
Bol, L., 7
Bondy, E., 178, 383
Bong, M., 298, 306
Borg, W., 14
Borgogni, L., 326
Borko, H., 6, 11, 14, 19, 22, 233
Borman, G. D., 114, 115, 116
Bornstein, M. H., 51, 63
Bortfeld, H., 32
Bos, C., 135, 420
Bos, C. S., 420
Bouchard, T., 127
Bourne, L., 255
Boyd-Zaharias, J., 65
Boyle, O., 52, 103, 104, 107, 491
Braaksma, M., 181, 182, 411
Bracey, G., 79, 457
Bradley, K. D., 358
Brainerd, C., 37
Bransford, J., 4, 7, 8, 9, 10, 11, 12, 13, 20, 21, 32, 33, 114, 127, 197, 203, 204, 210, 213, 221, 226, 232, 235, 238, 241, 242, 245, 248, 259, 262, 355, 391, 394
Bransford, J. D., 10, 238, 279
Braun, H., 441
Brehm, K., 116

Brehmer, Y., 213
Brekeimans, M., 372
Brendgen, M., 77
Brenner, M., 216
Brewer, D. M., 449
Bridgeman, B., 458
Brigham, M., 126
Brobst, K. E., 219, 268
Broer, K., 259
Bronfenbrenner, U., 62, 63, 66
Bronson, E., 149
Brookhart, S., 435, 458, 473, 475, 489, 493
Brookhart, S. M., 435
Brooks-Gunn, J., 65
Brophy, J., 7, 9, 11, 15, 16, 17, 22, 72, 89, 109, 116, 117, 130, 131, 132, 133, 153, 155, 169, 172, 184, 186, 214, 233, 243, 255, 285, 286, 288, 294, 299, 305, 309, 310, 327, 328, 329, 332, 333, 336, 338, 340, 343, 354, 355, 357, 358, 365, 366, 373, 382, 383, 394, 400, 401, 402, 403, 404, 405, 406, 408, 411, 412, 413
Brosvic, G. M., 402
Brouwers, A., 326
Brown, A., 7, 127, 226, 228, 394
Brown, C. M., 265
Brown, D., 356, 365
Brown, J., 229, 240
Brown, K., 113
Brown, R., 86, 114
Brown, S. P., 110
Brown-Chidsey, R., 140
Browne, D., 212
Bruce, B., 401
Bruer, J. T., 32
Bruner, J., 47, 254, 255
Bruning, R., 210, 268
Bruning, R. H., 7, 11, 22, 230, 260, 262, 271, 293, 327, 400
Bryan, C. L., 293
Buck, G., 340
Bukowski, W., 64
Bulgren, J., 212, 257
Bullough, R., Jr., 19
Burack, J., 75
Burbules, N., 401
Burden, R., 144
Burhans, K., 298
Burkam, D. T., 113, 114
Burke, L. A., 272
Burns, M., 434
Burns, M. S., 102
Burstyn, J., 383
Buzzelli, C. A., 87
Byars, B., 156
Byrnes, J., 33, 108, 346
Byrnes, J. P., 32, 33, 35, 46, 111, 270

Caldwell, M. S., 293
Cameron, J., 287, 292
Campbell, J., 70, 72
Campbell, W. K., 71
Campione, J., 127, 228
Campos, J., 85
Camras, L., 85
Candace, S., 135, 420
Canley, C. S., 293
Canter, A., 259
Canter, L., 375
Canter, M., 375
Caplan, N., 98
Caprara, G. V., 326
Cardinal, T. M., 165
Carey, B., 145
Carlson, C., 73
Carlson, N., 33
Carnine, D., 154, 409
Carpenter, B., 102
Carr, J. P., 268
Carr, M., 149
Carr, N., 494
Carrier, M., 199
Carroll, A., 141
Carter, K., 357, 358, 359, 360, 384
Carter, S., 304
Carver, S., 245
Case, R., 43
Caseau, D., 341
Cassady, J., 212
Cassady, J. C., 311, 313, 456
Castellano, J. A., 150–151
Castle, S., 131
Cattel, R., 127
Caulfield, R., 304
Cazden, C. B., 228
Cepello, M., 413
Chaffen, R., 216
Chandler, P., 240
Chao, R., 65
Chapman, J. W., 71
Chappuis, J., 8, 434, 435, 460
Chappuis, S., 460
Charles, C. M., 120, 324, 365
Charner-Laird, M., 86, 243, 344
Chatterji, M., 16
Chávez, O., 390
Chavous, T. M., 73
Chekley, K., 128
Chen, A., 310
Chen, J., 127
Chen, Z., 42
Cheng, L. R., 463
Cheung, A., 106
Chi, M. T. H., 236
Childs, R., 473
Chinn, C. A., 417
Chinn, P., 70, 96, 98, 102, 107
Choi, N., 71
Chomsky, N., 51, 177, 196
Chorzempa, B., 130, 131
Chowne, A., 421
Choy, M., 98
Christensen, L., 15, 17, 18
Christenson, S., 64, 78, 80
Christian, K., 130
Christou, C., 221
Chronicle, E., 260
Chumlea, W., 119
Chyung, S., 260
Cicchelli, T., 242, 264
Cicchetti, D., 64, 115
Cimera, R., 142
Ciofalo, J. F., 441
Cizek, G., 451
Clark, J., 210
Clark, K., 73
Clark, M., 73
Clark, R. C., 200, 201, 230, 257, 417
Clark, R. E., 411
Clarke, A., 5
Cleary, T., 298
Clough, M., 404
Cocchiarella, M., 256
Cochran-Smith, M., 243, 488
Cocking, R., 7, 226, 394
Coffield, F., 132
Cognition and Technology group at Vanderbilt, 265
Cohen, E., 419, 420
Coie, J., 76
Coiro, J., 268
Colangelo, N., 150, 151
Colbert, R. D., 115
Cole, D. A., 71
Cole, M., 7, 41, 42
Cole, P. M., 67
Cole, S. R., 7, 41
Coleman, M. C., 143, 144
Coles, G., 33
Coll, C., 130
Collins, A., 226, 229, 287
Collins, W. A., 63, 89
Comer, J., 65
Comstock, G., 63
Comunian, A. L., 84
Conchas, G., 346
Conti-Ramsden, G., 205
Conway, G., 172
Cook, B. G., 138, 154
Cook, M. J., 402
Cooper, D., 76
Cooper, H., 16, 17, 19, 20, 412, 413, 461
Cooper, J., 322
Cooter, R., 52, 53, 157
Corbett, D., 344, 345
Corbett, H. D., 86, 116, 117, 328, 344
Corcoran, C. A., 446
Corkill, A., 216
Cornelius-White, J., 289, 293
Corno, L., 127, 131
Cortina, K. S., 305, 323
Costa, D. S. J., 171
Coughlin, R., 73
Council for Exceptional Children, 137
Covington, M., 285, 287, 294, 295, 311, 320
Covington, M. V., 304
Craig, D., 31, 33
Craig, S. D., 182
Craik, F. I. M., 212
Crandall, C., 109
Craven, J., 6
Craven, R., 72
Crick, N. R., 75, 77
Crippen, K. J., 266
Crockett, C., 237
Cromley, J., 247
Crooks, T., 435, 458
Crosnoe, R., 114
Cross, T. L., 66
Crow, S. R., 293
Cruickshank, D., 402
Cuban, L., 53, 127, 200, 235, 414
Cummins, J., 104
Curran, M., 380
Curtindale, L., 207
Cushman, K., 120

d'Ailly, H., 309
D'Ambrosio, B., 304
D'Arcangelo, M., 33
Darden, E., 145
Darling-Hammond, L., 4, 8, 9, 11, 13, 114, 391, 487
Dauber, S., 478
Davidson, B., 116
Davidson, J., 260
Davies, K., 108
Davis, A., 33
Davis, E., 22
Davis, E. F., 276
Davis, G., 149, 150, 151, 264
Davis, H., 326
Davis, H. A., 293, 305, 354
Davis, M., 47, 167, 339, 417
Davis, S. D., 165
Davis-Kean, P. E., 70
Dean, D., Jr., 217, 417
Debus, R., 72
deCharms, R., 293
Deci, E., 21, 178, 189, 285, 286, 291, 293, 294, 323, 324, 325, 327, 332, 333, 344, 354, 366, 404
Deci, E. L., 293
De Corte, E., 275
DeCorte, E., 276
DeFinis, A., 204
de Haan, M., 31, 205
Delfino, R. J., 141
De Lisi, R., 41
Delpit, L., 102
Dembo, M., 117
Demetriou, A., 221
Dempster, R., 216
den Brok, P., 372
Denig, S. J., 127, 131
Deniz, C., 131
Dennis, T. A., 67
Denton, K., 81, 84
Denzin, N., 18
DePaepe, J., 449
Derry, S., 232, 241, 247
De Simone, C., 269
Deutsch, N., 71
DeVries, R., 227, 360
DeWall, C. N., 340, 344
Dewey, J., 226
Deyhle, D., 309, 490
Diamond, J., 113
Diaz, E., 150–151
Dick, J., 138
Dickens, C., 80
Dickson, S. M., 449
Dien, T., 309
Dihoff, R. E., 402

Dindia, K., 108, 109
Ding, M., 246
Dingle, M., 107
diSessa, A., 236
Do, S. L., 311
Dobler, E., 268
Dochy, F., 294
Dodge, K., 76, 77
Dodge, K. A., 75
Dolezal, S., 208, 333
Doll, B., 116
Dong, W., 63
Donovan, M. S., 10, 238, 279
Dori, Y. J., 265
Dougherty, L. A., 409
Douglas, N. L., 272
Dow, G. T., 263
Dowdy, C., 133
Downey, J., 115
Dowson, M., 306
Doyle, W., 353, 357, 358, 359, 360, 373, 374, 384
Draney, K., 451
Drasgow, E., 187
Drew, C., 133
Driscoll, M., 276
Dubois, D. L., 114
Duffett, A., 135
Duguid, P., 229
Duke, N., 408
Duncan, R. G., 417
Dunsmoore, K., 229
Duran, R., 201, 241, 417, 419
Durkin, K., 205
Dwairy, M., 259
Dweck, C., 71, 297, 303, 305, 309
Dweck, C. S., 298
Dwyer, K., 73
Dykens, E., 142
Dynarski, M., 117

Earl, B. L., 266
Eccles, J., 41, 71, 108, 297, 299, 300, 346, 355
Eccles, J. S., 71, 297, 299, 300, 309
Ecclestone, K., 132
Echevarria, J., 96, 101, 103, 104, 107, 119, 240, 491
Eckardt, N., 19
Ecken, L., 354, 359, 365
Edelin, K., 294
Educational Testing Service, 13, 488
Education Vital Signs, 112
Egan, W., 133
Eggen, P., 81, 107, 208, 235, 240, 243, 321, 334, 404, 408, 409, 413, 417, 450
Eilam, B., 247
Eisenberg, N., 64, 75, 76, 85, 207
Eisenman, L. T., 284, 293
Elbaum, B., 155
Elder, L., 264
Elias, M., 77, 78, 87
Elias, M. J., 354
Elik, N., 254
Elliot, A., 299, 304, 305
Elliot, J., 457
Emerson, M. J., 46
Emmer, E. T., 8, 11, 64, 172, 324, 354, 357, 358, 359, 360, 363
Enerick, D, 263
Engelberg, R., 462
Englehart, M., 392
Englert, C., 229
English, K., 113
Entwisle, D., 478
Epstein, J., 65
Epstein, M. L., 402
Ericsson, K. A., 263
Erikson, E., 67
Ertmer, P., 299
Evans, C., 131
Evans, E., 462
Evans, G. W., 113
Evans, L., 108
Evans, W., 86, 114
Evertson, C., 17, 411
Evertson, C. M., 8, 11, 64, 172, 353, 354, 357, 358, 359, 360, 361, 382
Exline, R., 293
Ezell, D., 450

Fabes, R., 64
Fabiano, G. A., 376
Fabrigar, L., 131
Faiman-Silva, S., 98
Fair Test, 479
Falk, B., 20
Farenga, S., 473
Farivar, S., 241
Farkas, R., 132
Fauth, R., 65
Feiman-Nemser, S., 8
Feldhusen, J., 151
Feldon, D. F., 201, 247, 404, 405, 412
Ferguson, R., 73, 344
Fernandez, S., 130, 161
Fernandez-Berrocal, P., 188, 197
Ferrara, R., 127
Ferrari, M., 254
Fields, L., 170
Fierros, E., 127
Fillmore, L. W., 103, 114
Finn, J., 65, 404
Finn, K., 457
Finney, S. J., 284
Fischer, K., 42
Fischer, K. W., 274
Fischer, L., 382, 488
Fishman, B., 22
Flavell, J., 39, 42, 219
Fleischman, S., 64, 103, 361, 412
Fleming, V., 228
Flint, J., 142
Flores, E., 115
Flores, M. M., 409
Florida Department of Education, 389, 395
Flowerday, T., 310
Ford, L., 127
Forget, J., 247, 412
Forness, S., 143
Forness, S. R., 135
Forzine, F., 19
Fouad, N., 298
Fowler, R., 49
Fox, N., 33
Franklin, S., 43
Franklyn-Stokes, A., 457
Fredericks, J. A., 71
Freed, J., 445
Freeman, J., 240
Freeman, K. E., 309
Freiberg, H. J., 288
Freiberg, J., 354, 362, 376
French, D., 446, 451
French, S., 73
Frey, B., 261, 446, 460
Fried, C., 99
Friedel, J. M., 305, 323
Friedman, J. A., 358
Frone, M., 457
Fuchs, D., 142, 291
Fuchs, L., 140
Fuchs, L. S., 276
Fujimura, N., 42
Furrer, C., 293
Furst, E., 392

Gagne, E. D., 203
Gagné, F., 247, 412
Gall, J., 14
Gall, M., 14, 17, 20
Gallagher, J. G., 115
Gallimore, R., 21, 228
Gallini, J., 306
Gallup, A. M., 15, 16, 80, 353
Gamoran, A., 233, 355
Gandara, P., 490, 491
Gao, H., 421
Garcia, E., 463
Gardner, H., 127, 128, 264
Gardner, R., III, 269
Garrahy, D., 108
Garver, K. E., 205
Gaskill, P. J., 219, 271
Gathercole, S. E., 205
Gay, B., 106
Gay, G., 106, 109, 357, 380
Gay, L., 18
Gearon, J., 439
Geban, Ö., 236
Gehlbach, H., 287, 326
Geisinger, K., 489, 491
Gelman, S., 52
Genessee, F., 53
Gentile, J., 165, 178
George, V., 451
Gerber, S., 65
Gersten, R., 107, 412
Gerwels, M. C., 357, 358
Gettinger, M., 358
Gholson, B., 182
Gielan, U. P., 84
Gijbels, D., 264
Gillies, R. M., 77
Gilligan, C., 85
Gillison, F. B., 293
Gimbel, P., 6
Ginsberg, A. E., 110
Giuliani, G., 153
Glasgow, D., 154
Glassman, M., 47
Gleason, P., 117
Gnagy, E. M., 376
Goddard, R. D., 326
Godley, A., 102
Goetz, T., 311
Goff, G., 172
Goicoechea, J., 227
Goldman, S., 130, 151
Goldstein, R. A., 14, 120, 309, 346, 364, 407, 408
Goleman, D., 86
Gollnick, D., 70, 96, 98, 102, 107
Gomez, K., 113
Gomez, L., 439
Gonzales, P., 395
Gonzalez, C., 235, 450
Good, C., 99
Good, T., 11, 15, 16, 17, 130, 131, 153, 155, 169, 172, 329, 354, 355, 357, 358, 373, 382, 383, 400, 401, 402, 403, 405, 406
Goodenow, J., 255
Goodman, J., 87
Goossens, L., 69
Gootman, M. E., 172
Gordon, P., 86
Gordon, T., 375
Gottfredson, P., 376
Gragg, C., 232
Gragg, C. I., 241
Graham, M., 219, 268
Graham, S., 119, 130, 131, 268, 292, 294, 303
Granby, C., 208, 405
Granqvist, M., 293
Grant, L. W., 8
Graves, A., 104, 107, 119, 240, 412, 491
Gray, T., 103
Gray-Little, B., 73
Gredler, M., 47
Green, C. L., 368
Green, S., 439
Greenberg, M., 383
Greene, J. A., 185
Greenfield, P., 97, 100, 101, 113
Greeno, J., 197, 221, 226, 227, 233, 276, 287
Greenough, W. T., 32
Greenwald, A., 109
Gregory, A., 383
Gresham, F., 478
Griffin, P., 102
Griffith, D., 144, 243
Grigorenko, E., 139, 140
Gronlund, N., 391, 392, 436, 441, 442, 444, 447, 479
Gronlund, N. E., 435, 436, 473
Grotpeter, J. K., 75
Gruber, H., 266
Gschwend, L., 117
Guan, J., 310
Gullo, D., 478, 494
Gurian, M., 109
Guskey, T., 454, 460, 462
Guthrie, J., 47, 339, 417

Gutiérrez, K., 105
Gutman, L. M., 309

Haager, D., 107
Hacker, D., 7
Hadjioannou, X., 419
Hadwin, A., 19, 269
Haertel, E., 451, 458
Hafdahl, A. R., 73
Hakuta, K., 53
Haladyna, T., 444
Haladyna, T. H., 461, 473
Hale, N., 457
Halford, G., 42
Hall, E., 132
Hallahan, D., 142, 143, 147, 152, 154
Halpern, D., 127
Halpern, D. F., 108, 109, 119, 340
Halpern, S., 32
Hamilton, R., 214
Hamilton, S. L., 269
Hammerness, K., 232
Hampton, J., 255
Hancock, D. R., 311
Hanich, L., 138
Hansbury, L., 345
Hansson, T., 293
Harackiewicz, J., 286, 304
Hardman, M., 119, 133, 134, 137, 138, 139, 140, 143, 145, 146, 147, 148, 151, 153
Hardre, P. L., 114
Hardy, L., 487
Hargrove, T., 473
Harkness, S., 304
Harnischfeger, A., 355
Harpalani, V., 73
Harriet, A. W., 358
Harris, K., 268
Harris, K. R., 267, 268, 273, 278, 279
Harrison, C., 438
Harry, B., 64, 151
Hatano, G., 262
Hatch, T., 128
Hattie, J., 141, 242, 341, 343, 402, 403
Hausser, R., 463
Havsy, L., 64, 78, 80
Hawkins, M., 106
Hawthorne, N., 80
Haycock, K., 117
Hayes, J. R., 259
Hayes, K., 106, 243
Heath, S. B., 18, 99, 228, 242
Hébert, T. P., 115
Hedges, L., 65
Heffner, T., 449
Hegarty, M., 210
Heiser, J., 210
Heller, J., 276
Hellerbran, V., 390
Helsing, D., 6, 8
Henker, B., 141
Henricsson, L., 383
Henson, R. K., 326
Herbert, J., 71
Hergenhahn, B. R., 174, 202
Herzig, A., 110
Hetherington, E. M., 63
Heubert, J., 463
Heward, W., 119, 135, 138, 139, 140, 142, 143, 144, 145, 146, 147, 148, 151, 153, 154
Hickey, D. T., 288
Hidi, S., 310, 337, 339, 346
Hiebert, E. H., 50
Hiebert, J., 21, 486
Higgins, A. T., 216
Higgins-D'Alessandra, M., 84
Hilbert, T. S., 269
Hilden, K., 43, 189, 217, 219, 346, 455
Hill, K., 311
Hill, L., 263
Hill, W., 392
Hill, W. F., 166, 174, 180
Hirsch, B., 71
Hirsch, E., 487
Hisley, J., 327
Hmelo-Silver, C. E., 264, 265, 417
Ho, H., 367, 368
Hodapp, R., 142
Hodell, M., 285, 293
Hofer, C., 207
Hoff, 473
Hoffman, J., 473
Hoffman, L., 14, 109
Hofstetter, C., 101, 463, 491
Hogan, T., 6, 372, 475, 479, 484
Hohn, R. L., 261
Hoke-Sinex, L., 113
Holahan, C., 149
Holloway, J., 113, 135
Holmquist, J. A., 362
Hong, S., 367, 368
Honora, D., 344
Hooper, K., 295
Hoover-Dempsey, K. V., 367, 368
Horgan, D., 7
Horn, S., 322
Horst, S. J., 284, 305
Hoskens, M., 451
Houts, R., 233
Howard, P., 31
Howard, T., 87, 242, 344
Howe, K., 248
Howe, M. L., 214
Hoy, A., 326
Hoy, W., 326
Hoy, W. K., 326
Huan, V. S., 208, 216
Huang, S., 120
Huba, M., 445
Huber, J. A., 271
Hübscher, R., 47, 48
Hughes, D., 73
Hughes, T. L., 140
Hunt, N., 140, 147
Huntsinger, C. S., 98
Hvitfeldt, C., 100
Hyman, I., 76, 78, 383

Igo, L. B., 210, 268
Ilg, T., 86, 115
Impara, J., 478
Imreh, G., 216
Ingersoll, R., 4, 8
Inhelder, B., 34, 39
Inzlicht, M., 99
Ittenbach, R. F., 142
Iwata, B., 172
Iwata, B. A., 176
Iyengar, S., 339
Izzard, C. E., 274

Jackson, D., 131
Jackson, P., 5
Jacobs, G. M., 273
Jacobs, J. E., 108, 109, 110, 309
Jalongo, R., 390, 394
Jamner, L. D., 141
Jefferies, D., 211
Jenkins, J., 419
Jennings, J., 487
Jesse, D., 115
Jetton, T., 268, 401
Jitendra, A., 258, 260, 265, 412
Johnson, A. P., 19, 21
Johnson, B., 15, 17, 18, 473
Johnson, D. D., 473, 489, 490
Johnson, D. W., 76, 77, 78, 341, 383, 419, 420
Johnson, E. S., 451
Johnson, J., 135
Johnson, K. E., 273
Johnson, L., 101, 172
Johnson, R., 76, 77, 78, 341, 383, 419, 420
Johnson, R. E., 311, 313, 456
Johnson, S., 8
Johnson, W., 127
Jonassen, D., 265
Jones, B., 473
Jones, G., 473, 489, 490, 491
Jones, L. S., 120, 358, 365, 378, 380
Jones, M., 73
Jones, N., 166
Jones, S. M., 108, 109
Jones, V. F., 120, 358, 365, 378, 380
Jong, Ton de, 421
Jongjohann, K., 409
Jordan, N., 138
Jordan, W., 116
Jorgenson, O., 33
Jose, P. E., 98
Jovanovic, J., 109
Joyce, S., 172
Joyner, E., 65
Judson, M., 407
Juniewicz, K., 450, 451
Juvonen, J., 293, 340, 344, 420

Kabboni, N., 478
Kafai, Y., 221
Kaff, M. S., 176, 357, 380
Kahlenberg, R., 112
Kahn, E., 441
Kahng, S. W., 176
Kakkarainen, O., 269
Kalish, C., 52
Kalyuga, S., 240
Kame'enui, E., 409
Kamil, 63
Kamil, M. L., 50
Kane, M., 479
Kang, J., 50, 53
Kaplan, A., 305
Kaplan, D., 138
Karateken, C., 200
Karnes, F., 150
Karten, T., 133, 152
Kastens, K., 233, 406
Kates, K., 176
Kato, T., 278
Katsiyannis, A., 175, 376
Kauchak, D., 107, 208, 321, 334, 404, 409, 413, 417
Kauffman, J., 126, 142, 143, 147, 152, 154
Kaufman, A. S., 476
Kaufman, J. C., 264
Kaufman, J. M., 376, 378
Kavale, K., 143
Kavale, K. A., 135
Kay, R., 260
Kaylor, M., 409
Kazden, A., 164, 167
Keating, D. P., 37
Keefer, M., 421
Kemenes, G., 166
Kempler, T., 327, 339
Kerman, S., 404
Kester, L., 233
Kibby, M. Y., 200
Kidron, Y., 64, 361
Kiewra, K., 210
Kim, E., 101
Kim, Y., 180
Kincheloe, J., 14, 86, 157, 346, 347
Kindler, A. L., 103
King-Friedrichs, J., 212
Kinkead, L., 103
Kirby, U., 131
Kirkpatrick, C., 86
Kirschner, P., 233
Kirschner, P. A., 411, 417
Kitsantas, A., 298, 326
Klahr, D., 265
Klatzky, R., 207
Klein, C., 450
Kliewer, C., 154
Klingner, J., 151
Klopfer, L., 227
Kluth, P., 135
Knapp, M. S., 115
Knight, J., 409
Knopik, S., 127
Kober, N., 65, 101
Koc, K., 87
Kodjo, C. M., 382
Kogan, L. R., 326
Kohlberg, L., 81, 82, 84
Kohler, K. M., 358
Kohlhardt, J., 80
Koning, E., 304
Kornhaber, M., 127
Korthagen, F., 181
Kostin, I., 340
Kounin, J., 172, 183, 354, 372, 378, 379, 381
Kozhevnikov, M., 210

Kozol, J., 65, 120, 243, 274, 491
Kozulin, A., 228
Krajcik, J., 264, 265, 339
Kramer, P. A., 5
Krapp, A., 346
Krashen, S., 106
Krathwohl, D., 390, 392, 393, 394, 405
Krathwohl, O., 392
Kratzig, G., 132
Krebs, D., 81, 84
Kress, J., 78
Kreuger, J., 70, 72
Kroesbergen, E. H., 409
Kroger, J., 68
Kuczka, K., 295
Kuhn, D., 43, 217, 236, 272, 274, 409, 417
Kuk, L. S., 69
Kulik, J., 414
Kulm, G., 246
Kumar, R., 304
Kunsch, C., 380
Kuther, T., 84

Labov, W., 102
Lajoie, S. P., 393
Lalli, J. S., 176
Lam, S-F., 333
LaMay, M., 127
Lambating, J., 436
Lambert, C., 449
Lambert, L., 449
Lambert, N., 186, 291
Lambert, S., 363
Lamkin, D. M., 213
Lan, W., 260
LaNasa, S. M., 404
Landrum, T. J., 376, 378
Landry, S., 63
Landsman, J., 344
Langer, J., 233
Lanzi, R. G., 130
Lareau, A., 113
Larrivee, B., 292
Larsen, S. L., 98
Larson, R., 71
Laurie-Rose, C., 207
Lave, J., 229, 240
Law, Y-K., 333
Lawless, E., 331
Lawson, A., 473
Lazar, N. A., 205
Lazonder, A. W., 421
Leaper, C., 109
LeCompte, M., 309
Lee, C., 221, 438
Lee, J., 260
Lee, J. D., 110
Lee, M., 268
Lee, R., 170, 171
Lee, V., 327
Lee, V. E., 113, 114
Lee, Y., 46
Leggett, E., 297, 305
Lehman, S., 309, 310, 339
Lei, J. L., 101
Leibham, M. E., 273
Leinhardt, G., 266, 401, 404
Lemke, M., 395
Lennon, R., 53
Leno, L. C., 409
Lens, W., 293, 309
Leonard, L. B., 205
Leont'ev, A., 46, 233
LePage, P., 4, 120, 364, 365
Lepper, M., 285, 293, 339
Lerner, R., 30, 130, 157
Letendre, G., 412
Levesque, C., 291
Levitt, H., 130
Lew, J., 101
Lewis, A., 101, 360, 486
Lewis, C. C., 274
Lewis, J. L., 101
Lewis, V., 137
Li, J., 126, 274, 309
Li, M., 491
Li, S-C., 213
Li, X., 246
Li, Y., 233, 419
Liben, L., 233, 406
Lictenberger, E. O., 476
Lidz, J., 52, 119
Lightfoot, C., 7, 41
Lillard, A. S., 309
Lin, J-R., 203
Lincoln, Y., 18
Linn, R. L., 435, 436, 473
Linnenbrink, E. A., 272, 311
Lippa, R. A., 108, 109
Lipson, M. Y., 271
Liston, D., 14, 19
Liu, X., 269
Lockl, K., 278
Lohman, D., 126, 127, 128
Lopes, P., 76, 86
Lopez, N., 108
Lopez del Bosque, R., 73
Lord, C., 101, 463, 491
Losh, S. C., 421
Loughran, J., 9
Lovelace, M., 132
Lowrie, T., 260
Loyens, S. M., 417
Lozano, J. M., 141
Lubinski, D., 151
Ludtke, O., 413
Luft, P., 265
Lumeng, J. C., 165
Luna, B., 205
Lundberg, U., 293
Lunenberg, M., 181
Luria, A. R., 274
Luther, S. S., 340
Lutz, S., 47, 339, 417
Luyckx, K., 69
Lynam, D., 76
Lynch, S., 144
Lytle, S., 243

Ma, X., 76, 77
Maag, J., 172
Mabry, L., 448
Maccoby, E. E., 63
MacGregor, J., 260
Macionis, J., 14, 70, 111, 113, 114, 120, 491
MacMillan, D., 478
MacNeil, M. S., 269
Macpherson, R., 272
Maehr, M., 178, 286, 304
Maehr, M. L., 293
Mager, R., 391
Magnusson, M., 293
Mahoney, J., 71
Maker, C. J., 151
Mandl, H., 266
Manning, M., 278
Manouchehri, A., 344, 346, 365
Mantz, M., 439
Manzo, K., 15, 242
Marchand, G., 292, 293, 295
Marcia, J., 69
Mariachi, R., 326
Marinoff, L., 34, 254
Marion, S., 447
Marks, W., 200
Marsh, H., 71, 72, 302
Marshall, B., 438
Marshall, K., 140, 147
Martin, A., 14
Martin, C., 70, 119
Martin, G., 164, 167
Martin, J., 216, 227
Martin, S., 63, 99
Martinussen, R., 141
Marzano, R. J., 336, 341, 358, 391, 402, 409, 412, 413, 461
Maslow, A., 288, 290, 291, 293, 327, 332
Mason, L., 228, 229
Massucci, J., 86, 115
Mastergeorge, A., 241
Mastropieri, M., 155
Maughan, A., 64
Maughan, B., 212
Mawhinney, T., 65, 89
Mayer, R., 7, 10, 11, 53, 197, 203, 210, 230, 235, 276, 339, 412, 417
Mayer, R. E., 200, 201, 212, 230, 257, 258, 259, 260, 261, 262, 266, 275, 417
Mazur, J. E., 172
McCartney, K., 62, 65
McCaughtry, N., 9
McCleery, J., 255
McCoach, D. B., 130
McCombs, B., 116, 186, 291, 307
McCombs, B. L., 291
McCombs, J., 395
McCrudden, M., 268
McCurdy, B. L., 380
McCutchen, D., 200
McDermott, R., 130, 151
McDevitt, T., 53
McDonough, P. M., 489
McDougall, D., 208, 405
McDowell, L., 294
McGee, K., 126
McGill-Franzen, A., 111
McGregor, H., 299, 304, 305
McGrew, K., 127
McInerney, D., 306
McIntosh, D. E., 140
McIntosh, S., 488, 489
McKeachie, W., 414
McLeod, J., 68, 69
McLoyd, V. C., 309
McMahon, S., 127
McManus, R. A., 271
McMillan, J., 434, 435, 484, 485, 493
McMillan, J. H., 16, 17, 18, 20
McNeil, L., 364
McNulty, J. K., 311
McPhail, J., 240
Md-Yunus, S., 264
Medin, D., 255, 256
Meece, J. L., 7, 22, 70, 108, 132, 165, 284, 323, 403, 435
Meek, C., 137
Mehta, J. D., 490
Meichenbaum, D., 185, 188
Meister, C., 412
Melloy, K. J., 173
Meltzer, L., 217, 219
Mendaglio, S., 87
Mercer, J., 490
Merisuo-Storm, T., 105
Merkley, D., 211
Mertler, C., 474, 475, 492
Merzenich, M. M., 31
Meter, P., 226, 228
Meyer, D. K., 284, 310, 323
Michael, R. S., 380
Middleton, M., 295, 304, 305
Middleton, M. J., 309
Midgley, C., 294, 295, 304, 305, 309
Mignano, A. J., Jr., 355, 361, 365, 368
Milham, M., 176, 357
Miller, A., 80
Miller, C. A., 205
Miller, G., 177, 200, 201
Miller, K. F., 346
Miller, L., 116
Miller, M. D., 435, 436, 441, 442, 447, 460, 462, 473, 474, 476, 478, 479, 483, 484, 485, 487, 489, 490, 492, 493
Miller, P., 37, 39, 40, 219
Miller, R., 457
Miller, S., 39, 219, 322
Mills, G., 18, 21
Milner, H. R., 345, 365, 366
Miltenberger, R., 172, 176
Minke, K., 370
Minnici, A., 102
Mislevy, R., 441
Mistry, R., 345
Mixutu, I., 67
Miyake, A., 46
Moll, L. C., 197
Moorman, M., 310
Moran, S., 127
Moreno, R., 22, 201, 241, 276, 339, 402, 417, 419
Morgan, P. L., 291
Morgan, R., 340
Morgan, S., 200
Morgan, S. L., 490
Morris, P., 62
Morrison, F., 233

Morrison, F. J., 130, 346
Morrone, A., 304
Mortimore, P., 212
Moseley, D., 132
Moshman, D., 247
Müeller, K. J., 304
Mulhall, P., 9
Mulholland, R., 413
Munakata, Y., 43
Munby, H., 14
Munk, D., 462
Murdock, T., 457
Murdock, T. B., 79, 80, 87
Murphy, J. C., 358, 360, 380
Murphy, P. K., 219, 271, 307
Murray, B., 76, 78
Myers, K. M., 167
Myers, M. E., 167

Naglieri, J., 46
Nagy, W., 52
Nansel, T. R., 383
Nardo, A. C., 380
Nashon, S., 217
Nasir, N., 221
Nasir, N. S., 327
National Assessment of Educational Progress, 109
National Center for Research on Teacher Learning, 7
National Commission on Excellence in Education, 486
National Council on Disability, 138
National Council on Measurement in Education, 489
National Education Association, 108, 110
National Excellence, 150
National Joint Committee on Learning Disabilities, 138
National Law Center on Homelessness and Poverty, 113
Needham, A., 276
Neill, M., 487
Neisser, U., 199
Neitzel, C., 113
Nelson, C., 31, 32, 205, 216
Nelson, S. C., 109, 110
Nesbit, J., 19, 269, 270
Ness, D., 473
New Commission on the Skills of the American Workforce, 119
Newman, R., 76, 78
Newstead, J., 457
Niaz, M., 41
Nichols, B., 493
Nichols, S., 15
Nilsson, L., 173
Nitko, A., 434, 444, 446, 473, 475, 489, 493
Noddings, N., 85, 327, 344
Noguera, P., 73, 86, 114, 346
Nokelainen, P., 142
Noll, E., 73
Norby, M. M., 7, 260, 327, 400
Northwest Regional Laboratory, 491
Norwood, P., 488, 489
Nosek, B., 109

Notar, C. E., 454
Nucci, L., 80, 81, 84, 87, 354, 355, 379
Nuthall, G., 210, 216, 226
Nuthall, G. A., 204
Nye, B. A., 65
Nystrand, M., 233, 355

Oakes, J., 130, 131
O'Brien, L., 109
O'Brien, T., 278
O'Connell, A., 130
O'Conner, C., 130, 161
O'Connor, E., 62, 65
Oden, M., 149
Odom, A. L., 404
O'Donnell, A., 119
Ogbu, J., 98, 101
Okagaki, L., 99, 100, 420
O'Leary, S., 172
Olson, J., 404
Olson, M. H., 174, 202
O'Mara, A., 72
Omelich, C., 311
Omerod, T., 260
Opdenakker, M. C., 404
Orr, A., 113
Osher, D., 73
Osterman, K. F., 328
Oura, Y., 262
Ousten, J., 212
Overman, L. R., 114, 115, 116
Owens, R. E., 101
Ozdas, A., 213

Paas, F., 199, 200, 266, 417
Packer, M., 227
Padilla, A., 96, 101, 102, 103, 104, 106
Page, E., 458
Paivio, A., 210
Pajares, F., 287, 309
Pajares, R., 298
Palincsar, A., 226, 227, 228, 332
Pan, J., 274, 309
Pannozzo, G., 404
Pape, S. J., 326
Parillo, V., 14, 113, 120
Paris, A. H., 185, 308, 451
Paris, S. G., 185, 308, 346, 451
Parish, J., 115
Parish, T., 115
Park, S.-H., 274
Parker, J., 64
Parks, M., 127
Parrett, W. H., 114, 115, 117, 120
Pascarella, J., 243
Pashler, H., 199
Pasley, J., 401, 404
Patall, E. A., 412
Patrick, B. C., 327
Patrick, H., 76, 294
Patterson, M., 439
Patton, J., 133
Patton, J. R., 142
Paul, R., 264
Pavlov, I., 165
Pear, J., 164, 167

Pearson, P. D., 208, 333
Peck, S. C., 327
Peevely, G., 65
Pekrun, R., 311
Péladeau, N., 247, 412
Pelham, W. E., Jr., 376
Pellegrini, A. D., 76, 383
Pellegrino, J., 447
Pepperling, J., 70
Peregoy, S., 52, 103, 104, 107, 491
Perini, M., 339
Perkins-Gough, D., 108, 114
Perry, M., 109
Perry, N., 285
Perry, N. E., 284, 287, 323, 327, 328, 341, 343, 344
Perry, R., 311
Peterson, C. C., 148
Peterson, D., 208, 333
Peterson, R., 175, 376
Peterson, R. L., 380
Peverly, S. P., 219, 268
Pfiffner, L., 172
Phelps, L., 127
Phelps, R., 473, 487
Phillips, D., 226, 247, 248
Phye, G., 275
Phye, G. D., 276
Piaget, J., 15, 20, 22, 34, 35, 39, 40, 45, 46, 81, 129, 226, 235, 287, 332, 359
Pianta, R., 233
Piccolo, D., 246
Pickering, D. J., 412, 413
Pickering, S. J., 205
Pierangelo, R., 153
Pierce, W. D., 287
Piercy, F. P., 165
Pintrich, P., 41, 304, 320
Pintrich, P. R., 7, 22, 70, 132, 165, 236, 272, 284, 311, 323, 403, 435
Pittman, K., 261
Placier, P., 14
Plake, B., 478
Plant, E. A., 263
Plata, M., 154
Platsidou, M., 221
Platt, R., 489, 490
Plucker, J. A., 263
Pokorny, N., 115
Pollica, L., 219
Polloway, E., 133
Pomerantz, E., 63
Popham, W., 487
Popham, W. J., 446, 449, 451, 463, 474, 476, 479, 487, 490, 492
Porter, L., 210
Potter, R. L., 271
Powell, R., 341
Prawat, R., 260
Premack, D., 169
Pressley, M., 43, 115, 189, 208, 217, 219, 267, 268, 273, 278, 279, 323, 333, 346, 401, 455
Pritchard, R., 274
Prochnow, J. E., 71
Proffitt, J., 255
Prosser, E., 73
Pulliam, J., 486

Puntambekar, S., 47, 48
Purdie, N., 141
Putnam, R., 6, 11, 22, 233
Pyryt, M., 87

Qian, G., 274, 309
Quihuis, G., 305
Quinn, P. C., 254
Quiocho, A., 21

Rabinowitz, M., 6
Rainwater, L., 113
Rakow, E., 7
Ramey, C. T., 130
Ramey, S. L., 130
Ramos-Ford, V., 264
Raphael, L., 115
Rapoport, J., 33, 140–141
Raskauskas, J., 79
Rawlings, M., 80
Reddy, R., 208
Reeve, J., 114
Reibstein, S., 380
Reigeluth, C. M., 260
Reiner, M., 236
Reis, S., 150
Reis, S. M., 115
Reisberg, D., 255
Renkl, A., 266, 269
Renninger, K. A., 310, 337, 346
Rentner, D., 487
Renzulli, J., 150
Repman, J., 260
Resing, W. C., 276
Resnick, L., 226, 227, 287
Resnick, L. B., 236
Rest, J., 84
Reutzel, D., 52, 53, 157
Reys, B., 390
Reys, R., 390
Rhodes, J., 208
Richards, T., 31, 32
Richardson, V., 14
Ridley, D., 307
Rieg, S., 390
Riehl, C., 19
Rikers, R. M., 268
Riley, M., 276
Rimm, S., 149, 150, 151, 264
Rimm-Kaufman, S. E., 344
Rittle-Johnson, B., 412
Ritts, V., 439
Roberts, S., 96
Robertson, J., 303
Robinson, J. C., 412
Robinson, T. R., 187
Roblyer, M., 200
Rodriguez, M., 208, 333
Roebers, C. M., 218
Roehrig, A. D., 323, 401
Roeser, R., 287
Roeser, R. W., 326, 327, 331, 332
Roger, B., 134
Rogers, C., 288, 289
Rogoff, B., 42, 43, 47, 49, 99, 108, 151, 197, 228, 229, 231, 274, 309, 332

Rogosch, F. A., 115
Roid, G., 476
Romboy, D., 103
Ronning, R. R., 7, 260, 327, 400
Rook, J. E., 217
Rose, D., 127
Rose, K., 439
Rose, L. C., 15, 16, 80, 353
Rosebery, A., 221
Rosen, L., 172
Rosenfield, P., 363
Rosenshine, B., 120, 403, 406, 409, 412, 413
Rosenthal, R., 330, 378
Roseth, C. J., 421
Ross, B., 255
Ross, S., 47
Roth, J., 65
Roth, W., 46
Rothstein, R., 112, 113, 114
Rotter, J., 293
Rotteveel, M., 311
Rowe, M., 406
Royer, J., 196
Rubie-Davies, Ch., 421
Rubin, K., 64, 65, 75
Rubinson, F., 14, 309, 340, 343, 344
Ruble, D., 70, 119
Rudolph, K. D., 68, 89, 293
Runco, M. A., 264
Russel, T., 14
Rutter, M., 212
Ryan, A., 294
Ryan, A. M., 76, 284, 297, 490, 494
Ryan, J., 444
Ryan, J. B., 175, 376
Ryan, K. E., 284, 297, 304, 311, 490, 494
Ryan, R., 21, 178, 189, 285, 286, 291, 293, 294, 323, 324, 325, 327, 332, 333, 344, 354, 366, 404
Ryan, S., 382
Rydell, A. M., 383

Saarni, C., 85
Sack-Min, J., 133, 137
Saddler, B., 445
Sadoski, M., 210
Safer, N., 412
Sagan, L., 65, 89
Sailor, W., 134
Salazar, J., 106
Saleh, Issa, 228
Saleh, M., 421, 423
Salovey, P., 76, 86
Salvia, J., 475, 476, 484
Salzfass, E., 78
Samuels, M., 284, 297, 494
San Antonio, D., 78
Sanders, J., 109, 110
Sandler, H. M., 70, 368
Sansone, C., 286
Santamaria, C., 188, 197
Santi, K., 434
Sapon-Shevin, M., 134
Sattler, J. M., 127
Sawyer, B. E., 344
Sawyer, R. K., 196
Scardamalia, M., 276, 391
Schacter, D., 201
Schallert, D. L., 311
Schank, R. C., 204
Scharrer, E., 63
Schellenberg, S., 81, 264, 278
Schiever, S., 151
Schimmel, D., 382, 488
Schlesinger, A., 105
Schlozman, S., 141
Schlozman, V., 141
Schmidt, H. G., 268, 417
Schmitt, V., 446, 460
Schneider, B., 46, 271
Schneider, W., 201, 278
Schnyder, I., 413
Schoenfeld, A. H., 278
Scholl, B. J., 226
Schommer, M., 7
Schraw, G., 262, 263, 309, 310, 339
Schraw, G. J., 7, 260, 327, 400
Schult, C. A., 75
Schumm, J., 135, 420
Schunk, D., 164, 181, 182, 183, 185, 254, 256, 298, 299, 322, 494
Schunk, D. H., 7, 8, 22, 70, 71, 132, 165, 185, 188, 284, 285, 286, 287, 288, 290, 291, 294, 296, 298, 300, 303, 304, 307, 323, 343, 403, 435, 456
Schutz, A., 157
Schwab, Y., 354
Schwartz, D., 78, 210, 260, 265, 275, 277, 279
Schwartz, H., 255
Schweinle, A., 310
Scott, J., 52
Scribner, J., 113
Scruggs, T., 155
Sears, K., 113
Sears, R., 149
Seegers, G., 309
Segall, A., 9
Seibert, M. A., 269
Seidman, E., 73
Selwyn, D., 13
Senter, G. W., 120, 324, 365
Serafino, K., 242, 264
Shahid, J., 302
Shapiro, A., 230–231
Shapiro, J. P., 110
Shaver, D., 102
Shaw, P., 33, 140–141
Shaywitz, B. A., 33, 138
Shaywitz, S. E., 33, 138
Shea, D., 151
Shea, T. M., 173
Sheehan, E., 53
Sheldon, S., 368
Shen, B., 310
Shen, E., 421
Shepard, L., 130, 444, 451, 460
Sheppard, J. A., 311
Shermer, M., 272
Shields, C., 47
Shields, P., 102
Shiffrin, R., 198, 199–200, 201
Shirin, A., 148
Short, D., 96, 101, 103, 104
Shuell, T., 16, 17, 212, 401, 405
Shulman, L., 8, 9
Shute, V. J., 242
Siegel, M., 10, 23
Siegler, R., 42, 43
Silbert, J., 409
Silver, H., 339
Simon, H., 210
Simons, H., 98
Simons, R., 65
Sinatra, G. M., 236, 237, 272
Singer, K., 493
Singh, N. N., 355
Skaalvik, E., 298
Skerry, S., 73
Skevington, S. M., 293
Skiba, R. J., 380
Skinner, B. F., 21, 51, 164, 167, 169
Skinner, D., 272
Skinner, E., 293
Skinner, E. A., 292, 293, 295
Slavin, R., 19, 106, 131, 182, 420
Sloane, F., 19
Slotta, J. D., 236
Smeedings, T., 113
Smith, A., 178, 212, 383
Smith, F., 112
Smith, J., 313, 449
Smith, K., 63, 451
Smith, K. S., 217
Smith, P., 298
Smith, T., 8, 111, 133, 152
Smith, T. W., 217
Smokowski, P., 99
Snary, J., 84
Snell, J., 76
Snow, C., 50, 53, 102
Snow, R., 131
Soenens, B., 63, 64, 69, 309
Solano-Flores, G., 491
Solley, B. A., 451
Solmon, M. A., 293
Southerland, S., 237, 246
Southerland, S. A., 237, 272
Spaans, M. A., 219, 267
Spalding, T., 255
Spanoudis, G., 221
Spearman, C., 127
Spencer, M. B., 73
Spies, R., 478
Spina, S. U., 99
Spinrad, T., 64
Spiro, R., 277
Spivey, N., 53
Spor, M., 271
Stahl, R., 406
Stahl, S., 132
Standage, M., 293, 295
Stanovich, K., 33
Stanovich, K. E., 272
Stanton-Salazar, R. D., 99
Staples, M., 402
Star, J., 204
Star, J. R., 204
Stark, R., 266
Steca, P., 326
Steele, M., 266, 404
Stein, B., 259
Steinberg, L., 63, 89, 309
Steiner, H. H., 149
Stellman, L., 382, 488
Stengel, B., 87
Stephens, K., 150
Sterberg, R., 260
Sternberg, R., 126, 127, 128, 129, 139, 140
Sternberg, R. J., 264
Stevens, K., 109
Stevens, R., 226, 228, 383, 406, 409
Stewart, E., 65, 65
Stiggins, R., 8, 186, 242, 294, 424, 434, 435, 441, 444, 445, 446, 448, 449, 451, 458, 460, 461, 473, 475
Stiggins, R. J., 8, 434, 435
Stigler, J., 21, 486
Stipek, D., 71, 185, 284, 285, 292, 294, 328, 330, 336, 403, 456, 461, 478, 494
Stoddard, E. R., 404
Stoltz, A., 79
Stoltzfus, J., 73
Story, R., 53
Stough, L. M., 324, 354
Strahan, D., 322
Straudt, J., 41
Strickland, B. B., 136
Stright, A., 113
Strong, R., 339
Struzynska-Kujalowicz, A., 165
Stuebing, K., 140
Sturmey, P., 170
Su, A. Y-L., 423, 424
Su, J.-M., 269
Sue, P-C., 269
Summerfield, J. P., 340
Sungur, S., 265
Sutherin, L. J., 265
Swank, P., 63
Swanson, C., 487
Swanson, J. M., 141
Swanson, T., 144
Sweeny, J. A., 205
Sweetland, J., 102
Sweller, J., 200, 201, 202, 203, 221, 240, 411
Swennen, A., 181
Szczesuil, S., 86

Talbert-Johnson, C., 269
Tamis-LeMonda, C. S., 51
Tannenbaum, A., 264
Tanner, D., 43
Tanner, L., 43
Tannock, R., 141
Taraban, R., 204
Tarter, C. J., 326
Tarver, S., 409
Taurer, J., 304
Taylor, B., 208, 333
Taylor, K., 307
Taylor, N., 259
Taylor, R., 412
Tekkaya, C., 236, 265
Tenenbaum, H., 109
Tennyson, R., 256

Terhune, K., 293
Terman, L., 149
Terry, S., 212, 213, 255
Terwilliger, J., 451
Texas Education Agency, 395, 396
Tharp, R., 228
Therriault, D., 270
Thiede, K. W., 270, 271
Thirunarayanan, M. O., 114
Thomas, K., 31, 205
Thorndike, E., 276
Thorndike, R. M., 475
Thousand, J., 135
Thrash, T., 304
Thurlow, M., 457
Tiegerman-Farber, E., 146
Tillema, H., 451
Timperley, H., 242, 341, 343, 402, 403
Tindal, G., 255
Tirosh, E., 216
Titsworth, S., 268
Titz, W., 311
Tollefson, N., 297
Tom, A., 87
Tomasello, M., 51, 52, 113, 119
Tomic, W., 326
Tomlinson, C., 462
Tomlinson, C. A., 153
Tomlinson-Clarke, S., 380
Tompkins, G., 52
Topping, D. H., 271
Torrens, A., 451
Tortora, M., 131
Townsend, B. L., 380
Trautwein, U., 413
Trawick-Smith, J., 68, 73, 100
Treasure, D. C., 295
Triona, L., 265
Trotter, A., 135
Troutman, A., 144, 172, 186, 378, 393
Trusty, J., 154
Trzesniewski, K., 70
Tschannen-Moran, M., 326, 327
Tseng, S-S., 269
Tubbs, M., 439
Tucker, M., 486
Tuculescu, G., 339
Tulving, E., 202
Tunmer, W. E., 71
Tunteler, E., 276
Turiel, E., 80, 81, 82, 84, 85
Turkanis, C., 228
Turnbull, A., 135, 136, 142, 143, 146, 148, 151, 152, 154, 155, 188, 409
Turnbull, R., 188
Turner, J. C., 284, 305, 310, 323
Turner, J. E., 421
Turner, M., 310
Turnure, J. E., 216
Twenge, J. M., 71
Twyman, T., 255
Tyler, R., 391

Ulanoff, S., 21
Uppal, S., 73
Urban, T. A., 205
Urdan, T., 305, 307, 320
Urdan, T. C., 293
U.S. Bureau of Census, 53, 97, 112
U.S. Department of Agriculture, 112
U.S. Department of Education, 113, 134, 138, 139, 143, 148
U.S. English, 105
Uygur, T., 213

Vacca, J., 270
Vacca, R., 270
Vacha-Haase, T., 326
Vadasy, P., 419
Valdez, A., 22
Valenzeno, L., 207
Valenzuela, A., 407
Valiante, G., 309
Van Damme, J., 404
van de Sande, C., 221, 233
VanDeWeghe, R., 264
Vang, C. T., 100
van Gelder, T., 34, 271, 272
van Gog, T., 266, 417
Van Horn, R., 14
van Luit, E. H., 409
van Merriënboer, J., 233, 240, 266
Van Patten, J., 486
Vansteenkiste, M., 293, 309
van Tartwijk, J., 372
Varenne, H., 130, 151
Vaughn, S., 135, 139, 140, 153, 154, 155, 157, 420, 434
Vavilis, B., 334
Vavilis, S., 334
Veenema, S., 127
Veenman, M. V., 219, 267
Veenman, S., 216
Venn, J. J., 462
Verkoeijen, P. P., 268
Vermeer, H. J., 309
Viadero, D., 76, 141, 243
Villa, R., 135
Villegas, A., 97
Vincent, M., 208, 333
Vogt, M., 104
Vohs, K., 70, 72
Volkow, N. D., 141
Von der Linden, N., 218
von Károlyi, C., 264
Vosniadou, S., 230, 236, 237
Vygotsky, L., 45, 46, 47, 197, 226, 227, 231, 233, 410, 419

Wadenmakers, E.-J., 311
Wadsworth, B. J., 20, 35, 36
Walberg, 63
Walberg, H., 75
Walker, H., 143
Walker, J. E., 173
Walker, J. M., 367, 368
Wallin, L., 293
Walpole, M., 489
Walsh, D., 33
Walsh, J. M., 435
Walsh, M., 227
Wang, Y., 47
Ware, H., 326
Warner, L., 144
Warren, B., 221
Waterhouse, L., 127
Watson, D., 86
Watson, M., 354, 359, 365, 376
Waxman, H., 120
Waxman, S., 52, 119
Way, N., 208
Wayne, A., 488
Wayne, S., 419
Wearing, H., 205
Webb, N., 241, 479
Webber, J., 143, 144
Weber, M., 457
Wechsler, D., 7, 476
Wehmeyer, M., 188
Weigel, D., 63, 99, 113
Weiland, A., 73
Weiner, B., 242, 294, 301, 302, 303
Weiner, L., 344, 358
Weinstein, C. S., 353, 354, 355, 361, 365, 368, 380
Weinstein, R., 329, 330, 383
Weinstein, T., 120
Weinstock, J., 302
Weismer, S. E., 205
Weiss, H., 113
Weiss, I., 401, 404
Weissberg, R., 75
Weissglass, S., 110
Welsh, L., 208, 333
Wenger, E., 240
Wenner, G., 113, 362
Wentzel, K., 77, 293, 305, 306
Wentzel, K. R., 293, 305, 306, 340
Wessler, S., 354
Whalen, C., 6
Whalen, C. K., 141
Wheeler, R., 102
Whitcomb, J., 14, 19
White, E. B., 80
White, P., 305
White, R., 292
Whitehurst, G., 32
Whitmore, J., 98
Whitmore, K., 197
Wigfield, A., 41, 108, 109, 116, 285, 293, 297, 299, 300, 306, 311, 340, 346, 355
Wilder, M., 328
Wiley, D., 355
William, D., 438, 461
Williams, C., 215, 216
Williams, J. M., 272
Williams, K., 439
Willingham, D. T., 33, 202, 271, 272
Willis, J., 33
Willoughby, T., 210
Wilson, B., 344, 345
Wilson, B. L., 86, 116, 117, 328, 344
Wilson, J. D., 454
Wilson, M., 451
Wilson, T., 100
Winitzky, N., 99–100
Winne, P., 185
Winsler, A., 46
Witherington, D., 85
Wittrock, M. C., 212, 230, 258, 259, 260, 261, 262, 266, 275, 417
Wixson, K. K., 271
Wolf, L., 313
Wolters, C., 295, 304
Wolters, C. A., 299, 304, 309, 320, 413
Wolz, D. J., 221
Wood, D., 47
Wood, E., 271
Wood, M., 70
Woolfolk Hoy, A., 326
Worsham, M. E., 8, 64, 172, 354
Wortham, S., 339
Worthy, J., 310
Wubbels, T., 372
Wylie, E. G., 441

Yates, L., 68, 69
Yeager, M., 15
Yearsley, T., 210
Yeh, Y.-C., 326
Yell, M. L., 187
Yeo, L. S., 208
Yeung, A. S., 71
Yip, D. Y., 236, 237, 241
Young, B., 111
Young, M., 113
Youngs, P., 488
Ysseldyke, J., 475, 476, 484
Yuan, R., 421
Yunker, B. D., 454

Zabel, R. H., 176, 357
Zacks, R., 215, 216
Zahn-Waxler, C., 67
Zahorik, J., 339, 341
Zambo, D., 139
Zan, B., 360
Zaragoza, N., 367
Zeelenber, R., 311
Zehr, M. A., 451
Zeidner, M., 313
Zhou, L., 172
Zhou, M., 309
Zhou, Q., 207
Zientarski, W. A., 435
Zimmerman, B., 185, 298, 322, 494
Zimmerman, B. J., 287, 288, 296, 298
Zins, J., 75
Zirkels, S., 106
Zirpoli, T. J., 173
Zucker, S., 116
Zuelke, D. C., 454
Zuiker, S. J., 288
Zull, J. E., 33
Zwiers, J., 114

subject index

ABA. *See* Applied behavior analysis (ABA)
Ability-focused goals, 304
Ability grouping, 130–131, 132, 423
Academic language proficiency, defined, 104
Academic learning time, 355
Acceleration, defined, 151
Accommodation
- conceptual change and, 236
- defined, 35
- Neo-Piagetian theory and, 43
- testing accommodations, 491, 493

Accountability
- constructivism and, 243
- defined, 13, 486
- formal assessment and, 451
- standardized testing and, 471, 473, 474, 475, 486–488
- standards and, 13, 395

Achievement
- ability grouping and, 131
- accountability and, 15
- assessment and, 435
- behavior disorders and, 143
- classroom management and, 354, 355
- cooperative learning and, 421
- correlational research on, 16, 17
- cultures and, 97–98, 100
- deliberate practice and, 263
- English Language Learners and, 103
- expectations and, 329, 330, 331
- gender differences and, 108–109
- goals and, 306–307
- identity achievement, 69
- learning styles and, 132
- note taking and, 268
- schema activation and, 212
- self-concept and, 71
- self-regulation and, 323
- socioeconomic status and, 111, 326–327
- students placed at risk and, 114
- teacher quality and, 13
- urban environments and, 87

Achievement motivation theory, 292
Achievement tests, 475
ACT, 473, 476–478, 479
Action research
- defined, 19
- guidelines for, 21
- professionalism and, 19–20, 21

Activities. *See also* Extracurricular activities
- attention and, 208
- feedback and, 341, 343
- hands-on activities, 341
- informal assessment during, 438–439
- introductory focus and, 336–338
- involvement and, 339–341
- knowledge construction and, 227, 238, 239
- motivation and, 322, 336–347
- personalization of, 338–339, 342
- preparing and organizing learning activities, 393–394
- sociocultural theory of development and, 46
- student input and, 332
- urban environment and, 366

Adaptation. *See also* Adaptive instruction
- defined, 35
- individualized education programs and, 137

Adaptive behavior
- assessment of, 153
- defined, 142
- learners with exceptionalities and, 157

Adaptive fit, defined, 134
Adaptive instruction
- attention-deficit/hyperactivity disorder and, 141
- collaborative consultation and, 152
- inclusion and, 153–154
- learners with exceptionalities and, 156
- learning disabilities and, 140
- mental retardation and, 143

Adolescence. *See also* High school students
- brain development and, 33
- characteristics of, 361–362
- identity and, 68, 69–70, 71
- self-concept and, 71
- self-esteem and, 70, 71
- social development and, 89

Adult–child interactions, 99–100
Adventures of Jasper Woodbury, The, 265
Affiliation, need for, 293
African Americans
- classroom management and, 380
- cultural attitudes and, 98–99, 101
- ethnic identity and, 73
- learner diversity and, 96
- motivation to learn and, 309
- need for belonging and, 344
- special education and, 151
- support of teachers and, 86

Aggression
- classroom management and, 382–384
- emotional intelligence and, 86
- long-term solutions to, 383–384
- peers and, 382
- social development and, 76–78

Algorithms, defined, 260
Allocated time, 355
Alternative assessment, defined, 462
Altruism, 84
American Association on Mental Retardation Adaptive Behavior Scale–Schools, 153
American Federation of Teachers, 488
American Sign Language, 148
Analogies
- concept learning and, 257
- defined, 212
- elaboration and, 212–213
- problem solving and, 261

Analytical dimension of intelligence, 128
Antecedents
- classroom use of, 177, 178
- defined, 173
- functional analysis and, 176
- operant conditioning and, 173–174

Anxiety
- defined, 311
- motivation to learn and, 311, 313
- test anxiety, 313, 456, 459

Appearances, misconceptions, 236
Application, guided discovery, 419
Applied behavior analysis (ABA)
- behavior disorders and, 144
- defined, 175
- functional analysis and, 176
- learners with exceptionalities and, 155, 175
- steps in, 175–176

Aptitude tests, 476–478
Arguments
- aggression and, 383
- avoiding, 373–374

Arizona, 103
Articulation disorders, 146
Asian Americans
- cultural attitudes and, 97–98
- learner diversity and, 96
- need for relatedness and, 309

Asperger syndrome, 145
Assertive discipline, 375
Assessment. *See also* Tests and testing
- achievement and, 435
- administration of, 457
- analyzing results, 457–459
- bias in, 463, 489–490, 493
- case studies on, 343, 431–433, 455, 457–458, 466–467
- classroom assessment, 434–436, 463
- concept mapping and, 269
- curriculum-based assessment, 153
- developmentally appropriate practice and, 465
- diagnostic assessment, 434–435, 474
- effective practices, 453–459
- effect on learning, 8
- feedback and, 294, 343, 435, 458, 459, 460, 463
- formal assessment, 242, 440–451
- formative assessment, 460
- grading and reporting, 459–464
- identifying learners with exceptionalities and, 152, 153
- informal assessment, 242, 437–440
- knowledge construction and, 242
- learner diversity and, 463
- as learning tool, 424–425
- motivation to learn and, 435
- planning for, 394, 424–425, 453–454, 459
- preparing students for, 454–456
- self-assessment, 186
- self-determination theory and, 293–294
- self-regulation and, 435
- standardized testing and, 474
- summative assessment, 460
- validity and, 435–436, 453

Assessment bias, 463, 489–490, 493
Assessment for learning, 242, 434, 458, 460
Assimilation
- conceptual change and, 236
- defined, 35
- Neo-Piagetian theory and, 43

Association, behaviorism, 165, 166
At-risk students. *See* Students placed at risk
Attainment value, 299–300
Attention
- attracting and maintaining, 207–208
- cognitive processes and, 207–208, 215
- constructivism, 239
- cues and, 174
- defined, 207
- developmental differences in, 216
- examples and, 240
- introductory focus and, 336–338
- meta-attention, 217, 219
- modeling and, 184, 189
- student involvement and, 172

Attention deficit/hyperactivity disorder (ADHD), 33, 140–141, 200, 216
Attitudes
- cultures and, 97–99, 274
- descriptive research and, 15
- essential teaching skills, 400–401, 407, 408
- peers and, 64–65
- socioeconomic status and, 113
- urban environments and, 407–408

Attributional statements, defined, 292

Attributions
beliefs and, 300–303, 312
characteristics of, 301
defined, 301
effort attributions, 327
emotions and, 311
hostile attributional bias, 77
Attribution theory
behavior and, 22
defined, 301
feedback and, 341
Attribution training, 303
Authentic tasks, 233
Authoritarian parenting style, 64, 77
Authoritative parenting style, 64
Autism spectrum disorders, 145
Automaticity
cognitive load and, 204, 206
defined, 201
procedural knowledge and, 204
retrieval and, 216, 247
Autonomous morality
defined, 81
promotion of, 87
Autonomy
adolescence and, 362
autonomy versus shame, 67
defined, 292
elementary students and, 359
motivation and, 285
need for, 292–293, 295, 296, 324, 334
order and safety, 332
portfolio assessment and, 450
self-regulation and, 324
socioeconomic status and, 113
Axons, defined, 31

Bandura, Albert, 179
Baseline, in applied behavior analysis, 175–176
Basic interpersonal communication skills, defined, 104
Basic Principles of Curriculum and Instruction (Tyler), 391
Behavior
consequences of, 167, 168
gender differences and, 109
ignoring inappropriate behavior, 378
inclusion and, 155
intervention for misbehavior, 371–381
learning disabilities and, 140
measuring changes in, 176
modeling and, 183
moral development and, 84
observable behavior, 180
praise for desired behavior, 378
rules governing, 77
standards for, 365
students placed at risk and, 114
target behaviors, 175–176
Behavior disorders
behavior management strategies, 144
defined, 143
teachers and, 144–145
types of, 143–144
Behaviorism
applications of, 189
applied behavior analysis and, 175–176
case studies on, 163–164, 165, 169, 171–172, 175, 177, 191–192
classical conditioning and, 164–167
defined, 164
emotions and, 164, 165, 166, 177, 190
interventions and, 376–377
language development and, 51
motivation and, 178, 286–287
operant conditioning and, 167–174
perspectives on, 176–178
principles of, 21, 22
social cognitive theory compared to, 180–181
views of learning, 164–178, 180, 196, 247
Behavior modification. *See* Applied behavior analysis (ABA)
Belief preservation, 272
Beliefs
attributions and, 300–303, 312
critical thinking and, 272
cultures and, 274
defined, 297
expectations and, 297, 302
intelligence and, 297
knowledge construction and, 237
moral development and, 80
motivation and, 287, 296–303
motivation to learn and, 296–303
personal teaching efficacy and, 326–327, 330
self-efficacy and, 298–299
self-regulation and, 323
societal beliefs, 236
values and, 299–300
Belonging, need for, 290, 291, 296, 327, 340, 344, 354, 362, 407
Between-class grouping, 130, 131
Bias
in assessment, 463, 489–490, 493
gender bias, 111
hostile attributional bias, 77
standardized testing and, 488, 489–490, 493
Bidialecticism, defined, 102
Bilingualism, defined, 105
Binet, Alfred, 34
Bioecological theory of development
additional systems in, 65
evaluation of, 65–66
microsystems and, 62–65, 86
Bipolar disorders, defined, 145
Black English, 102
Bloom's taxonomy, 392
Bodily-kinesthetic intelligence, 128
Boys. *See* Gender differences
Brain
cerebral cortex and, 32–33
cognitive development and, 31–33
gender differences and, 109
learning physiology of, 31–32
research on, 32–33
Brofenbrenner's bioecological theory of development, 62–66
Bronfenbrenner, Urie, 62
Bullies
defined, 76
informal assessment and, 439
parenting styles and, 77
responding to, 383
Bush, George W., 13, 487

California, 96, 103
Career choices
gender differences and, 110
identity development and, 68–69
learner diversity and, 119
modeling and, 185
Caring
communication of, 328
community of caring and trust, 354, 365, 380
defined, 327
morality of, 85
professional caring, 5
teachers and, 85, 117, 120, 289, 327–328, 330, 331, 344, 345, 354, 365, 400, 408
urban environments and, 344, 365
Case studies
on assessment, 343, 431–433, 455, 457–458, 466–467
on attribution, 300–301
on behaviorism, 163–164, 165, 169, 171–172, 175, 177, 191–192
on classroom management, 351–352, 356, 358, 360, 362, 364, 365, 385–386
on cognitive development, 29–30, 36, 42, 45, 48, 56–58
on cognitive learning theories, 195–196, 222–223
on cognitive processes, 214
communication with parents and, 368
on complex cognitive processes, 253–254, 280–281
on concept learning, 256
on content representation, 278
on cultures, 97, 99–100, 106–107
defined, 22
in educational psychology, 22–23
on essential teaching skills, 399–400
on ethnic identity, 73
on gender differences, 110
on goals, 303–304
on identity development, 68–69, 72
on instruction, 389–390, 426–427
on interventions, 372, 373–374, 376, 380, 381
on introductory focus, 336
on involvement, 340
on knowledge construction, 225–226, 227, 231–233, 234, 235, 240, 243, 244, 249–250
on learner diversity, 95–96, 121–122
on learners with exceptionalities, 125–126, 150, 158–160
on learning problems, 138, 141–142, 143, 144
on lecture-discussion, 414–417
on linguistic diversity, 103, 106–107
on memory, 202, 203, 220, 222–223
on moral development, 61–62, 82, 85, 87
on motivation, 283–284, 287, 289, 295, 303–304, 312, 315–316, 319–320, 330, 342, 348–349
on pedagogical content knowledge, 10
on perception, 208–209
on personal development, 61–62, 90–91
on personalization, 338–339
on problem solving, 258, 261–262, 266, 272–273
on professionalism, 3–4
on professional knowledge, 24–26
on research, 21
on rules, 366
on self-regulation, 322, 323–324
on social cognitive theory, 163–164, 179, 182, 186, 191–192
on social development, 61–62, 75, 77, 90–91
on standardized testing, 471–473, 478, 495–496
strategic learning and, 273
on students placed at risk, 114–117
on urban environments, 344, 364, 365
Caucasian Americans
classroom management and, 380
cultural attitudes and, 97–98, 99
motivation to learn and, 309
population of, 97
self-esteem and, 73
Causation
attributional statements and, 292
attributions and, 300–303
personal causation, 293
reciprocal causation, 180–181
Central executive
defined, 199
working memory and, 199, 200
Centration (centering), 38, 41
Cerebral cortex, 32–33
Challenge
motivation and, 333, 334, 335
urban environments and, 346–347
Characteristics, defined, 255
Charlotte's Web (White), 80
Charts, 208, 210
Cheating, 79, 80, 82–84, 457
Checklists, 449
Child development. *See* Cognitive development; Emotional development; Moral development; Personal development; Psychosocial development; Social development

Chinese Americans
cultural attitudes and, 98
ethnic identity and, 73
Chronosystem, defined, 65
Chunking, defined, 201
Cities. *See* Urban environments
Classical conditioning
in classrooms, 165–166, 190
defined, 164
discrimination and, 166
examples of, 166
extinction and, 166–167
generalization and, 166
operant conditioning compared to, 168
Classification
defined, 40
mental retardation and, 142, 490
Classroom assessment
assessment for student learning, 434
defined, 434
learner diversity and, 463
reliability and, 436
validity and, 435–436
Classroom connections
ability differences and, 132
assessment design and, 464
assessment practices and, 459
beliefs and, 302
Bronfenbrenner's bioecological theory and, 66
classical conditioning and, 166
climate variables and, 335
cognitive processes and, 215
communication with parents and, 371
concept learning and, 257
conceptual change and, 238
constructivism and, 245
Erikson's psychosocial development and, 74
essential teaching skills and, 407
gender differences and, 111
goals and, 308
informal assessment and, 440
instructional variables and, 345
interest and emotions promoting motivation to learn, 311
interventions and, 379
language development and, 54
learner diversity and, 105
learners with exceptionalities and, 156
memory stores and, 206
metacognition and, 218
models of instruction and, 422
moral development and, 88
needs and, 296
operant conditioning and, 178
Piaget's views applied in, 44
planning for classroom management and, 367
planning for instruction and, 398
problem solving and, 267
self-regulation and, 325
social cognitive theory and, 187
social development and, 78
standardized testing and, 485
strategic learning and, 275
students placed at risk and, 118
teacher characteristics and, 331
test bias and, 493
transfer and, 277
valid and reliable assessments, 453
Vygotsky's theory of development applied in, 50
Classroom management. *See also* Productive learning environments
authoritative style of, 64, 72
behaviorism and, 178
class size and, 65
communication with parents and, 367–371
complexities of classrooms and, 353
defined, 354
effectiveness of, 8
in elementary schools, 359–361
general pedagogical knowledge and, 11
goals of, 354–356
importance of, 352–356
influence on motivation and learning, 354
intervention for misbehavior, 371–381
learner diversity and, 380
learning disabilities and, 139–140
in middle and secondary schools, 361–364
moral development and, 87, 89
operant conditioning and, 167
planning for, 356–367
principles of planning, 356–358
public and professional concerns, 352–353
urban environments and, 364–366
violence and aggression, 382–384
Classrooms. *See also* Productive learning environments
action research in, 19–20
behaviorism and, 177, 178
classical conditioning and, 165–166, 190
complexity of, 353
constructivism in, 238–244
culture and, 97–101, 105
dialects in, 102
Erikson's psychosocial development and, 74
gender differences and, 109
master-focused environment and, 320–322
moral development and, 87, 88
motivation and, 332–335
order and safety in, 332–333, 335, 342, 353
organization of, 357–358
personalization of, 363–364
physical arrangement of, 361, 363
positive classroom climate, 332
small-school feeling in, 86
social development in, 77
structure in, 120, 366
students placed at risk in, 116–117
success and, 333, 335
time in, 355–356
Classwork, as punishment, 173
Cliques, defined, 65
Closure
essential teaching skills, 406, 408
guided discovery and, 419
Codes of power, 102
Cognition. *See also* Metacognition
situated cognition, 229–230, 233, 266, 267, 277
Cognitive activity, 213–214, 239, 269, 339, 416
Cognitive apprenticeships
defined, 229
knowledge construction and, 246
problem solving and, 267
verbalization and, 229, 233, 246
Cognitive behavior modification, defined, 188
Cognitive constructivism, 226–227
Cognitive development. *See also* Piaget's theory of cognitive development
brain and, 31–33
case studies on, 29–30, 36, 42, 45, 48, 56–58
current views of, 43–44
defined, 30
experience and, 30, 32, 35, 42–43, 44, 180
factors influencing, 30
social interaction and, 36–37, 44, 45, 48, 50
Cognitive domain
defined, 391
learning objectives in, 391–393
Cognitive learning theories
case studies on, 195–196, 222–223
concept mapping and, 269
defined, 196
direct instruction and, 410, 411, 413
guided discovery and, 417, 418
interventions and, 374–376
knowledge construction and, 197, 230
learning objectives and, 392
lecture-discussion and, 414, 415
memory and, 198
motivation and, 287
principles of, 196–198
problem solving and, 258
rules and, 361
schemas and, 35
Cognitive load
automaticity and, 204, 206
concepts and, 254
defined, 200
limitations of working memory and, 200–201, 239
organization and, 210
problem solving and, 262
reducing, 201
withitness and, 372–373
Cognitive modeling
defined, 182
knowledge construction and, 233
social cognitive theory and, 182, 189
Cognitive processes. *See also* Complex cognitive processes
attention, 207–208, 215
developmental differences in, 216–217
encoding, 209–214, 215
forgetting and, 214–216
in information processing model, 207
learning objectives and, 392
metacognition and, 217–219
perception and, 208–209, 215, 216
planning for instruction and, 398
retrieval, 214–216
social cognitive theory and, 180
Cognitive styles. *See* Learning styles
Cognitive tasks, information processing theory, 43–44
Cognitive tools, defined, 46
Collective efficacy
achievement and, 326–327
defined, 326
Collective self-esteem, defined, 73
Colorblindness, defined, 101
Columbine massacre of 1999, 76
Commercially prepared test items, 446
Communication
cooperative learning and, 421
essential teaching skills and, 401–402, 407, 408
verbal-nonverbal congruence, 374–375, 379, 381
Communication disorders
defined, 146
teachers and, 146–147
Communication with parents
benefits of, 368
classroom management and, 367–371
culture and, 101
grading and, 462–463
learner diversity and, 367
portfolio assessment and, 451
sample letter to parents, 369
solutions to aggression and, 383
strategies for involving parents, 368, 370
Community of caring and trust
classroom management and, 365, 380
defined, 354
Community of learners
characteristics of, 228–229, 354
defined, 228
motivation and, 288
Competence
assessment and, 294
autonomy and, 293, 295
challenge and, 333
defined, 291
feedback and, 341
modeling and, 185
need for, 291–292, 295, 329

Competence, *continued*
personal and social competence, 383
Completion, defined, 444
Complex cognitive processes
case studies on, 253–254, 280–281
concept learning and, 254–257
learner diversity and, 274
problem solving and, 258–267
strategic learning and, 267–273
transfer of learning and, 275–279
Comprehension monitoring, 270, 271, 416
Computer software. *See* Software
Concept learning
complex cognitive processes and, 254–257
examples and, 256–257
exemplar theories of, 256
prototype theories of, 255
rule-driven theories of, 255
theories of, 255–256
Concept mapping, 269–270
Concepts. *See also* Self-concept
in content areas, 255
defined, 254
preoperational stage and, 38
Conceptual change
examples and, 240
misconceptions and, 236–237
promotion of, 238
Concrete operational stage, 37, 39–40
Conditional knowledge
defined, 202
in long-term memory, 202, 203, 204
problem solving and, 259
Conditioned response, defined, 165
Conditioned stimulus, defined, 165
Conditioning
classical conditioning, 164–167, 190
operant conditioning, 167–174
Connected discourse, 401
Consequences
applying, 379–381
classroom management and, 366
defined, 167
logical consequences, 376, 379–380
moral development and, 81
nonoccurrence of expected consequences, 182, 184, 263
operant conditioning and, 167, 168, 172, 173
sample consequences for following/breaking rules, 377
Conservation
defined, 38
Neo-Piagetian theory and, 43
preoperational stage and, 38–39
Consistency
interventions and, 373, 381
reliability and, 436
Constructivism. *See also* Knowledge construction
characteristics of, 230–233
in classrooms, 238–244
cognitive constructivism, 226–227
concept learning and, 256
defined, 226
instruction and, 238, 240–242, 247–248
memory and, 238–239, 247
misconceptions and, 234–237
note taking and, 268
perspectives on, 245–248
Piaget's theory of cognitive development and, 43
social constructivism, 227–230, 354, 417, 421
Construct validity, 479
Content. *See also* Pedagogical content knowledge
bias in, 490
concepts in content areas, 255
high-quality examples and, 240, 245
knowledge of, 8–9
portfolio samples in content areas, 449
real-world experiences and, 240–241, 243, 245
representation of, 10, 241, 278
Content validity, 479
Continuous reinforcement schedules, 170–171, 176, 177
Conventional morality, 82–83
Cooperation
cultures and, 100
scripted cooperation, 421
Cooperative learning
defined, 419
effective use of, 422
features of, 420
introducing to students, 421
knowledge construction and, 197
learners with exceptionalities and, 155, 157
models of, 421
perspectives on, 421, 423–424
Correlation
defined, 16
positive and negative correlations, 16–17
Correlational research
defined, 16
evaluating, 17
quantitative representation of, 16–17
Cost
defined, 300
response cost, 172–173
Creative dimension of intelligence, 128
Creativity
defined, 263
enrichment and, 151
essays and, 444
motivation and, 285
in problem solving, 263–264
Crisis, defined, 67
Criterion-referenced grading, 461
Criterion-reference standardized tests, 474–475
Critical periods, 32
Critical thinking
advertising and, 271–272
challenge of, 272
cultures and, 274
defined, 271
essays and, 444
promoting, 272–273, 275
Criticism, competence, 292
Cross-age tutoring, 155
Crystallized intelligence, defined, 127
Cues
as antecedents, 174
indirect cues, 378
Culturally diverse students. *See* Learner diversity
Culturally responsive classroom management, 380
Cultural mismatch, 97, 100
Cultures
adult–child interactions and, 99–100
beliefs and, 272
case studies on, 97, 99–100, 106–107
classrooms and, 97–101, 105
cognitive development and, 42–43, 50
cognitive processes and, 216
complex cognitive processes and, 274
context of, 45–47, 48, 228
defined, 96
ethnicity and, 96–97
intelligence and, 126, 127
learner diversity and, 96–101
moral development and, 82, 84
parenting styles and, 64
role models and, 98–99, 190
self-esteem and, 73
social conventions and, 80
special education and, 151, 157
urban environment and, 86
Curriculum-based assessment, defined, 153

Deaf, defined, 148
Decision making
formal assessment and, 440
formative and summative assessment, 460
professionalism and, 5, 6
standardized testing and, 473–475, 478, 493
Declarative knowledge
defined, 202
direct instruction and, 411
in long-term memory, 202–204
problem solving and, 258
Defiant students, 383
Deficiency needs, defined, 291
Deliberate practice, 263
Demonstrations
attention and, 208
pedagogical content knowledge and, 10
Dendrites, defined, 31
Descriptive research
defined, 15
evaluating descriptive studies, 15–16
scientifically based research and, 19
Descriptive statistics
frequency distributions, 480–481
measures of central tendency, 481
measures of variability and, 481–482
normal distribution, 482
Desists
defined, 172, 378
intervention and, 378–379
Detention, 172
Development. *See also* Cognitive development; Emotional development; Moral development; Personal development; Psychosocial development; Social development
Bronfenbrenner's biological theory of, 62–66
culture and, 47
defined, 30
of language, 50–54, 55, 102, 105, 106, 107, 148
principles of, 30
social interaction and, 45–46
Developmental differences
in attention, 216
classroom management and, 356–357
defined, 12
in memory stores, 205
in metacognition, 218–219
in perception, 216–217
in self-efficacy, 299
thinking and, 12
Developmentally appropriate practice
assessment and, 465
behaviorism and, 189
classroom management and, 384
cognitive development and, 55
complex cognitive processes and, 278
constructivism and, 246
defined, 12
language development and, 55
learner diversity and, 119
learners with exceptionalities and, 157
memory and, 219
models of instruction and, 423
motivation to learn and, 313, 346
personal, social, and moral development and, 89
social cognitive theory and, 189
standardized testing and, 494
Diagnostic assessment
defined, 434
measuring understanding and, 434–435
standardized testing and, 474
Diagnostic tests, 475
Dialects, 101–102
Differences. *See* Developmental differences; Gender differences; Learner diversity
Direct instruction
defined, 409

developing understanding, 411–412
effective use of, 422
guided practice, 412
homework, 412–413
independent practice, 412
introduction and review, 411
phases of, 409–410
Direct modeling, 181
Disabilities. *See also* Individuals with Disabilities Education Act (IDEA); Learners with exceptionalities
defined, 126
hearing disabilities, 147–148
learning disabilities, 138–140
learning problems and, 137–138
visual disabilities, 147
Discipline. *See also* Classroom management
defined, 354
Discrepancy model of identification, defined, 140
Discrepant events, 208
Discrimination
bias in test interpretation and use, 490
classical conditioning and, 166
learners with exceptionalities and, 137
operant conditioning and, 174
self-esteem and, 73
Disorders
behavior disorders, 143–145
communication disorders, 146–147
defined, 137
Distracters, defined, 441
Divergent thinking, defined, 264
Diversity. *See* Learner diversity
Domain-specific knowledge, 264
Down Syndrome, 142
Drawing analogies, defined, 261
Dropout rates
behavior disorders and, 143
English Language Learners and, 103
need for belonging and, 340, 344
social development and, 75
socioeconomic status and, 111, 113, 114
Dual-coding theory, defined, 210
Due process, defined, 135

Economic status. *See* Socioeconomic status (SES)
Education. *See also* Special education
multicultural education, 106
standards-based education, 486
Educational psychology
case studies used in, 22–23
defined, 4
professionalism and, 4–6
Educational Testing Service, 13
Effective teaching
assessment and, 394
defined, 390
Egocentric speech, 46
Egocentrism, defined, 39
Ego-involved goals, 304
Elaboration
concept mapping and, 269
defined, 212
encoding and, 212–213, 215, 217
examples and analogies, 212–213
mnemonics and, 213
Elaborative questioning, 271
Elaborative rehearsal, 212, 217
Elementary and Secondary Education Act, 487
Elementary students
ability grouping and, 130, 132
assessment and, 453, 459, 464, 465
behaviorism and, 189
beliefs and, 302
bioecological theory of development and, 66
characteristics of, 359
classical conditioning and, 166
classroom climate variables and, 335
classroom management in elementary schools, 359–361, 367, 384
cognitive development and, 30, 44, 50, 55
cognitive processes and, 215
communication with parents and, 371
complex cognitive processes and, 278
concept learning and, 257, 278
conceptual change and, 238
constructivism and, 245, 246
developmental differences and, 12
emotions and, 311
Erikson's psychosocial development and, 74
essential teaching skills and, 407
gender differences and, 111
goals and, 308
informal assessment and, 440, 465
instructional variables and, 345
interest and, 311
interventions and, 379
language development and, 54, 55
learner diversity and, 105, 119
learners with exceptionalities and, 156, 157
memory and, 219
memory stores and, 206
metacognition and, 218, 219
models of instruction and, 422, 423
moral development and, 88, 89
motivation to learn and, 313, 331, 346
needs and, 296
operant conditioning and, 178
planning for instruction and, 398
problem solving and, 267, 278
self-regulation and, 325
social cognitive theory and, 187, 189
social development and, 78, 89
standardized testing and, 485, 493, 494
strategic learning and, 275, 278
students placed at risk and, 118
transfer and, 277
ELLs. *See* English language learners (ELLs)
Embarrassment, as punishment, 173
Emotional development
defined, 30
learner responsibility and, 355
self-concept and, 70
Emotional intelligence, defined, 86
Emotions
aggression and, 77
behaviorism and, 164, 165, 166, 177, 190
competence and, 292
episodic memory and, 202
gender differences and, 109
modeling and, 184
moral development and, 85–86
motivation to learn and, 310–311, 313
peers and, 65
test anxiety and, 456
Empathy
defined, 85
teacher caring and, 327, 345
Emphasis, 208, 401
Encoding
cognitive activity and, 213–214
cognitive processes and, 209–214, 215
constructivism and, 239
defined, 209
elaboration and, 212–213, 215, 217
imagery and, 210
meaningful learning and, 209, 210, 218
metacognition and, 218
organization and, 210–211
schema activation, 212
Engaged time, 355
English as a second language (ESL) pullout programs, defined, 104
English dialects, 101–102
English language learners (ELLs)
assessment and, 463
communication disorders and, 146
communication with parents and, 367
defined, 102
evaluating ELL programs, 105–106
high-quality examples and, 240
high-stakes tests and, 487
language development and, 53
population of, 102–103
standardized testing and, 490–491
testing accommodations for, 491, 493
types of ELL programs, 103–104
urban environments and, 120
Enrichment, 151, 156
Entity view of intelligence, 297–298, 305
Environment. *See also* Productive learning environments; Urban environments
aggression and, 77
bioecological theory of development and, 62–65
gender differences and, 108
language development and, 50–51
least restrictive environment, 133–135
mastery-focused environment, 320–322, 324
maturation and, 30
performance-focused environment, 320, 321, 343
standards-based environment, 395–398
Environmental conditions, as antecedents, 174
Episodic memory, defined, 202
Equilibrium
adaptation and, 35
defined, 34
knowledge construction and, 227, 272
misconceptions and, 236
motivation and, 287
order and safety, 332
organization and, 35
urban environments and, 366
Equitable distribution, in questioning, 404–405
Erikson, Erik, 66
Erikson's psychosocial development, 67–68
Essays
defined, 444
guidelines for preparing, 445
Essential teaching skills
attitudes and, 400–401, 407, 408
case studies on, 399–400
closure and, 406, 408
communication and, 401–402, 407, 408
defined, 400
feedback and, 402–403, 407, 408
focus and, 402, 407, 408
organization and, 401, 407, 408
questioning and, 404–405, 407, 408
reviews and, 406, 407, 408
in urban environments, 406–409
Ethics
classroom management and, 365
learner responsibility and, 355
moral development and, 80, 82–83
Ethnic identity, defined, 73
Ethnicity
assessment bias and, 489
cultures and, 96–97
defined, 96
ethnic identity, 73
Evaluation
of bioecological theory of development, 65–66
identity development and, 69
performance assessment and, 448–449
problem solving and, 261–262
program evaluation, 474
Examples
cognitive processes and, 216
concept learning and, 256–257

Examples, *continued*
direct instruction and, 412
elaboration and, 212–213
high-quality examples, 240, 242, 243, 245, 277
pedagogical content knowledge and, 10
quality of, 276
students placed at risk and, 117
variety of, 277
worked examples, 266
Exceptionalities. *See* Learners with exceptionalities
Exemplars, defined, 256
Exosystem, defined, 65
Expectancy X value theory, 297, 299
Expectations
beliefs and, 297, 302
cultures and, 97–98
defined, 297
gender differences and, 109
motivation and, 287, 289, 297
parenting styles and, 63–64
perception and, 208–209
social cognitive theory and, 180, 181, 182
socioeconomic status and, 113
students placed at risk and, 117, 118
of teachers, 328–331, 344, 345, 364, 400, 456
Experience
cognitive development and, 30, 32, 35, 42–43, 44, 180
cognitive learning theories and, 197
cognitive processes and, 216–217
diversity in, 216
intelligence and, 129, 130
knowledge construction and, 240
misconceptions and, 236
motivation and, 287
peak experiences, 291
with physical world, 36
prior knowledge and, 205
problem solving and, 260, 261
professionalism and, 5
professional knowledge and, 8, 12, 14
social cognitive theory and, 180
social experience, 36–37
socioeconomic status and, 112–113
urban environments and, 409
Experimental research
defined, 17
evaluating, 17–18
scientifically based research and, 19
Experts
defined, 262
problem solving and, 262–263
Explanations, constructivism, 241, 245
Explicit instruction, 52
Explicit knowledge, 202, 203
Expressive disorders, 146
Externalizing behavior disorders, 143–144
External morality, defined, 81
Extinction
classical conditioning and, 166–167
defined, 167, 171
ignoring inappropriate behavior and, 378
operant conditioning and, 171–172
Extracurricular activities
conditional regard and, 289
learners with exceptionalities and, 134
resilience and, 115
self-concept and, 71
urban environments and, 86
Extrinsic motivation, defined, 285

FAPE (free and appropriate education), 133
Feedback
assessment and, 294, 343, 435, 458, 459, 460, 463
defined, 402
essential teaching skills and, 402–403, 407, 408
formative assessment and, 460, 464
grading and, 460
modeling and, 184
motivation and, 341, 343, 345, 402
reflective practice and, 5
social cognitive theory and, 180
social development and, 77
students placed at risk and, 117
urban environments and, 408–409
First-letter method of mnemonic devices, 213
Fixed schedules, 170, 171
Fluency disorders, 146
Fluid intelligence, defined, 127
Focus
ability-focused goals, 304
essential teaching skills and, 402, 407, 408
introductory focus, 336–338, 345
mastery-focused environment, 320–322, 324
sensory focus, 402
task-focused goals, 304
Follow through, 373
Forgetting
defined, 214
as interference, 214–215
Formal assessment
assessment for learning and, 242
commercially prepared test items, 446
defined, 440
paper-and-pencil items, 441–446, 451, 458, 461
performance assessments, 446–449, 453, 454, 461, 462
perspectives on, 451
portfolio assessment, 449–451, 453, 461
reliability of, 440
Formal operational stage, 37, 40–42
Formative assessment, 460, 464
Free and appropriate education (FAPE), 133
Frequency distributions, 480–481
Frontal lobes, 32–33
Functional analysis, defined, 176
Gardner's theory of multiple intelligences, 127–128, 129
Gender bias, 111
Gender differences
assessment bias and, 489
attention-deficit/hyperactivity disorder and, 140, 141
autism spectrum disorders and, 145
behavior disorders and, 144
bullying and, 76
interest and, 340
Kohlberg's theory of moral development and, 85
learner diversity and, 108–111, 119
learning disabilities and, 140
motivation to learn and, 309
stereotypes and, 109–110
stereotype threat and, 99
Gender-role identities, 108
Generalization
antecedents and, 174
applied behavior analysis and, 176
defined, 166
overgeneralization, 51–52
undergeneralization, 52
General pedagogical knowledge
defined, 10
professionalism and, 10–11
General transfer, 275–276
Generativity versus stagnation, 67
Genetics. *See* Heredity
Geometric Supposer, The, 265
Germany, 473
"G" (general intelligence), 127
Gifts and talents. *See also* Students who are gifted and talented
defined, 126
Girls. *See* Gender differences
Goal monitoring, 307, 322, 323, 324, 325, 332
Goals
achievement and, 306–307
case studies on, 303–304
of classroom management, 354–356
cognitive learning theories and, 197
defined, 304
effective use of, 307–308
mastery goals, 304–305, 306, 309, 310, 311, 312, 323, 334
motivation to learn and, 303–308
performance goals, 304–305, 306, 309, 311
self-regulation and, 185, 322–325
social goals, 305–306
TARGET program and, 334, 335
types of, 306
work-avoidance goals, 306
Goal setting, 307, 322, 323, 325, 332
Golden Rule, 84
Grade-equivalent scores, 484
Grading
assigning grades, 462–464
considerations of, 459–460
cooperative learning and, 423–424
designing grading system, 460–462
informal assessment and, 439
mastery goals and, 323
performance goals and, 305
rubrics and, 445–446
scores and, 463–464
Graphic organizers, 257
Group differences. *See* Learner diversity
Grouping, by ability, 130–131, 132, 423
Growth needs, 290, 291
Guided discovery
application, 419
closure and, 419
convergent phase, 418–419
defined, 417
effective use of, 422
introduction and review, 418
open-ended phase, 418
phases of, 417–419
Guided notes, defined, 269
Guided practice, direct instruction, 412
Guilt
defined, 85
initiative versus guilt, 67

Handicaps. *See also* Learners with exceptionalities
defined, 137
disabilities and, 137–138
Hawaii, 96
Hearing disabilities, 147–148
Help, offers of, 292
Hemispheric specialization, 33
Heredity
aggression and, 77
bioecological theory of development and, 62, 65
gender differences and, 108
homosexuality and, 70
language development and, 50–51
maturation and, 30
mental retardation and, 142
Heuristics
defined, 260
problem solving and, 260–261, 262
Hierarchies
concept mapping and, 270
Maslow's hierarchy of needs, 288, 290–291, 296, 327, 332
organization and, 210
Higher-order functions, behaviorism and, 177
High-quality examples, 240, 242, 243, 245, 277
High school students
ability grouping and, 130, 132
assessment and, 453, 459, 464, 465
behaviorism and, 189
beliefs and, 302
bioecological theory of development and, 66
characteristics of, 361–362, 363
classical conditioning and, 166
classroom climate variables and, 335
classroom management and, 361–364, 367, 384

cognitive development and, 30, 44, 50, 55
cognitive processes and, 215
communication with parents and, 371
complex cognitive processes and, 278
concept learning and, 257
conceptual change and, 238
constructivism and, 245, 246
developmental differences and, 12
emotions and, 311
Erikson's psychosocial development and, 74
essential teaching skills and, 407
gender differences and, 111
goals and, 308
informal assessment and, 440
instructional variables and, 345
interest and, 311
interventions and, 379
language development and, 54, 55
learner diversity and, 105, 119
learners with exceptionalities and, 156, 157
memory and, 219
memory stores and, 206
metacognition and, 218, 278
models of instruction and, 422, 423
moral development and, 79, 88, 89
motivation to learn and, 313, 331, 346
needs and, 296
operant conditioning and, 178
planning for instruction and, 398
problem solving and, 267, 278
self-regulation and, 325
social cognitive theory and, 187, 189
social development and, 78, 89
standardized testing and, 485, 493, 494
strategic learning and, 275, 278
students placed at risk and, 118
transfer and, 277
High-stakes tests, 451, 487
Hispanics
ethnic identity and, 73
need for relatedness and, 309
parenting styles and, 64
population of, 96
special education and, 151
Hmong culture, 100
Homelessness, 113
Homework
action research on, 21
assessment options, 461–462
characteristics of effective homework, 413
direct instruction and, 412–413
grading and, 461
Homosexuality, 70
Hostile attributional bias, defined, 77
Hughes, Langston, 102
Humanistic psychology, 288–289, 332
Humiliation, as punishment, 173, 189

IDEA. *See* Individuals with Disabilities Education Act (IDEA)
Identity
adolescence and, 68, 69–70, 71
career choices and, 68–69
defined, 66
development of, 68–70, 72
Erikson's psychosocial development and, 66–67, 68
ethnic identity, 73
gender-role identities, 108
identity versus confusion, 67
promoting development of, 72
sexual identity, 70
Identity achievement, 69
Identity diffusion, 69
Identity foreclosure, 69
Identity formation, 69
Identity moratorium, 69
IEPs (individualized education programs). *See* Individualized education programs (IEPs)
Ill-defined problems, 259, 260–261, 265, 266
Imagery
concept mapping and, 269
defined, 210
I-messages, 375
Immersion programs, 103, 105
Immigration Act of 1965, 96–97
Implicit knowledge, 202, 203
Inclusion
behavior and, 155
collaborative consultation and, 152
controversies of, 135
defined, 134
identifying learners with exceptionalities, 152–153
modifying instruction and, 153–154
social integration and, 154–155, 156
teacher's role in, 152–155, 156
Incremental view of intelligence, 297–298, 302, 305, 327, 456
Independent practice, 412
Indirect cues, 378
Individual differences. *See* Learner diversity
Individualized education programs (IEPs)
adaptations and, 137
collaborative consultation and, 152
defined, 135
functions of, 135
grading and, 462
sample of, 136
Individuals with Disabilities Education Act (IDEA)
amendments to, 137
attention-deficit/hyperactivity disorder and, 140
due process and, 135
fair and nondiscriminatory education and, 135
free and appropriate education and, 133
individualized education programs and, 135–137
least restrictive environment and, 133–135
parent involvement and, 153
Industry versus inferiority, 67
Informal assessment
assessment for learning and, 242
defined, 437
elementary students and, 440, 465
as formative assessment, 460
in larger school context, 439
learning activities and, 438–439
reliability of, 439–440
Information processing
learning styles and, 131
Neo-Piagetian theory and, 43
Information processing theory
cognitive tasks and, 43–44
defined, 43, 198
model of, 198, 207, 218, 220, 239
Inhibitions, defined, 183
Initiative versus guilt, 67
Instruction. *See also* Adaptive instruction; Models of instruction
ability grouping and, 131
assessment and, 343, 394
case studies on, 389–390, 426–427
constructivism and, 238, 240–242, 247–248
direct instruction, 409–413, 422
effective instruction, 366, 379, 389
learning activities and, 393–394
learning objectives and, 391–393
learning styles and, 132–133
misconceptions of, 235
motivation and, 336–347
planning for, 390–398
social constructivism and, 227–228
topic selection, 390–391
transmission view of, 248
working memory and, 200
Instructional alignment
assessment and, 465
planning for, 394–395, 398, 453
self-determination and, 294
Instructional principles. *See* Theory to practice
Instructional strategies. *See* Strategies
Instructional time, 355
Instructional variables
classroom climate and, 342
feedback and, 341, 343, 345
introductory focus and, 336–338, 345
involvement and, 339–341, 345
personalization and, 338–339, 345
urban environments and, 343–347
Instrumental aggression, 76
Integrity versus despair, 67
Intelligence
ability grouping and, 130–131, 132
beliefs about, 297
defined, 126
entity view of, 297–298, 305
Gardner's theory of multiple intelligences, 127–128, 129
gender differences and, 109
goals and, 305
incremental view of, 297–298, 302, 305, 327, 456
issues and controversies of, 7
learners with exceptionalities and, 126–133
learning styles and, 131–133
nature versus nurture, 130
socioeconomic status and, 111
Sternberg's triarchic theory of intelligence, 128–129, 130
tests for, 126–127, 475–476
traits and, 127–129
Interactive Physics, 265
Interest
involvement and, 339–341
modeling of, 310, 327, 331
motivation to learn and, 309–310, 312
personal interest, 309–310
situational interest, 309–310
Interference
defined, 214
forgetting as, 214–215
Intermittent reinforcement schedules, 170, 171, 176, 177
Internalization, defined, 46
Internalizing behavior disorders, 143, 144
Interpersonal harmony stage, defined, 83
Interpersonal intelligence, 128
Interval schedules, 170, 171
Interventions
behavioral interventions, 376–377
cognitive interventions, 374–376
continuum of, 377–381
functional analysis and, 176
for misbehavior, 371–381
principles of successful interventions, 372–374
Intimacy versus isolation, 67
Intrapersonal intelligence, 128
Intrinsic motivation, defined, 285
Introductory focus
defined, 336
motivation and, 336–338, 345
tools and techniques for, 338
Involvement
defined, 339
hands-on activities and, 341
open-ended questions and, 339–341
strategies for promoting, 341, 345
urban environments and, 345–346
IQ scores
mental retardation and, 142
students who are gifted and talented and, 149

Japan, 274, 473
Jigsaw II, 421
Joplin plan, 130, 131

Keyboarding skills, 200, 201, 202
Key-word method of mnemonic devices, 213
Knowledge. *See also* Pedagogical content knowledge; Prior knowledge
  conditional knowledge, 202, 203, 204, 259
  of content, 8–9
  context-specific knowledge, 14
  creativity and, 264
  declarative knowledge, 202–204, 258, 411
  domain-specific knowledge, 264
  in long-term memory, 202–204
  organized bodies of, 413
  procedural knowledge, 202, 258, 262, 392
  professional knowledge, 6–12, 13, 14–22, 24–26
Knowledge construction. *See also* Constructivism
  case studies on, 225–226, 227, 231–233, 234, 235, 240, 243, 244, 249–250
  cognitive constructivism and, 226–227
  cognitive learning theories and, 197, 230
  lecture-discussion and, 417
  misconceptions and, 234–237, 246
  Piaget and, 49, 226, 272
  Piaget and Vygotsky compared, 49
  prior knowledge and, 230–231, 240
  rules and procedures and, 360
  social interaction and, 197, 227, 228, 231–233, 241, 245, 246
  urban environments and, 242–244
  Vygotsky and, 227, 233, 498
  working memory and, 199
Kohlberg, Lawrence, 81
Kohlberg's theory of moral development
  gender differences and, 85
  moral dilemmas and, 81–82, 84, 85
  perspectives on, 84
  stages of moral reasoning, 82–84

Labeling controversy, 138
LADs (language acquisition devices), 51
Language. *See also* English language learners (ELLs)
  assessment and, 463
  behaviorism and, 196
  cerebral cortex and, 32
  cultural influences on, 228
  development and, 46, 48
  linguistic diversity, 101–107
  misconceptions and, 236
  precise language, 401
  special education and, 151, 157
  working memory and, 205
Language acquisition
  critical periods and, 32
  preoperational stage and, 38
  research on, 18
  sociocultural theory of development and, 45
Language acquisition devices (LADs), 51
Language development
  dialects and, 102
  early childhood, 51–52
  hearing disabilities and, 148
  learner diversity and, 53, 105, 106, 107
  promotion of, 54, 55
  syntax and, 52–53
  theories of, 50–51
  vocabulary and, 52
Language disorders, defined, 146
Law and order stage, 83
Laws
  learners with exceptionalities and, 133–137
  learning problems and, 138
  moral development and, 84
  No Child Left Behind Act, 13, 15, 486–487, 491
Learned helplessness
  defined, 303
  learner diversity and, 309
  visual disabilities and, 147
Learner-Centered Psychological Principles, 333
Learner diversity
  assessment and, 463
  behaviorism and, 190
  case studies on, 95–96, 121–122
  classroom management and, 380
  cognitive processes and, 216
  communication disorders and, 146
  communication with parents and, 367
  complex cognitive processes and, 274
  cultures and, 96–101
  defined, 96
  equity in special education and, 151
  feedback and, 408–409
  gender differences and, 108–111, 119
  knowledge construction and, 237
  language development and, 53, 105, 106, 107
  linguistic diversity, 101–107
  motivation to learn and, 309
  personalization and, 340
  self-esteem and, 73
  social cognitive theory and, 190
  socioeconomic status and, 111–117
  standardized testing and, 489–491
  urban environments and, 14, 120, 364, 463
Learners. *See also* Learner diversity
  assessment's effect on, 8
  attributions' impact on, 301–302
  commitment to, 4–5
  community of learners, 228–229, 288, 354
  creativity in, 264
  dignity of, 373, 381
  knowledge of, 11
  meaningfulness and, 204
  responsibility of, 354, 355–356, 376, 384
  urban environments and, 86
Learners with exceptionalities
  applied behavior analysis and, 155, 175
  attention deficit/hyperactivity disorder, 33, 140–141
  autism spectrum disorders, 145
  behavior disorders and, 143–145
  bipolar disorders, 145
  case studies on, 125–126, 150, 158–160
  communication disorders, 146–147
  defined, 126
  developmentally appropriate practice and, 157
  grading and, 462
  hearing disabilities, 147–148
  identification of, 152–153
  intelligence and, 126–133
  labeling controversy and, 138
  laws regarding, 133–137
  learning disabilities, 138–140
  mental retardation and, 141–143
  population of students with disabilities, 138
  students who are gifted and talented and, 149–151
  students with learning problems and, 137–148
  teacher's role in inclusive classrooms, 152–155, 156
  visual disabilities, 147
Learning
  assessment and, 462, 464
  behaviorist views of, 164–178, 180, 196, 247
  classroom management and, 354
  cognitive perspectives on, 196–198
  constructivism and, 226, 246–247
  cultural contexts and, 45–47
  defined, 164, 180
  gender differences and, 108, 109
  knowledge of, 11–12
  language development and, 52–53
  Learning and Teaching Inventory, 7–8
  motivation for, 285–286
  social cognitive theory and, 180, 196, 247
  socioeconomic status and, 112–113
  vicarious learning, 182, 184, 187, 361, 378
  working memory and, 200
Learning contexts. *See also* Urban environments
  constructivism and, 242–244
  cultural context, 45–47, 48, 228
  informal assessment and, 439
  personal, social, and moral development in, 86–87
  real-world contexts and, 266
  transfer and, 230, 275, 277, 279
Learning disabilities
  causes of, 138–139
  characteristics of students with, 139
  defined, 138
  identifying and working with students, 139–140
Learning environment, productive. *See* Productive learning environments
Learning objectives
  assessment and, 435, 453
  in cognitive domain, 391–393
  criterion-referenced grading and, 461
  defined, 391
  formal assessment and, 441
  Gronlund's approach, 391–392
  Mager's approach, 391
  standards and, 395–398
Learning problems
  attention deficit/hyperactivity disorder, 33, 140–141
  autism spectrum disorders, 145
  behavior disorders and, 143–145
  bipolar disorders, 145
  case studies on, 138, 141–142, 143, 144
  communication disorders, 146–147
  disabilities and, 137–138
  hearing disabilities, 147–148
  labeling controversy and, 138
  learning disabilities, 138–140
  mental retardation and, 141–143
  visual disabilities, 147
Learning strategies
  cognitive load and, 201
  learners with exceptionalities and, 154, 156
  modeling of, 219
  motivation to learn and, 312
  self-regulation and, 187, 322
  work-avoidance goals and, 306
Learning styles
  defined, 131
  intelligence and, 131–133
  learning preferences and, 132
  teachers and, 132–133
Least restrictive environment (LRE)
  continuum of services for implementing, 134
  defined, 134
  Individuals with Disabilities Education Act and, 133–135
Lecture-discussion
  case studies on, 414–417
  effective use of, 422
  lectures and, 414
  organized bodies of knowledge and, 413
  overcoming weakness of lectures with, 414–415
Lesson plans, 395–398
Linguistic diversity, 101–107, 119. *See also* English language learners (ELLs)
Linguistic intelligence, 128
Link method of mnemonic devices, 213
Listening, 53
Lists, checklists, 449
Locus of control, 293
Logical consequences, 376, 379–380

Logical-mathematical intelligence, 128
Long-term memory
capacity of, 202
classroom application of, 206
conditional knowledge in, 202, 203, 204
declarative knowledge in, 202–204
defined, 201
dual-coding capability of, 210
encoding and, 209
perception and, 209
procedural knowledge in, 202, 203, 204–205
Louisiana, 96
LRE. *See* Least restrictive environment (LRE)

Macrosystem, defined, 65
Mainstreaming
defined, 133
least restrictive environment and, 133–134
Maintenance ELL programs, 103–106
Maintenance rehearsal
defined, 199
encoding and, 217
long-term memory and, 209
metacognition and, 218
working memory and, 199–200, 209
Maps, concept mapping, 269–270
Market exchange stage, 82
Maslow's hierarchy of needs, 288, 290–291, 296, 327, 332
Mastery-focused environment
defined, 320
motivation and, 320–322
performance-focused environment compared to, 321
self-regulation and, 324
Mastery goals, 304–305, 306, 309, 310, 311, 312, 323, 334
Matching format, defined, 443
Matrices, 210, 211, 454
Maturation
cognitive development and, 36
defined, 30
Mean, 481
Meaningful learning
assessment and, 465
concept learning and, 257
declarative knowledge and, 202–204
elaboration and, 212
encoding and, 209, 210, 218
implications for teachers and learners, 204
involvement and, 339
prior knowledge and, 205
promotion of, 206
situated cognition and, 233
social interaction and, 211
Meaningfulness
defined, 203
retrieval and, 216
Means–ends analysis, 260–261
Measurement, standard error of measurement, 485
Measures of central tendency, 481
Measures of variability, 481–482
Media, bioecological theory of development and, 63
Median, 481
Memory. *See also* Long-term memory; Sensory memory; Working memory
anxiety and, 313
case studies on, 202, 203, 220, 222–223
constructivism and, 238–239, 247
cultures and, 274
developmentally appropriate practice and, 219
direct instruction and, 410, 411
guided discovery and, 417
information processing theory and, 198
metamemory, 217–218, 219
modeling and, 184
model of human memory, 198, 207, 218, 220, 226, 239, 247
note taking and, 268–269
safe learning environment and, 332–333
social cognitive theory and, 180
Memory stores
characteristics of, 205
defined, 199
developmental differences in, 205
long-term memory and, 201–205
sensory memory and, 199, 205
working memory and, 199–201, 205
Mental Measurements Yearbook, 478n
Mental retardation
classification and, 142, 490
defined, 142
instruction for, 143
learning problems and, 141–143
levels of, 142
Mesosystem, defined, 65
Meta-attention, 217, 219
Metacognition
cognitive processes and, 217–219
critical thinking and, 272
defined, 217, 267
developmental differences in, 218–219
goals and, 308
in information processing model, 218
motivation to learn and, 312
problem solving and, 259
self-assessment and, 186
self-regulation and, 322
strategic learning and, 267–268
transfer and, 279
Metamemory, 217–218, 219
Metaphors, pedagogical content knowledge and, 10
Method of loci, mnemonic devices, 213
Mexican Americans. *See* Hispanics
Microsystems
bioecological theory of development and, 62–65, 86
defined, 62
Middle school students
ability grouping and, 130, 132
assessment and, 453, 459, 464, 465
behaviorism and, 189
beliefs and, 302
bioecological theory of development and, 66
characteristics of, 361–362
classical conditioning and, 166
classroom climate variables and, 335
classroom management and, 361–364, 367, 384
cognitive development and, 30, 44, 50, 55
cognitive processes and, 215
communication with parents and, 371
complex cognitive processes and, 278
concept learning and, 257
conceptual change and, 238
constructivism and, 245, 246
developmental differences and, 12
emotions and, 311
Erikson's psychosocial development and, 74
essential teaching skills and, 407
gender differences and, 111
goals and, 308
informal assessment and, 440
instructional variables and, 345
interest and, 311
interventions and, 379
language development and, 54, 55
learner diversity and, 105, 119
learners with exceptionalities and, 156, 157
memory and, 219
memory stores and, 206
metacognition and, 218, 219, 278
models of instruction and, 422, 423
moral development and, 88, 89
motivation to learn and, 313, 331, 346
needs and, 296
operant conditioning and, 178
planning for instruction and, 398
problem solving and, 267, 278
self-esteem and, 71
self-regulation and, 325
social cognitive theory and, 187, 189
social development and, 78, 89
standardized testing and, 485, 493, 494
strategic learning and, 275, 278
students placed at risk and, 118
transfer and, 277
Misconceptions
assessment and, 425, 458, 463
conceptual change and, 236–237
defined, 235
knowledge construction and, 234–237, 246
in learning theory, 235
multiple-choice items and, 441
origins of, 236
prior knowledge and, 197, 236
problem solving and, 258
resistance to change and, 236
Mississippi, 96
Mnemonic devices
defined, 213
types and examples of, 213
Mode, 481
Models and modeling
cognitive apprenticeships and, 229
cognitive modeling, 182, 189, 233
critical thinking and, 272
cultures and, 98–99, 190
defined, 181
direct instruction and, 410
effectiveness of, 184–185
effects of, 183–184
forms of, 181
inclusion and, 154, 155
incremental views of intelligence, 298, 327, 456
interest and, 310, 327, 331
mastery goals and, 310
metacognition and, 218, 219, 308
model responses to written assignments, 403
moral development and, 87
organization and, 210
pedagogical content knowledge and, 10
processes involved in learning from, 184
self-assessment and, 186
self-regulation and, 324, 330
social cognitive theory and, 181–185, 186, 187, 188, 189
social development and, 77
Models of instruction
cooperative learning, 155, 157, 197, 419–424
defined, 409
direct instruction, 409–413, 422
guided discovery, 417–419, 422
lecture-discussion, 413–417, 422
Monitoring
comprehension monitoring, 270, 271, 416
goal monitoring, 307, 322, 323, 324, 325, 332
self-regulation and, 186
Moral development
aggression and, 77
bioecological theory of development and, 62–66
case studies on, 61–62, 82, 85, 87
communities of caring and trust and, 354
defined, 62
emotional factors in, 85–86
informal assessment and, 439
interest increasing in, 79–80

Moral development, *continued*
moral, conventional, and personal domains, 80–81
promotion of, 87
Moral dilemmas
defined, 81
Kohlberg on, 81–82, 84, 85
teachers' use of, 87
Moral domains, 80
Motherese, 51
Motivation. *See also* Self-regulation
ability grouping and, 131
assessment and, 458
behaviorism and, 178, 286–287
case studies on, 283–284, 287, 289, 295, 303–304, 312, 315–316, 319–320, 330, 342, 348–349
classroom management and, 354
classrooms and, 332–335
cooperative learning and, 419
defined, 284
divergent thinking and, 264
extrinsic motivation, 285
feedback and, 341, 343, 345, 402
grading and, 462
instructional variables and, 336–347
intrinsic motivation, 285–286
introductory focus and, 336–338, 345
involvement and, 339–341
for learning, 285–286
learning styles and, 132
mastery-focused environment and, 320–322, 324
model for promoting, 321–322
modeling and, 184
pedagogical content knowledge and, 9
personalization and, 338–339, 342, 345
praise and, 8, 292, 333
standardized testing and, 494
stereotype threat and, 99
students placed at risk and, 114
teacher characteristics and, 325–331
test-preparation procedures and, 456
theoretical views of, 286–289, 332
urban environments and, 120, 343–347, 364, 366
Motivation to learn
assessment and, 435
beliefs and, 296–303
defined, 286
developmentally appropriate practice and, 313, 346
emotions and, 310–311, 313
goals and, 303–308
interest and, 309–310, 312
intrinsic motivation and, 285–286
learner diversity and, 309
needs and, 290–295
Multicultural education, defined, 106
Multiple-choice items
defined, 441
guidelines for preparing, 442
higher-level learning assessment and, 441–442
high-stakes testing and, 451
interpretive exercise in, 442
Multiple intelligences, 127–128, 129
Musical intelligence, 128
Myelination, 32

NAEP (National Assessment of Educational Progress), 15, 486
National Academy of Education, 13, 487
National Assessment of Educational Progress (NAEP), 15, 486
National norms, 473
Nation at Risk, A (National Commission on Excellence in Education), 486
Native Americans, 309
Nativist theory, defined, 51
Naturalist intelligence, 128
Nature view of intelligence, defined, 130
Need for approval, 293
Needs
defined, 290
growth needs, 290, 291
Maslow's hierarchy of, 288, 290–291, 296, 327, 332
motivation to learn and, 290–295
self-determination theory and, 291–294, 327, 334, 340, 344, 354
self-worth and, 294–295, 296
socioeconomic status and, 112–113
Negative correlations, 16–17
Negative reinforcement, 169–170, 235
Negligence, defined, 382
Neighborhoods
bioecological theory of development and, 63, 65
knowledge construction and, 242
Neo-Piagetian theory, defined, 43
Networks, defined, 270
Neurons
defined, 31
hemispheric specialization and, 33
research on, 32
Neutral stimulus, defined, 165
New Mexico, 96
No Child Left Behind Act (NCLB)
accountability and, 486–487
English language testing and, 491
public's attitude toward, 15
reforms and, 13
Nonoccurrence of expected consequences, 182, 184, 263
Nonverbal communication, 374–375
Normal distribution, of scores, 482
Norming groups, 473
Norm-referenced grading, 460–461
Norm-reference standardized tests, 474–475
Norms
in classrooms, 353
national norms, 473
North Carolina, 112
Note taking, 269–270
Nurture view of intelligence, defined, 130

Object permanence, 35, 38
Observation
identifying learners with exceptionalities and, 153
motivation and, 287
self-observation, 186
social cognitive theory and, 179, 180
systematic observation, 448–449
Open-ended questions
defined, 340
involvement and, 339–341
urban environments and, 408
Operant conditioning
antecedents and, 173–174
classical conditioning compared to, 168
defined, 167
punishment and, 172–173
reinforcement and, 168–172
Order and safety
in classrooms, 332–333, 335, 342, 353
defined, 332
in urban environments, 344–345
Organization
classroom organization, 357–358
concept mapping and, 269
defined, 35, 210, 357
encoding and, 210–211
essential teaching skills and, 401, 407, 408
guided notes and, 269
Organized bodies of knowledge, defined, 413
Outlines, 211
Overgeneralization
defined, 51
language development and, 51–52

Pacific Island culture, 99–100
Paper-and-pencil items
completion, 444
essays, 444–445
grading and, 461
item file and, 458
matching format, 443
multiple-choice items, 441–442, 451
rubrics and, 445–446
true-false, 443
Parenting styles
defined, 63
personal development and, 63–64
social development and, 77
Parents. *See also* Communication with parents
bioecological theory of development and, 63–64, 65
collaborative consultation and, 152
cultures and, 100–101
gender differences and, 109
learners with exceptionalities and, 135, 152, 153, 154
psychosocial development and, 67
resilience and, 115
socioeconomic status and, 113, 114
strategies for involving, 368, 370
urban environments and, 364
Partial hearing impairment, defined, 148
Pavlov, Ivan, 165
Peak experiences, 291
Pedagogical content knowledge
communication and, 401–402
defined, 9
professionalism and, 9–10
task analysis and, 393–394
topic selection and, 391
Peer mediation, aggression and violence prevention and, 78
Peers
aggression and, 382
basic interpersonal communication skills and, 104
bioecological theory of development and, 62, 64–65
high school students and, 361, 362, 384
identity and, 68
learners with exceptionalities and, 157
middle school students and, 361, 362, 384
need for approval and, 293
social development and, 65, 89
Peer tutoring, learners with exceptionalities and, 154, 155, 157
Peg-word method of mnemonic devices, 213
People-first language, defined, 138
Percentile bands, 484
Percentile ranks, 474, 483–484
Percentiles, 483–484
Perception
cognitive processes and, 208–209, 215, 216
constructivism and, 239
defined, 208
developmental differences in, 216–217
preoperational stage and, 38
Performance-approach goals, 304–305, 306
Performance assessments
as alternative assessment, 462
defined, 446
designing evaluation procedures, 448–449
elementary students and, 465
establishing criteria for, 454, 461
example of persuasive writing assessment, 447
grading and, 461
processes and products as components, 447
reliability and, 451
specifying performance components, 447

structuring evaluation setting, 448
validity and, 453
Performance-avoidance goals, 304–305, 306
Performance-focused environment
defined, 320
feedback and, 343
mastery-focused environment compared to, 321
Performance goals, 304–305, 306, 309, 311
Permissive parenting style, 64
Personal causation, 293
Personal development
bioecological theory of development and, 62–66
case studies on, 61–62, 90–91
defined, 30, 62
Erikson's psychosocial development theory and, 66–68
informal assessment and, 439
parenting styles and, 63–64
peers and, 64–65
Personal domain, 81
Personal interest, 309–310
Personalization
of classrooms, 363–364
defined, 339
learner diversity and, 340
motivation and, 338–339, 342, 345
Personal teaching efficacy
attitudes and, 400
beliefs and, 326–327, 330
defined, 326
Perspective taking
aggression and, 77
defined, 75
social development and, 75, 78, 89
Phi Delta Kappan/Gallup Poll of the Public's Attitude Toward the Public Schools, 15
Phonological loop
defined, 199
working memory and, 199–200, 201
Physical aggression, 76
Physical development, defined, 30
Physical punishment, 173, 189
Physical world, experience with, 36
Piaget, Jean, 34
Piaget's theory of cognitive development
behavior explained by, 22
descriptive research and, 15
egocentric speech and, 46
equilibrium and, 34
factors influencing development, 35–37
organization and adaptation and, 35
perspectives on, 42–43
stages of development, 37–42, 75
Vygotsky's views compared to, 49
Piaget's views
classroom application of, 44
on knowledge construction, 49, 226, 272
moral development theory, 81, 85
on motivation, 287
order and safety, 332
Pictures, 208
Placement, standardized testing used for, 474, 476
Planning
for assessment, 394, 424–425, 453–454, 459
for classroom management, 356–367
for cooperative learning, 421, 423, 424
for instruction, 390–398
in standards-based environment, 395–398
task analysis as tool of, 393–394
Portfolio assessment
defined, 449
features of, 450
grading and, 461
guidelines for, 451
self-regulation and, 453
Positive classroom climate, 332
Positive correlations, 16–17
Positive reinforcement, 169, 189
Postconventional morality, 83–84
Practical dimension of intelligence, 128
Practice. *See also* Developmentally appropriate practice; Theory to practice
automaticity and, 204, 206
deliberate practice, 263
guided practice, 412
independent practice, 412
modeling and, 184
reflective practice, 5–6
test-preparation procedures and, 456
wisdom of practice, 14
Praise
for desired behavior, 378
feedback and, 403
motivation and, 8, 292, 333
Praxis Series
components of, 488
reforms and, 13
Precise language, 401
Preconventional morality, 82, 83
Predictive validity, 479
Premack principle, defined, 169
Preoperational stage, 37, 38–39
Preparing Instructional Objectives (Mager), 391
Presentation punishment, defined, 172
Principles of Learning and Teaching (PLT) tests, 13
Prior knowledge
constructivism and, 230–231, 245
examples and, 212–213
feedback and, 402
forgetting and, 214–215
high-quality examples and, 240, 242, 245
introductory focus and, 338
knowledge construction and, 197
language and, 53
learner diversity and, 216
memory stores and, 205
misconceptions and, 197, 236
perception and, 209
personal interest and, 310
problem solving and, 258, 260, 261
self-concept and, 87
socioeconomic status and, 113, 216
strategic learning and, 268
urban environments and, 87, 242, 346, 364, 409
Private speech, defined, 46
Proactive aggression, 76
Proactive interference, defined, 214
Problem-based learning
defined, 264
problem solving and, 264–266
technology and, 265–266
Problems. *See also* Learning problems
attention and, 208
defined, 258
identification of, 260
ill-defined problems, 259, 260–261, 265, 266
representation of, 260
well-defined problems, 259, 266
Problem solving
action research and, 21
cerebral cortex and, 32
complex cognitive processes and, 258–267
cooperative learning and, 421
creativity in, 263–264
enrichment and, 151
expert-novice differences in, 262–263
imagery and, 210
model of, 259–262
problem-based learning and, 264–266
social problem solving, 76, 78, 89, 155
well-defined and ill-defined problems and, 259
Procedural knowledge
defined, 202
learning objectives and, 392
in long-term memory, 202, 203, 204–205
problem solving and, 258, 262
Procedures
bias in testing procedures, 490
classroom management and, 358
defined, 358
in elementary classrooms, 359–361, 384
in middle and secondary classrooms, 362–363
student input and, 332
test-preparation procedures, 456, 459, 492–493
Productive learning environments. *See also* Classroom management
behaviorism and, 175
creativity and, 264
defined, 352
interdependence of management and instruction, 357
physical arrangement of classroom and, 361
Professional caring, 5
Professionalism
action research and, 19–20, 21
case study on, 3–4
characteristics of, 4–6, 19
Professional knowledge
case study of, 24–26
decision making and, 6
learning to teach and, 6–12
reform and accountability, 13
research and, 14–22
Program evaluation, standardized testing, 474
Programs. *See* Software
Prompts
as antecedents, 174
questioning and, 405, 408
Prototypes, defined, 255
Psychosocial development
applying in classroom, 74
life-span stages, 67
personal development and, 66–68
perspectives on, 67–68
Puerto Ricans. *See* Hispanics
Punishers
applied behavior analysis and, 175–176
classroom use of, 178
defined, 172
effective use of, 172–173
misconceptions of, 235
social cognitive theory and, 180
Punishment
behavioral interventions and, 376, 377
defined, 172
effective use of, 172–173
humiliation as, 173, 189
ineffective forms of, 173
operant conditioning and, 172–173
social cognitive theory and, 180
Punishment-obedience stage, defined, 82

Qualitative research
defined, 18
quantitative research versus, 18–19
Quantitative research, qualitative research versus, 18–19
Questioning frequency, 404
Questions and questioning
cognitive levels of questions, 406
critical thinking and, 272
cultures and, 99–100
direct instruction and, 412
elaborative questioning, 271
encoding and, 214
essential teaching skills and, 404–405, 407, 408
guided discovery and, 417
involvement and, 339–341
lecture-discussion and, 416
misconceptions and, 237
operant conditioning and, 169
organization and, 211

Questions and questioning, *continued*
- perception and, 209
- procedural knowledge and, 204–205
- research on, 14–15, 16, 17
- students placed at risk and, 117
- thought-provoking questions, 208
- urban environments and, 242, 243, 408
- working memory and, 206

Random assignment
- defined, 17
- evaluating experimental research and, 17–18
- scientifically based research and, 19

Range, of scores, 481–482
Rating scales, 449, 450
Ratio schedules, 170, 171
Raw scores, 483
Reactive aggression, 76
Readiness tests, 478
Reading
- ability grouping and, 130, 131
- language development and, 53
- socioeconomic status and, 113

Real-world tasks
- content related to, 240–241, 243, 245
- defined, 233
- performance assessments and, 448
- problem solving and, 266, 267

Receptive disorders, 146
Reciprocal causation
- defined, 181
- social cognitive theory and, 180–181

Reciprocal questioning, 421
Reflective practice
- defined, 5
- professionalism and, 5–6

Reform movements, 463, 473, 486
Reforms, defined, 13
Reinforcement
- behavioral interventions and, 376
- defined, 168
- extinction and, 171–172, 378
- negative reinforcement, 169–170, 235
- operant conditioning and, 168–172
- positive reinforcement, 169, 189
- satiation and, 172
- shaping and, 170
- social cognitive theory and, 180

Reinforcement schedules
- applied behavior analysis and, 175–176
- classroom use of, 178
- effects on behavior and, 170–171
- examples of, 171

Reinforcers
- classroom use of, 177
- defined, 168
- motivation and, 286
- response cost and, 172–173
- social cognitive theory and, 180
- timing and spacing of, 170–171

Relatedness, need for, 293, 296, 309, 327–328, 332–333, 344, 354, 362, 408
Relational aggression, 76
Reliability
- in assessments, 436
- of formal assessment, 440
- of informal assessments, 439–440
- of portfolio assessment, 451
- relationship with validity, 436
- rubrics and, 445–446

Removal punishment, defined, 172
Reproduction, modeling and, 184
Research
- on ability grouping, 130–131
- action research, 19–20, 21
- on assessment, 458
- on attention-deficit/hyperactivity disorder and, 140
- on brain, 32–33
- on caring, 328
- on classroom management, 352–353, 354, 358
- on cooperative learning, 419–420
- correlational research, 16–17
- on cultural attitudes, 97–98
- defined, 14
- descriptive research, 15–16, 19
- on English Language Learner programs, 105–106
- experimental research, 17–18, 19
- on formal operational thinking, 41–42
- on grading, 462
- on guided discovery, 417
- on homework, 413
- on homosexuality, 70
- on introductory focus, 338
- on learning styles, 132–133
- on motivation, 285
- on neurons, 32
- on note taking, 268
- on problem-based learning, 265
- on problem solving, 259, 266
- professional knowledge and, 14–22
- qualitative research, 18–19
- scientifically based research, 19
- socioeconomic status and, 113, 114
- on standardized testing, 490–491
- test-anxious students and, 313
- theory development and, 20–22
- on transfer, 276
- urban environments and, 120
- on working memory, 200

Resilience
- defined, 115
- socioeconomic status and, 115–117

Resistance cultures, 98, 101
Response cost, 172–173
Response to intervention model of identification, defined, 140
Responsiveness, parenting styles and, 63–64
Retention, modeling and, 184
Retrieval
- automaticity and, 216, 247
- cognitive processes and, 214–216
- defined, 215

Retroactive interference, defined, 214
Reversibility, defined, 38–39
Reviews, essential teaching skills, 406, 407, 408
Rewards, as motivation, 286–287, 333
Ripple effect, 183
Rogers' person-centered therapy, 288–289
Role models
- cultures and, 98–99, 190
- teachers as, 181, 184, 185, 327, 330, 331, 400

Rote learning, 203, 209, 211
Rubrics
- defined, 445
- grading and, 445–446
- sample rubric for paragraph structure, 446

Rules
- behavior disorders and, 144
- classroom behavior and, 77
- classroom management and, 358, 359–363, 365
- communication with parents and, 370
- community of learners and, 228
- concept learning and, 255
- creating and teaching, 366
- defined, 358
- in elementary classrooms, 359–361, 384
- external morality and, 81
- inhibitions and, 183
- learner responsibility and, 354–355
- in middle and secondary classrooms, 362–363
- moral development and, 89
- nonoccurrence of expected consequences, 182
- sample consequences for following/breaking rules, 377
- student input and, 332, 360, 362

Safety
- classroom management and, 354, 366, 382
- interventions and, 373
- needs and, 291
- order and safety, 332–333, 335, 342, 344–345, 353

SAT, 473, 476–478, 479
Scaffolding
- challenge and, 333
- cognitive apprenticeships and, 229
- defined, 47
- formative assessment as, 460
- guided discovery and, 417
- informal assessment and, 439
- knowledge construction and, 233
- language development and, 51, 54
- learners with exceptionalities and, 156
- modeling and, 184
- motivation and, 288
- motivation to learn and, 297
- problem solving and, 262, 266, 267
- self-regulation and, 323
- teachers and, 47, 50
- urban environments and, 87
- Vygotsky's view of development and, 47, 48

Scarlet Letter, The (Hawthorne), 80, 222–223
Schema activation, defined, 212
Schemas
- cognitive learning theories and, 35
- defined, 202
- guided discovery and, 418
- knowledge construction and, 227, 233, 239
- lecture-discussion and, 416–417
- in long-term memory, 202–203, 206
- misconceptions and, 236
- problem solving and, 262
- as scripts, 204
- self-schemas, 300

Schemes
- defined, 35
- experience with physical world and, 36
- motivation and, 287
- social experience and, 36–37

Schools
- beginning of school year, 358–359
- bioecological theory of development and, 62, 65
- gender differences and, 108
- moral development and, 79–80
- resilience promoted by, 115–116
- violence and aggression in, 76–78

Scientifically based research, defined, 19
Scores
- descriptive statistics and, 480–482
- essays and, 444
- grade-equivalent scores, 484
- interpreting, 482–485, 493
- IQ scores, 142, 149
- norming groups and, 473
- percentiles, 474, 483–484
- points versus percentages, 463–464
- raw scores, 483
- reliability and, 436, 461
- social comparison and, 294
- standard error of measurement and, 485
- standardized testing, 474, 479–485
- standard scores, 484–485
- stanines, 484

Scripted cooperation, 421
Scripts, defined, 204
Secondary students. *See* High school students
Selection, standardized testing used for, 474, 476
Self-actualization, 288, 291
Self-concept
- defined, 66
- development of, 70–71
- promoting development of, 72, 74
- self-efficacy contrasted with, 298
- urban environments and, 87

Self-determination
defined, 291
self-regulation and, 322–325
Self-determination theory
assessment and, 293–294
classroom application of, 296
need for autonomy and, 292–293, 324, 332, 334
need for competence and, 291–292, 295, 329
need for relatedness and, 293, 327, 332–333, 340, 344, 354
Self-efficacy
defined, 298
developmental differences in, 299
expectations and, 330
factors influencing, 298
feedback and, 341
goals and, 307, 324
motivation to learn and, 299, 312
personal teaching efficacy, 326–327, 330
success and, 333
Self-esteem
ability grouping and, 131
defined, 70
emotional intelligence and, 86
extracurricular activities and, 71
learner diversity and, 73
resilience and, 115
students placed at risk and, 114
visual disabilities and, 147
Self-fulfilling prophecy
defined, 329
expectations and, 329–330
Self-handicapping behaviors, 294–295, 304–305
Self-instruction, 188
Self-regulation
aggression and, 77
assessment and, 435
cognitive behavior modification and, 188
defined, 185, 322
feedback and, 341
goals and, 185, 322–325
learning styles and, 132
mastery-focused environment and, 324
monitoring progress and, 186
moral development and, 87
portfolio assessment and, 453
private speech and, 46
self-determination and, 322–325
social cognitive theory and, 185–188, 189
strategy use and, 187
students placed at risk and, 117
Self-schemas, 300
Self-talk, 188
Self-worth. *See also* Self-esteem
beliefs and, 298
defined, 70, 294
need to preserve, 294–295, 296
Semantic memory, defined, 202
Semantics, defined, 52
Sensorimotor stage, 37–38
Sensory focus, 402
Sensory memory
characteristics of, 205
classroom application of, 206
defined, 199
Seriation, defined, 40
SES. *See* Socioeconomic status (SES)
Sexual identity, defined, 70
Sexual orientation, defined, 70
Shame, defined, 85
Shaping
classroom use of, 178
defined, 170
Sheltered English, defined, 104
Short-term memory, defined, 200
Similarity
modeling and, 185
transfer and, 276
Simulations
pedagogical content knowledge and, 10
performance assessment and, 448
Situated cognition, 229–230, 233, 266, 267, 277
Situational interest, 309–310
Skinner, B. F., 167
Social cognitive theory
applications of, 189
behaviorism compared to, 180–181
case studies on, 163–164, 179, 182, 186, 191–192
defined, 179
interventions and, 376
language development and, 51
modeling and, 181–185, 186, 187, 188, 189
motivation and, 287
perspectives on, 188
self-regulation and, 185–188, 189
vicarious learning and, 182, 184, 187, 361
Social comparisons, 294–295, 343
Social constructivism
cognitive apprenticeships and, 229
community of learners and, 228–229, 354
conceptual change and, 237
cooperative learning and, 421
defined, 227
guided discovery and, 417
situated cognition and, 229–230
social interaction and, 231–233, 241
sociocultural theory and, 228
transfer and, 277
Social contract stage, defined, 84
Social conventions, 80, 82, 83
Social development
bioecological theory of development and, 62–66
case studies on, 61–62, 75, 77, 90–91
defined, 30, 62
Erikson's psychosocial development and, 66–68
informal assessment and, 439
learner responsibility and, 355
peers and, 65, 89
perspective taking and, 75, 78, 89
promotion of, 77
self-concept and, 70
social problem solving, 76, 78, 89
tracking and, 131
violence and aggression in schools, 76–78
Social experience, 36–37
Social goals, 305–306
Social interaction
cognitive development and, 36–37, 44, 45, 48, 50
cooperative learning and, 419
guided discovery and, 418
inclusion and, 154–155, 156
knowledge construction and, 197, 227, 228, 231–233, 241, 245, 246
meaningful learning and, 211
problem solving and, 266, 267
social cognitive theory and, 188
urban environments and, 243–244
Social problem solving
aggression and violence prevention and, 78
defined, 76
modeling of, 155
social development and, 76, 78, 89
Social-responsibility goals, 305, 306, 312
Societal beliefs, misconceptions and, 236
Sociocultural theory of development
cultural context and, 45–47, 228
defined, 45, 228
motivation and, 288
Socioeconomic status (SES)
ability grouping and, 130
achievement and, 111, 326–327
assessment bias and, 489, 490
behavior disorders and, 144
characteristics of difference socioeconomic levels, 112
cognitive processes and, 216
communication with parents and, 367
defined, 111
impact of, 111–112
learner diversity and, 111–117
learning and, 112–113
resilience and, 115–117
special education and, 151
students placed at risk and, 114–115
Software
gender differences and, 108
problem solving and, 265
Spatial intelligence, 128
Special education
defined, 126
English Language Learners and, 103
equity in, 151, 157
inclusion and, 135
learning problems and, 138
least restrictive environment and, 134
Specific transfer, 275–276
Speech, hearing disabilities and, 148
Speech disorders, defined, 146
SQ3R, 271
STAD (Student Teams Achievement Divisions), 421
Standard deviation, 482
Standard English, 102
Standard error of measurement, 485
Standardized testing
accountability and, 471, 473, 474, 475, 486–488
administration of tests, 493
bias and, 488, 489–490, 493
case studies on, 471–473, 478, 495–496
defined, 473
developmentally appropriate practice and, 494
functions of, 473–475
learner diversity and, 489–491
scores, 474, 479–485
types of, 475–478
validity of, 478–479, 485, 489–490, 494
Standards
accountability and, 13, 395
for behavior, 365
defined, 395
planning in standards-based environment, 395–398
reform movement and, 463
resilience and, 115
Standards-based education, 486
Standard scores, 484–485
Stanford-Binet, 475–476
Stanines, 484
Status, modeling and, 185
Stereotypes
gender differences and, 109–110
learners with exceptionalities and, 154
test bias and, 488
urban environments and, 14, 120, 364, 407
Stereotype threat, defined, 99
Sternberg's triarchic theory of intelligence, 128–129, 130
Strategic learning
critical thinking and, 271–273
metacognition and, 267–268
study strategies and, 268–271
Strategies. *See also* Developmentally appropriate practice; Learning strategies; Study strategies
cognitive load and, 201
constructivism and, 246–247
defined, 267
general pedagogical knowledge and, 11
goals and, 308
interference and, 214–215
mastery goals and, 304
metacognition and, 218, 219
problem-based learning and, 264–266
for problem solving, 260–261
situational interest and, 310
students placed at risk and, 118
test-taking strategies, 455, 492

Structured immersion, defined, 103
Student artifacts, informal assessment and, 439
Student names
  attention and, 208
  caring and, 328
Students. *See* Learners
Students placed at risk
  case studies on, 114–117
  defined, 114
  socioeconomic status and, 114–115
Students who are gifted and talented
  characteristics of, 149–150
  enrichment for, 151, 156
  identification of, 150–151
  programs for, 151
Students with exceptionalities. *See* Learners with exceptionalities
Student Teams Achievement Divisions (STAD), 421
Study strategies
  concept mapping, 269–270
  defined, 268
  elaborative questioning, 271
  metacognition and, 218
  note taking, 269–270
  organization and, 211
  promoting, 275
  SQ3R, 271
  summarizing, 270
  text signals, 270
Substance abuse, social development and, 75
Success
  attributions and, 302
  classrooms and, 333, 335
  expectations and, 297, 330
  homework and, 413
  mastery goals and, 304
  motivation and, 284
  open-ended questions and, 340–341
  self-regulation and, 323
  urban environments and, 87
Summarizing, 270
Summative assessment, 460
Symbolic modeling, 181
Synapses
  defined, 31
  research on, 32
Synaptic pruning, 32
Syntax
  defined, 52
  language development and, 52–53
Synthesized modeling, 181
Systematic observation
  defined, 448
  performance assessment and, 448–449

Tables of specifications, 454
Tale of Two Cities, A (Dickens), 80
Target behaviors, 175–176
TARGET program and, 334, 335
Task analysis
  defined, 393
  as planning tool, 393–394
  sample of, 394
Task comprehension
  application of, 335
  defined, 334
Task-focused goals, 304
Task-involved goals, 304
Taxonomy, for cognitive objectives, 392–393
Teachers. *See also* Communication with parents
  ability grouping and, 130, 131
  accountability and, 488
  attributions and, 302
  authoritative teachers, 356
  behavior disorders and, 144–145
  caring and, 85, 117, 120, 289, 327–328, 330, 331, 344, 345, 354, 365, 400, 408
  characteristics of, 325–331, 400
  cognitive constructivism and, 227
  cognitive modeling and, 182
  collaborative consultation and, 152
  communication disorders and, 146–147
  conceptual change and, 237
  constructivism and, 238, 247–248
  cultural characteristics of, 110
  dialects and, 102
  expectations of, 328–331, 344, 345, 364, 400, 456
  Gardner's theory of multiple intelligences and, 127
  imagery and, 210
  learners with exceptionalities and, 152–155, 156
  learning styles and, 132–133
  meaningful learning and, 204
  modeling and, 181, 184, 185, 327, 330, 331, 400
  moral development and, 81
  motivation of students and, 285–286, 319–320, 321, 325–331
  parenting styles and, 64
  parents' communication with, 101
  positive reinforcement and, 169
  procedural knowledge and, 204–205
  psychosocial development and, 68
  quality of, 13
  research on, 19
  resilience and, 115, 117
  scaffolding and, 47, 50
  situational interest and, 310
  social cognitive theory and, 180
  social constructivism and, 227–228
  socioeconomic status and, 114
  standardized testing and, 473, 492–493
  students who are gifted and talented and, 149
  tests for, 487–488
  urban environments and, 86–87, 344–347, 364, 406–409
  withitness, 372–373, 379, 381
Teaching skills. *See* Essential teaching skills; Professionalism
Technology
  bioecological theory of development and, 65
  problem solving and, 265–266
  students who are gifted and talented and, 150
Temperament, defined, 62
Test anxiety, 313, 456, 459
Tests and testing. *See also* Assessment; Standardized testing
  accommodations for English Language Learners, 491, 493
  anxiety and, 313, 456, 459
  bias in testing procedures, 490
  bias in test interpretation and use, 490
  high-stakes tests, 451, 487
  intelligence tests, 126–127, 475–476
  for teachers, 487–488
  test-preparation procedures, 456, 459, 492–493
  test-taking strategies, 455
Texas, 96
Texas Assessment of Knowledge and Skills, 396
Text signals, 270
Theories
  comparison of, 247
  defined, 20
  research and, 20–22
Theory of mind, defined, 86
Theory to practice
  action research and, 21
  assessment and, 458
  behaviorism and, 177
  classroom climate and instructional variables and, 342
  concept learning and, 256
  constructivism and, 244
  essential teaching skills and, 408
  gender differences and, 110
  identity and self-concept development and, 72
  intervention for misbehavior, 381
  learner diversity and, 106
  learners with exceptionalities and, 155
  memory and, 220
  moral development and, 87
  motivation to learn and, 312
  needs and, 295
  Piaget's theory of cognitive development and, 42
  problem solving and, 266
  rules and, 366
  social cognitive theory and, 186
  social development and, 77
  strategic learning and, 273
  students placed at risk and, 116–117
  students who are gifted and talented and, 150
  teacher characteristics and, 330
  teacher's role in standardized testing, 492–493
  Vygotsky's theory of development and, 48
Thinking. *See also* Cognitive development; Cognitive processes
  assessment and, 424
  cerebral cortex and, 32
  critical thinking, 271–274, 275, 444
  developmental differences and, 12
  development of, 7
  divergent thinking, 264
  formal operational thinking, 40–42
  language and, 46
Thought-provoking questions, 208
Time
  classroom management and, 355–356
  cultures and, 99
  types of classroom time, 355–356
  wait-time, 405–406
Timeout, defined, 172
Topic selection, 390–391
Tracking
  defined, 130
  social development and, 131
Transfer
  complex cognitive processes and, 275–279
  defined, 229, 275
  factors affecting, 276–277, 279
  general transfer, 275–276
  guided discovery and, 419
  situated cognition and, 229–230
  specific transfer, 275–276
Transformation, defined, 38
Transitional ELL programs, 104, 105
Transition signals, 401
Transitivity, defined, 40
True-false, defined, 443
True scores, 485
Trust versus mistrust, 67
T-scores, 485

Unconditional positive regard
  defined, 288
  motivation and, 288–289
  need for relatedness and, 293
Unconditioned response, defined, 165
Unconditioned stimulus, defined, 165
Underachievers, 114
Undergeneralization, defined, 52
Uninvolved parenting style, 64
Universal principles stage, defined, 84
Urban environments
  classroom management and, 364–366
  essential teaching skills in, 406–409
  knowledge construction and, 242–244

learner diversity and, 14, 120, 364, 463
motivation and, 120, 343–347, 364, 366
personal, social, and moral development in, 86–87
teacher quality and, 13, 14
U.S. Department of Education, 19
Utility value, 300, 302, 334

Validity
assessment and, 435–436, 453
assessment bias and, 489–490
defined, 435
of formal assessment, 441
relationship with reliability, 436
standardized testing and, 478–479, 485, 489–490, 494
tables of specifications and, 454
Values
beliefs about, 299–300
challenge and, 333
cultures and, 97–99
defined, 299
peers and, 64–65
socioeconomic status and, 113
Variability, measures of, 481–482
Variable schedules, 170, 171
Verbalization, cognitive apprenticeships and, 229, 233, 246
Verbal-nonverbal congruence, 374–375, 379, 381
Vicarious learning
defined, 182
indirect cues and, 378
inhibitions and, 184
social cognitive theory and, 182, 184, 187, 361
Violence
classroom management and, 382–384
long-term solutions to, 383–384
social development and, 76–78
Visual disabilities, 147
Visual-spatial sketchpad
defined, 200
working memory and, 199, 200, 201
Voice disorders, 146
Vygotsky, Lev, 45
Vygotsky's view of development
applying, 48
cultural context and, 45–47
culture and, 47
knowledge construction and, 49, 227, 233
language and, 46
language development and, 51
Piaget's views compared to, 49
scaffolding and, 47, 48
social interaction and, 45–46
zone of proximal development, 47, 51, 288, 297

Wait-time, 405–406
Wechsler Intelligence Scale for Children–Fourth Edition, 7, 476
Wechsler Scales, 476, 477
Well-defined problems, 259, 266
Within-class grouping, 130
Withitness, 372–373, 379, 381
Work-avoidance goals, 306
Worked examples, 266
Working memory
classroom application of, 206
defined, 199
distributed processing and, 210
efficiency of, 205
Gardner's theory of multiple intelligences and, 128
limitations of, 200–201, 239
model of, 199–200
perception and, 209
Writing
language development and, 53, 55
persuasive writing assessment sample, 447
standardized testing and, 477–478
working memory and, 200
Written feedback, 403

Yearling, The (Rawlings), 80

Zone of proximal development
defined, 47
language development and, 51
motivation and, 288
motivation to learn and, 297
Z-scores, 485